AUFSTIEG UND NIEDERGANG
DER RÖMISCHEN WELT

II.17.1

AUFSTIEG UND NIEDERGANG DER RÖMISCHEN WELT

GESCHICHTE UND KULTUR ROMS
IM SPIEGEL DER NEUEREN FORSCHUNG

II

HERAUSGEGEBEN

VON

HILDEGARD TEMPORINI

UND

WOLFGANG HAASE

WALTER DE GRUYTER · BERLIN · NEW YORK
1981

PRINCIPAT

SIEBZEHNTER BAND
(1. TEILBAND)

RELIGION

(HEIDENTUM: RÖMISCHE GÖTTERKULTE,
ORIENTALISCHE KULTE
IN DER RÖMISCHEN WELT)

HERAUSGEGEBEN
VON

WOLFGANG HAASE

WALTER DE GRUYTER · BERLIN · NEW YORK
1981

Herausgegeben mit Unterstützung der Robert Bosch Stiftung, Stuttgart

CIP-Kurztitelaufnahme der Deutschen Bibliothek

Aufstieg und Niedergang der römischen Welt:
Geschichte u. Kultur Roms im Spiegel d. neueren Forschung /
hrsg. von Hildegard Temporini u. Wolfgang Haase – Berlin,
New York : de Gruyter.
NE: Temporini, Hildegard [Hrsg.)
2. Principat.
Bd. 17, Religion / Hrsg. von Wolfgang Haase.
1. Teilbd. – 1981.
    ISBN 3-11-008468-6
NE: Haase, Wolfgang [Hrsg.]

© 1981 by Walter de Gruyter & Co.,
vormals G. J. Göschen'sche Verlagshandlung · J. Guttentag, Verlagsbuchhandlung · Georg Reimer · Karl J. Trübner
Veit & Comp., Berlin 30 · Alle Rechte, insbesondere das der Übersetzung in fremde Sprachen, vorbehalten. Ohne
ausdrückliche Genehmigung des Verlages ist es auch nicht gestattet, dieses Buch oder Teile daraus auf photo-
mechanischem Wege (Photokopie, Mikrokopie) zu vervielfältigen.
Printed in Germany
Satz und Druck: Arthur Collignon GmbH, Berlin 30
Einbandgestaltung und Schutzumschlag: Rudolf Hübler
Buchbinder: Lüderitz & Bauer, Berlin
Reproduktionen: Terra-Klischee, Berlin

Vorwort

Mit dem vorliegenden Band II 17 wird im II. Teil ('Principat') des Gemeinschaftswerkes 'Aufstieg und Niedergang der römischen Welt' (ANRW) die Publikation der Rubrik 'Religion' fortgesetzt. Wie im Vorwort zum ersten Band (II 16,1 [Berlin–New York 1978] S. VIIf.) angekündigt, gliedert sich die Rubrik in mehrere Abschnitte, die aus den Bänden II 16–II 18 über die sog. heidnischen Religionen, II 19–II 21 über das Judentum, II 22 über Gnostizismus und verwandte Erscheinungen sowie II 23–II 28 über das vorkonstantinische Christentum bestehen. Aus jedem der drei größeren Abschnitte der Rubrik ist bereits ein Band erschienen: II 16,1 u. 2 (1978; der abschließende Teilband II 16,3 befindet sich noch in Vorbereitung), II 19,1 u. 2 (1979/80) und II 23,1 u. 2 (1979/80). Nachdem Bd. II 16 Beiträge zu verschiedenen Themenbereichen allgemeiner Art enthalten hat – vor allem zur Charakteristik der römischen Religion der Kaiserzeit, zu wichtigen literarischen Quellen späterer Kenntnis römischer Religion, zu einigen Grundbegriffen römischer Religion, zu den bedeutendsten römischen Priesterkollegien, zum Kaiserkult, zu Festen und Riten des römischen Staatskultes und zur Religion bestimmter sozialer Gruppen –, vereinigt Bd. II 17 in seinen beiden ersten Teilbänden (II 17,1 u. 2 [1981]) Beiträge zu einzelnen römischen Gottheiten und Kulten, in seinem dritten Teilband (II 17,3 [1982]) solche zu orientalischen Gottheiten und Kulten in der römischen Welt und ihrer Nachbarschaft. 'Römisch' heißen die Gottheiten und Kulte der ersten, größeren Gruppe hier deshalb ohne Einschränkung, weil sie alle, ungeachtet des größeren oder kleineren Anteils ursprünglich griechischer, etruskischer, altitalischer oder römisch-latinischer Elemente an ihrem Erscheinungsbild, in der Zeit der späten Republik und des Principats römisch 'eingebürgert' waren. Aus dieser Zeit werden sie teilweise bis zu ihren Ursprüngen zurückverfolgt, so daß hier öfters als in anderen Bänden des II. Teils von ANRW die Grenze zwischen den Perioden 'Von den Anfängen Roms bis zum Ausgang der Republik' (= Teil I) und 'Principat' (= Teil II) überschritten wird, wenn ein Thema, wie es häufig der Fall ist, im I. Teil (Bd. I 2 [1972]) seinerzeit noch nicht in der Weise behandelt werden konnte, daß sich jetzt einfach chronologisch daran anknüpfen ließe.

Zentrale Kapitel kaiserzeitlicher Kultgeschichte in ihrer Verbindung mit der politischen Geschichte, vor allem der politischen Ideen- und Ideologiegeschichte, aber auch mit Sozial-, Wirtschafts-, Literatur- und Kunstgeschichte sollen in diesem Band als Bausteine zu einer künftigen Gesamtgeschichte der römischen Religion und der Religionen der römischen Welt zusammengestellt werden. Zu dem Aspekt der kultgeschichtlichen und konzeptionellen Individualisierung aus dem Blickwinkel Roms als der Mitte des Reiches wird im anschließenden Band II 18 (ebenfalls in drei Teilbänden, II 18,1–3 [1982f.]) mit Beiträgen über die religiösen Verhältnisse in einzelnen Gebieten, in den Provinzen und bei den Nachbarn des römischen Reiches, der regionale Aspekt hinzutreten. Die drei 'heidnischen' Bände der Rubrik 'Religion' ergänzen sich aber nicht nur untereinander, sondern auch mit zahlreichen Beiträgen anderer Bände der gleichen Rubrik und anderer Rubriken wechselseitig. Hingewiesen sei beispielshalber zu dem Themenkreis des Bandes II 16 (1978) generell auf die Beiträge des Bandes II 23 (1979/80) über die Auseinandersetzung des römischen Staates mit dem Christentum, die Auseinandersetzung der christlichen Apologetik mit der heidnischen Religion und den Vergleich christlicher und nichtchristlicher religiöser Sachverhalte und Begriffe wie Opfer, Gebet, Mysterium, Vorzeichen u. a.; zu Bd. II 18 auf manche religionsgeschichtliche Kapitel und Absätze der Beiträge über 'Provinzen und Randvölker' in den Bänden II 3–II 11 (1975ff.) der Rubrik 'Politische Geschichte'; außerdem zu den Bänden II 16–II 18 im einzelnen auf Beiträge wie die von A. HULTGÅRD über 'Das Judentum in der hellenistisch-römischen Zeit und die iranische Religion – ein religionsgeschichtliches Problem' und von M. HADAS-LEBEL über 'Le paganisme à travers les sources rabbiniques des IIe et IIIe siècles. Contribution à l'étude du syncrétisme dans l'empire romain' in Bd. II 19 oder von I. M. BARTON über 'Capitoline Temples in Italy and the Provinces (especially Africa)' in der Rubrik 'Künste', Bd. II 12,1 (1982). – Ein thematisch wichtiger Beitrag zu Bd. II 17 von R. SCHILLING (Strasbourg) über 'Venus sous l'Empire' ist nicht rechtzeitig eingetroffen, um an passender Stelle aufgenommen zu werden; er wird nachträglich am Schluß entweder des zweiten oder des dritten Teilbandes veröffentlicht werden. Übrigens ist der Reihenfolge der Beiträge innerhalb der Teilbände 1 und 2 bzw. 3, für die sich kein einheitlicher, konsequent durchführbarer Gesichtspunkt außer dem irrelevanten alphabetischen hätte finden lassen, kein besonderes Gewicht beizumessen. Gesichtspunkte der Bedeutung für das religiöse Leben Roms und solche des Alters, der Herkunft und der wechselseitigen Beziehung haben zur Bildung locker verbundener Beitragsgruppen geführt. Orientieren wird sich der Leser statt an einem fragwürdigen System an der Inhaltsübersicht des Bandes.

Die Herausgabe des vorliegenden Bandes ist von der Robert Bosch Stiftung, Stuttgart, und vom Präsidenten der Eberhard-Karls-Universität Tübingen, ADOLF THEIS, materiell und ideell gefördert worden. Wertvolle Unterstützung haben auf unterschiedliche Weise die Direktoren des Althistorischen und des Philologischen Seminars der Universität Tübingen, KARL-ERNST PETZOLD und RICHARD KANNICHT, gewährt. Technische Hilfe haben KARIN GRAMER, URSULA SCHAFF und RUDOLF ROLINGER vom Althistorischen und LUISE BELTHLE vom Philologischen Seminar geleistet. Allen Genannten fühlen sich die Herausgeber, teilweise schon seit mehreren Jahren, zu lebhaftem Dank verpflichtet. Eine besondere Würdigung hätte die aufopfernde Mitwirkung ALEXANDER FRIEDEMANN WENSLERS an der redaktionellen Arbeit verdient; von seiner Sachkenntnis und unermüdlichen Aufmerksamkeit hat auch dieser Band wie viele andere profitiert. Helfer bei der Redaktion sind außerdem MICHAEL GROSS und ALFRED GRUBER gewesen. Die Betreuung des Bandes im Verlag de Gruyter lag in den bewährten Händen von LOTHAR UEBEL.

Tübingen, im Mai 1981 .   W. H.

Inhalt

RELIGION
(HEIDENTUM: RÖMISCHE GÖTTERKULTE, ORIENTALISCHE KULTE IN DER RÖMISCHEN WELT)

Band II. 17.1:

Band II. 17.2:

Band II. 17.3:

———————

NACHTRAG ZU BD. II. 17.1/2:

RELIGION

(HEIDENTUM: RÖMISCHE GÖTTERKULTE, ORIENTALISCHE KULTE IN DER RÖMISCHEN WELT)

The Cult of Jupiter and Roman Imperial Ideology[*]

by J. Rufus Fears, Bloomington, Indiana

Contents

[*] Like its companion pieces below in this same volume (ANRW II, 17,2), 'The Theology of Victory at Rome: Approaches and Problems' and 'The Cult of Virtues and Roman Imperial Ideology', this study was researched, written, and prepared for publication during my tenure as a Fellow of the John Simon Guggenheim Memorial Foundation (1976—77) and of the Alexander von Humboldt Stiftung (1977—78). I should like to express my profound gratitude to both these foundations; these studies could not have been written without the financial support and freedom from academic duties provided by their fellowships. A very special and a very personal debt of gratitude is owed to Dr. Heinrich Pfeiffer, Secretary General of the Alexander von Humboldt Foundation and to Professor Johannes Straub. Heinrich Pfeiffer's warm friendship and lively interest in my work added a very special quality to my stay in Germany; it is gratifying to have these studies appear in ANRW, a work which exemplifies that international scholarly cooperation to which the Humboldt Foundation is dedicated. My interest in imperial ideology was originally stimulated by Johannes Straub's 'Vom Herrscherideal in der Spätantike', Forschungen zur Kirchen- und Geistesgeschichte 18 (Stuttgart 1939); and it was an honor to have him sponsor my period of research in Germany as a Humboldt Fellow. All three essays were written in the stimulating atmosphere of his Seminar für Alte Geschichte at Bonn; all owe much to his advice, encouragement, and scholarly *exemplum*.

Abbreviations and Short Titles:

In the present essay, as well as in 'The Theology of Victory at Rome' and in 'The Cult of Virtues and Roman Imperial Ideology', below in this same volume (ANRW II, 17,2), the abbreviations used for periodicals are those found in 'L'Année Philologique'. For standard works of reference, the usual practice of abbreviating by initials has been followed.

AA	Archäologischer Anzeiger
AAP	Atti dell'Accademia Pontaniana.
AC	L'Antiquité Classique.
ACD	Acta Classica Universitatis Scientiarum Debreceniensis.
AFLN	Annali della Facoltà di Lettere e Filosofia della Università di Napoli.
AG	Archivio Giuridico.
AIIN	Annali dell'Istituto Italiano di Numismatica.
AJA	American Journal of Archaeology.
AJPh	American Journal of Philology
ALGP	Annali del Liceo classico G. Garibaldi di Palermo.
ANRW	Aufstieg und Niedergang der römischen Welt. Geschichte und Kultur Roms im Spiegel der neueren Forschung, ed. by H. TEMPORINI–W. HAASE (Berlin–New York 1972 ff.).
ANSMusN	The American Numismatic Society Museum Notes.
Année Epig.	L'Année Epigraphique.
ARW	Archiv für Religionswissenschaft.
A&R	Atene e Roma.
BAB	Bulletin de la Classe des Lettres de l'Académie Royale de Belgique.
BCAR	Bullettino della Commissione Archeologica Comunale in Roma.
BCH	Bulletin de Correspondance Hellénique.
BEFAR	Bibliothèque des Écoles Françaises d'Athènes et de Rome.
BJ	Bonner Jahrbücher des Rheinischen Landesmuseums in Bonn und des Vereins von Altertumsfreunden im Rheinlande.
BMC	Coins of the Roman Empire in the British Museum, I–V by H. MATTINGLY; VI by R. CARSON (London 1923 ff.).
BMIR	Bullettino del Museo dell'Impero Romano.
CAH	The Cambridge Ancient History, ed. by J. BURY and others (Cambridge 1923–39).
CE	Chronique d'Égypte.

CIG	Corpus Inscriptionum Graecarum, ed. by A. BOECKH and others (Berlin 1828–77).
CIL	Corpus Inscriptionum Latinarum, cons. et auct. Acad. Litt. Boruss. (Leipzig–Berlin 1862–1943), ed. altera (ibid. 1893 ff.).
CJ	The Classical Journal.
CPh	Classical Philology.
CQ	Classical Quarterly.
CR	Classical Review.
CRAI	Comptes Rendus de l'Académie des Inscriptions et Belles-Lettres.
CRAWFORD	M. CRAWFORD, Roman Republican Coinage I–II (Cambridge 1974).
CW	The Classical World (formerly Classical Weekly).
C&M	Classica et Mediaevalia.
D-S	Dictionnaire des Antiquités Grecques et Romaines, ed. by C. DAREMBERG–E. SAGLIO (Paris 1877–1919).
DOP	Dumbarton Oaks Papers.
FGrHist	Die Fragmente der griechischen Historiker, ed. by F. JACOBY (Berlin–Leiden 1923–58, rep. Leiden 1954 ff.).
GGA	Göttingische Gelehrte Anzeigen.
GNECCHI	F. GNECCHI, I medaglioni romani I–III (Milan 1912, rep. Bologna 1968).
GRUEBER, BMRR	Coins of the Roman Republic in the British Museum, ed. by H. GRUEBER (London 1910), rev. ed. (London 1970).
G&R	Greece and Rome.
HEAD, HN²	B. HEAD, Historia Numorum. A Manual of Greek Numismatics² (Oxford 1911).
HSCPh	Harvard Studies in Classical Philology.
HThR	Harvard Theological Review.
HZ	Historische Zeitschrift.
IG	Inscriptiones Graecae, cons. et. auct. Acad. Litt. Boruss., ed. maior (Berlin 1873–1939), ed. minor (ibid. 1913 ff.).
II	Inscriptiones Italiae, Acad. Italicae consociate ediderunt (Rome 1931 ff.).
IGRRP	Inscriptiones Graecae ad Res Romanas Pertinentes, ed. by R. CAGNAT and others (Paris 1906–28).
ILLRP	Inscriptiones Latinae Liberae Rei Publicae, ed. by A. DEGRASSI (Florence 1957–63).
ILS	Inscriptiones Latinae Selectae, ed. H. DESSAU (Berlin 1892–1916, rep. ibid. 1962).
JAW	Jahresbericht über die Fortschritte der klassischen Altertumswissenschaft.
JDAI	Jahrbuch des Deutschen Archäologischen Instituts.
JEH	Journal of Ecclesiastical History.
JHS	Journal of Hellenic Studies.
JNG	Jahrbuch für Numismatik und Geldgeschichte.
JOAI	Jahreshefte des Österreichischen Archäologischen Instituts.
JRGZ	Jahrbuch des römisch-germanischen Zentralmuseums Mainz.
JRH	Journal of Religious History.
JRS	Journal of Roman Studies.
MAAR	Memoirs of the American Academy in Rome.
MAL	Memorie della Classe di Scienze Morali e Storiche dell'Accademia dei Lincei.
MDAI(R)	Mitteilungen des Deutschen Archäologischen Instituts (Römische Abteilung).
MEFR	Mélanges d'Archéologie et d'Histoire de l'École Française de Rome.
MH	Museum Helveticum.
Myth. Lex.	Ausführliches Lexikon der griechischen und römischen Mythologie, ed. by W. H. ROSCHER (Leipzig 1884–1937, rep. Hildesheim 1965).

NAC	Numismatica e Antichità Classiche.
NC	Numismatic Chronicle.
NClio	La Nouvelle Clio.
NGG	Nachrichten von der Gesellschaft der Wissenschaften zu Göttingen.
Nilsson, GGR³	M. Nilsson, Geschichte der griechischen Religion, Hb. d. Altertumswiss. V, 2, 1/2, I³ (Munich 1967), II³ (ibid. 1974).
OGIS	Orientis Graeci Inscriptiones Selectae, ed. by W. Dittenberger (Leipzig 1903–5, rep. Hildesheim 1960).
PBA	Proceedings of the British Academy.
PBSR	Papers of the British School at Rome.
PCA	Proceedings of the Classical Association.
PCPhS	Proceedings of the Cambridge Philological Society.
PP	La Parola del Passato.
QS	Quaderni di Storia.
RA	Revue Archéologique.
RACF	Revue Archéologique du Centre [de la France].
RAL	Rendiconti della Classe di Scienze Morali, Storiche e Filologiche dell'Accademia dei Lincei.
RBPh	Revue Belge de Philologie et d'Histoire.
RCCM	Rivista di Cultura Classica e Medioevale.
RCl	Rivista Clasica.
RD	Revue Historique de Droit Français et étranger.
RE	Paulys Realencyclopädie der classischen Altertumswissenschaft, ed. by G. Wissowa and others (Stuttgart 1893 ff.).
REA	Revue des Études Anciennes.
REG	Revue des Études Grecques.
REL	Revue des Études Latines.
RFIC	Rivista di Filologia e di Istruzione Classica.
RH	Revue Historique.
RHD	Revue d'Histoire du Droit.
RhM	Rheinisches Museum.
RIC	Roman Imperial Coinage (London 1923 ff.), I–IV by H. Mattingly and E. Sydenham; V by P. Webb; VI by C. Sutherland; VII by P. Bruun.
RIC Hunter	Roman Imperial Coins in the Hunter Coin Cabinet, by A. S. Robertson (Oxford 1962 ff.).
RIL	Rendiconti dell'Istituto Lombardo, Classe di Lettere, Scienze Morali e Storiche.
RLAC	Reallexikon für Antike und Christentum, ed. by T. Klauser (Stuttgart 1941 ff.).
RPAA	Rendiconti della Pontificia Accademia di Archeologia.
RPh	Revue de Philologie.
SDHI	Studia et Documenta Historiae et Iuris.
SEG	Supplementum Epigraphicum Graecum, ed. by I. Hondius e.a. (Leiden 1923 ff.).
SIG³	Sylloge Inscriptionum Graecarum³, ed. by W. Dittenberger (Leipzig 1915–24, rep. Hildesheim 1960).
SMSR	Studi e Materiali di Storia delle Religioni.
SO	Symbolae Osloenses.
Strack I	P. Strack, Untersuchungen zur römischen Reichsprägung des zweiten Jahrhunderts, I. Die Reichsprägung zur Zeit des Traian (Stuttgart 1931).
Strack II	II. Die Reichsprägung zur Zeit des Hadrian (Stuttgart 1933).
Strack III	III. Die Reichsprägung zur Zeit des Antoninus Pius (Stuttgart 1937).
Stud Rom	Studi Romani.

I. Introduction

For Aristotle the collective political association of the *polis* provided the basis for civilized existence. For a writer of the second century A. D. like Celsus, civilization was rooted in theocratic monarchy, the kingship of the Roman emperor. For Celsus, only lawless and savage barbarians could live without a king. Peace, security, and justice existed because the Roman emperor ensured their existence. His authority and power to ensure these blessings derived directly from his investiture by Zeus.[1] Aristotle wrote as a man of the *polis*; Celsus as the citizen of a universal empire. In historical perspective, the Roman empire represents the culmination and resolution of the tension, inherent throughout the history of the ancient world, between the small autonomous political unit, like the *polis* based upon a conception of collective political authority, and large supranational empires, incorporating numerous smaller units. The Roman imperial structure of the high empire was a notably successful attempt to bring a large number of different ethnic groups and political units under a single government which ensured the rights and privileges as well as the burdens and responsibilities of members of the empire. Certainly the empire depended upon military strength; crucial also in securing continuity and stability was the network of personal alliances with the ruling classes throughout the empire. These were practical, material sinews of imperial rule. However, the continuance of any government is ultimately based upon a myth of supernatural character, a legitimization beyond military, economic, and socio-political bases of power.

Such a political myth is essential to any society. From KARL MARX and GEORGES SOREL to GEORG BRAND and JÜRGEN HABERMAS a series of distinguished social thinkers have taught us to recognize the significance of political mythology or ideology, to use its more common synonym. TALCOTT PARSONS provides a functional definition of ideology: a system of beliefs held in common by the members of a collectivity, a system of ideas that is oriented to the evaluative integration of the community. In these terms, ideology forms the matrix of social behaviour and provides the principal means for attaining social solidarity and integration. Through ideology a given state of political affairs can be rationalized, legitimatized, and perpetuated. Such a political myth binds a group of people together, taps their sentiments and emotions, and directs their energies towards specific objectives. As a shaper of political action ideology has a variety

TAPhA   Transactions and Proceedings of the American Philological Association.
WISSOWA RKR²   G. WISSOWA, Religion und Kultus der Römer², Hb. d. Altertumswiss. V, 4 (Munich 1912², rep. 1971).
WS   Wiener Studien.
YCS   Yale Classical Studies.

[1] Celsus as quoted by Origen Contra Celsum 8.68.

of complementary functions: legitimacy; identity; solidarity; agitation; communication; and goal specification. Thus social scientists rightly insist upon rec-
ognizing ideology as an essential instrument for leadership manipulation and
control of the masses. Indeed, as SOREL saw, one of the most important functions of any leadership group is to provide the appropriate political myth for its
society; and it is questionable whether any society can long endure without such
an ideology.

   This conceptualization of ideology, like the term itself, is modern. However, as defined by PARSONS and other social scientists, ideology was as much a
fact of ancient as it is of modern societies. Polybius (6.56) was as aware as SOREL
or PARSONS of the integrative function which a belief system could play in a
polity. The *theologia civilis* of the Roman exercised the same socio-political
function as do the ideas, formulae, and institutions of democracy, nationalism
and communism in a modern nation-state. At Rome, as throughout the ancient
world, political mythology was bound inextricably to the collective worship of
the community. This religious tincture may obscure parallels with modern ideol-
ogies such as democracy and nationalism, which we tend to regard in secular
terms. In part this is merely a question of perspective. To the Roman the
modern cult of the flag with its pledge of allegiance, national anthems, and
monuments like the Lincoln Memorial and the Altare della Patria, would differ
in no whit from his practice of cult offerings, hymns, and temples directed to
gods of the state, including deified rulers. Beyond this question of perspective,
there is a more fundamental issue. The modern dichotomy between sacred and
secular is of questionable validity in approaching the theme of ideology in the
ancient world. For the ancient, religion permeated every aspect of the state's life,
providing the very basis of the socio-political order. Of necessity political
ideology was formulated in theological terms and expressed through cult and
ritual. Religious imagery defined the ancient's conception of his socio-political
structures, and the cult life of the state mirrored each transformation in those
structures.[2]

   In short, the evolution of universal monarchy in the Greco−Roman world
demanded a new political mythology or ideology, an image of imperial rule to

---

[2] There is a tendency among students of ancient society to use the term 'ideology' in rather
   loose fashion. The foregoing remarks will serve at least to define the meaning of 'ideology'
   in the present essay and in its companion pieces in this volume. TALCOTT PARSON's
   definition of ideology, cited in the text, is taken from his 'The Social System' (Glencoe,
   Illinois 1956) 354−9. The best recent introduction to the nature of political mythology is
   G. BRAND, Welt, Geschichte, Mythos, und Politik (Berlin−New York 1978). On a
   theoretical level, P. BERGER, The Sacred Canopy (New York 1967) 3−52, explores the role
   of religion in the process of political and social legitimation. Both BERGER and more
   especially BRAND offer guides to the literature, particularly in the social sciences, dealing
   with the nature and social role of ideology and with related topics. An admirable outline of
   the history of the term 'ideology' is G. LICHTHEIM, The Concept of Ideology, History
   and Theory 4 (1965) 164−95. More recently, see E. KENNEDY, Ideology from Destutt de
   Tracy to Marx, JHI 40 (1979) 353−68; and K. RUDOLPH, Die Ideologiekritische Funktion
   der Religionswissenschaft, Numen 25 (1978) 17−39.

support the new and constantly developing political structure of oecumenical empire. In the Roman empire, as in other 'universal' empires, in Egypt, Mesopotamia, China, and India, this aura of supernatural legitimization came to be enshrined in and expressed through the figure of the monarch. The ideology of oecumenical empire was founded in an image of the ruler as the visible embodiment of cosmic order, divinely ordained to ensure the prosperity of the human race. In the Roman empire, this ideological need was supplied, in part, by the worship of the rulers, both living and departed; and it is the cult of the ruler which figures most prominently in treatments of the religious position of the Roman emperor, even as oriental cults tend to overshadow traditional Greco-Roman divinities in studies of religion in the imperial age. However, in the early Antonine age, that most creative period of imperial statecraft, Trajan and Hadrian turned to a Jovian theology of power as the central ideological element on which to establish their broadly conceived image of oecumenical empire. So too, after the most severe political and social crises, Diocletian sought to restore the Roman world on an ideological basis centered upon Jupiter and an image of the emperor as his divinely elected vicegerent. Neither effort was the result of mere traditionalism. Both are rather later chapters in the intermittently evolving portrait of the Roman Jupiter and its role in Roman political ideology. It was a process which endured with vigor for three-quarters of a millennium and which provides among the most fascinating chapters in the history of Roman religion. Its most creative and significant phases are three. One, already mentioned, occurs within the context of the Flavian and Antonine transformation of the imperial structure, marked by the adaptation of the Roman Jupiter to serve as the prototype of an omnipotent monarch of an oecumenical empire. The first two had occurred far earlier but within equally portentous political frameworks, the creation of the Roman *res publica*, and the rise of Rome to world dominion.

II. The Origins of the Roman Jupiter

1. Tarquinius Priscus and the Cult of Jupiter Optimus Maximus

The cult of the Capitoline Triad does not belong to the very earliest phase of the Roman state religion; it is conspicuously absent from the oldest Roman calendar.[2a] As Roman tradition recognized, it was not part of the religion of Numa. It was born in unconstitutional monarchy and fostered in political revolution. The great Capitoline temple was vowed by Tarquinius Priscus during the Sabine War. He laid the foundations of the temple, which was completed under

---

[2a] Scholarship on the Roman cult of Jupiter is surveyed below pp. 122—38. P. 138 n. 92 lists certain works which became available after the present essay went to press and which, although not dealing specifically with Jupiter, do relate to points raised in the texts and notes.

his son and dedicated in the first year of the republic.[3] For Tarquin it was a dynastic monument, of the father who made the vow and of the son who fulfilled it. The entire area of the temple was to be sacred to no god but Jupiter, and Tarquinius Superbus sought to remove other religious associations, secularizing a number of earlier sacred places on the Capitoline.[4] The temple was of massive proportions, fully comparable to such contemporary Hellenic structures as temple G at Selinus.[5] Indeed, comparison with the building history of the latter, begun in the mid-sixth century and still uncompleted at the time of the Carthaginian sack in 409, should relieve us of any doubts regarding the tradition that the erection of the great Capitoline temple endured over three reigns and for more than three-quarters of a century.[6]

The tyranny of Tarquinius Superbus made the title *rex* ever hateful to Roman ears; his violent expulsion marked the creation of the Roman republic.

---

[3] The chronology is traditional. With the exception of the attribution of the temple to Numa in Eusebius, p. 91 ed. HELM, ancient tradition was unanimous in ascribing the origins of the cult of the Capitoline Triad to Tarquinius Priscus; cf. Cic. Rep. 2.24.44, Verr. 5.19.48; Livy 1.38.7, 55.1; Pliny N.H. 3.5.70; Tac. Hist. 3.72; Auson. ord. nob. urb. p. 122 ed. PEIPER; Dion. Hal. 3.69, 4.59; Plut. Pop. 14. In the same way there was unanimity on the role of Tarquinius Superbus; cf. Cic. Rep. 2.24.44, Verr. 5.19.48; Livy 1.55; Pliny N.H. 3.70; Tac. Hist. 3.72. There is less unanimity on the date of the dedication. The majority view placed it in the first year of the republic; cf. Polyb. 3.22; Livy 2.8, 7.3; Val. Max. 5.10.1; Plut. Popl. 14. 507 B.C., the second consulate of Horatius, is given by Tac. Hist. 3.72 and Dion. Hal. 5.35. For the problem of the dedication date see, briefly, F. WALBANK, A Historical Commentary on Polybius I (Oxford 1957) 339—40; and, more recently, the sceptical treatment of T. PEKÁRY, Das Weihdatum des kapitolinischen Iupitertempels und Plinius N.H. 33.19, MDAI(R) 76 (1969) 307—12. For its connection with the date of the origin of the republic, F. DE MARTINO, Intorno all'origine della repubblica romana delle magistrature, ANRW I, 1 (1972) 219—21; R. BLOCH, Le départ des Étrusques de Rome selon l'annalistique et la dédicace du temple du Jupiter Capitolin, RHR 159 (1961) 141—56. R. WERNER, Der Beginn der römischen Republik. Historisch-chronologische Untersuchungen über die Anfangszeit der libera res publica (Munich 1963), collects the extensive literature. See further E. GJERSTAD, Discussions Concerning Early Rome, III, Historia 16 (1967) 264—7.

[4] Livy 1.55, with R. OGILVIE, A Commentary on Livy, Books 1—5 (Oxford 1965) ad loc. For an extremely perceptive discussion, see G. PICCALUGA, Terminus, Quaderni SMSR 9 (Rome 1974) 201—12.

[5] For the temple, E. GJERSTAD, Early Rome III, Fortifications, Domestic Architectures, Sanctuaries, Stratigraphic Excavations, Skrifter utgivna av Svenska Institutet i Rom 17,3 (Lund 1960) 168—90, supersedes all earlier studies. E. NASH, Pictorial Dictionary of Ancient Rome² (London 1968) s.v., collects the literature. However, problems remain; see more recently A. BOETHIUS, Nota sul Tempio Capitolino e su Vitruvio III, 3, 5, Arctos 5 (1967) 45—9; H. RIEMANN, Beiträge zur römischen Topographie, MDAI(R) 76 (1969) 110—21; and A. ALFÖLDI, Early Rome and the Latins (Ann Arbor 1965) 321—8 (rep. in: IDEM, Das frühe Rom und die Latiner [Darmstadt 1977] 284—289). ALFÖLDI and RIEMANN doubt the tradition of the monumentality of the sixth century structure.

[6] For the comparative size of the Capitoline temple, see A. BOETHIUS, in: A. BOETHIUS and J. WARD-PERKINS, Etruscan and Roman Architecture (Harmondsworth 1970) 42. For the building history of temple G at Selinus, see briefly I. BOVIO, Selinunte, in: Enciclopedia dell'Arte Antica VII (1966) 183.

Neither brought disrepute upon his great dynastic monument, the temple and cult of Jupiter Optimus Maximus. The first year of the republic witnessed M. Horatius Pulvillus dedicate the temple which would serve as the religious focus of Roman civic life. This is noteworthy rather than surprising. The parallel is not Ikhnaton and Akhetaton but rather Peisistratus and the cult of Athena on the Acropolis. The Age of Tyrants in the Greek world forms the proper institutional, as well as historical, context for the rule of the Tarquins and Servius Tullius at Rome.[7] The historical tradition drew a portrait of their characters and reigns which set them in strong contrast to their three immediate predecessors.[8] Like the Cypselids at Corinth and the Orthagorids at Sicyon,[9] their future kingship was divinely foretold by *omina imperii*.[10] Like Peisistratus at Athens,[11] political machinations and violence marked their seizure of power;[12] and like the Peisistratidai,[13] an act of violence precipitated their violent over-throw.[14] The parallel continues even to the attempt to return to power with foreign aid.[15] A false perspective has seen in these parallels cause to reject entirely the Roman historical tradition concerning the tyrants as mere fabrication spun out of models supplied by Greek historiography. The parallels are rather the legitimate consequences of similar economic and social conditions in an identical political context, the narrowly-based, clan-dominated city-state, occupying a limited territory of arable land and surrounded by aggressive neighboring states. Like the most successful of their Greek counterparts, the Roman tyrants sought to establish their rule upon a broad base of popular support, sponsoring public

[7] The following sketch of the historical context of the establishment of the Capitoline cult may seem naive in its reliance upon the portrait of the kings found in Roman historical tradition. I offer no apologies for it. Wholesale abandonment of the ancient tradition for modern hypothetical reconstructions will not bring us closer to the truth concerning early Roman institutions. A proper approach must combine a critical respect for the literary tradition with the evidence of archaeology and comparative history. Fundamental is re-cognition of the essential similarity of the social and political institutions of the Greek and Italic city states which characterized FUSTEL DE COULANGES' masterly 'La cité antique' (Paris 1888[12]). It would be out of place in so brief a discussion to attempt to survey the extensive modern literature on the history and institutions of the regal period. For the problems and earlier literature, see P. DE FRANCISCI, Primordia Civitatis, Pontif. Inst. Utriusque Iuris Stud. et Doc. 2 (Rome 1959). E. GJERSTAD, Innenpolitische u. militärische Organisation in frührömischer Zeit, ANRW I, 1 (1972) 136—88, touches upon the more important recent literature.

[8] Cf. the apt phrase of GJERSTAD: „Das usurpatorische Königtum der letzten drei Könige", ANRW I, 1 (1972) 166—69. Cf. T. GANTZ, The Tarquin Dynasty, Historia 24 (1975) 539—54; J. GAGÉ, La chute des Tarquins et les débuts de la république romaine (Paris 1976) 15—51.

[9] Herod. 5.92; Diod. 8.24.

[10] Livy 1.34; Dion. Hal. 3.47 (Tarquinius Priscus). Livy 1.41.3; Dion Hal. 4.4.2 (Servius Tullius).

[11] Herod. 1.59—64; Arist. Ath. Pol. 13—6.

[12] Livy 1.34—5, 41—2.

[13] Herod. 5.55—65; Thuc. 6.54—9; Arist. Ath. Pol. 18—9.

[14] Livy 1.57—60.

[15] Herod. 6.107; Livy 2.6, 10.

works programs and integrating into the state elements, such as yeoman hoplites and immigrants of whatever economic means, divorced from major civic rights under the earlier clan-based aristocratic state. This is the significance of the tradition of Tarquin's addition of one hundred new members to the Senate and of Servius' creation of the centuriate organization.[16] This latter sought to supersede the old political organization of the state by a new and more flexible conception of citizenship. Its timocratic organization and local tribes combine the major features of the Athenian reforms of Solon and Cleisthenes and sought the same inter-connected ends, weakening the political control of the traditional nobility, increasing the efficiency of the army, enfranchising the immigrants attracted to Rome by the new economic and political conditions brought by the tyranny, and giving more political power to these immigrants and to the yeoman hoplites.

The cult of Jupiter Optimus Maximus is the religious counterpart to the Servian constitutional reform. The traditional social organization, the *curia*, had religious as well as political functions; and in the early regal period, kinship determined membership in the religious as well as civic functions of the Roman state.[17] Under the new order, while the traditional gentilitial cults, like the po-litical organization of the *curiae*, were maintained, the worship of Jupiter Opti-mus Maximus offered a new pan-Roman divinity whose cult could serve as the religious focus for all elements in society. Although not his invention, the cult of Athena, carefully cultivated by the tyrant, served the same purpose for Peisi-stratus at Athens. Like the cult of Athena the worship of Jupiter Optimus Maxi-mus would endure after the expulsion of the tyrant and would continue to pro-vide the sacral foundations to the Roman commonwealth. In the republic, magistrates were elected by the people but could assume office only after confir-mation by Jupiter Optimus Maximus through the auspices.[18] In their magisterial oath, they swore by Jupiter and the Penates.[19] In the earliest period of the republic, consuls took office on the feast day of Jupiter Optimus Maximus, the ides of September. Even after the abandonment of this custom, the magisterial year began with a sacrifice to Jupiter and a meeting of the Senate in the Capitoline temple.[20] War, like every act of state, required the consent of Jupiter through

---

[16] Livy 1.35, 43.

[17] I am convinced that the passage of Laelius Felix ap. Gell. 15.27 implies that the *curiae* were based upon kinship; and this is the prevailing view. Cf. the literature in: F. DE MARTINO, Storia della costituzione romana I² (Naples 1958) 120–31; P. DE FRANCISCI, Primordia Civitatis 483–91, 572–83; and IDEM, La communità sociale e politica Romana primitiva, SDHI 22 (1956) 1–86; and GJERSTAD, ANRW I, 1 (1972) 147–53. A kinship basis has been denied. Cf. most recently A. MOMIGLIANO, An Interim Report on the Origins of Rome, JRS 53 (1963) 111; and R. PALMER, The Archaic Community of the Romans (Cam-bridge 1970) 67–75.

[18] Dion. Hal. 2.6.2; Cic. Div. 2.74.

[19] CIL I, 2, 582.

[20] The evidence for the beginning of the magisterial year in the early republic is collected by TH. MOMMSEN, Die römische Chronologie bis auf Caesar² (Berlin 1859) 86ff. See further, O. LEUZE, Die römische Jahrzählung (Tübingen 1909) 335–75; T. R. S. BROUGHTON, The Magistrates of the Roman Republic, Philological Monographs published by the American Philological Association 15 (New York 1951–2) II 637–8; and A. MICHELS,

the auspices interpreted by the augurs: *interpretes Iovis Optimi Maximi publici augures signis et auspiciis postea vidento.*[21] *Auspicium* and *imperium* were the twin pillars of the magistrate's power.[22] Only those magistrates who had the *maxima auspicia*, which were necessary to begin a war, had the right to celebrate a triumph. In the triumphal procession, the *triumphator* appeared, like a vice-gerent, bearing the *insignia* of Jupiter Optimus Maximus: *qui Iovis Optimi Maximi ornatu decoratus curru aurato per urbem vectus in Capitolium ascenderit.* The goal of the cavalcade was the temple of Jupiter Optimus Maximus, where the vicegerent dedicated the *spolia* to the true author of that victory which had augmented the power of the Roman People.[23] His election and his every state act having been confirmed by Jupiter Optimus Maximus, the magistrate of the Roman People was, in a very real sense, the representative of Jupiter on earth, carrying out his will in the service of the Roman commonwealth. However, this special relationship with Jupiter was not the sole prerogative of the magistrate nor did it belong to him by virtue of his personal charisma. It accrued to him only by virtue of his election by the Roman People. As a collective body, the Roman citizens stood under the patronage of Jupiter. Nowhere is this seen more clearly than in the custom that every Roman citizen, on the day on which he

The Calendar of the Roman Republic (Princeton 1967) 98. For the sacrifice to Jupiter and the meeting of the Senate *in Capitolio* in the later period, see TH. MOMMSEN, Römisches Staatsrecht³ (Leipzig 1887) 594–5. R. PALMER, Roman Religion and Roman Empire, Hanley Foundation Series 15, University of Pennsylvania (Philadelphia 1974) 140–2, discusses aspects of Jupiter worshipped on the Capitol.

[21] Cic. Leg. 2.8.20. Cf. Livy 1.36.6, 6.41.4; Cic. Div. 1.28.

[22] The development and meaning of *auspicium* is fully treated by P. CATALANO, Contributi allo studio del diritto augurale, Mem. Ist. Giurid. di Torino 107 (Turin 1960), with the critique of D. SABBATUCCI, SMSR 33 (1962) 129–53; cfr. also P. CATALANO, Aspetti spaziali del sistema giuridico-religioso romano. Mundus, templum, urbs, ager, Latium, Italia, ANRW II, 16, 1 (1978) 474–75. For full discussion and survey of the literature on the meaning and development of *imperium* and its relation to *auspicium*, see A. MAGDELAIN, Recherches sur l'imperium, Trav. et Rech. de la Fac. de Droit de Paris Sc. Hist. 12 (Paris 1968); R. COMBES, Imperator, Publ. de la Fac. des Lettres de Montpellier 26 (Paris 1966); and H. VERSNEL, Triumphus: An Inquiry into the Origin, Development, and Meaning of the Roman Triumph (Diss. Leiden 1970) 304–55.

[23] The quote regarding the *triumphator* is from Livy 10.7.10. VERSNEL, Triumphus, gives a critical survey of earlier discussions of the origin, development, and significance of the triumph. See the critique of VERSNEL by L. WARREN, Gnomon 46 (1974) 574–83; and her own contribution, EADEM, Roman Triumph and Etruscan Kings: The Changing Face of the Triumph, JRS 60 (1970) 49–66. More recently, see M. LEMOSSE, Les éléments techniques de l'ancien triomphe romain, ANRW I, 2 (1972) 442–53. Despite VERSNEL's somewhat caustic discussion, Triumphus 164–98, R. LAQUEUR's view of the triumph as an *honor deorum* and primarily a *voti solutio* (R. LAQUEUR, Über das Wesen des römischen Triumphs, Hermes 44 [1909] 215–36) remains extremely convincing. For Jupiter and *lustratio*, see J. GAGÉ, Les Quinctii, l'imperium capitolin et la règle du Champ de Mars, REL 52 (1974) 110–48. Cf. J. GAGÉ, Remarques sur le triomphe romain et sur ses deux principales origines, Revista de Historia 100 (1974) 1–28. Constitutional aspects are examined by J. RICHARDSON, The Triumph, the Praetors, and the Senate in the Early Second Century B.C., JRS 65 (1975) 50–63.

assumed the *toga virilis* and thus entered into the full rights of a citizen, offered sacrifice to Jupiter Optimus Maximus in the great Capitoline temple.[24]

Popular sovereignty was the ultimate consequence of the tyranny of the Peisistratidai at Athens and of the Tarquins and Servius Tullius at Rome; and into such a political framework the cults of Athena and Jupiter Optimus Maximus passed easily. Providing a sacral foundation for popular sovereignty under republics, they had served an analogous function under the tyrants, divine sanction for unconstitutional monarchy.[25] Tyrannies arose in archaic Greece and Italy as a response to a crisis, political, social, and economic, within the early city-state structure. The crisis was also, in a sense, spiritual. The early city-state rested upon the concept of blood relationship; kinship within the clan, brotherhood, and tribe provided the social nexus which held the political organization together. The traditional social nexus bent, even cracked, under a series of new and interrelated forces in the seventh and sixth centuries: increased capital and commerce, immigration, and the introduction of hoplite tactics with a concomitant transformation of the military structure of the state. The dictatorships, called forth by these crises in various city-states in Italy and Greece, could not find legitimization within the traditional order; and perforce they sought supernatural legitimization. The accession of Cypselus at Corinth was surrounded by tales of *omina imperii* by which Apollo at Delphi predestined his rule.[26] The stories of *omina imperii* seem to have circulated within the tyrant's own lifetime, representing his conscious cultivation of Delphic Apollo as a source of divine legitimization.[27] In the same way the story arose that the Lydian Gyges was forced to turn to Delphi for confirmation of his usurpation of kingship.[28] Although Delphi in no way sanctioned his rule, Peisistratus and his partisans made similar use of prophecy to give an aura of divine sanction to his seizure of power at Athens.[29] However, Peisistratus went beyond the vagueness of *omina imperii* and allowed himself to be represented quite literally as chosen by Athena to rule over her city. Having been expelled earlier and now seizing power for a second time, Peisistratus drove into the city accompanied by a statuesque beauty

[24] Serv. Ecl. 4.49.

[25] For the role of divine sanction in the early Greek tyrannies, see J. FEARS, Princeps A Diis Electus: The Divine Election of the Emperor as a Political Concept at Rome, Papers and Monographs of the American Academy at Rome 26 (Rome 1977) 29—43, with full bibliographical references. In the following brief discussion, references will be restricted largely to the ancient sources.

[26] Herod. 5.92; Diod. 8.24.

[27] For the view that the oracles are contemporary with Cypselus, see H. PARKE and D. WORMELL, The Delphic Oracle I (Oxford 1956) 114—25; W. FORREST, The First Sacred War, BCH 80 (1956) 47. This is denied by R. CRAHAY, La littérature oraculaire chez Hérodote, Bibl. de la Fac. de Philos. et Lettres de l'Université de Liège 138 (Paris 1956) 237—9; and H. BERVE, Die Tyrännis bei den Griechen II (Munich 1967) 522—3. Cf. W. DEN BOER, The Delphic Oracle Concerning Cypselus, Mnemosyne 4, 10 (1957) 339—40; E. WILL, Korinthiaka (Paris 1955) 451; S. OOST, Cypselus the Bacchiad, CPh 67 (1972) 18.

[28] Herod. 1.13.

[29] Herod. 1.62—3.

dressed in armor and by heralds urging the Athenians "to receive with honor Peisistratus, whom Athena honored above all other men and whom the goddess was bringing back to her citadel."[30] The elaboration of the Great Panathenaia, the Old Temple of Athena, and possibly the first issue of Athenian coinage bearing the portrait of Athena, all served as visual testimonies to the goddess who had bestowed power upon Peisistratus and who, like the tyrant, served as the focus of loyalty for all Athenians, regardless of ties of kinship and locale.[31]

Identical purposes and functions lay behind the Tarquins' cult of Jupiter Optimus Maximus at Rome, with its grandiose temple, its festival, the *ludi Romani*, and its tales of *omina imperii*.[32] The refusal of Terminus to abandon his place on the Capitoline and the discovery of a human head in the same spot foretold Rome's empire.[33] More to the point is the story, which possibly represents an early element in the tradition, that Jupiter had foretold the kingship of Tarquinius Priscus.[34] As Tarquin and Tanaquil stopped on the Janiculum on their journey to Rome, a great eagle carried away Tarquin's *pilleus* and, bearing it aloft, returned to place it gently upon his head, divine indication that Jupiter

---

[30] Herod. 1.60. Cf. Arist. Ath. Pol. 14.4; Cleidemus fr. 15; Val. Max. 1–2 ext. 2; Polyaenus 1.21.1. The story has been rejected as a mere legend by F. CORNELIUS, Die Tyrannis in Athen (Munich 1929) 41; P. URE, The Origin of Tyranny (Cambridge 1922) 60; F. SCHACHERMEYR, Peisistratos, RE XIX 1 (1937) 163; and, more recently, by V. EHRENBERG, From Solon to Socrates (London 1968) 400 n. 13. Its authenticity is rightly defended by, e.g., F. ADCOCK, The Persian Empire and the West. Chap. II: Athens under the Tyrannis, CAH IV (Cambridge 1926) 63; and BERVE (above n. 27) II 545. Herodotus' acceptance of the story and the inclusion of such details as the girl's name, her deme, and her father's name (in Cleidemus) also argue for the story's authenticity.

[31] For the interest of Peisistratus and his sons in the Greater Panathenaia, see J. DAVISON, Notes on the Panathenaea, JHS 78 (1958) 26–9; C. HIGNETT, A History of the Athenian Constitution (Oxford 1952) 330–1; BERVE (above n. 27) 551. For the modern literature on the old temple of Athena, see J. TRAVLOS, Pictorial Dictionary of Ancient Athens (New York–Washington 1971) 143. The dating to the reign of Peisistratus of the first issues portraying Athena was advanced by B. HEAD, Historia Numorum, A Manual of Greek Numismatics² (Oxford 1911) 368–9; and E. BABELON, Traité des monnaies grecques et romaines II (Paris 1907) 35; and was developed at length by C. SELTMAN, Athens, Its History and Coinage (Cambridge 1924) 48–52. More recent studies have argued for a later date. C KRAAY, The Archaic Owls of Athens: Classification and Chronology, NC 6, 16 (1956) 43–68, attempts to date the introduction of the owl to c. 525; an even later date, c. 510, is proposed by W. WALLACE, The Early Coinages of Athens and Euboia, NC 7, 6 (1966) 9–13; E. RAVEN, Problems of the Earliest Owls of Athens, in: C. KRAAY and G. JENKINS, Essays in Greek Coinage Presented to Stanley Robinson (Oxford 1968) 40–58; C. KRAAY, Archaic and Classical Greek Coinage (Berkeley 1976) 60–1.

[32] Livy 1.35. 9 attributes the establishment of the *ludi Romani* to Tarquinius Priscus. So too Cicero Rep. 2.20.36. Doubts have been raised but the tradition is rightly defended by SCHACHERMEYR, Tarquinius 6, RE IV A, 2 (1932) 2376. More recently, see W. QUINN-SCHOFIELD, Ludi Romani magnique varie appellati, Latomus 26 (1967) 96–103; VERSNEL, Triumphus 101–15, 255–70.

[33] Livy 1.55.

[34] Livy 1.34. 8–10; Dion. Hal. 3.47. 3–48.1. For the legend of the eagle and the *pilleus* of Tarquinius as an old element in the tradition, see R. OGILVIE, A Commentary on Livy, Books 1–5 (Oxford 1965) 413–4.

had chosen him for greatness. Tarquin was not alone among the petty dynasts of
Latium and Erutria in attempting to establish his tyranny upon a foundation of
divine sanction. Somewhat later, Thefarie Velianas of Caere erected at Pyrgi a
temple to Uni-Astarte, who had chosen him for kingship.[35]

Athena and Peisistratus, Juno and Thefarie Velianas, but Jupiter and
Tarquin. The Roman's choice and its contrast with that of the Athenian and the
Caeretan is not a matter for careless and easy assumptions.[36] Zeus-Jupiter represents the common Indo-European heritage of Greeks and the Latin-Faliscan
and Osco-Umbrian speakers of Italy. The divinity was early and easily equated
with the Etruscan Tinia. From the earliest period, Zeus-Jupiter is pre-eminently
the ruler, father, in the sense of master, of gods and men; and the same image
appears among the Etruscans. However, in not every Italic or Etruscan or
Greek city did Zeus rule as the peculiar patron divinity. Athena, not Zeus, ruled
the Acropolis and exercised her special patronage over her people. Juno, not
Tinia, ruled the *arx* at Veii and was divine patroness of Perusia and Falerii.[37]
Jupiter Latiaris served as the religious focus of the Latin League, like Poseidon
at Mycale for the Ionian League.[38] However, Jupiter was not the patron god of
every Latin city; Hercules enjoyed this distinction at Tibur, Juno Sospita at
Lanuvium.[39] Studies of the early cult of Jupiter at Rome and in Italy have
tended to concentrate upon his role as sky and weather god, while a search for

---

[35] This is based on a translation of the phrase *RSVBDY* in the Punic inscription from Pyrgi
as "[Astarte] has chosen him [Thefarie Velianas]." So J. HEURGON, The Inscriptions of
Pyrgi, JRS 56 (1966) 10—1; and, for the view of Velianas as the elect of Astarte-Uni,
A. PFIFFIG, Uni-Hera-Astarte, Österr. Akad. der Wiss., Phil.-hist. Kl., Denkschr. 88, 2
(Wien 1965) 30; and L. WARREN, Gnomon 46 (1974) 576 n. 5. J. FERRON, Un traité
d'alliance entre Caere et Carthage, ANRW I, 1 (1972) 189—216, admirably surveys the
literature on the tablets and their interpretation. For the character of the goddess, see
PALMER (above n. 20) 43—6.

[36] The complex recently excavated at Murlo suggests a secular structure, perhaps the residence of another of these petty dynasts. For the excavations, see E. NIELSEN and
K. PHILIPS, Bryn Mawr College Excavations in Tuscany, 1974, AJA 79 (1975) 357—66,
with references to the earlier literature, 357 n. 1. K. PHILLIPS, Poggio Civitate, Enciclopedia dell'Arte Antica, Supplemento (1973) 629, suggests a sanctuary or a civic complex
on the analogy of the Forum Romanum.

[37] Livy 5.21—22; Plut. Cam. 6.1 (Veii); App. B.C. 5.49 (Perusia); Ovid Am. 3.13.35, Fasti
6.49; Dion Hal. 1.21.2 (Falerii). Among Italic cities, Juno was the patron goddess at
Teanum Sidicinum (CIL I² 1573, X 4789—91) and Aeserina (CIL XI 2630). Cf. K. LATTE,
Römische Religionsgeschichte, Handbuch der Altertumswissenschaft 5,4 (Munich 1960)
166—7.

[38] For the cult of Jupiter Latiaris, the discussion of AUST, Juppiter, in: ROSCHER, Myth. Lex.
II, 1 (Leipzig 1890—1894, rep. Hildesheim 1966) 686—97, is still fundamental. The Latin
League itself is discussed in detail, with full bibliographical references, in: ALFÖLDI, Early
Rome and the Latins, passim (rep. in: IDEM, Das frühe Rom und die Latiner, passim).

[39] Macrobius Sat. 3.12.7; Serv. Aen. 8. 285; CIL XIV 3601, 3609, 3612, 3673, 3679, 3689
(Hercules at Tibur). For the cult of Juno Sospita at Lanuvium, see J. FEARS, The Coinage
of Q. Cornificius and Augural Symbolism on Late Republican Denarii, Historia 24 (1975)
594—604.

the origins of the triadic arrangement of the Capitoline cult has, at times,[40] over-shadowed the significance of the fact that Juno and Minerva were extremely minor partners in this association, a point clearly indicated by the official name of the temple *aedes Iovis Optimi Maximi*.[41] Jupiter was paramount on the Capi-toline, and he alone was patron of the Roman community. However, viewed without a priori assumptions there is no obvious reason why the Etruscan Tarquin or the nascent republic chose Jupiter as the central divinity in this new pan-Roman state cult. It was a portentous decision; and the question must be asked whether there is any light to be shed on this process by which the sky and weather god was transformed into the peculiar patron divinity of the Roman community and whether this evolution had its roots in the pre-Capitoline cult of Jupiter at Rome.

2. Fatherhood and Charisma: the Origins of the Capitoline Image of Jupiter

Little remains of the great edifice erected by comparative mythologists and philologists in the last century. However, this much remains fixed, the identity of the name of the highest god among the Greeks, the Romans, and the Aryan invaders of India: Zeus, Jupiter, Dyaus. Etymologically, the meaning of the common root is clear, "bright, shining," referring to the heavens as the source of light as well as to the day itself.[42] There is clear evidence for a conception of the Roman Jupiter as god of the bright sky. The ides of each month were sacred to him;[43] dedication dates of his temples generally fell upon the ides and

---

[40] The traditional view, based on Serv. Aen. 1.422 with Vitruv. 1.7.1, sought an Etruscan origin for the concept of a triad of divinities. So Wissowa RKR² 41; C. Thulin, Die etruskische Disziplin III, Göteborgs Högskolas Årsskrift 11/12 (Göteborg 1906) 43−4. However, the evidence for this is far from incontrovertible. For the lack of archaeological evidence, see L. Banti, Il culto del cosidetto 'tempio dell Apollo' a Veii e il problema delle triadi etrusco-italiche, Studi Etruschi 17 (1943) 187−224. Others have pointed to the triad of Zeus, Hera and Athena, at the federal sanctuary of Phokis (Paus 10.5.2), the sole Greek occurrence of such a triad of divinities, and suggested this as the model for the Capitoline Triad. Cf. F. Altheim, Römische Religionsgeschichte II (Berlin−Leipzig 1932) 59; G. Radke, Die Götter Altitaliens, Fontes et Commentationes 3 (Münster 1965) 158. Rome's alleged ties with Delphi in this early period are advanced to explain the choice of this rather obscure federal cult. According to T. Gantz, Divine Triads on an Archaic Etruscan Frieze Plaque, Studi Etruschi 39 (1971) 3−24, new light on this question may be shed by the representation of an assemblage of divinities on a recently discovered archaic Etruscan frieze plaque from Murlo near Sienna. However, for the moment, the non liquet of Latte, Römische Religionsgeschichte 151−2, and G. Dumézil, La religion romaine archaïque, Les Religions de l'Humanité 10 (Paris 1966) 305−6, still seems the wisest course.

[41] Livy 7.3.5; 40.51.3; 40.52.7; CIL III p. 846. See further the collection of material by Aust, Iuppiter, in: Roscher, Myth. Lex. II, 1, 720−1.

[42] See the comparative material in J. Pokorny, Indogermanisches etymologisches Wörter-buch I (Bern−Munich 1959) 183−6.

[43] Varro L.L. 6.29; Festus 187L; Ovid Fasti 1.56, 588; Macrobius Sat. 1.15.14. Johannes Lydus de Mensibus 3.10; Plutarch Quaest. rom. 24. Cf. A. Brelich, Iuppiter e le idus,

the two *epula Iovis* occurred on the ides of September and of November.[44]
Macrobius interpreted this in terms of Jupiter's role as 'giver of light', *lucis
auctor*; and the same conception lay behind the epithet *Lucetius* by which the Salii
invoked Jupiter.[45] 'Giver of light,' however, was only one aspect of Jupiter's
celestial *numen*; and the fact that Dyaus Pitar and Jupiter were homonymous
does not necessitate that they were also homologous. In the Vedic period,
Dyaus Pitar became increasingly remote, superseded by Varuna as sky god par
excellence and by Indra, god of the thunder which causes the rain to pour.[46]
The Roman Jupiter and the Greek Zeus were far more adaptable and enduring.
Indeed, so marked was the character of Zeus and Jupiter as *tempestatium divinarum potens* that it has been argued that the Indo-European sky god was totally
transformed into a weather god in Greece and Rome.[47] As *fulgur*, the Roman
Jupiter was the power which sent lightning.[48] Among both Greeks and Romans,
the thunderbolt was originally the pre-eminent attribute of Zeus and Jupiter;[49]

in: Ex Orbe Religionum, Stud. G. Widengren I, Studies in the History of Religions 21
(Leiden 1972) 299—306.

[44] The dedication day of the temple of Jupiter Optimus Maximus was 13 September, that of
Jupiter Victor was 13 April, that of Jupiter Invictus was 13 June, and that of Jupiter Stator
fell possibly on 13 January. The *epula Iovis* fell on 13 September and 13 November, while
the *ludi Capitolini* fell on 15 October. Summary of the evidence by AUST, in: ROSCHER,
Myth. Lex. II, 1, 654—56.

[45] Macrobius Sat. 1.15.

[46] Cf. J. GONDA, Die Religionen Indiens I, Die Religionen der Menschheit 11 (Stuttgart
1960) 94.

[47] LATTE, Römische Religionsgeschichte 79. Cf. NILSSON's remarks on Zeus, in: IDEM,
GGR³ I 391. For all aspects of the cult of Zeus and his image in the literature and philosophy
of Greece, see H. SCHWABL, Zeus, RE X A, 1 (1972) 253—76, and IDEM, RE Suppl. XV
(1978) 994—1481.

[48] The literary sources speak of Fulgur as the divinity which sends lightning by day,
Summanus as the power of lightning at night; Festus p. 254L: *Itaque Iovi Fulguri et
Summano fit quod diurna Iovis, Nocturna Summani Fulgura habentur.* Cf. Paulus p. 66;
Pliny N.H. 2.138; Augustine Civ. Dei. 4.23. The epigraphical evidence confirms this as a
matter of actual cult practice. Cf. CIL VI 206, 30879, 30880: *Fulgur Summanium
conditum.* However, it is generally thought that this distinction does not belong to the
earliest period. It is seen rather as the product of later speculation. Cf. LATTE, Römische
Religionsgeschichte 208—9; RADKE, Götter Altitaliens 157. According to Varro (L.L.
5.74) the cult of Summanus was established by Titus Tatius. Cf. Livy 32.29.1; Pliny N.H.
29.57. For the form *fulgur Summanium*, see A. MAIURI, Fulgur Conditum, o della
scoperta di un bidental a Pompei, Rend. Acc. Arch. Lett. e Belle Arti di Napoli 21 (1941)
68 n. 1; and C. PIETRANGELI, BMIR 13 (1942) 54. For Jupiter as Fulgur, see M. LEGLAY,
Fulgur conditu: un lieu consacré par la foudre en Grand Kabylie, Libyca 7 (1959)
101—19; R. SCHILLING, Iuppiter Fulgur, in: Mélanges de Philosophie, de Littérature et
d'Histoire Offerts à P. Boyancé, Coll. de l'École Franç. de Rome 22 (Paris 1974) 681—9;
R. PALMER, Jupiter Blaze, Gods of the Hills, and the Roman Topography of CIL VI
377, AJA 80 (1976) 47—9. For Summanus, see also S. WEINSTOCK, Summanus, RE IV A,
1 (1931) 897—9, arguing for an Etruscan origin; and C. KOCH, Der römische Juppiter,
Frankfurter Stud. zur Religion und Kultur der Ant. 14 (Frankfurt 1937) 101—3.

[49] A. COOK, Zeus II (Cambridge 1940) 1—833, collects the evidence. Jupiter bore the thunderbolt in his earliest cult statue at Rome, in the temple of Jupiter Optimus Maximus; cf. Ovid

and both people shared a common conviction that the welfare of the community depended upon the proper interpretation of the signs of the god[50]. At Athens, official interpreters expounded the *diosemeia*;[51] at Rome, certainly in the historical period, the augurs served as the interpreters to the Roman People of the will of Jupiter, manifested in heavenly signs like thunder, lightning, and the flight of birds.[52] In the *commentarii augurum* is found the proscription: *Iove tonante fulgurante comitia populi habere nefas*;[53] and we may well believe that this intimate dependence of the collective action of the Roman People upon the will of Jupiter Fulgur was characteristic of the earliest history of the Roman commonwealth.[54] The ancients also connected the epithet *Elicius* with Jupiter's role as thunderer.[55] It is more probable that it refers to his power to provide rain (*elicere aquam*) invoked in the ceremony of the *Aquaelicium*[56] and the later and distinct ceremony of the *Nudipedalia*.[57] A series of epithets, attested only in a later period, celebrated Jupiter's role as the giver of rain and general governor of the sky and weather: *Pluvialis*, *Imbricitor*, *Serenator*, and *Serenus*.[58]

Thus nothing could be clearer than the essential characteristic of Jupiter as a sky and weather god. However, by viewing him entirely in this fashion, we limit our understanding of the significance of his worship in the early Roman community. Among his earliest cults at Rome are those, particularly the *feriae Iovis* of the earliest calendar, which can not be easily derived from his status as

---

Fasti 1.201; Arnobius 6.25. Three centuries later the earliest full-figured representation of Jupiter on the Roman coinage (CRAWFORD no. 28) portrayed him with thunderbolt and sceptre.

[50] COOK, Zeus II 4–10.

[51] Pollux 8.124.

[52] Cicero Leg. 2.8.20: *Interpretes Iovis Optimi Maximi, publici augures, signis et auspiciis postea vidento*. In augural terminology a *signum ex caelo* was *auspicium maximum*, ranking as the most weighty of divine signs (Scholia Danielis Aen. 2.693; Dion. Hal. 2.5.5; Dio Cass. 38.13.3–4).

[53] Cic. Div. 2.18.42.

[54] For the literature on the institution of the auspices at Rome, see above n. 22. CATALANO's treatment is fundamental.

[55] For the fable, see Ovid Fasti 3. 285–392. Cf. Arnobius 5.1; Plutarch Numa 15; Pliny N.H. 2.140. Arnobius cites Valerius Antias as his source; Pliny gives Calpurnius Piso as his authority.

[56] For the ceremony of the *Aquaelicium*, Paulus p. 2L. For the *Lapis Manalis*, F. BÖMER, Der sogenannte Lapis manalis, ARW 33 (1936) 270–81. O. GILBERT, Geschichte und Topographie der Stadt Rom im Altertum (Leipzig 1883–90) II 154, seems originally to have made the suggestion. Despite the objections of M. MORGAN, Greek and Roman Rain-Gods and Rain Charms, TAPhA 32 (1900) 100, it has been generally accepted. Cf. AUST, in: ROSCHER, Myth. Lex. II, 1, 657–8; WISSOWA, RKR² 121 n. 5; LATTE, Römische Religionsgeschichte 79; DUMÉZIL, Rel. rom. 183.

[57] Petronius 44; Tertullian Apol. 40, 14, De ieiunio adversus psychicos 16.5. For the *Nudipedalia* as a quite separate ceremony from the *Aquaelicium*, see LATTE, Römische Religionsgeschichte 79.

[58] Apuleius De mundo 37; Anth. Lat. 395, 46 ed. RIESE; Tibullus 1.7.26; Statius Theb. 4.757; CIL VI 431; 433; IX 324; XI 6312. See further AUST, in: ROSCHER, Myth. Lex. II, 1, 750–52.

sky or weather god. Most importantly, neither theme appears in the epithet
which Tarquin chose to characterize his new pan-Roman cult of Jupiter: *Jupiter
Optimus Maximus*; and this very cult name may offer the clue to the process by
which the weather and sky god became divine king of the Romans and to the
significance of Tarquin's new cult. Jupiter Optimus Maximus, the name and title
evoke a dual image of the god as father and as charismatic preserver and augmenter of the Roman community. The simile was well known to Ennius (Ann.
v. 580 VAHL.) and represents among the earliest literary description of Jupiter:

> *divumque hominumque pater rex.*

The image itself belongs to the earliest stratum of the Roman cult. *Pater* is an
intrinsic part of the Latin name for Dion, the god of the bright sky, while the
concept of increase is the original significance of the epithet *optimus*. It is derived
from *ops* and has the same sense as in the original meaning of *optimae victimae*,
"endowed with a special, power-giving, fertilizing, dynamic energy."[59] Both
images are reflections onto the divine of the social and political order of the
human community. *Pater* points to the rigidly patriarchal social order of the early
Roman community; in its most profound and original sense *optimus* suggests the
fundamental concepts of the institution of sacral kingship.

The concept of Jupiter as *pater* clearly predates the Capitoline cult. Among
the Aryan invaders of India, the Greeks, and the Romans, Father is the most
common epithet of the great sky god. In Vedic and in Greek it stands as a
distinct epithet, *Dyaus Pitar*, *Zeus Pater*; in the Latin *Iuppiter* it has become an

---

[59] So rightly P. STEHOUWER, Étude sur Ops et Consus (Diss. Utrecht 1956) 76ff. See further,
A. ERNOUT and A. MEILLET, Dictionnaire étymologique de la langue latine³ (Paris 1951)
822—3; LEGLAY, Fulgur conditu 107. A. WALDE and J. B. HOFMANN, Lateinisches etymologisches Wörterbuch³ (Heidelberg 1954) 216—7; VERSNEL, Triumphus 306—13; and
especially J. MAROUZEAU, Iuppiter Optimus et Bona Dea, Eranos 54 (1956) 227—31;
IDEM, Sur le sens de Jovi Optumo, CRAI (1956) 347—8; IDEM, Compte Rendu des
Séances de la Société des Études Latines, Séance du Samedi 14 Janvier 1956, REL 34
(1956) 40—1. Other interpretations have been suggested. Pointing to the Homeric (Il.
2.412) *Zeu Kudiste Megiste*, LATTE, Römische Religionsgeschichte 151, suggests Greek
influence on the choice of cult titles. According to Cicero Dom. 57.144, Jupiter is called
Optimus propter beneficia et Maximus propter vim. R. SCHILLING argues that this 'ethical'
significance was the oldest meaning of the cult title (SCHILLING, À propos de l'expression
Iuppiter Optimus Maximus, in: Mél. N.I. Herescu, Acta Philologica 3, piae memoriae
N.I. Herescu [Rome 1964] 345—8). Earlier authors, e.g. W. FOWLER, The Religious Experience of the Roman People (London 1922) 238, and WISSOWA, RKR² 125, saw the title
as meant to elevate the Capitoline Jupiter above all other Jupiters in Latium. A. PARIENTE,
Optumus, Emerita 42 (1974) 111—20, would derive Jupiter's epithet *Optimus* from *ob*, in
its original sense of "before," hence, "first." RADKE, Götter Altitaliens 159, seeks to
revive, with adaptations, the view of TURCEWIČ (in a Russian article, Philologische Studien
und Notizen, summarized by J. LEZIUS, in: Wochenschrift für Klassische Philologie 24
[1907] 1225—26), based on Dig. 21.2.75 (*fundum uti optimus maximusque est*) and 50.16.
90 (*aedes uti optimae maximaeque sunt, tradere*), that the cult title indicates complete
freedom from any servitude.

intrinsic part of the name.[60] Moreover, it seems clear that the Italic people, like the Greeks, brought with them into their new homeland of Italy, not only the name of this great divinity, but also a conception of him as ruler embodied in the notion of *patria potestas*. The implication of the epithet Father is not generation but rather rule and dependence, the dependence of the human worshiper upon his divine protector who can supply his needs and protect him and under whose power he stands as one inferior in age and status.[61] Lactantius was near to the mark in writing:

> *Omnem Deum qui ab homine colitur, necesse est inter solennes ritus et precationes patrem nuncupari, non tantum honoris gratia, verum etiam rationis; quod et antiquior est homine, et quod vitam, salutem, victum praestat, ut pater. Itaque ut Iuppiter a precantibus pater vocatur . . .*[62]

Such a conception of divinity was natural to communities as strongly patriarchal as early Roman and Vedic society. In the patriarchal community of early Rome the father was supreme arbiter, exercising the power of life and death over the community. It was in this sense that the fathers of families came together to arbitrate a question of blood guilt in order to avoid the vendetta. The role of impartial arbiter to the community was an essential aspect of the power of the senatorial *patres*, to whom the auspices 'returned' during an interregnum and who, at this time, were responsible for arranging a new election and for governing in the meanwhile. In the early period, the father was supreme lawgiver to his family and represented it in its dealings with outsiders. This last is the significance of the title *pater* to designate the chief envoy of a fetial mission.[63]

---

[60] Of the roughly three hundred passages in Homer in which an epithet is given to Zeus, *patēr* is the choice in one hundred instances; cf. G. CALHOUN, Zeus the Father in Homer, TAPhA 66 (1935) 15 n. 30. On the sky god's fatherhood, see C. KERÉNYI, Zeus und Hera. Urbild des Vaters, des Gatten und der Frau, Studies in the History of Religions 20 (Leiden 1972) = IDEM, Zeus and Hera, Archetypal Image in Greek Religion 5, trans. C. HOLME (London 1976). Cf. H. G. GADAMER, Das Vaterbild in griechischem Denken, in: H. TELLENBACH, ed., Das Vaterbild in Mythos und Geschichte: Ägypten, Griechenland, Altes Testament, Neues Testament (Stuttgart 1976) 102–15.

[61] M. NILSSON, Vater Zeus, ARW 35 (1938) 156ff., rep. in: IDEM, Opuscula Selecta II, Skrifter utgivna av Svenska Institutet i Athen 2 (Lund 1952) 710ff., surveys the topic. F. DE COULANGES, La cité antique (Paris 1888¹², Librairie Hachette) 97, made this point concerning the meaning of *pater* in ancient cult titles; and it has long been accepted. See, e.g., A. VON DOMASZEWSKI, Abhandlungen zur römischen Religion (Leipzig 1909) 166; G. APPEL, De Romanorum precationibus, Religionsgeschichtliche Versuche und Vorarbeiten 7 (Giessen 1909) 102–3; L. PRELLER and H. JORDAN, Römische Mythologie (Berlin 1881–3) I, 155; and FOWLER, Religious Experience 155.

[62] Lact. Div. inst. 4.3.

[63] In general see T. MOMMSEN, Fabius und Diodor, in: IDEM, Römische Forschungen II (Berlin 1879) 249 n. 28; K. LATTE, Zwei Exkurse zum Römischen Staatsrecht, GGA 1,3 (1934) 66ff. (rep. in: IDEM, Kleine Schriften zu Religion, Recht, Literatur und Sprache der Griechen und Römer [Munich 1968] 347ff.). For the senatorial *patres*, see PALMER, Archaic Community of the Romans 197–202.

Certainly in this early period Jupiter was seen as the representative of the Roman community and as the source of its prosperity in dealing with foreigners. Primitive man throughout the world attributes to foreigners the possession of baleful power of an especial potency. Thus any relationship, of peace or war, conducted with foreigners must be surrounded by religio-magical precautions of a countervailing potency.[64] Bearing fire before invading armies is only one example which could be cited in ancient Greece.[65] In early Rome, as throughout Italy, a special group of priests, *fetiales*, conducted such relations with foreigners. The sphere of competence of the *fetiales* encompassed diplomacy (the attempt to obtain redress by peaceful means, *clarigatio*) as well as declaration of war and solemnization of peace. The character and implements of fetial ritual, for example the fire-hardened cornel spear, indicate that the institution was rooted very early in Italic history.[66] At Rome, in the historical period, the

---

[64] J. FRAZER's remarks on this, The Golden Bough³, The Dying God (London 1911–1927) III, 101–16, can still be read with profit. More comparative material is collected by P. HAMILTON-GRIERSON, Strangers, in: J. HASTINGS, ed., Encyclopaedia of Religion and Ethics XI (1920) 883–96. More recently, see, in general, H. WEBSTER, Taboo. A Sociological Study (London 1942) 230–6; and, for a specific case, O. RAUM, The Social Functions of Avoidances and Taboos among the Zulu, Monographien zur Völkerkunde 6 (Berlin–New York 1973) 114–5. Such taboos often co-exist with a rigid observance of the law of hospitality.

[65] Schol. Eur. Phoeniss. 1377 refers to a lighted torch thrown into the space, by men from both sides, before Greek armies joined battle, a rite which may be a relic of taboos on intercourse with strangers. These taboos were, of course, strongest at Sparta, which may suggest that they were more prevalent in an earlier period. Recent works on related topics in Greece tend to concentrate on the creation of institutions like *xenia* to facilitate intercourse with strangers. Cf. P. GAUTHIER, Symbola: les étrangers et la justice dans les cités grecques, Annales de l'Est publ. par l'Univ. de Nancy 2,42 (Nancy 1972) 17–61; F. GSCHNITZER, Proxenos, RE Suppl. XIII (1973) 638–43; and D. KIENAST, Presbeia, RE Suppl. XIII (1973) 581.

[66] For the *fetiales*, in addition to the treatments in general works such as SAMTER, Fetiales, RE VI (1909) 2259–2265; WISSOWA, RKR² 550ff.; and LATTE, Römische Religionsgeschichte 121ff., see J. BAYET, Le rite du fécial et le cornouiller magique, MEFR 52 (1935) 29–76, rep. in: IDEM, Croyances et rites dans la Rome antique (Paris 1971) 9–43, with the earlier literature; and A. HEUSS, Amicitia. Die völkerrechtlichen Grundlagen der römischen Außenpolitik in republikanischer Zeit, Klio Beiheft 18 (Leipzig 1933) 19–25. BAYET and HEUSS remain fundamental treatments of, respectively, the religious and the legal aspects of fetial ritual. A more recent survey is provided by OGILVIE, Livy 127ff. P. CATALANO, Linee del sistema sovrannazionale romano, Univ. di Torino, Mem. dell' Ist. Giuridico ser. 2, 119 (1965) 1ff., is an excellent introduction. See also L. HOLLAND, Janus and the Bridge, Papers and Monographs of the American Academy in Rome 21 (Rome 1961) 60–3. G. DUMÉZIL, Remarques sur le ius fétiale, REL 34 (1956) 93–111, discusses Indo-European parallels to Roman *ius fetiale*. H. LE BONNIEC, Aspects religieux de la guerre à Rome, in: J. BRISSON, Problèmes de la guerre à Rome, École Prat. des Hautes Études, VIᵉ Sec. Sc. Écon. et Soc., Centre de Recherch. Hist., Civilisation et Société 12 (Paris 1969) 103–4, provides a brief and undocumented survey. J. GAGÉ considers the problem of *hospes* and *ius fetiale*, GAGÉ, Diplomates inviolables ou magiciens de la Trêve?, Cahiers Internationaux de Sociologie 51 (1971) 252–62. See also K.-H. ZIEGLER, Das Völkerrecht der Römischen Republik, ANRW I,2 (1972) 82–108.

fetiales, while not technically priests of Jupiter, were intimately connected with him. Livy records the proceedings of the *clarigatio*: *Audi, Iuppiter, audite fines cuiuscumque gentis sunt, nominat, audiat fas; ego sum publicus nuntius populi Romani; iuste pieque legatus venio verbisque meis fides sit.* After a declaration of terms, Jupiter was again called to witness: *Si ego iniuste impieque illos homines illasque res dedier mihi exposco, tum patriae compotem me nunquam siris esse.*[67] If satisfactory restitution were not made after thirty days, the *pater patratus*, the fetial in charge of the embassy, declared:

> *Audi, Iuppiter et tu Iane Quirine diique omnes caelestes vosque terrestres vosque inferni audite; ego vos testor, populum illum — quicumque est, nominat — iniustum esse neque ius persolvere. Sed de istis rebus in patria maiores natu consulemus quo pacto ius nostrum adipiscamur.*[68]

Thus in fetial ritual, Jupiter appears as witness to the pious mission of the envoy of the Roman people and to the refusal of the enemy to make restitution. Indicative of the special role attributed to Jupiter in these relations with foreign communities is the fact that his name precedes Janus in the invocation. This is in contrast to the prayers at the ceremonies of *devotio*, *lustratio agri*, and the *piacula* of the Arval Brethren, in all of which the name of Janus precedes that of Jupiter.[69] Indeed, according to Cicero and others, Roman ritual prescribed that at all sacrifices Janus' name take first place in any full length invocation which addressed itself to all powers, great and small.[70] The fetial ritual is of course not a sacrifice. Jupiter is involved as witness and guarantor of the justness of the actions of the Roman community. In the same way, by the solemnization of peace the *pater patratus* invoked him as guarantor of the *fides* of the Roman people:

> *Audi, Iuppiter, audi, pater patrate populi Albani, audi tu, populus Albanus. Ut illa palam prima postrema ex illis tabulis cerave recitata sunt sine dolo malo, utique ea hic hodie rectissime intellecta sunt, illis legibus populus Romanus prior non deficiet; si prior defexit publico consilio dolo malo, tum ille dies, Iuppiter, populum Romanum sic ferito, ut ego hunc porcum hic hodie feriam; tantoque magis ferito, quanto magis potes pollesque.*[71]

Thus, in Livy's account, Jupiter is the only divinity called upon by the Roman envoys to sanction the treaty. His attribution of this practice to the regal period would not seem to be anachronistic. In Polybius' report of the oaths employed in the first treaty between Carthage and Rome, in the first year of the republic, Jupiter enjoys the same unique status.[72] It is a status which can

[67] Livy 1.32.6—7.
[68] Livy 1.32.9.
[69] Livy 8.9.6; Cato Agric. 134; Acta Frat. Arval. p. 144 ed. HENZEN.
[70] Cic. Nat. deor. 2.67; Ovid Fasti 1.171—72; Macrobius 1.9, Mart. 10.28; Arnobius 3.29; [Aurelius Victor] Origo Gentis Romanae 3.7.
[71] Livy 1.24.7.
[72] Polybius 3.25.6. WALBANK, A Historical Commentary on Polybius 351—53, is much the clearest statement of the problems involved in this passage. The problem of the treaty itself

not be explained summarily and entirely on the grounds of the sky god who sees all and thus punishes any breach of faith. In the Council Hall at Olympia, a statue of Zeus Horkios stood, by whom athletes, their relatives, and trainers swore to refrain from foul play at the games.[73] Elsewhere Zeus as guardian of oaths is a common literary and cult figure.[74] However, already in the 'Iliad,' Zeus is only one of a number of divinities invoked simultaneously in the ceremony of oath taking; and in the historical period in Greece international treaties were sanctioned by the invocation of the various patron divinities of the contracting states.[75] In the same way, Polybius records that in their treaties with Rome the Carthaginians swore by "their ancestral gods."[76] This comparative material is further indication that the unique status of Jupiter as sole guarantor of the treaty obligations of the Roman People points to a clear perception of him as the representative of the Roman commonwealth.

Furthermore, such a perception preceded the establishment of the cult of Jupiter Optimus Maximus. Fetial ritual was connected with the earlier cult of Jupiter Feretrius.[77] Roman tradition recognized that the cult of Jupiter Feretrius predated that of Jupiter Optimus Maximus.[78] No image of the divinity was to be found in the small shrine of Feretrius on the Capitoline. Instead men saw the image of Jupiter in the *silex* which was kept in the shrine, which was itself open to the heavens.[79] From this shrine of Jupiter Feretrius, the *fetiales* took *sceptrum*, *per quod iurarent, et lapidem silicem, quo foedus ferirent*.[80]

Jupiter Feretrius appears linked with Mars and Quirinus in a triad which clearly predates the establishment of the Capitoline Triad.[81] As Feretrius, Jupiter was the recipient of the *spolia opima*.[82] Jupiter Feretrius was not a war

is surveyed, with the earlier literature, by K.-E. PETZOLD, Die beiden ersten Römisch-karthagischen Verträge und das foedus Cassianum, ANRW I, 1 (1972) 364—411.

[73] Pausanias 5.24.9—11.

[74] COOK, Zeus II 722 n. 5, collects the passage. In general, see E. ZIEBARTH, De iureiurando in iure Graeco quaestiones (Göttingen 1892) 7,17ff.; and IDEM, Eid, RE V, 2 (1905) 2076ff.; L. OTT, Beiträge zur Kenntnis des griechischen Eides (Leipzig 1896) 39ff.; R. HIRZEL, Der Eid. Ein Beitrag zu seiner Geschichte (Leipzig 1902) 121ff., 145 n. 7, 147 n. 1, 155 n. 1; NILSSON, GGR³ I 139—42; E. SEIDL, Der Eid im ptolemäischen Recht (Diss. Munich 1929) 23—4; P. HERRMANN, Der römische Kaisereid, Hypomnemata 20 (Göttingen 1968) 45.

[75] Il. 3. 276—80, 19.258—60. For the historical period, see, e.g., SIG³ 526, 527. The material is fully collected in the works cited supra n. 74.

[76] Polybius 3.25.6.

[77] AUST, in: ROSCHER, Myth. Lex. II, 1, 674—79, collects the evidence. Cf. esp. Servius Aen. 12.206; Livy 1.24. See also HOLLAND, Janus and the Bridge 60 n. 33.

[78] Livy 1.10; Propertius 4.10; Dion. Hal. 2.34.4; Nepos Att. 20.3; Festus p. 302L; CIL I² p. 189. Cf. L. SPRINGER, The Cult and Temple of Jupiter Feretrius, CJ 50 (1954) 27—32.

[79] Servius Aen. 8.641.

[80] Paulus p. 81L.

[81] The fullest and most provocative discussion of this pre-Capitoline triad is DUMÉZIL, Rel. rom. 147—279.

[82] For the literary evidence, still very much worth reading are G. HERTZBERG, De spoliis opimis quaestio, Philologus 1 (1846) 331—9; and J. MARQUARDT, Römische Staatsverwal-

god; and it is misleading to speak of the development of an image of Jupiter Feretrius as a war god from his role as thunderer.[83] Jupiter Feretrius does not bring victory to the arms of the people. He rather receives the dedication of the *spolia opima*. Roman historical tradition saw in the institution of the *spolia opima* (the armor of a commander taken by a commander) the origins of the first temple at Rome.[84] Festus cites a *lex Numae* in which a distinction is made between *spolia opima, secunda, tertia*; and the ceremony is closely linked to the triad of Jupiter Feretrius, Mars, and Quirinus:

> *cuius auspicio classe procincta opima spolia capiuntur, Iovi Feretrio darier oporteat et bovem caedito, qui cepit aeris CC ⟨C⟩ . . . Secunda spolia, in Martis aram in campo solitaurilia utra voluerit caedito . . . Tertia spolia Ianui Quirino agnum marem caedito, C qui ceperit ex aere dato. Cuius auspicio capta, dis piaculum dato.*[85]

Numerous problems surround our account of the *spolia opima*. However, in its original significance, the ceremony was essentially magical, aimed at increasing the dynamic power of the community. The armor of the enemy commander is seen as especially potent, and like all such numinous implements it is filled with power which if used correctly can greatly benefit the community but if misused can be disastrous. Jupiter Feretrius could properly and beneficially channel this power. However, first a magically suitable vehicle must be found to transmit it safely into the sacred limits of the city. Such could be had only in the person of the Roman commander, whose own *mana* had been shown by his personal victory to be even stronger[86] than that of the enemy.

The very word *opima* suggests the fecundating aim of the ceremony. It is to be derived from *ops*; and it has the same significance in *spolia opima* as it did originally in *opimae victimae* "endowed with a special power-giving, fertilizing, dynamic energy." It is from this same root, that was to be drawn Jupiter's pre-eminent cult title at Rome: *Optimus*.[87] The image is one of Jupiter as the embodiment of that dynamic energy which preserves and nourishes the Roman com-

---

tung II, Handbuch der Römischen Alterthümer 5 (Berlin 1881–85) 580–1. More recently, see F. LAMMERT, Spolia RE III A,2 (1929) 1845–6; G. CH. PICARD, Les Trophées romaines, BEFAR 187 (Paris 1957) esp. 124–36; VERSNEL, Triumphus 306–13. Although serious reservations can be raised to VERSNEL's general approach to the Roman triumph, his interpretation of the *Spolia Opima* is convincing. See also WARREN, JRS 60 (1970) 53; A. PARIENTE, Opimus y la llamada lex de spoliis opimis, Emerita 42 (1974), 233–62.

[83] LATTE, Römische Religionsgeschichte 126, rightly doubts whether Jupiter Feretrius was conceived of as a war god in the earliest period. In general, see the apt comments of DUMÉZIL, Rel. rom. 172, 190–91; and LEMOSSE, ANRW I, 2 (1972) 446–47.

[84] Livy 1.10. For the actual date of the dedication of the temple, see L. SPRINGER, CJ 50 (1954/55) 27–32.

[85] Festus P. 204L. The best discussions of the value of Festus' account of this *lex* as a source are PICARD, Trophées romaines 131; and PARIENTE, Emerita 42 (1974) 233–62.

[86] Cf. VERSNEL, Triumphus 306–13.

[87] See above n. 59.

munity, protecting and representing it in relations with foreigners and causing it to be fertile and multiply.[88] It is this sense of 'increase' which lies behind the Latin *augere*.[89] In its original sense an *augurium* was a request for that *numen* which would increase the strength of the community of worshipers; and in an agrarian society like early Rome, the *augurium* would be aimed above all at obtaining the increased fertility of the land and its crops. It is to this world of the early Roman farmer that the rites of the *vernisera messalia auguria* belong. In the same way, it is indicative that among the *auguralia verba* there occur a number of phrases referring to perennial water supplies.[90]

The notion of 'increase' inherent in the ceremony of the *spolia opima* and in the cult title *optimus* permits the assumption that already in the regal period an intimate association existed between Jupiter, the act of the *augurium* and the augurs, *interpretes Iovis*. In private cult, Jupiter's association with fecundity was invoked in offerings to him (Jupiter Dapalis) before sowing and before harvest.[91] Epithets, most of them attested only in late sources, further suggest the significance of Jupiter's role as the nutritive force of the community: *Pecunia, Ruminus, Almus, Frugifer*.[92] More controversial is the significance of Jupiter's association with Liber. For WISSOWA, however, this association went back to the earliest period of Roman religion and was the product of this concept of Jupiter's dynamic fertilizing power, conveyed in the meaning of the word *liber* as "the one who assures fertility and increase."[93]

The image of Zeus as the guardian of fertility was well developed in Greece; and a similar concept lay behind the popular derivation of Jupiter's name from *iuvo quando mortales atque urbes beluasque omnis iuvat*. In late republican iconography Jupiter's thunderbolt and eagle are associated with cornucopiae and other symbols of fertility.

---

[88] Cf. W. PÖTSCHER, Flamen dialis, Mnemosyne 4,21 (1968) 233–34; and LEGLAY, Fulgur conditu 106–7.

[89] For the earlier literature, see H. WAGENVOORT, Roman Dynamism (Oxford 1947) 12 n. 1. More recent discussions include G. DUMÉZIL, Remarques sur augur, augustus, REL 35 (1957) 126; CATALANO, Contributi allo studio del diritto augurale I, 23–8.

[90] Cf. LATTE, Römische Religionsgeschichte 66–7.

[91] Cato Ag. 132, 134. So rightly, WISSOWA, RKR² 120.

[92] For *Almus* and *Ruminus*, cf. Augustine Civ. Dei 7.11; for *Frugifer*, CIL XII 336 and Apuleius De mundo 37; for *Pecunia*, Augustine Civ. Dei 7.12. For these epithets, see AUST, in: ROSCHER, Myth Lex. II, 1,658.

[93] WISSOWA, RKR² 120. This has been frequently doubted. See, e.g., LATTE, Römische Religionsgeschichte 70; RADKE, Götter Altitaliens 177; and F. BÖMER, Untersuchungen über die Religion der Sklaven in Griechenland und Rom, I, Die wichtigsten Kulte u. Religionen in Rom u. im latein. Westen, Abh. d. Geistes- u. Sozialwiss. Kl. d. Akad. Wiss. u. der Lit. in Mainz 1957, 7 (Wiesbaden 1957) 110–31 (484–505). However, in support of the view of WISSOWA, see AUST, in: ROSCHER, Myth. Lex. II, 1,661–65; and SCHUR, Liber Pater, RE XIII, 1 (1926) 68; and A. BRUHL, Liber Pater, BEFAR 175 (Paris 1953) 20–3. For the significance of Liber as « celui qui assure la naissance ou la croissance,» see also E. BENVENISTE, Liber et liberi, REL 14 (1936) 53.

Such a view of Jupiter offers the most consistent explanation of the taboos surrounding his special priest, the *flamen Dialis*.[94] Probably originally king as well as priest the *flamen Dialis* was a relic of sacral kingship at Rome. Embodying in his person the power of the god, the priest-king ensured the temporal prosperity of the community. This charismatic power flowed through him like an electric charge; and if proper care were not taken, it could be diminished with disastrous results for the community. Hence the elaborate set of sacral precautions, which were merely misunderstood relics in the historical period but which were originally intended to protect the sacred representative of Jupiter from magical forces which would diminish his life-giving power.[95] The prohibition on the use of iron and of horses indicates that the historical *flamen Dialis* preserved relics of Bronze-Age religio-political institutions. It may be that, in the earliest period, the priest king himself was divine; and the role of Jupiter may be secondary. What is significant is that, in the earliest recoverable phase of Roman religion, these taboos were associated with Jupiter's representative and thus provide further evidence for the image of Jupiter as the pre-eminent force securing the prosperity of the Roman community. He was the divine magistrate of the Roman People; his servant, the *flamen Dialis*, alone among Roman priests possessed the rights of a magistrate. The *flamen Dialis* was entitled to a *sella curulis* and to a seat in the Senate, and he wore the *toga praetexta*.[95a]

As the *rex Nemorensis* and the taboos of the *flamen Dialis* indicate, the institution of sacral kingship was at home in early Latium.[96] Predating the Capitoline cult, this image of Jupiter as sacral king, as the charismatic preserver and augmenter of the Roman community, is a reflection onto the divine of the social and political order of the human community. The same is true of the complementary image of Jupiter as father. The image of arbiter and augmenter come together clearly in the concept of Jupiter as Terminus, the *numen* which protects the frontiers of the Roman community and also the boundaries of the individual holdings of its own citizens. The disturber of a boundary stone became *Iovi sacer*; and the middle *cella* of the Capitoline temple encased a cult place of Terminus in the form of a boundary stone. The roof above it was

---

[94] Gellius N.A. 10.15; Plutarch Quaest. rom. 111.

[95] See, above all, the thorough and perceptive study of PÖTSCHER, Mnemosyne 4,21 (1968) 215—40. See further, A. BRELICH, Appunti sul flamen Dialis, ACD 8 (1972) 17—21; N. BOELS, Le statut religieux de la flaminica Dialis, REL 51 (1973) 77—100.

[95a] For the political privileges of the *flamen Dialis*, see Livy 1.20.2 (with OGILVIE [above n. 34] ad loc.) and 27.8.8; Festus 82L; Plut. Quaest. rom. 113. Cf. S. WEINSTOCK, Divus Julius (Oxford 1971) 307.

[96] The nature of early Roman kingship is, of course, extremely controversial. A detailed discussion of the questions, with bibliography, is offered by P. DE FRANCISCI, Primordia Civitatis (Rome 1959) 511—45. In particular, see E. MEYER, Römischer Staat und Staatsgedanke³ (Zurich 1975); S. MAZZARINO, Dalla monarchia allo stato romano (Catania 1949); U. COLI, Regnum, Studia et Documenta Historiae et Iuris 17 (Rome 1951); GJERSTAD, Early Rome V. The Written Sources, Skrifter utgivna av Svenska Institutet i Rom 17,5 (Lund 1973); and J. PRÉAUX, La sacralité du pouvoir royal à Rome, in: Le pouvoir et le sacré, Annales du Centre d'Étude des Religions 1 (Brussels 1962) 103—21.

open, pointing, like the very place in which it sat, to the intimate relationship between the sky father and the protection of the boundary stone.[97] It is a connection which appears clearly in the importance of the *pomerium* in augural ritual.[98]

The sacredness of the *pomerium* and the duty to expand it, both intimately connected with Jupiter, were vital aspects of the communal religion of the early Roman community.[99] Yet boundary stones can be divisive; and in the small agrarian community, disputes over the boundaries of individual holdings are a major source of internal friction between citizens. Hence the necessity to place the boundaries under the protection of the supreme arbiter. A second major potential source of discord is the marriage contract. As Jupiter guaranteed the contracts of the Roman People with foreigners, so he also guaranteed the marriage contract between fellow citizens. Notoriously exogamous, early Roman marriage of necessity involved relations between two *gentes*, each with its own *sacra*.[100] As Farreus, Jupiter was witness.[101] The ceremony of *confarreatio*, the earliest form of marriage, was presided over by the *flamen Dialis* and the *pontifex maximus*. The sacrifice involved a white sheep, the same animal sacrificed to Jupiter on the ides of each month and at the *Vinalia*. The

---

[97] Dion. Hal. 2.74.3; 3.69.5; Servius Aen. 9.446; Paulus p. 505L; Ovid Fasti 2.671—72. Wissowa, Terminus, in: Roscher, Myth. Lex. V (Leipzig 1916—24, rep. Hildesheim 1977) 381; Idem, RKR² 137, pointed to the prevailing interpretation of Terminus as an aspect of Jupiter: „*Ein staatlicher Vertreter aller Grenzsteine, der sich zu den zahllosen termini der Grundstücke ebenso verhält, wie die Vesta publica populi Romani zu den Herdstellen der einzelnen Häuser.*" See also A. Kirsop Lake, Lapis Capitolinus, CPh 31 (1936) 72; Latte, Römische Religionsgeschichte 80 n. 3; Dumézil, Rel. rom. 203—5; and Idem, Les dieux souverains des Indo-Européens (Paris 1977) 171—2. In a richly documented and persuasively argued study, Piccaluga (above n. 4) offers a fundamental reevaluation of the character of Terminus and of the relationship which existed between *termini*, Terminus, and Jupiter.

[98] For this relationship, see also Grom. Lat. I 350, 18. This is, of course, from the prophecy of Vegoia. For the date, see J. Heurgon, The Date of Vegoia's Prophecy, JRS 49 (1959) 42—45, who argues that it was composed shortly before 88 B.C. and reflects the hostility of the Etruscan aristocracy to the proposed reforms of M. Livius Drusus. More recently, W. Harris, Rome in Etruria and Umbria (Oxford 1971) 31—40, is skeptical of attempts to give the prophecy an exact date and emphasizes that in origin it was an Etruscan document and that most of it derives from that document. For an Etruscan source for the view of Jupiter as the author of the prevailing land system, see also R. Pettazzoni, La divinità suprema degli Etruschi, SMSR 4 (1928) 218—20; L. Zancan, Il frammento di Vegoia e il Novissimum Saeculum, A & R 3, 7 (1939) 212.

[99] Cf. the survey by A. von Blumenthal, Pomerium, RE XXI, 1 (1952) 1867—78, with the earlier literature, 1867—8. More recently see J. Gagé, La ligne pomériale et les catégoires sociales de la Rome primitive. À propos de l'origine des Poplifugia et des Nones Caprotines, RD 48 (1970) 5—27; and Holland, Janus and the Bridge 52—61.

[100] Plutarch Quaest. Rom. 289E.

[101] For *Farreus* as an epithet of Jupiter, see Gaius 1.112. The proper interpretation of this passage was first given by W. Studemund, Verhandlungen der Würzburger Philologenversammlung (1869) 25.

whole ceremony was in a sense dedicated to Jupiter.[102] As arbiter of the community as a whole, Jupiter could not be the special preserve of any particular *gens*, and there seems to be no direct evidence for Jupiter as a figure in any *sacra gentilicia*.[103]

This image of Jupiter as *pater* and *arbiter*, preserver and augmenter of the Roman community, may offer an insight into the seemingly curious role of Jupiter in the oldest Roman calendar. It is a problem which has proved strangely resilient to the traditional emphasis on Jupiter as a sky and/or weather god. In the earliest Roman calendar, the cult of Jupiter Optimus Maximus does not appear. The calendar thus predates the last period of the regal era at Rome. In it the ides of each month are sacred to Jupiter. Five other festivals are also designated as *feriae Iovis*: *Vinalia Rustica* (19 August), *Meditrinalia* (11 October), *Vinalia Priora* (23 April), a festival (almost certainly identical with the *Poplifugia*) falling on July 5, and another (perhaps identical with the *Larentalia*) on December 23. For Macrobius, the dedication of the ides to Jupiter was a function of the god's role as giver of light: *Hic dies . . . cuius lux non finitur cum solis occasu, sed splendorem diei et noctem continuat inlustrante luna*.[104] This speculative answer may not be the entire truth. Above all, the ides are the nights on which the moon is most prominent. In Celtic, Germanic, Slavonic, old Indian, and old Persian languages, the moon is masculine.[105] Regardless of whether this was ever the case among the early Italians, the dedication of the ides to Jupiter suggests an intimate connection between the divinity and the celestial body. Roman folk belief attributed to the moon great influence over the growth of plants and animals. As in Greece, the time of the full moon was the period of greatest dew fall, a phenomenon critical to the sustenance of plants, and an intimate relationship was seen between the moon and the provision of all moisture necessary for the growth of plants and animals.[106] Reference has

---

[102] Servius Georg. 1.31; Aen. 4. 374; Ulpian fr. 9; Gaius 1.112. See, in general, M. KASER, Das römische Privatrecht I, Handbuch der Altertumswissenschaft 10, 3,3 (Munich 1971) 76—7, with the earlier literature.

[103] For the significance of this, see KOCH, Juppiter 72—76. In view of the paucity of evidence concerning *gentilicia sacra* (cf. WISSOWA, RKR² 404 n. 4), this argument from silence should not be pushed too far. In the later republic, for example, the Aemilii regarded Jupiter as the father of the Aemilian gens; cf. Plut. Paul. 15.5, 17.5—6.

[104] Sat. 1.15.14—15.

[105] For speculation on the significance of this see H. USENER, Götternamen. Versuch einer Lehre von der religiösen Begriffsbildung (Bonn 1896) 36.

[106] The material is collected by ROSCHER, Mondgöttin, in: IDEM, Myth. Lex. II,2 (Leipzig 1894—97, rep. Hildesheim 1965) 3147—3163. See also E. TAVENNER, Roman Moon Lore, Washington University Studies (St. Louis 1920) 39—50; and IDEM, The Roman Farmer and the Moon, TAPhA 49 (1918) 67—82; and D. M. PIPPIDI, La lune dans les traditions romaines agricoles d'origine magique, RCl 1 (1929) 221—36, 344—68. For the cult of the moon in early Italy, see G. WISSOWA, Luna, RE XIII, 2 (1927) 1808—11; and C. KOCH, Gestirnverehrung im alten Italien, Frankfurter Stud. zur Rel. u. Kultur d. Antike 3 (Frankfurt 1933); and LATTE, Römische Religionsgeschichte 232. For a quite different view of Jupiter's association with the ides, see BRELICH (above n. 43) 299—306.

already been made to the connection of Jupiter with the provision of rain and other sources of water in augural rites and such ceremonies as the *Aquaelicium* and the *Nudipedalia*. A similar concept may lie behind this primeval association of Jupiter with the moon and its nutritive efficacy, which left its relic in the dedication of the full moon to the god.

In the oldest calendar three *feriae Iovis* were concerned with the production of wine. Jupiter's connection with the product of the vine is reflected clearly in the role of the *flamen Dialis*, who, *vindemiam auspicatus est*, cut the first grapes of the harvest.[107] Problems abound in regard to the three festivals, the *Vinalia Priora*, *Vinalia Rustica*, and the *Meditrinalia*.[108] This last was the day on which the must was drunk with the formula: *Novum vetus vinum bibo, novo veteri vino morbo medeor*. Like both *Vinalia* it was sacred to Jupiter.[109] Superficially at least, there is no reason why grapes should be of greater concern to a weather or sky god than other agricultural products.[110] In Greek cult, Zeus shows no such connection with the fruit of the vine. This points further to the fact that in these Roman festivals the concern is not with the grapes but with the product, wine. At the *Vinalia* libations of the new wine were poured out to Jupiter before the liquid was tasted by humans. At this point the wine was not yet called *vinum* but rather, for reasons of sacral caution, *calpar*.[111] The underlying concern in these rituals is with the magical potency of wine and in bringing this into proper relation with the community.[112] Among primitive man the sacral significance of wine is widespread.[113] With little imagination, the wine is viewed as the spirit and life force of the plant, as blood is to the body. In certain circumstances, the two fluids can be transposed, and, in particular, wine comes to be substituted for blood in cult functions. This no doubt accounts for its importance in rites of initiation. At Sparta bathing the newborn infant in wine

---

[107] Varro L.L. 6.16.

[108] For a survey of the problem, with the earlier literature, see W. EISENHUT, Vinalia, RE Suppl. X (1965) 1172–6; and DEGRASSI, II XIII, 2, 446–7. Much the best treatment of the question, thorough and perceptive, is R. SCHILLING, La religion romaine de Vénus depuis les origines jusqu'au temps d'Auguste, BEFAR 178 (Paris 1954) 97–155.

[109] Varro L.L. 6.21; Paulus p. 110L. Cf. EISENHUT 1176.

[110] Pace WISSOWA, RKR² 114–15; F. BÖMER, Juppiter und die römischen Weinfeste, RhM 90 (1941) 30–58; RADKE, Götter Altitaliens 157; LATTE, Römische Religionsgeschichte 75; EISENHUT (above n. 108) 1172–76, et al. It should, however, be noted that Pliny N.H. 18.284 expresses the same view. Nonetheless, SCHILLING, Vénus 97–115, is entirely convincing on this point.

[111] Festus p. 57L. Cf. Ovid Fasti 4.899–900; Pliny N.H. 18.287.

[112] For this view as the proper approach to an understanding of why wine festivals were sacred to Jupiter, see, briefly, H. ROSE, Religion in Greece and Rome (New York 1959, reprint with new introduction of IDEM, Ancient Greek Religion [London 1948]; and IDEM, Ancient Roman Religion [New York 1950] 241); J. BAYET, Histoire politique et psychologique de la religion romaine² (Paris 1973) 92; BRUHL, Liber Pater 19–20; DUMÉZIL, Rel. rom. 190; and especially SCHILLING, Vénus 124–55.

[113] See, in general, K. KIRCHER, Die sakrale Bedeutung des Weines im Altertum, Religionsgeschichtliche Versuche und Vorarbeiten 9,2 (Giessen 1910, rep. Berlin 1970); and SCHILLING, Vénus 131–7.

was the relic of such a rite.[114] The ritual and communal drinking of wine and/or blood is an important feature in initiations into brotherhood organizations.[115] The earliest socio-political organization at Rome, the *curia*, is best seen as such an organization, corresponding in this to the Athenian phratry.[116] Etymology points clearly to this interpretation, *curia* being derived from *co-viria*, i.e. a united body of men.[117] The *curiae* belonged to the earliest period of Roman social history as their connection with such festivals as the *Fornacalia* and the *Fordicidia* clearly indicates. As in other such brotherhoods in other cultures, each *curia* formed a closed corporation with its own cults and its own officers.[118] In such societies communal meals play an important role, and the meeting houses of the *curiae* at Rome were furnished with eating rooms in which the tables were spread for the gods with simple food in primitive earthenware dishes.[119] In the historical period at Rome, only slight traces remained of a ritual meal at the initiation of boys into Roman society.[120] However, in the very earliest period, the communal drinking of wine, perhaps as a substitute for blood, may have been the central element in the admission of a Roman youth into the ranks of citizens. However this may be, the key to the singularly important connection between Jupiter and the wine festivals in the early calendar is to be sought in the magical and sacral potency of wine and its role in the socio-religious rituals aimed at securing the fertility and incremental power of the primitive community of which Jupiter is the pre-eminent preserver and augmenter.[121] Nothing is known with certainty of the two other festivals of Jupiter in the oldest calendar, that which fell on July 5 and that which fell on December 23. Despite reservations, the former should be identified with the *Poplifugia*, the latter with the *Larentalia*.[122] The fanciful aetiological explanations offered for

---

[114] Cf. W. DEN BOER, Laconian Studies (Amsterdam 1954) 235—41.

[115] KIRCHER, Die sakrale Bedeutung 83—7.

[116] For the most recent and convincing treatment of a complex problem, see GJERSTAD, ANRW I,1 (1972) 147—53. For a different view and for a detailed discussion, see PALMER, Archaic Community of the Romans.

[117] Cf. PALMER, Archaic Community of the Romans 67.

[118] Dion. Hal. 2.7, 23; 2.50.5; 2.64.1; 2.65.4; Paulus p. 43 L; Servius Aen. 1.17; Varro L.L. 5.83, 6.46; Johannes Lydus Mag. 1.9; CIL VIII 1174.

[119] Dion. Hal. 2.23.

[120] Varro ap. Non. p. 108. Cf. H. WAGENVOORT, Initia Cereris, in: IDEM, Studies in Roman Literature, Culture and Religion (Leiden 1956) 150—68.

[121] So, rightly, SCHILLING, Vénus 124—55.

[122] Pace J. GAGÉ, RD 48 (1970) 13; and, earlier, W. OTTO, Iuno, Philologus 64 (1905) 189; and G. ROHDE, Die Kultsatzungen der röm. Pontifices, Religionsgeschichtliche Versuche und Vorarbeiten 25 (Berlin 1936) 96, the *Poplifugia* has generally and rightly been identified as a feast of Jupiter. R. MERKEL in his edition of Ovid's 'Fasti' (Berlin 1841) clviii ff. pointed to the identification on the basis of Cass. Dio 47.18.5, and he has been followed by, e.g., WISSOWA, RKR² 116; W. FOWLER, The Roman Festivals of the Period of the Republic (London 1899) 174—76; KOCH, Juppiter 92—97; H. ROSE, Two Roman Rites, CQ 28 (1934) 158; W. KRAUS, Poplifugia, RE XX,1 (1953) 74—78; DEGRASSI II XIII,2,477. By contrast it has been generally doubted that the *Larentalia* can be a festival of Jupiter, since it has been generally connected with a feast of the dead. Cf., e.g., WISSOWA, RKR²

the *Poplifugia* in antiquity reveal nothing more than that the meaning of the festival and of the word itself had wholly disappeared before the calendar began to be studied.[123] However, by its very name the *Poplifugia* suggests an intimate connection between Jupiter and the concept of the Roman *populus* whether conceived as the entire community or as the nation in arms. A proper understanding of the original significance of the *Poplifugia* may perhaps lie in viewing it as a ritual of initiation, a mock combat by which young males are admitted to the ranks of full citizens.[124] In this connection it is extremely important to note that an early and intimate cult relationship existed between Jupiter and Juventas. The *aedicula* of Juventas, ascribed to the period before the Capitoline temple, was built into that structure.[125] As the Capitoline Jupiter received a sacrifice from every Roman youth assuming the *toga virilis*, at the same time a tax was paid to *Juventas, dea novorum togatorum*.[126] In the earliest period Juventas was not an independent divinity; rather, like Terminus, Juventas was merely an aspect of Jupiter, marking his control over the entrance of new citizens into full membership into the community.[127] An equal number of problems is posed by the *Larentalia*. However, the most persuasive explanation would indeed connect it with Jupiter and interpret it as originally a festival in honor of the Mater Larum for the protection of the fields of the community.[128]

Perhaps no single point of view can convincingly explicate the role of Jupiter in the early Roman calendar. Nonetheless, it is possible to suggest that a partial answer may lie in a concept of Jupiter as preserver and augmenter of the Roman community, the embodiment of the dynamic energy which causes the community to prosper and safeguards the religio-social bonds which hold it together. This socio-political aspect would become the most characteristic feature of the Roman Jupiter in the historical period. For the early Roman, Jupiter was sky

---

116; THULIN, Larentalia, RE XII, 1 (1924) 805; A. VON BLUMENTHAL, Zur römischen Religion der archaischen Zeit, RhM 87 (1938) 275–77. Among those who have accepted the indentification of the *Larentalia*, G. RADKE, Acca Larentia und die Fratres Arvales, ANRW I, 2 (1972) 426–7; and LATTE, Römische Religionsgeschichte 92–94, doubt its original significance as a feast of the dead, while for KOCH, Juppiter 92–101, a connection of Jupiter with a festival of the dead is explicable as a relic of the chthonian aspect of the Italian Jupiter. Cf. DEGRASSI, II XIII, 544; and M. PALLOTTINO, Il culto degli antenati in Etruria ed una probabile equivalenza lessicale etrusco-latina, Studi Etruschi 26 (1958) 60.

[123] The various aetiological explanations centered upon the disappearance of Romulus (Dion. Hal. 2.56.5; Plutarch Romulus 29, Cam. 33), or an Etruscan or Latin attack in the wake of the Gallic sack (Macrobius Sat. 3.2.14; Varro L.L. 6.18; Plutarch Rom. 29, Cam. 33).

[124] So, although denying any connection with Jupiter, GAGÉ (above n. 99) 5–27.

[125] Dion. Hal. 3.69.5; Livy 5.54.7; Florus 1.7.8–9; Pliny N.H. 35.108.

[126] Dion. Hal. 4.15.5; Tertullian Ad nat. 2.11.

[127] The fullest treatment of Juventas is G. WISSOWA, Juventus, in: ROSCHER, Myth. Lex. II,1 (Leipzig 1890–1894, rep. Hildesheim 1965) 764–66. I have followed DUMÉZIL's stimulating and convincing interpretation: Rel. rom. 203–6. LATTE, Römische Religionsgeschichte 256 n. 1, among others, would reject it.

[128] LATTE, Römische Religionsgeschichte 92; and the full treatment of the problem by RADKE, ANRW I,2 (1972) 421–41.

god and weather god, but he was also king, preserver and augmenter of the Roman community; and this last aspect, embodied in the ephithet *Optimus*, was seminal for his future development. However, the seeds of this development already existed in the period before the establishment of the Capitoline cult of Jupiter Optimus Maximus. It is a development which presupposes a personal and concrete image of the divinity; and although the early Roman was wont to conceive of a multitude of incorporeal divine forces, it must not be forgotten that Latin possessed the word *deus*, which, with its cognates, is common to the Indo-European languages. In these as in Latin, *deiuos* and its derivatives represent an individualized being, personalized and fully constituted.[129] However we categorize the religion of the early Roman, he was fully capable of envisioning Jupiter as a divine king, who by his personal intervention could assure the prosperity of the Roman community. The establishment of the cult of Jupiter Optimus Maximus was a conscious political act; and in this too there may have been an earlier precedent. Early cults of Jupiter existed on the Esquiline, the Viminal, the Caelian and the Quirinal, all sites of early settlement.[130] The Quirinal was also the site of the Capitolium Vetus.[131] In this earliest period, the nutritive power of Jupiter and his role as arbiter and preserver of the Roman state were associated with the cult of Jupiter Feretrius, traditionally the oldest sanctuary at Rome and located on the Capitoline. In the same way, the Capitoline played an essential role in fetial and augural ritual.[132] There is no evidence for habitation on the Capitoline in this earliest period;[133] and the conjecture is plausible that the cult of Jupiter Feretrius, with its elevation of Jupiter to the role of chief god of the community, was a product of religio-political compromise. Perhaps during the period of 'Rome of the Four Regions', when the villages on the Palatine, Velia, Caelian, Esquiline, and Quirinal were united, there was a religious as well as a political compromise. Jupiter, a god common to the worship of all the villages, became the chief god and arbiter of the new community formed of separate villages and ethnic groups, Sabines and Latins. The compromise was reflected in the triadic arrangement which would continue to characterize the *flamines maiores*, Roman Jupiter as a dominant figure in a divine triad

---

[129] On this, contrast DUMÉZIL, Rel. rom. 44–5, and H. WAGENVOORT, Wesenszüge altrömischer Religion, ANRW I,2 (1972) 360–63.

[130] The *sacellum* of Jupiter Fagutalis lay on the Esquiline (Varro L.L. 5.152; Paulus p. 77L; Pliny N.H. 16.37; CIL VI 452). For Jupiter Viminus, see Varro L.L. 5.51; Festus p. 516L. For Jupiter Caelius, see CIL VI 334. For cult on the Quirinal, see Martial 5.22.4, 7.73.4.

[131] Varro L.L. 5.158. Cf. T. HACKENS, Capitolium Vetus, Bulletin de l'Institut Historique Belge de Rome 33 (Rome–Brussels–Paris 1961) 69–88.

[132] The *auguraculum* was, of course, on the *arx* (Verrius Flaccus ap. Paul. p. 17L: *Auguraculum appellabant antiqui, quam nos arcem dicimus, quod ibi augures publice auspicarentur*. Cf. Livy 1.18.6). So too the fetial *herbae* came from the *arx* (Livy 1.24. 4–6, 30.43.9). For the *auguraculum* at Rome, see most recently, A. MAGDELAIN, L'auguraculum de l'arx à Rome et dans d'autres villes, REL 47 (1969) 253–69.

[133] GJERSTAD, Early Rome III, 190–201, 206, argues that the Capitoline was not inhabited until the sixth century.

with the Latin Mars and the Sabine Quirinus.[134] A similar triad of Jupiter, Mars, and Vofionus existed at Umbrian Iguvium,[135] and such innovations in cult practice may have been a common product of political compromise between different elements in the various city-states of early Italy.

Thus by the late regal period, before the establishment of the Capitoline cult, the image of the Roman Jupiter as father and charismatic augmenter of the Roman community stood forth in the clearest colors, the product of the creative evolution of the Roman state and its institutions. The establishment of the cult of Jupiter Optimus Maximus under the Tarquins and its adoption by the nascent Roman republic represented the last stage in this development, creating a dynamic patron divinity, a divine image of power fully capable of reflecting the portentous evolution of the Roman commonwealth and its imperial mission.

III. The Evolving Image of Jupiter in the Later Roman Republic

1. Jupiter Victor and the Theology of Victory at Rome

In 295 B.C., the great victory at Sentinum was marked by the vow of a temple to Jupiter Victor by Q. Fabius Maximus.[136] Like Zeus Tropaios in Greece, Jupiter Feretrius and, later, Jupiter Optimus Maximus were clearly associated

---

[134] This view has frequently been advanced. See, most recently, GJERSTAD, Historia 16 (1967) 264; RADKE, Götter Altitaliens 158; and WAGENVOORT, Studies in Roman Literature, Culture and Religion 181.

   The arguments raised against it by J. POUCET are significant but not entirely decisive. See Recherches sur la légende sabine des origines de Rome, Univ. de Louvain, Rec. de Trav. d'Hist. et de Philos. 4,37 (Louvain-Kinshasa 1967) 22−70; together with a supplementary treatment of the term *collis Quirinalis* in: IDEM, L'importance du terme collis pour l'étude du développement urbain de la Rome archaïque, AC 36 (1967) 99−115; and, briefly, his treatment in: IDEM, Les Sabins aux origines de Rome, ANRW I,1 (1972) 104−5.

[135] Cf. G. DUMÉZIL, Remarques sur les dieux Grabouio− d'Iguvium, RPh 28 (1954) 225−34; and IDEM, Religion indo-européenne. Examen quelques critiques récentes, RHR 147 (1955) 265−7; R. BLOCH, Parenté entre religion de Rome et religion d'Ombrie: thèmes de recherches, REL 41 (1963) 115−22; A. PFIFFIG, Religio Iguvina, Österr. Akad. der Wiss., Phil.-hist. Kl., Denkschr. 84 (Vienna 1964) 11−31.

[136] Livy 10.29.14. G. LUGLI, Fontes ad topographiam veteris urbis romae pertinentes VIII (Rome 1962) 83−85, collects the sources. For the significance of the events surrounding the vow, contrast G. DUMÉZIL, La bataille de Sentinum, Annales: Economies, Sociétés, Civilisations 7 (1952) 145−55 (rep. with revisions in IDEM, Idées romaines [Paris 1969]) with J. BAYET, L'étrange omen de Sentinum et le celtisme en Italie, Hommages à A. Grenier, Collection Latomus 58 (Brussels 1962) 244−56. The location and dedication date of the *aedes Iovis Victoris* are uncertain. See, for the question of location, S. PLATNER and T. ASHBY, A Topographical Dictionary of Ancient Rome (London 1929) 306−07. For the dedication date, see BÖMER, Ovid II 261.

with the religio-magical aspects of warfare, battle, and victory.[137] Through the ceremonies of the erection of a trophy or the celebration of a triumph, their cults provided rituals by which the potent forces evoked by war could be safely channeled to the benefit of the community. In a sense, the cult of Jupiter Victor represents a development of this traditional association of Jupiter with victory in warfare. However, the circumstances of its introduction and its precise formulation bespeak the new political realities of Rome's struggle for dominion in Italy and, with it, the shaping of a new imperial ideology. It is not as sky and weather god, or even as war god, but rather as patron of the community that Zeus and Jupiter were intimately connected with the magic of warfare, one of the most critical collective acts of the primitive community.[138] For this reason Zeus was only one of various divinities which a particular community might invoke as gods of battle and triumph. *Nikephoros* and *Promachos* do not appear among his cult titles in Greece.[139] Both linguistically and conceptually the figure of Athena Nikephoros and Promachos offers the clearest parallel to the cults of Jupiter Victor, Jupiter Stator, and Jupiter Propugnator at Rome, guardian divinities who champion the cause of the commonwealth and who bring victory in war to their chosen people.

In the year following the consecration of the temple to Jupiter Victor, M. Atilius Regulus vowed a temple to Jupiter Stator.[140] The same year saw L. Postumius Megellus dedicate the first temple to Victoria at Rome, a structure on the Palatine, lying along side the Clivus Victoriae.[141] Earlier, in 296, Bellona,

---

[137] For Zeus Tropaius, see COOK, Zeus II, 110; E. FERHLE, Tropaios, in: ROSCHER, Myth. Lex. V (Leipzig 1916—1924, rep. Hildesheim—New York 1977) 1262—5; and PICARD, Trophées romaines 24—5. In general, for the literature and problems surrounding the significance of trophies and the triumph and their association respectively with Zeus and Jupiter, see most recently PICARD, Trophées romaines 14—136; VERSNEL, Triumphus; LEMOSSE, ANRW I,2 (1972) 442—53; and WARREN, Gnomon 46 (1974) 574—83.

[138] This point is made clearly by O. WASER, in: ROSCHER, Myth. Lex. VI, 691—2, and by LATTE, Römische Religionsgeschichte 126, and by DUMÉZIL, Rel. rom. 190—2.

[139] Cf. WASER, Zeus in: ROSCHER, Myth. Lex. VI (Leipzig—Berlin 1924—1937, rep. Hildesheim—New York 1977) 704, 707; and SCHWABL, Zeus, RE X A, 1 (1972) 340, 355.

[140] Livy 10.35.11, 37.15—16. Roman historical tradition traced the cult to Romulus; cf. Livy 1.12.6; Dion Hal. 2.50.3; Ovid Fasti 6.793; Cic. Catil. 1.33. In commenting on the dedication of the temple by M. Atilius Regulus, Livy notes: *ut Romulus ante voverat; sed fanum tantum, id est locus templo effatus, fuerat.* WISSOWA, RKR² 122—3; and AUST, in: ROSCHER, Myth. Lex. II,1, 682, accepted the possibility of an early *fanum* to Jupiter Stator. However, the tradition is rightly rejected by LATTE, Römische Religionsgeschichte 153 n. 5.

[141] Livy 10.33.9. LUGLI, Fontes VIII 103—106, collects the sources. The temple was begun at an earlier but uncertain date when Postumius Megellus was curule aedile; cf. MÜNZER, L. Postumius Megellus, RE XXII,1 (1953) 935. The tradition of a Romulean foundation of the cult of Victoria (Dion. Hal. 1.32.5; Plut. Rom. 24.5) is rightly rejected; cf. T. HÖLSCHER, Victoria Romana. Archäol. Untersuchungen zur Geschichte und Wesensart der röm. Siegesgöttin von den Anfängen bis zum Ende des 3. Jhrdts. (Mainz am Rhein 1967) 136.

closely identified with Victoria, received her first temple at Rome.[142] In 293, for
the first time, in celebration of their victories over the Samnites, those who had
been awarded crowns for heroism wore them at the games and the victors were
awarded palms, in accordance with Greek custom.[143] The theology of victory
had come to Rome from the Hellenistic East, and its introduction was marked
by a characteristic adaptation of the image of the Roman Jupiter.[144]

   In the eyes of their Greek subjects, the kingship of the Ptolemies and
Seleucids was neither territorial nor national but was rather a personal monarchy.
For the Greeks, Seleucus I was simply *Basileus Seleukos Nikator*, that is to say
Seleucus who was his own law and recognized no human authority above himself. In this context, then, understandably, the Diadochi, lacking national,
territorial, or dynastic claims, could base their rule only on right of conquest.[145]
The king was he who could be king and who testified to this ability by victory
on the field of battle. The entry on kingship in the 'Suda' recognizes this, stating
that "neither nature nor law gave kingship to men but rather the ability to lead
an army and to govern the commonwealth with understanding. Thus were
Philip and the successors of Alexander." The king was above all a soldier blessed
with divinely given good fortune; but the victory which gave him royal authority was not viewed in extralegal terms. Victory gave the conqueror legal right of
possession as well as divine sanction.[146] The theology of victory, the claim to
rule by virtue of victories gained in the field through the aid of patron deities,
was thus fundamental to the foundation of the successor kingdoms. Indeed the
establishment of these was in itself a witness to the validity of the theology of
victory, a concept basic to Near Eastern and Egyptian royal ideology and one
which had played an increasingly important role in later fifth and fourth century
Greece, culminating in Alexander's dramatic claim to rule the Persian empire in
virtue of his divinely granted victories over Darius.[147] The extermination of the
line of Alexander in 310 made it possible for the Diadochi to take the royal title.
However, as the first, Antigonus and Demetrius were hailed as kings only after
the naval victory at Salamis manifested the royal *eutychia* which qualified them
for kingship. Ptolemy became *basileus* only after his defeat of the invasion of
Antigonus. Similarly, Seleucus did not take the royal title until a victory in the

---

[142] Livy 10.19.17; Ovid Fasti 6.199—208. For the temple see, F. COARELLI, Il tempio di
   Bellona, BCAR 80 (1965—7) 37—72; and R. E. A. PALMER, The Neighborhood of Sullan
   Bellona at the Colline Gate, MEFR 87 (1975) 653.
[143] Livy 10.47.
[144] In a separate article in this same volume (ANRW II, 17,2), I treat the theology of victory
   at Rome.
[145] Cf. E. BIKERMAN, Institutions des Séleucides, Bibliothèque Archéologique et Historique
   26 (Paris 1938) 11—15.
[146] Xen. Cyrop. 7.5.73; Livy 34.57.7; Diod. 21.1.5; Polyb. 5.67.4, 28.1.4, 20.6, 18.51.4.
[147] Cf. Arr. 2.14. The earlier, pre-Hellenistic, history of the theology of victory in the Greek
   world is discussed in J. R. FEARS, The Theology of Victory at Rome: Approaches and
   Problems, below in this same volume (ANRW II, 17,2) ch. III. 1—2.

field certified his possession of divinely granted and victory-bearing charisma.[148] Tetradrachms of Lysimachus, issued after Ipsus, have on the obverse a portrait of the deified Alexander, gazing heavenward; the reverse proclaims Lysimachus as heir to Alexander's victory-giving *eutychia*, portraying Nike placing a victory wreath upon the name Lysimachus (Pl. I, 1).[149] In the same way, the circulation of tales of *omina imperii*, foreshadowing victory and the resultant kingship, clustered around such dynastic founders as Seleucus Nikator, whose very cognomen epitomizes the true basis of his kingship.[150]

The identical epithet distinguished the new cult of Jupiter Victor dedicated by Q. Fabius Maximus at the height of the great Samnite War in 295. In ideological aims, the introduction of the theology of victory at Rome corresponded entirely to contemporary developments in the nascent Hellenistic kingdoms. As Roman tradition recognized, the great Samnite War was a struggle for dominion over Italy. As Livy's Samnite spokesman said, "Let us decide, once and for all, whether Samnite or Roman is to govern Italy."[151] As fetial ritual indicates, from the earliest period Roman imperialism required justification.[152] The creation of an

---

[148] Cf. App. Syr. 54; Diod. 20.53.2—4; Justin 15.2.10; Plut. Dem. 17—8; Marmor Parium ep. 23. The evidence of the cuneiform documents in: A. SACHS and D. WISEMAN, A Babylonian King List of the Hellenistic Period, Iraq 16 (1954) 205; and A. AYMARD, Du nouveau sur la chronologie des Séleucides, REA 57 (1955) 105. In general, see BIKERMAN, Institutions des Séleucides 12; E. WILL, Histoire politique du monde hellénistique I, Ann. de L'Est publ. par l'Univ. de Nancy 30 (Nancy 1966) 59,64—6; G. COHEN, The Diadochi and the New Monarchies, Athenaeum n.s. 52 (1974) 177—9.

[149] B. HEAD, Historia Numorum² (Oxford 1911) 284. In general, see R. HADLEY, Deified Kingship and Propaganda Coinage in the Early Hellenistic Age (Diss. Univ. Pennsylvania 1964); and R. HADLEY, Royal Propaganda of Seleucus I and Lysimachus, JHS 94 (1974) 50—65; and IDEM, Seleucus, Dionysus, or Alexander, NC 7,14 (1974) 9—13.

[150] Diod. 19.90; App. Syr. 56; Justin 15.4; Plut. Dem. 29.1—2. Cf. R. HADLEY, Hieronymus of Cardia and Early Seleucid Mythology, Historia 18 (1969) 142—52.

[151] Livy 8.23.9. Livy's attribution of these sentiments may reflect the wisdom of hindsight; but it may also be that as early as the second Samnite war both Romans and Samnites had a conscious realization that their struggle was one for peninsular hegemony. See E. SALMON, Samnium and the Samnites (Cambridge 1967) 214.

[152] For a general discussion and a survey of the scholarship, see K.-H. ZIEGLER, ANRW I,2 (1972) 68—114; J. RICH, Declaring War in the Roman Republic in the Period of Transmarine Expansion, Collection Latomus 149 (Brussels 1976) 56—60.

The character of Roman imperialism has been the subject of a great deal of recent study. For discussion and literature, see W. HARRIS, War and Imperialism in Republican Rome (Oxford 1979). Specifically on religious aspects, see B. McBAIN, The Function of Public Prodigies and Their Expiations in Furthering the Aims of Roman Imperialism down to the Period of the Social War (Diss. Penn 1975). Other recent work which might be mentioned and which will provide reference to the literature includes R. WERNER, Das Problem des Imperialismus und die römische Ostpolitik im zweiten Jahrhundert v. Chr., ANRW I,1 (1972) 501—63; K. HOPKINS, Conquerors and Slaves, Sociological Studies in Roman History 1 (Cambridge 1977) 25—47; L. PERELLI, Punti di vista sull'imperialismo romano nel secondo secolo a.C., QS 3 (1976) 197—213; E. GABBA, Aspetti culturali dell'imperialismo romano, Athenaeum n.s. 65 (1977) 49—74; P. VEYNE, Y a-t-il eu un

imperium coterminus with Italy called forth a characteristic innovation, the Roman adaptation of the Hellenic concept of the theology of victory. The gods willed Rome's expansion, and they manifested this by granting Rome victories in the field. In the Hellenistic world, the numinous quality of victory adhered to the personality of the charismatic general and king, Alexandros Aniketos, Seleukos Nikator, and individual Ptolemies hailed as *Theoi Nikephoroi*. Roman victories, however, were not the product of a single charismatic individual; the *imperator*, under whose *imperium* and *auspicium* individual battles were won, received his acclaim in such ceremonies as the triumph, the *ovatio*, and the *triumphus in monte Albano*. However, the Roman commonwealth was rooted in a concept of collective political authority; its victories and its empire were the joint product of the Roman Senate and People. As earlier at Athens, the charisma of victory must be visualized as an attribute of the collective people or its divine patron. Hence arose the personification of Rome as a world-conquering Amazon, and hence the image and cult of Jupiter Victor.

The success of Roman arms confirmed this belief that Jupiter had willed victory and empire for the Roman People. An intimate personal union was forged between the concept of charismatic victory and Jupiter, divine king of the Roman People. In cult the personification of victory was assimilated to Jupiter. In the acts of the Arval Brethren, Jupiter Victor and Victoria are at times used interchangeably and, at another time, the two are joined together as a divine pair: *Iovi Victori bovem marem auratum et Victoriae bovem feminam auratam*.[153] This profound association of Jupiter and victory is also the theme which dominates the first extant representation of Jupiter in Roman art, a visual statement of the romanization of the theology of victory and its deep association with the cult of Jupiter. Rome's last issue of didrachms, the so-called *quadrigati* were first produced in 225 and continued to be struck in enormous bulk until 212. The obverse portrays a Janiform head of the Dioscuri; the reverse represents Jupiter in a quadriga driven by Victory. Jupiter holds a sceptre in his right hand, and with his left, he hurls a thunderbolt (Pl. I, 2). The first issue of *quadrigati* is rightly linked to the Gallic threat of 226 and the subsequent campaign of L. Aemilius Papus. The type then dominated the Roman coinage through the darkest period of the Punic War, ending a year before the captures of Syracuse, Capua, and the first issue of *denarii*.[154] The Roman prototype of the god in quadriga was the great image of Jupiter atop the pediment of the Capitoline temple, erected by the Ogulnii in 296 B.C. and believed to be intimately linked to the power of the Roman state.[155]

impérialisme romain, MEFR 87 (1975) 793–855; P. BRUNT, Laus Imperii, in: P. GARNSEY and C. WHITTAKER, Imperialism in the Ancient World (Cambridge 1978) 159–91; D. FLACH, Der sogenannte römische Imperialismus: Sein Verständnis im Wandel der neuzeitlichen Erfahrungswelt, HZ 222 (1976) 1–42.

[153] G. HENZEN, Acta. Frat. Arv. (Berlin 1874) pp. 86–7.

[154] The chronology is that of CRAWFORD 3–46. More recently, see W. STOECKLI, Bemerkungen zur Chronologie von Victoriat, Denar, Quinar und Sesterz, JNG 25 (1975) 73–90.

[155] Livy 10.23.12. Cf. H. MATTINGLY, The First Age of Roman Coinage, JRS 35 (1945) 73–4; and CRAWFORD 715 n.2. For the belief that the might of Rome was dependent upon

In Hesiod, Nike appears as the constant companion of Zeus, and the image of Nike driving the chariot of Zeus was a familiar theme in Greek art, particularly in portrayals of the Gigantomachy.[156] However, on the *quadrigati* Jupiter as victor appears as the Roman national badge, emblazoned by the legend ROMA. The obverse of the Dioscuri enforces this Roman national image of Jupiter Victor. At the most critical moment in the history of the infant republic, the sons of Jupiter, Castor and Pollux, championed the cause of Rome at Lake Regillus and then rode in haste to the Forum to announce the victory. Quite literally, the Dioscuri were the epiphany of Jupiter's victory-giving power and of his determination to preserve the republic.[157] The intimate connection of Jupiter and Victory was continued as a major numismatic theme on the *victoriatus*, introduced in 211 as part of the *denarius* system consisting of the *victoriatus, denarius,* and sextantal bronze. A laureate head of Jupiter decorates the obverse, while the reverse portrays Victory crowning a trophy (Pl. I, 3). The legend on the reverse reads ROMA.[158] The iconography is Greek. The laureate head of Zeus Hellanios appears on silver issues of Hicetas and the same obverse type was adopted by the Mamertines in Messana. The motif of Victory crowning a trophy appears, for example, on the reverse of issues of Agathocles and Seleucus (Pl. I, 4—5).[159] In fact, the imagery of these two neatly parallels that of the *victoriatus*. Persephone, the divine patroness of Sicily, appears on the obverse of the issue of Agathocles, while a portrait of Alexander Aniketos decorates the obverse of the Seleucid tetradrachms. As on the Roman *victoriatus*, victory is linked to the divine patron of the state. Together with the *denarius,* the *victoriatus* formed

the statue, see Festus pp. 340—1L. Servius Aen. 7.188; Plut. Pob. 13; Pliny NH 8.161, 28.16, 35.157. Cf. L. GERSCHEL, Structures augurales et tripartition fonctionnelle dans la pensée de l'ancienne Rome, Journal de Psychologie Normale et Pathologique (Janv.-Mars 1952) 58 ff.

[156] Theog. 383 ff. The evidence is summarized by HÖLSCHER, Victoria Romana 68—71. See also F. VIAN, Répertoire des gigantomachies figurées dans l'art grec et romain (Diss. Paris 1951) no. 392—4.

[157] Cicero ND 2.6, 3.11; Dion. Hal. 6.13; Florus 1.5.4; De Vir. Ill. 16; Val. Max. 1.8. 1; Frontinus Strat. 1.11. 8; Plut. Cor. 3; Paul 25. For the significance of the Dioscuri as a type, cf. CRAWFORD 715; and H. ZEHNACKER, Moneta: Recherches sur l'organisation et l'art des émissions monétaires de la République romaine (289—31 av. J. C.) BEFAR 222 (Paris 1973) I, 338—43. For the identification of the Dioscuri with the Penates Publici, see Dion. Hal. 1.68. 2 and CRAWFORD no. 312. For the significance of the archaic inscription from Lavinium, see F. CASTAGNOLI, Dedica arcaica lavinate a Castore e Polluce, SMSR 30 (1959) 109—17; R. SCHILLING, Les Castores romains à la lumière des traditions indo-européennes, in: Hommages à G. Dumézil, Collection Latomus 45 (Brussels 1960) 177—92; S. WEINSTOCK, Two Archaic Inscriptions from Latium, JRS 50 (1960) 112—18; ALFÖLDI, Early Rome and The Latins 268—71; and G. GALINSKY, Aeneas, Sicily and Rome, Princeton Monographs in Art and Archaeology 40 (Princeton 1969) 146 ff.

[158] Cf. CRAWFORD I, 3—46, esp. 7—8, 28.

[159] HEAD, Historia Numorum² 183, 156; 181, 757. Cf. R. THOMSEN, Early Roman Coinage I (Copenhagen 1957) 173—4. For the significance of the typology, cf. W. GROSS, Victoriatus, RE VIII A,2 (1958) 2555; and ZEHNACKER, Moneta I, 343—48, with the earlier literature. See further, FEARS, Theology of Victory, below in this same volume (ANRW II, 17,2) n. 162.

the Roman silver coinage in circulation during the heroic age of Rome's conquest of a Mediterranean empire, from the inception of the *denarius* system at the time of the capture of Syracuse until the lapse of the issue of *victoriati* in the 170's. The typology of the *denarius* completed that of the *victoriatus*, continuing the theme of Jupiter as the giver of victory to the Roman commonwealth. Until the first decade of the second century, the obverse head of Roma was consistently complemented by a reverse portraying the Dioscuri, sons of Zeus and saviour gods of Rome who, as at Lake Regillus, fought for Rome and continued to appear, manifestations of Zeus' victory-bearing power, to announce such great successes as Pydna (Pl. I, 6).[160] The same theme of Jupiter Victor was equally prominent on the brief issue of gold coinage struck during the period c. 211—207. The obverse type of Mars, divine sire of Rome, was complemented by a reverse of an eagle upon the thunderbolt.[161] In Ennius' 'Annales', Jupiter promises Mars that only one of his sons, Romulus, will rise to the stars as a divinity[162]. So too the coinage declares that Jupiter has willed victory for Rome alone.

As JOSEPH VOGT suggested, the belief in Rome's divine mission for world rule was born out of the desperate struggle with Carthage[163]. The political events, above all the inception of the Macedonian War immediately upon the conclusion of the Hannibalic War, bespeak a sense of 'manifest destiny,' and the ever-victorious march of Roman arms confirmed this belief that the gods had foreordained victory and empire for Rome.[164] This conviction of divine succor and imperative to conquest was crucial in persuading a reluctant Roman People to undertake the war with Philip of Macedon. As at other times during the Hannibalic War, in November of 201 an *epulum Iovis* was added to the plebeian games. His face reddened with *minium* as at a triumph, Jupiter lay on his couch at the feast of the outgoing plebeian magistrates. The practical advantages of conquest received emphasis with the distribution of African wheat, at a very low price, to the populace.[165] In March of the next year, on their first day of office, the consuls were directed by the Senate to sacrifice to such deities as they might select with a special prayer for the success of the projected war. Having examined the victims, the *haruspices* reported that the gods accepted the prayer and portended victory, triumph, and the extension of the frontiers of the Roman People: *renuntiassent consules rem divinam rite peractam esse et precationi annuisse deos haruspices*

---

[160] For the epiphany of the Dioscuri at Pydna, see Cicero ND 2.6; Val. Max. 1.8. 1; Pliny N. H. 7.86; Florus 1.28. 14. For their epiphany at Vercellae, see Florus 1.38. 19—21. For the identification of the obverse head as Roma, see CRAWFORD II, 721—5; and ZEHNACKER, Moneta I, 330—8, with full references to the earlier literature.

[161] CRAWFORD I, 28—9; and, for the typology, ZEHNACKER, Moneta I, 349—50. For the date, see also THOMSEN, Early Roman Coinage II, 243—319.

[162] Enn. Ann. 63—4 VAHL.

[163] J. VOGT, Vom Reichsgedanken der Römer (Leipzig 1942) 118—69.

[164] L. RADITSA, Bella Macedonica, ANRW I, 1 (1972) 564—76, surveys recent views of the second Macedonian War.

[165] Livy 31.4.

respondere laetaque extra fuisse et prolationem finium victoriamque et triumphum portendi . . .[166] When the People still doubted the wisdom of declaring war, the *consul* Sulpicius addressed them and, according to Livy, invoked the divine will to complement his political arguments: *Ite in suffragium, bene iuvantibus dis, et quae Patres censuerunt, vos iubete. Huius vobis sententiae non consul modo auctor est, sed etiam di immortales; qui mihi sacrificanti . . . laeta omnia prosperaque portendere.*[167] Finally convinced, the People voted for war; and the struggle began with consular vows of *ludi* and a special gift to Jupiter if the state should be whole and prosperous five years from that day.[168] The same divine sanctions were invoked to justify the war with Antiochus.[169]

Among the gifts dedicated to Jupiter to celebrate the triumph over Philip was a great statue of Jupiter Imperator brought from Macedonia by Flamininus and dedicated on the Capitoline: *Illud Flamininus ita ex aede sua sustulit ut in Capitolio, hoc est in terrestri domicilio Iovis, poneret.*[170] The action parallels the transportation to Rome of the statue of Victory at Tarentum almost a century earlier.[171] As in the ancient ceremony of *evocatio,* the charismatic image of the god had, by Roman invocation, abandoned his former people, their lands, their sanctuaries, their cities. Rome and its lands and sanctuaries would be more pleasing, would provide a proper home, and in turn would be nourished by the power of the god.[172] Victory and Jupiter Imperator as the personification of victory were quite literally brought to Rome by the action of Flamininus.

The imagery of the *victoriati* and *denarii* in this period confirmed the close association between Jupiter and Rome's mission of conquest. It was a theme which became a major element in the historical tradition. Jupiter's election of Rome for world rule was linked to the very establishment of his Capitoline temple. The stability and permanence of Rome was divinely portended in the refusal of Terminus, alone among the gods, to yield his shrine to the new cult. The discovery of a head with the features intact was a clear sign of the grandeur of Rome's empire and of the role of the Capitoline as the imperial citadel of the capital city of the world.[173] The theme received its most magisterial statement in Jupiter's speech to Venus in the 'Aeneid':

> *His ego nec metas rerum nec tempora pono:*
> *imperium sine fine dedi.*[174]

---

[166] Livy 31.5.

[167] Livy 31.7.

[168] Livy 31.8.

[169] Livy 36.1. FOWLER, Religious Experience 335–7, stresses the significance of these passages in Livy.

[170] Cic. Verr. 4.58.129.

[171] For the statue of victory from Tarentum, see most recently S. WEINSTOCK, Victoria, RE VIII A,2 (1958) 2512; PICARD, Trophées romaines 263–8; HÖLSCHER, Victoria Romana 6–17; and esp. H. POHLSANDER, Victory. The Story of a Statue, Historia 18 (1969) 588–601.

[172] Cf. Macrob. Sat. 3.9.7–8.

[173] Livy 1.55.

[174] Verg. Aen. 1.278–9.

In the 'Aeneid', Jupiter's promise is one of world rule, to be sure, but it is also one of civilizing power:

> aspera tum positis mitescent saecula bellis:
> cana Fides et Vesta, Remo cum fratre Quirinus
> iura dabunt; dirae ferro et compagibus artis
> claudentur Belli portae; Furor impius intus
> saeva sedens super arma et centum vinctus aënis
> post tergum nodis fremet horridus ore cruento.[175]

Like Jupiter Victor, the theme of the civilizing power of the Roman Jupiter was the product of a profound evolution and, again like Jupiter Victor, its development was of the greatest significance for the later role of Jupiter in the political ideology of the imperial age. As with the theology of victory, the major creative impulse came from Greece and the evolving image of Zeus in Greek literature and philosophy. Hesiod and Solon invoked Zeus as the guardian of social justice.[176] For Heraclitus, Zeus is the one primary being, who engenders and absorbs all things into himself. He is the universe as a unity, universal reason, law, and destiny.[177] In Aeschylus the universal power and justice of Zeus become twin attributes of the god or world ruler.[178] Developing this traditional image, the Stoics could give the name Zeus to the god of their pantheistic world view.[179] At times, almost all religious aspects were removed from the Stoic Zeus, as for example in Chrysippus' portrait of the god as mighty law, everlasting and eternal, which is our guide to life and which may be called Necessity, Fate, or the Everlasting Truth of Future Events.[180] However, for Cleanthes, in his magisterial hymn, this concept of the power and justice of Zeus evoked the deepest religious feelings:

"Greatest of the gods, eternal ruler of all things, Zeus, whose lawful government is over all. Man alone of all things can model himself upon god. The whole of the universe obeys the lead of Zeus and follows his will. All nature shudders beneath the might of his immortal thunderbolt; and by its majestic power Zeus has made one great law to rule in the universe, putting order into disorder, transforming love into hate. Zeus, giver of all things, save men from baneful ignorance and cleanse their souls. Father grant that men may discover that judgement and wisdom by which you govern all things. So honored he may truly honor you, for there is no

---

[175] Verg. Aen. 1.291—6.

[176] Hesiod Op. 27ff. Solon fr. 13 EDMONDS.

[177] Fr. 32 DIELS.

[178] Cf., e.g., Suppl. 90ff., 524ff.; Agam. 160ff., 355ff., 1563—4. In general for the evolving image of Dike in early Greek thought, see R. HIRZEL, Themis, Dike und Verwandtes (Leipzig 1907, rep. 1966); and H. LLOYD-JONES, The Justice of Zeus (Berkeley—Los Angeles—London 1971).

[179] Cf. M. POHLENZ, Die Stoa. Geschichte einer geistigen Bewegung³ (Göttingen 1964) 108—110; V. GOLDSCHMIDT, Le système stoïcien et l'idée de temps (Paris 1969) 79ff.

[180] SVF II fr. 937, 933, 1116, 1118, 1140, 1150.

reward greater than to sing the eternal praises of Zeus' rule over all things with justice and beneficence."[181]

This same pantheistic and moral conception of Zeus was basic to the theology of Panaetius and Posidonius, so important for the development of Stoicism at Rome.[182] Its impact is clear upon Cicero's image of Jupiter in 'De natura deorum.' Jupiter is truly *dominus rerum*, ruling all things with a nod, a deity omniscient and omnipotent. However, his power is used for good. The etymology of his name points to his role as 'helping father.'[183] The same is true of his epithets *Optimus Maximus*. Our ancestors, writes Cicero, were right to place *Optimus* ahead of *Maximus*, for universal beneficence is greater, or at least more permanent, than the possession of great wealth.[184]

Stoicism was not the only Greek philosophical current shaping the image of Jupiter in the later Republic. Long before Cicero, in the first extant lengthy literary portrait of Jupiter, Ennius described the great god in terms of the vision of Euhemerus.[185] Mortal not divine, Jupiter had come to world rule by a long and bloody path; having freed his father and mother from Titan, he restored kingship to his father. Predestined for rule by an *omen imperii*, he was betrayed by his own father, whom he was forced to drive into exile. Piety marked his attitude towards his grandfather and brother; beneficence charaterized his dealings with mankind. From Mount Olympus he dispersed law and inventions to aid the lot of man. Traveling around the world five times, he bequeathed to mortals laws and customs, the fruits of the earth and other blessings, binding to himself in friendship and hospitality the leaders of the peoples of every region. As a political allegory, the implications of Euhemerus' 'Holy History' complement the Stoic portrait of the world ruler as the beneficent king of mankind.

2. Jupiter and *Imperium* in the Later Republic

Thus under the influence of Rome's rise to world dominion and the concomitant cultural invasion of Hellenism the third and early second centuries saw the further evolution of the Roman Jupiter, an image combining Latin spirit with Greek subtlety, a warrior god who conquered to bring universal peace and

---

[181] SVF I fr. 537. There is an extensive literature on the 'Hymn to Zeus.' See esp. E. NEU-STADT, Der Zeushymnos des Kleanthes, Hermes 66 (1931) 387ff.; M. POHLENZ, Kleanthes' Zeushymnos, Hermes 75 (1940) 117ff. (rep. in: IDEM, Kleine Schriften [Hildesheim 1965] II, 87ff.); A. J. FESTUGIÈRE, La révélation d'Hermès Trismégiste II, Études Bibliques 31 (Paris 1949—54) 310ff. More recently, cf. M. TORTORELLI, Morfologia cleantea di Zeus, AAP 22 (1973) 327—42; A. JAMES, The Zeus Hymns of Cleanthes and Aratus, Antichthon 6 (1972) 28—38.

[182] Cf. POHLENZ, Stoa I 197—8, 233.

[183] Cicero ND 2.64.

[184] Cicero ND 2.64.

[185] Ennius' portrait of Jupiter, apart from the 'Holy History,' is briefly considered by DUMÉZIL, Rel. rom. 473—4.

prosperity. Withal, the god remained a Roman Jupiter, god of a chosen people called to world dominion:

> *tu regere imperio populos, Romane, memento*
> *(hae tibi erunt artes), pacisque imponere morem,*
> *parcere subiectis et debellare superbos.*[186]

Ennius' description of Jupiter in the 'Annales' as *divumque hominumque pater rex*[187] is manifestly patterned on the Homeric description of Zeus as father and lord of gods and men. But for Ennius, Jupiter is Rome's god; he stands on the Roman side:[188]

> *Non semper vestra evertit; nunc Iuppiter hac stat.*

Ennius' life spanned the rise of Rome to mistress of the Mediterranean world. Later generations saw in Scipio Africanus Maior the founder of Rome's world dominion, and Scipio's own career, like that of Ennius, represented a watershed in the history of Hellenistic cultural influences at Rome, including the sphere of political imagery. Verses of Ennius celebrated Scipio within the formula of Hellenistic panegyric which called for the widest possible geographic expanse for the hero's achievement:

> *A sole exoriente supra Maeotis paludes*
> *Nemo est qui factis aequiperare queat.*

The poet also dubbed his hero with the epithet *Invictus*, a panegyrical theme closely associated with Alexander in the Greek world. In the contemporary Hellenistic East it served as a royal epithet. At Rome, its association was with Jupiter and Hercules. Its attribution by Ennius to Scipio represents an early and major stage in the momentous process by which the theology of victory at Rome was 'personalized,' that is to say the charisma of victory was linked to the figure of the individual commander rather than to the supreme god of the community. The ultimate stage was the replacement of the god by the figure of the monarch as the source of those victories which ensured the commonwealth: Victoria Augusti. This was a development which lay far in the future of the Rome of Scipio and Ennius. Scipio rather presented himself as the representative of Jupiter, with whom he regularly communed in the Capitoline temple. Later tradition would represent him as the son of Jupiter, while his wax image was kept in the temple and thence carried to the funeral processions of the Cornelii. There was even a tradition that he had been voted, but refused to accept, the erection of his statue in the Capitoline temple and the honor of having his statue, garbed as *triumphator*, carried in the *pompa circensis* along with the images of the gods.[189]

---

[186] Verg. Aen. 6. 851–3. Cf. J. H. CROON, Die Ideologie des Marskultes unter dem Principat und ihre Vorgeschichte, below in this same volume (ANRW II, 17,1) 274.

[187] Enn. Ann. 580 VAHL.

[188] Enn. Ann. 258 VAHL.

[189] For Ennius' praise of Scipio, see Epig. 21–2; Scipio 3 VAHL. For *Invictus* as an epithet, see S. WEINSTOCK, Victor and Invictus, HThR 50 (1957) 211–47. For Scipio's conversations

The potential inherent in Scipio's personal association with Jupiter was not to be realized immediately.[190] His enormous prestige threatened the egalitarian working of the oligarchic government. His political disgrace was followed by the Senate's careful avoidance of great overseas commands. Symptomatically, as noted above, the imagery of the contemporary coinage proclaimed the association of Roman victory with the supreme god of the commonwealth. The intimate association of Jupiter with the *imperium* of the *res publica romana* continued to be a major theme on the Roman coinage for a generation after the destruction of Carthage removed the last external threat to Rome's dominion. First in 144 B.C. was the monotonous typology of the *denarius*, Roma, Dioscuri and Luna, broken by a new reverse type, Jupiter in a quadriga holding sceptre and reins in his left hand and hurling thunderbolt with his right hand (Pl. II, 7).[191] Over the next half century the increasingly variegated typology of the Roman *denarii* were dominated by the theme of triumph. Of the well over one hundred reverse types issued in the period, only a handful deal, in any sense, with peaceful themes. War and triumph are the almost exclusive concern of the numismatic symbolism. Within this, by far the dominant types are Victory, generally in triumphal chariot or crowning a trophy, and Jupiter in a quadriga. Sceptre, thunderbolt, and regalia of triumph are the attributes of the supreme god of the Romans, whose ornaments were worn by the *triumphator*.[192] On the issue

with Jupiter in the Capitoline temple, Polyb. 10.5; App. Iber. 23. For his divine descent, see Livy 26.19. 7; Gell. NA 6.1. 2–3; Sil. Ital. 13. 637ff. For the other aspects of his association with Jupiter mentioned in the text, see Val. Max. 8.15. 1; Livy 38.56. 12. T. MOMMSEN, Die Scipionenprozesse, in: IDEM, Römische Forschungen II (Berlin 1879) 502ff. (= first publ. in: Hermes 1 [1866] 161–216), argued that the list of honors in Livy was the invention of an anti-Caesarean pamphlet; cf. E. MEYER, Caesars Monarchie und das Principat des Pompejus. Innere Geschichte Roms von 66–44 v. Chr.² (Stuttgart 1918, rep. Darmstadt 1974) 531ff.; R. HAYWOOD, Studies on Scipio Africanus (Diss. Johns Hopkins 1932, pub. Baltimore 1933) 16ff.; W. HOFFMANN, Livius und der zweite punische Krieg, Hermes Einzelschriften 8 (Berlin 1942) 77; F. WALBANK, The Scipionic Legend, PCPhS n.s. 13 (1967) 56; WEINSTOCK, Divus Julius 36.

190 The association of Jupiter and Scipio was only one aspect in the charismatic elements which surrounded Africanus, his career, and legend. See further, E. MEYER, Kaiser Augustus, in: IDEM, Kleine Schriften I² (Halle 1924) 423–74 (= first publ. in: HZ 91 [1903] 385ff.); R. LAQUEUR, Scipio Africanus und die Eroberung von Neu-Karthago, Hermes 56 (1921) 131–225; W. SCHUR, Scipio Africanus und die Begründung der römischen Weltherrschaft (Leipzig 1927) 95–105; HAYWOOD, Studies on Scipio Africanus 90–2; HOFFMANN, Livius 71–102; C. J. CLASSEN, Gottmenschentum in der römischen Republik, Gymnasium 70 (1963) 315–21; WALBANK, PCPhS n.s. 13 (1967) 54–69; H. SCULLARD, Scipio Africanus: Soldier and Politician (London 1970) 18–23; R. ÉTIENNE, Le culte impérial dans la péninsule ibérique d'Auguste à Dioclétien, BEFAR 191 (Paris 1958) 85–92; PALMER (above n. 20) 141–2; R. SEGUIN, La religion de Scipion l'Africain, Latomus 33 (1974) 3–21.

191 CRAWFORD no. 221.

192 The relevant texts are Livy 10.7. 10; Juv. 10. 36–43; Suet. Aug. 94; Tert. Coron. 13.1; Pliny NH 33.111. For discussion of the problems and a survey of the extensive scholarship, see VERSNEL, Triumphus 56–93; and WARREN, JRS 60 (1970) 57–62; and EADEM, Gnomon 46 (1974) 574–83.

of C. Metellus in 125 B.C. the chariot is drawn by elephants, the heraldic badge
of the Metelli. A flying Victory crowns Jupiter (Pl. II, 8).[193] It will be recalled that
after his triumph in 146 B.C., Q. Caecilius Metellus Macedonicus dedicated a
second temple of Jupiter Stator at Rome.[194] Other issues of triumphant Jupiter in
this period may have been intended to evoke obliquely the military successes of the
moneyer's family. However, together with the consistent obverse type of Roma,
the message is equally a broad celebration of Rome's military dominion in a
period of almost constant military action against Celtiberians, Ligurians, and
Gauls. Victory is the predominant image but at least one type suggests a higher
purpose. Zeus warred against the Titans for a just cause; and his victory
was one of civilization over chaos.[195] The symbolism of an issue of Cn. Cornelius Sisenna rather explicitly linked Rome to the civilizing mission of Jupiter.
The helmeted head of Roma appears on the obverse; on the reverse Jupiter is
represented in a quadriga, holding a sceptre in his left hand and hurling the
thunderbolt with his right. On either side is a star; above is a head of Sol and a
crescent moon. Below trampled by Jupiter is an anguipede giant-demon (Pl.
II, 9).[196] The theme, enforced by the astral symbolism, is the external triumph of
the Roman god over the forces of chaos. The coin was struck during the period of
the great Gallic threat which began in 125 B.C. with the campaign of Flaccus, the
original aim of which was the defence of Massilia. On the great altar of Zeus at
Pergamum, the Gigantomachy symbolized the Attalid defense of Hellenism
against Celtic barbarism. Rome, through her god Jupiter, appears in the same guise
on the *denarii* of Cn. Cornelius Sisenna. Thus although the theme of victory dominates the numismatic typology of the last half of the second century, its significance was not a limited and brutal celebration of militarism. The representation
of Jupiter in quadriga hurling thunderbolts was closely associated with the Gigantomachy; and its frequent repetition on the coinage of the great period of Celti-
berian and Gallic wars (144–100 B.C.) may also be interpreted as symbolic of a
higher purpose of such warfare, the protection and spread of civilization, law,
and peace. Cleanthes hymned Zeus' power to bring order out of chaos, to trans-
form hate into love, and to unite all things under universal justice.[197] This exalted Stoic image of Zeus may not have been without effect upon the conception of the Roman Jupiter held by the aristocratic moneyers of the later half

---

[193] CRAWFORD no. 269. For the elephant's head on earlier issues of Caecilii Metelli, see CRAW-
FORD no. 262; and HEAD, Historia Numorum² 467. The reference was to the victory of
L. Caecilius Metellus at Panormus and his capture of Hasdrubal's elephants; cf. Polybius
1.40. 6–16.

[194] Vitr. 3.1.5; Macrob. Sat. 3.4.2.

[195] Cf. F. VIAN, La guerre des géants: le mythe avant l'époque hellénistique, Études et Commentaires 11 (Paris 1952); and, J. H. OLIVER, Demokratia, the Gods, and the Free World
(Baltimore 1960) 121–69.

[196] CRAWFORD no. 310. For the identification and significance of the anguipede figure, cf.
F. GOETHERT, Summanus, MDAI(R) 55 (1940) 233–6; and L. CURTIUS, Redeat narratio,
MDAI 4 (1951) 10–34, with the remarks of CRAWFORD pp. 318–9.

[197] SVF I fr. 537.

of the second century B.C., for it was in that very period that Stoicism began to exert its influence upon Roman political conceptions.[198]

Peace, order and prosperity flowed from Jupiter's victory over the Giants. The same result, the coins would say, marked the triumph of Roman arms. An issue of the same period, portrays on the reverse a cornucopiae superimposed on a thunderbolt, and surrounded by a wreath composed of ears of barley and wheat and of assorted fruits (Pl. II, 10).[199] *Frugifer* was among the epithets of Jupiter at Rome;[200] and a common etymology, already known to Ennius, associated his name with rejuvenation: *Iupiter . . . mortales atque urbes beluasque omnis iuvat.*[201] Furthermore, in astrological symbolism, the star of Jupiter was thought to bring fortune and health to mankind, a theme thoroughly familiar in the Rome of Cicero.[202]

His realm is infinitely wider, his actions carried out on a world-wide scale; but the image of Jupiter as champion and nourisher of the Roman commonwealth remained as vivid as in the early regal period.

3. Jupiter and the Roman Revolution

Cicero was well aware of Jupiter's universal benevolence but was equally convinced of Jupiter's pre-eminent concern for the Roman commonwealth and its institutions. For Cicero, titles like *Optimus Maximus, Stator, Hospitalis,* and *Salutaris,* indicate that the safety of the entire human race lies in Jupiter's hands.[203] The temples of the universal saviour are everywhere, but his earthly dwelling is the Capitoline.[204] The Roman commonwealth and its institutions are his special concern, and he sanctions those actions which preserve the Roman state. To those who ask by what law did Caius Cassius try to keep Dolabella out of Syria, Cicero answers "By that law which Jupiter has sanctioned, that all things salutary for the state should be held as lawful (*legitima*) and right (*iusta*), for law is nothing other than a principle of right derived from the divine will, commanding

---

[198] For the introduction and adaptation of Stoicism at Rome, see, among recent treatments, P. BOYANCÉ, Le stoïcisme à Rome, Association G. Budé, Actes du VIIe Congrès 1963 (Paris 1964) 218—55; A. ASTIN, Scipio Aemilianus (Oxford 1967) 294; and, with a survey of scholarship, G. VERBEKE, Le Stoïcisme, une philosophie sans frontières, ANRW I,4 (1973) 35—40. The classic accounts of E. ARNOLD, Roman Stoicism (Cambridge 1911) 99—127; and POHLENZ, Stoa 191—366, have still not been superseded. D. C. EARL, Terence and Roman Politics, Historia 11 (1962) 482—5, discusses the relation of Stoicism to traditional Roman aristocratic virtues. The influence of Stoicism upon Tiberius Gracchus has been discussed recently by J. B. BECKER, The Influence of Roman Stoicism upon the Gracchi Economic Land Reforms, PP 19 (1964) 125—34; and C. NICOLET, L'inspiration de Tiberius Gracchus. À propos d'un livre récent, REA 67 (1965) 142—158.

[199] CRAWFORD no. 265.
[200] CIL XII 336; Apul. De mundo 37.
[201] Enn. Epicharmus 54—8 VAHL.
[202] Cic. Rep. 6.17.17.
[203] Cic. Fin. 3.20. 66.
[204] Cic. Verr. 4.58. 129.

what is honest and forbidding the contrary."[205] For this reason the good *augur*, interpreter and assistant of Jupiter Optimus Maximus, should remember that it is his duty to come to the rescue of the state in great emergencies.[206] At such crises, Jupiter reveals himself as *Stator*, preserver and supporter of the Roman commonwealth. So at the time of the great Catilinarian conspiracy, Cicero convoked the Senate in the temple of Jupiter Stator, consecrated by Romulus with the same auspices as Rome itself and rightly called the foundation of Rome and its empire.[207] In the 'First Catilinarian,' Cicero invoked Jupiter Stator to repel Catiline and his ferocious band of miscreants:

> "Drive them, Jupiter, from your altars and from the other temples, from the houses and walls of the city, from the lives and fortunes of all citizens; overwhelm all these enemies of good men, these robbers of Italy, bound together by an infamous alliance of crimes, overwhelm them, now and after death, with eternal punishments."[208]

Throughout this great crisis of the state, Cicero portrays himself as the agent of Jupiter. The implication should not be borne that Cicero resisted the conspirators. Rome is governed by the power and authority of the gods; and only by their guidance did Cicero detect the plot. It was Jupiter himself who overthrew the Catilinarians. It was Jupiter who determined that the Capitoline should be safe; he saved the temples, he saved the city, he saved the citizens:

> *ille, ille Iuppiter restitit; ille Capitolium, ille haec templa, ille cunctam urbem, ille vos omnis salvos esse voluit.*[209]

Symbolically a great statue of Jupiter was being erected at the very moment Cicero had the conspirators and their accusers led through the Forum to the temple of Concordia. The statue had been vowed in 65 B.C. at the behest of the *haruspices* to appease the divine threat of civil destruction:

> *caedis atque incendia et legum interitum et bellum civile et domesticum et totius urbis atque imperi occasum appropinquare dixerunt, nisi di immortales omni ratione placati suo numine prope fata ipsa flexissent.*

---

[205] Cic. Phil. 11.12. 28.

[206] Cic. Leg. 3.19. 43.

[207] Cic. Cat. 1.5; 13. Commentators on 'In Catilinam I' have not really dealt with the question of why Cicero chose the temple of Jupiter Stator. Cf., e.g., K. HALM, Ciceros ausgewählte Reden III[14] (Berlin 1900) p. 26; G. LONG, M. Tulli Ciceronis orationes III (London 1856) p. 21; F. RICHTER and A. EBERHARD, Ciceros catilinarischen Reden (Leipzig 1887) p. 38; H. BORNECQUE and E. BAILLY, Budé edition (Paris 1965) p. 4. For Jupiter as Stator, see PICCALUGA (above n. 4) 246–50. For the significance of the epithet *Stator*, cf. A. PARIENTE, Stator, teóforo y nombre común, Duris 2 (1974) 57–66. R. GOAR, Cicero and the State Religion (Amsterdam 1971) 36–45, comments on the role of religion in the 'In Catilinam.'

[208] Cic. Cat. 1.13.

[209] Cic. Cat. 3.9.

The statue was to be erected, contrary to custom, facing east, looking upon the rising sun, the Forum, and the Senatehouse. So honored, the god would reveal to the Senate and the Roman People all plots secretly formed against the safety of the city and the empire.[210]

Thus in two of his greatest sets of public orations, the 'Catilinarians' and the 'Philippics' Cicero expressly linked Jupiter to the preservation of the Roman state against civil strife and specifically against individuals who seek violently to overthrow the institutions of the Roman commonwealth. Against such enemies of the Roman order, Jupiter justifies any action. Jupiter as the defender of the commonwealth against sedition and domestic discord is the dominant theme in the public, as opposed to philosophical, image of Jupiter in Cicero's writings. This same image offers the clue to and deepens the significance of the appearance of Jupiter on the coinage of the late republic. *Quinarii* of T. Cloulius in 98 B.C. portray a laureate head of Jupiter on the obverse, on the reverse Victory crowning a Gallic trophy (Pl. II, 11). Cloulius is probably to be identified with the Marian *legatus* Cloelius.[211] His celebration of Jupiter and victory marks the last of four such types struck from 101—98 B.C. in celebration of Marius' triumph over the Teutones and Cimbri.[212] After this issue of Cloulius, Jupiter does not appear again on the Roman coinage for a decade. An issue of *quinarii* of Cn. Lentulus in 88 B.C. portrays a laureate head of Jupiter on the obverse, Victory crowning a trophy on the reverse (Pl. II, 12).[213] As on the *quinarii* of Cloulius, the type is a revival of the imagery of the *victoriatus*. The typology of Lentulus' coins may be taken as a reference to the successful conclusion of the Social War. A sinister note, victory in brutal civil conflict, is perhaps to be seen in the types issued by L. Rubrius Dossenus in this same year, 88 B.C. The reverse on all is similar, Victory above a triumphal quadriga emblazoned with an eagle and thunderbolt. There are three obverse types, a laureate head of Jupiter with sceptre over shoulder (Pl. II, 13), a head of Juno, and a bust of Minerva.[214] *Denarii* of Cn. Blasio struck 112/111 B.C., had also invoked the Capitoline Triad at a moment of crisis for the Roman state, the renewal of the Gallic threat and the defeat of Carbo at Noreia (Pl. II, 14).[215] The safety of the Roman state was

---

[210] Cic. Cat. 3.8—9.

[211] CRAWFORD no. 332. For the identification of the moneyer with the Marian Cloelius, see T. WISEMAN, Cloelius of Tarracina, CR n.s. 17 (1967) 23. The *carynx* beside the trophy on the reverse points to a Gallic triumph.

[212] CRAWFORD no. 325, 326, 331. T. CARNEY, Coins Bearing on the Age and Career of Marius, NC 6,19 (1959) 79—88 discusses references on the coinage to Marius' triumphs.

[213] CRAWFORD no. 345.

[214] CRAWFORD no. 348, correctly identifying the vehicles on the reverse as triumphal quadrigas. We have no certain information about Dossenus' political associations. His possible connection with Minturnae, T. WISEMAN, New Men in the Roman Senate 139 B.C.— A.D. 14 (Oxford 1971) 257, might be used to support the argument that he was a follower of Marius (Plut. Marius 40—1).

[215] CRAWFORD no. 296. On the identification of the obverse portrait, P. Scipio Africanus or Cn. Cornelius Blasio cs. 270 and 257 or Mars, see M. VOLLENWEIDER, Das Bildnis des Scipio Africanus, MH 15 (1958) 27—45; E. ROBINSON, Punic Coins in Spain and Their

believed to be inextricably bound to the Capitoline cult. The typology of the
denarii of L. Rubrius Dossenus represents a similar invocation of the Capitoline
Triad at a moment of national crisis; however on this occasion the danger is
domestic sedition. As in Cicero's 'Catilinarians,' Jupiter is invoked on the *denarii*
of L. Rubrius Dossenus to save the commonwealth and its institutions from a
traitorous faction. The imagery of the triumph is best linked to a celebration of
the success of the Marian cause. Along with the Capitoline Triad, Dossenus' types
invoke Neptune amidst the symbolism of Victory; the allusion is both to Marius'
capture of Ostia and, in a more general sense, to the patronage of Neptune, whose
element bore Marius safely out of Italy, preserved him in Africa, and brought him
home again.

It has been argued that during the Marian civil war various divinities appear
on the coinage as factional symbols.[216] This is patently true of Venus, the divine
patroness of Sulla.[217] However, Jupiter, in this period, is invoked by all factions.
After the Marian capture of Rome, *denarii* struck in 86 B.C. celebrate Jupiter in
a quadriga, hurling the thunderbolt. The obverse represents Apollo, who on
an issue of 84 B.C. is portrayed with the thunderbolt.[218] The theme of the
denarius type of Jupiter in 86 B.C. is best taken as the triumph of *libertas*.[219]
Both Apollo and Jupiter were associated with *libertas*. In particular, Jupiter's
association with the struggle for *libertas* went back, at least in Roman historical
tradition, to the momentous period of the plebian-patrician conflict. At the very
end of the first Punic war, Ti. Sempronius Gracchus dedicated a shrine to Jupiter
Libertas on the Aventine. The shrine was built with money from fines; and like
most temples erected from this source it had plebian connotations, emphasized by
its location on the Aventine, traditionally associated with the plebs.[220] This cult of
Jupiter Libertas was originally quite distinct from the older cult of Jupiter

---

Bearing on the Roman Republican Series, in: Essays in Roman Coinage Presented to
H. Mattingly, ed. by R. CARSON and C. H. V. SUTHERLAND (Oxford 1956) 42; CRAW-
FORD I pp. 310–11; and ZEHNACKER, Moneta II, 977–80.

[216] Cf. T. LUCE, Political Propaganda on Roman Republican Coins circa 92–82 B.C., AJA 72
(1968) 25–39; CRAWFORD II, 731–3; ZEHNACKER, Moneta I, 565–77.

[217] See C. LANZANI, La Venere sillana, Historia 1 (1927) 31–55; H. LEOPOLD, Venus als
toekomstgodin in de eerste eeuw voor Christus, Mededeelingen van het Nederlandsch
Historisch Instituut te Rom 2, 6 (s'Gravenhage 1936) 1–19; J. P. V. D. BALSDON, Sulla
Felix, JRS 41 (1941) 8; SCHILLING, Vénus 272–96; C. KOCH, Venus, RE VIII A,1 (1955)
860–3; E. BADIAN, Forschungsbericht: From the Gracchi to Sulla (1940–1959), Historia
11 (1962) 228–9; B. WOSNIK, Untersuchungen zur Geschichte Sullas (Diss. Würzburg
1963) 25ff.

[218] CRAWFORD no. 350 A. This Apollonian god with thunderbolt (cf. no. 298; 354) has been
the subject of considerable discussion. Possible identifications include Vediovis or young
Jupiter as well as Apollo; cf. LUCE, AJA 72 (1968) 25–6; A. ALFÖLDI, Redeunt Saturnia
Regna III, Chiron 2 (1972) 215–30.

[219] For the association of Apollo with *libertas*, see Servius Ecl. 8.75; Macrob. Sat. 1.18.1–6,
8–9. Cf. LUCE, AJA 72 (1968) 25–39; and CRAWFORD I, 741.

[220] Livy 24.16.19; Festus p. 108 L. Cf. DEGRASSI, II XIII, 2, 440; and A. STYLOW, Libertas
und Liberalitas: Untersuchungen zur innenpolitischen Propaganda der Römer (Diss.
Munich 1972) 5.

Liber.[221] Its prototype was the Greek cult of Zeus Eleutherios.[222] Roman historical tradition preserved the patrician view that Jupiter had originally opposed plebian demands for admission to the consulship.[223] According to Livy, Appius Claudius Crassus warned of the consequences of plebian consuls, for only the patricians had the right to consult Jupiter through the auspices:

> *nobis adeo propria sunt auspicia. . . . Quid igitur aliud quam tollit ex civitate auspicia qui plebeios consules creando a patribus; qui soli ea habere possunt, aufert.*[224]

However, the plebians refused to permit the patricians to monopolize Jupiter, the god of the Roman commonwealth as a whole. Jupiter was the god honored at the *ludi plebei*, to which the *epulum Iovis* seems to have been originally attached.[225] In the historical tradition, at its very commencement, the plebian struggle was placed under the patronage of Jupiter.[226] The same Ti. Sempronius Gracchus dedicated the temple of Jupiter Libertas and saw to the trial and conviction of Claudia for her *verba incivilia* which had wounded the *maiestas* of the Roman People. However, domestic politics may not have been the entire impetus behind Gracchus' dedication of the shrine to Jupiter Libertas.[227] If, as seems likely, the shrine was vowed during his aedileship in 246, the temple is linked chronologically to the end of the Punic war.[228] In Greece, as at Syracuse, the cult of Zeus Eleutherios could have democratic associations, particularly the liberation of the city from a tyrant.[229] However, perhaps its most famous cult was at Plataia, where the cult of Zeus Eleutherios celebrated the liberation of Greece from the barbarian threat.[230] Gracchus' shrine of Jupiter Libertas is best taken as an offer of thanksgiving for the victory over Carthage and the continued freedom of the Roman state.[231] Secondarily it pointed to the role of the Roman People in achieving this victory.

With the issues of 86 B.C. the representation of Jupiter on the coinage is undeniably linked to Rome's self-destructive domestic turmoil. This is equally true of the appearance of Jupiter on *denarii* of C. Egnatius Maximus

---

[221] See above n. 93.

[222] For Zeus Eleutherios, see esp. WASER, in: ROSCHER, Myth. Lex. VI, 619–23.

[223] Cf. DUMÉZIL, Rel. rom. 195–201; J. BAYET in his Budé ed. of Livy, III (Paris 1942) 145–53; H. LE BONNIEC, Le culte de Cérès à Rome, Études et Commentaires 27 (Paris 1958) 347.

[224] Livy 6.40–1.

[225] Cic. Verr. 5. 36; Paulus p. 109L. Cf. WISSOWA, RKR² 127. The best discussion is still AUST, in: ROSCHER, Myth. Lex. II, 1, 734–6.

[226] Dion. Hal. 6.90.1.

[227] Livy per. 19; Val. Max. 8.1; Suet. Tib. 2.3; Gell. NA 10.6.

[228] Cf. BROUGHTON, Magistrates of the Roman Republic I, 216–7.

[229] For Syracuse, see Diod. 11.72 (the overthrow of the tyranny of Thrasybulus). Coins in honor of Zeus Eleutherios were issued after the overthrow of Dionysius II and Agathocles. HEAD, Historia Numorum² 179, 182. The earlier cult of Zeus Eleutherios at Samos arose after the overthrow of Polycrates; Herod. 3.142.

[230] Thuc. 2.71; Strabo 9.2.31; Plut. Arist. 19.8; 20.5; Paus. 9.2.5.

[231] For a different view, see STYLOW, Libertas 6.

in 75 B.C.[232] The decade of the 70's was marked by the insistent demand, in the name of *libertas*, for the restoration of the powers of the tribunate.[233] This was particularly true of the year 75 B.C., when the agitation was led by the tribune Q. Opimius. *Libertas* dominates the coin types of the year, which seek to link both Venus, formerly appropriated by Sulla, and Jupiter to the struggle.[234] *Denarii* of C. Egnatius Maximus portray Cupid on the obverse; on the reverse is represented the temple of Jupiter Libertas, identified by the combination of thunderbolt and *pilleus* as attributes (Pl. III, 15).

As in the earlier domestic strife of the patricians and plebians, Jupiter was invoked by all groups during the crisis of the Sullan epoch and its immediate aftermath. Sulla himself, according to Plutarch (Sulla 17), emphasized Jupiter's role in predestinating Sulla's victories in Greece. *Denarii* of L. Volumnius Strabo struck in 81 B.C. represent a laureate head of Jupiter on the obverse; on the reverse is portrayed Europa seated on the bull, with a winged thunderbolt and an ivy leaf in the field (Pl. III, 16).[235] Three years later *denarii* of M. Volteius portray the laureate head of Jupiter on the obverse and represent the Capitoline temple on the reverse (Pl. III, 17).[236] The great temple, believed to be linked intimately with the fate of the city, burned in 83 B.C., symbolic of the internal conflagration which threatened to destroy Rome. Expiation and renewal, as well as triumph, is the significance of the invocation of Jupiter on these two issues. The appearance of Jupiter on the issue of M. Volteius is one of a series honoring a variety of divinities. More interesting is the reverse type of L. Volumnius Strabo with its singular representation of Europa on the bull. The theme is renewal: *Mortalis atque urbes beluasque omnis iuvat [Jupiter]*.[237] The evergreen ivy combined with the thunderbolt, together with Europa, point to Jupiter's power eternally to bring order out of chaos and to renew the life of the state, even as the fecundity of Europa was responsible for the bountiful foilage of the ever-green plane tree under which the love of Zeus and Europa was consumated.[238]

The numismatic evidence thus complements Cicero's invocation of Jupiter in the 'Catilinarian' orations. The pre-eminent theme is Jupiter as preserver of the commonwealth and its institutions. The civil strife of the period is reflected in the discordant image of Jupiter. For one faction, he is linked with *libertas*, its preservation and triumph. On the coinage of 81 and 78 B.C., as in Cicero's 'Catilinarians,' the emphasis is on Jupiter's protection and renewal of the commonwealth against the forces of sedition. Unlike *libertas*, however, Jupiter did not become a catchword invoked by opposing factions during the last generation of the Roman republic.[239] Unlike Venus and Hercules, he did not become

---

[232] CRAWFORD no. 391.
[233] Cf. STYLOW, Libertas 12–20.
[234] So rightly CRAWFORD I p. 406.
[235] CRAWFORD no. 377.
[236] CRAWFORD no. 385.
[237] Enn. Epicharmus 58 VAHL.
[238] Theophrastus Hist. pl. 1.9.5; Varro R.R. 1.7.6.
[239] STYLOW, Libertas 12–33, is the best treatment of *libertas* as a political catchword in the late republic. His extensive consideration of the numismatic evidence effectively supple-

patron divinity of any of the great dynasts. Issues of P. Hypsaeus and M. Aemilius Scaurus in 60 and 58 B.C. return to the theme of Jupiter and foreign triumphs, but the emphasis is personal, celebrating the triumphs of the moneyer and his ancestors (Pl. III, 18; IV, 19).[240] Indeed, to a large degree, the religious propaganda of the period from Sulla through Octavian tacitly sought to usurp Jupiter's preeminent position as guardian of the Roman commonwealth and the dispenser of victory. The great charismatic generals, Sulla, Pompey, Caesar, each in turn celebrated Venus as the divine grantor of victory.[241] Sulla's coinage ostentatiously linked Venus to his triumph over Mithridates; and both Pompey and Caesar represented Venus as the source of those victories which made them masters of the *oikoumene*.[242] The personal divine patroness of the general replaced Jupiter as the dispenser of the charismatic power of victory which expanded the frontiers of the Roman People and restored domestic concord. This is revealed with particular clarity by the role of the augural symbolism in late republican numismatic iconography.[243] As symbol both of the magistrate's right of *auspicium* and of the individual's status as augur, the *lituus* was explicitly disassociated from Jupiter, traditional god of the state auspices. On the coinage from Sulla onward, the *lituus* was personalized, that is it was attached to the personal patron divinity of the charismatic general. It symbolized his personal auspices through which his divine patron and protector manifested the divine favor which brought success. Thus *denarii* of Faustus struck in honor of Sulla portray Aphrodite of Aphrodisias flying through the air in a biga and holding the *lituus* in her right hand; the same goddess was honored by Sulla with votive offerings, for she had appeared to him in a dream, fighting on his side and leading his troops to victory.[244] The Venus Victrix coinage of Caesar has the bust of the

ments such earlier treatments of the literary material as C. WIRSZUBSKI, Libertas as a Political Idea at Rome during the Late Republic and Early Principate (Cambridge 1950); J. BLEICKEN, Der Begriff der Freiheit in der letzten Phase der Römischen Republik, HZ 195 (1962) 1—20; G. CRIFÒ, Su alcuni aspetti della libertà in Roma, AG 6 (1958) 23 n. 154. See further, FEARS, Cult of Virtues, below in this same volume (ANRW II, 17,2) n. 67.

[240] CRAWFORD no. 420, 422.

[241] In general, see LEOPOLD (above n. 217) 1—19; SCHILLING, Vénus 272—346; KOCH, Venus, RE VIII A,1 (1953) 860—9; WEINSTOCK, Divus Julius 15—18, 80—2.

[242] CRAWFORD no. 359 (Sulla). For the significance of the type, see B. FRIER, Augural Symbolism in Sulla's Invasion of 83, ANSMusN 22 (1967) 111—8; and IDEM, Sulla's Priesthood, Arethusa 2 (1969) 182—201; E. BADIAN, Sulla's Augurate, Arethusa 1 (1968) 26—46; and FEARS, Historia 24 (1975) 598. CRAWFORD no. 426/3—4 (Pompey). For the types as a reference to Pompey, see A. ALFÖLDI, Komplementäre Doppeltypen in der Denarprägung der Römischen Republik, Schweizer Münzblätter 2 (1951) 5—6; J. RICHARD, Pax, Concordia et la religion officielle de Janus à la fin de la République romaine, MEFR 75 (1963) 316—7; and CRAWFORD I pp. 450—1. CRAWFORD no. 468; 480/3—5, 7—11 (Caesar). Cf. WEINSTOCK, Divus Julius 99—100. See further, FEARS, Theology of Victory, below in this same volume (ANRW II, 17,2) n. 261.

[243] For a detailed treatment, see FEARS, Historia 24 (1975) 592—602.

[244] CRAWFORD no. 426/2. The coin is part of a series, CRAWFORD no. 426/1—4. For Sulla's votive gift to Aphrodite of Aphrodisias, see App. B.C. 1.97. Cf. SCHILLING, Vénus 301 n. 1, for the identification of the reverse of no. 426/2 as Aphrodite of Aphrodisias. For the iconography of the entire issue, see ALFÖLDI, Schweizer Münzblätter 2 (1951) 1—7;

dictator on the obverse with the *lituus* behind his head. On the reverse, Venus Victrix stands, holding Victoria and a sceptre, her left arm resting on a globe.[245]

As in the Hellenistic monarchies, the charisma of victory has become personalized, attached to the patron divinity of the rule or to the person of the ruler himself. Thus Caesar became *synnaos* of Romulus Quirinus in the form of a statue of the *dictator* with the inscription *Deo Invicto*.[246] This displacement of Jupiter as Victor and Propugnator graphically portrays the replacement of *res publica* by monarchy. On the model of the Hellenistic monarchies, the ultimate step is to personalize the supreme god himself, associating him directly with the king with a cult epithet like *Zeus Seleukios*.[247] Among the honors bestowed upon Caesar in 44 B.C., Dio records that Caesar was openly addressed as Jupiter Julius.[248] Referring to Sulla, Cicero had compared the power of a Roman dictator to that of Jupiter Optimus Maximus.[249] In 44 B.C., the analogy became concrete political imagery. Caesar was equated with the Capitoline Triad, the pre-eminent divine patrons of the community. Only Jupiter, Juno, and Minerva possessed *tensae* in which their *exuviae* were borne to the Pulvinar. Other divinities had to be content with having their symbols carried in barrows, *fercula*.[250] In 44 B.C. Caesar was awarded the privilege of a *tensa*.[251] The act was a political statement of monarchy. It heralded the establishment of

---

L. LENAGHAN, Hercules-Melqart on a Coin of Faustus Sulla, ANSMusN 11 (1964) 131–50; HÖLSCHER, Victoria Romana 22, 148; CRAWFORD I, 450–1.

[245] CRAWFORD no. 480/3.

[246] Dio 43.45.3; Cic. Att. 13.28.3. The parallel was the statue of Alexander erected at Athens; cf. Hypereides Or. I col. 32. In general, see J. FEARS, The Stoic View of the Career and Character of Alexander the Great, Philologus 118 (1974) 120–1.

[247] Cf. OGIS 245. Cf. C. HABICHT, Gottmenschentum und griechische Städte², Zetemata 14 (Munich 1970) 158–9 n. 83. For the cult of Zeus Seleukios, see A. NOCK, Notes on Ruler-Cult, JHS 48 (1928) 41–42 (rep. in: IDEM, Essays on Religion and the Ancient World [Oxford 1972] I, 156–57); SEG XV 183; L. ROBERT, Bulletin épigraphique, REG 64 (1951) 133–4; P. M. FRASER, Zeus Seleukeios, CR 63 (1949) 92–4.

[248] Dio 44.6.4. Cf. L. TAYLOR, The Divinity of the Roman Emperor, Philological Monographs Published by the American Philological Assoc. 1 (Middletown Conn. 1931) 68–9; P. L. STRACK, Der augusteische Staat, in: Probleme der augusteischen Erneuerung, Auf dem Weg zum nationalpolitischen Gymnasium 6 (Frankfurt 1938) 21ff.; W. STEIDLE, Sueton und die antike Biographie, Zetemata 1 (Munich 1963)² 60ff. J. VOGT, Zum Herrscherkult bei Julius Caesar, in: Studies Presented to D. M. Robinson II (St. Louis 1953) 1138–46; P. LAMBRECHTS, César dans l'historiographie contemporaine, AC 23 (1954) 130–1; F. TAEGER, Charisma I–II (Stuttgart 1960) 70–1; WEINSTOCK, Divus Julius 287–317. H. GESCHE, Die Vergottung Caesars, Frankfurter Althist. Stud. 1 (Kallmünz 1968) 35–7; G. DOBESCH, Caesars Apotheose zu Lebzeiten und sein Ringen um den Königstitel (Wien, Österreichisches Archäologisches Institut 1966) 17–45; L. MORAWIECKI, The Power Conception of Alexander the Great and of Gaius Julius Caesar in the Light of the Numismatic Sources, Eos 63 (1975) 99–127, esp. 113–24.

[249] Cic. Rosc. Am. 131.

[250] In general, see C. KOCH, Tensa, RE V A,1 (1934) 533; and WEINSTOCK, Divus Julius 285.

[251] Dio 44.6.3; cf. WEINSTOCK, Divus Julius 285. Anth. Pal. 2.92–6 suggests that Caesar was celebrated in Italy as Novus Iuppiter.

an earthly master of the Roman commonwealth, who would tend the mortal concerns of the state, assuming those functions which had been the sole preserve of Capitoline Jupiter. This implication is made clear by Caesar's action when he realized that the time was not ripe for the consumation of this in political fact. When he refused the diadem at the *Lupercalia*, he had it placed in the Capitoline temple, stating that Jupiter alone was king of the Romans.[252]

In this context, added significance is attached to the appearance of Jupiter, the first in a decade, on an irregular military issue by the Optimates L. Cornelius Lentulus and C. Claudius Marcellus struck in 49 B.C. Three different types of *denarii* were struck. The first has the triskeles with winged head of Medusa on the obverse; the reverse represents Jupiter, standing and holding the thunderbolt in his right hand and an eagle in his left (Pl. IV, 20). The second type has a head of Apollo on the obverse; the reverse portrays Jupiter with thunderbolt and eagle. The third has a laureate head of Jupiter on the obverse; the reverse represents Artemis of Ephesus.[253] Jupiter forms the constant element in the series of types. As in Cicero's 'Catilinarians' and 'Philippics,' Jupiter is invoked as preserver of the Roman *res publica*. The supreme god of the *res publica* symbolizes constitutional government and its protection against the attacks of the would-be tyrants. Even more noteworthy is an issue struck by Pompey himself in 49 B.C. The obverse portrays a terminal bust of Jupiter, wearing a diadem. The reverse represents a sceptre, an eagle, and a dolphin (Pl. IV, 21).[254] Issues of Q. Metellus Scipio struck in Africa in 47—46 B.C. similarly celebrate Jupiter, his kingship, victory, and promise.[255] Both issues portray a laureate head of Jupiter on the obverse (Pl. IV, 22). By contrast, Jupiter plays no role on the coinage of Caesar or his adherents. The most prominent Caesarean type honors Venus, the divine patron and ancestress of the *dictator*. In 44 B.C. she was joined on the coinage by the obverse portrait of Caesar himself. The head of the new master of the Romans thus usurped that place which, on the *denarii* and the *victoriati* of the great age of the *res publica*, had been held by the personification of the Roman People, Roma, and by the divine patron of the commonwealth, Jupiter.

It is not coincidental that Jupiter plays no real role on the coinage of Julius Caesar's heir. Of course the supreme god of the Roman commonwealth is not subjected to open denigration. He is rather silently ignored. However, this very silence provides among the most eloquent statements of the monarchical and Hellenistic elements in the ideology of the Augustan principate.

---

[252] Dio 44.11.3. In Greek literature, it was commonplace to refer to the Persian king as the Zeus of the Persians. Cf. Herod. 7.56; Gorg. fr. 5a D—K; Aesch. Pers. 157. For the extensive literature on Caesar's honors in 44 B.C. and earlier and their significance, see, among recent studies, DOBESCH, Caesars Apotheose zu Lebzeiten; GESCHE, Die Vergottung Caesars; and WEINSTOCK, Divus Julius. For another aspect of the perception of Jupiter as divine patron of the republic, see R. MELLOR, The Dedications on the Capitoline Hill, Chiron 8 (1978) 319—30.

[253] CRAWFORD no. 445.

[254] CRAWFORD no. 447.

[255] CRAWFORD no. 459—60.

IV. Jupiter and the Ideology of Monarchy

1. Jupiter in Augustan Religious Policy

As with its constitutional forms, Augustus proceeded with deliberation in evolving an ideological foundation to support his new order. As the new principate became increasingly secure and as Octavian-Augustus matured from *dux* into *princeps* into *pater patriae*, outmoded or distasteful themes were discarded and new forms and associations evoked. Jupiter, like Romulus, was an early victim.[256] The supreme god of the *res publica* seems to have played an extremely insignificant role in the propaganda of the rabid young triumvir and son of Venus' deified darling.[257] Immediately after Actium there was a brief attempt to associate Jupiter directly with the victory which had established Augustus as master of the *oikoumene*. An issue of *denarii*, struck shortly after Actium, represents on the reverse an ithyphallic terminal figure of Augustus placed on a

---

[256] Sulla, Pompey, and Caesar preceded Octavian in the comparison of themselves with Romulus, the *Optimus Augur* who conducted the *augurium maximum* by which, in the historical tradition found in Livy and Dionysius (Livy 1.6.4; Dion. Hal. 1.86.1), the gods elected him to rule the new city. Octavian seriously considered adopting the name Romulus but finally decided upon Augustus (Suet. Aug. 7; Dio 53.16.7), and after 27 B.C. Romulus had little importance in Augustan ideology. In general, for the image and political use of Romulus in the first century B.C. see J. GAGÉ, Romulus-Augustus, MEFR 47 (1930) 138–81; A. ALFÖLDI, Die Geburt der kaiserlichen Bildsymbolik, MH 8 (1951) 190–215 (rep. in: IDEM, Der Vater des Vaterlandes im römischen Denken [Darmstadt 1971] 14–39), with the strictures on ALFÖLDI's use of the numismatic evidence in CRAWFORD II, 733 n. 2; WAGENVOORT, Studies in Roman Literature, Culture, and Religion 169–83; C. J. CLASSEN, Romulus in der römischen Republik, Philologus 106 (1962) 174–204; W. BURKERT, Caesar und Romulus Quirinus, Historia 11 (1962) 356–76; J. BAYET, Les sacerdoces romains et la prédivinisation impériale, BAB 5, 41 (1955) 487–510; W. KUNKEL, Über das Wesen des augusteischen Prinzipats, Gymnasium 68 (1961) 356–9; R. MERKELBACH, Augustus und Romulus (Erklärung von Horaz, Carm. I, 12, 37–40), Philologus 104 (1960) 149–53; DOBESCH, Caesars Apotheose zu Lebzeiten 11–7; WEINSTOCK, Divus Julius 177; H. J. KRÄMER, Die Sage von Romulus und Remus in der lateinischen Literatur, in: Synusia. Festgabe für W. Schadewaldt (Pfullingen 1965) 355–402.

[257] The only explicit reference to the Roman Jupiter on the republican coinage after Caesar's assassination is the issue of Petillius Capitolinus (CRAWFORD no. 487): ob: head of Jupiter; rev: Capitoline temple. The type has no political association but rather is a strictly personal reference to the moneyer. An eastern issue of Antony and P. Ventidius, struck in 39 B.C. (CRAWFORD no. 531), has on the reverse a nude male figure, holding a sceptre in his right hand and a branch in his left. He is generally identified as Jupiter Victor; cf. GRUEBER, BMRR II, 404; T. V. BUTTREY, The Denarius of P. Ventidius, ANSMusN 9 (1960) 96; CRAWFORD I p. 533. In light of the argument in the text that as a coin type Jupiter was associated with 'constitutional' government and the optimate cause in the late republic, the absence of Jupiter from the coinage of the Liberators is interesting. The central theme of their coinage is *libertas*; and since Jupiter could be associated with this theme (cf. above p. 50, his absence is significant.

thunderbolt.[258] The assimilation of the *princeps* to Jupiter, perhaps as Terminus, is clear. Similarly, a silver coin of the same period has a winged thunderbolt behind the obverse portrait of Augustus (Pl. IV, 23).[259] The iconography of an issue of *aurei*, struck in 27 B.C. and, like the other two types, at an eastern mint, was even more suggestive. The obverse legend, CAESAR COS VII CIVIBVS SERVATEIS, is complemented by a reverse type of an eagle holding an oak wreath in his claws with laurel branches in the background (Pl. IV, 24).[260] Jupiter is thus designated as the source of Augustus' victories and his salvation of the commonwealth, symbolized respectively by the laurel and by the oak wreath granted by senatorial decree.[261] The theme is emphasized by the simple reverse legend AVGVSTVS. Octavian's new name conveyed a mystique of numinous, increscent power and an aura of divine sanction manifest in the intervention of the gods through the auspices.[262]

The imagery was not confined to the official medium of the coinage. A gem, now in Vienna, has on its obverse a representation of Augustus in a quadriga drawn by Tritons, the two outermost holding globes. On the reverse Capricorn is portrayed in a laurel wreath; below is an eagle on a thunderbolt.[263] Capricorn, Augustus' natal sign, played a significant role on the Augustan coinage in the period from 22–12 B.C.[264] On the gem the divine foreordination of Augustus' world rule was explicitly linked to Jupiter, a theme which appears in

[258] BMC I no. 628. Cf. ALFÖLDI (above n. 218) 225; KRAFT (below n. 260) 207 n. 1.

[259] BMC I no. 637. Ephesus or Pergamum was the probable location of the mint of issue of both BMC no. 628 and 637; cf. ROBERTSON, RIC Hunter xlix. For the iconography, see L. LAFFRANCHI, Gli ampliamenti del pomerio di Roma nelle testimonianze numismatiche, BCAR 47 (1919) 25; K. SCOTT, The Imperial Cult under the Flavians (Stuttgart–Berlin 1936) 134; TAYLOR,. Divinity of the Roman Emperor 152.

[260] BMC I no. 656. Cf. C. H. V. SUTHERLAND, Coinage in Roman Imperial Policy, 31 B.C.– 68 A.D. (London 1951) 31–2; ROBERTSON, RIC Hunter I xlix. ROBERTSON (xlvi–li) follows MATTINGLY, BMC I cxxii–iv, in the view that no. 628, 637, and 656 were struck in Asia, probably at Ephesus and Pergamum. This is doubted by SUTHERLAND, The Emperor and the Coinage (London 1976) 49–53, who argues for an Italian mint. Cf. K. KRAFT, Zur Münzprägung des Augustus, Sitzungsberichte der Wissenschaftlichen Gesellschaft an der Johann-Wolfgang-Goethe-Universität Frankfurt/Main 7 = Jg 1968 (Wiesbaden 1969) with the review by M. CRAWFORD, JRS 64 (1974) 246–8. Important for all aspects of Augustan coinage are the catalogues of J. GIARD, Bibliothèque Nationale, Catalogue des monnaies de l'Empire romain I (Paris 1976) and C. KRAAY, Catalogue of the Coins of the Roman Empire in the Ashmolean Museum I (Oxford 1976).

[261] Res Gestae 34.

[262] For the significance of the name, the best treatment is H. ERKELL, Augustus, Felicitas, Fortuna: Lateinische Wortstudien (Diss. Göteborg 1952) 26–40, with the earlier literature. More recently see COMBES, Imperator 407; TAEGER, Charisma II, 118–9.

[263] Cf. F. EICHLER and E. KRIS, Die Kameen im Kunsthistorischen Museum Wien, Publikationen aus den kunsthist. Sammlungen in Wien 2 (Vienna 1927) 50–1.

[264] For the coins, see BMC I no. 305–8, 344–8, 655, 669, 679; cf. T. HÖLSCHER, Ein römischer Stirnziegel mit Victoria u. Capricorni, JRGZ 12 (1965) 57–71; K. KRAFT, Zum Capricorn auf den Münzen des Augustus, JNG 17 (1967) 17–27; E. DWYER, Augustus and the Capricorn, MDAI(R) 80 (1973) 59–67; FEARS, Princeps 208–11.

the Augustan panegyrics of such writers as Horace and Vergil.[265] According to
Suetonius, who mentions the coin type of Capricorn, Augustus gave wide circulation to Theogenes' prediction of future greatness based on his horoscope.
Furthermore on the day of Octavian's birth, the astrologer Publius Nigidius
Figulus proclaimed that the ruler of the world had been born.[266] This same
Publius Nigidius Figulus wrote that the gods of Egypt had placed Capricorn in
the sky to commemorate the liberation of the world from the tyranny of Typhon
and the re-establishment of divine order.[267] On the Gemma Augustea, Capricorn appears above the head of Augustus, who is himself represented as the
earthly counterpart of Jupiter, semi-nude, an eagle at his feet, a long sceptre in
his left hand and a *lituus* in his right.[268] The *lituus* symbolizes those auspices by
which the will of Jupiter is revealed to his earthly representative, triumphant
master of the world by land and by sea.

The imagery of the gems proclaimed that the fates and Jupiter had con-
spired to bring about the terrestrial golden age of Augustan rule. The same
theme appears in Vergil, Horace, and Ovid; and a desire to associate the
Augustan epoch with Zeus-Jupiter lay behind the decision of the eastern kings
and princes to complete the Olympieion at Athens and to dedicate it to the
Genius Augusti. The project, never actualized, was conceived shortly after
Actium, and commemorated by an Augustan coin type, issued in 27 B.C., portraying a hexastyle temple with the legend IOVI OLVM (Pl. V, 25).[269]

In all this, however, as in any attempt to follow the threads of imperial
ideology, it is essential to keep one dictum firmly in mind: we must distinguish
sharply between (a) the normal working theory of the principate and the implications of what the *princeps* officially says or does, as evidenced in such sources
as the imperial coinage or imperial inscriptions and official monuments and (b)
the metaphorical language used by *literati* and corresponding expressions in
art.[270] If we consider the implications of Augustus' official acts and of such

---

[265] Vergil Aen. 1.257—96; Horace Od. 1.2; 1.12; 4.2.

[266] Suet. Aug. 94.

[267] Figulus' comments on Capricorn are from his 'Sphaera graecanica.' For a text, see
Th. Hopfner, Fontes Historiae Religionis Aegyptiacae I, Fontes Historiae Religionum 2
(Bonn 1922) 84—6.

[268] There is a large bibliography on the Gemma Augustea (A. Furtwängler, Die antiken
Gemmen. Geschichte der Steinschneidekunst im klassischen Altertum I [Leipzig 1900]
pl. 56). The most significant contributions are Eichler and Kris (above n. 263) 52—4,
with the older literature; J. Gagé, La Victoria Augusti et les auspices de Tibère, RA 32
(1930) 1—35; L. Curtius, Ikonographische Beiträge VI, MDAI(R) 49 (1934) 119—56;
O. Brendel, The Great Augustus Cameo at Vienna, AJA 43 (1939) 307—8; C. Küthmann,
Zur Gemma Augustea, AA (1950—1) 89—103; and the excellent notes of H. Kähler to his
translation of A. Rubens, Dissertatio de Gemma Augustea, Monumenta Artis Romanae 9
(Berlin 1968), a study which itself is still of basic importance. Most recently see H. Jucker,
Der große Pariser Kameo. Eine Huldigung an Agrippina, Claudius und Nero, JDAI 91
(1976) 211—250.

[269] Suet. Aug. 60; BMC I no. 665—8. Cf. Mattingly, BMC I cxxiv; and Sutherland,
Coinage 44.

[270] Cf. A. Nock, HThR 23 (1930) 263—4 (rep. in: Idem, Essays on Religion and the Ancient
World, ed. by Z. Stewart [Cambridge, Mass. 1972] 262).

official testimony as the coinage, it becomes clear that after 27 B.C. Jupiter was relegated to a position of honored insignificance. The unimportance of Jupiter in Augustus' official religious policy was marked and intentional. The coinage offers our surest guide. A plethora of types honor Augustus and members of the imperial family, as well as such patron divinities as Mars Ultor, Apollo Actiacus, and Diana Sicula.[271] After 27 B.C. there is one significant reference to Jupiter on the imperial coinage for the duration of Augustus' reign. An issue of *aurei* and *denarii* from the period 19–16/15 B.C. portray on the reverse a hexastyle temple, in the center of which stands Jupiter, holding thunderbolt and sceptre.[272] The legend identifies the building as the temple of Jupiter Tonans dedicated on September 1, 22 B.C.[273] The cult and its context are suggestive. The type of Jupiter Tonans occurs within a series of types honoring Augustus and his victories, the divine foreordination of his principate, his divine father, and monuments which celebrate the Augustan achievement, including the altar to Fortuna Redux, the Capitoline temple of Mars Ultor, and the temple of Jupiter Tonans.[274] All three shrines celebrate the divine role in the preservation and success of Augustus: Mars Ultor at Philippi, Fortuna Redux during Augustus' stay in the East, and Jupiter Tonans during an incident in the Cantabrian Campaign described by Suetonius:

> *Tonanti Iovi aedem consecravit liberatus periculo cum expeditione Cantabrica per nocturnum iter lecticam eius fulgur praestrinxisset servumque praelucentem exanimasset.*[275]

In short neither the temple nor the type of Jupiter Tonans celebrates Jupiter as supreme god of the *res publica romana*. They honor Augustus and his *felicitas*.

According to Suetonius, Jupiter Optimus Maximus appeared in a dream to Augustus, complaining that the new shrine of Jupiter Tonans was stealing his worshipers.[276] Augustus replied that he had only wished to give Capitoline Jupiter a janitor, and upon awakening affixed bells to the temple of Tonans. The story may be apocryphal, an aetological anecdote to explain the bells. However, it may also have been taken from Augustus' autobiography, where it was intended to defend his attention to the new cult.[277] In either case, it accurately reflects the polite

---

[271] For all aspects of the imagery of the Augustan coinage, SUTHERLAND, Coinage 1–78, is still the best survey. For Mars Ultor cf. also J. H. CROON, Die Ideologie des Marskultes unter dem Principat und ihre Vorgeschichte, below in this same volume (ANRW II, 17,1) 246–275, esp. 250ff., for Apollo Actiacus H. GAGÉ, L'Apollon impérial, below (ANRW II, 17, 2).

[272] BMC I no. 362–5.

[273] For the dedication date, see DEGRASSI, II XIII, 2, 504. Cf. Suet. Aug. 29; Res Gestae 19; Dio 54.4.2. For inscriptions to Jupiter Tonans, see CIL IX 2162; XI 3773, 3778; XII 501.

[274] BMC I pp. 62–76.

[275] The quote is from Suetonius Aug. 29.1. The small domed shrine of Mars Ultor commemorated on BMC I no. 366–75 is the little temple dedicated on the Capitol in 20 B.C., not the great temple in Augustus' *forum*, which was dedicated in 2 B.C.; cf. Dio 55.10. Res Gestae 21, 29; Suet. Aug. 29.1–2. For the Ara Fortunae Reducis, see Res Gestae 11; Dio 54.10; CIL I² p. 332.

[276] Suet. Aug. 91.2.

[277] Cf. LATTE, Römische Religionsgeschichte 305–6.

manner in which the Capitoline cult was pushed into the background in the religious policy of the new principate. Nowhere is this seen more clearly than by the fashion in which the Augustan temples of Mars Ultor and Apollo Actiacus were intended to usurp the central role of Jupiter Optimus Maximus in public affairs and to become the sites of the most import events of public life, ceremonies which had previously been the prerogative of Jupiter. In the temple of Mars Ultor the Senate was to meet to discuss matters of war and peace, and there was to occur the formal granting of a triumph by the Senate. There the *triumphator* was to deposit the emblems of victory, as Augustus had so placed the standards recovered from the Parthians. Provincial governors were to take formal leave for their new provinces from the temple of Mars Ultor, and there the *censor* was to drive a nail after the completion of a *lustrum*. Mars Ultor was to witness the assumption of the *toga virilis* by all members of the imperial family.[278] No less significant was the transfer of the 'Sibylline books' from the custody of Jupiter Optimus Maximus to Apollo Actiacus. A treasury of advice for maintaining that *pax deorum* upon which the safety of the state depended and a potent source for political machinations, the 'Sibylline books' had been under the protection of Capitoline Jupiter since the first set had been brought to Rome under Tarquin. Filled with prophecies of kingship, they were now carefully edited and placed under the pedestal of the god who had brought world rule to Augustus.[279]

In conscious emulation of the Hellenistic monarchies, the political theology of the new principate was personal, dynastic, and exclusive. Mars Ultor and Apollo Actiacus celebrated the epochal victories which had established the new order. Their theme was the god-given *felicitas* of the charismatic dynast, sprung from divine ancestry and chosen by the gods for world rule. Both themes, the divine origin of the dynasty and its foundation in god-given victory, were central elements in the royal ideology of the Hellenistic monarchies. Now protesting filial piety and the triumph of Romans arms over the East, they appeared to bolster an Augustan monarchy.

Vowed on the eve of Philippi *pro ultione paterna*, the great temple of Mars Ultor was dedicated in 2 B.C., the centerpiece of the Augustan forum.[280] Its *cella* housed three gods, Mars Ultor, Venus Genetrix, and Divus Julius.[281] Mars

---

[278] Dio 55.10.2ff. For the deposition of the Parthian standards, see Res Gestae 29. In general for the significance of these provisions, see MOMMSEN, Römische Chronologie 179—80; IDEM, Staatsrecht II 407; WISSOWA, RKR² 78; LATTE, Römische Religionsgeschichte 303. J. H. C. CROON (above n. 272) 256ff.

[279] Suet. Aug. 31.1; Tibull. 2.5.17; Verg. Aen. 6.72; Servius Aen. 6.72.

[280] Suet. Aug. 29.2; cf. Ovid Fasti 5.545—98; Dio 55.10.1, 60.5.3; CIL I² p. 318.

[281] For the association of Venus in the cult, see Ovid Trist. 2.295; for Divus Julius, see CIL X 8373. Cf. G. WISSOWA, De Veneris Simulacris Romanis (Breslau 1882), in: IDEM, Gesammelte Abhandlungen zur römischen Religions- und Stadtgeschichte (Munich 1904) 50—1; T. KRAUS, Mars Ultor und Kultbild, in: Fest. E. v. Mercklin (Waldsassen 1964) 73. Mars and Venus appeared together on the pediment of the temple; cf. the relief in the Villa Medici (P. HOMMEL, Studien zu den römischen Figurengiebeln [Berlin 1954] 22ff.; pl. 2; I. S. RYBERG, Rites of the State Religion in Roman Art, MAAR 22 [1955] 69—70;

and Venus were the ancestors of the Julian house,[282] as Dionysos had been the
ancestor of the Attalids and the Ptolemies and Apollo of the Seleucids.[283] Divus
Julius fully corresponds to Seleukos Nikator, Ptolemaios Soter, and Philetairos,
enrolled among the gods of the state, their mortal remains enshrined as the
object of cult. Divus Julius had been the watchword at Philippi,[284] and like the
Spartans with the bones of Orestes and Ptolemy with the corpse of Alexander,[285]
Octavian won fair requital from gods and men by his honors to his deified father;
but lest the implication be lost Julius' divine status became part of his heir's
official nomenclature.[286] The temple of Mars Ultor enshrined the victory-
bearing *felicitas* of the Julian *gens* which had brought blessings to the entire Roman
commonwealth. The day of its dedication was the first day of Augustus' own
month, August, officially labeled by the Senate as the most propitious month
for the Roman state. In that month Augustus had assumed his first consulship
and in that month he had thrice entered Rome in triumph, had ended the civil
wars, and had brought Egypt under the power of the Roman People.[287] In the
republic, the charisma of victory was narrowly associated with the Roman
People, its god Jupiter and its personification, Roma. Now it is inextricably
linked with the person of the *princeps*. The theme was continued in the decoration of the Forum Augustum with statues of the great *triumphatores* from Aeneas

P. ZANKER, Forum Augustum: Das Bildprogramm., Monum. Artis Antiquae 2 [Tübingen
1970] 18—9).

[282] The exact construction of the genealogy poses problems. In his funeral oration for his aunt
(Suet. Caes. 6), Caesar referred only to the descent of the Iulii from Venus. At Pharsalus
he sacrificed to Mars and Venus (App. B.C. 2.68); and after the battle he was called
son of Ares and Aphrodite (SIG 760). More significantly, the Feriale Cumanum (CIL X
8375) associates his birthday with sacrifices to Mars Ultor and Venus Genetrix.
WEINSTOCK, Divus Julius 17, 129, 183, argues that the connection with Mars arose
through the alleged descent of the Iulii from Romulus. However, see the objection of
LATTE, Römische Religionsgeschichte 302 n. 6.

[283] For the Ptolemies' descent from Dionysos, see P. M. FRASER, Ptolemaic Alexandria (Ox-
ford 1972) 44—5, 202—3. For Apollo and the Seleucids, see G. DOWNEY, A History of
Antioch in Syria (Princeton 1961) 68. For Dionysos and the Attalids, see E. HANSEN, The
Attalids of Pergamum², Cornell Studies in Classical Philology 36 (Ithaca 1971) 461; and
TAEGER, Charisma I, 346.

[284] Cf. R. SYME, The Roman Revolution (Oxford 1939) 470—1.

[285] Diod. 18.28.4.

[286] For the adoption of the title *Divi Filius* and its propaganda value, see TAYLOR, Divinity of
the Roman Emperor 78—150; K. SCOTT, The Sidus Iulium and the Apotheosis of Caesar,
CPh 36 (1941) 257—72; E. SJÖQVIST, Kaisareion: A study in Architectural Iconography,
in: Opuscula Romana I. A. Boethius gewidmet, Acta Inst. Rom. Regni Sueciae, Ser. in
4°, 18 (Lund 1954) 86—108; A. ALFÖLDI, Studien über Caesars Monarchie, Bull. Soc. des
Lettres de Lund 1952—1953, 1 (Lund 1953) 38—82; TAEGER, Charisma II, 82—8, 97—100;
J. C. RICHARD, Énée, Romulus, César et les funérailles impériales, MEFR 78 (1966)
67—78; GESCHE, Vergottung Caesars 89—90; A. ALFÖLDI, La divinisation de César dans la
politique d'Antoine et d'Octavien entre 44 et 40 av. J.-C., Revue Numismatique 6,15
(1973) 99—128.

[287] Cf. DEGRASSI, II XIII, 2, 490; Macrob. Sat. 1.12.35 purports to give the senatorial decree
recording the reasons for the change of name.

to the present.[288] The implications were dynastic as well as patriotic, forming an Augustan counterpart to the *area Capitolina* with its statues of *triumphatores* and their *spolia*. The sculptural survey of Rome's military greatness in the Forum Augustum began with Aeneas, like Mars, ancestor of the Roman state and the Julian *gens*. Centering upon the temple of Mars Ultor, it portrayed the Augustan achievement as the culmination of Rome's collective triumph and linked it inextricably with the *felicitas* of the dynasty. On the Capitoline, sacrifices were offered to the collective Genius of the Roman People, in the form of the cult of Genius Publicus.[289] Now, in the Forum Augustum, Genius Augusti was joined in cult with Mars Ultor, Venus Genetrix, and Divus Julius.[290]

The Augustan Palatine formed a second counterpart to the Jovian Capitolium with its republican associations of Jupiter as the preserver and augmenter of the Roman commonwealth. Jupiter Imperator stood on the Capitoline, symbolic of those victories by which Jupiter had raised Rome to mistress of the world.[291] Apollo Actiacus openly proclaimed that victory by which Augustus had been elevated to master of the *oikoumene*. According to Propertius, the struggle at Actium witnessed the epiphany of Apollo, who hailed Augustus as *Salvator Mundi* and *Princeps*, bidding him to conquer by sea and promising him world rule. Apollo promised to be at Augustus' side, his bow would fight for him, his every arrow would favor the *princeps*, upon whom the safety of Rome depended.[292] Like Athena and Zeus on the acropolis of Pergamum, Palatine Apollo symbolized the divinely granted victory to which the monarch owed his position; and like the Attalids, Augustus dwelt beside his patron divinities.[293] Like those of the Attalids, it was a modest residence.[294] However, this should not lead us to underestimate the implications of the Augustan complex on the Palatine. After 12 B.C., part of the house was *locus publicus*, as residence of the *pontifex maximus*.[295] By senatorial decree, the cult of Vesta, so central to the public worship of the commonwealth, was brought into the closest association with the emperor and his house. Augustus erected an altar to Vesta in his own home, and the new imperial shrine came to overshadow the public cult in the

---

[288] In general see ZANKER, Forum Augustum, with the earlier literature.

[289] DEGRASSI, II XIII, 2, 518.

[290] Cf. CIL VI 2042, 29; 2051, 88; Acta Frat. Arv., ed. HENZEN 84, 87.

[291] Cic. Verr. 4.58.129.

[292] Prop. 4.6.23,37—54.

[293] In general, for the charismatic significance of the Augustan Palatine, see FEARS, Princeps 214—5; and FEARS, Vergilius 22 (1976) 49. Cf. N. DEGRASSI, La dimora di Augusto sul Palatino e la base di Sorrento, RPAA 39 (1966—7) 77—116.

[294] Suet. Aug. 72. On the modest nature of the residences of the Hellenistic Monarchs, see A. VON GERKAN, Griechische Städteanlagen. Untersuchungen zur Entwicklung des Städtebaus im Altertum (Berlin—Leipzig 1924) 109. For the identification of the house of Augustus, see G. CARETTONI, I problemi della zona augustea del Palatino alla luce dei recenti scavi, RPAA 39 (1966—67) 55—75; F. C. GIULIANI, Note sull'architettura delle residenze imperiali dal I al III secolo d. Chr., ANRW II, 12,1 (1981).

[295] Dio 54.27.3; 55.12.5.

Forum.[296] *Phoebus habet partem, Vestae pars altera cessit, / quod superest illis, tertius ipse [Augustus] tenet*, wrote Ovid.[297] The imperial Vesta (Caesarea Vesta) and the imperial Apollo shared the Palatine with Augustus. However unpretentious the actual living quarters of the emperor, his Palatine home included the temple of Actian Apollo built at divine command: *templum Apollinis in ea parte Palatinae domus excitavit, quam fulmine ictam desiderari a deo haruspices pronuntiarant.*[298] Here Augustus received foreign delegations; and here, particularly in his later years, the Senate frequently met.[299] His immediate neighbor to the southwest was Romulus, in the form of the Casa Romuli and the little shrine which marked the spot on which Romulus had taken those auspices by which the gods elected him to be king over his new city.[300] Those same auspices sanctioned the very name Augustus, adopted by Octavian, who had also considered Romulus a suitable name for the new *princeps*.[301] Further to the west was the temple of the Magna Mater, who in Vergil's account had blessed the departure from Troy of Augustus' ancestor Aeneas.[302] The whole area, probably set off from the rest of the Palatine by the Arcus Octavii, thus formed an architectural statement and unification of three major charismatic aspects of the Augustan principate: the divine origin of the dynasty, the theology of victory, and the assimilation of Augustus to Romulus, elect of the gods and inaugurator of a golden age.

In all this, Jupiter had no place. His most important function in the religious ideology of the new principate was as the recipient of *vota* on behalf of the emperor.[303] The participation of all four priestly colleges emphasized the importance of the ceremony for the entire commonwealth.[304] An Augustan innovation, the *vota* were monarchic in implication and Hellenistic in origin. The motivating concept was the belief that the safety of the community depended utterly upon the well-being of the ruler.[305] Jupiter best performed his duty

---

[296] Cf. Fast. Caer., Ap. 28. See A. DEGRASSI, Esistette sul Palatino un tempio di Vesta, MDAI(R) 62 (1955) 144–54; and IDEM, II XIII, 2, 452; N. DEGRASSI, La dimora di Augusto sul Palatino e la base di Sorrento, RPAA 39 (1966–67) 77–116; CARETTONI, RPAA 39 (1966–67) 57; B. TAMM, Auditorium and Palatium, Stockholm Studies in Class. Arch. 2 (Lund 1963) 47–8.

[297] Ovid Fasti 4.949–54.

[298] Suet. Aug. 29.

[299] Dio 49.15.5–6, 55.33.5; Suet. Aug. 29.3; Verg. Aen. 8.720.

[300] NASH, A Pictorial Dictionary of Ancient Rome I², s.v., collects the evidence.

[301] Suet. Aug. 7.

[302] Verg. Aen. 2.801–3; cf. T. KÖVES, Zum Empfang der Magna Mater in Rom, Historia 12 (1963) 332–3; P. LAMBRECHTS, Cybèle, divinité étrangère ou nationale, Bull. Soc Roy. Belge d'Anthrop. et de Préhist. 2 (1951) 45, 50. For the identity of the temple, see NASH, Pictorial Dictionary I² s.v.

[303] For the imperial *vota* in general, see below pp. 97–100.

[304] Cf. LATTE, Römische Religionsgeschichte 305.

[305] For this concept in Hellenistic and Roman political thought and panegyric, see J. BÉRANGER, Recherches sur l'aspect idéologique du principat, Schweizer. Beiträge zur Altertumswissenschaft 6 (Basel 1953) 169–218; E. DOBLHOFER, Die Augustuspanegyrik des

towards the Roman People by preserving the person of Augustus: *non te [Iovem] distringimus votis. Simplex cunctaque ista complexum omnium votum est, salus principis.*[306] The supreme god of the *res publica Romana* had his place in official Augustan religious policy: to hear the prayers of the Roman People and to preserve their saviour Augustus. For Cicero, Jupiter directly intervened to save the commonwealth. In the ideology of the Augustan principate, this role was reserved for Augustus. Suggestive are the *omina imperii* which foretold Augustus' rise to world mastery. In a dream his father saw him, wearing the garb of Jupiter Optimus, crowned with a radiate diadem, wielding thunderbolt and sceptre, and riding in a belaurelled chariot drawn by twelve white horses.[307] So too the young Octavian was said to haunt the dreams of Q. Catulus after the dedication of the Capitoline temple. In one, he saw Jupiter place the *signum rei publicae*, which the god had held, into the hands of Octavian. In a second, the boy appeared in the lap of the god, who forbad Catulus to remove him, proclaiming that Octavian was being reared to be the guardian of the Roman commonwealth.[308]

The great god was thus honored and ignored, his central role as preserver and augmenter of the Roman commonwealth usurped by divinities linked to the new patron of the Roman People. Thus the first day of the *ludi saeculares* began with a sacrifice to Jupiter Optimus Maximus, the second to Juno, but the third to Apollo and Diana.[309] In the 'Carmen saeculare,' Apollo and Diana are in-

Horaz in formalhistorischer Sicht, Bibl. der klass. Altertumswiss. 2,16 (Heidelberg 1966) 52–6,116–21; IDEM, Horaz und Augustus, ANRW II, 31, 3 (1981) 1949–61; R. NISBET and M. HUBBARD, A Commentary on Horace: Odes, Book I (Oxford 1970) 167–8.

[306] Pliny Pan. 94, of Trajan, of course, but the idea parallels Hor. Epist. 1.16.27–9. To this last Porphyrio notes: *sunt notissimo ex panegyrico Augusti.* The panegyric mentioned by Porphyrio was probably that of L. Varius Rufus; cf. H. BARDON, La littérature latine inconnue II (Paris 1956) 32–3; DOBLHOFER, Augustuspanegyrik 14–5; and W. WIMMEL, Der Augusteer Lucius Varius Rufus, ANRW II, 30,2 (1982).

[307] Suet. Aug. 94.

[308] Suet. Aug. 94, with a similar dream attributed to Cicero. The dream of Cicero, with slight variations also appears in Plut. Cicero 44; in Dio 45.2, also with a version of the dream of Catulus; and in Tertullian De anima 46.7, ed. J. WASZINK, p. 494. WASZINK argues rightly that the story of Cicero's dream already appeared in the commentarii on the gens Vitellia written for Q. Vitellius, *quaestor* under Augustus.

[309] The best general treatments of the Augustan *ludi Saeculares* are M. NILSSON, Saeculares ludi, RE I A, 2 (1920) 1710–1717; L. R. TAYLOR, New light on the History of the Secular Games, AJPh 55 (1934) 101–20; J. GAGÉ, Apollon romain, BEFAR 182 (Paris 1955) 622–37. See also G. PIGHI, De ludis saecularibus populi romani quiritium libri VI² (Amsterdam 1965). For the role of Apollo and Diana in the 'Carmen Saeculare', see esp. the perceptive treatment of J. GAGÉ, Recherches sur les jeux séculaires (Paris 1934) 25–43; and IDEM, Observations sur le Carmen saeculare d'Horace, REL 9 (1931) 290–308; L. HERRMANN, À propos du chant séculaire d'Horace, REL 15 (1937) 308–15; A. LA PENNA, Orazio e l'ideologia del principato (Turin 1963) 106–08; G. K. GALINSKY, Sol and the Carmen Saeculare, Latomus 26 (1967) 619–33; H. RAHN, Zum Carmen Saeculare des Horaz, Gymnasium 77 (1970), 467–79. See also E. FRAENKEL, Horace (Oxford 1957) 364–82, the most sensitive interpretation of the poem as a whole and its circumstances. See, most recently, P. BRIND'AMOUR, L'origine des jeux séculaires, ANRW II, 16, 2 (1978) 1334–1417.

voked to inaugurate the golden age. They were responsible for Rome's rise to greatness, and now under their auspices Augustus rules the *oikoumene* with stern justice and prosperity for all. Jupiter is confidently invoked to give his blessing to the Latonigenae's assumption of the welfare of Rome as their special charge. Suggestive too is Augustus' comment in the 'Res Gestae.'[310] Jupiter appears first in the list, but the fact remains that he now shares the honor of the *spolia* with the patron divinities of Augustus: *dona ex manibiis in Capitolio et in aede divi Juli et in aede Apollinis et in aede Vestae et in templo Martis Ultoris consacravi quae mihi constiterunt HS (sestertium) circiter milliens.*

In short, the minor role of Jupiter in Augustan religious policy was the product of the conscious intent of the new *princeps*. He followed a pattern already set by Julius Caesar and, to a lesser degree, by Pompey and Sulla. Historically, deeply linked with the fate of the Roman commonwealth, Jupiter was closely identified by Cicero and the Optimates with the free *res publica* and its institutions, above all constitutional government and the prerogatives of the Senate. As such, he stood in opposition to the claims of the great charismatic generals, who associated their own cause with the divine sanction of personal patron divinities, particularly Venus and, later for Octavian, Mars Ultor and Apollo. The triumph of their cause was reflected in the displacement of Jupiter from the coinage and the dominance of their divine patrons. Augustus claimed to have restored the republic, and in a certain sense he did.[311] However, he realized that the republic could only function in the presence of a permanent *rector*, who incorporated in his person and prerogatives all real power in the state. The position of the *princeps* was obvious to all; and no less openly Augustus sought to establish his new order upon a political myth which identified divine concern for the well-being of the state with the *princeps* and his personal patron divinities. As the political institutions of the republic were honored but in fact totally subordinated to the omnipotence of Augustus, so the supreme god of the republic was honored but in fact relegated to a minor position besides the patron gods of Augustus. It was a policy followed by his immediate Julio-Claudian successors. Jupiter has no place upon the coinage of Tiberius and Gaius.[312] Their types celebrate the emperor, his virtues, and the imperial family. For divine legitimization, they invoke the charisma of the dynasty embodied in the person of Divus Augustus Pater, now assimilated to Jupiter.[313] The relegation of Jupiter to a subordinate position was subtle; but its

---

[310] Res Gestae 21.

[311] For a discussion of the sincerity of Augustus' claim to have restored the republic, see, among recent studies, W. KUNKEL, Gymnasium 68 (1961) 353—70; M. HAMMOND, The Sincerity of Augustus, HSCPh 69 (1965) 139—62; F. MILLAR, Two Augustan Notes, CR n.s. 18 (1968) 265—6; H. W. BENARIO, Augustus Princeps, ANRW II, 2 (1975) 79—80.

[312] For Gaius and Jupiter, see below pp. 71—3.

[313] For the assimilation of Augustus to Jupiter on the coinage of Tiberius, see BMC I no. 155—8. For Divus Augustus as Jupiter on Spanish issues, see A. HEISS, Description générale des monnaies antiques d'Espagne (Paris 1870) p. 124, 196, 401. A Roman issue, properly dated to 42 A.D., portrays the thunderbolt in the field of a portrait of Divus Augustus; cf. C. SUTHERLAND, Divus Augustus Pater, NC 6,1 (1941) pl. I. For the

dynastic and monarchic implications were not lost upon contemporaries. When Gaius was assassinated, those senators who sought to restore the republic refused to meet in the Curia with its Julian name. Instead they convoked the Senate in the Capitoline temple of Jupiter Optimus Maximus.[314]

2. The Evolution of a Jovian Theology of Imperial Power

a) The Julio-Claudian Background

The literature of the Augustan age offers a contrast to the insignificance of Jupiter in the official religious policy of the period. Vergil associated Jupiter directly with the fate of Rome and Augustus: *imperium sine fine dedi . . . . Sic placitum . . . . Nascetur pulchra Troianus origine Caesar, imperium Oceano, famam qui terminet astris, Iulius a magno demissum nomen Iulo.*[315] Ovid and Manilius celebrated Augustus as the earthly counterpart of Jupiter.[316] Manilius hailed Augustus as *rector Olympi* and *deus ipse*, who had come down from heaven whither he would return to rule with Jupiter as his associate.[317] In the 'Tristia' Ovid hailed Augustus as Jupiter on earth, whose safety assures the pro-

---

bronze statue, now in Naples, of Augustus as Jupiter, see R. WEST, Römische Porträt-plastik I (Munich 1933) pl. 38 no. 162. On the Julio-Claudian dynastic relief from Ravenna, Augustus was portrayed as Jupiter; cf. J. BERNOULLI, Römische Ikonographie II (Stuttgart 1882—94) 254—60, with the earlier literature. For the view that Augustus is portrayed as an unbearded Mars, with lance and sword, see E. PETERSEN, Ara Pacis Augustae, Sonderschriften des Österr. Archäolog. Institutes zu Wien 2 (Vienna 1902) 183. More recently on the Ravenna relief, see V. H. POULSEN, Studies in Julio-Claudian Iconography, Acta Arch 17 (1946) 32—9; L. CURTIUS, Ikonographische Beiträge zum Porträt der römischen Republik und der julisch-claudischen Dynastie, MDAI 1 (1948) 59—63, 81—4; HOMMEL, Studien 27; RYBERG, Rites of the State Religion 91; WEINSTOCK, Divus Julius 129.

[314] Suet. Gaius 60.

[315] Verg. Aen. 1.279, 283, 286—8. R. SCHILLING, Le Romain de la fin de la République et du début de l'Empire en face de la religion, AC 41 (1972) 540—62, stresses the importance of this passage within the general context of Roman religious thought in the late republican and Augustan age. For the scene between Jupiter and Venus and the god's promise, see also, among recent studies, A. WLOSOK, Die Göttin Venus in Vergils Aeneis, Bibl. der klass. Altertumswiss. N.F. 2,21 (Heidelberg 1967) 11—74; H. STAHL, Verteidigung des 1. Buches der Aeneis, Hermes 97 (1969) 346—61, esp. 352—6.

[316] For the assimilation of the emperor to Jupiter in the literary sources, P. RIEWALD, De imperatorum Romanorum cum certis dis et comparatione et aequatione, Dissertationes Philologicae Halenses 20,3 (Halle 1912) retains its value. See also M. WARD, The Association of Augustus with Jupiter, SMSR 9 (1933) 203—24. On Augustus and Jupiter in Horace, there is discussion along with more recent literature in: R. MUTH, Horaz Parcus deorum cultor et infrequens: zu Carm. 1.34, Grazer Beiträge 4 (1975) 171—206; A. DUNSTON, Horace, Ode 1,12 Yet Again, Antichthon 7 (1973) 54—9; T. OKSALA, Religion und Mythologie bei Horaz, Comm. Hum. Litt. 51 (Helsinki 1973); D. INNES, Gigantomachy and Natural Philosophy, CQ n.s. 29 (1979) 165—71.

[317] Manil. 1.9,916. Cf. E. FLORES, Augusto nella visione astrologica di Manilio ed il problema della cronologia degli Astronomicon libri, AFLN 9 (1960—61) 5—66.

tection of the gods for the whole of the Ausonian race.[318] The same theme appears at the close of the 'Metamorphoses.' Destined to join the gods, Augustus is Jupiter's earthly counterpart. Both are *pater* and *rector*; Jupiter's watches over the heavens, while Augustus guards the earth.[319] The same motif is invoked by Horace in the fifth Roman ode:

> *Caelo tonantem credidimus Iovem*
> *regnare: praesens divus habebitur*
> *Augustus adiectis Britannis*
> *imperio gravibusque Persis.*[320]

However, in Horace there is a subtle emphasis on the subordination of Augustus to Jupiter, supreme ruler of gods and men (Od. 3.1.5—8):

> *regum timendorum in proprios greges,*
> *reges in ipsos imperium est Iovis,*
> *clari Giganteo triumpho,*
> *cuncta supercilio moventis.*

Jupiter has appointed Augustus to expiate the crimes of Rome and the resultant divine wrath.[321] By divine will Augustus is leader and father of the Roman state and militant augmenter of its frontiers. Father and guardian of the human race, Jupiter rules all things; but he has chosen Augustus to serve as his vicegerent on earth:

---

[318] Ovid Tr. 5.2.47—8.

[319] Ovid Metam. 15. 858—70. A recent study of the structure of Metam. 15. 622—870 is A. HOLLEMAN, Ovidii Metamorphoseon liber XV, 622—870, Latomus 28 (1969) 42—60; cf. C. SEGAL, Myth and Philosophy in the 'Metamorphoses'. Ovid's Augustanism and the Augustan Conclusion to Book XV, AJPh 90 (1969) 257—92.

[320] Hor. Od. 3.5.4—8. The literature on Augustus and Horace is enormous. Recent treatments of the question, with discussions of earlier literature, include A. LA PENNA, Orazio; V. PÖSCHL, Horaz und die Politik², Heidelb. Akad. d. Wiss., Phil.-hist. Kl., Sitz. 1956, 4 (Heidelberg 1963); W. WILI, Horaz und die augusteische Kultur² (Basel 1965) 131—50; DOBLHOFER, Augustuspanegyrik 11—6; IDEM, Horaz und Augustus (above n. 305); C. STARR, Horace and Augustus, AJPh 90 (1969) 58—64; D. KIENAST, Horaz und die erste Krise des Prinzipats, Chiron 1 (1971) 239—51; C. CARTER, God, King, Law — and Augustus? — in Horaces Odes I—III, PCA 70 (1973) 39—40; T. GESZTELYI, Mercury and Augustus, Horace, Ode I, 2, ACD 9 (1973) 77—81. G. WILLIAMS, Horace Odes 1, 12 and the Succession of Augustus, Hermathena 18 (1974) 147—55; J. KORPANTY, Les vertus d'Auguste dans les odes d'Horace, Meander 30 (1975) 61—75 (in Polish with French summary); D. PIETRUSIŃSKI, Identifications épiphaniques de la divinité avec Octave Auguste chez Virgile et Horace, Eos 66 (1978) 249—66.

[321] Hor. Od. 1.2. Recent studies include G. NUSSBAUM, A Postscript on Horace, Carm. I, 2, AJPh 82 (1961) 406—17; P. JAL, Les dieux et les guerres civiles dans la Rome de la fin de la république, REL 40 (1962) 170—200; LA PENNA, Orazio 81—8; NISBET and HUBBARD, Commentary I, 16—40; L. A. MACKAY, Horace, Augustus, and Ode I,2, AJPh 83 (1962) 168—77; S. COMMAGER, Horace, Carmina I, 2, AJPh 80 (1959) 37—55; F. CAIRNS, Horace, Odes 1,2, Eranos 69 (1971) 68—88; and H. WOMBLE, Horace, Carmina I,2, AJPh 91 (1970) 1—30.

> *Gentis humanae pater atque custos,*
> *orte Saturno, tibi cura magni*
> *Caesaris fatis data: tu secundo*
> > *Caesare regnes.*[322]

As the subordinate of the divine father, Augustus rules the earth in his behalf, the warrior vicegerent of Jupiter who holds the barbarians at bay. Augustus sees to the tasks of men, freeing Jupiter to look after the concerns of the gods:

> *Ille seu Parthos Latio imminentis*
> *egerit iusto domitos triumpho*
> *sive subiectos Orientis orae*
> > *Seras et Indos,*
>
> *Te minor latum reget aequos orbem:*
> *tu gravi curru quaties Olympum,*
> *tu parum castis inimica mittes*
> > *fulmina lucis.*[323]

The prominence of the association of Jupiter and *princeps* in Augustan pan-egyric may have been largely literary in origin. "Kings are from Zeus," wrote Hesiod; and the tradition of Zeus-nutured kings was a familiar one in Greek literature.[324] In the 'Iliad' Zeus bestowed kingship upon Agamemnon, investing him with the sceptre, his symbol of authority, with the right to render justice and with the obligation to take counsel for his subjects.[325] Other kings are Zeus-nurtured and Zeus-sprung; but to Agamemnon alone has Zeus bestowed the heaven-wrought sceptre, in virtue of which Agamemnon leads the Achaean host.[326] Echoes of the Homeric tradition of the divine election of kings appear in Pindar, Aeschylus, Sophocles and, in the Hellenistic period, in Theocritus and in Callimachus' 'Hymn to Zeus.'[327] Zeus played a prominent role in the royal ideology of all the great Hellenistic monarchies; and the association of Zeus and king seems to have been an important *topos* of Hellenistic royal pan-egyrics. In his own lifetime, panegyrists sought to associate closely Alexander and Zeus; and on decadrachms struck towards the end of his life, Alexander was portrayed wielding the thunderbolt of Zeus.[328] In the same way, the memory of

---

[322] Hor. Od. 1.12.49—52.

[323] Hor. Od. 1.12.53—60.

[324] Hesiod Th. 94—6. For a detailed discussion, with full bibliography, of the concept of divine election in Greek literature and political life, see FEARS, Princeps 29—83.

[325] Il. 2. 203—6.

[326] Il 2.100—8.

[327] Pind. Nem. 4.67; Pyth. 4. 106, 5.12; Aeschylus Agam. 42.4; Eum. 625; Pers. 762; Soph. Philoc. 135—43; Call. Zeus 73—4; Theocritus Idyl 17.71—5.

[328] For the association of Alexander and Zeus, see Callisthenes, FGrHist 124 F 14a. Apelles portrayed Alexander wielding the thunderbolt; cf. Pliny NH 35.92; Plut. Alex. 4.2; De fort. Alex. 2.2.; Is. 24. See also D. MICHEL, Alexander als Vorbild für Pompeius, Caesar und Marcus Antonius, Coll. Latomus 94 (Brussels 1967) 28—9. For the decadrachms portraying Alexander with the thunderbolt, see HEAD, Historia Numorum² 833. For the

Alexander played an important role in forming a second major theme of Hellenistic royal panegyric, the image of the king as ruler of the *oikoumene*, who, by his government of earth, frees Zeus to devote his attention entirely to heaven.[329]

Hellenistic encomiastic tradition exercised a marked influence on Augustan panegyric; and together with the Homeric tradition of the divine election of kings, it was the primary literary model for the celebration of Augustus as the divinely chosen earthly counterpart of Jupiter. This is also true for Horace; but the intensity of his emphasis on Augustus' subordination to Jupiter suggests a personal statement as well, a subtle caution against the minor role of Jupiter in the political theology of the new principate and a harbinger of Augustus' own misgivings expressed in nocturnal admonitions from Jupiter Optimus Maximus.

The significance of the association of *princeps* and Jupiter in Augustan writers was more than literary. It contained the seeds of a theocratic monarchy at once more broadly based and more absolutist than the Augustan principate, an image of oecumenical autocracy based not on the charisma of a single dynasty but upon the eternal image of the emperor as the divinely chosen vicegerent of the supreme king of gods and men. The argument of Seneca's 'De Clementia' rests upon the assumption of absolutism.[330] *Clementia* in its truest form is only possible when the sovereign, by virtue of his absolute power, stands above the

date and the occasion of issue, see G. HILL, Decadrachm Commemorating Alexander's Indian Campaign, BMQ 1 (1926) 36–7; W. KAISER, Ein Meister der Glyptik aus dem Umkreis Alexanders des Großen, JDAI 77 (1962) 227 n. 3; and A. BELLINGER, Essays on the Coinage of Alexander the Great, Num. Studies 11 (New York, American Num. Soc., 1963) 27. For a detailed discussion, see FEARS, Theology of Victory, below in this same volume (ANRW II, 17, 2) ch. III. 1c.

[329] Cf. Anth. Plan. 120. For the dates and authorship, see A. GOW and D. PAGE, The Greek Anthology: Hellenistic Epigrams II (Cambridge 1965) 590,146–7. For the concept of the ruler as cosmocrator in astrological thought, see Firmicus Maternus I p. 108, 16; p. 123,29, ed. KROLL and SKUTSCH, and the treatise attributed to Hermes Trismegistos in: W. GUNDEL, Neue astrologische Texte des Hermes Trismegistos, Abhandlungen der bayerischen Akademie der Wissenschaften, Phil.-hist. Abt. NF 12 (Munich 1936) p. 73, 22; p. 84, 31. In general, see F. CUMONT, L'Égypte des astrologues, Fondat. égyptol. Reine Élisabeth (Brussels 1937). A Ptolemaic royal petition is extant in which reference is made to the monarch's kingship over the entire *oikoumene* (PSI V 541).

[330] For this aspect of the 'De clementia' see J. FEARS, Nero as the Vicegerent of the Gods in Seneca's De Clementia, Hermes 103 (1975) 486–96, with the earlier literature. The 'De clementia' is generally dated to between December 55 and December 56 (cf. 1.9.1). See further H. FUCHS, Zu Seneca De Clementia I, 9, RhM 108 (1965) 378; F. GIANCOTTI, Il posto della biografia nella problematica senechiana, IV 1: Sfondo storico e data del De clementia, RAL 9 (1954) 329–44; L. HERMANN, La date du De clementia, REL 7 (1929) 94ff. and IDEM, Encore le De clementia, REA 36 (1934) 353ff.; F. PRÉCHAC, La date et la composition du De clementia, REL 10 (1932) 91ff.; and IDEM, Notulae Vaticane sur le De clementia de Sénèque, MEFR 59 (1957) 49ff.; W. RICHTER, Das Problem der Datierung von Seneca De clementia, RhM 108 (1965) 146–70; and T. ADAM, Clementia Principis: Der Einfluß hellenistischer Fürstenspiegel auf den Versuch einer rechtlichen Fundierung des Principats durch Seneca, Kieler hist. Stud. 11 (Stuttgart 1970) 9 n. 1. For a study of the structure of the 'De clementia' see B. MORTREUX, Recherches sur le De clementia de Sénèque, Collection Latomus 128 (Brussels 1973).

capabilities of human institutions to punish him.[331] For Seneca in the ʿDe Clementia,ʾ such sovereignty is the gift of the gods.[332] The gods have transferred
into the hands of the young Nero power over the entire human race; and he
rules as the earthly vicegerent of the gods.[333] True monarchy is an imitation of
the divine, and the good ruler invites comparison with Jupiter.[334] The same
theme appears in the poetry of Calpurnius Siculus, who directly associates Nero
with Jupiter and wonders if Nero is not in fact Jupiter on earth.[335] In both
Seneca and Calpurnius Siculus, the influence of Hellenistic treatises on kingship
and royal panegyrics is apparent.[336] However, in the Neronian period, the association of *princeps* and Jupiter served as more than a literary and philosophical
topos. At a critical moment in the reign, its appearance on the coinage marks its
re-entry into the mainstream of official imperial ideology. Divine protection of
the emperor was fulsomely invoked to celebrate Nero's escape from the
Pisonian conspiracy.[337] General offerings and thanksgivings were decreed to the
gods, and especially to Sol, whose divine power revealed the conspiracy. A
temple was erected to. Salus and the dagger of Scaevinus was dedicated to
Jupiter Vindex.[338] The commemoration was continued on the coinage, and gold
and silver issues were struck in honor of Salus and Jupiter Custos.[339] On the last
Jupiter is portrayed seated on a throne, holding thunderbolt and sceptre (Pl. V,
26). Appearing along with types of Roma and Vesta,[340] Salus and Jupiter Custos
celebrate a theme central to Hellenistic and Augustan royal panegyric: god
preserves the state by preserving the emperor:

---

[331] Sen. Clem. 1.11.2.

[332] Sen. Clem. 1.5.6−7; 1.21.1−2. Cf. Sen. Thyest. 607−8.

[333] Sen. Clem. 1.1.

[334] Sen. Clem. 1.19.8, 1.7.2.

[335] Calp. Sic. Ec. 4.92−4, 142−4.

[336] For Seneca, see ADAM (above n. 330); FEARS (above n. 330) 491−6; and G. AALDERS,
Political Thought in Hellenistic Times (Amsterdam 1975) 19. E. CHAMPLIN, The Life and
Times of Calpurnius Siculus, JRS 68 (1978) 95−110, suggests that Severus Alexander was
the object of Calpurnius' panegyric. For the traditional dating to the Neronian age, see,
e.g., W. SCHMID, Panegyrik und Bukolik in der neronischen Epoche, BJ 153 (1953)
63−96; D. KORZENIEWSKI, Zur ersten und siebten Ekloge des Calpurnius Siculus, MH 33
(1976) 248−53; M. L. PALADINI, Osservazioni a Calpurnio Siculo, Latomus 15 (1956)
330−46, 521−31; M. SPARADO, Sulle eloghe politiche di Tito Calpurnio Siculo (Catania
1969); E. LEACH, Corydon Revisited, Ramus 2 (1973) 53−97. In general, see E. CIZEK,
L'époque de Néron et ses controverses idéologiques, Roma Aeterna 4 (Leiden 1972), with
the review by M. GRIFFIN in: JRS 66 (1976) 229−30.

[337] A general study of Neronian propaganda is W. HUSS, Die Propaganda Neros, AC 47
(1978) 129−48.

[338] Tac. Ann. 15.74. On the Pisonian conspiarcy, see B. BALDWIN, Executions, Trials, and
Punishment in the Reign of Nero, PP 22 (1967) 425−39; K. BRADLEY, Suetonius' Life of
Nero: An Historical Commentary, Collection Latomus 153 (Brussels 1978); CIZEK (above
n. 336) 184−93.

[339] BMC I no. 67−76. For the connection with Nero's escape from the conspiracy of Piso, see
also P. HILL, Aspects of Jupiter on Coins of the Roman Mint, NC 6,20 (1960) 120; and
SUTHERLAND, Emperor and Coinage 118.

[340] For Salus, BMC I no. 87−100; Vesta, no. 100−06; Roma, no. 81−6.

Tene magis salvum populus velit an populum tu
servet in ambiguo qui consulit et tibi et urbi
Iuppiter.[341]

By his care, the emperor preserves the commonwealth. His subjects, cognizant of this fact pray Jupiter to protect the emperor; and, in so doing, they pray for their own safety. The emperor stands in a double stream of care, prayed for from below and protected from above.

Later in the reign of Nero, during the trip to Greece, Jupiter again appears on the coinage, on an issue of *aurei* in honor of Jupiter Liberator, portraying a seated Jupiter, holding thunderbolt and sceptre (Pl. V, 27).[342] The type commemorates Nero's liberation of Greece, by which Achaea as a whole obtained autonomy and immunity from taxation. In gratitude, the town of Acraephiae erected an altar and a statue of Nero Zeus Eleutherios. The assimilation of Nero to Zeus Eleutherios also appears on an issue of copper coins, struck in Greece.[343] In contrast to the Jupiter Custos type, with its emphasis on the god's protection of Nero, the Jupiter Liberator type commemorates the emperor's role as performer of the functions of Jupiter on earth. As Zeus Eleutherios had earlier delivered Greece from peril, so his earthly counterpart Nero now had liberated Greece from her burdens. This dual theme, the emperor as vicegerent of Jupiter and Jupiter as protector of his vicegerent, were to form the two pillars of a Jovian theology of imperial power at Rome.

The reign of Nero then was central in the re-establishment of Jupiter as the dominant divine figure in official imperial ideology. Under Nero he appears on the Roman coinage for the first time since early in the principate of Augustus; and his reappearance is explicitly associated with the protection of the emperor as the surest means to preserve Rome itself. In the last years of his reign, Nero was moving towards a Jovian theology of imperial power, the establishment of the principate upon an ideological foundation deriving the emperor's power directly from Jupiter.

As a predecessor in this aim, he may have had Caligula. Among the acts of Gaius the monster, Suetonius records that the emperor sought to associate himself with Jupiter by a variety of actions. He adopted the title: *Optimus Maximus Caesar*; and he sought to have his own head placed upon the statue of Zeus at Olympia. He extended the palace into the Forum, converting the shrine of Castor and Pollux into a vestibule. Those who visited to worship him, on occasion, called him Jupiter Latiaris. He would frequently hold conversations with Capitoline Jupiter. At length he announced that Jupiter had asked him to

---

[341] Hor. Epist. 1.16.27–9. See above n. 306.

[342] BMC I no. 110. The coin is rightly accepted as genuine by M. GRANT, Nero (New York 1970) 232; E. SMALLWOOD, Documents Illustrating the Principates of Gaius, Claudius, and Nero (Cambridge 1967) 37. K. BRADLEY treats: The Chronology of Nero's Visit to Greece A.D. 66/67, Latomus 37 (1978) 61–72.

[343] SIG 814; for the coin and its attribution to Sicyon, see COOK, Zeus II, 97 n. 3. G. BARBIERI, Liberator, in: E. DE RUGGIERO, Dizionario Epigrafico di Antichità Romane IV fasc. 28 (1958) 889–90, collects the epigraphical and numismatic evidence.

share his home, and he forthwith began to build a house within the precincts of
the Capitol.[344]

Dio too records that Caligula was called Jupiter and Olympios;[345] and in the
East he was celebrated as Zeus Epiphanes Neos Gaios.[346] However, none of this
is corroborated in the epigraphical or numismatic evidence.[347] That is, as far as
the extant sources permit a judgement, the association of Gaius with Jupiter
received official encouragement. However, such encouragement did not, in the
brief period of Gaius' reign, reach the level of a broadly based program utilizing
the wide variety of propaganda media available to the emperor, including the
coinage. Moreover, if Suetonius' comments are regarded objectively, they loose
much of their appearance of the actions of a megalomaniac. Augustus, after
all, was called Jupiter by poets, and in the Greek East he too was identified
with Zeus.[348] Claudius, like Trajan later, was addressed as Optimus;[349] and

---

[344] Suet. Gaius 22: *Compluribus cognominibus adsumptis — nam et pius et castrorum filius et
pater exercituum et optimus maximus Caesar uocabatur — cum audiret forte reges, qui
officii causa in urbem aduenerant, concertantis apud se super cenam de nobilitate generis,
exclamauit* (Hom. Il. 2,204):

εἷς κοίρανος ἔστω, εἷς βασιλεύς.

*nec multum afuit quin statim diadema sumeret speciemque principatus in regni formam
conuerteret. uerum admonitus et principum et regum se excessisse fastigium, diuinam ex eo
maiestatem asserere sibi coepit; datoque negotio, ut simulacra numinum religione et arte
praeclara, inter quae Olympii Iouis, apportarentur e Graecia, quibus capite dempto suum
imponeret, partem Palatii ad forum usque promouit, atque aede Castoris et Pollucis in
uestibulum transfigurata, consistens saepe inter fratres deos, medium adorandum se
adeuntibus exhibebat; et quidam eum Latiarem Iouem consalutarunt. templum etiam
numini suo proprium et sacerdotes et excogitatissimas hostias instituit. in templo simulacrum
ṣtabat aureum iconicum amiciebaturque cotidie ueste, quali ipse uteretur. magisteria
sacerdotii ditissimus quisque et ambitione et licitatione maxima uicibus comparabant.
hostiae erant phoenicopteri, pauones, tetraones, numidicae, meleagrides, phasianae, quae
generatim per singulos dies immolarentur. et noctibus quidem plenam fulgentemque lunam
inuitabat assidue in amplexus atque concubitum, interdiu uero cum Capitolino Ioue secreto
fabulabatur, modo insusurrans ac praebens in uicem aurem, modo clarius nec sine iurgiis.
nam uox comminantis audita est* (Hom. Il 23, 724):

ἤ μ' ἀνάειρ' ἤ ἐγὼ σέ,

*donec exoratus, ut referebat, et in contubernium ultro inuitatus super templum Diui
Augusti ponte transmisso Palatium Capitoliumque coniunxit. mox, quo propior esset, in
area Capitolina nouae domus fundamenta iecit.*

[345] Dio 59.26; 28.8.

[346] Philo Leg. ad Gai. 43.346, 29.188; Jos. AJ 19.1.4, 19.2.11. Cf. S. Eitrem, Zur Apotheose,
SO 10 (1932) 54ff; A. Aiardi, Optimus Maximus Caesar. Considerazioni sull'interesse di
Caligola per il culto di Giove, Atti Istituto Veneto di Scienza, Lettere ed Arti 136 (1977—78)
99—108.

[347] As has often been pointed out, the coinage offers no evidence for the excesses of Gaius
alleged by the literary sources; see Mattingly, BMC I cxli; Taeger, Charisma II,289—
90; J. Balsdon, The Principates of Tiberius and Gaius, ANRW II,2 (1975) 94.

[348] Ward, SMSR 9 (1933) 203—24, collects the evidence.

[349] See the senatorial decree cited by Pliny Ep. 8.6.10; cf. CIL X 1401. In general, see M.
Hammond, Imperial Elements in the Formula of the Roman Emperors during the First
Two and a Half Centuries of the Empire, MAAR 25 (1957) 42.

Nerva adopted Trajan before the altar of Jupiter Optimus Maximus.[350] Suetonius' record of Gaius' action might be viewed as the malicious distortion by Suetonius or his source of a serious attempt by Gaius and his entourage to foster an image of the emperor as the divinely elected vicegerent of Jupiter, a policy which would come to fruition under Trajan.[351] Trajan, as will be seen, proceeded cautiously. First he used a member of his entourage, Pliny, verbally to proclaim this doctrine before the Senate; and only some years later did he permit himself to appear on the coinage as the vicegerent of Jupiter. Suetonius specifically notes that the association of Gaius with Jupiter arose within his entourage. Furthermore this association derived directly from Gaius' quotation of that famous Homeric verse (Il. 2.204) which under Trajan would be used by writers like Dio Chrysostom to justify the doctrine that the emperor ruled as the elect of Zeus. This concept was absolutist; it raised the emperor above human institutions like the Senate. Who could criticize a ruler whose power came from god? Again Suetonius specifically links Gaius' quotation of the Homeric verse to his plan to assume the diadem and to do away with the pretense that he was chief executive of a republic.[352] The Senate under Gaius recognized this and feared it, its historians transforming Gaius' actions from far sighted statesmanship into pure megalomania. Domitian would seek to revive Gaius' policy and would likewise fail. It would remain for Trajan to reconcile the Senate to a Jovian theology of imperial power.

Trajan's accomplishment in this respect might be viewed as an aspect of that reconciliation of *libertas* and *principatus* which Tacitus lauded.[353] In the later Julio-Claudian period, specifically under Gaius and Nero, there is evidence that Jupiter became a figure of partisan conflict between supporters of *principatus* with its absolutist implications and the senatorial opposition to the principate. The former sought to associate Jupiter with the emperor as the earthly image of the god. The senatorial opposition took *libertas* as its battle cry and looked back to Cicero, Cato the Younger, and those Optimates who had revered Jupiter as the preserver of the free *res publica*.[354] Thus Gaius' evocation of Jupiter was repudiated by those senators, who wishing to restore the republic

---

[350] Pliny Pan. 8.

[351] For a similar distortion, see Cic. Dom. 92: *inducis etiam sermonem urbanum . . . me dicere solere esse me Iovem.* The allegation of Clodius must have arisen out of Cicero's claim, during the Catilinarian conspiracy, to have acted as the agent of Jupiter. Cf. WEINSTOCK, Divus Julius 303

[352] Suet. Gaius 22.

[353] Tac. Agricola 3.

[354] G. BOSSIER's classic 'L'opposition sous les Césars' (Paris 1905) has been followed by a large literature dealing with various aspects of opposition. See, among more recent studies, WIRSZUBSKI, Libertas 124—71; R. MACMULLEN, Enemies of the Roman Order (Cambridge, Mass. 1966) 1—94; ADAM, Clementia Principis 56—82; K. BECKER, Studien zur Opposition gegen den römischen Prinzipat (Diss. Tübingen 1950); A. BERGENER, Die führende Senatorenschicht im frühen Prinzipat, Habelts Diss. Drucke, Reihe Alte Geschichte 4 (Diss. Bonn 1965); J. MELMOUX, C. Helvidius Priscus, disciple et héritier de Thrasea, PP 30 (1975) 23—40; A. BREEBAART, The Freedom of the Intellectual in the Roman World, Talanta 7 (1975) 55—75; P. A. BRUNT, Stoicism and the Principate, Papers of the British School at Rome 43 (1975) 6—35.

after his assassination, convoked the Senate in the Capitoline temple of
Jupiter.[355] Nero commemorated Jupiter as the *Custos* who saved him from a
senatorial conspiracy and celebrated his own role as the earthly image of Jupiter
Liberator. Dying at the command of Nero for their alleged opposition, Seneca
and Thrasea Paetus offered their blood as a libation to Jupiter Liberator. They
perished, they would say, as sacrifices for the concept of *libertas*.[356]

With Nero perished the last of the Julio-Claudian line. The image of
Augustus remained a political talisman, and Nero's ultimate successor Vespasian
sought to evoke the memory of the founder of the principate.[357] However, the
parvenu Vespasian did not link himself to the Julio-Claudian line. Nor was such
an association desirable. The excesses, failure, and violent death of Nero had
rendered a mortal blow to the *felicitas* of his dynasty. The gods had given rule
and divine sanction to the Julio-Claudian line; and now they took it away.
Official history recorded the theme in the form of the *omina* which were said to
have surrounded the fall of the Julio-Claudians.[358] In the year of Nero's death, a
peculiar grove of laurels and flock of chickens both died. Their origin went back
to Livia, into whose lap an eagle had dropped a white hen carrying a laurel
branch in its beak. Livia raised the hen, from which issued a large flock of
chickens, and planted the laurel, from which grew a large grove. From the latter
the Caesars cut their laurels when they were to celebrate a triumph and planted
other laurels to replace them. It was noted that before the man died, the laurels
which he had planted died. Shortly after the utter demise of both flock and
grove, lightning struck the temple of the Caesars; the heads fell from all the
statues of the Caesars, and the sceptre was knocked from the hand of Augustus.
Jupiter had given offspring, rule, and victory to the house of Augustus; now he
took it away.

b) The Role of Domitian

The rapid succession of emperors in 68—69 demanded a new emphasis on
divine sanction in imperial ideology. The pliant role of the Senate was not
sufficient to grant legitimacy to emperors who so clearly owed their position to
the praetorians or the legions. Unlike Claudius and Augustus, they could not
appeal to the charisma of the dynasty or to a divine father. Like the Diadochi
they sought to surround themselves with an aura of divine sanctions and in
particular their followers circulated tales of omens which indicated that the gods
had foreordained them for rule. Such *omina imperii* formed a potent source of

---

[355] Suet. Gaius 60.
[356] Tac. Ann. 15.64, 16.35.
[357] Cf. H. NISSEN, Die Stadtgründung der Flavier, RhM 49 (1894) 279—80; WEYNAND, T.
   Flavius Vespasianus, RE VI,2 (1909) 2675; MATTINGLY, BMC II xlix; M. HAMMOND, The
   Antonine Monarchy, Papers and Monographs of the American Academy in Rome 19
   (Rome 1959) 60. The numismatic evidence is treated by T. V. BUTTREY, Vespasian as
   Moneyer, NC 7,12 (1972) 89—109.
[358] Suet. Galba 1.

propaganda and were used with particular efficaciousness by the Flavian sympathizers.[359] Suetonius seems to preserve an 'official' record of these divine phenomena, carefully edited after Vespasian's ultimate success. Of the four emperor's of 68–69 A.D., *omina imperii* cluster around only Galba, whom Vespasian regarded as his legitimate predecessor, and around Vespasian himself.[360] A number of these *omina imperii* were extremely vague, their implications becoming clear only after the recipient had become emperor. Others were more dramatic, and for both Galba and Vespasian *omina* were circulated in which Jupiter himself had clearly foreordained them for rule.[361]

Indeed, the same circumstances brought Jupiter into a new prominence in imperial ideology. In contrast to the last great civil conflict, a century earlier between Antony and Ovtavian, Jupiter played a role on the coinage of 68–69 which, if not dominant, was at least significant. Several issues of the civil war coinage, i.e. lacking imperial portraits, invoke Jupiter in suggestive contexts.[362] A series of coins, associated with the revolt of Vindex and its catchword "freedom from the Tyrant," have various reverse types honoring Jupiter as OPTIMVS MAXIMVS, CAPITOLINVS, LIBERATOR, and CVSTOS. The obverse types associate Jupiter with ROMA RESTITVTA and with GENIVS P(*opuli*) R(*omani*), thus clearly invoking him as the guardian and *liberator* of the Roman

---

[359] In general, see SCOTT, Imperial Cult 1–20; and IDEM, The Role of Basilides in the Events of A.D. 69, JRS (1934) 138–40; R. LATTIMORE, Portents and Prophecies in Connection with the Emperor Vespasian, CJ 29 (1933–34) 441–49; W. WEBER, Josephus und Vespasian. Untersuchungen zu dem jüdischen Krieg des Flavius Josephus (Berlin–Stuttgart–Leipzig 1921) 40–54, 256–8; TAEGER, Charisma II, 210–16; 329–33; R. SYME, Tacitus, I (Oxford 1958) 518–27; R. SCOTT, Religion and Philosophy in the Histories of Tacitus, Papers and Monographs of the American Academy in Rome 22 (Rome 1968) 53–70, 79–95. Specifically on the extremely significant miracles of healing, see S. MORENZ, Vespasian, Heiland der Kranken. Persönliche Frömmigkeit im antiken Herrscherkult?, Würzburger Jahrbücher für die Altertumswissenschaft 4 (1949–50) 370–8; CH. PICARD, Protohistoire de la thaumaturgie royale, RA 38 (1951) 68–9; P. DERCHAIN, La visite de Vespasien au Sérapéum d'Alexandrie, CE 28 (1953) 261–79; L. HERRMANN, Basilides, Latomus 12 (1953) 312–5. For the rumours of a king from Judaea, see J. GAGÉ, Basiléia. Les Césars, les rois d'Orient et les Mages (Paris 1968); and esp. A. SCHALIT, Die Erhebung Vespasians nach Flavius Josephus, Talmud und Midrasch. Zur Geschichte einer messianischen Prophetie, ANRW II,2 (1975) 208–327 with the earlier literature.

[360] Cf. Tac. Hist. 3.7. See further J. GAGÉ, Vespasien et la mémoire de Galba, REA 54 (1952) 290–315. FEARS, Princeps 171–6, discusses the role of *omina imperii* in Suetonius' biographies.

[361] Suet. Galba 4; 8; 9. See further H. JUCKER, Hispania Clunia Sul. Zu einem Sesterz des Kaisers Galba, Schweizer. Münzblätter 15 (1965) 94–11. For Vespasian, see Suet. Vesp. 5 with F. KRAUSS, An Interpretation of the Omens, Portents, and Prodigies Recorded in Livy, Tacitus, and Suetonius (Diss. Philadelphia 1930) 152–3; SCOTT, Imperial Cult 5.

[362] There is still considerable uncertainty over the purpose and origin, of these several series of coins lacking an imperial portrait. Cf. H. MATTINGLY, The «Military» Class in the Coinage of the Civil Wars of A.D. 68–69, NC 6,12 (1952) 72ff.; C. KRAAY, Revolt and Subversion: The So-called «Military» Coinage of A.D. 69 Re-Examined, NC 6,12 (1952) 78ff.; ROBERTSON, RIC Hunter I xcii; P. MARTIN, Die Anonymen Münzen des Jahres 68 n. Chr. (Mainz 1974); E. NICOLAS, De Néron à Vespasien (Paris 1979) II, 1299–1465.

commonwealth.[363] The same theme appears on 'military' issues, linked to the German legions in revolt against Galba.[364] The obverse type celebrates VESTA P. R. QVIRITVM; the reverse portrays Jupiter in his Capitoline temple with the legend IVPITER OPTIMVS MAXIMVS CAPITOLINVS. Disaffected from Galba, the Upper Army broke his images and took an oath to the Senate and the Roman People, honored on this coinage along with the Capitoline guardian of Rome.[365] Quite different is the significance of Otho's type portraying Jupiter Custos (Pl. V, 28).[366] The type intentionally recalled the Neronian issue to commemorate the god's salvation of the emperor. Otho permitted himself to be hailed as Nero and restored the latter's statues.[367] He followed his model in associating the great god directly with the person of the emperor. An issue of Vitellius celebrates Jupiter Victor, representing the god seated holding Victory in his right hand and a sceptre in his left (Pl. V, 29).[368] The type does not commemorate the victory of Roman arms over a foreign foe or even the quelling of a revolt by a disloyal general. It rather celebrates the battle of Bedriacum in which the army of Vitellius defeated Otho, the legitimate emperor, recognized by the Senate.[369] Victory at Bedriacum gave Vitellius his throne; and by honoring Jupiter Victor on the coinage after this victory over fellow citizens, Vitellius clearly sought to claim Jupiter as the source of his imperial power.

As in other constitutional and ideological aspects, the early Flavian period, before Domitian, was a transitional one in the evolution of a Jovian theology of imperial power. Vespasian and Titus as *Caesar* issued a type portraying a standing Jupiter, sacrificing out of a *patera*. The legend reads IOVIS CVSTOS (Pl. V, 30).[370] The type appears along with a series of other types commemorating Pax Augusti, Victoria Augusti, Annona Augusti, and Ceres Augusti.[371] Jupiter is thus here quite clearly Custos Augusti, and, as under Nero, the god of the Roman state is intimately linked to the person of the emperor. The theme is Neronian but typically the Flavians have personalized it. The type and the archaic form of the legend disassociate it from Nero's issue of a seated Jupiter labeled IVPPITER CVSTOS.[372] Nero, like Augustus and Tiberius, had used the globe on his

---

[363] BMC I pp. 294–5.

[364] BMC I p. 307. Cf. MATTINGLY, BMC I cxcviii, which is still the most plausible attribution of this issue.

[365] Tac. Hist. 1.55.

[366] BMC I no. 10.

[367] Suet. Otho 7.

[368] BMC I no. 8–9; 22.

[369] Cf. MATTINGLY, BMC I ccxxiii–iv; HILL, NC 6,20 (1960) 126.

[370] BMC II p. 49 no. 276–9, p. 53 no. 305–9.

[371] BMC II pp. 49–52.

[372] Cf. MATTINGLY, BMC II xxxix; HILL, NC 6,20 (1960) 120. The suggestion that the coin commemorates Jupiter's protection against a conspiracy seems plausible. For such plots, see Suet. Vesp. 25. Cf. J. M. C. TOYNBEE, Dictators and Philosophers in the First Century A.D., G & R 13 (1944) 51–8; WIRSZUBSKI, Libertas 146–50; MACMULLEN, Enemies 55–6.

coinage to symbolize his status as *cosmocrator*.[373] Now on a series of Vespasianic issues the globe is associated with Jupiter. First struck in 71 A.D., bronze issues portray on the reverse an eagle holding a globe in his claws (Pl. V, 31).[374] Later Hadrian issued types representing an eagle bringing the sceptre to him and others with Jupiter handing him the globe.[375] Although less explicit, the message of these early Vespasianic issues is the same: Jupiter has bestowed world rule upon Vespasian and his son Titus.

As emperor, the coins of Titus celebrated the dynastic theme of the foresight of Divus Vespasianus in transferring world rule to Titus.[376] It was only with Domitian that this Jovian theology of power fully emerged as a central element in official imperial ideology. It was a development founded in Domitian's deep personal piety towards Jupiter and shaped by his keen perception of the necessity for a new mythology of imperial power to suit a new oecumenical vision of the Roman commonwealth. The young emperor was a religious man. He worshipped Minerva with an almost superstitious awe;[377] and there is no reason to doubt that he sincerely believed that Jupiter had saved his life in order to elevate him to the purple. After Vespasian's victory, Domitian built a shrine to Jupiter Conservator to commemorate his salvation when the Vitellians fired the Capitol. The altar in the shrine depicted his own adventures in escaping. Later, after his own accession, he consecrated a large temple to Jupiter Custos, with an effigy of himself sitting in the lap of the god.[378] The rebuilding of the Capitolium was begun with elaborate ceremony by Vespasian.[379] The new temple was again destroyed by fire in 80 A.D. and rebuilt by Domitian along even more magnificent lines. Having done so, he permitted only his name to be

---

[373] Cf. BMC I p. 41, p. 42 no. 217. The coins, it should be noted, are triumphal issues of Augustan moneyers. For the coins of Nero with the globe as an imperial attribute, see BMC I pp. 259ff., 398—9. In general for the globe as an imperial attribute in the first century A.D., see A. SCHLACHTER, Der Globus: Seine Entstehung und Verwendung in der Antike, nach den literarischen Quellen und den Darstellungen in der Kunst, hrsg. v. F. GISINGER, ΣΤΟΙΧΕΙΑ 8 (Berlin 1927) 69—76; A. ALFÖLDI, Insignien und Tracht der römischen Kaiser, MDAI(R) 50 (1935) 37 (rep. in: IDEM, Die monarchische Repräsentation im römischen Kaiserreiche [Darmstadt 1970]); HÖLSCHER, Victoria Romana 22—3. Under Augustus and Tiberius the globe as a coin type was used particularly to link the *princeps'* world rule with the workings of Providence and the fulfillment of the divine plan for the universe. Thus Augustus associated the globe with his natal sign Capricorn (BMC I p. 56 no. 305—8; p. 62 no. 344—8; p. 80 no. 465—6; p. 107 no. 664, above p. 58). Tiberius paid hommage to Augustus' providential foresight and celebrated his own status as heir to the Augustan charisma and destiny with the type of an eagle on the globe (BMC I p. 145 no. 155—6, above n. 313) and of a globe and rudder, attributes of Providentia and Fortuna (BMC I p. 135 no. 104—5).

[374] BMC II p. 132, 138, 142, 155, 201, 205, 210.

[375] BMC III no. 1203, 1236, 242.

[376] BMC II no. 178.

[377] Suet. Dom. 15. Cf. J.-L. GIRARD, La place de Minerve dans la religion romaine au temps du principat, below in this same volume (ANRW II, 17,1) 203ff., esp. 227, and IDEM, Domitien et Minerve: une prédilection impériale, below pp. 233—245.

[378] Tac. Hist. 2. 74.

[379] Tac. Hist. 4. 53.

inscribed on the new structure.[380] On the model of the Olympic games, in 86
A.D. Domitian instituted the *agon Capitolinus*.[381] It was to be celebrated every
four years with competitions in music, public speaking, horsemanship, and
gymnastics.[382] He presided at the events wearing a purple robe and a gold
crown engraved with the images of Jupiter, Juno, and Minerva; and at his side
sat the *flamen Dialis* and the priest of the Deified Flavians, both dressed like the
emperor except that their crowns bore the imperial image.[383] The public
celebration of the new Capitoline festival was a dramatic statement of the central
role of Jupiter in imperial ideology and of his profound association with the
emperor and with the charisma of the Flavian dynasty. By contrast with
Augustus,[384] Domitian sought to establish his new order upon a Jovian theology
of imperial power which was complemented, not opposed, by his private
devotion to Minerva and by his celebration of the dynasty. Extremely significant
in this regard is Domitian's transformation in the *sodales Flaviales*. Under Titus
the organization of the *sodales Flaviales* was similar to that of the *Augustales*;
but under Domitian the cult activities of the group were transferred to Jupiter as
the protector of Domitian.[384a]

  Like Actian Apollo for Augustus, Minerva was the personal divine
patroness of Domitian. He celebrated her on his coinage; and he built a *forum* in
her honor. However, her worship was not permitted to usurp the supreme
position of Jupiter Optimus Maximus. Thus a new festival was instituted in her
honor, but it was celebrated as a private act at Domitian's Alban villa.[385] She
rather complements the great god, serving, like the emperor, as his warrior
vicegerent on earth. To this end, she appears on the coinage bearing the
thunderbolt of Jupiter.[386] Domitian's deep piety towards Jupiter and the god's
central role in imperial ideology is a dominant theme on the coinage. The
coinage of Domitian as emperor honors Jupiter in a long series of issues, from
84—96 A.D., as CONSERVATOR, CVSTOS, and VICTOR. It began before
Domitian's accession to the purple on issues of Domitian as Caesar, portraying a

---

[380] Dio 66.24; Suet. Dom. 5; Plut. Popl. 15. Cf. Mart. 13.74; Stat. Silv. 4.1.20; 3.16; 1.6.102.
[381] Suet. Dom. 4; Censorin. De Die natali 18.11.
[382] L. Friedländer, Darstellungen aus der Sittengeschichte Roms in der Zeit von August
   bis zur Ausgang der Antonine II (Leipzig 1889) 481—3, 630—5, collects the evidence. The
   prize was an oak wreath; Stat. Silv. 5.3. 231; Mart. 4.54. 4, 9.23. 5; Juv. 6. 387.
[383] Suet. Dom. 4.
[384] Augustus' institution of the Actia (Dio 51.1. 2) is significant in this regard.
[384a] A. Momigliano, Sodales flaviales titiales e culto di Giove, BCAR 63 (1935) 165—71.
[385] Suet. Dom. 4; Dio 67.1. 2.
[386] Cf. BMC II p. 447. Note the story, recorded in Suet. Dom. 15, that late in his reign
   Minerva appeared to Domitian and told him that she could no longer protect him *quod exarmata esset a Iove*. The type of Minerva with the thunderbolt reappears after Domitian
   only on a few issues of Hadrian (BMC III p. 298, 379, 564). However, especially under
   Antoninus Pius, Minerva, as the vicegerent of Jupiter, became closely linked with the
   Caesar, the vicegerent of the *Augustus*; cf. Strack III, 30—2; and Beaujeu, La religion
   romaine à l'apogée de l'empire, La politique religieuse des Antonins (96—192) (Paris
   1955) 301—03. Cf. M. Lestaw, The Symbolism of Minerva on the Coins of Domitian,
   Klio 59 (1977) 185—93.

goat standing in a laurel wreath with the legend PRINCEPS IVVENTVTIS (Pl. V, 32).[387] The reference is to Amalthea, foster nurse of the infant Jupiter; and the theme is the rejuvenescence of the world in a new golden age of peace and prosperity — under Jupiter's earthly counterpart, the emperor-to-be Domitian. However, Jupiter's rule over mankind and its blessings were secured only after struggle, above all the great battle with the Giants and with Typhoeus, friends of chaos and enemies of civilized life. The conflict was won only with the aid of a mortal, Hercules, destined to be deified for his *virtus* and labors on behalf of mankind. As Hercules once served Jupiter and the gods, so Domitian now serves as the warrior vicegerent of Jupiter on behalf of mankind. Such is the message of a striking type, first issued in 85 A.D. in celebration of the victory over the Chatti and repeated in issues from 86—96.[388] The emperor is pictured standing left wearing military garb and holding a spear in his left hand and a thunderbolt in his right hand. He is crowned by Victory.

In defeating the Chatti, Domitian had fought a *bellum Iovis*. He had restored peace to a portion of the empire, which had been threatened by disorder. As Jupiter had destroyed the Giants with his thunderbolt, so his warrior vicegerent Domitian wielded thunderbolt and lance against the Chatti. The *fulmen* symbolized the position of Jupiter as sovereign and preserver of the universe.[389] On the Column of Trajan, Jupiter is portrayed hurling this thunderbolt against the Dacians, who, like the Giants, represent disorder.[390] The *fulmen* thus represents the rule of order and further Jupiter's power to protect and preserve, as on later imperial types on which a gigantic figure of Jupiter holds a thunderbolt over a tiny figure of an emperor. Domitian wields the thunderbolt to signify that Jupiter has delegated all these powers and functions to him. The role of the emperor as the warrior vicegerent and subordinate of Jupiter is emphasized iconographically by the fact that he wears military garb and holds a spear, not the long sceptre, the supreme attribute of the king of gods and men.

Together with the celebration of Jupiter as *Conservator* and *Victor*, the role of Domitian as the vicegerent of Jupiter was a constant numismatic motif for the last decade of the reign. The themes are complementary: Jupiter protects and gives victory to Domitan, who in turn protects the human race. Like Hercules, he will win deification for his labors on behalf of mankind, whom he serves as

---

[387] BMC II pp. 47, 66, 237, 239, 249, 251.

[388] BMC II pp. 372, 377, 381, 386, 389, 399, 403, 406. For the Gigantomachia and Hercules' role in it as a theme in contemporary panegyric, see Silius Italicus 17.648—54; Martial 8.50. In general, see W. SPEYER, Gigant, in: RLAC X (1978) 1247—64, esp. 1254—5, together with the literature cited in FEARS, Theology of Victory, below in this same volume (ANRW II, 17,2) n. 405.

[389] Cf. ZIEGLER, Zeus, in: ROSCHER, Myth. Lex. VI (Berlin—Leipzig 1924—37; rep. Hildesheim—New York 1977) 565—7; P. JACOBSTAHL, Der Blitz in der orientalischen und griechischen Kunst. Ein formgeschichtlicher Versuch (Berlin 1906); COOK, Zeus III 945—6; L. CAMPBELL, Mithraic Iconography, Ét. Prélimin. aux Relig. Orient. dans l'Emp. Rom. 11 (Leiden 1968) 377—8.

[390] Scene 24 (after C. CICHORIUS, Die Reliefs der Trajanssäule [Berlin 1896—1900]).

the mediator of the supreme god. It is a major *topos* of the panegyrical literature
of the period. Domitian chose to crown the great arch built at Cumae with a
representation of him wielding the thunderbolt, there at the very entrance to
Phlegra, where traditionally Zeus did battle with the Giants.[391] In the speech of
the Sibyl, celebrating the great highway of Domitian, in connection with which
the arch was cut, Statius forcefully portrays the emperor as a supernatural
beneficent power, appointed by Jupiter to rule as his vicegerent on earth:

> *En! hic est deus, hunc iubet beatis*
> *pro se Iuppiter imperare terris.*[392]

Silius Italicus writes of the divine predestination of the Flavians. Vespasian,
Titus, and Domitian are foreordained by Jupiter in his speech of promise to
Venus before the Second Punic War.[393] The warrior *gens* of the Flavians is
destined to rule Rome. Each of them, after performing glorious deeds on earth,
will rise to the heavens. For the sake of the earth, Jupiter will deliver Domitian
from the sacrilegious flames which will devour the Capitoline temple:

> *Tunc, o nate deum divósque dature, beatas*
> *imperio terras patrio rege.*[394]

In their panegyrics, both Silius Italicus and Statius devote considerable space to
the deeds of Domitian in war. Jupiter's promise of Flavian rule in Silius Italicus
is filled with the martial deeds and territorial expansion of the Flavians.
Quintilian celebrates Domitian as *Germanicus,* whom the gods have ordered to
assume the governance of the entire world.[395] Martial and Statius hail Domitian
as *Jupiter Noster* and *Tonans,*[396] while Statius lauds him as Jupiter's warrior
vicegerent:

> *tu [Domitiane] bella Iovis, tu proelia Rheni,*
> *tu civile nefas, tu tardum in foedera montem*
> *longo Marte domas . . .*[397]

c) *Traianus ab Iove electus*

The reign of Domitian was thus pivotal in the evolution of a Jovian
theology of imperial power at Rome. Like the later and rather different concept
of *regnum gratia Dei,* it is a political concept autocratic in its implications. The

---

[391] Cf. J. R. FEARS, Cumae in The Roman Imperial Age, Vergilius 21 (1975) 8.
[392] Stat. Silv. 4.3. 128—9.
[393] Sil. Pun. 3. 570—629. For Silius' attitude towards Domitian, see W. McDERMOTT and
A. ORENTZEL, Silius Italicus and Domitian, AJPh 98 (1977) 24—34.
[394] Sil. Pun. 3. 625—6.
[395] Quint. 10.1 91.
[396] Mart. 4.8. 12, 7. 99; Stat. Silv. 1. praef., 1.6. 39—50, 4.4. 58. Cf. F. SAUTER, Der römische
Kaiserkult bei Martial und Statius, Tüb. Beiträge zur Altertumswiss. 21 (Stuttgart—Berlin
1934) 54—78.
[397] Stat. Silv. 1.1. 79—81.

emperor and his policies are above human criticism because his power is rooted not in human institutions but in his election by the supreme god of the state. It is representative of the degree to which Domitian perceived the ideological needs of the next century of Roman imperial rule; and it is fully consistent with much of Trajanic policy that Trajan exploited to its fullest the image of the emperor as the divinely elected vicegerent of Jupiter.[397a] Domitian's reign ended in tragedy because of his incapacity to cultivate a vital segment of public opinion within the senatorial class. Trajan's genius lay in a singular ability to follow closely Domitian's policy in many areas, to provide the necessary autocratic leadership, and yet to convince the 'senatorial opposition' that *libertas* and *principatus* were now truly reconciled. His adoption of the Jovian theology of imperial power is an excellent case in point. There is considerable reason to assume that this aspect of imperial power, before it was transformed by the magic of Trajan, was closely associated with the image of Domitian the tyrant and was extremely suspect to the 'senatorial opposition'. Jupiter is conspicuously absent from the coinage of Nerva, who ostentatiously portrayed the Senate as the source of his *imperium* and whose types commemorate LIBERTAS PVBLICA, FORTVNA POPVLI ROMANI, and SALVS PVBLICA. It is suggestive that Trajan, in the third year of his principate, would chose a senator to deliver an oration which would, at the same time, vilify Domitian, praise the constitutional qualities of Trajan's reign, and hail Jupiter, not the Senate and not Nerva, as the source of Trajan's imperial power.

Pliny's panegyric of Trajan's reign is built around the central theme of Jupiter's election of the *princeps* to serve as his vicegerent on earth.[398] The speech begins with an invocation to Jupiter in which Pliny declares that Trajan has been chosen not by a blind act of fate but clearly and openly by Jupiter:[399]

> *non enim occulta potestate fatorum, sed ab Iove ipso coram ac palam re-*
> *pertus electus est.*

In adopting Trajan, Nerva was simply the agent of Jupiter.[400] Jupiter's choice was made clear by an extraordinary *omen imperii*, in which the crowds at the Capitoline temple mistook Trajan for Jupiter and prematurely saluted him as *imperator*.[401] The adoption of Trajan took place not in the marriage chamber but in the Capitoline temple, not before the marriage bed but before the altar of Jupiter Optimus Maximus.[402] Now by divine foresight Jupiter has given the whole of the earth into the hands of Trajan; freed by the excellent government of his subordinate, he now need tend only to heaven:

[397a] Cf. K. Waters, Traianus Domitiani Continuator, AJPh 90 (1969) 385–405; A. Garzetti, La politica amministrativa di Traiano, Stud. Rom. 8 (1960) 125–39; and B. Jones, Domitian's Attitude to the Senate, AJPh 94 (1973) 79–91.

[398] Cf. D. Kienast, Nerva u. das Kaisertum Trajans, Historia 17 (1968) 51–71; Fears, Princeps 145–54.

[399] Pliny Pan. 1. 3–5.

[400] Pliny Pan. 5–8.

[401] Pliny Pan. 5. 2–9.

[402] Pliny Pan. 8.

Talia esse crediderim, quae ille mundi parens temperat nutu, si quando oculos demisit in terras et fata mortalium inter divina opera numerare dignatus est; qua nunc parte liber solutusque tantum caelo vacat, postquam te dedit, qui erga omne hominum genus vice sua fungereris.[403]

By his great deeds and virtues, Trajan has become the benefactor of the human race. He has made a pact with Jupiter; the god will preserve him as long as he governs the commonwealth well and for the benefit of all. His continued well-being is proof substantial of his good government; and his subjects pray to Jupiter for his safety as the best means of preserving their own.[404]

Pliny's 'Panegyric' is rightly regarded as an official publicity notice of the new regime;[405] and its emphasis on Trajan as the elect of Jupiter was continued throughout the reign in the various media of official propaganda and by such official acts as the request that public thanks for imperial benevolence be addressed not to his Genius but rather to *Numen Iovis Optimi Maximi*.[406] At the time of the second Dacian war Trajan revived the Domitianic type of the emperor in military garb, wielding the thunderbolt and crowned by victory.[407] Iconographically the type is identical with the Domitianic issue. As a whole, it differs only in the addition of the legend SPQR OPTIMO PRINCIPI (Pl. V, 33). The adaptation is subtle yet enormously significant. Unlike Domitian, Trajan does not arrogate the thunderbolt to himself. Rather the Senate and the Roman People recognize him as the warrior vicegerent of Jupiter and gratefully dedicate the coin to him. The title *Optimus* further emphasized the status of Trajan as the earthly counterpart of Jupiter Optimus Maximus. In his 'Panegyric'

---

[403] Pliny Pan. 80. 4.

[404] Pliny Pan. 67.

[405] Cf. J. BEAUJEU, Pline le Jeune 1955–1960, Lustrum 6 (1961) 290; KIENAST, Historia 17 (1968) 56; M. DURRY, Les empereurs comme historiens d'Auguste à Hadrien, Fond. Hardt, Entretiens 4 (Vandœuvres–Genève 1956) 231–4; and R. SYME, The Senator as Historian, Fond. Hardt. Entretiens 4 (Vandœuvres–Genève 1956) 238. In general on the value of panegyrics for official ideology, see M. SCHANZ and C. HOSIUS, Geschichte der römischen Literatur bis zum Gesetzgebungswerk des Kaisers Justinian, III. Die Zeit von Hadrian 117 bis auf Constantin 324, Handbuch der Altertumswiss. VIII, 3 (Munich 1922³, rep. 1959) 150–2; J. STRAUB, Vom Herrscherideal in der Spätantike, Forsch. zur Kirchen- u. Geistesgesch. 18 (Stuttgart 1939) 146–59; D. ROMANO, Per una nuova interpretazione del panegirico latino in onore dell'imperatore, ALGP 2 (1965) 327–38; S. DABROWSKI, O panegiryku, Przeglad humanistyczny 9, 3 (1965) 101–10; L. K. BORN, The Perfect Prince According to the Latin Panegyrists, AJPh 55 (1934) 20; J. BÉRANGER, L'expression de la divinité dans les Panégyriques latins, MH 27 (1970) 242–54 (rep. in: IDEM, PRINCIPATVS. Études de notions et d'histoire politiques dans l'Antiquité gréco-romaine, Université de Lausanne, Publ. de la Faculté des Lettres 20 [Genève 1975] 429–444); G. DOWNEY, Justinian and the Imperial Office, in: Lectures in Memory of Louisa Taft Semple (University of Cincinnati 1968) 9.

[406] Pliny Pan. 52.6: *Simili reverentia, Caesar, non apud genium tuum bonitati tuae gratias agi, sed apud Numen Iovis Optimi Maximi pateris: illi debere nos quidquid tibi debeamus, illius, quod bene facias, muneris esse qui te dedit.*

[407] BMC III no. 825, 899.

Pliny indicates that the Senate had already by 100 A.D. bestowed this epithet upon Trajan:

> *Nec magis distincte definiteque designat, qui Traianum quam qui Optimum adpellat . . . Nec videri potest optimus, nisi qui est optimis omnibus in sua cuiusque laude praestantior . . . Ideoque ille parens hominum deorumque Optimi prius nomine, deinde Maximi colitur. Quo praeclarior laus tua, quem non minus constat optimum esse quam maximum.*[408]

The same theme of Trajan as the earthly counterpart of Jupiter forms the centerpiece of the great arch dedicated in 114 A.D. at Beneventum to mark the beginning of the *via Traiani*.[409] The arch was an official statement of the program and achievement of the principate of Trajan, and its reliefs form a visual 'Res Gestae Traiani'.[410] The crown of the arch and of the 'Res Gestae' is formed, on both sides of the arch, by attic reliefs portraying Jupiter's bestowal of the thunderbolt upon Trajan. On the city side of the arch the *traditio fulminis* occurs at Rome. Trajan appears on the right attic side, wearing *toga* and standing amidst such personifications as Roma and Penates Populi Romani, who, like the diminutive consuls who stand before him, gaze admiringly at the emperor (Pl. XI, 70b). The left side of the attic completes the scene. Jupiter is flanked by Juno and Minerva; and Hercules, Liber Pater, Ceres and Mercury are portrayed in the background. In his left hand, Jupiter holds his sceptre, and with his right, he extends the thunderbolt towards Trajan (Pl. XI, 70a). On the Campagna side Jupiter was originally also portrayed on the left attic, standing amidst Silvanus, Liber Pater, Diana, and Ceres, deities all closely associated with

---

[408] Pliny Pan. 88. For the stages by which *Optimus* was incorporated into the official nomenclature of Trajan, see HAMMOND, Imperial Elements 41—5; SYME, Tacitus I, 36; R. HANSLIK, M. Ulpius Traianus, RE Suppl. X (1965) 1097; T. FRANKFORT, Trajan Optimus, recherche de chronologie, Latomus 16 (1957) 333—4; and F. RÖMER, Das Senatus Consultum bei Plinius, Paneg. IV.1, WS N.F. 4 (1970) 181—8.

[409] The most important studies of the arch of Trajan at Beneventum are A. MEOMARTINI, I monumenti e le opere d'arte della città di Benevento (Benevento 1889); E. PETERSEN, L'arco di Traiano a Benevento, MDAI(R) 7 (1892) 239—64; A. VON DOMASZEWSKI, Die politische Bedeutung des Trajansbogens in Benevent, JÖAI 2 (1899) 173—92, rep. in: IDEM, Abhandlungen zur römischen Religion (Leipzig 1909) 25—42; S. SNIJDER, Der Trajansbogen in Benevent, JDAI 41 (1926) 94—128, with the critique by F. KOEPP, Kritische Bemerkungen zum römischen Relief, NGG (1926) 322—50; P. HAMBERG, Studies in Roman Imperial Art with Special Reference to the State Reliefs of the Second Century (Uppsala & Copenhagen 1945); J. TOYNBEE, JRS 36 (1946) 178—85; BEAUJEU, Rel. rom. 431—7; F. HASSEL, Der Trajansbogen in Benevent, ein Bauwerk d. röm. Senates. Archäol.-hist. Untersuchungen z. seiner Chronologie u. kunstgeschichtl. Stellung (Mainz am Rhein 1966); A. LEPPER, JRS 59 (1969) 250—61; P. VEYNE, Une hypothèse sur l'arc de Bénévent, MEFR 72 (1960) 191—219; M. ROTILI, L'arco di Traiano a Benevento (Rome 1972); I. RICHMOND, Roman Archaeology and Art (London 1969) 229—38; K. FITTSCHEN, Das Bildprogramm des Trajansbogens zu Benevent, AA 87 (1972) 742—788; W. GAUER, Zum Bildprogramm des Trajansbogens von Benevent, JDAI 89 (1974) 308—35.

[410] The interpretation of the imagery of the arch presented here is defended at length in FEARS, Princeps 228—37.

the new province of Dacia (Pl. XI, 71a). Again Jupiter, now missing from the relief, was portrayed in the act of extending the thunderbolt towards Trajan, represented on the right side of the attic standing in military cloak and with his entourage at his side and suppliant Dacia at his feet (Pl. XI, 71b).

Iconographically the reliefs of the arch must be viewed as a unified propaganda statement. The four lower reliefs of the arch on the Campagna side are devoted to the military aspects of Trajan's principate: the recruitment of soldiers, a peace with the Germans, the inspection of the northern frontier, and the introduction of the *alimenta* system, the main purpose of which was to supply Italian recruits. The lower reliefs on the city side represent Trajan's provisions for Ostia, the establishment of colonies, and the *princeps'* modest entry into Rome in 99 A.D. and his reception by representatives of the Roman People, the Senate, and the Equestrian Order, a general statement then of the constitutional nature of Trajan's principate. Jupiter's bestowal of the thunderbolt on Trajan, located at Rome, crowns the relief celebrating the peaceful accomplishment; and in the same way the *traditio fulminis* amidst the empire's newest province forms the center piece of Trajan's military deeds. *Domi militiaeque*, Trajan ruled in virtue of his election by Jupiter to serve as the vicegerent of the gods on earth. The imagery of the attic scenes thus presents a visual official statement of Trajan's divine election and a clear parallel to the verbal proclamation in Pliny's 'Panegyric:'

> *Ad te imperii summam et omnium rerum tum etiam tui potestatem di transtulerunt . . . Ille mundi parens . . . te dedit, qui erga omne hominum genus vice sua fungereris.*[411]

In all this it is essential to note the caution with which Trajan proceeded in his campaign to establish the imperial position upon an ideological foundation rooted in a vision of the emperor as the divinely chosen vicegerent of Jupiter. The theme first appears in Pliny's 'Panegyric', a verbal statement before the emperor and a senatorial audience. The theme is first reflected on the coinage in 105/06 A.D. The actual investiture of Trajan by Jupiter never appeared on the coinage but was reserved for the arch at Beneventum. In all this Trajan was careful to use senatorial media, in a speech by a senator, on a type on the bronze coinage, traditionally a senatorial prerogative, here emphasized by the legend SPQR OPTIMO PRINCIPI, and on an arch erected by the Senate and Roman People and dedicated to Trajan. Trajan thus sought to establish the Jovian theology of imperial power as an ideological feature of good, i.e. constitutional government.

Pliny had celebrated Jupiter's protection of his vicegerent as proof of Trajan's good government. *Vota* were the expression of this idea in cult.[412] Trajan's departure for the Parthian campaign called forth a *vota extraordinaria* in connection with which a new coin type was issued, strikingly portraying

---

[411] Pliny Pan. 56.3, 80.4.
[412] For *vota*, see below pp. 98—101.

Jupiter's protection of Trajan, who in turn preserves the commonwealth (Pl. VI, 34).[413] An enormous figure of Jupiter is represented holding a thunderbolt over a diminutive Trajan, who holds in his hand a branch, an attribute which links the scene to the *vota* undertaken on behalf of the emperor.

A comparison with the iconography of the attic of the arch at Beneventum reveals the clarity of which imperial iconography was capable. On the attic the theme is Trajan's elevation to serve as Jupiter's earthly counterpart. Hence he is portrayed as equal in size to the gods and divine personifications like Roma and the Penates Populi Romani and considerably larger than such mortals as the consuls. The coin type emphasizes Trajan's dependence upon Jupiter, and he is accordingly portrayed as a tiny child-like figure at the feet of the supreme god. The theme is complemented by the legend CONSERVATORI PATRIS PATRIAE. Trajan is Jupiter's mediator on earth; but at critical moments the supreme god materalizes on earth to aid his vicegerent. During an earthquake at Antioch, a supernatural being led Trajan from a building just before it collapsed.[414] On the reliefs of the Trajanic column, dominated by the image of the emperor, Jupiter appears at a crucial moment to hurl his thunderbolts against the Dacians.[415]

d) Hadrian and the Hellenization of the Jovian Theology of Imperial Power

Firmly reconciled with 'constitutional government' by the propaganda of Trajan, the Jovian theology of imperial power was further integrated into the official ideology of the principate under Hadrian. Before his accession, Hadrian was moved to a poetic declaration of the emperor's role as vicegerent of Jupiter:

> "Trajan, son of Aeneas, did dedicate these pleasing gifts to Casian Zeus, the lord of men to the lord of immortals: two cups richly-wrought and the horn of a urus, curiously fashioned in all-gleaming gold. These precious things from the best part of the spoils were gained when he unbending with spear overthrew the haughty Getae. But do you, O cloudwrapped Zeus, grant that he gloriously execute this war with the Achaemenids so that double spoils, that of the Getae and that of the Arsacids, may doubly gladden your heart as you gaze upon them."[416]

---

[413] BMC III no. 493. For the occasion of issue, see STRACK I, 216; BEAUJEU, Rel. rom. 77.

[414] Dio. 68.24; cf. R. LONGDEN, Notes on the Parthian Campaigns of Trajan, JRS 21 (1931) 1—8. Contrast BEAUJEU, Rel. rom. 76.

[415] Scene 28, CICHORIUS, Die Reliefs der Trajanssäule. Cf. also G. BECATTI, La Colonna Traiana, espressione somma del rilievo storico romano, ANRW II, 12,1 (1981); A. MALISSARD, Une nouvelle approche de la colonne Trajane, ibid., and G. KOEPPEL, Official State Reliefs of the City of Rome in the Imperial Age. A Bibliography, ch. VII, ibid.

[416] Anth. Pal. 6. 332. The traditional attribution of the poem to Hadrian has generally been accepted; cf. B. W. HENDERSON, The Life and Principate of the Emperor Hadrian (London

After his accession, Hadrian went beyond Domitian and Trajan and used the imperial coinage to portray his actual investiture by Jupiter. Accession issues of Titus celebrated the foresight of Divus Vespasianus in transferring the globe into the hands of his son. Nerva and Trajan commemorated the foresight of the Senate and represented the Genius Senatus in the act of handing them the globe. So did Hadrian in 117 A.D.[417] However, after his return to Rome, in 119 A.D. he portrayed Jupiter bestowing the globe upon him (Pl. VI, 35).[418] Another type, with the legend PROVIDENTIA DEORVM, represents an eagle bringing the sceptre to Hadrian (Pl. VI, 36).[419] His deathbed adoption doubted by some,[420] having broken with Trajan's expansionist policy,[421] and his relations with the Senate poisoned by the execution of four senators,[422] Hadrian dramatically placed his accession and policies above human institutions and a deified father. The coin types proclaim that he acceded to the purple by the direct intervention of Jupiter and by the foresight of the gods. The theme and the motives were the same as for Trajan in 100 A.D.; only the medium was different.

Throughout the reign of Hadrian, Jupiter played a major role on the coinage. As an infant suckling the goat Amalthea (Pl. VI, 37), he was invoked in association with the theme of a new golden age, celebrated in other Hadrianic types such as TEMPORVM FELICITAS and TELLVS STABILITA.[423] He is

---

1923) 127—8; BEAUJEU, Rel. rom. 75—6; GAGÉ, Basiléia 198; H. BARDON, Les empereurs et les lettres latines d'Auguste à Hadrien³ (Paris 1968) 423.

[417] BMC II no. 178 (Titus); BMC III p. 21 (Nerva); BMC III no. 53, GNECCHI I p. 44 no. 22 (Trajan); BMC III no. 1, 1101 (Hadrian).

[418] BMC III no. 242. P. HILL, The Undated Coins of Rome A.D. 98—148 (London 1970) 157, would date this issue to late 121 A.D. However, a study of the portrait together with the significance of the type best suits a date of 119.

[419] BMC III nos. 1203, 1236.

[420] Dio 69.1; SHA Had. 3—4; Eutropius 8.6; Victor 13; Cf. M. PRÉVOST, Les adoptions politiques à Rome sous la République et le Principat, Publ. Inst. de Droit Rom. de l'Université de Paris 5 (Paris 1949) 50—2; J. CARCOPINO, L'hérédité dynastique chez les Antonins, REA 51 (1949) 280—5 (rep. in: IDEM, Passion et politique chez les Césars [Paris 1961] 166—71); M. HAMMOND, The Transmission of the Powers of the Roman Emperor from the Death of Nero in A.D. 68 to that of Alexander Severus in A.D. 235, MAAR 24 (1956) 90—2; SYME, Tacitus I 40; B. PARSI, Désignation et investiture de l'empereur romain (Ier et IIe siècles après J.C.), Publ. Inst. de Droit Rom. de l'Univ. de Paris 21 (Paris 1963) 20—1; M. THORNTON, Hadrian and his Reign, ANRW II,2 (1975) 443 n. 28. Cf. H. TEMPORINI, Die Frauen am Hofe Trajans. Ein Beitrag zur Stellung der Augustae im Principat (Berlin—New York 1978) 120—125.

[421] SHA. Had. 9; Dio. 69.5.1; Fronto p. 206 ed. NABER; Jerome Chron. s.a. 118 p. 197 ed. HELM; Suda s.v. Dometianos; cf. J. GUEY, Essai sur la guerre parthique de Trajan, Bibl. d'Istros 2 (Bucarest 1937) 145—6; N. DEBEVOISE, A Political History of Parthia (Chicago 1938) 240—1; F. LEPPER, Trajan's Parthian War (Oxford 1948) 148—50; and K. ZIEGLER, Die Beziehungen zwischen Rom und dem Partherreich. Ein Beitrag zur Geschichte des Völkerrechts (Wiesbaden 1964) 105—10; THORNTON, ANRW II,2 (1975) 435.

[422] Dio 69.1.5; cf. A. VON PREMERSTEIN, Das Attentat der Konsulare auf Hadrian im Jahre 118 n. Chr., Klio Beiheft 8 (Leipzig 1908); E. M. SMALLWOOD, Palestine c. 115—118, Historia 11 (1962) 500—20.

[423] BMC III pp. 438, 442, 444. For the theme of the golden age on Hadrianic coinage, see BMC III pp. 332—4, 362, 477, 486—7. Cf. BEAUJEU, Rel. rom. 128—60; H. CASTRITIUS,

honored as *conservator* with issues portraying him holding his thunderbolt over
Hadrian.[424] A variety of types portray the figure of Jupiter, at times standing
holding an eagle or with his hand on a shield; at times he is portrayed seated,
holding sceptre and Victory (Jupiter Victor) or sceptre and thunderbolt (as
Capitolinus).[425]

Among the most cosmopolitan and philhellenic of the emperors, Hadrian
did not limit his emphasis on Jupiter to Roman cult; and during his principate
there was a resurgence of attention to the cult of Zeus in the Greek East.[426]
Significant is Hadrian's insistence on the completion of the temple of Olympian
Zeus at Athens.[427] Under Augustus the eastern kings and princes had planned to
pay to complete the structure, begun under Peisistratus, and to dedicate it to the
Genius Augusti.[428] Hadrian took the work in hand, dedicating the *cella* in
128—29 and the *temenos* complex during his third stay in 131—32. The
decoration of the *peribolos* witnessed to the pre-eminent status of Zeus Olympios
as the panhellenic deity, guardian of a peaceful and united Hellas, the giver of
life and blessings, the common father and saviour of mankind, Zeus the king,
the city-god, the god of friendship, the god of the suppliant and the stranger.[429]
The statues in the enclosure, erected by a large number of cities in Greece and
Asia Minor, were dedicated not to Zeus Olympios but to Hadrian as *Olympios*,
Soter, and *Panhellenios*.[430] Behind the temple, the Athenians erected a colossal
statue of Hadrian.[431] The epithets *Olympios*, *Soter*, and *Panhellenios* celebrate
Hadrian as the earthly counterpart of Zeus, fulfilling all his functions as guardian
of Greece and her culture. The subjects, Zeus Olympios and Hadrian Olympios,

---

Der Phoenix auf den Aurei Hadrians und Tacitus' Annalen, JNG 14 (1964) 89—95;
J. MARTIN, Hadrien et le phénix, in: Mél. d'histoire ancienne offerts à W. Seston, Publ.
de la Sorbonne Sér. Études 9 (Paris 1974) 327—37.

[424] BMC III p. 323.

[425] BMC III p. 585. For the interpretation of the types, see HILL, NC 6, 20 (1960) 113—28.

[426] This is treated with considerable perception by BEAUJEU, Rel. rom. 176—206. See further,
more recently, B. FORTE, Rome and The Romans as the Greeks Saw Them, Papers and
Monographs of the American Academy in Rome 24 (Rome 1972) 294—326; A. BENJAMIN,
The Altars of Hadrian in Athens and Hadrian's Panhellenic Program, Hesperia 32 (1963)
57—86.

[427] Dio 69.16. 1—2; Paus. 1. 18—19. In general, see P. GRAINDOR, Athènes sous Hadrien
(Cairo 1934) 218ff. The literature on the structure is collected by TRAVLOS, Pictorial
Dictionary of Ancient Athens 403. For other aspects of Hadrian's benefactions towards
Athens, see J. OLIVER, The Athens of Hadrian, in: A. PIGANIOL, ed., Les empereurs
romains d'Espagne (Paris 1965) 121—33; and IDEM, Marcus Aurelius. Aspects of Civic
and Cultural Policy in the East, Hesperia Suppl. 13 (Princeton 1970) 48, 54, 130; FORTE,
Rome 294—5. Cf. also D. J. GEAGAN, Roman Athens: Some Aspects of Life and Culture,
I. 86 B.C.—A.D. 267, ANRW II, 7, 1 (1979) 389ff., 426ff.

[428] Suet. Aug. 60.

[429] The titles of Zeus are from Dio Chrysostom Or. 12. 74—77.

[430] For the statues, see Paus. 1.18. 6. For the statue bases, see IG II² 3289—3310; cf. GRAINDOR,
Athènes sous Hadrien 50—1; A. BENJAMIN and A. RAUBITSCHEK, Arae Augusti, Hesperia
28 (1959) 65—85; BENJAMIN, Hesperia 32 (1963) 57—86; C. VERMEULE, Roman Imperial
Art in Greece and Asia Minor (Cambridge, Mass. 1968) 430—1.

[431] Pausanias 1.18. 6.

and the setting, Athens, are complementary; Zeus Olympios, god of law and Hellenic civilization, receives his earthly manifestation in the political world through Hadrian and in the cultural world through Athens. As Aelius Aristides proclaimed, the true empire of Athens was one of civilization and education, an empire of the *logos* and a spiritual bastion against barbarism. Like Theseus and Hercules, Athens and the emperor are partners in a great civilizing mission. The emperor as guardian of the military defences of the *oikoumene* and Athens as leader of the *poleis* in civilization. Like the emperor, Athens is a mediator between Zeus and mankind, a model for human life.[432]

To foster further this sense of panhellenic unity under the common fathership of Zeus and the emperor, Hadrian established a sanctuary called the Panhellenion at Athens.[433] Elsewhere the cult of Zeus received assiduous attention under Hadrian, both from the emperor and from individual cities. Thus Zeus took on new importance as a coin type on the issues of Greek cities in Asia Minor.[434] The role of Hadrian as the earthly counterpart to Zeus was honored in cult by the attribution to him of local epithets of Zeus: *Sotēr* at Sparta, *Archēgetēs* at Aegina, *Boulaios* at Abea, *Dōdōnaios* at Dodona.[435] As Zeus' vicegerent, he fulfilled these functions on earth.

The assimilation of the emperor to Zeus was no innovation in the Greek world.[436] The practice is attested for Augustus, Nero, Domitian, and Trajan.[437] The question is rather different with Hadrian, however. It is not merely a question of municipal honors granted to the emperor. The epithets *Olympios* and *Panhellenios* became part of Hadrian's official titles in the Greek world.[438] The parallel is Trajan's adoption of *Optimus* as an official agnomen. It is to be taken together with Hadrian's sponsorship of the cult of Zeus Olympios at Athens, with the importance of Zeus on Greek imperial issues under Hadrian, and with the significant role of Jupiter on his Roman imperial coinage. As a whole this material indicates the central role of Zeus-Jupiter in the imperial ideology of Hadrian. It marks the culmination of a conscious policy, initiated

---

[432] Ael. Arist. Or. XIII passim. In general see the excellent discussion of J. H. OLIVER, The Civilizing Power: A Study of the Panathenaic Discourse of Aelius Aristides Against the Background of Literature and Cultural Conflict, Transactions of the American Philosophical Society, n.s. 58 (1968) 35—44.

[433] The shrine is attested both in the literary sources (Paus. 1.18. 9; Dio 69.16. 1) and in the epigraphical material (IG II² 3872 = SIG³ 842). For its location, see G. KRUSE, Opfer, RE XVIII, 1 (1939) 593; GRAINDOR, Athènes sous Hadrien 52ff., 102ff., 126ff.; COOK, Zeus II, 1119ff.; BEAUJEU, Rel. rom. 178—181. See further BENJAMIN, Hesperia 32 (1963) 59—60, 71; OLIVER, Marcus Aurelius 129—30. In general for the Panhellenion in the second century A.D., see OLIVER, Marcus Aurelius 92—138.

[434] Cf. BEAUJEU, Rel. rom. 190—8.

[435] For a complete list, see BENJAMIN, Hesperia 32 (1963) 57—86.

[436] Cf. BEAUJEU, Rel. rom. 201—02. The treatment of W. METCALF, Hadrian Jovis Olympios, Mnemosyne 4, 27 (1974) 59—66, is misconceived.

[437] For Augustus, see WARD, SMSR 9 (1933) 213—220. For Nero, SIG³ 814; BMC Lydia p. 75. For Domitian, IG II² 1996. For Trajan, IG IV 701; IG II² 3322; BMC Lydia p. 320.

[438] Cf. GRAINDOR, Athènes sous Hadrien 41; L. PERRET, La titulature impériale d'Hadrien (Paris 1929) 31—2; BEAUJEU, Rel. rom. 200—01; BENJAMIN, Hesperia 32 (1963) 59.

under Nero and conscientiously developed by Domitian and Trajan, aimed at establishing a new ideological foundation for the imperial structure, one which was neither narrowly Roman nor linked to a single dynasty, but which could instead elicit the understanding and loyalty of the empire as a whole. It centered upon the image of the emperor as the divinely elected vicegerent of Jupiter-Zeus, who fulfills the earthly functions of Zeus and serves as the mediator between man and the common father of the human race.

e) Jupiter and the Evolving Image of the Principate

The association of *imperator* and Jupiter went back to the earliest period of Roman history. In Augustan literature, the image of the emperor as the vicegerent of Jupiter was already fully developed along the lines of Hellenistic panegyric. However, a deeper significance is attached to the emphasis placed on this Jovian theology of imperial power in the official imperial ideology of the late Flavian and early Antonine period. The reigns of Domitian, Trajan, and Hadrian represented a critical period in the transformation of the Augustan principate into the Antonine monarchy. This process, an inevitable consequence of the Augustan system itself, saw the *princeps* become the ultimate source of all administrative, judicial, and legislative power and the figure to whom all agencies of government, all citizens, and all subjects looked for authority. A centralized, enlightened autocracy replaced the Augustan ideal of the *princeps* as a special agent of the Senate and Roman People. At the same time and as part of this development, a broad imperial vision of empire superseded a more narrowly Romano-Italian outlook. The new emphasis on a Jovian origin of imperial power was another product of this great transformation. The new imperial structure was to be established upon an ideological basis which could not be shaken by the failure of a lone emperor or an entire dynasty and which could appeal to all areas and all segments of the empire.

The choice of Jupiter-Zeus as the pre-eminent and central divine support of this new imperial ideology was a natural but not an inevitable choice; and its origins, significance, and ramifications are worth examining. The customary explanation sees it entirely in terms of the traditional republican association of the *imperator* with the cult of Jupiter Optimus Maximus.[439] This background certainly did nothing to hinder the evolution of a Jovian theology of imperial power. However, it is hardly the whole story. Furthermore, in the late republic and in the Augustan period, this association was tenuous indeed. As was argued above, the charisma of victory had become disassociated from Jupiter and attached to the person of the individual *imperator* and his patron divinities. It is thus a question of a revival of interest in Jupiter and a renewed association between *imperator* and Capitoline deity in the later part of the first century A.D. A variety of factors lay behind this 'resuscitation' of Jupiter; but they are best understood within the context of the image of Jupiter in Roman national

---

[439] So BEAUJEU, Rel. rom. 69—71.

ideology, in popular philosophy and literature in the Greco-Roman world, and in the religious currents of the imperial age.

As with Hadrian and the cult of Zeus in the Greek East, the association of the *princeps* and Jupiter could be interpreted in the broadest terms. It could also be viewed from a narrowly Roman perspective, linked to the Capitoline and the traditional guarantee of Rome's imperial power. *Pignus imperii* Tacitus called it; and his comments on the burning of the Capitoline temple by the Vitellians indicate how profoundly the cult place of Jupiter still symbolized Roman imperial might.[440] The destruction of the Capitoline filled the Gauls with courage and led them to believe that the end of the Roman Empire was at hand. The Druids declared that this disaster revealed the wrath of the gods and portended the end of Rome and the birth of a Gallic world empire. The Gauls recalled that their earlier occupation of the city had ended in failure because they had been unable to take the Capitolium itself.[441] For Tacitus the destruction by the Vitellians epitomized the suicidal character of the struggles of 68–69 A.D. Assailed by no foreign enemy and with the gods willing to be propitious, had Roman vices not interfered, the seat of Jupiter Optimus Maximus, founded to be the assurance of Rome's empire, was burned by Roman hands. *Id facinus post conditam urbem luctuosissimum foedissimumque rei publicae populi Romani accidit.*[442] The disaster is not to the emperor but to the commonwealth as a whole. For Tacitus, two themes are central to the role of the Capitoline temple in the history of the Roman commonwealth, *imperium* and *libertas*. Such was true in its earliest period. Tarquinius Priscus, Tacitus writes, had vowed its erection during his war with the Sabines and laid its foundations on a scale commensurate with the hope of future greatness. Servius Tullius and Tarquinius Superbus, with the spoils from conquered Suessa Pometia, raised the super-structure. But the glory of its completion was reserved for the inauguration of Rome's liberty: *gloria operis libertati reservata.*[443] As did those senators who, after the murder of Gaius, proclaimed their intention to restore the free republic by meeting in the Capitoline temple, Tacitus continued the association of Jupiter Optimus Maximus and *libertas*.

Both themes, *pignus imperii* and *libertas* were symbolized in the new emphasis on Jupiter in Flavian and early Antonine imperial ideology. *Pignus imperii* may have dominated Flavian intentions: Capitoline Jupiter as the assurance of Rome's continued world dominion and triumph over civil enemies and rebellious Gauls and Germans. Under Trajan, the prominence of Jupiter in imperial art and cult could also epitomize that reconciliation between *libertas* and *principatus* which Tacitus himself lauded. As such, Jupiter was not limited to a narowly Roman interpretation. A *princeps* chosen by Jupiter-Zeus to serve as his earthly viceroy was an assurance of just government for all mankind. Such was the theme of Dio Chrysostom's 'Four orations on kingship'. For Dio, the

[440] Tac. Hist. 3.72.
[441] Tac. Hist. 4.54.
[442] Tac. Hist. 3. 72.
[443] Tac. Hist. 3. 72.

belief that true kings receive their power from Zeus and are his earthly reflection is a hoary tradition in the Greek world, sanctioned by the authority of Homer. The ideal king is "him to whom the son of crafty Cronus has given the sceptre and the authority that he may take counsel for his subjects."[444] Homer, to paraphrase Dio's speech, was correct in implying that not every king derives his sceptre and his role from Zeus. Only the good king is elected by Zeus, receiving his office on the grounds that he will take counsel for and care of those he rules. The king elected by Zeus does not use his office as a license for lawlessness and tyranny.[445] The Zeus-chosen king is pious towards the gods and watchful for the welfare of his subjects, like a true good shepherd.[446] His position gives him a larger portion not of wealth and pleasure but rather of care and worry. By his deeds and virtues he gains the title 'father'. King not for his own sake but for the sake of all men, his greatest pleasure is in bestowing blessings upon those he rules. He is warlike when necessary but desires peace. Above all, he is a man whom good men can freely praise and who desires the praise only of men who are free and noble. The good king must always seek to imitate Zeus, the first and greatest king. It is for this reason that Homer describes true kings as "Zeus-nurtured" and "like unto Zeus in counsel."[447] Zeus alone of the gods is called father, king and protector-god of cities, of friends, of comrades, of the race, of suppliants, of guests, the god of property and the god who makes the earth to blossom forth. All these duties are a part of the title and functions of a true king.[448] The vicegerent of Zeus conforms to and governs in the manner of his sovereign Zeus and is assured of a long and prosperous reign. But that ruler will come to a bad end who refuses to mold his rule after Zeus and dishonors him who bestows the stewardship upon him. The bad ruler, having proved himself unworthy of his trust, will be remembered like Phaethon, who disregarded his status and attempted to drive the divine chariot but failed. He should rather emulate Heracles, who sought to do the greatset good for the greatest number, who chose to follow the precepts of his father, and to chastise savage and wicked men and to crush and destroy the power of overweening tyrants.[449]

Dio's eulogy on good kingship was fully in the tradition of Hellenistic political thought with its emphasis on true royalty as the imitation of the divine.[450] His portrait of Zeus closely parallels the image of the god in Stoic

---

[444] Dio Or. I 11.
[445] Dio Or. I 13.
[446] Dio Or. I 15—20.
[447] Dio Or. I 21—38.
[448] Dio Or. I 38—41.
[449] Dio Or. I 42—84.
[450] Elsewhere in his orations on kingship, Dio returns to the same themes; cf. III 7—9, 45—6, 55, 62; IV 10—28, 39—46. For his political thought, see V. VALDENBERG, La théorie monarchique de Dion Chrysostome, REG 40 (1927) 142—62, a summary of his longer study in Russian in: IDEM, Izvestija Akademii Nauk SSR, Otdelenie Hum. 6, 20 (1926) 943—74, 1281—1302, 1523—54; and F. DVORNIK, Early Christian and Byzantine Political Philosophy, Dumbarton Oaks Studies 9 (Washington 1966) II, 537—42.

philosophy. To the Stoic the *logos*, the Reason that permeates all things, was the mind of Zeus-Jupiter. Seneca lists the names which a Stoic might give to God, Fate, Providence, Nature, Universe, but he starts with Jupiter.[451] As a Stoic, Epictetus held God to be immanent, permanently pervading the universe; and Zeus is the name by which he most frequently refers to this god. Zeus, for Epictetus, is the common father of gods and men, who out of the goodness of his nature cares for his children.[452] "Dwell with the gods," Marcus Aurelius admonished himself. He dwells with the gods who at all times exhibits to them a soul satisfied with its apportioned lot, a soul which in its actions follows the command of the inner spirit, that fragment of himself that Zeus has given to every man as his guardian and guide.[453] Whether in the personal image of Cleanthes or the abstract conception of Marcus Aurelius, the Stoic identified Zeus with the all-pervading reason which governed the universe; and in so doing Stoicism provided a profound philosophical and ethical basis for the association of the emperor with Zeus.[454]

A complementary basis in the religious thought of the period was found in the tendency towards monotheism, which by the second century A.D. had become pervasive among all elements of society in the Greco-Roman world.[455] Zeus-Jupiter was carried along in the monotheistic current. Syncretism was an aspect of this development, identifying Zeus-Jupiter with numbers of supreme local gods. As with monotheism, this was not a new development, but it was one which reached a new pitch of intensity in the second century A.D. At times, such syncretism was sponsored by official imperial ideology. This was particularly true of the identification of Jupiter with Sarapis. Since Caligula, Sarapis had played an icreasingly important role as a divine protector of the emperors, and their imperial protégés lavished attention on the cults of Sarapis and Isis at Rome and throughout the empire.[456] With the aid of Sarapis, Vespasian performed miracles of healing at Alexandria.[457] Soldiers of the Third Cyrenaic Legion made a dedication for Trajan's health and safety to Jupiter-Sarapis;[458] and coins of Alexandria portray Sarapis crowning Trajan with a laurel

---

[451] Sen. Q.N. 2. 45; cf. Lucan 9.580: *Iuppiter est quodcumque vides quodcumque moveris.*

[452] Cf. esp. Epict. Diss. 1.3, 1.12, 1.19, 2.17.23, 3.7.36, 3.8, 3.11, 3.22.56, 3.24, 4.4, 4.8.30.

[453] Marc. Aur. 5. 27.

[454] Cf. J. FERGUSON, The Religions of the Roman Empire, Aspects of Greek and Roman Life (Ithaca 1970) 40.

[455] The best single discussion of religious syncretism in the imperial age is NILSSON, GGR³ II 581—701.

[456] Since the 'invention' of Sarapis by Ptolemy I Soter, Sarapis, like Isis, stood in a particularly close patronage relationship with the sovereigns of Egypt and with the city of Alexandria. For this phenomenon under the Ptolemies and the Romans, see J. STAMBAUGH, Sarapis under The Early Ptolemies, Ét. Prélimin. aux Relig. Orient. dans l'Emp. Rom. 25 (Leiden 1972) 93—8; F. DUNAND, Le culte d'Isis, Ét. Prélimin. aux Relig. Orient. dans l'Emp. Rom. 26 (Leiden 1973) 27—45; R. E. WITT, Isis in the Graeco-Roman World (Ithaca 1971) 212—42; J. GAGÉ, L'empereur romain devant Sérapis, Ktema 1 (1976) 145—66.

[457] Tac. Hist. 4. 81. See above n. 359.

[458] L. VIDMAN, ed., Sylloge Inscriptionum Religionis Isiacae et Sarapiacae, Religionsgeschicht-liche Versuche und Vorarbeiten 28 (Berlin 1969) 362.

wreath.[459] Under Hadrian, for the first time, the Alexandrian coinage represents the emperor standing in the Sarapeum and receiving the globe from Zeus-Sarapis.[460] Before marching against the Parthians, Trajan consulted the oracle of Jupiter Heliopolitanus, the Syrian sun god and only one of several instances of the assimilation of Zeus-Jupiter to a solar deity.[461] After his victory over the Parthians, Trajan issued *aurei* in honor of the sun god, who like the emperor rises in eternal triumph.[462]

"It makes no difference," wrote Clesus, "whether the supreme God is called Zeus or Adonaios or Sabaoth or Ammon as by the Egyptians or Papaios as by the Scythians."[463] All gods are in reality one and the same manifestations of the supreme power which governs the universe. Here theology went hand in hand with political reality and ideology. Despite the plethora of cities, tribes, officials, races, and tongues within the Roman empire, there was but one supreme power, the Roman emperor, who by his force governed the whole. One supreme god in heaven, one emperor and one empire on earth.[464] Popular philosophy, religion, and imperial ideology thus complemented each other. The image of the emperor and the image of Zeus came not only to mirror but to ennoble each other. Bearded from Hadrian onward and wearing a laurel crown and carrying an eagle-tipped sceptre, the emperor increasingly resembled physically the most-famed portrayal of Zeus, the statue of Pheidias at Olympia.[465] "Of all images on earth," Dio Chrysostom called it, "The most beautiful and the dearest to heaven . . . so that none of its beholders can easily acquire another conception."[466] Since the Sullan reconstruction, the image of Capitoline Jupiter had been fundamentally shaped by the influence of the Pheidian statue,

---

[459] J. Vogt, Die alexandrinischen Münzen II (Stuttgart 1924) 32.

[460] A. El-Mohsen El-Khachab, Ho Karakallos Kosmokrator, JEA 47 (1961) 129. A Roman issue of *aurei* under Hadrian bears the legend ADVENTVI AVG. ALEXANDRIAE and portrays the emperor and Sarapis clasping right hands (BMC III p. 339).

[461] Macrob. Sat. 1.23. 12–16; cf. Gagé, Basiléia 179–205. For the cult of Jupiter Heliopolitanus, Cook, Zeus I, 550–76; S. Ronzevalle, Jupiter Heliopolitain, Mél. de l'Univ. Saint-Joseph 21,1 (Beirut 1937) with the review by O. Eissfeldt, Der Alte Orient 40 (1941) 46–50.

[462] BMC III no. 592. The type, with the addition of the legend ORIENS, reappears under Hadrian in 117 (BMC III no. 35) and in 125–28 A.D. (no. 377–8). For the significance of the type and its connection with Giessen papyrus 20, see E. H. Kantorowicz, Oriens Augusti – Lever du Roi, DOP 17 (1963) 117–78, esp. 122–3; Thornton, ANRW II, 2 (1975) 456–8; Fears, Princeps. 238–42. For its association with Alexander the Great, see Fears, Princeps 249–50.

[463] Celsus ap. Orig. Cont. Celsum. 5.41. Cf. W. Schäfke, Frühchristlicher Widerstand, ANRW II, 23, 1 (1979) 633 with n. 1208.

[464] This has been treated in a fine and justly famous study by E. Peterson, Der Monotheismus als politisches Problem. Ein Beitrag zur Geschichte der politischen Theologie im Imperium Romanum (Leipzig 1935). See further Dvornik, Early Christian and Byzantine Political Philosophy II, 611ff.

[465] For the fame of Pheidias' statue, see L. Farnell, The Cults of the Greek States I (Oxford 1896) 128–39; and Waser in: Roscher, Myth. Lex. VI, 724–34.

[466] Dio Chrysostom Or. 12. 53–4.

and the same was true of the second most important cult statue of Jupiter represented on the Roman coinage, Jupiter Victor.[467] For such second century writers as Dio Chrysostom and even the sober Pausanias, the statue conveyed a profound philosophical statement of god and his goodness and the moral character of his rule over gods and men. "His power and kingship are displayed by the strength and majesty of the whole image, his fatherly care for men by the mildness and loving kindness in the face; the solemn austerity of the work marks the god of the city and the law, . . . he seems like one giving and abundantly bestowing blessings."[468] The supreme artistic effort was devoted to the eyes, brows, and hair of the statue in an effort to capture that sense of the majesty and power conveyed in the Homeric verse: "The son of crafty Kronos spoke and he nodded assent with his gleaming eyebrows; and from the immortal head of the king the deathless locks waved down and great Olympus was shaken with his nod."[469]

Homer's Zeus wielded the thunderbolt, an attribute conspicuously absent from the Pheidian statue. For Dio Chrysostom and Pausanias the omission was significant. Pheidias rejected all imagery of terror; it was beyond his skill and counter to his will to portray that ferocious aspect of Zeus, symbolized by the thunderbolt, which sent painful strife upon mankind.[470] By contrast the thunderbolt was pre-eminent among the Jovian attributes adopted by Domitian and Trajan. The difference is suggestive. On the arch at Beneventum, Jupiter bestows the thunderbolt upon Trajan. As Pliny wrote, the supreme god is now free of such cares. The thunderbolt symbolizes struggle and thus epitomizes the enormous task which Jupiter has laid upon his vicegerent. As in Seneca's 'Hercules Oetaeus', the thunderbolt is the emblem of the hero's struggle, ultimate triumph, deification, and consequent intercession on behalf of mankind:

> Sed tu domitor magne ferarum
> orbisque simul pacator, ades;
> nunc quoque nostras respice terras,
> et si qua novo belua voltu
> quatiet populos terrore gravi,
> tu fulminibus frange trisulcis
> fortius ipso genitore tuo
> fulmina mitte.[471]

---

[467] Cf. Aust, in: Roscher, Myth. Lex. II, 1, 757—9; Platner and Ashby, Topographical Dictionary 299.

[468] Dio Chrysostom Or. 12. 77; Paus. 5. 11.9.

[469] Cf. Macrob. Sat. 5.13. 23; Strabo 8. 3.30.

[470] Dio Chrysostom Or. 12. 78.

[471] Sen. Herc. Oet. 1989—96. Of equal importance for the significance of the thunderbolt in imperial imagery is a passage in the fragmentary treatise on kingship attributed to Diotogenes (ap. Stob. Anth. 4.7. 62, p. 270 ed. Hense): ἔχοντι γὰρ τὰς διαθέσιας τοιαύτας καὶ οἱ θεοὶ καὶ μάλιστα ὁ κρατέων πάντων Ζεύς· καὶ γὰρ οὗτος σεμνὸς μέν ἐντι καὶ τίμιος διά τε τὰν ὑπεροχὰν καὶ τὸ μέγεθος τᾶς ἀρετᾶς, χραστὸς δὲ διὰ τὸ εὐεργετικός τε ἦμεν καὶ ἀγαθοδότας, ὅκως δὴ καὶ λέγεται ὑπὸ τῶ Ἰωνικῶ ποιητᾶ ὥς κ' εἴη 'πατὴρ

The imagery of the vault of the Trajanic arch at Beneventum completes the theme of the attic. In the vault Trajan was portrayed wearing military garb and crowned by Victory. In his left hand he carries a spear, in his right he wields the thunderbolt. He has fought the good fight, and by his *virtus* he has raised himself to the stars.

The surging current of monotheism in the high empire had as its corollary a belief in a divine mediator who stood between mankind and the supreme god of the universe, who would save the human race and whose victory would bring the blessings of a golden age to all. "There is one god and one mediator between god and man, the man Christ Jesus, who gave himself as a ransom for all."[472] So Paul to Timothy, but the idea was not limited to Christian circles; Mithra was called *mesitēs*.[473] As dramatically on the arch at Beneventum, Trajan appears as the divine mediator. Jupiter has entrusted him with care over mankind. His *virtus* will carry him to the stars; for the moment it has brought about the triumph of the new era of blessings attested in the lower reliefs on the arch, a golden age which Trajan will continue to assure even after his departure from earth.

ἀνδρῶν τε θεῶν τε·· δεινὸς δὲ διὰ τὸ κολάζεν τὼς ἀδικέοντας καὶ κρατὲν καὶ κυριεύεν πάντων· ἔχει δὲ καὶ τὸν κεραυνὸν μετὰ χεῖρα, σύμβολον τᾶς δεινότατος· ἐπὶ πᾶσι δὲ τούτοις μναμονεύεν δεῖ ὅτι θεόμιμόν ἐντι πρᾶγμα βασιλῆα.

The date of this treatise, like the companion pieces attributed to Sthenidas and Ecphantus, remains controversial. E. R. GOODENOUGH, The Political Philosophy of Hellenistic Kingship, YCS 1 (1928) 55–102, who first emphasized the importance of these fragments, argued for a Hellenistic date, a position developed by W. TARN, Alexander the Great and the Unity of Mankind, PBA 19 (1933) 128, and by W. THEILER, Das Musengedicht des Horaz, Schrift d. Königsberger Gel. Ges. 12 (Halle 1935) 268. In 1942, L. DELATTE prefaced his edition of these fragments (IDEM, Les traités de la royauté d'Ecphante, Diotogène, et Sthénidas, Bibl. Fac. de Philos. et Lettres de l'Univ de Liège 97 [Liège 1942]) with a detailed treatment of the question of their date, arguing especially on linguistic grounds that the treatises must have been written in the first or second centuries A.D. His view won considerable support; cf. e.g., FESTUGIÈRE, REG 55 (1942) 375–7; DE STRYCKER, RBPH 25 (1946–7) 223–9; LANA, RFIC 27 (1949) 136–40; MARCUS, CJ 44 (1949) 500–2; LEMERLE, RPh 25 (1951) 102; TAEGER, Charisma II, 623–5. More recently, three independent studies have strongly argued, on the basis of content and language, for a Hellenistic date; see DVORNIK, Early Christian and Byzantine Political Philosophy I, 245–61; DOBLHOFER, Augustuspanegyrik 57–65; H. THESLEFF, An Introduction to the Pythagorean Writings of the Hellenistic Period, Acta Acad. Aboensis, Hum. 24,3 (Abo 1961). However, the debate continues; see most recently, W. BURKERT, Zur geistesgeschichtlichen Einordnung einiger Pseudopythagorica, and H. THESLEFF, On the Problem of the Doric Pseudo-Pythagorica, both contributions: in Fond. Hardt, Ent. sur l'Antiquité Classique 18 (Vandœuvres–Genève 1971) 23–102; and AALDERS (n. 336) 27–38.

For the association of the thunderbolt with Alexander the Great and the significance of *imitatio Alexandri* in imperial propaganda in the late Flavian and early Antonine periods, see FEARS, Princeps 56–60, 249–50.

[472] 1. Tim. 2.5
[473] Cf. F. CUMONT, Les mystères de Mithra³ (Paris 1913) 129; A. D. NOCK, Conversion (London 1933) 235–6.

By the intimate association of the emperor with Jupiter, the imperial arrogation of the thunderbolt was transformed from an act of *hybris* into a symbol of selfless devotion to humanity.[474] The process coincided and perhaps influenced the culmination of a far older transformation of the image of Zeus from a lecherous and capricious master into the creator and ruler of the universe, eternal perfection and goodness. Its origins can be seen as early as Hesiod's invocation of Zeus as the guardian of social justice. However, its ultimate formulation, among extant sources, is in Aristides' panegyric to Zeus, composed early in the reign of Antoninus Pius.[475]

To begin his hymn of praise to Zeus, the orator celebrates the creation. Zeus created the universe and everything in it. The rivers, the earth, the sea, the heavens and everything in them, under them, and above them, are his handiwork. He created gods and men and everything which can be seen with the eye or grasped with the mind. First of all, he created himself. There was no Cronus nor was Zeus hidden in a cave on Crete. These tales are no more possible than for a son to be older than his father or a creature to be older than its creator. Zeus is the first and the oldest and the origin of all, who created himself out of himself. No one can say when he came into being, for he was in the beginning and shall be forevermore. As he brought Athena forth from his own forehead without the benefit of a partner, so he conceived and bore himself, father and son in the same person.

Thus Zeus is the beginning of all things and all things came from him. Beginning with the foundations he built the earth so that the universe could rest upon it. With nails, with stone, with foundations without limit, he made it fast. In the middle he placed the ocean and rivers and streams so that there might be communication between all parts. Above he placed the air and above it the ether and over everything the universe. Here he gave full reign to his artistic power, decorating the heaven with stars as the sea with islands. All this he did in the blink of an eye. To every region he gave its characteristic features and nature. To everything he assigned a place, the gods in heaven and man on earth. To the gods he gave the special task of caring for mankind. He established man as master of all things on earth; and to man he gave life, cities, civilization, laws, art, and all blessings. So rightly he is honored and invoked by mankind as source of all things, creator, leader and guardian of all. His epithets tell of his countless undertakings on behalf of mankind, Zeus, who is the saviour of mankind — Zeus, father and ruler of all, who brings all things to perfection.

Considerable significance attaches to the image of Zeus in Aristides' 'Eis Dia.' Aristides was not a profound thinker and moreover an oration of this

---

[474] For the arrogation of the thunderbolt as an act of *hybris*, see, e.g., Plut. Is. 24; Lucan. 7.457–8; Polyb. 12.12.

[475] The best discussion of the 'Eis Dia', together with German translation and commentary, is J. AMANN, Die Zeusrede des Ailios Aristeides, Tübinger Beiträge zur Altertumswissenschaft 12 (Stuttgart 1931), who dates it (p. 236) to the period of Aristides' stay in Egypt, 142–43 A.D. For a later date, 149 A.D., see C. A. BEHR, Aelius Aristides and the Sacred Tales (Amsterdam 1968) 72–3.

sort was not the place for philosophical innovation. The audience expected and received platitudes, commonplace ideas which could be elaborately dressed for the occasion, without taxing the mind of speakers or hearers. Hence it is not rash to assume that this exalted image of Zeus had so penetrated popular thought in the mid-second century Roman empire that it was part of the intellectual equipment of the average man of some education, perhaps of the common mass of humanity. Certainly the idea that Zeus-Jupiter bestows power upon earthly rulers appears in a variety of popular sources, such as rhetorical speeches in historians, the oration on kingship preserved in the 'Corpus Herme-ticum,' and in romancers like Pseudo-Callisthenes and Achilles Tatius.[476] Thus clearly in the Antonine Age, in popular thought and in political ideology, Zeus-Jupiter enjoyed an unprecedented pre-eminence as divine patron of that un-equalled era of oecumenical peace, prosperity, and civilization eulogized by Aelius Aristides. The question remains whether the importance of Zeus-Jupiter as guardian of the political order was in any sense representative of the vitality of the cult of the Roman Jupiter as a religious expression in this period.

3. Aspects of the Roman Cult of Jupiter in the Imperial Age

Particularly in the Hellenistic East, the emperor was at times directly assim-ilated to Zeus in cult. Thus Augustus received cult honors as Zeus Olympios and, as did later Nero and Domitian, as Zeus Eleutherios.[477] Cult statues of emperors adorned with Jovian attributes are extant and are also known from the coinage.[478] Such assimilations of the emperor to Zeus-Jupiter belong rather to the topic of the ruler cult; and in terms of the role of Jupiter in public cult in the

---

[476] Cf. Arr. Anab. 4.20.3; Herod. 4.5.7; Galen. ed. KÜHN vol. XIV p. 217; Celsus ap. Orig. Contra Celsum 8.68; Corp. Herm. XVIII 8–10; 15–16; Pseudo-Callisthenes 1.12; 24; Achilles Tatius 2.1. In general see FEARS, Princeps 121–88.

[477] See above n. 437.

[478] For Augustus see above n. 313. Other examples of cult statues which might be cited include a statue of Tiberius, nude and holding a sceptre (WEST, Römische Porträtplastik I p. 147 no. 210); a statue of Claudius, naked except for a cloak and wearing oak wreath and holding sceptre and *patera*, with an eagle at his feet (G. LIPPOLD, Die Skulpturen des vaticanischen Museums III,1 [Berlin–Leipzig 1936] no. 558); Galba as Jupiter (W. HELBIG, Führer durch die öffentlichen Sammlungen klassischer Altertümer in Rom 4 [Tübingen 1972] I no. 42); and, for the later period, statues from Athens of Balbinus and Pupienus as Jupiter (C. VERMEULE, Roman Imperial Art in Greece and Asia Minor [Cambridge, Mass. 1968] 310–11). Such cult statues are also represented in minor arts. See, e.g., the cameo of Claudius as Jupiter Optimus Maximus (FURTWÄNGLER, Die antiken Gemmen pl. 55 no. 48) and gems showing either Titus or Domitian as Jupiter (FURTWÄNGLER pl. 48). For a cult statue of Trajan with the attributes of Zeus see also the coins from Traianopolis in Cilicia (BMC Lycaonia, Isauria, and Cilicia p. 143). References to such statues are known from the literary sources; cf. Lucan. 7.457–9. A statue of Julius Caesar wearing the aegis and holding a thunderbolt is mentioned among the bronze statues in the Zeuxippos in Constantinople described by Christodorus (Anth. Pal. 2.92–6; MICHEL, Alexander als Vorbild 72–3).

imperial period the most significant aspect is his status as recipient of *vota* undertaken on behalf of the emperor. Under the republic *vota pro reipublicae salute* were regularly made for a set period of time, and after its completion the vows were both fulfilled and undertaken again for the same period of time. Along with these, *vota* were undertaken by the chief magistrates at the beginning of the magisterial year. In addition to these regular *vota*, *vota extraordinaria* were undertaken to mark an extraordinary and perilous situation for the state, such as the beginning of a campaign. In such situations *vota quinquennalia* or *decennalia* could be undertaken to see the state safely beyond the possible limits of the danger. Private individuals could also, of course, undertake *vota*; and in both private and public cult, prayers and sacrifices, not invariably accompanied by *vota*, were made at the beginning of some critical period or of some important enterprise and again at its successful completion. In the imperial period, such sacrifices, prayers, and *vota* were closely associated with the person of the emperor. *Vota pro salute imperatoris*, replacing the republican *vota pro reipublicae salute*, were undertaken at the commencement of each calendar year and for longer periods of five, ten, and twenty years. *Vota extraordinaria* and other forms of special sacrifices occurred at critical moments such as a departure of an emperor on campaign or in thanksgiving for an emperor's escape from an assassination attempt. As already mentioned, the underlying concept is that the safety of the state depends upon the well-being of the emperor. The chief divine recipient of all such *vota* and sacrifices was Jupiter Optimus Maximus. At the annual *vota pro salute imperatoris*, vows were made and fulfilled to Jupiter, Juno, Minerva, Salus, and, at times, to other deities.[479] *Vota extraordinaria* could include a variety of divinities. Thus Nero's escape from the Pisonian conspiracy was commemorated by the offer of sacrifice to Jupiter, Juno, Minerva, Mars, Providentia, Genius Augusti, Honos, and Aeternitas.[480] Domitian's safe return from the Dacian campaign saw sacrifices to Jupiter, Minerva, Mars, Salus, Fortuna, Victoria Redux, and Genius Populi Romani.[481] Trajan's departure for the first Dacian war was marked by sacrifices to Jupiter Optimus Maximus, Juno Regina, Minerva, Iovis Victor, Salus Rei Publicae Populi Romani Quiritum, Mars Pater, Mars Victor, Victoria, Fortuna Redux, Vesta Mater, Neptunus Pater, Hercules Victor.[482]

The tradition of imperial *vota* began with Augustus and represented a natural evolution from the republican custom of undertaking and fulfilling vows on the occasion of the departure and return of a general. Augustan imperial imagery placed some emphasis on the *vota* undertaken in his behalf. In the 'Res

---

[479] A basic collection of material for the study of the imperial *vota* is H. MATTINGLY, The Imperial Vota, PBA 36 (1950) 155—95 and 37 (1953) 219—68. In general, see HAMMOND, Antonine Monarchy 31—3, 49—51; and W. EISENHUT, Votum, RE Suppl. XIV (1974) 964—73. For the republican antecedents, WISSOWA, RKR² 382—3. For the ritual. A. PIGANIOL, Recherches sur les jeux romains, Publ. de la Fac. des Lett. de l'Univ. de Strasbourg 13 (Strasbourg 1923) 79, 145, 149.

[480] Acta Frat.Arv., ed. HENZEN lxxxi.

[481] Acta Frat.Arv., ed. HENZEN cxxii.

[482] Acta Frat.Arv., ed. HENZEN cxl—iii; 124.

Gestae,' Augustus refers to the Senate's decree that vows for his health be offered every fifth year.[483] *Vota* are commemorated on two Augustan issues, both probably struck in 16 B.C.[484] The imperial *vota* have little prominence in the propaganda of his Julio-Claudian and Flavian successors; and it is only with Trajan that the commemoration of *vota* on behalf of the emperor emerges as a major element in the imperial image. After the Augustan issues, the next explicit reference to the *vota* occurs on *aurei* of Trajan struck in 115/16 A.D.[485] The reverse portrays Genius Senatus and Genius Populi Romani, the last in the act of sacrificing, at a lighted altar. The legend reads VOTA SVSCEPTA. Earlier, on the Column of Trajan, *vota* and special sacrifices for the emperor were given particular emphasis, accounting for five of the eight sacrificial scenes represented among the reliefs. All five are portrayed in the course of the first campaign of the second Dacian war, dramatically invoking Jupiter's aid and protection of the emperor at this critical period in a campaign which was no mere border war but was rather a struggle on behalf of civilization against the forces of destruction and chaos, a *bellum Iovis* like the Gigantomachy.[486] Under the later Antonines the imperial *vota* played an extremely important role in imperial propaganda, appearing with ever increasing frequence on the coinage and as an important motif in monumental art.[487]

Indeed the very prominence of representations of *vota publica* in the official art of the second century is indicative of the importance of the Jovian theology of imperial power in the Antonine imperial image and of how significantly this image differed, in this charismatic aspect, from that of the Julio-Claudian period. Among extant monuments, scenes portraying sacrifices to the Genius of the emperor and to the Divi, both aspects of the ruler cult, are popular themes on imperial monuments of the first century and more particularly of the Julio-Claudian period. They play no role in official art of the Antonine period. In the second century the only scenes which can be connected with the worship of the Genius of the living emperor and of the Divi are found on provincial monuments following artistic currents no longer in fashion in the mainstream of imperial art. Such scenes give way to representations of *vota publica*, of *suovetaurilia*, and the celebration of the triumph and the closing of a *lustrum*.[488] These ceremonies all belonged to the hoary traditions of the state

---

[483] Res gestae 9.
[484] BMC I no. 437–42; cf. MATTINGLY, PBA 36 (1950) 156–7.
[485] BMC III no. 587, 612.
[486] Cf. RYBERG, Rites of the State Religion 122–7.
[487] For the numismatic evidence, see MATTINGLY, PBA 36 (1950); STRACK, I, 227; II, 184–6; BEAUJEU, Rel. rom. 74, 84, 92–3, 313, 360–1, 367, 374, 395; F. FERRARIO, Vota publica pro salute felicitate aeternitate Augusti, AIIN 7/8 (1960–61) 39–57; R. MATHISEN, The Periodic Vota of the Later Roman Empire, Journal of the Society of Ancient Numismatics 4 (1972–73) 43–5. RYBERG, Rites of the State Religion 120–40, collects the monumental evidence. Recent additions to the epigraphical material include J. REYNOLDS, Vota Pro Salute Principis, PBSR 30 (1962) 33–6; L. MĂRGHITAN and C. PETOLESCU, Vota Pro Salute Imperatoris in an Inscription at Ulpia Traiana Sarmizegetusa, JRS 66 (1976) 84–6.
[488] Cf. RYBERG, Rites of the State Religion 81–162, esp. 102–3.

cult, but in the imperial age they centered upon the person of the emperor as the charismatic force which ensured the safety of the commonwealth. However, unlike the cult of the imperial Genius or Numen or of the Divi, Jupiter Optimus Maximus and the divinities of the Roman state, not some aspect of the imperial personage, was the recipient of their sacrifices. The difference is significant. The celebration of a *vota publica pro salute imperatoris* proclaims that the emperor depends upon the protection of the gods, above all Jupiter Optimus Maximus. Behind the care which the emperor exercised for the Roman state lay the abiding protection of Jupiter, a concern which was eternal and unchanging, removed from any temporary harm inflicted on the state by the failure and excesses of any one particular emperor or any one particular dynasty.

The central role of Jupiter in the imperial ideology of the Antonine Age was not a mere political fabrication devoid of any real religious feeling. It was not a political mythology erected upon the expiring corpse of an outworn and dying creed. A sincerely religious belief in the Roman Jupiter par excellence, Jupiter Optimus Maximus, was a major theme in the cult life of the Antonine Age. Among all classes and throughout the Latin-speaking parts of the empire the conviction existed that the Roman Jupiter was a personal deity who intervened as a saviour not merely in state affairs but also in the private life of his individual worshipers. From emperor to slave, Jupiter's devotees have left us their witness to their living faith.

Few would doubt that an actual religious experience played some role in Constantine's favorable attitude towards Christianity. Would we deny the same of Domitian's efforts to restore Jupiter to a dominant position in imperial ideology? There is no reason to doubt that Jupiter's salvation of him, memorialized in shrines to Jupiter Custos and Jupiter Conservator, was any less significant as a personal religious encounter than was Christ's aid to Constantine during the civil wars with Maxentius and Licinius. Suetonius specifically states that Domitian was a man of deep piety, bordering on superstition, whose divine patrons appeared to him in dreams.[489] With regard to later emperors, such divine visitations actually appear on the columns of both Trajan and Marcus Aurelius.[490] One hesitates to dismiss them as merely the result of artistic tradition. The scenes differ in the two cases. On Trajan's column, Jupiter intervenes to hurl his thunderbolt during the critical first large battle with the Dacians. On Marcus' column, Jupiter brings water to the parched troops. This last passed into the literary tradition, which ascribed the intervention directly to the prayers of Marcus: *Fulmen de caelo precibus suis contra hostium machinamentum extorsit, suis pluvia impetrata cum siti laborarent.*[491]

---

[489] Suet. Dom. 15.

[490] CICHORIUS, Die Reliefs der Traianssäule, Scene 28; E. PETERSEN, A. VON DOMASZEWSKI, and G. CALDERINI, Die Marcussäule auf Piazza Colonna in Rom (Munich 1896) Scene 16.

[491] SHA Marc. 24. According to Dio 71.8—10, the storm was sent by Hermes at the behest of an Egyptian magician. A Christian legend (Xiphilinus in Dio 71.9) held that the rain came in answer to the prayers of the Twelfth Legion, the *Fulminata*, composed of Christians.

Commodus exhibited a nearly neurotic piety towards Jupiter and other divinities. This is particularly evident in the number of *vota extraordinaria* which were undertaken during his reign, marking almost every year and extensively commemorated on the coinage.[492] Like Domitian, Commodus sought to associate Jupiter intimately with the official image of the emperor, instituting a new era in the role of Jupiter in imperial ideology.[493]

A survey of the importance of Jupiter in private cult in the imperial age only increases the conviction that religious feeling was central to the pre-eminent role of Jupiter in the imperial ideology of the high empire. Interest in such exotic deities as Mithras, Sarapis, and Jupiter Dolichenus should not obscure the fact that in the Latin West, with the exception of Africa, private dedications to Jupiter vastly outnumber those to any other god. A partial survey of dedications to Jupiter in Dacia reveal 112 to Jupiter Optimus Maximus alone. His nearest competitor among Roman gods is Mars with slightly more than fifteen.[494] Roughly sixty such dedicatory inscriptions to Mithra are known.[495] In Spain dedications to Jupiter Optimus Maximus outnumber those to his nearest competitors, like Mars, Hercules, and Minerva by more than a four-to-one margin.[496] The fact that Spain and Dacia were so different as provinces only increases the significance of the dominance of the cult of Jupiter Optimus Maximus.

The miracle of the rain has been the subject of an extensive scholarly literature. For earlier studies, see W. ZWIKKER, Studien zur Markussäule I (Amsterdam 1941) 206 n. 166; A. ROOS, Het regenwonder op de zuil van Marcus Aurelius, Mededeelingen der Koninklijke Akademie van Wetenschappen, Afdeeling letterkunde n.s. 6,1 (Amsterdam 1943); J. GUEY, Encore la «pluie miraculeuse», RPh 22 (1948) 16–62; and IDEM, La date de la «pluie miraculeuse», MEFR 60 (1948) 105–27, 61 (1949) 93–118; BEAUJEU, Rel. rom. 342–9; G. BARTA, Legende und Wirklichkeit – Das Regenwunder bei Marcus Aurelius, ACD 4 (1968) 85–91; D. BERWIG, Marc Aurel und die Christen (Diss. Munich 1971).

[492] Cf. BEAUJEU, Rel. rom. 373–84, who labels this aspect of Commodus' character *«la piété exubérante. »*

[493] See below pp. 107–14.

[494] The figures are from L. JONES, The Cults of Dacia, University of California Publications in Classical Philology 9, 8 (Berkeley 1929) 245–305. A survey of inscriptions which have come to light since 1929 changes the numbers but not the overwhelming numerical dominance of Jupiter. The epigraphical evidence for the worship of Jupiter is collected and briefly analyzed on a province-by-province basis by R. BARTOCCINI, Iuppiter, in: E. DE RUGGIERO, Dizionario Epigrafico di Antichità Romane IV (Rome 1941) 240–62. For methodological reasons, the evidence presented in this essay was assembled and evaluated independently of BARTOCCINI's excellent study.

[495] Cf. M. J. VERMASEREN, Corpus inscriptionum et monumentorum religionis Mithriacae I (Den Haag 1956). The number mentioned in the text includes only dedications, properly so-called, to the divinity.

[496] The figures for Jupiter are based on the model collection of material by F. PEETERS, Le culte de Jupiter en Espagne d'après les inscriptions, RBPh 17 (1938) 157–193, 853–86 (rep. as Le culte de Jupiter en Espagne d'après les inscriptions [Brussels 1938]). For the Capitoline divinities in Spain see also, for the epigraphical and numismatical evidence, G. HEUTEN, Les divinités capitolines en Espagne, RBPh 12 (1933) 549–68; IDEM, Les divinités capitolines en Espagne, II: La numismatique, RBPh 14 (1935) 709–23.

The prevalence of epigraphical evidence for the cult of Jupiter Optimus Maximus in the Latin provinces has frequently been recognized. Its significance, however, has been underestimated by a tendency to assume that the dedicants were almost invariably Roman officials and soldiers and that the dedications were little more than manifestations of patriotic loyalty.[497] Neither assumption is entirely valid. Again in provinces as dissimilar as Spain and Dacia the Roman cult of Jupiter Optimus Maximus cut across all social grades. Only nineteen per cent of 166 dedications to Jupiter Optimus are from Roman officials and soldiers. Dedicants who are clearly Roman citizens account for thirty-seven per cent more, but in many cases these are members of the municipal aristocracy. However, Jupiter Optimus Maximus was also the recipient of four of the five dedications by known slaves and freedmen. Jupiter could be identified with such native divinities as Anderonus, Solutorius, Ladicus, and Candamius. However, natives also worshipped Jupiter as Optimus Maximus, and twenty-six per cent of all such dedications come from natives.[498] The cult of Jupiter Optimus Maximus had the same wide appeal in Transalpine and Cisalpine Gaul.[499] In Gallia Cisalpina, for example, of those donors who can be adequately identified, eight were military, six were connected with the imperial bureaucracy or the imperial cult, while two senators, two equestrians, and six *seviri* and *Augustales* are known. Twenty-two other dedications are identified as being from freeborn citizens, while ten are clearly from freedmen, eight certainly from slaves, and ten from unassimilated natives and slaves.[500] In the military provinces of the Danubian and Rhine regions the vast majority of dedications to Jupiter Optimus Maximus are from military men and imperial officials.[501] This itself is not in-

---

[497] This is the view of J. TOUTAIN, Les cultes païens dans l'empire romain I, Bibliothèque de l'École des Hautes Études, Sciences Religieuses 20 (Paris 1907) 199, 210; and, perhaps because the cult of Jupiter in the provinces in the imperial period has been the subject of so little attention, it continues to be repeated. See, e.g., C. PASCAL, The Cults of Cisalpine Gaul (Brussels 1964) 14–5; K. PRÜMM, Religionsgeschichtliches Handbuch für den Raum der altchristlichen Umwelt. Hellenistisch-römische Geistesströmungen und Kulte mit Beachtung des Eigenlebens der Provinzen (Rome 1954) 750, 778.

[498] For the figures see PEETERS, RBPh 17 (1938) 157–93.

[499] Examples of dedications to Jupiter by natives, slaves and freedmen in Tres Galliae include the following: CIL XIII 37, 1674, 163, 234, 235, 1741, 6396. Dedications from women include CIL XIII 234, 235, 387, 571. Dedications by slaves and freedmen in Gallia Narbonensis include CIL XII 499, 1563, 5752; E. ESPÉRANDIEU, Inscriptions latines de Gaule (Narbonnaise) (Paris 1929) no. 77.

[500] Cf. PASCAL, Cisalpine Gaul 15–6.

[501] Dedications from military personnel and imperial officials include Germania, CIL XIII 6213, 6397, 6509, 6525, 6526, 6620, 6643, 6644, 6645, 7609, 7714, 7896, 8198, 8197. Dacia, CIL III 822, 845, 886, 887, 892, 946, 1293, 947, 1034, 1037, 1038, 1041, 1042, 1295, 1298, 1044, 1045, 1052, 1056, 1058, 1074, 1347, 7754, 7755, 7850, 12671. Moesia, CIL III 1643, 1674–76, 8099, 8162, 8249. Dalmatia, CIL III 1780, 1907, 1918, 2759, 2823, 3114, 9790, 9862, 10050, 13229, 13847. Pannonia, CIL III 3220, 3306, 3344, 3386, 3434, 3275, 3435, 3444, 3446, 3451, 3453, 3454, 3669, 3900–02, 3915–6, 3938, 3948–50, 4147, 4235, 4406–07, 4553, 4559, 4787, 10198, 10247, 10360, 10389, 10370, 10411, 10413, 10415, 10417, 10420, 10423, 10580, 10787, 10799, 10839, 10979, 10981, 10982, 10983,

significant if it is remembered that it was precisely at this class that much of the numismatic propaganda of the third-century emperors was aimed. Moreover, in Dacia, Pannonia, Moesia, Raetia, Noricum, and Germania the worship of Jupiter was not confined to soldiers and imperial officials. Dedications by freeborn citizens and by members of the municipal aristocracy are not infrequent,[502] while donors also include slaves, freedmen, women, and natives.[503]

Furthermore, these numerous dedications are not to be dismissed as mere manifestations of *romanitas* and loyalty to emperor and state. The bulk of our evidence for the worship of Jupiter is in the form of simple inscriptions, and in these circumstances it is not always possible to judge whether such a memorial is a testimony to true religious feelings. The surest guide is the presence of an ex-voto formula, "the touchstone of piety in antiquity as . . . made in recognition of supposed deliverance in some invisible manner from sickness or other peril."[504] Considering Britain, the Gallic provinces, Spain, the Germanies, Noricum, Raetia, Pannonia, Dacia, and Moesia, a considerable proportion of extant private dedications to Jupiter Optimus Maximus contain ex-voto formulas. In Dacia sixty-six of one hundred and twelve inscriptions to Jupiter Optimus Maximus are ex-votos.[505] The same proportion, roughly half, is true of the dedications in Cisalpine Gaul.[506] A substantial proportion of the dedications from Moesia, Dalmatia, Pannonia, and Noricum and Raetia fall into this category.[507] The proportions for Spain, Gaul and Britain are smaller but still

10984, 10985, 10987, 10988, 11118, 11123, 11124, 11697, 11918, 12385. Noricum, CIL III 5178, 5180, 5184, 5690, 5161−74, 5177, 5179, 5181. Raetia, CIL III 5942.

[502] Dedications by free-born Roman citizens are far too extensive to be listed here. A list of dedications by members of the municipal aristocracy would include Dacia, CIL III 983, 1051, 1282, 1407, 7910, 8043; Dalmatia, CIL III 1942, 8301, 8366, 12747. Pannonia, CIL III 3220, 3230, 3291, 3436, 3438, 3449, 10267, 10334. Noricum, CIL 5182; Moesia, 8141, 8189, 8247, 12466.

[503] Dedications by natives, slaves, and freedmen include: Germania, CIL XIII 5411, 5990, 5991, 6075, 6144, 6204, 6395, 6703, 7565a, 7896, 8540, 8541, 8542. Dalmatia, CIL III 9810. Moesia, A. and J. ŠAŠEL, Inscriptiones Latinae quae in Iugoslavia inter annos MCMXL et MCMLX repertae et editae sunt (Ljubljana 1963) no. 22; CIL III 7535, 8142. Pannonia, CIL III 4020, 4023, 4024, 4029, 14069. Dacia, CIL III 7823, 7825, 8025. Dedications by women include CIL III 4026 (Pannonia), 8025 (Dacia).

[504] The quote is from A. NOCK, The Augustan Empire 44 B.C. − A.D. 70, Chapter XV: Religious Developments from the Close of the Republic to the Death of Nero, CAH X (Cambridge 1934) 481. PASCAL, Cisalpine Gaul 16−17, rightly emphasizes the significance of ex-voto dedications as indicators of true personal piety on the part of the dedicator.

[505] CIL III 845, 855, 883, 885, 887, 888, 891, 946, 947, 983, 1031, 1034, 1035, 1036−7, 1039, 1044−8, 1050−2, 1057−8, 1074, 1260, 1283, 1295, 1297, 1301, 1301a, 1301b, 1344−7, 1349−50, 1406, 1408, 1430, 1574, 6260, 7658, 7674, 7675−77, 7755−6, 7758, 7823, 7852, 7848−9, 7881, 7890, 7909, 7910, 8015, 12600, 13768, 14472.

[506] Cf. PASCAL, Cisalpine Gaul 16−7.

[507] A list of ex-votos from the Danubian and Rhine Provinces would include the following: Moesia, CIL III 8084, 8106, 8149, 8150, 8171, 8185, 8246; ŠAŠEL (above n. 503) no. 22. Pannonia, CIL III 3220, 3229, 3230, 3254, 3270, 3275, 3291, 3386, 3391, 3432, 3433, 3434−7, 3439, 3440−2, 3444, 3446−54, 3619, 3648, 3669, 3839, 3900−2, 3916−7, 3938−40, 3947−50; 4020, 4022, 4024, 4025−8, 4132, 4157, 4293−4, 4404−5, 4407, 4409,

considerable.[508] Another bit of evidence for the intensity of religious feeling is the record that the dedication was made as the result of a personal order by the god to his devotee. In the imperial period divine appearances in dreams were associated with traditional divinities as well as oriental 'saviour' gods like Sarapis.[509] In Cisalpine Gaul three dedicants made their offerings to Jupiter at his direct behest.[510] In Spain, Dacia, Germania Superior, Germania Inferior, Dalmatia and Moesia, dedicants commemorated the intense personal religious feeling involved in a dedication inspired by a vision of the god or some other form of divine command.[511]

Religious feeling and patriotism are not mutually exclusive; and without denying the importance of the religious aspect, it is also proper to interpret the pre-eminence of Jupiter Optimus Maximus in the private cult of the Latin provinces as evidence of romanization and in individual cases, as manifestations of political loyalty to emperor, Rome, and the entire concept of *romanitas*. A further suggestion of this is found in the degree to which Optimus Maximus, the Capitoline form of Jupiter, dominates the dedications. Relatively uncommon are dedications in which Jupiter is invoked by another epithet such as *Victor, Stator, Conservator, Defensor et Tutator*, and *Depulsor*. In such cases the epithet is most frequently added to the full title *Jupiter Optimus Maximus*. Similarly it was as Jupiter Optimus Maximus that the Roman god was most frequently associated with native gods and with oriental divinities.[512]

4559, 4588, 10198, 10217, 10247, 10267, 10307, 10334, 10360, 10389, 10370, 10411—17, 10420, 10422—3, 10580—1, 10763, 10787, 10799, 10839, 10840, 10889, 10902, 10980, 10982—9, 11117—20, 11546, 11697—8, 11918, 13362, 13387, 13388, 13437, 14069, 14087. Dalmatia, CIL III 1736, 1777—80, 1907, 1918, 1943, 2759, 3114, 8302, 8366, 8367, 8110, 8671a, 9809, 9811, 9861—2, 9899, 9901, 9933, 9958, 9959, 9968, 10050, 12747, 13236, 13269, 13356, 13847. Šašel (above n. 503) 327—31; 337—8.
Noricum, CIL III 4752, 4788, 5120, 5161—5, 5167—73, 5175, 5177—81, 5184, 5690. Raetica, CIL III 5894, 5903, 5919, 5975.
Germania, CIL XIII 5002, 5330, 5356, 5473, 5990, 6081—2, 6092, 6128, 6144, 6147, 6204, 6214, 6215, 6323, 6325, 6361, 6386b.; 6395—7, 6419, 6445, 6509, 6554, 6620, 6622, 6644—5, 6702, 7341, 7409, 7565a, 7609, 7672, 7784, 7896, 8012, 8162, 8163, 8515, 8540, 8605, 8614, 8615, 8618, 8715, 8715—7, 8778, 11708, 11711, 11728—9.

[508] A list of ex-votos to Jupiter from Spain, Gaul, and Britain would include the following: Spain, CIL II 151, 755, 926, 2376, 2386, 2388, 2389, 2394, 2466—8, 2537, 2571, 2608, 2774, 2817, 2850, 2851, 5640, 5644.
Tres Galliae, CIL XIII 3586, 3645, 3647, 4302, 4548, 4570, 11154. P. Wuilleumier, Inscriptions latines des Trois Gaules, Gallia Suppl. 17 (Paris 1963) no. 39.
Britannia, CIL VII 3775, 3835, 385, 3865, 3875, 435, 881.

[509] Cf. S. Newhall, Quid de somnis censuerint quoque modo eis usi sint antiqui quaeritur (Diss. Harvard 1913). More recently, see A. J. Festugière, Personal Religion among the Greeks (Berkeley 1954) 95—104; E. R. Dodds, Pagan and Christian in an Age of Anxiety (Cambridge 1965) 38—53.

[510] CIL V 3251, 5597, 6503a. Cf. Pascal, Cisalpine Gaul 17.

[511] CIL II 1015; CIL III 855, 1057, 1294, 2821, 7939, 7756, 8015, 8510, 10108; CIL XIII 6144, 8162; An. Ép. (1944) 62; (1950) 14; (1964) 158. Cf. Bartoccini, Iuppiter, in: De Ruggiero, Dizionario Epigrafico 250—1.

[512] Cf. CIL XIII, v. p. 114—5; CIL III p. 2515—7. See also Peeters, RBPh 17 (1938) 182—3;

Sincere religious belief and patriotism were combined in the *vota publica*; and the same perfectly laudable feelings were combined in the large number of private dedications to Jupiter Optimus Maximus *pro salute imperatoris*.[513] Perhaps the most spectacular extant monument of such dedications is the Jupiter column at Mainz.[514] It was erected by the *canabarii* and dedicated to Jupiter Optimus Maximus *pro salute Neronis Claudii Caesaris Augusti imperatoris*. From a double plinth rose a shaft and capital supporting a pedestal on which stood a bronze statue of Jupiter. The plinth and shaft are decorated with figures, and the iconographical message celebrates Jupiter as the eternal guardian of the peace and prosperity brought about by Nero and those blessings and virtues which he embodies: *Abundantia, Honos, Virtus, Victoria*. Such isolated columns dedicated to Jupiter Optimus Maximus and, at times, Juno Regina, were erected particularly in the second and first part of the third century over a wide area in Roman Germany.[515] Whatever native concepts lie behind the idea of erecting such columns and behind the significance of the various iconographical elements, the columns were dramatic testimony to Jupiter Optimus Maximus as the guardian of the divine and human order. The reconciliation of native and Roman forms in the Jupiter columns is itself significant evidence of popular recognition, at all levels of society, of the identification of Jupiter with the political order.

JONES, Cults of Dacia 249–51; BARTOCCINI, Iuppiter, in: DE RUGGIERO, Dizionario Epigrafico 241.

[513] A list of such private dedications to Jupiter *pro salute imperatoris* would include ŠAŠEL (above n. 503) 331; CIL III 453, 1043, 1675, 3431, 8185, 10360, 13457; CIL XIII 4302. These are proportionately most common in Africa. See CIL VIII 2467, 4510, 16439, 23326, 25894.

[514] The best recent treatment is H. INSTINSKY, Kaiser Nero und die Mainzer Jupitersäule, JRGZ 6 (1959) 128–41.

[515] Still extremely valuable for the Jupiter columns, their significance and iconography is F. HERTLEIN, Die Juppitergigantensäulen (Stuttgart 1910). See further COOK, Zeus II, 50–100; HAUG, Gigantensäulen, RE Suppl. IV (1924) 689–96; F. DREXEL, Die Götterverehrung im römischen Germanien, Bericht Röm.-Germ. Komm. 15 (Frankfurt 1923) 53ff.; F. HEICHELHEIM, Gigantensäulen, RE Suppl. VII (1940) 220–2; F. BENOÎT, Les mythes de l'outre-tombe: le cavalier à l'anguipède et l'écuyère Epona, Coll. Latomus 3 (Brussels 1950); P. LAMBRECHTS, Divinités équestres celtiques ou défunts héroïsés, AC 20 (1951) 107–28; J. MOREAU, Colonnes du dieu cavalier au géant anguipède dans le territoire de la Sarre, NClio 4 (1952) 219–45; P. FOURNIER, Le dieu cavalier à l'anguipède dans la cité des Arvernes, RACF 1 (1962) 105–27; E. VON MERCKLIN, Antike Figuralkapitelle (Berlin 1962) no. 420, 430, 437, 440; M. P. NILSSON, Zur Deutung der Juppitergigantensäulen, ARW 23 (1925) 175–83 (rep. in: IDEM, Opuscula Selecta, Skrifter utgiv. av Svenska Instit. i Athen II,1 [Lund 1951] 399–409); R. NIERHAUS, Ein Viergötterstein aus Sinsheim an der Elsenz, Bad. Fundber. 23 (1967) 111–5; G. CH. PICARD, Le vulcain à la proue de Vienne-en-Val (Loiret), RACF 8 (1969) 195–210; and IDEM, Les fouilles de Vienne-en-Val (Loiret), CRAI (1970) 176–91; J. MERTENS, Le cavalier à l'anguipède de Tongres, RA (1972) 175; M. TAILLANDIER, Un nouveau dieu-cavalier en Auvergne, RACF 12 (1973) 11–20; W. MUELLER, Die Jupitergigantensäulen und ihre Verwandten, Beiträge zur klassischen Philologie 66 (Meisenheim am Glan 1975).

If native and Roman elements fused in the Jupiter columns of Roman Germany, such was certainly not the case in that aspect of the cult of Jupiter which in Africa came to symbolize the divine sanction of the Roman political order. At Rome, in terms of imperial ideology, the cult of Jupiter centered upon the great Capitoline temple. Significantly, representations of the Capitoline temple are absent from the coinage of the Julio-Claudians. First in the year 68–69 does the Capitoline appear on the imperial coinage, becoming a prominent motif under Vespasian. Its characteristic triple doors are prominent in monumental representations of *nuncupatio votorum* in the Antonine period.[516] The same era marked the beginning of the large-scale construction of Capitolia throughout the provinces of the Latin West and especially in the Roman cities of Africa.[517] In republican Italy the erection of tripartite temples on the model of the Roman Capitolium was a product of Roman expansion. The earliest group of such Capitolia were erected in the second century B.C., all in cities, like Cosa and Signia, which were Roman *coloniae*.[518] In the first century of the imperial age Capitolia continued to be built, again largely in cities which were *coloniae*. The Flavian epoch in particular was marked by the erection or reconstruction of Capitolia in a number of *coloniae* in Italy. In the second and the beginning of the third centuries, however, Capitolia were built in cities with the most diverse municipal constitutions. The movement was especially characteristic of Africa, the only province of the Latin West for which there is little evidence for Jupiter as an important figure in private cult. Two Capitolia are known in Spain, three in Gaul, three in the Danubian provinces and as many as thirty-eight in Africa. In the Antonine Age, it was not necessary for a city to possess colonial status in order to erect a Capitolium. The essential qualification was a community of interest with Rome, marked by the assimilation, in some degree, of Roman religious and civil institutions. The Capitoline Triad was the national cult of Rome par excellence; and its adoption was a mark of romanization. By contrast, such assimilation to Roman civil and religious institutions was lacking in the cities of the East, excluding of course actual Roman colonies; and in the East the cult of Zeus Capitolinus lacked the patriotic intensity which was a hallmark

---

[516] BMC II pp. 123, 133, 144, 155, 158, 160, 168, 173, 178, 210, 216, 261, 280. For representations in Antonine art, see RYBERG, Rites of the State Religion 128, 157, 143, 150, 175, 180–1, 189.

[517] In the following treatment of Capitolia in the imperial period, I have closely followed the excellent study of U. BIANCHI, Disegno storico del culto capitolino nell'Italia romana e nelle provincie dell'impero, MAL 8,2 (1950) 349–415. More recently, U. BIANCHI, I Capitolia, and G. RADKE, Il valore religioso e politico delle divinità del Campidoglio, both in: Atti del Convegno Internazionale per il XIX Centenario della Dedicazione del Capitolium e per il 150 Anniversario della sua Scoperta, I Suppl. ai Comment. dell'Ateneo di Brescia (1975) 63–76, 245–53. See also H. GABELMANN, Das Kapitol in Brescia, JRGZ 18 (1971) 124–45 and in the near future I. M. BARTON, Capitoline Temples in Italy and the Provinces (especially Africa), ANRW II, 12, 1 (1981).

[518] The excavators of Cosa, excavated after BIANCHI's larger study, argue that it is the earliest extant Capitolium outside Rome; cf. F. BROWN, E. RICHARDSON, and L. RICHARDSON, Cosa II: The Temples of the Arx, MAAR 26 (Rome 1960) 102–8. They would date it to c. 150 B.C.

of the worship of the Capitoline Triad in the West. By building a Capitolium a city demonstrated its loyalty to the fundamental institutions of the empire and to the emperor. The formula *pro salute imperatoris* was a part of every dedicatory inscription. The structure was often dedicated by the highest imperial official of the province. The individual worshippers, who have left a record, were largely imperial officials and military. Few real provincials are attested. The cult was in the hands of the municipal *flamines perpetui*. All Capitolia were dedicated to Jupiter Optimus Maximus, Juno Regina, and Minerva; and in contrast to the cult of Jupiter Optimus Maximus, which could be assimilated to native or eastern divinities, no barbarian elements contaminated the worship of the Capitoline Triad in the provinces.

Together with the epigraphical evidence for the other provinces of the Latin West, the circumstances of the construction of Capitolia in Africa indicate how strongly in the Antonine Age the cult of Jupiter Capitolinus had come to represent the concept of *romanitas* and to serve as the religious foundation of the civil institutions of the *imperium Romanum*. This is further seen in the actual placing of Capitolia not on an *arx* but in the *forum*, in the very center of civic life. It is further revealed by the role of Capitolia during the persecution of Christians. These enemies of the state were taken to the Capitolium in the various cities to offer those sacrifices which would prove their loyalty to Rome.[519] For the Christian the concept of Capitolium represented the totality of Roman religion: *sciant ergo Romani Capitolium suum id est summum caput religionum publicarum*.[520] Cyprian contrasted *ecclesia* with *Capitolium*; and his choice is suggestive.[520a] Like the concept of *romanitas* itself, the worship of Jupiter Optimus Maximus was a Roman national cult and at the same time a universal cult, transcending other national traditions and uniting worshipers and fellow Romans throughout the empire. The cults of the ancient Greco-Roman world traditionally served sociological as well as religious functions, providing for the well-being of the community as well as the individual. On both levels, the cult of Jupiter Optimus Maximus remained a vital religious force throughout the second and third centuries, and it is only with this realization that we can attempt to understand its role in the imperial ideology during the great third-century crisis of the Roman imperial structure.

4. The Jovian Theology of Imperial Power and the Crisis of the Roman Order

a) Commodus

As in many other aspects of the imperial structure, the principates of Antoninus and Marcus were a period of assimilation for the Jovian theology of imperial power formulated by Domitian, Trajan, and Hadrian. Jupiter retained his central role in imperial ideology. He appears frequently on the coinage, but

---

[519] Cyp. De lapsis 8.19; Ep. 59.13.
[520] Lact. Div. inst. 1.11.49.
[520a] Cyp. Ep. 59.18.

generally on fairly banal types (Pl. VI, 38—41).[521] Occasionally he is invoked on
the coinage by a particular epithet, *Victor, Latius,* and *Stator.*[521a] The direct
association of the emperor with Jupiter on the coinage was infrequent. A single
issue of *aurei,* struck in 171—2 during the great northern war, portrays Marcus
wielding the thunderbolt and crowned by Victory.[522] Issued shortly after the
victory which gained Marcus his sixth imperatorial acclamation and along with
a type commemorating VICTORIA GERMANICA,[523] the reverse of Marcus
Keraunophorus conveys the image of the emperor as the warrior vicegerent of
Jupiter, wielding divinely granted power against the forces of chaos.[524] However, a portrayal of the actual investiture of the emperor by Jupiter, such as
occurs under Hadrian, does not appear on the imperial coinage of Antoninus,
Marcus, or Lucius Verus, and its absence is suggestive. The legend PROVI-
DENTIA DEORVM had marked a Hadrianic issue portraying the emperor's
election by Jupiter (Pl. VI, 36). Antoninus disassociated this legend from an explicit portrayal of his investiture by Jupiter. On an issue of 140—42 A.D., the
legend is linked with the simple reverse type of a thunderbolt (Pl. VI, 42) and
issued along with a series in honour of the army, the emperor, Rome itself,
Concordia, and Genius Senatus.[525] In short, the foresight of the gods is thus

---

[521] Standing front, holding sceptre, hand on hip; to the right stands an eagle: BMC IV
pp. 259, 262 (Pl. VI, 38).
Standing front, holding sceptre and thunderbolt: BMC IV pp. 32, 200, 272, 329, 340,
341, 346, 347 (Pl. VI, 39).
Seated, holding thunderbolt and sceptre: BMC IV pp. 69, 72, 259, 260, 460, 462, 463,
589, 616 (Pl. VI, 40).
Seated, holding Victory and sceptre: pp. 262, 491, 495, 497, 627, 630, 631, 633—6, 680,
682, 683 (Pl. VI, 41).
HILL, NC 6,20 (1960) 113—28, attempts to reduce the numerous and complicated Jupiter
types of the Roman mint in imperial times to five main types: *Capitolinus, Victor,
Conservator, Propugnator,* and *Latius.*

[521a] BMC IV p. 32 no. 210—2, p. 200 no. 1247, p. 272 no. 1687, p. 329 IOVI STATORI
(Antoninus Pius); BMC IV p. 262 IOVI VICTORI (Antoninus); BMC IV p. 262 IOVI
LATIO (Antoninus). MATTINGLY, BMC IV lvi, associates the type of Jupiter Stator with
warfare in Britain. However, the significance of Jupiter's role as Stator was not limited to
the field of military action. Indeed that may not have been even its primary significance.
As discussed in the text, Cicero emphasizes the role of Jupiter Stator as preserver of the
commonwealth and its institutions (Cat. 1.13). Antoninus' type no. 210—2 appears within
an issue largely concerned with Rome, honoring APOLLO AVGVSTVS (Palatinus) (no.
186—90), OPS (no. 221) *in cuius tutela urbs Roma est* (Macrob. 3.9.4—5); ROMA
AETERNA (p. 34); GENIVS SENATVS (no. 204), and GENIO POPVLI ROMANI
(no. 207). It is in the sense of 'preserver of Rome', not in reference to any external
warfare, that the Jupiter Stator type of Antoninus should be interpreted.

[522] BMC IV no. 566.

[523] BMC IV no. 563.

[524] The divine aspect is celebrated on a bronze issue of Marcus, dated to 176—77, on which
Jupiter appears hurling his thunderbolt at the foe and with the legend PROPVGNATOR;
BMC IV p. 665.

[525] BMC IV no. 225—228 (PROVIDENTIA DEORVM). The issue is part of that discussed
above n. 521. The types include Ops (no. 221); APOLLO AVGVSTVS (no. 186—90);
ROMA AETERNA (p. 34); ROMVLVS AVGVSTVS (no. 232, cf. no. 1286), GENIVS

only one of the forces which lie behind the accession of the new emperor.[526] Intentional was the avoidance of the strident Hadrianic iconography of divine election. Hadrian's relations with the Senate, never entirely amicable, deteriorated increasingly towards the end of his reign; and only with difficulty and concessions did Antoninus secure the confirmation of Hadrian's work and his consecration. Antoninus' reign thus commenced in a context of requisite compromise. The essentially autocratic concept of rule by divine election, acceptable under Trajan, may have been viewed with increasing distrust by the Senate under Hadrian. Jupiter retained his central role in imperial ideology; but the emperor's association with him was placed on a more indirect level. Another restraining influence was the increasing importance of the dynastic theme in the later Antonine Age.[527] Although not mutually exclusive, the election of the emperor by Jupiter and the image of the emperor as heir of his deified predecessor were alternate modes of viewing the transmission of the imperial power.[528] The contrast is nicely illustrated by a comparison of the imagery of the attic reliefs of the arch at Beneventum with the adoption relief from the Antonine monument from Ephesus.[529] This tension between the dynastic and the Jovian origin of imperial power would never be entirely reconciled and would pass on into the Christian empire.

Associated in the imperial power since 177 A.D., Commodus' accession to sole power was sanctioned by the charisma of the dynasty. However, like Hadrian, the very beginning of his reign was marked by the abandonment of his father's foreign policy.[530] On medallions issued in 180 and again in 183 and 184,

---

SENATVS (no. 204), GENIO POPVLI ROMANI (no. 207) and CONCORDIA AVG. (no. 196). For this type of PROVIDENTIA DEORVM, see, with a different emphasis, STRACK, III,127. FEARS, Princeps 270—8, discusses the significance of *Providentia Deorum* as a type on the imperial coinage.

[526] For the Stoics, of course, Jupiter was identified with divine providence; cf. Sen. Q.N. 2.45.

[527] On the dynastic character of the principate in general, see M. PRÉVOST, Les adoptions politiques à Rome sous la République et le Principat (Paris 1949); HAMMOND, Antonine Monarchy 4—5; L. WICKERT, Princeps, RE XXII,2 (1954) 2179—80; and IDEM, Neue Forschungen zum römischen Principat, ANRW II,1 (1974) 46—59, with a survey of the more recent literature. R. SYME, Emperors and Biography. Studies in the Historia Augusta (Oxford 1971) 78—88, examines the role of the *nomen Antoninorum*. Cf. J. BLÁZQUEZ, Propaganda dinástica y culto imperial en las acuñaciones de Hispania, Numisma 23—24 (1974) 311—29; H. GESCHE, Die Divinisierung der römischen Kaiser in ihrer Funktion als Herrschaftslegitimation, Chiron 8 (1978) 377—90; E. CHAMPLIN, Notes on the Heirs of Commodus, AJPh 100 (1979) 283—306.

[528] Cf. FEARS, Princeps 270—8, 294—6, 308—9.

[529] For the Antonine relief from Ephesus, see VERMEULE, Roman Imperial Art 95—123. The relief in question commemorates the adoption of Antoninus by Hadrian, who are portrayed as priests, side by side with Lucius Verus between them. Marcus Aurelius stands to the left of Antoninus and Hadrian. A long sceptre is in the background between Antoninus and Hadrian. The whole import of the monument is the dynastic, rather than Jovian, legitimization of the imperial office.

[530] G. ALFÖLDY, Der Friedensschluß des Kaisers Commodus mit den Germanen, Historia 20 (1971) 84—109, examines Commodus' peace with the Germans.

Commodus appealed to a higher authority.[531] The type represents Jupiter seated
and holding a thunderbolt in his left hand. With his right hand he presents a
globe to the togate Commodus standing before him. Earlier, while Caesar,
Commodus had issued coins which portrayed him standing under the protective
thunderbolt of Jupiter Conservator, a type avoided by his father and grandfather (Pl. VII, 43).[532] The medallions, which portrayed Jupiter's bestowal of
the globe upon Commodus, were thus a second step in a propaganda campaign
aimed at a dramatic transformation and elevation of the imperial office and its
association with Jupiter. Issued for small, select audiences, these medallions are
to be differentiated in significance from coin types.[533] As a propaganda media,
they are comparable to Pliny's 'Panegyric,' advancing a new motif in imperial
ideology, first before a select audience and only later introducing it into the
general stream of official propaganda.[534]

The coinage of the period 180—85 was replete with references to Jupiter,
portrayed seated with thunderbolt and sceptre or thunderbolt and Victory.[535]
An issue of 181 repeated the Jupiter Conservator type of Commodus under the
protective thunderbolt of Jupiter.[536] The issues of 185—86 began a series of new
types and legends in honor of Jupiter, which parallels a new insistence on the
theme of the inauguration of a golden age.[537] Jupiter is portrayed standing with
thunderbolt and sceptre; the legend reads IOVI IVVENI (Pl. VII, 44).[538] A
medallion of 189 portrays Iuppiter Iuvenis standing beside an altar on which the

---

[531] GNECCHI, II, nos. 64, 66, 143, 146, 156.

[532] BMC IV p. 643 no. 1524, p. 644 no. 1525. The legend reads IOVI CONSERVATORI.

[533] In treating the numismatic evidence for imperial ideology, it is essential to realize that
medallion types were issued for a different audience and thus had a quite different
significance from the regular currency. Cf. J. M. C. TOYNBEE, Roman Medallions, The
American Numismatic Society, Numismatic Studies 5 (New York 1944) 119—20: "The
content of the large bronze medallions proper reveals no less strikingly than do their
structure and style a genuine independence of the regular currencies . . . In their wealth
and variety of interest the types unmistakably affirm the primary role of medallions as gift
pieces presented to special persons on special occasions."

[534] BEAUJEU, Rel. rom. 371—2, rightly emphasizes 185—6 and 190—1 A.D. as marking
significant stages in the evolution of imperial ideology under Commodus. The dates, of
course, coincide, with changes in the government, the replacement of Perennis by
Cleander, and subsequently the replacement of Cleander by Eclectus, Q. Aemilius Laetus,
and Marcia. However, this scheme should not be pushed too far. MATTINGLY, BMC IV
clxiv, rightly points to the new impulses on the coinage of 188—9, when Cleander was still
in power. Cf. R. STORCH, Cléandre: une autre vue, AC 47 (1978) 501—15; M. RAISS, Die
stadtrömische Münzprägung des Commodus (Diss. Frankfurt 1976); H. CHANTRAINE, Zur
Religionspolitik des Commodus im Spiegel seiner Münzen, Römische Quartalschrift für
christliche Altertumskunde und für Kirchengeschichte 70 (1975) 1—31.

[535] BMC IV pp. 785, 787, 781, 782, 712, 716, 705, 709, 778, 704, 780, 781.

[536] BMC IV pp. 771, 775.

[537] Cf. BEAUJEU, Rel. rom. 369—70; MATTINGLY, BMC IV clxiv. Perhaps it might best be
suggested that the theme appears already in 186 but it only became a dominant motif in
188—9.

[538] BMC IV pp. 736, 738, 810, 819, 821, 823.

god is represented hurling his thunderbolt at a Giant.[539] The type celebrates
RENOVATIO TEMPORVM, a new age for the world under its youthful Jovian emperor.[539a] Another new type of the period portrays Jupiter seated holding
branch and sceptre; the legend reads IOVI EXSVPER (Pl. VII, 45).[540] Jupiter
Exsuperatorius or Zeus Hypsistos was one name by which the supreme god, of
which all other gods were mere emanations, was known in monotheistic
thought.[541] As Apuleius described him, he resides in the highest heights and
by his power he makes to move the sun and moon and turns the entire sphere
of the sky, assuring, through his intermediaries, the well-being of the human
race.[542] Although lacking the epithet *Exsuperatorius*, an identical image of Jupiter
appears on the arch of Dativius Victor in Mainz. A figure of Jupiter as *cosmocrator*, his foot resting upon a globe, is portrayed as the apex of a series of representations of the signs of the zodiac. Jupiter decorates the keystone, while
signs of the zodiac are arranged along the extrados. Zeus is also portrayed admidst
the signs of the zodiac on Antonine and Severan Greek imperial issues from
Perinthus, Tium, Nikaia, and Amastris.[542a] On the arch of Dativius Victor, the
theme of Jupiter as *arbiter fatorum* is directly associated with his role as guardian
of the imperial order. The arch is dedicated to *IOM Conservatori in honorem
Domus Divinae*. Whether late Antonine or Severan in date, its imagery offers
an important clue to the significance of Jupiter Exsuperatorius in the imperial
imagery of Commodus. Jupiter Exsuperatoruis (or Exsuperantissimus) is also
known from inscriptions;[543] and one dedication from Dacia gives a clear idea of

[539] GNECCHI, II, pl. 81 no. 3.

[539a] BMC Mysia p. 151 shows a bronze issue of Pergamum under Commodus on which a
youthful Jupiter is associated with astral symbolism. COOK, Zeus II, 1185—6; and
BEAUJEU, Rel. rom. 390—1, argue for the assimilation of Commodus to Jupiter on this coin.

[540] BMC IV pp. 728, 808, 812, 821. Like the theme of *Jupiter Juvenis* (BMC IV p. 810),
IVPITER EXSVPERATORIVS first appears in 186/87 and then is absent on the coinage
of 187/88 only to reappear with the new emphasis on RENOVATIO TEMPORVM on
the coinage of 188/9.

[541] See esp. F. CUMONT, Jupiter Summus Exsuperantissimus, ARW 9 (1906) 323 ff., who
argues that Jupiter Exsuperatorius represents the Semitic Ba'al šamin, adapted to certain
Hellenic, especially Platonic, concepts. See further BEAUJEU, Rel. rom. 388—91.

[542] Apul. De mundo 27.

[542a] The most detailed publication and discussion of the arch of Dativius Victor is H. VON
GALL, Bemerkungen zum Bogen des Dativius Victor in Mainz, JRGZ 15 (1968) 98—119.
However, reservations are possible concerning various points in his analysis. There is no
strong evidence to support his dating of the arch to the first half of the third century. The
letter forms are inconclusive; and the form *In h(onorem) d(omus) d(ivinae)* already appears
in the mid-second century (cf. M.-TH. RAEPSAET-CHARLIER, La datation des inscriptions
latines dans les provinces occidentales de l'Empire Romain d'après les formules «IN
H(ONOREM) D(OMUS) D(IVINAE)» et «DEO, DEAE», ANRW II,3 [1975] 232—82).
The inscription, the iconography, and the provincial style of the reliefs are all consistent
with a date any time in the period from Antoninus Pius until the fourth century. More
importantly, his interpretation of the iconography overemphasizes alleged Mithraic and
'oriental' influence.

[543] CIL VI 416; IX 784, 948; XI 2600; XIII 8812.

his popular image: *Iovi Summo Exsuperantissimo divinarum humanarumque rerum rectori fatorumque arbitro.*[544] As Apuleius notes, he worked his will on earth through intermediaries. Commodus, the coinage would proclaim, serves as such an intercessor. His will was the well-being of the human race; and on an issue of 191 Commodus dramatically portrayed Jupiter's role in the new Commodian golden age. Jupiter is portrayed standing, brandishing a thunderbolt and holding a sceptre. The seven stars in the field proclaim the astral associations of Jupiter, hailed on the coin as DEFENSOR SALVTIS AVGVSTI (Pl. VII, 46).[545] In 192 Commodus associated himself even more closely with the supreme god by taking the epithet *Exsuperatorius.*[546] Another type, struck in 191, portrays Jupiter holding a thunderbolt and standing with his hand on the shoulder of Commodus, who is togate and holding a sceptre. The legend reads IOM SPONSOR SECVRITATIS AVGVSTI (Pl. VII, 48).[547]

Coins of the same year portray Hercules with his hand on the shoulder of Commodus (Pl. VII, 47).[548] A Hercules type of 189 A.D. has the legend HERCVLI COMITI.[549] Jupiter is the guardian of the young prince and his new order; Hercules is his more immediate companion, who shares with him the great work of bringing a new golden age into existence.[550] The image of Hercules was a natural model for the emperor, who like the hero would win deification for his great labors on behalf of mankind. The association of Hercules with the emperor is the central theme of the frescoes in the Collegiate House of the *Augustales* at Herculaneum; and it played a rather significant role in the imperial ideology of Domitian and more particularly Trajan and the later Antonines.[551] With Commodus new heights were reached culminating in issues of 192, on which appear the attributes of Hercules or the god himself with the features of Commodus, elucidated by the legend HERCVLES ROMANVS AUG (Pl. VII, 49–50).[552] The transition from association to identification is complete, as it

---

[544] CIL III 1090.
[545] BMC III p. 754 no. 349; p. 833 no. 679.
[546] Cassius Dio 73.15; Herodian 1.14.8.
[547] BMC III p. 754 nos. 347–8; p. 833 no. 678.
[548] BMC III p. 746 no. 306.
[549] BMC IV p. 816.
[550] For the significance of *Comes* as a divine title, see A. D. NOCK, The Emperor's Divine Comes, JRS 37 (1947) 102–16 (rep. in: NOCK, Essays II, 653–75).
[551] In general, see STRACK, II, 94–104, 133–6, 217–8; W. DERICHS, Herakles, Vorbild des Herrschers in der Antike (Diss. Cologne 1951); BEAUJEU, Rel. rom. 80–7, 398–410; W. H. GROSS, Herakliskos Commodus, Nachrichten der Akademie der Wissenschaften in Göttingen 1973, 4 (Göttingen 1973). For the frescoes at Herculaneum, Neronian in date, see FEARS, Theology of Victory, below in this same volume (ANRW II, 17, 2) ch. IV. 2 with n. 427. Cf. also M. JACZYNOWSKA, Le culte de l'Hercule romain au temps du Haut-Empire, ibid., and esp. J. GAGÉ, La mystique impériale et l'épreuve des 'jeux'. Commode–Hercule et l'anthropologie héracléenne, ibid.
[552] BMC IV pp. 752–3 no. 339–42, p. 842 no. 711: rev: club with legend HERCVLI ROMANO AVGVSTO; p. 842 no. 714–6: rev: Hercules with the features of Commodus, placing right hand on trophy with legend HERCVLI ROMANO AVGVSTO. (For this as the correct full form of the legend see p. 842 no. 713).

appears on the richly symbolic bust of Commodus as Hercules in the Museo dei Conservatori.[553] The identification of the emperor with Hercules only added a new emphasis to the Jovian associations of the imperial order. Hercules was Jupiter's own son, and it was Jupiter who bestowed immortality upon him when his deeds on earth were done.

Whatever excesses marked other aspects of Commondus' imperal ideology, there was little in his association with Jupiter which did not have ample precedents under Trajan and Hadrian. His adoption of the Jovian title *Exsuperatorius* corresponds to Trajan's use of *Optimus* and Hadrian's title *Olympios* in the East. His coins represent him in the same scene with the god, but Trajan and Hadrian also appear in the same fashion. He is portrayed roughly equal in size to the god on certain types, but then so is Hadrian on the coinage and Trajan on the arch at Beneventum. In terms of the history of the Jovian theology of imperial power at Rome, Commodus' reign merely represents a renewal of its central importance established under Trajan and Hadrian and permitted to slide into a certain abeyance by Antoninus and Marcus Aurelius. Indeed, it is questionable to what extent terms like orientalism should be used to describe the imperial imagery of Commodus' reign. Particularly relevant is the degree to which this term is applicable to the new elements which marked Commodus' Jovian theology of imperial power. Granted an eastern source may be suggested for the original impetus behind astral associations for Zeus-Jupiter and his image as *arbiter fatorum*. However, this last was not alien to Greco-Roman tradition; and indeed already in the 'Iliad' the question of Zeus' relation to *moira* is raised.[554] Similarly republican Rome was no stranger to astral associations for Jupiter. Cicero recorded that Jupiter's star brings fortune and health to mankind;[555] and on a republican coin of the late second century B.C., Jupiter hurls his thunderbolt against a Giant, while Sol and a crescent are portrayed above his chariot with a star on either side.[556] Similarly on another republican issue of the late second century, the thunderbolt is associated with the *cornucopiae*;[557] and Ennius joined Jupiter's name with renewal and youth.[558] The title *Exsuperatorius* merely reflects that concept of Zeus-Jupiter as the supreme god, creator of all, which Aelius Aristides hymned and which belonged among the commonplace ideas of the second century A.D. By celebrating Jupiter as *Exsuperatorius* and by taking the title himself, Commodus directly associated imperial ideology with

---

[553] For a description, see H. STUART JONES, A Catalogue of the Ancient Sculptures Preserved in the Municipal Collections of Rome, The Sculptures of the Palazzo dei Conservatori (Oxford 1926) 139—42. Its symbolism is treated by J. AYMARD, Commode-Hercule fondateur de Rome, REL 14 (1926) 361—4; BEAUJEU, Rel. rom. 406—08. Further bibliography in: HELBIG, Führer⁴ II, no. 1486. See also FEARS, Theology of Victory, below in this same volume (ANRW II, 17, 2) ch. IV. 2, for a general discussion of the implications of Hercules as an imperial exemplum under Commodus and his predecessors. Pl. XII, 49 of that article illustrates the bust of Commodus—Hercules.

[554] NILSSON, GGR³ I, 361—8, summarizes the problem.

[555] Cic. Rep. 6.17. 17.

[556] CRAWFORD no. 310.

[557] CRAWFORD no. 265.

[558] Ennius Epicharmus 54—8 VAHL.

this, the most creative aspect of the popular philosophical and religious currents of his age. Astral imagery and the concept of youthful renewal were linked to Jupiter on the coinage of Pergamum as well as Rome under Commodus, suggesting a wider and more serious program for Commodus' imperial ideology than has sometimes been admitted. The imperial titles *Optimus, Olympios,* and *Exsuperatorius* represent three stages in the integration of the Jovian theology of imperial power into the political life of the empire. In a strictly Roman context, *Optimus* proclaimed Trajan's reconciliation of *principatus* and *libertas. Olympios* heralded that new role which the Greek speaking parts of the empire would play in the later Antonine age. *Exsuperatorius* proclaimed that association of emperor and supreme god which would receive its ultimate formulation in the Christian empire.

The full implications of Commodus' title *Exsuperatorius* only become clear in the light of Constantinian propaganda. Coins of Constantine portray the emperor seated, his right hand resting on the zodiac; Victory crowns him. The legend reads RECTOR TOTIVS ORBIS (RIC VII p. 368 no. 54). A passage in Firmicus Maternus (Math. 2.30) elucidates the typology of the coinage. No astrologer is able to learn anything true about the destiny of the emperor, for the emperor alone is not subject to the course of the stars, and in his fate alone the stars have no power to decree. Master of the world, the emperor is subject only to the decree of the supreme god, whose viceroy he is. The coins proclaim Constantine as *rector totius orbis,* recalling the designation of Jupiter Exsuperantissisimus as *divinarum humanarumque rerum rector.* Like Jupiter on the Arch of Dativius Victor, Constantine is *arbiter fatorum.* Like Jupiter on the Arch of Dativius Victor, he rules the zodiac; he is thus free from the shackles that bind mankind to the unalterable decrees of destiny. By taking the agnomen *Exsuperatorius,* Commodus proclaimed himself the viceroy of god and the possessor of god-given power over fate itself. He is the earthly image of Hercules, the son of god. The bust of Commodus-Hercules portrays him holding the golden apples of the Hesperides, symbols of immortality: like Hercules, he will conquer even death. As *arbiter fatorum* he will lead mankind into a new golden age. His official proclamation of a Commodan golden age (Cassius Dio 73.15) both looks back to the imagery of the Augustan principate with its celebration of the good tidings of a new era of peace (SEG IV 490) and forward to Constantine's declaration of himself as God's chosen instrument for the salvation of mankind (Eusebius Vita Const. 2.28–9). *Rector totius orbis,* Constantine would champion a faith that claimed the power to release man from the most terrifying of all the decrees of fate, death itself (Eusebius Laud. Const. 2).

b) The Third Century Crisis

After his death, Commodus was adopted and rehabilitated by Septimius Severus, who sought thereby to associate himself with the charisma of the *nomen Antoninorum.*[559] However, as the first emperor to come to the throne by

[559] Dio 76.7.4; 77.9.4. Cf. HAMMOND, Imperial Elements 98; A. McCANN, The Portraits of Septimius Severus, MAAR 30 (Rome 1968) 50–1.

force of arms since Vespasian, Septimius needed an even more forceful and less ambiguous ideological support. Like Commodus, he sought to establish his new order securely upon the premise of a Jovian origin of his imperial power. After his victory over Niger, Severus issued a type in honor of Jupiter Victor who had proclaimed Severus' election on the field of battle (Pl. VII, 51).[560] *Aurei* of the same year, 194 A.D., portray Jupiter clasping hands with Septimius, who wears military garb and holds a spear.[561] Another issue of *aurei* in the same year adds a significant detail to the *adventus* scene. A globe rests upon the clasped hands of emperor and god; Jupiter welcomes his warrior vicegerent to a partnership of rule (Pl. VII, 52).[562] The *aurei* of 194 had proclaimed Septimius as Jupiter's warrior vicegerent. On the arch at Leptis Magna, Septimius appears in a peaceful sacrificial scene, togate and holding a small thunderbolt in his right hand (Pl. XII, 71).[563] Septimius carefully used the coinage to emphasize his unique relationship with Jupiter. After 196 A.D., only Septimius issued Jupiter types; Geta and Caracalla were not permitted to do so. They were rather linked with Hercules and Bacchus-Liber, the gods of Septimius' home town of Leptis Magna. By connecting Jupiter with himself and associating Hercules and Bacchus with his designated successors, Septimius foreshadowed the Jovius-Herculius arrangement of Diocletian.[564]

The Jovian theology of power provided the basic ideological foundation for Diocletian's reorganization of the imperial structure. This did not represent a mere sop to traditionalism. It rather reflected the continued vitality of the cult of Jupiter as a religious force, so evident from the inscriptions. Equally importantly, it was the culmination of almost a generation of renewed insistence upon the emperor's election by Jupiter, a policy which arose in the wake of Valerian's capture by the Persians and which received explicit formulation by Aurelian.[565] A series of distinct but not mutually exclusive elements can be discerned within the Jovian theology of imperial power. The emperor, both personally and *ex officio* as chief magistrate of the Roman state, stands under the protection of Jupiter, a concept exemplified by coin types of Jupiter Custos and Jupiter Con-

[560] BMC V no. 68, 74.

[561] BMC V p. 31 no. 67.

[562] BMC V p. 31 no. 67 with note.

[563] On the Severan arch at Leptis Magna, see R. BARTOCCINI, L'arco quadrifronte dei Severi a Lepcis (Leptis Magna), Africa Italiana 4 (1931) 32—152; P. TOWNSEND, The Significance of the Arch of the Severi; at Lepcis, AJA 42 (1938) 512—24; J. WARD-PERKINS, Severan Art and Architecture at Lepcis Magna, JRS 38 (1948) 59—80; M. FLORIANI SQUARCIAPINO, Le sculture severiane di Leptis Magna, VIII Cong. Intern. di Arch. Class. I ‹Paris 1963› (Paris 1965) 229—33; R. BRILLIANT, The Arch of Septimius Severus, MAAR 29 (Rome 1967) 39, 84; McCANN, Portraits of Severus 73—8. Doubts about BARTOCCINI's identification of the object in Severus' right hand as a thunderbolt may be alleviated by familiarity with COOK's discussion of the variety of ways in which the thunderbolt can be represented, Zeus II, 722—85.

[564] I. MUNDLE, Untersuchungen zur Religionspolitik des Septimius Severus (Diss. Freiburg 1958) 48—9.

[565] This has been treated in detail by FEARS, Princeps. The following remarks offer a summary and citation will be limited to the ancient sources.

servator. The emperor conquers in the field with the aid of Jupiter, typified by coin types of Jupiter Victor. Neither of these concepts represents Jupiter as the bestower of imperial power. As under the republic, the god can aid and protect a magistrate chosen by human institutions like the Senate and the Roman People. Jupiter's election of the emperor was visualized by coin types of the emperor receiving *insignia* of power from the god. Although an important literary motif from the earliest period of the principate, its importance in official imperial ideology was quite spasmodic for the first three hundred years of imperial history. First under Domitian did it emerge as an important theme in official imperial ideology, and under Trajan and Hadrian for the first time Jupiter's investiture of the emperor appeared on official monuments and the coinage. After Hadrian it sank again into relative unimportance, appearing as a numismatic theme again under Commodus and Septimius Severus. Septimius' type portraying his actual investiture by Jupiter ceased after 194 A.D., and the type does not appear again on the imperial coinage until the sole reign of Gallienus.

In the intervening years Jupiter's protective concern for the emperor was a fairly constant numismatic theme. The Jupiter Conservator type was issued by Septimius Severus, Macrinus, Elagabalus, Severus Alexander, Severus Alexander and Mamaea, Balbinus, Pupienus, Gordian III, Aemilianus, Philip, Valerian, and Gallienus. At times the reverse is a simple image of the god, but frequently the type is the more dramatic scene of Jupiter holding his thunderbolt or cloak over the diminutive emperor.[566] Types of the period also celebrate Jupiter as *Victor, Ultor, Propugnator,* and *Stator.*[567] The avoidance of types portraying Jupiter's investiture was conscious. Macrinus, party to the death of the popular Caracalla and the first emperor who was not a member of the senatorial order, might well have represented his election by higher authority. Instead his first coin issue was marked by a pious modesty. A gigantic figure of Jupiter dwarfs the tiny figure of Macrinus, over whom he holds a thunderbolt; the legend reads VOTA PVBLICA (Pl. VII, 53).[568]

---

[566] BMC V p. 356 no. 1: Jupiter stands above Caracalla and Geta, issued under Septimius Severus. Other issues of the Jupiter Conservator type portraying Jupiter standing above the emperor are Macrinus BMC V no. 1; Severus Alexander BMC VI no. 688; Gordian III RIC IV,3 no. 255; Aemilianus RIC IV,3 nos. 4, 14, 45—6.
Other issues which commemorate Jupiter Conservator by a simple type representing an image of the god include: Septimius Severus BMC V pp. 60, 77, 176, 286; Macrinus BMC V pp. 497—8, 506, 524—6; Elagabalus BMC V p. 550; Severus Alexander BMC VI nos. 55—61; Balbinus no. 22—4; Pupienus no. 44—5; Gordian III RIC IV, 3, nos. 2, 50, 136, 211, 255; Philip II RIC IV,3 no. 213; Aemilian no. 57; Valerian RIC V,1 no. 92; Gallienus p. 149.

[567] IOVI VLTORI: Severus Alexander BMC VI nos. 231—42, 974. Gallienvs RIC V,1 pp. 85, 135, 150, 164, 167. IOVI VICTORI: Valerian RIC V,1 p. 39. IOVIS PRO-PVGNATOR: Severus Alexander BMC VI nos. 799—801. Gallienus RIC V,1 pp. 134, 139, 149. IOVI STATORI: Severus Alexander BMC VI nos. 697—8. Gordian III RIC IV,3 pp. 25, 26, 48. Philip RIC IV,3 p. 80. Valerian RIC V,1 p. 46. Gallienus RIC V,1 pp. 134, 139, 150, 173, 188.

[568] BMC V no. 1.

Jupiter's election of the emperor appears only on medallions in this period and indeed only under Severus Alexander. On one medallion type, with the legend FELICITATI POPVLI ROMANI, Alexander in military dress receives a globe from Jupiter. Behind Jupiter is a soldier; behind Alexander is Mars leaning on a shield.[569] On another medallion, with the same legend, Jupiter gives the globe to Alexander, who is wearing military garb and standing in front of a soldier bearing a standard.[570] On these medallions, for the first time, Jupiter's election of the emperor is explicitly connected with the *felicitas* of the commonwealth, a concept closely linked to the themes of renewal and eternity.[571] Another medallion has the legend PERPETVITAS IMP. AVG. and portrays Jupiter bestowing the globe upon Alexander, standing in front of two soldiers with spears.[572] The military emphasis on these themes contrasts with the pacific character of those types of Hadrian and Commodus portraying Jupiter's investiture of the togate emperor.[573] Their model is rather the issues of Severus in which, clad as a warrior, he shares the globe with Jupiter.

In their militaristic imagery and in their association of the themes of *Renovatio Temporum* and *Aeternitas* with Jupiter's investiture of the emperor, these medallions were the harbinger of a vigorous numismatic propaganda campaign instituted by Aurelian and aimed at establishing the revitalized imperial structure firmly upon a vision of the emperor as the elect of Jupiter. The immediate prototypes were two issues of Gallienus struck in the East by unknown officials immediately in the wake of Valerian's capture. The types portray Jupiter bestowing the globe upon Gallienus, with the legend IOVI CONSERVATORI, and upon Saloninus, with the legend DII NVTRITO-RES (Pl. VII, 54; VIII, 55).[574] The theme does not reappear on the coinage of Gallienus or of Claudius. It remained for Aurelian to seize upon the type; and in conjunction with the first stage in his monetary reform, mints throughout the empire celebrated the emperor's investiture by Jupiter with legends such as IOVI

[569] GNECCHI, II, no. 4.

[570] GNECCHI, II, no. 5.

[571] Cf. H. U. INSTINSKY, Studien zur Geschichte des Septimius Severus, Klio 35 (1942) 218; J. GAGÉ, Recherches sur les jeux séculaires 107—11; IDEM, Elagabal et les pêcheurs du Tibre, in: Mél. d'Archéologie, d'Épigraphie et d'Histoire offerts à J. Carcopino (Paris 1966) 403—18; IDEM, Felicitas, RLAC VII (1969) 711—23.

[572] GNECCHI no. 10.

[573] Severus Alexander's concern over the loyalty of his soldiers is treated by H. THIERFELDER, Die römische Reichspolitik von Septimius Severus bis zum Senatskaisertum (193—238 n. Chr.) im Spiegel der Münzen, Wissenschaftliche Zeitschrift der Universität Leipzig 6 (1956—7) 280, while R. STORCH, The "Absolutist" Theology of Victory: Its Place in the Late Empire, C & M 29 (1968) 197—206, examines the increasing militarism of the third century coin types.

[574] RIC V,1 no. 440 (Gallienus); RIC V,1 no. 35 (Saloninus). The legend DII NVTRITORES should be compared with the types of Gallienus as Caesar linking Jupiter to renewal; RIC V,1 p. 70 no. 20 portraying a child Jupiter on a goat. The legend reads IOVI CRESCENTI. The same type was issued by Valerian II, RIC V,1 p. 116 no. 1. An identical type issued by Valerian II (RIC V,1 p. 119 no. 32) has the legend IOVI EXORIENTI.

CONSERVATORI, FIDES MILITVM, and CONCORDIA MILITVM (Pl. VIII, 56—60). Sol dominates the coinage of the last years of Aurelian's reign; but this should not be seen as an attempt to displace the Jovian theology of imperial power. Jupiter, the supreme god, Exsuperatorius, makes all things come into being by his power and rules the universe through his intermediaries. Having elected Aurelian his vicegerent, Jupiter recedes into the heights; and imperial ideology can focus upon the new era which has dawned under the direct guidance of Sol and Aurelian, *Oriens Augusti*, rising eternally to dispel the darkness and ensure peace and prosperity.

Under Aurelian's Illyrian compatriots and imperial successors, Tacitus and Probus, Jupiter's election of the emperor dominated the coinage of the eastern mints of the empire linking the divine bestowal of the globe with the themes of *Clementia Temporum* and *Providentia Deorum* (Pl. IX, 61—62). Under Carus, who was not an Illyrian and had two sons to associate in the imperial power, a dynastic motif reappears in the form of Carus sharing the globe with his sons (Pl. IX, 63). The failure of the dynasty was vividly portrayed on the last issue of Carinus, on which Jupiter reappears as the imperial elector (Pl. IX, 64). Diocletian had already laid claim to the purple by appealing to his election by Jupiter; his first issues from Antioch and Tripolis show him receiving the globe from the god (Pl. IX, 65—66).[575]

The victory of Diocletian assured the continued importance of a Jovian theology of imperial power in official imperial ideology. Critical moments in the evolution of the new state structure, such as the elevation of Maximian and the creation of the Tetrarchy, saw the emission of types proclaiming Jupiter's election of the emperors (Pl. X, 67—68).[576] Diocletian's choice of the titles *Jovius* for himself and *Herculius* for his colleagues implied their divine election and status as the vicegerents of Jupiter and his deified son and helper Hercules.[577] Jupiter was the author and preserver of the Diocletianic order.[578] His presence sanctioned the representation of the Tetrarchical system on the Arch of Galerius at Thessalonica and on the monument to the Tetrarchy in the Forum Romanum.[579] Dio-

---

[575] For a detailed discussion, with full treatment of the numismatic evidence, see FEARS, Princeps 279—310.

[576] RIC V,2 no. 324, 328 (mark the accession of Diocletian); no. 325, 329 (the elevation of Maximian); RIC VI pp. 283, 355, 358, 465, 531, 580, 621, 667 (the divine origin of the Tetrarchy).

[577] For the significance of the titles, see H. MATTINGLY, The Roman 'Virtues', HThR 30 (1937) 113; TAEGER, Charisma II, 460; W. SESTON, Diocletianus, RLAC III (1957) 1041—3.

[578] Cf. Pan. Lat. III. 3, VI. 12.

[579] For the arch of Galerius at Thessalonica, see K. KINCH, L'arc de triomphe de Salonique (Paris 1890); VERMEULE, Roman Imperial Art 336—52; M. POND, The Arch of Galerius (Diss. Michigan 1970). For the role of Jupiter on the arch (pl. VI in: KINCH) see W. SESTON, Dioclétien et la tétrarchie (Paris 1946) 252; and IDEM, Diocletianus, in: RLAC III (1957) 1038—45; and STRAUB, Herrscherideal 76—90. The role on Jupiter as the basis

cletian's speech of abdication and his investiture of Maximinus Daia with his own purple robe took place before a statue of Jupiter.[580] As the emperor represented by his image watched over all legal acts of his subordinates,[581] so Jupiter watched over the deeds of his earthly vicegerent.

The center of Roman imperial ideology in 306 A.D., within eighteen years Jupiter would disappear entirely from the imperial coinage and all official monuments. Ironically the immediate cause was his profound association with the Tetrarchical system. The rebels Maxentius and Constantine ostentatiously displaced Jupiter as the source of their imperial power.[582] Coins of Maxentius portray Mars, divine founder of his bastion Rome, bestowing the globe upon him (Pl. X, 69).[583] After his victory over Maxentius, Constantine permitted himself to appear on the coinage in the act of receiving the globe from Sol.[584] By contrast, Licinius emphasized his status as the protégé of Jupiter. The legend IOVI CONSERVATORI, with types representing Jupiter in a variety of poses dominates his coinage.[585] *Conservator* as an epithet for Jupiter contrasts with Constantine's celebration of Sol as *Comes*, a title suggesting a more immediately personal divine patron. Constantine commemorated his special relationship with Sol and that of his rival with Jupiter on gold medallions struck at Ticinum in 320—21. The medallion with an obverse of Licinius portrays on the reverse Jupiter in the act of crowning the emperor. On the reverse of the Constantinian medallion, Sol appears bestowing the imperial wreath.[586] According to Eusebius, the final campaign against Licinius took the form of a holy war, a struggle to the death between *Ecclesia* and *Capitolium*.[587] With Constantine's victory, Jupiter, shortly to be followed by Sol, disappears forever from the Roman coinage.[588]

of the tetrarchical system was also represented on the monument in the Forum Romanum, which is portrayed on the left side passage on the north side of the Arch of Constantine. Five columns are shown, four bearing statues of the emperors, and the one in the middle having a statue of Jupiter. See H. L'Orange, Tetrarchisches Ehrendenkmal auf dem Forum, MDAI(R) 53 (1938) 1—34; and H. Kähler, Das Fünftsäulendenkmal für die Tetrarchen auf dem Forum Romanum (Cologne 1964). L'Orange's essay is reprinted in: Idem, Likeness and Icon (Odense 1973) 131—57.

[580] Lact. De Mort. Pers. 19.

[581] Cf. H. Kruse, Studien zur offiziellen Geltung des Kaiserbildes im römischen Reiche (Paderborn 1934); H. Niemeyer, Studien zur statuarischen Darstellung der römischen Kaiser (Berlin 1968) 17—26.

[582] Cf. Sutherland, RIC VI pp. 110—1; and D. de Decker, La politique religieuse de Maxence, Byzantion 38 (1968) 550—2.

[583] RIC VI pp. 401—2. Cf. A. Alföldi, Numizmatikai Közlöny 44—45 (1945—6) 12—16.

[584] RIC VII pp. 375, 397, 468, 500.

[585] RIC VII 741—2.

[586] Cf. RIC VII p. 374.

[587] Euseb. Vita Cons. 2. 1—42.

[588] An issue of *solidi*, from the mint at Antioch, struck in late 324 or early 325, represents Sol handing the globe to Constantine (RIC VII p. 685); cf. P. Bruun, The Disappearance of Sol from the Coins of Constantine, Arctos n.s. 2 (1958) 15.

V. Epilogue

The disappearance of Jupiter from cult and imperial ideology is to be seen of course as only one aspect of the triumph of Christianity. In the Christian version of history, Licinius himself has given his blessing to the abandonment of the ancestral gods of Rome. According to Eusebius, before engaging Constantine in battle, Licinius told his soldiers that the battlefield would prove whether he or Constantine worshipped the true gods. If Constantine should triumph, then it would be manifest that the hoary gods of Rome were false and that the God of Constantine, having proved superior to the Roman deities, was the true Saviour and Helper of mankind.[589] The story is an edifying fabrication, but it accurately reflects the view of the event held by Christians, Constantine, and not a few pagans. For an age which worshipped *dynamis*,[590] no more dramatic testimony of true divinity could exist than triumph in such a trial by combat. Eusebius eulogized Constantine's victory as the gift of God;[591] and in his edict to the inhabitants of Palestine, Constantine presented himself as the chosen instrument of the sole true God, the possessor of almighty and eternal power, who had granted victory to Constantine.[592] From its earliest period, the cult of Roman Jupiter had been intimately linked to the prosperity of the Roman commonwealth. In the imperial age, Jupiter and the emperor were closely associated, in cult and in imperial imagery, as partners in the struggle against the forces of chaos and evil. Now, for Constantine, the worship of Jupiter itself is linked to these forces of evil. His earlier refusal to participate in the traditional sacrifices on the Capitoline had aroused the hatred of the Senate and the people at Rome, according to pagan sources.[593] Now after his victory over Licinius, he proclaimed that the true God

[589] Euseb. Vita Cons. 2.5.
[590] This is the subject of an admirable discussion by P. BROWN, The Rise and Function of the Holy Man in Late Antiquity, JRS 61 (1971) 80—101.
[591] Euseb. H.E. 10.9. See further, FEARS, Theology of Victory, in this same volume (ANRW II, 17, 2) ch. IV. 2.
[592] Euseb. Vita. Cons. 2. 28—9. I accept the documents cited by Eusebius as authentic proclamations of Constantine. The evidence of A. H. M. JONES, and T. C. SKEAT, Notes on the Genuineness of the Constantinian Documents in Eusebius' Life of Constantine, JEH 5 (1954) 196—200, seems decisive on this point. The problem of the authenticity of the documents and the 'Vita' as a whole is surveyed by J. QUASTEN, Patrology III (Westminster, Maryland—Utrecht—Antwerp 1960) 319—24. For further discussion of the authenticity of the documents, see N. BAYNES, Constantine The Great and The Christian Church, PBA 15 (1929) 378—87, still the clearest introduction to the problem; F. WINKELMANN, Zur Geschichte des Authentizitätsproblems der vita Constantini, Klio 40 (1962) 187—243; H. DRAKE, In Praise of Constantine, University of California Publications, Classical Studies 15 (Berkeley—Los Angeles 1976) 8—10.
[593] Zosimus 2.29. For the problems surrounding this passage and the question of the date of Constantine's refusal to carry out the sacrifices on the Capitoline, see J. STRAUB, Konstantins Verzicht auf den Gang zum Kapitol, Historia 4 (1955) 297—313 (rep. in: IDEM, Regeneratio imperii. Aufsätze über Roms Kaisertum und Reich im Spiegel der heidnischen

had chosen him and given him the power utterly to remove every form of evil in the hope that mankind might be recalled to the due observance of the holy laws of God and that the most blessed faith might prosper.[594]

Certainly in terms of imperial ideology, epoch-making was the Christian God's revealed ability to wrench away from Jupiter the guarantee of victory and prosperity for the Roman commonwealth. Augustine grasped the critical importance of this fact. Christians might inveigh against the scandalous deeds attributed to Jupiter in mythology;[595] but as Augustine was aware, the pagans themselves had outgrown these crude stories.[596] Far more telling against their beliefs, argues Augustine, is their need to call upon a vast number of supplementary deities to aid the so-called king of the gods. Why, if he is truly king, do the pagans not address all their supplications to him alone? Most decisive of all is their patently false conception of Victory and Jupiter.[597] If, as the pagans believe, Jupiter were responsible for the establishment and growth of the Roman Empire, why need they also worship Victory? If they contend that Jupiter sends Victory on her missions, then they speak falsely. It is the true God, king of the ages, who dispatches his angel to grant victory to the just:

> *An forte dicunt, quod deam Victoriam Iuppiter mittat atque illa tamquam regi deorum obtemperans ad quos iusserit veniat et in eorum parte considat? Hoc vere dicitur non de illo Iove quem deorum regem pro sua opinione confingunt, sed de illo vero rege saeculorum, quod mittat non Victoriam, quae nulla substantia est, sed angelum suum et faciat vincere quem voluerit; cuius consilium occultum esse potest, iniquum non potest.*[598]

Appropriating the central role of Jupiter Optimus Maximus in the theology of victory, the Christian god passed easily into his pre-eminent position in the imperial ideology of the Christian Empire. By the second century A.D., a philosophical image of Zeus-Jupiter was well established at the popular level, conceiving of him as the creator of the universe, who was in the beginning and will be for evermore. Able to control all things by a simple nod, he works his will on earth by a series of intermediaries. Pliny's 'Panegyric' and the imperial coinage had portrayed Trajan as such an intermediary and as the veritable image

---

und christlichen Publizistik [Darmstadt 1972] 100–118). F. PASCHOUD, Zosime 2.29 et la version païenne de la conversion de Constantin, Historia 20 (1971) 334–53.

[594] Euseb. Vita Cons. 2.28.

[595] Attacks on Jupiter's immorality or on the absurd stories of his birth, as evidenced by pagan mythology, were a standard element in Christian polemic. Cf., e.g., Arnobius Adv.Nat. 1.34; Athenagoras Leg. pro Christ. 20; Tatian Ad Graecos 8; Commodian Inst. 1.4.7–1.6.26. For Commodian, see E. HECK, Iuppiter-Iovis bei Commodian, Vigiliae Christianae 30 (1976) 72–7. On Christian criticism of pagan myth in general cf. R. P. C. HANSON, The Christian Attitude to Pagan Religions up to the Time of Constantine the Great, ANRW II, 23, 2 (1980) 910–973, esp. 290ff.; C. A. CONTRERAS, Christian Views of Paganism, ibid. 974–1022, esp. 974ff., 988ff.

[596] Aug. Civ. Dei 4.26.

[597] Aug. Civ. Dei 4.9–34.

[598] Aug. Civ. Dei 4.17.

of Jupiter on earth. Like the theology of victory, the theme of the royal office as an *imitatio Dei* was easily Christianized. Eusebius lauded Constantine and Crispus, in the final struggle with Licinius, as worthy earthly images of God the Father and Christ the Son.[599] It is precisely in this association of emperor with the high god that we observe most clearly that continuity between pagan and Christian imperial ideology which was such a crucial element in securing the continuity of the imperial structure and with it of classical culture. In a real sense it represents the culmination of the evolving portrait of the Roman Jupiter as an image of the Roman state.

Appendix:

The Cult of Jupiter and Roman Imperial Ideology:
A Bibliographical Survey, 1918–1978[*]

Apart from mention within general surveys of scholarly work on Roman religion,[1] no bibliographical treatment of scholarship on the cult of Jupiter has appeared; and thus such an essay might appropriately begin with the fundamental encyclopaedia articles of AUST and THULIN, which, along with WISSOWA's discussion in: 'Religion und Kultus der Römer,' summarized the approach and scholarship of the nineteenth and early twentieth centuries and

---

[599] Euseb. H.E. 10.9.

[*] This bibliographical survey is limited to studies dealing with the Roman cult of Jupiter and its role in imperial ideology. Hence I have systematically excluded discussion of works treating Jupiter Dolichenus, Jupiter Poeninus, and other oriental and indigenous culture figures assimilated to Jupiter.

[1] Surveys of scholarship on Roman religion include L. DEUBNER, ARW 23 (1925) 298–317, and IDEM, ARW 33 (1936) 100–36 (for the period 1915–33); F. PFISTER, JAW 129 (1930) 373–86 (1918–30); N. TURCHI, BCAR 68 (1940) 203–09 (1936–40); IDEM, Stud Rom 2 (1954) 570–77 (1940–50); A. BRELICH, Doxa 2 (1949) 136–66 (1939–48); H. ROSE, JRS 50 (1960) 161–72 (1910–60). More recent surveys include N. TURCHI, Stud Rom 6 (1958) 591–4; U. BIANCHI, Stud Rom 9 (1961) 301–07; 11 (1963) 581–9; 15 (1967) 70–8; 19 (1971) 315–22; 23 (1975) 195–205. Mention might also be made of the surveys which ROSE did for 'The Year's Work in Classical Studies' (1920) 47–60; (1921–22) 47–58; (1922–23) 45–54; (1923–24) 47–56; (1924–25) 45–54; (1925–26) 53–62; (1926–27) 49–58; (1927–28) 55–64; (1928–29) 51–62; (1930) 53–64; (1931) 67–78; (1932) 65–76; (1933) 53–60; (1934) 53–60; (1935) 63–70; (1936) 63–72; (1937) 73–82; (1939–45) 113–34; (1945–7) 85–94. The earlier surveys in 'The Year's Work in Classical Studies' were by W. W. FOWLER (1906) 53–55; (1907) 64–9; (1908) 77–80; (1909) 65–70; (1910) 59–64; (1912) 71–6; (1913) 139–46; (1915) 81–90; (1917) 103–10; and by C. BAILEY (1911) 73–8; (1914) 117–24. Surveys of limited periods include, for the early Republic, A. MICHELS, CW 48 (1955) 25–35, 41–5; and for the entire republican period, R. SCHILLING, ANRW I, 2 (1972) 319–47 (cf. below n. 8), for the time of the principate, J. BEAUJEU, Le paganisme romain sous le Haut Empire, ANRW II, 16, 1 (1978) 3–26.

which remain the only comprehensive surveys of Jupiter.[2] AUST's treatment was far more extensive, a monograph in its own right; but the two articles, published almost a generation apart, were extremely similar in outlook and in arrangement. Like WISSOWA, and indeed like MOMMSEN in his 'Staatsrecht,' AUST and THULIN collected a variety of evidence from all periods and systematized it into a comprehensive delineation of Jupiter as a party in Roman cult action, aiming, like a legal code, not at a historical analysis tracing the process of the development but rather at a description of status at an ideal moment in time. Their concern throughout was with the position of Jupiter in cult. By an analysis of the epithets of Jupiter and Roman cult practice they sought to describe the god's functions in the religion of the Roman state. Within these limits, both articles were masterly presentations. The wider implications of the comparative methods were eschewed, but both treated in detail the various Italic cults of Jupiter. Properly considering such evidence as irrelevant to cult aspects, neither AUST nor THULIN was concerned with theological and literary speculations about Jupiter in ancient authors or specifically with the political or philosophical image of Jupiter apart from its role in cult. However neither was unaware of the importance of the cult of Jupiter in the political ideology of the Roman commonwealth; and both touched upon the political significance of the Capitoline cult and, for the early empire down to Trajan, the importance of the worship of Jupiter in the religious policies of the emperor. However the basic approach of AUST and THULIN excluded an analytical approach to these problems or an attempt to present a more organic picture of the evolution of the cult of Jupiter; and in both the worship of the Roman Jupiter in the provinces of the imperial age received almost no attention.

Together with THULIN's briefer discussion, AUST's extensive study will long remain of fundamental importance, particularly for its collection and critical evaluation of the literary evidence. Both articles are less out-of-date than many companion pieces in ROSCHER's 'Lexikon' and in the earlier volumes of the 'Pauly-Wissowa,' because in the intervening years since 1917 the cult of Jupiter has received less attention than a good many areas of Roman religion. The early history of the Roman Jupiter continues to serve as the focus of scholarly interest; and it bulks largest in the treatment given to Jupiter in general histories of Roman religion. Of these, perhaps the most significant, in terms of a discussion of Jupiter, are ALTHEIM's 'Römische Religionsgeschichte,'[3] which seeks to place the cult of Jupiter within its Italic context, and LATTE's 'Römische Religionsgeschichte,' which argues that at Rome the Indo-European god of the

---

[2] E. AUST, Iuppiter, in: W. ROSCHER, ed., Ausführliches Lexikon der griechischen und römischen Mythologie II,1 (Leipzig 1890–94, rep. Hildesheim 1966) 618–762; C. THULIN, Iuppiter, RE X,1 (1918) 1126–44.

[3] F. ALTHEIM, Römische Religionsgeschichte, originally published at Berlin–Leipzig, 1931– 33, in 'Sammlung Göschen' (no. 1035, 1052, 1072); English translation by H. MATTINGLY (London 1938); rev. German edition (Baden-Baden 1951); 2. rev. ed. (Berlin 1956); French translation of 1. rev. ed. (Paris 1955).

bright sky was transformed entirely into a weather god.[4] In his dictionary-like survey of 'Die Götter Altitaliens,' RADKE returns to the earlier view of WISSOWA and others which seeks to distinguish, on the basis of epithets, Jupiter's functions as god of the bright sky, weather god, war god, god of certain agricultural phenomena, and guardian of such political concepts as *libertas*.[5] COOK's exhaustive series of volumes devoted to Zeus as god of the bright and dark sky contains much of interest to students of the Roman cult and mythology of Jupiter, treating such diverse aspects as the *Aquaelicium*, Jupiter Terminus, Jupiter's relation to Dius Fidius, and the assimilation of emperors to Zeus and to Jupiter.[6]

Apart from inclusion in such general studies, the image of Jupiter in early cult has been the subject of two extended discussions, both controversial. KOCH's 'Der römische Juppiter' is a notable attempt to trace, in the period predating the establishment of the Capitoline cult, the evolution of a specifically Roman conception of Jupiter as an expression of peculiarly Roman political and social concepts.[7] The work is extraordinarily perceptive, only sparingly documented, and almost philosophical in tone, replete with references to such no longer fashionable concepts as '*die Seele des Volkes*.' For KOCH, the Roman Jupiter of the late republic was the last stage in a long process of creative development by which the divinity had been rigorously depersonalized, being deprived of such attributes as parenthood and chthonic associations which were characteristic of him elsewhere in Italy. So fashioned, the cult of Jupiter Optimus Maximus could stand at the very heart of Roman state life, inextricably bound to the concept of the commonwealth, *„die allen Parteiungen der Bürgerschaft übergeordnete Idee schicksalshafter Zusammengehörigkeit.“*

GEORGES DUMÉZIL is also intensely interested in the image of Jupiter in archaic Roman religion. The figure of Jupiter, of course, stands at the center of DUMÉZIL's structural interpretation of Indo-European religious institutions and mythologies, which he argues reflect a tripartite ideology and conception of society, divided into three superposed zones corresponding to three functions: sovereignty, warrior force, economic prosperity.[8] Each function corresponds to a socio-political group in human society, which assumes responsibility for its actualization (respectively kings or priests, warriors, and peasants) and to a specific type of godhead in the divine sphere (at Rome Jupiter, Mars, Quirinus).

---

[4] K. LATTE, Römische Religionsgeschichte, Handbuch der Altertumswissenschaft 5, 4 (Munich 1960).

[5] G. RADKE, Die Götter Altitaliens, Fontes et Commentationes 3 (Münster 1965).

[6] A. J. COOK, Zeus: A Study in Ancient Religion (Cambridge 1914—40).

[7] C. KOCH, Der römische Juppiter, Frankfurter Stud. zur Religion und Kultur der Antike 14 (Frankfurt am Main 1937).

[8] For an introduction and critical discussion of DUMÉZIL's theories, see C. SCOTT LITTLETON, The New Comparative Mythology: An Anthropological Assessment of the Theories of G. Dumézil (Berkeley—Los Angeles 1966). A sensitive appreciation of DUMÉZIL's work in Roman religion is offered by R. SCHILLING, La situation des études relatives à la religion romaine de la République (1950—1970), ANRW I,2 (1972) 328—32. DUMÉZIL's ideas continue to evolve, and a guide to his more recent work may be found in the introduction to IDEM, Les dieux souverains (below n. 9).

However, one need not accept DUMÉZIL's general thesis to profit from the insight and erudition which characterizes the treatment of Jupiter in his 'La religion romaine archaïque' and his 'Les dieux souverains des Indo-Européens'.[9] Throughout these stimulating volumes DUMÉZIL is concerned less with cult than with theology, that is the ideas and representations of divinity. In his view, in the earliest period at Rome Jupiter had emerged as the complex figure of a personal god, head of a divine triad, sky god and thunderer but also king, a god who manifests himself in the areas of power and law but not warfare and not agriculture. The establishment of the Capitoline cult represented a new and even grander stage in the figure of Jupiter at Rome. The new social classifications instituted by Servius Tullius had obscured the third element in the ancient Jupiter-Mars-Quirinus triad; and Jupiter now became "the great god" rather than merely first among the great gods of the state, his majesty augmented by the expulsion of the kings. Now the god became the only king Rome knew, the sole survivor of a vanished time and ideology. Associated with Rome's imperial mission, he served a dual role, Jupiter Rex as heavenly model of royal power, and Jupiter Liber as guardian of the free commonwealth.

The origins of the Capitoline cult have been the subject of several specialized studies. From the vantage point of 1931, RYBERG re-examined the question and concluded that, although the earlier association of Jupiter, Mars, and Quirinus may have afforded inspiration, the Capitoline Triad was in the strictest sense an Etruscan invention.[10] Within the context of an examination of the evidence for a cult of a triad of divinities at Veii, BANTI seeks to define rigorously the concept of a triad as a union of divinities associated in a permanent common cult located within the same sacred area.[11] Examining the evidence for divine triads at Rome, Iguvium, and Etruria, she argues that, while the architectural form of the tripartite temple arose in Etruria, the concept of a triad of divinities was Italic and borrowed by the Etruscans. At Rome, although earlier tendencies towards triadic arrangements existed, the true triad of Capitoline divinities was introduced by the Etruscans. By contrast, pointing to the fact that the Capitoline temple is the oldest known tripartite temple and to the absence of any clear evidence for a similar cult in pre-Roman Italy, BIANCHI rejected the view that the Capitoline cult and the grouping Jupiter-Juno-Minerva were imported to Rome from Etruria.[12] The Capitoline cult was rather a Roman invention, independent from outside influences. BIANCHI's conclusion remains the most generally accepted view, despite the recent attempt of GANTZ to find triads of deities represented on a newly discovered archaic Etruscan frieze

---

[9] La religion romaine archaïque (Paris 1966); new edition, revised and annotated by DUMÉZIL, translated into English by P. KRAPP (Archaic Roman Religion [Chicago 1970]); IDEM, Les dieux souverains des Indo-Européens (Paris 1977).

[10] I. RYBERG, Was the Capitoline Triad Etruscan or Italic?, AJPh 52 (1931) 145–56.

[11] L. BANTI, Il culto del cosidetto 'tempio dell'Apollo' a Veii e il problema delle triadi etrusco-italiche, Studi Etruschi 17 (1943) 187–224.

[12] U. BIANCHI, Questions sur les origines du culte capitolin, Latomus 10 (1951) 413–18.

plaque from Murlo.[13] GANTZ argues that two separate pairs of triads can be identified, one consisting of Zeus-Hera-Athena, and another related to the Roman triad of Ceres-Liber-Libera. Similarly, more recent archaeological work has not definitely controverted BIANCHI's assertion of the Capitoline temple as the earliest extant tripartite temple. The first clear example of an Etruscan temple with three *cellae* is temple A at Pyrgi, dated to the first quarter of the fifth century B.C.[14] For BRELICH, the Capitoline cult was a purely Roman creation and along with the calendar represents the most significant stages in the religious history of archaic Rome.[15] Following HANELL, BRELICH argues that the dedication of the Capitoline temple occurred within the monarchical period but that the image of the god carried in itself the seeds of revolution. The Capitoline god was divine king of the Roman commonwealth, and by establishing his cult the Romans transferred sovereignty to the god, theoretically for the moment, in fact after the expulsion of the kings. Under the influence of DUMÉZIL, BASANOFF also rejects the view of an Etruscan origin of the Capitoline Triad.[16] Rather he argues for the progressive substitution, under Greek, Etruscan, and Italic influences, of a triad of Jupiter-Juno-Minerva for the primitive Indo-European triad of Jupiter-Mars-Quirinus. He also finds evidence for an intermediary stage of a triad of Jupiter-Janus-Juno. TERNES considers the problem of triads of gods at Rome within the general context of ancient Mediterranean religions.[17]

Apart from the question of the origins of the Capitoline Triad, particular interest has centered upon the epithets chosen for the new cult figure: *Optimus Maximus*. MAROUZEAU points to the derivation of *optimus* from *ops* to stress the concept of 'bestower of abundance' as the original significance of Jupiter's new cult title. SCHILLING cautions that the ethical significance of *optimus* is older than MAROUZEAU admits.[18] However, PARIENTE would discard entirely the derivation of *Optumus*, as an epithet for Jupiter, from *ops*. Instead, he would derive it from *ob* in its original sense of 'before,' and, hence, 'first,' in the case of its significance as an epithet for Jupiter. Using the same methodology, PARIENTE has examined another epithet of Jupiter, that of *Stator*. The epithet is derived from *sto*, not from *sisto*; a *stator* was a magistrate's attendant or an

---

[13] T. GANTZ, Divine Triads on an Archaic Etruscan Frieze Plaque, Studi Etruschi 39 (1971) 3–24.

[14] Cf. G. COLONNA, Il santuario di Pyrgi alla luce delle recenti scoperte, Studi Etruschi 33 (1965) 191–219.

[15] A. BRELICH, Deux aspects religieux de la Rome archaïque, AC 20 (1951) 335–42.

[16] V. BASANOFF, La triade capitoline, in: Studi in Onore di V. Arangio-Ruiz II (Naples 1953) 323–32.

[17] C.-M. TERNES, L'apport romain aux traditions religieuses de l'Occident, Nouv. Rev. Luxembourgeoise Academia (1961) 45–55.

[18] J. MAROUZEAU, Iuppiter Optimus et Bona Dea, Eranos 54 (1956) 227–31; R. SCHILLING, À propos de l'expression Iuppiter Optimus Maximus, in: Acta philologica 3, piae memoriae N. I. Herescu (Rome 1964) 343–48.

orderly. Hence, PARIENTE argues, as a divine epithet it was invoked to indicate Jupiter's role as custodian of the city and its citizens.[19]

Among the other republican cults of Jupiter at Rome, Jupiter Feretrius, the history of the cult and its temples, is the subject of a brief survey by SPRINGER.[20] LAKE argues that the sacred stone in the *cella* of Jupiter in the Capitolium, thought by the ancients to represent the god Terminus, was in fact an aniconic representation of Jupiter worshipped on the Capitoline hill before the Etruscan introduction of images.[21] Jupiter Fulgur and the location of his temple is discussed by PALMER, who argues that in the mid-third century B.C. a roofless temple was built for Jupiter Fulgur at the junction of the Vicus Portae Collinae and the Vicus Montanus and thus disputes the generally accepted view that the temple lay in the Campus Martius.[22] In passing, PALMER considers the ceremony of *fulgur conditum*, which has been the topic of a special study by LEGLAY.[23] In separate and complementary studies, H. LE BOURDELLÈS and R. SCHILLING have examined the view which archaic Roman law took of a mortal struck by lightning.[24] Such an unfortunate was, to use LE BOURDELLÈS' term, '*interdit*;' as SCHILLING argues, he was regarded as having become the untouchable property of Jupiter, whose death-dealing action was conceived in quite concrete and personalized terms.

Of divine forms related to Jupiter, recent scholarship has done most to illuminate Terminus and Vediovis. In an extremely important monograph, G. PICCALUGA has investigated the conception and function of *termini* in Roman cult and religious thought. Combining a critical reassessment of the literary tradition with insights from comparative religion and anthropology, she offers a fundamental reevaluation of Terminus as a divine entity at Rome, his relation to Jupiter, and the connection which both deities bore to the sanctity of boundary marks.[25]

In his essays on 'Roman Religion and Roman Empire,' R. PALMER touches upon a number of aspects of Roman Jupiter, especially the Capitoline cults, including Feretrius and Summanus. More detailed is his treatment of Vediovis, in the god's aspect both as a young Jupiter and as an anti-Jupiter. As PALMER emphasizes, our sources indicate a real confusion in the beliefs and cults of Jupiter and Vediovis. Vediovis was, in PALMER's words, a hellish counterpart of

---

[19] A. PARIENTE, Optumus, Emerita 42 (1974) 111−20; IDEM, Stator, teóforo y nombre común, Duris 2 (1974) 57−66.

[20] L. SPRINGER, The Cult and the Temple of Jupiter Feretrius, CJ 50 (1954) 27−32.

[21] A. LAKE, Lapis Capitolinus, CPh 31 (1936) 72−3.

[22] R. PALMER, Jupiter Blaze, Gods of the Hills, and the Roman Topography of CIL VI 337, AJA 80 (1976) 43−56.

[23] M. LEGLAY, Fulgur conditu. Un lieu consacré par la foudre en Grande Kabylie, Libyca 7 (1957) 101−09.

[24] H. LE BOURDELLÈS, La loi du foudroyé (Festus, p. 295 Lindsay, G. L.), REL 51 (1973) 62−76; R. SCHILLING, Iuppiter Fulgur: À propos de deux lois archaïques, in: Mél. P. Boyancé, Collection de l'École Française de Rome 22 (Paris 1974) 681−9.

[25] G. PICCALUGA, Terminus: I segni di confine nella religione romana, Quaderni SMSR 9 (Rome 1974).

Jupiter, representing Jupiter's capacity to deny what he normally bestowed. He was a god of the netherworld, the very antithesis of the god of light, Jupiter.[26] A variety of studies have been devoted to Vediovis. SCHUSTER provides a reliable survey of the problems connected with this obscure figure in Roman cult;[27] WEINSTOCK examines his relation to the gens Iulia;[28] ALFÖLDI paints an evocative picture of the evolution which the figure of Vediovis underwent in the late republic and which permitted him to emerge as the symbolic 'Anführer' of a return to the golden age;[29] GJERSTAD argues that Vediovis was pre-Indo-European in his origins.[30]

Whatever his relation to Vediovis, Jupiter was indeed a god of heavenly light, and BRELICH has sought to explain when and how the idea became associated with him. Although his conclusions are admittedly tentative, BRELICH suggests that Jupiter's connections with the ides are more artificial than those of Juno with the calends. The association of Jupiter with the ides predates the creation of the Capitoline cult; but the politically sophisticated conception of the godhead, inherent in his association with the ides, suggests that the connection was not made earlier than the beginnings of the urban period at Rome. As BRELICH points out, various feriae Iovis occur on days other than the ides.[31] The feriae mentioned in the Roman calendar have each received a brief but excellent treatment by DEGRASSI in his admirable edition and commentary of the Roman Fasti.[32] Among the feriae Iovis and other ceremonies connected with Jupiter, the Vinalia is the subject of a re-examination by BÖMER, which seeks to place Jupiter's association with the wine festivals within the context of viniculture in early Italy and among the Indo-Europeans.[33] The most valuable part of his essay is his careful collection and discussion of the sources for the Vinalia rustica, Vinalia priora, and the *Meditrinalia. Much more valuable is SCHILLING's detailed discussion of the Vinalia, arguing that Jupiter's association is not with the vine itself but with its product, wine. The aim of the ceremonies, according to SCHILLING, is to place the potent magic inherent in the wine under the protection of Jupiter and thus to render it beneficial to the community.[34] A more recent survey of the problems of the Vinalia is provided by EISENHUT, who, without dealing with SCHILLING's convincing arguments to the contrary,

---

[26] R. E. A. PALMER, Roman Empire and Roman Religion: Five Essays, Hadley Foundation Series 15 (Philadelphia 1974) 137—49.

[27] M. SCHUSTER, Veiovis, RE VIII A, 2 (1955) 600—10.

[28] S. WEINSTOCK, Divus Julius (Oxford 1971) 8—12.

[29] A. ALFÖLDI, Redeunt Saturnia Regna III: Juppiter-Apollo-und Veiovis, Chiron 2 (1972) 215—30.

[30] E GJERSTAD, Veiovis: A Pre-Indo-European God in Rome, Opuscula Romana 9 (1973) 35—42.

[31] A. BRELICH, Iuppiter e le idus, in: Ex orbe religionum: Studia G. Widengren oblata, Numen Suppl., Stud. in the Hist. of Religions 21 (Leiden 1972) 299—306.

[32] A. DEGRASSI, II XIII, 2 (Rome 1963).

[33] F. BÖMER, Juppiter und die römischen Weinfeste, RhM 90 (1941) 30—58.

[34] R. SCHILLING, La religion romaine de Vénus depuis les origines jusqu' au temps d'Auguste, BEFAR 178 (Paris 1954) 92—155.

derives Jupiter's association with these festivals from his role as weather god, vines being especially fragile and subject to damage by storms.[35]

The other *feriae Iovis* of the calendar, that on July 5 and that on December 23, have at times been identified with the *Poplifugia* and the *Larentalia*. The most recent study of the *Poplifugia*, by GAGÉ, denies any connection between that festival and the *feriae Iovis* mentioned in the calendar under the same date.[36] Earlier scholars, like WISSOWA, summarily dismissed any association between Jupiter and the *Larentalia* on the grounds that the latter was a festival of the dead and that Jupiter's priest and hence the god shunned all contact with death. This view has been attacked on two sides by more recent work. KOCH, supplemented by a short note by VON BLUMENTHAL,[37] argues that chthonic associations were not originally foreign to the nature of the Roman Jupiter,[38] while LATTE denies that the *Larentalia* was a festival of the dead, suggesting instead that it was a rite to secure the fertility of the fields of the community.[39] Similarly RADKE argues that Larentia signifies 'das Grüne' and suggests that the bearer of this name was not a goddess of death but rather a fertility divinity. He further argues for the existence of an original goddess Larentia Dia, i.e. "Larentia who carries out her functions within the sphere of Jupiter's competence." To this original association of Larentia and Jupiter is to be traced the fact that the *Larentalia* is labeled *feriae Iovis* In his exemplary commentary, DEGRASSI[40], like KRAUS in his survey of the *Poplifugia*,[41] identifies the *Poplifugia* as a *feriae Iovis* but suspends judgement on the *Larentalia*.

Of other ceremonies associated with the worship and image of Jupiter, particular attention has been devoted to the triumph and to the relationship of the *triumphator* to Jupiter. Recently, VERSNEL has provided a full summary of the problems and the various theories which have been proposed concerning the triumph and the *Ludi Romani*. His own contribution has been supplemented by the work of WARREN, LEMOSSE, and GAGÉ.[42] As with the *Larentalia* and the *Poplifugia*, doubts have been cast on Jupiter's association with the *Aquaelicium* and the use of the *lapis manalis* to elicit rain. SAMTER argued that the *lapis*

[35] W. EISENHUT, Vinalia, RE Suppl. X (1965) 1172—6.

[36] J. GAGÉ, La ligne pomériale et les catégoires sociales de la Rome primitive. À propos de l'origine des Poplifugia et des Nones Caprotines, RD 48 (1970) 5—27.

[37] A. VON BLUMENTHAL, Zur römischen Religion der archaischen Zeit, RhM 87 (1938) 266—77; IDEM, Zur römischen Religion der archaischen Zeit II, RhM 90 (1941) 313—34.

[38] KOCH, Der römische Juppiter 90—103, esp. 92.

[39] LATTE, Römische Religionsgeschichte 92.

[40] DEGRASSI, II XIII, 2, 426—7, 543—5; G. RADKE, Acca Larentia und die Fratres Arvales. Ein Stück römisch-sabinischer Frühgeschichte, ANRW I, 2 (1972) 421—41.

[41] W. KRAUS, Poplifugia, RE XXII, 1 (1953) 74—8.

[42] H. VERSNEL, Triumphus: An Inquiry Into the Origin, Development, and Meaning of the Roman Triumph (Diss. Leiden 1970); cf. the review by L. WARREN, Gnomon 46 (1974) 574—83; and her essay, in: EADEM, Roman Triumph and Etruscan Kings: The Changing Face of the Triumph, JRS 60 (1970) 49—66; M. LEMOSSE, Les éléments techniques de l'ancien triomphe romain, ANRW I, 2 (1972) 442—53; J. GAGÉ, Les Quinctii, l'imperium capitolin et la règle du champ de Mars, REL 52 (1974) 110—48; and IDEM, Remarques sur le triomphe romain et sur ses deux principales origines, Revista de Historia 100 (1974) 1—28.

manalis had nothing to do with the cult of Jupiter but was rather in some way associated with the *manes*, the dead being frequently in other cultures held responsible for rain.[43] BÖMER argues that the *lapis manalis* had nothing to do with any ceremony to invoke rain, such a rain-stone never existed but was rather the etymological invention of antiquarians.[44] Along these same lines, RUBENS denies any connection between Jupiter's cult title *Elicius* and the rite of the *Aquaelicium*.[45] RUBENS argues that the true interpretation of his name was suggested by Livy, who ascribes to him the drawing forth of rules and rituals from the gods; Jupiter Elicius is the god from whom man could draw forth from heaven knowledge of those rituals which would maintain the *pax deorum*.

More recently, Jupiter's priest, the *flamen Dialis*, and the curious restrictions which surrounded his person have been the subject of considerable scholarly attention. Within the context of his structural approach, DUMÉZIL has examined the differences and the similarities in the status of the *rex sacrorum* and the three *flamines maiores*.[46] PÖTSCHER carefully re-examines the ancient evidence concerning the *flamen Dialis* and offers an encompassing interpretation of the taboos. The *flamen Dialis*, according to PÖTSCHER, is the representative of Jupiter on earth and above all he embodies the fecundating power of Jupiter which the *flamen* must preserve by avoiding contact with all harmful forces and substances.[47] BOELS offers a similar interpretation of the restrictions surrounding the *flaminica Dialis*, which arise from her status as the spouse of the representative on earth of Jupiter's nutritive force.[48] This would seem to be an extremely fruitful approach which might bear further investigation. Along similar lines, BRELICH sees the *flamen Dialis* as a reflection of an earlier worship of Jupiter as supreme king of the sky.[49] ALBANESE attempts to explain the *trinoctium continuum* of the *flamen Dialis* on the parallel of the *usurpatio trinoctii* of a wife, arguing that the status of the *flamen* is one of the absolute subjugation to the power of Jupiter like that of a wife to her husband. Such an absence of the *flamen* from the sacred bed would place in jeopardy the entirety of his attachment to Jupiter.[50] Rather more inconclusive is PALMER's attempt to explain the prohibition *capram et carnem incoctam et hederam et fabam neque tangere Diali mos est neque nominare*.[51] He rejects the view of JOHNSON and HAMP that *hedera* might be a corruption;[52] and on the assumption that the

[43] E. SAMTER, Altrömischer Regenzauber, ARW 21 (1922) 317–339.

[44] F. BÖMER, Der sogenannte Lapis manalis, ARW 33 (1936) 270–81.

[45] M. RUBENS, A New Interpretation of Jupiter Elicius, MAAR 10 (1932) 85–102.

[46] G. DUMÉZIL, Le rex et les flamines maiores, in: The Sacral Kingship: Contributions to the Central Theme of the VIIth International Congress for The History of Religions, Rome 1955 (Leiden 1957) 407–17.

[47] W. PÖTSCHER, Flamen dialis, Mnemosyne 4, 21 (1965) 215–40.

[48] N. BOELS, Le statut religieux de la Flaminica Dialis, REL 51 (1973) 77–100.

[49] A. BRELICH, Appunti sul flamen Dialis, ACD 8 (1972) 17–21.

[50] B. ALBANESE, Il trinoctium del flamen Dialis, SDHI 35 (1969) 73–98.

[51] R. PALMER, Ivy and Jupiter's Priest, in: Homenaje a Antonio Tovar (Madrid 1972) 341–7.

[52] V. JOHNSON, The Prehistoric Roman Calendar, AJPh 84 (1963) 28–35; and E. HAMP, Hedera is not 'ivy', AJPh 90 (1969) 464.

flamen Dialis did not touch what Jupiter might not eat, he suggests that ivy was interdicted as possibly harmful to human and therefore divine consumption. LEMOSSE considers the problem raised by the remark of Dio Cassius that all subsequent acts are annulled should the censor see a cadaver before the *lustratio*, suggesting that the prohibition arose because the ceremony was dedicated to Jupiter, whose priest, the *flamen Dialis*, could not be associated with death.[53] The civil *lustratio* arose at the time of the Etruscan kings but before the creation of the Capitoline cult; as heir to military lustrations in honor of Mars it joined the *suovetaurilia* to rites in honor of Jupiter.

Turning to the Roman cult of Jupiter in the imperial age, scholarly attention has tended to concentrate on two themes, Jupiter and the Capitoline cult in the provinces and the association of the emperor with Jupiter in religio-political ideology. This last is surveyed in a masterly fashion by BEAUJEU in his admirable 'La religion romaine à l'apogée de l'Empire, I. La politique religieuse des Antonins.'[54] Skillfully weaving together the literary, numismatic, and archaeological sources, BEAUJEU provides, within the context of his more general treatment of official religion, a reign-by-reign summary of the role of Jupiter in imperial ideology. Treating in particular Trajan's creation of a Jovian theology of imperial power and the role of Zeus in the Hadrianic imperial image, BEAUJEU argues that the profound association of Jupiter and emperor in the Antonine Age was the product of the traditional association of the republican *imperator* with the god, and that it arose naturally out of the constantly enormous prestige which Jupiter had enjoyed earlier in the empire. Concentrating on official ideology, BEAUJEU treats the role of Jupiter in imperial imagery without any real discussion of the cult of Jupiter in private cult or in the provinces; and this lacuna is not filled by the much briefer discussion of Jupiter in FERGUSON's 'The Religions of the Roman Empire.' Sketching the significance of the sky father in the religious currents of the imperial age, FERGUSON mentions the importance of the cult of Jupiter in the Danubian provinces and comments in slightly more detail on such topics as the assimilation of Jupiter and Zeus to foreign deities, the continued activity of the cult of Zeus in the Greek world, and on the association of the emperor with Jupiter in literature as well as official imperial ideology.[55]

WEINSTOCK examines the problems involved in the statement of Dio Cassius that Caesar was called Iuppiter Iulius, and in the process he surveys the association of the ruler with Olympian Zeus in Greece and in the Roman Republic.[56] ALFÖLDI has recognized Jovian symbolism on a series of gems depicting an eagle bearing what he labels a sceptre (in reality a *thyrsus*) or, at times, a crown, to a sleeping woman. The scene depicts, he argues, the dream of Rhea and Jupiter's promise of kingship for Romulus and empire and a golden

[53] M. LEMOSSE, Mort et lustratio à propos de Dion Cass. 54.28. 4, RHD 36 (1968) 519–24.
[54] J. BEAUJEU, La religion romaine à l'apogée de l'empire, I: La politique religieuse des Antonins (96–192), (Paris 1955).
[55] J. FERGUSON, The Religions of the Roman Empire (Ithaca 1970) 32–43.
[56] S. WEINSTOCK, Divus Julius (Oxford 1971) 270–317.

age for Rome, an allegorical statement of political propaganda in the late
republic in which the charismatic dynasts like Pompey, Caesar, and Octavian
compared themselves to Romulus.[57] SIMON has accepted AFÖLDI's general view
but interprets certain of the gems as a reference to Atia's conception of Octavian
and Jupiter's promise of kingship.[58] The central importance of Jupiter's promise
of world rule in Augustan literature is discussed by SCHILLING within the
context of Roman attitudes toward religion in the late republic.[59]

Treated more briefly in general accounts of the ruler cult at Rome, most
notably in CERFAUX-TONDRIAU, TAEGER, and DVORNIK,[60] the association of
Augustus with Jupiter is the subject of a detailed study by WARD.[61] Examining
instances of comparison as well as actual identification, WARD considers the
association both as a literary theme in the Augustan poets and the evidence for
the equation of Augustus with Zeus in the Hellenistic East and the Latin West.
The conquests of Augustus inspired in the poets a vision of the *princeps* as the
victor of a contemporary Gigantomachia. Egypt, delivered from Antony and
Cleopatra, hailed Augustus as Zeus Eleutherios: but, WARD argues, the absence
of a tradition of deified rulers together with Augustus' own policy prevented the
West, with few exceptions, from following the Greek East in conferring the
epithets of Zeus upon the *princeps*. BUCKLER examines the attribution of the
epithet *Patrōos* to Augustus at Pergamum and suggests that it was chosen to
equate Augustus with Zeus, so prominent on the great altar, and with Athena,
Theoi Patrioi of the city.[62] While more recent studies of Augustan literature
have examined the variety of fashions in which panegyrists associated Augustus
with Jupiter,[63] a general survey of assimilation of emperors to Jupiter in the
literary sources remains a desideratum. Such assimilation is found, of course in
art, in the numismatic material and in the inscriptions, as well as in literature. It
is a rich and significant theme, warranting a major study. RIEWALD's 1912
Halle dissertation 'De imperatorum romanorum cum certis dis et comparatione
et aequatione,' while admirable, did not by any means exhaust the theme.
However, despite the relative wealth of material studies of the emperors'
assimilation to Jupiter, as well as the figure of Jupiter in Roman art, remain

---

[57] A. ALFÖLDI, Die Geburt der kaiserlichen Bildsymbolik I. Der Traum der Rea, MH 7
    (1950) 1–13, rep. in: IDEM, Der Vater des Vaterlandes im römischen Denken, Libelli 211
    (Darmstadt 1971).
[58] E. SIMON, Die Portlandvase (Mainz 1957) 17–20.
[59] R. SCHILLING, Le Romain de la fin de la République et du début de l'Empire en face de la
    religion, AC 41 (1972) 540–62.
[60] L. CERFAUX and J. TONDRIAU, Le culte des souverains dans la civilisation gréco-romaine
    Bibl. de Théol. Sér. 3,5 (Paris 1957) 334; F. TAEGER, Charisma (Stuttgart 1957–60) II,
    169; F. DVORNIK, Early Christian and Byzantine Political Philosophy, Dumbarton Oaks
    Studies 9 (Washington 1966) II, 495–6.
[61] M. WARD, The Association of Augustus with Jupiter, SMSR 9 (1933) 203–24.
[62] W. BUCKLER, Augustus, Zeus Patroos, RPh 9 (1935) 177–88.
[63] See the literature collected above p. 66–7, n. 316–20. D. PIETRUSINSKI, L'Apothéose
    d'Octavien Auguste par le parallèle avec Jupiter dans la poésie d'Horace, Eos 68 (1980)
    103–22, is a detailed and illuminating study.

1. Tetradrachm, Lysimachus (HEAD, HN² p. 284); n. 149 — 2. Didrachm, Rome (CRAWFORD no. 28/3); n. 154 — 3. Victoriatus, Rome (CRAWFORD no. 57/1); n. 158 — 4. Tetradrachm, Agathocles (HEAD, HN² p. 181); n. 159 — 5. Tetradrachm, Seleucus (HEAD, HN² p. 757); n. 159 — 6. Denarius, Anonymous (CRAWFORD no. 44/5); n. 160

PLATE II   FEARS

7. Denarius, Annius Rufus (CRAWFORD no. 221); n. 191 — 8. Denarius, C. Metellus (CRAWFORD no. 269); n. 193 — 9. Denarius, Cn. Cornelius Sisenna (CRAWFORD no. 310); n. 196 — 10. Denarius, Q. Fabius Maximus (CRAWFORD no. 265); n. 199 — 11. Quinarius, T. Cloulius (CRAWFORD no. 332); n. 211 — 12. Quinarius, Cn. Lentulus (CRAWFORD no. 345/2); n. 213

13. Denarius, L. Rubrius Dossenus (CRAWFORD no. 348/1); n. 214 − 14. Denarius, Cn. Blasio (CRAW-
FORD no. 296); n. 215 − 15. Denarius, C. Egnatius (CRAWFORD no. 391/2); n. 232 − 16. Denarius,
L. Volumnius Strabo (CRAWFORD no. 377); n. 235 − 17. Denarius, M. Volteius (CRAWFORD no. 385/1);
n. 236 − 18. Denarius, P. Hypsaeus (CRAWFORD no. 420/1); n. 240

PLATE IV   FEARS

19. Denarius, P. Hypsaeus − M. Aemilius Scaurus (CRAWFORD no. 422); n. 240 − 20. Denarius, L. Lentulus − C. Marcellus (CRAWFORD no. 445/1); p. 55 − 21. Denarius, Cn. Pompeius Magnus (CRAWFORD no. 447); n. 254 − 22. Denarius, Q. Metellus Pius Scipio (CRAWFORD no. 459); n. 225 − 23. Denarius, Augustus (BMC no. 637); cast of piece in Kunsthistorisches Museum, Vienna; n. 259 − 24. Aureus, Augustus (BMC no. 656); cast of piece in Kunsthistorisches Museum, Vienna; n. 260

25. Denarius, Augustus (BMC no. 665); n. 269 — 26. Aureus, Nero (BMC no. 67); n. 339 — 27. Aureus, Nero (BMC no. 110); n. 342 — 28. Denarius, Otho (BMC no. 10); n. 366 — 29. Denarius, Vitellius (BMC no. 8); n. 368 — 30. Denarius, Vespasian (BMC no. 276); n. 370 — 31. As, Vespasian (BMC no. 612); n. 374 — 32. Denarius, Domitian Caesar (BMC Titus no. 88); n. 387 — 33. Sestertius, Trajan (BMC no. 825); n. 407

PLATE VI   FEARS

34. Aureus, Trajan (BMC no. 493); n. 413 — 35. Aureus, Hadrian (BMC no. 242); n. 418 — 36. Sestertius, Hadrian (BMC no. 1203); n. 419 — 37. As, Hadrian (BMC no. 1362A); n. 423 — 38. As,
Antoninus Pius (BMC no. 1632); n. 521 — 39. Aureus, Antoninus Pius (BMC no. 210); n. 521 —
40. Aureus, Antoninus Pius (BMC no. 490); n. 521 — 41. Denarius, Marcus Aurelius (BMC no. 728);
n. 521 — 42. Denarius, Antoninus Pius (BMC no. 225); n. 525

43. Sestertius, Commodus Caesar (BMC Marcus Aurelius no. 1524); n. 532 — 44. Denarius, Commodus (BMC no. 253); n. 538 — 45. Aureus, Commodus (BMC no. 215); n. 540 — 46. Sestertius, Commodus (BMC no. 679); n. 545 — 47. Silver quinarius, Commodus (BMC no. 306); n. 547 — 48. Sestertius, Commodus (BMC no. 678); n. 548 — 49. Denarius, Commodus (BMC no. 341); n. 552 — 50. Sestertius, Commodus (BMC no. 714); n. 552 — 51. Aureus, Septimius Severus (BMC no. 68); n. 560 — 52. Aureus, Septimius Severus (BMC no. 67 with note); n. 562 — 53. Denarius, Macrinus (BMC no. 1); n. 568 — 54. Antoninianus, Saloninus, Antioch? (cf. Kunsthistorisches Museum, Vienna Inv. No. 20241); n. 574

PLATE VIII   FEARS

55   56   57

58   59   60

55. Antoninianus, Gallienus, Cyzicus (cf. Kunsthistorisches Museum, Vienna Inv. No. 84275); n. 574 –
56. Antoninianus, Aurelian, Cyzicus (cast of piece in Kunsthistorisches Museum, Vienna Inv. No. 63383);
p. 118. For the significance of this issue from Cyzicus, see Fears, Princeps p. 282 – 57. Antoninianus,
Aurelian, Cyzicus (cf. Kunsthistorisches Museum, Vienna Inv. No. 63428); p. 118 – 58. Antoninianus,
Aurelian, unattributed eastern mint (cast of piece in Kunsthistorisches Museum, Vienna Inv. No.
21349); p. 118 – 59. Antoninianus, Aurelian, Siscia (cf. Kunsthistorisches Museum, Vienna Inv. No.
75868); p. 118 – 61. Antoninianus, Aurelian, Rome (cast of piece in Kunsthistorisches Museum,
Vienna Inv. No. 54996); p. 118

61. Antoninianus, Probus, Antioch (cf. Kunsthistorisches Museum, Vienna Inv. No. 47618); p. 118 –
62. Antoninianus, Probus, Tripolis (cf. Kunsthistorisches Museum, Vienna Inv. No. 49371); p. 118 –
63. Antoninianus, Carus, Tripolis (cf. Kunsthistorisches Museum, Vienna Inv. No. 84020); p. 118 –
64. Antoninianus, Carinus, Siscia (cf. Kunsthistorisches Museum, Vienna Inv. No. 23108); p. 118 –
65. Antoninianus, Diocletian, Antioch (cf. Kunsthistorisches Museum, Vienna Inv. No. 86371);
p. 118 – 66. Antoninianus, Diocletian, Antioch (cf. Kunsthistorisches Museum, Vienna Inv. No. 57855); p. 118

PLATE X   FEARS

67. Radiate fraction, Diocletian, Ticinum (RIC VI p. 283 no. 25); n. 576 – 68. Antoninianus, Diocletian, Heraclea (RIC V, 2 no. 284); n. 576 – 69. Aureus, Maxentius, Rome (RIC VI p. 401 no. 6); n. 583

70b

70a

70, a, b. Attic reliefs, city-side, Arch of Trajan, Beneventum; photograph courtesy of Deutsches Archäologisches Institut, Rom; p. 83

PLATE XII   FEARS

71b

71a

71, a, b. Attic reliefs, Campagna-side, Arch of Trajan, Beneventum; photograph courtesy of Deutsches Archäologisches Institut, Rom; p. 84

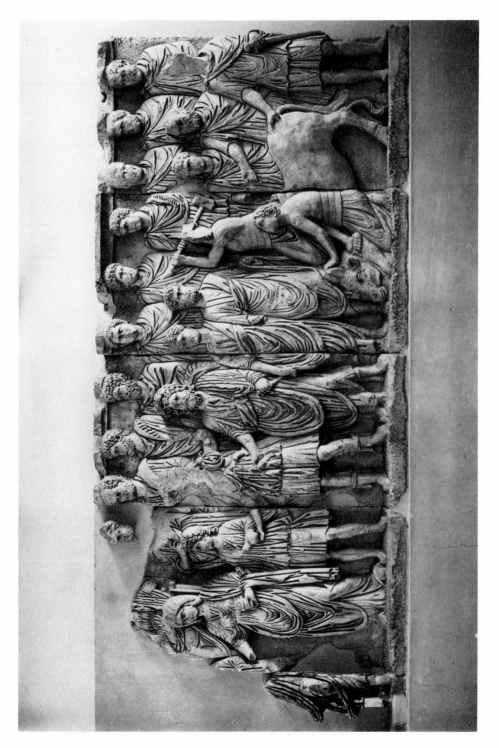

72. Attic, Arch of Septimius Severus, Leptis Magna; photograph courtesy of Deutsches Archäologisches Institut, Rom; n. 563

limited to points of detail. Thus BUCKLER (above n. 62) has argued that Trajan's willingness to permit his worship as Zeus Philios at Pergamum arose out of the Augustan precedent but emphasized Trajan's own quality of benevolence. METCALF discusses Hadrianic cistophoric tetradrachms which portray Jupiter on the reverse with the legend IOVIS OLYMPIVS. He associates the issue with Hadrian's visit to Ephesus in 129 and argues that it provides the first positively datable evidence for Hadrian's divine pretensions.[64]

MOMIGLIANO's treatment of the *sodales Flaviales* casts light upon the importance of Jupiter in Domitian's imperial ideology, arguing that under Titus the organization of the *sodales Flaviales* was similar to that of the *Augustales* but that under Domitian they were transferred to Jupiter as protector of Domitian.[65] A similar development in imperial art is pointed to by RYBERG, who shows how the sacrifice to the Genius of the emperor, common on first century reliefs, was replaced in the second century by representations of the *vota publica* and other sacrifices to Jupiter on behalf of the emperor.[66]

AUST's treatment of Jupiter in Roman art has not been replaced, although limited and now very much out-of-date. NAPOLI's article in the 'Enciclopedia dell'Arte Antica' is a disappointingly brief survey.[67] The image of Jupiter on the coinage, however, has been the subject of a study by HILL, who attempts to reduce the numerous and complicated Jupiter types of the Rome mint in imperial times to five main types: Capitolinus, Victor, Conservator, Propugnator, and Latius.[68] HACKENS briefly treats the coin types illustrating the Capitoline temple and its history.[69]

The concept of Jupiter's election of the emperor as his earthly vicegerent, a theme central to the imperial image of the Antonine Age and the third century, is the subject of a monograph by FEARS, who traces the history of the idea of

---

[64] W. METCALF, Hadrian, Iovis Olympius, Mnemosyne 4, 27 (1974) 59—66. Much more significant than METCALF's unconvincing effort are the series of articles which W. DEN BOER has devoted to exploring Pap. Giss. 3 and other evidence for Hadrian's use of religion, including the deification of Trajan, for political advantage: Religion and Literature in Hadrian's Policy, Mnemosyne n. s. 8 (1955) 123—44; Trajans Vergottung (P. Giss. 3, Inv. 20), Kurzbericht aus der Giessener Papyrussammlung no. 34 (1975); Trajan's Deification and Hadrian's Succession, Ancient Society 6 (1975) 203—12. The first and third are reprinted in IDEM, Syggrammata. Studies in Greco-Roman History, ed. by H. PLEKET and others (Leiden 1979) 197—218, 277—86.

[65] A. MOMIGLIANO, Sodales flaviales titiales e culto di Giove, BCAR 63 (1935) 165—71. The highly significant question of Domitian's emphatic association of himself with Jupiter receives no illumination at the hands of T. WISEMAN, Flavians on the Capitol, American Journal of Ancient History 3 (1978) 167—75. An understanding of the nuances and implications of Tacitus' narrative fail entirely in this unconvincing attempt to locate the actual site of the siege of the Flavians on the Capitol.

[66] I. SCOTT RYBERG, Rites of the State Religion in Roman Art, MAAR 22 (Rome 1955) 81—162.

[67] M. NAPOLI, Giove, Enciclopedia dell'Arte Antica III (1960) 911—3.

[68] P. HILL, Aspects of Jupiter on Coins of the Roman Mint, NC 6, 20 (1960) 113—28.

[69] T. HACKENS, De Tempel en de goden van het Kapitool op de Romeinse munten, Société Royale de Numismatique de Belgique, Exposition Numismatique, Bruxelles, Bibliothèque Albert I, 30 Avril—29 Mai 1966 (Brussels 1966) 33—6.

rule by divine election in the ancient Near East and in Greece and argues that it was a familiar theme at Rome by the late republic.[70] The ultimate expression of this concept in the imperial titles, Diocletian's adoption of *Jovius*, is the subject of a special study by MATTINGLY, who argues that Diocletian, in his new system of Jupiter and Hercules, meant to offer an interpretation of paganism which might be so far acceptable to the Christians as to induce them to pay a modest but satisfactory modicum of conformity.[71] The association of Jupiter and Hercules in the imperial age, which MATTINGLY argues was implicitly similar to the Christian concept of God the father and Christ the son, is the subject of an essay by COSTA.[72]

No general study has appeared to replace the first volume of TOUTAIN's 'Les cultes païens dans l'empire romain;' and this has perhaps hampered a reassessment of his view, still repeated, that the cult of Jupiter Optimus Maximus in the provinces was limited almost entirely to imperial officials and soldiers and that it was a manifestation of patriotic loyalty rather than a vital religious force. This is not entirely supported by the epigraphical evidence; and the single most pressing desideratum for our topic is a detailed examination of the cult of Jupiter in the Roman provinces. This has been treated as part of general surveys of Roman cults in particular provinces, such as JONES for Dacia and PASCAL for Cisalpine Gaul.[73] However, only for Spain has a comprehensive study of the cult of Jupiter been made. The preliminary studies by HEUTEN on the epigraphical and numismatic evidence for the worship of the Capitoline divinities in Spain[74] have been followed by PEETERS' monographic treatment of the cult of Jupiter in Spain as evidenced by the inscriptions.[75] HEUTEN shows that while Jupiter became assimilated in Spain, including the adoption of indigenous epithets and dedications by natives, and was worshipped throughout the Spanish provinces, Juno and Minerva and the Capitoline Triad as an entity remained purely Roman and localized in the romanized provinces of the South and East, an impression confirmed by both the epigraphical and the numismatic material. More extensive and more significant still is PEETERS' analysis of the epigraphical evidence, which shows that the worship of Jupiter cut across all social grades.

[70] J. R. FEARS, Princeps A Diis Electus: The Divine Election of the Emperor as a Political Concept at Rome, Papers and Monographs of the American Academy in Rome 26 (Rome 1977).

[71] H. MATTINGLY, Jovius and Herculius, HThR 45 (1952) 131—4.

[72] G. COSTA, Giove ed Ercole: Contributo allo studio della religione romana nell'impero (Rome 1919).

[73] L. JONES, The Cults of Dacia, University of California Publications in Classical Philology, vol. 9, no. 8 (Berkeley 1929) 245—305; C. PASCAL, The Cults of Cisalpine Gaul, Coll. Latomus 75 (Brussels 1964).

[74] G. HEUTEN, Les divinités capitolines en Espagne, RBPh 12 (1933) 549—68, and IDEM, Les divinités capitolines en Espagne, II. La numismatique, RBPh 14 (1935) 709—23.

[75] F. PEETERS, Le culte de Jupiter en Espagne d'après les inscriptions, RBPh 17 (1938) 157—93, 853—86, rep. as monograph (Brussels 1938).

Equally important is BIANCHI's careful analysis of the history of the Capitoline cult in Roman Italy and in the provinces in the imperial age.[76] BIANCHI shows that expansion of the Capitoline cult in Italy was the product of Roman expansion and that the earliest Capitolia outside of Rome arose in colonies in the second century B.C. Only in the second century A.D. did Capitolia begin to be erected in cities with the most diverse municipal constitutions, above all in Africa, but always in cities which had assimilated Roman civil and religious institutions, for, as BIANCHI argues, the Capitoline cult came to epitomize the religious aspects of *romanitas*. More recently, the celebration of the 1900th anniversary of the dedication of the Capitolium at Brescia has provided the opportunity for BIANCHI to supplement these earlier remarks. The same occasion was marked by RADKE's wide ranging and evocative discussion of the political and religious significance of the Capitoline cult.[77]

Other studies of the cult of Jupiter in the imperial age tend to be more limited or to focus upon the assimilation of indigenous divinities to Jupiter. This question of assimilation is of considerable import for an understanding of the phenomenon of the diffusion and transformation of Greco-Roman culture in the imperial age. The evidence, particularly epigraphic and monumental, for individual cults of Jupiter in the provinces is rich and is constantly augmented by archaeological research. It is no easy task for the historian of religion to remain abreast of these new developments; even the keenest peruser of 'L'Année Philologique' will miss much that is published only in archaeological reports. At the present any attempt at a systematic bibliographical survey is premature. The subject of the cults of Jupiter in the provinces will be put on an entirely new level by the essays to appear in ANRW II, 18, 1–3 and by that of I. M. BARTON, Capitoline Temples in Italy and the Provinces (especially Africa), in ANRW II, 12, 1 (1981).

The study of the cult of Jupiter in the imperial period, particularly in the provinces, offers the most obviously fruitful path for future research into our topic. As indicated briefly in the text, careful collation of the mass of epigraphical material would do much to dispel the still current notion that the cult of Jupiter Optimus Maximus in the provinces was observed almost entirely by imperial officials and soldiers and that such observation was a manifestation of patriotic loyalty rather than a sign of true piety and devotion to the godhead. Such a study can build upon BARTOCCINI's excellent but seldom cited collection of inscriptions relating to the worship of Jupiter in the Roman world.[78] In his summary of the material BARTOCCINI has indeed already pointed to the main conclusions which will emerge from a more complete listing and analysis of the

---

[76] U. BIANCHI, Disegno storico del culto capitolino nell' Italia romana e nelle provincie dell' impero, MAL 8, 2 (1950) 349–415.

[77] U. BIANCHI, I Capitolia, and G. RADKE, Il valore religioso e politico delle divinità del Campidoglio, both in Atti del Convegno Internazionale per il XIX Centenario della Dedicazione del Capitolium e per il 150 Anniversario della sua Scoperta, Suppl. ai Comment. dell' Ateneo di Brescia (1975) I, 63–76, 245–53.

[78] R. BARTOCCINI, Iuppiter, in: E. DE RUGGIERO, Dizionario Epigrafico di Antichità Romane IV (1941) 240–62.

epigraphical material; he stresses the importance of Jupiter in the popular cult life of the Latin West and the sincere piety with which the god was worshipped at all levels of society. As does BARTOCCINI, a detailed study of the cult of Jupiter in the provinces of the Roman empire might best proceed with a province-by-province examination, giving careful attention to such matters as the social grades and origins of dedicants of inscriptions to Jupiter, the degree to which the quantity and content of inscriptions in honor of Jupiter reflect regional and chronological variations, and the extent to which the cults of Jupiter Optimus Maximus and the Capitoline Triad were assimilated to native and to eastern religious elements. Particular attention should be focused on the evidence which these inscriptions offer for the intensity of religious feeling, making careful note of the percentage of inscriptions which are ex-votos and of those which refer to some direct encounter of the worshipper with Jupiter, which inspired the dedicant to erect the inscription. Such a study should concentrate equally on the private and public cult of Jupiter in the imperial period, and it would do well to consider at length the cult of Zeus in the Greek world of the imperial age, for which a mass of numismatic material offers a useful supplement to the epigraphical evidence. Some of the questions likely to be raised by such an essay can be anticipated. Is the importance of Jupiter-Zeus in public cult, imperial propaganda, and popular philosophy of the imperial age, a reflection of a deeply rooted and sincerely religious belief in Jupiter at the private level? To what extent had the cult of Jupiter Optimus Maximus come to absorb the cults of such hypostases as Jupiter Victor, Jupiter Propugnator, and Jupiter Stator? Why was the cult of Jupiter Optimus Maximus readily adopted by natives in Gaul and Spain but not in Roman Africa and Britain? To what degree was the Christian doctrine of God the Father and Christ the Mediator preceded in popular religious belief by the image of Jupiter as the supreme creator and the emperor as his earthly vicegerent? Indeed such an examination might well reveal that the cult of Jupiter in the imperial period is at least as important for an understanding of the rise and triumph of Christianity as is the worship of Isis and Mithras.

The Christian image of God the father was indelibly impressed by the notions and formula inherent in the worship and in the popular and philosophical conceptions of Zeus and Jupiter. Until we possess a study of Jupiter, thorough in coverage, broad in historical scope, and analytical in approach, a fundamental element will be missing from our portrait of the historical process by which Christianity became the established religion of the Roman empire and the dominant and characteristic intellectual statement of the late ancient world. Even apart from this, the pre-eminent god of the Roman state over a period of a millennium simply deserves a detailed treatment of at least the same order as SCHILLING has provided for Venus, GAGÉ for Apollo, and BRUHL for Liber Pater. The time is overdue for such a work of synthesis. Our sources, archaeological, epigraphical, literary, and numismatic, are abundant; the main outlines are clear. Certainly the evidence at our disposal will be supplemented, primarily through archaeology. And as recent work has shown, important points of detail remain to be clarified. For example, the question of the origin of the Capitoline Triad is reconsidered in the course of BLOCH's treatment of religious developments and innovations in Rome of the Etruscan kings.[79] DUMÉZIL's concepts continue to increase our understanding of early Roman religion and to stimulate further research. Thus his view of the divine triad at Iguvium serves as the framework for BRIQUEL's examination of the military aspects of the Umbrian divinity Fiscus Sancius and of the association at Rome of Jupiter and Dius Fidius.[80] BRELICH's article on the ides and the remarks in the present essay indicate that Jupiter's association with the moon continues to be a source of scholarly interest and puzzlement.[81] A collection of material which can be brought to bear on this problem is provided by LUNAIS' study of the treatment in Latin authors of the moon's influence on plant and animal life.[82] In early Rome and throughout Roman history, the image of Jupiter's power and supremacy was closely associated with the social and legal concept of *pater*. WLOSOK's survey of the idea of father in Roman culture considers the relationship between the traditional Roman conception of fatherhood and the role of Jupiter and later the Christian God as father.[83] The pre-eminent Roman cult place of the father of gods and men, the Capitoline temple, figures on coins of the republic and on imperial issues. These numismatic representations of the Capitoline temple are discussed by BASTIEN in the course of his remarks on a previously unpublished coin of Vitellius, the reverse of which portrays the temple.[84] JOBST considers the evidence, primarily epigraphical, for the worship of Jupiter Capitolinus at Carnuntum.[85] Recent issues of 'L'Année Épigraphique' continue to add evidence in support of the view that Jupiter was the object of widespread and sincere popular piety at all levels of society in the provinces of the Latin West in the imperial age.[86] The reception of the cult of Jupiter in Roman Germany is put into clearer perspective by MUELLER's comprehensive survey of Jupiter columns.[87]

Of course, Rome, Italy, and the Latin West will remain the prime focus for research on the cult of Roman Jupiter. Nonetheless, any attempt at a broad understanding of the significance of the worship of Jupiter in the imperial age must go beyond the Latin material and beyond the mere collection of evidence for cult practice. It must take into account fully the worship of Zeus throughout

---

[79] R. BLOCH, Recherches sur la religion romaine du VIᵉ siècle avant J.C., CRAI (1978) 669–87.

[80] D. BRIQUEL, Sur les aspects militaires du dieu ombrien Fiscus Sancius, MEFR 90 (1978) 133–52.

[81] See above p. 128 n. 31 and p. 29.

[82] S. LUNAIS, Recherches sur la lune I. Les auteurs latins, Ét Prélimin. aux Relig. Orient. dans l'Emp. Rom. 72 (Leiden 1979), esp. 49–74.

[83] A. WLOSOK, Vater und Vatervorstellungen in der römischen Kultur, in: H. TELLENBACH, ed., Das Vaterbild im Abendland I (Stuttgart 1978) 18–54, 191–200.

[84] P. BASTIEN, Vitellius et le temple de Jupiter Capitolin. Un as inédit, NAL 7 (1978) 181–202.

[85] W. JOBST, Jupiter Kapitolinus oder Jupiter Karnuntinus, in: J. FITZ, ed., Limes. Akten des XI. Internationalen Limeskongresses (Budapest 1979) 155–64.

[86] Année Épig. (1975) 153, 545, 690, 720, 732, 734, 951; Année Epig. (1976) 198, 224, 296, 334, 336, 424, 502, 543, 297, 321.

[87] W. MUELLER, Die Jupitergigantensäulen und ihre Verwandten, Beiträge zur klassischen Philologie 66 (Meisenheim am Glan 1975).

the Roman East in the imperial age, and it must give the most careful consideration to the theology and to the popular, philosophical, and literary image of Jupiter/Zeus. The 'Olympian Oration' of Dio Chrysostom and the 'Eis Dia' of Aelius Aristides are fundamental sources for elucidating the significance attached by Trajan, Hadrian, and a wide range of their subjects to the association of the emperor and Jupiter, which was such a marked characteristic of imperial ideology in the Antonine age. It is precisely this wide vision of Roman religion and this use of all our sources, archaeological as well as literary, which gives such enduring importance to BEAUJEU's 'La religion romaine à l'apogée de l'empire.'[88] It is precisely the absence of both of these essential qualities which makes the recent book by LIEBESCHUETZ such a disappointing and misguided attempt at understanding 'Continuity and Change in Roman Religion.'[89] Dio and Aelius Aristides belong as much to the world of Roman religion as do the elder and younger Pliny. Studies of Dio's twelfth oration by HARRIS and CHIRASSI indicate approaches which can considerably expand our understanding of the popular conception of Zeus in the imperial age.[90] More recently, SCHWABL's encyclopaedic survey of Zeus has placed every student of classical religion in his debt.[91] From a comparative point of view, the student of Jupiter and early Roman cult can learn much from SCHWABL's treatment of Zeus' role as guardian of the social order in Greece, while his assemblage and evaluation of the literary sources provide a comprehensive survey of the evolution of the image of Zeus in Greek literature and philosophy.[92]

---

[88] See above n. 54. For a survey of recent scholarship, see J. BEAUJEU, Le paganisme romain sous le Haut Empire, ANRW II, 16, 1 (1978) 3—26.

[89] J. LIEBESCHUETZ, Continuity and Change in Roman Religion (Oxford 1978). See the review by J. R. FEARS, Gnomon (in press).

[90] B. HARRIS, The Olympian Oration of Dio Chrysostom, JRH 2 (1967) 85—97; I. CHIRASSI, Il Significato religioso del XII discorso di Dione Crisostomo, RCCM 5 (1963) 266—85.

[91] H. SCHWABL, Zeus, RE X A, 1 (1972) 253—76, and IDEM, Suppl. XV (1978) 994—1481.

[92] Attention is drawn to the following works, which became available after 'The Cult of Jupiter and Roman Imperial Ideology' went to press but which might usefully be referred to in connection with questions discussed in the text and notes:

n. 8:   For the impact of the Etruscan kings upon early Roman society, see J. RICHARD, Les origines de la plèbe romaine, BEFAR 232 (Rome 1978) 287—600.

n. 17:   On the nature of the *curiae*, see RICHARD, Plèbe romaine 197—222.

n. 31:   F. KOLB discusses 'Die Bau-, Religions- und Kulturpolitik der Peisistratiden', JDAI 92 (1977) 99—138.

n. 42:   J. SCHINDLER, Zeus, RE Suppl. XV (1978) 999—1001, is an important collection of material relating to the etymology of the name 'Zeus.'

n. 268:   For discussion and literature on major aspects of Augustan historical imagery in the visual arts, see J. POLLINI, Studies in Augustan 'Historical' Relief (Diss. California, Berkeley 1978).

n. 271:   For aspects of Augustan numismatic propaganda, see L. CONSIGLIERE, 'Slogani' Monetari e poesia augustea, Publ. Ist. di Filol. class. e medioev. dell'Università di Genova 56 (Genoa 1978).

n. 275:   C. SIMPSON, The Date of the Dedication of the Temple of Mars Ultor, JRS 67 (1977) 91—4, reconsiders the accepted chronology and the identification of the temple represented on BMC I, p. 65 no. 366.

List of Illustrations

Unless otherwise noted, all photographs of coins are from casts of pieces in the British Museum. The photographs of these casts were made by Dr. O. VON VACANO, using the facilities of the Seminaı für Alte Geschichte, Universität Düsseldorf. I should like to express my deep appreciation to Dr. VON VACANO and to Professor KIENAST for this gesture of friendly cooperation. I am also extremely grateful to Mr. R. A. G. CARSON and his staff at the British Museum for the alacrity and skill with which they have responded to my numerous requests for casts. I particularly wish to thank the American Council of Learned Societies and the Penrose Fund of the American Philosophical Society for grants which made possible the collection of the numismatic and archaeological material.

I 1. Tetradrachm, Lysimachus (HEAD, HN² p. 284); n. 149.
   2. Didrachm, Rome (CRAWFORD no. 28/3); n. 154.
   3. Victoriatus, Rome (CRAWFORD no. 57/1); n. 158.

n. 279: Apollo's role in the Augustan order is discussed by E. SIMON, Apollo in Rom, JDAI 93 (1978) 202–27.

n. 280: The ideological implications of the temple of Mars Ultor and the Augustan Forum are considered by P. GROS, Aurea Templa. Recherches sur l'architecture religieuse de Rome à l'époque d'Auguste, BEFAR 231 (Rome 1976) 15–52. M. SAGE examines 'The Elogia of the Augustan Forum and the de viris illustribus', Historia 28 (1979) 192–210.

n. 313: On the Ravenna relief, see H. JUCKER, Die Prinzen auf dem Augustus-Relief in Ravenna, Mélanges à P. Collart, Cah. d'archeol. rom. 5 (Lausanne–Paris 1976) 237–67.

n. 319: R. SYME, History in Ovid (Oxford 1978) 169–84, discusses the relationship of Ovid and the Augustan poets in general to the princeps.

n. 405: K. SCHWARTE, Trajans Regierungsbeginn und der 'Agricola' des Tacitus, Bonner Jahrbücher 179 (1979) 139–75, places Pliny's 'Panegyric' within the context of the early period of Trajan's principate.

n. 420: For the circumstances surrounding the accession of Hadrian, see E. MERTEN, Die Adoption Hadrians, in: Bonner Festgabe J. Straub, ed. A. LIPPOLD and N. HIMMELMANN (Bonn 1977).

n. 427: On Hadrian and Athens, see S. FOLLET, Athènes au IIᵉ et au IIIᵉ siècle. Études chronologiques et prosopographiques (Paris 1977) 107–35.

n. 486: On the Column of Trajan, see W. GAUER, Untersuchungen zur Trajanssäule, I. Darstellungsprogramm und künstlerischer Entwurf, Monum. artis Rom. 13 (Berlin 1977).

n. 487: K. SCHWARTE, Salus Augusta Publica. Domitian und Trajan als Heilbringer des Staates, in: Festgabe Straub 225–46, discusses the role of the vota in the imperial propaganda of Domitian and Trajan.

n. 491: Three recent studies of Marcus Aurelius and the rain miracle are: I. TOTH, Marcus Aurelius' Miracle of the Rain and the Egyptian Cults in the Danube Region, Studia Aegyptiaca 2 (1976) 101–13; W. JOBST, 11. Juni 172 n. Chr. Der Tag des Blitz- und Regenwunders im Quadenland, Sitzungsberichte Österreichische Akademie der Wissenschaften, phil.-hist. Klasse 335 (Vienna 1978); H. RUBIN, Weather Miracles under Marcus Aurelius, Athenaeum 57 (1979) 357–80.

n. 515: The question of native and Roman elements in the iconography of the Jupiter columns is discussed by M. GREEN, The Worship of the Roman-Celtic Wheel-God in Britain seen in Relation to Gaulish Evidence, Latomus 38 (1979) 345–67.

4. Tetradrachm, Agathocles (HEAD, HN² p. 181); n. 159.
5. Tetradrachm, Seleucus (HEAD, HN² p. 757); n. 159.
6. Denarius, Anonymous (CRAWFORD no. 44/5); n. 160.

II 7. Denarius, Annius Rufus (CRAWFORD no. 221); n. 191.
8. Denarius, C. Metellus (CRAWFORD no. 269); n. 193.
9. Denarius, Cn. Cornelius Sisenna (CRAWFORD no. 310); n. 196.
10. Denarius, Q. Fabius Maximus (CRAWFORD no. 265); n. 199.
11. Quinarius, T. Cloulius (CRAWFORD no. 332); n. 211.
12. Quinarius, Cn. Lentulus (CRAWFORD no. 345/2); n. 213.

III 13. Denarius, L. Rubrius Dossenus (CRAWFORD no. 348/1); n. 214.
14. Denarius, Cn. Blasio (CRAWFORD no. 296); n. 215.
15. Denarius, C. Egnatius (CRAWFORD no. 391/2); n. 232.
16. Denarius, L. Volumnius Strabo (CRAWFORD no. 377); n. 235.
17. Denarius, M. Volteius (CRAWFORD no. 385/1); n. 236.
18. Denarius, P. Hypsaeus (CRAWFORD no. 420/1); n. 240.

IV 19. Denarius, P. Hypsaeus − M. Aemilius Scaurus (CRAWFORD no. 422); n. 240.
20. Denarius, L. Lentulus − C. Marcellus (CRAWFORD no. 445/1); p. 55.
21. Denarius, Cn. Pompeius Magnus (CRAWFORD no. 447); n. 254.
22. Denarius, Q. Metellus Pius Scipio (CRAWFORD no. 459); n. 225.
23. Denarius, Augustus (BMC no. 637); cast of piece in Kunsthistorisches Museum, Vienna; n. 259.
24. Aureus, Augustus (BMC no. 656); cast of piece in Kunsthistorisches Museum, Vienna; n. 260.

V 25. Denarius, Augustus (BMC no. 665); n. 269.
26. Aureus, Nero (BMC no. 67); n. 339.
27. Aureus, Nero (BMC no. 110); n. 342.
28. Denarius, Otho (BMC no. 10); n. 366.
29. Denarius, Vitellius (BMC no. 8); n. 368.
30. Denarius, Vespasian (BMC no. 276); n. 370.
31. As, Vespasian (BMC no. 612); n. 374.
32. Denarius, Domitian Caesar (BMC Titus no. 88); n. 387.
33. Sestertius, Trajan (BMC no. 825); n. 407.

VI 34. Aureus, Trajan (BMC no. 493); n. 413.
35. Aureus, Hadrian (BMC no. 242); n. 418.
36. Sestertius, Hadrian (BMC no. 1203); n. 419.
37. As, Hadrian (BMC no. 1362A); n. 423.
38. As, Antoninus Pius (BMC no. 1632); n. 521.
39. Aureus, Antoninus Pius (BMC no. 210); n. 521.
40. Aureus, Antoninus Pius (BMC no. 490); n. 521.
41. Denarius, Marcus Aurelius (BMC no. 728); n. 521.
42. Denarius, Antoninus Pius (BMC no. 225); n. 525.

VII 43. Sestertius, Commodus Caesar (BMC Marcus Aurelius no. 1524); n. 532.
44. Denarius, Commodus (BMC no. 253); n. 538.
45. Aureus, Commodus (BMC no. 215); n. 540.
46. Sestertius, Commodus (BMC no. 679); n. 545.
47. Silver quinarius, Commodus (BMC no. 306); n. 547.
48. Sestertius, Commodus (BMC no. 678); n. 548.
49. Denarius, Commodus (BMC no. 341); n. 552.
50. Sestertius, Commodus (BMC no. 714); n. 552.
51. Aureus, Septimius Severus (BMC no. 68); n. 560.
52. Aureus, Septimius Severus (BMC no. 67 with note); n. 562.

53. Denarius, Macrinus (BMC no. 1); n. 568.

54. Antoninianus, Saloninus, Antioch? (cf. Kunsthistorisches Museum, Vienna Inv. No. 20241); n. 574.

VIII 55. Antoninianus, Gallienus, Cyzicus (cf. Kunsthistorisches Museum, Vienna Inv. No. 84275); n. 574.

56. Antoninianus, Aurelian, Cyzicus (cast of piece in Kunsthistorisches Museum, Vienna Inv. No. 63383); p. 118. For the significance of this issue from Cyzicus, see FEARS, Princeps p. 282.

57. Antoninianus, Aurelian, Cyzicus (cf. Kunsthistorisches Museum, Vienna Inv. No. 63428); p. 118.

58. Antoninianus, Aurelian, unattributed eastern mint (cast of piece in Kunsthistorisches Museum, Vienna Inv. No. 21349); p. 118.

59. Antoninianus, Aurelian, Siscia (cf. Kunsthistorisches Museum, Vienna Inv. No. 75868); p. 118.

60. Antoninianus, Aurelian, Rome (cast of piece in Kunsthistorisches Museum, Vienna Inv. No. 54996); p. 118.

IX 61. Antoninianus, Probus, Antioch (cf. Kunsthistorisches Museum, Vienna Inv. No. 47618); p. 118.

62. Antoninia, Probus, Tripolis (cf. Kunsthistorisches Museum, Vienna Inv. No. 49371); p. 118.

63. Antoninianus, Carus, Tripolis (cf. Kunsthistorisches Museum, Vienna Inv. No. 84020); p. 118.

64. Antoninianus, Carinus, Siscia (cf. Kunsthistorisches Museum, Vienna Inv. No. 23108); p. 118.

65. Antoninianus, Diocletian, Antioch (cf. Kunsthistorisches Museum, Vienna Inv. No. 86371); p. 118.

66. Antoninianus, Diocletian, Antioch (cf. Kunsthistorisches Museum, Vienna Inv. No. 57855); p. 118.

X 67. Radiate fraction, Diocletian, Ticinum (RIC VI p. 283 no. 25); n. 576.

68. Antoninianus, Diocletian, Heraclea (RIC V, 2 no. 284); n. 576.

69. Aureus, Maxentius, Rome (RIC VI p. 401 no. 6); n. 583.

XI 70, a, b. Attic reliefs, city-side, Arch of Trajan, Beneventum; photograph courtesy of Deutsches Archäologisches Institut, Rom; p. 83.

XII 71, a, b. Attic reliefs, Campagna-side, Arch of Trajan, Beneventum; photograph courtesy of Deutsches Archäologisches Institut, Rom; p. 84.

XIII 72. Attic, Arch of Septimius Severus, Leptis Magna; photograph courtesy of Deutsches Archäologisches Institut, Rom; n. 563.

Aperçu critique de travaux relatifs au culte de Junon

par Geneviève Dury-Moyaers, Liège,
et Marcel Renard, Bruxelles*

Table des matières

* Geneviève Dury-Moyaers, Aspirant au Fonds National de la Recherche Scientifique; Marcel Renard, Membre de l'Académie Royale de Belgique.

Abréviations:

A.J.A.	American Journal of Archaeology
A.N.R.W.	H. Temporini—W. Haase (éd.), Aufstieg und Niedergang der Römischen Welt. Geschichte und Kultur Roms im Spiegel der neueren Forschung, Berlin—New York, 1972 ss.
C.I.L.	Corpus Inscriptionum Latinarum
C.R.A.I.	Comptes Rendus des Séances. Académie des Inscriptions et Belles Lettres

Notre propos n'est pas de faire œuvre originale mais bien de présenter et d'opposer certains travaux[1] consacrés à Junon ainsi qu'à des cultes dans lesquels elle intervient. Nous étudierons ainsi « à la file » diverses virtualités de Junon, certains cultes, quelques relations entretenues avec d'autres divinités, italiques ou étrangères. Pour chaque point ainsi envisagé, nous avons rappelé des opinions souvent divergentes des modernes qui confrontent leurs points de vue et se critiquent. Nous n'avons que très rarement exprimé un avis personnel qui ne trouverait pas sa place ici mais que nous formulerons ultérieurement. Puisque l'éditeur nous avait donné toute latitude, nous avons fait la part la plus large aux publications consacrées à la Junon des époques anciennes, car c'est à ce moment que la déesse présente le plus d'intérêt. Du reste cet aspect de sa personnalité est celui qui a été de loin le plus étudié.

I. Le nom de Junon et la valeur de la déesse

L'étymologie du nom *Iūnō* semble bien définitivement élucidée. On ne peut plus rapprocher ce nom que des termes de la famille *iuuenis*. Les autres hypothèses ne sont plus défendables. Au XIXe siècle, on rapprochait le nom de Junon de celui de son parèdre Jupiter; les savants, emmenés par Buttmann[2],

D.E.	A. Ernout—A. Meillet, Dictionnaire étymologique de la langue latine, Paris, 1932
H.Th.R.	Harvard Theological Review
I.L.L.R.P.	Inscriptiones Latinae Liberae Rei Publicae, éd. A. Degrassi
I.L.S.	Inscriptiones Latinae Selectae, éd. H. Dessau
J.R.S.	Journal of Roman Studies
Lex.	W. Roscher (éd.), Ausführliches Mytholog. Lexikon, Berlin—Leipzig, 1884ss.; réimpr. Hildesheim—New York, 1965ss.
M.E.F.R.(A).	Mélanges d'Archéologie et d'Histoire de l'Ecole Française de Rome (Antiquité)
P.M.A.A. Rome	Papers and Monographs of the American Academy at Rome
R.B.Ph.	Revue Belge de Philologie et d'Histoire
R.E.	F. Pauly—G. Wissowa (éd.), Realencyclopaedie der classischen Altertumswissenschaft
R.E.L.	Revue des Etudes Latines
R.H.R.	Revue de l'Histoire des Religions
St.Etr.	Studi Etruschi
T.A.P.A.	Transactions and Proceedings of the American Philological Association

[1] Cette contribution ne prétend pas à l'exhaustivité: d'une part, le trop court délai qui nous a été imparti pour mener à bien cette recherche ne le permettait pas; d'autre part, la bibliographie est fort abondante. Nous avons donc tenté de mettre en évidence certaines publications qui nous paraissaient renouveler l'optique d'une question ou apporter des données nouvelles.

[2] P. K. Buttmann, Mythologus, I, Berlin, 1828, p. 22ss.; J. A. Hartung, Die Religion der Römer, II, Erlangen, 1836, p. 62; L. Preller—H. Jordan, Römische Mythologie, I, 3e

comparaient, phonétiquement, *Dione* et *Iuno* : *Iuppiter* et *Iuno* formaient un couple équivalant à celui de Zeus et Dioné.

En 1904, W. SCHULZE établit l'indépendance de *Iuno* et de la racine *Diovi-*[3]. L'année suivante, W. OTTO conteste tout lien étymologique entre *Iuppiter* et *Iuno* et propose de voir en Junon une déesse infernale dont le nom serait formé sur le radical de *iuuenis* et que l'on pourrait dès lors traduire par „*junge Frau*"[4]. Les anciens, Varron, Cicéron, Plutarque, avaient déjà rapproché le nom de *Iuno* de *īuuando* ou de *iuuenescendo*[5], mais Plutarque attribue ce rapport avec *iuuenescendo* à la nature de la nouvelle lune croissante; Junon, dans leur optique, demeurait donc déesse lunaire. En 1912, WISSOWA[6] adhéra à la nouvelle étymologie tandis que d'autres la contestaient encore ou persistaient à défendre la relation Jupiter-Junon[7]. Pourtant, comme l'a rappelé tout récemment R. E. A. PALMER[8], la forme étrusque du nom de *Iuno*, *Uni*, récuse tout rapprochement avec **diouin-*, car elle est due − tout comme *Ani*, issu de *Ianus*[9] − à la chute d'un *i-* (ou d'un *y-*) initial et non d'un *di-*. Finalement, nombreux furent les historiens qui adoptèrent la théorie de SCHULZE et OTTO[10]. Mais tout n'était pas expliqué.

éd., Berlin, 1881, p. 271; W. H. ROSCHER, Studien zur vergleichenden Mythologie der Griechen und Römer. II: Juno und Hera, Leipzig, 1875, p. 43; ID., Lex., II,1, 1890−7, art. Iuno, col. 578−9; G. WISSOWA, dans la première édition de: Religion und Kultus der Römer, Handb. d. klass. Altertumswiss., V, 4, Munich, 1902, p. 113−4, analysait encore *Iuno* en tant que *Iouino* formé sur *Iou-*.

[3] W. SCHULZE, Zur Geschichte lateinischer Eigennamen, Abhandlungen der Königlichen Gesellschaft der Wissenschaften zu Göttingen, Philologisch-historische Klasse, V, 2, Berlin, 1904, p. 470−1.

[4] W. F. OTTO, Iuno. Beiträge zum Verständnisse der ältesten und wichtigsten Thatsachen ihres Kultes, dans: Philologus, 64, 1905, p. 161−223 = IDEM, Aufsätze zur römischen Religionsgeschichte, Beiträge zur klassischen Philologie, 71, Meisenheim am Glan, 1975, p. 1−63, spéc. p. 17s. et p. 60s.

[5] Varron, L.L., 5, 67 et 69; Cic., N.D., 2, 66; Plut., Qu. Rom., 77.

[6] G. WISSOWA, R. u. K. d. R., Handb. d. klass. Altertumswiss., V, 4, 2e éd., Munich, 1912, p. 181−2.

[7] A. ZIMMERMANN, Zur Etymologie des Namens Juno, dans: Wochenschr. für klass. Philol., 36, 1905, p. 990−2; J. WHATMOUGH, The Iouilae Dedications from S. Maria di Capua, dans: Class. Quart., 16, 1922, p. 181ss. Défenseurs de la relation Jupiter − Junon: W. WARDE FOWLER, dans: J. HASTINGS, Encyclopedia of Religion and Ethics, X, 1918, art. Roman Religion, p. 825; à sa suite, E. L. SHIELDS, Juno. A Study in Early Roman Religion, Northampton, Massachusetts, 1926, p. 6 et passim, où l'on trouvera également la bibliographie antérieure; H. USENER, Götternamen. Versuch einer Lehre von der religiösen Begriffsbildung, Francfort, 1948, 3e éd. (simple réimpression).

[8] R. E. A. PALMER, Roman Religion and Roman Empire. Five Essays, The Haney Foundation Series, 15, Univ. of Pennsylvania, Philadelphia, 1974, p. 4; cf. aussi G. RADKE, Die Götter Altitaliens, Fontes et Commentationes. Schriftenreihe des Instituts für Epigraphik an der Universität Münster, 3, Münster, 1965, p. 152−155. Contra: J. WHATMOUGH, op. cit. et E. L. SHIELDS, op. cit.

[9] C. THULIN, Die Götter des Martianus Capella und der Bronzeleber von Piacenza, Religionsgeschichtl. Versuche und Vorarbeiten, 3, Giessen, 1906, p. 22ss.

[10] H. EHRLICH, Zur Mythologie. I: Juno, dans: Zeitschr. für Vergl. Sprachforschung, 41, 1907, p. 283ss.; K. BRUGMANN, Senex Iuuenis, dans: Archiv für lat. Lex., 15, 1908, p. 4s.; G. GIANNELLI, Juno, dans: Mem. R. Ist. Lombardo, 23 = 14 (sér. III), 1915, p. 174; C.

Grâce aux études d'E. Benveniste[11], M. Renard[12] et G. Dumézil[13] on peut aller plus avant et éclairer la nature de Junon. Le rapprochement établi par E. Benveniste entre le nom indo-européen de la «durée» et les mots du type *iuuenis* permet de mieux préciser encore le sens du nom de Junon et la nature essentielle de ses fonctions. En effet, le thème **yuwen-* comprend la racine **yu-* au degré zéro et le suffixe *-wen-*[14]. Or le sens initial de cette racine **yu-* est celui de «force vitale» que l'on retrouve dans le védique *áyuh* «force vitale», gén. *áyusah*, loc. *áyuni; āyúh* «génie de la force vitale» et aussi dans le grec αἰών «durée féconde» et le latin *aeuum*.

Un *iuuenis* est donc un être en possession de toute sa force vitale. Et pour M. Renard[15], Junon «a été primitivement le *numen* de la force de vie dans ce que cette force a de fécond et de durable». Quant à G. Dumézil, il s'interroge sur ce que «Jūnō met, ou a d'abord mis en évidence: la simple notion abstraite de jeunesse? la force vitale ou le moral pétulant des jeunes? Les jeunes comme classe d'âge, comme division sociale? Il n'est pas possible de décider, et l'existence d'une *Iuuentas* personnifiée, sans doute plus récente, ne simplifie pas les choses»[16].

Reste encore le problème de la flexion en *-o, -onis*, elle n'est pas unique comme le pensait Otto[17]. G. Dumézil[18] et R. E. A. Palmer[19] font remarquer qu'elle n'est pas courante au féminin. Palmer songe aux cas analogues de *Ceres* et de *Venus* (un nom neutre à l'origine, dont le genre a changé) et il imagine une origine semblable pour *Iuno "a *iuveno, meant merely deity of youth(fulness), without assigning that physical state to men or women"*.[20]

Ces considérations étymologiques nous amènent tout naturellement à nous interroger sur la valeur propre de la déesse Junon. Voilà bien, selon G. Dumézil, «l'une des questions les plus difficiles de la théologie des peuples latins, l'une de

Thulin, dans: R.E., X,1, 1917, art. Iuno, col. 1114s.; N. Turchi, La religione di Roma antica, Storia di Roma, XVIII, Istituto di Studi Romani, Bologne, 1939, p. 168; A. Walde—J. B. Hofmann, Lateinisches etymologisches Wörterbuch I³, Indogerman. Bibliothek I,2,1, Heidelberg, 1938, art. Iuno. Pour l'histoire de la controverse, cf. Shields, op. cit., p. 3—11 et V. Basanoff, Evocatio. Etude d'un rituel militaire romain, Bibl. Ecole des Hautes Etudes, 61, Paris, 1947, p. 6 s.

[11] E. Benveniste, Origines de la formation des noms indo-européens, Paris, 1935, p. 110s.; Id., Expression indo-européenne de l'éternité, dans: Bull. Soc. Linguistiq. Paris, 38, 1937, p. 103—112. Toutefois, R. Schilling, Janus. Le dieu introducteur, le dieu des passages, dans: M.E.F.R.(A.), 72, 1960, p. 106, n.1, rapporte une lettre d'E. Benveniste où il lui écrit qu'il doute de la possibilité d'un rapprochement entre *Iuno* et la famille *iuuenis*.

[12] M. Renard, Le nom de Junon, dans: Phoibos, 5, Bruxelles, 1950—1 (= Mél. J. Hombert), p. 141—3.

[13] G. Dumézil, La religion romaine archaïque, 2e éd., Paris, 1974, p. 299—300.

[14] E. Benveniste, Origines de la formation des noms indo-européens, p. 110s.

[15] M. Renard, op. cit., p. 142.

[16] G. Dumézil, Rel. rom. arch.², p. 210—211, 299—300.

[17] W. F. Otto, op. cit., p. 61—2.

[18] G. Dumézil, Rel. rom. arch.², p. 299.

[19] R. E. A. Palmer, Roman Religion . . ., p. 4.

[20] R. E. A. Palmer, ibidem.

celles qui paraissent le plus irrémédiablement abandonnées aux préférences des écoles, aux inspirations des savants »[21].

Au XIXe siècle, on reconnaissait en Junon, apparentée à Jupiter, une déesse céleste; la lumière venant des ténèbres et la naissance amenant au jour, on expliquait ainsi que, divinité du ciel, elle était devenue en un second temps déesse des femmes et de la naissance[22]. La nouvelle étymologie admise, on vit en Junon (*„die Jugendliche"*)[23] une déesse féminine, un type de déesse-mère, fécondante et chthonienne[24]. De là, le problème qui se pose à V. BASANOFF: comment établir une « délimitation des zones entre la déesse indo-européenne du ciel lumineux et la déesse au serpent et à la chèvre »[25]. Pour très longtemps, seules les fonctions féminines de la déesse devaient apparaître comme caractéristiques de la Junon romaine[26].

En 1948, P. NOAILLES apportait un correctif et mettait en cause un des aspects majeurs de la Junon romaine, déesse des femmes: « l'Héra grecque n'a pas été sans influence sur la vocation de Junon à devenir la déesse matrimoniale des Romains »[27]. ROSCHER[28] et ALTHEIM[29] entrevoient cette influence hellénique dès l'époque ancienne, quand, – à la faveur de l'ascendant étrusque, – fut introduite la triade capitoline protectrice de la cité. Mais l'influence grecque « a été plus grande à l'époque classique, lorsque l'Olympe grec eut conquis le panthéon romain »[30]. « Si c'est parce qu'elle est l'épouse qu'elle est la déesse du mariage à Rome et si cette vocation n'y est pas originaire, c'est que, sans doute, elle n'y a pas protégé les noces avant que Jupiter ne soit lui-même devenu le dieu protecteur de la cité »[31].

A part cela, et il faut y revenir, les virtualités de fécondité et de maternité de la Junon latine sont réelles et originelles. « La maternité de Junon est partout présente »[32]. Mais, si cet aspect est essentiel, il n'est pas unique. On le sait et on

---

[21] G. DUMÉZIL, Iuno S.M.R., dans: Eranos, 52, 1954, p. 111.

[22] Cf. SHIELDS, Juno, p. 3 et notre note 2.

[23] W. F. OTTO, op. cit., p. 60ss.; EHRLICH, op. cit., p. 283ss.; WISSOWA, R.u.K. d. R.², p. 181, etc.

[24] Les Anciens parvenaient à intégrer cette nature chthonienne au sein de la relation Jupiter – Junon: selon les principes stoïciens, les principales divinités sont le ciel et la terre. Jupiter est le ciel ou l'air, Junon, sa femme, est la terre: cf. H. J. ROSE, Ancient Roman Religion, Londres, 1948, p. 110.

[25] V. BASANOFF, Evocatio, p. 73. Rappelons ici la réserve de G. DUMÉZIL, Jupiter, Mars, Quirinus³, Paris, 1941, p. 146: « Nous ne pouvons certes accepter de voir dans les ʽcultes chthoniensʼ de Rome la survivance exclusive du substrat méditerranéen, alors que les Indo-Européens n'auraient apporté en propre que ʽle culte du cielʼ».

[26] ROSE, op.cit., p. 63, 68–9; K. LATTE, Römische Religionsgeschichte, Handb. d. Altertumswiss., V, 4, Munich, 1960, p. 168.

[27] P. NOAILLES, Junon, déesse matrimoniale des Romains, dans: IDEM, Fas et Ius. Etude de droit romain, Coll. d'Et. Anc., Paris, 1948, p. 33–4, 43.

[28] ROSCHER, Juno und Hera, p. 62.

[29] F. ALTHEIM, Römische Religionsgeschichte, II, Berlin–Leipzig, 1932, p. 59–60.

[30] P. NOAILLES, Junon, déesse matrimoniale des Romains, p. 33.

[31] P. NOAILLES, op. cit., p. 43.

[32] M. RENARD, Le nom de Junon, p. 143.

le verra, certaines Junons – du Latium et de l'Etrurie, car c'est moins perceptible à Rome – peuvent afficher une vocation militaire et exercer un patronage politique. Comment les auteurs adeptes de la Junon des femmes concilient-ils ces virtualités antinomiques? Certains auteurs envisagent une influence de l'Héra argienne, déesse polyvalente, féconde, guerrière et politique[33]. D'autres admettent l'idée d'un développement spontané, ainsi K. Latte: „*daß die Göttin zunächst als Frauengöttin für die Vermehrung der Bevölkerung und damit auch für die kriegerische Macht der Gemeinde angerufen wurde*"[34].

Ces tentatives d'explication par accroissement de potentialités nous semblent artificielles et nous partageons les vues de G. Dumézil quand il écrit: «On souhaiterait connaître au moins un autre cas où la protection de la fécondité féminine aurait ainsi évolué en ardeur militaire et en patronage politique»[35]. Il propose lui-même une solution éclairante que R. Bloch accepte[36] et à laquelle nous adhérons. Dès les origines, Junon est multivalente, «trivalente» même: féconde, guerrière, politique. Ces trois aspects – son côté guerrier est peu apparent à Rome (cf. infra) – seraient fondamentalement irréductibles et c'est leur réunion même qui caractériserait la déesse réalisant en sa personne la synthèse des trois fonctions[37]. La Junon *Seispes, Mater, Regina* de Lanuvium est l'expression théologique la plus claire de cette trivalence. Cette titulature lanuvienne «donne le premier rang à la deuxième fonction, à Junon en tant que protectrice armée et combattante: ne serait-ce pas là le centre germinatif de la déesse? On s'expliquerait ainsi son nom qui la rattache sûrement aux *iuuenes*, aux *iuniores* des sociétés italiques»[38]. Car, selon notre auteur, le radical *iuuen-* sur

---

[33] G. Giannelli, Culti e miti della Magna Grecia. Contributo alla storia più antica delle colonie greche in Occidente, Florence, 1924, p. 165–170 (2e éd., Univ. Napoli, Centro di Studi per la Magna Grecia, 2, Naples, 1963), ouvrage utilisé par J. Bayet, Les origines de l'Hercule romain, Bibliothèque des Ecoles Franç. Athènes et Rome, Fasc. 132, Paris, 1926, p. 75, 115, 170–1, qui semble accepter l'existence d'une Junon guerrière latine assimilée dans un second temps à l'Héra Argienne; J. Bérard, Les origines historiques et légendaires de Posidonia à la lumière des récentes découvertes archéologiques, dans: Mél. Ec. Fr. Rome, 57, 1940, p. 21; Id., La colonisation grecque de l'Italie méridionale et de la Sicile dans l'Antiquité. L'histoire et la légende, Public. Fac. Lettres Paris, 4, Paris, 1957, p. 400, 474; A. Grenier, Les religions étrusque et romaine, dans: Les Religions de l'Europe Ancienne, III, Coll. Mana. Intr. à l'Hist. des Religions, 2, Paris, 1948, p. 139.

[34] K. Latte, Röm. Religionsgesch., p. 168; Rose, op. cit., p. 69, se contente de considérer les aspects guerriers de la déesse comme anormaux et marginaux.

[35] G. Dumézil, Rel. rom. arch.², p. 306.

[36] R. Bloch, Interpretatio. II: Héra, Uni, Junon en Italie centrale, dans: Recherches sur les Religions de l'Italie Antique, Centre de Recherches d'Histoire et de Philologie de la IVe Sect. de l'Ec. Prat. Hautes Et., III, Hautes Etudes du Monde Gréco-Romain, 7, Genève, 1976, p. 15.

[37] G. Dumézil, Rel. rom. arch.², p. 307ss.

[38] Sur la Junon de Lanuvium, on consultera, à côté de l'article de G. Dumézil, Iuno S.M.R., dans: Eranos, 52, 1954, p. 105–119, l'étude très complète de A. E. Gordon, The Cults of Lanuvium, Univ. of California Publications in Classical Archaeology, II,2, Berkeley, 1938, p. 21–58; spéc. p. 23–37 consacrées à *Iuno Sospita*; p. 24–25 (notes 22–26) sur les inscriptions (dates et titulature); p. 33–34 (notes 64–71) sur les monnaies; p. 26–32, sur

lequel est formé *Iuno* est orienté non pas vers la fécondité, mais plutôt vers la vitalité vigoureuse, agissante c'est-à-dire vers les *iuuenes* non vers les *matres*[39].

R. E. A. PALMER, dans un chapitre complexe consacré à 'Juno in Archaic Italy'[40], développe une hypothèse analogue à celle de G. DUMÉZIL — sans jamais citer le comparatiste français[41]. Il insiste sur l'importance de la Junon guerrière, sans toutefois tomber dans l'erreur des tenants de la thèse de la féminité: Junon n'a pu être originellement une déesse de la guerre et de l'Etat, car une déesse de la guerre ne peut devenir divinité du mariage pas plus que le contraire. Et PALMER de poursuivre: *"The sense of iuno that fits all circumstances is the deity or spirit of youthfulness. After all, both women and men dwell on the retention of their youth. At war, Juno protected the man eligible to bear arms, the iuvenis, a word often used for soldier; thence she assumed the function of the tutelary deity of sovereign peoples. For the woman capable of bearing children, Juno from the time of puberty oversaw childbirth and marriage"*[42].

La conception d'une Junon, déesse essentiellement féminine, a contribué à encourager une autre hypothèse, liée à la théorie du *numen*[43]. La grande déesse féminine serait née de la multitude des *iunones* individuelles, expressions, esprits de la nature féconde de chaque femme[44]. Pourtant si le *genius* des hommes est déjà attesté chez Plaute[45], on ne rencontre pas la mention d'une *iuno* de chaque femme avant Tibulle[46]. ROSE, en l'absence de témoignages anciens, doute de l'antiquité de la *iuno*[47]. Pour témoigner de l'antiquité de la *iuno* féminine, K. LATTE, en dernier lieu, rappelle la *Iuno Deae Diae* du rituel des Arvales[48]; d'époque impériale, ce rituel a pu subir des modifications modernisantes au

les fouilles. Cet auteur corrige notamment la thèse proposée en 1913 par Miss E. M. DOUGLAS, Iuno Sospita of Lanuvium, dans: J. R. S., 3, 1913, p. 61–72, qui reconnaissait en *Iuno Sospita* une déesse italienne indigène, déesse-mère assez barbare dont les virtualités se seraient accrues au cours de son développement et dont le culte évolua sous les influences étrusque et hellénique. On verra aussi A. GALIETI, Intorno al culto di 'Iuno Sispita Mater Regina' in Lanuvium, dans: Bull. Comm. Archeol. Com. Roma, 44, 1916, p. 3–36 et J. C. HOFKES-BRUKKER, Iuno Sospita, dans: Hermeneus, 27, 1956, p. 161–169.

[39] G. DUMÉZIL, Iuno S.M.R., p. 105–119, spéc. p. 118, n.2.

[40] R. E. A. PALMER, Roman Religion . . ., p. 3–56.

[41] Il s'agit d'un parti pris, car PALMER écrivait dans: The archaic Community of the Romans, Cambridge, 1970, p. X: *"Finally, I have all but ignored the many years of work by G. Dumézil, for it seems founded on no Roman evidence whatsoever where it touches on subjects treated here."*

[42] R. E. A. PALMER, Roman Religion . . ., p. 39.

[43] Sur le *numen*, cf. G. DUMÉZIL, Rel. rom. arch.², p. 37–48.

[44] W. F. OTTO, op. cit., p. 19; WISSOWA, R. u. K. d. R.², p. 182; N. TURCHI, La religione di Roma antica, p. 169; V. BASANOFF, Les dieux des Romains, Coll. Mythes et Religions, Paris, 1943, p. 38; A. GRENIER, Les religions étrusque et romaine, p. 115; M. RENARD, Le nom de Junon, p. 142; K. LATTE, Röm. Religionsgesch., p. 105.

[45] Plaute, Stich., 622; Pers., 263; Aul., 724–6; Capt., 879; Curc., 301; Men., 138.

[46] Tibulle, 3, 19, 15 et 3, 6, 48.

[47] ROSE, op. cit., p. 45–6.

[48] K. LATTE, Röm. Religionsgesch., p. 105; cf. W. HENZEN, Acta fratrum Arvalium quae supersunt, Berlin, 1874, 144.

moment où Auguste restaura les cérémonies et les rites du passé. Or, à l'époque d'Auguste, la *iuno* des femmes équilibrait bien le *genius* des hommes[49]. G. Dumézil combat le processus d'une *Iuno* issue de l'ensemble des *iunones* parce qu'il «n'a aucun appui dans les faits et, en soi, n'est pas vraisemblable: des *Genii* multiples, par exemple, s'est-il jamais dégagé un dieu appelé Genius?»[50]. Wissowa[51] dont les arguments sont repris notamment par Turchi[52], répondait anticipativement à G. Dumézil: la vie, globale, de la femme, diffère de celle de l'homme partagée entre diverses activités politiques, guerrières, agricoles; de même, Junon, au contraire du *Genius*, est devenue une représentation divine unitaire, une grande déesse des fonctions féminines. Si l'on admet que Junon intervient, nous le verrons, dans les affaires politiques et militaires, l'explication de Wissowa devient caduque.

II. Iuno Lucina

Nous examinerons d'abord les cultes de Junon déesse de la fécondité et des femmes, et les études qu'ils suscitèrent. Le plus célèbre est celui de *Iuno Lucina*. Les anciens déjà étaient partagés entre deux explications étymologiques de *Lucina*. Le temple de la déesse s'élevait sur le Cispius dans un bois qui lui était consacré (*lucus*), ainsi Pline dérive l'épithète de la déesse du *lucus*[53]. D'autres, tels que Varron[54], considéraient *Iuno Lucina* comme une déesse de la lumière (*lux*) à laquelle elle amenait les nouveaux-nés. Tout comme les Anciens, les modernes demeurent divisés entre ces deux solutions[55]. Une minorité adhère à la solution de Pline. Ernout-Meillet admettent la possibilité de rapprocher *Lūcina* et *lūcus*[56]. R. E. A. Palmer, adversaire quasi systématique des fonctions féminines de Junon, soutient la filiation *lucus* > *Lucina* et minimise la part des femmes dans le culte à la déesse[57].

---

[49] G. Dumézil, Rel. rom. arch.², p. 300. A cette époque, «à Délos comme à Pompéi nous trouvons couramment le *genius* du père de famille et la *juno* de la maîtresse de maison, associés autour de l'autel familial aux Pénates et aux Lares.» A. Grenier, Le génie romain dans la religion, la pensée et l'art, Paris, 1925, p. 451.

[50] G. Dumézil, Rel. rom. arch.², p. 300.

[51] Wissowa, R. u. K. d. R.², p. 182.

[52] Turchi, op. cit., p. 169.

[53] Pline, N.H., 16, 235; avant lui, Ovide, Fastes, 2, 435–6; 449.

[54] Varron, L.L., 5, 69; Cic., N.D., 2, 68; Ov., Fastes, 2, 450; 3, 255; Plut., Qu. Rom., 77; les témoignages anciens sur *Lucina* sont cités par Thulin, dans: R.E., X,1, 1918, art. Iuno. col. 1115–6.

[55] Cf. Radke, Die Götter Altitaliens, art. Lucina.

[56] A. Ernout–A. Meillet, D.E., art. lucus; hésitation chez Y.-M. Duval, Les Lupercales, Junon et le printemps, dans: Annales de Bretagne, 83, 2, 1976, p. 258–9.

[57] R. E. A. Palmer, Roman Religion, p. 19–21; M. Leumann, Zwei lateinische Wortbedeutungen: Lucina und bubo, dans: Die Sprache, 6, 1960, p. 156ss. et Id., Lateinische Laut- und Formenlehre 1955–1962, dans: Glotta, 42, 1964, p. 112, estime lui aussi que

La majorité des modernes relient *Lucina* à *lux*, mais les conséquences qu'ils tirent de cette étymologie diffèrent. Au XIXe siècle, dans la tradition de la Junon céleste, l'épithète *Lucina* évoque Junon déesse de la lumière et non encore la symbolique de la venue au jour des nouveaux-nés. Mais comme toutes les déesses de la lumière en général, elle préside à la naissance et aux phénomènes propres à la femme; la lune réglant la gestation, toutes les divinités lunaires sont divinités de l'enfantement[58]. On n'explique plus cette double valeur de Junon par une nature lunaire — qui appartient à Diane[59]; c'est en tant que «force vitale» que Junon favorise le «travail» de la jeune lune comme celui de la parturiente[60].

L'interprétation puerpérale de l'épithète *Lucina* est désormais la mieux admise[61]. Un autre problème se pose; «Diane, qui, tout en passant pour être *opifera* aux femmes, était par excellence *lucifera*, dispensatrice de la lumière astrale, a été confondue avec *Iuno Lucina*, mais cette confusion ne date pas des origines»[62], car primitivement, l'épithète appartient exclusivement à Junon. J. GAGÉ observe ce qui se passait dans les esprits romains à l'époque classique: «. . . dans la poésie latine, dans la vulgate mythologique, on ne sait trop si *Lucina* est un aspect de Junon ou de cette vierge déesse; il semble bien que le doute n'atteignit guère le plan cultuel, où l'on invoque *Iuno Lucina*»[63]. L'invocation ancienne est bien *Iuno Lucina*, on la trouve plusieurs fois dans le théâtre de Plaute

---

l'appellation de *Iuno Lucina* vient de *lucus* et différenciait la déesse de l'Esquilin de celle du Capitole. Ses attributions de déesse assistant aux naissances qui ont fait voir dans *Lucina* une dérivation de *lux* sont secondaires.

[58] Cf. DAREMBERG et SAGLIO, III,1, 1899, art. Juno, p. 683 (HILD); L. PRELLER, Römische Mythologie[3], I, Berlin, 1881, p. 271.

[59] Cf. S. LUNAIS, Recherches sur la Lune, I, Etudes Prélim. aux Relig. Orient. dans l'Empire Rom., 72, Leiden, 1979.

[60] R. SCHILLING, Janus. Le dieu introducteur. Le dieu des passages, dans: M.E.F.R.(A.), 72, 1960, p. 108, article consacré à Janus, mais où les remarques originales concernant Junon sont nombreuses. Article repris dans: R. SCHILLING, Rites, cultes, dieux de Rome, Etudes et Commentaires, 92, Paris, 1979, p. 220ss.

[61] V. BASANOFF, Les dieux des Romains, p. 39; J. BAYET, La religion romaine. Histoire politique et psychologique, Paris, 1976, p. 92; J. GAGÉ, Matronalia. Essai sur les dévotions et les organisations cultuelles des femmes dans l'ancienne Rome, Coll. Latomus, 60, Bruxelles, 1963, p. 73 — l'ouvrage n'est pas spécialement consacré à la fête des *Matronalia*, mais à toutes les manifestations matronales; G. DUMÉZIL, Rel. rom. arch.[2], p. 301.

[62] R. SCHILLING, Janus . . ., p. 106—107; pour *Diana Opifera*, cf. les inscriptions citées par WISSOWA, dans: R.E., V,1, 1903, art. Diana, col. 329. Jadis, on jugeait l'épithète *Lucina* réellement commune à Diane et à Junon, car toutes deux président à l'empire de la lumière nocturne et, en tant que divinités féminines de la lumière, à la naissance et aux phénomènes féminins, cf. J. A. HILD, dans: DAREMBERG et SAGLIO, art. Juno, col. 683; comme le montre R. SCHILLING, Janus . . ., p. 106, n.5: «Le passage de Cicéron (N.D., II, 68), tout en distinguant *Diana lucifera* de *Iuno Lucina*, montre le glissement de sens qui a fait confondre *lucifera* («qui dispense la lumière») et *lucina* («qui met au jour»): *Dianam autem et lunam eandem esse putant, cum . . . luna a lucendo nominata sit. Eadem est Lucina. Itaque, ut apud Graecos Dianam eamque Luciferam, sic apud nostros Iunonem Lucinam in pariendo inuocant.*

[63] J. GAGÉ, Matronalia, p. 73.

et de Térence. Les poètes influencés par Artémis Eileithyia s'adressent de préférence à Diane pour cet office, mais il est significatif que Catulle, tout en s'adressant à Diane, l'appelle encore *Iuno Lucina*[64].

Iuno Lucina est particulièrement à l'honneur aux *Matronalia femineae kalendae* du 1er mars, *dies natalis* de son temple de l'Esquilin dédié en 375[65]. Les fondations junoniennes sont toujours rapportées à des Calendes, car elles lui étaient consacrées (cf. infra)[66]. Mais le 1er mars est aussi l'ancien jour de l'An neuf auquel Mars était fortement associé. Ainsi, à l'époque classique, les Calendes de Mars étaient marquées par deux fêtes, l'une en l'honneur de Mars, mobilisant les hommes; l'autre, en l'honneur de Junon, matronale par définition[67]. Les explications de la fête font état de la naissance de Romulus[68] ou de l'éveil printanier de la fécondité[69].

Le temple de *Lucina* fut dédié par les matrones en 375, dans le bois sacré de la déesse sur l'Esquilin, déjà fréquenté précédemment par les matrones et sans doute voué à Junon[70]. D'après Varron, le bois sacré de *Iuno Lucina* était voisin de celui de *Mefitis*, sinon commun aux deux divinités[71]. Dès lors, pour J. GAGÉ — après d'amples développements — «si quelque culte indigène et local a devancé sur l'*area* du Cispius, dès le Ve siècle par exemple, le temple de *Iuno Lucina*, comme on aurait le droit de le supposer a priori, il aurait pu être rendu (. . .) à un couple de nymphes cathartiques, plus tard divisé entre une *Mefitis* et une *Lucina*»[72]. Or le culte de *Lucina* a pu entretenir certains rapports avec celui de Méfitis, déesse des émanations sulfureuses. Les dédicaces lucaniennes de Rossano di Vaglio qui mettent en évidence un nouveau lien entre Méfitis et Caprotine[73] viennent confirmer cette hypothèse qui ne manque peut-être pas d'une certaine

---

[64] R. SCHILLING, Janus . . ., p. 106—7, n. 5; Horace, Odes, 3, 22, 1s.; sur l'influence grecque, cf. JESSEN, dans: R.E., V, 2, 1905, art. Eileithyia, col. 2109; Catulle, 34, 13s.

[65] Juvenal, 5, 93; J. GAGÉ, Matronalia, p. 66—80; G. DUMÉZIL, Rel. rom. arch.[2], p. 301—302.

[66] R. SCHILLING, Janus . . ., p. 107; G. DUMÉZIL, Rel. rom. arch.[2], p. 302.

[67] J. GAGÉ, Matronalia, p. 66—7.

[68] Ovide, Fastes, 3, 233.

[69] Ibidem, 235—244.

[70] G. DUMÉZIL, Rel. rom. arch.[2], p. 301; R. E. A. PALMER, Roman Religion, p. 21.

[71] Varron, L.L., 5, 49.

[72] J. GAGÉ, Matronalia, p. 80.

[73] M. LEJEUNE, Notes de linguistique italique, XXIII: Le culte de Méfitis à Rossano di Vaglio, dans: R.E.L., 45, 1967, p. 202—221. Il s'agit d'inscriptions osques de graphie grecque, des IIIe—IIe siècles, où se manifestent les premiers signes de la romanisation, particulièrement l'emprunt au latin des noms de Vénus et, semble-t-il, de Caprotine. Ces documents mettent en évidence un nouveau lien entre Méfitis et Caprotine. Inscription n° 06 (= n° de l'édition de M. LEJEUNE, dans: Mem. Lincei, sér. VIII, 16, 1971, p. 47ss.; R. Lincei, sér. VIII, 26, 1971, p. 663ss.); interprétation proposée: [μ]εfίτηι/καπορotινν-(ιαις), «A Méfitis, le jour de la fête de Caprotine». Cf. aussi R. LAZZERONI, Contatti di lingue e di culture nell' Italia antica: i dati delle iscrizioni posteriori alla Silloge di E. Vetter, dans: La Cultura Italica, Atti del Convegno della Società Italiana di Glottologia, Pisa, 1977, Orientamenti Linguistici, 5, Pise, 1978.

audace. Par ailleurs, Ovide[74] rapporte un épisode oraculaire lié au culte de *Lucina* dans son *lucus* de l'Esquilin — sans négliger la possibilité que cet oracle, et ses suites, servant d'*aition* aux Lupercales (cf. infra), peut aussi avoir lieu par l'intermédiaire de Faunus[75]. Les Sabines, frappées de stérilité, se rendirent au bois sacré pour prier la déesse. Il y avait dans le *lucus* un arbre oraculaire[76], et dans un bruissement de feuilles l'on entendit ces mots:

Italidas matres sacer hircus inito.

Un augure interpréta l'oracle de façon moins littérale et l'on soumit les Sabines à une flagellation appliquée au moyen de lanières taillées dans la peau d'un bouc. Ce remède mit fin à leur stérilité.

Selon E. GJERSTAD[77], ce récit étiologique, où interviennent arbre sacré et bouc, permet clairement d'identifier *Iuno Lucina* à la divinité au figuier et à la chèvre des Lupercales et des Nones Caprotines[78] — auxquelles nous nous intéresserons bientôt. V. BASANOFF ne limite pas, lui non plus, le rôle de *Iuno Lucina* à celui d'une adjuvante des parturientes. Tout comme E. GJERSTAD, il la

---

[74] Ovide, Fastes, 2, 425—452:

> *Nupta, quid expectas? Non tu pollentibus herbis*
> *nec prece nec magico carmine mater eris;*
> *excipe fecundae patienter uerbera dextrae,*
> *iam socer optatum nomen habebit aui.*
> *Nam fuit illa dies, dura cum sorte maritae*
> *reddebant uteri pignora rara sui . . .*
> *Monte sub Esquilio multis incaeduus annis*
> *Iunonis magnae nomine lucus erat.*
> *Huc ubi uenerunt, pariter nuptaeque uirique*
> *suppliciter posito procubuere genu,*
> *cum subito motae tremuere cacumina siluae*
> *et dea per lucos mira locuta suos.*
> *„Italidas matres" inquit, „sacer hircus inito".*
> *Obstipuit dubio territa turba sono.*
> *Augur erat nomen longis intercidit annis:*
> *nuper ab Etrusca uenerat exul humo;*
> *Ille caprum mactat; iussae sua terga puellae*
> *pellibus exsectis percutienda dabant.*
> *Luna resumebat decimo noua cornua motu,*
> *uirque pater subito nuptaque mater erat.*
> *Gratia Lucinae! dedit haec tibi nomina lucus,*
> *aut quia principium tu, dea, lucis habes.*
> *Parce, precor, grauidis, facilis Lucina, puellis,*
> *maturumque utero molliter aufer onus.*

[75] A. BRELICH, Tre variazioni sul tema delle origini. II: I primi re latini, Univ. Roma Pubblic. Scuola St. Storico-Religiosi, 2, Nuovi Saggi, 14, Rome, 1955, p. 59 s.

[76] Il ne s'agit pas d'un figuier comme aux Nones Caprotines, mais plutôt d'un orme, cf. Pline, N.H., 16, 235 et E. GJERSTAD, Early Rome, V, The Written Sources, Acta Inst. Rom. Regn. Sueciae, 17, 5, Lund, 1973, p. 30.

[77] E. GJERSTAD, Early Rome, V, p. 30—31.

[78] Identifications parmi lesquelles s'intégreraient parfaitement les données épigraphiques de Rossano di Vaglio.

relie à « l'ombre divine de la grotte du Cermalus », à cette force vivante du rituel fertilisant des Luperques[79].

Il nous semble heureux de ne pas confiner, dès l'origine, *Iuno Lucina* dans ce rôle d'auxiliaire lors des accouchements, mais « il est difficile », observe J. GAGÉ, « dans les cultes féminins de ce genre, de distinguer nettement, parmi les compétences de la déesse, entre celles dont dépend la fécondité, et celles qui veillent sur la délivrance »[80]. Pourtant dès une époque relativement ancienne − selon GAGÉ au IVe siècle, − *Iuno Lucina* tendit spécialement à devenir patronne des parturientes, assumant les attributions de l'Eileithyia des Grecs[81]. M. ELIADE a noté de semblables évolutions de rites de fécondation en rites d'accouchement[82].

III. Les Lupercales

La fête des Lupercales du 15 février a été l'objet, ces dernières années, de controverses et d'études intéressantes. On reconnaît généralement dans la course des Luperques qui parcourent la ville en flagellant les femmes avec des lanières en peau de bouc, un rite où se mêlent intentions purificatrice et fécondante. D. PORTE a donné en 1973 un article en marge de l'opinion la plus couramment reçue[83]. Notre auteur conteste la logique d'un symbolisme de fécondation le 15 février, c'est-à-dire en plein mois de clôtures et quinze jours avant la symbolique de l'accouchement[84] − le 1er mars, fête de *Lucina* qui, pourtant, nous l'avons vu, intéresse la fécondité toute entière. Elle insiste exclusivement

---

[79] V. BASANOFF, Evocatio, p. 74; selon cet auteur (ibidem, p. 76), et nous ne le suivons pas, ce côté fécondant de la déesse n'appartient pas à son passé indo-européen, il résulte de l'assimilation à une divinité méditerranéenne dont elle gardera parfois des attributs. Sur les limites du fond religieux « méditerranéen », cf. les remarques de G. PUGLIESE CARRATELLI, Culti e dottrine religiose in Magna Grecia, dans: Atti Quarto Conv. Studi sulla Magna Grecia, Taranto, 1964, Naples, 1965, p. 29−30.

[80] J. GAGÉ, Matronalia, p. 73.

[81] Ibidem.

[82] M. ELIADE, Traité d'histoire des religions, Paris, 1977, p. 194, rapporte un exemple grec d'un tel déplacement dans la signification d'un rite: « A Athènes, les femmes enceintes se rendaient sur la colline des Nymphes et se laissaient glisser sur le rocher tout en invoquant Apollon, afin de s'assurer un heureux accouchement (V. HARTLAND, Primitive Paternity. The Myth of Supernatural Birth in Relation to the History of the Family, I, Londres, 1909, p. 130). » C'est là un bon exemple de changement de signification d'un rite, la pierre de fécondation devenant pierre d'accouchement.

[83] D. PORTE, Le devin, son bouc et Junon (Ovide, Fastes, II, 425−452), dans: R.E.L., 51, 1973, p. 171−189. Les principaux textes anciens traitant de la fête des Lupercales sont donnés par D. PORTE, op. cit., p. 172, n. 1. La bibliographie sur les Lupercales est citée par D. PORTE, op. cit., p. 172, n. 2 et par L. FOUCHER, Flagellation et rite de fécondité aux Lupercales, dans: Annales de Bretagne, 83, 2, 1976, p. 273, n. 2; autres informations bibliographiques encore: G. DUMÉZIL, Rel. rom. arch.², p. 352, n. 2.

[84] D. PORTE, op. cit., p. 173.

sur la valeur purificatrice des coups de fouet. Selon D. PORTE, l'orientation des Lupercales vers la fécondité n'est pas antérieure à Auguste qui «remit à l'honneur les Lupercales abandonnées depuis 44, et se soucia grandement de repeuplement et de natalité»[85]. Ovide, rompant avec la tradition antérieure, se fait l'écho de cette propagande impériale et crée le conte lupercalien de *Iuno Lucina* afin qu'il serve d'*aition* aux *Lupercalia*. A partir d'Ovide *Iuno Lucina* se substituerait donc à *Iuno Februlis* indiquée par Verrius Flaccus, son contemporain[86]. Et pourtant, «quoiqu'on en dise, les *Fastes* d'Ovide sont un bon monument de la mythologie romaine»[87]. Cet article fait appel à une logique, à une rationalité peu conciliables avec la pensée religieuse. On lira avec profit les études d' Y.-M. DUVAL et de L. FOUCHER consacrées aux Lupercales qui jugent ainsi l'article de D. PORTE[88]: «Il y a là toute une série d'affirmations qui manquent d'appui ferme et surtout une dissociation excessive de données très souvent conjointes dans les religions antiques»[89]. On reprochera surtout à cette thèse de rendre inconciliables les aspects purificateurs et fécondants du rite.

L. FOUCHER donne une signification plus harmonieuse aux Lupercales: «acte de purification magique qui a pour conséquence d'écarter tout ce qui peut nuire à une heureuse fécondité»[90]. La même idée s'exprime chez Y.-M. DUVAL: «La purification ne vise pas à restaurer un état neutre. La source qui est obstruée et que l'on purifie se met à couler naturellement avec abondance»[91]. Pour lui, février a d'ailleurs davantage pour fonction d'ouvrir une année nouvelle que de terminer la précédente[92].

Quant à G. DUMÉZIL, il résout ce voisinage des contraires que veut nier D. PORTE: aux Lupercales, «... l'équilibre entre le monde réglé ... et le monde sauvage se rompait ... une liaison nécessaire et inquiétante [s'établissait] entre deux mondes, celui des vifs et celui des morts: fin d'hiver, approche du printemps et du "nouvel an" dans le plus ancien comput, ces jours remettaient rituellement en question les cadres même de l'organisation sociale et cosmique.

---

[85] Ibidem, p. 180.

[86] Paul. Fest., De sign. Verb., p. 75 L.

[87] G. DUMÉZIL, Le problème des Centaures. Etude de mythologie comparée indo-européenne, Min. Instr. Publiq. et Beaux-Arts, Ann. Musée Guimet, Bibliothèque d'Etudes, 41, Paris, 1929, p. 197; p. 203.

[88] YVES-MARIE DUVAL, Les Lupercales, Junon et le printemps, dans: Annales de Bretagne, 83, 2, 1976, p. 253-272 et L. FOUCHER, op. cit.

[89] Y.-M. DUVAL, op. cit., p. 258, n. 25.

[90] L. FOUCHER, op. cit., p. 276: La flagellation purifiante et apotropaïque purge les femmes des maux qui peuvent provoquer la stérilité; par exemple, dans le mythe de la stérilité des Sabines, épouses mal acquises, cf. G. DUMÉZIL, Rel. rom. arch.², p. 354, car contrairement à l'opinion de D. PORTE, op. cit., p. 181, la stérilité des Sabines ne nous semble pas invraisemblable.

[91] Y.-M. DUVAL, Des Lupercales de Constantinople aux Lupercales de Rome, dans: R.E.L., 55, 1977, p. 222−270, spéc. p. 266.

[92] Y.-M. DUVAL, Des Lupercales de Constantinople ..., p. 267; cf. aussi A. BRELICH, Tre variazioni sul tema delle origini, p. 72, 99.

Rites de liquidation et rites de préparation s'y mêlaient en se retrempant dans leur source commune: ce qui est au-delà de l'expérience quotidienne »[93].

Quelle place occupe Junon dans cette fête débridée où *Faunus* est partout présent[94]? De ce voisinage de Faunus et de Junon, G. MARTORANA a émis récemment l'hypothèse douteuse d'une hiérogamie[95]. Pour Y.-M. DUVAL, il serait erroné de ne placer à la tête de cette fête qu'un seul dieu − *Dis, Faunus* ou Junon, − mais il s'en tient quant à lui à Junon et nous l'imiterons[96]. Une famille de mots formée sur le verbe *februare* («purifier»)[97] revient souvent dans les notices, elle a notamment déterminé le nom du mois *februarius*[98]. Les anciens appelaient *februum*[99] la peau de bouc dans laquelle on taillait des lanières en vue de constituer le fouet des Luperques (*amiculum Iunonis*)[100]. La *Iuno* de ce jour porte l'epithète *Februalis*, mais, semble-t-il, seulement chez les auteurs savants[101]. Pour D. PORTE, mais aussi pour R. E. A. PALMER [102], la *Iuno Februlis* (ou *Februa, Februata, Februalis*)[103], des Lupercales n'entretient aucun lien avec la fécondité. Et pourtant, *Februlis* nourrit d'excellents rapports avec *Fluonia* : *Februlis* favorisant la délivrance des femmes [104], *Fluonia*, la grossesse[105]. Voici donc une conception un peu étroite de la fécondité qui voudrait que les divinités de la maturation et de la délivrance soient incapables de favoriser la fécondation.

Et *Iuno Lucina*, intervient-elle aux Lupercales? Selon G. DUMÉZIL[106] et L. FOUCHER[107] − en réponse à D. PORTE, qui voit chez Ovide une participation de *Lucina* aux Lupercales qui ne sont pas sa fête, − son rôle au moment des Lupercales, est envisagé seulement dans l'avenir quand le rite aura eu son effet

---

[93] G. DUMÉZIL, Rel. rom. arch.², p. 352.

[94] Ibidem.

[95] G. MARTORANA, Un'ipotesi sui Lupercalia, dans: Studi di storia antica offerti dagli allievi a Eugenio Manni, Rome, 1976, p. 241−258.

[96] Y.-M. DUVAL, Les Lupercales, Junon et le printemps, p. 270.

[97] Jean Lyd., Mens., 4, 20.

[98] Plut., Rom., 21, 7; Ovide, Fastes, 2, 19ss.

[99] Serv., ad Aen., 8, 343; Varron, L.L., 6, 13, traduit *februum* par *purgamentum*.

[100] Paul. Fest., De sign. Verb., p. 75s. L.

[101] Cf. L. FOUCHER, op. cit., p. 277: Paul. Fest., De sign. Verb., p. 75 L.; Mythographi Romani, 3, 3; Martianus Capella, 2, 149.

[102] R. E. A. PALMER, Roman Religion . . ., p. 18−9.

[103] Sur les différentes formes de l'épithète cf. RADKE, Die Götter Altitaliens, art. Februa, Februata.

[104] *Februlis* s'emploit à délivrer les femmes de la membrane placentaire: Mythographi Romani, 3, 3.

[105] *Fluonia* est la déesse qui retient le sang dans le corps pendant la grossesse, Paul. Fest., p. 82 L.; cf. également Mart. Cap., 2, 149; Arnobe, 3, 30. Selon R. E. A. PALMER, Roman Religion . . ., p. 19, *Fluonia* (ou *Fluvionia* ou *Fluvonia*, cf. RADKE, op. cit., art. Fluonia) est déesse d'une rivière, de l'eau courante, *fluvius*. Attribuer à Junon cette épithète, c'est évoquer les purifications de la déesse dans l'eau courante et non son influence sur la menstruation.

[106] G. DUMÉZIL, Le problème des Centaures, p. 217.

[107] L. FOUCHER, op. cit., p. 277.

fécondant, c'est-à-dire quand commence la grossesse. Mais alors quelle serait cette
Junon de l'Esquilin que les Sabines s'en vont consulter dans son bois sacré?
Toutes ces interprétations prennent les textes à la lettre mais en modifient l'esprit.
Un auteur nous semble donner une interprétation satisfaisante, échappant à un
schématisme et à un formalisme abusifs. Y.-M. DUVAL observe que février tout
entier est placé sous le signe de Junon[108]: du 1er février, *dies natalis* du temple de
Iuno Sospita sur le Palatin, au 1er mars, fête des *Matronalia* [109]. G. DUMÉZIL
estimait également qu'entre le 1er février et le 1er mars on assistait à trois fêtes de
«Junons sauvages»[110]. Nous touchons ici à l'essentiel, comme l'écrit Y.-M.
DUVAL[111], quelle que soit l'épithète qu'on lui donne, février est consacré à une
divinité féminine, Junon. Nombreux sont, dès WISSOWA, les auteurs qui notent
des similitudes entre la Junon des Lupercales et la Junon de Lanuvium[112],
essentiellement parce que toutes deux sont en rapport avec la chèvre symbole de
fécondité. Pour Y.-M. DUVAL, c'est *Iuno Sospita* que l'on fête aux *Lupercalia*.
C'est elle encore que l'on retrouve le 1er mars[113]. Nous préférons, quant à nous,
songer à une Junon romaine aux virtualités similaires. Dans cette fête, où les rites
sont les uns purificatoires, les autres fécondants, une incertitude entre deux
dénominations de Junon, − l'une, évoquant la purification (*Februalis*) l'autre, la
fécondité (*Lucina*) − doit-elle surprendre? Comme le suggère Y.-M. DUVAL, en
recourant au passage d'Ovide[114] qui explique la fête des *Matronalia* par un lien
entre Junon et le renouveau du printemps, ce qui est valable pour le 1er mars l'est
aussi pour le 15 février. «Le début d'un nouveau cycle ne peut, dans la mentalité
qui est celle de ces temps anciens, s'opérer sans l'accord de la ou des divinités qui
détiennent l'empire sur cette nature et, par le fait, sur les morts comme sur les
vivants et leurs forces vives. Les cultes et rites de nos fêtes de février tendent tous,
dans leur multiplicité apparente, à cette fin unique, même si le temps et l'évolution
des mentalités l'ont morcelée et diversifiée»[115].

«Purificatoire, fécondante, cette fête avait en outre quelque rapport avec le
pouvoir politique». C'est ainsi que G. DUMÉZIL[116] évoque un dernier aspect des
Lupercales.

Les Anciens ne nous ont laissé à ce sujet aucune information claire, mais cet
aspect inhérent aux rites se dégage pourtant de leur témoignage. A la fin de la
République, les Lupercales donnèrent lieu à cette célèbre manifestation
monarchique au cours de laquelle Antoine offrit la couronne royale à Jules
César[117]. S'agit-il d'une «reconstitution d'une vieille scène, susceptible de flatter
l'imagination nationale et de contrebalancer les préjugés républicains? Et s'il n'en

---

[108] Y.-M. DUVAL, Les Lupercales, Junon et le printemps, p. 255ss.
[109] Ibidem.
[110] G. DUMÉZIL, Le problème des Centaures, p. 209, n. 7.
[111] Y.-M. DUVAL, Les Lupercales, Junon et le printemps, p. 257−8.
[112] WISSOWA, R. u. K. d. R.², p. 185.
[113] Y.-M. DUVAL, Les Lupercales . . ., p. 255ss.
[114] Ovide, Fastes, 3, 235−248.
[115] Y.-M. DUVAL, Les Lupercales . . ., p. 271−2.
[116] G. DUMÉZIL, Le problème des Centaures, p. 219.
[117] Plut., Caes., 61, 2−3; Nicolas de Damas, Caes., 21.

avait pas été ainsi, les spectateurs auraient-ils si rapidement compris le sens politique du geste? »[118]. Sous César encore, l'institution d'une troisième section de Luperques sous le nom de *Luperci Iulii*, au moment où s'installait la dynastie julienne, apparaît comme un acte politique motivé[119]. De même nature encore, le lien puissant et multiple entre les *Lupercalia* et la vie de Romulus, le premier roi[120]. Y.-M. DUVAL a publié récemment une étude tout à fait séduisante, qui éclaire les liens entre Lupercales et pouvoir politique[121]. Partant d'un chapitre du 'Livre des Cérémonies' de Constantin VII Porphyrogénète qui concerne une course de Lupercales à l'hippodrome de Constantinople et qui mentionne un hymne au Printemps, il établit le pont avec les rites du début de notre ère qui mettent en rapport les Lupercales et les diverses activités ou conditions du renouveau printanier. Il apparaît qu'à cette fête le chef en exercice, de Romulus à l'empereur de Constantinople, devait se soumettre à l'acclamation du peuple qui renouvelait son approbation à longueur d'année. Les Lupercales de Constantinople révèlent peut-être la quintessence des Lupercales romaines: elles attestent l'importance agricole et politique d'un événement naturel qui survient à proximité de leur célébration: le printemps. Et Junon? Elle y jouait peut-être un rôle plus complexe qu'on ne le perçoit, en intervenant dans les implications politiques des rites.

IV. Les Nones Caprotines

C'est encore cette divinité liée à la chèvre que l'on retrouve aux Nones Caprotines du 7 juillet dont les rites, écrivait G. DUMÉZIL en 1974, «reposent peut-être sur un mythe perdu de Junon: on ne l'entrevoit même pas »[122]. Depuis, P. DROSSART[123] a donné un article proposant une nouvelle solution à laquelle adhère G. DUMÉZIL qui l'a publiée pour l'essentiel dans ses 'Dix questions romaines'[124]. Cette fête sur laquelle, malgré tout, le jour n'est pas fait, a été l'objet d'autres études, intéressantes mais souvent inconciliables.

[118] G. DUMÉZIL, Le problème des Centaures, p. 221.

[119] Dion Cassius, 44, 6; 45, 30; Denys, 1, 80; cf. G. DUMÉZIL, ibidem.

[120] G. DUMÉZIL, Le problème des Centaures, p. 215 ss. et 221. Cet auteur remarque encore (p. 222, n. 1): «Est- ce aussi un hasard qu' Ovide ait placé en tête du second livre des *Fastes* (*février*) son éloge d'Auguste comme «chef» et son parallèle entre Auguste et Romulus? N'est-ce pas une façon de reprendre (et de réussir) le geste manqué du consul Antoine, de «couronner César» aux *Lupercalia*? »

[121] Y.-M. DUVAL, Des Lupercales de Constantinople aux Lupercales de Rome, dans: R.E.L., 55, 1977, p. 222−270. ID., La victoire de Rémus à la course des Lupercales chez Ovide (Fastes, II, 359−380), dans: Caesarodunum, 7, 1972, p. 201−19.

[122] G. DUMÉZIL, Rel. rom. arch.², p. 72−3.

[123] P. DROSSART, Nonae Caprotinae: La fausse capture des Aurores, dans: R.H.R., 185, 2, 1974, p. 129−139.

[124] G. DUMÉZIL, Fêtes romaines d'été et d'automne suivi de Dix questions romaines. IX: Les Nones Caprotines, Bib. Sc. Humaines, Paris, 1975, p. 271−283.

Avant d'aborder les analyses qui ont été tentées, rappelons-en, comme le fait P. Drossart, le récit étiologique et les rites:

« Les Latins campent sous les murs de la ville, et exigent des Romains qu'ils leur livrent des jeunes filles et des femmes de naissance libre. Peu soucieux de céder à cette exigence, mais incapables de soutenir un siège, les magistrats tergiversent. Une esclave nommée par les uns Philôtis et par les autres Tutula (ou Tutela) leur propose alors de se livrer en otage à la place des femmes libres, avec un certain nombre de ses compagnes dans la fleur de l'âge. Vêtues et parées comme des dames, elles se rendent dans le camp des assiégeants, sous la conduite de Philôtis. Macrobe précise ici que les pseudo-matrones, réparties dans le camp, *uiros plurimo uino prouocauerunt*. Pendant la nuit (νύκτωρ) une fois les hommes endormis, elles leur volent leurs épées. Philôtis se hisse sur un figuier sauvage et brandit un flambeau dont (précise le seul Plutarque) elle dissimule la lumière aux ennemis en déployant de leur côté son manteau (ἱμάτιον, Cam., 33, 5), peut-être même un écran et des tentures (προκαλύμματι καὶ παραπετάσμασιν, Rom., 29, 8). C'est le signal convenu avec les magistrats, à l'insu des autres citoyens. Tirés du sommeil, les Romains font une sortie désordonnée (étiologie des *Poplifugia*), et vont massacrer sans gloire les ennemis toujours endormis. La fête des nones de juillet commémore l'événement. ʿOn la commence en franchissant en foule la porte de la ville et en criant beaucoup de prénoms les plus communs dans le pays . . . pour imiter les soldats qui, dans leur précipitation, s'interpellaient alors les uns les autres. Ensuite les servantes, brillamment parées, se promènent en folâtrant et en lançant des railleries à ceux qu'elles rencontrent. Elles se livrent aussi entre elles une sorte de combat, pour marquer la part qu'elles prirent alors à la lutte contre les Latins. Enfin, elles s'installent et festoient, à l'ombre des branches de figuier. On appelle ce jour les Nones Caprotines, à cause, pense-t-on, du figuier sauvage d'où la jeune esclave éleva sa torche; car le figuier sauvage s'appelle en latin *caprificus*ʾ (Cam., 33, trad. R. Flacelière) »[125].

En 1949, V. Basanoff établit un rapport entre les rites des Nones Caprotines et le rituel d'*euocatio*: « Le danger de l'évocation de la déesse tutélaire – Junon symbolisée par les esclaves, les *iunones* et leur représentante Tutela – est le point central, inévitable et nécessaire dans les circonstances de l'*aition*. » « . . . L'intimation de Postumius Livius réclamant dans son camp les matrones et les jeunes filles, assume un sens particulier. Dans les termes d'un récit historicisé, dont les acteurs sont, par définition, les humains, c'est l'unique moyen d'exprimer le rite d'évocation. Le nom de Tutela en est d'ailleurs garant »[126]. Comme beaucoup, Basanoff reconnaît dans la divinité des Nones, Junon des Lupercales, Junon de Lanuvium. Plus encore, l'arbre, le *caprificus*, dont les fruits évoquent le

---

[125] Cf. P. Drossart, Nonae Caprotinae . . ., p. 130–1; Macr. Sat., 1, 11, 35–40; Plut., Cam., 33; Rom., 29; Varron., L.L., 6, 18.

[126] V. Basanoff, Nonae Caprotinae, dans: Latomus, 8, 1949, p. 209–216; spéc. p. 214–215.

pudendum féminin et le suc laiteux, les seins de la femme, est en rapport direct avec la déesse «non seulement en ce qui concerne la fonction physiologique des organes correspondants, mais encore leurs propriétés religieuses spécifiques. Les seins, comme les *genitalia*, ont des vertus particulières (apotropaïques) dans le ressort de la déesse guerrière protectrice»[127]. Voici un point de vue astucieux, audacieux sans doute. L'auteur nous met en présence d'une divinité sans titulature mais analogue à *Iuno, Seispes, Mater, Regina*, qualifiée dans les trois fonctions de la vieille idéologie indo-européenne, puisque *Iuno Caprotina* serait à la fois guerrière, fécondante, protectrice et tutélaire[128].

E. GJERSTAD donne une explication de la fête uniquement située dans le cadre de la fécondité et placée sous le signe du *caprificus* (figuier sauvage qui, en plus de sa sève laiteuse, a comme particularité de libérer des insectes soucieux de féconder les figuiers des alentours). Cette «caprification» — fécondation des figuiers — avait lieu fin juin et coïncidait, presque, avec le festival de *Iuno Caprotina*. Dès lors la symbolique des rites féminins sous le figuier fécondant est aisée à comprendre. Et l'auteur d'expliquer ces rites par l'identification de Junon avec une ancienne déesse méditerranéene . . .[129].

D. PORTE interprète également ce rituel dans le sens «d'une symbolique de la fécondation féminine»[130]. Son explication utilisant l'étude linguistique de *Caprotina* de M. LEJEUNE[131] peut sembler fantaisiste. «Nous pouvons raisonnablement imaginer à l'origine de la fête, un oracle — en fait, l'auteur invoque pour les Nones Caprotines l'oracle qu'Ovide donne pour *aition* des Lupercales![132] — enjoignant, pratique fort courante dans l'Antiquité, une hiérogamie des femmes avec le bouc sacré»[133], symbolisant la déesse. Mais ce rapport avec le bouc sacré dut se transformer en contact probablement symbolique, avec un *phallus* en figuier[134]. Selon l'auteur, les mots eux-mêmes

---

[127] V. BASANOFF, Nonae Caprotinae, p. 212—3, a montré pour *Iuno Moneta* la valeur apotropaïque des seins. Il en est de même des *genitalia* comme en témoignent des pratiques tardives d'Asie Mineure.

[128] V. BASANOFF, Nonae Caprotinae, p. 214, évoque la situation où les deuxième et troisième fonctions voisinent en la personne des femmes représentatives de Junon: «La fête se déroule au surlendemain des *Poplifugia* (cf. BASANOFF, Regifugium, ch. III: Regifugium et Poplifugia, Paris, 1943). Le *populus*, citoyens en armes, s'était enfui, frappé par la disparition du *rex*, par l'éclipse de la puissance lumineuse de Jupiter. Il ne reste que les *patres* et les femmes. Et, tandis que les *patres* délibèrent, les femmes, représentatives de *Juno*, s'entraînent au cours de la fête dans des combats, se lancent des pierres et des coups, en un mot, mettent en scène le combat, en invoquant par leur langage obscène les images familières et concrètes chargées de la force de la déesse; chacune de ces *iunones* recrée par ses actes la présence de la *Juno*». Selon Y.-M. DUVAL, Les Lupercales, Junon et le printemps, p. 269, n. 87, il y a là «un simulacre de bataille, à fins de fécondité.»

[129] E. GJERSTAD, Early Rome, V, p. 28 ss.

[130] D. PORTE, op. cit., p. 183 ss.

[131] M. LEJEUNE, Notes de linguistique italique. XXII: Caprotina, dans: R.E.L., 45, 1967, p. 194—202.

[132] D. PORTE, op. cit., p. 188.

[133] D. PORTE, op. cit., p. 186.

[134] RADKE, Die Götter Altitaliens, art. Caprotina et Tutula: *Caprotina* dériverait d'un mot signifiant le *phallus*, selon l'auteur, cette étymologie répond bien au caractère obscène des

appellent cette explication (*fircus* = le bouc en sabin[135], *caper, fircus* = le bouc[136], *caprificus* = le figuier): le *hircus inito* de l'oracle d'Ovide aura été transformé par l'augure en *ficus inito*[137]. «Et voilà pourquoi, lors d'une fête dite 'Fête du bouc', les femmes romaines utilisaient des branches de figuier»[138]. Cette exégèse caricature, en les mélangeant, les témoignages des Anciens.

R. E. A. PALMER[139] a consacré un paragraphe important à Junon Caprotine. Il donne de l'épithète une explication toponymique: les deux formes *Caprotina* et *Capratina*[140] dérivent d'un lieu-dit issu du nom de la chèvre[141]. Selon lui, rien ne prouve l'origine romaine de la déesse, il s'agirait plutôt de la déesse tutélaire de Fidènes — cité assaillant Rome dans le récit étiologique — évoquée par les Romains, et transportée à Rome où des femmes étrangères, esclaves, la célébraient le 7 juillet. L'auteur envisage donc un processus opposé à celui de BASANOFF, mais moins justifié. Les cérémonies de la Junon Caprotine comportent des rites de fécondité qui ne vont pas à l'encontre de son rôle de protectrice du *populus* de Fidènes. Par ailleurs selon cet auteur, Junon Caprotine porterait la *toga praetexta* . . .[142] "*(that) reflects an archaic robing in the trappings of the chief magistrates*".

L'exégèse de P. DROSSART[143] a le mérite d'embrasser tous les éléments du récit des Nones et de les mettre en oeuvre en une interprétation cohérente, aboutissant à une action de Junon tout à fait plausible et conforme à son image. La fête des Nones se célébrait dans le calendrier lunaire au premier quartier suivant le solstice d'été, donc au début de la saison à dominance des nuits. Elle est ainsi une continuation inversée des rites qui, en juin, à l'approche du solstice, ont prétendu

rites — qui ne le sont que dans les interprétations dont ils sont l'objet! cf. R. E. A. PALMER, Roman Religion . . ., p. 16. Selon Varron, L.L., 6, 18, aux Nones, les femmes utilisaient une branche du *Caprificus*, l'usage qui en était fait n'est pas précisé; on sait par ailleurs (Horace, Sat., 1, 8) qu'on fabriquait des *phallus* en figuier.

[135] Varron, L.L., 5, 97: *Hircus, quod Sabini Fircus.*

[136] V. BASANOFF, Nonae Caprotinae, p. 212; selon lui, le *Caprificus* et *Caprotina* sont liés, «il s'agit de la chèvre et non du bouc — *hircus*, mot latin. *Caper* dans le sens de bouc est tardif. D'autre part, *caper*, comme bouc châtré, n'a évidemment rien à voir avec les qualités prolifiques de l'arbre. Ainsi, la chèvre de l'arbre est la chèvre de la déesse. C'est celle de *Juno Lanuuina*, celle aussi des Luperques.»

[137] Ovide, Fastes, 2, 441.

[138] Selon M. LEJEUNE, op. cit., p. 199—200, dans ces rites, il s'agit d'une Junon *Caprōta, c'est-à-dire «pourvue d'attributs de bouc», «assimilée à un bouc». Les Nones Caprotines auraient été, conjointement, la fête d'une déesse *Caprōta et de fidèles *Caprātae . . . (déesse-bouc fertilisant des fidèles-chèvres). Cf. D. PORTE, op. cit., p. 187.

[139] R. E. A. PALMER, Roman Religion . . ., p. 7—17.

[140] Plut., Rom., 29; Cam., 33; C.I.L., IV, 1555.

[141] R. E. A. PALMER, Roman Religion . . ., p. 16.

[142] Pour désigner le manteau de Philôtis, Plut., Cam., 33, 5, emploie ἱμάτιον, terme grec pour signifier *toga* (Plut., Cam., 10; Brut., 17; Cor., 14) . . . cf. PALMER, Roman Religion . . ., p. 13.

[143] P. DROSSART, Nonae Caprotinae: La fausse capture des Aurores, dans: R.H.R., 185, 2, 1974, p. 129—139.

fortifier, encourager les Aurores menacées ou fatiguées (*Matralia* du 11 juin)[144]. Cette fête dans ses rites et dans le récit étiologique dont le thème central est la substitution des femmes esclaves aux dames romaines appelle donc une interprétation lunaire. Dans la scène du signal, Philôtis — Tutela, — juchée sur un figuier brandit un flambeau tout en déployant derrière elle son manteau: ses attributs sont en fait ceux que l'iconographie classique prête à la lune[145]. Elle représente en un tableau vivant le partage de l'orbe lunaire dont la moitié seulement, la nuit des Nones, dispense ses rayons. Cette interprétation est la seule à rendre compte solidairement, de la servante, du figuier, de l'écran et de la torche. Laissons la conclusion à l'auteur: «Il ne s'agit pas ici d'avancer l'existence de quelque ʿculte de la lune' dans la Rome archaïque. C'est en tant que régulatrice des saisons, mais aussi de la sexualité féminine que la lune, dans le complexe ʿjunonien' des Nones Caprotines, joue un rôle qu'établit de toute manière la place de la fête dans le calendrier[146]. A l'intersection du mythe et du rite, le *caprificus*, support de la lumière nocturne (dans le mythe) et instrument d'initiation gynécologique (dans le rite), est aussi le point de rencontre symbolique des plans astronomique et sexuel.» «Travesties en aurores, les lunes, leurs complices, se sont laissé capturer par les ténèbres, qui ne peuvent rien sur elles, et qu'elles dissipent au lieu de s'y engloutir. La déroute des ténèbres sort de leur apparente victoire sur les aurores»[147]. Ainsi juste après le solstice d'été ces rites sont destinés à renforcer la lumière nocturne[148].

V. Iuno Cur(r)itis

Un autre aspect de Junon présente des analogies avec la divinité de Lanuvium, des Lupercales, des Nones. Il s'agit de la *Iuno Cur(r)itis* (ou *Quiritis*

---

[144] G. DUMÉZIL, Déesses latines et mythes védiques, ch. I: Mater Matuta, Coll. Latomus, 25, Bruxelles, 1956; ID., Rel. rom. arch.², p. 66—71; ID., Mythe et épopée. III: Histoires romaines, deuxième partie: La saison de l'Aurore, Bibl. des Sciences Hum., Paris, 1973.

[145] P. DROSSART, Nonae Caprotinae, p. 134—5 et n. 3.

[146] ROSCHER, Lex., art. Iuno, col. 587, considérait la Junon Caprotine comme lunaire, car le sacrifice de la chèvre est habituel pour les déesses lunaires. Elle avait dès lors une influence sur le climat. De plus des rites concernant les femmes s'attachèrent à ce culte car, écrivait P. M. A. EHRENREICH, Die allgemeine Mythologie und ihre ethnologischen Grundlagen, Mytholog. Bibliothek, 4, 1, Leipzig, 1910, p. 40—1, une divinité lunaire est aussi divinité de la terre, de la végétation, de la naissance et de la mort; cf. aussi SHIELDS, Juno, p. 49—50. Cette ancienne théorie est à la fois proche et lointaine de l'explication des Nones par DROSSART ou de celle de la *Iuno* des Calendes par DUMÉZIL ou par SCHILLING (cf. supra). De même que pour SCHILLING, Janus . . ., p. 108, Junon ne se confond pas avec la lune parce que, grâce à sa «force vitale», elle favorise le «travail» de la jeune lune, P. DROSSART n'envisage pas de culte de la lune: simplement, les hommes par leurs gestes symboliques et leurs prières à Junon, force motrice céleste, stimulent la nature pour qu'elle suive son cycle habituel. Cf. aussi G. DUMÉZIL, Fêtes romaines d'été et d'automne suivi de Dix questions romaines, p. 281.

[147] P. DROSSART, Nonae Caprotinae, p. 136.

[148] G. DUMÉZIL, Fêtes romaines . . ., p. 281.

ou *Curis*)[149] de Faléries[150], de Tibur[151] et de Rome qui, nous dit G. Dumézil, est «figurée et invoquée dans des conditions très voisines de ce que nous savons pour Iuno Sospita»[152]. Elle est armée (*Iuno Curritis, tuo curru clipeoque tuere meos curiae uernulas*[153] et *Curitis quae utitur curru et hasta*[154]); des éléments de fécondité interviennent dans son culte; elle devait jouer à Faléries le rôle de divinité tutélaire avantageant l'ensemble de la société[155]. De plus, là encore la chèvre intervient dans le culte: tandis qu'elle sert d'égide à *Iuno Sospita,* que le bouc est sacrifié aux Lupercales, à Faléries, on chasse la chèvre à coups de pierres[156]. La *Iuno Curritis* de Faléries était, on le voit, aussi complexe que la *Seispes* de Lanuvium, tripartie, peut-être, mais alors sans titulature triple[157]. Les Anciens ont proposé de nombreuses explications pseudo-étymologiques[158]. On a dérivé cette épithète du nom de la ville sabine de *Cures*[159], du mot sabin *curis* pour désigner la lance[160], de *currus,* «le char»[161], de *quirites* (en raison de la graphie *Quiritis*[162]), de *curiae,* car Denys d'Halicarnasse rapporte que dans chaque curie, Tatius dédia des Tables à Junon appelée *Curritis* qui existent toujours à l'époque de l'historien[163]; d'autre part, on se rappelle cette phrase citée par Servius: *tuere meos Curiae uernulas* (Serv., Aen., 1, 17).

Les modernes hésitent entre ces diverses étymologies et en ont même imaginé d'autres[164]. Mommsen et Wissowa tendaient à voir dans *Curitis* une

---

[149] Les références aux auteurs anciens sont données par E. Aust, dans: R.E., IV, 2, 1901, art. Curritis, col. 1845–6 et par W. Eisenhut, art. Quiris, Quiritis, Curis, Cur(r)itis, dans: R.E., XXIV, 1, 1963, col. 1324–33 (information très actuelle). La bibliographie sur cette divinité est citée par J. Poucet, Recherches sur la légende sabine des origines de Rome, Recueil de Travaux d'Hist. et de Philol., 4e sér., Fasc. 37, Louvain, 1967, p. 60, n. 229.

[150] C.I.L., XI, 3100; 3125; 3126.

[151] Serv., ad Aen., 1, 17.

[152] G. Dumézil, Iuno S.M.R., p. 117, note.

[153] Serv., ad Aen., 1, 17.

[154] Serv., ad Aen., 1, 8.

[155] V. Basanoff, Junon falisque et ses cultes à Rome, dans: R.H.R., 124, 1, 1941, p. 110–141.

[156] Description de la *Iuno Sospita* chez Cicéron, Nat. deor., 1, 82: . . . *illam uestram Sospitam, quam tu numquam . . . uides nisi cum pelle caprina, cum hasta, cum scutulo, cum calceolis repandis.* Allusion à la chasse à la chèvre de Faléries chez Ovide, Am., 3, 13, 16ss.

[157] G. Dumézil, Iuno S.M.R., p. 117, note.

[158] Cf. Daremberg – Saglio, IV, 1, 1905, art. Quirinus, Quirinalia, p. 807 (J. A. Hild); Shields, Juno, p. 51–6; Radke, Die Götter Altitaliens, art. Cur(r)itis.

[159] Schol. Pers. Sat., 4, 26; Steph. Byz., art. Κυρίς; Fest., p. 302 L. Cette étymologie remonte sans doute à Varron.

[160] Paul. Fest., p. 43, 5; 55, 6 L.; Serv., ad Aen., 1,8; Plut., Rom., 29; Qu. Rom., 87; Ovide, Fastes, 2, 477; c'est Reitzenstein (cf. W. Eisenhut, op. cit.) qui suggéra en 1901 de lire le nom de la lance, *curi* au lieu de *curru* dans Serv., 1, 17.

[161] Cf. Serv., ad Aen., 1, 8: *quae utitur curru et hasta.*

[162] Cf. Radke, op. cit., art. Cur(r)itis.

[163] Denys, 2, 50, 3.

[164] On a voulu, notamment, expliquer *Curritis* par le nom de ville *Currium* ou *Curria* qui aurait existé . . .; cf. E. Bickel, Beiträge zur römischen Religionsgeschichte, I. Flamen curialis und Iuno Curritis, dans: Rhein. Mus., 71, 1916, p. 560 et Radke, op. cit., art. Cur(r)itis.

forme dérivée de *curia*[165], cette étymologie fait difficulté en raison de la longueur du '*u*' dans *Cŭrītis* et *cūria*[166]. En 1920, P. KRETSCHMER relança une étymologie déjà ancienne: *Quirinus* apparenté à *Quirites* est dérivé d'un **co-uirio* ou d'une **co-uiria* qui désigne un rassemblement d'hommes, de *uiri*. *Quirinus* serait le dieu des hommes réunis en communauté, les *Quirites,* les membres de cette communauté, les Romains considérés dans leur organisation civile et politique[167]. *Curia* est un mot de la même famille[168]. Mais en ce qui concerne *Iuno Curritis,* G. DUMÉZIL est moins affirmatif: «Ce vocable est écrit de diverses façons et chacune des orthographes se fonde sur une étymologie différente. Il se peut donc que Junon n'ait été mise en rapport avec les *curiae* que par jeu de mots»[169]. Selon J. GAGÉ par contre, le nom de la déesse «ne peut être séparé du vocabulaire des *curiae* elles-mêmes», mais il donne une toute autre étymologie du terme *curia*: «un vocable concret, sabin ou non, tel que **quiri(s)*, **quiru* avait réellement désigné une lance sacrée, celle qui peut-être avait donné le nom initial à cette unité primitive que les Romains appelaient une *curia*» . . .[170]. R. VERDIÈRE et E. PARATORE sont les auteurs d'une contribution commune[171] dans laquelle R. VERDIÈRE donne pour *curia* la même étymologie que J. GAGÉ[172]. De plus, suite à la découverte à Sulmone d'un sanctuaire d'Hercule *Curinus,* E. PARATORE approuve Varron quand il affirme «l'origine sabine d'Hercule et de Junon dans le Latium préromain»[173]. Selon R. VERDIÈRE, «Les Sabins, émigrant à Rome pour venir s'y installer sur le *Collis Quirinalis,* ont tenu à emporter avec eux leur *Hercules Curis* (. . .). Il n'est pas étonnant que l'on représente à Rome une Junon combattant de concert avec Hercule ou contre lui, puisqu'il y eut une *Iuno Curis*»[174] c'est-à-dire

---

[165] Cf. SHIELDS, Juno, p. 55.

[166] W. WARDE FOWLER, Confarreatio: A Study of Patrician Usage, dans: J.R.S., 6, 1916, p. 189; SHIELDS, Juno, p. 54; V. BASANOFF, Junon falisque et ses cultes à Rome, p. 125; M. RENARD, Aspects anciens de Janus et de Junon, dans: R.B.Ph., 31, 1953, p. 14.

[167] A. POTT, Etymol. Forsch. auf d. Gebiete der Indo-Germanischen Sprache, II, Lemgo, 1836, p. 493 et 533; KRETSCHMER, Lat. 'Quirites' und 'Quiritare', dans: Glotta, 10, 1920, p. 147−157; V. PISANI, Mytho-etymologica, dans: Rev. des Et. Indo-Européennes, 1, 1938, p. 230−3; E. BENVENISTE, Symbolisme social dans les cultes gréco-italiques, dans: R.H.R., 129, 1945, p. 7−9; G. DUMÉZIL, Jupiter, Mars, Quirinus, IV, Paris, 1948, p. 161s.

[168] G. DUMÉZIL, Rel. rom. arch.², p. 271.

[169] Ibidem, p. 303.

[170] J. GAGÉ, Les autels de Titus Tatius. Une variante sabine des rites d'intégration dans les curies?, dans: Mél J. Heurgon. L'Italie préromaine et la Rome républicaine, I, Coll. Ec. Franç. Rome, 27, 1976, p. 316.

[171] E. PARATORE et R. VERDIÈRE, Varron avait raison, dans: L'Ant. Class., 62, 1, 1973, p. 49−63.

[172] Ibidem, p. 54 ss.

[173] Ibidem, p. 50 ss.; sur les découvertes de Sulmone: E. PARATORE, Hercule et Cacus chez Virgile et Tite-Live, dans: Vergiliana. Recherches sur Virgile, publ. par H. BARDON et R. VERDIÈRE, Roma Aeterna, 3, Leiden, 1971, p. 260 ss. = ID., Romanae Litterae, Rome, 1976, p. 425 ss., spéc. p. 433 ss. et IDEM, Le tradizioni popolari abruzzesi su Ovidio alla luce delle nuove esperienze, dans: Atti del VII Congresso nazionale delle tradizioni popolari (Chieti, 1957), Florence, 1959, p. 30 ss.

[174] R. VERDIÈRE, Varron avait raison, p. 59−60.

«Junon Doryphore»[175]. Au sujet de cette intégration de *Iuno Curitis* dans le cycle sabin et du lien établi entre le culte de Junon dans les curies et Titus Tatius, J. POUCET écrit: «ils étaient inscrits dans la logique des choses: le surnom *Curitis* devait à plus ou moins longue échéance introduire dans le cercle sabin le culte rendu par les curies à Junon»[176].

C'est précisément ce culte dans les curies qui a retenu l'attention de R. SCHILLING. Il rappelle que dans les curies, Junon était invoquée comme protectrice de la jeune épouse, lors de la conclusion du mariage: «les *curiae ueteres* de Rome devaient jouir, à cet égard, d'une compétence analogue à celle des phratries grecques. En tout cas, les épouses étaient censées être 'sous la protection de Junon Curitis'»[177]. R. SCHILLING rappelle le témoignage de Festus: . . . *quia matronae Iunonis curitis in tutela sint, quae ita appellabatur a ferenda hasta quae lingua Sabinorum curis dicitur*[178]. «Il s'agit de la *caelibaris hasta*, qui servait à coiffer la nouvelle épouse ominis causa»[179]. Ce dernier point n'est pas aussi évident. Car *Iuno Curritis* est décrite comme une divinité réellement guerrière. On trouve une interprétation analogue chez PRELLER: dans le nom de *Curitis*, «la lance était le symbole de l'homme en tant qu'il doit être le protecteur de sa femme, de la mère de ses enfants»[180]. Et pourtant on a vu trop d'exemples de Junons aux virtualités féminines présentant aussi des aspects guerriers pour que ce rapprochement surprenne encore.

R. E. A. PALMER, bien sûr, insiste sur l'appareil guerrier dans lequel nous est décrite la *Iuno Curitis*[181]. Primordiale également selon cet auteur, l'intervention de cette Junon dans les curies. Les rites de *Iuno Quiritis* étaient célébrés dans les trente curies et consistaient en repas frugaux. Denys, qui en fut témoin, admirait les curies d'avoir su maintenir au temps de la magnificence de la Rome d'Auguste, l'archaïque sobriété[182]. R. E. A. PALMER relie la divinité des curies aux rites d'évocation: *"The rites of curias, like most curias themselves, originated outside of the Roman communities, presumably, then, these sacra, had been evoked from several places and transported to old curias on the Palatine"*[183]. La divinité évoquée était une Junon[184] devenant, à la suite de son entrée dans les curies, une *Iuno Curitis*[185]. Plus tard, *"although the Romans ceased to incorporate the conquered into curias, they scrupulously observed the protocol of bringing Junos from Etruscan and Latin towns and that god or goddess under whose protection*

---

[175] Ibidem, p. 58.

[176] J. POUCET, Recherches sur la légende sabine des origines de Rome, p. 322.

[177] R. SCHILLING, Janus, p. 111.

[178] Paul. Fest., p. 55 L.

[179] R. SCHILLING, Janus, p. 111, n. 4.

[180] L. PRELLER, Les dieux de l'ancienne Rome. Mythologie romaine, 3e éd., Paris, 1884, p. 186.

[181] R. E. A. PALMER, Roman Religion, p. 5.

[182] Denys, 2, 23; 2, 50, 3.

[183] R. E. A. PALMER, The Archaic Community of the Romans, Cambridge, 1970, p. 180−1 et p. 168−9.

[184] Ibidem, p. 180.

[185] R. E. A. PALMER, Archaic Community . . ., p. 168, rejette donc l'étymologie qui ferait de *Curitis* un dérivé du mot sabin pour désigner la lance.

the army and citizens of Carthage lived"[186]. On le voit, R. E. A. PALMER insiste à juste titre sur le rôle de Junon dans la vie politique et militaire, mais, encore une fois, ne lui reconnaît aucune intervention dans la vie des femmes. Ici aussi nous penchons à admettre l'opinion de G. DUMÉZIL qui, tout en décelant la divinité combattante, n'est pas contraint par parti pris d'en nier les virtualités féminines[187].

VI. Iuno Moneta

Nous nous arrêterons maintenant à la *Iuno Moneta* dont le culte a des origines assez obscures. Comme l'écrit H. J. ROSE: *"we do not know why she was worshipped on the Arx . . . under the title Moneta, 'the adviser or warner'"*[188]. Nous l'étudierons à la suite de *Iuno Curitis*, la combattante, car les informations que les Anciens nous ont laissées à son sujet se situent dans un contexte guerrier[189]. Pour G. DUMÉZIL, ces deux Junons — *Curitis* et *Moneta* — manifestent, à côté de *Iuno Regina* et de *Iuno Lucina*, le troisième aspect de Junon, l'aspect guerrier, peu représenté à Rome[190]. Cicéron[191] et ses sources nous ont conservé une étymologie du nom: *Moneta* proviendrait du verbe *monēre*; cette Junon serait donc «avertisseuse». Certains modernes ont accepté cette étymologie antique, d'autres l'ont rejetée sans rien soumettre de plus convaincant[192]. Dernièrement, R. E. A. PALMER a proposé de nouvelles explications de l'épithète: *moneta* serait formé sur le même etymon que les mots *mons, e-mineo, monile* en référence à la colline capitoline où se tenait le culte à la divinité. Mais selon lui, *Moneta* pourrait également être un terme gaulois adopté après la victoire de 349. Puisque le temple de *Moneta* abritait les *libri lintei*, PALMER suggère une troisième explication: *moneta* dériverait bien de *monēre* mais avec le sens de *"recorder"*, car Livius Andronicus voit en *Moneta* la Mémoire (Mnémosyne)[193]. Pour M. VAN DEN BRUWAENE, en une hypothèse très douteuse, *Moneta* ne serait qu'une transcription de *Minerva* primitive[194].

---

[186] R. E. A. PALMER, Archaic Community . . ., p. 169.

[187] Sur les aspects fécondants de cette déesse, cf. V. BASANOFF, Junon falisque et ses cultes à Rome, passim.

[188] H. J. ROSE, Ancient Roman Religion, p. 71.

[189] Schol. à Lucain Pharsale, 1, 379: attaque gauloise de 390 et oies du Capitole; Suid., art. Μονῆτα (III, p. 408 ADLER): assurance donnée aux Romains pendant la guerre contre Pyrrhus et les Tarentins; Cic., De div., 1, 45, donne un *aition* différent: l'annonce d'un tremblement de terre. Cf. G. DUMÉZIL, Iuno S.M.R., p. 116, n. 3 et R. E. A. PALMER, Roman Religion, p. 29—30.

[190] G. DUMÉZIL, Iuno S.M.R., p. 116 et n. 3.

[191] Cic., De div., 2, 69.

[192] Pour la bibliographie antérieure, cf. SHIELDS, Juno, p. 59—62 et M. MARBACH, dans: R.E., XVI, 1, 1933, art Moneta, col. 114—119.

[193] Livius Andronicus, fgt. n° 23 (MOREL) = Cic., Nat. deor., 3, 47.

[194] M. VAN DEN BRUWAENE, L'épithète de Iuno Moneta, dans: Hommages M. Niedermann, Coll. Latomus 23, Bruxelles, 1956, p. 329—32.

Le *natalis* de Junon *Moneta* était fêté aux Calendes de juin, son temple sur le sommet du Capitole n'aurait été voué et construit qu'au milieu du IVe siècle, soit une génération après le sac gaulois. Tite-Live a noté cette fondation avec une précision qui suppose un enregistrement effectif dans les annales: «Au cours d'une guerre contre les Aurunques, le dictateur L. Furius Camillus — plus probablement un fils du héros de la prise de Véies et de la libération de Rome que le personnage lui-même, — en 348 avant J.-C., fait voeu d'élever un temple à Junon Monéta »[195]. Mais ce culte est certainement d'origine plus ancienne et des constructions plus vétustes ont sans doute précédé ce temple du IVe siècle[196]. Pourtant G. DUMÉZIL considère que le vocable *Moneta* n'est peut-être pas aussi ancien que ceux de *Lucina* et de *Regina*[197].

Ce culte, pour M. GUARDUCCI[198], aurait une origine bien plus ancienne et étrangère: *Iuno Moneta*, 'l'avertisseuse', identifiée à Mnémosyne[199], voisine sur le Capitole de l'*auguraculum,* et qui annonça à Rome divers périls, peut être considérée comme une déesse oraculaire, elle serait une traduction romaine de l'Héra de Cumes introduite à Rome au VIIe siècle. L. A. MAC KAY considère ce culte comme beaucoup plus ancien que toutes les explications étymologiques que nous en avons conservé. Il rappelle le témoignage de Valère-Maxime[200] affirmant qu'elle est la Junon venue de Véies; si cela était, son épithète ne serait pas romaine . . .[201]

Pour V. BASANOFF, «le culte de Juno Moneta fut introduit dans la citadelle dès la première époque royale et (. . .) ce culte était celui de Juno Curitis qui, adoptée par les Sabins, était arrivée à Rome par l'intermédiaire de Cures[202]. A Cures cette Junon se montre déjà en sa nouvelle qualité de divinité protectrice du chef militaire, qu'elle n'a jamais connu dans son milieu latin. Cette nouvelle qualité ressort de l'emplacement du *fanum*, du surnom de la déesse, du rôle dérivé qui lui revient d'après la tradition. 1° Son autel se trouvait sur la place de la Regia de T. Tatius[203]; 2° *Moneta*, de *moneo* (conseiller) fait apparaître la déesse sous les mêmes traits que la divinité féminine — Egérie — d'un autre prince de souche sabine, Numa; 3° Dans le récit de Denys, les tables-autels sont consacrées à Junon qui s'appelle là *Curitis*, afin de justifier l'étymologie notoirement fausse *Cŭrītis* de *cūria*. Ces tables dans les curies assurent la présence du *numen* protecteur du roi dans ces curies, où la déesse apparaît comme conseillère, – *Moneta*»[204].

Ce qui reste de tout ceci, c'est l'intervention de *Moneta* en des circonstances guerrières, les arguments à l'appui d'une association avec le pouvoir royal nous

[195] Tite-Live, 7, 28; cf. J. GAGÉ, Matronalia, p. 206 ss., spéc. p. 207–8.

[196] Cf. V. BASANOFF, Les dieux des Romains, p. 151, où il cite M. MANCINI.

[197] G. DUMÉZIL, Iuno S.M.R., p. 116, n. 3.

[198] M. GUARDUCCI, Un antichissimo responso dell' oracolo di Cuma, dans: Bull. Comm. Archeol. Com. Roma, 72, 1946–8, p. 129–141.

[199] Liv. Andr., fgt. n° 23.

[200] Valère Maxime, 1, 8, 3.

[201] L. A. MAC KAY, Janus, University of California Publications in Classical Philology, 15, 4, Berkeley, 1956, p. 157–181, spéc. p. 175.

[202] V. BASANOFF, Junon falisque et ses cultes à Rome, p. 110–141.

[203] Cic., De domo sua ad pontifices, 38, 101.

[204] V. BASANOFF, Les dieux des Romains, p. 151–2.

semblent moins probants, d'autant que dans ce rôle, nous allons le voir, elle bénéficie peut-être d'une certaine confusion avec la *Iuno Regina*[205].

VII. Iuno Martialis

Avant d'en terminer avec les «Junons guerrières», nous devons évoquer le cas de la *Iuno Martialis*, uniquement représentée sur des monnaies du IIIe siècle après J.-C., émises durant les règnes de princes d'origine étrusco-ombrienne (Trébonien Galle, Volusien, Hostilien)[206] qui malgré les siècles demeuraient fidèles à leur passé. Il s'agirait donc d'une réminiscence archaïsante d'un culte issu de la religion étrusco-ombrienne et resté jusqu'alors inconnu pour nous[207]. La dénomination même de *Iuno Martialis* offre un indice sûr de sa provenance. «La relation de parenté ou de subordination qu'elle implique entre Junon et Mars (. . .) est exactement de celles qui unissent les familles divines dans la théologie primitive de l'Italie», ombrienne surtout[208]. Tout porterait alors à croire qu'à l'époque archaïque cette divinité a pu présenter des traits guerriers[209].

[205] Sur le lien entre *moneta* et la monnaie, qui demeure obscur, on verra L. A. Mac Kay, Janus, p. 175: "*The commercial importance of the Kalends, Juno's especial day, suggests that the placing of the mint under her protection can be most plausibly explained on the supposition that Moneta was, or was at the time thought to be, the monthgoddess*"; J. Gagé, Matronalia, p. 206 ss.: les oies de *Iuno Moneta* sont symboles des matrones, par ailleurs, les oies passent pour avoir relation avec l'or. Sur les oies de *Iuno Moneta*: V. Basanoff, Les dieux des Romains, p. 151 ss., ne leur reconnaît qu'un rôle apotropaïque.

[206] J. Heurgon, Traditions étrusco-italiques dans le monnayage de Trébonien Galle, dans: St. Etr., 24, 1955–1956, p. 91–105; G. Marchetti-Longhi, La Juno Martialis nelle monete di Treboniano Gallo e di Volusiano, dans: Annali Ist. Italiano Numismatica, 3, 1956, p. 65–82.

[207] J. Heurgon, op. cit., p. 91 ss.

[208] Nombreuses, chez les Osques et les Ombriens, sont ces appellations doubles qui déterminent le nom d'une divinité – ou d'une notion divinisable – par un adjectif dérivé du nom d'un autre dieu ou par ce nom même au génitif (cf. G. Devoto, Gli antichi Italici⁴, Florence, 1969, p. 187 ss; J. Heurgon, Recherches sur l'histoire, la religion et la civilisation de Capoue préromaine, des origines à la deuxième guerre punique, Bibl. Ec. Franc. d'Ath. et de Rome, 46, Paris, 1942, p. 386 [2e éd., 1970]). Par cette sorte de surnom, il était précisé que le premier dieu appartenait au second, qu'un *numen* inférieur était entré dans le cercle d'une divinité plus importante, cf. J. Heurgon, op. cit., p. 96 qui cite notamment le cas de *Nerio Martis* qui était d'abord 'le courage de Mars' avant de devenir Nerio, épouse de Mars. L'auteur (n. 21) rappelle certaines coïncidences; le 1er mars, on célébrait l'antique fête de Mars mais aussi celle de *Lucina* aux *Matronalia*, d'autre part, le 1er juin était le jour de fondation des temples de Mars à la porte Capène et de *Iuno Moneta*. Ces rencontres ont créé un lien entre Junon et Mars, exploité par les poètes au siècle d'Auguste (Ovide, Fastes, 5, 229 s.; Paul. Fest., p. 86 L.) qui comme dans la légende grecque d'Héra et d'Arès, ont fait de Mars le fils de Junon (cf. Wissowa, R.u.K. d. R.², p. 147; G. Hermansen, Stud. über den ital. u. den röm. Mars, Copenhague, 1940, p. 25). Selon J. Heurgon (ibidem), «Il ne pouvait, à la rigueur, sortir de là qu'un Mars Junonius, non une Juno Martialis.»

[209] G. Dumézil, Rel. rom. arch.², p. 305.

A la faveur de réflexions sur la *Iuno Martialis*, J. GAGÉ[210] établit un lien entre la figure guerrière de Junon et le caractère martial et brutal des cultes matronaux[211] et de l'éducation des filles[212] à l'époque ancienne. Aux temps classiques, les Romains n'en avaient plus d'idée, dès lors, à Rome, l'aspect guerrier de Junon finit par s'estomper.

Selon G. DUMÉZIL, il est possible que l'évolution romaine ait tendu à éliminer l'élément guerrier de la *Regina*[213]; on observe qu'en latin, les noms d'origine indo-européenne de 'la fonction guerrière', du 'pouvoir reposant sur la force' ont disparu, toutes les notions guerrières ont reçu à Rome des noms nouveaux, soit indigènes[214].

VIII. Iuno Regina

A Rome, Junon est *Regina* sur le Capitole très certainement[215] et sur l'Aventin. Quelle est la nature de la déesse? Quelles sont ses origines? Autant de questions auxquelles les modernes apportent des réponses variées. Selon G. DUMÉZIL, «au Capitole, Junon est certainement *Regina* et ce n'est pas là un titre que des Italiques, en particulier les premières générations de la *libertas* romaine, pouvaient donner ou accepter à la légère. De plus, c'est la *regina sacrorum* qui offre à Junon le sacrifice des Calendes[216]. Comme, dans ce sacrifice, sûrement ancien, la déesse est envisagée, on l'a vu, comme 'faisant naître' le mois, l'intervention de la *regina* donne à penser que, dès avant la République et le culte capitolin, Junon, même en tant que mère, intéressait la royauté»[217]. Le titre de *Regina* présente Junon comme maîtresse politico-religieuse de la cité[218].

Si pour G. DUMÉZIL, «Junon Regina siégeait déjà depuis longtemps à Rome sur le Capitole quand son double véien − sans doute une *Uni* − (. . .) vint

---

[210] J. GAGÉ, Matronalia, p. 55, n.2 et p. 273−6.

[211] J. GAGÉ, Matronalia, p. 273, souligne le peu d'éléments guerriers subsistant à la fin de la République lors des *Matronalia* et des Nones Caprotines, malgré l'*aition* militaire. On rappellera tout de même le combat à coups de pierres auquel se livrent les esclaves le jour des Nones. Cf. Macr., Sat., 1, 11, 35−40; Plut., Cam., 33; Rom., 29.

[212] Ce caractère brutal de l'éducation des filles serait en rapport avec des rites d'initiation, cf. J. GAGÉ, Matronalia, p. 276 et aussi p. 9, 22, 36−7, 99 et passim.

[213] G. DUMÉZIL, Iuno S.M.R., p. 116 et note.

[214] Cf. G. DUMÉZIL, 'Ner-' et 'viro' dans les langues italiques, dans: R.E.L., 31, 1953, p. 180, n.1.

[215] G. DUMÉZIL, Rel. rom. arch.², p. 303; R. BLOCH, Héra, Uni, Junon en Italie centrale, dans: Recherches sur les Religions de l'Italie Antique, p. 15.

[216] G. DUMÉZIL, Rel. rom. arch.², p. 184.

[217] G. DUMÉZIL, Rel. rom. arch.², p. 303.

[218] «Ainsi s'explique que ce soit le plus haut magistrat de Lanuvium, le dictateur, qui nomme son flamine (Cic., Mil., 17, 45) et que depuis le condominium respectueux que Rome s'est arrogé en 388 sur la déesse lanuvienne (Tite-Live, 8, 14, 2), ses plus hauts magistrats aussi, *omnes consules*, soient tenus de lui sacrifier (Cic., Mur., 41, 90).» Cf. G. DUMÉZIL, Rel. rom. arch.², p. 305.

s'installer sur l'Aventin »[219], pour V. BASANOFF, quand *Iuno Regina* de Véies arriva à Rome, « elle n'était pas une inconnue. Sa souveraineté avait déjà animé celle de Junon capitoline »[220].

R. E. A. PALMER nous propose pour ce culte un exposé riche et fouillé qui très honnêtement laisse apparaître les incertitudes[221]. A son avis, la *Iuno Regina* serait la *"iuno of the king"*, les rois de Rome ayant leurs Junons. A la suite d'une inscription de Dacie qui donne à Junon les deux titres de *Regina* et de *Populonia* — déesse politique et militaire sans lien avec la vénération féminine[222] —, R. E. A. PALMER conçoit que le *templum* de *Populona* était situé dans le temple capitolin *"instead of the intended Regina of the king"*. Ainsi l'identité entre Junon *Populona* et Junon du Capitole lui semble assurée. La cause et la date de la prise de l'épithète *Regina* restent pour lui incertaines: cette appellation est peut-être due à une identification avec l'Héra Basiléia ou avec Jupiter *rex*. Mais l'épithète *Regina* a pu arriver avec la Junon de Véies[223]. Laissons s'exprimer l'auteur: *"I have assumed that the cult title is a Latin rendition of the Etruscan. Etruscan Junos certainly had epithets. Moreover, Regina could have been continuously applied to a Juno at Rome other than to Juno of the Aventine, for the Roman priest-king and his queen were responsible for a monthly sacrifice to Juno. Finally, the pre-republican Junos could have been royal"*[224].

J. GAGÉ exprime une opinion plus tranchée: « le culte de cette Regina a été apporté du dehors: la tradition unanime le fait amener vers 395, de Véies vaincue par Camille. Si Junon portait le même titre en d'autres sanctuaires, c'était par extension à partir de celui-là. Rien non plus ne permet de penser, malgré quelques apparences, ni que le surnom provienne d'un culte de l'époque royale — il n'y a pas de Jupiter Rex qui lui eût pu réellement correspondre — ni inversément qu'on se soit contenté de transposer en latin le titre grec d'une Héra. L'Héra Basiléia des cultes helléniques a pu contribuer à former, hors de Rome, le modèle de cette Junon encore n'est-ce point sûr »[225].

R. BLOCH n'envisage pas le problème de l'antiquité à Rome de la *Iuno Regina* mais renvoie et adhère aux pages où G. DUMÉZIL défend la polyvalence originelle de Junon[226]. On doit à Y. ROE D'ALBRET l'étude la plus récente sur

---

[219] G. DUMÉZIL, Rel. rom. arch.², p. 426.

[220] V. BASANOFF, Les dieux des Romains, p. 87.

[221] R. E. A. PALMER, Roman Religion . . ., p. 21–29.

[222] C.I.L., III, 1074–1076 = I.L.S., 3085–87; trois dédicaces à Jupiter, à Junon et à Minerve offertes à l'époque de Commode par un légat stationné en Dacie: *I(ovi) O(ptimo) M(aximo)*; *Iunoni Reginae Populoniae deae patriae*; *Minervae Iovis consiliorum participi*, la graphie *Populonia* n'a pas d'importance, cf. R. E. A. PALMER, Roman Religion, p. 6–7 et p. 22–23.

[223] R. E. A. PALMER, Roman Religion . . ., p. 21ss.

[224] R. E. A. PALMER, Roman Religion . . ., p.29; ibidem, p. 31: la *Iuno Sispes* pourrait avoir été une autre *Regina*, sur le Palatin, centre civique à l'époque royale, tombée en désuétude quand le dernier roi eut installé la vénération de sa *iuno* sur le Capitole et que le culte de *Iuno Regina* fut transféré à la *Regia*.

[225] J. GAGÉ, Matronalia, p. 80–81.

[226] R. BLOCH, Héra, Uni, Junon en Italie centrale, dans: Recherches . . ., p. 15–18.

Iuno Regina[227]. Il ne semble pas envisager la présence à Rome d'une Junon Reine avant l'époque de Camille alors qu'il la discerne en de nombreuses cités étrusques et latiales[228]. A Rome, c'est *Iuno Moneta* qu'il considère comme divinité équivalente de la divinité poliade de Véies.

A notre avis, *Iuno Regina* à Rome est une personnalité divine ancienne. Le titre de la divinité de Véies exprimait très certainement une réalité approchante du culte romain, mais qui conserva toujours des caractères originels étrangers[229].

Interrogeons-nous un moment sur le nom sous lequel *Iuno Regina* était vénérée à Véies: il ne nous est pas connu[230]. Il s'agit sans doute d'une *Uni*[231] – c'est le moment de rappeler «que Uni, avant tout, est bien cette Juno italique dont son nom est sans doute une déformation»[232]. Nous ne savons pas si la traduction de la déesse de Véies par *Iuno* – même spécifiée par *Regina* – est exhaustive[233], ni à quelle notion étrusque correspond le nom de *Regina*[234], «vieux titre italique, qu'il est arbitraire de considérer comme une traduction de l'étrusque»[235].

La venue de la *Iuno Regina* de Véies à Rome en 396 est, comme l'écrit G. DUMÉZIL, le seul cas certain d'*euocatio* que cite l'annalistique[236], ce qui ne veut pas dire que le rite était exceptionnel: Macrobe en rapporte de nombreux exemples[237]. Peut-on dire comme J. LE GALL que le rite était banal[238]?

---

[227] Y. ROE D'ALBRET, Recherches sur la prise de Véies et sur Juno Regina, dans: Annuaire de l'Ec. Prat. des Hautes Et., IVe sect., 1975–6, p. 1093–1103, spéc. p. 1099, thèse déposée en 1974 et dirigée par R. BLOCH.

[228] Visentium (cf. L. ROSS TAYLOR, Local Cults in Etruria, dans: P. M. A. A. Rome, 2, 1923, p. 166), Tarquinia (ibidem, p. 143–4), Ardée (Tite-Live, 5, 43–5).

[229] J. BAYET, Tite-Live livre V. Appendice III: Véies: réalités et légendes, éd. des Belles Lettres, Paris, 1954, p. 127.

[230] On lira à ce sujet l'article brillant, mais qui n'a pas emporté notre adhésion de S. FERRI, La 'Iuno Regina' di Vei, dans: St. Etr., 24, 1955–1956, p. 107–113: c'est *Uni* c'est-à-dire **Veni–Turan* transportée jadis de l'Ida, la „*Dea Madre-Signora*".

[231] G. DUMÉZIL, Rel. rom. arch.[2], p. 426.

[232] G. DUMÉZIL, Mythe et épopée, III, p. 168.

[233] Ibidem, p. 171.

[234] J. GAGÉ, Matronalia, p. 278.

[235] G. DUMÉZIL, Rel. rom. arch.[2], p. 307.

[236] G. DUMÉZIL, Rel. rom. arch.[2], p. 426; cf. Tite-Live, 5, 21 et 5, 22, 3–7.

[237] Macrobe, Sat., 3, 9, cf. J. LE GALL, Evocatio, dans: Mél. J. Heurgon, I, p. 524: «Toute *devotio* d'une ville était nécessairement précédée par l'*evocatio* de ses dieux, comme le rappelle Macrobe. La liste des dévotions anciennes qu'il fournit, sans avoir la prétention d'être exhaustive, est donc en même temps une liste d'évocations.»

[238] J. LE GALL, op. cit., p. 519–524, montre la minceur du dossier à partir duquel on pouvait étudier l'évocation (principalement Tite-Live et Macrobe). A ces témoignages est venue s'ajouter une inscription découverte par A. HALL, New Light on the Capture of Isaura Vetus by P. Servilius Vatia, dans: Akten des VI. Internationalen Kongresses für Griechische und Lateinische Epigraphik, Munich 1972, Vestigia, 17, Munich, 1973, p. 568–571, qui révèle que l'évocation a été pratiquée à l'encontre d'une ville barbare d'Asie Mineure; ainsi, l'évocation n'était pas réservée aux divinités poliades des villes italiennes. En conséquence, il n'y a plus aucune raison de rejeter les indications fournies par Macrobe à propos du siège de Carthage. On doit admettre la loyauté de son témoignage lorsqu'il affirme avoir fait une

L'évocation est une opération de droit religieux qui, contrairement à l'opinion de certains auteurs — ROSE, GAGÉ, BASANOFF (de façon plus nuancée)[239], — se distingue de l'acte magique et contraignant désigné par le verbe *excantare*[240]. L'évocation est «une proposition de pacte que l'évocateur juge si séduisante pour les dieux auxquels il l'adresse qu'il n'envisage pas leur refus (...) du même coup, il devient probable que n'étaient ainsi évoquées que des divinités recevables à Rome, communes — au *cognomen* près — aux Romains et à leurs ennemis ou bien qu'une interprétation précoce et solide, ou un jeu de sons, identifiait à une divinité romaine»[241]. Or, nonobstant les réserves que nous devons faire sur les difficultés qui se dressent quand on veut mieux cerner la déesse de Véies, tous les auteurs s'accordent au moins pour reconnaître qu'à Rome elle est bien connue, familière même, issue d'un milieu topographiquement proche et d'un climat psychologique et religieux comparable[242].

Les auteurs insistent beaucoup sur le rôle de Camille. Y. ROE D'ALBRET a relevé entre Camille et *Iuno Regina* un lien personnel unissant la déesse à son prêtre-magistrat tel que G. DUMÉZIL l'a montré entre Camille et *Mater Matuta*[243]. Camille dans ses rapports avec la déesse se substitue au roi de Véies[244]. Ce lien entre le roi et la déesse suscite dans nos esprits le «roi» Thefarie Velianas de Caere qu'un lien difficile encore à préciser rapproche d'Uni-Astarté ainsi qu'en témoignent les lamelles d'or de Pyrgi (cf. infra).

Par ailleurs, l'inscription d'une lamelle de bronze de Pyrgi a permis à R. BLOCH de faire une découverte importante puisqu'elle a révélé le nom de *Thesan*, l'Aurore étrusque[245]. Ainsi, l'on sait désormais qu'à Pyrgi des attaches, qui demeurent obscures, unissaient *Thesan* et *Uni,* c'est-à-dire les divinités que les Grecs identifiaient à Leucothée et Ilithyie et les Latins à *Mater Matuta* et *Iuno Lucina* ... G. DUMÉZIL tire de ces révélations des conclusions qui nous séduisent[246]: «comment ne pas être frappé par cette coïncidence: le héros que

enquête sérieuse pour retrouver le souvenir des «dévotions» de villes auxquelles on avait procédé autrefois. V. BASANOFF, Evocatio, voit trop souvent le recours à cette opération là où, peut-être, on ne la reconnaîtrait pas.

[239] ROSE, Ancient Roman Religion, p. 84; J. GAGÉ, Matronalia, p. 81; V. BASANOFF, Evocatio, p. 33—41, spéc. p. 40: «Dès ses débuts, l'*evocatio* ne doit pas être confondue avec des opérations purement magiques. Mais le secret jaloux, dont sont entourés les noms de l'*urbs* et de la divinité de l'*urbs*, montre que les notions que comporte *excantare* n'ont pas été sans influencer les pratiques du rite».

[240] G. DUMÉZIL, Rel. rom. arch.², p. 426.

[241] Ibidem.

[242] Cf. spéc. J. BAYET, Tite-Live, livre V, Appendice III: Véies: réalités et légendes, p. 125—140; R. BLOCH, Héra, Uni, Junon en Italie centrale, dans: Recherches . . ., p. 16—7.

[243] Y. ROE D'ALBRET, Recherches sur la prise de Véies et sur Iuno Regina, p. 1103; G. DUMÉZIL, Mythe et épopée. III, 2e partie: La saison de l'Aurore, Paris, 1973, p. 93—199.

[244] J. GAGÉ, Matronalia, p. 80ss.; Y. ROE D'ALBRET, op. cit., p. 1099s.; cf. Tite-Live, 5, 21, 8 et Plut., Cam., 5, 6.

[245] La question des découvertes de Pyrgi sera reprise plus loin, nous nous bornerons à donner ici la référence de la dernière contribution de R. BLOCH sur ce sujet: Figures divines de Pyrgi, dans: Recherches . . ., p. 1—9.

[246] G. DUMÉZIL, Mythe et épopée, III, p. 171.

l'épopée romaine présente comme le dévot et le protégé de l'Aurore latine, Mater Matuta, et qui, avant de quitter Rome à la conquête de Véies, vient de se confier à Mater Matuta, ce héros, une fois dans son camp devant Véies, lorsqu'il prépare l'assaut final, s'adresse par *euocatio* à une déesse étrusque que rien, jusqu'alors ne nous préparait à considérer comme la divinité la plus importante de cette ville, et qui, en un autre point du domaine étrusque – Pyrgi –, était soit assimilée, soit étroitement associée à Θesan, l'Aurore, elle-même interprétée par les Latins en Mater Matuta (. . .). Ainsi prendrait un sens plus riche l'exécution simultanée, aussitôt après le triomphe, des voeux faits successivement aux deux déesses la nationale et l'étrangère: «Pour *Iuno Regina* il fixa l'emplacement de son temple sur l'Aventin et il fit la dédicace de celui de Mater Matuta»[247]. Quatre siècles plus tard, lors du siège de Pérouse, Octave répéta les gestes de Camille: suite à un rêve, il fit transporter à Rome la statue de Junon – *Regina* vraisemblablement[248] – que l'on vénérait dans cette ville[249].

　　Iuno Regina, évoquée de Véies, au cours de circonstances guerrières et même en quelque sorte, politiques, diplomatiques, reçoit paradoxalement, dès son arrivée à Rome, les hommages des femmes[250].

　　Selon R. E. A. PALMER, en Etrurie, Junon était une déesse politique à laquelle était associé un culte de la sexualité féminine, ce qui suscita ces manifestations féminines lors de sa venue à Rome, et par la suite[251]. L'auteur souligne les traits étrangers qui marquent encore la dévotion des matrones envers *Iuno Regina* durant la seconde guerre punique[252] et en 17 avant J.-C., lorsque Auguste fait revivre les jeux séculaires. Auguste transforma considérablement la liturgie de ces jeux marqués par l'idéologie religieuse étrusque[253]. Pourtant à cette époque encore, les jeux restaient imprégnés d'éléments étrusques, selon PALMER, spécialement, dans les interventions féminines des sacrifices à Junon du

---

[247] Tite-Live, 5, 23, 7.

[248] L. Ross TAYLOR, Local Cults in Etruria, Am. Ac. Rome, 1923, p. 182–190.

[249] Dion Cassius, 43, 14, 5–6. De même, en vertu du souvenir de Camille qui évinça le roi véien dans le culte de *Iuno Regina* grâce à un rite que l'histoire romaine a transformé en anecdote: le rapt des entrailles sacrifiées par le *rex* sur la citadelle de Véies (Tite-Live, 5, 21, 8; Plut., Cam., 5, 6), Octave, au siège de Pérouse (ville étrusque), abandonna sans regret aux mains de l'ennemi les entrailles de la victime qu'il venait de sacrifier et qui donnait des signes défavorables qui retomberaient ainsi sur l'ennemi (Suet., Aug., 96). Cf. J. BAYET, Tite-Live livre V, p. 133, n.3; R. BLOCH, Religion romaine et religion punique à l'époque d'Hannibal: Minime romano sacro, dans: Mél. J. Heurgon, L'Italie préromaine et la Rome républicaine, I, Coll. Ec. Franç. Rome, 27, 1976, p. 37; Y. ROE D'ALBRET, op.cit., p. 1100.

[250] J. GAGÉ, Matronalia, p. 64–5; p. 80ss.; Y. ROE D'ALBRET, op. cit., p. 1101; cf. Tite-Live, 5, 23, 3; 5, 31, 3.

[251] R. E. A. PALMER, Roman Religion . . ., p. 25.

[252] Ibidem; cf. Tite-Live, 22, 1, 17–9, sacrifices à *Iuno sospita* de Lanuvium, lectisterne offert à *Iuno Regina* de l'Aventin grâce à l'argent récolté par les matrones, Macr., Sat., 1, 6, 12–14.

[253] J. BAYET, La religion romaine, histoire politique et psychologique, Paris, 1976, p. 136; p. 178; R. E. A. PALMER, Roman Religion . . ., p. 27.

Capitole[254]. L'auteur en conclut que ce culte féminin rendu à *Iuno Regina* avait une origine non romaine.

J. GAGÉ et Y. ROE D'ALBRET constatent qu'une fois transférée à Rome, *Iuno Regina* vit s'accentuer son aspect matronal[255] au point que, écrit J. GAGÉ, malgré ses origines étrangères, «à la fin de la République, Junon Reine est probablement la plus matronale de toutes les déesses romaines»[256]. Pour J. GAGÉ, «aucune influence hellénique n'a été nécessaire pour faire d'elle, par excellence, la protectrice des *matronae*», par ailleurs même si ce rôle avait été le sien à Véies, «il resterait à savoir si les 'matrones' eurent réellement besoin du modèle»[257]. J. GAGÉ pose la question de savoir pourquoi les Junons reçurent le privilège d'encadrer la dévotion des matrones et analyse l'exemple modèle de la préhistoire du culte de *Iuno Regina* de l'Aventin où M. Furius Camillus joue un rôle personnel. A Rome, primitivement, les dévotions matronales étaient mises sous le nom de *Fortuna*. Quand Camille dont la dévotion pour les déesses matronales (*Matuta, Fortuna*) était notoire[258], ramena de Véies *Iuno Regina*, les femmes romaines connaissaient déjà plusieurs Junons, mais les anciens rites de *Fortuna* commençaient sans doute à péricliter[259]. Dès lors, songe J. GAGÉ, en installant Junon Reine sur l'Aventin, Camille, objet de l'hostilité plébéenne, a voulu «créer un culte où les femmes trouveraient de hauts symboles en dehors du cadre habituel des oppositions sociales»[260]. Cette dévotion matronale pour *Iuno Regina* s'intègre sans heurt à l'ensemble de la personnalité junonienne définie par G. DUMÉZIL qui reconnaît d'ailleurs primitivement à *Iuno Regina*, un rôle de mère[261].

G. DUMÉZIL, reprenant une théorie parfois contestée, souligne très justement l'influence de l'épopée troyenne sur les récits de la guerre de Véies[262]. Désormais, les Romains entrevoient Junon à travers la figure de son homologue

---

[254] Cf. Horace, C.S.; E. FRAENKEL, Horace, Oxford, 1957 (ch. 7: étude des cérémonies); I. B. PIGHI, De ludis saecularibus populi Romani Quiritium, Pubbl. Univ. Catt. S. Cuore, Sér. 5, Vol. 35, Milan, 1941, p. 107–119; p. 201–221.

[255] J. GAGÉ, Matronalia, p. 64–5; Y. ROE D'ALBRET, op. cit., p. 1101.

[256] J. GAGÉ, Matronalia, p. 80.

[257] J. GAGÉ, Matronalia, p. 64–5.

[258] Cf. G. DUMÉZIL, Servius et la Fortune, Essai sur la fonction sociale de louange et de blâme et sur les éléments indo-européens du cens romain, Coll. Les Mythes Romains, Paris, 1943; J. BAYET, Tite-Live livre V, p. 154 et notes.

[259] J. GAGÉ, Matronalia, p. 86.

[260] Ibidem.

[261] G. DUMÉZIL, Rel. rom. arch.², p. 303.

[262] G. DUMÉZIL, Rel. rom. arch.², p. 463; contra J. BAYET, Tite-Live livre V, p. 133–4, pour qui les éléments homériques sont occasionnels et sporadiques; ils peuvent constituer «des embellissements tout superficiels dus à un poète hellénisant – Ennius par exemple – qui mettrait en forme sur des poncifs d'école la tradition annalistique.» Voir aussi sur ce problème: J. GAGÉ, Huit recherches sur les origines italiques et romaines, ch. IV: Véies et le thème des origines troyennes à Rome, Paris, 1950, p. 73s.; F. BÖMER, Rom und Troia, Untersuchungen zur Frühgeschichte Roms, Baden-Baden, 1951, critiqué par J. PERRET (dont on connaît le système de datations basses: Les origines de la légende troyenne de Rome [281–31], Thèse Paris, 1942) dans: R.E.L., 30, 1952, p. 488–491.

grecque. Dix ans durant, elle protégea les ennemis de Rome qui n'obtint la victoire qu'après l'avoir évoquée: «moyennant de grandes promesses, elle avait abandonné son peuple et accepté de devenir, sur l'Aventin, une Regina du peuple romain plus actuelle que la Regina jointe à Jupiter sur le Capitole»[263].

Après Véies, les Romains pouvaient croire Junon conciliée à jamais, mais, nous dit G. DUMÉZIL, «une nouvelle *interpretatio* replaça Junon dans le camp du plus redoutable ennemi: la grande déesse, la reine de Carthage ne pouvait être rendue que par les noms grec et latin de la déesse reine, Héra, Junon»[264]. R. BLOCH conteste la suggestion de DUMÉZIL d'une nouvelle *interpretatio*. Junon – Héra n'a pu passer aussi tardivement dans le camp de l'ennemi carthaginois, elle s'y trouvait, en vérité depuis longtemps, car *Iuno Regina* et *Iuno Caelestis* sont en fait les deux divinités – Uni et Astarté – assimilées dans le traité entre le roi de Caere et Carthage ainsi qu'en témoignent les inscriptions du Ve siècle sur lamelles d'or de Pyrgi (cf. infra)[265].

La position de R. BLOCH fondée sur le réseau d'interprétations qui relie, dès l'époque archaïque, ces divinités homologues nous semble justifiée; néanmoins, nous ne le suivons plus quand il conçoit qu'au temps de l'alliance divine scellée à Pyrgi (Ve siècle avant J.-C.), Rome aurait entrevu dans ces deux peuples unis religieusement, la menace d'ennemis futurs soutenus par deux grandes déesses dans lesquelles elle devait reconnaître peut-être dès la haute époque, sa propre Junon[266]. G. DUMÉZIL ne nie nullement le témoignage exceptionnel de l'interprétation précoce des quatre noms Junon – Uni – Astarté – Héra à Pyrgi, seulement, il n'attribue pas le même impact à une assimilation qui aura besoin d'être repensée au temps d'Hannibal.

Le souvenir de cette alliance conclue à Caere au Ve siècle n'amena peut-être pas Rome à redouter la déesse de Carthage, par contre, durant la «guerre contre la ville de Didon, tout ce qui paraît indiquer un mécontentement, une hostilité de Junon, d'avance suspecte de punisme, trouve les Romains sensibles»[267]. De là, le souci évident des Romains de se la concilier par des mesures exceptionnelles, spécialement aux moments dramatiques de 217 et de 207[268]. Y. ROE

---

[263] G. DUMÉZIL, Rel. rom. arch.[2], p. 463.

[264] Ibidem.

[265] R. BLOCH, Hannibal et les dieux de Rome, dans: Recherches . . ., p. 32–42, spéc. p. 34 = C.R.A.I., 1975, p. 14–25.

[266] R. BLOCH, Héra, Uni, Junon en Italie centrale, dans: Recherches . . ., p. 9–19, spéc. p. 19; exposé analogue dans: C.R.A.I., 1972, p. 384–395.

[267] G. DUMÉZIL, Rel. rom. arch.[2], p. 667, p. 481.

[268] A. ABAECHERLI-BOYCE, The Expiatory Rites of 207 B.C., dans: T.A.P.A., 68, 1937, p. 157–171; J. COUSIN, La crise religieuse de 207 av. J.-C., dans: R.H.R., 126, 1943, p. 15–41; P. GRIMAL, Le siècle des Scipions. Rome et l'hellénisme au temps des guerres puniques, ch. III: Les années terribles et la montée des héros, Coll. Historique, Paris, 1953, spéc. p. 70ss.; J. BAYET, La religion romaine, p. 149–152; K. LATTE, Röm. Religionsgeschichte, p. 257, n.3, explique les nombreuses manifestations rituelles en l'honneur de Junon, pour lui, déesse essentiellement féminine, par les pertes humaines subies par Rome et par le découragement qui en résulta chez les femmes; G. DUMÉZIL, Rel. rom. arch.[2], IIIe partie, ch. VII: La religion pendant la seconde guerre punique, p.

D'ALBRET et G. DUMÉZIL présentent ces années comme cruciales dans l'évolution du culte de Junon[269] «de par l'assimilation à Héra, elle est depuis longtemps devenue l'épouse de Jupiter, le mot *Regina* recevant désormais tout son sens. Mais elle commence officiellement, en cette année difficile (217 avant J.-C.), l'étonnante carrière mythologique dont l'ʻEnéideʼ, dont Horace donnent la plus riche expression: protectrice de Rome, mais protectrice qui mérite des soins particuliers et incessants parce qu'elle ne l'a pas toujours été, parce qu'elle a, dans sa mémoire de déesse grecque ennemie de Troie, des raisons de ne pas l'être»[270]. L'Enée de Virgile se comporte envers la déesse tout comme Camille ou les Romains du temps des guerres puniques. Laissons P. BOYANCÉ nous révéler l'évolution de la Junon virgilienne qui finit par renoncer à son hostilité envers les Troyens: «Si elle y renonce, c'est sans doute en grande partie parce qu'Enée, conformément aux ordres qu'il a reçus des oracles à plusieurs reprises, n'a cessé de chercher à la fléchir et à l'apaiser. On songe aussitôt à la conception officielle de la *pax deorum* qui joue un si grand rôle dans la religion romaine. On songe aussi à ce rite fameux de l'*evocatio* par lequel on se flatte de transférer chez soi le dieu de l'adversaire. Quand s'est écroulé l'Empire troyen, c'est parce que les dieux qui faisaient sa grandeur ont quitté leurs sanctuaires et abandonné leurs autels»[271].

Hannibal comprend tout le parti à tirer de l'interprétation Junon-Tanit (à Carthage, Tanit prend rapidement la place d'Astarté[272]), et entreprend de vénérer Junon-Héra; on connaît ses ʻdémêlésʼ avec *Iuno Lacinia*[273]. Comme l'exprime R. BLOCH: «La vieille inimitié de l'Héra grecque, ennemie des Troyens, doit à ses yeux venir renforcer la haine de Tanit contre Rome»[274].

Le passage de l'ʻEnéideʼ où devant la promesse d'un culte brillant à Rome, Junon change d'humeur à l'égard d'Enée et de son peuple[275] suscite ce commentaire de Servius qui voit dans cet épisode divin la transposition d'un fait historique: *sed constat bello Punico secundo exoratam Iunonem*[276]. Cette notice donne à croire que Junon a été l'objet d'une *exoratio* à la fin de la deuxième

457ss.; R. BLOCH, Hannibal et les dieux de Rome, dans: Recherches . . ., p. 32ss., CH. GUITTARD, Recherches sur la nature de Saturne des origines à la réforme de 217 avant J.C., dans: Recherches . . . p. 43—71.

[269] Y. ROE D'ALBRET, op. cit., p. 1101; G. DUMÉZIL, Rel. rom. arch.², p. 463.

[270] G. DUMÉZIL, Rel. rom. arch.², p. 463.

[271] P. BOYANCÉ, La religion de Virgile, Coll. Mythes et Religions, 48, Paris, 1963, p. 35—6; voir aussi V. BUCHHEIT, Vergil über die Sendung Roms. Untersuchungen zum Bellum Poenicum und zur Aeneis, Gymnasium Beih., 3, Heidelberg, 1963, p. 11—150: „Juno's Kampf gegen Rom und ihre Versöhnung"; p. 173—189: „Carthago-Rom als Antithese in Aeneis 1—7".

[272] R. BLOCH, Héra, Uni, Junon en Italie centrale, dans: Recherches . . ., p. 18.

[273] Cic., De div., 1, 24, 48; Tite-Live, 28, 46, 16. J. BAYET, Herclé. Etude critique des principaux monuments relatifs à l'Hercule Etrusque, Paris, 1926, p. 215; V. BASANOFF, Evocatio, p. 206; G. DUMÉZIL, Rel. rom. arch.², p. 464; Y. ROE D'ALBRET, op. cit., p. 1101.

[274] R. BLOCH, Hannibal et les dieux de Rome, dans: Recherches . . ., p. 34.

[275] Virgile, Enéide, 12, 841.

[276] Serv., ad Aen., 12, 841.

guerre punique[277]. Mais Servius de poursuivre: . . . *tertio uero bello a Scipione sacris quibusdam etiam Roman translatam*. Ce transfert de la déesse à Rome semble bien supposer son évocation à la fin de la troisième guerre punique avant la destruction de Carthage[278]. Le *carmen* dont Macrobe a conservé le texte d'après un contemporain de Scipion, Furius, reproduit peut-être les termes de cette évocation où l'absence de nom divin est frappante[279]. On ne connaît point de temple dédié à cette divinité évoquée. F. Cumont et V. Basanoff estiment que son image a pu être abritée dans le temple de *Moneta* jusqu'à ce que, en 122 avant J.-C., la *Colonia Iunonia* ressuscitant une Carthage romaine sur le sol africain, un nouveau temple y soit bâti pour la *Iuno Caelestis*[280]. Selon J. Le Gall, un culte a pu lui être rendu dans le temple de *Iuno Regina*, divinité qui lui avait été assimilée. Pourtant, l'empereur Elagabal amènera à Rome *Iuno Caelestis* de la Carthage romaine, il ne pouvait ignorer qu'il s'agissait de la 'Junon' punique[281]. L'auteur conclut: «On doit (. . .) se demander si les promesses de l'*evocatio* n'étaient pas tenues dans le pays même, devenu romain par la conquête»[282].

IX. Junon dans la triade capitoline

Avant d'abandonner *Iuno Regina*, il reste à considérer son intégration au sein de la triade capitoline. Varron rappelle l'existence d'un *Capitolium uetus* qui aurait déjà réuni sur le Quirinal Jupiter, Junon, Minerve[283]. Certains auteurs

---

[277] V. Basanoff, Evocatio, p. 63–65: Iuno Caelestis de Carthage, I, Exoratio; G. Dumézil, Rel. rom. arch.², p. 468.

[278] V. Basanoff, Evocatio, p. 65–6: Iuno Caelestis de Carthage, II, Evocatio; G. Ch. Picard, Les religions de l'Afrique antique, Paris, 1954, p. 568.; G. Dumézil, Rel. rom. arch.², p. 468; R. Bloch, Hannibal et les dieux de Rome, p. 35.

[279] Macr., Sat., 3, 9: *Si deus si dea est cui populus ciuitasque Carthaginiensis est in tutela, teque maxime, ille qui urbis huius populique tutelam recepisti, precor uenerorque ueniamque a uobis peto, ut uos populum ciuitatemque Carthaginiensem deseratis, loca templa sacra urbemque eorum relinquatis, absque his abeatis, eique populo ciuitati metum formidinem obliuionem iniciatis, proditique Romam ad me meosque ueniatis, nostraque uobis loca templa sacra urbs acceptior probatiorque sit, mihique populoque Romano militibusque meis praepositi sitis, ut sciamus intellegamusque, si ita feceritis, uoueo uobis templa ludosque facturum.* On verra les réflexions de J. Le Gall, Evocatio, dans: Mél. Heurgon, I, p. 521ss. et de R. Bloch, Hannibal et les dieux de Rome, spéc. p. 34–5.

[280] F. Cumont, dans: R.E., III,2, 1899, art. Caelestis, col. 1248; V. Basanoff, Evocatio, p. 66; Plut., C. Gracchus, 11, cf. Solin, 28, 11.

[281] J. Le Gall, Evocatio, p. 523, n. 17: «Elagabal et non Septime Sévère, comme l'a démontré J. Mundle, *Dea Caelestis in der Religionspolitik des Septimius Severus und der Iulia Domna* dans *Historia*, 10, 1961, p. 228–237 ».

[282] J. Le Gall, Evocatio, p. 523.

[283] Varr., L.L., 5, 158: *Cliuus proximus a Flora susus uersus Capitolium uetus, quod ibi sacellum Iouis, Iunonis, Mineruae, et id antiquius quam aedis quae in Capitolio facta*; cf. Mart., Epigr., 5, 22, 4; 7, 73, 4.

ne voient en ce témoignage qu'une invention a posteriori tendant à vieillir et à nationaliser l'œuvre étrangère[284]. Ainsi que le remarque K. Latte, ce terme de *Capitolium uetus* sur le Quirinal ne peut être antérieur au moment où le 'Capitole' devint synonyme de temple de la triade capitoline[285]. Pourtant, E. Gjerstad persiste à croire en une triade antérieure qui aurait été fondée entre 575 et 509[286]. Quant à J. Bayet, il semble accepter la mention de cette triade plus ancienne tout en considérant qu'elle ne fait que reporter le problème de l'origine de ce groupement divin[287].

On a songé à une influence grecque. Cependant on ne connaît qu'en Phocide un groupe cultuel Ζεύς, Ἥρα, Ἀθηνᾶ[288], mais, il est vrai, «dans des conditions remarquablement analogues à celles du culte capitolin»[289]. Par ailleurs, la mythologie grecque a conçu des épisodes légendaires rapprochant Zeus, Héra, Athéna (enfance d'Héraclès; ruine de Troie voulue par ces trois divinités) qui touchèrent très tôt l'Italie[290]. Pourtant, G. Dumézil n'envisage pas la possibilité que ce modèle grec ait pu être connu aussi tôt (VIe siècle) à Rome[291]. Il ne nous semble pas que l'argument soit déterminant. On a eu la preuve, ces vingt dernières années, que des cultes grecs ont pu pénétrer au Latium dès le VIe siècle, directement, sans médiation étrusque; nous ne citerons que le cas des Dioscures[292].

L'origine étrusque semble bien la plus vraisemblable, mais on lira avec grand profit les réserves d'U. Bianchi: en fait, «il n'existe aucune triade étrusque dont l'existence soit réellement démontrée»[293]. Pour combler cette lacune, E. Gjerstad[294] accorde beaucoup de poids à la découverte faite en 1967 à Poggio Civitate (Murlo): il s'agit d'une terre cuite du VIe siècle qui

---

[284] G. Dumézil, Rel. rom. arch.², p. 313; T. Hackens, Capitolium vetus, dans: Bull. Inst. Hist. Belge Rome, 33, 1961, p. 69ss.

[285] K. Latte, Röm. Religionsgeschichte, p. 150, n.3.

[286] E. Gjerstad, Early Rome, V, p. 63—4; R. E. A. Palmer, Roman Religion . . ., p. 22, rappelle que Varron est notre seule source à l'appui.

[287] J. Bayet, La religion romaine, p. 40.

[288] Pausanias, 10, 5, 1—2.

[289] G. Dumézil, Rel. rom. arch.², p. 313—4.

[290] G. Dumézil, Rel. rom. arch,², p. 316—7.

[291] G. Dumézil, Rel. rom. arch.², p. 316.

[292] Sur une inscription du VIe siècle découverte à Lavinium (Pratica di Mare), au sanctuaire des treize autels, Castor et Pollux portent des noms tirés du grec sans médiation étrusque: *Castorei Podlouqueique Qurois*. F. Castagnoli, Dedica arcaica lavinate a Castore e Polluce, dans: Studi Mat. St. Relig., 30, 1959, p. 109—117; St. Weinstock, Two Archaic Inscriptions from Latium, dans: J.R.S., 50, 1960, p. 112ss.; G. Radke, Zu der archaischen Inschrift von Madonnetta, dans: Glotta, 42, 1964, p. 214ss.; cette découverte épigraphique a suscité une bibliographie abondante que l'on trouvera dans: F. Castagnoli et alii, Lavinium II. Le tredici are, Ist. Topografia Antica Univ. Roma, Rome, 1975, p. 443.

[293] U. Bianchi, Disegno storico del culto Capitolino nell' Italia romana e nelle provincie dell' Impero, dans: Acc. Lincei, Memorie, Sér. VIII,2, 1949 [1950], p. 347—415; Id., Questions sur les origines du culte capitolin, dans: Latomus, 10, 1951, p. 413—418, spéc. p. 415; voir aussi Luisa Banti, Il culto del cosiddetto „Tempio dell' Apollo" a Veii e il problema delle triadi etrusco-italiche, dans: St. Etr., 17, 1943, p. 187—224.

[294] E. Gjerstad, Early Rome V, p. 64 et p. 192.

représenterait Jupiter, Junon et Minerve[295]. Pour G. Dumézil, il s'agit certainemement d'une illusion[296]. Malgré les interrogations et les incertitudes, J. Bayet, G. Dumézil et même F. Altheim acceptent l'origine étrusque[297]. J. Bayet regarde cette fondation comme un acte politique: «contre la 'masculinité divine' des Latins (. . .) en faveur de déesses volontiers protectrices de cités dans l'Etrurie du Sud (Junon Reine) ou les peuplements italiques influencés par elle (Faléries honorait spécialement Minerve)»[298]. G. Dumézil pense lui aussi à une manœuvre politique: la légende d'Enée connue très tôt au Latium[299] aurait pu servir au réveil du patriotisme latin, italique contre les Etrusques. En ce cas, l'appel lancé par les «Tarquins» pour protéger leur Rome au groupement des divinités grecques qui avaient renversé Troie et persécuté les Troyens se comprendrait comme une défense idéologique[300].

On ne peut négliger l'opinion d'U. Bianchi estimant que l'absence de cultes similaires dans l'Italie préromaine «autorise à admettre l'originalité *relative* du culte romain du Capitole par rapport à la religion et aux cultes locaux des villes de l'ancienne Italie avec lesquelles Rome a été en contact direct pendant les premiers siècles de la République»[301].

---

[295] K. M. Phillips Jr., Bryn Mawr College Excavations in Tuscany 1967, dans: A.J.A., 72, 1968, p. 120−4; Id., Poggio Civitate, dans: Archaeology, 21, 1968, p. 252−261; Id., Poggio Civitate (Murlo, Siena). Il santuario arcaico. Catalogo della Mostra. Firenze-Siena, 1970, Min. P. I. Soprint. Antichità d'Etruria, Florence, 1970, p. 55ss., pl. XXXVII; T. N. Gantz, Divine Triads on an Archaic Etruscan Frieze Plaque from Poggio Civitate, dans: St. Etr., 39, 1971, p. 3−24.

[296] G. Dumézil, Rel. rom arch.², p. 669−70, n.5: «Il ne s'agit sans doute même pas de dieux, et il y a quatre personnages, un masculin avec un serviteur, un féminin avec une servante. Les autres figures de la même terre cuite ne sont pas davantage une variante étrusque de la «triade infernale», préfiguration supposée de la triade Cérès, Liber, Libera.»

[297] F. Altheim, Römische Religionsgeschichte, II. Von der Gründung des kapitolinischen Tempels bis zum Aufkommen der Alleinherrschaft, Berlin−Leipzig, 1932, p. 59−60 et passim; J. Bayet, La religion romaine, p. 40; G. Dumézil, Rel. rom. arch.², p. 314ss.; G. Pugliese−Carratelli, Lazio, Roma e Magna Grecia prima del secolo quarto A.C., dans: Par. Pass., 23, 1968, p. 331, considère que dans l'introduction de la triade capitoline par les Etrusques l'influence grecque a joué très tôt un rôle, car il ne faut pas oublier qu'Athéna et Héra figurent parmi les premières divinités grecques à avoir atteint l'Italie, dès la «précolonisation» de la fin de l'époque mycénienne.

[298] J. Bayet, La religion romaine, p. 40.

[299] Sur le problème des origines de la légende d'Enée au Latium on pourra voir G. Moyaers, Enée et Lavinium à la lumière des découvertes archéologiques récentes, dans: R.B.Ph., 55, I, 1977, p. 21−50 et pl. V−VIII; G. Dury-Moyaers, Enée et Lavinium. A propos de découvertes archéologiques récentes, Coll. Latomus, 174, Bruxelles, 1981 250 p. et 37 pl.

[300] G. Dumézil, Rel. rom. arch.², p. 317, n.1.

[301] U. Bianchi, Questions . . ., p. 416: «. . . on doit admettre la probabilité que la formule cultuelle capitoline s'appuyait sur des traditions locales préexistantes; dans ce cas, elle devrait être séparée de l'ensemble des éléments artistiques, cultuels et rituels qui ont pu avoir été empruntés à l'Etrurie, lors de l'édification du grand sanctuaire du mont capitolin. Ce ne serait peut-être pas le premier cas, dans l'histoire de Rome, où l'on aurait tiré des conséquences injustifiées de la constatation de l'emprunt d'un élément formel dans le domaine religieux et politique».

La triade qui deviendra le symbole de la grandeur de Rome, « ne forme pas une structure conceptuelle »[302]. A l'époque ancienne, même les formules cultuelles associant les trois divinités sont peu nombreuses. Les siècles passant, à l'époque augustéenne, les deux divinités Junon et Minerve ont acquis quelque consistance et l'on trouve leurs deux noms associés à celui de Jupiter dans les invocations des personnages de Tite-Live[303]. Dans la pratique, seule la présence de Jupiter, maître de Rome, semble vraiment compter; la présence de Minerve au côté du couple Jupiter-Junon, surtout, demeure fort obscure[304].

X. Junon et Jupiter

Ce couple Jupiter-Junon, il est vrai, n'a pris toute sa signification que sous l'influence de la mythologie grecque. A l'exemple d'Héra, Junon devint la déesse matrimoniale, la *Pronuba,* patronne des femmes mariées et de l'union conjugale[305]. Selon P. NOAILLES, elle joue ce rôle en sa qualité d'épouse de Jupiter: quand s'affirma la vocation de Jupiter, dieu du Capitole et de la cité, elle entraîna le rôle de Junon dans le mariage des citoyens[306]. Cette vision nous semble excessive, Junon, déesse matronale dans son essence, dut, de tout temps, être concernée par cet aspect de la féminité, mais l'influence grecque vint préciser cette virtualité en faisant de la déesse l'Epouse par excellence. Pour P. NOAILLES, l'intervention de Junon dans les rites nuptiaux proprement dits est tardive. Les *dii nuptiales*[307] sont de beaucoup plus anciens, la déesse a pris leur place, elle se les a incorporés, car les rites étaient déjà constitués au moment où elle a assumé la protection du mariage. Nous n'adhérons pas à ce schéma évolutif, car « dans les cas les mieux connus, les listes d'*indigitamenta* apparaissent en position subordonnée »[308] à une divinité autonome de type Cérès[309] ou Junon: « ce que nous

---

[302] G. DUMÉZIL, Rel. rom. arch.², p. 316; voir aussi V. BASANOFF, La triade capitoline, dans: Studi-Arangio-Ruiz, II, Naples, 1953, p. 323–332 et G. RADKE, Il valore religioso e politico delle divinità del Campidoglio, dans: Atti del convegno Internazionale per il XIX Centenario della Dedicazione del 'Capitolium' Bresciano e per il 150° anniversario della sua scoperta, I, Suppl. ai Comment. dell' Ateneo di Brescia, Brescia, 1975, p. 245ss.

[303] Tite-Live, 6, 16, 2; 38, 51, 9; cf. G. DUMÉZIL, Rel. rom. arch.², p. 298.

[304] G. DUMÉZIL, Rel. rom. arch.², p. 313.

[305] Voir notamment J. GAGÉ, Matronalia, p. 80; P. NOAILLES, Junon, déesse matrimoniale des Romains, dans: ID., Fas et Ius. Etude de Droit Romain, Paris, 1948, p. 33 et passim.

[306] P. NOAILLES, op. cit., p. 34.

[307] Ces *dii nuptiales*, qui ont fait la joie des Pères de l'Eglise (Tertullien, Ad Nationes, 2, 11 et surtout saint Augustin, Civ. dei, 6, 9), sont sans doute toujours restés confinés dans la liturgie, sans jamais intervenir dans la religion vivante, cf. G. DUMÉZIL, Rel. rom. arch.², p. 53.

[308] G. DUMÉZIL, Rel. rom. arch.², p. 53.

[309] Cf. la liste des entités divines, spécialistes chacune d'un moment de la culture du sol dont le flamine de Cérès récite les noms quand il sacrifie à Tellus et à Cérès. Cette liste vient des 'Libri iuris pontificii' de Fabius Pictor par l'intermédiaire de Varron cité lui-même par Servius, Géorg, 1, 21; saint Augustin, 4, 8, en a connu une variante.

savons de Junon, protectrice des mariages comme de l'accouchement, donne à penser que c'est d'elle aussi que la série Virginiensis, Subigus, etc. (. . .) détaillent l'opération»[310]. Sans que l'on puisse suspecter l'antériorité dans le temps des *indigitamenta*[311].

Si l'on revient au couple Jupiter-Junon, il est peut-être abusif de n'y reconnaître qu'un apport grec. Il ne faut pas négliger la possibilité de leur rapprochement dans la plus ancienne théologie latine[312]: à Préneste, «il paraît (. . .) probable que les bébés allaités par Fortuna (. . .) ont possédé de tout temps „l'individuazione nominativa", probable aussi que, nommés de toujours, ils n'ont pas, en cours de carrière, changé de noms: ils s'appellent Jupiter et Junon quand nous les connaissons, or Jupiter et Junon étaient, dans toutes les cités latines, des divinités du plus ancien lot»[313]. Un postulat domine l'étude moderne des religions latines écrit G. DUMÉZIL: ces religions auraient ignoré les filiations, les généalogies et aussi les «enfances» divines et là où on en observe elles résulteraient nécessairement d'une influence grecque ou gréco-étrusque. Il est vrai qu' «à Rome il n'y a pas de mythes divins. Mais les résultats de l'enquête comparative (. . .) ont conduit à rectifier cette formule et à dire il n'y a plus de mythes divins»[314]. «Préneste peut donc avoir conservé ici un théologème — filiation et enfances — que Rome aura perdu»: «le dieu souverain et la déesse de son niveau, Junon (. . .) ont une mère qui est la déesse primordiale»[315].

[310] G. DUMÉZIL, Rel. rom. arch.², p. 54.

[311] Ibidem. p. 53.

[312] G. DUMÉZIL, Déesses latines et mythes védiques. III: Fortuna Primigenia, Coll. Latomus, 25, Bruxelles, 1956, p. 71−98.

[313] Ibidem, p. 84; cf. Cic., De div., 2, 85−6: ... *Is est hodie locus saeptus religiose propter Iouis pueri, qui lactens cum Iunone Fortunae in gremio sedens, mammam appetens, castissime colitur a matribus.* A Préneste, des statuettes de terre cuite ont été découvertes, elles représentent une femme allaitant un enfant (E. FERNIQUE, Etude sur Préneste, Paris, 1880, p.78−9). Une de ces images évoque vraiment la description de Cicéron puisqu'elle figure la Fortune passant le bras autour du cou de deux enfants de sexe différent, qui de la main, lui touchent le sein; cf. F. LENORMANT, dans: DAREMBERG et SAGLIO, I,1, 1887, art. Ceres, fig. 1307, p. 1062 et M. RENARD, Junon, la Fortune et Ilithyie, dans: Mél. I. Lévy, Bruxelles 1955 = Ann. Inst. Philol. Or. et. Sl., 13, 1953, p. 531−537, pl. I, spéc. p. 534, pour qui il ne s'agit nullement de Déméter portant ses deux enfants comme le pensait LENORMANT. En plus du texte de Cicéron, on disposait d'inscriptions votives à F(ortuna) P(rimigenia) (réunies dans C.I.L., XIV, la plupart des nᵒˢ 2849 à 2888) et de deux dédicaces qui semblaient bien associer la déesse au *Iuppiter puer* dont parle Cicéron; l'une disait *Fortunae Ioui puero* ..., l'autre, apparemment fautive, *Fortunae Iouis puero* ... (C.I.L., XIV, 2868, 2862). En 1882, M. R. MOWAT, Inscription latine sur plaque de bronze acquise à Rome par M. A. Dutuit, dans: Mémoires de la Société nationale des Antiquaires de France, 5ème sér., 3 (= 43), 1882, p. 200, publia une inscription qui changeait tout; C.I.L., XIV, 2863: *ORCEVIA NVMERI / NATIONV CRATIA / FORTVNA DIOVO FILEA / PRIMO CENIA / DONOM DEDI;* de mère de Jupiter qu'elle était, *Fortuna* devenait ainsi sa fille, cf. G. DUMÉZIL, Déesses latines . . ., p. 71ss.

[314] G. DUMÉZIL, Déesses latines . . ., p. 85.

[315] Cf. G. DUMÉZIL, Déesses latines . . ., p. 96ss., où l'on trouvera également l'exégèse de cette théologie prénestine. On se reportera aussi à A. BRELICH, Tre variazioni romane sul tema delle origini. I: Roma e Preneste. Una polemica religiosa nell'Italia antica, Università di

XI. *Junon et la Fortune*

On ne peut négliger les liens très anciens qui unissent Junon et la Fortune. « A l'époque classique, la religion romaine accorde une place encore superstitieuse à la notion de Fortuna »[316]. On rappellera le rôle joué par la *Fortuna Augusti* dans le culte impérial. Elle a absorbé des éléments du culte républicain et assimilé le contenu des cultes hellénistiques de la *Tychè* des rois. Cette identification avec la *Tychè* grecque fait de *Fortuna* la divinité de la chance[317]. Pourtant les vieilles divinités latines, la *Fortuna Virgo* du *Forum Boarium*, la *Fortuna Muliebris* du sanctuaire de la Voie Latine, la *Fortuna Virilis*[318], la *Fortuna Mammosa*[319], la Fortune d'Antium[320] ou encore la Fortune de Préneste avaient peu de points communs avec cette *Tychè* grecque et avec la notion de hasard — on fera la distinction avec le culte de Préneste où « la distributrice dès sorts a été identifiée avec la déesse primordiale, mère de Jupiter, et c'est elle qui est devenue le terme féminin de l'énigme des origines »[321].

Selon Cicéron, le sanctuaire de *Fortuna Primigenia* est l'objet d'une grande dévotion de la part des mères[322]. Pourtant, selon J. GAGÉ, «sa première apparence (. . .) est plutôt d'une divinité des hommes, voire d'une puissance androgne »[323]. Les deux Fortunes Antiates semblent présenter l'une, une apparence «guerrière», l'autre, un aspect plus «matronal» correspondant à deux caractères de la puissance féminine; ceci confirme la dualité de la déesse[324], «protectrice (. . .) des destinées respectives de l'homme et de la femme, et de leurs relations entre eux »[325]. Ce portrait divin ne manque pas de similitude avec la

Roma, Pubblicazioni della Scuola di Studi Storico-Religiosi, 2, Nuovi Saggi, 14, Rome, 1955, p. 9—14, qui reconnaît pareillement dans la *Primigenia* la divinité primordiale tout en donnant une explication moins convaincante.

[316] J. GAGÉ, Matronalia, p. 24.

[317] Ibidem.

[318] Références dans: WISSOWA, R. u. K. d. R²., p. 257—8; voir aussi M. RENARD, Junon, la Fortune et Ilithyie, p. 534.

[319] Cf. L. PRELLER—H. JORDAN, Römische Mythologie³, Berlin, 1863, p. 187 et J. A. HILD, dans: DAREMBERG et SAGLIO II,2, 1896, art. Fortuna, p. 1275.

[320] E.g. Hor., Odes, 1, 35.

[321] Cic., De div., 2, 85—6; cf. G. DUMÉZIL, Déesses latines . . ., p. 71—98. spéc. p. 97.

[322] Cic., De div., 2, 85—6.

[323] J. GAGÉ, Matronalia, p. 25.

[324] J. GAGÉ, Matronalia, p. 62—3: « La représentation monétaire des deux Fortunes d'Antium ne permet pas d'affirmer que l'une d'elles ait été, à proprement parler, « guerrière »; il y en a cependant quelques apparences, par comparaison avec l'aspect «matronal» de sa compagne. Même si le culte d'une Fortuna Equestris à Antium, connu par un passage de Tacite, Ann., 3, 71, ne peut servir d'indice sûr, il y a lieu de considérer que les deux Fortunes Antiates avaient réellement correspondu à deux aspects de la puissance féminine, exprimés pratiquement par la *virgo* vigoureuse et vaillante et par la femme, féconde ou non ».

[325] J. GAGÉ, Matronalia, p. 95.

personnalité de Junon, d'autant que si l'on suit J. GAGÉ «nous discernons une tendance générale de l'évolution, par laquelle ces anciens cultes [de Fortuna . . .] se sont en partie transformés, soit en cultes de Junon, soit aux cultes de Vénus, cette dernière veillant surtout sur les relations entre les deux sexes, la première plutôt sur les fonctions même de l'épouse et de la mère de famille»[326].

A Préneste, Fortuna est déesse-mère, mais l'expression est trop vague, sa maternité n'était pas simplement signifiée par deux bébés anonymes. Ses poupons ne sont autres que Jupiter et Junon[327]. Dès lors, on peut penser que le lien qui unit Junon à *Fortuna* est de même nature que celui qui existe entre Jupiter et la *Primigenia*. A Préneste, cette présence de Junon à côté de *Fortuna* n'est pas unique puisqu'on connaît encore un *Iunonarium*[328] et qu'un mois lui était consacré en propre[329].

On n'oublia pas cette rencontre de *Fortuna* et de Junon, divinités maternelles; c'est ce que montre M. RENARD par la publication d'un monument de l'époque d'Hadrien représentant une déesse de la fécondité. L'inscription est étonnante: *IUNONI. FORTUN(ae). HELITIA[e]*[330]. Elle témoigne de l'identification de trois déesses maternelles, sujettes, depuis les temps anciens à de telles assimilations: on a vu les liens qui unissent Junon et la Fortune; par ailleurs l' Εἰλείθυια grecque – que M. RENARD reconnaît dans *Helitia*, transcription incorrecte[331] – a été de longue date identifiée à Héra-*Iuno Lucina*: notamment à Pyrgi et à l'Héraion du Sélé où l'on a découvert une statuette du IVe siècle avant notre ère considérée comme une Héra-Ilithyie[332].

XII. *Junon et Janus*

Junon entretenait également certains liens anciens avec Janus: «Il y a deux manières en effet de concevoir les commencements: ou bien ils sont 'naissance', et alors ils appartiennent à Junon, ou ils sont 'passage' d'un état à un autre, et ils relèvent de Janus»[333]. M. RENARD explique aussi cette rencontre: «les deux notions que représentent Janus et Junon correspondent à deux idées primitives et

---

[326] Ibidem.
[327] G. DUMÉZIL, Déesses latines . . . p. 83.
[328] C.I.L., XIV, 2867.
[329] Ovide, Fastes, 6, 62; PRELLER–JORDAN, Röm. Myth.³, p. 191, n. 1; M. RENARD, Junon, la Fortune et Ilithyie, p. 535.
[330] M. RENARD, Junon, la Fortune et Ilithyie, p. 531ss.
[331] M. RENARD, Junon, la Fortune et Ilithyie, p. 532.
[332] Cf. CH. P[ICARD], dans: Rev. Arch., VI,7, 1939, 1, p. 136 et M. RENARD, Junon, la Fortune et Ilithyie, p. 533–534; U. ZANOTTI BIANCO et P. ZANCANI MONTUORO, Capaccio. Heraion alla foce del Sele, dans: Atti della reale Accademia nazionale dei Lincei, 334 ème année, 6ème sér., 15, 1937 (= Notizie degli scavi di Antichità vol. XIII), p. 223 et fig. 8.
[333] G. DUMÉZIL, Rel. rom. arch.², p. 334.

complémentaires qui sont fondamentales dans la psychologie de l'humanité: l'agent féminin de la fécondité et l'agent masculin du mouvement sont étroitement liés, l'action de celui-ci permettant la manifestation de celui-là»[334].

Junon et Janus se rencontrent essentiellement en deux occasions: pour le patronage des Calendes et pour le rite du *Tigillum Sororium*.

«Parallèlement à Junon, qui en est la véritable maîtresse, Janus est présent au premier jour de chaque mois, aux Calendes»[335]. Cette attribution à Janus, dieu initial[336] est logique. Cette association se manifeste dans l'épithète *Iunonius* sous laquelle on invoquait Janus[337]. Ainsi, au lever de la nouvelle lune — plus tard, au début de chaque mois du calendrier solaire — le *rex sacrorum,* aidé du pontife mineur, préposé à l'observation de l'astre, sacrifiait à Janus dans la *curia calabra* tandis que la *regina sacrorum* offrait un sacrifice à Junon dans la *Regia*[338]. Ensuite, le pontife convoquait la plèbe pour lui annoncer le nombre de jours avant les nones. S'il restait cinq jours, il répétait cinq fois le verbe *calo,* s'il en restait sept, il le répétait sept fois[339]. Varron nous apprend qu'en cette occasion on invoquait nommément *Iuno Couella*[340]. Cette épithète, a fait couler beaucoup d'encre; le texte de Varron dont l'établissement scientifique n'est pas certain en donne l'unique mention[341]. On a proposé une lectio facilior *NOVELLA* qui ne repose sur aucune tradition sûre; d'autre part, la leçon *COVELLA* n'offre aucun sens satisfaisant[342].

---

[334] M. RENARD, Aspects anciens de Janus et de Junon, dans: R. B. Ph., 31, 1953, p. 20.

[335] G. DUMÉZIL, Rel. rom. arch.², p. 336; SCHILLING, Janus, p. 102ss; cf. Macr., Sat., 1, 9, 16; 15, 18—20; Ovide, Fastes, 1, 55.

[336] M. RENARD, Aspects anciens de Janus et de Junon, p. 7; R. SCHILLING, Janus, p. 102ss.

[337] Cf. Macr., Sat., 1, 15, 19; G. CAPDEVILLE, Les épithètes cultuelles de Janus, dans: M.E.F.R(A.), 85, 1973, 2, p. 426—7.

[338] Macr., Sat., 1, 15, 10, donne seulement: . . . *sacrificio a Rege et minore pontifice celebrato* . . . Mais selon R. SCHILLING, Janus, p. 103, n. 2 et 3, les circonstances et la qualité du *Rex* ne permettent pas de douter sur la désignation du dieu, d'autant que Macr., Sat., 1, 15, 19, ajoute *Romae quoque Kalendis omnibus, praeter quod pontifex minor in curia Calabra rem diuinam Iano (Iunoni codd.) facit, etiam Regina sacrorum, id est Regis uxor, porcam uel agnam in regia Iunoni immolat.* WISSOWA, dans: R.E., X,2, 1919, art. Kalendae, col. 1560, a proposé avec justesse la correction *Iano:* il s'agit de deux sacrifices symétriques et le texte poursuit: *A qua etiam Ianum Iunonium cognominatum diximus* . . ., ce qui suppose une allusion préalable à Janus.

[339] Macr., Sat., 1, 15, 9—10.

[340] Varr., L.L., 6, 27: *Primi dies mensium nominati Kalendae, quod his diebus calantur eius mensis Nonae a pontificibus, quintanae an septimanae sint futurae, in Capitolio in curia Calabra sic dicto quinquies „Kalo Iuno Couella" septies dicto „Kalo Iuno Couella".* Ce texte est celui de GOETZ—SCHOELL, cf. M. RENARD, Iuno Couella, dans: Mél. H. Grégoire, IV, Bruxelles, 1953 = Ann. Inst. Philol. Or. et Sl., 12, 1952, p. 401—408, spéc. p. 402, n.2.

[341] Pour l'établissement du texte, cf. M. RENARD, Iuno Couella, p. 402, n.1 et R. SCHILLING, Janus, p. 103, n.4.

[342] Pour les interprétations antérieures, cf. SHIELDS, Juno, p. 13—18; M. RENARD, Iuno Couella, p. 402—405; G. RADKE, Die Götter Altitaliens, art. Covella; R. SCHILLING, Janus p. 103, n.4; R. E. A. PALMER, Roman Religion . . ., p. 24, n. 149.

Chez les Laurentins, se pratiquaient les mêmes rites: Junon surnommée *Kalendaris* était honorée à toutes les Calendes de mars à décembre[343], ce qui, montre M. RENARD, prouve l'antiquité du rite qui remonte «à un moment où l'année était encore de dix mois, c'est-à-dire à une époque antérieure − et sans doute de beaucoup − à la réforme du calendrier attribuée à Numa»[344].

On expliquait le plus souvent cette intervention de Junon à la nouvelle lune par sa nature lunaire[345]. WISSOWA accepte cette explication lunaire mais sans y reconnaître la nature fondamentale de Junon[346]. M. RENARD a voulu résoudre l'énigmatique *Couella* en la rapprochant des termes remontant au nom générique indo-européen désignant le bovin, d'autant qu'on rapproche le nom de Junon de *iunix* (génisse), *iuuencus − iuuenca* (taureau-génisse), *iuuenis* (jeune)[347]. «Cette interprétation de *Couella* permet de saisir Junon, divinité de la fécondité terrestre, animale et lunaire au moment où elle devient déesse lunaire»[348]; la déesse de la fécondité et des femmes dont les phénomènes physiologiques ainsi que la gestation sont liés aux phases de la lune se vit consacrer les Calendes, jours de la nouvelle lune[349].

D'autres historiens considèrent qu'il n'est point besoin d'envisager à proprement parler une nature lunaire de Junon. *Iuno Couella* est invoquée en cette circonstance au même titre que *Iuno Lucina* par les futures mères: la déesse de l'enfantement préside aussi au début du mois à la renaissance de la lune. Ainsi la collaboration de Junon avec Janus s'explique: Janus patronne le passage d'un mois à l'autre et Junon facilite le passage grâce à la vitalité exaltée dont elle est la dépositaire[350]. Selon R. SCHILLING, cette union rappelle «la collaboration qui existe entre Janus et Junon sur le plan humain, s'il est vrai que la clef, attribut de Janus, «est donnée aux femmes en couches pour faciliter leur travail»[351]. P. DROSSART adoptait une position analogue dans son interprétation des Nones Caprotines. Il semblerait que Junon exerçât, tout en étant étrangère, une espèce de

---

[343] Macr., Sat., 1, 15, 18.

[344] M. RENARD, Iuno Couella, p. 408: l'institution de la cérémonie est même attribuée à Romulus par Serv., ad Aen., 8, 654. R. E. A. PALMER, Roman Religion . . ., p. 24, explique cette donnée par le fait que seuls les mois durant lesquels la végétation est en éveil lui seraient consacrés.

[345] Les Anciens ont souvent identifié Junon à la Lune, Varr., L.L., 5, 69; Macr., Sat., 1, 15, 20; Jean le Lydien, De Mensibus, 3, 10.

[346] WISSOWA, R. u. K. d. R.², p. 187.

[347] M. RENARD, Juno Couella, p. 405; çontra: G. DUMÉZIL, Juno S.M.R., p. 118, n.2. S. FERRI, Esigenze archeologiche, dans: Studi Class. e Orient., 6, 1957, p. 231−242; ID., Esigenze archeologiche, IV, dans: Studi Class. e Orient., 9, 1960, p. 161−178, estime que le nom de *Iuno Couella* vient de Lydie ou il désigne Cybèle.

[348] M. RENARD, Iuno Couella, p. 408.

[349] M. RENARD, Aspects anciens de Janus et de Junon, dans: R.B.Ph., 31, 1953, p. 10.

[350] G. DUMÉZIL, Rel. rom. arch.², p. 302; R. SCHILLING, Janus, p. 107s.; G. CAPDEVILLE, op. cit., p. 426.

[351] Paul. Fest., p. 49 L.: *Clauim consuetudo erat mulieribus donare ob significandam partus facilitatem*, cf. R. SCHILLING, Janus, p. 108.

tutelle et d'impulsion sur la lune: dans le complexe junonien des Nones Caprotines, la lune intervient en tant que régulatrice des saisons et de la sexualité féminine, mais il n'y a pas de culte de la lune[352]. De même, G. DUMÉZIL rappelle qu'à Rome, il n'y a de fête ni du Soleil ni de la Lune; après le solstice d'été, il y a un rituel destiné à renforcer la lumière nocturne; la lune en son premier quartier est figurée, non nommée, aux Nones Caprotines où c'est une Junon patronne de la fécondité des femmes qui est à l'honneur[353].

Le 1er octobre, on retrouve au culte du *Tigillum Sororium* — célébré à l'origine par la *gens Horatia,* plus tard par l'Etat — *Ianus Curiatius* rapproché de *Iuno Sororia,* rites de purification perpétuant le souvenir de l'expiation d'Horace meurtrier de sa soeur[354]. G. DUMÉZIL a montré dans 'Horace et les Curiaces' que ce récit est la transcription historicisée de rites d'initiation guerrière et de réintégration dans la vie civile du jeune héros débarrassé de son *furor*[355]. Rites tout à fait à leur place en ce mois riche en célébrations mettant fin aux activités militaires[356].

Les critiques modernes sont divisés quant à l'explication des épithètes de *Iuno Sororia* et de *Ianus Curiatius.* Pour certains, c'est à la légende même que les deux divinités doivent les épithètes qu'elles portent en cette occasion; face aux incertitudes étymologiques que nous entreverrons, c'est l'opinion pondérée et sage sans être définitive, exprimée dernièrement par G. CAPDEVILLE[357].

---

[352] P. DROSSART, Nonae Caprotinae, p. 136, n. 1, parle de Junon «lunaire» invoquée aux Calendes sous le nom de *Iuno Couella.*

[353] G. DUMÉZIL, Fêtes romaines d'été et d'automne suivi de Dix questions romaines. IX: Les Nones Caprotines, Paris, 1975, p. 281. R.E. A. PALMER, Roman Religion . . ., p. 24—25, s'est penché sur le problème de *Iuno Couella* qu'il veut solutionner en métamorphosant le texte de Varron (L.L., 6, 27): c'est *calo lunam nouellam* que crie chaque mois le pontife mineur (en plus de la correction de SCALIGER *Couella>Nouella,* selon PALMER, Varron substitua *Iuno* à *Lunam* . . .). Quant au sacrifice de la *Regina sacrorum,* il était destiné à la *iuno* de son mari afin qu'il conserve sa jeunesse au passage de chaque mois. Ce sacrifice de la 'reine du roi' à chaque Calende, suggéra aux Romains de lui consacrer ce jour. A son tour, cette suggestion influença les Romains quant au choix d'une date pour dédier les temples à Junon; jusqu'à ce que Varron et d'autres reconnaissent la Lune en Junon. Ce système explicatif montrera combien dans l'ouvrage très intéressant de R. E. A. PALMER, il y a du bon et du moins bon.

[354] Denys, 3, 22, 7—9; Fest., p. 380, 5 L.; Schol. Bob in: Cic. Mil., 7; Tite-Live, 1, 26,13; Paul. Fest., p. 399,2 L.; Ps. Aur. Vict., Vir., 4; cf. G. CAPDEVILLE, op. cit., p. 428ss.

[355] G. DUMÉZIL, Horace et les Curiaces, Coll. Les Mythes Romains, Paris, 1942; ID., Aspects de la fonction guerrière chez les Indo-Européens, Bib. Ec. Hautes Et., Sciences religieuses, 68, Paris, 1956, p. 15—61, reproduit dans: ID., Heur et malheur du guerrier, Coll. Hier, Paris, 1969, p. 11—50; ID., Mythe et épopée, I. L'idéologie des trois fonctions dans les épopées des peuples indo-européens, Bib. Sc. Humaines, Paris, 1968, p. 278ss.

[356] N. TURCHI, La religione di Roma antica, Storia di Roma, Vol. XVIII, Bologne, 1939, p. 99ss.; M. RENARD, Aspects anciens de Janus et de Junon, dans: R.B.Ph., 31, 1953, p. 13.

[357] G. CAPDEVILLE, op. cit., p. 430ss.; cf. RADKE, Die Götter Altitaliens, art. Curiatius et Sororia.

H. J. Rose avait proposé une explication de *sororia*[358] qui a convaincu plus d'un historien qui l'adaptèrent dans des sens divergents[359]. Selon Rose, d'après Festus, *sororia* issu de *sororiare* *"is used of the swelling breasts of an adolescent girl"*[360]. A partir de cette étymologie, à laquelle il ne croit plus, M. Renard proposait une explication qui ne manquait pas de vraisemblance: «*sororiare* marquant que deux objets sont identiques et vont par paire[361], ne faut-il pas comprendre ici *sororius* dans un sens voisin de „jumelé, apparié, double, parallèle" (. . .). Nous songeons (. . .) à l'équivalence des termes et à l'équivalence matérielle que cette interprétation permettrait d'établir entre le *Ianus Geminus* de l'Argilète et notre *Tigillum Sororium* constitué par deux jambages de bois analogues aux deux *postes* de la maison et surmontés d'un entrait, d'une poutre de charpente horizontale. Festus nous le dit clairement: Horace *duo tigilla tertio superiecto . . . subit* »[362]. Dès lors, «Janus préside au passage, [. . . mais] c'est Junon qui est la divinité de l'arc, du joug proprement dit»[363]. Pour *Curiatius*, M. Renard établit un parallèle avec l'épithète de *Iuno Curitis*, «Junon a prêté une de ses épithètes à Janus, d'ailleurs appelé parfois Janus Iunonius»[364]. Pour M. Renard, ces pratiques tiennent à la fois du rite de passage sous l'égide de Janus et du rite de désacralisation et de fécondation auquel participe la déesse. «Ce rite permettait, au *retour* de la guerre de rendre les *iuuenes* à leur état *fécond* d'éleveurs et d'agriculteurs. Au *Tigillum Sororium,* le *rite* est devenu un *mythe,* et celui-ci s'est fait *histoire*»[365].

R. Schilling explique *Curiatius* par *curia*[366]: Janus présidait au sein de la curie au rite d'initiation des jeunes gens accédant à la vie militaire. Quant à *Iuno Sororia,* on connaît le culte de Junon à l'intérieur des curies, on peut donc lui prêter un rôle d'initiatrice lors de la «formation» de la jeune fille. La présence simultanée de leurs deux autels au *Tigillum Sororium* donne à penser qu'il était

---

[358] H. J. Rose, Mana in Greece and Rome, dans: H.Th.R., 42, 1949, p. 165–69; Id., Ancient Roman Religion, Londres, 1948, p. 69. H. J. Rose avait exprimé cette idée, dont il lui avait été fait part personnellement par J. Whatmough, dès 1925 dans: De religionibus antiquis quaestiunculae tres, dans: Mnemosyne, N.S., 53, 1925, p. 407–410 et p. 413–414; Id., Two Roman Rites, dans: Class. Quart., 28, 1934, p. 157.

[359] M. Renard, Aspects anciens de Janus et de Junon, p. 14s.; J. Gagé, La poutre sacrée des Horatii. A propos du «tigillum sororium», dans: Hommages Deonna, Coll. Latomus, 28, Bruxelles, 1957, p. 235ss.; K. Latte, Röm. Religionsgeschichte, p. 133; R. Schilling, Janus, p. 108. Contra, H. Wagenvoort, Roman Dynamism, Oxford, 1947, p. 155; G. Dumézil, Déesses latines . . ., p. 13ss.; Id., Mythe et épopée, III, p. 308ss.

[360] Fest., p. 380, 25 L. = Paul. Fest., p. 381, 2 L.: *Sororiare mammae dicuntur puellarum cum primum tumescunt, ut fraterculare puerorum,* cf. Rose, Ancient Roman Religion, p. 69.

[361] Ernout–Meillet, D.E. art. Soror.

[362] M. Renard, Aspects anciens de Janus et de Junon, p. 14–5; cf. Fest., p. 380 L.

[363] Ibidem, p. 15.

[364] Ibidem, p. 14.

[365] Ibidem, p. 20.

[366] R. Schilling, Janus, p. 109; rapprochement admis par R. H. Klausen, Aeneas und die Penaten, Hambourg, 1839–40, p. 714, rejeté, notamment, par M. Renard, Aspects anciens de Janus et de Junon, p. 14; cf. G. Radke, Die Götter Altitaliens, art. Curiatius.

l'endroit privilégié pour un double rite de passage pour les jeunes gens mais aussi pour les jeunes filles. Par ailleurs le passage sous la poutre du *Tigillum Sororium* correspond à un rite de sortie au retour de la guerre; ce qui justifie le voisinage de l'autel de *Ianus Curiatius*: le *miles* redevient *quiris* et réintègre les *curiae*[367]. Cette théorie est séduisante, mais on lira les réserves de G. CAPDEVILLE qui note sur combien peu d'éléments traditionnels elle repose[368].

J. GAGÉ accepte lui aussi l'hypothèse de ROSE, mais lui donne une valeur arbustive. Le *Tigillum Sororium* aurait été à l'origine une pièce de bois ayant une propriété «ruminale». Junon intervient dans des rôles d'allaitement mytho-logique (cf. infra); d'autre part, on connaît dans la religion égyptienne une déesse allaitante dont les seins faisaient partie d'une branche d'arbre[369]. On peut donc rapprocher cette hypothèse de J. GAGÉ et le problème du *ficus ruminalis* et de *Iuno Rumina* et même la question de *Iuno Caprotina* et du *Caprificus* – dont on utilisait une branche et dont Macrobe mentionne le lait[370]. Les anciens interpré-taient *Rumina* à partir de *rumis* («mamelle»)[371]. A l'initiative de WISSOWA, suivi par LATTE, approuvés par G. DUMÉZIL et maintenant par PALMER, on reconnaît dans les noms *Rumina, Ruminalis ficus, Iuppiter Ruminus*, le nom de Rome[372] avec un vocalisme étrusque (cf. *Rumaχ*, «Romain») scrupuleusement conservé par la langue sacrée[373]. Dès lors, pour PALMER, les seules offrandes de lait à *Rumina* ne suffisent pas pour identifier un culte de la fécondité[374]. Remarquons pourtant que le *ficus ruminalis* était proche du Lupercal, que sa sève ressemblait au latex du *ficus caprotinus*, que son branchage présentait des protubérances, tout cela devait concourir à évoquer une symbolique sexuelle, à engendrer des rites fécondants, à provoquer l'étymologie populaire[375]. Nous acceptons néanmoins la conclusion de PALMER concernant *Iuno Caprotina* et *Iuno Rumina*: *"Although fertility rites might be attached to such cults, they do not impose an exclusive interpretation that the deities were originally and principally gods of (female) sexuality and procreation"*[376]. Cet excursus nous a été suggéré par la connotation

---

[367] R. SCHILLING, Janus, p. 108–113.

[368] G. CAPDEVILLE, Les épithètes cultuelles de Janus, p. 431: par exemple, aucun auteur ne parle de rites d'initiation pour les jeunes filles, les cérémonies du 1er octobre ne sont pas une initiation mais une purification des combattants, etc.

[369] J. GAGÉ, La poutre sacrée des Horatii . . ., p. 235–6; ID., Matronalia, p. 88ss.

[370] Varr., L.L., 6, 18; Macr., Sat., 1, 11, 40.

[371] Varr., R.R., 2, 11, 4–5; Varr., ap. Non., 246 L.; Aug., Civ. dei, 4, 11; 4, 21; 4, 34.

[372] WISSOWA, R. u. K. d. R.², p. 242; K. LATTE, Röm. Religionsgeschichte, p. 111; G. DUMÉZIL, Rel. rom. arch.², p. 193; R. E. A. PALMER, Roman Religion, p. 17.

[373] G. DUMÉZIL, Rel. rom. arch.², p. 193; voir H. RIX, Das etruskische Cognomen, Wiesbaden, 1963, p. 232.

[374] *Iuppiter Latiaris* recevait également des offrandes de lait: Denys, 4, 49, 3; Cic., De div., 1, 11, 18; cf. R. E. A. PALMER, Roman Religion, p. 17, n. 91.

[375] J. GAGÉ, La poutre sacrée des Horatii . . ., p. 236 et ID., Matronalia, p. 89, considère l'arbre comme «ruminal» en lui-même, c'est-à-dire nourricier; il «n'avait pas besoin, pour être ainsi appelé, que la louve aux mamelles pleines vînt chercher à son pied les fils de la vestale». Dès lors, J. GAGÉ rapproche *Iuno Sororia* de *Iuno Rumina*.

[376] R. E. A. PALMER, Roman Religion . . ., p. 17.

nourricière de *Iuno Sororia* proposée par J. GAGÉ: elle nous apparaît plus aléatoire encore que celle de *Iuno Rumina*.

Pour en revenir aux liens qui unissent Junon et Janus, ils peuvent être interprétés avec plus ou moins d'insistance. Pour M. RENARD, «Délaissant son premier compagnon [Janus] et devenant déesse lunaire, elle [Junon] en arrive à nouer dans le ciel avec Jupiter une idylle qui a sa conclusion au temple du Capitole»[377]. G. CAPDEVILLE conteste cette vision: pour lui, «chacune des deux divinités a des raisons particulières de patronner telle ou telle des fêtes où elles se rencontrent, en raison de sa propre définition (. . .) G. DUMÉZIL a montré que la déesse agissait dans les trois fonctions auxquelles président à Rome Jupiter, Mars et Quirinus; une extension toute naturelle, aidée par des coïncidences — les naissances, par exemple, sont des commencements — a dû la mettre également en rapport avec Janus, qui s'ajoute, en tant que dieu initial, à la triade fonctionelle»[378].

R. SCHILLING a bien montré pourquoi, avec l'établissement de l'Empire, quand Rome a charge de la paix dans le monde, le rôle de *Ianus Quirinus*, protecteur de la paix — les portes de son temple sont solennellement fermées par Octave — éclipse les cultes où Junon et Janus étaient honorés conjointement et qui n'avaient une réelle importance qu'au sein d'une société plus archaïque (succession des lunaisons, rituel du *Tigillum Sororium*)[379].

XIII. Junon et Hercule

Junon rencontre un autre compagnon encore: Hercule, héros de la Grèce mais intégré au monde italien archaïque au point que l'on puisse parler de dieu italique, irradié à travers la Campanie et jusqu'au Bruttium et la Sabine[380]. Héraclès, «la seule figure mythologique qui paraisse avoir possédé en Etrurie, outre son bagage traditionnel, une mythologie originale»[381]. Héraclès, dieu grec, qui chemine à partir des colonies grecques d'Italie méridionale jusqu'à Rome, au centre de commerce du *Forum Boarium*, est souvent associé par les auteurs à l'itinéraire de la grande Héra Argienne[382]. On considère le plus souvent

[377] M. RENARD, Aspects anciens de Janus et de Junon, p. 21.

[378] G. CAPDEVILLE, Les épithètes cultuelles de Janus, p. 427, n.1.

[379] R. SCHILLING, Janus, p. 129ss.

[380] U. BIANCHI, Gli dei delle stirpi italiche, dans: Popoli e civiltà dell'Italia antica, VII, Rome, 1978, p. 221; A. PROSDOCIMI, Le religioni dell' Italia antica, dans: G. CASTELLANI (éd.), Storia delle religioni, II⁶, Turin, 1971, p. 708.

[381] G. DUMÉZIL, Rel. rom. arch.², p. 664—5.

[382] J. BAYET, Les origines de l'Hercule romain, passim; G. GIANNELLI, Culti e miti della Magna Grecia. Contributo alla storia più antica delle colonie greche in Occidente, 2e éd., Naples, 1963, passim; J. HEURGON, Rome et la Méditerranée occidentale jusqu'aux guerres puniques, Coll. Nouvelle Clio, 7, Paris, 1969, p. 147 et p. 180; G. DUMÉZIL, Rel. rom. arch.², p. 434; U. BIANCHI, Gli dei delle stirpi italiche, p. 221. Sur Héraclès en Italie, on

Herculanum comme le centre de la diffusion étrusco-campanienne[383]. A. DE NIRO, plutôt qu'à Herculanum pour laquelle joue la relation étymologique, songe à l'Héraion du Sélé où Héraclès, le serviteur d'Héra, occupait une place importante dans l'iconographie des métopes archaïques et probablement dans le culte[384].

C'est l'étude de J. BAYET sur 'Les origines de l'Hercule romain' (elle date pourtant de 1926) qui fournit la solution la plus satisfaisante au problème de l'alliance Hercule-Junon. Cette union semble assez tardive, postérieure à ses rencontres avec la Bona Dea et la Diane aventine; pourtant dès le Ve siècle l'expansion d'Héra Lacinia a pu dans certains centres (peut-être Lanuvium) préparer cette union[385].

Quels faits de détail témoignent de cette rencontre des deux divinités[386]? Un miroir 'étrusque' représente Jupiter (*Iouei*) prêt à unir Hercule (*Hercele*) et Junon (*Iuno*). Notons la forme latine des noms[387]. Selon Servius, à la naissance des enfants, dans les grandes familles, on dressait dans l'atrium un lit pour Junon Lucina et une table pour Hercule[388]. Ce rapprochement est également connu à Tusculum où Hercule et Junon Lucina étaient vénérés conjointement[389]. J. BAYET

verra: M. DETIENNE, Héraclès, héros pythagoricien, dans: R. H. R., 158, 1960, p. 19–53; P. M. MARTIN, Héraclès en Italie d'après Denys (A.R., I, 34–44), dans: Athenaeum, 60, 1972, p. 252–275; F. VAN WONTERGHEM, Le culte d'Hercule chez les Paeligni. Documents anciens et nouveaux, dans: L'Ant. Class., 42, 1973, p. 36–48 (sur le culte d'Hercule à caractère pastoral chez les Péligniens). J. BAYET, Hercule romain, p. 456, avait noté une influence orientale et remarqué les liens unissant l'Hercule romain au Baal-Melqart tyrien. Mais récemment est née une véritable théorie phénicienne des origines d'Hercule. A. PIGANIOL, Les origines d'Hercule, dans: Hommages A. Grenier, Coll. Latomus, 58, Bruxelles, 1962, p. 1261–1264, a montré que l'Hercule romain avait été apporté au *Forum Boarium* par les marchands phéniciens. D. VAN BERCHEM, Hercule-Melqart à l'Ara Maxima, dans: Rend. Pont. Acc. Archeol., 32, 1959–60, p. 61–8; ID., Sanctuaires d'Hercule-Melqart, dans: Syria, 44, 1967, p. 73–109; p. 307–338, a fait semblable rapprochement. Plus encore R. REBUFFAT, Les Phéniciens à Rome, dans: M.E.F.R.(A.), 78, 1966, p. 7–48, pense à l'installation très ancienne au *Forum Boarium* d'une colonie tyrienne, fondatrice et administratrice de l'*Ara Maxima* jusqu'en 312 ... On lira également à ce sujet les réserves de J. HEURGON, op. cit., p. 147–8; de G. DUMÉZIL, Rel. rom. arch.², p. 434, n. 1; de J. BAYET, La religion romaine, p. 289.

383 G. DEVOTO, Gli antichi Italici⁴, Florence, 1969, p. 198–9; U. BIANCHI, Gli dei delle stirpi italiche, p. 221.

384 A. DE NIRO, Il culto di Ercole tra i Sanniti e Frentani. Nuove testimonianze, Salerne, 1977; P. ZANCANI MONTUORO, Un mito italiota in Etruria, dans: Ann. Scuola Archeol. Atene, N.S., VIII, 10, 1950 (Mél. della Seta) p. 85–98.

385 J. BAYET, Hercule romain, p. 389; p. 75; p. 115; p. 170–1; p. 379ss.

386 Sur ce dossier, cf. J. BAYET, Hercule romain: Hercule et Junon, p. 379ss.

387 E. GERHARD, Etruskische Spiegel, II, Berlin, 1845, pl. 147. On reconnaîtra dans cette scène la réconciliation d'Hercule et de Junon au seuil des demeures divines et non une représentation d'Hercule et de Junon en tant que dieux conjugaux ainsi que le proposait REIFFERSCHEID, cf. J. BAYET, Hercule romain, p. 380ss.

388 Serv., Schol. Bern. Verg. Ecl., 4, 62; donnée analogue chez un mythographe tardif, Mythogr. Vatic., 1, 177.

389 C.I.L., I², 1581 (= X, 3807 = I.L.S., 3099 = I.L.L.R.P., 165); C.I.L., I², 1582 (= X, 3808 = I.L.S., 3099a = I.L.L.R.P., 139).

constate le caractere tardif de ces documents: le miroir ne peut être antérieur au
IIe siècle et «la substitution d'Hercule—Junon à Pilumnus-Picumnus comme
protecteurs du nouveau-né est forcément postérieure à la décadence de l'ancienne
religion nationale et au triomphe des idées grecques»[390]. «L'Hercule évoqué par
ces documents n'est pas un dieu primitif italique, mais un substitut hellénique à de
vieilles divinités oubliées»[391]. Mais le dossier nous réserve encore un document
qui permet certainement d'entrevoir une union plus ancienne de Junon et
d'Hercule; à Lanuvium, les deux divinités sont honorées ensemble dans une
dédicace[392]. L'inscription est tardive, il est vrai, mais l'on sait par ailleurs que le
culte d'Hercule en cette cité est important et fort ancien: «les ruines de son
temple, qui était le plus important après celui de Junon, nous font remonter au
moins jusqu'au IIe ou IIIe siècle avant notre ère»[393]. Dans ce sanctuaire, tout
comme à l'*Ara maxima* à Rome — où aucun texte n'atteste son union avec *Iuno
Sospita* mais que certains recoupements permettent d'envisager[394] — les femmes
ne participaient pas à la consommation des victimes; l'exclusion des sexes est une
pratique caractéristique du culte des divinités fécondantes[395]. Ainsi, Junon-
Hercule ont été substitués à Pilumnus-Picumnus pour leurs caractères propres de
déesse accoucheuse et de dieu apotropaïque protecteur de l'enfance mais aussi
pour leur virtualité commune de divinités fécondantes[396]: c'était le cas à Tusculum
et à Rome notamment où l'on connaît un culte de Junon Lucina et d'Hercule.

Par contre, à Lanuvium et à Rome peut-être, leur alliance plus ancienne
repose sur leurs caractères fécondant mais aussi guerrier[397]. On l'a vu, certaines
Junons latines présentent des traits nettement guerriers, à Lanuvium, Faléries,
Tibur, Rome, sans doute. Ces caractères pouvaient suggérer la comparaison avec
les Héras grecques, armées, telles qu'on les rencontre dans le sud de l'Italie au cap
Lacinion et à l'embouchure du Sélé, divinités voisines des Héras guerrières d'Elis
et d'Argos ce qui leur a valu l'épithète d'«Argiennes»[398]. L'Héra argienne recevait
un culte au cap Lacinion où elle est l'alliée d'Héraclès qui passait pour avoir fondé

---

[390] J. BAYET, Hercule romain, p. 383.

[391] J. BAYET, Hercule romain, p. 383—4.

[392] Eph. Epigr., IX, 605: *Herculi San[cto] et Iunoni Sispit[i]*.

[393] J. BAYET, Hercule romain, p. 387; cf. LANCIANI, Storia degli scavi, Rome, 1902—1912, III,
p. 22 et 31; D. VAGLIERI, Civita Lavinia. Scoperte di antichità nel territorio del Comune,
dans: Atti della reale Accademia nazionale dei Lincei, 304ème année, 5ème sér., 1907 (=
Notizie degli scavi di Antichità, vol. IV), p. 125; GALIETI, dans: Bull. Assoz. Archeol.
Rom., 1911, p. 21—43.

[394] *Iuno Sospita* est depuis 193 avant J.-C. au *Forum Holitorium*, près de la porte Carmentale:
un des lieux de la légende héracléenne à Rome; la fête de la déesse, le 1er février, coïncide
avec un *natalis* d'Hercule célébré par des jeux de cirque, cf. WISSOWA, R.u.K.d.R.²,
p. 276, n. 5; J. BAYET, Hercule romain, p. 387—8; Properce, El., 5, 9, 71 écrit: *Sancte
Pater salue, cui iam fauet aspera Iuno*, à la fin de la pièce qu'il consacre à la légende de
Bona Dea et du Grand Autel.

[395] Tertull., ad Nat., 2, 7; cf. J. BAYET, Hercule romain, p. 387.

[396] J. BAYET, Hercule romain, p. 388.

[397] Ibidem.

[398] Notamment, J. BAYET, Hercule romain, p. 170.

son sanctuaire[399]. De là, leur culte fut transporté par des colons (cf. infra) aux bouches du Sélé. Dès lors, à la faveur des contacts avec l'Italie centrale (cf. infra), cette ressemblance entre les déesses militaires latines et leurs homologues grecques favorisa une certaine assimilation: la déesse italique acquiert une coloration grecque et connaît, à ce moment, l'union avec Hercule qui ne peut, évidemment, avoir une origine latine.

Certains historiens[400], nous l'avons déjà vu, reconnaissent simplement en ces Junons de Faléries, de Tibur et de Lanuvium l'Héra grecque sans envisager la

---

[399] Serv., ad Aen., 3, 552: *Iunonis Laciniae templum secundum quosdam a rege conditore dictum, secundum alios a Latrone Lacinio, quem illic Hercules occidit, et loco expiato Iunoni templum constituit.* Cette union d'Hercule et de sa marâtre ennemie pouvait surprendre, en fait «l'immortalité d'Héraclès semble à l'origine plutôt due à Héra qu'entravée par elle.» Cf. J. BAYET, Hercule romain, p. 170.

[400] Pour M. TORELLI, Il santuario greco di Gravisca, dans: Par. Pass., 32, 1977, p. 435 s., la présence samienne a donné une connotation argienne aux cultes d'Héra en Italie. Faléries subit une forte hellénisation à l'époque archaïque responsable des caractéristiques argiennes de l'Héra (sic) falisque, cf. M. TORELLI, Tre studi di storia etrusca, dans: D. d'A., 8, 1974–5, p. 56 s. Le culte argien de Tivoli est peut-être une importation falisque, cf. S. WEINSTOCK, dans: R.E., VI A, 1, 1937, art. Tibur, col. 832 s. Selon G. PUGLIESE CARRATELLI, Prime fasi della colonizzazione greca in Italia, dans: Greci e Italici in Magna Grecia, Atti del Iº Convegno di Studi sulla Magna Grecia, Tarente, 4–8/XI/1961, Naples, 1962, p. 137 ss et la bibliographie qui y est citée; ID., Achei nell'Etruria e nel Lazio?, dans: Par. Pass., 17, 1962, p. 24; ID., Santuari extramurani in Magna Grecia, dans: Par. Pass., 17, 1962, p. 241–6; ID., Culti e dottrine religiose in Magna Grecia, dans: Santuari di Magna Grecia, Atti del IVº Convegno di Studi sulla Magna Grecia, Tarente – Reggio de Calabre, 11–16/X/1964, Naples, 1965, p. 19–45 = ID., dans: Par Pass., 20, 1965, p. 1 ss.; ID., Lazio, Roma e Magna Grecia prima del secolo quarto A.C., dans: Par. Pass., 23, 1968, p. 321–47, spéc. p. 331, cette Héra en Italie, au Latium et en Etrurie notamment, est d'origine «précoloniale», mycénienne. Ainsi s'exprime-t-il dans 'Culti e dottrine religiose', p. 42: „'Precoloniale' appare il culto di una dea greca, alternativamente identificata con Eiléithyia o con Hera, a Pyrgi porto di Caere; 'precoloniale' il culto di Hera 'Argoa' (o 'Iuno Argiva') la dea del santuario posidoniate, nel Lazio meridionale, ove una tradizione riferita da Strabone (V, 233) collocava, a Caieta e a Formiae, colonie laconiche". Dans cette même étude, p. 26, il rappelle la tradition qui attribue à Jason la fondation de l'Héraion du Sélé, il fait remarquer que les itinéraires des Argonautes semblent bien correspondre aux routes méditerranéennes des métaux au début de l'Age du Fer. Et l'auteur de poursuivre: „resistendo alla suggestione del tema, mi limiterò a ricordare la singolare circostanza che la dea del Silaro si ritrova nel Lazio lungo la via verso la zona mineraria dell' Italia centrale, a Lanuvium, Tibur, e Falerii." J. HEURGON, Rome et la Méditerranée occidentale, p. 180, accepte la progression de Héra argienne de Métaponte et Crotone à l'Héraion du Sélé et à Posidonia, puis à Capoue, Lanuvium, Tibur, Caere, Faléries. R. E. A. PALMER, Roman Religion, p. 40–1, qui, on l'a remarqué diverses fois, voit en Junon une figure essentiellement guerrière, est frappé par sa ressemblance avec *Hera Lacinia Hoplosmia* (Lyc., Alex., 856–8, 614): "*Hera's great sanctuary in the Greeks' New World apparently had old ties with the northern people of Latium, strong enough to hang a Roman mythology therefrom.*" J. BÉRARD, Les origines historiques et légendaires de Posidonia à la lumière des récentes découvertes archéologiques, dans: Mél. Arch. Hist. Ec. Fr. Rome, 57, 1940, p. 7–31, spéc. p. 25–6; ID., La colonisation grecque de l'Italie méridionale et de la Sicile dans l'Antiquité, Paris, 1957, spéc. p. 393–4: *Héra Argeia* «se retrouve (. . .) non seulement au Silaris et chez les Vénètes, mais en trois villes de l'Italie centrale: à Lanuvium, où son culte

possibilité d'un culte indigène primitif de Junon guerrière. On ne peut qu'approuver G. Dumézil quand il s'élève contre ces «invérifiables hypothèses qui ont contre elles de ne rien laisser pratiquement d'original dans une déesse pourtant bien italique et, aussi loin qu'on remonte, importante»[401]. Mais il vise excessivement J. Bayet qui, contrairement à d'autres, laisse la place à la Junon italique guerrière, car, si nous l'entendons bien, il prétend seulement que les «Junons militaires latines» ont subi, à un certain moment, l'influence des Héras Lacinienne et du Sélé ce qui leur valut l'épithète d'«Argiennes» et une certaine coloration grecque[402]. Il est vrai que des trois qualités de *Iuno Sospita*, guerrière, mère et reine, il reconnaît celle de mère fécondante comme primitive[403].

A la formation de l'Hercule romain se sont mêlées les influences de Grande-Grèce, de centres religieux importants tels Lanuvium, probablement aussi des influences sabines[404]. La découverte à Sulmone d'un sanctuaire d'*Hercule Curinus*[405] et l'existence bien connue de *Iuno Quiritis* confirme pour E. Paratore le témoignage de Varron qui attribue une origine sabine aux cultes d'Hercule et de Junon dans le Latium préromain[406]. Une introduction sabine du

voisine avec la légende du Diomède, à Tibur et à Faléries.» *Héra Argolis* à Lanuvium: Aelian., Nat. an., 11, 16; *Juno Argeia* à Tibur: C.I.L., XIV, 3556; *Héra Argeia* ou *Juno Argiva* à Faléries: Denys, 1, 21, 1—2; Ovide, Amor., 3, 13, 31; légende de Diomède à Lanuvium: Appien, B.C., 2, 20 (la cité avait le héros pour oeciste légendaire). Sur les origines de l'Héra Argienne, J.Bérard, op. cit., passim: étant donné le caractère thessalien de la légende des Argonautes, le nom d'Argienne évoque l'Argos de Thessalie; d'autre part, le culte d'Héra du Sélé, qui aurait précédé la colonisation historique, aurait été amené par les Aminéens, populations pélagiques issues de Thessalie (Denys, 1, 17, 2 et 89, 2). A l'époque de la colonisation historique, au milieu du VIIe siècle, les Trézéniens, populations doriennes du Péloponnèse (Argolide) (Hérodote, 8, 43; Pausanias, 3, 30, 10) chassés de Sybaris par les Achéens, s'installèrent sur le golfe de Posidonia où ils reprirent ce sanctuaire établi par leurs prédécesseurs. Sur les données archéologiques de l'Héraion du Sélé: P. Zancani Montuoro et U. Zanotti Bianco, Heraion alla foce del Sele, I—II, Rome, 1951 et 1953; P. C. Sestieri, Paestum. La ville, la nécropole préhistorique dans la région de Gaudo, le sanctuaire de Héra Argiva à l'embouchure du Sélé, Rome, 1953; Id., Ricerche posidoniate, dans: M.E.F.R.(A.), 67, 1955, p. 35—48; U. Zanotti Bianco, Heraion alla foce del Sele, Rome, 1954; P. Zancani Montuoro, Heraion alla foce del Sele, I—II, dans: Atti e Mem. Soc. Magna Grecia, 8, 1967, p. 7—28. G. Pugliese Carratelli, Culti e dottrine religiose in Magna Grecia, p. 25—6, croit résolument en l'origine achéenne des cultes d'Héra Lacinienne et d'Héraclès, son compagnon; il note, par exemple, que les étapes du voyage mythique d'Héraclès en Occident coïncident avec les points où des établissements mycéniens ont été localisés par l'archéologie. Pour les cultes eubéens d'Héra en Occident: M. Guarducci, Un antichissimo responso dell'oracolo di Cuma, dans: Bull. Comm. Archeol. Com. Roma, 72, 1946—1948, p. 129ss.; N. Valenza Mele, Hera ed Apollo nella colonizzazione euboica d'Occidente, dans: M.E.F.R.(A.), 89, 1977, p. 493—524.

[401] G. Dumézil, Rel. rom. arch.², p. 307.

[402] J. Bayet, Hercule romain, p. 170—1.

[403] J. Bayet, Hercule romain, p. 386.

[404] J. Bayet, Hercule romain, p. 305—321.

[405] Cf. supra et J. Bayet, dans: Gnomon, 33, 1961, p. 523 et E. Paratore, Varron avait raison, dans: L'Ant. Class., 67, 1973, p. 49.

[406] Varr., L.L., 5, 66; 5, 74; cf. le commentaire de J. Collart, Varron, de Lingua Latina, livre V, Publ. Fac. Lettr. de l'Univ. de Strasbourg, 122, Thèse complém., Paris, 1954, p. 185—6.

culte? peut-être pas, mais certaines influences sabines sont possibles. « Conclusion aussi vague qu'on peut l'imaginer »[407].

On évoquera aussi le monde étrusque qui a connu le couple Junon-Hercule. On s'attardera au mythe de l'allaitement d'Herclé par Uni[408]. La scène de l'allaitement varie d'un monument à l'autre: sur certains documents, Hercule est un enfant en âge d'être nourri au sein, ailleurs c'est un jeune garçon impubère ou encore un adulte imberbe ou même un homme en pleine maturité et barbu[409]. Selon J. BAYET, les deux conceptions, allaitement d'Héraclès enfant ou adulte ont existé en Grèce et l'une n'apparaît pas sensiblement avant l'autre. La tradition de l'allaitement d'Héraclès enfant remonterait à Lycophron (fin IVe siècle)[410]. L'allaitement à l'âge d'homme nous est attesté au IIIe siècle avant J.-C.[411]: en fait, Diodore ne parle que de l'accouchement simulé par lequel, persuadé par Zeus, Héra, sa marâtre, adopta Héraclès, fils adultérin de Zeus et d'Alcmène, mais, selon J. BAYET, le premier allaitement fictif s'en suit[412]. Pour W. DEONNA, cette conclusion de J. BAYET ne s'impose pas: le mythe grec d'Héra allaitant Héraclès enfant a été modifié sous l'influence étrusque: Hercule est devenu adulte, barbu même, sur les monuments des IVe—IIIe siècles avant J.-C.[413]. M. RENARD envisage un processus différent, plus conforme à l'évolution: «En fait, l'allaitement d'Hercule adulte apparaît nettement comme une sorte de *lectio difficilior*: cette version est irrationnelle et par là même paraît plus archaïque dans sa substance que l'autre, attestée cependant un peu plus tôt. On peut se demander si nous n'avons pas affaire à un processus analogue à celui que nous constatons dans le mythe d'Eros, d'abord imaginé comme dieu primordial président à la naissance d'Aphrodite, ensuite comme le tout jeune enfant de la déesse »[414].

XIV. *Héra en Etrurie*

Les pages qui précèdent ont déjà mis en évidence l'influence qu'a pu exercer la déesse Héra en Italie centrale dès l'époque archaïque. Les découvertes archéologiques des dix dernières années à Gravisca ont révélé plus encore: l'Héra

[407] J. BAYET, Hercule romain, p. 312.
[408] J. BAYET, Herclé. Etude critique des principaux monuments relatifs à l'Hercule Etrusque, Paris, 1926, p. 150—4; W. DEONNA, Deux études de symbolisme religieux. I: La légende de Pero et de Micon et l'allaitement symbolique, Coll. Latomus, 18, Bruxelles, 1955, p. 15 ss.: Junon et Hercule; M. RENARD, Hercule allaité par Junon, dans: Hommages J. Bayet, Coll. Latomus, 70, Bruxelles, 1964, p. 611—8.
[409] Références aux divers documents littéraires et iconographiques dans W. DEONNA, op. cit., p. 15—19.
[410] Lyc., Alex., 39 et schol.; Diod., 4, 9; Hygin, Poet. astr., 2, 43; Paus., 9, 25, 2.
[411] Eratosthène, Katast., 44, appuyé par Diod., 4, 39, 2.
[412] J. BAYET, Herclé, p. 152.
[413] W. DEONNA, op. cit., p. 50.
[414] M. RENARD, Hercule allaité par Junon, p. 617—8.

grecque est vénérée dès le VIe siècle dans le sanctuaire d'un emporium grec établi au coeur de la péninsule. Les fouilles dans l'ancien port de Tarquinia, à Gravisca, ouvertes en 1969 ont rapporté l'existence d'un véritable emporium centré sur un sanctuaire grec. En 1971, dans le premier rapport des fouilles[415], M. TORELLI parlait de l'Héraion de Gravisca, on a dû abandonner cette dénomination, car depuis lors, de nouvelles découvertes, épigraphiques surtout, ont fait apparaître qu'Héra était loin d'être la seule divinité vénérée dans ce sanctuaire[416].

Il semble bien que la présence grecque dans cette zone (fin VIIe siècle – début VIe siècle) soit contemporaine de l'établissement étrusque.

Dès la première moitié du VIe siècle, la présence d'Aphrodite-Turan est attestée par des dédicaces sur tessons. D'autres cultes viennent bientôt s'y adjoindre: des dédicaces à Héra et à Déméter attestent leur présence durant la seconde moitié du VIe siècle. Enfin, toujours au VIe siècle, des inscriptions manifestent la dévotion à Apollon[417].

La totalité des dédicaces à Héra sont rédigées en caractères ioniens[418]. Mais quelle ville d'Ionie est à l'origine du culte? Phocée, Samos, un autre centre? M. TORELLI, sur la base d'arguments que nous ne pouvons expliciter ici, penche pour Samos dont la présence en Occident est constante durant toute la seconde moitié du VIe siècle et à laquelle le cas de Naucratis fait songer[419]. Par ailleurs, les autres fondations grecques italiotes ne peuvent être restées étrangères au grand développement de ce culte à Gravisca; les fouilles n'apportent pas de précisions, mais comment ne pas penser aux grands sanctuaires du Cap Lacinion et de Posidonia à l'embouchure du Sélé?

Après l'efflorescence du VIe siècle, le culte d'Héra dans le port de Tarquinia connaît un déclin; du moins, on le constate sur le plan des dédicaces: pour les IVe et IIIe siècles, on dispose uniquement d'une dédicace mentionnant la correspondante étrusque d'Héra, Uni.

Quel rôle, M. TORELLI, soucieux d'intégrer les cultes dans le contexte sociologique, entrevoit-il pour Junon dans cet emporium[420]? Dans ce port, Aphrodite et Héra, divinités lunaires, ont pu être vénérées en tant que protectrices des navigations[421]. Mais le culte d'Héra semble plutôt avoir été introduit par réaction contre celui d'Aphrodite. Le culte à la déesse de Paphos n'a pu manquer d'être lié à des phénomènes propres aux installations portuaires, telle la prostitution. Héra-Uni, par contre, divinité de grands emporia (Crotone,

---

[415] M. TORELLI, Il santuario di Hera a Gravisca, dans: Par Pass., 26, 1971, p. 44–67.

[416] M. TORELLI, Il santuario greco di Gravisca, dans: Par. Pass., 32, 1977, p. 398–458. En attendant la publication des fouilles, les pages qui suivent reposent essentiellement sur les deux articles de M. TORELLI, nous nous abstiendrons donc parfois de les citer.

[417] M. TORELLI, dans: Par. Pass., 32, 1977, p. 427 ss.

[418] J. et L. ROBERT, dans: Rev. Et. Grecq., 84, 1971, p. 534, n° 730 du Bull. Epigr.; M. TORELLI, dans: Par. Pass., 32, 1977, p. 435.

[419] M. TORELLI, dans: Par. pass., 26, 1971, p. 62 ss.

[420] M. TORELLI, dans: Par. Pass., 32, 1977, p. 436; p. 449 ss.

[421] Cf. ROSCHER, Studien zur vergleichenden Mythologie der Griechen und Römer. II: Juno und Hera, Leipzig, 1875, p. 106 ss.

Posidonia, Pyrgi), était aussi la souveraine du mariage légitime, son nom évoquait la patrie et la sacrosainteté de la famille dans cette colonie et pour cette société nouvelle à la recherche d'un équilibre.

Avant les remarquables découvertes de Gravisca, la présence d'Héra était attestée depuis fort longtemps en Etrurie, à Caere[422] où l'on avait découvert dans le sanctuaire dit «del Manganello» des dédicaces à Héra des IVe et IIIe siècles, peintes sur tessons. Contrairement à ce que l'on croit pouvoir dire de l'emporium grec bien réel de Gravisca, à Caere le culte ne semble pas uniquement aux mains de Grecs[423].

A Castrum Nouum (Santa Marinella) à une dizaine de kilomètres seulement de Caere, on a découvert au XVIIIe siècle une dédicace à *Iuno Historia*[424]. M. RENARD a trouvé une explication pour cette épithète inattendue dans la légende grecque d'Historis, fille de Tirésias, qui déjoua les desseins d'Héra et permit à Alcmène d'accoucher d'Hercule[425]. *Iuno Historia* a pu se développer à partir de ce mythe où Héra et Historis apparaissent côte à côte. Toutes deux sont liées aux notions de fécondité et de naissance, elles ont en commun une capacité prophétique ou magique[426] et un pareil caractère lunaire[427]. Le parallélisme est continu et l'antinomie qui paraît résulter de l'hostilité d'Héra à l'égard d'Historis s'explique par les oppositions ou les contradictions, parfois apparentes, qui peuvent se manifester dans la personnalité d'une même divinite[428]. Ce mythe a été repris par Ovide dans ses 'Métamorphoses'[429]. Mais il a gagné bien plus tôt l'Italie, peut-être en raison de la popularité dont jouit Hercule et ses légendes en Italie et en Etrurie particulièrement. Pourtant le culte de Junon et d'Héra est

---

[422] R. MENGARELLI, Il luogo e i materiali del tempio di Ἥρα a Caere, dans: St. Etr., 10, 1936, p. 84ss.; M. TORELLI, dans: Par. Pass., 26, 1971, p. 63.

[423] M. TORELLI, dans: Par. Pass., 26, 1971, p. 63.

[424] C.I.L., XI, 3573.

[425] M. RENARD, Iuno Historia, dans: Latomus, 12, 1953, 2, p. 137–154, où l'auteur examine aussi les interprétations précédemment émises. Sur la légende d'Historis: Pausanias, 9, 11, 3.

[426] Historis est la fille du devin Tirésias et la soeur de la prophétesse Manto (cf. M. RENARD, Iuno Historia, p. 144) tandis qu'Héra et Junon, qui à l'époque classique ont beaucoup perdu de leur caractère oraculaire, ont pourtant joué un rôle prophétique. Héra est oraculaire à Cumes (cf. M. GUARDUCCI, Un antichissimo responso dell' oracolo di Cuma, p. 129ss), son sanctuaire d'Akraia près de Corinthe était un μαντεῖον (Strabon, 8, 380), elle a une place près de l'oracle de Trophonios à Lébadée (Paus., 9, 39, 4–5). Autres indices du caractère prophétique d'Héra dans: M. GUARDUCCI, op. cit. Quant à Junon, on rappellera notamment qu'elle est *Moneta* «avertisseuse» sur l'*Arx* du Capitole (cf. M. GUARDUCCI, op. cit., et M. RENARD, Iuno Historia, p. 144).

[427] Dans un récit analogue à celui rapporté par Pausanias et recueilli dès le IIe siècle avant notre ère par Nicandre (au IVe livre de ses Ἑτεροιούμενα) et transmise en résumé dans la compilation réunie au IIe–IIIe siècle après J.-C. par Antoninus Liberalis sous le titre de Μεταμορφώσεων συναγωγή (Ant. Liberalis, 29) après avoir été préalablement repris par Ovide (Mét. 9, 281–323), Galinthias joue le rôle d'Historis et la fable se continue ainsi: Galinthias est métamorphosée en belette et Hécate, divinité infernale et lunaire, fait d'elle sa servante; cf. M. RENARD, Iuno Historia, p. 140–1, p. 144–5.

[428] M. RENARD, Iuno Historia, p. 146.

[429] Ovide, Mét., 9, 281–323.

également général en Etrurie[430]. On rappellera les cultes dont elle est l'objet à Pérouse[431], à Cortone[432], dans la région de Sienne[433], peut-être à Populonia[434], à quelque distance de Visentium[435]; plus encore en Etrurie méridionale à Véies, à Faléries, à Tarquinia[436], à Gravisca, à Caere, à Pyrgi (comme on va le voir). Dans ces conditions, il n'est pas étrange qu'à Santa Marinella toute proche de Pyrgi et de Cerveteri «soit mentionnée — sur un hermès qui fait songer aux *xoana* de la divinité bienfaisante de Caere[437] — une *Iuno Historia* c'est-à-dire une Junon courotrophe et salutaire, peut-être même sage-femme et à coup sûr guerrisseuse puisque les fouilles qui l'ont révélée ont livré un lot d'instruments de chirurgie»[438]. Dans une région où le culte d'Héra est solidement implanté, l'épithète d'origine grecque de la *Iuno* est bien explicable.

XV. *Les divinités de Pyrgi*

Nous nous devons maintenant d'évoquer les importantes découvertes épigraphiques de Pyrgi (Santa Severa), un des ports de Caere. Les fouilles menées dès 1956 sous la direction de M. PALLOTTINO et de G. COLONNA révèlent une aire sacrée qui connut une vie intense à la fin du VIe siècle. Dès le début de l'entreprise, on a découvert deux tessons de la fin du VIe siècle, portant les dédicaces *uni, unial* (génitif) qui indiquèrent l'identité de la divinité tutélaire locale[439]. En 1964, les fouilles débouchèrent sur une révélation au retentissement

---

[430] Appien, B.C., 5, 49; sur la Junon étrusque, cf. J. BAYET, Herclé, p. 146ss. et ID., Hercule romain, p. 115ss.

[431] Cf. L. ROSS TAYLOR, Local Cults in Etruria, p. 85, où l'on trouvera le détail des sources relatives aux cultes étrusques que nous citons.

[432] Ibidem, p. 192; cf. aussi A. NEPPI MODONA, Cortona etrusca e romana nella storia e nell' arte, Pubbl. R. Univ., Fac. Lett. e Filos., N.S., 7, Florence, 1925, p. 139ss.

[433] Ibidem, p. 202.

[434] Ibidem, p. 207ss. Pour ce culte, M. RENARD, Iuno Historia, p. 148, n. 8, fait de prudentes réserves.

[435] Ibidem, p. 166.

[436] Ibidem, p. 143ss.

[437] Un sanctuaire anonyme de Caere, fouillé à 380m. à l'Ouest du sanctuaire où l'on a découvert les dédicaces à Héra (cf. R. MENGARELLI, dans: St. Etr., 9, 1935, p. 83–94; L. ROSS TAYLOR, op. cit., p. 118, pour les trouvailles anciennes), était dédié à une divinité de même type que Junon comme le font penser certains ex-voto (statuettes courotrophes, ex-voto anatomiques) et d'autres offrandes: hermès féminins cylindriques dont les seules mains posées à plat font saillie sur le corps en forme de gaine. Tel était aussi l'aspect de Junon véienne (Denys, 13, 3); cf. M. RENARD, Iuno Historia, p. 152.

[438] M. RENARD, Iuno Historia, p. 152.

[439] M. PALLOTTINO, Scavi nel santuario etrusco di Pyrgi. Relazione preliminare della prima campagna, 1957, dans: Archeol. Class., 9, 1957, p. 222; ID., Scavi nel santuario etrusco di Pyrgi. Relazione preliminare della seconda campagna, 1958, dans: Archeol. Class., 10, 1958, p. 319, pl. CXI, 3; G. COLONNA, Santa Severa (Roma). Scavi e ricerche nel sito dell' antica Pyrgi (1957–1958), dans: Not. Scavi, 13, 1959, p. 225ss., fig. 79–81.

international: trois lamelles d'or couvertes d'inscriptions. L'une porte un texte punique, les deux autres, un texte étrusque. Ces inscriptions datent du Ve siècle, de la première moitié peut-être, même du premier quart[440]. Il s'agit d'une quasi-bilingue, le texte punique (P) est la version originale que les Étrusques durent traduire dans leur langue (E1). Le second texte étrusque (E2) reproduit partiellement E1, peut-être à l'occasion d'une commémoration anniversaire[441]. Le texte punique est clair mais le texte étrusque ne laisse pas de poser des problèmes. Voici la traduction du texte punique[442]:

> « [1]A la Dame Astarté. Ce lieu saint, [2]c'est ce qu'a fait et ce qu'a donné [3]Tebarie Velianas, roi sur [4]Kayišraie [c'est-à-dire Cisra, Caere], au mois du sacrifice [5]au Soleil, comme son (propre) don, comprenant le temple et son haut-lieu, [6]parce qu'Astarté a favorisé son fidèle: [7]en l'an 3 de son régne, au mois de [8]KRR, au jour de la Sépulture [9]de la Déesse.
>
> Et puissent les années où la statue de la Déesse résidera [10]dans son temple être des années aussi nombreuses que ces étoiles-[11]là! »

Il ressort de la confrontation des deux textes punique et étrusque que le nom d'Astarté est rendu par celui d'Uni. Cette découverte a suscité une bibliographie plus qu'abondante. Nous nous limiterons aux conclusions qui font l'unanimité ainsi qu'à certaines idées originales[443]. Cette nouvelle équivalence

---

[440] G. GARBINI, Scavi nel santuario etrusco di Pyrgi. Relazione preliminare della settima campagna, 1964, e scoperta di tre lamine d'oro iscritte in etrusco e in punico, dans: Archeol. Class., 16, 1964, p. 76, propose le début du Ve siècle, vers 500; M. PALLOTTINO, Scavi nel santuario etrusco di Pyrgi, dans: Archeol. Class., 16, 1964, p. 106, les date des années 500−490. Certains auteurs ont voulu abaisser cette date: A. I. KHARSEKIN, dans: Vestnik Drevnei Istorii, 3, 1965, p. 108ss., spéc. p. 115, songe au troisième quart du Ve siècle; A. J. PFIFFIG, Uni-Hera-Astarte. Studien zu den Goldblechen von S. Severa-Pyrgi mit etruskischer und punischer Inschrift, dans: Österr. Akad. der Wissenschaften, Philol.-Hist. Kl., 88,2, Vienne, 1965, p. 22; p. 40ss., pense à la fin du Ve siècle à l'époque de la guerre du Péloponnèse. J. HEURGON, The Inscriptions of Pyrgi, dans: J.R.S., 56, 1966, p. 7−8, tranche et accepte la datation haute. Quant à J. FERRON, Quelques remarques à propos de l'inscription phénicienne de Pyrgi, dans: Oriens Antiquus, 4, 1965, p. 194, à partir du texte punique, il propose la seconde moitié du VIe siècle.

[441] J. HEURGON, The Inscriptions of Pyrgi, p. 11ss.

[442] Traduction de A. DUPONT-SOMMER, L'inscription, punique récemment découverte à Pyrgi, dans: Journ. Asiat., 252, 1964, p. 292, à laquelle il n'avait rien changé au moment de la seconde édition de 'La religion romaine archaïque' de G. DUMÉZIL, 1974, p. 665, n. 6.

[443] M. PALLOTTINO, G. COLONNA, G. GARBINI, L. VLAD BORELLI, Scavi nel santuario etrusco di Pyrgi e scoperte di tre lamine d'oro iscritte in etrusco e in punico, dans: Archeol. Class., 16, 1964, p. 39−117. Les textes étrusques et punique ont été établis par J. HEURGON, Les inscriptions de Pyrgi et l'alliance étrusco-punique de 500 av. J.C., dans: C.R.A.I., 1965, p. 89−103; ID., The Inscriptions of Pyrgi, dans: J.R.S., 56, 1966, p. 1−15 et par A. DUPONT-SOMMER, L'inscription punique récemment découverte à Pyrgi, dans: Journ. Asiat., 252, 1964, p. 289−302. Deux ans déjà après la découverte, on sentit la nécessité de publier la bibliographie consacrée à ce sujet: G. COLONNA, M. CRISTOFANI, G. GARBINI, Bibliografia delle pubblicazioni più recenti sulle scoperte di Pyrgi, dans: Archeol. Class., 18, 1966, p. 279ss.; G. GARBINI, Riconsiderando l'iscrizione punica di Pyrgi, dans: Annali dell' Istituto Orientale di Napoli, 18, 1968, donne la bibliografia postérieure; Le lamine di Pyrgi, dans:

(Uni = Astarté) – que pourtant l'on trouvait déjà chez saint Augustin: *Iuno Astarte uocatur* mais que l'on avait négligée, «la Junon carthaginoise étant bien plutôt Tanit»[444] – s'intègre dans un «réseau» dense d'interprétations que les études récentes de R. BLOCH ont particulièrement éclairé[445].

A l'occasion du récit de la destruction du sanctuaire de Pyrgi en 384 avant J.-C. par la flotte syracusaine, les auteurs anciens mentionnent la déesse du lieu, mais donnent deux interprétations différentes de son appellation indigène: tantôt Εἰλήθυια (Εἰλείθυια), Ilithye[446], tantôt Λευκοθέα, Leucothée[447]. On reconnaîtra dans le premier nom une traduction courante de *Lucina* et dans le second, le rendu canonique de *Mater Matuta*. Or on connaît, depuis les découvertes de Pyrgi, le nom indigène de la déesse: *Uni*. Dès lors, a posteriori, les deux formes de l'*interpretatio graeca* surprennent, on aurait attendu Héra[448].

Mais voici qu'une autre découverte épigraphique de Pyrgi vient compléter encore ce noeud d'interprétations: sur une lamelle, de bronze cette fois, mise au jour aux abords de la vasque aux feuilles d'or, après une longue restauration, on a pu lire une inscription du Ve siècle contenant notamment, le nom étrusque de l'Aurore, *Thesan*[449]! On doit à R. BLOCH d'avoir intégré cette donnée dans

Problemi attuali di scienza e di cultura, Accademia nazionale dei Lincei, quaderno 147 (367 ème année), Rome, 1970, p. 9–67, l'ouvrage comporte une bibliographie, p. 64–67; signalons encore les articles et la bibliographie qu'ils comportent de J. FERRON, Un traité d'alliance entre Caere et Carthage contemporain des derniers temps de la royauté étrusque à Rome ou l'événement commémoré par la quasi-bilingue de Pyrgi, dans: A.N.R.W., I, 1, 1972, p. 189–216 et V. TUSA, La civiltà punica nelle altre regione d'Italia, dans: Popoli e civiltà dell'Italia antica, III, Rome, 1974, p. 88–9; p. 135.

[444] Aug., Quaest. in Heptateuchum, 7, 16; cf. G. DUMÉZIL, Rel. rom. arch.², p. 665.

[445] R. BLOCH, Ilithye, Leucothée et Thesan, dans: C.R.A.I., 1968, p. 365–375; ID., Un mode d'interprétation à deux degrés: de l'Uni de Pyrgi à Ilithye et Leucothée, dans: Archeol. class., 21, 1969, p. 58–65; ID., Figures divines de Pyrgi, dans: Recherches sur les Religions de l'Italie Antique, Centre de Recherches d'Histoire et de Philologie de la IVe Section de l'Ecole Pratique des Hautes Etudes, III, Hautes Etudes du Monde Gréco-Romain, 7, Genève, 1976, p. 1–9; ID., Processus d'assimilations divines dans l'Italie des premiers siècles, dans: Les syncrétismes dans les religions de l'Antiquité, Colloque de Besançon (22–23 octobre 1973), Etudes Préliminaires aux Religions Orientales dans l'Empire Romain, 46, Leiden, 1975, p. 112–122; ID., Héra, Uni, Junon en Italie centrale, dans: C.R.A.I., 1972, p. 384–395; ID., Héra, Uni, Junon en Italie centrale, dans: Recherches . . ., p. 9–19. On verra aussi ID., Hannibal et les dieux de Rome, dans: C.R.A.I., 1975, p. 14–25; ID., Hannibal et les dieux de Rome, dans: Recherches . . ., p. 32–42; ID., Religion romaine et religion punique à l'époque d'Hannibal, dans: Mél. J. Heurgon, I, p. 33–40.

[446] Strabon, 5, 2, 8.

[447] Ps.-Aristote, Economiques, 2, 2, 10; Polyen, Traité des ruses de guerre, 5, 2, 21; Elien, Histoire variée, 1, 20; cf. G. DUMÉZIL, Mythe et épopée, III, p. 166ss.; R. BLOCH, dans: Recherches . . ., p. 2.

[448] R. BLOCH, dans: Recherches . . ., p. 2.

[449] M. PALLOTTINO, Scavi nel santuario di Pyrgi. Relazione delle attività svolte nell'anno 1967. Un'altra laminetta di bronzo con iscrizione etrusca recuperata dal materiale di Pyrgi et G. COLONNA, L'ingresso del santuario, la via Caere-Pyrgi ed altri problemi, dans: Archeol. Class., 19, 1967, p. 332–348. Une autre inscription encore, fragmentaire, trouvée à Pyrgi porte les noms d'Uni et probablement de Tinia, cf. M. PALLOTTINO, I frammenti di lamina di bronzo con iscrizione etrusca scoperti a Pyrgi, dans: St. Etr., 34, 1966, p. 175–209.

son «interprétation à deux degrés»[450]; *Uni-Thesan* de Pyrgi, matronale et
aurorale, deviendra aux yeux des Romains *Iuno Lucina* et *Mater Matuta*.
«L'assimilation grecque s'est faite, non pas directement, mais d'après ces
premières interprétations sans doute courantes à l'époque. Ainsi Uni devenue
Juno Lucina, enfanteuse à la lumière et présidant aux Matronalia du 1er Mars,
a-t-elle pu apparaître, comme l'atteste Strabon, sous le nom de l'homologue de
Juno Lucina, c'est-à-dire Eileithuia, ainsi Uni devenue Mater Matuta, maîtresse
de la lumière naissante et présidant aux Matralia du 11 juin, a-t-elle pris le nom
de l'homologue de Mater Matuta, c'est-à-dire Leucothée»[451]. Nous ferons une
seule réserve, d'importance, à l'égard du processus proposé: R. BLOCH envisage
Thesan comme une autre qualification d'*Uni* elle-même. Il nous semble qu'il
s'agirait plutôt de deux personnalités divines bien distinctes qu'un lien étroit
unissait dans ce lieu de culte[452].

A ces multiples interprétations, vient encore s'ajouter l'Astarté carthaginoise! Quelle est la signification de cet acte religieux par lequel le «roi» ou le
magistrat suprême de Caere, Thefarie Velianas, dédie un lieu consacré à la déesse
Astarté? En tout cas, comme l'écrit R. BLOCH, cette assimilation de Pyrgi
remontant au Ve siècle — peu de temps après la victoire étrusco-punique de
l'Alalia (540/535) et quasi contemporaine du plus ancien traité entre Rome et
Carthage[453] — témoigne d'«une familiarité plus intime qu'on ne le suppose
généralement des Etrusques avec la religion phénico-punique»[454]. Rome
elle-même a pu connaître ces apports religieux et retrouver dans ces déesses sa
propre Junon[455].

Ceci dit, les documents témoignent de «l'extrême malléabilité de la
théologie étrusque, prête aux assimilations, prête à accueillir sous un nom étrusque, à la faveur d'un nom divin étranger considéré comme équivalent, toute une
matière, mythique et rituelle»[456]. L'inscription punique donne l'impression
d'une adoption intégrale du culte sémitique par le roi étrusque; les inscriptions
étrusques, toujours obscures, confirmeront-elles cette impression[457]? Une chose
pourtant ne laisse pas de surprendre: ces inscriptions réalisées sur lamelles d'or,
c'est-à-dire sur le support le plus précieux qui soit, semblent, paradoxalement,
avoir été composées à la hâte, ce qui, écrit M. PALLOTTINO, confirme
l'impression d'un fait improvisé en rupture avec la tradition, en rapport avec la
tyrannie de Thefarie Velianas soutenue par les Carthaginois en ce début du Ve
siècle quand se fait pressante la menace des Massaliotes vainqueurs à

---

[450] R. BLOCH, Figures divines de Pyrgi, dans: Recherches . . ., p. 1ss.

[451] Ibidem, p. 7.

[452] G. DUMÉZIL, Mythe et épopée, III, p. 171, n'est pas sûr que Thesan, l'Aurore à Pyrgi, soit
une désignation d'Uni. Il constate que l'Aurore comme personne divine était assez
consistante chez les Etrusques.

[453] Polybe, 3, 22, 119; cf. J. HEURGON, Rome et la Méditerranée occidentale, p. 386ss.

[454] R. BLOCH, Héra, Uni, Junon en Italie centrale, dans: Recherches . . ., p. 18.

[455] Ibidem, p. 19.

[456] G. DUMÉZIL, Rel. rom. arch.², p. 667.

[457] A. DUPONT-SOMMER, L'inscription punique récemment découverte à Pyrgi, dans: Journ.
Asiat., 252, 1964, p. 298.

l'Artémision et des Syracusains, à la veille de la bataille d'Himère[458]. Mais cet engouement sera aussi bref que brutal: jusqu'à preuve du contraire, on ne note pas une influence punique dans la physionomie monumentale de Pyrgi; l'Etrurie et Caere reviendront à leur philhellénisme; cette civilisation déterminera bien davantage l'évolution de l'Etrurie. En ce qui concerne les cultes du sanctuaire, cet apport punique n'a été probablement qu'un épisode passager de nature politique[459].

Ces inscriptions n'en attestent pas moins dès le début du Ve siècle, l'interprétation qui eut tant d'impact dans la politique étrangère de Rome. Comme le sentent très bien G. DUMÉZIL et R. BLOCH[460]: «cette identification trouvera sa plus belle illustration dans l'*Enéide* de Virgile» où la déesse tient de la Junon latine, de l'Héra grecque, de la divinité de Carthage. L'oeuvre de Virgile constitue l'achèvement d'une identification qui avait dû se poursuivre au cours des siècles[461] — les dédicaces à Astarté et Tanit d'époque hellénistique découvertes au *Fanum Iunonis* de l'île de Malte en témoignent[462]. Virgile

---

[458] J. HEURGON, The Inscriptions of Pyrgi, dans: J.R.S., 56, 1966, p. 15; M. PALLOTTINO, dans: St. Etr., 34, 1966, p. 208−9; voir aussi M. PALLOTTINO, Rapporti fra Greci, Fenici, Etruschi ed altre popolazioni italiche alla luce delle recenti scoperte, dans: Problemi attuali di scienza e di cultura, Accademia nazionale dei Lincei, quaderno 87 (363 ème année), Rome 1966, p. 13 ss. (paru aussi dans: Saggi di Antichità, I: Alle origini dell' Italia antica, Rome, 1979, p. 391 ss.).

[459] M. PALLOTTINO, dans: St. Etr., 34, 1966, p. 209; G. DUMÉZIL, Rel. rom. arch.[2], p. 667. Un point dans l'interprétation de la quasi-bilingue reste obscur: pourquoi Thefarie Velianas a-t-il fait un don à Astarté? A partir du texte punique de Pyrgi, plusieurs 'sémitisants', avec des nuances sur lesquelles nous ne pouvons nous arrêter ici, estiment que l'offrande du roi appartient à la célébration de l'hiérogamie, du mariage sacré entre le roi Thefarie et la déesse Astarté. Notamment dans certaines études de J. FERRON, Quelques remarques à propos de l'inscription phénicienne de Pyrgi, dans: Oriens Antiquus, 4, 2, 1965, p. 181−198; ID., Précision supplémentaire relative à la datation contenue dans le texte phénicien de Pyrgi, dans: Oriens Antiquus, 5, 2, 1966, p. 203−6; ID., La dédicace à Astarté du roi de Caere Tibérie Velianaš, dans: Le Muséon, 81, 1968, p. 523−546; ID., Toujours Pyrgi, dans: Annali dell'Istituto Universitario Orientale di Napoli, 30, 4, 1970, p. 425−437; ID., Un traité d'alliance entre Caere et Carthage contemporain des derniers temps de la royauté étrusque à Rome ou l'événement commémoré par la quasi-bilingue de Pyrgi, dans: A.N.R.W., I, 1, 1972, pp. 189−216; de J. G. FÉVRIER, L'inscription punique de Pyrgi, dans: C.R.A.I., 1965, p. 9−15; ID., Remarques sur l'inscription punique de Pyrgi, dans: Oriens Antiquus, 4, 1965, p. 175−180; ID., A propos du hieros gamos de Pyrgi, dans: Journ. Asiat., 253, 1965, p. 11−13; de M. DELCOR, Une inscription bilingue étrusco-punique récemment découverte à Pyrgi. Son importance religieuse, dans: Le Muséon, 81, 1968, p. 241−254; E. LIPIŃSKI, La fête de l'ensevelissement et de la résurrection de Melqart, dans: Actes de la XVIIe Rencontre Assyriologique Internationale, Bruxelles, 1969, Bruxelles 1970, p. 30−58.

[460] G. DUMÉZIL, Rel. rom. Arch.[2], p. 463; R. BLOCH, Héra, Uni, Junon en Italie Centrale, dans: Recherches . . ., p. 18.

[461] R. BLOCH, A propos de l'Enéide de Virgile: réflexions et perspectives, dans: R.E.L., 45, 1967, p. 336.

[462] G. GARBINI et B. PUGLIESE, Le iscrizioni puniche, dans: Missione Archeologica a Malta, Centro di Studi Semitici, Ist. del Vicino Oriente, Ser. Archeol., 5, Rome, 1964, p. 83−104 où l'on trouvera l'édition des dédicaces à Astarté et Tanit découvertes dans le *Fanum Iunonis* de Tas-Silg à Malte. Voir aussi S. MOSCATI, La prima campagna di scavi della

représente « la synthèse [religieuse] qu'il trouvait constituée autour de lui et qui lui paraissait toute naturelle, et non le produit d'une sédimentation plus ou moins hétéroclite. Ce qui importe ce n'est pas ce qu'il y a dans sa Junon de l'Héra grecque et de la Juno latine, mais bien que, pour lui, l'une est identique à l'autre »[463].

XVI. En guise de conclusion

Sous l'Empire, Junon va demeurer l'expression de la fécondité féminine; Auguste, à la faveur de sa politique nataliste, exalte la déesse tandis que des syncrétismes de plus en plus larges l'identifient aux 'déesses-mères' étrangères bien plus vivantes dans la dévotion populaire. Elle fut très tôt assimilée à Héra, dont elle prend les attributs et les mythes, mais aussi à Diane[464]. En tant que *Iuno Caelestis*, elle est Astarté ainsi que Tanit. Mais on connaît aussi, par exemple, une *Caelestis Brigantia*, déesse régionale, tutélaire des *Brigantes* identifiée à *Iuno Caelestis*[465]. Ovide assimile *Iuno Lucina* à Isis[466], il est vrai que cette dernière est décrite sur une inscription comme « ayant dix mille noms » . . .[467] Syncrétismes sans fin.

Pourtant sous l'Empire, le culte de Junon, abstraction faite de la vénération dont la déesse est l'objet en tant que membre de la triade capitoline, n'est que relativement peu attesté dans le monde romain[468]. Il apparaît dans les dédicaces à Jupiter Optimus Maximus, à Junon Reine, à Minerve, témoignages de civisme à l'égard de l'Empire, et pas beaucoup plus. Dès l'époque augustéenne, des temples capitolins sont édifiés en de nombreuses villes d'Italie mais aussi dans les

Missione archeologica italiana a Malta. I: Lo scavo di Tas-Silg fino all'età romana, dans: Rend. Pontif. Acc. Archeol., 36, 1963−4, p. 23−35.

[463] P. BOYANCÉ, La religion de Virgile, Coll. Mythes et Religions, Paris, 1963, p. 19; R. BLOCH, A propos de l'Enéide de Virgile, p. 334−337, montre le double visage de la Junon de Virgile l'un italique, l'autre carthaginois; il insiste sur le fait que dans l'étude de la religion chez Virgile, à la suite de l'œuvre de P. BOYANCÉ, « il faut faire intervenir ce sentiment juste et profond qu' avait le poète du parallèle ou de l'identification de divinités appartenant à des mondes différents et que le rapprochement des peuples qui les vénéraient a pu amener à s'unir, parfois à se confondre ». On lira également V. BUCHHEIT, Vergil über die Sendung Roms, p. 11−150: Juno's Kampf gegen Rom und ihre Versöhnung; p. 173−189: Carthago−Rom als Antithese in Aeneis 1−7. On citera encore W. S. ANDERSON, Juno and Saturn in the Aeneid, dans: Studies in Philology, 55, 4, 1958, p. 519−532; C. W. AMERASINGHE, Saturnia Iuno, dans: Greece and Rome, 22, 1953, p. 61−9; L. A. MacKAY, Saturnia Iuno, dans: Greece and Rome, 2de sér., 3, 1956, p. 59−60.

[464] Cf. supra; e. g. Catulle, 34, 13ss. qui tout en s'adressant à Diane, l'appelle *Iuno Lucina*.

[465] Cf. J. FERGUSON, The Religions of the Roman Empire, Coll. Aspects of Greek and Roman Life, Londres, 1970, p. 216.

[466] Ovide, Amor., 2, 13.

[467] I.L.S., 4361 et C.I.L., X, 3800 = I.L.S., 4362; cf. ROEDER, dans: R.E., IX,2, 1914, art. Isis, col. 2114.

[468] J. TOUTAIN, Les cultes païens dans l'Empire romain, I, Paris, 1907, p. 289; M. RENARD, Iuno Historia, p. 147−8.

provinces[469]. A côté des *Capitolia*, les inscriptions votives, particulièrement celles à caractère patriotique qui mentionnent souvent les noms des divinités de la triade capitoline, nous fournissent une autre source de documentation. Les noms de Jupiter, Junon, Minerve y sont souvent cités à côté d' autres divinités protectrices de l'Etat[470]. En milieu provincial, on admet d'énormes dépenses pour doter les cités d'un Capitole; par contre, on ne connaît que de très rares témoignages de piété individuelle: le culte capitolin représente, plus qu'un élément de religiosité personnelle, le culte officiel de l'Empire, un acte publique d'hommage à la religion nationale et à l'Empereur[471]. Dans les milieux des militaires et des fonctionnaires, on connaît davantage de manifestations individuelles à l'égard des divinités de la triade[472]. Ainsi, les inscriptions du type de celle dédiée à *Iuno Regina Populonia* par un légat stationné en Dacie (cf. p. 169) sont extrêmement intéressantes: il faudrait encore dresser l'inventaire des autres épigraphes de ce genre afin d'affiner la connaissance du culte de Junon sous l'Empire, considéré exagérément peut-être comme formaliste à l'extrême. Nous devons constater aussi combien dans ces pages les images archéologiques entrent peu en ligne de compte, elles permettraient pourtant de préciser le tableau.

---

[469] U. BIANCHI, Disegno storico del culto capitolino nell'Italia romana e nelle provincie dell'Impero, dans: Acc. Naz. Lincei, Memorie, Ser. VIII,2, 1949 [1950], p. 349−414; p. 373: c'est de 44 avant J.-C. que date la première mention d'un culte publique à la triade Capitoline dans une ville hors d'Italie, en Espagne cf. C.I.L., I², 594.

[470] Un exemple caractéristique: une inscription de 66 après J.-C. dédiée à la fois à la triade Capitoline, à *Felicitas*, à Rome et à Auguste (C.I.L., XI, 1331); dans cette dédicace sont donc réunis les deux cultes nationaux par excellence, celui à la triade Capitoline et celui à Rome et à Auguste, cf. U. BIANCHI, op. cit., p. 376.

[471] U. BIANCHI, op. cit., p. 383−4.

[472] U. BIANCHI, op. cit., p. 380ss.

La place de Minerve dans la religion romaine au temps du principat

par Jean-Louis Girard, Strasbourg

Table des matières

Introduction

Avec la restauration augustéenne s'instaure en matière religieuse un nouvel équilibre. Le *cultus deorum* regagne, après le déclin de la fin de la République, en dignité et en vigueur. L'antique religion s'élargit aux dimensions de l'Empire. La nudité des conceptions archaïques se pare des ornements de la poésie et des allégories de la philosophie. Les productions de l'art religieux se multiplient et atteignent une qualité inégalée.

Antique divinité du culte romain sans être liée exclusivement à Rome, revêtue du riche héritage d'Athéna par une *interpretatio* promptement et universellement acceptée, dotée d'une iconographie caractéristique, prêtant à la spéculation intellectuelle par la variété de ses fonctions, Minerve se trouve au temps du principat dans des conditions idéales pour tenir une place de choix dans le panthéon, et, de fait, nous allons la voir largement bénéficier de l'évolution religieuse en cours.

I. Les sanctuaires romains

1. Constructions d'époque républicaine

A la fin de la République, Minerve est richement dotée en lieux de culte, dont on peut suivre l'histoire au cours de la période qui nous intéresse.

Abréviations:

A.E.	= L'Année Epigraphique.
AJA	= American Journal of Archeology.
ANRW	= Aufstieg und Niedergang der römischen Welt. Geschichte und Kultur Roms im Spiegel der neueren Forschung, H. Temporini et W. Haase (éd.), Berlin–New York, 1972 ff.
BMC	= H. Mattingly, Coins of the Roman Empire in the British Museum, t. I–IV, Londres, 1923–1940.
CIL	= Corpus inscriptionum Latinarum.
Degrassi	= A. Degrassi, Fasti anni Numani et Iuliani, Rome, 1963.

D'abord, elle occupe une des *cellae* du grand temple capitolin, à la droite de Jupiter[1]. Ce sanctuaire, le plus important de Rome, a eu une histoire agitée. Déjà incendié au cours des guerres civiles entre Marius et Sylla puis rebâti, il sera encore deux fois victime d'un incendie. En 69 après Jésus-Christ, Flauius Sabinus et Domitien y sont assiégés par les partisans de Vitellius, qui livrent l'édifice aux flammes[2]. Vespasien le restaure, mais, sous Titus, un autre incendie, accidentel celui-là, réduit de nouveau ces efforts à néant[3]. C'est Domitien qui devait reconstruire et dédier un quatrième Capitole, dont il ne subsiste plus que les fondements. Nous pouvons nous faire une idée de son architecture, caractéristique de l'époque flavienne, par la description de Plutarque[4].

Il existe à Rome un autre sanctuaire de la triade capitoline, connu sous le nom de *Capitolium uetus*[5] ou *antiquum*[6]. Cette dénomination ne doit pas nous abuser, en nous faisant prêter à cette chapelle une prodigieuse antiquité. Lorsque

ESPÉRANDIEU	= E. ESPÉRANDIEU, Recueil général des bas-reliefs, statues et bustes de la Gaule romaine, continué par. R. LANTIER, t. I–XIV, Paris, 1908–1949.
ESPÉRANDIEU, Germ.	= E. ESPÉRANDIEU, Recueil général des bas-reliefs, statue et bustes de la Germanie romaine, Paris–Bruxelles, 1931.
HELBIG[4]	= W. HELBIG, Führer durch die öffentlichen Sammlungen klassischer Altertümer in Rom, remanié par H. SPEIER, B. ANDREAE, T. DOHRN, E. SIMON e.a., t. I–IV, [4]Tübingen, 1963–72.
MDAI	= Mitteilungen des Deutschen Archaeologischen Instituts; M: Madrider Abteilung; R: Römische Abteilung.
PLATNER–ASHBY	= S. B. PLATNER & T. ASHBY, A Topographical Dictionary of Ancient Rome, Londres, 1929.
RE	= F. PAULY–G. WISSOWA (éd.), Realencyclopaedie der classischen Altertumswissenschaft, Stuttgart 1892ff.
RIC	= H. MATTINGLY–E. A. SYDENHAM–V. SUTHERLAND, Roman Imperial Coinage, t. I–III, Londres, 1926–1948.
ROSCHER	= W. ROSCHER, Ausführliches Lexicon der griechischen und römischen Mythologie, Leipzig, 1884–1937, réimpr. Hildesheim, 1965/67.
STRACK	= P. L. STRACK, Untersuchungen zur römischen Reichsprägung des 2. Jahrhunderts, t. I–III, Stuttgart, 1931–1937.
VALENTINI– ZUCCHETTI	= R. VALENTINI–G. ZUCCHETTI, Codice topografico della città di Roma, Fonti per la Storia d'Italia, LXXXI e LXXXVIII, I, Rome, 1940; II Rome, 1941.

[1] Liv., 7,3,5: *dextro lateri Iouis optimi maximi, ex qua parte Mineruae templum est.*

[2] Cass. Dio, 64,17: Οἵ τε ὕπατοι (. . .) καὶ Σαβῖνος (. . .) ἔς τε τὸ Καπιτώλιον ἀνέφυγον (. . .) Ἐμπρησθέντων δὲ τῶν περὶ τὸ Καπιτώλιον ἀνεκόπησαν διὰ τοῦ πυρός.

[3] Plut., Publ., 15,2: Ἅμα τῷ τελευτῆσαι Οὐεσπασιανὸν ἐνεπρήσθη τὸ Καπιτώλιον.

[4] Plut., Publ., 15,4: Οἱ δὲ κίονες ἐκ τοῦ Πεντελῆσιν ἐτμήθησαν λίθου, κάλλιστα τῷ πάχει πρὸς τὸ μῆκος ἔχοντες — εἴδομεν γὰρ αὐτοὺς Ἀθήνησιν, ἐν δὲ Ῥώμῃ πληγέντες αὖθις καὶ ἀναξυσθέντες. . .

[5] Varr., L.L., V,158: *Cliuus proximus a Flora susus uersus Capitolium uetus, quod ibi sacellum Iouis Iunonis Mineruae.*

[6] Curiosum Vrbis Romae regionum XIIII: *Regio VI*: (. . .) *Capitolium antiquum* (VALENTINI-ZUCCHETTI, t. I, p. 107).

Varron écrit: *Et id antiquius quam aedes quae in Capitolio facta*[7], il pense au grand temple capitolin qu'il connaît, et qui est de facture récente puisqu'il vient d'être rebâti au Ier siècle avant Jésus-Christ. Ce qui le prouve, c'est l'appellation même de *Capitolium uetus*. Capitole est d'abord une désignation géographique, et ne s'est appliqué qu'ensuite, par métonymie, à un «temple de la triade honorée sur le Capitole». Mais, pour que la triade capitoline ait pu prendre ce nom, il faut bien qu'elle ait été honorée d'abord sur le Capitole. Dans toutes les cités de province où l'on construit, à l'imitation de Rome, un temple à trois *cellae*, ce temple porte également le nom de *Capitolium*.

En l'absence de renseignements plus précis sur le *sacellum*, nous ne pouvons rien dire de la raison qui a fait bâtir, à Rome même, un deuxième lieu de culte de la triade capitoline. En tout cas, la chapelle a subsisté jusqu'à la fin de l'Antiquité, puisqu'elle est mentionnée dans les listes des curiosités de la ville de Rome[8].

Minerve était honorée, en qualité de patronne des corporations, dans un temple sur l'Aventin, dont la date précise de fondation n'est pas connue[9]. Ce temple figure parmi ceux qu'Auguste se fait, dans son testament, honneur d'avoir restauré[10]. Un fragment de la 'Forma Vrbis Romae', d'époque sévérienne, nous a conservé ses caractéristiques, qui sont celles d'un hexastyle périptère[11]. Nos sources indiquent comme le *dies natalis templi* tantôt le 19 mars, premier jour des *Quinquatrus*[12], tantôt le 19 juin[13]. Cette discordance a fait supposer que la deuxième date pouvait être celle d'une restauration du temple[14]. Mais il est clair que cette hypothèse repose sur des bases extrêmement fragiles.

Sur les pentes du Caelius, se dressait encore, à l'époque d'Ovide[15] le petit sanctuaire de *Minerua Capta*. De cette épithète bizarre, le poète a donné plusieurs explications. Une seule a quelque probabilité, et se trouvait d'ailleurs, semble-t-il, confirmée par une inscription à l'intérieur du temple[16]: le culte a été introduit à Rome venant de Faléries, après la prise de cette ville en 241. Cela

---

[7] Varr., L.L., 5,158.

[8] Voir note 6 ci-dessus.

[9] Il ressort de Fest., pp. 446—7 L. que ce temple existait déjà à l'époque de la deuxième guerre punique: *Cum Liuius Andronicus bello Punico secundo scribsisset carmen quod a uirginibus est cantatum, publice adtributa est ei in Auentino aedis Mineruae, in qua liceret scribis histrionibusque consistere et dona ponere.*

[10] J. GAGÉ, Res gestae diui Augusti[2], Paris, 1950, § 19,2: *aedes Mineruae.*

[11] G. CARETTONI—A. M. COLINI—L. COZZA—G. GATTI, La pianta marmorea di Roma antica, Rome, 1960, p. 79 & pl. 23, fr. 22.

[12] Fest., p. 306 L.: *Mineruae autem dicatum eum diem* (sc. Quinquatrus) *existimant quod eo die aedis eius in Auentino consecrata est.*

[13] Ov., F., 6,728: *Coepit Auentina Pallas in arce coli.*

[14] PLATNER—ASHBY, p. 342.

[15] Ov., F., 3,835—7:

> *Caelius ex alto qua mons descendit in aequum*
>
> . . .
>
> *Parua licet uideas Captae delubra Mineruae.*

[16] Ov., F., 3,844: *Hoc ipsum littera prisca docet.*

nous fournit, du même coup, une date pour le sanctuaire. Celui-ci, qu'on désigne parfois sous le nom de *Mineruium*[17], devait occuper l'emplacement de l'actuelle église des Quatre-Saints-Couronnés. Un relief de l'époque des Antonins[18], où l'on aperçoit une statue de Minerve à travers l'arc d'Isis, semble faire allusion à cet édifice[19]. On rapporte en tout cas à ce site une inscription trouvée sur les pentes du Caelius[20], et l'on a supposé qu'un torse mutilé, portant l'égide, trouvé en 1923 via Celimontana, et conservé au Musée des Thermes[21], était celui de la statue cultuelle. Si l'identification est exacte, ce serait une présomption en faveur du caractère guerrier de la *Minerua Capta*.

Tout différent est le culte de *Minerua Medica*, dont la fonction guérisseuse nous est déjà attestée à la fin de la République par une plaisanterie de Cicéron[22], mais de la popularité croissante de laquelle témoignent, sur les pentes de l'Esquilin, de nombreux ex-voto d'époque impériale. Une inscription vient confirmer la localisation du sanctuaire, à l'ouest de la via Merulana[23].

On ne sait rien de l'emplacement d'un sanctuaire de Minerve que Pompée aurait édifié sur le produit de ses prises de guerre, ni de l'histoire de ce culte, sur lequel on peut supposer une forte influence de la guerrière Athéna[24].

2. Constructions nouvelles

Comme, par leur abondance, les lieux de culte d'époque républicaine pouvaient suffire à la piété publique ou privée, on comprend que le rythme des créations ait tout d'abord été modéré. On ne doit pas, semble-t-il, attribuer à Auguste la consécration à Minerve du *Chalcidicum* (sorte de cryptoportique) attenant à la Curie. Dans son testament, il signale bien la réfection de ce monument, mais sans faire allusion à Minerve[25]. Et si Dion Cassius, dans sa liste des monuments restaurés par Auguste, place «l'Athénéum qu'on appelle Chalcidique»[26], c'est qu'il se réfère à la situation de son temps, où ce promenoir a été consacré à Minerve, probablement par Domitien.

C'est peut-être le même monument qu'à partir de cette époque on appelle l'*Atrium Mineruae*[27]. Il sera ensuite englobé dans les constructions de la curie de

[17] Varr., L.L., 5,47: *circa Mineruium qua in Caelio monte itur in tabernola*.
[18] Monumenti Antichi Inediti, pubblicati dall'Istituto di Corrispondenza Archeologica, Rome, 1829–1885, V,7.
[19] PLATNER-ASHBY, p. 344.
[20] CIL, VI,524: *Miner[uae] / donum[dat] / conlegi[um cor] / nicin[um]*.
[21] HELBIG⁴, t. III, n° 2368.
[22] Cic., Div., 2,123: *sine medico medicinam dabit Minerua*.
[23] CIL, VI,10133: *D(is) M(anibus) / Cn(aeus) Vergilius / Epaphroditus / magister odararius / a Minerua / Medica uixit annos / septuaginta et . . .*
[24] Plin., N.H., 7,97: *in delubro Mineruae quod ex manubiis dicabat*.
[25] J. GAGÉ, Res gestae diui Augusti², Paris, 1950, § 19,1: *curiam et continens ei chalcidicum*.
[26] Cass. Dio., 51,22: Τὸ Ἀθήναιον τὸ ὠνομασμένον Χαλκιδικόν.
[27] Curiosum Vrbis Romae regionum XIIII: *Regio VIII (. . .) Atrium Mineruae* (VALENTINI–ZUCCHETTI, t. I, p. 114).

Dioclétien[28]. On ne doit pas, sous prétexte que Minerve est la patronne des corporations, le confondre avec l'*Atrium sutorium*[29].

Ce n'est pas davantage un lieu de culte que la bibliothèque du Palatin, dans laquelle Auguste avait placé une statue de Minerve, patronne des activités intellectuelles. Martial y fait encore allusion dans une épigramme adressée à son ami le bibliothécaire Sextus[30]. Domitien, dont la dévotion pour Minerve est connue, n'a pas consacré moins de trois temples à la déesse: celui de *Minerua Chalcidica* sur le Champ de Mars, un temple sur le Forum entre l'*aedes Castorum* et le *templum nouum diui Augusti*, et le temple du *Forum transitorium*[31]. A cela, il faut ajouter la restauration du temple capitolin, dont la *cella* de droite était consacrée à Minerve, et sans doute la transformation du *Chalcidicum* de la Curie en *Atrium Mineruae*.

Après le règne de Domitien, on ne relève plus de nouveaux sanctuaires en l'honneur de Minerve. L'*Athenaeum* construit par Hadrien est un bâtiment destiné à abriter les activités intellectuelles, et non un temple[32].

II. Le calendrier liturgique

1. Quinquatrus

La principale fête de Minerve est celle des *Quinquatrus*, qui se déroule du 19 au 23 mars. Les témoignages divergents de nos sources permettent de soupçonner qu' à l'origine, Mars jouait un rôle dans cette fête, et peut-être un rôle plus important que celui de Minerve[33]. Quoiqu'il en soit, à l'époque où nous nous plaçons, les *Quinquatrus* sont indubitablement la fête de Minerve. Elle est célébrée par des jeux, et, pour l'époque d'Auguste, Ovide[34] nous signale que les combats de gladiateurs sont proscrits le premier jour, *dies natalis* de Minerve. Cela nous permet de supposer que l'aspect guerrier n'était pas primordial dans l'hommage rendu à la déesse. De fait, les *Quinquatrus* semblent être essentiellement la fête des artisans, dont le même Ovide nous décrit le cortège bigarré, partant en procession[35].

[28] PLATNER—ASHBY, p. 111.

[29] Varr., L.L., 6,14: *Dies tubulustrium appellatur, quod eo die in atrio sutorio sacrorum tubae lustrantur.*

[30] Mart., 5,5,1: *Sexte, Palatinae cultor facunde Mineruae.*

[31] Voir ci-après J.-L. GIRARD, Domitien et Minerve: une prédilection impériale.

[32] Aur.-Vict.., Caes., 14,1—3: *Aelius Hadrianus (. . .) doctores curare occepit, adeo ut ludum ingenuarum artium, quod Athenaeum uocant, constitueret.*

[33] O. HENTSCHEL, Quinquatrus, in: RE, XXIV,1 (1963), c. 1149—1160.

[34] Ov., F., 3,812—3:

> *Sanguine prima (sc. dies) uacat nec fas concurrere ferro.*
> *Causa, quod est illa nata Minerua die.*

[35] Ov., F., 3,821—2:

> *Hanc cole, qui laesis maculas de uestibus aufers.*
> *Hanc cole, uelleribus quisquis aëna paras.*

Cela contribue à donner à cette fête un caractère populaire et privé, que vient renforcer une autre circonstance: les maîtres d'école se plaçaient sous la protection de Minerve, et les classes vaquaient pendant les *Quinquatrus*[36]. Est-ce pour cette raison que ces cinq journées étaient vouées à la distraction? Auguste, dans une lettre à Tibère, révèle qu'il a passé les *Quinquatrus* à jouer aux dés[37]. Ces quelques jours au début du printemps étaient pour les Romains une occasion de s'échapper de Rome. Néron était à Baïes, lors des *Quinquatrus* de l'année 59, lorsqu'il saisit l'occasion de ce voyage pour attenter à la vie d'Agrippine, plus à l'abri des regards que dans les palais de la capitale[38]. L'événement valut à la fête un regain de notoriété, à vrai dire d'assez fâcheux aloi. Néron, non content de faire dresser une statue d'or à Minerve dans la Curie, ordonna de célébrer par des jeux la découverte de la prétendue conjuration d'Agrippine[39]. Il va de soi que cette célébration indécente fut interrompue par la mort de l'empereur.

Domitien quittait également Rome pour sa propriété d'Albe pendant les *Quinquatrus*. Ce dévot de Minerve avait donné à la fête une solennité particulière, instituant un *collegium Mineruae* dont le président était tiré au sort, et chargé d'organiser des jeux[40]. Le rôle de ce collège, qui n'est pas attesté épigraphiquement, reste assez obscur. Son président devait suppléer à l'absence du prince, en organisant, pour la foule des *humiliores* restés à Rome, les jeux qu'Ovide signale déjà à l'époque d'Auguste. Mais, d'autre part, il est certain qu'à Albe se déroulaient des concours poétiques. Stace se vante d'y avoir participé, et d'avoir été couronné de la main de Domitien[41]. On ne trouve plus trace des *ludi Albani* après la disparition de cet empereur.

2. Quinquatrus minusculae

Le calendrier officiel comporte également une autre fête de Minerve, celle des *Quinquatrus minusculae* ou *minores*, le 13 juin. La corporation des joueurs

---

[36] Hor., Ep., 2,2,197–8:

> Puer ut festis Quinquatribus olim,
> Exiguo gratoque fruaris tempore raptim.

[37] Suet., Aug., 71,5: *Nos, mi Tiberi, Quinquatrus satis iucunde egimus; lusimus enim per omnis dies forumque aleatorum calfecimus.*

[38] Tac., An., 14,4,1: *Placuit sollertia, tempore etiam iuta, quando Quinquatruum festos dies apud Baias frequentabat.*

[39] Tac., An., 14,12,1: *utque Quinquatrus, quibus apertae insidiae essent, ludis annuis celebrarentur, aureum Mineruae simulacrum in curia et iuxta principis imago statuerentur.*

[40] Suet., Dom., 4,4: *Celebrabat (sc. Domitianus) et in Albano quotannis Quinquatria Mineruae, cui collegium instituerat, ex quo sorte ducti magisterio fungerentur ederentque eximias uenationes et scaenicos ludos superque oratorum et poetarum certamina.*

[41] Stace, S., 4,2,66–7:

> Cum modo Germanas acies, modo Daca sonantem
> Proelia Palladio tua me manus induit auro

et 3,5,28–9:

> Me nitidis Albana ferentem
> Dona comis.

de flûte célèbre la déesse par une procession de carnaval. Tite-Live, Ovide et Plutarque donnent pour occasion à cette fête un événement historique[42]. Ce qui nous intéresse ici est qu'ils en parlent comme de quelque chose de contemporain. Au IIème siècle après Jésus-Christ, on pouvait donc voir encore se dérouler dans les rues de Rome cette procession.

3. L'*Agon Capitolinus*

Domitien créa également, sur le modèle des grands jeux helléniques, l'*Agon Capitolinus*, qui se célébrait tous les quatre ans. Il était dédié au seul Jupiter Capitolin, mais Minerve n'en était pas absente, la triade y jouant un rôle. Sur la couronne de l'empereur, qui préside aux jeux, sont représentés Jupiter, Junon et Minerve, ainsi que sur les couronnes du flamine de Jupiter et du collège des Flaviens, à côté, cette fois, de l'effigie de Domitien.[43] Les jeux capitolins ont survécu jusqu'à la fin du paganisme, mais sans que les couronnes en or, témoignage de la démesure de Domitien, aient continué d'être en usage.

4. La question de l'*Agon Mineruae*

L'institution d'un *Agon Mineruae* est prêtée à Gordien III par le Chronographe de 354[44]. D'autre part, Aurélius Victor déclare que cet empereur a « agrandi et confirmé le concours lustral que Néron avait introduit à Rome »[45], alors que la célébration des *Neronia* avait été interrompue. Il y a lieu de soupçonner une confusion. Il ne paraît pas probable qu'elle ait eu lieu avec l'*Agon Capitolinus*, dédié à Jupiter et dont la création par Domitien n'avait pu être oubliée. En revanche, si l'on se rappelle que Néron avait ordonné que l'on célébrât les *Quinquatrus*, on comprend qu'Aurélius Victor ait pu lier son nom aux jeux qui se célébraient à l'occasion de cette fête. L'*Agon Mineruae* se confondrait donc avec les *Quinquatrus*.

---

[42] Liv., 9,30,5–10; Val. Max., 2,5,4; Ov., F., 6,657–69; Plut., Q.R., 55. Cf. G. DUMÉZIL, Mythe et épopée. III: Histoires romaines, Paris, 1973, pp. 174–94.

[43] Suet., Dom. 4,3: (*Domitianus*) *instituit et quinquennale certamen Capitolino Ioui triplex, musicum, equestre, gymnicum. Certamini praesedit* (. . .) *gestans coronam auream cum effigie Iouis ac Iunonis Mineruaeque, adsidentibus Diali sacerdote et collegio Flauialium pari habitu, nisi quod illorum coronis inerat et ipsius imago.*

[44] Chronica minora saeculorum IV, V, VI, VII (= Monumenta Germaniae historica, Auctores antiquissimi, IX), ed. TH. MOMMSEN, p. 149: *Gordianus* (. . .) *agonem Mineruae instituit.*

[45] Aur. Vict. Caes, 27,7: *Eoque anno* (il s'agit de 238), *lustri certamine, quod Nero Romam induxerat, aucto firmatoque, Persas profectus est.*

5. La question de l'*Epulum Mineruae*

Les ménologes rustiques indiquent en septembre un *Epulum Mineruae*[46]. Il s'agit d'un banquet, auquel participaient, au témoignage de Valère Maxime, les trois membres de la triade capitoline, assises sur des sièges, tandis que Jupiter était couché[47]. La préférence accordée à Minerve par ces calendriers zodiacaux tardifs vient peut-être de ce que le mois de septembre était placé sous le signe de la Vierge.

III. La diffusion du culte dans l'Empire romain

Il s'agit ici du culte de Minerve seule. Une place à part (VII,1: Le culte capitolin) est réservée au culte de la triade, qui revêt une signification particulière.

1. La péninsule italique

Minerve n'est pas une déesse exclusivement romaine. Varron lui attribue même une origine sabine[48]. Le « sabinisme » bien connu de cet auteur affaiblit ici la portée de son témoignage. Mais il est certain qu'à Orvinium, Minerve possède un temple très ancien, de l'importance duquel témoigne Denys d'Halicarnasse[49]. Cette importance du culte de Minerve en Sabine explique en partie la dévotion qu'eurent pour la déesse les empereurs de la dynastie flavienne, originaire du pays sabin, et particulièrement Domitien.

A Préneste, une inscription que date précisément le nom martelé de Domitien commémore l'érection d'une statue de Minerve par Q. Flauius Eulogus, peut-être un affranchi de la maison impériale[50].

En dehors du Latium, des dédicaces attestent un culte de Minerve, qui est généralement le fait des artisans, dans de nombreuses cités d'Italie et de Gaule cisalpine. Contentons-nous de relever quelques particularités locales intéressantes:

A Caverzago, dans les environs de Plaisance, se dressait un temple où de nombreuses inscriptions sont dues à la reconnaissance de fidèles guéris par *Minerua Cabardiacensis*, *Minerua medica Cabardiacensis*, *Minerua Memor*

---

[46] CIL, I², I, p. 281; DEGRASSI, Menologium Vallense, Menologium Colotianum: *Epulum Mineruae*.

[47] Val. Max., 2,1,2: *Iouis Epulo ipse in lectulum, Iuno et Minerua ad cenam inuitabantur, quod genus seueritatis aetas nostra diligentius in Capitolio quam in suis domibus conseruat.*

[48] Varr., L.L., 5,74: *Minerua a Sabinis.*

[49] Denys d'Halic., A.R., 1,14,3: Ὀρουΐνιον (. . .) ἔνθα καὶ νεὼς Ἀθηνᾶς ἐστιν ἀρχαῖος ἱδρυμένος ἐπὶ τῆς ἄκρας.

[50] CIL, XIV,2897: *Signum Minerua[e] / ///////// August[i] / Q. Flauius Eulogus . . .*

(*Cabardiacum* est le nom antique de Caverzago)[51]. Ce culte local est manifestement celui d'une Minerve guérisseuse, que nous avons déjà rencontrée à Rome avec l'épithète de *Minerua Medica*, mais qui peut-être s'est substituée ici à une divinité locale.

En d'autres emplacements d'une Italie romanisée, Minerve semble avoir pris la place d'Athéna, et donné naissance à des appellations géographiques. C'est le cas de la Minerve de Sorrente, dont le temple, édifié sur le *Promuntorium Mineruae*, dominait le golfe de Campanie[52]. C'est également le cas à *Arx* ou *Castrum Mineruae*, en Calabre, où Virgile fait apercevoir pour la première fois l'Italie à Enée[53], et qui va devenir la *Colonia Mineruia Neruia Augusta Scolacium*[54].

A Pesaro, en Emilie, un laraire enfantin contient une statuette de Minerve, patronne des études. C'est un témoignage émouvant de la diffusion du culte, dans tous les milieux[55].

Les épithètes de *Minerua Nortina* à Bisenzio[56], de *Minerua flanatica* à Monsalice[57] recouvrent certainement l'*interpretatio* de divinités locales.

Enfin, en 228, on voit apparaître à Bénévent, dans un contexte taurobolique d'offrandes à Attis et à la Mère des Dieux, une *Minerua Berecynthia*[58].

2. Les provinces

Le culte de Minerve fut souvent répandu aux frontières par des soldats, qui adoraient la guerrière déesse, protectrice des destinées de Rome. C'est surtout à partir du IIème siècle que leurs dédicaces se multiplient dans les garnisons du Rhin, du Danube et en Afrique[59].

Mais il faut tenir compte aussi du fait que, dans un certain nombre de régions d'Occident, la dévotion à la déesse avait rencontré un terrain parti-

---

[51] CIL, XI, 1297–1305.

[52] Stace, S., 5,3,166: *Tyrrheni speculatrix uirgo profundi*.

[53] Verg., A., 3,530–1:
> Portusque patescit
> Iam propior, templumque apparet in arce Mineruae.

[54] CIL, X, 103: *Imp(erator) Caesar T(itus) Aelius Hadri/anus Antoninus Aug(ustus) Pius Pontif(ex) / Maxim(us) trib(unicia) potest(ate) VI, co(n)s(ul) III, p(ater) p(atriae), imp(erator) II / Coloniae Mineruiae Neruiae Aug(ustae) / Scolacio aquam dat.*

[55] L. Mercando, Il larario puerile del Museo Oliveriano di Pesaro, in: Studia Oliveriana, Pesaro, XIII–XIV (1965–6), pp. 129–150.

[56] L. Gasperini, Nuove iscrizioni etrusche e latine in Visentium, in: Epigraphica, XXI (1959), pp. 31–50. Id., Minerua Nortina, in: Giornale Italiano di Filologia, (1957), pp. 193.7.

[57] A. Degrassi, Minerua flanatica, in: Rivista di Filologia e d'Istruzione Classica, n.s., X (1932), pp. 87–94.

[58] Pour l'interprétation de cet adjectif, voir ci-après p. 217.

[59] A. von Domaszewski, Die Religion des römischen Heeres, in: Westdeutsche Zeitschrift für Kunst und Geschichte (Trèves), XIV (1895), pp. 29–33; E. Birley, The Religion of the Roman Army (1895–1977), in: ANRW, II 16,2 (1978), p. 1512.

culièrement favorable, à cause de la présence de divinités locales que la pratique de l'*interpretatio* permettait d'assimiler à Minerve.

Le phénomène s'observe d'abord en Espagne où, dès la période républicaine, Tarragone a donné les traits de Minerve à sa déesse poliade[60]. Mais la plus célèbre des Minerves espagnoles est honorée avec Hercule à Gadès (où la déesse et le demi-dieu ont sans doute succédé à l'Allat et au Melqart phéniciens) et, bénéficiant de la dévotion des Espagnols Trajan et Hadrien, apparaît fréquemment sur leur monnayage[61]. La faveur de Minerve auprès des peuples sémitiques est peut-être aussi à l'origine de l'importation en Afrique de statues de la déesse, comme on en retrouve, par exemple, à Hippone[62].

Mais c'est en milieu celtique que l'*interpretatio* a trouvé son terrain le plus favorable. Déjà, en décrivant la religion des Gaulois, César notait la présence dans le panthéon celtique d'une déesse qu'il assimilait à Minerve[63].

Le culte de Minerve qui a donné leur nom à une ville et à une région de France (*Minerve* et le *Minervois*) est célèbre[64]. Mais, ces dernières années, des statues de Minerve ont également été découvertes à Pontailler, dans la Côte-d'or[65], à Rezé, en Loire-Atlantique[66], et à Vienne-en-Val, dans le Loiret[67]. La Minerve d'Avenches semble bien se rattacher au culte capitolin, connu dans cette cité[68].

[60] Ch. B. Rueger, Eine Weihinschrift aus Tarraco, in: MDAI (M), IX (1968), pp. 259–262; W. Grünhagen, Bemerkungen zum Minerva-Relief in der Stadtmauer von Tarragona, in: MDAI (M), XVII (1976), pp. 209–225. On vient de déchiffrer sur ce site une inscription qui prouve l'ancienneté de l'identification du culte local à celui de Minerve.

[61] Strack, t. II, n° 490–2, p. 88; J. Beaujeu, La religion romaine à l'apogée de l'Empire, t. I: La politique religieuse des Antonins (96–192), Paris, 1955, pp. 94 & 216.

[62] J. Formigé, Les officines romaines de marbrerie artistique à Carrare, in: Revue Archéologique, XLI (1953), pp. 204–6; J. Formigé, Officines romaines de marbrerie artistique à Carrare, in: Bulletin de la Société Nationale des Antiquaires de France, 1952/3, pp. 130–2; G. Ch. Picard, Rapport sur l'archéologie romaine en Tunisie dans le premier sémestre 1950, in: Bulletin Archéologique du Comité des Travaux Historiques, 1950, pp. 154–62.

[63] Caes., B.G., 2,17,1–2: *Deorum maxime Mercurium colunt (. . .) Post hunc Apollinem et Martem et Iouem et Mineruam. De his eandem fere quam reliquae gentes habent opinionem: (. . .) Mineruam operum atque artificiorum initia tradere.*

[64] H. de Gérin-Ricard, La Minerve de Rognac, in: Revue des Etudes Anciennes, XXIV (1922), pp. 149–50.

[65] R. Joffroy, Statuette de Minerve en bronze trouvée à Pontailler (Côte-d'or), in: Revue Archéologique de l'Est et du Centre-Est, XV (1964), pp. 118–122.

[66] J. Bousquet, Informations archéologiques. Circonscriptions de Bretagne et Pays de la Loire, in: Gallia, XXV (1967), pp. 225–238; A. Plouhinec, Bronzes de Rezé (Loire-Atlantique), in: Notices d'Archéologie Armoricaine, Extrait des Annales de Bretagne, 1967, pp. 155–166.

[67] G. Ch. Picard, Les fouilles de Vienne-en-Val (Loiret), in: Comptes Rendus de l'Académie des Inscriptions et Belles-Lettres, 1970, pp. 176–191; G. Debal, Vienne-en-Val, Sanctuaires et divinités, in: Revue Historique et Archéologique de l'Orléanais, V, 42 (1973), pp. 3–84.

[68] H. Boegli, Ein bedeutender Neufund aus Aventicum, in: Antike Welt, III, 3 (1972), pp. 49–52; H. Boegli, Il Capitolium di Aventicum, in: Atti del Convegno Internazionale per il XIX° Centenario della Dedicazione del Capitolio, t. II, Brescia, 1973, pp. 145–9.

En Bretagne, c'est un aspect particulier de la personnalité de Minerve qui a favorisé son assimilation à une divinité locale. Solin[69] nous parle d'un temple de Minerve situé au centre de l'île, qui peut être avec beaucoup de vraisemblance rapproché des imposantes constructions élevées auprès des sources chaudes de Bath, où Minerve est assimilée à la déesse *Sul*[70]. Les pouvoirs de *Minerua medica* peuvent expliquer sa présence auprès de ces sources thermales, sans qu'il soit besoin de faire de la déesse une divinité des eaux[71]

Le degré d'assimilation entre Minerve et *Belisama* (s'agit-il d'une identification ou d'une simple juxtaposition?), sur une inscription de Saint-Bertrand de Comminges[72] reste obscur.

IV. *Les types iconographiques*

C'est dans le domaine des arts plastiques que s'était exercé le plus tôt, et de la façon la plus exclusive, l'influence de la Grecque Athéna sur Minerve. Encore qu'à l'origine l'aspect guerrier de la déesse n'ait dû représenter qu'une faible partie de ses fonctions, le casque et la lance sont devenus des accessoires presque obligés de son costume, au point qu'un casque corinthien posé sur un siège en arrive à symboliser un *sellisternium* de Minerve[73]. L'art de notre période prend ses racines dans cette influence, mais en tire parti pour la création de quelques types originaux.

1. Types traditionnels

Le type de l'*Athéna Promachos*, casquée, brandissant une lance, revêtue de l'égide, et en marche pour le combat, reste de loin le plus courant. C'est lui qui figure ordinairement sur les monnaies, où la présence de Minerve garantit une

---

[69] Sol., 22,10: *In quo spatio* (sc. *Britanniae*) *magna et multa flumina, fontes calidi opiparo exculti apparatu, ad usus mortalium, quibus fontibus praesul est Mineruae numen, in cuius aede perpetui ignes.*

[70] H. J. Croon, The Cult of Sul-Minerva at Bath-Somerset, in: Antiquity, XXVII (1953), pp. 79–83; B. Cunliffe, The Temple of Sulis-Minerva at Bath, in: Antiquity, XL (1966), pp. 199–204; I. A. Richmond & J. M. C. Toynbee, The Temple of Sulis-Minerva at Bath, in: Journal of Roman Studies, XCV (1957), pp. 97–105. CIL, VII, 43 (= A. G. Collingwood–R. P. Wright, The Roman Inscriptions of Britain, t. I, Oxford, 1965, n° 146): *Deae / Suli Mi/neruae / Sulinus / Matu/ri fil(ius) / V(otum) s(oluit) l(ibens) m(erito).*

[71] F. Jenkins, Romano-Gaulish Figurines as Indications of the Mother-Goddess Cults in Britain, in: Hommages à A. Grenier, Coll. Latomus, LVIII, Bruxelles, 1962, pp. 836–852. L'association de Neptune et de Minerve sur une stèle de Chichester (S. E. Winbolt, The Neptune and Minerva Stone, Chichester, 1935) est inspirée par la légende grecque.

[72] *Mineruae Belisamae sacrum / Q(uintus) Valerius M[ontanus, ?].* Cf. Steuding, in: Roscher, t. I (1884), c. 757, s.v. Belisama.

[73] BMC, t. II, p. 240, n° 97 (pl. 46,12).

protection vigilante des frontières de l'Empire. Domitien l'a employé avec une particulière abondance[74], mais on le retrouve pendant tout le IIème siècle, avec un regain de faveur sous le règne de Commode[75].

Un peu moins fréquent est le type plus pacifique de l'*Athéna Parthénos*, qui s'appuie sur son bouclier placé à côté d'elle, type qui a surtout tenté les sculpteurs[76].

Une affectation d'archaïsme signifie le désir de rappeler le souvenir du Palladium. Sur six antéfixes d'époque flavienne, cinq évoquent ce *xoanon* armé de la lance, revêtu de l'égide et d'un péplos retenu par une ceinture[77], le même qu'on retrouve sur toutes les monnaies où la remise du Palladium à un prince signifie sa prise en main des destinées de l'Etat[78]. L'imitation d'une œuvre de Crésilas est à l'origine d'un type représentant Minerve tournant la tête, la lance dans la main droite, qu'on retrouve dans une statue d'époque flavienne conservée au Musée du Capitole[79]. F. CASTAGNOLI[80] a proposé d'y voir le type de *Minerua Chalcidica*.

Enfin, c'est à un original d'époque hellénistique que remonte le geste de Minerve vers son casque sur un cippe d'époque sévérienne où la triade capitoline est représentée à côté de divinités guérisseuses[81].

2. Innovations

Tout à fait exceptionnel est le type d'une colossale statue de porphyre, conservée au Musée des Thermes[82], qui représente Minerve, reconnaissable à son égide, assise, couverte d'un manteau et la tête voilée. Le style en est de l'époque julio-claudienne. S'agit-il de la statue dans le giron de laquelle Caligula déposa sa fille Drusilla[83]? Il est certain que la déesse a toute la dignité d'une matrone, mais on hésite à reconnaître dans cette œuvre, avec R. ENKING[84], l'attestation d'un hypothétique culte de *Minerua Mater*.

C'est aussi une statue colossale, trouvée à Ostie, pourvue d'ailes, qui constitue l'incarnation plastique de *Minerua Victrix*[85]. Elle date sans doute du

---

[74] BMC, t. II, pl. 65, 12, 14 & 18.

[75] BMC, t. IV, p. 706, n° 103.

[76] HELBIG[4], t. II, n° 1945.

[77] HELBIG[4], t. II, n° 1022.

[78] BMC, t. II, p. 126, n° 586; pl. 23,1 (Vespasien).

[79] HELBIG[4], t. II, n° 1395.

[80] F. CASTAGNOLI, Minerva Calcidica, in: Archeologia Classica, XII (1960), p. 91.

[81] HELBIG[4], t. III, n° 2411 (illustration n° I). Pour l'interprétation du geste, cf. E. SIMON, Zu den flavischen Reliefs der Cancelleria, in: Jahrbuch des Deutschen Archäologischen Instituts, LXXV (1960), p. 147, avec une datation légèrement trop haute du monument.

[82] HELBIG[4], t. III, n° 2244.

[83] Voir ci-après VII, 3: Minerve et les détenteurs du pouvoir.

[84] R. ENKING, Minerua mater, in: Jahrbuch des Deutschen Archäologischen Instituts, LIX–LX (1944)–5), p. 11.

[85] L. SAVIGNONI, Minerva Vittoria, in: Ausonia, V (1910), pp. 69–108; C. W. KEYES, Minerva Victrix? Note on the Winged Goddess of Ostia, in: AJA, 2nd ser., XVI (1912), n°

IIème siècle, mais le type ailé apparaissait déjà sur des monnaies de Domitien[86]. Il s'agit d'une création originale du génie romain, du moins dans l'application du type à Minerve. Le type de *Minerua Pacifera*, caractérisé par un rameau d'olivier, se rencontre sur de nombreuses monnaies, réalisant une sorte de symétrie avec l'*Athéna Promachos*, en insistant sur les résultats heureux qu'a la vigilance de Minerve pour l'Empire préservé, et sur la paix intérieure que la déesse garantit en inspirant au prince et à ses collaborateurs la sagesse[87].

Plus étranges sont quelques représentations isolées ou exceptionnelles: Minerve tenant une corne d'abondance n'est peut-être qu'un prolongement du thème précédent, la sécurité et la paix étant des facteurs d'abondance[88]. Minerve, tenant lance et bouclier, lève la main au-dessus d'un candélabre[89], en un geste qu'on a interprété comme un geste d'hommage symbolisant la *pietas* de Minerve envers Jupiter[90]. Enfin, Minerve peut chevaucher un sphinx, symbole de sagesse[91].

Cette multiplicité de types témoigne a la fois de la richesse de la personnalité de Minerve et de la capacité de la Rome impériale à renouveler son inspiration artistique.

V. *Les épithètes cultuelles*

Parmi les épithètes de la déesse, les unes sont fréquemment répétées, tandis que d'autres semblent liées à des lieux déterminés.

1. Epithètes fréquentes

Ces épithètes présentent évidemment un plus grand caractère de banalité, mais ce n'est pas à dire qu'elles ne nous apprennent rien sur la déesse et ses adorateurs.

4, pp. 490−4. Contra: C. ANTI, Atena marina e alata, in: Atti della Accademia Reale dei Lincei, Memorie, Classe di Scienze Morali, Storiche e Filosofiche, Ser. 3°, XXVI (1920), pp. 269−318.

[86] BMC, t. II, pl. 69,1.

[87] BMC, t. IV, p. 418, n° 245; p. 501, n° 769 (Marc-Aurèle).

[88] STRACK, t. II, n° 644; J. M. C. TOYNBEE, The Roman Medallions, Numismatic Studies, V, New York, 1944, pl. XXV, 1.

[89] STRACK, t. II, p. 90, n° 96 (Hadrien), t. III, p. 160, n° 665 (Marc-Aurèle César).

[90] J. BEAUJEU, La religion Romaine à l'apogée de l'Empire, t. I: La politique religieuse des Antonins (96−192), Paris, 1955, p. 303, n. 4.

[91] J. M. C. TOYNBEE, The Roman Medallions, Numismatic Studies, V, New York, 1944, pl. XXIV, 7.

Ainsi, l'épithète de *Minerua Victrix* témoigne du rôle guerrier de la déesse, et de l'entrée de la Victoire dans sa sphère[92]. L'épithète n'est pas propre à Minerve. Elle a été au contraire libéralement dispensée, tant à des dieux qu'à des empereurs, des généraux ou des légions, surtout dans l'atmosphère d'exaltation des valeurs militaires qu'engendre la montée des périls[93]. Mais dans le cas de Minerve, nous assistons en même temps à la création d'un type iconographique original, celui de Minerve ailée.

L'épithète de *Minerua Augusta*[94] paraît elle aussi passablement conventionnelle. C'est un fait courant que le rappel par cette épithète de la protection accordée par les dieux aux empereurs. Peut-être, dans le cas de Minerve, est-elle particulièrement appropriée, en raison du rôle de la déesse inspirant la sagesse aux princes[95]. Une dédicace d'Argenton-sur-Creuse confirme le rapprochement entre Minerve et l'idée impériale[96]. Sur une monnaie d'Alexandrie, à l'époque de Domitien, ᾿Αθηνᾶ Σεβαστή est la traduction grecque de *Minerua Augusta*[97].

De l'épithète *Sancta* appliquée à Minerve aussi bien qu'à d'autres divinités, il y a peu à dire, sinon qu'on a observé qu'elle se rencontre surtout en Afrique[98].

2. Epithètes occasionnelles

L'épithète de *Minerua Supera* est exceptionnelle. On la rencontre sur un autel des environs d'Apulum, qui fait pendant à un autre autel dédié à *Saturnus Securus*[99]. Elle témoigne peut-être d'un désir de mettre l'accent sur le caractère de divinité céleste de Minerve. Sur des monuments de l'époque flavienne, une étoile figure sur le vêtement de la déesse[100]. Toute spéculation plus poussée serait hasardeuse.

Minerua Berecynthia figure sur cinq inscriptions de Bénévent commémorant des offrandes tauroboliques à Attis[101]. L'orthographe est d'ailleurs déformée en *Paracentia* sur quatre de ces inscriptions[102], et la *scriptio* de la cin-

---

[92] A.E., 1968, n° 228: *Ioui Optimo Maximo / Iunoni Reginae / Mineruae Victrici / P(ublius) Ael(ius) P(ublii) f(ilius) Hilarianus / proc(urator) Aug(usti) / cum liberis pro salute / Commodi Aug(usti) / Pii Felicis.*

[93] Cf. S. WEINSTOCK, Victor, Victrix, in: RE, VIII A, 2 (1958), c. 2485–2500.

[94] A.E., 1973, n° 635: *Mineruae / Aug(ustae) Pomponius / Venustus Saturni/nus sacerdos / iussus l(ibenti) a(nimo) pos⟨i⟩uit.*

[95] Voir ci-après, p. 226.

[96] *[Numini]bus Aug(ustorum) et Mineruae*, A. E., 1973, n° 340; G. CH. PICARD, Les sanctuaires d'Argentomagus, in: Comptes Rendus de l'Académie des Inscriptions et Belles-Lettres, 1971, pp. 621–33.

[97] J. VOGT, Die alexandrinischen Münzen. Grundlegung einer alexandrinischen Kaisergeschichte, t. I, Stuttgart, 1924, p. 47.

[98] A.E., 1957, n° 81: *Mineruae / Sanctae / T(itus) Aelius Sil/uanus a tri/bus militiis / fl(amen) perp(etuus) / coloniae / Thamug (ensis) / uot(um) sol(uit) / cum Siluano [et Vrba]no / filis.*

[99] A.E., 1962, n° 206: *Mineruae Superae. Saturno Securo.*

[100] HELBIG⁴, t. I, n° 1022.

[101] CIL, IX, 1538–1542.

[102] CIL, IX, 1539–1542.

quième[103] est déficiente (*Berecint*). Mais la lecture, dans un pareil contexte, n'est pas douteuse. R. DUTHOY[104] a bien montré que Minerve n'est pas confondue avec la mère des Dieux, d'ailleurs nommée à côté d'elle sur l'une des inscriptions[105]. *Berecynthia* est ici synonyme de *Phrygia*, et c'est l'origine phrygienne de Minerve, incarnée dans le Palladium, qui a autorisé son introduction dans ces dédicaces. Deux des dédicantes sont des artistes, la *cymbalistria* Concordia Ianuaria[106] et la *tympanistra* Trebulana Iustina[107], qui ont pu vouloir concilier, par le choix heureux de cette épithète, la dévotion à leur patronne traditionnelle et leur nouvelle ferveur taurobolique.

La question de l'épithète de *Minerua Chalcidica* est liée à celle du temple, bâti par Domitien, où la déesse est désignée de ce nom. L'influence du *chalcidicum* attenant à la curie, transformé en *atrium Mineruae*, paraît pouvoir expliquer cette épithète sans qu'il soit nécessaire de recourir à un souvenir de l'Ἀθάνα Χαλκίοικος dorienne[108]. Pour *Minerua Capta*, voir p. 206.

On a découvert sur le site de Visentium un cippe qui porte l'inscription *Minerua Nortina*[109]. *Nortinus* est déjà connu comme cognomen[110]. Il renvoie à la déesse volsinienne *Nortia*. Il est difficile de dire s'il s'agit d'une assimilation syncrétiste entre Minerve et *Nortia*, ou s'il existe entre les deux déesses un rapport précis, qui ne nous est pas connu. Le seul parallèle connu, *Mercurius Matutinus*, suscite le même doute[111]. *Minerva* et *Nortia* ont déjà été mises en rapport par Tite-Live, à propos de la fixation annuelle d'un clou dans le mur qui sépare, dans le temple capitolin, la *cella* de Jupiter de celle de Minerve[112].

Une dédicace mutilée à *Minerua Flanatica* a été trouvée en 1928 à Monsalice, en Istrie[113]. La restitution et l'interprétation de l'épithète sont dues à

---

[103] CIL, IX, 1538.

[104] R. DUTHOY, La Minerua Berecynthia des inscriptions tauroboliques de Bénévent (CIL, IX, 1538−1542), in: L'Antiquité Classique, XXXV (1966), pp. 548−61.

[105] CIL, IX, 1538.

[106] CIL, IX, 1538.

[107] CIL, IX, 1542.

[108] F. CASTAGNOLI, Minerva Calcidica, in: Archeologia Classica, XII (1960), pp. 91−5.

[109] L. GASPERINI, Nuove iscrizioni etrusche e latine in Visentium, in: Epigraphica, XXI (1959), pp. 31−50. ID., Minerua Nortina, in: Giornale Italiano di Filologia, X (1957), pp. 193−7.

[110] CIL, XI, 2690: *C(aius) Callius / Nortinus / decurio / ex uoto / posuit.*

[111] CIL, XIII, 5235: *Mercurio / Matutino / iuris / ex uoto.*

[112] Liv., 7,3,6−7: *Eum clauum, quia rarae per ea tempora litterae erant, notam numeri annorum fuisse ferunt, eoque Mineruae templo dicatam legem, quia numerus Mineruae inuentum sit. Volsinis quoque clauos indices numeri annorum fixos in templo Nortiae, Etruscae deae, comparere, diligens talium monumentorum auctor Cincius adfirmat.* Nous avons étudié la question du *clauus annalis* dans une communication au Groupe strasbourgeois des études latines (J.-L. GIRARD, Nortia et le rite du clauus annalis, in: Revue des Etudes Latines, LIV [1976], pp. 23−4).

[113] Notiziario archeologico, in: Atti e Memorie della Società Istriana di Archeologia, XL (1928), p. 400: *[M]ineruae [Fl]anaticae / sacrum [. . .] dius Bassus [ex] uoto / quot a dea pet [iit] consecutus.*

l'ingéniosité d'A. DEGRASSI[114], qui a rapproché l'adjectif du nom des *Flanates*, habitants de la côte orientale de l'Istrie, cités par Pline, qui ont donné leur nom au *Flanaticus sinus*, actuellement golfe de Canaro[115]. Il s'agit donc d'un culte local, où Minerve n'est que l'*interpretatio* d'une déesse illyrienne. En l'absence de renseignements sur le véritable nom et la personnalité de cette déesse, nous ne pouvons rien soupçonner des raisons qui appuyaient le rapprochement.

C'est aussi, bien évidemment, d'une *interpretatio* que proviennent les dédicaces à *Minerua Suliuia Idennica*, trouvées en milieu celtique[116]. La deuxième épithète reste obscure, mais il est tentant de rapprocher la première de *Sul*, qui veille sur les eaux chaudes de Bath et a été assimilée à Minerve[117].

L'épithète de *Minerua Medica* est attestée à Rome par une dédicace d'époque impériale, trouvée auprès du temple où la déesse dispensait ses bienfaits de guérisseuse[118]. Elle est attestée également à Plaisance, où l'on trouve des dédicaces à *Minerua Medica Cabardaciensis*[119], *Minerua Cabardaciensis*[120] et *Minerua Memor*[121]. *Cabardaciensis* renvoie à *Cabardiacum*, site des environs de Plaisance (aujourd'hui Caverzago). La présence de l'épithète *Memor* est particulièrement intéressante. Elle nous indique ce qui a pu faciliter l'attribution de fonctions guérisseuses à Minerve. Déesse des arts qui se transmettent de génération en génération par tradition, Minerve est par excellence dotée de mémoire[122]. Arnobe, d'ailleurs, en une étymologie populaire, fait dériver le nom de Minerve du verbe *memini*[123]. Cette mémoire permet à la déesse de conserver des recettes, du pittoresque desquelles on aura une idée en lisant à Plaisance une inscription où une femme rend grâce pour la repousse de ses cheveux[124].

L'épithète *Regina*, d'ordinaire réservée à Junon, est attribuée une fois à Minerve, en Aquitaine[125]. L'influence d'un culte local peut être soupçonnée derrière cette qualification inhabituelle.

---

[114] A. DEGRASSI, Minerva Flanatica, in: Rivista di filologia e d'Istruzione Classica, n.s., X (1932), pp. 87−94.

[115] Plin., N.H., 3, 21, 139: *Ius Italicum habent Flanates, a quo sinus nominatur.*

[116] CIL, XII, 2974: *Suliuiae Idennicae / Mineruae uotum.*

[117] Voir ci-dessus, p. 214.

[118] Voir note 23.

[119] CIL, XI, 1306: *Mineruae / Medicae / Cabardiac(ensi) / Valeria / Summonia / Vercellens(is) / u(otum) s(oluit) l(ibens) m(erito).*

[120] CIL, XI, 1301: *Mineruae / Cabardiacensi.*

[121] CIL, XI, 1297: *Mineruae / Memori / Caelia Iuliana / indulgentia / medicinarum / eius infirmitati graui liberatam d(edit) p(erpetuum).* La graphie est très souvent défective: *M(ineruae) M(emori).*

[122] M. BOLLINI, Minerua medica memor, in: Atti del III° Congresso di Studi Veleiati, Milan, 1969, pp. 147−150.

[123] Arn., 3,31: *Ipsius (sc. Mineruae) esse summam dicerunt memoriam nonnulli, unde ipsum nomen Minerua quasi quaedam Meminerua formatum est.*

[124] CIL, XI, 1305: *Mineruae / Memori / Tullia / Superiana / restitutione / facta sibi / capillorum / u(otum) s(oluit) l(ibens) m(erito).*

[125] CIL, XIII, 177: *Mineruae / Reginae / Auctus / Antisti l(ibertus) / u(otum) s(oluit) l(ibens) m(erito).*

VI. *Associés et protégés*

1. Association de Minerve à d'autres divinités

Minerve, à cause des multiples aspects de sa personnalité, se prête à être rapprochée de nombreuses divinités. Certains groupements sont traditionnels, d'autres apparaissent plus épisodiquement.

En tout premier lieu, il faut bien entendu citer la triade capitoline, qui jouit d'un statut tout à fait particulier[126]. Les trois divinités qui la composent sont très fréquemment invoquées ou représentées ensemble, soit seules, soit en compagnie d'autres divinités. Leur présence garantit la protection de ce qu'il y a de plus puissant dans le panthéon national.

A l'intérieur de la triade capitoline, Minerve semble entretenir des relations plus spécialement étroites avec Jupiter. Dans un groupe d'inscriptions d'Apulum dédié aux trois membres de la triade capitoline, celle qui concerne Minerve la dit *Iouis consiliorum particeps*[127]. Et, sur un fragment de moule de céramique sigillée en provenance d'Autun, Jupiter et Minerve sont représentés côte à côte[128].

Une autre association traditionnelle est celle de Minerve et de Neptune. Appuyée sur la légende attique de la rivalité d'Athéna et de Poseidon, elle s'est introduite très tôt à Rome, puisque, lors du lectisterne de 217, Neptune et Minerve figuraient sur le même *puluinar*[129]. La même association semble évoquée, à l'aide de symboles, sur un denier de Titus[130]. En tout cas, Minerve et Neptune sont indubitablement représentés côte à côte sur une monnaie de Marc-Aurèle[131] et sur une stèle de Chichester[132]. Un troisième personnage peut intervenir: J. GAGÉ a montré comment l'honneur de la victoire d'Actium avait été partagé entre Minerve, Neptune et Apollon[133].

Le couple formé par Minerve, protectrice des héros, et Hercule est fréquent sur les monuments figurés. Sur une monnaie d'Alexandrie, Domitien est figuré en Héraclès tenant le Palladium[134].

---

[126] Voir ci-après, p. 223.

[127] CIL, III,1076: *Mineruae / Iouis consili/orum partici/pi C(aius) Caerellius / Sabinus leg(atus) Aug(usti) / leg(ionis) XIII G(eminae) / et Fufidia Pollitta / ei[u]s uoto.* Mart., 6,10,9 appelle la déesse *conscia uirgo Tonantis*.

[128] R. MAJUREL, Un fragment de moule de céramique sigillée en provenance d'Autun, in: Ogam, XXI (1969), pp. 227–232.

[129] Liv., 22,10,9: *Sex puluinaria in conspectu fuere (. . .), alterum Neptuno ac Mineruae.*

[130] BMC, t. II, p. 234, n° 71.

[131] STRACK, t. III, p. 109, n° 577.

[132] S. E. WINBOLT, The Neptune and Minerva Stone, Chichester, Chichester, 1935.

[133] J. GAGÉ, Actiaca, in: Mélanges d'Archéologie et d'Histoire de l'Ecole Française de Rome, V (1936), pp. 37–100.

[134] J. VOGT, Die alexandrinischen Münzen. Grundlegung einer alexandrinischen Kaisergeschichte, t. I, Stuttgart, 1924, pp. 54–5.

Minerve, déesse des arts, est associée au forgeron Vulcain sur un médaillon d'Antonin[135], et les armuriers de la légion *II Antoniniana* honorent en même temps Mars et Minerve[136], association qui semble le dernier vestige d'un rapport qui a dû être bien plus étroit à l'époque archaïque.

L'association avec la Fortune est plus surprenante, mais elle est bien attestée[137]. Pour l'expliquer, il faut sans doute recourir à l'évolution qui a fait dans certains cas de Minerve une distributrice d'abondance[138].

La même explication rend compte d'une couple de braseros où Minerve est figurée avec l'Abondance et Mercure, dieu du commerce[139]. Ces contacts avec le monde des biens matériels préparent à lire avec moins de surprise une curieuse inscription, où le prêtre Tullus s'acquitte d'un voeu envers Minerve et Mercure « à l'aide d'une somme d'argent reçue d'un certain Boccius Copo, afin que ne soit pas intentée contre celui-ci l'action pour injures, en vertu d'un décret du proconsul Marcellus, qui avait flétri ce Boccius comme calomniateur »[140].

Très caractéristiques de la frontière germanique sont les monuments appelés « stèles à quatre dieux », qu'on trouve le plus souvent au pied des colonnes aux géants anguipèdes[141]. Le groupement le plus fréquent est celui qui comprend Junon, Minerve, Hercule et Mercure[142]. Junon est parfois remplacée par une inscription[143] ou par Jupiter[144]. Le sens de ces groupements nous échappe, lié qu'il est sans doute à la personnalité des divinités celtiques dont les dieux romains sont ici l'*interpretatio*.

2. Les fidèles de Minerve

Les témoignages du culte officiel, inspirés par le désir de célébrer les splendeurs militaires ou artistiques du principat, ne donneraient qu'une idée incomplète de la personnalité de la déesse. Une plus juste proportion entre ses

---

[135] Strack, t. III, p. 55, n° 544, pl. XXI; F. Gnecchi, I medaglioni romani, Milan, 1912, pl. 52,7.

[136] CIL, III, 10435: *Marti et Mineruae / Aug(ustis) coll(egium) / armatura[e] / leg(ionis) II Adi(utricis) P(iae) F(idelis) / Antoninia/nae.*

[137] CIL, VI, 527: *Mineruae et Fort [unae] / sacr(um) / C(aius) Manlius Euhodus hon(oratis) et decurionibus q(uin)q(uennali) d(ono) d(edit) / dedicauit XI Kal(endas) Iun(ias) / P. Iuuentio Celso III / L. Neratio Marcello II / co(n)s(ulibu)s.* Les hypothèses hardies de C. Thulin, Minerva auf dem Capitol und Fortuna in Praeneste, in: Rheinisches Museum, LX (1905), pp. 256—261, ne sont guère étayées par les faits.

[138] Voir ci-dessus IV: Types iconographiques. IV, 2: Innovations.

[139] R. Lantier, Deux braseros romains, in: Bulletin de la Société Nationale des Antiquaires de France, 1950/1, pp. 89—90.

[140] AE, 1954, n° 215. Date du règne d'Antonin le Pieux. J. B. Reynolds et J. B. Ward Perkins, Inscriptions of Roman Tripolitania, Paris—Londres, s.d. [=1952], n° 304.

[141] H. B. Wiggers, Viergöttersteine, in: RE, Sptbd. XIV (1974), c. 854—864.

[142] J. J. Hatt, Découverte d'une stèle à quatre dieux (Junon, Minerve, Hercule et Mercure), in: La Revue des Arts, IV (1954), pp. 239—241.

[143] Espérandieu, Germ., n° 31.

[144] Espérandieu, VII, n° 5887.

différents aspects peut être rétablie par la considération des hommages privés qui s'adressent à elle.

Nous avons vu quelle place tenaient les pratiquants des *artes* (au sens large, puisque le mot s'applique aussi bien aux médecins et aux maîtres d'école) dans le culte des *Quinquatrus*[145]. Les dédicaces privées confirment cet intérêt. Elles sont souvent le fait de corporations d'artistes ou d'artisans. C'est le cas, par exemple, de l'inscription, trouvée sur les pentes du Caelius, qui rappelle une offrande faite à Minerve par la corporation des joueurs de cor[146].

Sur un cippe d'époque augustéenne[147], où sont représentés des instruments symbolisant les professions artisanales, hommage est rendu à Minerve par les «ministres du deuxième lustre». Le culte avait donc été organisé (ou réorganisé par Auguste?) depuis peu de temps. Il est dommage que nous ne soyons pas mieux renseignés à ce sujet. Ceux qui interviennent dans ce culte se nomment Erilis, esclave de Marcus Antonius Andronicus, et Utilis, esclave de Gaïus Fictorius Flaccus[148]. Leur humble condition ne doit pas nous étonner, car peu d'hommes libres pratiquaient des métiers manuels, et certainement le rôle des esclaves au sein des corps de métiers était devenu prépondérant.

Au sein de l'armée, on observe une liaison plus particulière de la déesse avec les corps de techniciens.[149]. Certes, les dédicaces de militaires peuvent faire allusion aux aspects guerriers et victorieux de la déesse[150], mais ce sont surtout les «administratifs» qui placent leurs activités intellectuelles sous sa protection. Citons en exemple une dédicace du bureau des corniculaires d'Aquincum[151].

Les guérisons opérées par Minerve lui attirent aussi de nombreux fidèles. En principe, en ce domaine, le métier ne devrait plus entrer en ligne de compte. On notera pourtant que ce sont les protégés naturels de Minerve qui recourent le plus volontiers à ses services, plutôt qu'a ceux d'Esculape. Le dédicataire d'une inscription reconnaissante à *Minerua Medica* est un maître de chant, qui fait honneur de sa longévité à sa patronne[152].

De la même façon, parmi les auteurs des dédicaces à *Minerua Berecynthia*, on relève deux musiciennes, la *cymbalistria* Concordia Ianuaria,[153] et la *tympanistria* Trebulana Iustina[154].

---

[145] Voir plus haut II, 1: Quinquatrus.

[146] CIL, VI, 524: *Miner[uae] / donum [dat] / conlegi [um cor]/nicin[um].* De nombreux exemples de dédicaces corporatives sont donnés par G. WISSOWA, Minerua, in: ROSCHER, II (1897), c. 2991.

[147] HELBIG⁴, t. II, n° 1238. Illustration n° II.

[148] CIL, VI, 30982: *Erilis M(arci) Antoni Andronic[i] / Vtilis C(ai) Fictori Flacci* (face C, pl. III, 2 c); *Ministri lustri secun[di]* (face A, pl. II, 2 a).

[149] I. BERCIU & A. POPA, Exceptores consularis in Dacia, in: Latomus XXIII (1964), pp. 302–310.

[150] CIL, X, 10433: *Mineruae / Victrici / C(aius) Valerius Pudens / leg(atus) Aug(usti) pr(o) pr(aetore).*

[151] CIL, III, 10437: *Mineruae Aug(ustae) officium / cornicul/ariorum / u(otum) s(oluit) l(ibens) m(erito).*

[152] Voir note 23.

[153] CIL, IX, 1538.

[154] CIL, IX, 1542.

Enfin, Minerve est honorée par ceux qui s'occupent des chevaux. Le buste de la déesse orne fréquemment le manche des boutoirs, instruments qui servent à tailler l'ongle du sabot[155]. C'est moins, sans doute, par un lointain souvenir de l''Aθηνᾶ 'Ιππία[156] que par l'application aux chevaux des compétences médicales de la déesse, et parce que la profession de maréchal-ferrant et de vétérinaire est aussi un art.

VII. Minerve et l'Empire romain

1. Le culte capitolin

Minerve est, aux côtés de Jupiter et de Junon, une des divinités de la triade capitoline, qui tient, dans la religion de l'époque du principat, une place essentielle. Dans ces longues litanies, si caractéristiques de la piété romaine, qui servent à placer les entreprises officielles sous la protection du plus grand nombre de divinités possible, les trois divinités du Capitole sont toujours nommées en premier lieu, comme le recours le plus sûr du peuple romain. Les exemples seraient innombrables. Contentons-nous de citer, parce que l'occasion en est particulièrement solennelle et particulièrement bien connue, les *vota extraordinaria pro salute et reditu et uictoria imperatoris Traiani*, que prononcent le 25 mars 101, à la veille de la première campagne contre les Daces, les frères arvales, et où sont successivement invoqués: *Iuppiter Optimus Maximus, Iuno Regina, Minerua, Iouis Victor, Salus rei publicae populi Romani Quiritium, Mars pater, Mars Victor, Victoria, Fortuna Redux, Vesta mater, Neptunus pater, Hercules Victor*[157].

Cette place d'honneur assigne un caractère privilégié au culte capitolin, qui apparaît, de fait, aux populations de l'Empire, comme le culte par excellence du peuple romain. Aussi, le loyalisme à l'égard de Rome s'exprime, dans le cités provinciales de la Méditerranée occidentale, par la construction d'un temple à trois *cellae*, bâti sur le modèle du temple capitolin et qui reçoit, lui aussi, le nom de *Capitolium*; tandis que l'Orient hellénophone, choisissant une solution différente, inscrit la référence au culte romain dans l'épithète de Ζεὺς Καπετώλιος, qui est honoré seul, et non au sein d'une triade. Cette divergence entre les deux parties de l'Empire est intéressante, en ce qu'elle nous confirme le caractère original et proprement italique de la triade capitoline, alors que le

---

[155] J. HEURGON, Note sur un boutoir antique découvert à Amiens, in: Mélanges Louis Jacob (= Revue du Nord, XXXVI [1954]), pp. 147–9.

[156] Cf. N. YALOURIS, Athena als Herrin der Pferde. Archaeologische Untersuchung zu Pindars dreizehnter Olympie, Bâle, 1950.

[157] G. HENZEN, Acta fratrum Arualium, Berlin, 1874, pp. CXL sqq & 124; A. PASOLI, Acta fratrum Arualium, Bologne, 1950, p. 85. On notera que le souci de ne pas séparer les trois membres de la triade capitoline a fait séparer *Iouis Victor* de *Iuppiter Optimus Maximus*, alors que *Mars Victor* est invoqué immédiatement après *Mars pater*.

rapprochement de Zeus, Héra et Athéna dans un même sanctuaire est accidentel et isolé dans le monde grec[158].

U. BIANCHI, qui a fait l'inventaire détaillé de ces Capitoles bâtis à l'imitation du grand temple romain[159], a bien marqué les caractères propres du culte capitolin, en l'opposant au culte impérial, qui connaît dans les provinces une diffusion parallèle, et témoigne, lui aussi, d'un attachement à l'autorité centrale: *„Il culto capitolino fu un culto nazionale, il culto proprio del popolo romano, mentre il culto imperiale fu solo un culto statale, cioè un culto reso direttamente a chi impersonava, o aveva impersonato, il potere summo nel mondo romano"*[160].

La représentation ou l'invocation de la triade capitoline va souvent de pair, comme nous l'avons vu, avec celle d'autres divinités. Le choix de ces divinités ne semble pas fait en fonction de leurs affinités avec la triade capitoline, qui n'a d'autre rôle que d'assurer pleine efficace, par sa présence, à la protection recherchée. Peut-être cependant le rôle de Minerve dans les guérisons est-il pour quelque chose dans l'association de la triade avec des divinités guérisseuses sur un cippe d'époque sévérienne[161].

La présence même de Minerve au sein de la triade, quelle qu'en ait été l'explication aux origines, apparaît à ce moment comme liée à la protection que la déesse étend sur Rome. La diffusion du culte capitolin dans les provinces a sans doute fait beaucoup pour rapprocher l'image de Minerve de celle d'Athéna Polias, avec laquelle elle avait une affinité que venait renforcer l'importance prise par le culte du Palladium.

2. Le Palladium

Seruius Danielis[162] cite le Palladium parmi les sept gages de survie de l'Empire romain. A l'époque du principat, on ne met pas en doute l'identité entre ce précieux gage et un *xoanon* archaïque d'Athéna, conservé dans le *penus* du

---

[158] Paus., 10,5,2: Ἔστιν οἰκοδόμημα καλούμενον Φωκικόν (. . .) Διὸς δὲ ἄγαλμα καὶ Ἀθηνᾶς καὶ Ἥρας (sc. ὁρᾶται).

[159] U. BIANCHI, Disegno storico del culto capitolino nell'Italia romana e nelle provincie dell' Impero, in: Accademia Nazionale dei Lincei, Memorie, Classe die Scienze Morali, Storiche e Filosofiche, Serie 8ᵃ, II (1949–1950), pp. 349–415. Une table des Capitoles italiens et provinciaux se lit pp. 406–8. Seuls sont antérieurs à Auguste, en Italie les Capitoles de Signia, Brescia, Minturnes, peut-être Capoue et Bénévent, et en Espagne celui de Colonia Iulia Genetiua Ursonensis, C'est dire l'étendue des créations de l'époque impériale.

[160] U. BIANCHI, op. cit., p. 411.

[161] HELBIG⁴, III, n° 2411. Pl. I, 1.

[162] Serv. Dan., ad A. 7,188: *Septem fuerunt pignora, quae imperium Romanum tenent: lapis matris Deum, quadriga fictilis Veientanorum, cineres Orestis, sceptrum Priami, uelum Ilionae, Palladium, ancilia.*

temple de Vesta[163]. Tout au plus discute-t-on la façon dont il serait parvenu à Rome[164]. La complexité même des traditions sur ce point prouve l'intérêt qui s'attachait à ce précieux objet. Si l'on tient compte du fait que la première mention sûre de la présence du Palladium à Rome est du Ier siècle avant Jésus-Christ,[165] on s'explique facilement qu'il soit fait allusion à une miraculeuse invention du Palladium sur le site de la Nouvelle Ilion, lors des guerres contre Mithridate[166]. Mais des légendes plus flatteuses n'ont pas tardé à se faire jour. Il était normal que l'on liât la présence du Palladium en Italie au voyage d'Enée vers les rives du Latium[167]. On se heurtait alors à une tradition, remontant à la 'Petite Iliade' de Leschès, qui faisait précéder la chute de Troie du vol du Palladium par Diomède et Ulysse. Aussi, certaines versions font-elles intervenir ces deux personnages, Enée n'entrant en possession du Palladium qu'en Italie[168]. De plus, on s'est efforcé de rattacher davantage la *Minerua Troiana* − qui est en fait une Athéna − à l'histoire primitive du Latium, en lui assignant à Lauinium un culte ayant pour prêtre le Troyen Nautès, compagnon d'Enée, dont prétendait descendre la *gens Nautia*.[169] Cette reconstruction, qui paraissait absolument artificielle, est aujourd'hui moins étonnante, après la récente découverte, lors des fouilles à Pratica di Mare, site de l'antique Lauinium, de statues d'Athéna du Vème siècle avant Jésus-Christ.[169a]

On sait que le règne d'Auguste a vu l'édification d'un temple de Vesta sur le Palatin, à côté du palais d'Auguste. Il semble bien que ce temple ait aussi comporté un Palladium. C'est en tout cas ce que donne à croire la base de Sorrente, où un temple de Vesta, situé à l'emplacement du temple palatin, abrite

---

[163] F. CHAVANNES, De Palladii raptu, Berlin, 1891; K. GROSS, Die Unterpfänder der römischen Herrschaft, Berlin, 1935; L. ZIEHEN, Palladium, in: RE, XVII,3 (1949), c. 171−201.

[164] J. BEAUJEU, La religion romaine à l'apogée de l'Empire, t.I: La politique religieuse des Antonins (96−192), Paris, 1955, p. 142.

[165] Cic., Scaur., 48: *Palladium illud quod quasi pignus nostrae salutis atque imperi custodiis Vestae continetur.*

[166] Serv., ad A. 2,166: *Quamquam alii dicant, simulacrum hoc a Troianis absconditum fuisse intra extructum parietem, postquam agnouerunt Troiam esse perituram, quod postea bello Mithridatico dicitur Fimbria quidam Romanus inuentum indicasse. Quod Romam constat aduectum.*

[167] Plut., Cam., 20,6: Τὸ Τρωϊκὸν ἐκεῖνο Παλλάδιον (. . .) δι' Αἰνείαν κομισθὲν εἰς Ἰταλίαν.

[168] Ov., F., 6,424; 433−4:
> *Pallada Roma tenet*
> (. . .)
> *Seu genus Adrasti, seu furtis aptus Ulixes*
> *Seu pius Aeneas eripuisse ferunt.*

[169] Denys d'Halic. A.R., 6,69,1: Ἀνίσταται Σπόριος Ναύτιος, οἰκίας ἐν τοῖς πάνυ λαμπροτάτης διάδοχος. Ὁ γὰρ ἡγεμὼν τοῦ γένους Ναύτιος, ἀπὸ τῶν σὺν Αἰνείᾳ στειλάντων τὴν ἀποικίαν εἰς ἣν Ἀθηνᾶς ἱερεὺς Πολιάδος καὶ τὸ ξόανον ἀπηνέγκατο τῆς θεᾶς.

[169a] F. CASTAGNOLI, Il culto di Minerva a Lavinium in: Problemi attuali di scienza e di cultura, Accademiá Nazionale dei Lincei, anno CCCLXXVI (1979), quaderno n° 246, pp. 3−14.

une statue d'Athéna[170]. Cet illogisme de la reproduction d'un talisman par définition irremplaçable heurte notre mentalité. Il ne posait sans doute pas le même problème aux Romains, que la multiplicité des images divines devait avoir préparés à admettre l'idée d'une imitation du Palladium authentique.

La faveur remarquable que connaît le Palladium dans les monnayages impériaux s'explique aisément par le fait qu'il symbolise l'éternité de Rome. De plus, la remise du Palladium à un empereur, souvent représentée sur les revers, exprime la légitimité de son pouvoir[171].

Le Palladium figure souvent aussi sur la cuirasse de celui qui a en charge les destinées de Rome. On le trouve, flanqué de deux Victoires, sur la poitrine d'une statue d'Auguste[172], ou au dessus de la louve qui allaite les jumeaux, sur la cuirasse d'Hadrien[173].

Le Palladium devait connaître, à la fin du Haut-Empire, deux nouvelles mésaventures. Sous Commode, un incendie l'exposa aux regards profanes[174]. Puis Héliogabale songea à l'impliquer dans une hiérogamie avec le dieu qu'il adorait[175]. Hérodien, qui nous rapporte les deux incidents, insiste sur la vénération que continuait à inspirer la statue. C'est dire que, par son assimilation au Palladium, Minerve se trouvait symboliser d'une manière privilégiée la confiance dans les destinées de l'Empire romain.

3. Minerve et les détenteurs du pouvoir

Il y a lieu de consacrer une étude particulière à la sollicitude que certains empereurs ont attendue de Minerve à leur égard. Si l'invocation d'une déesse qui est la sagesse même est fort naturelle de la part d'un détenteur de hautes responsabilités, elle a été particuliérement le fait de certains princes, non d'ailleurs toujours de ceux qui se sont montrés les plus sages.

Un curieux épisode de la vie de Caligula témoigne du désir de rechercher d'une façon plus personnelle la protection de la puissante déesse. Lorsque Caesonia donne une fille à l'empereur, celui-ci la mène dans les temples de tous les dieux, mais c'est à Minerve qu'il la confie, « pour la nourrir et l'élever »[176]. H. P. L'ORANGE a rapproché la présentation à tous les dieux de coutumes

---

[170] G. E. Rizzo, La base di Augusto, Naples, 1933, pl. I.

[171] BMC, II, p. 260, n° 188 (pl. 49,7) (Titus).

[172] E. Hübner, Augustus. Marmorstatue des Berliner Museums, 28. Winckelmannsprogramm, Berlin, 1868, pl. I.

[173] A. H. Smith, A Catalogue of Sculpture in the Department of Greek and Roman Antiquities, British Museum, Londres, 1882—1904, t. I, n° 1466.

[174] Hérodien, 1,14,4: Καὶ τῆς Ἑστίας τοῦ νεὼ καταφλεχθέντος, ὑπὸ τοῦ πυρὸς γυμνωθὲν ὤφθη τὸ τῆς Παλλάδος ἄγαλμα, ὃ σέβουσί τε καὶ κρύπτουσι Ῥωμαῖοι κομισθὲν ἀπὸ Τροίας.

[175] Hérodien, 5,6,3: Τῆς τε Παλλάδος τὸ ἄγαλμα, ὃ κρυπτὸν καὶ ἀόρατον σέβουσι Ῥωμαῖοι, ἐς τὸν ἑαυτοῦ θάλαμον μετήγαγε (. . .) Καὶ πρὸς γάμον δὴ ἐς τὴν βασίλειον αὐλὴν τῷ θεῷ ἀνήγαγεν.

[176] Suet., Cal., 25,7: Infantem autem, Iuliam Drusillam appellatam, per omnium deorum templa circumferens, Mineruae gremio imposuit alendamque et instituendam commendauit.

pharaoniques[177]. L'épisode témoignerait de la fascination de Caligula pour le rituel des monarchies orientales. Il nous paraît que l'intervention de Minerve, en tout état de cause, ne peut relever de cette explication, mais s'inscrit dans une tradition authentiquement italique, ou du moins enracinée depuis longtemps en Italie: celle qui fait de Minerve une *'Kindespflegerin'*, une protectrice du développement des enfants. Peut-être des légendes grecques, où l'on voit Athéna prendre soin d'Erichthonios, ont-elle joué leur rôle[178], mais des monuments étrusques, d'interprétation difficile[179], témoignent déjà d'une sollicitude de la déesse pour les enfants.

Nous avons observé, à propos des *Quinquatrus*, comment Néron a voulu qu'on reconnût l'effet de la protection de Minerve dans la découverte de la conjuration qu'il attribuait à sa mère[180]. Quant à Domitien, sa prédilection pour la déesse atteint de telles proportions qu'elle nous a paru mériter une étude séparée[181].

Le mauvais souvenir de cette dévotion «tapageuse»[182] rendit plus circonspects Trajan et Hadrien qui, tout en honorant Minerve, se gardèrent de paraître revendiquer sa protection à titre personnel. En revanche, la déesse apparaît sur un quinaire de Plotine[183], où peut-être elle symbolise les vertus domestiques de l'impératrice, ou son esprit de conseil.

Mais c'est le monnayage d'Antonin et de Marc-Aurèle qui fournit sur les rapports de la déesse et des détenteurs du pouvoir les indications les plus intéressantes. A partir de 147, Minerve, qui a figuré jusque-là sur les monnaies d'Antonin, commence d'apparaître sur le monnayage de son César[184]. Or c'est en 147 qu'Antonin atteint l'âge de soixante ans, et, renonçant désormais à commander les troupes en personne, en confie le soin à Marc-Aurèle associé au pouvoir impérial. On en conclura, avec J. BEAUJEU, que «Minerve assume à l'égard du César le rôle que tient Jupiter à l'égard de l'Empereur; fille et associée du dieu suprême de même que le César est le fils et l'associé du *Princeps*, elle est sa protectrice et la source divine de son pouvoir surnaturel»[185]. Du même

---

[177] H. P. L'ORANGE, Das Geburtsritual der Pharaonen am römischen Kaiserhof, in: Symbolae Osloenses, XXI (1941), pp. 105—116.

[178] Ov., Met., 2,553:

> *Pallas Erichthonium, prolem sine matre creatam,*
> *Clauserat Actaeo texta de uimine cista.*

[179] E. GERHARD, Etruskische Spiegel, t. III, Berlin, 1863, pp. 158—9, pl. 166; t. IV, Berlin, 1867, pp. 215—6, pl. 257 B. L'idée, émise par R. ENKING, Minerua mater, in: Jahrbuch des deutschen Archäologischen Instituts, LIX—LX (1944—5), pp. 111—124, d'une maternité de Minerve doit être envisagée avec circonspection.

[180] Voir plus haut, II, 1: *Quinquatrus*.

[181] Voir l'article suivant J.-L. GIRARD, Domitien et Minerve, une prédilection impériale.

[182] L'expression est de J. BEAUJEU, La religion romaine à l'apogée de l'Empire, t. I: La politique religieuse des Antonins (96—192), Paris, 1955, p. 93.

[183] STRACK, t. II, n° 262.

[184] STRACK, t. III, n° 170, 189, 200.

[185] J. BEAUJEU, op. cit., p. 302. Front. Ep., I, 10 (ed. VAN DEN HOUT, Leyde, 1954, p. 22): Ὁ μέν ἐστιν μέγας βασιλεὺς ἄρχων πάσης τῆς γῆς καὶ θαλάττης, ὁ δὲ ἕτερος υἱὸς μεγάλου βασιλέως, ἐκείνου μὲν οὕτω παῖς ὥσπερ Ἀθάνα τοῦ Διός.

coup, s'éclaire l'intérêt particulier d'une protection de Minerve pour le pouvoir impérial, à qui elle peut inspirer, pour le triomphe des desseins de Jupiter auxquels elle est associée, vigueur et sagesse pour le salut de l'empire romain.

Conclusion

L'extrême diversité des hommages rendus à Minerve répond à la multiplicité des compétences et des interventions de la déesse. Mais, derrière cette diversité, et sous un vêtement grec de plus en plus envahissant, se laisse reconnaître l'unité d'une personnalité divine authentiquement romaine.

C'est l'ingéniosité mise au service de l'efficacité qui appelle, outre la vénération des artisans, celle des généraux et des princes. C'est l'intelligence toujours en éveil que récompensent les succès littéraires ou musicaux. C'est une mémoire gardienne de la tradition qui guérit les malades par des recettes éprouvées et redresse le pied des chevaux. Mais, dans un Empire qui s'interroge sur son avenir, le costume guerrier, que Minerve, protectrice de l'art militaire comme de tous les autres arts, a emprunté à Athéna, inspire confiance en la protection de son égide, et en tous les effets heureux qui peuvent en découler pour le bien de l'Empire. Enfin, la prospérité de celui-ci dépend en dernière analyse de la sagesse que les conseils de Minerve peuvent inspirer à ceux qui sont responsables du destin de Rome, sur laquelle veillent la triade capitoline et le Palladium.

La prière adressée à Minerve à propos d'activités si diverses est inspirée par une conception unique, toute romaine: travail, art, victoire et sagesse ne sont-ils pas tous le fruit des efforts de l'esprit humain?

Bibliographie

1. Ouvrages généraux:

J. BEAUJEU, La religion romaine à l'apogée de l'Empire, t. I: La politique religieuse des Antonins (96–192), Paris, 1955.

J. FERGUSON, The Religions of the Roman Empire, Londres, 1970.

K. LATTE, Römische Religionsgeschichte, Handbuch der Altertumswissenschaft, V, 4, Munich, 1960.

G. WISSOWA, Religion und Kultus der Römer², Handbuch der Altertumswissenschaft, V, 4 Munich, 1912.

2. Sources documentaires:

G. CARETTONI–A. M. COLINI–I. COZZA–G. GATTI, La pianta marmorea di Roma antica, Forma Vrbis Romae, Rome, 1960.

A. DEGRASSI, Inscriptiones Italiae, XIII: 1: Fasti et elogia; 2: Fasti anni Numani et Iuliani, Rome, 1963.

E. ESPÉRANDIEU, Recueil général des bas-reliefs, statues et bustes de la Gaule romaine, continué par R. LANTIER, t. I–XIV, Paris, 1908–1949.

E. Espérandieu, Recueil général des bas-reliefs, statues et bustes de la Germanie romaine, Paris–Bruxelles, 1931.

F. Gnecchi, I medaglioni romani, I–III, Milan, 1912.

W. Helbig, Führer durch die öffentlichen Sammlungen klassischer Altertümer in Rom[4], remanié par H. Speier, B. Andreae, T. Dohrn, E. Simon e.a., t.I–IV, Tübingen, 1963–72.

G. Lugli, I monumenti antichi di Roma. Il suburbio, Rome, 1936.

G. Lugli, Roma antica. Il centro monumentale, Rome, 1946.

H. Mattingly, Coins of the Roman Empire in the British Museum, I: Augustus to Vitellius, Londres, 1923; II: Vespasian to Domitian, Londres, 1930; III: Nerua to Hadrian, Londres, 1936; IV: Antoninus Pius to Commodus, Londres, 1940.

H. Mattingly–E.-A. Sydenham–V. Sutherland, The Roman Imperial Coinage, I: Augustus to Vitellius[2], Londres, 1948; II: Vespasian to Hadrian, Londres, 1926 ([2]1972); III: Antoninus Pius to Commodus, Londres, 1930.

E. Nash, Bildlexikon zur Topographie des antiken Rom, I, Tübingen, 1961; II, Tübingen, 1962.

S. B. Platner–I. Ashby, A Topographical Dictionary of Ancient Rome, Londres, 1929.

P.L. Strack, Untersuchungen zur römischen Reichsprägung des 2. Jahrhunderts, I: Die Reichsprägung zur Zeit des Traian, Stuttgart, 1931; II: Die Reichsprägung zur Zeit des Hadrian, Stuttgart, 1933; III: Die Reichsprägung zur Zeit des Antoninus Pius, Stuttgart, 1937.

E. Strong, La scultura romana di Augusto a Costantino, I, Florence, 1924; II, Florence, 1926.

J. M. C. Toynbee, Roman Medallions, Numismatic Studies, V, New York, 1944.

R. Valentini–G. Zucchetti, Codice topografico della città di Roma, Fonti per la storia d'Italia, LXXXI e LXXXVIII, I, Rome, 1940; II, Rome, 1941.

J. Vogt, Die alexandrinischen Münzen. Grundlegung einer alexandrinischen Kaisergeschichte, I, Stuttgart, 1924.

W. Wruck, Die syrische Provinzialprägung von Augustus bis Trajan, Stuttgart, 1931.

3. Notices encyclopédiques:

F. Altheim, Minerua, in: RE, XVII,2 (1932), c. 1874–1802.

F. Coarelli, Minerua, in: Enciclopedia dell'Arte Antica, V (1963), pp. 37–8.

F. Heichelheim, Minerua (keltisch), in: RE, XVII,2 (1932), c. 1802–5.

O. Hentschel, Quinquatrus, in: RE, XXIV,1 (1963), c. 1149–62.

A. Hermann–F. J. Dölger, Capitolium, in: Reallexikon für Antike und Christentum, IV (1954), c. 847–861.

G. Radke, Minerua, in: Der kleine Pauly, III (1969), c. 1317–9.

S. Weinstock, Victor, uictrix, in: RE, VIII A,2 (1958), c. 2485–2500.

H. B. Wiggers, Viergöttersteine, in: RE, Sptbd. XIV (1974), c. 854–864.

G. Wissowa, Minerua, in: Roscher, II (1897), c. 2982–2992.

L. Ziehen, Palladion, in: RE, XVIII,3 (1949), c. 171–201.

4. Monographies et études de détail:

A. Audin, Le Palladium de Rome, in: Revue Archéologique, XXX (1929), pp. 46–57.

J. Beaujeu, Politique religieuse et propagande numismatique sous le Haut-Empire, in: Mélanges d'archéologie et d'histoire offerts à A. Piganiol, Ecole Pratique des Hautes Etudes, VIe Section, Centre de Recherches Historiques, I–III, Paris, 1966, III, pp. 1529–40.

I. Berciu & A. Popa, Exceptores consularis in Dacia, in: Latomus, XXIII (1964), pp. 302–10.

U. Bianchi, Disegno storico del culto capitolino nell'Italia romana e nelle provincie del Impero, in: Accademia Nazionale dei Lincei, Memorie, Classe di Scienze, Storiche e Filosofiche, Serie 8[a], II (1949–1950), pp. 349–415.

E. Birley, The Religion of the Roman Army (1895–1977), in: ANRW, 16,2 (1978), pp. 1506–1541.

H. Boegli, Ein bedeutender Neufund aus Auenticum, in: Antike Welt, III,3 (1972), pp. 49–52.

H. Boegli, Il Capitolium di Auenticum, in: Atti del Convegno Internazionale per il XIX° Centenario della Dedicazione del Capitolio, Brescia, 1973, pp. 145–9.

M. Bollini, Minerua medica memor, in: Atti del III° Convegno di Studi Veleiati, Piacenza, 31.5.–2.6.1967, Milan, 1969, pp. 347–50.

S. Boucher, Figurations de bronze. Grèce et Gaule, in: Revue Archéologique, LXIII (1975), pp. 251–266.

J. Bousquet, Informations archéologiques. Circonscriptions de Bretagne et Pays de la Loire, in: Gallia, XXV (1967), pp. 225–238.

D. F. Brown, Temples of Rome as Coin Types, Numismatic Notes and Monographs, XC, New York, 1940.

A. Brückner, Römischer Balkenkopf aus dem Rhein bei Wardt-Lüthringen, Kreis Moers, in: Bonner Jahrbücher des rheinischen Landesmuseums, CLXIII (1963), pp. 11–16.

Ch. Callmer, Athenaeum, in: Opuscula Romana, VII (1969), pp. 277–284.

G. Caputo, Leptis Magna e l'industria artistica campana in Africa, in: Rendiconti dell'Accademia di Archeologia di Napoli, XXXV (1960), pp. 11–27.

F. Castagnoli, Minerva Calcidica, in Archeologia Classica, XII (1960), pp. 91–5.

F. Castagnoli, Il culto di Minerva a Lavinium, in: Problemi attuali di scienza e di cultura, Accademia nazionale dei Lincei, anno CCCLXXVI (1979), quaderno n° 246, pp. 3–14.

H. J. Croon; The Cult of Sul-Minerva at Bath-Somerset, in: Antiquity, XXVII (1953), pp. 79–83.

B. Cunliffe, The Temple of Sulis-Minerva at Bath, in: Antiquity, XL (1966), pp. 199–204.

G. Debal, Vienne-en-Val. Sanctuaires et divinités, in: Revue Historique et Archéologique de l'Orléanais, V,22 (1973), pp. 3–84.

A. Degrassi, Minerva flanatica, in: Rivista di Filologia e d'Istruzione Classica, X (1932), pp. 87–91.

A. von Domaszewski, Die Religion des römischen Heeres, in: Westdeutsche Zeitschrift für Geschichte und Kunst (Trèves), XIV (1895), pp. 1–128.

R. Duthoy, La Minerua Berecynthia des inscriptions tauroboliques de Bénévent (CIL, IX, 1538–42), in: L'Antiquité Classique, XXXV (1960), pp. 548–561.

P. M. Duval, Observations sur les dieux de la Gaule, in: Revue d'Histoire des Religions, CXLV (1954), pp. 5–17.

F. Eichler, Signum pantheum, in: Jahreshefte des österreichischen Archäologischen Instituts XXXIX (1952), pp. 21–7.

F. El-Fakharani, The Library of Philadelphia or the So-Called Temple on the Citadel Hill of Amman, in: Wissenschaftliche Zeitschrift der Universität Rostock, Gesellschafts- und Sprachwissenschaftliche Reihe, XXIV (1975), pp. 553–4.

R. Enking, Minerua mater, in: Jahrbuch des deutschen Archäologischen Instituts in Rom, LIX–LX (1944–5), pp. 111–124.

R. Fleischer, Antike Bronzestatuetten aus Carnuntum, Graz–Köln, 1966.

J. Formigé, Les officines romaines de marbrerie antique à Carrare, in: Revue Archéologique, XLI (1953), pp. 204–6.

J. Formigé, Officines romaines de marbrerie antique à Carrare, in: Bulletin de la Société Nationale des Antiquaires de France, 1952/3, pp. 130–2.

J. Gagé, Actiaca, in: Mélanges d'Archéologie et d'Histoire de l'Ecole Française de Rome, LIII (1936), pp. 37–100.

L. Gasperini, Nuove iscrizioni etrusche e latine di Visentium, in: Epigraphica, XXII (1959), pp. 31–50.

L. Gasperini, Minerva Nortina, in: Giornale Italiano di Filologia, X (1957), pp. 193–7.

H. DE GERIN-RICARD, La Minerve de Rognac, in: Revue des Etudes Anciennes, XXIV (1922), pp. 149—50.

K. GROSS, Die Unterpfänder der römischen Herrschaft, Berlin, 1935.

W. GRÜNHAGEN, Bemerkungen zum Minerva-Relief in der Stadtmauer von Tarragona, in: Mitteilungen des deutschen Archäologischen Instituts, Madrider Abteilung, XVII (1976), pp. 209—225.

J.-J. HATT, Strasbourg. Découverte d'une stèle à quatre dieux (Junon, Minerve, Hercule et Mercure), in: La Revue des Arts, IV (1954), pp. 239—241.

J.-J. HATT, Strasbourg. Découverte d'une stèle à quatre dieux (Junon, Minerve, Hercule et Mercure), in: Cahiers d'Archéologie et d'Histoire d'Alsace, 1954, CXXXIV, pp. 57—70.

M. HENIG, A New Cameo from Lincolnshire, in: The Antiquarian Journal, 1970, pp. 338—340.

J. HEURGON, Note sur un boutoir antique découvert à Amiens, in: Mélanges L. Jacob (= Revue du Nord, XXXVI [1954]), pp. 147—9.

J. HEURGON, Deux objets de bronze récemment découverts à Amiens, in: Bulletin de la Société Nationale des Antiquaires de France, 1952—3, pp. 31—2.

G. HEUTEN, Les divinités capitolines en Espagne, in: Revue Belge de Philologie et d'Histoire, 1933, pp. 548—563 & 1935, pp. 709—723.

F. JENKINS, Romano-Gaulish Figurines as Indications of the Mother-Goddess Cults in Britain, in: Hommages à A. Grenier, Collection Latomus, LVIII, Bruxelles, 1962, pp. 836—52.

R. JOFFROY, Statuette de Minerve en bronze trouvée à Pontailler (Côte-d'or), in: Revue Archéologique de l'Est et du Centre-Est, XV (1964), pp. 118—22.

E. J. JORY, Associations of Actors in Rome, in: Hermes, XCVII (1970), pp. 224—253.

C. W. KEYES, Minerva Victrix? A note on the Winged Goddess of Ostia, in: American Journal of Archaeology, 2nd ser. XVI (1912), n° 4, pp. 490—4.

P. LAMBRECHTS, L'œuvre religieuse d'Auguste, in: Latomus, VI (1949), pp. 177—91.

R. LANTIER, Deux braseros romains, in: Bulletin de la Société Nationale des Antiquaires de France, 1950/1, pp. 89—90.

H. P. L'ORANGE, Das Geburtsritual der Pharaonen am römischen Kaiserhof, in: Symbolae Osloenses, XXI (1941), pp. 105—116.

V. LUNDSTROM, Chalcidicum och Minerva Chalcidica?, in: Strena philologica Upsaliensia (= Festskrift P. Persson), Uppsala, 1922, pp. 369—392.

R. MAJUREL, Un fragment de céramique sigillée en provenance d'Autun, in: Ogam, XXI (1969), pp. 227—232.

L. MERCANDO, Il larario puerile del Museo Oliveriano di Pesaro, in: Studia Oliveriana, Pesaro, XII—XIV (1965—6), pp. 129—150.

J. H. OLIVER, Julia Domna as Athena Polias, in: Athenian Studies Presented to W. S. Ferguson, Harvard Studies in Classical Philology, Suppl. I, Cambridge, 1940.

W. C. PHILIPPS, Numismatic Typology of Antoninus Pius, in: Journal of the Society of Ancient Numismatic, 1971, pp. 52—3.

G. CH.-PICARD, Rapport sur l'archéologie romaine en Tunisie dans le premier semestre 1950, in: Bulletin Archéologique du Comité des Travaux Historiques, 1950, pp. 154—62.

G. CH.-PICARD, Les fouilles de Vienne-en Val (Loiret), in: Comptes Rendus de l'Académie des Inscriptions et Belles-Lettres, 1970, pp. 176—191.

E. PLANSON—A. LAGRANGE, La Minerve des Bolards, in: Revue Archéologique, LX (1970), pp. 81—92.

A. PLOUHINEC, Bronzes de Rezé (Loire-Atlantique), in: Notices d'Archéologie Armoricaine. Annales de Bretagne, 1967, pp. 157—166.

I. A. RICHMOND & J. M. C. TOYNBEE, The Temple of Sulis-Minerva at Bath, in: Journal of Roman Studies, XCV (1955), pp. 97—105.

G. E. RIZZO, La base di Augusto, Naples, 1933 (et in: Boll. della Comm. Arch. Com. di Roma, LX [1932], pp. 7—109).

CH. B. RUEGER, Eine Weihinschrift aus Tarraco, in: Mitteilungen des deutschen Archäologischen Instituts, Madrider Abteilung, IX (1968), pp. 259—262.

H. SAUER, Die Kapitolinische Trias. Zu einem Relief in der Sammlung des archäologischen Instituts in Kiel, in: Archäologischer Anzeiger, 1950/1, pp. 73—89.

L. SAVIGNONI, Minerva Vittoria, in: Ausonia, V (1910), pp. 69—108.

L. SGOBBO, Thespis l'auleta raffigurato in un bronzo di Ercolano, in: Rendiconti dell'Accademia di Archeologia, Lettere e Belle Arti di Napoli, XLV (1970), pp. 132—158.

G. STÉGEN, Vénus et Minerve, in: Les Etudes Classiques, XXVII (1959), pp. 28—30.

M. STETTLER, St. Gereon in Köln und der sogenannte Tempel der Minerua medica in Rom, in: Jahrbuch des römisch-germanischen Zentralmuseums, Mainz, IV (1957), pp. 123—8.

E. THÉVENOT, Le monument de Mavilly (Côte-d'or), in: Latomus, XV (1955), pp. 75—99.

R. THOUVENOT, Sur deux inscriptions récemment découvertes à Poitiers, in: Akten des IV. internationalen Kongresses für griechische und lateinische Epigraphik, Vienne, 1964, pp. 391—7.

R. VERDIÈRE, Contribution à un commentaire de CIL II, 954, in: Rivista di Cultura Classica e Medioevale, XII (1970), pp. 28—30.

S. E. WINBOLT, The Neptune and Minerva Stone, Chichester, Chichester, 1935.

Domitien et Minerve: une prédilection impériale

par JEAN-LOUIS GIRARD, Strasbourg

Table des matières

Introduction

C'est un fait bien avéré que la dévotion de Domitien pour Minerve. En témoignent, sur le ton de la flatterie, Quintilien lorsqu'il écrit, en louant les talents d'écrivain de l'empereur: «A qui Minerve, sa divinité familière, pourrait-elle préférer dévoiler les secrets des arts qu'elle patronne?»[1], Martial quand, énumérant les motifs de reconnaissance que peuvent avoir envers Domitien les dieux de la triade capitoline, il s'écrie: «Je laisse de côté Pallas; elle t'est toute acquise»[2]. Suétone, quoique dans un esprit bien différent, ne dit pas autre chose: «Minerve, qu'il honorait jusqu'à la superstition»[3].

Ce choix d'une divinité de prédilection ne laisse pas de surprendre, de la part d'un prince dont la conduite, surtout dans les dernières années de sa vie, paraît bien éloignée de l'idéal de modération et de sérénité intellectuelle qu'on s'attendrait à voir la dévotion à Minerve lui inspirer. Une étude plus détaillée de la question peut-elle nous éclairer sur la signification de cette préférence, illustrant les détours d'un caractère complexe et la richesse d'une personnalité divine?

I. Edifices religieux

Encore que l'étude de l'œuvre de bâtisseur religieux de Domitien soit obscurcie par l'habitude de ce prince, signalée par Suétone[4], de s'attribuer la construction de sanctuaires qu'il n'avait fait que restaurer, il est clair que Minerve occupe dans les préoccupations du règne une place de tout premier choix.

1. Le temple capitolin

C'est à Domitien que revint la charge d'élever et de dédier pour la quatrième fois le temple capitolin, détruit à nouveau en 80 par un incendie[5]. A l'importance officielle prise par le culte de la triade capitoline, devenu à l'époque impériale le véritable culte national de Rome[6], s'ajoutait pour l'empereur le poids d'un souvenir personnel. Il avait échappé heureusement à l'incendie, allumé en 69 par les Vitelliens, de ce même temple capitolin, où il s'était réfugié

Abréviations: v. supra pp. 204—5.

[1] Quint., Inst. Or., 10,1,91: *Cui magis artes suas aperiret familiare numen Mineruae?*

[2] Mart., 9,3,10: *Pallada praetereo; res agit illa tuas.*

[3] Suet., Dom., 15,3: *Mineruam, quam* (sc. *Domitianus*) *superstitiose colebat.*

[4] Suet., Dom., 5,1: *plurima et amplissima opera incendio absumpta restituit, sed omnia sub titulo suo, ac sine ulla pristini auctoris memoria.*

[5] Plut., Publ., 15,3: Ἅμα τῷ τελευτῆσαι Οὐεσπασιανὸν ἐνεπρήσθη τὸ Καπιτώλιον. Ὁ δὲ τέταρτος οὗτος ὑπὸ Δομετιανοῦ καὶ συνετελέσθη καὶ καθιερώθη.

[6] U. Bianchi, Disegno storico del culto capitolino nell'Italia romana e nelle provincie dell'Impero, in: Accademia Nazionale dei Lincei, Memorie, Classe di Scienze Morali, Storiche e Filologiche, Ser. 8ª, II (1949—1950), p. 411. J. R. Fears, The Cult of Jupiter and Roman Imperial Ideology, ci-dessus, pp. 3—141; I. M. Barton, Capitoline Temples in Italy and the Provinces (especially Africa), ANRW, II 12, 1 (1981).

avec son oncle Flauius Sabinus. Or, de ce salut, on le voit faire honneur à la protection du seul Jupiter, à qui il dédie, du vivant de Vespasien, une chapelle sous l'invocation de *Conseruator*, puis, après son accession à l'empire, un temple sous celle de *Custos*[7]. Minerve n'est donc pas, dans cette restauration du temple capitolin, l'objet d'une attention particulière. Cela rend assez peu probable l'hypothèse de H. SAUTER[8], selon laquelle la dévotion de Domitien pour Minerve aurait son origine dans quelque important service rendu par la déesse au fidèle menacé.

2. L'*Atrium Mineruae*

La curie comportait, en annexe, un cryptoportique, du type spécial appelé *Chalcidicum*, qui se trouve peut-être, à date tardive, désigné sous le nom d'*Atrium Mineruae*[9]. Auguste rappelle qu'il a restauré ce monument, sans faire aucune allusion à la présence de Minerve[10]. En revanche, Dion Cassius, qui écrivait sous les Sévères, signalant cette même restauration, parle de «l'Atheneum nommé Chalcidique».[11] Le monument s'est donc trouvé, entre le début du Ier et le début du IIIème siècle, voué à Minerve. On a supposé[12] − non sans vraisemblance − que Domitien, qui a restauré la Curie en 94, avait consacré cet édifice à sa déesse favorite, appelant la sagesse de Minerve á présider aux délibérations du Sénat.

3. Le temple de *Minerua Chalcidica*

La chronique de 354 nous apprend que Domitien a fait construire le temple de *Minerua Chalcidica*[13], sur le Champ de Mars, où une inscription très mutilée portant le nom de la déesse a été découverte[14] à l'emplacement de l'actuelle église de Santa Maria sopra Minerva. L'épithète est curieuse. Il est peu probable qu'elle

---

[7] Tac., H., 3,74: *Domitianus prima irruptione apud aedituum occultatus, sollertia liberti lineo amictu turba sacricolarum immixtus ignoratusque, apud Cornelium Priscum paternum clientem iuxta Velabrum delituit. Ac, potiente rerum patre, disiecto aeditui contubernio, modicum sacellum Ioui Conseruatori, aramque posuit casus suos in marmore expressam, mox, imperium adeptus, Ioui Custodi templum ingens seque in sinu dei sacrauit.* J. R. FEARS, ci-dessus, pp. 74−80, spéc. 77−8.

[8] H. SAUTER, Der römische Kaiserkult bei Martial und Statius, Stuttgart−Berlin, 1934, p. 92.

[9] Curiosum Vrbis Romae regionum XIIII, in: VALENTINI−ZUCCHETTI, t. I, p. 114.

[10] Res gestae diui Augusti, éd. J. GAGÉ, ⁴Paris, 1950, § 19: *curiam et continens ei chalcidicum.*

[11] Cass. Dio. 51,22: τό τε Ἀθήναιον τὸ Χαλκιδικὸν ὠνομασμένον.

[12] PLATNER−ASHBY, p. 144.

[13] Chronica minora saeculorum IV, V, VI, VII (= Monumenta Germaniae historica, Auctores antiquissimi, IX), ed. MOMMSEN, p. 146: *Domitianus* (. . .) (sc. *aedificauit*) (. . .) *Mineruam Chalcidicam.*

[14] F. CASTAGNOLI, Minerva Calcidica, in: Archeologia Classica, XII (1960), pp. 91−5.

ait été entraînée par une confusion avec *Athéna Chalkioikos*. Ce culte dorien[15] ne devait pas être très connu à Rome, et le rapprochement, qui serait frappant paléographiquement, perd beaucoup de sa valeur quand il s'agit de rendre compte d'une déformation phonétique. Il paraît bien plus probable que l'épithète a été transférée par la foule du *Chalcidicum*, devenu *Atrium Mineruae*, à la déesse, et a accompagné Minerve dans son nouveau lieu de culte[16].

L'emplacement du temple laisse supposer le culte d'une Minerve guerrière, à laquelle Domitien confiait sans doute la protection des armes romaines. L'hypothèse de S. B. PLATNER[17], selon laquelle ce temple aurait été édifié sur l'emplacement du sanctuaire que Pompée avait voué à une Minerve de caractère également guerrier avec la dîme de son butin[18] est ingénieuse, mais ne repose sur aucun témoignage.

4. Le temple de Minerve sur le Forum

A partir de 86 après Jésus-Christ, les diplômes militaires portent la mention *Descriptum et recognitum ex tabula aenea quae fixa est Romae in muro post templum diui Augusti ad Mineruam*[19]. Par ailleurs, le Chronographe de 354 écrit, dans l'énumération des constructions de Domitien: *templum Mineruae et Castorum.*[20] Le rapprochement de ces deux témoignages permet d'en déduire l'existence d'un temple de Minerve sur le Forum, construit par Domitien, et qui aurait occupé l'emplacement situé devant l'église Santa Maria Antica, entre le temple des Dioscures et le *templum nouum diui Augusti. Ad Mineruam* ne peut désigner l'*Atrium Mineruae*, trop éloigné, et l'idée d'un culte de Minerve dans le temple des Dioscures, qui n'a pas paru étrange à TH. MOMMSEN, méconnaît que le chroniqueur a pu s'exprimer, comme souvent, par brachylogie. Une allusion à ce temple semble d'ailleurs se rencontrer sous la plume de Martial[21]. Malheureusement, nous n'avons aucun indice sur la nature du culte.

5. Le temple du *Forum transitorium*

La *damnatio memoriae* a privé Domitien de l'honneur des constructions qu'il avait élevées entre le Forum d'Auguste et celui de Vespasien. Mais toute la

---

[15] Ar., Lys., 1300, où un Spartiate invoque Χαλκίοικον ἄνασσαν; Liv., 35,36,9: *Aetoli circa Chalcioecon — Mineruae aereum est templum — congregati caeduntur.*

[16] V. LUNDSTRÖM, Chalcidicum och Minerva Chalcidica?, in: Strena philologica Upsaliensia (= Festskrift P. Persson), Uppsala, 1922, pp. 369−382.

[17] PLATNER−ASHBY, p. 344.

[18] Plin., N.H., 7,97: *Pompeius (. . .) in delubro Mineruae quod ex manubis dicabat.*

[19] CIL, III, Suppl., pp. 1965−2005; Ephemeris epigraphica, V, pp. 652−6.

[20] Chronica minora saeculorum IV, V, VI, VII (= Monumenta Germaniae historica, Auctores antiquissimi, IX), ed. MOMMSEN, p. 146.

[21] Mart., 4,53,1−2:

Hunc, quem saepe uides inter penetralia nostrae
Pallados et templi limina, Cosme, noui.

1. La triade capitoline sur un cippe sévérien

2b

2a

2a.b. Autel votif à Minerve d'un culte d'artisans

2 c.d. Autel votif à Minerve d'un culte d'artisans

2 c

2 d

3. Minerve dans le cortège triomphal de Domitien, Bas-relief du Palazzo della Cancelleria

conception de cet ensemble monumental remonte à son règne, et Nerva trouva pratiquement achevé le Forum qui porte aujourd'hui son nom, et qu'il n'eut plus qu'à dédier[22].

Or, le rôle capital tenu sur le Forum d'Auguste par le temple de Mars Ultor revenait sur ce *Forum transitorium* à un temple de Minerve. Des vestiges importants en ont d'ailleurs subsisté jusqu'au XVIème siècle, où ils ont été sacrifiés à des embellissements entrepris par le pape Paul V, et l'inscription dédicatoire nous a été transmise[23]. Il ne reste plus aujourd'hui de cet ensemble qu'un imposant fragment de portique, que les Romains désignent sous le nom de Le Colonnacce. Il est orné d'une statue de Minerve et de bas-reliefs assez mal conservés, mais dont le sens discernable ne permet pas de douter que c'était la déesse des arts qu'on honorait dans le temple disparu.

II. Monuments d'apparat

1. Les reliefs de la Chancellerie Apostolique

On a découvert en 1939, lors de travaux entrepris dans le voisinage de la chancellerie apostolique, des bas-reliefs de style flavien, mais, malheureusement, dans un contexte d'époque républicaine, qui ne peut donner une idée exacte de leur véritable destination[24]. Malgré des tentatives de datation plus basses[25], leur attribution à l'époque de Domitien ne paraît pas douteuse, même si la tête de Nerva a été substituée à celle d'un Domitien frappé de *damnatio memoriae*. Séduisante est l'hypothèse qui voit dans ces morceaux de sculpture, représentant l'entrée de Vespasien à Rome en 70 et le triomphe de Domitien sur les Chattes en 94, une histoire de la dynastie telle que Domitien voulait qu'on se la représentât, et les destine à orner un monument que la mort a empêché le prince d'édifier, et qui aurait été l'équivalent flavien de l'*Ara pacis Augustae*. Or, dans la longue théorie de divinités, d'allégories et de personnages historiques qui se déploie sur cette frise, la proximité de Domitien et de Minerve est absolument frappante, assez pour faire déclarer à un commentateur: „*Auch hier ist sie ihm*

---

[22] Suet., Dom., 5,2: (*Domitianus*) *excitauit* (. . .) *Forum quod nunc Neruae uocatur.*

[23] CIL, VI, 953: *Imp(erator) Nerua Caes(ar) Aug(ustus)* (sc. *Gemanicus*) *pont(ifex) max(imus)* / *trib(uniciae) pot(estatis) II co(n)s(ul) IIII [p(ater) p(atriae) aedem Mi]neruae fecit.*
Les conditions de transmission de l'inscription rendent incertaine l'étendue de la lacune. *Aedem* est une restitution plus probable que *Forum. Forum Palladium* (Mart., 1,2,78) n'est qu'une licence poétique.

[24] W. Helbig, Führer durch die öffentlichen Sammlungen klassischer Altertümer in Rom, remanié par B. Andreae, T. Dohrn, E. Simon e.a., I–IV, ⁴Tübingen 1963–1972. I, n° 12 (pl. IV,3).

[25] H. Rumpf, Römische historische Reliefs, I: Die Reliefs von der Cancelleria, in: Bonner Jahrbücher des rheinischen Landesmuseums, CLV–VI (1955–6), pp. 112–9.

näher als alle anderen, sie erscheint ihm allein"[25a]. Dans ce contexte triomphal, l'attitude de Minerve ne permet pas de douter que c'est à sa protection que Domitien doit les victoires éclatantes qu'il s'attribue et à la glorification desquelles il entendait consacrer ce monument.

2. Le Colonnacce

Les bas-reliefs qui ornent la partie qui nous a été conservée du portique du *Forum transitorium* sont malheureusement mutilés au point d'être en partie incompréhensibles. Néanmoins, les deux plus importants ont pu être interprétés grâce à la perspicacité de H. BLÜMNER[26] et de E. PETERSEN[27]. Sur le premier, au milieu de scènes de tissage, Minerve, reconnaissable à son costume, frappe une silhouette féminine agenouillée devant elle. Il s'agit indubitablement de la légende grecque d'Arachné, et plus précisément du moment, décrit par Ovide[28], où Athéna châtie la présomption de sa rivale en la touchant de sa navette pour la métamorphoser en araignée. Le choix de cet épisode est particulièrement riche de sens, puisqu'il met en scène la déesse à la fois comme protectrice des arts et comme vengeresse de la majesté divine.

Le deuxième bas-relief nous la montre assise au milieu du choeur des Muses. Celles-ci sont plus fréquemment représentées en compagnie d'Apollon, mais peuvent aussi bien, elles qui patronnent chacune un art particulier, être rapprochées de la protectrice de tous les arts en général[29].

Les autres bas-reliefs sont dans un piètre état de conservation[30]. E. STRONG[31], pour y voir des scènes d'initiation aux différents arts, se place plus sur le terrain de la vraisemblance que sur celui de l'observation.

3. La statue équestre de Domitien

Dans la première de ses 'Silves', Stace nous décrit la statue équestre colossale que Domitien s'était fait ériger sur le Forum, en face du temple de Jules

---

[25a] HELBIG[4], I, n° 12, p. 11.

[26] H. BLÜMNER, Il fregio del portico del Foro di Nerva, in: Annali del Instituto di Corrispondenza Archeologica, XLIX (1877), pp. 5–36.

[27] E. PETERSEN, Mitteilungen des kaiserlichen deutschen archäologischen Instituts, Römische Abteilung, IV (1886), Sitzungsprotokolle, p. 88.

[28] Ov., Mét., 6,132–3:

> *Vtque Cytoriaco radium de monte tenebat,*
> *Ter quater Idmoneae frontem percussit Arachnes.*

[29] Front., Ep., 2,12 (ed. VAN DEN HOUT, Leyde, 1954, p. 33): Ἡ Ἀθηνᾶ τέχνας ἁπάσας, κέκτηταί τε καὶ ἐπίσταται (. . .) οἷος ὁ τῶν Μουσῶν ἔπαινος ἐκ μιᾶς τέχνης καὶ καθ' ἑκάστην διῃρημένος.

[30] P. H. VON BLANCKENHAGEN, Die flavische Architektur und ihre Dekoration, untersucht am Nervaforum, Berlin, 1940.

[31] E. STRONG, La scultura romana d'Augusto a Costantino, I, Florence, 1924, p. 132.

César, monument de ses victoires. Nous apprenons ainsi que la main gauche de l'empereur tenait une statuette de la « vierge Tritonienne » brandissant la tête de Méduse[32]. Le sens de cette référence à la Gorgone n'est pas douteux: Minerve frappe de terreur les ennemis de l'empereur et lui garantit la fortune des armes.

III. Fêtes et rites

1. Les jeux capitolins

Par la création des *ludi Capitolini*, célébrés tous les quatre ans à Rome, Domitien témoigne de son intérêt pour les arts et les lettres[33]. Sans doute, pour établir un parallèle avec Ζεὺς Ὀλύμπιος, Jupiter Capitolin est-il seul dédicataire de ces jeux, mais la triade n'en est pas absente, puisque Domitien préside en portant sur sa couronne l'effigie de Jupiter, Junon, Minerve. Le flamine de Jupiter et le collège des Flaviens portent des couronnes semblables, ornées en outre de l'effigie de Domitien[34]. Si les jeux capitolins ont duré jusqu'à la fin du paganisme, l'usage des couronnes, trop liées au souvenir de l'empereur honni, disparaît à partir de 96.

2. Les Quinquatries

A côté des jeux capitolins, où Minerve ne tient qu'une place subalterne, Domitien célébrait également dans son domaine d'Albe des jeux annuels dédiés à la seule Minerve, à l'occasion de la fête des Quinquatries (19–23 mars)[35].

---

[32] Stace, S., 1,1,37–8:
   Dextra uetat pugnas, laeuam Tritonia uirgo
   Non grauat et sectae praetendit colla Medusae.

[33] I. Lana, I ludi Capitolini di Domiziano, in: Rivista di Filologia e d'Istruzione Classica, n.s., XXIX (1951), pp. 145–160; S. J. Simon, Domitian, Patron of Letters, in: The Classical Bulletin, LI (1975), pp. 58–9.

[34] Suet., Dom., 4,1–3: *Instituit et quinquennale certamen Capitolino Ioui triplex, musicum, equestre, gymnicum. Certamini praesedit crepidatus, purpureaque amictus toga Graecanica, capite gestans coronam auream cum effigie Iouis ac Iunonis Mineruaeque, adsidentibus Diali sacerdote et collegio Flauialium pari habitu, nisi quod illorum coronis inerat et ipsius imago.* Cf. J. R. Fears, ci-dessus, p. 78.

[35] Suet., Dom., 4,3–4: *Celebrabat et in Albano quotannis Quinquatria Mineruae, cui collegium instituerat, ex quo sorte ducti magisterio fungerentur ederentque eximias uenationes et scaenicos ludos superque oratorum et poetarum certamina.* Cass. Dio, 67,1,2: Τὰ Παναθήναια μεγάλως ἑώρταζε, καὶ ἐν αὐτοῖς ἀγῶνας καὶ ποιητῶν καὶ λογογράφων μονομάχων τε κατ' ἔτος ὡς εἰπεῖν ἐν τῷ Ἀλβάνῳ ἐποίει. Τὰ Παναθήναια est une *interpretatio Graeca* de *Quinquatria*.

Stace, qui échoua à l'*agon Capitolinus*[36], remporta en revanche trois fois[37] la victoire aux jeux albains[38]. Le rôle du *collegium Mineruae*, institué à l'occasion de ces fêtes, et qui n'est pas attesté épigraphiquement, est peu clair. Plutôt que de faire intervenir son président à Albe, où Domitien devait, naturellement, tenir le premier rôle, il est plus naturel de lui attribuer l'organisation des jeux qui se déroulaient traditionnellement à Rome lors des Quinquatries[39], et que le prince, absent, ne pouvait plus célébrer en personne.

On ne trouve plus de mention des jeux albains au-delà du règne de Domitien.

3. Le culte impérial

Domitien lia-t-il la dévotion qu'il portait à Minerve au culte impérial? Outre la présence de la triade capitoline sur la couronne des Flaviens aux jeux capitolins, que nous venons de relever, le témoignage de Philostrate peut, si nous lui prêtons crédit, inciter à le croire[40]. Le biographe d'Apollonius de Tyane fait rencontrer au thaumaturge un exilé qui, magistrat à Tarente, n'a pas voulu ajouter aux prières publiques que Domitien était fils de Minerve[41]. K. Scott a remarqué avec finesse[42] que, la dynastie julio-claudienne ayant eu *Venus Genetrix* pour protectrice, Domitien peut avoir voulu donner à la dynastie flavienne, originaire de Sabine, où le culte de Minerve était ancien[43], une protectrice semblable.

---

[36] Stace, S., 3,5,31−3: (à sa femme Claudia):

> *Tu cum Capitolia nostrae*
> *Infitiata lyrae, saeuum ingratumque dolebas*
> *Mecum uicta Iouem.*

[37] Stace, S., 3,5,28−9:

> *Ter me nitidis Albana ferentem*
> *Dona comis.*

[38] Il subsiste des vestiges du théâtre où avaient lieu ces concours. Cf. F. Magi, I marmi del teatro di Domiziano a Castelgandolfo, in: Rendiconti della Pontificia Accademia di Archeologia, XLVI (1973/4), pp. 63−77.

[39] Ov., F., 3,811−3:

> *Sanguine prima uacat, nec fas concurrere ferro.*
> *Causa, quod est illa nata Minerua die.*
> *Altera tresque super rasa celebrantur harena.*

[40] Sur l'utilisation de la 'Vie d'Apollonius de Tyane', cf. F. Grosso, La Vita di Apollonio di Tiana come fonte storica, in: Acme, VII (1954), pp. 441−491; E. Lyall Bowie, Apollonius of Tyana, Tradition and Reality, in: ANRW II, 16,2 (1978), pp. 1652−1699.

[41] Philostr., Vit. Apoll., 7,24: Ἑτέρου δ᾽ αὖ φήσαντος γραφὴν φεύγειν, ἐπειδὴ θύων ἐν Τάραντι, οὗ ἦρχε, μὴ προσέθηκε ταῖς δημοσίαις εὐχαῖς, ὅτι Δομετιανὸς Ἀθηνᾶς εἴη παῖς, "σὺ μὲν ᾠήθης," ἔφη, "μὴ ἂν τὴν Ἀθηνᾶν τεκεῖν, παρθένον οὖσαν τὸν ἀεὶ χρόνον, ἠγνόεις δ᾽, οἶμαι, ὅτι ἡ θεὸς αὕτη Ἀθηναίοις ποτὲ δράκοντα ἔτεκε."

[42] K. Scott, The imperial Cult under the Flavians, Stuttgart, 1936, p. 186.

[43] Varr., L.L., 5,74: *Minerua a Sabinis*; Denys d'Halic., A.R., 1,14,3: Ὀρουΐνιον (. . .) ἔνθα καὶ νεὼς Ἀθηνᾶς ἐστιν ἀρχαῖος.

4. Le culte privé de Domitien pour Minerve

Domitien gardait une statue de Minerve dans sa chambre à coucher. Nous le savons grâce au récit que fait Suétone d'un rêve prémonitoire de l'empereur, un peu avant sa mort: «Il rêva que Minerve, qu'il honorait jusqu'à la superstition, sortait de sa chapelle (*sacrarium*), et lui disait ne plus pouvoir le protéger, parce que Jupiter l'avait désarmée»[44]. Le *sacrarium* dont il est question ici est probablement le laraire placé dans la chambre à coucher de l'empereur[45], puisque Dion Cassius, rapportant ce rêve d'une manière un peu différente, place la statue de la déesse ἐν τῷ κοιτῶνι[46]. C'est d'ailleurs, en dépit des avertissements de la déesse, Minerve que Domitien appellera à son secours lorsqu'il sera assassiné, à ce que rapporte Philostrate[47].

Il est possible qu'il y ait eu dans le palais de Domitien une deuxième statue de la déesse, car lorsqu'Apollonius de Tyane rencontre pour la première fois l'empereur, celui-ci vient de sacrifier à Minerve «dans la cour d'Adonis»[48]. Mais ce lieu est tout à fait inconnu par ailleurs.[49]

IV. Symboles et emblèmes

1. Le monnayage

Minerve et les symboles qui rappellent Minerve jouent, d'une manière générale, un rôle important dans le monnayage des Flaviens. Vespasien et Titus portent fréquemment l'égide[50]. Tous deux sont représentés recevant le Palladium, symbole des destinées de l'Empire et de la légitimité de leur pouvoir, le premier des mains de la Victoire, sur un sesterce de 71[51], le deuxième des mains de Rome, sur un sesterce de 80—81[52]. Déjà, pendant son consulat de 80, Domitien avait symbolisé Minerve sur son monnayage de bronze par un casque corinthien placé sur un siège, allusion peut-être à un *sellisternium*[53]. Mais, avec son accession au pouvoir, le nombre des types monétaires consacrés à Minerve

---

[44] Suet., Dom., 15,3: *Mineruam, quam superstitiose colebat, somniauit sacrario excedere negantemque ultra se tueri eum posse, quod exarmata esset a Ioue.*

[45] K. Scott, Le sacrarium Mineruae de Domitien, in: Revue Archéologique, VI (1935), pp. 69—72.

[46] Cass., Dio, 67,16: Τὴν Ἀθηνᾶν, ἣν ἐν τῷ κοιτῶνι ἱδρυμένην εἶχε, τὰ ὅπλα ἀποβεβληκέναι καὶ ἐπὶ ἅρματος ἵππων μελάνων ἐς χάσμα ἐσπίπτειν ἔδοξεν.

[47] Philostr., Vit. Apoll, 8,25: Ἐκάλει δὲ (sc. ὁ Δομετιανὸς) τὴν Ἀθηνᾶν ἀρωγόν.

[48] Philostr., Vit. Apoll., 7,32: (Ὁ Δομετιανὸς) ἄρτι μὲν τῇ Ἀθηνᾷ τεθυκὼς ἐτύγχανεν ἐν αὐλῇ Ἀδώνιδος.

[49] PLATNER—ASHBY, p. 1.

[50] BMC, II, pp. 121—2 (Vespasien), p. 175 (Titus).

[51] BMC, II, p. 126, n° 586 (pl. 23,1).

[52] BMC, II, p. 260, n° 188 (pl. 49,7).

[53] BMC, II, p. 240, n° 97 (pl. 46,12).

s'accroît. H. MATTINGLY a justement observé; *"Rarely has one divinity received such numismatic honours from a votary"*[54].

On peut rapporter à la commémoration des *ludi Albani* un *semis* portant l'image de Minerve accompagnée d'une chouette[55] et une pièce avec Minerve au droit et une branche d'olivier au revers[56], à cause du caractère pacifique de ces symboles. Mais la plupart des types renvoient à une Minerve guerrière. On en distingue cinq principaux: Minerve combattante, tournée vers la droite[57]; Minerve, tenant une lance, tournée vers la gauche[58]; Minerve combattante, tournée vers la droite, montée sur une proue[59]; Minerve, tenant un foudre, tournée vers la gauche[60]; Minerve ailée, tournée vers la gauche, tenant une lance dans la main droite et un bouclier rond dans la main gauche[61]. Le premier et le deuxième type n'appellent pas de commentaire. Le troisième signifie sans doute que les flottes de Rome, aussi bien que ses armées, sont mises sous la protection de Minerve; le quatrième se rattache à une vieille tradition italique qui place Minerve parmi les dieux appelés par Jupiter à se prononcer sur l'envoi de la foudre[62]; le dernier, enfin, postérieur à la conclusion en 94 de la guerre contre les Chattes, représente la première apparition du type de *Minerua Victrix*, qu'incarnera, au début du IIème siècle, une colossale statue en marbre d'Ostie, et qui représente une création originale du génie romain.[63] L'intérêt de Domitien pour Minerve se marque particulièrement en ce qu'à partir de 83 l'image de la déesse est réservée au monnayage d'argent, frappé par le seul empereur[63a].

La prépondérance des aspects guerriers dans les types monétaires n'a rien qui doive étonner, la propagande impériale ayant pris de préférence pour sujet les efforts et les victoires militaires. La confiance dans le destin de Rome s'exprime également par le recours au symbole du Palladium: sur un sesterce de 81, Domitien le tient dans la main droite[64]; et l'on peut reconnaître l'empereur sur une monnaie d'Alexandrie où il est représenté en Héraclès, toujours tenant le Palladium dans la main droite[65].

[54] BMC, II, p. 151.

[55] BMC, II, p. 409, n° 487 (pl. 81,10).

[56] BMC, II, p. 410, n° 490 (pl. 81,1).

[57] BMC, II, p. 306, n° 39. L. MORAWIECKI, The Symbolism of Minerva on the Coins of Domitianus, in: Klio, LIX (1977), pp. 185–193, fig. 1.

[58] BMC, II, p. 307, n° 44. L. MORAWIECKI, op. cit., fig. 3.

[59] BMC, II, p. 306, n° 40. L. MORAWIECKI, op. cit., fig. 2.

[60] BMC, II, p. 306, n° 42. L. MORAWIECKI, op. cit., fig. 4.

[61] BMC, II, pl. 67,1.

[62] Sen., Q.N., 2,41: *Fulmina dicunt a Ioue mitti et tres illi manubias dant (. . .) Secundam mittit quidem Iuppiter, sed ex consilii sententia; duodecim enim deos aduocat.*

[63] C. W. KEYES, Minerua Victrix? Note on the Winged Goddess of Ostia, in: American Journal of Archeology, 2nd ser., XVI (1912), n° 4, pp. 490–4. L. SAVIGNONI, Minerva Vittoria, in: Ausonia, V (1910), pp. 69–108. Contra: C. ANTI, Atena marina e alata, in: Atti dell'Accademia Reale dei Lincei, Memorie, Classe di Scienze Morali, Storiche e Filologiche, Ser. 5ª, XXVI (1920), pp. 269–318.

[63a] L. MORAWIECKI, op. cit., pp. 189–190.

[64] BMC, II, pl. 68,9.

[65] J. VOGT, Die alexandrinischen Münzen. Grundlegung einer alexandrinischen Kaisergeschichte, I, Stuttgart, 1924, pp. 54–5.

2. La *legio I Flauia Mineruia*

C'est par Domitien que fut instituée, au moment de la guerre contre les Chattes, la *legio I Mineruia*[66]. Cette légion avait pour enseigne une statue de Minerve, qui figure sur une pièce de Gallien avec la légende LEG*(io)* I MIN*(eruia)*[67]. L'emblème en était le bélier, qui apparaît sur la colonne Trajane[68]. Or, c'est au cours de la période où le soleil est dans le signe du Bélier que se célèbrent les *Quinquatrus*[69]. Ces symboles doivent avoir été choisis en même temps que le nom de la légion par Domitien, et ne peuvent être attribués à ses successeurs, qui n'ont pas porté à Minerve le même intérêt.

Conclusion

Après avoir tracé du dernier des Flaviens ce portrait sans indulgence: «Pour Domitien, il était violent et coléreux, mais il était aussi perfide et dissimulé, en sorte que, partagé entre la vivacité et la ruse, souvent il opprimait avec la brutalité de la foudre qui s'abat, souvent aussi il nuisait de propos délibéré», Dion Cassius poursuit: «C'est que, parmi les dieux, il honorait particulièrement Minerve»[70].

Peu flatteur pour la déesse ce raccourci saisissant ne manque pas de pénétration psychologique. Domitien est, comme Tibère, un être complexe, qui veut donner une certaine image de lui-même; par sa référence à la sagesse guerrière, il se veut le prince des décisions foudroyantes et des desseins longuement mûris. Troisième empereur flavien, comme Minerve est la troisième dans la triade capitoline et la conseillère de Jupiter[71], il proclame que les succès de son père et de son frère n'ont été dus qu'à ses conseils[72]. Fondateur des jeux

---

[66] Cass. Dio, 55,24: Δομιτιανὸς τὸ πρῶτον τὸ Ἀθηναῖον τὸ ἐν Γερμανίᾳ τῇ κάτω (sc. ἔκτισεν).

[67] RIC, V,1, p. 93, n° 322.

[68] C. CICHORIUS, Die Reliefs der Traianssäule, Berlin, 1896, pp. 227–8, pl. XLVIII.

[69] E. RITTERLING, Legio, in: RE, XII,2 (1925), c. 1421.

[70] Cass., Dio, 67,1: Δομιτιανὸς δὲ ἦν μὲν καὶ θρασὺς καὶ ὀργίλος, ἦν δὲ καὶ ἐπίβουλος καὶ κρυψίνους, ὥστε ἀφ' ἑκατέρων τῶν μὲν τὸ προπετές, τῶν δὲ τὸ δολιὸν ἔχων, πολλὰ μὲν ὥσπερ σκηπτὸς ὀξέως ἐμπίπτων τισὶν ἐλυμαίνετο, πολλὰ δὲ καὶ ἐκ παρασκευῆς ἐκακούργει, θεῶν μὲν γὰρ τὴν Ἀθηνᾶν ἐς τὰ μάλιστα ἤγαλλε.
Ce passage ouvre le livre 67 dans l'état où nous l'avons conservé. Comme nous ne disposons, pour cette partie de l'œuvre, que du résumé de Xiphilin, il serait hasardeux de tirer trop de conséquences de cette place privilégiée. En revanche, il ne paraît pas douteux que la suite des idées exprimée par μὲν γάρ ne reflète la pensée de Dion Cassius.

[71] CIL, III, 1076: *Mineruae / Iouis consili/orum partici/pi C(aïus) Caerellius / Sabinus leg(atus) / Aug(usti) leg(ionis) XIII / G(eminae) et Fufidia / Pollitta ei[u]s / uoto.*

[72] Quint., Inst. Or., 10,1,91: reflétant la version officielle des événements, écrit: *Quid tamen his ipsis eius operibus, in quae, donato imperio, iuuenis secesserat, sublimius, doctius, denique omnibus numeris praestantius?*

capitolins, auteur de poèmes sur les combats de Judée et du Capitole, il se proclame le protecteur des lettres et des arts[73]. Fils de la Sabine, il tente d'assurer à une dynastie dont il ne peut prévoir qu'il sera le dernier représentant un patronage aussi prestigieux que celui de *Venus Genetrix*. Aucune divinité ne pouvait offrir à Domitien autant de traits propres à illustrer les aspects de son personnage et les ambitions de son règne que Minerve lui en offrait.

Bibliographie

1. Généralités

P. E. ARIAS, Domiziano, Catane, 1945.
A. DEGRASSI, Domiziano, Dodici Cesari, Quaderni della Radio, XL, Turin, 1955.
K. GROSS, Domitianus, in: Reallexikon für Antike und Christentum, IV (1959), c. 91–109.
S. GSELL, Essai sur le règne de l'empereur Domitien, Paris, 1893.
E. WEYNAND, T. Flauius Domitianus, in: RE, VI,2 (1909), c. 2541–2596.

2. Etudes de détail

G. BENDINELLI, I rilievi domizianei del Palazzo della Cancelleria in Roma, Turin, 1949.
P. H. VON BLANCKENHAGEN, Die flavische Architektur und ihre Dekoration, untersucht am Nervaforum, Berlin, 1940.
I. LANA, I ludi Capitolini di Domiziano, in: Rivista di Filologia e d'Istruzione Classica, n.s., XXIX (1951), pp. 145–160.
H. LAST, On the Flavian Reliefs from the Palazzo della Cancelleria, in: Journal of Roman Studies, XXVIII (1948), pp. 9–14.
V. LUNDSTRÖM, Chalcidicum och Minerva Chalcidica?, in: Strena philologica Upsaliensia (= Festskrift P. Persson), Uppsala, 1922, pp. 369–392.
M. McCRUM–A. G. WOODHEAD, Select Documents of the Principates of the Flavian Emperors, Cambridge, 1961.
F. MAGI, I rilievi flavi del Palazzo della Cancelleria, Rome, 1945.
F. MAGI, I marmi del teatro di Domiziano a Castelgandolfo, in: Rendiconti della pontificia Accademia di Archeologia, XLVI (1973–4), pp. 63–77.
L. MORAWIECKI, The Symbolism of Minerva on the Coins of Domitianus, in: Klio, LIX (1977), pp. 185–193.
A. RUMPF, Römische historische Reliefs, I. Die Reliefs von der Cancelleria, in: Bonner Jahrbücher des Rheinischen Landesmuseum, CLV–VI (1955–6), pp. 112–119.
H. SAUTER, Der römische Kaiserkult bei Martial und Statius, Tübinger Beiträge zur Altertumswissenschaft, XXI, Stuttgart–Berlin, 1934.
K. SCOTT, Le Sacrarium Mineruae de Domitien, in: Revue Archéologique, VI (1935), pp. 69–72.
K. SCOTT, The Imperial Cult under the Flavians, Stuttgart, 1936.
E. SIMON, Zu den flavischen Reliefs von der Cancelleria, in: Jahrbuch des Deutschen Archäologischen Instituts, LXXV (1960), pp. 134–156.
S. J. SIMON, Domitian, Patron of Letters, in: The Classical Bulletin, LI (1975), pp. 58–9.

[73] S. J: SIMON, Domitian, Patron of Letters, in: The Classical Bulletin, LI (1975), pp. 58–9.

Liste des illustrations
(pour les deux articles de J.-L. GIRARD, supra, pp. 203—32 et 233—44)

Die Ideologie des Marskultes unter dem Principat und ihre Vorgeschichte

von Johan H. Croon, Amstelveen*

Inhalt

I. Mars und die augusteïsche Restauration

Augustus hat sich bestrebt, Neugründer des römischen Staates zu werden,[1] und sich somit in die Reihe der großen politischen Schöpfer der Vorzeit gestellt,

---

* An dieser Stelle möchte ich Herrn Dr. W. Haase herzlich danken für viele sprachliche und stilistische Verbesserungen im Text dieses Beitrags.

[1] Im Einklang hiermit steht es, daß er daran gedacht haben soll, sich Romulus nennen zu lassen: Suet., Aug. 7; Cass. Dio 53,16,7; Ovid, Fasti II,133—144 läßt ihn den Romulus weit übertreffen:

> Romule, concedes. facit hic tua magna tuendo
> moenia: tu dederas transilienda Remo.
> te Tatius parvique Cures Caeninaque sensit:
> hoc duce Romanum est solis utrumque latus.
> tu breve nescio quid victae telluris habebas:
> quodcumque est alto sub Iove, Caesar habet.
> tu rapis, hic castas duce se iubet esse maritas.
> tu recipis luco, reppulit ille nefas.
> vis tibi grata fuit: florent sub Caesare leges.
> tu domini nomen, principis ille tenet.
> te Remus incusat: veniam dedit hostibus ille.
> caelestem fecit te pater, ille patrem.

freilich in etwas versteckter Weise: denn unter die Fahne der *libertas restituta* konnte eine allzu öffentliche Neuordnung schwerlich passen. Neugründer also, aber auf alten, teilweise uralten Fundamenten. Zu der wesentlich monarchischen, aber hinter einer republikanischen Fassade versteckten Verfassung stimmte es, daß vor allem auf die republikanische Zeit zurückgegriffen wurde, daß aber auch Elemente der Königszeit nicht ganz fehlten. Es war ja möglich, gerade die ersten Jahrhunderte der Königszeit auch unter dem Blickwinkel der Ideologie der *libertas* einzubegreifen. Die unverhüllte Alleinherrschaft, die leicht in eine Gewaltherrschaft übergehen konnte und geradezu mit dem Begriff der Tyrannis identisch zu sein neigte[2], an der der Diktator Caesar zugrunde gegangen war, wurde namentlich mit der Regierung der etruskischen Könige assoziiert.

Nun hat die augusteïsche Neuordnung sich bekanntlich allmählich vollzogen[3]. Dabei ist es eine auffallende Begleiterscheinung, daß das ideologische Fundament der neuen Staatsordnung schon sehr früh in voller Kraft erscheint und daß in dieser Hinsicht kaum eine allmähliche Entwicklung sichtbar wird.

Damit kommen wir auf die augusteïsche Restauration der altrömischen Religion zu sprechen, ein Kapitel der römischen Religionsgeschichte, dem von jeher in der Wissenschaft besondere Aufmerksamkeit gewidmet worden ist[4]. Man hat dabei mit Recht betont, daß das großartige Restaurationsprogramm nur bei oberflächlicher Betrachtung ein steriles Unternehmen gewesen zu sein scheint. Zwar hatte im letzten Jahrhundert der Republik der alte Staatsgottesdienst viel von seiner Bedeutung verloren, aber ein positiver Atheïsmus war noch nicht verbreitet[5], und schon in den ersten Jahren von Octavians politischer Betätigung spürte man überall eine Neigung zu neuem Glauben und tiefer Religiosität. Die Jahre der Bürgerkriege hatten ein tiefes Trauma hinterlassen, und das Gefühl war allgemein verbreitet, daß die Sünden der Väter (*delicta maiorum*: Hor., Od. III, 6, 1) gesühnt werden könnten durch Wiederherstellung der von ihnen

---

[2] Cicero, De Rep. I,65—68; vgl. L. Wickert, Neue Forschungen zum römischen Principat, ANRW II, 1, hrsg. v. H. Temporini (Berlin—New York 1975), 3—76, insbes. 21—23; 34—37.

[3] Vgl. Tac. Ann. I,2,1: *insurgere paulatim*.

[4] Ausführliche Behandlung bei K. Latte, Römische Religionsgeschichte (München 1960), 294—311; kürzer und sachlicher bei G. Wissowa, Religion und Kultus der Römer (München ²1912), 73—78; mit manchen theoretischen Darlegungen bei F. Altheim, Römische Religionsgeschichte III (Berlin—Leipzig 1933), 26—67; 67—100 (der letzte Abschnitt, 'Die Religion der augusteïschen Zeit', ist die Wiedergabe einer früheren Rede); knappe, aber klare Zusammenfassung bei H. J. Rose, Ancient Roman Religion (London 1948), 106—124; R. M. Ogilvie, The Romans and their Gods (London 1969), 112—123; vgl. außerdem W. W. Fowler, The Religious Experience of the Roman People (London 1911, Nachdr. 1933), 428—451; A. D. Nock, The Augustan Restoration (Class. Review 39, 1925, 60—67), in: Ders., Essays on Religion and the Ancient World I (Oxford 1972), 16—25; R. Syme, The Roman Revolution (Oxford ²1952), 446—449; H. H. Scullard, From the Gracchi to Nero (London ³1972), 223—224; 235—236; 241—244; J. Beaujeu, Le paganisme romain sous le Haut Empire, ANRW II, 16,1, hrsg. v. W. Haase (Berlin—New York 1978), 10f.; W. Fauth, Römische Religion im Spiegel der 'Fasti' des Ovid, ebd. 170ff.

[5] Rose, a.a.O. 108.

vernachlässigten Kulte[6]. Außerdem war der Princeps selber kein (oder besser: in seinem tiefsten Wesen nicht ein) zynischer Intellektueller, sondern innerlich überzeugt von einer Mission. Und wenn es schon wahr sein mag, daß die Gebildeten größtenteils sich den philosophischen Strömungen zuwandten und daß große Massen des Volkes in orientalischen Kulten ihr Heil suchten[7], so bleibt es doch merkwürdig, daß der vermeintlich tote und begrabene Staatskult noch über 400 Jahre weitergelebt hat und, wichtiger noch, daß die christlichen Schriftsteller ihre schärfsten Angriffe gerade gegen die altrömischen Religionsformen richteten[8].

Das großartige Restaurationsprogramm hatte verschiedene Aspekte und verzweigte sich auf verschiedene Gebiete. Zu nennen wäre der Wiederaufbau von 82 Tempeln in der Stadt Rom[9], die Wiederbelebung alter Kulte und der Priesterschaft der Fratres Arvales[10], die Wiedereinführung der Ludi Saeculares[11] und daneben insbesondere die Hervorhebung von zwei Göttern, die jeder für sich einen besonderen Aspekt der augusteïschen Religion vertreten: Apollo[12] und Mars.

Apollo war natürlich der Gott von Actium, der Octavian den Sieg versprochen hatte[13]. Ihm wurde der Tempel auf dem Palatin geweiht, bei dem die berühmte Bibliothek eingerichtet wurde (hier schon *in solo privato*!). Aber Augustus' Verehrung des Apollo läßt sich sicher früher datieren. Schon 40 v. Chr. erscheint Apollo bei einer Zwölfgöttermahlzeit[14], und Verg. Ecl. IV, 10: *Casta fave Lucina, tuus iam regnat Apollo* wurde laut dem Kommentar des Servius in dem Sinne verstanden, daß Lucina Octavia sei, deren Bruder Octavian

---

[6] OGILVIE, a. a. O. 113; ALTHEIM, a. a. O. 26.

[7] Übrigens protestiert ALTHEIM, a. a. O. 73 gegen eine scharfe Trennung zwischen den Neigungen von Gelehrten einerseits und der Masse andererseits.

[8] FOWLER, a. a. O. 429.

[9] Mon. Ancyr. 20: *Duo et octoginta templa deum in urbe consul sextum ex auctoritate senatus refeci.* NOCK, a. a. O. 23—24 zählt auch noch eine ganze Reihe von restaurierten Heiligtümern außerhalb Roms auf.

[10] Vgl. J. SCHEID, Les prêtres officiels sous les empereurs julio-claudiens, ANRW II, 16,1, hrsg. v. W. HAASE (Berlin—New York 1978), 610—654, bes. 623f., und E. OLSHAUSEN, „Über die römischen Ackerbrüder". Geschichte eines Kultes, ebd. 820—832.

[11] Vgl. P. BRIND'AMOUR, L'origine des Jeux Séculaires, ANRW II, 16,2, hrsg. v. W. HAASE (Berlin—New York 1978), 1334—1417.

[12] Zu Apollo vgl. nach J. GAGÉ, L'Apollon Romain, bes. DERS., L'Apollon impérial, garant des 'Fata Romana', unt. in diesem Band (ANRW II, 17,2).

[13] Propertius 4,6,15—58.

[14] Suet. Aug. 70,1—2: (eine Notiz, die freiich aus einer Verspottung dieses Vorgehens stammt, ALTHEIM a. a. O. 65): *Cena quoque eius secretior in fabulis fuit, quae vulgo δωδεκάθεος vocabatur; in qua deorum dearumque habitu discubuisse convivas et ipsum pro Apolline ornatum non Antoni modo epistulae . . . exprobrant, sed et sine auctore notissimi versus: . . .* (es folgt ein anonymes Schimpfgedicht). Vgl. O. WEINREICH, Art. Zwölfgötter, Ausführliches Lexikon der griechischen und römischen Mythologie VI (1924—1937), 764ff., bes. 804ff. = DERS., Ausgewählte Schriften II. 1922—1937, hrsg. v. G. WILLE (Amsterdam 1973), 555ff., bes. 606ff.

also Apollo[15]. Nachher spielt der palatinische Tempel eine bedeutende Rolle in den Ludi Saeculares von 17 v. Chr., wobei sonst die capitolinischen Götter Jupiter und Juno im Mittelpunkt standen. Jedenfalls konnte Apollo als der Gott der kosmischen Ordnung, der bisher in der römischen Religion einen ziemlich geringen Platz eingenommen hatte, sehr wohl in den Vordergrund geschoben werden im Rahmen der staatlichen Neuordnung. Wieder ist es hier auffallend, daß die ideologischen Grundlagen der faktischen politischen Neugestaltung lange vorausgehen.

Griechisches Wesen wurde hier also mit römischer Staatsräson verknüpft. In diesem Zusammenhang lohnt es sich, R. SYME zu zitieren[16]: *"Though the national spirit of Rome was a reaction against Hellas[17], there was no harm, but every advantage, in invoking the better sort of Greek deities on the right side, . . .".* Der Apollokult kann demnach als die griechisch-hellenistische Komponente in der augusteischen Religion betrachtet werden[18].

Wie steht es aber mit der zweiten in den Vordergrund gerückten Gottheit, mit Mars? Dabei geht es hier in erster Linie um den Kult des Mars Ultor, dem der Princeps sein eigenes Forum geweiht hat. Auch hier hat man in der modernen Forschung an eine griechische Komponente gedacht, sogar an eine Umbeugung des altrömischen Marskultes zu einer Verehrung, die weit mehr mit dem griechischen Ares als mit dem italisch-römischen Mars zu tun gehabt habe[19]. Der wichtigste Grund für diese Annahme war die Verbindung von Mars und Venus in diesem Kult; die Verbindung an sich ist schon spätestens 217 v. Chr. bei einem *lectisternium* für zwölf Götter bezeugt[20] und gehört da dem *Graeco*

---

[15] Außerdem datiert OGILVIE a.a.O. die Gründung des palatinischen Tempels schon auf 36 v. Chr.

[16] The Roman Revolution 448.

[17] Ganz zu schweigen davon, daß die orientalischen Kulte aus dem *pomerium*, ja aus dem Stadtgebiet hinausgedrängt wurden: Cass. Dio 53,2,4: καὶ τὰ μὲν ἱερὰ τὰ Αἰγύπτια οὐκ ἐξεδέξατο εἴσω τοῦ πωμηρίου; 54,6,6: τά τε ἱερὰ τὰ Αἰγύπτια ἐπεσιόντα αὖθις ἐς τὸ ἄστυ ἀνέστειλεν, ἀπειπὼν μηδένα μηδὲ ἐν τῷ προαστείῳ ἐντὸς ὀγδόου ἡμισταδίου ποιεῖν. Vgl. dazu R. M. KRILL, Roman Paganism under the Antonines and Severans, ANRW II,16,1, hrsg. v. W. HAASE (Berlin—New York 1978), 29.

[18] Gleichwie in der eigentlichen politischen Sphäre die heroisierende Tendenz des Augustustitels und die ersten Ansätze zu einer Kaiserverehrung an hellenistische Vorbilder anknüpfen.

[19] HERMANSEN (s. die Bibliographie unten S. 275; hier und im folgenden werden Werke, die dort verzeichnet sind, nur mit Autornamen angedeutet) schreibt (24f.): „Eine wirkliche Hellenisierung ist der Mars Ultor-Kult, wo Mars in gleicher Weise wie an einzelnen anderen Stätten mit Venus gepaart ist. Dies ist durch und durch griechisch, eine von der Literatur abhängige Neuschöpfung des gleichen Ursprungs wie das Verhältnis zwischen Mars und Juno, wo man Ares—Hera kopiert, und zwischen Mars und Pavor—Pallor, was Deimos—Phobos und Ares wiedergibt. Aber all dies hat nicht den stadtrömischen und italischen Marskult berührt" (Sperrung von mir, J. H. C.). Bezeichnenderweise schreibt derselbe Autor (18): „Aber was im Übrigem über den Tempel und den Kult des Mars Ultor bekannt ist, verrät keinen griechischen Einfluß".

[20] Livius 22,10,9: *sex pulvinaria in conspectu fuerunt, Iovi ac Iunoni unum, alterum Neptuno ac Minervae, tertium Marti ac Veneri, quartum Apollini ac Dianae, quintum Volcano ac Vestae, sextum Mercurio et Cereri.* SCHOLZ 34.

ritu vollzogenen Kult zu, ist aber sonst eigentlich literarischen Ursprungs. Daneben hatten natürlich auch dynastische Erwägungen eine Rolle gespielt. Die *gens Iulia* stammte ja von Venus ab, und insbesondere hatte Caesar „Ares und Aphrodite" als seine Voreltern genannt[21]. Nun war Mars aber auch der Urvater des Römertums in der literarischen Tradition und im Kult ein uralter italischer und stadtrömischer Gott. Es lohnt sich daher, erneut die Frage aufzuwerfen, warum denn Augustus diesen Gott so offensichtlich ins Zentrum gestellt hat, und dies sogar im Herzen der Stadt, auf dem Kapitol und in seinem eigenen Forum. Dazu wollen wir die Zeugnisse über den Kult des Mars Ultor, insbesondere die zwei Hauptzeugnisse, einer genaueren Untersuchung unterwerfen.

II. Die Hauptzeugnisse für den Mars Ultor-Kult

Im Jahre 42 v. Chr. hatte Octavian bei Philippi dem Mars einen Tempel gelobt, in dem der Gott als Ultor verehrt werden sollte, wenn er seiner, 'der besseren' Sache Gnade verleihen würde[22]. Daß das Gelübde nicht gleich in Erfüllung ging, wäre zu erklären aus den politischen Wirren der Folgezeit, obwohl in der verhältnismäßig ruhigen Periode nach den Verträgen von Brundisium und Tarent, als er sich, gestützt von Agrippa und Maecenas, daran machte, die Ziegelstadt in eine Marmorstadt zu verwandeln, dafür Gelegenheit hätte gefunden werden können. Eine neue Gelegenheit war vorhanden, als er kurz nach Actium anfing, die 82 Tempel zu restaurieren (s. o. Anm. 9). Indessen gab es einen neuen Anlaß, als die im Jahre 53 von den Parthern erbeuteten Feldzeichen zurückgegeben wurden. Die Rückgabe wurde wie ein regelrechter Sieg gefeiert[23]; offenbar konnte die Idee der Rache von dem Geschehen des Jahres 42 auf das des Jahres 53 übertragen werden. Und nun wurde wirklich 20 v. Chr. ein Tempel für Mars Ultor auf dem Kapitol geweiht[24]. Danach dauerte es wieder viele

[21] Syll³. 760 (Ephesus 48 v. Chr.): αἱ πόλεις αἱ ἐν τῇ Ἀσίᾳ καὶ οἱ [δῆμοι] καὶ τὰ ἔθνη Γάϊον Ἰούλιον Γαΐο[υ υἱ]ὸν Καίσαρα, τὸν ἀρχιερέα καὶ αὐτοκράτορα καὶ τὸ δεύτερον ὕπατον τὸν ἀπὸ Ἄρεως καὶ Ἀφροδε[ί]της θεὸν ἐπιφανῆ καὶ κοινὸν τοῦ ἀνθρωπίνου βίου σωτῆρα. Latte (oben Anm. 4) 302. Die Verbindung von Mars und Venus im Tempel des Mars Ultor bei Ovid, Tristia II, 295—296: *venerit in magni templum, tua* (sc. *Augusti*) *munera, Martis: stat Venus Ultori iuncta, vir* (= *coniunx*, sc. *Vulcanus*) *ante fores.* Die gleiche Verbindung im Pantheon des Agrippa: Cass. Dio 53,27,2: προσαγορεύεται δὲ οὕτω τάχα μὲν ὅτι πολλῶν θεῶν εἰκόνας ἐν τοῖς ἀγάλμασι, τῷ τε τοῦ Ἄρεως καὶ τῷ τῆς Ἀφροδίτης, ἔλαβε, . . . CIL X, 8373 (Feriale Cumanum) erwähnt eine *supplicatio Marti Ultori Veneri* [*Genetrici*] anläßlich des Geburtstages des Caesar.

[22] Suetonius, Aug. 29,2 (u. S. 257); vgl. Ovid, Fasti, V,571—577 (u. S. 252).

[23] Augustus hebt die Wiedergewinnung der *signa* als eine imponierende persönliche Leistung hervor: Mon. Ancyr. 29 (s. u. Anm. 36); Cassius Dio (s. nächste Anm.).

[24] Cassius Dio 54,8,2—4: καὶ αὐτοὺς (sc. τοὺς αἰχμαλώτους) ἐκεῖνος ὡς καὶ πολέμῳ τινὶ τὸν Πάρθον νενικηκὼς ἔλαβε· καὶ γὰρ ⟨ἐπὶ τούτοις⟩ ἐφρόνει μέγα, λέγων ὅτι τὰ πρότερόν ποτε ἐν ταῖς μάχαις ἀπολόμενα ἀκονιτὶ ἐκεκόμιστο. ἀμέλει καὶ θυσίας ἐπ' αὐτοῖς καὶ νεὼν Ἄρεως Τιμωροῦ ἐν τῷ Καπιτωλίῳ, κατὰ τὸ τοῦ Διὸς τοῦ Φερετρίου ζήλωμα,

Jahre, bis der ursprüngliche Plan zur Ausführung gelangte. Am 1. August 2 v. Chr. wurde der große Tempel des Mars Ultor auf dem dafür bestimmten Augustusforum eingeweiht[25]. Über dieses Heiligtum und dem ihm verliehenen Statut gibt es ausführliche Mitteilungen in zwei Hauptzeugnissen, die wir jetzt genauer besprechen wollen: eines aus den 'Fasten' des Ovid, wobei der große moderne Kommentar von BÖMER zur Verfügung steht, das andere aus Cassius Dio, bei dem ein solches Hilfsmittel leider fehlt.

Ovidius, Fasti V, 545–598:

545   *Sed quid et Orion et cetera sidera mundo*
      cedere festinant noxque coartat iter?
    quid solito citius liquido iubar aequore tollit
      candida Lucifero praeveniente dies?
    fallor, an arma sonant? non fallimur, arma sonabant:
550   *Mars venit et veniens bellica signa dedit.*
    Ultor ad ipse suos caelo descendit honores
      templaque in Augusto conspicienda foro:
    et deus est ingens et opus, debebat in Urbe
      non aliter nati Mars habitare sui.
555   *digna Giganteis haec sunt delubra tropaeis:*
      hinc fera Gradivum bella movere decet,
    seu quis ab Eoo nos impius orbe lacesset,
      seu quis ab occiduo sole domandus erit.
    perspicit armipotens operis fastigia summi
560   *et probat invictos summa tenere deos,*
    perspicit in foribus diversae tela figurae
      armaque terrarum milite victa suo.
    hinc videt Aenean oneratum pondere caro
      et tot Iuleae nobilitatis avos,
565   *hinc videt Iliaden umeris ducis arma ferentem,*
      claraque dispositis acta subesse viris;
    spectat et Augusto praetextum nomine templum
      et visum lecto Caesare maius opus.
    voverat hoc iuvenis tunc, cum pia sustulit arma:
570   *a tantis princeps incipiendus erat.*

πρὸς τὴν τῶν σημείων ἀνάθεσιν καὶ ψηφισθῆναι ἐκέλευσε καὶ ἐποίησε. καὶ προσέτι καὶ ἐπὶ κέλητος ἐς τὴν πόλιν ἐσήλασε καὶ ἁψῖδι τροπαιοφόρῳ ἐτιμήθη. ταῦτα μὲν ἐπ' ἐκείνοις ὕστερον ἐπράχθη. Es ist dieser Tempel, der auf den Münzen des Augustus dargestellt ist (weiteres unten S. 270ff.), wie schon CHAMBALU 730 mit Recht betont hat, denn diese stammen von 20 v. Chr.; außerdem ist auch ein kleiner Rundtempel abgebildet. Vgl. aber auch unten Anm. 30.

[25] Mon. Ancyr. 21: *In privato solo Martis Ultoris templum forumque Augustum ex manibiis feci . . . Dona ex manibiis in Capitolio et in aede divi Juli et in aede Apollinis et in aede Vestae et in templo Martis Ultoris consecravi.*

ille manus tendens hinc stanti milite iusto,
       hinc coniuratis talia dicta dedit:
'si mihi bellandi pater est Vestaeque sacerdos
       auctor et ulcisci numen utrumque paro,
575 *Mars, ades et satia scelerato sanguine ferrum,*
       stetque favor causa pro meliore tuus!
templa feres et me victore vocaberis Ultor.'
       voverat et fuso laetus ab hoste redit.
nec satis est meruisse semel cognomina Marti:
580   *persequitur Parthi signa retenta manu.*
gens fuit et campis et equis et tuta sagittis
       et circumfusis invia fluminibus.
addiderant animos Crassorum funera genti,
       cum periit miles signaque duxque simul.
585 *signa, decus belli, Parthus Romana tenebat,*
       Romanaeque aquilae signifer hostis erat!
isque pudor mansisset adhuc, nisi fortibus armis
       Caesaris Ausoniae protegerentur opes.
ille notas veteres et longi dedecus aevi
590   *sustulit. agnorunt signa recepta suos.*
quid tibi nunc solitae mitti post terga sagittae,
       quid loca, quid rapidi profuit usus equi?
Parthe, refers aquilas, victos quoque porrigis arcus:
       pignora iam nostri nulla pudoris habes.
595 *rite deo templumque datum nomenque bis ulto,*
       et meritus voti debita solvit honor.
sollemnes ludos Circo celebrate, Quirites!
       non visa est fortem scaena decere deum.

545 „Doch warum eilen Orion und die anderen Sterne, den Himmel zu
verlassen, und (warum) kürzt die Nacht ihren Weg? Warum erhebt
der helle Tag, und vor ihm der Morgenstern, sein strahlendes Licht
schneller als gewöhnlich aus der karen Flut? Täusche ich mich? Oder
klirren (da) Waffen? Ich täusche mich nicht, es klirrten (da) Waffen!
550 Mars kommt, und im Kommen gab er Kriegssignale. Der Rächer
steigt selbst vom Himmel herab, um sein Fest und seinen Tempel auf
dem Forum des Augustus anzuschauen. Gewaltig ist Mars und gewaltig sein Tempel. Anders hätte er (auch) in der Stadt seines Sohnes
nicht wohnen dürfen. Zu diesem Heiligtum gehören Trophäen aus
555 Gigantenkämpfen; Gradivus mag von hier aus wilde Kriege beginnen,
sei es, daß ein ruchloser (Feind) uns im Osten reizt, sei es, daß einer
im Westen unterworfen werden muß. Der Waffengott erhebt den
Blick zu den Zinnen seines Tempels, und er ist damit zufrieden, daß
die unbesiegten Götter die höchsten Stellen innehaben. An den Türen
560 sieht er Waffen von verschiedener Gestalt und aus (allen) Ländern
Rüstungen, die durch seine Soldaten erbeutet (besiegt) wurden. Hier

565 sieht er Aeneas, mit seiner teueren Last beladen, und so viele Ahnen
des julischen Adels; hier sieht er den Sohn der Ilia, wie er die Waffen
des (besiegten feindlichen) Führers auf den Schultern trägt und wie
die Ruhmestaten der Reihe nach unter jedem Helden (in einer Inschrift aufgezeichnet) sind. Er sieht auch, daß die Front des Tempels
mit dem Namen des Augustus versehen ist, und wenn er den Namen
des Caesar gelesen hat, scheint ihm das Heiligtum (noch) wertvoller.
(Der Kaiser) hatte es als junger Mann gelobt, als er aus Pietät (für
seinen Vater) zu den Waffen griff. Mit einem solchen Werk mußte
570 der Princeps (seinen Weg) beginnen. Hier standen die Soldaten der
gerechten Sache, dort die Verschworenen, (da) erhob er seine Hände
und rief: „Wenn (Caesar als) mein Vater und (als) der Priester der
Vesta mich zum Kampfe ruft und ich mich aufmache, beide Gott-
575 heiten zu rächen, (dann,) Mars, steh mir bei und sättige das Eisen mit
Verbrecherblut. Deine Gnade stehe auf der Seite der besseren Sache!
Einen Tempel wirst du erhalten, und wenn ich siege, wirst du den
Beinamen 'Rächer' (*Ultor*) erhalten." (Dies) war sein Gelübde, und
nach seinem Siege über den Feind kehrte er im Jubel heim.
Es genügte ihm aber nicht, für Mars den Beinamen einmal verdient
580 zu haben; er ging aus auf die Feldzeichen, die von der Hand der
Parther zurückgehalten wurden. Diese waren ein Volk, das sicher
war durch seine (weiten) Ebenen, seine Pferde und seine Pfeile, und
das unerreichbar war durch die Flüsse, die es umgeben. Der Tod des
Crassus und seines Sohnes hatte dem Volke den Mut gestärkt, als zu
gleicher Zeit die Truppen, der Feldherr und die Zeichen untergingen.
585 Römische Feldzeichen, die Sinnbilder der Waffenehre, besaß der
Parther, und ein Feind war der Feldzeichenträger des römischen
Legionsadlers! Und diese Schmach hätte bis heute angedauert, wenn
das Reich des Abendlandes nicht von Caesars tapferen Waffen ge-
schützt würde. Er hat die alte Schande und die Schmach eines (gan-
590 zen) langen Zeitalters getilgt; die zurückgewonnenen Feldzeichen er-
kannten ihre (alten) Besitzer wieder. Was haben dir, Parther, die
Pfeile nun genützt, die ihr gewöhnlich von hinten (auf den Gegner)
schießt, was das Gelände, was der Gebrauch der schnellen Pferde?
Du gibst die Adler wieder, und du reichst auch die besiegten Bogen
her. Jetzt besitzest du keine Zeichen unserer Schande mehr!
595 Mit Recht wurde der Tempel und der Name dem Gotte gegeben, der
(uns) zweimal rächte. Die Verpflichtung des Gelübdes wurde durch
verdiente Ehrung getilgt. Begeht im Circus die feierlichen Spiele,
Quiriten; die Bühne schien nicht zu dem Kriegsgott zu passen."

(Übersetzung: F. BÖMER).

Die Partie enthält fünf Teile:
Erstens (545—552) die Epiphanie des Gottes. Dann (553—568) die Beschreibung des Tempels, erst (—558) durch die Augen des Dichters, darauf
durch die des Gottes. Sodann (569—578) das Gelübde bei Philippi und der

zweite Stiftungsgrund, die Wiedergewinnung der Feldzeichen (579–594); schließlich eine Zusammenfassung mit Aufruf an die Bürger, den Spielen beizuwohnen (595–598). Zu jedem Teil einige Bemerkungen (Weiteres im Kommentar von BÖMER):

Die Epiphanie mit Waffengeklirr bei Sonnenaufgang ist rein literarisch ausgearbeitet. Hier liegt das traditionelle Bild des Kriegsgottes vor, der auf Erden erscheint, um sich von den Menschen ehren zu lassen.

Im zweiten Teil ist 555 eine schwierige Zeile: bedeutet *Giganteis* nur „gigantisch"[26], und handelt es sich um Trophäen an den Türen, oder war an dem Giebel ein Gigantenkampf dargestellt? – Über *Gradivus* (556) s. u. S. 267. – In *impius* (557) klingt schon das Thema des *iustum bellum* auf; der Kriegsgott ist nicht der Patron der Waffengewalt ohne weiteres, sondern erscheint als der Beschützer der gerechten Sache; auch in auswärtigen Kriegen sollte die römische Seite die *causa melior* (576) vergegenwärtigen; freilich wird dies wieder abgeschwächt durch *domandus* (558). – In der zweiten Hälfte dieses Teiles, wo der Gott selber der Zuschauer wird, erscheinen die Gottheiten, denen neben Mars an den Zinnen Platz eingeräumt ist[27], und dann verweilt der Blick auf der Außenseite des Forums, wo die große Ahnengalerie zu sehen ist, versehen mit Inschriften über ihre Taten[28], anfangend mit Aeneas, der auf seinen Schultern seinen Vater Anchises trägt, dem Inbegriff der Treue gegenüber dem Vaterland, und endend mit einem nach dem Tempel zurückkehrenden Blick: „wenn er den Namen des Caesar gelesen hat, scheint ihm das Heiligtum (noch) wertvoller" (568, Übersetzung BÖMER). Das Bild wird hiermit ganz verschoben von *fera bella movere* zu einer Darstellung des Mars als Beschützers der augusteïschen Neuordnung, gestützt auf nationale Tradition.

Im dritten Teil herrscht durchaus der Gedanke des *iustum bellum* (*pia arma, miles iustus, causa melior*) vor. In erster Linie wird natürlich der Name Ultor begründet durch die Rache für den Tod des Vaters, aber bemerkenswerterweise wird gleich hinzugefügt: *numen utrumque* (574), wobei wohl Divus Iulius und Vesta zu verstehen sind. Es ist also zugleich eine Rache für das geschändete Vaterland.

Der vierte Teil bringt eine Überraschung. Für die von den Parthern zurückgegebenen Feldzeichen war doch schon der Rundtempel auf dem Kapitol geweiht (s. o. Anm. 24). Nun ist das Einweihungsdatum dieses Tempels nicht

---

[26] So übersetzt von W. GERLACH (München 1960).

[27] G. B. PIGHI, Le 'dee invitte' del tempio di Marte Ultore, Atti Accad. delle Scienze dell' Istituto di Bologna, Cl. di Sc. Mor., Redinconti 59 (1970–71), 39–46 (ein Artikel, den ich nur nach einem Auszug kenne) will in 560 *deas invictas* (= Victorien) lesen: eine für die Beseitigung des *dedecus*, die andere für die des *scelus*.

[28] Ausführliche Behandlung bei A. VON PREMERSTEIN, Art. Elogium, RE V, 2 (1905), 2444–2449: Die Elogien auf dem Augustusforum in Rom. CIL I², S. 186ff. Zu vergleichen wären Verg., Georg. III, 12–39 (insbesondere 34 *spirantia signa*) und Verg., Aen. VII, 177–182. Kaum richtig hat man hierbei auch Aen. I,453ff. und VI,20ff. herangezogen; denn bei dem Junotempel in Carthago sind es sicherlich Arbeiten am Gebäude selbst, bei dem Tempel von Cumae ist es die Türdekoration.

bekannt[29], aber es ist auffallend, daß Ovid den Passus unter den 12. Mai gestellt hat, während andererseits der 1. August als Datum des Tempels auf dem Forum überliefert ist, ein Tag, der mit Pferderennen gefeiert wurde[30]. Weil nun auch Ludi Martiales für den 12. Mai bezeugt sind[31], konnte man denken, daß Ovid das Stiftungsdatum des Tempels von 20 v. Chr. mit dem des Tempels von 2 v. Chr. verwechselt, ja sogar die beiden Tempel verwechselt habe[32]. Dies letztere ist allerdings kaum vorstellbar. Wie sollte denn ausgerechnet dieser Mann die Baugeschichte seiner eigenen Stadt nicht kennen? Dabei taucht die Frage auf, ob vielleicht die Feldzeichen im Jahre 2 v. Chr. von dem älteren Tempel in den neuen überführt worden sind. Was Augustus im 'Monumentum Ancyranum' (c. 29) darüber schreibt[33], läßt dies vermuten, da er in c. 21 (s. o. Anm. 25) nur über den Tempel von 2. v. Chr. redet; außerdem hat der neue Tempel, natürlich durch seine großartige Anlage, den älteren nachher ganz überschattet[34]. Über diese Vermutung werden wir aber bei dem zur Verfügung stehenden Material wohl nicht hinauskommen.

Im kurzen Schlußteil fällt erstens die Zusammenfassung mit den Worten *bis ulto* auf; der offenbare Unterschied zwischen den beiden Stiftungsgründen wird ganz beiseite geschoben: einerseits die Rache mit Waffengewalt bei Philippi und

[29] Latte 303 Anm. 7.

[30] Cassius Dio 60,5,3: ἐν γὰρ δὴ τῇ τοῦ Αὐγούστου νουμηνίᾳ, ἐν ᾗ ἐγεγέννητο, ἠγωνίζοντο μὲν ἵπποι, οὐ δι' ἐκεῖνον δέ, ἀλλ' ὅτι ὁ τοῦ Ἄρεως ναὸς ἐν ταύτῃ καθιέρωτο καὶ διὰ τοῦτο ἐτησίοις ἀγῶσιν ἐτετίμητο. Meistens wird angenommen, daß die Spiele, die Augustus in einem Brief an Livia erwähnt, mit diesen identisch sind: Suet. Claud. 4,1: *Collocutus sum cum Tiberio, ut mandasti, mea Livia, quid nepoti tuo Tiberio* (sc. *Claudio*) *faciendum esset ludis Martialibus.* L. Morawiecki, Le Monoptère sur les monnaies de bronze du temps d'Auguste, EOS 64, 1976, 59—82 sucht zu erweisen, daß es nur einen einzigen Tempel des Mars Ultor gegeben habe, nämlich den aus dem Jahre 2 v. Chr., für den zwei Daten wichtig sind, der 12. Mai als Einweihungsdatum und der 1. August als Eröffnungsdatum. S. 66 bemerkt er, daß, wenn der 12. Mai das Datum der Übertragung der Feldzeichen in einen (gleich welchen) Tempel auf dem Kapitol gewesen wäre, dies erst der 12. Mai 18 v. Chr. gewesen sein könnte, da Augustus erst am 12./13. Oktober 19 zurückkehrte. Nach Morawiecki's Ansicht haben die Münzen mit dem kleinen Tempel (vgl. oben Anm. 24 und unten Anm. 87) überhaupt nichts mit einem Mars Ultor-Tempel auf dem Kapitol zu tun, sondern zeigen einen Tempel in Ephesos, der einer Anfangsstufe eines Kultus des Augustus zugehört. (Zum Augustuskult in Ephesos vgl. jetzt D. Knibbe, Ephesos vom Beginn der römischen Herrschaft in Kleinasien bis zum Ende der Principatszeit, ANRW II, 7,2, hrsg. v. H. Temporini [Berlin—New York 1980], 785 f.) Ich möchte noch bemerken, daß Morawiecki zwar das Zeugnis des Cassius Dio 54,8,3 (oben Anm. 24) nennt, daß er aber, nachdem er die numismatische Unterstützung dieses Zeugnisses zu entkräften versucht hat, im weiteren gar nicht das Zeugnis zu widerlegen versucht. Er notiert bloß, daß die anderen Testimonien alle nur einen Tempel voraussetzen.

[31] P. Herz, Kaiserfeste der Prinzipatszeit, ANRW II, 16,2, hrsg. v. W. Haase (Berlin—New York 1978), 1149 gibt den 12. Mai als Dedikationsdatum des Mars Ultor-Tempels an. Ebenso C. J. Simpson, The Date of Dedication of the Temple of Mars Ultor, Journal of Roman Studies 67, 1977, 91—94.

[32] Chambalu 731.

[33] S. u. Anm. 36.

[34] Chambalu 731.

andererseits die Rache (die gar keine eigentliche Rache war) für den Tod des Crassus und für die Schmähung durch die Erbeutung der römischen Feldzeichen. Das führt zu der Frage, welche Bedeutung der Rachegedanke noch in der Friedenszeit von 2 v. Chr. hatte. Mit dieser Frage werden wir uns aber im nächsten Abschnitt (unten S. 259–268) zu beschäftigen haben.

Das zweite Thema, der Aufruf zur Beiwohnung der Spiele im Circus, bietet einen Übergang zum zweiten Hauptzeugnis, der Überlieferung des Tempelstatuts bei Cassius Dio 55, 10, 2–8:

(2) . . . Ἄρει, ἑαυτὸν δὲ καὶ τοὺς ἐγγόνους, ὁσάκις ἂν ἐθελήσωσι, τούς τε ἐκ τῶν παίδων ἐξιόντας καὶ ἐς τοὺς ἐφήβους ἐγγραφομένους ἐκεῖσε πάντως ἀφικνεῖσθαι, καὶ τοὺς ἐπὶ τὰς ἀρχὰς τὰς ἐκδήμους στελλομένους ἐκεῖθεν ἀφορμᾶσθαι, (3) τάς τε γνώμας τὰς περὶ τῶν νικητηρίων ἐκεῖ τὴν βουλὴν ποιεῖσθαι, καὶ τοὺς πέμψαντας αὐτὰ τῷ Ἄρει τούτῳ καὶ τὸ σκῆπτρον καὶ τὸν στέφανον ἀνατιθέναι, καὶ ἐκείνους τε καὶ τοὺς ἄλλους τοὺς τὰς ἐπινικίους τιμὰς λαμβάνοντας ἐν τῇ ἀγορᾷ χαλκοῦς ἵστασθαι, (4) ἄν τέ ποτε σημεῖα στρατιωτικὰ ἐς πολεμίους ἁλόντα ἀνακομισθῇ, ἐς τὸν ναὸν αὐτὰ τίθεσθαι, καὶ πανήγυρίν τινα πρὸς τοῖς ἀναβασμοῖς αὐτοῦ ὑπὸ τῶν ἀεὶ ἱλαρχούντων ποιεῖσθαι, ἧλόν τε αὐτῷ ὑπὸ τῶν τιμητευσάντων προσπήγνυσθαι, (5) καὶ τήν τε παράσχεσιν τῶν ἵππων τῶν ἐς τὴν ἱπποδρομίαν ἀγωνιουμένων καὶ τὴν τοῦ ναοῦ φυλακὴν καὶ βουλευταῖς ἐργολαβεῖν ἐξεῖναι, καθάπερ ἐπί τε τοῦ Ἀπόλλωνος καὶ ἐπὶ τοῦ Διὸς τοῦ Καπιτωλίου ἐνενομοθέτητο. (6) ἐπὶ μὲν τούτοις τὸ μέγαρον ἐκεῖνο ὁ Αὔγουστος ἐθείωσε, καίτοι τῷ τε Γαΐῳ καὶ τῷ Λουκίῳ πάντα καθάπαξ τὰ τοιαῦτα ἱεροῦν ἐπιτρέψας ὑπατικῇ τινι ἀρχῇ κατὰ τὸ παλαιὸν χρωμένοις. καὶ τήν γε ἱπποδρομίαν αὐτοὶ τότε διέθεσαν, τήν τε Τροίαν καλουμένην οἱ παῖδες οἱ πρῶτοι μετὰ τοῦ Ἀγρίππου τοῦ ἀδελφοῦ αὐτῶν ἵππευσαν. (7) καὶ λέοντες ἑξήκοντα καὶ διακόσιοι ἐν τῷ ἱπποδρόμῳ ἐσφάγησαν. ὁπλομαχία τε ἐν τοῖς σέπτοις καὶ ναυμαχία ἐν τῷ χωρίῳ ἐν ᾧ καὶ νῦν ἔτι σημεῖά τινα αὐτῆς δείκνυται Περσῶν καὶ Ἀθηναίων ἐποιήθη· ταῦτα γὰρ τὰ ὀνόματα τοῖς ναυμαχοῦσιν ἐτέθη, καὶ ἐνίκων καὶ τότε οἱ Ἀθηναῖοι. (8) καὶ μετὰ τοῦτο ἔς τε τὸν Φλαμίνιον ἱππόδρομον ὕδωρ ἐσήχθη, καὶ ἐν αὐτῷ κροκόδειλοι ἓξ καὶ τριάκοντα κατεκόπησαν. οὐ μέντοι καὶ διὰ πασῶν τῶν ἡμερῶν τούτων ὁ Αὔγουστος ὑπάτευσεν, ἀλλ' ἐπ' ὀλίγον ἄρξας ἄλλῳ τὸ ὄνομα τῆς ὑπατείας ἔδωκε.

(2) . . . (Er hatte einen Tempel geweiht) für Ares, (und dabei die Bestimmungen getroffen,) daß er selbst und seine Enkel, sooft sie nur wollten, und überhaupt diejenigen, die aus den Reihen der Knaben austräten und in die jüngeren militärischen Ränge eingeschrieben würden, Zutritt haben sollten; daß diejenigen, die zu ihren auswärtigen Kommandos auszögen, von dort aufbrechen sollten, (3) daß der Senat seine Beschlüsse über Triumphe dort fassen sollte, daß diejenigen, die diese Triumphzüge gehalten hätten, diesem Ares sowohl ihr Zepter als auch ihren Kranz weihen sollten und daß sie wie auch die anderen, welche die Triumphalehren erhalten würden, für sich eherne Statuen im Forum aufstellen lassen sollten;

(4) und wenn jemals vom Feinde eroberte Feldzeichen wiedergewonnen würden, daß diese in dem Tempel aufgestellt werden sollten; daß ein Fest bei den Stufen des Tempels von den jeweiligen Schwadronführern gefeiert werden sollte, und daß ein Nagel von denen, die das Zensoramt innegehabt hätten, daran geschlagen werden sollte; (5) daß es auch Senatoren gestattet sein sollte, an der Lieferung der Pferde für die Rennen und an der Überwachung des Tempels mitzuwirken, wie das entsprechend für den Tempel des Apollo und den des Jupiter Capitolinus gesetzlich bestimmt worden war. (6) Unter diesen Bestimmungen weihte Augustus jenen Tempel ein; freilich hatte er sowohl dem Gaius als auch dem Lucius es ein für allemal überlassen, solche Weihungen zu vollziehen, wobei sie eine Art von Konsulswürde nach alter Sitte ausübten. Sie waren es auch, die das Pferderennen damals organisierten, und zusammen mit deren Bruder Agrippa führten die vornehmsten Knaben das sogenannte Troia-Spiel zu Pferd aus. (7) Ferner wurden zweihundertsechzig Löwen im Circus niedergemacht. Es wurde ein Gladiatorenkampf in den Septa gehalten sowie eine Seeschlacht an der Stelle, wo sich auch jetzt noch gewisse Merkmale davon zeigen; es war eine Schlacht zwischen den Persern und Athenern: diese Namen wurden nämlich den Seekämpfern gegeben, und es siegten auch damals die Athener. (8) Darauf wurde Wasser in den Circus Flaminius eingelassen, und darin wurden sechsunddreißig Krokodile erschlagen. Freilich übte Augustus nicht während aller dieser Tage das Konsulat aus, sondern gab nach kurzer Amtsführung einem anderen den Konsulstitel."

(Übersetzung vom Autor).

In dieser Passage bietet der zweite Paragraph (10, 2) eine Schwierigkeit. Soll man den Satzteil τούς τε ... ἐγγραφομένους als nähere Bestimmung zu ἐγγόνους nehmen? Aber Gaius Caesar hatte doch schon im Jahre 5 v. Chr. die *toga virilis* angenommen, und Lucius Caesar hatte dies gerade im Jahre 2 v. Chr. getan; also konnte es für die Folgezeit nur für Agrippa Postumus gelten. Oder ist es ein selbständiger Zusatz? Es ist jedoch kaum anzunehmen, daß weiterhin alle Verleihungen der *toga virilis* in dem Tempel des Mars Ultor vollzogen werden sollten. Allerdings folgen erst hiernach die wichtigen Verordnungen. Zu dem Rest des zweiten Paragraphen und zu Paragraph 3 soll noch auf die kürzere Wiedergabe bei Suetonius, Augustus 29, Bezug genommen werden:

> *Aedem Martis bello Philippinensi pro ultione paterna suscepto voverat; sanxit ergo, ut de bellis triumphisque hic consuleretur senatus, provincias cum imperio petituri hinc deducerentur, quique victores redissent, huc insignia triumphorum conferrent.*

Bei den Bestimmungen über Triumphatoren und Empfänger der *insignia triumphorum* muß man in erster Linie an kriegerische Zusammenhänge denken, wie auch öfters die ganze Funktion des Mars Ultor-Kultes in solchem Zusammenhang gesehen wird[35]. Wie steht es aber mit τὰς ἀρχὰς τὰς ἐκδήμους? Dabei kämen

---

[35] CHAMBALU 733: „Unter August und Tiber war also der Tempel des Mars Ultor der Mittelpunkt für Alles, was mit dem Kriegswesen zusammenhing".

zuerst die *legati Augusti pro praetore* in Betracht, die über die militärisch über-
aus wichtigen kaiserlichen Provinzen walteten. Aber die Wiedergabe bei Sueton,
provincias cum imperio petituri, setzt eine umfassendere Bedeutung voraus;
hierunter sind sicherlich auch die Statthalter der senatorischen Provinzen zu verstehen. Unter diesem Gesichtspunkt erscheint Mars Ultor nicht nur als Beschützer des Kriegswesens, sondern der Reichsordnung überhaupt.

Im vierten Paragraphen handelt es sich zuerst um künftige Wiedergewinnung von Feldzeichen, die im Tempel aufbewahrt werden sollen. Das ist also
eine Fortsetzung dessen, was Augustus selbst mit früher zurückeroberten Feldzeichen getan hat[36]. Hier sind wir ganz in der kriegerischen Sphäre. Über das
Fest, das an den Stufen des Tempels von den *severi equitum* gefeiert werden
soll, läßt sich nichts Genaueres sagen. Mit den in den Paragraphen 6—8 be-
schriebenen Einweihungsfeiern hat es offensichtlich nichts zu tun. Mit dem von
den Censoren angeschlagenen Nagel sind wir wieder in der bürgerlichen Sphäre.
Das Auffallende hierbei ist, daß die Zeremonie der Versöhnung des Schicksals,
ehemals vollzogen von dem *dictator clavi figendi causa* am Tempel des Jupiter
Capitolinus, jetzt auf die Censoren und auf den Mars Ultor-Tempel übertragen
wird, ebenso wie die Vorschriften für den Triumph und die Bestimmungen von
Paragraph 5 eine Übertragung von Jupiter Optimus Maximus auf Mars Ultor
andeuten. Dabei ist zwar zu bemerken, daß die Funktionen von Triumph und
Censur nun grundsätzlich dem kaiserlichen Haus vorbehalten waren[37]. Das aber
verstärkt noch die Stellung des Mars Ultor als Beschützers der kaiserlichen
Familie, die selber den Anspruch erhob, das römische Volk zu repräsentieren.
Darauf könnte übrigens auch die hervorragende Rolle der Enkel des Augustus
bei den Einweihungsfeierlichkeiten deuten.

In Paragraph 5 wird die ἱπποδρομία erwähnt, für die die Besorgung von
Pferden auch[38] Senatoren gestattet wurde. Handelt es sich hier um Pferderennen
im allgemeinen, um die Equirria vom 27. Februar und 14. März und das Equus
October-Fest vom 15. Oktober, Feste, die besonders mit dem Marskult verbunden waren, oder insbesondere um die ἱπποδρομία von Paragraph 6? Ich
vermag es nicht zu entscheiden. Jedenfalls ist die gewichtige Rolle von Pferderennen sowohl im Tempelstatut wie auch bei der Einweihungsfeier von Bedeutung. Bei diesem Fest, beschrieben in den Paragraphen 6—8, wird der Schauplatz vom Augustusforum auf den Campus Martius verlegt. Der Platz der ἱπποδρομία von Paragraph 6 ist doch wohl als identisch mit dem ἱπποδρόμος der
Paragraphen 7 und 8, also mit dem Circus Flaminius, zu betrachten. Die σέπτα
von Paragraph 7 sind die Saepta Iulia, beschrieben von Cassius Dio 53, 23, 1—2,

---

[36] Mon. Ancyr. 29: *Signa militaria complura per alios duces amissa devictis hostibus reciperavi
ex Hispania et Gallia et a Dalmateis. Parthos trium exercit(u)um Romanorum spolia et
signa reddere mihi supplicesque amicitiam populi Romani petere coegi. Ea autem signa in
penetrali, quod est in templo Martis Ultoris, reposui.* Unter *ea signa* sind meiner Ansicht
nach nicht nur die parthischen, sondern auch die vorher genannten Feldzeichen zu verstehen.

[37] Vgl. dazu die bedeutenden Anmerkungen von LATTE 303.

[38] E. CARY (Loeb-Ausg.) übersetzt „sogar" (*"even"*), vermutlich in der Meinung, daß es hier
etwas ganz Außerordentliches betrifft.

ein Bauwerk auf dem Marsfeld, geweiht von Agrippa, erbaut von Lepidus und umgeben mit Wandelhallen für die *comitia tributa*. Die Verbindung der Einweihung auf dem Augustusforum mit dem Fest an der von alters her bekannten Kultstätte des Mars ist hier von Bedeutung.

Es wird inzwischen deutlich geworden sein, daß, abgesehen von der Verbindung Mars—Venus, die offensichtlich aus dynastischen Gründen in den Mars Ultor-Kult hineingebracht worden ist, nur national-römische Aspekte vorhanden sind (s. o. Anm. 19); weiters, daß zwar die kriegerische Sphäre nicht abwesend ist, aber eingebettet in dem viel weiteren Kontext einer Nationalreligion; und ferner, daß die Neigung hervortritt, Ehrungen von Jupiter Capitolinus auf den neuen Marskult zu übertragen. Das leitet zu der Frage über, mit welchen Vorstellungen die Gestalt des Mars in dieser Zeit verknüpft war, warum gerade diese Gestalt eine so hervorragende Stellung im augusteïschen Restaurationsprogramm erhielt und warum Mars an diesem Ort in der Mitte der Stadt sein großes Heiligtum bekam.

III. Die Ideologie des Marskultes um die Jahrtausendwende und ihre Vorgeschichte

Das Epitheton ʻDer Rächerʼ war Mars aus zwei Gründen gegeben worden, und bei beiden Gründen kann man die Frage stellen, ob der Gedanke der Rache noch wirklich lebendig war.

Erstens: Zwischen dem Gelübde *pro ultione paterna* und der Einweihung im Jahre 2 v. Chr. waren vierzig Jahre vergangen. Es mag nun sein, daß an dem Forum viele Jahre gearbeitet worden ist; daß es inzwischen schon für das Publikum geöffnet wurde, bezeugt Suetonius[39]. Aber in dieser langen Zeit hatte sich das Weltbild geändert. Konnte noch im Jahre 42 bei der julischen Partei der Gedanke der blutigen Rache im Vordergrund stehen, so war danach die *pax Augusta* eingetreten. Die vorherrschende Ideologie war jetzt die der Friedensherrschaft geworden, die auch später noch, sogar für republikanisch gesonnene Gebildete, dem Principat seine Rechtfertigung gab[40]. Nicht viele Jahre nach der Einweihung des Mars Ultor-Tempels bricht die Zeit an, von der Tacitus später schrieb[41]: *iuniores post Actiacam victoriam, etiam senes plerique inter bella civium nati: quotus quisque reliquus, qui rem publicam vidisset?* Für die jüngere Generation um die Jahrtausendwende war Philippi schon eine alte Geschichte, und für die ältere (freilich durch diese auch für viele der jüngeren) waren die Bürgerkriege, wie schon oben gesagt, ein traumatisches Erlebnis, ähnlich wie die Wirtschaftskrise der dreißiger Jahre unseres Jahrhunderts es für die ältere Gene-

---

[39] Suet. ʻAug. 29.
[40] Tac. Hist. I,1,1: *Postquam bellatum apud Actium atque omnem potentiam ad unum conferri pacis interfuit,* . . .
[41] Tac. Ann. I,3,7.

ration von heute ist. Mit dem Gedanken einer Rache, mag dieser auch für den Princeps selber noch einigermaßen lebendig gewesen sein, konnte man die Menge kaum mehr begeistern.

Zweitens: Der Begriff der *ultio* in Zusammenhang mit den von den Parthern zurückgewonnenen Feldzeichen ist etwas sehr Merkwürdiges. Bei einer *ultio* würde man eigentlich eher an einen Partherfeldzug mit blutigen Schlachten und gewaltsamer Wiedergewinnung denken. Aber obwohl die Rückgabe unter politischem Druck erzwungen wurde, beruft sich Augustus stolz gerade darauf, daß es „ohne den Staub des Schlachtfeldes"[42] geschehen war. Auch hier wieder wollte er sich als der Friedensherrscher im Vergleich z. B. mit Crassus und Marcus Antonius absetzen. Obwohl also in diesem Fall der Rachegedanke 20 v. Chr. noch größere Virulenz gehabt haben könnte[43], erscheint die Bedeutung der *ultio* selber nun abgeschwächt.

Dazu kommt noch eine weitere Erwägung, die ich allerdings mit Zurückhaltung vorbringen möchte. Bei Cassius Dio wird Ultor mit Τιμωρός wiedergegeben. Aber in dem griechischen Text des 'Monumentum Ancyranum', der doch wohl eine offiziell inspirierte Übersetzung darstellt, steht dafür 'Αμύντωρ[44]. Nun können die beiden Bezeichnungen natürlich einfach Synonyme sein. In ἀμύντωρ klingt jedoch sicher auch die Nebenbedeutung von 'Helfer' oder 'Beschützer' mit.

Das führt dann wieder zu der Frage nach dem Wesen der Gottheit Mars, wie sie dem Römer im Anfang der Kaiserzeit erschienen ist. Ich werde mich hier nicht in „die große Auseinandersetzung"[45] einlassen. In der modernen Literatur ist der Stand der Diskussion ausführlich und klar wiedergegeben[46]. Hier seien nur einige Hauptkomponenten erwähnt: Gegenüber den alten Vegetationstheorien von ROSCHER und MANNHARDT hatte WISSOWA behauptet, daß Mars in historischer Zeit für die Römer[47] nie etwas anderes als der Kriegsgott gewesen

---

[42] ἀκονιτί Cass. Dio 54,8,3 (s. o. Anm. 24).

[43] Dabei mag auch gelten, daß für das römische Volk das *dedecus* des Feldzeichenverlustes größere Realität gehabt haben wird als das *scelus* der Caesarmörder, das für manche Bürger in Wirklichkeit sogar als ein *pulcherrimum facinus* (Tac. Ann. I,8,6) erscheinen konnte.

[44] Die Stelle Mon. Ancyr. 21 (o. Anm. 22): ἐν ἰδιωτικῷ ἐδάφει "Αρεως 'Αμύντορος . . . ἐπόησα. Desgleichen 29 (o. Anm. 32): ταύτας δὲ τὰς σημέας ἐν τῷ "Αρεως τοῦ 'Αμύντορος ναοῦ ἀδύτῳ ἀπεθέμην.

[45] «*Le grand débat*»: DUMÉZIL 1966, 215.

[46] SCHOLZ 9—17. Sehr klare Übersicht auch bei BALKESTEIN 1—5. Dieses Buch ist leider wenig beachtet worden, obwohl es ein französisches Résumé enthält; ich habe jedenfalls in der 'Année Philologique' keine Rezension finden können. Es enthält nach dem Buch von HERMANSEN zwar nicht sehr viele ganz neue Gesichtspunkte, aber es zeichnet sich durch die auf phänomenologischer Grundlage erarbeitete Methode aus. SCHOLZ nimmt freilich ernsthaft Rücksicht auf dieses Werk. Eine knappe ältere Übersicht der Auseinandersetzung ist neulich in einem Wiederabdruck erschienen: P. BOYANCÉ, Études sur la religion romaine (Rom 1972), 310—321. Im republikanischen Teil von ANRW (I, 2 [1972] 364—366) gibt H. WAGENVOORT, Wesenszüge altrömischer Religion, einen Überblick.

[47] WISSOWA wollte nach seinen apodiktischen Ausführungen in 'Religion und Kultus der Römer' später (Rez. E. BICKEL, Der altrömische Gottesbegriff [Leipzig 1921], Phil. Wochenschr. 41, 1921, 994—995) zugeben, daß im italischen Marskult die agrarische Komponente

sei, eine These, die bis in jüngste Zeit von DUMÉZIL energisch verteidigt worden ist. Demgegenüber hat eine ganze Reihe von Gelehrten, gestützt auf das Lustralgebet bei Cato (De Agri Cultura 141), auf das 'Carmen Arvale' und auf den Ritus des Oktoberrosses und das daraus gewonnene Bild mit mannigfachen anderen Argumenten ergänzend, das agrarische Wesen des Mars betont. Dabei wären insbesondere die Namen von WIDE und NILSSON, von FOWLER (s. u.), HERMANSEN, BALKESTEIN, WAGENVOORT und ROSE zu nennen. Hierbei gibt es freilich noch allerhand Nuancierungen, je nachdem ob Mars beschrieben wird als ein ursprünglich unspezialisierter 'high god', der unter verschiedenen Umständen verschiedene Funktionen erhalten konnte (z. B. ROSE), oder als ein ursprünglich chthonischer oder Todesgott (HERMANSEN, BALKESTEIN), oder als ein Agrargott, der erst unter dem Einfluß des Ares zu einem Kriegsgott geworden ist[48]. Eine Zwischenstellung nimmt gewissermaßen MARBACH in seiner ausgezeichneten Zusammenfassung des Materials und der Probleme ein[49]. Er beschreibt Mars als „die Urkraft des Italertums". In anderem Sinn gilt das gewissermaßen auch für FOWLER und sicher für LATTE, indem der erstere in Mars den „Herr der Wildnis" sieht (doch mit Nachdruck auf dem agrarischen Aspekt), der letztere den „Exponenten der unheimlichen unvertrauten Welt draußen", dessen Macht eine schützende und helfende, aber auch eine der Abwehr bedürftige Wirkung haben konnte, und zwar für den Agrarier ebenso wie für den Krieger[50]. Eine neue Position nimmt SCHOLZ[51] ein, der in Mars eine große Schutzgottheit sieht, deren Macht durch die Konsolidierung des römischen Staatswesens in der späteren Königszeit in Verfall geraten war und die daher später ein zwiespältiges Bild aufweist.

Die große Kontroverse ist hier nur kurz angedeutet, weil der Zweck dieses Kapitels nicht ist, die ursprüngliche Bedeutung des Gottes Mars zu erforschen. Es geht vielmehr darum zu zeigen, welche Bedeutung der Gott für die Römer im Anfang des Principats noch haben konnte. Aber wir können dabei auch die Frage nach dem ursprünglichen Sinn nicht ganz außer acht lassen. Wenn nämlich Mars in Rom früher nie etwas anderes als der Kriegsgott gewesen ist, so trifft dies wohl auch für die Zeit des Augustus (und seiner Nachfolger) zu. Wenn dagegen sein ursprünglicher Sinn ein ganz anderer gewesen ist oder wenn

---

nicht wegzudeuten ist. Diese scharfe Unterscheidung zwischen einem römischen und einem italischen Mars ist aber schwer zu verstehen. Vor der Etruskerherrschaft war doch Rom eine italische Siedlung, und in frührepublikanischer Zeit ist es überwiegend wieder italisch geworden. Warum dann diese Gottheit in Rom ein grundsätzlich anderes Wesen erhalten haben sollte als im übrigen Italien, bleibt völlig ungeklärt. Daß Mars in Etrurien einen ganz eigenen Charakter gehabt hat, halte ich durchaus für möglich, aber ich wage es nicht, mich darüber genauer auszusprechen. Für die italischen Marskulte vgl. insbes. HERMANSEN 26—107 und in der älteren Literatur ROSCHER 2385—2395; s. außerdem BÖMER's Kommentar zu Ovids Fasti II,184.

[48] Neuerdings noch bei M. D. PETRUŠEVSKI, L'évolution du Mars italique d'une divinité de la nature à un dieu de guerre, Acta Antiqua Academiae Scientiarum Hungaricae 15, 1967, 417—422. (Ich kenne diesen Artikel nur aus einem Auszug.)

[49] MARBACH 1937.

[50] LATTE 18; 114.

[51] Zusammenfassend SCHOLZ 78—79.

er jedenfalls eine viel weitere Wirkungssphäre umfaßt hat, dann besteht allerdings die Möglichkeit, daß entweder etwas davon die Entwicklung der Zeit überstanden hat oder (was ich eher annehmen möchte) durch eine offiziell inspirierte Ideologie darauf zurückgegriffen werden konnte. Ich möchte nun von vornherein MARBACH beipflichten, wenn er schreibt[52]: „Es scheinen mir aber diese Deutungen (gemeint sind die, die in Mars nur das kriegerische Wesen sehen wollten) dem Charakter der betreffenden Feste (gemeint sind die Ambarvalien und das Oktoberroß), vor allem auch dem Wortlaut der bei Cato überlieferten Gebete . . . und auch dem Arvalliede . . . zu wenig gerecht zu werden". Meines Erachtens sind auch mehr gezwungen als natürlich die eindrucksvollen Bemühungen von DUMÉZIL[53], den zweiten Teil des Gebetes an Mars bei Cato, De Agri Cultura 141[54], als dem ersten Teil, in dem von *defendere* und *averrucare*, potentiell kriegerischen Tätigkeiten, die Rede ist, gänzlich untergeordnet zu erklären.

Nun könnte man fragen, in welchem Maße die Vorstellungen, die bei Cato anzutreffen sind, noch zur Zeit des Augustus lebendig waren. Wurde z. B. Cato noch gelesen, abgesehen von Gelehrten oder speziell an der Agrarwirtschaft Interessierten? Die Frage läßt sich wahrscheinlich nicht mit einiger Sicherheit beantworten. Anders steht es mit dem Arvallied, das in den 'Acta Fratrum Arvalium' (von 218 n. Chr.) überliefert ist, also den Akten gerade einer Priesterschaft, die von Augustus restauriert worden war. Es wurde bei der Lustration der Felder gesungen; anderseits ist in den Worten *neve lue rue Marmar sins incurrere in pleores, satur fu, fere Mars, limen sali, sta berber,* wie man nun auch im Einzelnen diese Worte verstehen mag[55], Mars die schützende und abwehrende (in *enos Marmor iuvato* auch die helfende) Kraft und nicht eigentlich die segnende und schenkende, wie im Gebet des Landmannes bei Cato. Nun wird in diesem Zusammenhang auch öfters das Ambarvalgedicht des Tibull (II, 1) erwähnt. Wenn SCHOLZ[56] dazu schreibt: „Viel deutlicher als im Arvallied werden hier die Sorgen und Erwartungen des Landmannes laut", so trifft das gewiß zu; wenn er aber fortfährt: „der Lustralakt wendet sich an die Laren . . ., und vermutlich auch an Mars, den Gott der *Ambarvalia*", dann muß doch daran erinnert werden, daß es sich nur noch um eine Vermutung handelt.

---

[52] A. a. O. 1935.

[53] DUMÉZIL (1966), 232—235.

[54] *utique tu fruges frumenta vineta virgultaque grandire beneque evenire siris, pastores pecuaque salva servassis, duisque bonam salutem valetudinemque mihi domo familiaeque nostrae.*

[55] Um nur einiges zu nennen: ist *fere Mars* wirklich „wilder Mars"? Bedeutet *limen sali* „springe auf die Schwelle (des Saatfeldes, um es zu verteidigen)" oder vielleicht „springe von draußen auf die Schwelle (und nähere dich uns nicht weiter)"? Bedeutet *sta berber* „halt die Geißel an", oder „bleib stehen, Geißel (= unheimliche Macht)", oder ist *berber* gar nicht identisch mit *verber*, sondern bedeutet „da, da", oder ist es ein ungeklärtes Wort? Vgl. E. NORDEN, Aus altrömischen Priesterbüchern, Skrifter utgivna av kungliga humanistiska Vetenskaps-samfundet i Lund 23 (Lund 1939), 109—280 (weiteres bei SCHOLZ 14 Anm. 31; 64—67).

[56] A. a. O. 68—69.

Festeren Boden erreichen wir bei dem Opfer des Oktoberrosses, dem SCHOLZ die Hälfte seines Buches widmet[57]. Eine kurze Beschreibung der Daten sei hier gegeben: Am 15. Oktober wurden auf einem Teil des Marsfeldes, der Ad Nixas[58] hieß, Pferderennen gehalten. Das rechte Pferd (d. h. das Pferd, das die größten Anstrengungen überstanden hatte) des gewinnenden Gespannes wurde dem Mars geopfert. Der Kopf und der Schwanz wurden abgehauen. Über den Kopf entbrannte einmal ein Streit zwischen den Bewohnern der Subura und denen des Viertels um die Sacra Via, indem die ersteren ihn an die Turris Mamilia (ein Gebäude auf dem Mons Caelius), die letzteren an die Regia anheften wollten. Der Schwanz wurde immer nach der Regia gebracht, und zwar mit solcher Geschwindigkeit, daß dort noch das Blut auf den Herd tropfen konnte[59]. Außerdem wird – obwohl erst in karolingischer Zeit – berichtet, daß man den Kopf des geopferten (oder für das Opfer mit *mola salsa* bestreuten) Tiers mit Broten (?) umwickelte (umhing?).

Zunächst einige Bemerkungen zu der Quellenüberlieferung und einige kritische Randnotizen über die Deutungen von SCHOLZ. Die Überlieferung geht fast ganz auf das Werk des augusteïschen Freigelassenen und Gelehrten Verrius Flaccus, 'De verborum significatu' zurück. Damit ist festgestellt, daß das Opfer noch in augusteïscher Zeit gehalten wurde, und zwar auf dem Campus Martius; im vorigen Abschnitt ist schon hervorgehoben worden, daß dieser Ort auch der Schauplatz der Spiele aus Anlaß der Einweihung des Mars Ultor-Tempels war. Der Epitomator Festus (2. Jhdt.) schreibt noch *immolatur*, während im Auszug des Paulus Diaconus (8. Jhdt.) *immolabatur* steht. Vermutlich blieb der Brauch noch einige Jahrhunderte bestehen, ist aber am Ende des Altertums außer Übung geraten. Nun hat SCHOLZ mit Recht betont[60], daß auffallenderweise der Streit um den Kopf gerade von Festus mit *solebat* angedeutet wird. Das würde also besagen, daß dieser Teil des Opferbrauches schon in der Zeit des Festus (aber auch in der des Verrius Flaccus?) außer Übung gekommen war[61]. Übrigens ist dabei von einiger Bedeutung, daß Plutarch in seiner kurzen Schilderung des Opfers doch das Präsens gebraucht (διαμάχονται)[62]. Daß das Opfer

---

[57] 81–167; vgl. BALKESTEIN 61–86; beide mit reichlichen Angaben der älteren Literatur.

[58] Im Philocalus-Kalender zum 15. Oktober: *Idib. Ludi Equus ad Nixas fit.*

[59] Daß dasselbe, bald getrocknete, Blut aufbewahrt wurde, um im April noch bei den Parilia verwendet zu werden, halte ich mit SCHOLZ 97–99 für unerwiesen.

[60] A. a. O. 93.

[61] Festus 190 L: *October equus appellatur, qui in Campo Martio mense Octobri immolatur quotannis Marti, bigarum victricum dexterior. De cuius capite non levis contentio solebat esse inter Suburanes et Sacravienses, ut hi in regiae pariete, illi ad turrim Mamiliam id figerent; eiusdemque coda tanta celeritate perfertur in regiam, ut ex ea sanguis distillet in focum participandae rei divinae gratia. Quem hostiae loco quidam Marti bellico deo sacrari dicunt, non, ut vulgus putat, quia velut supplicium de eo sumatur, quod Romani Ilio sunt oriundi et Troiani ita effigie in equi sint capti.* Für die Deutungen der *quidam* und des *vulgus* vgl. auch Paulus 71 L: *equus Marti immolabatur, quod per eius effigiem Troiani capti sunt vel quod eo genere animalis Mars delectari putaretur.*

[62] Plut. Quaest. Rom. 97: Διὰ τί ταῖς Δεκεμβρίαις (Fehler, vermutlich entstanden, weil die unmittelbare Quelle „im zehnten Monat" formulierte) εἰδοῖς ἱπποδρομίας γενομένης ὁ

ein staatliches Fest war, erfahren wir aus Plinius dem Älteren[63]. Ob es nun zusammen mit den Arvalriten und dem Gebet bei Cato einen Beleg für die agrarische Funktion des Mars darstellt, hängt mit ab von dem Zeugnis in der Epitome des Paulus, wo von den „Broten" (?) gesprochen wird[64]. Daß die Deutung dieser „Brote" in der Passage in zwei Sätzen sich selber widerspricht, indem erstens der Brauch erklärt wird *ob frugum eventum* und gleich darauf das Pferd als kriegerisches Wesen gedeutet wird, ist wohl unklarem Verständnis bei Paulus zuzuschreiben. Wichtiger ist die Frage, ob eigentlich „Brote" gemeint seien. SCHOLZ hat versucht zu zeigen, daß *panibus*: „mit Tüchern" bedeutet, da *pannus* („Tuch") noch Spuren eines *u*-Stammes im Altlatein hat und *pannibus* vielleicht *panibus* geschrieben werden konnte; und das könnte dann für Verrius Flaccus, der ja seltene und altertümliche Wörter erklären wollte, der Anlaß gewesen sein, dieses Wort als Lemma aufzuführen. Diese Annahme hängt aber von einer ganzen Kette von Hypothesen ab: Die Begründung *ob frugum eventum* müßte dann ein Mißverständnis des Paulus sein, die Mitteilung über das Umwinden aber würde noch von Festus (und Verrius Flaccus) stammen. Die Begründung müßte von Verrius Flaccus in anderer Weise gegeben sein, weil er doch erläutern müßte, wie und warum man so etwas mit dem Pferd machte; diese Begründung wäre dann verloren gegangen, und so wäre nichts von dem bei Festus und Paulus bewahrt. Dann fragt man sich, warum das geschehen sein sollte. Hierbei müßte die Form *panibus* für *pannibus*, i.e. *pannīs*, in irgendeiner Weise in augusteischer Zeit noch lebendig oder befriedigend verständlich gewesen sein. Das alles erscheint nun zwar fein gesponnen, geht aber meiner Meinung nach etwas zu weit. Daß *panibus* (= „mit Broten") ein zu gewöhnliches Wort war, um als Lemma gebraucht zu werden, leuchtet mir nicht ein, da verschiedene andere Paulus-Stellen mit ganz gewöhnlichen Wörtern anfangen. In der Deutung von SCHOLZ entfällt nun der ganze umstrittene Fruchtbarkeitsritus; damit fallen die Erklärung, die er Verrius Flaccus zumutet, und die der *quidam* im Festus-Text (s. o. Anm. 61) zusammen, indem sie beide das Opfer als Kriegsbrauch auffassen. Auffallend ist dabei, daß SCHOLZ das Testimonium des Timaios, das von den Anhängern der Mars-nur-Kriegsgott-Theorie gern als ältestes Zeugnis angeführt wird[65], da hier ausdrücklich von

---

νικήσας δεξιόσειρος Ἄρει θύεται, καὶ τὴν μὲν οὐρὰν ἀποκόψας τις ἐπὶ τὴν Ῥηγίαν καλουμένην κομίζει καὶ τὸν βωμὸν αἱμάσσει, περὶ δὲ τῆς κεφαλῆς οἱ μὲν ἀπὸ τῆς ἱερᾶς ὁδοῦ λεγομένης οἱ δ' ἀπὸ τῆς Συβούρης καταβάντες διαμάχονται;

[63] Plin. N.H. 28, 146: . . . *flamini sacrorum equum tangere non licet, cum Romae publicis sacris equus immoletur.*

[64] Paulus 246 L, 277 Th, 220 M: *Panibus redimibant caput equi immolati Idibus Octobribus in Campo Martio, quia id sacrificium fiebat ob frugum eventum; et equus potius quam bos immolabatur, quod hic bello, bos frugibus pariendis est aptus.* Hierzu SCHOLZ 101–102.

[65] Timaios Fr. Gr. Hist. 566 F 36 apud Polyb. 12, 4 b: (φησὶ τοὺς Ῥωμαίους) ἐν ἡμέρᾳ τινὶ κατακοντίζειν ἵππον πολεμιστὴν πρὸ τῆς πόλεως ἐν τῷ Κάμπῳ καλουμένῳ διὰ τὸ τῆς Τροίας τὴν ἅλωσιν διὰ τὸν ἵππον γενέσθαι τὸν δούριον προσαγορευόμενον, πρᾶγμα πάντων παιδαριωδέστατον· οὕτω μὲν γὰρ δεήσει πάντας τοὺς βαρβάρους λέγειν Τρώων ἀπογόνους ὑπάρχειν· σχεδὸν γὰρ πάντες, εἰ δὲ μή γ' οἱ πλείους, ὅταν ἢ πολεμεῖν μέλλωσιν ἐξ ἀρχῆς ἢ διακινδυνεύειν πρός τινας ὁλοσχερῶς, ἵππον (ms. ἵππῳ) προ-

einem Kriegsroß gesprochen wird, gerade verwirft; es handelt sich seiner Meinung nach um einen Frühjahrsritus, vielleicht um die Märzequirrien. Er behauptet mit Recht, daß es hier offensichtlich um einen Ritus gehe, der Bezug auf einen bevorstehenden Kampf habe; demgegenüber steht erstens, daß schon hier die merkwürdige Begründung durch das Trojanische Pferd auftritt, die schon Polybius für Unsinn hält und die bei Festus (Anm. 61) als Mißdeutung wiederkehrt (im Kontext des Oktoberrituals), und zweitens, daß bei keinem anderen Ritus in Rom ein Pferdeopfer bekannt ist. Die Verwerfung des Timaioszeugnisses steht anscheinend in Zusammenhang mit der Auffassung von SCHOLZ, daß das Pferd mit Tüchern erstickt wurde[66], während Timaios als einziger die Tötung durch einen Speer (durch Speere?) erwähnt. Dies alles macht die Kette von Hypothesen noch unsicherer.

In zweiter Linie sucht SCHOLZ zu erweisen, daß der abgehauene Schwanz das Geschlechtsteil des Tieres war[67]. Wenn man dies buchstäblich versteht, gibt es eine Schwierigkeit: Es müßte immer ein Hengst gewesen sein. Was wäre aber geschehen, wenn das Rennen von einem Stutenpaar gewonnen worden wäre? Wurde in diesem Fall der Schwanz als Symbol für einen Phallos verwendet? Das scheint eingeräumt zu werden mit den Worten: „Dabei spielt es keine entscheidende Rolle, ob beim Pferdeopfer wirklich das Geschlechtsteil oder der Schwanz abgeschnitten wurde; die Begriffe sind auswechselbar, ohne daß sich dabei am Ritual etwas ändern würde". Aber es bleibt doch eine merkwürdige Sache, daß der Schwanz einer Stute möglicherweise die rituelle Funktion eines Hengstphallos sollte erfüllen können, zumal das Blut von SCHOLZ als Samen gedeutet wird[68]. Ist es nicht viel natürlicher, den Kopf und den Schwanz, die extremen Körperteile also, als transportierbare Verkörperung des gewinnenden, dem Gotte geweihten Tieres, der Urkraft also, zu deuten? In dieser Richtung weiterdenkend, kann ich trotzdem dem Hauptschluß des Buches von SCHOLZ durchaus beipflichten. Das Blut des stärksten Pferdes − man braucht dies überhaupt nicht als Samen zu deuten −, das vom Marsfelde, dem Sitz nicht nur eines bedeutenden Marskultes, sondern auch sehr wichtiger staatlicher Anstalten, in das Zentrum der Stadt übertragen wurde und auf den Herd in der Regia tropfte, konnte für die Teilnehmer des Ritus immerhin die Urkraft des Römertums vertreten. Daß all dies sogar auf die frühe Königszeit zurückgeht, mag als annehmbar gelten; aber darauf wollen wir hier nicht näher eingehen, weil es ja hier in erster Linie darum geht, die Vorstellungen zu ermitteln, die man zu Anfang des Principats haben konnte.

In Zusammenhang damit steht eine andere Streitfrage, die Frage nach der Funktion des Gottes als des „Exponenten der unheimlichen, unvertrauten Welt draußen" (o. S. 261). Die Kultstätten des Mars befanden sich bekanntlich in republikanischer Zeit *extra pomerium*, nämlich auf dem Marsfelde (die *ara*

θύονται καὶ σφαγιάζονται, σημειούμενοι τὸ μέλλον ἐκ τῆς τοῦ ζῴου πτώσεως. Mit „beinahe alle" sind wohl „beinahe alle *barbaroi*" gemeint.
[66] SCHOLZ 118.
[67] Ibidem 126; dabei schließt er sich den Ansichten von EITREM und WAGENVOORT an.
[68] Ibidem 139.

Martis in Campo und spätere Tempel sowie der Schauplatz der Equirria) und bei der Porta Capena. Die theoretische Grundlage findet sich in einer Vitruvstelle und in zwei Notizen bei Servius[69]. Es bleibt fraglich, woher Servius seine Kenntnis hat, aber aus Vitruv wird klar erstens, daß spätestens in der augusteïschen Zeit die Lage der Kultstätten, offensichtlich als der eines Kriegsgottes, außerhalb der Stadt für richtig angesehen wurde; zweitens, daß diese Lokalisierung etruskischer Religionsgelehrsamkeit zugeschrieben wurde. Das *sacrarium Martis in regia* und die *curia Saliorum* auf dem Palatin lassen die Gelehrten, die, wie Wissowa, der Lage *extra pomerium* außerordentlich viel Wert beilegen, außer acht, da diese keine eigentlichen Kultstätten waren. Demgegenüber sind von den Forschern, die nicht an einen 'Mars des Draußen' glauben wollen[70], Spuren älterer Kultstätten innerhalb des *pomerium* erschlossen worden. Hierzu schreibt Balkestein[71]: „Außerdem würde ausgerechnet Augustus die Staatsordnung schwer übertreten haben, indem er seinen Tempel für Mars Ultor innerhalb des Pomoeriums stiftete". Da kann man sich jedoch die Frage stellen, ob vielleicht die Stiftung an dieser Stätte, nicht nur innerhalb des Pomeriums, sondern sogar im Herzen der Stadt, nur wenige Schritte von der Regia entfernt, absichtlich geschehen sei. Ich bin geneigt zu meinen, daß Augustus sich der Neuerung in der Lokalisierung bewußt war und daß er den Gott als einen (freilich 'martialischen') Beschützer seiner Friedensordnung einen sorgfältig gewählten Platz innerhalb des Pomeriums einnehmen ließ. Man wird einwerfen, daß nirgends in der Überlieferung über den Mars Ultor-Kult der Name Quirinus auftaucht[72], obwohl Quirinus gerade in dem Kontext der *pax Augusta* von Augustus selber[73] als Beiname des Janus gebraucht wird; und weiter, daß an der Ovidstelle (o. S. 251) sogar Gradivus als ein Name des Mars gebraucht wird (556). Dem steht gegenüber, daß in spätrepublikanischer Zeit die Lage der Kultstätten geradezu auffallend war, und die Zeugnisse des Servius und

---

[69] Vitruv. I,7,1: *Aedibus vero sacris, quorum deorum maxime in tutela civitas videtur esse . . . areae distribuantur: . . . Marti extra urbem, sed ad Campum . . . Id autem etiam Etruscis haruspicibus scripturis ita est dedicatum, extra murum Veneris, Volcani, Martis fana ideo conlocari, ut . . .* (hier folgen erst die Gründe für Venus und Vulkan) *Martis vero divinitas cum sit extra moenia dedicata, non erit inter cives armigera dissensio, sed ab hostibus ea defensa a belli periculo conservabit.*
  Servius ad Aen. I,292: *Mars enim cum saevit Gradivus dicitur, cum tranquillus est Quirinus. Denique in urbe duo eius templa sunt: unum Quirini intra urbem, quasi custodis et tranquilli, aliud in Appia via extra urbem prope portam, quasi bellatoris, id est Gradivi.*
  Servius ad Aen. VI,860: *Quirinus autem est Mars qui praeest paci et intra civitatem colitur, nam belli Mars extra civitatem templum habuit.*
[70] Scholz 18—33; S. 105—116 sucht er zu erweisen, daß der Campus Martialis auf dem Caelius der ursprüngliche Ort des Oktoberfestes gewesen sei. Noch Ovid (Fasti III,519—522) berichtet, daß bei Überschwemmungen des Campus Martius die Märzequirrien auf den Caelius verlegt wurden.
[71] Balkestein 95: Übersetzung aus dem Holländischen von mir.
[72] Schon längst ist erkannt, daß bei Servius der Gegensatz zwischen einem tobenden Mars Gradivus (draußen) und einem ruhigen Mars Quirinus (innen), nicht zwischen einem 'kriegerischen' Mars und einem 'friedlichen' Quirinus besteht.
[73] Mon. Ancyr. 13.

vor allem Vitruvs beweisen, daß diese Lage in der augusteïschen Zeit als Norm angesehen wurde. Daß Ovid Mars ῾Gradivus᾽ nennt, braucht kein Hindernis zu sein. Er hat den Beinamen sicher (vgl. *fera bella movere*) im Sinne von „in den Kampf schreitend" verstanden, obwohl das kaum die ursprüngliche Bedeutung gewesen sein kann[74]. Doch das stimmt ganz mit seinem Bild der Epiphanie unter Waffengeklirr, dem traditionellen poetischen Bild, überein.

Damit sind wir an unseren Ausgangspunkt zurückgekehrt. Es geht natürlich nicht darum, die Funktion des Mars als Kriegsgott in der augusteïschen Ideologie zu beseitigen. Das wäre unangebracht. Es geht darum, sie einzuschränken. Wenn man mit SCHOLZ das Timaioszeugnis verwirft, so bleibt von einem kriegerischen Ritus im Oktoberroßopfer nicht viel übrig, oder man müßte das Pferd an sich als kriegerisches Symbol deuten[75]. Es sollte aber die Möglichkeit nicht außer acht gelassen werden, daß mit dem Pferd ursprünglich auch ganz andere Vorstellungen verbunden sein konnten[76] und daß jedenfalls für den Römer der augusteïschen Zeit das Ritual den Eindruck machen mußte, einer großen allgemein schützenden Gottheit geweiht zu sein. Denselben Eindruck

---

[74] Wegen der Länge des *ā* wird die Herleitung von *gradior* meistens verworfen (s. WALDE–HOFFMANN s. v.; RADKE 139–140: „wegen der Quantität ausgeschlossen"). Die Anhänger der ῾agrarischen᾽ Theorie postulieren einen Zusammenhang mit *grandio* (Cato, De agri cult. 141: *utique tu fruges . . . grandire . . . siris*). Übrigens hat W. F. OTTO, Römische Sagen III. Larentalia und Acca Larentia, Wiener Studien 35 (1913), 64f. auf Längewechsel in Lāres/Lārentalia, *pāx/păg-* (*pango*) und *lēx/lĕg-* (*lego*) hingewiesen. Dies sei hier nur nebenbei bemerkt; es geht wieder nicht darum festzustellen, was die ursprüngliche Bedeutung ist, sondern wie man das Wort später verstanden hat.

[75] Es fällt mir immer schwer zu verstehen, warum für die Römer, die ihre Kampfkraft immer überwiegend im Fußvolk hatten, das Pferd ein so ausgesprochen kriegerisches Wesen sein sollte. Ich kann allerdings auch nicht von den immer wieder zitierten Vergil- und Justinstellen absehen, nämlich Verg., Aen. III, 539–543:

> *et pater Anchises: „bellum, o terra hospita, portas:*
> *bello armantur equi, bellum haec armenta minantur;*
> *sed tamen idem olim curru succedere sueti*
> *quadrupedes et frena iugo concordia ferre:*
> *spes et pacis", ait.*

(– Hier wird übrigens auch die Möglichkeit angedeutet, das Pferdsymbol friedlich zu verstehen, anders als in der Justinstelle: –) und Justin. 18,5,15 (bei der Stiftung von Carthago): *in primis fundamentis caput bubulum inventum est, quod auspicium fructuosae quidem, sed laboriosae perpetuoque servae urbis fuit; propter quod in alium locum urbs translata; ibique* (ms. *ibi quoque**) *equi caput repertum, bellicosum potentemque populum futurum significans, urbi auspicatam sedem dedit.* (Wenn man die Lesung *ibi quoque* beibehält, sollte man erklären: „auch hier wurde ein Kopf gefunden, und zwar der eines Pferdes, und der bedeutete . . .") Die Lösung liegt vielleicht darin, daß diese Vorstellungen auf die Zeit zurückgehen, wo die *equites* (in der ursprünglichen Bedeutung) durch ihr gesellschaftliches Prestige eine überragende Rolle im Kriegswesen spielten. Vgl. aber auch H. J. ROSE, Ancient Roman Religion 66: *"chariots, a vehicle which was never used, as far back as our records go, by Italians for actual war, though no doubt it once had been, but was retained for sport, as it was in Greece also."*

[76] HERMANSEN 72–78; 166–173 und BALKESTEIN 68–70 heben insbesondere die (nach ihrer Meinung) chthonische Bedeutung des Pferdes hervor und verbinden diese mit der Interpretation des Wettkampfes als Totenritual.

wird man von dem Ritual der Arvalbrüder erhalten haben und außerdem von dem Marsbild, wie es aus dem Werk des Cato hervortrat, falls dieses noch in dem Bewußtsein gegenwärtig war. Das steht wiederum ganz im Einklang mit dem ovidischen Hauptzeugnis über den Mars Ultor-Kult, in dem neben dem traditionellen Waffengeklirr die Funktion des Mars als Beschützer der staatlichen Neuordnung erkennbar ist. Vor allem stimmt es zu der Cassius Dio-Stelle, die bezeugt, wie eine beträchtliche Anzahl von Privilegien von Jupiter Capitolinus auf Mars Ultor übertragen wurde. Jupiter Capitolinus war ja auch der *custos imperii*. Nun hat SCHOLZ, m. E. nicht ohne schwerwiegende Gründe, zu erweisen versucht, daß Mars als Schutzgottheit unter etruskischem Einfluß schon in der späteren Königszeit von Jupiter Capitolinus zurückgedrängt und überschattet worden ist[77]. In diesem Zusammenhang ist es eine naheliegende Vermutung zu glauben, daß Augustus bewußt über die republikanische und etruskische Zeit auf Vorstellungen der älteren latinischen Königszeit zurückgreifen wollte. Mehr als eine Vermutung kann dies jedoch nicht sein.

Was blieb inzwischen übrig von der Idee der Rache? Nicht sehr viel, wie wir schon oben (S. 260) gesehen haben, aber wenigstens doch der Anlaß. Auch dieser war jedoch schon ideologisch untergraben. Das kann man aus der Propaganda schließen, die den Princeps in Kontrast zu seinen Kollegen im Triumvirat gerne schon von Anfang an als den Friedfertigen schildern möchte, ja, die ihn ausgerechnet bei Philippi als den versöhnlichen Sieger darstellen will[78].

Alle diese Überlegungen führen zu dem Schluß, daß Mars in der Ideologie des Principats natürlich als der Kriegsgott gelten konnte, aber älteren Vorstellungen gemäß noch als weit mehr; daß er, da der Krieg vor allem ein *iustum bellum* sein sollte, zugleich Beschützer der *pax Augusta* wurde; und daß im Mars Ultor-Kult der Rachegedanke allmählich abgeschwächt wurde und ideologisch kaum mehr zur Geltung kam[79].

IV. Die weitere Entwicklung; das Zeugnis der Münzen

Während der Jahrzehnte des julisch-claudischen Hauses sind die Erwähnungen des Mars Ultor-Kultes nicht sehr häufig. Die Seltenheit der

---

[77] SCHOLZ 157.

[78] Tac. Ann. I,9,4 (die Lobredner des Augustus sprechen): *multa Antonio, dum interfectores patris ulcisceretur, multa Lepido concessisse*; besonders Velleius Paterculus in seinem Epilog über die Schlacht bei Actium II,86,2: *Ex qua lenitate ducis colligi potuit, quem aut initio triumviratus sui aut in campis Philippiis, si ei licuisset, victoriae suae facturus fuisset modum.* Dabei ist es natürlich unwichtig, daß es hier um Geschichtsfälschung geht; wichtig ist nur, daß man dieses Bild des versöhnlichen Herrschers als glaubhaft hinstellen konnte.

[79] Es ist bemerkenswert, daß auch MORAWIECKI (s. o. Anm. 30) in seinem Artikel, der zu meiner Kenntnis gekommen ist, als der vorliegende Beitrag schon nahezu vollendet war, dem Kult des Mars Ultor eine viel weitere Bedeutung zuspricht als bloß die eines Gottes der Rache. Nach seiner Auffassung ist er die Personifikation von Roms Siegeskraft im allgemeinen.

inschriftlichen Zeugnisse ist auffallend; und bei denen, die vorliegen, handelt es sich meist um kurze Dedikationen, kaum oder gar nicht datierbar und ohne weitere Information[80]. In der Literatur gibt es einige Erwähnungen. Anläßlich der Apotheose des Augustus wurde seine goldene Totenmaske im Marstempel (wohl dem des Mars Ultor) aufgestellt[81]. Im Jahre 19 wurden Bogen für Germanicus und Drusus an den Seiten des Tempels errichtet, und zwar wieder im Zusammenhang mit der Bewahrung der *pax Augusta*[82]. Kurz darauf jedoch zeigten im Gefolge des Prozesses gegen Calpurnius Piso[83] gewisse Senatoren, daß auch der Gedanke der *ultio* noch einige Bedeutung hatte. Dasselbe tat Caligula, als er Dolche von Verschwörern in dem Tempel weihte. Ein Verschwörer gegen Claudius wollte ihn bei einem Opfer in diesem Tempel angreifen[84]. Nimmt man noch die beiläufigen Notizen in den 'Acta Fratrum Arvalium' hinzu (s. o. Anm. 80), dann ist das Material wohl erschöpft, und der Eindruck besteht, daß der großartig begonnene Kult auf dem Augustusforum in den ersten Jahrzehnten des Principats wenig Anklang gefunden hat.

Dieser Eindruck wird zuerst bestätigt, aber im weiteren Verlauf doch wesentlich modifiziert, wenn wir uns nun einer anderen Quelle, den kaiserlichen Münzen, zuwenden; da wird sich nach der Zeit des julisch-claudischen Hauses ein gewandeltes Bild herausstellen. Die Münzen sind völlig die Träger der kaiserlichen Ideologie und Propaganda, ungefähr wie die Briefmarkenausgaben mancher modernen Staaten, zumal in den letzten Jahrzehnten, es sind. Außerdem sind sie meistens genau datierbar. Nun könnte man einwenden, daß die Münzbilder nur traditionell gewesen seien und somit keine spezifische Bedeutung für die ideologischen Bestrebungen der einzelnen Kaiser hätten. Das trifft jedoch nicht zu. Man braucht nur in den großen Sammelwerken von

---

[80] In der großen Übersicht der italischen Kulte bei HERMANSEN findet man nur 92 (Aequiculi) CIL IX, 4108 (= DESSAU 3158, in ROSCHER's Liste Nr. 14): *Marti Ultori*, und 95 (Volcei, Lucania) CIL X, 1, 403 (in ROSCHER's Liste Nr. 39): *Iovi Conservatori et Marti Ultori ordo populusque Volceianus*. In den 'Acta Fratrum Arvalium' werden noch Opfer für Mars Ultor zu Ehren einiger Kaiser erwähnt (HENZEN S. 72; 121: Vitellius; 84: Nero; 86: Hadrianus, Antoninus Severi filius [= Caracalla]). Man würde erwarten, daß insbesondere in den Inschriften aus den Kreisen des römischen Heeres Mars einen wichtigen Platz einnehmen würde. Nun hat aber A. VON DOMASZEWSKI, Die Religion des römischen Heeres, Westdeutsche Zeitschrift für Geschichte und Kunst 14, 1895, 34 nachgewiesen, daß dies erst nach 250 der Fall ist, wobei sich außerdem vermuten läßt, daß dann *interpretatio Romana* eines germanischen Kriegsgottes vorliegt.

[81] Cass. Dio 56,46,4: ἐν ᾧ δ᾽ οὖν τὸ ἐν τῇ Ῥώμῃ ἡρῷον ἐγίγνετο, εἰκόνα αὐτοῦ χρυσῆν ἐπὶ κλίνης ἐς τὸν τοῦ Ἄρεως ναὸν ἔθεσαν.

[82] Tac. Ann. II,64,1: *Structi et arcus circum latera templi Martis Ultoris cum effigie Caesarum* (sc. *Germanici aque Drusi), laetiore Tiberio, quia pacem sapientia firmaverat, quam si bellum per acies confecisset.* S. über Tac. Ann. II,22 unt. Anm. 108.

[83] Tac. Ann. III,18: *Atque idem* (sc. *Tiberius), cum Valerius Messalinus signum aureum in aede Martis Ultoris, Caecina Severus aram ultionis statuendam censuisset, prohibuit, ob externas ea victorias sacrari dictitans, domestica mala tristitia operienda.*

[84] Suet. Calig. 24: *Tres gladios in necem suam praeparatos Marti Ultori addito elogio consecravit.* Cass. Dio 59,22,7: καὶ ξιφίδια τρία τῷ Ἄρει τῷ Τιμωρῷ ἐς τὴν Ῥώμην ἔπεμψε. Suet. Claud. 13: . . . *alter ut sacrificantem apud Martis aedem adoreretur.*

COHEN und MATTINGLY e.a. (s. u. Anm. 87) zu blättern, um das Gegenteil fest-
zustellen[85]. Die Münzprägungen bringen im allgemeinen den Charakter einer
Regierung klar zum Ausdruck. Dabei ist immer zu bedenken, daß es um Propa-
ganda geht; die Akzente werden daher so gesetzt, wie es der Regierung genehm
ist. Die paradoxe Erscheinung tritt dabei auf, daß der Kaiser manchmal den
Anspruch erhob, gerade das zu verwirklichen, was er nicht vollbringen konnte.
Der berüchtigtste Fall ist wohl das UBIQUE PAX auf einem Münztypus des
Gallienus, als das Reich in Wahrheit völlig zerrissen war[86].

Mars Ultor erscheint auf den Münzen des Augustus[87]. Wie schon oben
(Anm. 24) bemerkt ist, wird hier der kleine kapitolinische Tempel aus dem Jahre
20 v. Chr. dargestellt. Unter dem julisch-claudischen Hause gibt es keine
weiteren Mars Ultor-Typen mehr, was mit dem oben bemerkten verhältnismäßig geringen Anklang der Konzeption übereinstimmt. Auffallender ist noch,
daß auch andere Marstypen fehlen. Es läßt sich vermuten, daß dies mit der
geringen Rolle des Mars als Gott des römischen Heeres in Zusammenhang steht
(s. o. Anm. 80). Dann fällt ein Neubeginn in das Vierkaiserjahr[88]. Galba und
Vespasian machen wieder mit Mars Ultor Propaganda. Warum? Die Antwort
von CHAMBALU[89] war, daß diese Kaiser damit symbolisch auf das schlechte
Andenken ihrer Vorgänger reagieren, an ihnen „Rache nehmen" wollten: Das
schlechte Benehmen jener war wie eine Verschwörung gegen das römische Volk,
dergegenüber man die gleiche Haltung einnehmen konnte wie Caligula, als er
die Dolche der Verschwörer dem Mars Ultor schickte. Das ist gewiß eine

---

[85] Vgl. dazu die wichtigen Bemerkungen von H. MATTINGLY, Roman Coins (London [2]1960),
139—144; insbes. 143: "A picture of the government is built up, as it wished itself to be
seen"; 144: "The general shape of a reign is known from history; the coins give the added
colouring that was chosen by the Emperor". Einige Beispiele: Claudius I: DE BRITAN-
NIS; die Kaiser von 68—69 und dann wieder die Soldatenkaiser: FIDES MILITUM und
FIDES EXERCITUUM; Traianus: OPTIMO PRINCIPI; Hadrianus: RESTITUTOR
ACHAIAE, AFRICAE; Aurelianus: RESTITUTOR ORBIS. Vgl. D. MANNSPERGER,
ROM. ET AVG. Die Selbstdarstellung des Kaisertums in der römischen Reichsprägung:
ANRW II, 1, hrsg. v. H. TEMPORINI (Berlin—New York 1974), 919—946.

[86] MATTINGLY (s. vorige Anm.); COHEN (s. nächste Anm.) 1015—1019.

[87] Hier und in den folgenden Anmerkungen werden die Münztypen angeführt nach dem
Sammelwerk von H. COHEN, Description historique des monnaies frappées sous l'empire
romain I—VI (Paris [2]1930): hiernach angegeben mit C. Das zweite Sammelwerk von H.
MATTINGLY—E. A. SYDENHAM—C. H. V. SUTHERLAND—P. H. WEBB, The Roman Imperial
Coinage I (London 1923)—IV,3 ([2]1968); V (1927—1933) gibt nur in einzelnen Fällen Er-
gänzungen oder Verbesserungen; grundsätzlich wird das Bild durch Einbeziehung dieses
Werkes (hiernach angegeben mit M) nicht verändert. Im Rahmen dieser Arbeit werde ich
mich grundsätzlich auf die unter dem Principat geprägten Münzen beschränken. Die Mars
Ultor-Münzen des Augustus: C 189—204; vgl. auch 255—265 mit der Legende SIGNIS
(PARTHICIS) RECEPTIS (davon 258—262 mit Marsbild).

[88] Galba C 378, 380, 382, 384 (ULTOR); 376—377 (ADSERTOR); 138 (VICTOR); Vitellius
56, 58 (VICTOR); Vespasianus 270—271 (ULTOR); 264 (CONSERVATOR); 265, 268
(VICTOR); da Mars an sich von dieser Zeit an bei fast allen Kaisern vorkommt, wird im
allgemeinen hier auf Numerierung der einzelnen Typen, bei denen ein Epitheton fehlt, ver-
zichtet.

[89] CHAMBALU 733.

interessante Theorie. Aber liegt es nicht näher anzunehmen, daß diese Kaiser nichts anderes wollten als ein neuer Augustus, ein *optimus princeps* zu sein? Bemerkenswert ist dabei, daß Galba auch MARS ADSERTOR ('Befreier' oder 'Beschützer') und Vespasian MARS CONSERVATOR auf seinen Münzen prägen läßt[90]. MARS CONSERVATOR kehrt unter dem Principat nur noch bei Gallienus wieder[91] und wird nachher unter der Tetrarchie geläufig.

Übersieht man nun insgesamt die Beinamen des Mars auf den Münzen[92], dann ergibt sich folgendes: Einige Epitheta sind 'neutral', wie Augustus[93], Invictus[94], Pater[95], und kommen nur spärlich vor. Der einzige 'aggressive' Beiname, der auch mit einer aggressiven Darstellung des Gottes im Münzbild verbunden wird, ist Victor, und dieser ist weit verbreitet. Man findet ihn bei Galba, Vitellius und Vespasian[96], dann wieder bei verschiedenen der sogenannten Adoptivkaiser[97] und bei den meisten der Soldatenkaiser[98], bei denen das Epitheton sehr häufig vorkommt, worüber man sich nicht wundern wird. Auffallender ist, daß der defensive Aspekt des 'Beschützers' im Epitheton Propugnator im 3. Jahrhundert bei einer Reihe von Kaisern wieder hervortritt[99]. Dazu gesellt sich gleichzeitig ein anderer auffallender Beiname, Pacifer, bei dem der Gott mit einem Oelzweig dargestellt wird[100]. Dasselbe geschieht bei einem anderen Epitheton, Pacator, das sonst eine mehr aggressive Bedeutung ('Unterwerfer') haben konnte, das aber nach dem Symbol des Ölzweiges mit Pacifer gleichzusetzen ist[101]. Es wirkt fast wie eine Ironie, daß die Kaiser, die am

---

[90] Auf den Münzen von Anhängern des Civilis findet man in diesen Jahren ULTOR ADSERTOR: M I 192; allerdings ist die Echtheit zweifelhaft.

[91] Gallienus C 608.

[92] Ein bequemes Hilfsmittel ist dabei die alphabetische Registrierung in: M. BERNHART, Handbuch zur Münzkunde der römischen Kaiserzeit (Halle/Saale 1926), 51; 199 ff. (allerdings bei weitem nicht vollständig).

[93] Pescennius Niger C 48; Gallienus C 604; Tetricus I C 79.

[94] Pescennius Niger C 49; Aurelianus C 123–126.

[95] Septimius Severus C 311–314; Albinus C 45.

[96] Galba C 138; Vitellius C 56, 58; Vespasianus 265, 268.

[97] Trajanus M II 262; Antoninus Pius C 207 (d. h. der Münztypus ohne Erwähnung des Beinamens); M. Aurelius C 431–432; Commodus C 853 (wie bei Antoninus Pius).

[98] Pescennius Niger C 50–52; Septimius Severus C 319; Caracalla C 147, 217, 254 (die letzte wie bei Antoninus Pius Anm. 97); Geta C 76; Elagabal C 108–117; Severus Alexander C 177; Gallienus C 630; Postumus C 191; Victorinus C 74–76; Tetricus I C 80; Tetricus II C 26; Claudius II C 154, 170; Tacitus C 55–58; Florianus C 42; Probus C 347, 367; Numerianus C 18–24; Carinus C 51–53.

[99] Caracalla C 150–153; Severus Alexander M IV, 2, 68, 88; Gordianus III C 155–161; Herennius Etruscus C 7–8; Hostilianus C 10–16; Trajanus Decius M IV, 3, 144–145; Trebonianus C 70; Volusianus C 60; Aemilianus C 25; Gallienus C 623–629; Macrianus I C 2; Macrianus II C 9; Quietus C 9.

[100] Septimius Severus C 315–318; Caracalla C 260–262 (mit Ölzweig, aber ohne Beinamen); Severus Alexander C 172–176; Maximinus I C 28–29; Gordianus III C 162; Trebonianus C 71–73; Volusianus C 61; Aemilianus C 21–24; Valerianus I C 125; Gallienus C 609–622; Claudius II C 161–169; Quintillus C 47–50; Aurelianus C 127–133; Tacitus C 60–62; Florianus C 40–41; Probus C 350–366.

[101] Commodus C 349–353 (nach BERNHART: s. o. Anm. 92; man könnte hier auch PAC(I-FERO) lesen); Septimius Severus C 308–310; Caracalla 149; Quintillus C 46.

meisten gegen ständige Bedrohungen zu kämpfen hatten, den 'Friedensbringer' in der Propaganda besonders hervorhoben[102]. Man kann sich dem Eindruck nicht entziehen, daß diese Kaiser die Friedenspropaganda so intensiv betrieben, weil sie das Reich vor äußeren und inneren Drohungen schützen wollten, aber in der Tat nicht mehr die Kraft der 'Friedensherrscher' aus früheren Zeiten des Principats besaßen. Je mehr sie jene erfolglos nachzuahmen suchten, desto mehr glichen sie sich ihnen in der Ideologie an. Wenn man nun die Münzen mit der Aufschrift Mars Ultor überblickt[103], dann ergibt sich dasselbe Bild. Nach Augustus, Galba und Vespasian kehrt der Beiname erst bei Antoninus Pius und Marcus Aurelius wieder, die sicher mit ihrer Propaganda von *felicitas saeculi, hilaritas, libertas publica, pax, pietas* usw. die goldene Zeit der Ruhe und Wohlfahrt unter Augustus nachahmen und sogar noch übertreffen möchten; nachher tritt der Beiname ungefähr bei denselben Kaisern auf, die auch Mars Pacator und Pacifer führen, mit einem gewissen Übergewicht in der zweiten Hälfte des 3. Jahrhunderts. Aus der Übersicht der Münzen tritt also das merkwürdige Phänomen hervor, daß der Mars Ultor-Kult im ersten Jahrhundert im Hintergrund bleibt, um dann im zweiten Jahrhundert in gewissem Umfang, im dritten weit stärker in den Vordergrund zu treten und daß parallel dazu die Popaganda mit Mars Pacifer und Pacator sich entwickelt. Andererseits fehlt Gradivus als Beiname auf Münzen völlig, wie übrigens auch Mars Quirinus nicht anzutreffen ist. Mars Gradivus ist einige Male inschriftlich bezeugt[104]. Im allgemeinen ist es speziell ein poetischer Beiname, und es ist vielleicht kein Zufall, daß das interessanteste (und gut datierbare) inschriftliche Zeugnis eine Versinschrift ist, die im übrigen auch religionsgeschichtlichen Wert hat. Es handelt sich hier um eine Inschrift auf einem Tempel des Aesculapius und der Salus in Lambaesis in Numidien, wo ein *consul designatus,* dessen Name wegen der *damnatio memoriae* getilgt worden ist, um 167 unter Marcus Aurelius bezeugt, daß er den Heilgott Medaurus aus Dalmatien nach Afrika überführt hat, und von sich sagt, daß er als alter Krieger „dem Gradivus wohlbekannt" war[105]. Gradivus ist hier, wie öfters, einfach synonym für Mars.

Im Anfang des zweiten Jahrhunderts gibt es noch einen Fall, wo man glaubhaft machen kann, daß Mars Ultor noch wirklich „der Rächer" ist, sogar in stärkerem Maße, als er es meiner Meinung nach 20 v. Chr. und 2 v. Chr. gewesen war. Im Jahre 108/109 ließ Trajan in Dacia, bei dem heutigen Adamklissi

---

[102] Mars Pacifer ist auch inschriftlich bezeugt: CIL IX, 5060 (Interamnia, Picenum: *[M]arti Pacife[ro]*); HERMANSEN 41 (leider undatierbar); weiter DESSAU 3162 (Ribchester, Britannia).

[103] Antoninus Pius C 549—550; M. Aurelius C 430; Commodus C 346—348; Septimius Severus M IV, 1, 134; Albinus C 46; Caracalla C 148, 154; Severus Alexander C 157—170; Gallienus M V, 188; Claudius II C 155—160; Quintillus C 44—45; Tacitus C 59; Probus C 348—349; Carus C 39; Carinus C 49—50; auch in dem britannischen Teilreich unter Carausius findet man noch MARS ULTOR und MARS PACIFER: M V, 470, 533.

[104] DESSAU 3152 (Tusculum), 3153 (Aquileia), 3154 (Drobeta, Dacia), 9240 (Asturia).

[105] CIL VIII 2581:

> 9   *Notus Gradivo belli vetus ac tibi, Caesar*
> 10   *Marce, in primore [cl]arus* (?) *ubique acie.*

(Dobrudja), ein großes Siegesdenkmal aufrichten mit einer Inschrift[106], von der Stücke zu verschiedenen Zeiten wiedergefunden worden sind. Der rekonstruierte Text meldet, daß das Denkmal Mars Ultor geweiht ist. Es wird nun angenommen, daß es errichtet worden ist, um der Rache Trajans für die schmächliche Niederlage, die Domitians Truppen hier erlitten hatten, zu gedenken. Diese Auffassung stimmt mit den Reliefbildern überein, auf denen der Kaiser die Barbaren erbarmungslos verfolgt und eine Parade von Kriegsgefangenen vorführt, Kriegsgefangenen, die im oberen Register an Bäume gebunden gezeigt werden[107]. Zufällig ist auch der Name *Ultor* auf zwei Inschriftfragmenten verschiedener Zeiten gefunden worden: *VL* und *OR*, wobei die Rekonstruktion *VLTORI* sich auf winzige Spuren eines T[108] gründet. Das ist das einzige Beispiel einer buchstäblichen Deutung des Namens *Ultor*, das mit einem wirklichen und rücksichtslos unternommenen Rachefeldzug verbunden ist, das ich gefunden habe.

V. Schlußbetrachtung

Wir haben im Vorhergehenden die Entwicklung des Marskultes in den ersten drei Jahrhunderten unseres Zeitalters zu überblicken versucht, dabei ausgehend von der literarischen, der epigraphischen und, zumal im Fall der weiteren Entwicklung, der numismatischen Überlieferung. Dabei haben wir insbesondere die ideologischen Gesichtspunkte in den Vordergrund gerückt. Hiermit ist die Gefahr verbunden, daß man von Voraussetzungen ausgeht, die nicht jedem sofort einleuchten werden und die immer wieder überprüft werden müssen. In der Beurteilung des Mars Ultor-Kultes sind viele auch von der Annahme ausgegangen, daß Ultor ja „der Rächer" bedeutet und daß daher das Vorkommen dieses Beinamens in irgendeiner Weise mit einer wirklichen Rache zusammenhängen müsse. Ich bin dagegen von der Frage ausgegangen, wie es möglich war, daß dieser Mars Ultor-Kult, der bedeutendste Marskult unter dem Principat, ausgerechnet in einer Zeit eingerichtet wurde, in der die vorherr-

---

[106] CIL III Suppl. 12 467; F. B. FLORESCU, Das Siegesdenkmal von Adamklissi. Tropaeum Trajani (Bukarest—Bonn 1965), 61—67: *Marti Ultori / Imp(erator) Caesar divi / Nervae f(ilius) Nerva / Trajanus Aug(ustus) Germ(anicus) / Dacicus pont(ifex) max(imus) / trib(unicia) potest(ate) XIII / imp(erator) VI, co(n)s(ul) V, p(ater) p(atriae), / ? per exerc]itu[m . . .*

[107] I. A. RICHMOND, Adamklissi, Papers of the British School at Rome 35 (1967), 29—39.

[108] G. G. TOCILESCU, Monumentul de la Adamklissi (Bukarest 1895); DERS. unter Mitwirkung von O. BENNDORF u. G. NIEMANN, Das Monument von Adamklissi (Wien 1895). Unter vergleichbaren Umständen weihte Germanicus 16 n. Chr. einen Tempel *Marti et Jovi et Augusto* (Tac., Ann. II,22); nur der Kuriosität wegen erwähne ich hier, daß O. HIRSCHFELD, Augustus und sein Mimus vitae, Wiener Studien 5 (1883), 124 an dieser Stelle die Emendation *Marti Ultori et Augusto* vorgeschlagen hat; vgl. den Kommentar von E. KOESTERMANN I, 290.

schende Ideologie die der *pax Augusta* und des Konservativismus in militärischen Angelegenheiten geworden war. In dieser Richtung weiterdenkend habe ich zu erweisen gesucht, daß Ultor von der Zeit des flavischen Kaiserhauses an in Parallele mit Conservator, Propugnator, Pacator und Pacifer erscheint. Auch ich bin also an meinem Ausgangspunkt von einer bestimmten Voraussetzung ausgegangen, von der nämlich, daß eine in der Vorgeschichte nachweislich umfassendere Funktion des Gottes Mars noch um die Jahrtausendwende im Bewußtsein anwesend sein konnte. Für diese Voraussetzung gibt es gute Gründe, aber es läßt sich, soweit ich sehe, nicht schlüssig beweisen, daß ein alter Gedankeninhalt von Mars als Beschützer der Gemeinschaft von vornherein in der offiziell inspirierten Ideologie realisiert worden ist. Daher habe ich meine Schlüsse mit Zurückhaltung vorgetragen.

Ein Mißverständnis soll schließlich noch ausgeräumt werden. Es könnte der Eindruck entstehen, daß in diesem Beitrag gewissermaßen das Bild einer pazifistischen Ideologie im Rahmen des Marskultes gezeichnet werden sollte. Davon kann natürlich nicht die Rede sein. Es sollte niemals vergessen werden, daß der Augustusfriede ein schwer erkämpfter und noch dauernd zu erkämpfender Friede gewesen ist. Mars der Beschützer konnte zu jeder Zeit Mars der Angreifer werden, wie ja im Wesen fast jeder Gottheit eine Ambivalenz eingeschlossen liegt. Gerade da, wo Augustus in seinem Tatenbericht sich rühmt, das Tor des Janus geschlossen zu haben, unterstreicht er, daß dies von alters her üblich war bei einem durch Siege errungenen Frieden[109]. Und wo von der ideologischen Begründung der *pax Augusta* die Rede ist, sollte niemals die prägnante Formulierung Vergils, Aeneis VI, 851–853 außer acht gelassen werden:

> *Tu regere imperio populos, Romane, memento –*
> *hae tibi erunt artes –, pacique imponere morem,*
> *parcere subiectis et debellare superbos*[110].

Noch in der Zeit, als die *pax Augusta* von einer Realität zum Inhalt einer realitätsfernen, künstlichen Propaganda geworden war, gesellte sich zu Mars Ultor, Propugnator, Conservator, Pacifer und Pacator noch immer das Bild von Mars Victor mit Speer und Trophäe.

---

[109] Mon. Ancyr. 13: *Ianum Quirinum, quem claussum esse maiores nostri voluerunt cum per totum imperium populi Romani terra marique esset parta victoriis pax, cum priusquam nascerer a condita urbe bis omnino clausum fuisse prodatur memoriae, ter me principe senatus claudendum esse censuit.*

[110] Vgl. H. E. STIER, Augustusfriede und römische Klassik, ANRW II, 2, hrsg. v. H. TEMPORINI (Berlin–New York 1975), 3–54 und H. W. BENARIO, Augustus Princeps, ebd. 75–85 (insbes. 83 über die hier zitierte Vergilpassage). Vgl. auch W. HAASE, „Si vis pacem, para bellum". Zur Beurteilung militärischer Stärke in der römischen Kaiserzeit, Akten des XI. Internationalen Limeskongresses, Székesfehérvár 30.8.–6.9.1976, Budapest 1977, 721–755 (insbes. 742); vgl. ferner V. PÖSCHL, Virgil und Augustus, ANRW II, 31,2, hrsg. v. W. HAASE (Berlin–New York 1981), 709–727 (insbes. 716f.) und R. RIEKS, Vergils Dichtung als Zeugnis und Deutung der römischen Geschichte, ibid., 728–868 (insbes. 742 mit Anm. 61, 798, 835ff., 841 mit Anm. 540).

Bibliographie

A. CHAMBALU, Flaviana, Philologus 51 (1892), 720ff.; darin 730–734: 'Der Cultus des Mars Ultor von August bis Vespasian'. Diese ältere Arbeit ist, die betreffenden Abschnitte in den Handbüchern nicht mitgerechnet, die einzige Monographie, in der der Mars Ultor-Kult in seinem historischen Verlauf eingehend untersucht wird.

W. ROSCHER, Art. Mars, in: Ausführliches Lexikon der griechischen und römischen Mythologie II (Leipzig 1894–1897), 2385–2438; der ausführliche Artikel stützt sich auf eine frühere Arbeit: Apollon und Mars (Leipzig 1873). Diese Arbeit ist in manchen Hinsichten noch immer unentbehrlich, weil sie das gesamte damals zur Verfügung stehende Material enthält.

G. WISSOWA, Religion und Kultus der Römer, Handbuch der klassischen Altertumswissenschaft V 4, München ²1912.

E. MARBACH, Art. Mars, in: RE XIV, 2 (Stuttgart 1930), 1919–1937; 2582–2584. Sehr knappe, besonders klare Zusammenfassung aller Aspekte und Probleme.

G. HERMANSEN, Studien über den italischen und den römischen Mars, Kopenhagen 1940.

G. DUMÉZIL, Jupiter, Mars, Quirinus I–II, Paris 1941–1944.

H. WAGENVOORT, Studies in Roman Literature, Culture and Religion, Leiden 1956.

H. J. ROSE, Some Problems of Classical Religion, Eitrem Lectures 1, Oslo 1958.

K. LATTE, Römische Religionsgeschichte, Handbuch der Altertumswissenschaft V 4, München 1960.

J. BALKESTEIN, Onderzoek naar de oorspronkelijke zin en betekenis van de Romeinse god Mars, Assen 1963 (Diss. Leiden).

G. RADKE, Die Götter Altitaliens, Fontes et commentationes 3, Münster 1965 (2., durchgesehene und ergänzte Auflage Münster 1979).

G. DUMÉZIL, La religion romaine archaique, Paris 1966.

U. W. SCHOLZ, Studien zum altitalischen und altrömischen Marskult und Marsmythos, Bibliothek der klass. Altertumswiss., N.F., 2. Reihe, Bd. 35, Heidelberg 1970.

Quirinus.
Eine kritische Überprüfung der Überlieferung und ein Versuch

von GERHARD RADKE, Berlin

Inhalt

Abkürzungen:

AC	L'Antiquité Classique, Louvain
AJPh	American Journal of Philology, Baltimore
ANRW	Aufstieg und Niedergang der römischen Welt. Geschichte und Kultur Roms im Spiegel der neueren Forschung, edd. H. TEMPORINI—W. HAASE, Berlin—New York 1972ff.
ARW	Archiv für Religionswissenschaft, Leipzig—Berlin
BCAR	Bullettino della Commissione Archeologica Comunale in Roma, Roma
BN	Beiträge zur Namenforschung, Heidelberg
CGlL	Corpus Glossariorum Latinorum, edd. G. LOEWE—G. GÖTZ, Leipzig 1888—1923, ND Amsterdam 1964
CIL	Corpus Inscriptionum Latinarum, Leipzig—Berlin 1862ff., ed altera 1893ff.
CR	Classical Review, Oxford
GL	Grammatici Latini, ed. H. KEIL, Leipzig 1855—80, ND Hildesheim 1961
ILLRP	Inscriptiones Latinae Liberae Rei Publicae[2], ed. A. DEGRASSI, Firenze 1966
ILS	Inscriptiones Latinae Selectae, ed. H. DESSAU, Berlin 1892—1916, ND Berlin 1954/55
JRSt	Journal of Roman Studies, London
Kl.Pauly	Der kleine Pauly. Lexikon der Antike, Stuttgart 1964—75

I. Der Kult des Gottes

Quirinus ist eine jener Gottheiten aus der Frühzeit Roms, deren Wesen in den Schatten[1] des Vergessens zurückgefallen ist; nur vereinzelt lassen sich bruchstückhafte[2] Spuren mehr erraten als erkennen. Sie sind durch willkürliche Änderungen der Kultinhalte[3] schon im Altertum verfremdet und durch moderne Fehlinterpretationen[4] mehr oder weniger verfälscht worden. Mit dem Anwachsen des Schrifttums verfestigten sich bedauerlicherweise gerade diese.

LEC	Les Études Classiques, Namur
LEW	A. WALDE–J. B. HOFMANN, Lateinisches etymologisches Wörterbuch[3], Heidelberg 1938/53
MDAI(R)	Mitteilungen des Deutschen Archäologischen Instituts Rom, Mainz
MEFR	Mélanges d'Archéologie et d'Histoire de l'École Française de Rome, Paris
Myth.Lex.	W. H. ROSCHERS Ausführliches Lexikon der griechischen und römischen Mythologie, Leipzig 1884ff., ND Hildesheim 1965
Philol.	Philologus. Zeitschrift für klassische Philologie, Berlin
PID	R. S. CONWAY–J. WHATMOUGH–S. E. JOHNSON, The Prae-Italic Dialects of Italy, Cambridge 1933, ND Hildesheim 1968
PMAA	Papers and Monographs of the American Academy in Rome, Rome
RE	PAULYS Realencyclopädie der classischen Altertumswissenschaft, Stuttgart 1893ff.
REL	Revue des Études Latines, Paris
Rhein.Mus.	Rheinisches Museum für Philologie, Frankfurt a. M.
RHR	Revue de l'Histoire des Religions, Paris
RIL	Rendiconti dell'Istituto Lombardo, Classe di lettere, scienze morali e storiche, Milano
SCO	Studi Classici e Orientali, Pisa
SE	Studi Etruschi, Firenze
SMSR	Studi e Materiali di Storia delle Religioni, Roma
ZRGG	Zeitschrift für Religions- und Geistesgeschichte, Köln

[1] W. BURKERT, Historia 11, 1962, 359: „Quirinus eine der schattenhaftesten Gestalten unter den Göttern Roms"; vgl. F. BÖMER, Die Fasten Ovids II S. 116.

[2] C. KOCH, Religio 18: „Was wir an Überlieferung über den Quirinus-Kult besitzen, gleicht Mauerstücken einer vielgestaltigen, ungemein verfallenen Ruine".

[3] C. KOCH a. O. 17: „vordem eine Gestalt, die die Überlieferung als Patron des sabinischen Bevölkerungsteils der Stadt betrachtet, später der vergöttlichte conditor urbis, Romulus".

[4] Vgl. beispielsweise P. KRETSCHMER, Glotta 10, 1920, 151: „der zur Gesamtmännerschaft gehörige Gott, der Gott der Bürgerschaft". F. MULLER, Altitalisches Wörterb., 1926, 108: „Männergenossenschaftsgott". M. G. BRUNO(-TIBILETTI), I Sabini e la loro lingua, RIL 95, 1961, 508 „dio della curia, dell'assemblea". G. DUMÉZIL, Rel.Rom.Arch., 1966, 246: «le patron des hommes considérés dans leur totalité organique». Weil griech. πρῖνος vermutlich vorgriechischer Herkunft ist (J. B. HOFMANN, Etymologisches Wörterbuch des Griechischen, München 1950 [²1966] 284), entfällt die Deutung als 'Eichengott' (A. B. COOK, CR 18, 1904, 368f.). Auch die verbreitete Herleitung von einem fiktiven Ortsnamen *Quirium (G. WISSOWA, Rel., ²1912, 154, 1; DERS., Myth.Lex. IV [1909–1915], 11. L. DEUBNER, MDAI(R) 36/7, 1921/2, 14ff. C. KOCH, Rel. 26f. K. LATTE, Röm.

Eine Bestandsaufnahme ergibt:

Nach dem Gotte Quirinus[5] sind sein Priester, der *flamen Quirinalis*[6], und sein Fest, die *Quirinalia*[7] am 17. Februar[8], benannt. Ein *sacellum* des Quirinus gab der nahegelegenen *Quirinalis porta*[9], der Tempel des Gottes zuerst dem eigentlichen *collis Quirinalis*[10] und später dem ganzen Höhenzug den Namen. Wird dieser demnach dem Gotte verdankt, erübrigen sich die Versuche, aus der Siedlungsgeschichte den Kult erklären zu wollen[11]. Die Aufnahme des Festes in den ältesten römischen Kalender sichert dieses für das 6. Jhdt. v. Chr.[12], während der Name des Tores zum Bau der vermutlich nach dem Galliereinfall errichteten Mauer des frühen 4. Jhdts. v. Chr. gehört und für das Heiligtum ein entsprechend höheres Alter voraussetzt. Der *flamen Quirinalis* konnte seine Stellung zusammen mit den beiden anderen *flamines maiores* zwischen *rex sacrorum* und *pontifex maximus*[13] erst nach der Vertreibung des politischen Königs und Übertragung von dessen priesterlichen Aufgaben auf den Opferkönig einnehmen, d. h. also um die Wende vom 6. zum 5. Jhdt. v. Chr.; seine Obliegenheiten als Priester des Quirinus dürfte er freilich unabhängig davon schon früher erfüllt haben.

Rel.Gesch. 113: „Gottheit vom Quirinal") oder *Currium* (W. Otto, Philol. 64, 1905, 201) wird von J. Poucet, Recherches sur la légende sabine des origines de Rome, 1967, 45 abgelehnt. Zu hethit. *kuirwanas* vgl. LEW 1, 169.

[5] Quirinus führt häufig das Epitheton *pater*: Enn.ann. 117. Lucil. 22 M. Liv. 5,52,7. Verg. Aen. 6,859. Sil. 8.696.

[6] Fest. 198,31 L. Cic.Phil. 2,110. Liv. 1,20,2. Gai. 1,112. Plut.Numa 7.

[7] Varro l.l. 6,13. Fest. 304,5 f. L. *Quirinalia mense Februario dies quo Quirini fiunt sacra.* Paul.Fest. 305,1 L. Fest. 418,33 ff. L. Paul.Fest. 419,5 ff. L. – Wenn D. Porte 320 die Quirinalia als Fest der *curiae* anspricht, kann ich dem aus sprachlichen Gründen (s. u. Anm. 89.90.91) nicht folgen; zum Inhalt sagt D. Porte a. O. selbst, daß der *curio maximus* vor den Quirinalia tätig war, sein Wirken für die *curiae* also nicht mit den Quirinalia zu verbinden ist.

[8] Ov.fast. 2,511. Fast.Caer.CIL I² p. 212. Maff. p. 223. Farn. p. 250. Philocal. p. 258. Polem.Silv. p. 259 *quo die Romulus occisus a suis*. Fast.Ant.vet.(ILLRP 9).

[9] Paul.Fest. 303,5 f. L. *Quirinalis porta dicta, sive quod ea in collem Quirinalem itur seu quod proxime eam est Quirini sacellum*; vgl. die Namen der *portae Salutaris, Sanqualis* und *Lavernalis* nach den jeweils den Toren nahegelegenen Heiligtümern.

[10] Varro l.l. 5,51. Fest. 304,11 ff. L. *quod in eo factum sit templum Quirini, est dictum.* Paul. Fest. 305,6 f. L. Ov.met. 14,836 f. mit einer etymologischen Anspielung auf den Namen des Quirinal (*qui viret*). J. Paoli, in: Studi in onore di U. E. Paoli, 1955, 527 ff., lehnt die Annahme ab, der Hügel sei nach dem Gotte benannt; ihm pflichtet J. Gagé, Mél. Piganiol III, 1966, 1591 f. bei. Aus Varro ergibt sich jedoch, daß ursprünglich nur der nördlich des *vicus Salutaris* gelegene Teilhügel *collis Quirinalis* hieß; der Name wurde später (vgl. Cic. rep. 2,20 *in eo colle . . . qui nunc Quirinalis vocatur*) ausgedehnt.

[11] Der Name *Quirinalis* ist nicht von fiktivem *Quirium*, sondern erst von dem des *Quirinus* abgeleitet; vgl. F. Altheim, Röm.Rel.Gesch. I, 1931, 67. G. Radke, RE XXIV 1 (1963), 1299 f.

[12] Vgl. G. Wissowa, Rel.² 31. F. Altheim, Röm.Rel.Gesch. I, 1931, 28. C. Koch, Rel. 28 f. K. Latte, Röm.Rel.Gesch. 2. E. J. Bickerman, Chronologie², Leipzig 1963, 25. Ders., Chronology of the Ancient World, London 1968 (²1969), 44 f. A. Kirsopp Michels, The Calendar of the Roman Republic, Princeton 1967, 207 ff.

[13] Fest. 198,29 ff. L.

Seit wann und warum Quirinus mit Mars[14] — immerhin mit deutlicher Unterscheidung des besonderen Wirkungsfeldes[15] — identifiziert wurde und seit wann und warum man glaubte, Romulus[16] sei unter dem Namen des Quirinus zu verehren, wird nur mit unsicheren Hypothesen beantwortet. Die Glaubwürdigkeit sabinischer Herkunft des Gottes[17] wächst, wenn er mit Mars, und sinkt, wenn er mit Romulus gleichgesetzt wird. Ob schließlich die tribus Quirina ihren Namen nach Quirinus[18] hat, ist höchst ungewiß, da man nicht begreift, daß unter 35 römischen tribus nur diese eine nach einem Gotte heißen sollte.

Die aedes[19] Quirini auf dem Quirinal, nach Plin. n.h. 15, 120 eines der antiquissima delubra Roms, wurde — umstritten[20], ob am Platze der ara[21], des

[14] Serv.Aen. 6,859 *Quirinus autem et Mars.* Macr. 1.9.16. Serv. auct. Aen. 7,610. Schol. Turon.Serv.Aen. 7,612. Lyd.mens. 4,1. Ov.met. 14,828. fast. 375.796; vgl. L. PRELLER— H. JORDAN, Röm.Myth. I³, 334.369. Weder Serv.Aen. 1,292. 6,859 noch Mart.Cap. 1,46. 50 erweisen einen Doppelnamen *Mars Quirinus.* Vor D. PORTE 323 hat schon SCHOLZ 19 auf ein Gegenüber Mars Gradivus — Mars Quirinus bei Serv.Aen. 1,292 hingewiesen. Der Doppelname Mars Gradivus kommt nur auf späten außerrömischen Inschriften (WISSOWA, Rel.² 146 Anm. 1), bei Liv. 1,20,4. 5,52,7 und Auson. LXVII 4 p. 337 PEIPER vor, während in den übrigen Beispielen bei Verg., Ovid., Sen., Germanicus, Lucan., Valer.Flacc., Stat., Iuven., Sil., Avien., Manil., Claudian. und Mart.Cap. nur Gradivus allein — meist als Vokativ *Gradive* — genannt wird (vgl. auch Paul.Fest. 86,15 L. *Gradivus Mars appellatur*); besonders kennzeichnend sind Sil. 4,222. 9,290. Und dennoch ist nicht auszuschließen, daß Mars Quirinus, der Mars der Umfriedung, von den Griechen als Ares Enyalios mißdeutet wurde und so eine Identifikation von Quirinus und Enyalios entstand. Seit Polyb. 3,25,6 wird Quirinus in griechischer Sprache meist Enyalios (vgl. Monum.Anc. 13) genannt; demnach muß schon im 2. Jhdt. v. Chr. Quirinus als Kriegsgott vorstellbar gewesen sein: Er hat offenbar eine Bedeutungsentwicklung durchgemacht, die der des Mars entspricht.

[15] Serv.Aen. 1,292 *cum tranquillus est, Quirinus.* 6,859 *qui praeest paci.* Claudian. IV cons. Hon. 8 *positisque parumper bellorum signis sequitur vexilla Quirini.* Varro bei Dion.Hal. ant. 2,48,2, woraus BRELICH, Quirinus, SMSR 31, 1960, 74 auf die Absicht einer bewußten Unterscheidung von Mars schließt.

[16] Cic.rep. 2,20. leg. 1,3. 2,19. nat.deor. 2,62. off. 3,41. Hor.ep. 16,13. c.3,3,15. Elog.CIL I² p. 189; Zweifel an der Identität bei Tertull.spect. 9.

[17] L. PRELLER—H. JORDAN a. O. 278.334.369. K. J. BELOCH, Römische Geschichte, Berlin 1926, 264. A. v. BLUMENTHAL, Rhein.Mus. 90, 1941, 310ff. H. WAGENVOORT, Studies etc. 181 (sabinischer Kriegsgott der vorkapitolinischen Trias, aber auch Fruchtbarkeitsgott). F. BÖMER, Die Fasten Ovids II S. 115. Ablehnung bei J. POUCET, a. O. 70f.

[18] Fest. 304,16f. L. *a Curensibus Sabinis.* Cic.Quint. 24. CIL I² 546 (= ILLRP 1249). 1259 (= ILLRP 802). 1855 (= ILLRP 531); vgl. jedoch C. KOCH, Rel. 23 „von Quirina kann man Quirinus und Quirites nicht trennen"; L. ROSS TAYLOR, The Voting Districts of the Roman Republic, PMAA 20, Roma 1960, 63f. leitet den Namen der Tribus von dem des M'. Curius Dentatus her.

[19] Varro l.l. 5,52. Liv. 4,21,9. 10,46,7. Monum.Anc. 19. Vitruv. 3,2,7. Plin.n.h. 7,123. 15,120. Bei Fest. 304,16L. Paul.Fest. 305,4L. Ov.fast. 2,511. 6,796 heißt es *templum* oder *templa.*

[20] O. RICHTER, Topogr.² 286,1 gegen G. WISSOWA, Der Tempel des Quirinus in Rom, Hermes 26, 1891, 138f. = DERS., Gesammelte Abhandlungen zur römischen Religions- und Stadtgeschichte, München 1904, 146.

[21] Varro l.l. 5,74 (der Begriff einer *ara* kann an dieser Stelle symbolisch für 'Kult' gemeint sein).

19*

fanum[22] und des *sacellum*[23] oder an einer weiter südlich gelegenen Stelle – i.J. 293 v.Chr. geweiht[24], i.J. 206 v.Chr. vom Blitz getroffen[25], i.J. 49 v.Chr. durch Feuer zerstört[26], konnte jedoch i. J. 46 v. Chr. schon wieder eine Statue Caesars aufnehmen, deren Sockelinschrift in griechischer Überlieferung als θεῷ ἀνικήτῳ erhalten ist[27]; der Neubau des Augustus i.J. 16 v.Chr.[28] zeigte im Giebelfeld die Zwillinge Romulus und Remus beim *augurium augustum*[29].

Am 29. Juni[30] wurden dem Quirinus, an den Volcanalia des 23. August dem Quirinus in colle[31] und der Hora Quirini[32] Opfer gebracht; in einem Kalender des 4. nachchristl. Jhdts.[33] gilt der 3. April als *natalis dei Quirini*. Im Bereich des Quirinus wirken Ianus[34], Hora[35] und die Virites[36] sowie nach den unsicheren Zeugnissen je einer Weihung[37] Iupiter und Hercules.

Die *arma*[38] *Quirini* wurden vom *flamen Portunalis* an einem nicht bekannten Tage[39] unter Verwendung eines *persillum*[40] eingeschmiert; wie und

---

[22] Varro l.l. 5,51.

[23] Paul.Fest. 303,6 L.

[24] Liv. 10,46,7.

[25] Liv. 28,11,4.

[26] Cass.Dio 41,14,3.

[27] Cass.Dio 43,45,2. Cic.Att. 12,45,3. 13,28,3.

[28] Cass. Dio 54,19,4. Monum.Anc. 19. Vitruv. 3,2,7. Ov.fast. 6,796.

[29] MDAI(R) 19,1904, Taf. 4; vgl. W. BURKERT a. O. 358. Die Zwillinge als *Quirini* bei Iuven. 11,105.

[30] Fast.Venus. CIL I² 221. Ov.fast. 6,706. Dieser Tag ist erst von Caesar dem Kalender hinzugefügt worden.

[31] Fast.Arv.CIL I² p. 215 *QUIR.IN COLLE*.

[32] Fast. Ant.vet. (= ILLRP 9) *[H]ORAE QUI[R]* (so!).

[33] Philocal. CIL I² p. 262 *n. dei Quirini*.

[34] Liv. 1,32,9 *tu, Iane Quirine* (codd. bieten *Iuno*!). Monum.Anc. 13. Suet.Aug. 22. Macr. 1,9,16. Lyd.mens. 4,1 (bei Lyd. mens. 4,2 wird nur Ianus, nicht Ianus Quirinus genannt); vgl. R. SCHILLING, MEFR 72, 1960, 166f.

[35] Enn.ann. 117. Fast.Ant.vet. (= ILLRP 9) zum 23. Sext. Ov.met. 14,851. Gell. 13,23,2. Plut.qu.Rom. 46 p. 275F.

[36] Gell. 13,23,2.

[37] CIL IX 3303 aus Superaequum/Castel d'Ieri *[IO]VI QUIRINO* und *IOVI CYRIN[O]*; zu Hercules vgl. ST. WEINSTOCK, JRSt 51, 1961, 212. J. POUCET, Recherches 68 Anm. 249.

[38] Verg.georg. 3,27 *victorisque arma Quirini* wird immer wieder als Beispiel des *armiferi . . . Quirini* (Sil. 16,76 kaum zitiert) genannt; einer beruft sich auf den anderen: So zitiert W. BURKERT a. O. 360 Anm. 26 WISSOWA, KOCH und LATTE für die Vorstellung von den *arma Quirini*, ohne daß an den genannten Stellen reichere Auskunft zu finden wäre. Berufung auf die Schilde (Liv. 5,52,7. Stat.silv. 5,2,125ff.) ist ganz unzuverlässig; man könnte nur daran erinnern, daß Quirinus bei Arnob. 4,3 seine Lanze vom Aventin zum Palatium hinüberwarf, was sonst dem Romulus zugeschrieben wird (Serv.Aen. 3,46. Plut. Rom. 20,6); ein 'Lanzenfetisch' (L. DEUBNER, ARW 8, 1905 [Usener-Beiheft] 75; DERS., in: CHANTEPIE DE LA SAUSSAYE, Lehrb.d.Rel.Gesch.⁴II, 440) ist er deshalb noch nicht.

[39] A. BRELICH, Quirinus, SMSR 31, 1960, 67. C. KOCH, Rel. 21 weisen auf die Frist von sechs Monaten zwischen Quirinalia und Portunalia hin, jedoch liegt das letztgenannte Datum zu früh, um der Wintervorbereitung irgendeines Gerätes dienen zu können.

[40] Fest. 238,7ff. L. *persillum vocant sacerdotes rudiculum picatum, quo unguine flamen Portunalis arma Quirini unguet*. Paul.Fest. 239,2f. L. *persillum dicebant vas quoddam pica-*

womit das geschah, was *persillum* bedeutet und was unter den *arma* zu verstehen ist, läßt sich nicht eindeutig bestimmen. Der *flamen Quirinalis* wurde bei Kultakten für Acca Larentia im April[41], für Robigo (so!) an den Robigalia des 25. April[42] und zusammen mit den *virgines* an den Consualia des 21. August[43] tätig[44], woraus einleuchtend auf agrarische Funktionen des Gottes geschlossen wurde[45]. Eine Beziehung zu den *virgines Vestales* läßt sich darüber hinaus auch bei Gelegenheit der Bergung der *sacra* beim Galliereinfall beobachten[46].

Man konnte bei Quirinus schwören[47].

Quirinus soll mit einem aboriginischen Mädchen, das in seinem Heiligtum tanzen wollte, den Modius Fabidius, späteren Gründer der Stadt Cures, gezeugt haben[48].

Das älteste[49] inschriftliche Zeugnis ist auf dem Quirinal gefunden: Eine Weihung des Prätors *L. Aemilius L.f.* aus der Wende vom 3. zum 2. Jhdt. v. Chr.[50]

II. Quirinus gehört zu keiner Trias

Die verbreitete Annahme, Quirinus habe zusammen mit Iupiter und Mars einer vorkapitolinischen Trias angehört[51], stützt sich besonders auf die Rolle der zu diesen Göttern gehörigen drei *flamines maiores*[52], für deren Stellung nach

tum in quo unguentum, unde arma Quirini unguebantur. Der Hinweis von D. PORTE 310 auf die Verwendbarkeit von Pech für Holz und Leder ist sehr bedeutsam.

[41] Gell. 7,7,7. Plut.Rom. 4,5. qu.Rom. 35 p. 272F; vgl. G. RADKE, ANRW I, 2 (1972), 424 (Datierungen auf den Dezember widersprechen den Angaben Plutarchs, finden sich aber bei vielen Forschern, mitunter sogar mit der abwegigen Ansetzung auf den 25. Dezember).

[42] Ov.fast. 4,910.

[43] Tertull.spect. 5,8 (Angaben sind nicht identisch mit denen bei Varro l.l. 6,21) *sacrificant apud eam nonis Iuliis sacerdotes publici, XII kalend. Septembres flamen Quirinalis et virgines*; für den *flamen Quirinalis* gilt also eindeutig nur das Augustdatum, was oft übersehen wird.

[44] K. LATTE, Röm.Rel.Gesch. 114 Anm. 1 bezweifelt die Nachricht m. E. zu Unrecht.

[45] A. PIGANIOL, Essai sur les origines de Rome, 1917, 114. G. DUMÉZIL, Héritage indoeurop. à Rome, 1949, 92. J. PAOLI, Quirinus, in: Studi U. E. Paoli 1956, 530 Anm. 2. E. C. EVANS, Cults of the Sabine Territory, PMAA 11, 1939, 224. A. BRELICH a. O. 80ff. W. BURKERT a. O. 360.

[46] Liv. 5,40,7. Val.Max. 1,1,10. Plut.Cam. 21,2. Strab. 5,220.

[47] Paul.Fest. 71,17L. *equirine*. Cass.Dio frg. 4,7M. πρὸς τοῦ Κυρίνου.

[48] Dion.Hal.ant. 2,48,2ff. vgl. J. POUCET a. O. 56.

[49] Angebliche Erwähnung in einer *lex Numae* (Fest. 204,12L. Serv. Aen. 6,859) ohne chronolog. Wert; zu zwei Münzen vgl. POUCET a. O. 42f.

[50] CIL I² 803 (= ILLRP 251).

[51] Vgl. G. WISSOWA, Rel.² 154. A. BRELICH a. O. 64f. J. POUCET a. O. 23. G. DUMÉZIL, Rel.Rom.Arch. 272ff. P. GRIMAL, Dict. 405. R. SCHILLING, The Rom.Rel. 458. K. LATTE, Röm.Rel.Gesch. ignoriert diese Trias mit Recht.

[52] Paul.Fest. 137,1L. Gai. 1,112. Aug.civ. 2,15. Bei Liv. 1,21,4 bleiben die Namen der einzelnen *flamines* im Fides-Kult unerwähnt, so daß diese Stelle nicht auswertbar ist; vgl. K. LATTE a. O. 237 Anm. 4.

dem *rex sacrorum* und vor dem *pontifex maximus* sich im Vorausgehenden (ob.
S. 278) ein ziemlich spätes Datum hatte finden lassen; da den Gottheiten der
sicheren Triaden auf dem Kapitol und am Fuße des Aventin keine besonderen
Dreiergruppen von Priestern zugeordnet werden, ist diese Argumentation wenig
überzeugend. Auch der Hinweis[53] auf die im umbrischen Iguvium unter dem
Übernamen Grabovius vereinigten Götter Iupiter, Mars und Vofionus spricht
sogar eher gegen die Annahme einer solchen Trias, da man dem Iupiter Grabovius an der *porta Trebulana*[54], dem Mars Grabovius an der *porta Tessinaca*[55]
und dem Vofionus Grabovius an der *porta Veia*[56] opferte, die drei Götter also
nicht an einem gemeinsamen Kultplatze verehrt wurden; gerade das aber müßte
doch für eine Trias vorauszusetzen sein[57]. Eine Bedeutungsidentität von
Vofionus mit Quirinus[58] läßt sich nicht nachweisen.

Die Nennung der drei Götter zusammen mit einer Reihe anderer Gottheiten innerhalb der Devotionsformel[59] besagt ebensowenig wie ihre gemeinsame Erwähnung bei Lucil. frg. 20−22 M., wo neben dem *pater optumus divum*
die Götter Neptunus, Liber, Saturnus, Mars, Ianus und Quirinus genannt
werden, weil ihnen allen die Anrede *pater* zusteht[60]. Daß die Fetialen ihren Eid
bei der angeblichen Trias Iupiter, Mars und Quirinus zugleich leisteten[61], ist der
Überlieferung nicht zu entnehmen. Die Angabe, die Salier stehen *in tutela Iovis
Martis Quirini*[62], ist nach LATTE 113, Anm. 3 „sicher falsch", dem ich bei-
pflichte: Salier Iupiters sind sonst unbekannt ebenso wie Salier im Ianuskult[63],
die unter dem Eindruck der Übereinstimmung ihrer Zwölfzahl mit der der
Monate erfunden wurden.

---

[53] Vgl. R. BLOCH, REL 41, 1963, 115ff. A. J. PFIFFIG, Rel.Iguv., 1964, 1ff. G. DUMÉZIL,
Rel.Rom.Arch., 1966, 155f.

[54] Tab.Iguv. I a 2f.

[55] Tab.Iguv. I a 7f.

[56] Tab.Iguv. I a 11.

[57] Sowohl die kapitolinische Trias Iuppiter O.M., Iuno Regina und Minerva wie auch die
aventinische Trias Ceres, Liber und Libera werden in jeweils einem Tempel verehrt; das gilt
selbst für die zweifelhafte Trias des Capitolium vetus auf dem Quirinal (Varro l.l. 5,158).

[58] Vgl. A. BRELICH a. O. 118. E. C. EVANS, The Cult of the Sabine Territory, PMAA 11,
Rome 1939, 225. W. MEID, BN 8, 1957, 106.

[59] Liv. 8,9,6.

[60] Demnach kann der Schlußfolgerung bei D. PORTE 312 (« *la première attestation de ce ianus
quirinus remonte à Lucilius* ») nicht zugestimmt werden.

[61] Von den Fetialen werden bei Liv. 1,32,9 Iuppiter und Ianus Quirinus angerufen; Polyb. 3,
25,6 bezeugt für den ersten Karthagervertrag den Eid bei Ζεὺς λίθος, für die späteren Verträge jedoch bei Ares und Enyalios. A. BRELICH, Quirinus 65, nennt zu Unrecht alle drei
Götter nebeneinander.

[62] Serv.Aen. 8,663. Lyd.mens. 4,2 p. 64,17 W. nennt allein Ianus. Nach J. POUCET, Rech.
28,96 gehören Salier nur zu Mars; vgl. DERS., ANRW I 1 (1972), 105f.

[63] Nachdem Lyd.mens. 4,1 eine lange Reihe von Beinamen des Ianus aufgezählt hat (Κον-
σίβιος, Κήνουλος, Κιβούλλιος, Πατρίκιος, Κλουσίβιος, ᾿Ιουνώνιος, Κυρῖνος, Πατούλ-
κιος, Κλούσιος, Κουριάτιος, Αἰωνάριος), geht er in 4,2 auf die Beziehungen des Ianus
(nicht des Ianus Quirinus) zum Kalender ein und sagt, wegen der Zwölfzahl der Monate
habe Numa auch die zwölf Salier ὑμνοῦντας τὸν ᾿Ιανόν eingesetzt.

Obwohl ein letztes Argument bis in die Anfangszeit Roms zurückzureichen scheint, bringt es keinen Nachweis für die Zugehörigkeit des Quirinus zu einer Trias: Die *opima spolia*, die ein römischer Feldherr dem Führer der Feinde abgewann, wenn er ihn im Zweikampf tötete, wurden dem Iupiter Feretrius geweiht[64]; das geschah – jeweils unter ausdrücklicher Namensnennung nur dieses Gottes – dreimal in der römischen Geschichte und wurde ein viertes Mal für Caesar als Fiktion eingeräumt[65]. Auch Ablehnungen bei Nichterfüllung der Voraussetzung eigener Auspizien sind bekannt[66]. Die nicht mehr sicher kenntlichen Regeln eines angeblichen Gesetzes des Numa Pompilius[67], wonach lediglich *spolia prima* dem Iupiter Feretrius, *spolia secunda* jedoch dem Mars und *spolia tertia* dem Ianus Quirinus[68] darzubringen seien, sind schwer auslegbar und beruhen vermutlich auf einem Mißverständnis der Überlieferung, dem schon Verg. Aen. 6, 859 verfiel und das auch durch D. PORTE 308 nicht gelöst wird. Selbst wenn eine Unterscheidung hinsichtlich der Zuständigkeit der genannten drei Götter vorläge, wäre sie nicht beweiskräftig für eine Trias Iupiter, Mars, Quirinus. Wieder wiegen die trennenden Faktoren schwerer als die verbindenden: Der Tempel des Iupiter Feretrius steht auf dem Kapitol[69]; Mars soll die ihm gebührende Weihung an seiner *ara* auf dem *campus* erhalten[70]; bei Ianus Quirinus bleibt es ungewiß, ob der Ianusbogen auf dem Forum Romanum oder der heilige Bezirk auf dem Quirinal gemeint ist. Wie dem auch sei, jedenfalls sind drei in ihrer Art unterschiedliche – *aedes, ara, arcus* oder *fanum* – und regional voneinander getrennte Kultstätten schlecht geeignet, die Annahme einer Trias zu bestärken. Aus der unbewiesenen Vermutung, Quirinus habe einer solchen angehört, läßt sich demnach für das Verständnis seines Wesens keine Auskunft gewinnen.

---

[64] Fest. 202,23 ff. L. *unde spolia quoque quae dux populi Romani duci hostium detraxit.* Serv. Aen. 6,859. 10,449.

[65] Es werden Romulus, Cossus und Marcellus genannt; vgl. Fest. 204,1 ff. L. Serv. Aen. 6,859. Liv. 1,10,7. 4,20,2 f. Prop. 4,10,45 f. Val. Max. 3,2,3 ff. Plut. Rom. 16,7. Marc. 8; zu Caesar vgl. Cass. Dio 44,4,3.

[66] Ablehnungen bei T. Manlius Torquatus, Valerius Corvinus und dem jüngeren Scipio (Val. Max. 3,2,6. Flor. 1,33) und Licinius Crassus (Cass. Dio 51,24,4). Als Grund für die Zurückweisung wird für die drei Erstgenannten bei Val. Max. a. O. angegeben, *quia sub alienis auspiciis rem gesserant, spolia Iovi Feretrio non posuerunt consecranda*, für Licinius Crassus (Cass. Dio a. O.), daß er nicht αὐτοκράτωρ στρατηγός war. Nach der Theorie bei LATTE 205 (vgl. DUMÉZIL, Rel. Rom. Arch. 173) wären das Beispiele für eine Weihung an Mars, während die Weihung des Marcellus an Quirinus bei Verg. Aen. 6,859 danach diesen zum *manipularis* degradiert. Die vorgenannten vier Beispiele nehmen auch der grundsätzlich einleuchtenden Argumentation bei D. PORTE 309 ihre Überzeugungskraft.

[67] Fest. 204,11 ff. Serv. Aen. 6,859. Plut. Marc. 8; zu den *libri pontificum* vgl. Fest. 204,9 ff. L.

[68] Die altertümliche Form *Ianui Quirino* (Fest. 204,17 L.) spricht für Originalität des Doppelnamens gegenüber der einfachen Nennung des Quirinus bei Serv. und Plut. a. O.

[69] Monum. Ancyr. 19. Liv. 1,10,5 f. 4,20,4. Nepos Att. 20,3. Dion. Hal. ant. 2,34.

[70] Fest. 204,16 L.

III. Antike und moderne Namensdeutungen

Schon im Altertum hat man versucht, aus dem Namen des Quirinus Rückschlüsse zu ziehen, und diesen entweder mit dem der sabinischen Stadt Cŭres[71] oder mit dem sabinischen Worte *cŭris*[72] 'Lanze' oder mit griechisch κοίϱανος[73] bzw. κύϱιος[74] oder mit dem Namen der Quirites[75] oder mit *quĭrītare*[76] verbunden; da Cŭres[77] und *cŭris*[78] auch zur Erklärung des Namens der Iuno Curitis[79] herangezogen wurden, wozu noch die Herleitungen aus *cūria*[80] und *currus*[81] kommen, wird dieser Komplex zwar nicht inhaltlich, wohl aber sprachlich unter einheitlichen Gesichtspunkten betrachtet werden müssen. Von modernen Deutungen − soweit sie nicht antike wiederaufgreifen[82] − hat sich die Herleitung aus einem hypothetischen Ortsnamen **Quirium* für die Siedlung auf dem Quirinal[83] nicht durchzusetzen vermocht[84], während die Rückführung auf ein ebenfalls hypothetisches Wort **cŏ-u̯ir-iom* 'die vereinigte Männerschaft'[85], die 'Männergemeinschaft', nicht nur für den Gottesnamen, sondern auch für den der Quiriten und sogar für den der *cūria* fast[86] uneingeschränkt Zustimmung gefunden hat[87].

Soweit diese Herleitung allein den Namen des Quirinus betrifft, schien sie unter der Annahme möglich, die Namensbildung sei vor Einsetzen der Anfangsbetonung, d.h. vor dem Ende des 5. Jhdts. v. Chr., aus **cŏ-u̯ir-ínŏ-* erfolgt;

---

[71] Fest. 200,2 L. Paul.Fest. 43,3 L. Varro l.l. 5,51. Ov.fast. 2,480. Lyd.magistr. 1,5.

[72] Paul. Fest. 43,1 f. L. Macrob. 1,9,16. Serv.Aen. 1,292. Ov.fast. 2,477. CGIL 5,140,49. 238,18. GLSuppl. 241,3 ff. K. Fast.Praen. DEGRASSI I.I.XIII p. 119. Schol.Tur. bei Serv. Aen. 7,612. Plut.qu.Rom. 87 p. 285 C.

[73] Serv.Aen. 1,292.

[74] Lyd.magistr. 1,5.

[75] Varro l.l. 5,51.73. Ov.fast. 2,479.

[76] Varro frg. 174 FUN. (Tertull.nat. 2,9).

[77] Schol.Pers. 4,26.

[78] Paul.Fest. 43,5. 55,6 f. L. Serv.Aen. 1,8. Mart.Cap. 2,149. Plut.qu.Rom. 87 p. 285 C.

[79] Die Quantität der ersten Silbe von Curitis ist unbekannt.

[80] Paul.Fest. 56,21 L. Serv.Aen. 1,17. Dion.Hal.ant. 2,50,3.

[81] Serv.Aen. 1,8. Serv.auct.Aen. 1,17.

[82] Vgl. L. PRELLER−H. JORDAN a.O. I, 278. 369 (Herleitung von *curis*).

[83] Vgl. o. Anm. 4.

[84] Vgl. J. POUCET, Rech. 45.

[85] P. KRETSCHMER, Glotta 10, 1920, 147 ff. folgt in dieser Herleitung A. POTT, Etym.Forschungen I, 1836, 123. A. SCHWEGLER, Römische Geschichte I, Tübingen−Berlin 1853, 498. L. LANGE, Römische Altertümer I³, Berlin 1876, 91. R. VON PLANTA, Anz.f.indogerman. Sprach- und Altertumskunde 10, 1899, 57.

[86] Ablehnung bei C. KOCH, Rel. 26 f.

[87] Vgl. E. BENVENISTE, RHR 129, 1945, 6 ff. M. G. BRUNO(-TIBILETTI) a. O. 508. W. MEID a. O. 80.101. F. MULLER a. O. 108. V. PISANI, Lingue e culture 283 f. H. RIX, BN 8, 1957, 135 f. H. J. ROSE, Anc.Rom.Rel. 1949, 68. J. POUCET, Rech. 83 f. A. BRELICH a. O. 113 (mit Einschränkungen). G. DUMÉZIL, Rel.Rom.Arch. 246. G. RADKE, RE XXIV 1 (1963), 1301.

dabei mußte jedoch eine analoge Erklärung für das Wort *cūria* oder gar eine solche von Quirinus aus *cūria*[88] ausgeschlossen werden[89]. Das Wort *cūria* nämlich ließe sich aus **cŏ-u̯(ĭ)r-ia* gerade nur unter Anfangsbetonung[90] erklären; diese wirkte während des 4. Jhdts. v. Chr., was für die Benennung einer Institution der ältesten Gesellschaftsordnung Roms jedoch zu spät sein dürfte. Auch inhaltlich hat die *cūria* nichts mit den *viri* zu tun, sondern setzt sich aus Sippen zusammen[91].

Die aus lautlichen Gründen trotz vorgebrachter Bedenken[92] immerhin annehmbare Herleitung des Gottesnamens Quirinus aus einem Worte **cŏu̯ĭriom* muß aufgrund von dessen inhaltlicher Aussage hingegen entschieden abgelehnt werden: Eine deverbative Bildung wie bei den Wörtern *concilium, concubium, confugium, colloquium, compluvium, conubium, convivium* liegt nicht vor, da die angenommene Zurückführung auf *vir* eine denominative Herleitung voraussetzt. Für eine solche bieten sich die Beispiele *confinium, coniugium, collegium, commercium, consortium, contubernium* an und gestatten eine Analyse ihrer Aussage; sie bedeuten den Zustand, daß jemand mit einem anderen eine gemeinsame Grenze, ein gemeinsames Joch, eine gemeinsame Satzung, eine gemeinsame Handelsware bzw. einen gemeinsamen Handel, ein gemeinsames Los oder eine gemeinsame Hütte besitzt: Folgerichtig müßte **cŏu̯ĭriom* demnach den gemeinsamen Besitz eines Mannes, d. h. eine Art Vielweiberei, bedeuten! Das ist ebenso unsinnig für den Namen des Gottes wie für den der Quirites[93]. So verlockend und so Rom-gemäß diese Herleitung auch zu sein schien, sie hat sich als unannehmbar erweisen lassen und darf nicht mehr als Grundlage sprachgeschichtlicher oder religionswissenschaftlicher Deutungen dienen.

IV. Sprachliche Grundlagen des Namens

Der sprachliche Befund gestattet folgende Feststellungen:
1. Der Name *Quirīnus* ist adjektivisch gebildet[94], was eine sprachliche Aufschlüsselung als möglich erscheinen läßt; da das Ableitungssuffix *-īnŏ-* jedoch

---

[88] M. G. Bruno(-Tibiletti) a. O.; vgl. auch F. Coarelli, Rom (übers. von A. Allroggen-Bedel, Freiburg 1975), 220: „der einigende Schutzgott der Kurien".

[89] G. Radke, RE XXIV 1 (1963), 1301.

[90] F. Muller, Altital.Wörterb. 108: „mit durch den Akzent bedingter anders gerichteter lautl. Entwicklung"; vgl. W. Burkert a. O. 361 Anm. 30.

[91] G. Radke, RE XXIV 1 (1963) 1301. K. D. Fabian, Aspekte einer Entwicklungsgeschichte der römisch-latinischen Göttin Iuno, Diss. Berlin 1978, 95f.

[92] G. Radke, RE XXIV 1 (1963) 1301; Ders., Die Götter Altitaliens 269.

[93] Fest. 304,2 L. *Quiris* ließe sich nach der Kretschmerschen Herleitung nicht verständlich machen.

[94] Wie im Namen der *dei Penates* gibt es auch die Formulierung *deus Quirinus* bei Philocal. CIL I² p. 262 und in der konstantin. Stadtbeschr. bei Richter, Topogr. ²372 (*templum dei Quirini*); vgl. ferner *Ianus Quirinus* neben *Ianus Quirini* (Hor. c. 4,15,9) und ἐν τῷ

nur allgemein sowohl denominativ wie deverbativ die Zugehörigkeit[95] wiedergibt, kann daraus noch kein Rückschluß auf den Charakter des Grundwortes oder gar seine Bedeutung gezogen werden.

2. Zwischen *Quirīnus* und *cūria* besteht weder sprachlich noch inhaltlich bzw. sachlich irgendeine Verbindung. *Quirites* sind nicht die Mitglieder der *curia*.

3. Sprachliche Zusammengehörigkeit von *Quirīnus* und *Quirītes* wird angenommen werden dürfen.

Es ist auffällig, daß sowohl der Name der Iuno Curitis wie der Ortsname Cures und das sabinische Wort *curis* in recht unterschiedlicher Orthographie bezeugt sind, deren jeweilige Besonderheiten jedoch nicht nur bei jedem dieser drei Wörter, sondern auch bei einer Reihe anderer auftreten, die ebenfalls Anspruch auf ein hohes Alter erheben können:

– Neben *Curitis*[96] *Curis*[97] – vgl. den Namen des faliskischen *pater Curris*[98] –, *Curritis*[99], *Curretis*[100] und *Quiritis*[101],

– neben *Cures*[102] *Curres*[103] und *Quirres*[104],

– neben *curis*[105] *curris*[106] und *quiris*[107],

– neben älterem *Ecurria*[108] *Equirria*[109] und *Equiria*[110],

– neben *clivus Urbius*[111] in Rom *clivus Virbii*[112] in Aricia,

---

λόφῳ Κυρίνᾳ (Plut.Rom. 29,2) neben Κυρίνου λόφος (Plut.Numa 14); vgl. K. LATTE a. O. 113. A. BRELICH a. O. 115.

[95] Denominativ: *Latīnus, Reatīnus* von *Latium* und *Reate, Sābīnus* und *libertīnus* von *Sābus* und *libertus, sobrīnus* zu *soror, bovīnus, equīnus* zu *bos* und *equus*, deverbativ: *cortīna* zu **qert-* 'flechten' und *Furrīna* zu **ghers-* 'starren'.

[96] Paul.Fest. 43,5 L. Serv.Aen. 1,8. 4,59. 8,84. Serv.auct.Aen. 1,17. 2,614. Myth.Vat. 3,4,3. Mart.Cap. 2,149.

[97] Paul.Fest. 56,21 L.

[98] Tertull.apol. 24.

[99] CIL XI 3100 *IUN.CU[.* 3126 (= ILS 5374). Serv.Aen. 8,84 (cod. L). Serv.auct.Aen. 1,17 (cod. D). Fast.Arv.CIL I² p. 214.

[100] Serv.Aen. 1,9 (codd. BL).

[101] CIL I² 396 (= ILLRP 169). XI 3125 (ILS 3111). Fast.Ant.vet. (ILLRP 9) zum 7. Okt. *IUNON.QUIR. Quiritis* dürfte eine volksetymologische Umformung von *Curritis* sein.

[102] Ov.fast. 2,480. Varro l.l. 5,51. Verg.Aen. 6,811. 8,638. 10,345. Dion.Hal.ant. 2,48,4. Strab. 5,228.

[103] Fest. 302,33 L.

[104] Varro l.l. 5,1 (cod. G).

[105] Ov.fast. 2,477. ILS 8744a. Paul.Fest. 43,1. 55,8 L. Serv.Aen. 1,292. Macrob. 1,9,16. Polem.Silv. CIL I² p. 259. Plut.Rom. 29,1. qu.Rom. 87. Strab. 5,228.

[106] Serv.Aen. 1,8 (cod. K).

[107] GLSuppl. 241,3 ff. K. Serv.Aen. 1, 292 (cod. L). Macrob. 1,9,16 (codd. TVA).

[108] Varro l.l. 6,13 (cod. H: *Ecuria*). Tertull.spect. 5 *ecuriaquis* (d. h. *Ecuria ⟨ab e⟩quis*).

[109] Paul.Fest. 71,15. 117,26 L. Ov.fast. 2,859. 3,519. Fast.Vat.CIL I² p. 241 *[E]QVIRR*. Fast.Verul. zum 14. März, DEGRASSI, I.I.XIII, p. 166 *E[Q]VIRR*.

[110] Paul.Fest. 71,15 L. (cod. IT). Fast.Ant.vet. (ILLRP 9) *EQVIR*. Fast.Verul. zum 27. Febr., DEGRASSI, I.I.XIII, p. 164 *EQVIR*.

[111] Liv. 1,48,6. Solin. 1,25; *clivus Orbius*: Fest. 196,1 ff. L. Dion.Hal.ant. 4,39,3.

[112] Pers. 6,56 mit Schol.

– neben *Ortona*[113] (= **Urtona*) in Latium Βιρτῶνα[114] (= *Virtona*)
– und vermutlich aus **cŭrcur* über **quircur*[115] *quirquir* in der Auguralformel[116].

Bei allen diesen vorgenannten Formen fällt auf, daß jeweils -*ŭr*- vor Konsonant als -*u̯ĭr*- ausgesprochen und demnach auch geschrieben werden konnte[117], wobei eine aus -*rs*- herzuleitende Doppelschreibung -*rr*- wie in anderen Beispielen gerade innerhalb des religionsgeschichtlichen Rahmens unbeachtet blieb[118]. Man muß sich jedoch davor hüten zu übersehen, daß im Bereiche der Volksetymologie willkürliche Angleichungen in der Schreibweise an ähnlich klingende, aber keinesfalls zugehörige Wörter zustande gekommen sein können. So läßt sich etwa für *curis* 'Lanze' trotz der Schreibweise *curris* keine sprachgeschichtliche Herleitung[119] finden, bei der die -*ur*- vor Konsonant steht: Da aber gerade diese Voraussetzung erst den angenommenen Lautvorgang zu veranlassen vermag, wird man aus dem Nebeneinander von *curis* und *quiris* keine weiteren Schlußfolgerungen zu ziehen haben; das macht auch die antike Herleitung des Gottesnamens von dem sabinischen Wort für Lanze und damit sowohl die Vorstellung eines Lanzenfetischs[120] wie die sprachlich zu begründende sabinische Herkunft[121] des Gottes unwahrscheinlich. Selbst bei Vergleichbarkeit lautlicher Vorgänge läge keine Aussage über Zusammenhang und Inhalt der jeweiligen Wörter vor.

V. *Quirinus und der* primigenius sulcus

Für *Quirinus* gibt es zwar keine Schreibung **Quirrinus*, doch läßt sich die Annahme[122], griechisch Κυρῖνος stehe für lateinisch *Curinus*[123], nicht von der Hand weisen, so daß unter dem Eindruck des Nebeneinanders von *Ecurria* und *Equirria-Equiria* eine Herleitung aus **cursīnŏ-*, **korsīnŏ-* möglich scheint. Sie setzt als Grundlage die Formen **qr̥s-īnŏ-* oder **kr̥s-īnŏ-* voraus. Von diesen

---

[113] Liv. 2,43,2. 3,30,8.

[114] Dion.Hal.ant. 10,26,2 (cod. A) Βιρτῶνα.

[115] G. Radke, Romanitas 11, 1972, 208 Anm. 136.

[116] Varro l.l. 7,8.

[117] Vgl. auch *urvat* (Fest. 514,22 L.) neben *vervat* (Paul.Fest. 515,10 L.). Dazu *Vervactor* (G. Radke, Die Götter Altitaliens 320).

[118] Zur Schreibung von Cerus < **cerso*- vgl. LEW I, 207 (Zweifel bei G. Radke, Die Götter Altitaliens 92), von Cerialia < **cersialia* Leumann ⁶180. Vgl. auch Curitis zu *curia* < **coursia*.

[119] LEW I,315.

[120] G. Wissowa, in: Myth.Lex. IV (1909–1915), 12. L. Preller–H. Jordan, Röm.Mythol. I,339. II,227. G. Rohde, Die Kultsatzungen der röm. Pontifices 121. L. Deubner, in: Chantepie de la Saussaye, Lehrb.d.Rel.Gesch. ⁴II,440.

[121] Vgl. L. Deubner, ARW 8, 1905 (Usener-Beiheft), 75. W. Burkert a. O. 361 Anm. 28.

[122] Vgl. Ornella Terrosi-Zanco, SCO 10, 1961, 205, die Curinus, Curinalis, Curites für die „*grafia originale*" hält. Häufiges griech. Κυρῖνος kann = Curinus sein.

[123] Griech. ου in Κουρῖται u. ä. entspricht latein. -*u*-.

beiden Möglichkeiten läßt sich allein die erstgenannte in eine inhaltliche Beziehung zu dem setzen, was man von Quirinus weiß: Auf *qṛs- gehen nämlich altindisch kṛṣáti 'er pflügt', kṛṣíḥ 'das Pflügen' und kṛṣuḥ 'die Furche' zurück[124]. Da der mit Quirinus identifizierte Romulus den *primigenius sulcus* bei der Gründung Roms gezogen hat[125], also der erste Furchenzieher oder Pflüger ist, eröffnet sich ein neues Verständnis für die Aussage des Gottesnamens wie für die Gleichsetzung des Gottes mit dem Stadtgründer: Was Romulus tat, ist die Funktion des Quirinus. Die Römer «*ne choisirent pas au hasard le dieu destiné à récupérer le personnage humain de Romulus*» (D. PORTE 302). Die mythographische Nachricht, Numa Pompilius habe den *flamen Quirinalis* für den Kult des Romulus eingesetzt (Plut. Numa 7. Aug. civ. 2, 15), wäre demnach inhaltlich annehmbar.

Zum Namen des Romulus vermag ich mich auf frühere Studien zu stützen[126]: Die lange propagierte Herleitung aus dem Etruskischen[127] hat sich widerlegen lassen[128]. *Rōmulus* < *r̄m-lŏ- stellt unter einer im Griechischen wie im Venetischen − ich möchte formulieren: im Aboriginischen[129] − zu beobachtenden Lautgebung -rō- für -r̄- eine suffixbetonte Ableitung zum Namen des *Rĕmus* dar: Romulus heißt 'der zu Remus Gehörige'. Unter dem gleichen Lautgesetz ist *Rōma* < *r̄m-nā́ als 'die Stadt des Remus' anzusehen[130], während 'die Leute des Remus' mit einem einheimischer italischer Lautgesetzlichkeit folgenden Namen, in dem -rā- für -r̄- steht, *Rāmnenses* < *r̄m-n-enses* heißen. Daraus konnte auf ein Zusammentreffen von 'Aboriginern' und Italikern auf dem Boden

---

[124] Vgl. W. D. WHITNEY, The Roots, Verb-Forms and Primary Derivates of the Sanskrit Language, Bibliothek indogerman. Grammatiken II 2, Leipzig 1885 (Nachdruck: American Oriental ser. 30, New Haven, Conn. 1945), 23. C. C. UHLENBECK, Kurzgefaßtes etymologisches Wörterbuch der altindischen Sprache, Amsterdam 1898/9 (Nachdruck Osnabrück 1973), 47.64. M. MAYRHOFER, Kurzgefaßtes etymologisches Wörterbuch des Altindischen, I, Indogerman. Bibliothek II 4, Heidelberg 1956, 176f.263. E. LEUMANN, Indica, Leipzig 1907, 58, W. NEISSER, Zum Wörterbuch des Rgveda, Abhandlungen für die Kunde des Morgenlandes 16,4, Leipzig 1930 (Nachdruck Nendeln 1966), 64.

[125] Plut.Rom. 11,3ff. Fest. 270,36L. Paul.Fest. 271,3L.

[126] G. RADKE, Die Götter Altitaliens 273f.

[127] W. SCHULZE, Zur Geschichte lateinischer Eigennamen, Berlin 1904 (Nachdruck Zürich 1966), 579f.; vgl. noch C. J. CLASSEN, Historia 12, 1963, 457 Anm. 49.

[128] Es läßt sich nicht nachweisen, daß *Romilius* erst nach etrusk. *rumlna* gebildet wurde; der umgekehrte Weg ist mindestens ebenso wahrscheinlich. Vgl. die scharfe Ablehnung einer Ableitung aus dem Etruskischen schon durch W. FRÖHNER, Rom und die Ramnes, Philol. 10, 1855, 552ff.: „Kein Mensch läugnet heutzutag mehr, daß alles, was man von einer tuskischen Herkunft des Namens, von *rumis* = *mamma* und ähnlichem gefabelt hat, unbrauchbarer Plunder sei".

[129] Vgl. G. RADKE, Klass. Sprachen u. Literaturen 6, 1971, 82ff.

[130] Statt Remus nennen die griechischen Autoren meist Ῥῶμος. Das kann eine Verkürzung gegenüber Romulus sein, aber auch einem *r̄m-nŏ́s seine Entstehung verdanken. Zum Wandel -mn- zu -m- nach langem Vokal vgl. F. SOMMER, Handbuch der lateinischen Laut- und Formenlehre³, Indogerman. Bibliothek I 3, 1a, Heidelberg 1948, 232 (= F. SOMMER − R. PFISTER, Handbuch der lateinischen Laut- und Formenlehre, Indogerman. Bibliothek Reihe I, Heidelberg 1977, 175).

Roms während des 8. Jhdts. v. Chr. geschlossen werden[131], was mit früheisen-
zeitlichen Spuren vereinbar ist.

Die trotz der erst verhältnismäßig späten[132] Bezeugung primäre Stellung
des Namens Remus wird durch eine Reihe alter Ortsnamen in Rom und seiner
Umgebung bestätigt: Remens[133], Remona[134], Ῥεμώνιον[135], Remoria[136], Remu-
ria[137], *ager Remurinus*[138], zu denen auch der auf dem Palatium inschriftlich
bezeugte Name der Göttin Remureina[139] gehört. Man kann mit Sicherheit sagen,
Remus sei am Tiberufer beheimatet.

Italisches *Rĕmŏna* beruht auf den gleichen sprachlichen Elementen –
Wortstamm *rĕm-* bzw. *r̄m-* und Erweiterung durch *n*-Suffix – wie unlatei-
nisches *Rōma* < *r̄m-nā̊*[140] oder venetisch *ruma.n.-*[141] < *r̄m-n-*. Hat sich der
Name des Romulus als eine 'aboriginische' Ableitung zu dem italischen Namen
Remus erkennen lassen – seit E. Norden[142] wird man nicht mehr so ängstlich
die Geschichtlichkeit der Aboriginer abstreiten wollen –, ist es auffällig, daß der
mit Romulus gleichgesetzte Quirinus in der Zeugungsgeschichte des Modius
Fabidius – trotz mancher Zweifel[143] – als ein Gott der Aboriginer angesehen
wird. Unter diesen Voraussetzungen läßt sich sein Kult schon für das 8. Jhdt.
v. Chr. annehmen, als die Veneter-Aboriginer im Besitze des Eisens vermutlich
zuerst bis zu den von Varro bei Dion. Hal. ant. 1, 14 genannten Plätzen und
dann kurzfristig bis in den Raum von Rom vordrangen.

[131] Vgl. G. Radke, Archaisches Latein, Darmstadt 1981, 41 f.

[132] G. Radke, Romulus, Kl. Pauly IV (1972), 1455. Ῥέμος wird erstmalig Mitte des 3. Jhdts.
v. Chr. inschriftlich auf Chios genannt (Kontoleon, Prakt.Arch.Hel. 1953, 271, Z. 24ff.);
vgl. C. J. Classen a. O. 452.

[133] Liv. 42,2,4 *in Veienti apud Rementum lapidatum.*

[134] Paul.Fest. 345,11 L. *Remona habitatio Remi.* Enn.ann. 82 *certabant urbem Romam Re-
m⟨on⟩amve vocarent.* Diese schon ältere Ergänzung der Lücke wurde freilich von Th.
Mommsen, Die Remuslegende, Hermes 16, 1881, 16 f. = Ders., Gesammelte Schriften IV,
Berlin 1906, 15 mit der Begründung abgelehnt, man müsse dann **Remĭna* erwarten; bei
seinem Vorschlag *Rem⟨or⟩amve* müßte es dann auch **Remĕra* lauten.

[135] Plut.Rom. 9,4; K. Ziegler liest in seiner Ausgabe Ῥεμωρία.

[136] Remoria ist der Platz, an dem Remus bestattet wurde (Plut.Rom. 11,1 Ῥεμωρία. Dion.
Hal.ant. 1,87 Ῥεμορία), oder auch ein Ort 30 Stadien von Rom (Dion. Hal. 1,85) oder ein
anderer Name für den Aventin (Dion.Hal. 1,86).

[137] Steph.Byz. s. v. Ῥεμουρία· πόλις πλησίον Ῥώμης; vgl. Ov.fast. 5,479 mit dem Festnamen
Remŭria zu Ehren des Remus.

[138] Paul.Fest. 345,10 L. *Remurinus ager dictus quia possessus est a Remo.*

[139] ILLRP 252.

[140] Eine Verbindung mit dem Tibernamen *Rŭmōn* (**srou-mōn*) ist abzulehnen; vgl.
jedoch die *porta Romanula* (Varro l.l. 5,164) oder *Romana* (Fest. 318,25 ff. L.),
nach Richter, Topogr.² 34 f. 'Flußtor'.

[141] Der venetische Frauenname *ruma.n.na* (M. Lejeune, Manuel de la langue vénète, Indo-
german. Bibliothek Reihe I, Heidelberg 1974, nr. 30.31 = PID nr. 21.22) ist von einem
Stamm *rŭmņ-* mit Gamonym *-na* 'Frau des *rŭm-nŏ-*' gebildet. Vgl. auch *Rāmĕnia* (W.
Schulze, Zur Geschichte lateinischer Eigennamen 218) < **r̄m-ņ-iă*.

[142] E. Norden, Alt-Germanien. Völker- und namengeschichtliche Untersuchungen, Leipzig–Berlin 1934, 111,1. 288.

[143] J. Poucet, Rech. 57.

Unter den *arma Quirini* wären bei Herleitung des Gottesnamens von *qrs-'pflügen' weder Schild[143a] noch Lanze zu verstehen, sondern man könnte in ihnen den Pflug wiedererkennen, der freilich primär nicht nur zum Vollzug des *primigenius sulcus*, sondern überhaupt zur Bearbeitung des Ackers benutzt wurde: Das bestätigt die auch sonst beobachteten Beziehungen des Quirinus zum agrarischen Bereich (s. ob. S. 281), ohne daß man in ihm einen Repräsentanten der 'dritten Funktion'[144] sehen müßte, da der besondere Akt seines Wirkens die Gründung einer Stadt mit allen ihren Bürgern beinhaltet. Wie der alte Bauerngott Mars das Ackerlos 'zuteilt'[145], umpflügt Quirinus diesen Acker und schafft eine kultisch umfriedete[146] Siedlung. Da im Altindischen durch Verbindung des Stammes *qrs- 'pflügen' mit dem Suffix -*ti*- das Wort *kṛṣṭiḥ* 'Volk, Stamm' aus der ursprünglichen Bedeutung 'umpflügtes Land'[147] gebildet werden konnte, dürfte die Ableitung mit Suffix -$i\breve{o}$- als *qrs-$i\breve{o}m$ in der Sprache, die den Namen des Quirinus schuf, eine mit kultisch gezogener Furche umgebene Siedlung bedeuten, deren Bewohner *Quirites* heißen können. Ich komme damit auf den hypothetischen Namen *$Quirium$ zurück, ohne ihn jedoch einer prähistorischen Quirinalstadt zuschreiben zu wollen; ich halte das Wort *$quirium$ vielmehr für die Bezeichnung einer durch die Umpflügung charakterisierten Siedlungsform[147a]. Varro l.l. 5, 143 sieht darin einen etruskischen Ritus; das ist hinsichtlich der ethnologischen Aussage nicht bindend, spricht aber für Übernahme des Brauchs aus der Fremde. Da man sich den Vollzug des Furchenziehens mit Stier und Kuh vor dem Pfluge rings um den Abhang des zerklüfteten Palatium kaum vorstellen kann, darf angenommen weden, daß der Vorgang und damit auch der Name des Umpflügens aus anderen geographischen Verhältnissen stammen; dem entspräche am ehesten Herkunft aus den Ebenen des 'aboriginischen' Venetien. Der *ritus Gabinus*, den der Pflüger hinsichtlich seiner eigenen Kleidung beachten muß[148], hat sich als aboriginisch erweisen lassen[149]. Spuren des altindischen Vokabulars im Venetischen wurden noch nicht gesucht.

[143a] Bei Liv. 5.52,7 spricht Camillus von den *ancilia* des Mars Gradivus und des Quirinus pater, bekundet also die Auffassung, daß die Salii Palatini und die Salii Collini (inschriftliche Zitate bei LATTE 115 Anm. 1) den beiden Göttern zuzuordnen seien; da bei Stat.silv. 5,2,129ff. gerade wegen der vorausgehenden Nennung des Mavors mit Quirinus stellvertretend Mars gemeint sein kann, böte Liv. a. O. das einzige Zeugnis für Salier des Quirinus, während die Einsetzung von Saliern für Mars bei Liv. 1,20,4. Ovid.fast. 3,259f. Lucian.salt. 20. Porph.Hor. c. 1,36,12. vir.ill. 3,1 erwähnt wird.

[144] G. DUMÉZIL, Rel.Rom.Arch. 161ff. und passim; vgl. auch E. BENVENISTE, RHR 129, 1945, 7.

[145] G. RADKE, Die Götter Altitaliens 199ff.; DERS., Mars, Kl.Pauly III (1969), 1046ff.

[146] Cato frg. 18P. Varro l.l. 5,143. r.r. 2,1,10. Ov.fast. 4,825f. Isid.or. 15,2,3. Serv.Aen. 1, 12. Serv.auct.Aen. 4,212. Plut.Rom. 11,3. qu.Rom. 27 p. 271A.

[147] C. C. UHLENBECK (Zitate s. Anm. 124) a. O. 64. W. NEISSER a. O. 64. M. MAYRHOFER a. O. 263.

[147a] Damit komme ich der Auffassung von D. PORTE 325 sehr nahe, die im Begriff der Bürgergemeinde («*cité*») das Verbindende zwischen Romulus und Quirinus sieht.

[148] Cato frg. 18P.

[149] Vgl. G. RADKE bei F. ALTHEIM–R. STIEHL, Die Araber in der alten Welt IV, 526f.; DERS., Klass. Sprachen u. Literaturen 6, 1971, 84f. Abbildungen bei PID I Tafel VIIa. R. BIAN-

VI. Die umpflügte Stadt

Die Bezeichnung einer Siedlungsform als *quirium* läßt sich mit dem Begriff der *urbs* vergleichen, ohne daß man dabei der − sehr an die vorgetragene Deutung erinnernden − varronischen Etymologie *oppida . . . circumducta aratro ab orbe et urvo urbes* (l.l. 5, 143) zu folgen braucht. Das Umpflügen des Areals einer künftigen Siedlung unter Beobachtung kultischer Maßnahmen hat nicht nur den praktischen Wert einer Umgrenzung, sondern verfolgt auch eine apotropäische Absicht[150]. Da Romulus jedoch den Pflug immer dann angehoben, die Furche also nicht durchgezogen haben soll, wenn er die Lage eines Tores markieren wollte[151], hätte er den magischen Schutz an diesen Stellen jeweils unterbrochen; diese Lücken im *primigenius sulcus* mußten daher unter die Obhut eines besonderen Gottes gestellt werden, der seinen Namen vom 'Durchgang der Umpflügung' erhielt: *Ianus Quirinus*. Dieses Tor kannte schon Enn. ann. 267 als *belli ferratos postes portasque* und nennt das Monum. Ancyr. 13 ausdrücklich πύλη Ἐνυάλιος. Die Gleichsetzung von Quirinus und Enyalios ist erstmalig bei Polyb. 3,25,6 bezeugt, geht aber auf − noch nicht geklärte − Voraussetzungen zurück, die schon Ennius a.O. vorlagen (vgl. ob. Anm. 14). Von da aus ist auch die spätere Benennung als πύλη Ἐνυάλιος (Monum. Anc. 13) verständlich; sie setzt lediglich die seit Polyb. 3,25,6 bezeugte Gleichsetzung von Quirinus und Enyalios voraus[152].

Die Hŏra[153] Quirini (s. ob. S. 280) wird von Enn. ann. 117, den vorcaesarischen 'Fasti Antiates veteres' zum 23. August[153a], von Ov. met. 14,851 (*quae nunc dea iuncta Quirino est*) und alten Priesterbüchern bei Gell. 13,23,2

CHI−A. GIULIANO, Etrusker und Italiker vor der römischen Herrschaft, Universum der Kunst, München 1974, Abb. 47 mit Hinweis von G. RADKE, Gnomon 51, 1979, 54.

[150] L. DEUBNER, ARW 16, 1913, 128.

[151] Plut.Rom. 11,3. qu.Rom. 27 p. 271A. Cato frg. 18P.

[152] Im Monum.Anc. wird sorgfältig zwischen πύλη Ἐνυάλιος (13) und ναὸς Κυρείνου (19) unterschieden.

[153] Plut.qu.Rom. 46 p. 275F sagt ausdrücklich, Hora werde 'jetzt' mit verlängerter erster Silbe Ὥρα genannt − unter analogischer Anlehnung an die Orthographie der griechischen Horen −, woraus eine ursprünglich kurze Quantität der ersten Silbe entnommen werden darf, wie sie bei Ov.met. 14,851 und nach der notwendigen Änderung in *vener⟨ab⟩or* auch bei Enn.ann. 117 vorliegt (überliefertes *veneror Horam* läßt sich nicht halten). K. LATTE, Röm.Rel.Gesch. 55 Anm. 3 hält zu Unrecht für Enn.ann. 117 an *Hōram* ebenso wie ann. 104 an *Hērem* (überliefert *Herclem*!) fest. Warum Non. 120,1 M. Hora als *dea iuventutis* erklärt, läßt sich leicht erkennen. Mit den Gottheiten, die nach den Fast.Arv. CIL I² p. 215 am 23. August (für den die Fast.Ant.vet. *[H]ORAE QUI[R]* verzeichnen) ein Opfer erhalten, ist Hora nicht zu verbinden.

[153a] Während in den Fast.Antiat.vet. a. O. Volkanus, Hora Quirini und eine Gottheit *supra comitium* als Empfänger von Opfern genannt werden, geben die Fast.Arval. a. O. *Volcanus (in circo Flaminio), (Iuturna) nymphae in campo, Ops Opifera, Quirinus in colle* und *Volkanus in comitio* an. Das berechtigt nicht zur Annahme funktioneller Verwandtschaft (D. PORTE 316) zwischen den genannten Gottheiten.

erwähnt; ob die Göttin Horta, deren Tempel nach Auskunft des M. Antistius Labeo[154] ständig offen stand, mit Hora identisch ist, läßt sich nicht mehr entscheiden[155]. Beide Namen dürften auf den gleichen Stamm *ĝhĕr- zurückzuführen sein, der sowohl ʿGefallen finden, begehren, zum Wollen veranlassen, Lust machen' (vgl. lat. *horior*, osk. *herest*, umbr. *heri*, altind. *háryati*)[156] wie auch ʿumfassen, einfassen, umhegen' (vgl. lat. *hortus, cohors*, osk. *húrz*, griech. χόρτος, altind. *hárati*)[157] bedeutet. Ich hatte mich früher[158] unter dem Eindruck älterer Deutungen[159] für die erstgenannte Möglichkeit entschieden, ohne damit eine sinnvolle Klärung herbeiführen zu können; deshalb sehe ich jetzt im Zusammenhang mit der neuen Auslegung des Quirinus-Namens die letztere für die zutreffende an, nach der *Hŏra* (wie *tŏga* zu *tegere*) *Quirini* ʿdie Einhegung beim Umpflügen' zum Ausdruck bringt. *Horta < *ĝhr-tā́* (vgl. *Morta, -u̯orta*) hält die Tür ihres Tempels offen, um anzuzeigen, daß sie fähig ist aufzunehmen, zu umschließen und zu hegen[160]. Die *Virites* sind sicherlich nicht die ʿMännergenossen'[161]; ihre Bedeutung bleibt dunkel, da sonst nichts über sie bekannt ist[161a].

Die Identifikation des *praediatus*[162] Quirinus mit Romulus, *aptus aratris*[163], hat demnach ein anderes Gewicht erhalten. Beide sind ursprünglich einander gleich; beide Namen bezeichnen nur jeweils eine andere Seite der gleichen göttlichen Potenz und entsprechen einer religiösen Vorstellung, die charakteristisch ist für eine primitive Bauerngesellschaft[164] zum Zeitpunkt des Übergangs zu städtischer Siedlungsform und bürgerlicher Lebensweise[164a]. Von dieser ʿidentità originaria' (A. BRELICH a.O.) ist die spätere Gleichsetzung durch Apotheose zu unterscheiden[165]. Diese ist das Ergebnis griechischer Vorstellungen, die aus der nicht mehr verstandenen Entsprechung einen mytho-

---

[154] Antist.Labeo frg. 20 HUSCHKE b.Plut.qu.Rom 46 p. 276A.

[155] G. WISSOWA, Hora Quirini, in: Myth.Lex. I,2 (1806—1890), 2712 lehnt Identifikation von Hora und Horta als ʿPhantasie' ab; zurückhaltender W. DEECKE, Horta, ebd. 2749.

[156] LEW I, 657f.

[157] LEW I,242f.,660.

[158] G. RADKE, Die Götter Altitaliens 145.

[159] Vgl. K. LATTE, Röm.Rel.Gesch. 113.

[160] Vgl. P. PRELLER—H. JORDAN a. O. I,174: „Horta, weil man sie sich immer segnend und tätig dachte", stehen die Türen ihres Tempels offen.

[161] F. MULLER, Altital.Wörterb. 108.

[161a] Ohne daß dafür ein Beweis geboten werden könnte, ließe sich *Virites* oder *Urites*, das durch *[i]urites* des cod. γ empfohlen wird, formal wie *Ancītes* (RADKE, Götter 64) aus *u̯r̥s-ītes* zum Stamme *u̯ers-, *u̯r̥s- ʿbenetzen, befruchten, zeugen' herleiten, so daß als *Virites Quirini* die guten Geister angerufen würden, die für die ʿBefruchtung' des umgepflügten Ackers sorgen sollen.

[162] Mart.Cap. 1,46. Vgl. das besondere Verhältnis des Quirinus zum *rusticus* (Iuven. 3,67).

[163] Prop. 4,10,19.

[164] A. BRELICH, Quirinus, SMSR 31, 1960, 111.

[164a] Vgl. D. PORTE 324f.

[165] Cic.leg. 1,3 verbindet die Apotheose des Quirinus mit der der Orithyia.

logisch deutbaren Vorgang herstellten: Menschen werden nach ihrem Tode durch ihre Verdienste zu Lebzeiten in den Rang von Göttern erhoben[166]. So fand diese Erscheinung auch ihren ausschließlichen Niederschlag in der Literatur – in gewissem Sinne (s. u.) auch in der politischen Propaganda –, nicht jedoch im Kult.

VII. Romulus wird Quirinus

Da die uralten Zusammenhänge im Bewußtsein der Öffentlichkeit längst in Vergessenheit geraten waren, schuf die Apotheose, für die Ennius der älteste Zeuge ist, und die später sich anschließende Gleichsetzung dieses vergöttlichten Romulus mit Quirinus eine neue Vorstellung: Aus der ursprünglich göttlichen Einheit wurden ein menschlicher König und ein vom Menschsein zum Halbgott aufgestiegener Heros. Das wird durch das augusteische Romulus-Elogium[167] ausdrücklich bestätigt. Wann dieser Prozeß begonnen hat, ist umstritten; Cic. nat. deor. 2,62 sagt *quem quidem eundem esse Quirinum putant*, so daß C. KOCH, Rel. 31f. durch irriges *quidam* statt *quidem* an dieser Stelle zu Unrecht eine Spätdatierung erschließt. Dagegen spricht auch Ciceros ohne Einschränkung vorgetragene frühere Schilderung des dem Iulius Proculus gegenüber geäußerten Anspruchs des Romulus auf göttliche Verehrung unter dem Namen des Quirinus[168].

Wie unklar die Vorstellungen durch die Apotheose geworden sind, erkennt man an der Äußerung des Horaz, der im Romulus-Grab *ossa Quirini* wähnt[169]: Der Gott ist zum Sterblichen geworden. Besonders deutlich wird das bei Formulierungen wie *geminos sub rupe Quirinos* für die Zwillinge bei Iuven. 11, 105 und bei der Benennung des Romulus[169a] als Quirinus im Mutterleibe (Ov. fast. 3,41) oder als Säugling (Sidon. c. 2,119), zu Zeiten also, in denen die Vergöttlichung noch nicht erfolgt war. Die Statue Caesars im Quirinus-Tempel (s. ob. S. 280) kann nicht als Gleichstellung[170] mit dem Gotte gewertet werden; Cic. Att. 12,45,3 nennt Caesar ausdrücklich distanzierend σύνναον Quirino.

---

[166] Cic.nat.deor. 2,62. leg. 3,19. Hor. c. 3,3,15. Ov.amn. 3,8,51.

[167] CIL I² p. 189.

[168] Cic.rep. 2,20. leg. 1,3.

[169] Hor.ep. 16,13.

[169a] Man hatte den Eindruck, daß ihm der Name Romulus ganz lieb gewesen wäre, politische Erwägungen ihn jedoch von der Annahme abhielten (Cass.Dio. 53,16,7). Daß bei seinem *funus* ein Romulusbild mitgeführt wurde (Cass.Dio 56,34,2), besagt weniger, als D. PORTE 337 annimmt, da dem Leichenzug offenbar die *imagines* der durch die *elogia* vor dem Marstempel geehrten *maiores* von Romulus angefangen (ἀπ' αὐτοῦ τοῦ Ῥωμύλου) vorangetragen wurden.

[170] W. BURKERT, a. O. 357.

VIII. Namenswahl für Augustus

Versuche zu einer politischen Propaganda mit dem Namen des Quirinus beginnen erst in den frühen Jahren des Augustus; es gibt darüber auseinanderklaffende Nachrichten: Unter Berufung auf Sueton wird behauptet, man habe dem Herrscher die Namen Quirinus, Caesar oder Augustus (Serv. Aen. 1,292) bzw. Quirinus, Augustus oder Caesar (Serv. georg. 3,27) angeboten, worauf er, um niemanden zu kränken, sich zuerst Quirinus, dann Caesar und schließlich Augustus genannt habe, wobei es geblieben sei. Klarer wird diese Angabe durch die Auskunft, die einen haben ihn Quirinus bzw. Romulus (Κυρῖνον οἱονεὶ ῾Ρωμύλον), die anderen Caesar genannt, worauf er bei gemeinsamer Abstimmung der Priesterschaft und des Senats den Namen Augustus erhalten habe[171]. Zweifelhaft ist dabei das Angebot, sich Caesar zu nennen, da das ja sein durch die Adoption ererbter Name war. Dem trägt Suet. Aug. 7,2 Rechnung: *postea Gai Caesaris et deinde Augusti cognomen assumpsit, alterum testamento maioris avunculi, alterum Munati Planci sententia*; er fährt fort, man habe diesen Namen vorgezogen, obwohl es auch Leute gab, die ihn Romulus zu nennen für nötig hielten *quasi et ipsum conditorem urbis*. Dieses echte Sueton-Zitat straft die angeblichen Nachrichten bei Servius Lügen und verweist die Gleichsetzung des Kaisers mit Quirinus in den Bereich der Dichtung: Mit einer nicht zu übersehenden Anspielung spricht Verg. georg. 3,27 von *victorisque arma Quirini*; das bleibt aber auch der einzige Hinweis — und das bezeichnenderweise in der Zeit der Diskussion um einen neuen Namen —, aus dem die pseudosuetonischen Zitate herausgesponnen wurden. Späte Inschriften aus der Gallia Narbonensis[172] mit Weihung an Quirinus Augustus drehen das Verhältnis um und besagen nichts über Augustus selbst, der wohl nie daran gedacht hat, sich Quirinus nennen zu lassen[173].

Außer auf den genannten beiden Inschriften aus Vienna in der Gallia Narbonensis wird in der Kaiserzeit dem Quirinus lediglich eine private Weihung auf einer Inschrift aus Amiternum zuteil[174]; zweimal wird noch ein *flamen Quirinalis* erwähnt[175]. Nur die Dichter behalten die Gewohnheit bei, von Quirinus zu sprechen, wenn sie Romulus meinen[176]; sonst zitieren seinen

---

[171] Lyd.mens. 4,111 p. 150,22ff.W. Flor. 2,34 *tractatum etiam in senatu, an, quia condidisset imperium Romulus vocaretur, sed sanctius et reverentius visum est nomen Augusti*; vgl. Suet.Aug. 7,2.

[172] CIL XII 2201.2202.

[173] Vgl. G. RADKE, Klass. Sprachen u. Literaturen 5, 1970, 29. An die Möglichkeit, sich Quirinus nennen zu lassen, hat Augustus wohl nie gedacht; Romulus hingegen hätte er gern geheißen (Cass.Dio 53,16,7).

[174] DESSAU ILS 3150.

[175] BCAR 1915, 292 (Zeit des Tiberius). CIL IX 3154 (Zeit Hadrians).

[176] Vgl. Verg.Aen. 1,292 *Remo cum fratre Quirinus*; besonders deutlich wird das an dem Nebeneinander von Verg.georg. 1,498 (*di patrii indigetes et Romule*) einerseits und Ov. met. 15,862f. (*dique indigetes genitorque Quirine urbis*) sowie Sil. 9,294 (*indigetesque dei*

Namen gelegentlich die Grammatiker[177] und die Glossographen[178]. Wer eine Geschichte des Quirinus in der Prinzipatszeit schreiben will, müßte sich mit diesen dürftigen Beispielen rückschauender Erwähnung begnügen oder muß einen Grund zu nennen suchen, warum der in augusteischer Zeit noch so berufene Gott offenbar völlig vergessen wurde.

IX. Verlust der Göttlichkeit

Ich sehe die Veranlassung für das Schwinden jeden Interesses und auch nur des geringsten Kultes darin, daß durch die Apotheose des Romulus der göttliche Begriff des Quirinus auf diesen überging und damit seinen eigentümlichen Wert einbüßte. Romulus als Stadtgründer war eine verehrungswürdige Gestalt der Geschichte; Quirinus war ein Gott, der Kult in verschiedener Form erhielt, auch als man sein ursprüngliches Wesen nicht mehr verstand; die auf Gleichheit beruhende Identifikation beider schadete diesem Verhältnis nicht. Als man aber erfand, daß Romulus ein Gott wurde und als solcher Quirinus heißen sollte, weil er als Mensch auf Erden besondere Verdienste erworben hatte, rückten beide in die gleiche Vorstellungssphäre ein, in der man den Divus Augustus verehrte: Seit dieser sich *C. Iulius Divi filius* nannte[179] und selbst nach seinem Tode konsekriert wurde[180], folgten ihm Caligula[181], Livia[182], der Divus Claudius[183], die nach viermonatigem Leben verstorbene Nerotochter Diva Claudia[184] und schließlich der Divus Nero[185], um nur die ersten vergöttlichten Kaiser und Mitglieder der *domus divina*[186] zu nennen. Man wird sich kaum vorstellen können, daß in allen diesen Fällen die Gläubigkeit der Römer gegenüber diesen Göttern ernsthaft in Anspruch genommen worden sein kann. Damit aber wurde auch jene am Anfang der Entwicklung des Kaiserkults stehende Apotheose des

---

Faunusque satorque Quirinus) andererseits. Vgl. ferner Hor. c. 1,2,46 *populus Quirini*. Ov.met. 14,607 *turba Quirini*. trist. 1,3,33 *urbs Quirini*. Stat.silv. 3,5,112 *tecta Quirini*. Sil. 11,118 *sedes Quirini*. Lucan. 1,197 *rapti secreta Quirini* u. a.

[177] Als Beispiele seien Serv.Aen. 1,292. Isid.or. 9,2,84. Macrob. 1,9,16 genannt.

[178] CGlL 2,167,42. 300,58. 3,236,47 u. a.; vgl. 5,238,18 *Quirinus Sabinorum lingua asta, unde et postea Romulus dictus est, Quirinus, quia Sabinos subegit.*

[179] Die Namensform *Imp. Caesar Divi f.* in den Fast.cons.Amitern. (CIL I² p. 61) seit 43 v. Chr., in den Fast.triumph.Capit. (CIL I² p. 50) seit 40 v. Chr., in den Fast.cons.Capit. (CIL I² p. 28) seit 37 v. Chr.; vgl. G. RADKE, Klass.Sprach.u.Lit. 5, 1970, 25.

[180] Suet.Aug. 100,4. Fast.Amitern. CIL I² p. 244. Antiat. ebd. p. 248.

[181] Suet.Cal. 22,3; vgl. Drusilla als Πανθέα (Cass.Dio 59,11,3).

[182] Suet.Claud. 11,2.

[183] Suet.Claud. 45.

[184] Tac.ann. 15,23,3. 16,6,2.

[185] Tac.ann. 15,74,3.

[186] K. LATTE, Röm.Rel.Gesch. 316. Zu den *divi* und *divae* des 1. Jh. und zur *domus divina* vgl. jüngst auch H. TEMPORINI, Die Frauen am Hofe Trajans. Ein Beitrag zur Stellung der Augustae im Principat, Berlin–New York 1978, 27ff. 36ff. et passim.

Romulus in die Gestalt des Quirinus entwertet. Hatte man Romulus geachtet und an einen Gott Quirinus geglaubt – nach den Erfahrungen der so leicht vollziehbaren *consecrationes* mußte man Romulus-Quirinus in solchen Vorgang einordnen: Für die Dichter mochte diese Vorstellung als mythologisches Motiv weiterleben, für den Kult war sie gegenstandslos geworden.

Bibliographie

Aus der umfangreichen Literatur zu Quirinus sei folgende Übersicht gegeben:

S. ACCAME, I re di Roma nella leggenda e nella storia[2], Napoli 1965, 137.203.

DERS., Le origini di Roma[2], Napoli 1969, 330.

A. ALFÖLDI, Hasta – summa imperii, AJPh 63, 1959, 13 (*"boar-god"*).

F. ALTHEIM, Römische Religionsgeschichte I, Berlin 1931, 28.67.

DERS., Römische Religionsgschichte II, Berlin 1933, 20.109.

DERS., Römische Religionsgeschichte II, Berlin 1956, 14.

C. BAILEY, Phases in the Religion of Ancient Rome, Sather Classical Lectures 10, Berkeley 1932, 69.155.

L. BANTI, Il culto del cosidetto tempio dell'Apollo a Veii e il problema delle triadi etrusco-italiche, SE 17, 1943, 187–224.

V. BASANOFF, Les dieux des Romains, Paris 1942, 16f.

J. BAYET, Histoire politique et psychologique de la religion romaine, Paris 1957, 118.

E. BENVENISTE, Symbolisme social dans les cultes Gréco-Italiques, RHR 129, 1954, 6–9.

E. BICKEL, Beiträge zur römischen Religion, Rh.Mus. 71, 1916, 558ff.

G. BINDER, Aeneas und Augustus. Interpretationen zum 8. Buch der Aeneis, Beiträge zur klass. Philologie 38, Meisenheim 1971, 167ff.

R. BLOCH, Parenté entre religion de Rome et religion d'Ombrie, REL 41, 1963, 115–122.

A. VON BLUMENTHAL, Zur römischen Religion der archaischen Zeit II, Rhein.Mus. 90, 1941, 310ff.

F. BÖMER, Ahnenkult und Ahnenglaube im alten Rom, ARW Beiheft 1, 1943, 75ff.

DERS., P. Ovidius Naso, Die Fasten II, Heidelberg 1956, 116.

A. BRELICH, Tre variazioni sul tema delle origini, Roma 1955, 113ff.

DERS., Quirinus. Una divinità romana alla luce della comparazione storica, SMSR 31, 1960, 63.119.

M. G. BRUNO(-TIBILETTI), I Sabini e la loro lingua, RIL 95, 1961, 501ff.

W. BURKERT, Caesar und Romulus-Quirinus, Historia (Wiesbaden) 11, 1962, 356–376.

V. CALESTANI, Aborigini e Sabini, Historia (Studi storici per l'antichità classica, Milano/Roma) 7, 1933, 374–401.

P. CATALANO, Populus Romanus Quirites, Memorie dell'istituto giuridico. Università di Torino, ser. 2, memoria 156, Turin 1974, 3ff.

C. J. CLASSEN, Zur Herkunft der Sage von Romulus und Remus, Historia (Wiesbaden) 12, 1963, 447–457.

A. B. COOK, Zeus, Jupiter, and the Oak, CR 18, 1905, 368f.

L. DEUBNER, Die Devotion der Decier, ARW 8, 1905 (Usener-Beiheft), 74ff.

DERS., Lustrum, ARW 16, 1913, 127–136.

DERS., Zur römischen Religionsgeschichte, MDAI(R) 36/7, 1921/2, 14ff.

DERS., Die Römer, in: P. D. CHANTEPIE DE LA SAUSSAYE, Lehrbuch der Religionsgeschichte II[4], Tübingen 1925, 439f.

G. Devoto, Nomi propri, in: Ders., Scritti minori 2, Firenze 1967, 282.284.

Ders., Altitalien, in: Historia Mundi 3, München 1954, 372.

G. Dumézil, Jupiter, Mars, Quirinus. Essai sur la conception indo-européenne de la société et sur les origines de Rome, Paris 1941, 90.

Ders., Id., II. Naissance de Rome, Paris 1944, 194–221.

Ders., L'héritage indoeuropéen à Rome. Introduction aux séries 'Jupiter, Mars, Quirinus' et 'Les Mythes romains', Paris 1949, 92.

Ders., Jupiter, Mars, Quirinus et les trois fonctions chez les poètes latins du Iᵉʳ siècle av. J.C., REL 29, 1951, 318–330.

Ders., Iuppiter, Mars, Quirinus et Ianus, RHR 139, 1951, 208–215.

Ders., Ner- et viro- dans les langues Italiques, REL 31, 1953, 181 ff.

Ders., A propos de Quirinus, REL 33, 1955, 105–108.

Ders., Remarques sur les armes des dieux de troisième fonction chez divers peuples indo-européens, SMSR 28, 1957, 1–10.

Ders., La religion romaine archaïque, Les religions de l'humanité 10, Paris 1966, 246–271.

A. Ernout, Sur quelques noms de dieux Sabins, in: Studies presented to Joshua Wathmough, 's-Gravenhage 1957, 26 Anm. 2.

E. C. Evans, The Cults of the Sabine Territory, PMAA 11, Rome 1939, 211–226.

J. Gagé, Quirinus, fut-il le dieu des Fabii?, in: Mél. d'archéol. et d'Hist. offerts à A. Piganiol III, Paris 1966, 1591–1605.

Ders., Le témoignage de Julius Proculus sur l'assomption de Romulus-Quirinus et les prodiges fulguratoires dans l'ancien ritus comitialis, AC 41, 1972, 49–77.

Ders., Enquêtes sur les structures sociales et religieuses de la Rome primitive, Coll.Latomus 152, Bruxelles 1977, 137 ff.

L. Gerschel, Saliens de Mars et Saliens de Quirinus, RHR 138, 1950, 145-151.

P. Grimal, Dictionnaire de la mythologie grecque et romaine³, Paris 1963, 405.

M. Guarducci, Hora Quirini, BCAR 64, 1936, 31–36.

J. A. Hartung, Die Religion der Römer, I, Erlangen 1836, 296 f.

J. Adams Holland, Janus and the Bridge, Rome 1961, 110 f. 166 ff. 285 Anm. 88.

O. Immisch, Crimen, Glotta 13, 1924, 35 Anm. 1.

C. Koch, Bemerkungen zum römischen Quirinuskult, ZRGG 5, 1953, 1–25 = Ders., Religio. Studien zu Kult und Glauben der Römer, hrsg. v. O. Seel, Erlanger Beiträge zur Sprach- und Kunstwiss. 7, Nürnberg 1960, 17 ff.

Ders., Quirinus, in: RE XXIV 1 (1963), 1306–1321.

P. Kretschmer, Lateinisch quirites und quiritare, Glotta 10, 1920, 147–157.

L. Labruna, Quirites, Labeo (Napoli) 8, 1962, 340–348.

K. Latte, Römische Religionsgeschichte, Handbuch d. Altertumswiss. V 4, München 1960 (1967²), 113.114.

M. Leumann, Lateinische Laut- und Formenlehre⁶ = Leumann–Hofmann–Szantyr, Lateinische Grammatik I, Handbuch d. Altertumswiss. II, 2,1, München 1977.

W. Meid, Das Suffix -no- in Götternamen, BN 8, 1957, 135.

P. Mingazzini, L'origine del nome di Roma etc., BCAR 78, 1961/2, 3–18.

F. Muller, Altitalisches Wörterbuch, Göttingen 1926, 108.

W. F. Otto, Iuno. Beiträge zum Verständnisse der ältesten und wichtigsten Thatsachen ihres Kultes, Philologus 64, 1905, 201 = Ders., Aufsätze zur römischen Religionsgeschichte, Beiträge zur klassischen Philologie 71, Meisenheim am Glan 1975, 41.

Ders., Ianus, RE Suppl. III (1918), 1181.

R. E. A. Palmer, The Archaic Community of the Romans, Cambridge, Mass. 1970, 160 ff.

Ders., Roman Religion and Roman Empire, The Haney Foundation Ser. Publ. 15, Philadelphia 1974, 132 f.

J. PAOLI, Autour du problème de Quirinus, in: Studi U. E. Paoli, Firenze 1956, 525—537.

A. J. PFIFFIG, Religio Iguvina, Wien 1964, 37ff.

A. PIGANIOL, Les origines d'Hercule, in: Hommages à A. Grenier, III, Coll.Latomus 58, Bruxelles 1962, 1261—1264.

DERS., Essai sur les origines de Rome, Bibl. des Écoles franç. d'Athènes et de Rome 110, Paris 1917, 114.

G. B. PIGHI, La religione romana, Lezioni A. Rostagni 3, Turin 1967, 31ff.

V. PISANI, Mytho-Etymologica, in: DERS., Lingue e culture, Brescia 1969, 283f.

R. VON PLANTA, Rezension von FR. STOLZ, Laut- und Stammbildungslehre (1894) und von W. M. LINDSAY, The Latin Language (1894), Anz.f.Indogerman.Sprach- und Altertumskunde 10, 1899, 57.

D. PORTE, Romulus-Quirinus, Prince et dieu, dieu des princes (Étude sur le personnage de Quirinus et sur son évolution, des origines à Auguste), unt. in diesem Band (ANRW II, 17,1, hrsg. v. W. HAASE), 300—342.

A. POTT, Etymologische Forschungen auf dem Gebiete der indogermanischen Sprache, Lemgo 1836, I, 123: II, 493.533.

J. POUCET, Les origines mythiques des Sabins à travers l'œuvre de Caton, de Cn. Gellius, de Varro, d'Hygin et de Strabon, in: Études étrusco-italiques. Mélanges pour le 25e anniversaire de la chaire d'étruscologie à l'Univ. de Louvain, Univ. de Louvain, Rec. de trav. d'hist. et de philol., 4e sér. 31, Louvain 1963, 188.

DERS., Recherches sur la légende sabine des origines de Rome, Kinshasa 1967, 22—74.

DERS., Romains, Sabins et Samnites, AC 40, 1971, 146.

DERS., Les Sabins aux origines de Rome: Légende ou histoire?, LEC 39, 1971, 139f.

DERS., Les Sabins aux origines de Rome, in: ANRW I, 2, Berlin—New York 1972, 103ff.

L. PRELLER—H. JORDAN, Römische Mythologie I³, Berlin 1881, 369—375.

G. RADKE, Quirinalis collis, in: RE XXIV 1 (1963), 1301.

DERS., Varro, l.l. V 74 zu sabinischen Gottheiten, Romanitas 7, 1965, 290—313.

DERS., Zu einem Buch A. Alföldis, in: F. ALTHEIM—R. STIEHL, Die Araber in der alten Welt, IV, Berlin 1967, 515—538.

DERS., Das imperium des Augustus, seine politischen und sozialen Grundlagen, in: Klass. Sprachen u. Literaturen 5, München 1970, 19—41.

DERS., Res Italae Romanorumque triumphi, in: Klass. Sprachen und Literaturen 6, München 1971, 78—104.

DERS., Die Überlieferung archaischer lateinischer Texte in der Antike, Romanitas 11, 1972, 189—264.

DERS., Acca Larentia und die fratres Arvales, in: ANRW I, 2, Berlin—New York 1972, 421—441.

DERS., Die Götter Altitaliens², Fontes et Commentationes 3, Münster 1979.

O. RICHTER. Topographie der Stadt Rom², München 1901.

H. RIX, Sabini, Sabelli, Samnium, BN 8, 1957, 135ff.

G. ROHDE, Die Kultsatzungen der römischen Pontifices, RVV 25, Berlin 1936.

H. J. ROSE, Ancient Roman Religion, London 1949, 68.

E. T. SALMON, Samnium and the Samnites, Cambridge 1967, 246.

G. DE SANCTIS. Storia dei Romani I², Firenze 1956, 265f.; IV, 2,1, ibid. 1953, 139.

R. SCHILLING, Ianus le dieu introducteur, le dieu des passages, MEFR 72, 1960, 166f.

DERS., Romulus l'élu et Rémus le réprouvé, REL 38, 1960, 182—199.

DERS., The Roman Religion, in: J. BLEEKER—G. WIDENGREN, Historia Religionum 1, Leiden 1969, 442—494.

DERS., Les études relatives à la religion romaine, in: ANRW I, 2, Berlin—New York 1972, 325f.

U. W. SCHOLZ, Studien zum altitalischen und altrömischen Marskult und Marsmythos, Bibl. der klass. Altertumswiss. 2. R., 35, Heidelberg 1970, 18ff.

K. Scott, Identification of Augustus with Romulus-Quirinus, Cleveland 1925, 82–105.

J. Scott-Ryberg, Was the Capitoline Triad Etruscan or Italic?, AJPh 52, 1931, 145–153.

F. Sommer, Handbuch der lateinischen Laut- u. Formenlehre³, Indogerman.Bibliothek I 3, 1a, Heidelberg 1948 (cf. F. Sommer–R. Pfister, Handbuch der lateinischen Laut-und Formenlehre, Heidelberg 1977).

O. Terrosi-Zanco, Varrone l.l. V 74. Divinità sabine o divinità etrusche, SCO 10, 1961, 204f.

K. F. Thormann, Der doppelte Ursprung der Mancipatio, Münchener Beiträge zur Papyrusforschung und antiken Rechtsgeschichte 33, München 1943, 81f. (*flamen Quirinalis* Abbild des Gottes).

H. Wagenvoort, Studies in Roman Literature, Culture and Religion, Leiden 1956, 178ff. 293.

Ders., Wesenszüge altrömischer Religion, in: ANRW I, 2, Berlin–New York 1972, 365.

A. Walde–J. B. Hofmann, Lateinisches etymologisches Wörterbuch³, Heidelberg 1938, II, 409.

St. Weinstock, Rez. Latte, Römische Religionsgeschichte, JRSt 51, 1961, 212.

G. Wissowa, Gesammelte Abhandlungen zur römischen Religions- und Stadtgeschichte, München 1904.

Ders., Quirinus, in: W. H. Roscher, Ausführliches Lexikon der griechischen und römischen Mythologie IV (1909–1915, Nachdruck 1977), 10–18.

Ders., Religion und Kultus der Römer², Handbuch der Altertumswiss. V 4, München 1912 (Nachdruck ibid. 1972).

Romulus-Quirinus, prince et dieu, dieu des princes.
Etude sur le personnage de Quirinus et sur son évolution, des origines à Auguste

par Danielle Porte, Paris

Table des matières

Abréviations:

AC   L'Antiquité Classique, Louvain.

AJA   American Journal of Archaeology, New York.

ANRW Aufstieg und Niedergang der römischen Welt. Geschichte und Kultur Roms im Spiegel der neueren Forschung, hrsg. v. W. Haase u. H. Temporini, Berlin/New York, 1972 sqq.

ARW   Archiv für Religionswissenschaft, Leipzig.

Ath   Athenaeum. Studi periodici di Letteratura e Storia dell' Antichità, Pavia.

C.I.L.   Corpus Inscriptionum Latinarum, consilio et auctoritate Acad. Litt. (Regiae) Boruss. ed., Leipzig/Berlin, 1862−1943. Ed. alt., ibid. 1893 sqq.

Introduction

Quirinus est sans doute la figure la plus paradoxale de tout le panthéon romain.

Il fut un très grand dieu, puisqu'il constitue la troisième composante de la Triade archaïque Jupiter-Mars-Quirinus — et nul ne sait plus qui il est[1]. On le trouve cité partout et par tous, pourtant, son personnage originel disparaît complètement derrière un autre nom, celui de Romulus, qui vient interposer entre le dieu primitif et nous sa puissante résonance historique. Les déboires de Quirinus proviennent au premier chef de l'intérêt tout particulier que César, puis Auguste, lui portèrent. Condamné à prêter son nom au Fondateur divinisé, d'abord pour innocenter le Sénat du meurtre de Romulus[2], puis pour cacher ce que la déification directe d'un roi aurait eu de trop novateur aux yeux des Romains traditionalistes[3], Quirinus dut abdiquer toute personnalité pour devenir Romulus, au point que les écrivains de la fin de la République et du début de l'Empire ne savent plus nous donner sur lui que des renseignements squelettiques et contradictoires. Quirinus, dans la plupart de nos textes, c'est Romulus. Aussi, tenter de retrouver la figure originelle de Quirinus à travers Romulus peut sembler, comme le pense A. BRELICH, *„un'impresa disperata"*[4].

CR   Classical Review, Oxford.

I.L.S.   Inscriptiones Latinae Selectae, ed. H. DESSAU, Berlin, 1892 sqq.

JRS   Journal of Roman Studies, London.

MDAIR   Mitteilungen des Deutschen Archäologischen Instituts, Röm. Abt., Mainz.

MEFR(A)   Mélanges d'Archéologie et d'Histoire de l'École Française de Rome, Paris (Mélanges de l'école française de Rome [Antiquité], Paris).

MSL   Mémoires de la Société de linguistique de Paris, Paris.

MusHelv   Museum Helveticum. Revue Suisse pour l'Étude de l'Antiquité classique, Bâle.

REL   Revue des Études Latines, Paris.

RHR   Revue de l'Histoire des Religions, Paris.

RIL   Rendiconti dell'Istituto Lombardo, Classe di Lettere, Scienze morali e storiche, Milano.

SMSR   Studi e materiali di storia delle religioni, Roma.

TAPhA   Transactions and Proceedings of the American Philological Association, Cleveland, Ohio.

WS   Wiener Studien. Zeitschrift für klassische Philologie und Patristik, Wien.

[1] W. BURKERT, Caesar und Romulus-Quirinus, Historia, 11, 1962, 356—376, p. 359, estime qu'il est *„eine der schattenhaftesten Gestalten unter den Göttern Roms"*. Il est significatif que l'étude consacrée à Quirinus par G. RADKE, dont je viens d'avoir connaissance et que l'on trouvera p. 276 à 299 de ce même volume, commence par une même observation désabusée, assortie de la même citation de W. BURKERT! Au moins, le mystère de Quirinus ne fait de doute pour personne.

[2] Ovide, Fast., II, 497—499; Plutarque, Rom., 43; Tite-Live, I, 16.

[3] Auguste marque une préférence pour le surnom de Romulus, d'après Dion Cassius, LIII, 16, 7, mais juge plus prudent de se faire appeler Quirinus: Suétone, Aug., 7; Servius, Ad Aen., I, 292.

[4] Quirinus. Una divinità romana alla luce della comparazione storica, SMSR, 30, 1, 1960, 63—119, p. 80.

Les écrivains modernes s'y sont essayés tour à tour, et leurs recherches s'orientèrent selon deux directions successives: on fit fond, d'abord, sur les interprétations anciennes, et l'on considéra Quirinus comme un dieu guerrier, d'origine sabine, un 'Mars sabin'. Puis vint G. Dumézil, qui, privilégiant d'autres textes méconnus par ses prédécesseurs, étudia les fonctions du prêtre attaché à Quirinus, le *Flamen Quirinalis*, et établit la vocation agricole du dieu. Sabin? Guerrier? Fondateur? Paysan? Il ne serait peut-être point mauvais de dresser une sorte de bilan, et d'essayer d'utiliser et de comprendre tous les textes. La figure de Quirinus peut en sortir quelque peu éclaircie.

Afin de travailler sur du matériel solide, il nous faut rassembler d'abord les données antiques touchant notre dieu, et tâcher, s'il se peut, de séparer le bon grain de l'ivraie.

I. *Quirinus dans les spéculations antiques*

L'ivraie, c'est peut-être justement l'omniprésence de Romulus, que nous essayerons plus tard de justifier, persuadée que nous sommes du solide bon sens des Romains, qui ne choisirent pas au hasard le dieu destiné à récupérer le personnage humain de Romulus. Lorsque Ovide nous propose des étiologies relatives au nom de Quirinus, il le fait en partant des traits caractéristiques de Romulus, ce qui constitue un progrès par rapport à ses devanciers, Varron et Verrius Flaccus[5], préoccupés, eux, de la seule étymologie:

> *Qui tenet hoc nomen, Romulus ante fuit,*
> *Siue quod hasta 'curis' priscis est dicta Sabinis,*
> *Bellicus a telo uenit in astra deus,*
> *Siue suo regi nomen posuere Quirites,*
> *Seu quia Romanis iunxerat ille Cures*[6].

Après lui, Plutarque et Servius suivent cette voie avec enthousiasme, et jouent sans hésiter la carte de l'assimilation entre Romulus et Quirinus, favorisée par les idées du Régime[7]. A la fin du Paganisme, la confusion est si bien faite que le *Flamen Quirinalis* est donné dans les textes comme Flamine « de Romulus »[8].

Pour qui pratique un peu l'étiologie romaine, le manque total de logique dont font preuve les chercheurs latins et grecs de la fin de la République est

---

[5] On peut écrire, grâce aux textes, l'histoire de l'assimilation. Ennius atteste la divinisation, Ann. I, 74—78, chez Cicéron, Rep., I, 16, 25, mais pas encore l'assimilation; Tite-Live nomme 'Romulus-dieu' en I, 16, pas encore 'Quirinus'; l'assimilation date des dernières années de la République, et ne soulève pas l'enthousiasme de Cicéron, Leg., I, 1, 3, Nat. Deor., II, 63, Rep., II, 10, 20, ni de Varron, cf. p. 323 sqq.

[6] Ovide, Fast., II, 476—480. Cf. W. Fauth, Römische Religion im Spiegel der 'Fasti' des Ovid, ANRW, II, 16, 1, 1978, p. 170.

[7] Plutarque, Rom., 48; Servius, Ad Aen., I, 292; Probus, Ad Georg., III, 27.

[8] Augustin, Ciu. Dei, II, 15.

devenu un dogme. Comment s'étonner alors de voir Quirinus, tenu pour Romulus, fondateur de Rome, expliqué à l'aide d'étymologies dont on souligne à l'envi la coloration sabine: *curis*, la lance sabine[9], *Cures*, la capitale des Sabins[10]? Sans hésiter, Verrius Flaccus écrit même que Quirinus est un dieu de Cures: *Curibus ascito Quirino*[11].

Si quelque esprit plus critique s'avise de la contradiction évidente qui fait surnommer le roi de Rome à l'aide de vocables empruntés au dialecte d'un peuple vaincu par lui, il explique ce phénomène avec la mentalité d'un Romain, et voit dans Quirinus un surnom triomphal octroyé à Romulus vainqueur de Cures, tout comme l'on saluait du nom de Germanicus le vainqueur des Germains, ou d'Africanus le vainqueur de Carthage: c'est la justification la plus rationnelle, donnée par Ovide[12]. Ce qui n'empêche pas, après la sienne, d'autres explications singulièrement embrouillées! Ainsi, pour Servius, à la suite du synoecisme latino-sabin, les anciens Sabins furent dénommés *Romani*, du nom de leur vainqueur, Romulus, tandis que les anciens Romains s'appelaient désormais *Quirites*, d'après *Cures*, la capitale vaincue, ces échanges linguistiques peu convaincants répondant à un souci guère plus satisfaisant de diplomatie envers les Sabins écrasés[13]. Il trouvait déjà cette idée en germe chez Tite-Live: *ut Sabinis tamen aliquid daretur*[14]. On sent, dans ces échafaudages laborieux, la gêne que l'on ressentait à expliquer *Quirites*, mot qui contient l'essence même de la qualité de Romain, à l'aide du nom sabin de *Cures*: bien qu'on analyse leur nom comme un nom sabin, les *Quirites* sont toujours sentis comme les authentiques anciens Romains, et l'inadéquation de l'étymologie embarrasse les philologues.

Quirinus apparaît donc fortement teinté de couleurs sabines; mais ce n'est pas tout. Conséquence, sans doute, de son assimilation avec Romulus, dont l'annalistique romaine, soucieuse de symétrie et d'antithèse, exagérait le caractère belliqueux afin de l'opposer plus nettement au pacifique Numa[15], il se voyait considérer aussi comme un dieu guerrier, aspect que nous étudierons en détail. Mais avec tout cela, les érudits romains restaient tout de même sensibles à un rapprochement linguistique dont l'évidence crève les yeux[16]: Quirinus était

[9] Paulus-Festus, p. 43 L.; Servius, Ad Aen., I, 292; Macrobe, Sat., I, 9; Plutarque, Rom., 48.

[10] Paulus-Festus, p. 43 L.; p. 198 L.; et le texte d'Ovide déjà cité.

[11] P. 198 L.

[12] Fast., II, 480.

[13] Ad Aen., VII, 710: *Vnde et Romani Quirites dicti sunt, quod nomen Sabinorum fuerat, a ciuitate Curibus, et Sabini a Romulo Romani dicti sunt.*

[14] I, 12: *nec pacem modo sed ciuitatem unam ex duabus faciunt; regnum consociant: imperium omne conferunt Romam. Ita geminata urbe, ut Sabinis tamen aliquid daretur, Quirites a Curibus appellati.*

[15] Tite-Live, I, 21: *duo deinceps reges, alius alia uia, ille bello, hic pace, ciuitatem auxerunt.* En I, 16, le testament de Romulus est indéniablement guerrier: «Qu'ils s'exercent assidûment dans le métier de la guerre; qu'ils sachent et qu'ils apprennent à leurs enfants que nulle puissance sur la terre ne pourra résister aux armes romaines».

[16] Remarque de C. KOCH, Bemerkungen zum römischen Quirinuskult, dans: IDEM, Religio. Studien zu Kult und Glauben der Römer, hrsg. v. O. SEEL, Erlanger Beitr. zur Sprach- und Kunstwiss., 7, Nuremberg, 1960, 17–39, p. 35.

forcément lié aux *Quirites*, aux «Romains de souche»: *siue suo regi nomen posuere Quirites*[17], écrit sagement Ovide, après Varron: *Quirinus a Quiritibus*[18]. Et afin de ne sacrifier aucune trouvaille étymologique, on soutenait alors que *Quirites* venait de *Cures*[19]. A moins que l'on n'appliquât le processus inverse, en supposant que *Quirites* avait été formé sur Quirinus, lui-même nommé à partir de *curis*[20]! Il est vrai que la religion des auteurs varie entre plusieurs passages d'une seule œuvre . . . Le même Festus ne nous affirme-t-il pas ailleurs: *Quiritibus, quod est Curensibus, quae ciuitas Sabinorum potentissima fuit*[21]! Et si nous faisons intervenir enfin le nom du *Quirinal*, nommé pour les uns d'après *Quirinus* qui y avait son temple[22], mais pour les autres d'après *Cures*[23], nous nous sentons saisis d'une légitime angoisse devant ce qui finit par nous paraître un autre noeud gordien. L'opposition s'établit, et semble irréductible, entre Varron, qui admet une dérivation *Quirites* → *Quirinus*, et Verrius Flaccus qui, lui, prône une étymologie *Quirinus* → *Quirites*. Au point qu'Ovide, soucieux de logique, s'inspire de Tite-Live, lorsqu'il écrit: *Cures* a donné *Quirites*, de Varron, lorsqu'il écrit: *Quirites* a donné *Quirinus*, et de Cicéron, lorsqu'il écrit: *Quirinus* a donné le nom du *Quirinal*. Le tableau ci-dessous[24] permettra d'apprécier à loisir les méandres de la question.

[17] Fast., II, 479.
[18] L.L., V, 73.
[19] L.L., VI, 68; Festus, p. 59 L.; Tite-Live, I, 12, etc.
[20] Paulus-Festus, p. 43 L.
[21] P. 59 L.; aussi, p. 304 L.
[22] Varron, L.L., V, 45; Festus, p. 304 L.; Ovide, Fast., II, 511, etc.
[23] Festus, p. 304 L.
[24]

Varron, L.L., V, 73:	*Quirites* ⟶	*Quirinus*
VI, 68:	*Cures* ⟶	*Quirites*
V, 45:	*Quirinus* ⟶	*Quirinal*
Verrius, p. 198 L.:	*Cures* ⟶	*Quirinus*
p. 43 L.:	*Cures* ⟶	*Quirinus*
p. 43 L.:	*curis* ⟶	*Quirinus*
	Quirinus ⟶	*Quirites*
p. 59 L.:	*Cures* ⟶	*Quirites*
p. 304 L.:	*Cures* ⟶	*Quirina tribus* et *Quirinal*
	Quirinus ⟶	*Quirinal*
Ovide, Fast., II, 479:	*Quirites* ⟶	*Quirinus*
II, 480:	*Cures* ⟶	*Quirinus*
II, 478:	*curis* ⟶	*Quirinus*
IV, 855:	*Quirinus* ⟶	*Quirites*
Servius, Ad Aen., I, 292:	*Koiranos* ⟶	*Quirinus*
VII, 710:	*Cures* ⟶	*Quirinus*
I, 292:	*curis* ⟶	*Quirinus*
VIII, 635:	*Cures* ⟶	*Quirites*
Tite-Live, I, 13:	*Cures* ⟶	*Quirites*
Macrobe, Sat., I, 9, 16:	*curis* ⟶	*Quirinus*
Plutarque, Rom., 48:	*curis* ⟶	*Quirinus*
	Quirites ⟶	*Quirinus*
Rom., 30:	*Cures* ⟶	*Quirites*
Num., 6:	*Cures* ⟶	*Quirites*

Voilà donc comment les Romains comprenaient Quirinus: un dieu sabin, venu de Cures, régnant sur les *Quirites* romains, et doté d'un caractère guerrier, sans doute à cause de son étymologie par *curis*, la lance, interprétation favorisée par son assimilation avec Romulus.

II. Examen des thèses antiques

1. Quirinus – dieu guerrier

Ce Quirinus guerrier ne heurtait pas le bon sens pourtant reconnu à la race romaine. On acceptait sans frémir que Janus, surnommé *Quirinus*[25], puisque le mot *Quirinus* est une épithète, devînt un dieu belliqueux[26] (*Ianum Quirinum quasi bellorum potentem*), lui, le dieu paisible par excellence. On traduisait couramment ce *Quirinus* par le grec *Enyalios*, surnom d'Arès[27], et Servius, tiraillé entre les interprétations qui, contre toute vraisemblance, en faisaient un autre Mars[28], et son caractère de paisible dieu des *Quirites*, en arrive à nous livrer des définitions savoureuses et antithétiques: *Mars qui praeest paci*[29], ou *Mars tranquillus*[30].

On allègue pourtant que le caractère guerrier de Quirinus n'est pas fondé seulement sur une étymologie par *curis*, la lance. Il existe, en effet, d'autres indices: Quirinus possède des Saliens, ceux dits «de la Colline», des armes, des boucliers sacrés ou *ancilia*, des prêtres Fétiaux. Tout cela n'est plus de l'interprétation, mais appartient au domaine du rite. C'est ce qui a motivé l'interprétation résolument guerrière qu'un bon nombre de savants adoptent au sujet du dieu[31].

Certains de ces faits sont troublants, si d'autres se laissent comprendre sans trop de peine. Le plus limpide est l'affectation à Quirinus de Fétiaux, prêtres chargés des rites de la déclaration de guerre. Elle n'est peut-être qu'une déduction gratuite de Polybe, notre unique source, à partir de la formule que

---

[25] Res Gestae diui Augusti, II, 42.

[26] Macrobe, Sat., I, 9, 16.

[27] Sur cette traduction, voir p. 311 sq.

[28] N'oublions pas que, précisément, Romulus est le fils de Mars dans la légende romaine! Les interprétations romaines négligent à la fois le fait que, dans la Triade archaïque, Mars et Quirinus sont deux personnages différents, ce qui devrait interdire d'affecter à l'un le surnom exprimant la qualité dominante de l'autre; et celui que le fils pourrait difficilement être assimilé à un personnage divin qui se révélerait être en réalité son propre père sous un autre nom! Sans compter le fait que *Enyalios* = Mars guerrier est affecté à Quirinus, compris comme Mars tranquille, pour un Romulus on ne peut plus guerrier!

[29] Ad Aen., VI, 859.

[30] Ad Aen., I, 292.

[31] En particulier, C. KOCH, Bemerkungen zum römischen Quirinuskult, dans: IDEM, Religio, Nuremberg, 1960, 17–39, p. 20; F. ALTHEIM, Römische Religionsgeschichte, II, Baden-Baden, 1953, p. 14.

prononce le *Pater Patratus* aux frontières ennemis, et dans laquelle sont invoqués Jupiter et Janus *Quirinus*[32], ce qui n'entraîne pas de relations particulières des Fétiaux avec le troisième dieu.

Pour les Saliens, le cas est plus complexe[33]. Il ne faut pas arguer, pour s'en débarrasser, du petit nombre de textes existants, comme le fait J. POUCET[34]. Il existe tout de même le texte de Tite-Live[35]: *Quid de ancilibus uestris, Mars Gradiue, tuque, Quirine pater?*, paroles où, certes, Tite-Live «a glissé des idées de son temps», mais qui sont prononcées par Camille. Tite-Live n'aurait pas risqué un aussi grave anachronisme institutionnel. Denys d'Halicarnasse, lui aussi, évoque des Saliens de la Colline, créés par Tullus Hostilius, et précise qu'ils sont affectés «aux dieux armés», pas au seul Mars[36]. Dans les 'Laudes Crispini'[37], un Salien de la Colline est décrit par Stace, et les expressions qu'il emploie («la science des combats, Mars et Minerve te l'enseigneront; Castor t'apprendra à dompter les chevaux, *Quirinus* à lancer le javelot, ce Quirinus qui t'a permis déjà de porter des boucliers fabriqués dans les cieux, et un glaive encore intact de carnage»), nous montrent sans équivoque un Quirinus guerrier indépendant de Mars. A cette époque, la figure de Romulus a sans doute influencé la vision qu'on a de Quirinus. Néanmoins, ce qui nous importe, c'est la mention des anciles et du glaive saliens, en rapport avec Quirinus. Enfin, Servius nous affirme que les Saliens sont *in tutela Iouis Martis Quirini*[38], soit de la Triade archaïque dans l'ordre, et Jean le Lydien attribue ces mêmes Saliens à *Ianus Quirinus*[39].

Avant d'envisager plus loin une explication de ces Saliens, notons que leur institution n'est pas contemporaine de celle des *Salii Palatini*[40], voués au culte de Mars, mais postérieure. On l'attribue en effet à Tullus Hostilius, après la mort de Romulus, et, une fois encore, ces Saliens peuvent avoir été sentis comme voués au culte d'un guerrier divinisé. De toute façon, leur action cultuelle se situant à la charnière entre les deux périodes-clefs de l'année, la période guerrière (mars—octobre) et la période paisible (octobre-mars), ils peuvent ouvrir une

---

[32] Polybe, III, 25, 8; Tite-Live, I, 32, 9: *Audi, Iuppiter, et tu, Iane Quirine, dique omnes caelestes, uosque terrestres uosque inferni, audite!*; aussi Aulu-Gelle, N.A., XVI, 4.

[33] Lire W. HELBIG, Sur les Attributs des Saliens, Mém.Acad.Inscr.et Belles-Lettres, 37, 2, 1906, 205—276; R. BLOCH, Sur les Danses armées des Saliens, Annales Econ.Soc.Civ., 13, 1958, 706—715; R. CIRILLI, Les prêtres-danseurs de Rome, Paris, 1915.

[34] Recherches sur la légende sabine des origines de Rome, Univ.de Louvain, Rec.de trav. d'hist.et de philos., IVᵉ Sér., 37, Kinshasa, 1967, p. 28—29.

[35] Tite-Live, V, 52.

[36] Denys, II, 70: τῶν ἐνόπλων θεῶν; aussi, II, 48, 4: δαιμόνων πολεμιστῶν.

[37] Stace, Silv., V, 2, 128—131:

> *Monstrabunt acies Mauors Actaeaque uirgo,*
> *Flectere Castor equos, humeris quatere arma Quirinus*
> *Qui tibi tam tenero permisit plaudere collo*
> *Nubigenas clypeos, intactaque caedibus aera.*

[38] Ad Aen., VIII, 663.

[39] Mens., IV, 2.

[40] P. LAMBRECHTS, Mars et les Saliens, Latomus, 5, 1946, 113—114.

saison paisible aussi bien qu'une saison guerrière, fait observer G. Dumézil[41];
aussi, la présence de prêtres Saliens dans le culte n'est pas une preuve décisive du
caractère foncièrement guerrier de Quirinus.

Restent les *spolia*, les *arma*, et peut-être aussi la traduction de *Quirinus* en
langue grecque par le mot *Enyalios*, épithète d'Arès.

La question des *spolia* ne se laisse pas résoudre simplement. Deux thèses
sont en présence dès l'Antiquité. Celle qui fait offrir les *spolia opima* uniquement à *Iupiter Feretrius*, les définit comme des dépouilles conquises par un
chef sur le cadavre du chef ennemi, et s'appuie sur trois exemples historiques:
Romulus vainqueur d'Acron de Caenina, Cornélius Cossus vainqueur du chef
véien Lar Tolumnius, Marcellus, enfin, vainqueur de l'Insubre Viridomare; et
celle qui cite trois catégories de dépouilles opimes, les *prima*, qui, selon une loi
de Numa, appartiennent à *Jupiter Feretrius*, sont consacrés par le sacrifice d'un
bœuf et rapportent 300 pièces à celui qui les consacre; les *secunda*, voués à Mars,
consacrés par un suovetaurile, et récompensés par 200 pièces; les *tertia*, enfin,
offerts à *Ianus Quirinus*, consacrés par le sacrifice d'un agneau, et habilitant leur
possesseur à recevoir 100 pièces[42].

Comment comprendre les termes *prima, secunda, tertia*? Les premiers *spolia*
dans l'histoire, ou les premiers en importance? Chronologiquement, ou quantitativement? L'interprétation chronologique semble dominer dans nos textes.
Festus comprend que les *prima spolia* furent ceux conquis par Romulus, les
seconds ceux de Cornélius Cossus, les troisièmes ceux de Marcellus. Ainsi font
Plutarque, chez qui Marcellus lui-même s'écrie qu'il est «le troisième», et Servius[43]. Toutefois, il faudrait alors que Cornélius Cossus ait offert ses *spolia* à
Mars et que Marcellus ait offert les siens à Quirinus, ce qui n'est pas le cas, tous
s'adressant à Jupiter. D'autre part, il aurait fallu, c'est une remarque intéressante
de G. Dumézil[44], un don de voyance extraordinaire au roi Numa pour savoir,
dès l'aube de l'histoire romaine, qu'il y aurait en tout et pour tout trois chefs
ennemis tués de la main de généraux de Rome. Aussi, G. Dumézil revient-il, de
son propre aveu, sur ses vues antérieures, et adopte-t-il les conclusions de K.

---

[41] La Religion romaine archaïque, Bibl.hist., Coll.Les religions de l'humanité, Paris, 1966,
p. 261. G. Dumézil adopte là les conclusions de L. Gerschel, Saliens de Mars et Saliens
de Quirinus, RHR, 138, 1950, 145–151.

[42] Festus, p. 202–204 L.: *Vnde spolia quoque quae dux populi Romani duci hostium detraxit;
quorum tanta raritas est ut intra annos paulo . . . trina contigerint nomini romano: una
quae Romulus de Acrone, altera quae Cossus Cornelius de Tolumnio, tertia quae M. Marcellus (Ioui Feretrio) de Viridomaro fixerunt. M. Varro ait opima spolia esse, etiam si manipularis miles detraxerit, dummodo duci hostium. (. . .) non sint ad aedem Iouis Feretri
poni, testimonio esse libros Pontificum, in quibus sit „Pro primis spoliis boue, pro secundis,
solitaurilibus, pro tertiis, agno, publice fieri debere“. Esse etiam Pompilii regis legem
opimorum spoliorum talem: „Cuius auspicio classe procincta opima spolia capiuntur, Ioui
Feretrio darier oporteat, et bouem caedito, qui cepit aeris CC(C); secunda spolia in Martis
ara in campo solitaurilia utra uoluerit caedito . . . Tertia spolia Ianui Quirino agnum
marem caedito, C qui ceperit ex aere dato; cuius auspicio capta, dis piaculum dato“.* Texte
cité également par Plutarque.

[43] Plutarque, Marc., 7; Servius, Ad Aen., VI, 859.

[44] Rel.rom.arch., p. 173.

LATTE[45] avec une interprétation quantitative. Varron écrivant que les dépouilles opimes ne sont pas forcément conquises par un chef[46], K. LATTE interprète ainsi le texte de Festus: les dépouilles premières sont conquises par un chef sur un chef, et vouées à Jupiter; les secondes par un officier sans *ius auspicii* personnel, et vouées à Mars; les troisièmes, enfin, par un soldat de la masse, mais toujours sur le cadavre du chef ennemi, et vouées à *Ianus Quirinus*. Cette solution satisfait G. DUMÉZIL, car il y retrouve «la distinction fonctionnelle des trois dieux»[47].

Mais alors, comment concilier cette thèse avec les circonstances historiques, et les grades des trois hommes, Romulus, Cornélius, Marcellus, que la tradition nomme à propos des dépouilles opimes?

La difficulté n'arrête pas G. DUMÉZIL, qui s'en défait grâce à une note rapide: «Peu importent ici les discussions des Anciens sur le titre et le commandement exacts de Cossus»[48]. En effet, le vainqueur de Lar Tolumnius est présenté par Tite-Live non pas comme le chef suprême, mais comme un tribun militaire, le dictateur du moment étant Mamercus Aemilius[49].

La difficulté n'est pas, pourtant, dans le cas de Cornélius Cossus. Le point épineux, que G. DUMÉZIL n'examine pas, est en effet celui de Marcellus, qu'il faut absolument considérer, si l'on poursuit le même type de raisonnement, comme un ʿsoldat de la masseʾ, s'il est vrai qu'il dédie ses *spolia* à Quirinus! Ce à quoi l'histoire romaine se refuse catégoriquement: Marcellus est consul et triomphateur.

La sagesse nous invite à envisager les choses ainsi: Romulus offrit des *spolia opima ʿprimaʾ* à Jupiter Férétrien, et, pour cette première dédicace, tous nos textes sont d'accord. Cornélius Cossus, selon Tite-Live, consacra également à Jupiter les dépouilles conquises[50]: c'étaient donc aussi des *opima ʿprimaʾ*; Marcellus, enfin, selon Plutarque[51], offrit lui aussi les *spolia* à Jupiter, encore une fois, donc, des *opima ʿprimaʾ*.

Mais le chiffre trois, commun aux trois catégories de dépouilles et aux trois exemples recensés, causa une confusion dans les textes postérieurs. En contradiction avec Tite-Live, Servius assigne à Mars les dépouilles conquises par Cornélius Cossus, et les désigne comme des *secunda*; au mépris du texte de Plutarque, il attribue à Quirinus les *spolia* arrachés sur Viridomare par Marcellus, et les désigne comme des *tertia*. En fait, la loi de Numa, transcrite par Festus et Plutarque, garde tout son effet, simplement, il ne faut appliquer aux trois chefs

---

[45] Römische Religionsgeschichte, Handb.d.Altertumswiss., V, 4, Munich, 1960, p. 204–205.
[46] Dans le texte de Festus cité ci-dessus: *opima spolia esse, etiam si manipularis miles detraxerit*: il y a «dépouilles opimes» même si elles sont conquises par un simple soldat d'infanterie.
[47] Op.cit., p. 173.
[48] Ibid.; quelques manuscrits de Festus ajoutant au nom le titre de *consul*.
[49] Tite-Live, IV, 17; IV, 19.
[50] Tite-Live, IV, 20.
[51] Marc., 8, et Rom., 25; voir CH. PICARD, Les trophées romains, Paris, 1937, p. 131, qui critique une étude de J. CARCOPINO, MEFR, 54, 1937, 373–376; pour J. CARCOPINO, Plutarque a interprété à rebours la loi de Numa; il faudrait supposer que Tite-Live en a fait autant, ce qui serait étonnant.

connus, Romulus, Cossus, Marcellus, que son premier paragraphe, celui qui décrit les *spolia opima prima*. Il est vraisemblable que les *spolia secunda* et *tertia* revenaient à Mars et à Quirinus; seulement, nous n'avons conservé le nom d'aucun dédicant, ce qui a amené les auteurs postérieurs à faire 'descendre' de deux paragraphes Cossus et Marcellus, pour avoir un exemple à citer à propos de chacun des trois cas prévus par Numa. Un schéma simplifiera l'explication:

Loi de Numa originelle			
Spolia opima prima	Jupiter *Feretrius*	sacrifice: bœuf	300 pièces
Spolia opima secunda	Mars	suouetaurile	200 pièces
Spolia opima tertia	Quirinus	agneau	100 pièces

Application historique (Tite-Live, Plutarque)		
Spolia opima prima	Jupiter *Feretrius*	Romulus sur Acron Cossus sur Tolumnius Marcellus sur Viridomare
Spolia opima secunda	Mars	?
Spolia opima tertia	Quirinus	?

Application historique (Servius)		
Spolia opima prima	Jupiter *Feretrius*	Romulus sur Acron
Spolia opima secunda	Mars	Cossus sur Tolumnius
Spolia opima tertia	Quirinus	Marcellus sur Viridomare

La rareté seule des *spolia opima prima* a fait que l'on s'est soucié de conserver le souvenir des trois chefs qui les offrirent, et il convient de considérer la loi de Numa comme quantitative, en accord avec le texte de Varron, mais de laisser 'en blanc' les exemples de *spolia opima secunda* et *opima tertia*, en remettant à leur place, c'est à dire dans le cas des *opima prima*, aussi bien Marcellus que Cornélius.

Si nous lisons attentivement, du reste, le texte de Festus, nous ne pouvons qu'être confortés dans cette opinion. La loi de Numa est donnée par lui seulement en fin de texte, une fois que les noms des trois chefs ont été cités, avec une triple consécration, tout à fait normale, à Jupiter *Feretrius*. Autrement dit, Festus nous a donné d'abord un aperçu historique et trois noms; puis nous cite une notice de Varron, contenant une autre définition des *spolia opima*, et introduisant une notion de hiérarchie dans les dédicaces de dépouilles; enfin, une justification de cette opinion grâce à une réglementation pontificale et à une loi de Numa, mais sans se référer aux trois exemples cités d'abord, et pour cause! La confusion existe seulement dans le texte de Servius, qui, au mépris des traditions antérieures, fait offrir des dépouilles secondes à Mars par Cossus, et troisièmes à Quirinus par Marcellus. Mais le vœu de Marcellus s'adressa bien, selon la loi religieuse, à Jupiter, les textes historiques le disent expressément. Influencé par la correspondance entre trois chefs et trois séries de dépouilles, Servius rapprocha Cornélius Cossus de Mars et Marcellus de Quirinus, brouillant ainsi pour la postérité une question en définitive bien simple.

La question des 'armes' de Quirinus pose également un problème irritant. Un seul texte en fait mention, celui de Verrius Flaccus, rapporté d'une part par Festus: *Persillum uocant sacerdotes rudiculum picatum, quo unguine Flamen Portunalis arma Quirini unguet*[52], et, un peu plus tard, par Paulus: *Persillum dicebant uas quoddam picatum, in quo erat unguentum, unde arma Quirini unguebantur*[53]. «La nature de ces armes, le sens de l'opération, ainsi que le rapport exact entre Portunus et Quirinus nous échappent absolument», note J. Poucet[54]. Si absolument, qu'on a corrigé les textes: K. Latte préfère lire *Flamen Quirinalis* au lieu de *Flamen Portunalis*[55], ce qui est évidemment aller au plus simple! L. A. Holland suppose une inversion ayant altéré le texte originel, qui serait: *Flamen Quirini arma Portuni unguet*, ces *arma Portuni* étant un gouvernail[56].

Cernons d'un peu près les deux textes. La recherche moderne les utilise ainsi: elle emprunte à Festus le détail qui concerne le Flamine de Portunus, et laisse le reste de la définition de côté, pour demander la description des opérations au texte de Paulus, évidemment de tout repos: «un vase contenant un onguent qui servait à graisser les armes de Quirinus»: on peut toujours supposer n'importe quel amalgame graisseux destiné à protéger le métal contre la rouille! Le texte que Paulus abrège était un peu plus détaillé. Le *persillum*, nous dit-il, «était un *rudiculum* enduit de poix». Il ne s'agit donc pas d'un récipient, puisque le mot *uas* du texte de Paulus est absent de celui de Festus; en l'absence d'autres renseignements, le mot *rudiculum* étant un *hapax*, nous pouvons comprendre qu'il s'agit d'une spatule enduite de poix (*rudicula, -ae* existe chez Caton, Agr., 95 et l'instrument ainsi désigné sert à remuer une préparation dans un chaudron). Ce serait donc à l'aide de la poix que le Flamine procéderait à l'onction des armes, et l'on peut supposer que Paulus, ne comprenant pas l'usage de la poix ni le mot archaïque *persillum*, est allé au plus simple, et a défini le mot comme désignant un récipient contenant de la graisse, à cause, sans doute, du verbe *unguere*. Mais il faut noter que les définitions de Festus et de Paulus sont tout à fait différentes sur le même objet. Le *persillum* nous demeure encore à présent mystérieux, malgré une étude récente de G. B. Pighi[57], et le recours à l'ombrien *persontrum*. Est-ce un récipient enduit de poix, et contenant une préparation graisseuse, destinée à protéger de la rouille l'objet enduit? Est-ce au contraire une baguette servant à étendre la poix sur les armes, probablement alors pour les imperméabiliser, ce qui se comprend dans le cas d'armes archaïques en bois et cuir? Nous ne pouvons entrer ici dans les méandres de la question, et nous réservons d'y revenir ultérieurement.

---

[52] Verb.Sign., p. 238 L.

[53] P. 239 L.

[54] Op.cit., p. 28.

[55] Römische Religionsgeschichte, Munich, 1960, p. 37, n. 1.

[56] The Attribute of Portunus and the Verona Scholia on Aeneid V, 241, dans: Hommages à A. Grenier, éd. par M. Renard, Coll.Latomus, 58, Bruxelles, 1962, 817–823, passim.

[57] De Romanorum persillo et Umbrorum persontro, Latinitas, 2, 1954, 18–25.

Un autre fait tout aussi mystérieux est la mention du Flamine de Portunus[58]. Puisque Quirinus possède un Flamine, c'est bien lui qu'on attendrait, en une occasion où son dieu est directement impliqué! Or, le Flamine de Quirinus paraît s'occuper de bien d'autres services liturgiques indifférents à Quirinus, ceux d'Acca Larentia, de Consus, de Robigo, mais négliger complètement celui de Quirinus lui-même, nous aurons encore l'occasion de le constater[59]. Il est possible que la mention du Flamine de Portunus soit due à l'une de ces confusions dont nous avons des exemples reconnus. Portunus est un peu le même dieu que Janus, aux yeux des Anciens, s'il faut en croire la description de sa statue dotée de clefs: *qui clauim manu tenere fingebatur*[60], et il étend sa protection sur les portes: *et deus putabatur esse portarum*, poursuit Festus. On sait que Janus est surnommé *Quirinus*; que les auteurs latins confondent volontiers Janus et Quirinus, par exemple lorsqu'ils attribuent les *spolia tertia* à Janus *Quirinus*[61], ou les Saliens de la Colline à Janus[62]. Janus entre ainsi dans l'orbe de la Triade archaïque[63], et l'on peut supposer (prudemment) dans le cas qui nous occupe une méprise du même genre: aurait-on écrit quelque jour: «le Flamine de Janus-Quirinus enduit les armes de Quirinus», tout comme on avait écrit: «il dédia les Saliens de la Colline à Janus-Quirinus» au lieu de «à Quirinus» tout seul, et, puisqu'il n'existe pas de Flamine de Janus, remplacé ensuite ce Flamine fantôme par celui de Portunus, dieu assez proche de Janus pour être souvent confondu avec lui, et qui, lui, possède un Flamine? Il est en tout cas singulier que le *Flamen Quirinalis* ne s'acquitte pas de ce service concernant étroitement son dieu.

Venons-en à la traduction de *Quirinus* dans les textes grecs, dont les auteurs recourent à l'épithète du dieu Arès: *Enyalios*, épithète guerrière.

Comment expliquer ce curieux emploi? G. DUMÉZIL songe à une approximation fautive des traducteurs, en quête d'un adjectif recevable pour traduire des expressions comme *Mars tranquillus*, et séduits par l'adjectif Ἐνυάλιος ordinairement accolé au nom de Arès, sans s'aviser que cet adjectif signifie 'guerrier'[64]. Il est tout de même paradoxal que des Grecs aient rendu l'idée de paix par l'idée de guerre, et lorsque Denys d'Halicarnasse commente ce surnom, il le fait en se fondant sur l'idée de guerre qu'il voit sciemment dans le personnage de Quirinus[65].

Une autre explication serait possible. On sait que le *ianus* de l'Argilète, le fameux passage qui gouverne rituellement la guerre et la paix, est désigné par

---

[58] Que G. ROHDE explique par un échange entre prêtres latins et dieux sabins, Die Kultsatzungen der römischen Pontifices, Religionsgesch.Versuche u.Vorarbeiten, 25, Gießen, 1963, p. 121.

[59] Voir p. 316 sqq.

[60] Festus, Verb.Sign., p. 48 L.; Scholie de Vérone, Ad Aen., V, 241.

[61] Festus, p. 204 L.

[62] Jean le Lydien, Mens. IV, 2; voir G. CAPDEVILLE, Les épithètes cultuelles de Janus, MEFRA, 85, 1973, 395–436.

[63] Lire G. DUMÉZIL, Jupiter Mars Quirinus – et Janus, RHR, 139, 1951, 208–215.

[64] Religion romaine archaïque, Paris, 1966, p. 263.

[65] A.R., II, 48, 2; aussi Polybe, III, 25, 6; Macrobe, Sat., I, 9, 15.

deux expressions: *ianus geminus*, et *ianus quirinus*. La première attestation de ce *ianus quirinus* remonte à Lucilius et peut se relever dans divers autres textes[66]. Pour sa part, la poésie désignait le passage fatidique par l'expression «les portes de la Guerre»; d'abord Ennius, et son *Belli ferratos postes portasque*[67], puis Virgile, qui le reprend textuellement: *Belli ferratos rumpit Saturnia postis*[68]. Il s'établit donc une équivalence entre l'expression *ianus quirinus*, ou, selon Horace, *ianus Quirini*[69], et l'expression *Belli portae*. Comment pouvait-on rendre en grec ce *Belli portae*? Nous le savons grâce à l'inscription des 'Res gestae diui Augusti', rédigée à la fois en grec et en latin. Or, en face de l'expression: *ianum quirinum (clausi)*, nous trouvons en grec: Πύλην Ἐνυάλιον κε-κλεῖσθαι . . .[70]. Il est donc clair que les traducteurs grecs, confrontés à la difficulté de traduire l'expression *ianus quirinus*, qu'ils comprenaient, dans le texte des 'Res Gestae', comme se rapportant au temple et non au dieu, éprouvaient le besoin d'employer une épithète différente de celle qu'ils utilisaient pour traduire *Quirinus* en son nom propre, et qui est tout simplement Κυρῖνος[71]; ils durent songer alors à la formule voisine *Belli portae*, que les poètes emploient pour évoquer le *ianus quirinus*, et la transposer dans leur langue. Ils traduisirent alors *ianus = portae* par Πύλη, et *quirinus = belli* par Ἐνυάλιος, ce mot signifiant tout bonnement 'de la guerre', comme on le voit dans un exemple de Théocrite[72], en même temps que dans d'autres situations il se trouve qualifier le dieu Arès. Par ricochet, on en vint également à traduire *Quirinus* par Ἐνυάλιος, même indépendamment de Janus, une fois que les étymologies eurent montré en lui un dieu guerrier, à cause du rapprochement entre son nom et la *curis* sabine. Habitué qu'on était à voir voisiner Mars et Quirinus à l'intérieur de la Triade archaïque, on fut amené tout naturellement à rendre cette suite connue *Mars-Quirinus* par une autre suite connue *Arès-Enyalios*. *Quirinus* étant à leurs yeux une épithète au même titre qu'*Enyalios*, les Grecs hésitent même à dissocier Mars de Quirinus, et Denys d'Halicarnasse ne sait même plus trop s'il s'agit d'un seul dieu ou de deux dieux distincts! Il nous semble que cette explication est un moyen bien simple de rendre compte de la genèse de la traduction grecque affectée à Quirinus.

Après tout cela, il reste que le temple de Quirinus fut érigé à l'intérieur du *pomoerium*, celui de Mars restant prudemment relégué à l'extérieur des murailles[73]: toutes les étymologies guerrières ne prévalaient pas contre la croyance générale, qui n'analysait pas Quirinus comme un dieu foncièrement guerrier.

---

[66] Lucilius, chez Lactance, Diu.Inst., IV, 3, 12; aussi Tite-Live, I, 32, 9; Festus, Verb.Sign., p. 204 L.

[67] Ann., VIII, 258.

[68] Aen., VII, 622.

[69] Odes, IV, 15, 9.

[70] Res Gestae, II, 13; l'expression latine exacte est: *(Ianum) Quirin. claudendum esse censui(t)*.

[71] Entre autres, Plutarque, Rom., 28; 29.

[72] XXV, 279.

[73] Servius, Ad Aen., I, 292; VI, 859.

2. Quirinus – dieu sabin

Nous nous attarderons beaucoup moins sur la nationalité prétendûment sabine du dieu, pour l'excellente raison que le dossier a été fort bien traité par G. DUMÉZIL et par J. POUCET.

Rappelons rapidement les éléments de ce dossier: le choix, pour l'édification du temple, du Quirinal, colline tenue pour «sabine»[74], et la présence de notre dieu dans la liste que Varron dresse des divinités sabines importées par Titus Tatius[75], le roi sabin.

L'emplacement de son temple a contribué à faire de Quirinus le dieu du Quirinal, donc un dieu sabin[76]. Mais le texte de Festus que nous venons de citer nous montre que la colline ne s'est pas toujours appelée de ce nom (l'ancien nom était *Agonus*), et J. POUCET aboutit à la conclusion qu'elle n'a pas toujours admis Quirinus comme son dieu principal[77]. Nous ajouterons que la présence d'une divinité en un lieu de culte réputé sabin n'est pas prégnante pour sa nationalité sabine. Varron nous affirme ainsi que la Triade Capitoline, avant de se fixer sur le Palatin, occupa elle aussi le Quirinal: *cliuus proximus a Flora susus uersus Capitolium uetus, quod ibi sacellum Iouis Iunonis Mineruae, et antiquius quam aedis quae in Capitolio facta*[78]. Nul n'irait s'aviser pour autant de déclarer cette triade sabine!

La liste varronienne des dieux sabins n'est guère plus inébranlable, puisqu'elle comprend des divinités pour lesquelles Varron lui-même a proposé des étymologies latines[79]. On peut songer aussi à la légende de Modius Fabidius, habitant de Cures et fils de Quirinus, selon la légende relatée par Denys d'Halicarnasse. Mais avant de fonder Cures, Modius était indiscutablement un Aborigène, l'auteur grec le précise lui-même[80]. Il en résulte que Quirinus, père du héros fondateur de Cures, pourrait difficilement être Curète et sabin avant que son fils ait posé la première pierre de la capitale sabine!

En fait, on voit aisément que c'est l'étymologie, et elle seule, avec ses rapprochements séduisants et fallacieux *Quirinus/Quirites/Curetes/Cures* qui a donné naissance au caractère sabin de Quirinus, secondée, du reste, par le sens

---

[74] Festus, p. 304 L.: *Quirinalis collis qui nunc dicitur, olim Agonus appellabatur, ante quam in eum commigrarent fere Sabini . . .*

[75] Varron, L.L., V, 168.

[76] E. EVANS, The Cults of the Sabine Territory, Papers & Monogr.of the American Acad.in Rome, 9, Rome, 1939, p. 152 sq.; G. WISSOWA, Religion u. Kultus der Römer, Hb.d. klass.Altertumswiss. IV, 5, 2° éd., Munich, 1912, p. 156; C. KOCH, op.cit., p. 15; J. PAOLI, Autour du problème de Quirinus, dans: Studi in onore di U. E. Paoli, Florence, 1955, 525–537; L. DEUBNER, Zur römischen Religionsgeschichte, MDAIR, 36–37, 1921–1922, 14–33.

[77] Op.cit., p. 44–45.

[78] Varron, L.L., V, 68.

[79] V, 74; étude par J. POUCET, op.cit., p. 72.

[80] Denys, A.R., II, 48.

historique des Romains, toujours prêts à rattacher une institution à un événement ou à un lieu fameux. On sentait bien la dépendance qui liait *Quirinal* et
Quirinus. Une fois découverte l'étymologie par *Cures*, il était fatal que, pour la
justifier, on affectât au Quirinal un caractère sabin, sans s'aviser de l'étrangeté
d'une dérivation qui faisait venir le nom des purs Romains d'une ville ennemie et
vaincue[81]. Pour sa part, G. DUMÉZIL estime que la version sabinisante serait née
aux alentours de l'an 293 av. J.-C., date à laquelle fut érigé le sanctuaire sur le
Quirinal, résidence nouvelle des Sabins incorporés à la tribu *Quirina*, en 290[82],
et il fait remarquer que l'existence d'une triade parallèle à Iguvium, qui renferme
le dieu *Vofionos Grabovios*, au nom symétrique de celui de Quirinus, interdit de
considérer le dieu comme sabin. Nous ajouterons au dossier le simple fait que
Quirinus possède un Flamine majeur, ce qui prouve que les Romains ne le
concevaient pas comme un dieu importé, et d'autre part son identification avec
Romulus, incompréhensible dans le cas d'un dieu sabin. Si l'on adopte les vues
des historiens modernes, pour qui les guerres sabines de 293 furent le modèle *a
posteriori* des guerres sabines de Romulus, le temple voué à Quirinus par le père
de Papirius Cursor en 325 av. J.-C. l'aurait été a v a n t que les Sabins occupent le
Quirinal. Voici le résumé que donne des événements J. POUCET: «L'introduction du Quirinal dans la légende sabine serait due à l'influence d'une étymologie très ancienne: *Quirites a Curibus*. Basée comme c'est souvent le cas dans
l'Antiquité sur une simple ressemblance extérieure entre les deux mots, elle aurait
d'abord sabinisé en partie le terme *Quirites*, qui finit par désigner les Sabins
venus de Cures avec Titus Tatius. La réaction en chaîne était alors amorcée.
Quirinalis et *Quirinus*, phonétiquement voisins de *Quirites* et étroitement liés
par le fait même à *Cures*, allaient à leur tour glisser dans la sphère sabine». Et
l'auteur de conclure: «On se trouve là en présence d'un très beau cas d'étymologie créatrice d'histoire légendaire»[83].

Le tour d'horizon est terminé, en ce qui concerne les textes qui nous ren-
seignent directement sur Quirinus, hormis les fragments livrés par Ennius et
Aulu-Gelle[84], qui ne nous apprennent rien de très utile, puisqu'on ignore encore
ce que sont réellement les personnages désignés par les mots *Hora, Virites,
Heries, Moles*. Nous n'avons là que des fragments de litanies composés de noms
divins énumérés à la file, sans qu'aucune précision nous soit apportée: les formules sont très anciennes, voilà tout ce qu'on en peut dire.

---

[81] Remarques sur l'influence de l'étymologie, par J. POUCET, op.cit., p. 72.
[82] Op.cit., p. 249. Au sujet des sacrifices iguviens, voir G. RADKE, op.cit., p. 282 notes 53
à 58.
[83] Op.cit., p. 72.
[84] N.A., XIII, 22 d'Aulu-Gelle: *Comprecationes quae ritu romano fiunt diis expositae sunt in
libris sacerdotum populi romani, et in plerisque antiquis orationibus; in iis scriptum est:
„Luam Saturni, Salaciam Neptuni, Horam Quirini, Virites Quirini, Maiam Volkani,
Heriem Iunonis, Moles Martis, Nerienemque Martis"*. Ennius, Ann., I, au vers 116: *Teque
Quirine pater ueneror, Horamque Quirini.*

III. Quirinus et l'agriculture

1. Thèse de G. DUMÉZIL

Il est temps d'aborder d'autres textes, et de consacrer une analyse à la thèse de G. DUMÉZIL lui-même.

Il est difficile de donner de cette thèse une définition unique, puisque la pensée de son auteur semble avoir évolué depuis sa première expression. Dans l'"Héritage indo-européen à Rome"[85], Quirinus était un dieu résolument paysan:

> « Le Quirinus du *Flamen Quirinalis* et des Quirinalia nettoie, enfouit, torréfie le grain, et il s'intéresse au sous-sol; les divinités auxquelles on le voit associé lui-même ou son flamine attaché, sont Ops, Consus, Robigo, Larentia. C'est à dire que le vieux Quirinus est, cette fois centralement et dans tous les sens du mot, pour le mode d'action comme pour le point d'application, un dieu 'agraire' ».

D'autres textes pourtant, influencés par l'étymologie reconnue de Quirinus, à laquelle nous consacrerons bientôt une analyse[86], modulent cette définition, pour mettre en avant l'idée de 'communauté', de 'masse populaire', mais sans jamais sacrifier, toutefois, l'idée d'abondance, de fécondité, de ravitaillement. Quirinus veille alors « à la subsistance, au bien-être, à la durée de cette classe sociale . . . prosaïquement, par le soin qu'il prend des grains, lui ou son flamine, depuis la veille de leur maturité jusqu'à leur torréfaction, en passant par leur mise en réserve[87] ». Quirinus devient alors une sorte de nourricier du peuple.

Quoi qu'il en soit, plus agraire ou plus communautaire, Quirinus représenterait pour Rome la troisième fonction indo-européenne, abondance et fécondité. Rome a conservé l'ancienne triade indo-européenne, sous les noms de Jupiter, Mars et Quirinus; Jupiter correspond à la première fonction védique, la souveraineté et la magie; Mars représente la seconde, la guerre. Il semble fatal que Quirinus doive occuper la troisième, nourriture, richesse, fécondité. Ainsi se reconstitue l'ordre social et divin de l'Inde ancienne: les prêtres, les guerriers, les paysans. G. DUMÉZIL a posé lui-même l'équation qu'il se propose de résoudre: « le lecteur a pressenti que notre hypothèse de travail va consister à voir originellement dans le troisième dieu de la Triade le dieu de la troisième fonction sociale, — fécondité, abondance —, associé ou plutôt subordonné au magicien Jupiter et à Mars combattant[88] ». Mais une hypothèse de travail a ceci de dangereux qu'elle mobilise l'attention du chercheur sur le résultat à obtenir, et l'amène donc à privilégier les faits qui permettent d'y aboutir au détriment des

---

[85] Paris, 1949², p. 92.

[86] Voir p. 321 sq.

[87] Religion romaine archaïque, Bibl.hist., Paris, 1966, p. 246.

[88] Jupiter, Mars, Quirinus. Essai sur la conception indo-européenne de la société et sur les origines de Rome, Coll.La Montagne Sainte-Geneviève, 1, Paris, 1941, p. 85.

textes contradicteurs, dont on minimise les informations. Ainsi a-t-on schématisé la pensée de G. DUMÉZIL, en l'accusant de forcer les textes pour justifier le patronage de Quirinus sur sa troisième fonction vacante[89].

Voyons d'abord les éléments de la démonstration. Elle a le mérite de faire entrer en ligne de compte les occupations du prêtre de Quirinus, le *Flamen Quirinalis*, dont on s'était, il faut le reconnaître, assez peu soucié jusqu'alors. Sa participation à trois cérémonies romaines ne pouvait que déconcerter son interprétation comme dieu guerrier, de la même façon que le service agraire des Arvales, prêtres de Mars, déconcerte la présentation guerrière de ce dieu.

2. Examen de cette thèse

a) Fêtes en liaison avec le Flamine de Quirinus

Trois fêtes, donc. Les *Consualia*, pour lesquels Tertullien atteste un service assuré par le *Quirinalis* et les *Vestales*[90]; les *Robigalia*, lors desquels, selon Ovide, le *Quirinalis* conduit le cortège et préside au sacrifice; il répond d'ailleurs de bonne grâce aux questions que le poète vient lui poser[91]. Enfin, le sacrifice offert, au Vélabre, sur la tombe d'Acca Larentia, transmis par Aulu-Gelle[92]. Ajoutons, pour compléter le dossier, une dédicace à Quirinus, à Ops, aux Nymphes[93]; et, bien sûr, la fête des *Quirinalia*, le 17 février.

Nous ne possédons, pour chacune de ces fêtes, qu'une seule attestation. Mais que les témoignages soient isolés, obscurs, douteux même (songeons à l'impossibilité qu'avait Ovide, venant de Nomentum comme il l'écrit, de rencontrer le Flamine sur la via Claudia où s'ouvre le bois sacré de Robigo[94]!), ne nous autorise pas à les récuser, comme le fait K. LATTE[95]. Mais il ne faut pas non plus les exploiter exagérément dans une seule direction.

---

[89] Héritage . . ., p. 99; Tarpéia. Essais de philologie comparative indo-européenne, Paris, 1947, p. 27. Citons l''Héritage': «On entend parfois résumer ainsi ma démarche quant à Quirinus: «M. DUMÉZIL pense avoir montré que Jupiter et Mars représentent les deux plus hautes fonctions; il faut donc que Quirinus représente la troisième». Je n'opère pas ainsi . . .».

[90] Spect., 5, 7: *Exinde, ludi Consualia dicti qui initio Neptunum honorabant; eundem enim et Consum uocant; et nunc ara Conso illi in Circo demersa est ad primas metas sub terra cum inscriptione eius modi: „Consus consilio, Mars duello, Lares †coillo† potentes". Sacrificant apud eam nonis Iuliis sacerdotes publici XII kalend. septembres Flamen Quirinalis et Virgines.*

[91] Fast., IV, 905—942. Cf. W. FAUTH, ANRW, II, 16, 1, p. 161 sq.

[92] Noct.Att., VI, 7: *Sed Acca Larentia corpus in uolgus dabat, pecuniamque emeruerat ex eo quaestu uberem. Ea testamento in Antiatis historia scriptum est, Romulum regem, ut quidam autem alii tradiderunt, populum Romanum bonis suis heredem fecit. Ob id meritum, a Flamine Quirinali sacrificium ei publice fit, et dies e nomine eius in Fastos additus.*

[93] C.I.L., I², 1, p. 326.

[94] Discussion chez F. BÖMER, édition commentée des Fastes, II, Heidelberg, 1958, p. 287.

[95] Römische Religionsgeschichte, Handb.d.Altertumswiss., V, 4, Munich, 1960, p. 114, n. 1.

Ce n'est pas un hasard, estime G. Dumézil, si le Flamine intervient par trois fois dans des opérations «agricoles». Cette épithète est à nuancer, après examen des textes, et nous proposerons plus loin une explication de cette triple participation liturgique autrement que par un caractère agraire du dieu[96].

Que les *Robigalia* du 25 avril aient été une fête agricole, c'est certain. Il s'agit alors de préserver le grain de dangers présentés par la rouille, à un moment critique de sa croissance[97]. Varron couple Robigo (ou Robigus) avec Flora: *Quarto Robigum ac Floram, quibus propitiis, neque Robigo frumenta atque arbores corrumpit, neque non tempestiue florent*[98].

Que les *Consualia* du 21 août aient été une fête agricole, c'est également une certitude, Consus n'étant, malgré les fantaisies des Anciens, ni un dieu du *consilium*, ni un Neptune équestre, mais le dieu des silos; sa fête correspond, du reste, à l'engrangement du blé[99]. Prenons garde, toutefois, que l'inscription de son autel ne nous conduise aussi à faire de Mars un dieu agraire, thèse contre laquelle G. Dumézil mobilise toutes ses énergies[100], puisque, si on utilise la présence de Quirinus, par l'intermédiaire de son flamine, aux *Consualia*, pour affirmer le caractère agraire du dieu, on doit affecter le même caractère au dieu Mars, dont le nom se trouve gravé sur la pierre de l'autel! De la même façon, si nous prenons en compte l'inscription qui unit, le 23 août, Quirinus à Ops, pour en tirer argument en faveur d'un caractère agricole du dieu, il serait injuste de frustrer les Nymphes, présentes sur la même inscription, de ce même caractère agraire. Utilisons les textes, soit, mais avec tous leurs détails; et puisque les Vestales officient aux côtés du *Flamen Quirinalis*, tenons également Vesta pour une divinité essentiellement agraire . . .

En revanche, rien ne nous obligera à concéder un caractère agraire à la fête d'Acca Larentia, le 23 décembre. Nous ne savons rien sur Acca Larentia[101], et, confesse A. Brelich, ce rien ne suffit pas pour lui attribuer un caractère agraire[102], ce qui est l'évidence même. G. Dumézil essaie d'attirer Acca Larentia

---

[96] P. 36—37.

[97] Etude par L. Delatte, Recherches sur quelques fêtes mobiles du calendrier romain, AC, 5, 1936, p. 93—103 et 381—404.

[98] Res rust., I, 1, 6.

[99] Etude de G. Dumézil, Consus et Ops, dans: Idem, Idées romaines, Bibl.des sc.hum., Paris, 1969, p. 289—304.

[100] Religion romaine archaïque, p. 215—241.

[101] Malgré l'acharnement des Modernes à pressurer les textes: Th. Mommsen, Die echte und die falsche Acca Larentia, dans: Idem, Römische Forschungen, II, Berlin, 1879, p. 1—22; V. Scialoia, Il testamento di Acca Larentia, Rend.Accad.Lincei, 14, 1905, 141—160; W. F. Otto, Römische Sagen, WS, 35, 1913, 62—74; E. Tabeling, Mater Larum, Frankf.Studien z.Rel.u.Kult.d.Antike, 1, Francfort, 1932, 39—68; U. Pestalozza, Mater Larum u. Acca Larentia, RIL, 56, 1, 1933, 905—960; A. Momigliano, Misc.Fac.Lett. Univ. Torino, 1938, 16—23; A. H. Krappe, Acca Larentia, AJA, 46, 1942, 490—499; P. Mingazzini, Due pretese figure mitiche, Ath, 25, 1947, 140—165; D. Sabbatucci, Il mito di A. Larentia, SMSR, 29, 1958, 41—76; G. Radke, Acca Larentia, ANRW, I, 2, 1972, 421—441.

[102] Quirinus. Una divinità romana alla luce della comparazione storica, SMSR, 30, 1, 1960, 61—119, p. 102.

du côté de la troisième fonction. Elle paraît avoir été, dit-il, «un génie de la fécondité, de la volupté et de la richesse généreuse[103]». En fait, la célébration est une *parentatio*, c'est à dire un service mortuaire qui se déroule sur un tombeau[104]. Cette *parentatio*, à laquelle A. MOMIGLIANO consacre quelques bonnes remarques[105], nous est présentée par les Anciens comme une commémoration reconnaissante offerte à une Romaine pétrie de sens civique, à défaut de vertu. Parler, à propos de la fable un peu leste, où Acca est l'enjeu d'une partie de dés entre Hercule et le sacristain de son temple, de «contes de fécondité[106]» nous paraît une interprétation pré-orientée. Ne confondons pas l'Acca Larentia courtisane avec la mère des douze Arvales, puisque les Romains ne les confondaient pas[107]: la courtisane n'est pas connue pour sa progéniture mais pour sa générosité envers ses concitoyens. La situation de cette *parentatio* au mois de décembre ne nous oriente guère non plus vers des idées de fécondité. Non plus que la répétition de la même légende, pourvue du même dénouement, à propos de la déesse Flora[108], qui ne se voit pas pour autant honorée d'une fête, et n'intéresse nullement le Flamine de Quirinus. Mais surtout, Macrobe précise par deux fois que les *Larentinalia* concernaient Jupiter: *Decimo Kalendas feriae sunt Iouis quae appellantur Larentinalia, et ideo ab Anco in Velabro loco celeberrimo urbis, sepulta est, ac sollemne sacrificium eidem constitutum, quo dis Manibus eius per Flaminem sacrificaretur, Iouique feriae consecratae, quod aestimauerunt Antiqui animas a Ioue dari, et rursus post mortem eidem reddi*[109]. Peu importe l'étiologie de fantaisie qui nous est offerte: la dédicace de la fête au dieu souverain, patron de la première fonction indo-européenne, n'est pas compatible avec un classement d'Acca Larentia dans le cadre de la troisième fonction.

Si, de plus, nous gratifions Quirinus d'un caractère agraire à cause de la venue de son Flamine sur la tombe d'Acca Larentia, nous sommes tenus d'en faire autant pour le dieu Mars, dont le Flamine est chargé de la même cérémonie en faveur de la même divinité, au mois d'avril. «Le prêtre de Mars, écrit Plutarque[110], lui offre au mois d'avril les libations de vin et de lait habituelles pour les funérailles». Cette ingérence de Mars dans un culte qu'il souhaite agraire ne convient pas davantage à G. DUMÉZIL que sa présence sur l'inscription dédiée à Consus. S'il ne faisait pas état de cette inscription pour le culte de Mars, il esquive cette fois la présence du *Flamen Martialis* aux *Larentalia* grâce à un

---

[103] Héritage . . ., p. 90.

[104] Varron, L.L., VI, 24: *cui sacerdotes nostri publice parentant, e sexto die qui ab ea* (corr. sur *atra*) *dicitur, dies Parentalium* (corr. sur *Tarentum*) *Accas Larentinas. Hoc sacrificium fit Velabro, qua in Nouam Viam exitur, ut aiunt quidam ad sepulcrum Accae ut quod ibi prope faciunt diis Manibus seruilibus sacerdotes.*

[105] Tre figure mitiche, cit.supra, p. 16–18.

[106] J. BAYET, Hist.pol.et psychologique de la religion romaine, Paris, 1969, p. 65.

[107] Aulu-Gelle, loc. cit. n. 92, d'ap. Masurius Sabinus.

[108] Lactance, Div.Inst., I, 20.

[109] Macrobe, Sat., I, 10, 11, et I, 10, 15.

[110] Rom., 4, 5 . . . καὶ χοὰς ἐπιφέρει τοῦ Ἀπριλίου μηνὸς ὁ τοῦ Ἄρεως ἱερεύς. G. RADKE ne prend pas ce texte en compte lorsqu'il s'efforce de prouver, Die Götter Altitaliens, Fontes & Commentationes, 3, Munster, 1965, p. 165, que la fête n'est pas une *parentatio*.

argument qui n'en est pas un: «Plutarque nomme le prêtre d'Arès, ce qui est sûrement faux, mais pourrait se comprendre comme un à-peu-près grec pour celui
d'*Enyalios*, de Quirinus[111]». L'appréciation première sur le témoignage de Plutarque est aussi gratuite que celle de K. LATTE supprimant sans explication le
Flamen Quirinalis des *Robigalia*; la seconde explication n'est pas rationnelle:
pourquoi Plutarque, qui désigne ordinairement Quirinus par la transcription
Κυρῖνος l'aurait-il appelé cette fois-là *Enyalios*? Et pourquoi confondrait-il Mars-
Arès et Quirinus, dont il connaît parfaitement l'identification avec Romulus fils
de Mars[112]?

Pour ce qui nous occupe, donc, le texte qui concerne Acca Larentia ne doit
pas être tiré ni dans un sens ni dans l'autre: nous nous bornons à enregistrer la
présence du *Quirinalis* lors d'une fête funéraire, le 25 décembre, sur un tombeau
du Vélabre. C'est tout ce que nous pouvons en dire.

b) Les *Quirinalia*

Venons-en maintenant à la fête de Quirinus, les *Quirinalia* du 17 février, où
nous avons toutes les raisons d'attendre la présence du Flamine de Quirinus.
Saisissant paradoxe: le prêtre officiellement chargé du culte de Quirinus ne
s'occupe pas des *Quirinalia*!

Et voici qu'en une fête capitale, puisqu'elle concerne l'usinage du grain et sa
torréfaction, aboutissement d'un cycle agricole sur lequel, nous dit-on, veille
Quirinus depuis les *Robigalia* et les *Consualia*, ce n'est plus le Flamine de
Quirinus qui officie, mais le Grand Curion (*Curio Maximus*) . . . Lorsque G.
DUMÉZIL écrit: «le Quirinus du *Flamen Quirinalis* et des *Quirinalia* torréfie le
grain», c'est inexact. Ni Quirinus ni son Flamine ne sont concernés par l'usinage
du grain.

Rappelons les faits. «les *Quirinalia*, dit Festus[113], sont appelés *Stultorum
Feriae* ('Fête des Sots') parce que ce jour-là sacrifient (à la déesse du Four,
Fornax), ceux qui n'ont pu accomplir ce rite au jour qui leur était officiellement
assigné (*sollemni die*), ou qui ne se sont pas avisés qu'ils avaient à le faire».

Selon Ovide[114], les citoyens torréfient leur grain et sacrifient à *Fornax*,
déesse du Four, en observant la division par curies, selon les indications du

---

[111] Religion romaine archaïque, p. 268−269.
[112] Rom., 28, 3: Ἐγὼ δ' ὑμῖν εὐμενὴς ἔσομαι δαίμων Κυρῖνος.
[113] P. 419 L.: *Stulto(rum feriae appellaban)tur Quirina(lia) . . . Quirini qu(od eo die omnes
sa)crificant ii q(ui sollemni die aut) non potuer(unt rem diuinam face)re aut ign(orauerunt).*
Le texte de Paulus garantit les restitutions.
[114] Fast., II, 525−532:   *Facta dea est Fornax; laeti Fornace, coloni
              Orant ut fruges temperet illa suas.
        Curio legitimis nunc Fornacalia uerbis
              Maximus indicit, nec stata sacra facit.
        Inque Foro, multa circum pendente tabella,
              Signatur certa curia quaeque nota.
        Stultaque pars populi quae sit sua curia nescit,
              Sed facit extrema sacra relata die.*

Grand Curion, car il s'agit d'une fête mobile; mais les «Sots», ceux qui ignorent
à quelle curie ils sont rattachés, et ne peuvent donc tirer aucune indication des
tablettes suspendues sur le Forum à seule fin de publier les dates pour chaque
curie, se voient réserver en bloc le jour des *Quirinalia*, où ils peuvent accomplir
leurs dévotions à *Fornax* sans distinction de Curie.

Ce texte est limpide, mais il n'est jamais exploité correctement. En effet, il
interdit de comprendre que Quirinus monopolisait à sa fête, pour le service du
grain, l'ensemble du peuple. G. DUMÉZIL, par exemple, en a tiré les conclusions
suivantes: «Il ressort de tous les témoignages anciens que les *Quirinalia* coïnci-
daient avec les *Stultorum Feriae* non seulement pour le temps, mais pour le
fond; que les *Quirinalia* achevaient les *Fornacalia*; qu'ils les achevaient par une
opération collective, synthétique, par opposition aux opérations fragmentaires
qui avaient précédé. Il semble qu'il y ait là une convenance profonde: Quirinus
préside à un rassemblement des hommes dans une fonction particulière, la
préservation du grain[115]».

C'est là une simplification excessive: les *Quirinalia* ne coïncident avec les
Fornacalia que pour les Sots! Les citoyens 'sensés', c'est à dire tout de même la
large majorité des Romains, correctement informés de leur appartenance curiate,
ont célébré le grain et *Fornax* à celle des dates que le Grand Curion a assignée à
leur curie par un écriteau suspendu au Forum, mais forcément avant les *Quirinalia* du 17 février. Les *Quirinalia* ne récupèrent que les citoyens étourdis, et
c'est le dernier jour seul des *Fornacalia* que l'on fait coïncider avec les *Quirinalia*: la grande masse des Romains a fêté la torréfaction du grain sans autrement
s'occuper de Quirinus, puisque à des dates variables de février avant le 17.

Pourquoi cette coïncidence entre *Quirinalia* et *Fornacalia* pour les Romains
étourdis? En aucune façon parce que Quirinus protégeait leur alimentation, car
il faudrait comprendre alors que Quirinus ne s'intéresse qu'à la nourriture des
«Sots»! Mais parce que les *Quirinalia* étaient la fête des Curies, et se trouvaient
donc parfaitement habilités à récupérer ceux qui ne connaissaient pas leur curie,
lors d'une fête collective. C'est si vrai que la présidence en revient au Grand
Curion, responsable des curies, et non au Flamine de Quirinus, chargé du
service de ce dieu. Quirinus n'est pas concerné. Bien que Varron écrive: *Quirinalia: quod ei deo feriae*[116], on serait bien en peine de citer un seul rite faisant
intervenir d'une façon ou d'une autre la liturgie de Quirinus, dont nous ne
savons pas un traître mot. Ovide lui-même n'a rigoureusement rien à dire sur les
Quirinalia, et se tire d'affaire en racontant l'apothéose de Romulus. Or, la date
de cette apothéose n'est pas le 17 février, mais le 5 juillet, jour des *Poplifugia*[117]. La présence de Quirinus-Romulus aux *Quirinalia* dans les 'Fastes' n'est
qu'une ingénieuse fiction littéraire. Une fois de plus Romulus a trahi Quirinus,
en empêchant Ovide, obnubilé par l'histoire du Fondateur, de s'intéresser à la
liturgie ancienne propre de Quirinus.

---

[115] L'Héritage . . ., p. 91.

[116] L.L., VI, 13: *quod ei deo feriae, et eorum hominum qui Fornacalibus suis non fuerunt
    feriati.*

[117] Plutarque, Rom., 29, 2: ἡ δ' ἡμέρα ἧ μετήλλαξεν «ὄχλου φυγὴ» καλεῖται.

c) L'étymologie de *Quirinus*

Mises à part les activités de son Flamine, Quirinus n'apparaît jamais en personne dans les opérations concernant le grain, ni même dans aucun texte traitant de l'agriculture en général. Quelque oblitéré qu'il fût par le personnage de Romulus, il devrait nous rester quelques traces de sa vocation originelle, comme il nous reste des traces des occupations de Cérès avant son absorption par Déméter. Nous avons rencontré Mars à deux reprises, aux *Consualia* et aux *Larentinalia*, lui dont G. DUMÉZIL dénie les attaches avec l'agriculture. Nous le voyons encore présider la fête du Cheval d'Octobre, qui concernait le *bonus euentus*[118] du grain. Lorsque Caton nomme les dieux protecteurs de l'agriculture, il énumère Mars, pour les bœufs, Janus, Jupiter, Cérès, pour les moissons, Janus, Jupiter et Mars pour les champs[119], soit . . . la Triade archaïque, précédée, comme il est de règle dans toute prière romaine, par Janus, mais amputée de Quirinus, ce qui serait le comble s'il était réellement un dieu agricole. G. DUMÉZIL accorde beaucoup d'importance au sentiment des Romains qui, lorsqu'ils évoquaient Mars, le comprenaient comme un dieu des guerriers, non un dieu agricole. Il nous faut donc accorder toute son importance à l'opinion romaine qui faisait de Quirinus le dieu des *Quirites*, tout simplement. De fait, si l'on confronte aux textes les deux idées ensemble, c'est à dire Quirinus dieu paysan, ou Quirinus dieu des *Quirites* (qui ne sont pas des paysans), c'est sans conteste la seconde qui triomphe chaque fois de l'épreuve.

En effet, l'étymologie de *Quirinus*[120] ne parle aucunement d'agriculture, mais de communauté. P. KRETSCHMER[121], après A. POTT[122] et R. VON PLANTA[123], l'écrit: **co-uiri-nos*, correspondant à **co-uiri-tes*, pour *Quirites*, forme rendue plausible par l'existence aux côtés de Quirinus de *Virites*, entités divines au reste mal définies[124]. Lorsqu'on hésite à l'accepter, on lui objecte la rareté du passage de **co* à **Cu*. Mais l'hésitation entre ces deux graphies paraît monnaie courante. Songeons à une divinité dont nous aurons à reparler: Junon *Quiritis*. Son nom connaît diverses orthographes: *Curis*[125], *Curitis*[126], en face de *Quiri-*

---

[118] Festus, p. 246 L.

[119] Respectivement, Agr., § 83, 134, 141.

[120] Admise généralement, sauf par C. KOCH, op.cit., p. 27; A. ERNOUT et A. MEILLET, Dict. Etym., Paris, 3ᵉ éd., 1951, p. 160, admettent **co-wiri-yà* pour *curia*, mais jugent « insoutenable » p. 559 **co-uiri* pour *Quirinus*. G. RADKE discute longuement cette étymologie p. 284 sq., aux notes 88 à 93; nous maintiendrons toutefois le lien entre *Quirinus*, *Quirites* et *curia*, car il ressort des rites eux mêmes, inséparables de l'organisation curiate.

[121] Lat. *quirites* und *quiritare*, Glotta, 10, 1920, 147−157.

[122] Etymologische Forschungen auf dem Gebiet der Indogermanischen Sprache, 2, Lemgo, 1836, p. 493.

[123] Anzeiger für indogermanische Sprach- u. Altertumskunde, 10, 1899, p. 57.

[124] Voir note 84.

[125] Paulus, Verb.Sign., p. 56 L.

[126] Servius, Ad Aen., II, 614; I, 8; IV, 59; VIII, 84; Festus, Verb.Sign., p. 380 L.; Denys, II, 4; Martianus Capella, II, 149; Paulus, p. 43 L. *Curritis*: C.I.L., XI, 3126. Etude détaillée des différentes formes du nom dans G. RADKE, op.cit., p. 286 notes 96 à 107.

tis[127]. Quant aux noms de *Curia, Quirites, Quirinus,* ils s'orthographient en grec: Κουρία, Κυρῖται, Κυρῖνος[128]: pour des oreilles grecques, le problème d'une différence entre *Quirinus* et *Curia* ne se posait apparemment pas.

S'il est vrai que l'adjectif *Quirinus* sert d'épithète à d'autres noms divins, son emploi doit faire réfléchir. Dans la Triade iguvienne, qui correspond à la Triade romaine, c'est le mot *Grabovios* (identique à *Gradiuus*, surnom de Mars, à Rome?) qui sert d'épiclèse aux trois divinités Jupiter, Mars et Vofionos. Néanmoins, à Rome, le nom du troisième dieu de la triade est incontestablement une épithète, qui s'est vue utiliser comme telle pour qualifier d'autres dieux, à la différence des formules ombriennes, où *Grabovios* n'est pas l'un des trois noms unis en triade mais un vocable indépendant. Quirinus est ainsi accolé au nom de Janus, et la tentation est grande de considérer un autre surnom de ce même dieu, *Curiatius,* comme une forme alternante de *Quirinus,* tous deux étant bien proches de *curia!* Toutefois Varron, dans L.L. 7, 26, d'après l'un des manuscrits, écrit *cusiatii.* (Voir G. RADKE, Götter . . ., s. v. Curiatius). On rencontre aussi ce *Quirinus* près de Jupiter[129], de Mars[130], voire d'Hercule[131]. Naturellement, témoignages tardifs, isolés, douteux. Néanmoins, tous ces dieux n'ont, à première vue, aucun rapport avec l'agriculture, tout particulièrement Jupiter ou Hercule. Il convient donc d'accorder à l'épithète *Quirinus* une extension sémantique aussi considérable que possible, afin qu'elle puisse s'appliquer sans invraisemblance à des personnages divins aussi opposés. Si elle signifie: «de la Cité», ou «de la Communauté», elle se révèle on ne peut plus satisfaisante, puisque applicable à la majorité des dieux romains. Le plus connu, *Ianus Quirinus,* est très fortement lié à la Cité, de par le fameux rite d'ouverture et de fermeture auquel il préside, et qui, déterminant le passage de l'état de paix à l'état de guerre, commande en fait toute la vie de la Cité[132].

C. KOCH estimait que Janus devenait, à cause de cette épithète, un dieu guerrier, ce qui lui permettait de sauver son interprétation de Quirinus, mais contredisait formellement les textes: *nil mihi cum bello,* déclare Janus chez Ovide, *pacem postesque tuebar*[133]. G. DUMÉZIL ne fait pas de Janus un dieu agricole; il pense seulement qu'on a rapproché Janus et Quirinus simplement parce qu'ils contiennent tous deux l'idée de paix[134]. Mais alors, la contre-épreuve

---

[127] C.I.L., XI, 3125; Pseudo-Acron, Ad Hor.Ep., I, 6, 7; C.I.L., IX, 1547; Fasti Paulini au 7 octobre; *Curris:* Tertullien, Apol., 24, 8.

[128] Respect.: Denys, A.R., II, 7, 3; Denys, II, 46; Plutarque, Rom., 29.

[129] H. DESSAU, I.L.S., 3036: *Ioui Quirino.*

[130] Servius, Ad Aen., I, 292; Martianus Capella, I, 46 et I, 50.

[131] Inscription signalée par ST. WEINSTOCK dans son commentaire du livre de K. LATTE, Röm. Religionsgeschichte, Hb.d.Altertumswiss., V, 4, Munich, 1960, paru dans JRS, 51, 1961, 206–215, p. 212.

[132] Pour L. DEUBNER, Zur römischen Religionsgeschichte, MDAIR, 36, 1920–1923, 14–33, p. 17, le *ianus* serait le «passage vers *Quirium*», la cité imaginée sur le Quirinal par B. G. NIEBUHR. La désignation *quirinus,* ajouterons-nous, vaut même dans le cas de *ianus* nom commun: le *ianus quirinus* serait alors un «passage public».

[133] Fast., I, 253.

[134] Religion romaine archaïque, p. 264.

doit être probante, et faire accréditer un Jupiter paisible, un Mars paisible, un Hercule paisible . . .

Prenons le cas de Mars. Le texte de Servius est souvent interprété d'une façon peu satisfaisante. Que nous dit Servius? *Mars enim cum saeuit Gradiuus dicitur, cum tranquillus est, Quirinus*[135]. On accepte bien le mot *Gradiuus* comme une épithète indissociable de Mars, mais on fait toujours de *Quirinus* un dieu indépendant: «il existe un Mars combattant: *Mars Gradiuus*». Soit. Pourtant, au lieu de comprendre la seconde partie de la phrase de la même façon que la première, et traduire «Mars apaisé se nomme *Mars Quirinus*», on comprend ensuite: «Quirinus est un Mars paisible», ce qui n'est pas satisfaisant.

d) L'assimilation de Romulus à Quirinus

A un Mars agraire, à des Jupiter, Janus, Hercule, paysans, nous préférons donc des dieux protecteurs de la Cité romaine.

La pierre de touche la plus sûre est encore l'assimilation de Romulus à Quirinus, qui ne peut s'interpréter que dans un seul sens. G. DUMÉZIL est le premier à reconnaître que cette assimilation ne cadre pas du tout avec son Quirinus nourricier des masses: «On ne voit pas qu'il (Romulus) ait rien à faire avec la fécondité et la richesse que patronnait primitivement Quirinus[136]». Les justifications apportées à ce paradoxe semblent toutes des expédients: Quirinus serait lié avec l'Au-delà, de par ses rapports avec Larenta, Consus, Véjovis, et à cause de la disparition de Romulus lui-même. Ainsi, comme d'autres rois mythiques, Romulus devient-t-il un «Roi de l'Au-delà», c'est à dire un dieu du sous-sol, Quirinus[137]. Se fondant sur les thèses duméziliennes, A. BRELICH, au terme d'une longue et déconcertante démonstration, fournit l'explication que voici: l'assimilation de Romulus à Quirinus étant un phénomène mystérieux, il convient de s'en débarrasser «comme par magie[138]», et donc de supposer qu'à l'origine Romulus et Quirinus ne faisaient qu'un. Ils étaient 'le' déma, personnage divin fondateur de cités chez les Kikuyu du Kénya. Le propre de tout déma, c'est d'abord de fonder une ville, ensuite, d'être massacré par son peuple, enfin, de donner naissance, après dépeçage, à une plante nourricière utile à la Cité, tout comme des tubercules coupés en quatre et enterrés naît un tubercule nouveau. Lors, donc, de la formation des mythes, ce déma unique fut scindé en deux personnages distincts, l'un baptisé Quirinus, récupérant la caractéristique agricole, l'autre, Romulus, chargé de la fondation de Rome, et victime du peuple. Ainsi, le mythe est transposé dans l'histoire romaine: Romulus est égorgé par les Sénateurs, et ressuscite en une plante, ou plutôt, car on n'en est plus à ce détail près, en un dieu agricole, ce qu'est Quirinus selon la thèse de G. DUMÉZIL, mais seulement selon cette thèse . . .

---

[135] Ad Aen., I, 292.
[136] Jupiter, Mars, Quirinus, p. 183.
[137] Ibid., p. 185—187.
[138] „*In tal caso, le difficoltà scompaiono come per incanto*" (Quirinus, SMSR, 30, 1, 1960, 63—119, p. 103).

Ne discutons point pareil monument d'ingéniosité. Une seule remarque anodine: le chassé-croisé qui se produit dans le destin des deux divinités était-il prévu à l'origine? Romulus fonde la Ville, mais ne porte pas un nom forgé sur la notion de cité, celui de *Quirinus*, par exemple; tandis que Quirinus hérite du caractère agricole, tout en portant un nom mieux en rapport avec la fondation de la ville. Distraction du destin, sans doute . . .

La dernière explication est fournie plus récemment par G. DUMÉZIL: la vie de Romulus peut se scinder selon trois phases:

> Romulus 1 = le Berger
> Romulus 2 = le Guerrier
> Romulus 3 = le Souverain,

le cours de sa vie lui faisant assumer successivement, en somme, les trois fonctions indo-européennes mais à l'envers! C'est, dit G. DUMÉZIL, Romulus 1 qui fut assimilé à Quirinus, en tant que berger promu dieu-paysan; puis, Quirinus reçut par ricochet le caractère guerrier inhérent à Romulus 2, ce qui explique les textes où on le voit pourvu d'armes et de Saliens, et assimilé à Mars[139].

Les objections surgissent immédiatement. Lorsque Romulus est divinisé, il y a beau temps qu'il est roi, et que ses antécédents agricoles sont passés à l'arrière-plan. Ensuite, Romulus fut un pasteur, non pas un cultivateur, tandis que Quirinus s'occupe du grain, nous dit-on, mais pas de troupeaux. Si, enfin, le glissement de Romulus 1 à Romulus 2 est, malgré les différences fonctionnelles, si aisé, il devrait y avoir également glissement de Romulus 2 à Romulus 3, et donc attribution à Quirinus de la royauté magique, ce qui ne se trouve jamais réalisé.

En fait, Romulus aurait pu être assimilé, sans heurter le bon sens, avec Jupiter, en tant que roi et prêtre; ou avec Mars, en tant que guerrier. Mais il serait curieux que les Romains aient choisi un dieu agricole pour en travestir le personnage divin de leur roi, qui jamais ne fit pousser de blé. Il est évident que le caractère exceptionnel qui a rendu Romulus unique aux yeux de la postérité, c'est la fondation de Rome.

Son œuvre de législateur est maintes fois soulignée[140], et Denys n'emploie pas moins de vingt six chapitres à décrire son œuvre administrative. Ce qu'a fait Romulus, et que personne d'autre n'a fait dans l'histoire romaine, c'est transformer un ramassis d'individus venus d'un peu partout en une communauté de citoyens: *uocata ad consilium multitudine*, écrit Tite-Live[141], *quae coalescere in populi unius corpus nulla re praeterquam legibus poterat, iura dedit*. Romulus est d'abord le protecteur de la communauté, le patron et le gardien de la patrie: *O Romule, patriae custodem!* s'écrie Ennius[142]. Et lisons son testament politique

---

[139] Religion romaine archaïque, p. 255—256.

[140] Il est significatif qu'il disparaisse un jour où, précisément, il « donne des lois à son peuple »! (Ovide, Fast., II, 492).

[141] I, 8.

[142] Ann., II, 118—119; On lira deux études: C. J. CLASSEN, Romulus in der römischen Republik, Philologus, 106, 1962, 174—204, et E. MANNI, Romulus e *parens patriae* nell'ideologia politica e religiosa romana, Il Mondo classico, 4, 1934, 106—118.

chez Plutarque: «Après avoir bâti une cité qui en gloire et en puissance sera la première du monde, il a plu aux dieux que je m'en retournasse demeurer au ciel. Je vous serai désormais dieu protecteur et patron[143]». Chez Tite-Live, mêmes résonances: «Romulus, le père de notre Cité, m'est apparu» «et ils acclamèrent Romulus-dieu, né d'un dieu, roi et père de la ville de Rome[144]». C'est donc bien cette vocation de fondateur de cité, d'ouvrier de la cohésion civique romaine, qui, incarnée exclusivement en Romulus, va faire de lui un dieu; en sorte que l'assimilation paraît un phénomène quasi fatal:

$$\text{Romulus} = \text{la Cité}$$
$$\text{Quirinus} = \text{la Cité}$$
$$\text{donc: Romulus} = \text{Quirinus.}$$

Non point un dieu agricole qui récupère on ne sait trop comment un roi occupé à tout autre chose que l'agriculture, mais le dieu de la Cité, qui récupère, sur le plan divin, le premier citoyen de Rome. Si Quirinus est un dieu agricole, l'assimilation de Romulus à Quirinus demeure un point d'interrogation; si Quirinus est le dieu de la Cité, l'assimilation se justifie d'elle-même.

Nous pensons également à l'influence grecque. L'apothéose est évidemment un phénomène grec et non romain[145]. Cicéron fait voisiner, un peu malignement, l'apothéose de Romulus avec l'enlèvement d'Orithye par Aquilon[146]. Sans songer à mal, Plutarque ajoute à son récit deux notules qui se réfèrent à des précédents hellènes: «ces propos-là, certainement, ressemblent fort aux contes que les Grecs font d'Aristéas de Proconnèse et de Cléomède d'Astypalée». Les historiens grecs, dont on sait le rôle dans la formation des légendes primitives, ne pouvaient que rapprocher du κύριος, ou κοίρανος Romulus, un dieu qu'ils rencontraient sous la forme *Quirinus*, et traduisaient eux-mêmes par Κυρῖνος. *Kurinos, Kurios, Koiranos*, le rapprochement phonique vaut à lui seul une étymologie.

IV. *Quirinus et la Cité romaine*

Quirinus serait donc le dieu de la Cité, des Curies, des *Quirites*: il s'agit de préciser ces idées-là, et de les confronter également à nos documents, afin de replacer notre dieu dans son contexte liturgique et social.

---

[143] Plutarque, Rom., 44.
[144] I, 16.
[145] J. POUCET, note, op.cit., p. 34, que nous possédons un seul exemple romain, celui, précisément, de Romulus. Il faudrait évoquer également celui d'Enée, devenu, sur le plan divin, Jupiter Indigète; néanmoins, il est exact que le seul cas d'assimilation entre un mortel et un dieu préexistant, avant les folles prétentions d'un Antoine, est celui de Romulus.
[146] Leg., I, 1, 3.

1. Les *Quirites*: gens en paix?

Les *Quirites*, d'abord, s'ils ne sont pas forcément des paysans, ne sont pas non plus des 'gens en paix'.

L'idée originelle contenue dans le mot est simplement celle de «membre de la communauté romaine», de «citoyen romain», sans référence à une fonction, à une occupation, à une classe. Toujours influencés par l'état social hindou, dans lequel la classe des producteurs occupe le dernier rang de l'échelle, d'aucuns voudraient que les *Quirites* se confondent peu ou prou avec la plèbe. C'est ce qui ressort d'expressions telles que «le dieu de la masse», ou même le «dieu du Tiers-Etat[147]». En fait, si imprécise que soit notre documentation, il semble bien que la division en curies, premier stade dans l'organisation de l'état romain, ait été réalisée par référence au système des *gentes*[148], donc, en tenant compte aussi bien des patriciens que des plébéiens ou que des clients qui gravitent dans la sphère d'une *gens*. Il semble même qu'à l'origine les curies aient été purement patriciennes, et que le peuple y ait obtenu le droit de vote plus tard que dans les comices centuriates[149]. *Quirites* est donc une dénomination indépendante de toute attache sociale, signifiant simplement «qui participe à la vie de la communauté romaine», et un texte de Festus nous remet en mémoire le seul emploi que l'on faisait du mot au singulier, pour désigner un défunt par sa qualité de citoyen: *Vt indicio est praeco qui in funeris indictione ita pronuntiare solet: „Ollus Quiris leto datus"*[150]. Ainsi, lorsque Juvénal déplore l'envahissement de Rome par une tourbe grecque, le mot *Quirites* a-t-il dans ses vers le sens de «pur Romain de Rome[151]». Je ne sache pas que les *Patres* aient été exclus de la désignation par *Quirites*, qui, dans les discours officiels, s'adresse tout de même à tous les Romains sans exception. Toutes les indications que nous pouvons recevoir convergent vers l'idée de citoyenneté, de civisme, d'ensemble politique cohérent, de lien patriotique. Ainsi, le verbe *quiritare*, employé déjà par Lucilius[152], signifie-t-il: «en appeler à la bonne foi des *Quirites*», c'est à dire à la conscience publique. *Quiritium fidem clamans implorat*[153]: il supplie les assistants de se souvenir qu'ils appartiennent à la même communauté que lui, et

---

[147] Expression de V. BASANOFF, Les Dieux des Romains, Paris, 1954, p. 17; aussi G. DUMÉZIL, Jupiter, Mars, Quirinus, p. 194: «Juxtaposé à la fois au Sénat comme inférieur, et aux *Quirites* comme supérieur, le *Populus romanus* a sans doute désigné d'abord la *pubes romana*, c'est à dire la partie vigoureuse, combattante, de la nation ... Tel Mars, entre Jupiter et Quirinus, le 'peuple' paraît ainsi encadré à égale distance et par les 'Pères' et déjà par une sorte de 'plèbe'». Il faut supposer alors que les Patriciens n'étaient pas des *Quirites* ...

[148] TH. MOMMSEN, Le Droit public romain, trad. P. F. GIRARD, Paris, 1889, p. 100.

[149] Ibidem, p. 102.

[150] Verb.Sign., p. 304 L.

[151] Sat., III, 58 sqq.

[152] Sat., II, 273 WARM.

[153] Varron, L.L., VI, 68; Nonius, I, 31, 18; Diomède, dans G.L., 1, p. 381, 23; Voir O. IMMISCH, *Crimen*, Glotta, 13, 1927, 32–42, p. 34.

donc de le secourir pour cette seule raison. Le *ius Quiritium* n'était-il pas un peu la 'Déclaration des Droits de l'Homme', dans la communauté romaine? Quant à la formule *Populus Romanus Quiritium*, ou *Quirites*[154], elle unit, pense TH. MOMMSEN, «les citoyens pris en masse et les citoyens pris individuellement[155]».

G. DUMÉZIL a mis l'accent sur l'idée de paix présente, croit-il, dans le mot *Quirites* et dans les fonctions-mêmes de Quirinus. Il sait bien que les paysans, à Rome, et les soldats, sont les mêmes hommes, au point que Mars soit parfois confondu avec Quirinus, ou que ce dernier possède des armes[156]. Aussi détermine-t-il une alternance entre l'état de *Quiris*, «civil entre deux appels», et de *miles*, «soldat entre deux congés[157]». Néanmoins, il songe toujours à un état primitif, où les deux classes des *milites* et des *Quirites* étaient distinctes. C'est ce qui ressort de la phrase: «. . . le fait notamment que, à Rome, les *milites* sont rigoureusement identiques aux *Quirites* a-t-il entraîné l'identification des dieux qui, primitivement, présidaient à chacune des deux classes distinctes[158]». Primitivement: avant Rome? Il n'y avait alors ni Mars ni Quirinus; à l'aube de Rome? Paysans et soldats ne font déjà qu'un, et l'armée de métier n'est pas une institution originelle.

L'éloquente alternance *Quirites* en temps de paix / *milites* en temps de guerre, les uns protégés par Quirinus, les autres protégés par Mars, n'est elle-même pas infaillible. On connaît, bien sûr, l'apostrophe de César à ses soldats rebelles: *Quirites!* c'est à dire: «Bourgeois[159]!», où l'écrasant mépris du chef pour ceux en qui il refuse désormais de voir des «compagnons d'armes» assimile ses anciens *commilitones* à de simples civils, et suffit pour faire reprendre leurs armes à ses hommes humiliés. Mais cette distinction populaire a-t-elle valeur technique et officielle?

Pour l'établir, G. DUMÉZIL a pris en compte un texte de Varron, extrait des Tables des Censeurs. Il montre d'après lui que les soldats futurs sont désignés avant l'enrôlement par le terme de *Quirites*, et par celui de *milites*, ou d'*exercitus*, une fois leur engagement signé: *Qui exercitum imperaturus erit, accenso dicito: „C. Calpurni, uoca inlicium omnes Quirites huc ad me"* . . . *Dein, consul eloquitur ad exercitum*[160].

Si l'on se reporte, cependant, aux premières lignes de ce texte, dont G. DUMÉZIL n'a pas fait usage, on tombe sur une donnée capitale, et qui appartient, elle, à la langue ancienne, et formulaire de Rome:

---

[154] Etude par P. CATALANO, *Populus romanus Quirites*, Univ.di Torino, Mem.dell'Istituto giuridico, Sér. II, Mém. 156, Turin, 1974, IDEM, Aspetti spaziali del sistema giuridico-religioso romano. Mundus, templum, urbs, ager, Latium, Italia, ANRW, II, 16,1, 1978, p. 443 sqq., 505 sq. et L. LABRUNA, *Quirites*, Labeo, 8, 1962, 340–348.

[155] Op.cit., p. 4.

[156] Jupiter, Mars, Quirinus, p. 187.

[157] Religion romaine archaïque, p. 259.

[158] Jupiter, Mars, Quirinus, p. 187.

[159] Suétone, Diu.Iul., 70.

[160] Varron, L.L., VI, 88.

22*

> *Omnes Quirites pedites armatosque priuatosque*
> *Curatores omnium tribuum*
> *Si quis pro se siue pro altero rationem dari uolet,*
> *Voca inlicium huc ad me*[161].

Quirites pedites armatosque priuatosque: il existe donc des *Quirites arma-tos*, prêts, par conséquent, à partir en campagne, soit, très exactement, des sol-dats sous les drapeaux!

Si *Quirites* signifie «gens en paix», l'expression «Quirites armés» ne s'ex-plique plus. On ne peut concevoir, puisqu'elle existe, que le Quirite soit le soldat de retour au foyer qui a suspendu ses armes au-dessus du seuil, et va reprendre sa charrue. Les *Quirites*, dans ce texte des Censeurs, ce sont des hommes qui, au moment où ils se présentent en armes devant des autorités militaires, et peuvent donc se prévaloir du titre de *milites*, perdent, certes, leur qualité de gens en paix, mais demeurent, même armés, des *Quirites*, parce qu'ils ne perdent pas, bien au contraire, leur qualité de c i t o y e n s.

Si bien que désigner un soldat comme 'Quirite' est un contresens si *Quiris* signifie «Romain en temps de paix», mais point du tout s'il signifie «citoyen romain», car on est citoyen en paix comme en guerre, on peut être, comme dit Varron, 'Quirite' *armatus* ou 'Quirite' *priuatus*. Si le mot *milites* ne peut s'étendre à la catégorie des gens en paix, ce qui le cantonne dans une sphère 'fonctionnelle', le mot *Quirites* peut s'étendre à la catégorie des gens en armes, ce qui montre bien que l'idée de paix n'y est pas fondamentale ni primitive, et qu'il échappe à toute notion de «fonction».

C'est ce que nous enseignent divers emplois du mot dans l'histoire ou les institutions romaines. Lorsque Tite-Live fait prononcer à Camille le fameux dis-cours dans lequel il s'efforce de retenir les Romains décidés à quitter les ruines de Rome pour émigrer à Véies[162], il commence d'emblée son discours non par *Romani!*, «gens de Rome», mais par *Quirites*, qui souligne mieux l'idée d'union ethnique, d'association profonde entre ressortissants d'une même communauté. Il ne s'adresse pas alors ni à des gens 'en paix', ni à des producteurs, ni à la plèbe urbaine, mais à tous les hommes n é s s u r l e s o l r o m a i n, et dont la cité romaine a été jusque-là le centre des préoccupations, quelles que fussent par ailleurs leurs fonctions dans cette cité. A un autre moment de l'histoire de Rome, nous voyons un chef offrir sa vie pour le salut des siens, en pleine bataille. Pour qui se dévoue-t-il alors? Pour le «peuple romain des *Quirites*[163]». Ces *Quirites* ne sont pas des gens en paix, ce ne sont pas les Romains de Rome, p u i s q u e c e s o n t s e s p r o p r e s s o l d a t s!

A côté de *Populus romanus*, expression désignant l'ensemble de ce qui est romain, anciens ennemis intégrés, immigrants divers dotés du droit de cité, etc., les *Quirites* apparaissent comme les représentants de la pure Romanité originelle,

---

[161] Ibidem, 86.
[162] Tite-Live, V, 51.
[163] Tite-Live, VIII, 6, 13: *comparant inter se ut ab utra parte cedere Romanus exercitus coe-pisset, inde se consul deuoueret, pro populo Romano Quiritibusque.*

ceux qui formaient les curies, à l'origine de Rome. 'Quirite' semble donc vouloir dire 'Romain par excellence'.

2. Quirinus et la Cité dans l'histoire et les institutions romaines

Quand voyons-nous intervenir Quirinus dans l'histoire romaine? Toujours dans des occasions solennelles, intéressant la vie de l'Etat en divers domaines.

L'un des premiers épisodes est naturellement le geste du Flamine de Quirinus et des Vestales, se chargeant des objets sacrés, dans le sauve-qui-peut général devant l'avancée gauloise. Le Flamine enterre les objets sacrés tout près de sa demeure, ce qui prouve, pour G. DUMÉZIL, les rapports de Quirinus avec le sous-sol[164]. Le même G. DUMÉZIL s'étonne que ce ne fût pas le *Dialis*, principal prêtre de l'Etat, qui s'en vît chargé. En fait, le principal prêtre de l'Etat, ce n'est pas le *Dialis*, monopolisé au service de Jupiter, mais plutôt le Grand Pontife. Le *Quirinalis* n'agit pas comme prêtre d'un dieu chargé du ravitaillement (le moment ne s'y prête guère), pas plus que d'un dieu de la paix (nous sommes en pleine déroute militaire), mais comme prêtre du dieu représentant la Cité romaine sur le plan divin, et sa demeure devient le réceptacle des *sacra publica*, parce que nul autre dieu, mieux que Quirinus, ne pouvait veiller, en la personne de son prêtre, sur des objets représentant matériellement la notion de Cité.

Nous voyons aussi le roi Tullus vouer les Saliens «de la Colline» (ou *Agonenses*), *in re trepida*[165], essayant donc de fléchir le dieu de la cité pour l'amener à secourir son peuple en danger; dans ce contexte, la promesse de créer un sacerdoce guerrier en l'honneur de Quirinus se justifie pleinement.

De même que les curies sont les divisions administratives du peuple, par opposition aux militaires centuries, de même que la Curie est le bâtiment officiel où se discutent tous projets, pacifiques ou militaires, relatifs à la vie de l'*Vrbs*, de même que la *lex curiata* est nécessaire à l'investiture de tout magistrat, de même Quirinus est un dieu civique et 'social'. Aussi, lorsqu'on installe à Rome le premier cadran solaire, est-ce le temple de Quirinus, emplacement point très central mais symbolique, que l'on choisira pour l'accueillir: cette innovation, destinée à améliorer la vie quotidienne de chaque citoyen, ne pouvait être mieux placée que devant le temple du dieu «des citoyens[166]».

Mieux encore: c'est devant le temple de Quirinus, également, que l'on avait planté deux myrtes, l'un représentant la classe patricienne, l'autre la classe plébéienne: *inter antiquissima namque delubra habetur Quirini, hoc est Romuli. In eo sacrae fuere murti duae, ante aedem ipsam per longum tempus, altera patricia appellata, altera plebeia; patricia multis annis praeualuit, exuberans ac laeta;*

---

[164] Jupiter, Mars, Quirinus, p. 95; texte: Tite-Live, 40.
[165] Tite-Live, I, 27.
[166] Pline, H.N., VII, 213; *Princeps Romanis solarium horologium statuisse ante undecim annos quam cum Pyrrho bellatum est ad aedem Quirini, L. Papirius Cursor, cum eam dedicaret a patre suo uotam, a Fabio Vestale proditur.*

quamdiu Senatus quoque floruit, illa ingens, plebeia retorrida ac squalida. Quae postquam eualuit, flauescente patricia, a Marsico bello, languida auctoritas Patrum facta est, ac paulatim in sterilitatem emarcuit maiestas[167]. Le dieu arbitre donc l'ensemble des corps politiques romains, aussi bien le patriciat que la plèbe, et ne restreint pas seulement sa protection au Tiers-Etat des producteurs campagnards. Ce qui intéresse Quirinus, c'est le gouvernement de la Ville.

3. Quirinus dans la Triade

C'est par la même idée-force qu'on peut expliquer l'action personnelle de Quirinus au sein de la Triade archaïque. Dans les formules qui mentionnent la Triade, on peut toujours supposer que Quirinus intervient de façon automatique, parce qu'on a l'habitude de le nommer à la suite de Jupiter et de Mars, mais c'est une solution stérile. Les auteurs qui transcrivent les invocations ne savent plus nous dire à quel titre il intervient au sein de la Triade, et c'est aux Modernes d'étudier le contexte de ses manifestations. Les trois dieux sont toujours invoqués ensemble dans des occasions solennelles, où l'Etat se voit concerné en tant que tel. Il est vraisemblable qu'alors, chacune des trois divinités apportait son efficacité propre: Jupiter, la garantie du serment, la certitude que le domaine divin était présent, attentif au correct déroulement d'une entreprise humaine, à laquelle il se réservait d'apporter sa sanctioñ. Mars, la puissance de Rome, offensive ou défensive, la certitude que la Cité saurait défendre ses intérêts comme sa vie propre. Quirinus, nous semble-t-il, devait compléter cet ensemble solennel, en représentant Rome en tant que Cité organisée. Il apportait, lui, la certitude que Rome, ensemble constitutionnel, juridique et moral, se sentait concernée. A côté des forces sacrées et militaires, Quirinus serait donc la force politique de Rome.

Ainsi voyons-nous la Triade invitée à se manifester dans le cas de la *deuotio*, où il s'agit de sauver l'existence même du peuple romain en sauvant l'existence de ses combattants menacés d'extermination. *Iane, Iupiter, Mars pater, Quirine, Bellona, Lares, Diui Nouensiles, Di Indigetes, Diui quorum est potestas nostrorum hostiumque, Dique Manes*[168]: une expression bien connue se répète obstinément dans ce même texte: *Populus Romanus Quiritium*, appliquée aux hommes en train de se battre obstinément, donc à des soldats, et destinée à sauver en même temps qu'eux la patrie dont ils sont citoyens. D'autres occasions tout aussi solennelles et tout aussi belliqueuses voient intervenir les trois dieux: la déclaration du Fétial aux frontières ennemies, prélude obligatoire et inexorable à l'ouverture des hostilités[169], ou la consécration aux Infernaux d'une ville ennemie détruite[170]. Lors du sacrifice offert à la déesse Fides, et qui réclame la

---

[167] H.N., XV, 120.
[168] Tite-Live, VIII, 9, 6.
[169] Tite-Live, I, 32; Polybe, III, 35, 6: τὸν δὲ ὅρκον ὀμνύειν ἔδει τοιοῦτον ἐπὶ μὲν τῶν πρώτων συνθηκῶν Καρχηδονίους μὲν τοὺς θεοὺς τοὺς πατρῴους Ῥωμαίους δὲ διὰ λίθων κατά τι παλαιὸν ἔθος. ἐπὶ δὲ τούτων τὸν Ἄρην καὶ τὸν Ἐνυάλιον.
[170] Macrobe, Sat., III, 9, 6–13.

participation des trois Flamines majeurs, Quirinus représente encore la participation unanime des *co-uiri*, des hommes réunis dans une seule cité, pour laquelle l'idée de *fides publica* est le fondement moral et civique indispensable à une existence et à un fonctionnement réguliers[171].

C'est la constitution même de la cité romaine qui nous fait mesurer l'évolution qu'ont connue les structures indo-européennes adaptées au sol latin. Lorsque E. Benveniste définit Quirinus comme un dieu incarnant «la classe des citoyens et l'activité d'un tiers-état essentiellement rural[172]» il nous propose une définition bâtarde, écartelée entre l'étymologie de *Quirinus* et la pensée dumézilienne. En effet, les citoyens ne sont pas une «classe», et d'autre part, les ruraux ne sont pas les seuls à être citoyens! Quirinus ne peut être à la fois le dieu d'une classe et celui de l'ensemble du peuple. Un prêtre est quirite, un soldat l'est aussi, un magistrat également; un plébéien peut l'être au même titre qu'un patricien; et tous ne sont pas des paysans! Dès l'aube de l'histoire romaine, on est citoyen romain si on habite Rome et si on est libre. Tout non-citoyen ne peut être qu'un esclave, un étranger, un ennemi. Dans Rome même, l'immense majorité des résidents peut s'enorgueillir du titre de *ciuis romanus*, même si elle n'a jamais touché une bêche. Donc, si l'on imagine que la troisième classe, celle des producteurs, est patronnée par Quirinus, dieu des citoyens à en croire son étymologie, il faut comprendre que les autres classes, celle des soldats et celle des prêtres, ne jouissent pas de la *ciuitas*, ce qui est un non-sens.

En effet, et G. Dumézil le sait bien, il n'existe pas de différence, à Rome, entre les producteurs et les combattants, puisque l'armée de métier n'apparaît que tardivement dans les institutions romaines. En allant plus loin, il n'existe pas non plus d'incompatibilité entre la prêtrise et d'autres ativités laïques. Pour nous contenter de noms célèbres, Scipion est général en chef et Salien, Antoine consul et Luperque, Cicéron est avocat et Augure, Auguste *imperator* et Grand-Pontife. Nous voyons même le Flamine de Mars se disposer à partir pour la guerre, puisqu'il est aussi consul, malgré l'opposition du Grand-Pontife[173]. Les trois fonctions originelles ont été brassées en profondeur. Dès les origines, nous entendons parler de paysans pour la guerre, le plus fameux d'entre eux étant Cincinnatus. La puissante notion de Cité, qui sous-tend toute la vie et oriente toute la religion de Rome, causant l'effacement de l'acte personnel devant l'acte communautaire, a donc pu se substituer sans heurt à une notion de fécondité qui pouvait apparaître comme secondaire[174].

Quirinus n'est donc pas un dieu de classe sociale, mais un dieu des structures civiques de Rome, en particulier de la *curia*, à laquelle le rattache son nom.

La *curia* est une division politique et religieuse très ancienne. Elle possède des prêtres, les *Flamines Curiales*, présidés par le *Curio Maximus*, des fonds

---

[171] Sacrifice à Fides: Tite-Live, I, 20—21. Cf. G. Piccaluga, Fides nella religione romana di età imperiale, ci-dessous (ANRW, II, 17, 2).

[172] Le symbolisme social dans les cultes gréco-italiques, RHR, 129, 1945, 5—16, p. 7.

[173] Tite-Live, periochae, § 19.

[174] Et qui était patronnée par une autre triade ancienne, celle de Cérès, Liber et Libera.

particuliers, le *curionium aes*, pour assurer les dépenses inhérentes à son fonctionnement religieux, une fête annuelle, celle des *Quirinalia*, des tables sacrificielles, les *mensae curiales*, sur lesquelles on sacrifiait à sa déesse particulière, *Iuno Quiritis* ou *Curitis*[175]. La proximité des noms, la coïncidence des *Quirinalia*, fête des curies et de Quirinus, semble appeler auprès de cette *Iuno Quiritis* un *deus Quirinus*. S'il est vrai que Janus fait souvent couple avec Junon, qu'il existe un *Ianus Curiatius* et un *Ianus Quirinus* de la même façon qu'existent *Iuno Curitis* et *Iuno Quiritis*, il nous paraîtrait possible, d'autant que *Ianus Quirinus* est nommé parfois à la place de *Quirinus* seul, d'envisager un *Ianus Quirinus* dieu des curies. L'éventualité d'une triade Jupiter Mars et Janus a déjà été envisagée, du reste, avant nous[176].

Resteraient à justifier, dans le cadre d'activités que nous avons délimité pour Quirinus, les occupations 'agricoles' de son Flamine, grâce à d'autres raisons que l'appartenance de son dieu au domaine agricole, puisque nous ne croyons pas à cette appartenance. Nous ne croyons pas davantage, d'ailleurs, au Flamine à tout faire de G. WISSOWA[177], chargé de services multiples sous prétexte qu'au fil des ans le service unique de Quirinus, restreint avec l'effacement du dieu lui-même, lui aurait laissé des loisirs trop copieux.

Nous avons songé que le Flamine attaché au dieu «de la communauté» pourrait bien représenter en quelque sorte physiquement cette communauté aux lieux de culte situés hors du *pomoerium*, ce qui est justement le cas du tombeau de Larentia, sis au Vélabre[178] ce qui est le cas aussi du bois de Robigo, très loin au nord de Rome[179], et le cas également de l'autel de Consus, enfoui dans le Grand Cirque[180].

De même que dans les formules officielles Quirinus apporte le poids de la présence romaine, son Flamine pourrait, lors de certaines cérémonies officielles, rendre présente la ville de Rome, là où il est nécessaire d'affirmer plus nettement que dans son enceinte même la prise en charge d'un culte par le peuple romain.

Dans les trois cultes dissociés du dieu Quirinus qui réclament la présence du *Quirinalis*, un mot apparenté ressort avec insistance des descriptions rituelles, celui de *publicus*. Le Flamine offre ainsi à Larentia la *parentatio* funèbre *publice* «au nom du peuple». Aux *Consualia*, Tertullien désigne le *Flamen Quirinalis* et les Vestales à l'aide de l'expression *sacerdotes publici*. Quant aux *Robigalia*, comme, du reste, les *Floralia*, ils sont un culte «public», comme en témoigne Varron: *itaque, publice Robigo feriae Robigalia, Florae ludi Florales, instituti*[181].

---

[175] Tous ces détails nous sont connus par Festus, p. 42, p. 56, p. 113, et par Denys d'Halicarnasse, A.R., II, 50.
[176] G. DUMÉZIL, Jupiter, Mars, Quirinus – et Janus, RHR, 139, 1951, 209–215.
[177] Religion und Kultus der Römer, Hb.d.Altertumswiss. IV, 5, 2e éd., Munich, 1912, p. 155.
[178] Aulu-Gelle, N.A., VI, 7, 7: Varron, L.L., VI, 24: *qui uterque locus extra urbem antiquam fuit; non longe a porta Romanula.*
[179] C.I.L., I², 1, p. 316–317.
[180] Tertullien, Spect., 5, 7.
[181] Varron, R.R., I, 1, 6.

Il était par conséquent normal que de telles cérémonies « publiques », offertes au nom du peuple et à ses frais, fussent confiées au Flamine de Quirinus, le *populus* et les *Quirites* semblant, dans un contexte religieux, des termes équivalents[182].

V. *Quirinus et la* gens Iulia

Cette même définition de Quirinus comme « gardien de l'Etat » peut éclairer assez bien la prédilection des *Iulii* pour ce dieu si obscur. Il est hors de doute que seule une orientation politique ou sociale pouvait intéresser un Jules César, par exemple, aux yeux duquel un dieu agricole ne représenterait aucun soutien d'idéologie. Cet intérêt même est un puissant facteur dans l'essai de compréhension du dieu. Le choix des *Iulii* est paradoxal, et il faut se demander quel trait particulier, dans ce personnage inconnu, pouvait retenir l'attention d'hommes politiques avisés, à la fin de la République romaine.

Cet éclairage soudain de Quirinus ne remonte pas exactement à Jules César, mais se décèle un peu avant lui. Plusieurs solides études modernes, dues à A. ALFÖLDI, à C. KOCH, à W. BURKERT, à C. J. CLASSEN, à H. J. KRÄMER[183] ont tenté de comprendre les circonstances de l'assimilation de Romulus à Quirinus, dans divers contextes idéologiques et politiques. Tous s'accordent sur le rôle primordial joué dans l'affaire par la *gens Iulia*. Selon C. KOCH, par exemple, l'identification de Romulus-dieu et du vieux Quirinus serait une initiative des *Iulii*, soucieux de redorer le blason du Fondateur, un peu noirci par les opposants à la dictature, sous les gouvernements de Marius et de Sylla, lorsqu'on présentait le premier roi de Rome comme un tyran justement assassiné par le parti sénatorial[184]. En réponse à ces calomnies, les *Iulii* auraient sanctifié le héros discuté en l'incarnant dans le personnage révéré de Quirinus. Le souverain dont on conteste l'excellence perdait ainsi sa composante humaine pour acquérir une dimension métaphysique, ce qui doit faire taire les discussions autour de son passé humain. On avance un premier nom, celui de Métellus le Pieux, Grand Pontife entre les années 82 et 64 av. J.-C. Faisant son apprentissage politique dans l'ombre d'un pareil personnage, le jeune César dut profiter sans aucun doute de ces emprunts de la politique à la religion.

---

[182] Dans la définition, par exemple, des *Quiritium fossae*, nous trouvons les deux mots: *Et quia populi opera eas fecerat, appellauit Quiritium*, Paulus-Festus, p. 304 L.

[183] A. ALFÖLDI, Die Geburt der kaiserzeitlichen Bildsymbolik, Mus.Helv., 8, 1951, 190 sqq.; C. KOCH, Bemerkungen zum Römischen Quirinuskult, dans: IDEM, Religio, Nuremberg, 1960, p. 167 sqq.; W. BURKERT, Caesar und Romulus-Quirinus, Historia, 11, 1962, 356 sqq.; C. J. CLASSEN, Romulus in der römischen Republik, Philologus, 106, 1962, 174 sqq.; H. J. KRÄMER, Die Sage von Romulus und Remus in der lateinischen Literatur, dans: Synusia. Festgabe f. W. Schadewaldt i. Namen seiner Tübinger Schüler hrsg. v. H. FLASHAR u. K. GAISER, Pfullingen, 1965, 355–402.

[184] Bemerkungen . . ., dans: IDEM, Religio, p. 17–39; ici, p. 35–37.

W. Burkert a excellemment démontré le mécanisme de l'apothéose et de l'assimilation[185]. Il est impossible, certes, de ne pas attacher d'importance au nom de ce Proculus Julius, venu se porter garant devant le Sénat de l'ascension céleste de Romulus[186], authentifiée par la bouche du Fondateur lui-même. Proculus Julius, originaire, qui plus est, d'Albe[187], fondation julienne[188], quel nom inquiétant! Le premier à l'écrire, ce nom, c'est Cicéron, et tous les passages de son œuvre où l'on rencontre Proculus Julius sont ironiques[189]. En fait, il fallait toute la crédulité du peuple romain d'alors, pour ajouter foi à une mise en scène aussi grossière, et se fier à la parole d'un seul 'témoin' pour authentifier l'apothéose du fondateur. On admire, du reste, qu'à peine quelques décennies plus tard, Livie ait osé recourir au même stratagème, lorsqu'elle fit attester par un préteur que l'âme d'Auguste avait, sous ses yeux, gagné les hauteurs célestes, sans soulever d'autres protestations que quelques insinuations d'esprits forts affirmant, avec quelle raison, que l'Impératrice avait payé le préteur[190]. Ce Proculus Julius, on le croyait toujours, «même quand il affirmait les choses les plus invraisemblables»; cette remarque perfide apparaît sous la plume de Tite-Live, qui ajoute même: «c'est une chose étonnante que de voir une telle confiance accordée au récit de ce personnage[191]».

Si la fiction de l'apothéose romuléenne et de l'identification du roi à *Quirinus* est l'œuvre des *Iulii*, comme cela semble bien être le cas, on s'étonne alors, à juste titre, de voir la tradition officielle signer, si l'on peut dire, le crime, en appelant précisément 'Julius' l'homme qui porte la responsabilité de ce mensonge. L'intérêt de César n'était certes pas que l'identification du premier roi de Rome à l'un des anciens dieux parût un ouvrage de sa main! L'introduction dans la légende officielle de ce Proculus Julius nous paraît, venant d'un César, si maladroite, qu'elle peut difficilement lui être imputée. Nous songerions plutôt à une perfidie de ses adversaires, et, en première ligne, de Cicéron, qui, attribuant le miracle à un ancêtre, fictif ou non, des *Iulii*, ramènerait l'événement à de plus modestes proportions, en y faisant voir aux braves Romains crédules ce qu'ils n'y avaient pas vu tout seuls, c'est à dire une manipulation julienne. Ainsi, l'orateur insinue-t-il que Proculus Julius était payé par le Sénat: *impulsu Patrum, quo illi a se inuidiam interitus Romuli pellerent*[192]; dans un autre texte, un

---

[185] Op.cit., p. 371 sqq.

[186] On n'en fera pas pour autant le Frontiac étrusque occupé de brontoscopie qu'en fait J. Gagé, Le témoignage de Julius Proculus sur l'assomption de Romulus-Quirinus et les prodiges fulguratoires dans l'ancien *ritus comitialis*, AC, 41, 1972, 49—77.

[187] Ovide, Fast., II, 499: *Sed Proculus Longa ueniebat Iulius Alba.*

[188] Virgile, Aen., I, 267sqq.:

> *At puer Ascanius, cui nunc cognomen Iulo*
> *. . . regnumque ab sede Lauini*
> *Transferet, et longam multa ui muniet Albam.*

[189] Rep., II, 10, 20; Nat.Deor., II, 24; Leg., I, 1, 3.

[190] Suétone, Diu.Aug., 100; Dion Cassius, LVI, 46, 2.

[191] I, 16: *Et consilio etiam unius hominis addita rei dicitur fides . . . Mirum quantum illi uiro nuntianti haec fides fuerit, quamque desiderium Romuli apud plebem exercitumque facta fide immortalitatis lenitum sit.*

[192] Rep., II, 10, 20.

perfide *Quidam* semble bien insinuer que «certaines gens», évidemment les *Iulii*, n'étaient pas étrangers à la déification surprenante du Fondateur[193]. Chez Varron, à une époque où, pourtant, l'assimilation de Romulus à Quirinus semblait chose acquise, c'est à dire où l'on comprenait Quirinus comme le prolongement divin de Romulus mort, Quirinus se voit inclure dans la liste que dresse le polygraphe des divinités sabines importées par Titus Tatius: cela équivaut à le faire exister à Rome a v a n t la mort et la déification de Romulus, et c'est donc le refus implicite de la thèse officielle. Nous percevons ici les réticences des Romains éclairés à cette falsification religieuse, autant que l'importance qu'avait prise, dans les luttes des clans politiques au cours du premier siècle, le personnage de Quirinus.

Quelles ressources présentait donc pour César et pour les *Iulii* un dieu archaïque aussi fossilisé que Quirinus?

Si Quirinus est un dieu de l'agriculture, nous l'avons dit, pas le moindre. S'il est un dieu de la paix, pas beaucoup plus.

Mais s'il est le dieu des *Quirites*, alors s'enchaîne sous nos yeux un subtil calcul.

Selon une tradition que les *Iulii* se sont donné bien du mal à établir, Romulus est l'un des ancêtres de la *gens Iulia*; en lui se rencontrent deux lignes généalogiques, celle des *Iulii*, depuis le premier *Iulius*, Ascagne-*Iulus*, et celle de Rome, grâce au dieu Mars et à Rhéa Silvia. Dans le domaine divin, c'est la rencontre entre Vénus, mère d'Enée, et Mars, père de Romulus. Les *Iulii* s'annexent donc le Fondateur, et Rome leur devient en quelque sorte une propriété de famille[194]. Souvenons-nous de l'apologie prononcée par César lors des obsèques de *Julia*: «Ma famille unit à la majesté des rois qui sont les maîtres des hommes, la sainteté des dieux qui sont les maîtres des rois[195]».

Comment mettre mieux en lumière l'intérêt que présente pour César le personnage de Romulus-Quirinus, à l a f o i s r o i e t d i e u?

L'assimilation de Romulus, récent divinisé, à Quirinus, dieu vénérable des anciens Romains, donnait au nouveau dieu des lettres de noblesse, et permettait de faire mieux accepter l'innovation que représentait pour la mentalité romaine la canonisation d'un être humain.

César pouvait ainsi se réclamer de Mars, dieu du peuple romain; de Romulus, fondateur du peuple romain; de Quirinus, incarnation divine du peuple romain. L'ensemble se révèle d'une remarquable cohérence. La *gens Iulia* se trouve ainsi liée de façon indéfectible au peuple romain, qu'elle fonde,

---

[193] Nat.Deor., II, 24: c'est du reste l'avis de F. BÖMER, Gymnasium, 64, 1957, 112–135, p. 132. Sur Proculus Julius, on possède également le texte de Dion Cassius, I, frg. 6, 1, aa: l'intervention de Proculus enraye une émeute παρασσομένων καί τι παρασκευαζομένων δρᾶσαι (αὐτῶν).

[194] Ovide, Fast., IV, 19–58, dont surtout:

Ille suos semper Venerem Martemque parentes
Dixit, et emeruit uocis habere fidem.

[195] Suétone, Diu.Iul., 6: *Est ergo in genere et sanctitas regum, qui plurimum inter homines pollent, et caerimonia deorum, quorum ipsi in potestate sunt reges.*

gouverne, protège et agrandit. Elle possédait déjà un ancêtre divinisé, Enée,
devenu Jupiter Indigète; il faut croire que cela ne lui suffisait pas, puisqu'elle
éprouve le besoin de favoriser la divinisation d'un autre ancêtre; et de fait, Enée
ne la rattachait pas au peuple romain.

Si les *Iulii* ont travaillé à l'assimilation entre Romulus et Quirinus, c'est
parce qu'ils désiraient rendre tangible aux yeux de tous que la cité romaine,
incarnée dans Quirinus, son représentant divin, s'incarnait également dans son
fondateur Romulus, ancêtre des *Iulii*. Que le dieu de «tous les citoyens unis en
communauté», les *co-uiri*, pouvait recevoir en lui l'homme qui avait le premier
œuvré pour la confection de l'unité romaine. Donc, que l'apothéose, récom-
pense décernée à Romulus leur ancêtre, exaltait ses mérites envers le peuple
romain, puisqu'elle investissait Romulus des insignes de Quirinus, le premier
Citoyen de Rome; et qu'elle pouvait alors à nouveau, dans la même famille,
récompenser d'autres grands serviteurs du peuple romain, soucieux de sa réuni-
fication après les guerres civiles.

Sous ce rapport, un geste de César lui-même est significatif. Lorsqu'il se
fait élever une statue, en 45 av. J.-C., comme au *Deo Inuicto*, ce n'est pas le
temple de Vénus Genetrix qu'il choisit pour son emplacement, bien qu'il l'ait
consacré lui-même le 26 septembre 46: dans le temple de la Vénus julienne,
l'honneur rendu à César serait resté une affaire quasi gentilice. C'est le temple de
Quirinus[196], le sanctuaire aux deux myrtes abritant le dieu commun aux patriciens et aux plébéiens, dont la coexistence était symbolisée par les deux arbres
sacrés qui ombrageaient ses portes. Dans le temple de Quirinus, dieu d'union,
l'hommage devenait un geste de toute la Cité adressé au chef de la Cité. Les résonances sont alors bien différentes! Plus ou moins à l'ombre du dieu, César
lui-même, nouveau patron de la Cité romaine, présidait, comme Quirinus, aux
destinées de l'ensemble du peuple. Peut-on rêver plus riche imagerie pour le sub-
conscient populaire, qui, vénérant Quirinus dans son temple, y rencontrait César,
et assimilait plus ou moins les deux hôtes du sanctuaire . . .

Dans cette quête idéologique, César s'arrêta en chemin. Il ne fit que
suggérer la possibilité d'une divinisation des *Iulii* par Rome, à l'aide d'un
exemple heureux, celui de Romulus, qu'il mettait sous les yeux des Romains,
sans en tirer lui-même de conclusions trop franches, sans oser insinuer qu'il
pouvait lui-même être ce nouveau Romulus. Dans les honneurs quasi divins
qu'il s'octroie, et que nous énumère Suétone[197], «prérogatives qui l'élevaient

---

[196] Dion Cassius, XLIII, 45, 3: ἄλλην τέ τινα εἰκόνα ἐς τὸν τοῦ Κυρίνου ναὸν θεῷ ἀνικήτῳ
ἐπιγράψαντες. On connaît la pointe ironique de Cicéron sur César σύνναος Quirini, Att.,
XII, 45, 3 ou *contubernalis Quirini*, Att., XIII, 28, 3. Le temple sera reconstruit par
Auguste en 16 (Res gestae, IV, 5; VI, 32), et orné de 76 colonnes (Dion, LIV, 19, 4). Nombreux détails sur le sanctuaire de Quirinus dans l'article de G. RADKE, déjà cité (ci-dessous
p. 279 à 280), aux notes 19 à 29.

[197] Suétone, Diu.Iul., 76: *Sed et ampliora etiam humano fastigio decerni sibi passus est, sedem auream in Curia et pro tribunali, tensam et ferculum circensi pompa, templa, aras,
simulacra iuxta deos, puluinar, Flaminem, Lupercos* etc. . . . *Insuper praenomen Imperatoris, cognomen Patris Patriae*. On lira E. MANNI, Romulus e parens patriae nell'ideologia
religiosa romana, Il Mondo classico, 4, 1934, 106–118.

même au-dessus de l'humanité», nous trouvons des temples, des autels, des statues jouxtant celles des dieux, un lit de parade, etc., mais pas encore de surnom trop parlant. Le seul qu'il se laisse décerner, c'est celui de Père de la Patrie, encore suffisamment anonyme.

Pourtant, si l'on y regarde d'un peu près, qui était le véritable 'Père de la Patrie', sinon Romulus? Il est évident que ce titre, recherché obstinément par César, puis par Auguste, était à leurs yeux inséparable de l'idéologie romuléenne et quirinienne, partant, de l'apothéose. Le Père de la Patrie, c'est, sur le plan humain, Romulus, et sur le plan divin, Quirinus, qui la porte dans son nom même. Ce surnom, en quelque sorte 'fonctionnel', faisait à lui seul de César l'homologue de celui qu'il avait lui-même contribué à élever au rang des dieux.

Mais César ne franchit jamais le pas, laissant ouverte la conclusion prévisible: Romulus, père de la patrie, avait été divinisé en Quirinus; César, Père de la Patrie, et voisin de Quirinus en son temple, devait aussi bénéficier du même privilège. Nul ne tira cette conclusion, ou plutôt, Rome en tira une autre, hors de ce beau contexte, celle que César, nouveau Romulus, pouvait subir le même sort que le premier roi, massacré par les Sénateurs[198].

C'est sans doute le sort de César qui arrêta Auguste, lorsque désireux de parachever l'œuvre idéologique césarienne, il songea à mettre en clair ce que le dictateur n'avait fait qu'insinuer. Il est symptomatique qu'il ait songé d'abord à *Romulus*, et que cette prédilection l'ait marqué jusqu'à sa mort, puisqu'il ordonnera de faire porter dans son cortège funéraire la statue du premier roi[199]. C'est sans doute cette préférence que certains souhaitaient officialiser le jour où l'on discuta au Sénat de l'opportunité d'appeler le Prince *Romulus*[200]. On justifia aussitôt cette opportunité grâce aux mérites du Fondateur, qui se retrouvaient dans le programme augustéen, avec d'une part la fondation de la cité, et de l'autre la fondation d'une ère nouvelle de stabilité, favorisée par l'installation d'un nouveau régime: *quasi et ipsum conditorem Vrbis . . .*

Ce ne fut pourtant pas le surnom de *Romulus* qui prévalut, encore que par caprice Auguste se fît parfois appeler ainsi[201]. Sans doute, ce nom éveillait-il trop de dangereux souvenirs, dans l'esprit des Romains déjà spectateurs du

---

[198] C'est ainsi qu'on interprète l'allusion de Cicéron, Att. XIII, 28, 3: *malo eum σύνναον Quirini quam Salutis.*

[199] Dion, LVI, 34, 2: καὶ μετὰ ταύτας αἵ τε τῶν προπατόρων αὐτοῦ καὶ αἱ ἄλλων συγγενῶν τῶν τεθνηκότων, πλὴν τῆς τοῦ Καίσαρος (ὅτι ἐς τοὺς ἥρωας ἐσέγεγραπτο) αἵ τε τῶν ἄλλων τοῦ Ῥωμύλου ἀρξάμεναι, ἐφέροντο.

[200] Suétone, Diu.Aug., 7, 4: . . . *quibusdam censentibus Romulum appellari oportere, quasi et ipsum conditorem Vrbis.*

[201] Lydus. Mens., IV, 72: οἱ μὲν γὰρ αὐτὸν ὠνόμαζον Κυρῖνον οἱονεὶ Ῥωμύλον, et cf. n. 209 (*omnibus usus est*). Dans le fameux *Remo cum fratre Quirinus*, il est évident que Virgile pense à Romulus, frère de Rémus, c'est à dire, comme le veut Servius, comm. ad loc., à Auguste et à son gendre et co-régent Agrippa. Il est d'autre part significatif qu'au chant VI, Virgile fasse se succéder, en un raccourci saisissant, les règnes de Romulus et d'Auguste, comme s'ils se suivaient immédiatement dans le temps (VI, 777—807). Cf. R. RIEKS, Vergils Dichtung als Zeugnis und Deutung der römischen Geschichte, ANRW, II, 31,2, 1981, p. 742, 841 e. a.

meurtre de César. Romulus étant aussi *Quirinus*, c'est sous ce nom-là qu'on désigna couramment Auguste[202].

Qu'apportait de plus, par rapport à *Romulus*, cet autre surnom? D'abord, il éloignait toute idée de royauté, par essence hostile à l'esprit national, et inhérente au personnage de Romulus, comme l'a bien compris Dion Cassius[203]. Dans la légende de Romulus, il y avait encore trop de caractères contestables, peut-être trop de sang. Quirinus apportait au contraire la caution d'une antiquité d'autant plus sainte qu'on ne savait plus trop qui il était, et rappelait opportunément, de par son nom seul, à une Rome épuisée par les luttes fratricides du premier siècle av. J.-C., une idée de communauté civique passée à l'arrière-plan des préoccupations générales. Cette idée de concorde est une des idées-fondamentales du régime institué par Auguste. On connaît, bien sûr, sa préférence pour la déesse Concordia[204], mais d'autres initiatives parlent dans le même sens: l'érection de statues, sur l'argent produit par la fonte de ses propres images[205], à la Santé publique, à la Concorde (ὁμόνοια) et à la Paix; ou encore, la réponse à la salutation sénatoriale et populaire de *Pater patriae*, par le seul vœu d'un *consensus* durable entre tous les citoyens[206]. L'action de *Concordia*, c'est essentiellement de *iungere*[207]; le chef qui la réalisait dans son peuple se plaisait donc à incarner son œuvre, en se parant d'un nom qui lui-même parlait d'union, celui de **Co-uirinus* bien sûr. Ainsi l'entend la poésie virgilienne[208] qui nous rappelle avec insistance que, sur le plan allégorique, le Prince se confondait avec le dieu Quirinus. Et le commentaire de Servius nous est, à ce titre, précieux[209].

---

[202] Virgile, Georg., III, 27 et II, 171: *In foribus pugnam ex auro solidoque elephanto / Gangaridum faciam uictorisque arma Quirini*, et: *Et te maxime Caesar / qui nunc extremis Asiae iam uictor in oris / imbellem auertis Romanis arcibus Indum,* qui donne la clef de la première désignation.

[203] LIII, 16, 7: Auguste souhaite être nommé Romulus (ὁ Καῖσαρ ἐπεθύμει ἰσχυρῶς Ῥωμύλος ὀνομασθῆναι) mais se ravise, en songeant qu'on pourrait lui imputer des prétentions à la royauté (αἰσθόμενος δὲ ὅτι ὑποπτεύεται ἐκ τούτου τῆς βασιλείας ἐπιθυμεῖν, οὐκέτ' αὐτοῦ ἀντεποιήσατο, ἀλλὰ Αὔγουστος ὡς καὶ πλέον τι ἢ κατὰ ἀνθρώπους ὢν ἐπεκλήθη. On lira K. Scott, The Identification of Augustus with Romulus-Quirinus, TAPhA, 56, 1925, 85−105.

[204] Ovide, Fast., VI, 637:

> Te quoque, magnifica, Concordia, dedicat aede
> Liuia: Quam caro praestitit ipsa uiro.

Aussi, I, 637, VI, 91−96.

[205] Dion, LIV, 35, 2.

[206] Suétone, Diu.Aug., 58.

[207] Ovide, Fast., VI, 96: *his iunctis.* Aussi 94: *coisse.*

[208] Aen., I, 292: *Remo cum fratre Quirinus / iura dabunt.*

[209] *Vera tamen hoc habet ratio, Quirinum Augustum esse, Remum uero pro Agrippa positum, qui filiam Augusti duxit uxorem, et cum eo pariter bella tractauit; nam adulans populus Romanus Octauiano tria obtulit nomina, utrum uellet Quirinus an Caesar an Augustus uocari. Ille ne unum eligendo partem laederet quae aliud offerre cupiebat, diuerso tempore omnibus usus est.*

En un troisième temps, le Prince adopte décidément le nom d'Auguste, sous lequel la postérité le connaît seulement, et qui l'auréole, de son vivant, d'un rayonnement sacré. Ce n'est point ici le lieu de rappeler les discussions interminables sur le sens actif ou passif de *Augustus*[210]. Il suffit de dire que ce nouveau surnom établit plus fermement encore l'essence déjà divine du chef de Rome, en le préparant directement à l'apothéose, parce que marqué déjà d'un sceau divin. En même temps, cette décision marque un progrès par rapport au surnom de *Quirinus*. *Augustus* appartient en propre à Octave, et l'individualise en tant que dieu, ce que ne faisait pas suffisamment le nom de *Quirinus*, qui l'obligeait, en quelque sorte, à partager sa divinité avec un autre personnage humain. *Quirinus* était encore et trop Romulus, *Augustus* sera le dieu-Octave seul, mais les deux surnoms précédents lui auront préparé savamment et patiemment le chemin, en faisant ressortir sa qualité de fondateur, puis sa qualité d'unificateur divin. *Augustus*, c'est en somme le but suprême auquel tendait tout le travail idéologique précédent. Il y avait eu l'étape *Romulus*, correspondant à la conquête du pouvoir par Octave, dans la guerre et le massacre, aboutissant pourtant à la réédification de l'*Vrbs*. Il y a ensuite l'étape *Quirinus*, marquant une transition, invitant les anciens ennemis à se réunir sous les auspices de *Quirinus* et de *Concordia*. Une fois suffisamment assuré pour pouvoir se passer de ses références divines antérieures, et affirmer sa divinité personnelle, il faudra que le Prince aborde l'ultime étape, celle de l'*Augustus*, organisant Rome pour la paix, lui rendant des structures morales et civiques mais surtout religieuses. Au despotisme tyrannique et arbitraire qui fut celui d'Octave succédait la monarchie éclairée d'Auguste *princeps*; le pouvoir temporel de Romulus cédait la place au pouvoir spirituel de Quirinus et d'Augustus. Il ne restait plus qu'à souffler aux Romains encore hésitants que la divinisation était réservée à Auguste par les dieux eux-mêmes, et c'est ce à quoi le Prince s'emploiera, lorsqu'un mystérieux et bénéfique hasard aura fait effacer le C sur les inscriptions portant le titre de *Caesar*: les interprètes de prodiges déclarèrent alors que c'était là un présage de divinisation, puisque *AESAR* signifie « dieu » en langue étrusque! *ictu fulminis ex inscriptione statuae eius prima nominis littera effluxit. Responsum est ... futurum ut inter deos referretur, quod AESAR, id est reliqua pars e Caesaris nomine, etrusca lingua deus uocaretur*[211]. L'homme « augmenté par les dieux », *Augustus*, allait devenir un dieu tout court. Ainsi se réalisait ce que César, dans son imparfaite connaissance de la psychologie romaine, avait, pour son malheur,

---

[210] On trouvera de nombreuses remarques utiles dans les études suivantes: K. Scott, Notes on Augustus' Religious Policy, ARW, 35, 1938, 121–130; A. Levi, Il tempo di Augusto, Florence, 1951, passim; J. Béranger, Recherches sur l'aspect idéologique du Principat, Schweizer.Beitr.z.Altertumswiss., 6, Bâle, 1953; F. Haverfield, The Name Augustus, JRS, 5, 1915, 249–250; L. Ross Taylor, Livy and the Name Augustus, CR. 32, 1918, 159–161; A. Ernout, Augur-Augustus, MSL, 22, 1921, 234–238; J. Gagé, Romulus-Augustus, MEFR, 47, 1930, 138–187; M. A. Koops, De Augusto, Mnemosyne, sér. III, 5, 1937, 34–39; G. Dumézil, Remarques sur Augur-Augustus, REL, 35, 1957, 149–150.

[211] Suétone, Diu.Aug., 97.

tenté d'imposer aux Romains récalcitrants, et qu'Auguste faisait accepter en
douceur par une série d'insinuations subtiles dont il laissait apparemment au
peuple l'initiative d'adopter les effets: la sacralisation anticipée d'un homme,
préludant à sa réception au nombre des dieux.

Pater patriae, Romulus, Quirinus, Augustus: chaque surnom marque un
progrès sur celui qui le précède, fait avancer d'un pas l'homme providentiel de
Rome sur le chemin qui mène, lentement mais sûrement selon la devise
d'Auguste lui-même, jusqu'à l'accession au rang des dieux. Le hasard n'a pas
place dans de tels calculs; et l'enchaînement se réalise si harmonieusement qu'on
peut y reconnaître les effets d'une réflexion approfondie de cerveaux hors du
commun. Jusqu'au moment où, le nouveau dieu couché sur son bûcher
funéraire, Livie pourra 'boucler la boucle', et ressusciter, pour l'époux défunt, le
même cérémonial dont on usa pour Romulus devenu dieu, et faire jurer par un
témoin digne de foi qu'il avait vu de ses yeux l'âme du héros en marche vers les
hauteurs célestes: par delà la tombe, Auguste restait fidèle à l'idéologie mûre-
ment réfléchie par d'autres membres de la *gens Iulia*.

Conclusions sur Quirinus

L'utilisation concertée de Quirinus par les deux *Iulii* fondateurs de l'empire
romain, César et Auguste, nous confirme dans l'opinion que l'assimilation de
Romulus à Quirinus n'était pas plus ou moins le fait d'un hasard inexplicable,
rompant avec sa figure originelle de dieu des approvisionnements pour mettre en
valeur une caractéristique secondaire du dieu, rapproché de Romulus on ne sait
trop pourquoi. Nous croyons au contraire que seule une continuité impeccable
entre les fonctions de Quirinus à l'époque archaïque et la façon dont on le comprenait à Rome aux siècles historiques put favoriser sa confusion avec Romulus
et sa résurrection inattendue à l'époque républicaine et impériale. Une idéologie
ne peut s'imposer à un peuple que si elle a la force de conviction nécessaire pour
lui apparaître comme une aspiration fondamentale dont il peut avoir l'initiative.
Une telle idéologie doit donc appartenir au fonds de croyances commun à tout le
peuple, et non lui apparaître comme une innovation plus ou moins gratuite.

Quirinus nous est apparu comme le dieu des *Quirites*. Les *Quirites* sont des
privilégiés, ce privilège consistant en une appartenance commune aux plus vieux
cadres religieux de Rome, ceux des curies. Ainsi affirment-ils en face des
ennemis, des étrangers, des futurs immigrants, la pureté de leurs origines. Un
Quirite est un membre de la communauté romaine, qu'elle soit en paix, qu'elle
soit en guerre, qu'il occupe en son sein n'importe quelle fonction. Le dieu qui le
protège est un dieu d'allure paisible, puisque les activités juridiques et gouver-
nementales, autant que toutes les opérations qui peuvent se dérouler *intra
muros*, se satisfont davantage de l'idée de paix, et puisque son collègue Mars
prend en charge les activités guerrières. Néanmoins, Quirinus peut suivre ses
ressortissants sur le champ de bataille, et protéger ses «Quirites armés» lorsqu'ils
quittent l'enceinte de la Ville sans abandonner pour autant leurs droits de
citoyens: à cet effet, il possède des armes, et peut intervenir, le cas échéant, dans

des formes solennelles, lorsque la vie de ses citoyens est en balance. Et s'il s'occupe un instant de la nourriture de son peuple, ce n'est pas en tant qu'agriculteur, c'est pour prêter sa fête à ceux des membres de la communauté trop peu soucieux de leurs devoirs civiques.

Bien que Quirinus apparaisse comme un civil, comme un dieu de paix, il n'empêche que sa caractéristique principale n'est pas la paix, sans quoi l'on ne comprendrait plus son assimilation à Romulus, roi essentiellement belliqueux. Cette assimilation nous prouve à l'évidence que, malgré l'effacement de la curie devant d'autres structures plus modernes, malgré l'effacement de Quirinus devant Mars, dû à la vocation guerrière de Rome − *horridus miles amatur!* −, le sens originel de *Quirinus* était encore bien vivant dans les esprits romains aux deux premiers siècles avant Jésus-Christ, puisque le créateur des curies, Romulus, fondateur de Rome, pouvait s'incarner divinement en lui. Il est significatif que ce cas unique de confusion entre un homme et une divinité ait été engendré par le souci principal de tout Romain à toute époque: œuvrer au bénéfice de sa Cité, et en exalter les réalisations. Cette résurrection d'un dieu perdu, à l'époque de l'apogée romaine, est due à la permanence obstinée à travers son histoire de l'idée communautaire.

Symbole inerte et impersonnel de la Cité romaine, Quirinus acquérait, de par son assimilation avec Romulus, une personnalité, une histoire, une vie. Mais il se voyait par là-même victime de la politique qui le tirait de son néant, victime de Romulus. Car, habitués à ne le considérer que comme Romulus, les historiens de la religion ne se préoccupèrent pas de nous conserver sa liturgie propre, sinon à l'aide de misérables fragments. Que se passait-il réellement le 17 février, aux *Quirinalia*, si l'on excepte une reprise du service liturgique de *Fornax* à l'intention des Romains distraits? Nous l'ignorons complètement. Ovide, au lieu de nous narrer l'apothéose de Romulus, que nous connaissons par au moins quatre autres auteurs, et qu'il avait déjà relatée dans ses 'Métamorphoses', aurait bien mieux fait de nous décrire le rituel des *Quirinalia*, et de réserver l'apothéose de Romulus pour le 5 juillet! Certes. Mais à son époque, Romulus était devenu un personnage beaucoup plus considérable, jouissant qui plus est de la faveur impériale, qui, au lieu de rendre vie au malheureux Quirinus à qui il empruntait son nom, l'étouffait.

Et l'on se prend à rêver: si Auguste avait choisi comme surnom personnel ce nom de *Quirinus* qu'il porta un moment, peut-être quelque historien aurait-il exhumé pour nous du fond des siècles quelques détails liturgiques propres à Quirinus . . .

Et quel destin que celui de Quirinus aux débuts de la dynastie julienne! Conquérant entre les conquérants, Jules César ne choisit pas Mars comme son homologue céleste pour protéger son image, mais ce dieu oublié qu'est Quirinus, anonyme, de réputation paisible. N'est-ce pas parce que seul il pouvait faire comprendre que les ambitions du dictateur n'avaient pour but que le bonheur de la Cité, dont il s'instaurait le représentant terrestre, comme Quirinus en était le représentant divin? *Princeps* et non pas *dominus*, premier citoyen de Rome mais seulement citoyen, Auguste applique un moment ce même principe, et ses deux surnoms de *Romulus* et de *Quirinus*, celui-là préféré par Virgile, suggèrent discrètement que le nouveau responsable de Rome est parfaitement conscient de ses devoirs envers la Cité, que les honneurs particuliers qui lui échoient ne s'adressent pas à l'homme mais au citoyen.

Romulus, prince et dieu, Quirinus, dieu des Princes: ainsi se réunissaient les deux vocations de Rome, guerrière et constituante, sous une main unique, celle de César, puis celle d'Auguste. Un nouveau régime s'ancrait, conformément aux habitudes romaines, dans un cadre ancien; l'idée impériale, jouant sur d'anciens symbolismes, s'appuyait sur une idéologie venue du fond des âges.

Die *dei penates* und Vesta in Rom

von GERHARD RADKE, Berlin

Inhalt

Einleitung

Die *dei penates* gehören sowohl nach der Bildung ihres Namens (s. u. S. 355 ff.) wie nach der Art ihres Kultes zur ältesten Schicht römischer Gottes-

Abkürzungen:

ANRW	Aufstieg und Niedergang der römischen Welt. Geschichte und Kultur Roms im Spiegel der neueren Forschung, edd. H. TEMPORINI—W. HAASE, Berlin—New York 1972 ff.
ARW	Archiv für Religionswissenschaft, Leipzig—Berlin
CIL	Corpus Inscriptionum Latinarum, Leipzig—Berlin 1862 ff., ed. altera 1893 ff.
FGrH	Die Fragmente der griechischen Historiker, ed. F. JACOBY, Berlin—Leiden 1923—58, ND Leiden 1954 ff.
GCS	Die griechischen christlichen Schriftsteller der ersten Jahrhunderte, Leipzig—Berlin 1897 ff.

verehrung. So unbestimmte Vorstellungen man sich von ihnen machte[1], waren sie·doch im römischen Leben allgegenwärtig[2] und stellten Wahrzeichen alter römischer Gläubigkeit dar[3]. Ihr Kult in Lavinium wurde von Rom als ein römischer Gottesdienst in Anspruch genommen, obwohl sie auch dort an der Velia einen Tempel besaßen (s. u. S. 349); eine Verbindung zwischen beiden Plätzen im Sinne einer Kultübertragung läßt sich nicht erkennen. Von besonderer Bedeutung war jedoch ihre Verehrung in jedem Hause eines Römers; wenn auch gerade darüber sehr ungenaue Angaben vorliegen, beweist doch allein schon die metonymische Verwendung ihres Namens für den Begriff 'Haus'[4] bis in die Gegenwart die Wichtigkeit und Nachhaltigkeit dieser Verehrung. Große Verwirrung bestand bereits im Altertum hinsichtlich ihrer Verbindung mit dem Kult der Vesta; fraglich bleibt, ob und wie sich sowohl bei dieser Göttin wie auch bei den Penaten die Verehrung aus dem Einzelhaus in den Staatskult verlagert habe[5].

II	Inscriptiones Italiae, Roma 1931 ff.
ILLRP	Inscriptiones Latinae Liberae Rei Publicae², ed. A. DEGRASSI, Firenze 1966
ILS	Inscriptiones Latinae Selectae, ed. H. DESSAU, Berlin 1892−1916, ND Berlin 1954/55
JÖAI	Jahreshefte des österreichischen Archäologischen Instituts, Wien
JRSt	Journal of Roman Studies, London
Kl.Pauly	Der kleine Pauly. Lexikon der Antike, Stuttgart 1964−75
LEW	A. WALDE−J. B. HOFMANN, Lateinisches etymologisches Wörterbuch³, Heidelberg 1938/53
MDAI(R)	Mitteilungen des Deutschen Archäologischen Instituts Rom, Mainz
Myth.Lex.	W. H. ROSCHERS Ausführliches Lexikon der griechischen und römischen Mythologie, Leipzig 1884 ff., ND Hildesheim 1965
REA	Revue des Etudes Anciennes, Bordeaux
RFIC	Rivista di Filologia e di Istruzione Classica, Torino
Rhein.Mus.	Rheinisches Museum für Philologie, Frankfurt a. M.
RVV	Religionsgeschichtliche Versuche und Vorarbeiten, Gießen−Berlin
SMSR	Studi e Materiali di Storia delle Religioni, Roma

[1] Vgl. L. DEUBNER, in: CHANTEPIE DE LA SAUSSAYE, Lehrb. d. Rel.Gesch. II⁴, 435: „Gestalten ohne individuelle Bestimmtheit, deren Kreis später aus irgendwelchen dem Hause nahestehenden Göttern zusammenzusetzen in jedermanns Belieben stand". P. GRIMAL, Dictionnaire de la Mythologie Grecque et Romaine³, 1963, 355 *« puissances invisibles, simples abstractions »*. K. LATTE, RRG, 89.

[2] Vgl. Serv.auct.Aen. 3,12 *quod praesentissimi sentiantur.*

[3] Vgl. Cic.Catil. 4,18 *vobis arcem et Capitolium, vobis aras penatium, vobis illum ignem Vestae sempiternum . . . commendat.* har.resp. 12 *de deorum penatium Vestaeque matris caerimoniis.* dom. 144 *patriique penates familiaresque, qui huic urbi et rei publicae praesidetis.* Aug.civ. 3,28 *nihil apud Romanos templo Vestae sanctius habebatur*; vgl. 7,16.

[4] Man kann heute noch von seinem Hause als seinen Penaten, nicht aber als seinen Laren oder seiner Vesta sprechen.

[5] Vgl. G. WISSOWA, Rel.², 164f. K. LATTE, RRG, 108.

I. Die Penaten in Lavinium

Die Überlieferung berichtet, Aeneas habe die Penaten nach Lavinium gebracht[6]. In den bildlichen Darstellungen der Flucht aus Troia trägt Anchises oft einen Kasten in den Händen, der nach der Beischrift auf der 'Tabula Iliaca' τὰ ἱερά enthält[7]. Dem Timaios (FGrH 566 F 59) hatten Einheimische mitgeteilt, die im ἄδυτον des Tempels[8] in Lavinium liegenden ἱερά seien eiserne und bronzene Heroldstäbe sowie troische Irdenware, worin man später die von den Römern Penaten genannten θεοὶ πατρῷοι wiedererkennen zu dürfen glaubte[9]. In anderen Nachrichten wird von hölzernen, irdenen, steinernen oder marmornen *sigilla*[10] oder *simulacra*[11] − Bildwerken also − gesprochen, die im Traume erscheinen[12], was sich kaum für anikonische Gegenstände wie Heroldstäbe hätte verstehen lassen. Naevius und Vergil unterscheiden zwischen *sacra* und *penates*[13]; offenbar sind in diesem Rahmen die Vorstellungen austauschbar, wie die Formulierung bei Verg. Aen. 3,148 lehrt: *effigies sacrae divom Phrygiique penates*.

Nach langer Irrfahrt[14] in Lavinium angekommen, widersetzen sich die Penaten erfolgreich jedem Versuch, sie nach Alba Longa[15] oder nach Rom[16] zu bringen. Darin ist offenbar die Mythisierung einer religionshistorischen Aussage

---

[6] Nach Critolaus (unbekannter Zeit) b. Fest. 439,4 ff. L. aus Samothrake, nach Val. Max. 1, 8,7 aus Troia. Es gibt eine ganze Literatur in der antiken Überlieferung (vgl. Hygins 'De deis penatibus') über die Wanderfahrt der Penaten: Nach Varro b. Serv. auct. Aen. 1,378. 3,148. Schol. Veron. Aen. 2,717 brachte Dardanos die Penaten von Samothrake nach Troia und Aeneas von Troia nach Italien; vgl. Dion. Hal. ant. 2,66,5. Plut. Cam. 20,6. Daneben gibt es auch abweichende Berichte, die aber die römischen Penaten nicht betreffen. Ob Cassius Hemina frg. 6 P. die Penaten in Lavinium oder in Rom (so J. PERRET, Orig. 342) meint, ist ungewiß.

[7] Vgl. F. BÖMER, Rom u. Troia 17. K. SCHAUENBURG, in: Gymn. 67, 1960, 176 ff., bes. S. 190 f. G. LIPPOLD, Tabula Iliaca, in: RE IV A 2 (1932), 1887.

[8] Ein Penatentempel in Lavinium wird von Serv. auct. Aen. 3,12 anläßlich des prodigiösen Todes einer der *ambae virgines* erwähnt, die in ihm schliefen.

[9] Dion. Hal. ant. 1,67,3.

[10] Serv. auct. Aen. 1,378. 3,148. Schol. Veron. Aen. 2,717.

[11] Orig. g. Rom. 11,3. 12,5. 13,3. 17,2.

[12] Serv. auct. Aen. 3,148. orig. g. Rom. 12,5. Ein ἐπιχώριος δαίμων erscheint dem Latinus im Traume, die πατρῷοι θεοί dem Aeneas und geben beiden jeweils den Rat zu friedlichen Vereinbarungen (Dion. Hal. ant. 1,57,4). Traumerscheinung als Grund für den Kult (Serv. auct. Aen. 3,148).

[13] Verg. Aen. 2,293 *sacra suosque tibi commendat Troia penates*. ebd. 717 *tu genitor, cape sacra manu patriosque penatis*. Naev. frg. 3,2 MOR. *sacra in mensa penatium ordine ponuntur*.

[14] Nach Sil. 2,604 (*et prisca advectos Rutulorum ex urbe penates*) kamen die Penaten der Rutuler nach Saguntum; die Penaten von Tyros kamen nach Theben (Ov. met. 3,539. Stat. Theb. 11,216.368). Das sind in Analogie zu den 'troischen' Penaten erfundene Formulierungen, aus denen für den Inhalt der Penaten in Lavinium oder Rom nichts zu gewinnen ist.

[15] Val. Max. 1,8,7. orig. g. Rom. 17,2 f. Dion. Hal. ant. 1,67,1 f. Schol. Lykophr. 1332.

[16] Serv. auct. Aen. 1,270. 3,12.

zu erkennen. Der Kult der bildlosen *sacra* und der mit ihnen verbundenen oder gleichgesetzten *dei penates* ist von Anchises und Aeneas – schon der Aeneas-Sohn Ascanius hatte ihre Gefolgschaft verloren, wie die Weigerung, mit ihm nach Alba Longa zu gehen (s. ob.), veranschaulicht – auf den Ort Lavinium übergegangen; die dortige Penaten-Verehrung wird von den Römern erstaunlicherweise als eine nationale Aufgabe angesehen, obwohl sich dafür kein angemessener Grund finden läßt[17], da ja doch die Gründer Roms nicht aus Lavinium, sondern aus Alba Longa kamen, wohin die Penaten nicht zu gehen bereit waren. Man bescheidet sich daher mit der schlichten Feststellung: *ibi dii penates nostri*[18].

Dieser Glaube steht in Verbindung damit, daß die römischen Oberbeamten, d. h. Konsuln und Prätoren sowie gegebenenfalls der Diktator, bei Amtsantritt[19] in Lavinium ein Opfer – *sacrificium sollemne* angeblich schon in der Zeit des T. Tatius[20] – bringen: *sacrificia publica populi Romani deum penatium, quae Lavini fierent*[21]. Diese Opfer sind unter namentlicher Erwähnung der Konsuln C. Hostilius Mancinus für das Jahr 137 v. Chr.[22] und M. Aemilius Scaurus für das Jahr 115 v. Chr.[23] bezeugt.

Ob zu diesen *sacra principia*[24] auch das von *pontifices* zusammen mit *consules* vollzogene Opfer im Tempel des Aeneas Indiges in Lavinium[25] und die dortige Anwesenheit von *flamines*[26] gehören, läßt sich nicht entscheiden. Die Gewohnheit jedenfalls, einen Machtantritt sozusagen unter den Schutz der in Lavinium befindlichen 'römischen' Penaten zu stellen, erhielt sich lange Zeit;

[17] Die Gemeinsamkeit des Kultes der Iuno zwischen Rom und Lanuvium (Liv. 8,14,2. Ascon. Cic.Mil. p. 31 CL.) ist nicht vergleichbar, obwohl auch dort die *consules* ein jährliches Opfer bringen (Cic.Mur. 90).

[18] Varro l.l. 5,114 *oppidum quod primum conditum in Latio stirpis Romanae Lavinium; nam ibi dii penates nostri.* Inhaltlich stimmt damit die Angabe bei Plut.Coriol. 29,2 überein, wo von den θεῶν ἱερὰ Ῥωμαίοις πατρῴων gesprochen wird. Die Entstehung der 'historischen Legende' von Coriolan setzt SCHUR, Marcius Nr. 51, in: RE Suppl. V (1931), 654, in die zweite Hälfte des 4. Jhdts. v. Chr.; vgl. H. G. GUNDEL, Coriolanus, in: Kl.Pauly I (1964), 1306.

[19] Nach Macr.sat. 3,4,11 (*cum adeunt magistratum*) ist die aus der gleichen Quelle stammende Angabe bei Serv.auct.Aen. 2.296 (*cum . . . abeunt magistratu*) zu berichtigen, wie das Beispiel des Mancinus (s. u. Anm. 22) lehrt; vgl. auch Serv.auct.Aen. 3,12 *quod imperatores in provincias ituri apud eos primum immolarint.*

[20] Liv. 1,14,2; vgl. Plut.Rom. 23,3. Dion.Hal.ant. 2,52,3; auch in der Mahnung des Camillus (Liv. 5,52,8) werden die Opfer in Lavinium genannt.

[21] Ascon.Cic.Scaur. p. 21,7f. CL.

[22] Val.Max. 1,6,7. Prodigien beim Opfer in Lavinium auch nach Cato frg. 55 P. (b.Serv. auct.Aen. 10,541).

[23] Dem Aemilius Scaurus wurde vorgeworfen *sacra publica populi Romani deum penatium, quae Lavini fierent, opera eius minus recte casteque fieri* (Ascon.Cic.Scaur. p. 21 CL.).

[24] In einer Inschrift aus der Zeit des Kaisers Claudius – das *v* als umgekehrtes Digamma geschrieben – wird ein ⟨*praif.*⟩ *sacrorum principiorum p. R. Quirit. nominisque Latini, quai apud Laurentes coluntur* genannt (CIL X 797= ILS 5004).

[25] Schol.Veron.Aen. 1,259 (Ascanius) *Aeneae Indigeti templum dicavit, ad quod pontifices quotannis cum consulibus [iri solent sacri] ficaturi.*

[26] Serv.Aen. 8,664 *cum sacrificarent Laurolavini.*

noch als Kaiser Marcus Aurelius im November 176 n. Chr. seinen Sohn Commodus zum Mitregenten einsetzte[27], ging er nach Lavinium[28].

Hält man die angegebene Teilnahme von *dictatores* für historisch, muß die Festsetzung der Opferhandlung vor der letzten ordnungsmäßigen Diktatur *rei gerundae causa* im Jahre 216 v. Chr.[29] erfolgt sein. Da ferner die hypothetische Benennung der ältesten Oberbeamten als *praetores* außer acht bleiben kann, bietet sich das Jahr 366 v. Chr., in dem erstmalig ein *praetor* neben den beiden *consules* eingesetzt wurde, als Datum der frühesten Regelung an[30]. Damit käme man für die Einrichtung der Opfer römischer Magistrate für die 'römischen' Penaten in Lavinium in die Mitte des 4. vorchristl. Jhdts., d. h. in die Zeit des Latinerfriedens, was annehmbar erscheint[31]. Damals dürfte auch die Vorstellung aufgekommen sein, die Anwesenheit der römischen Magistrate in Lavinium diene der Erneuerung des *foedus* zwischen Aeneas und Latinus[32].

Dazu paßt auch, daß der Name Lavinium literarisch nicht vor Cato belegt ist[33] und die Erwähnung dieser Stadt — unter welcher Umschreibung auch immer[34] — lediglich durch Vergleich von Lykophr.Al. 1259 mit Varro r.r. 2,4, 18 und Lykophr.Al. 1262 mit Dion.Hal.ant. 1,67,4 für Timaios[35] erschlossen

---

[27] Vgl. P. VON ROHDEN, Annius Nr. 94, in: RE I 2 (1894), 2302.

[28] Hist.Aug.v.Marc.Aurel. 27,4.

[29] Vgl. W. LIEBENAM, Dictator, in: RE V 1 (1904), 388; die letzte Diktatur *comit. habend. causa* war im Jahre 202 v. Chr.

[30] Vgl. Liv. 6,42,11 *concessumque ab nobilitate plebi de consule plebeio, a plebe nobilitati de praetore uno, qui ius in urbe diceret, ex patribus creando*; ein solcher Prätor trat erstmalig i. J. 366 v. Chr. sein Amt an (Liv. 7,1,1f.). Vermutlich nahm dieser — später *praetor urbanus* genannte — Beamte am Vollzug der Kulthandlungen in Lavinium teil; andernfalls könnte man auch an die Einsetzung des sogenannten *praetor peregrinus* i. J. 245 v. Chr. denken (vgl. G. RADKE, Sprachliche und historische Beobachtungen zu den Leges XII tabularum, in: Sein und Werden im Recht. Festgabe f. U. von Lübtow, Berlin 1970, 240f.; vgl. Liv.epit. 19. Lyd.magistr. 1,38).

[31] Vgl. TH. MOMMSEN, Römisches Staatsrecht III, Handb.d.röm.Altertümer III 1, Leipzig 1887, 579,3.

[32] Vgl. Liv. 1,14,2 *foedus inter Romam Laviniumque urbes renovatum est.* ebd. 8,11,15 *cum Laurentibus renovari foedus iussum renovaturque ex eo quotannis post diem decimum Latinarum,* Serv.auct.Aen. 3,148 *monitu nam eorum* (scil. *deorum penatium*) *per quietem iussum cum Latino foedus fecisse*; zum Zustandekommen des *foedus* auf göttlichen Rat vgl. Dion.Hal.ant. 1,57,4. CIL X 797 (= ILS 5004) wird ein Sp.Turranius Proculus Gellianus genannt, der neben anderen Ämtern auch das des *pater patratus populi Laurentis foederis ex libris Sibullinis percutiendi cum p. R.* innehat; es ist der ob. Anm. 24 genannte ⟨*praef.*⟩ *sacrorum principiorum p. R. Quirit. nominisque Latini, quai apud Laurentis coluntur*; vgl. ST. WEINSTOCK, Penates, in: RE XIX 1 (1937), 430.

[33] Cato frg. 55 P. Serv.Aen. 10,541 *Cato in originibus ita ait: Lavini boves immolatos, priusquam caederentur, profugisse in silvam*; die nächsten Zeugnisse sind erst Varro l.l. 5,144. r.r. 2,4,18; vgl. aber auch Enn.ann. 34 *Laurentis terra.* Cato frg. 58 P. *populus Laurens.* frg. 8 P. *inter Laurentum et castra Troiana.* Cic.de or. 2,22 *Laurentum.* Polyb. 3,22,11 αϱεντινων wird m.E. zu Unrecht in Λαυϱεντίνων verändert.

[34] J. PERRET, Orig. 354, glaubt, es sei Alba Longa gemeint. Dion.Hal.ant. 1,56,2 jedoch gibt die Entfernung des Hügels vom Landeplatz mit 24 Stadien an, orig.g.Rom. 12,5 nennt ihn „Platz des späteren Lavinium".

[35] Tim. FGrH 566 F 59.

werden kann, wodurch eine Verbindung mit Aeneas zustande kommt. In der
zweiten Hälfte des 4. vorchristl. Jhdts., der gleichen Zeit also, die sich auch von
den *sacrificia* her hatte errechnen lassen, wurden die Ereignisse bei der Gründung der Stadt Lavinium durch Aeneas zusammen mit der dortigen Penaten-
verehrung den Griechen bekannt[36].

Aber schon ein Jahrhundert früher wußten sie durch Hellanikos und Damastes[37], Rom sei von Aeneas gemeinsam mit Odysseus gegründet worden. Es
ist mit großer Wahrscheinlichkeit angenommen worden[38], die Römer haben bei
der Gründung ihres Staates um die Wende vom 6. zum 5. Jhdt. v. Chr. begonnen, ihre eigene Geschichte zu gestalten — ich kann hinzufügen: wie sie damals auch ihr Verhältnis zu den Göttern und zu den Menschen anderer Völker
klärten und festlegten[39] — und sich als Gründerheros für den ihnen literarisch
kurz vorher bekannt gewordenen Aeneas entschieden. Diese Vorstellung wurde
jedoch aufgegeben, seit Lavinium Aeneas und die Penaten für sich in Anspruch
nehmen konnte, da sich in Rom die Auffassung von der Gründung der Stadt
durch Romulus[40] durchsetzte, die vermutlich aus einheimischer Überlieferung
stammt[41]. So bewahrte man in Rom den Aeneas lediglich noch als Vater oder
Großvater[42] des Stadtgründers und überließ man Lavinium die Penaten mit der
einschränkenden Behauptung, eigentlich seien es die römischen: *ibi dii penates
nostri.*

Wesen, Namen und Zahl dieser von Aeneas nach Italien gebrachten Penaten
war schon im Altertum unbekannt[43], was zu unterschiedlichen Spekulationen

---

[36] Stesich. FGrH 840 F 6 b nennt als Ziel der Flucht lediglich Ἑσπερία; obwohl Anchises die
Kiste mit den ἱερά trägt, scheint es fraglich, ob schon eine Verbindung mit der laviniatischen Überlieferung möglich ist.

[37] Hellanik. FGrH 4 F 84; vgl. Damastes FGrH 5 F 3; vgl. ferner Prokop Goth. 4,22,7, wo
Aeneas als Gründer Roms (τοῦ τῆς πόλεως οἰκιστοῦ) bezeichnet und von der Erhaltung
seines Schiffes als θέαμα gesprochen wird.

[38] F. BÖMER, Rom u. Troia 40: „daß aber die Römer sich für Aeneas entschieden, war
wiederum eine römische Tat"; ebd. „Die Entscheidung für Aeneas ist vielmehr eine römische Entscheidung, und mit 510 hat Rom begonnen, seine eigene Geschichte zu gestalten."

[39] Vgl. G. RADKE, in: Klass.Sprachen u.Literaturen 6, 1971, 93: „in diesem Jahre 508 ordnet
. . . der junge Staat sein Verhältnis mit den anderen Mächten und zugleich mit den Göttern".

[40] Es spielt dabei keine Rolle, ob in der Überlieferung (FGrH 840) von Romulus oder
Ῥῶμος, Sohn des Aeneas (F 21) oder des Odysseus (F 17) oder des Latinus (F 14a) oder
von einer Ῥώμη (Troerin F 14a) gesprochen wird, die auch Tochter des Askanios (F
18/9ab) oder des Italos oder des Telephos (F 40) heißt.

[41] Die Namen *Roma* und *Romulus* lassen sich mit den Lautvorgängen einer in Italien gespro-
chenen Sprache aus *r̄m-nā́ und *r̄m-lṓ- als zugehörig zu *Rḗmus* erklären; vgl. G. RADKE,
Die Götter Altitaliens², 1979, 273; DERS., in: Klass.Sprachen u.Lit. 6, 1971, 84.

[42] Aeneas galt als Vater des Romulus dem Alkimos (FGrH 840 F 12), dem Hegesianax (ebd.
F 21), dem Apollodor (ebd. F 40b) sowie Plut.Rom. 2,2. Dion.Hal.ant. 1,73,3 und als
Großvater des Romulus dem Eratosthenes (FGrH 840 F 20), dem Naev.frg. 25 MOR., dem
Ennius (b.Serv.auct.Aen. 1,273. Serv.Aen. 6,777) sowie Plut.Rom. 2,3. Dion.Hal.ant.
1,76,6.

[43] Macr.sat. 3,4,7 *qui sint autem di penates in libro quidem memorato* (i.e. *humanarum
secundo*) *Varro non exprimit.* Varro b.Serv.auct.Aen. 3,12 *quod eorum nomina nemo sciat*

führte[44]. Auch die moderne Annahme, es handele sich bei den laviniatischen Penaten um die Dioskuren[45], die durch eine hocharchaische Inschrift für Lavinium nachgewiesen sind[46], stößt auf verschiedene Schwierigkeiten: Waren die später als Penaten angesprochenen Kultgegenstände zur Zeit des Timaios noch anikonisches Gerät, dürften sie zweihundert Jahre früher im frühen 5. Jhdt. kaum mit den Namen der Zeussöhne angesprochen worden sein. Die Gleichsetzung der Götterbilder im römischen Penatentempel an der Velia mit den Dioskuren wird trotz aller Ähnlichkeit von Varro abgelehnt (s. u. S. 350). Das Verhältnis zwischen den laviniatischen und den römischen Penaten gestattet kaum einen Rückschluß von den einen auf die anderen, zumal die Überlieferung von der Weigerung der laviniatischen Gottheiten, nach Rom zu gehen, das verbietet. Der Annahme derartiger Vorstellungen steht auch der Kult der Castores am Forum Romanum im Wege.

II. Die aedes deum penatium in Rom

Daß es trotz der starken und nie bezweifelten Bindung der Penaten an Lavinium[47] auch in Rom einen Tempel dieser Gottheiten gab, kann nicht als eine der — mehrfach bekannten[48] — Kultübertragungen aus anderen Orten nach Rom ausgelegt werden[49], da sonst weder das Opfer der römischen Magistrate in Lavinium noch der Ausspruch *ibi dii penates nostri* (s. o.) verständlich wären. Die *aedes deum penatium* in Rom lag am Abkürzungsweg zu den Carinae zwischen höheren Gebäuden versteckt nahe dem Westhang der Velia[50] dort, wo

(vgl. ST. WEINSTOCK, a. O. 424 „namenlos"). Varro b.Arnob. 3,40 *nec eorum numerum nec nomina sciri.*

[44] Dazu gehören die Spekulationen des Nigidius Figulus, denen sich Cornelius Labeo anschloß (Serv.auct.Aen. 1,378 *Nigidius et Labeo deos penates Neptunum et Apollinem tradunt.* ebd. 2,325. 3,119. Macr.sat. 3,4,6. Arnob. 3,40).

[45] A. ALFÖLDI, Early Rome and the Latins, 268ff. = DERS., Das frühe Rom und die Latiner, 241ff. F. CASTAGNOLI, Dedica arcaica lavinate a Castore e Polluce, in: SMSR 30, 1959, 109ff. DERS., Lavinium I, 1972, 109. ST. WEINSTOCK, Two Archaic Instcriptions from Latium, in: JRSt 50, 1960, 112ff. DERS., in: RE XIX 1 (1937), 451.

[46] A. DEGRASSI, ILLRP nr. 1271a *Castorei Podlouqueique qurois.*

[47] Lucan. 7,394 *Laurentinosque penates.* Serv.Aen. 3,12 *penates vero apud Laurolavinium.*

[48] Aus Veii und Lanuvium wurden Kulte der Iuno, aus Falerii der Minerva, aus Tarracina der Fortuna und aus Aricia vielleicht der Diana (hier kann auch der Kult auf dem Aventin unabhängig von dem aricinischen Kulte sein) nach Rom übertragen; ebenso ungewiß ist die Herleitung des Kultes der Castores am Forum Romanum aus Tusculum (ST. WEINSTOCK, a. O. 450).

[49] Die Verehrung der Iuno Sospita aus Lanuvium in Rom (dort heißt sie bekanntlich Iuno Matuta [Liv. 34,53,3; vgl. G. RADKE, in: Rhein.Mus. 106, 1963, 329ff. DERS., Die Götter Altitaliens², 1979, 206]) kann nicht zum Vergleich herangezogen werden.

[50] Dion.Hal.ant. 1,68,1ff. Varro l.l. 5,54. vit.pop.Rom.frg. 7 RIPOSATI (b.Non. p. 531M.). Solin. 1,22. H. RIEMANN, Pacis Ara Augusti/Pacis Forum, in: RE XVIII 2 (1942), 2091.

später SS. Cosma e Damiano verehrt wurden[51], was offenbar ein Weiterleben des Kultes unter anderen Namen am gleichen Platze erkennen läßt. Die Treppe, die zu dem Tempel führte, ist vermutlich von den Censoren des Jahres 179 v. Chr. aus den Strafgeldern gebaut worden, die N.Equitius Cuppes und M'. Macellus zu zahlen hatten[52]; der Bau des Tempels selbst liegt dann noch weiter zurück: Seine Erwähnung in der Argeerurkunde[53] läßt darauf schließen, daß er im 3. Jhdt. v. Chr. schon bestand. Aus Anlaß von Prodigien wird er in den Jahren 167 v. Chr.[54] und 165 v. Chr.[55] erwähnt; Augustus ließ ihn erneuern[56].

In diesem Tempel befanden sich τῶν Τρωϊκῶν θεῶν εἰκόνες, sehr altertümliche Bilder angeblich zweier sitzender speertragender Jünglinge[57], wie sie in anderen alten Heiligtümern auch vorhanden gewesen sein sollen[58]. Ihnen konnte man offenbar nicht mehr ansehen, wen sie darstellten: Sie für Castor und Pollux[59] oder für die ithyphallischen Gottheiten vor den Toren von Samothrake[60] zu halten, lehnt Varro ab[61], wenn ihm auch eine Übereinstimmung mit dem Kult der dortigen *magni di* möglich erscheint, zumal sie in den Schriften der *augures* als *divi qui potes* bezeichnet werden[62]. Auch soll an der Basis des

2116. F. CASTAGNOLI, Il tempio dei Penati e la Velia, in: RFIC 24, 1946, 157ff. G. LUGLI, Roma antica. Il centro monumentale, Roma 1946, 226. F. COARELLI, Rom (übers. von A. ALLROGGEN-BEDEL), Freiburg—Basel—Wien 1975, 94.

[51] L. DEUBNER, Kosmas und Damian, Leipzig 1907, 52ff. O. RICHTER, Topographie der Stadt Rom², Handb.d.klass.Altertumswiss. III 3,2, München 1901, 161. S. B. PLATNER—TH. ASHBY, A Topographic Dictionary of Ancient Rome, Oxford 1929, 388f.

[52] Vgl. Varro b. Donat.Ter.Eun. 356 mit Cato frg. 90 P. und Paul.Fest. 42,9ff. 112,14ff. L.

[53] Vgl. ST. WEINSTOCK, a. O. 449.

[54] Liv. 45,16,5.

[55] Obsequ. 13.

[56] Monum.Anc. 19.

[57] Dion.Hal.ant. 1,68.

[58] R. H. KLAUSEN, Aeneas und die Penaten, II, 1840, 660. „Hierbei kann man wohl an nichts anderes denken als an die Heiligtümer einzelner römischer Familien. Die unter diesen von echt römischem oder latinischem Ursprung waren, betrachteten ihre Penaten, soviel wir sehn, als mit denen des römischen Volkes im Wesentlichen gleichartig“; das überzeugt mich nicht.

[59] G. WISSOWA, Rel.² 165: „In diesem Tempel erfuhr die Vorstellung von den Staatspenaten eine eigentümliche Veränderung und Verflachung. Der Wunsch, nach griechischem Vorbilde die verehrten Götter im Bilde darzustellen, nötigte, an die Stelle des undarstellbaren allgemeinen Begriffes von Gottheiten des Staatswohles bestimmte göttliche Individuen zu setzen; wie die Privatleute nach Ausweis der pompejanischen Bilder sich einzelne Götter zu Penaten ihres Hauses wählten, so mußte auch der Staat unter den von ihm anerkannten Göttern zu diesem Zwecke eine Wahl treffen, und diese fiel auf die Dioskuren.“

[60] Herod. 2,51. Serv.auct.Aen. 3,12 *simulacra duo virilia*. Hippolyt.ref.haeres. 5,8, ed. P. WENDLAND, GCS, Leipzig 1916 (Nachdr. Hildesheim 1977), 26.

[61] Varro l.l. 5,58 *terra enim et caelum, ut Samothracum initia docent, sunt dei magni, et hi quos dixi multis nominibus, non quas Samothracia ante portas statuit duas virilis species aeneas dei magni, neque ut volgus putat, hi Samothraces dii, qui Castor et Pollux, sed hi mas et femina et hi quos augurum libri scriptos habent sic „divi qui potes" pro illo, quod Samothraces „theoe dynatoe".*

[62] Vgl. Prob.ecl. 6,31 *Varro in logistorico qui inscribitur Curio de deorum cultu: tres arae sunt in circo medio ad columnas, in quibus stant signa: in una inscriptum Diis magnis, altera*

Götterbildes *magnis diis* gestanden haben[63]. Das könnte für Verg.Aen. 3,12. 8, 678 der Anlaß für die Zusammenstellung *penatibus et magnis dis* gewesen sein. Varro sieht in den Denkmälern des römischen Tempels eine männliche und eine weibliche Gottheit, die er in verschiedener Weise zu deuten versucht[64]. Eine Ähnlichkeit mit den Bildern der Dioskuren muß dennoch bestanden haben, da auch Münzen mit den Legenden DEI PENATES, DDP oder PP[65] zwei Jünglingsköpfe mit Attributen der Zeussöhne aufweisen; ferner könnte man die Nachricht *alii hastatos esse et in regia positos tradunt*[66] als Verwechslung zwischen der Regia und dem nahegelegenen Penatentempel ansehen; zu dieser Frage gehört auch die Auskunft, die *sacra penatium* werden von Saliern betreut[67]. Welche Priester den Penatenkult besorgten, ist freilich unbekannt[68], da weder die o.g. *flamines* und *pontifices* in Lavinium noch der *sacerdos deum penatium*, der in zwei Inschriften am Volusierdenkmal genannt wird[69], geeignet erscheinen.

Die Zweizahl der in der *aedes deum penatium* an der Velia verehrten Gottheiten — wer auch immer sie waren — schließt aus, Vesta[70] oder Ianus[71] zur Zahl der Penaten zu rechnen; ebenso wird die Deutung auf mehr als zwei Gottheiten — mindestens im öffentlichen Kult — ausgeschlossen[72].

Diis potentibuis, tertia (vgl. G. Wissowa, Ges.Abh., 116) *Diis ⟨valentibus, hoc est⟩ terrae et caelo;* vgl. Tertull.spect. 8.

[63] Varro b.Serv.Aen. 3,12 *unum esse dicit penates et magnos deos; nam et in basi scribebatur magnis diis.* Dion.Hal.ant. 1,68,1 heißt es: ἐν δὲ τούτῳ κεῖνται τῶν Τρωϊκῶν θεῶν εἰκόνες, ἃς πᾶσιν ὁρᾶν θέμις, ἐπιγραφὴν ἔχουσαι δηλοῦσαν τοὺς Πενάτας. Es macht den Eindruck, als sei der Wortlaut der genannten Inschrift ausgefallen; in diesem Falle müßte sie sinngemäß wie die bei Serv. a. O. genannte *magnis diis* gelautet haben, was Dion.Hal. a. O. als Hinweis auf die Penaten ansieht.

[64] Varro l.l. 5,58f. Da am Anfang von Serv.auct.Aen. 3,12 unter Zitat Varros eine Angabe steht, die dem authentischen Varrotext l.l. 5,58 widerspricht (*Varro et alii complures magnos deos adfirmant simulacra duo virilia, Castoris et Pollucis, in Samothracia ante portam sita*), wird man erst den nachfolgenden Satz (*alii deos magnos Caelum ac Terram putant ac per hoc Iovem et Iunonem*) als varronisch ansehen dürfen, zumal dessen erster Teil mit Varro l.l. 5,58 übereinstimmt.

[65] St. Weinstock, a. O. 449f.

[66] Serv.auct.Aen. 2,325 *alii hastatos esse et in regia positos tradunt.*

[67] Serv.auct.Aen. 2,325 *namque Samothraces horum penatium antistites Saos vocabant, qui postea a Romanis Salii appellati sunt; hi enim sacra penatium curabant: quos tamen penates alii Apollinem et Neptunum volunt, alii hastatos esse et in regia positos tradunt.*

[68] Nach Cic.har.resp. 12 kümmert sich der *pontifex maximus de deorum penatium Vestaeque matris caerimoniis.* Nach Dion.Hal.ant. 1,67,2 heißt der Führer der zur Betreuung der schließlich in Lavinium zurückgelassenen Leute Aigestos.

[69] CIL VI 2266 = 7283 *sacerdos [. . .] penatium.* 2267 = 7283a *sacer [. . .] deum penat [. . .].*

[70] Serv.auct.Aen. 2,296 *quaeritur, utrum Vesta etiam de numero penatium sit.* Macr.sat. 3, 4,11 *Vestam, quam de numero penatium aut certe comitem eorum esse manifestum est.*

[71] Prokop.Goth. 1,25,19.

[72] Nach Serv.auct.Aen. 2,325. Arnob. 3,40 sind Ceres, Fortuna und Pales, nach Serv.Aen. 3,12. 8,679. Serv.auct.Aen. 2,296. Macr.sat. 3,4,8. Arnob. 3,40 Iupiter, Iuno, Minerva und Mercurius, nach Mart.Cap. 1,41. Arnob. 3,40 die *di consentes* gemeint. Nigidius Figulus (b.Arnob. 3,40) *in libro sexto exponit et decimo, disciplinas Etruscas sequens, genera esse penatium quattuor et esse Iovis* (vgl. Mart.Cap. 1,41) *ex his alios, alios Neptuni, inferorum tertios, mortalium hominum quartos.*

Eine Verehrung der *dei penates* als personenhaft vorgestellter Gottheiten in der *aedes Vestae*[73] hat es m. E. nicht gegeben; wohl aber wäre es denkbar, daß die dort bezeugten ἱερὰ ἀπόρρητα[74] als Penaten gedeutet wurden[75], wofür die ähnlichen Verhältnisse im Tempel von Lavinium (s. o.) sprechen könnten. Es liegt in der Art der Kulthandhabung im Tempel der Vesta, daß die in ihm ruhenden *sacra* zwar unbekannt blieben, sich jedoch mannigfache Gerüchte um sie bildeten[76]; die Bezeichnung der dort aufbewahrten Kultmittel als *penus Vestae* (s. u.) kann aus sprachlichen Gründen dazu verführt haben, sich 'Penaten' im römischen Vestatempel vorzustellen.

Die *dei penates* wurden bei öffentlichen Maßnahmen[77] und in privaten Angelegenheiten[78] zusammen mit Iupiter als Schwurhelfer angerufen. Die Bauern opferten ihnen im Januar[79]; ein Staatsopfer erhielten sie am 14. Oktober[80], ohne daß die näheren Umstände bekannt sind. Daß ihnen die Arvalbrüder am 11. September 59 n. Chr. *pro salute et reditu Neronis* eine Kuh opferten[81], widerspricht

---

[73] Tac.ann. 15,41,1 *Numaeque regia et delubrum Vestae cum penatibus populi Romani exusta*; diese Stelle hat zu der Auffassung geführt, im Vestatempel seien die Bilder der Penaten aufgestellt (und das im Tempel eines bildlosen Kultes!): L. DEUBNER, in: CHANT. II, 435 „auch der Staat hatte seine Penaten; sie wurden im Vestatempel verehrt". Irreführende Erfindung behauptet: „verschmelzen die Penaten, die doch zunächst eher zu Consus gehörten," – auch das findet keinen Rückhalt in der Überlieferung! – „mit Vesta zu einer Einheit, die im Atrium Vestae verehrt wird" (K. LATTE, RRG, 108). Daß Nero Penatenbilder aus Edelmetall raubte, behauptet Suet.Nero 32,4 ohne Nennung der Herkunft.

[74] Dion.Hal.ant. 2,66,3 εἰσὶ δέ τινες, οἵ φασιν ἔξω τοῦ πυρὸς ἀπόρρητα τοῖς πολλοῖς ἱερὰ κεῖσθαί τινα ἐν τῷ τεμένει τῆς θεᾶς, ὧν οἵ τε ἱεροφάνται τὴν γνῶσιν ἔχουσι καὶ αἱ παρθένοι, wobei man nicht übersehen sollte, daß γνῶσις 'Kenntnis' und nicht 'Anblick' bedeutet; die Geschichte von der Erblindung des Pontifex L.Caecilius Metellus, der die *sacra* anläßlich ihrer Errettung aus der Feuersbrunst zu Gesicht bekommen hatte, spricht für eine Einschränkung des Zugangs allein auf die Vestalen. Das *sacrarium* der Ops durften nur die Vestalen und der *sacerdos publicus* betreten (Varro l.l. 4,21).

[75] G. WISSOWA, Rel.², 165 Varro „leugnete ausdrücklich, daß die im Tempel an der Velia dargestellten Götter die wahren Penaten seien; diese wären vielmehr in gewissen geheimnisvollen Symbolen, die im Penus Vestae aufbewahrt würden, enthalten". Die in der Anm. hierzu beigebrachten Stellen beziehen sich – mit Ausnahme der ersten – auf die laviniatischen Penaten, die von Aeneas mitgebracht worden waren.

[76] Dion.Hal.ant. 1,68,3 f. 69,2.4. 2,66,5. Strab. 6,264. Lucan. 9,994 nennen das Palladium, Plin.n.h. 28,39 einen *fascinus*.

[77] Vgl. die Lex Latin.Bant. CIL I² 582 Z. 17f.24 (ca. 100 v. Chr.), die Lex Iul.Genet.sive Urson. CIL I² 594 tab. 2 col. 3 Z. 19 (44 v. Chr.), die Lex Salpens. CIL II 1963 (= ILS 6088) col. 1 Z. 30/2 und die Lex Malacit. CIL II 1964 (= ILS 6089) col. 3 Z. 13/7 (beide 81/84 n. Chr.).

[78] Hor.epist. 1,7,94 *per genium dextramque deosque penates*; vgl. serm. 2,3,176.

[79] Menologia rust. CIL I² p. 280.

[80] Fast.viae Ardeat. bei A. DEGRASSI, I.I.XIII 2, p. 154 (den deutlich erkennbaren Worten *penat. in Velia* geht der Rest einer senkrechten Hasta voraus, worin DEGRASSI die letzte Spur von *[dis mag]n.* erkennen möchte); die Zuweisung zum 14. Dezember bei K. LATTE, RRG, 416. 416,8 ist irrig.

[81] W. HENZEN, Acta fratrum Arvalium, Berlin 1874 (Nachdr. Berlin 1967), LXXV . . . *magister collegii fratrum Arvalium nomine immolavit in Capitolio pro salute et reditu Neronis Claudi Caesaris Aug(usti) Germanici Iovi bovem marem, Iunoni vaccam, Minervae vaccam,*

der üblichen Regel *diis feminis feminas, mares maribus hostias immolare*[82]. Da die offizielle[83] griechische Übersetzung die im Tempel an der Velia verehrten Penaten θεοὶ κατοικίδιοι[84] nennt, liegt die Annahme einer Übertragung aus dem Kult des Einzelhauses in den Staatskult nahe, so daß ihnen erst dann als den *diis pub(licis) p(enatibus) p(opuli) R(omani) Q(uiritium)* geopfert wurde[85].

III. Die Penaten des römischen Einzelhauses

Der Name der Penaten soll darauf hinweisen, daß sie *in penetralibus aedium* verehrt wurden[86], wonach die *penetralia* auch als *penatium deorum sacraria* galten[87]. Sie sind die Gottheiten, *qui domi coluntur*[88], deren Altar die Herdstätte ist[89]. Ob ihre Verehrung mit der angeblich einmal üblichen Bestattung der Toten im Hause zusammenhängt, war im Altertum eine umstrittene Frage[90], die man jedoch wird verneinen müssen.

Die *dei penates* des Hauses wurden als *sigilla* verehrt, die auf einer *patella*[91] standen; literarische Berühmtheit erfuhren die kostbaren *penates hospitalesque dei* im Hause des Römers Cn.Pompeius Philo in Tyndaris, die Verres nach dem Mahle einfach an sich nahm und stahl[92]. Von Gesetzen zur Einschränkung von Luxus waren diese *sigilla* ausgenommen[93]. Den Penaten gaben die jungen Männer *deposita pueritia* ihre *bulla*[94], was einen festen Standort im Hause vor-

item in foro Augusto Genio ipsius taurum, Saluti vaccam, ante domum Domitianam dis penatibus vaccam. Da die *domus Domitiana* nach W. HENZEN, a. O. LXXVI *in sacra via* liegt, könnte der Platz der nahegelegenen *aedes deum penatium* gemeint sein; W. HENZEN, a. O. 85 hält diese Götter für die *penates domus imperatoris*.

[82] Arnob. 7,19. Vgl. G. WISSOWA, Rel.², 413.
[83] Bei Dion.Hal.ant.1,67,3 werden weitere griechische Übersetzungen genannt: θεοὶ πατρῷοι (vgl. auch Hygin.b.Macr.sat. 3,4,13 und Mon.Ancyr., Appendix, 2), κτήσιοι, γενέθλιοι, μύχιοι, ἑρκεῖοι; vgl. auch δυνατοί b.Varro l.l. 5,58.
[84] Mon.Ancyr. 19.
[85] Feriale Cuman. CIL I² p. 229 zum 6. März, dem Tage, an dem Augustus im Jahre 12 v. Chr. *pontifex maximus* wurde: *supplicat⟨i⟩o Vestae dijs pub(licis) p(enatibus) p(opuli) R(omani) Q(uiritium).*
[86] Serv.auct.Aen. 3,12; zur Formulierung vgl. Arnob. 3,40 *Varro qui sunt introrsus atque in intimis penetralibus caeli deos esse censet.*
[87] Paul.Fest. 231,1 L.
[88] Serv.Aen. 2,514; vgl. ebd. 469 *singula enim domus sacrata sunt diis: ut culina penatibus.*
[89] Serv.auct.Aen. 3,134. 11,211 u. a.
[90] Serv.Aen. 5,64 *ut et penates colantur in domibus*; jedoch Serv.Aen. 6,152 *nam di penates alii sunt.*
[91] Val.Max. 4,4,3; vgl. ST. WEINSTOCK, a. O. 427.
[92] Cic.Verr. 4,48.
[93] Liv. 26,36,6; zur Herstellung aus Edelmetall vgl. Suet.Nero 32,4 *ultimo templis compluribus dona detraxit simulacraque ex auro vel argento fabricata conflavit, in iis penatium deorum.*
[94] Schol.Pers. 5,31.

aussetzt. Man grüßte sie, wenn man das Haus verließ[95] und wenn man heimkehrte[96]. So ist es nicht verwunderlich, daß *penates* auch metonymisch für 'Haus'[97] gesagt werden konnte: *penates hominum sunt, deorum templa*[98]. In diesem privaten Bereiche, der keiner kultischen oder gesetzlichen Regelung unterworfen war, sondern sich nach den Vorstellungen des Einzelnen entwickeln konnte, bahnte sich eine Angleichung an andere Gottheiten des häuslichen Lebens und eine Vermischung mit den diesen eigentümlichen Formen an. Besonders nahe liegt die Verwechslung mit den Laren, deren ursprüngliches Wesen freilich völlig anderer Art ist: *Lar* kann in der Einzahl bestehen, hat einen substantivischen, aussagefähigen Namen[99] und gehört eher zum Grundstück[100] als zum Hause, von dessen Bewohnern eher zur *familia* als zum Hausherrn, während die *dei penates* nie in der Einzahl auftreten (s. u.) und in ihrem adjektivisch gebildeten Namen eine Abhängigkeit zum Ausdruck bringen (s. u. S. 355 ff.). Dennoch darf man wohl annehmen, daß in den Lararien auch Penaten verehrt wurden, ohne daß diese noch dem ursprünglichen Bilde entsprochen zu haben brauchen, das man sich von den *dei penates* machte: Daß sie auch *Gabino cinctu* dargestellt worden sein sollen[101], läßt diese Verwechslung deutlich erkennen.

Die Bindung der Penaten an das Einzelhaus dürfte trotz der späteren Entwicklung erst sekundär vom Hausherrn auf dessen Wohnsitz und seine Herdstätte übertragen sein. Das läßt sich aus der zweitältesten literarischen Bezeugung des Namens der Penaten schließen. Im 'Mercator' des Plautus (196 v. Chr.) verabschiedet sich Charinus mit den Worten (vv. 734 ff.):

> *Di penates meum parentum, familiai Lar pater,*
> *vobis mando, meum parentum rem bene ut tutemini.*
> *Ego mihi alios deos penates persequar, alium Larem,*
> *aliam urbem, aliam civitatem.*

Wenn er neue Penaten finden kann, haften sie an seiner Person, wie die, von denen er sich verabschiedet, nicht die des Hauses, sondern die Penaten seiner Eltern sind. Diese Personenbezogenheit, die von Anchises und Aeneas aus dem mythischen Rahmen geläufig ist, wird besonders deutlich, wenn arme, aber fromme Leute, aus ihrem Hause vertrieben, bei ihrem Fortgang als kostbarstes Gut ihre *dei penates* mit sich nehmen[102]. Diese Bindung gilt jedoch offenbar in hervorragendem Maße für *cives Romani*, zu denen die *dei penates* demnach eine besondere Beziehung haben[103].

---

[95] Plaut.Merc. 834 (aus dem Jahre 196 v. Chr.).
[96] Ter.Phorm. 311 (aus dem Jahre 161 v. Chr.); vgl. Colum. 1,8,20. Cic.prov.cons. 35.
[97] Vgl. G. Wissowa, Rel.², 162,1. St.Weinstock, a. O. 423 u. a.
[98] Schol.Stat.Theb. 1,643.
[99] Vgl. G. Radke, Die Götter Altitaliens², 1979, 171.
[100] Vgl. K. Latte, RRG, 90 ff.; ein besonderer Platz der Larenverehrung ist das *compitum*; vgl. G. Radke, a. O. 168.
[101] Schol.Pers. 5,31; vgl. jedoch auch Serv.Aen. 3,174 *nam dii, qui erant apud Laurolavinium, non habebant velatum caput.*
[102] Porph.Hor.c. 2,18,26; vgl. auch Cic.Sest. 145 u. a.
[103] Cic.Sest. 30; vgl. St. Weinstock, a. O. 425.

Nach der politischen Tätigkeit auf dem Forum zieht sich der Hausherr *intra domesticos penates* zurück[104]; bei der Rückkehr ins Haus nimmt man seine *dii penates* wieder in Besitz[105]. Wie offen hinsichtlich der personalen Vorstellung das Bild dieser häuslichen Penaten werden konnte, lehren Weihungen, die *dijbus et deabus penatibus familiaribus et Iovi ceterisve dijbus*[106] oder *I.O.M.dis deabusque hospitalibus penatibusque*[107] gelten. Die Penaten halfen in allen Lebenslagen; auch das geht aus den Inschriften hervor: *ob conservatam salutem suam suorumq(ue)*, weshalb *P.Ael.Marcianus praef. coh.* einen Altar errichten läßt[108], oder *dibus penatibus ob rem militarem votum solvit l.m.*[109] Man erwartet ihre Zuneigung, wenn man sich ordentlich verhält: *ita mihi deos penates propitios, ut ego hoc monimentum non violabo*[110]. Unter dieser Gewohnheit nahm der Name der Penaten in manchen Fällen die allgemeine Bedeutung von 'Götter' an[111].

IV. Der Name der dei penates

Zur Deutung der ursprünglichen kultischen Vorstellung kann die sprachliche Analyse des Namens der *dei penates* herangezogen werden. Er ist − von gelegentlichem Gebrauch vorwiegend der Dichter abgesehen[112] − so gestaltet, daß *penates* als adjektivisches Attribut an den Begriff *dei* gefügt wird[113]; ferner begegnet er ausnahmslos[114] im Plural, was zur Zweizahl im römischen Staatskult ebenso paßt wie zu der unbestimmten Zahl[115] im Kult von Lavinium oder im Einzelhause. Das Suffix *-āti-* bezeichnet eine Herkunft[116] oder Zugehörigkeit[117].

---

[104] Colum. 12 praef. 6 *ad requiem forensium exercitationum omni cura deposita patribus familias intra domesticos penates se recipientibus.*

[105] Cic.dom. 142.

[106] CIL VI 30991 (= ILS 3597).

[107] CIL VII 257 (= ILS 3598).

[108] CIL VII 257 (= ILS 3598).

[109] CIL XI 1920 (= ILS 3600).

[110] CIL XI 1286 (= ILS 3601).

[111] F. BÖMER, Rom u. Troia, 54; vgl. CIL II 172 *di deaeque omnes.*

[112] Vgl. Verg.Aen. 1,68.378.527.704. 2,293.514.747. 3,15 u. a. Hor.c. 2,4,15. 3,14,3. 23.19 (jedoch serm. 2,3,176 *per divos oratus uterque penatis.* epist. 1,7,94 *per genium dextramque deosque penates*) u. a.; vgl. aber auch Tac.ann. 15,41,1 *cum penatibus populi Romani*).

[113] Vgl. ST.WEINSTOCK, a. O. 418.

[114] Antistius Labeo (b.Fest. 298,18 ff. L.; vgl. Paul.Fest. 299,7 ff. L.) erörtert rein theoretisch die sprachliche Möglichkeit eines Singulars: *Penatis singulariter Labeo Antistius posse dici putat, quia pluraliter Penates dicantur; cum patiatur proportio etiam Penas dici, ut optimas, primas, Antias.*

[115] Arnob. 3,40 *nec eorum numerum nec nomina sciri.*

[116] M. LEUMANN, Lateinische Laut- und Formenlehre[6] = LEUMANN−HOFMANN−SZANTYR, Lateinische Grammatik I, Handb. d. Altertumswiss. II 2,1, München 1977, 345.

[117] ST. WEINSTOCK, a. O. 419.

Cic.nat.deor. 2,68 bietet eine Alternativlösung zum Verständnis des Namens: *sive a penu ducto nomine — est enim omne, quo vescuntur homines, penus — sive ab eo, quod penitus insident; ex quo etiam penetrales a poetis*[118] *vocantur.* Für die Verbindung mit *penitus* gibt es mehrere Zeugen bei jeweils unterschiedlicher Auslegung[119], während die erstgenannte Deutung lediglich[119a] im Spott des Firmicus Maternus (error. 14,1) einen Widerhall findet: *qui nihil aliud putant esse vitam nisi vescendi et potandi licentiam, hos* (scil. *deos penates*) *sibi deos ex cupiditatis suae humilitate finxerunt.*

Das Wort *penus* — seit Plautus[120] bezeugt — hat die antiken Grammatiker[121] wegen der dreifachen Möglichkeit seiner Flexion und die Juristen[122] wegen der damit bezeichneten Inhalte interessiert, so daß reichhaltiges Material zum Verständnis vorliegt. Alle[123] antiken Zeugnisse stimmen darin überein, daß *penus* 'Vorrat' — und zwar *esculenta et poculenta*[124] wie auch *ligna, carbones* und sogar *iumenta*[125] — bedeute, der in der *cella pen(u)aria*[126] oder an einem *locus penarius*[127] lagere. Da man den Vorrat *quasi penitus et in penetralibus*[128] aufbewahrte, kam es dazu, *ipsum penetral penus* zu nennen[129]. Keinesfalls[130] jedoch kann dem Worte *penus* die Bedeutung 'Vorratskammer' oder 'Speicher'

---

[118] Sen.Oed. 265. Phoen. 340 geht anscheinend auf ältere, nicht erhaltene Vorbilder zurück.

[119] Serv.auct.Aen. 3,12 *quos Romani penitus in cultu habent* (vgl. Gell. 4,1,17. Paul.Fest. 20, 19ff.L. Non. p. 51,3M.) und Serv.auct.Aen. 2,296 *per quos penitus spiramus* (= Macr. sat. 3,4,8).

[119a] Man könnte freilich auch bei Verg.Aen. 1,704 (*penum struere et flammis adolere penates*) eine Anspielung auf die Verbindung von *penates* mit *penus* sehen.

[120] Plaut.Capt. 472.771.920. Men. 120. Pers. 178.228.608. Trin. 253.

[121] Vgl. Gell. 4,1,2ff. Donat.Eun. 310. Serv.Aen. 1,703. Non. p. 51,3M. Charis. p. 94,21B. Folgende Formen sind belegt: Der *u*-Stamm ist feminin und begegnet in den Formen *penus* (nom.sg. Lucil. 1205.1350M. Dig. 33,9,1ff.), *penus* (gen.sg. Dig. 33,9,1,3), *penum* (acc. sg. Verg.Aen. 1,703f. Dig. 33,9,7; weitere Beispiele lassen das Geschlecht nicht erkennen: Lucil. 519M. Ter.Eun. 310), *penu* (abl.sg. Plaut.Capt. 472.920. Pers. 3,74. Dig. 33,9,2ff.), *penus* (acc.pl. Hor.epist. 1,16,72); der *s*-Stamm liegt vor in *penus omne* (Plaut.Pseud. 228), *penoris* (Dig. 33,9,1,5 pr.), *penori* (Dig. 33,9,3,5. 9) und *penora* (Paul.Fest. 231,8L.). Es gibt ferner einen *o*-Stamm (Plaut.Pseud. 178 *penus annuōs.* 608 *procurator peni*; vgl. nom. sg.ntr. *penum legatum* bei Dig. 33,9,4 pr.

[122] Vgl. Ulpian.Dig. 33,9,2.4. Paul.Dig. 33,9,5. Scaevola bei Gell. 4,1,19. Serv.Sulpicius ebd. 20. Masurius Sabinus ebd. 21.

[123] Nach Paul.Fest. 231,8f. L. (*penora dicuntur res necessariae ad victum . . . et locus earum penarius*) notwendige Wiederherstellung bei Serv.auct.Aen. 2,508 *et pen⟨ari⟩um dicimus locum, ubi conduntur, quae ad vitam sunt necessaria.*

[124] Vgl. Gell. 4,1,17. Dig. 33,9,3,1.

[125] Vgl. Gell. 4,1,20ff.

[126] Cic.Verr. 2,5 *cellam penariam.* Varro l.l. 5,162 *penariam ubi penus.* Charis. p. 140,19B.; jedoch Suet.Aug. 6. Dig. 33,9,3,8.11 *cella penuaria.*

[127] Paul.Fest. 231,9L. Serv.auct.Aen. 2,508.

[128] Serv.auct.Aen. 3,12.

[129] Serv.auct.Aen. 3,12.

[130] Die einzige, jedoch nur scheinbare Ausnahme bildet die Formulierung *penus Vestae*; dazu s. u. S. 359f.

zugeschrieben werden[131]; dementsprechend gibt es auch keine Beziehung der Penaten zu dem Gotte Consus[132]. In seiner vierten Rede gegen M'.Acilius Glabrio im Jahre 190 v. Chr. gebrauchte Cato das Wort *penatores*[133], das in Analogie zu *caduceator, gladiator* oder ähnlichen Bildungen nur die Bedeutung „wer *frumenta penusque*[134] trägt" haben kann; es handelt sich um Leute, die den Vorrat, nicht die Vorratskammer tragen.

Die Berichterstatter unterscheiden sich in der näheren Festlegung des Begriffes 'Vorrat': Während die einen in *penus* das erkennen, was für eine längere Zeit aufgehoben werden soll[135], bezeichnen die anderen *penus* als den für den Hausherrn, den *pater familias* bzw. *dominus*, und seine nächste Umgebung aufbewahrten Vorrat[136]. Da der zur Präposition erstarrte Lokativ *penes* 'bei' als Ausdruck für *dominium* und *potestas*[137] verstanden wurde oder als Bezeichnung für den Zustand der *potestas*[138] galt, ist die Zusammengehörigkeit von *penus* im Sinne des dem Hausherrn vorbehaltenen Vorrats und *penes* nicht zu übersehen. In gewissem Sinne läßt sich die Bestimmung für eine langdauernde Aufbewahrung in der Beziehung zum Hausherrn und von da aus zum Hause einbeziehen. Die Zugehörigkeit von *penes* ist zur Erklärung des Penatennamens mit Recht betont worden[139].

Obwohl sich eine sprachliche Herleitung dieser Wörter einschließlich des Namens der *dei penates* von *potis* schon wegen ihrer Nähe zum *dominus* wahrscheinlich machen ließe[140], wird man bei der Klarheit der Sachlage und der Überzeugungskraft der vorgebrachten Aussagen der Juristen auf Hypothesen zur Verdeutlichung des komplizierten Lautvorgangs verzichten dürfen. Es muß jedoch bewußt bleiben, daß der Name der *dei penates* unmittelbar weder von *penus* 'Vorrat' noch von *penes* 'bei, im Hause von' gebildet werden konnte[141], sondern auf einen auch in diesen beiden Wörtern enthaltenen Wortstamm zurückgeht, der − mindestens inhaltlich − von *potis* 'Herr' nicht zu trennen ist. Es scheint berechtigt, sie „Geister des sich selbst versorgenden Hausstandes"[141a]

---

[131] Vgl. G. Wissowa, Rel.², 162. F. Bömer, Rom u. Troia, 52. K. Latte, RRG, 89. G. Dumézil, Rel.rom.arch., 346 u. a.; Zweifel bei P. Boyancé, in: REA 54, 1952, 112f.

[132] K. Latte, RRG, 108.

[133] Fest. 268,22f. L. *penatores qui penus gestant* mit Zitat von Cato or.frg. 66 Malc. = or.frg. XIII J.; *caduceator* bei Cato (Paul.Fest. 41,11f. L.). Petron. 108,12.

[134] Hor.epist. 1,16,72 *portet frumenta penusque.*

[135] Plaut.Pers. 178 *penus annuŏs.* Gell. 4,1,17 *longae usionis gratia.* ebd. 23 *quae satis sint usui annuo.* Serv.Aen. 1,703 *penus vero temporis longi.* Paul.-Fest. 231,8 *ad victum ⟨non⟩ cotidianum.*

[136] Ter.Eun. 310. Gell. 4,1,17.21. Dig. 33,9,3,1.3.4.6.4,2.

[137] Paul.Fest. 20,19ff. L. *apud et penes in hoc differunt, quod alterum personam cum loco significat, alterum personam et dominium ac potestatem.*

[138] Fest. 296,30L. (= Paul.Fest. 297,10L.) *penes nos, quod in potestate nostra est.*

[139] E. Norden, Alt-Germanien, Leipzig–Berlin 1934, 98,4.

[140] Vgl. G. Radke, Die Götter Altitaliens², 1979, 249.

[141] Die Formulierung bei St. Weinstock, a. O. 420 „*penates* ist nur indirekt, d. h. durch ein hypothetisches adverbiales Zwischenglied mit *penus* zu verbinden" reicht nicht zur Klarstellung des Verhältnisses aus.

[141a] R. H. Klausen, Aeneas u. die Penaten, 647.

zu nennen, sofern die Stellung des Hausherrn gebührend berücksichtigt wird.
Nach Varro l.l. 5,58 heißen die Penaten in den Auguralbüchern *divi qui potes*;
er hält das für eine Übersetzung des griechischen Namens der samothrakischen
θεοὶ δυνατοί. Man kann die Formulierung aber auch als einen Bezug auf die
eigentliche Bedeutung dieser Gottesvorstellung ansehen, zumal das für die Etymologie benötigte Wort *potis* vorliegt. Bei der Deutung der Penaten als der
Götter des Hausherrn kann man sich auf ihr Verhältnis zu Anchises berufen[142].

Schwierig gestaltet sich die Frage der Beziehung von *penus* zu *penitus*, den
beiden Begriffen, die Cicero alternativ einander gegenüberstellt. Mit Sicherheit
kann man jedoch wohl sagen, daß *penitus* nicht von *penus* und *penus* nicht von
penitus abgeleitet, sondern allenfalls beide auf eine gemeinsame Wurzel zurückzuführen sind; aber selbst das ist nicht sicher[143]. Die − sachlich berechtigte −
Verbindung zwischen *penetralia* und *penatium deorum sacraria*[144] dürfte auf
volksetymologischer Grundlage vertieft worden sein; sonst wären Ausdrücke
wie *avi penetralia Turni* (Sil. 1,668) oder *penetrale parentum* (Sil. 13,62) für die
Penaten nicht verständlich.

V. *Der* penus Vestae

Wenn es möglich war, *ipsum penetral* nach dem dort lagernden Vorrat
penus zu nennen (s. o.), bereitet das eine von der bisher üblichen[145] Deutung
abweichende Beurteilung der Formulierung vor: *et ipsum penetral penus dicitur,
ut hodie quoque penus Vestae claudi et aperiri dicitur* (Serv.auct.Aen. 3,12). Die
Hervorhebung eines gegenwärtigen Zustandes läßt erkennen, daß es früher
anders war, daß es sich bei dieser Verwendung des Namens um das Ergebnis
einer jüngeren Entwicklung handelt. Der Vorgang, den das um des Sprach-

---

[142] Vgl. J. Götte, Vergil, Aeneis³, München 1971, 774 „(Radke) versteht daher unter den P.
die Götter, die sich um die Dinge in der *potestas* des Hausherrn kümmern. Diese Auffassung wird u. E. dem Wesen der in der 'Aeneis' wirkenden Penaten . . . eher gerecht als die
anderen Deutungen. Denn Vorratsgötter wirken nicht mit der . . . sich offenbarenden geheimnisvollen Macht. Für Radke spricht auch die von Weinstock betonte Tatsache, daß
nur ein *dominus, pater familias, civis Romanus* Penaten hat".

[143] Vgl. Walde−Hofmann, LEW II, 281.283. Die von St. Weinstock, a. O. 418 angenommene Entwicklung von *penus* 'das Innere' über *penus* 'Vorratsraum' zu *penus* 'Vorrat'
bzw. 'Speisevorrat' übersieht nicht nur die entscheidende Beziehung zum Hausherrn,
sondern vertauscht auch die beiden letzten von ihm angenommenen Glieder der Entwicklung: Konnte man statt *penetral* einfach *penus* sagen (Serv.auct.Aen. 3,12), so bedeutet
das, die Vorstellung 'Vorrat' impliziere auch den Raum, in dem dieser aufbewahrt wird.
Vgl. die Entwicklung von lat. *officium* zu ital. *ufficio*, engl. *office*.

[144] Paul.Fest. 231,1 L. *penetralia sunt penatium deorum sacraria.*

[145] Vgl. G. Wissowa, Rel.², 159. C. Koch, Vesta, in: RE VIII A 2 (1958) 1727. St. Weinstock, a. O. 444.

cum penatibus populi Romani besser verstehen und gewinnt die bei Serv.auctus und Macrobius gestellte Frage ein anderes Gewicht: Sie ist natürlich weder von dem Verfasser des Vergilkommentars noch von Macrobius selbständig aufgeworfen worden, sondern geht auf eine gemeinsame Quelle zurück. Das könnte ein Ovidkommentar des 3. nachchristl. Jhdts.[169], der die Metamorphosenstelle (15,864f.) mißvertanden hatte, oder aber auch des Augustus Bibliothekar Iulius Hyginus selbst sein, dem man zutrauen darf, daß er in seinem Buche 'De dis penatibus'[170] ein solches Problem erörterte; das wird um so wahrscheinlicher, als Macr.sat. 3,4,12 ihn gerade im Anschluß an den Bericht über die Opfer in Lavinium zitiert und dabei hervorhebt, Hyginus habe noch hinzugefügt, die Penaten heißen — man muß annehmen: bei diesem Kultakt — θεοὶ πατρῷοι.

Dementsprechend wird man auf die Vorstellung verzichten dürfen, Vesta und die Penaten seien aufgrund ihrer Beziehungen zum Herde miteinander verbunden worden[171]. Hinsichtlich der Göttin ist die Zugehörigkeit zum Herd des Einzelhauses schon längst bezweifelt worden[172]; andererseits passen die Penaten als Götter des für den Hausherrn aufbewahrten Vorrats wenig zu Vesta, zu der man um die *salus publica populi Romani* betet[173]. Erst als diese Grundbedeutungen in Vergessenheit geraten waren — ein Vorgang, den das Geheimnis um die *sacra* besonders gefördert hat —, konnte man Vesta und Penaten zusammenstellen, weil sich um beide der *pontifex maximus* zu kümmern hatte. Seit das Augustus war, konnte eine solche Auslegung in die offizielle Vorstellung eingehen.

VII. Das Bild der Vesta

Aus den Kalendern wird bekannt (s. o.), daß im Hause des Augustus ein *signum* der Vesta geweiht war; sie sagen aber nichts darüber aus, daß es einen Tempel oder eine *aedicula*[174] auf dem Palatium gegeben habe. Das erwähnte

---

[169] G. Radke bei F. Altheim, Literatur und Gesellschaft im ausgehenden Altertum II, Halle 1950, 280–299.

[170] Hygin.b.Macr.sat. 3,4,13.

[171] A. Brelich, Vesta, 75.

[172] G. Wissowa, Rel.², 157. G. Dumézil, Rel.Rom.Arch. 311. H. Hommel, ANRW I 2 (1972), 399 „nichts anderes als der Herd"; vgl. jedoch U. von Wilamowitz-Möllendorff, Glaube der Hellenen I², Berlin 1955, 155 „Hestia ist der Herd, Vesta das Herdfeuer".

[173] Gell. 1,12,14.

[174] A. Degrassi, MDAI(R) 62, 1955, 144ff. hat nachgewiesen, daß in den Fast.Praen. zum 28. April 1. die Lücke zwischen *di[* und *]et* nicht groß genug ist, um die Buchstaben *[e aedicula]* aufnehmen zu können, und 2. der vor *et* erhaltene Buchstabenrest eindeutig als eine senkrechte Hasta zu erkennen ist und daher nicht zu *ą*, wohl aber zu *ṃ* ergänzt werden kann. In Übereinstimmung mit den Fast.Caer. zum gleichen Tage (s. ob., Anm. 164) schreibt er daher *eo di[e signu]ṃ et [ara] Vestae* usw. Damit ist eine große Reihe von Schlußfolgerungen in fast allen neueren Bearbeitungen des Vestakultes hinfällig geworden, die von einem Vestatempel oder einer Vestakapelle auf dem Palatium ausgehen.

Götterbild außerhalb eines geweihten Kultraumes steht jedoch nicht allein: Unter den vergoldeten Bildern der zwölf *dei consentes*[175] befand sich nach dem Zeugnis des Enn.ann. 62 auch ein solches der Vesta. Ihr Bild wurde ferner ebenfalls anläßlich des Zwölfgötter-Lectisterniums im Jahre 217 v. Chr. neben dem des Volcanus verehrt und herumgetragen[176]. Über die Existenz eines Kultbildes in der *aedes Vestae* selbst war man sich noch in ciceronischer Zeit im Unklaren: Das zeigt sich in den Schilderungen der Ermordung des Q.Mucius Scaevola auf Befehl des jüngeren Marius im Jahre 82 v. Chr. Als Platz des Mordes werden μικρὸν πρὸ τοῦ βουλευτηρίου[177], *ante penetrale deae*[178], *in vestibulo*[179], und *in templo*[180] angegeben; hier soll Scaevola noch den Altar umfaßt haben[181]. Am weitesten geht die Darstellung Ciceros: Das *simulacrum* der Göttin sei vom Blute des Opfers bespritzt worden[182]. Mag Cicero auch daran geglaubt haben, die genaue Aussage Ov.fast. 6,295 ff. widerspricht dem:

> *Esse diu stultus Vestae simulacra putavi,*
> *mox didici curvo nulla subesse tholo:*
> *Ignis inextinctus templo celatur in illo,*
> *effigiem nullam Vesta nec ignis habet.*

Damit stimmen Darstellungen republikanischer Münzen — freilich mit dem Bilde einer *sella curulis* — sowie solche augusteischer Zeit überein; erst nach dem neronischen Brande im Jahre 64 n. Chr. erkennt man auf den Münzen ein Kultbild im Innern des Tempels[183]. Das Vestabild bei dem vorgenannten Lectisternium kann unabhängig davon gezeigt worden sein, daß im Tempel selbst kein Kultbild stand; man hat auch an eine Vesta-Büste gedacht[184].

Der Unterschied zwischen den Vorstellungen, die das Fehlen eines Bildwerkes in der *aedes Vestae* begründen[185], und dem Gottesbild unter den *dei consentes* auf der anderen Seite des Forums lassen sich nur durch griechischen Einfluß — Vorbild der Hestia[186] — erklären, der jedoch auf den eigentlichen Kult keine Einwirkung hatte. Da Augustus den uraltheiligen Vestatempel nicht auf das Palatium umsetzen konnte, stellte er wenigstens ein *signum* der Göttin auf, wofür er sich auf das Bild unter den *dei consentes* hätte berufen können, wenn jemand Anstoß nehmen wollte. Daraufhin konnte beim Neubau nach dem

---

[175] Varro r.r. 1,1,4.
[176] Liv. 22,10,9.
[177] Appian.civ. 1,88.
[178] Lucan. 2,126.
[179] Liv.epit. 86.
[180] Comment.Lucan. 2,126.
[181] Flor. 2,9. Augustin.civ. 3,28.
[182] Cic. de or. 3,10. nat.deor. 3,80; vgl. Adnot.Lucan. 2,126.
[183] Vgl. C. KOCH, in: RE VIII A 2 (1958), 1725.
[184] Vgl. C. KOCH, in: RE VIII A 2 (1958), 1728 nach Liv. 40,59,7.
[185] Vgl. F. BÖMER, Rom u. Troia, 68 ff. 113 ff.
[186] Vgl. Süss, Hestia, in: RE VIII 1 (1912), 1293 ff. Nach Verg.Aen. 2,296 holt Aeneas das Vestabild aus Troia.

Brande besten Gewissens auch ein Kultbild der Vesta in ihrem Tempel errichtet werden.

Anderer Art sind die Statuetten, die nach Ausweis von Münzen republikanischer wie augusteischer Zeit auf der Spitze des kegelförmigen Daches standen[187]. Für sie gibt es noch ein sehr spätes Zeugnis bei Alberic.imag.deor. 17: *supra pinnaculum autem templi depicta erat ipsa Vesta in formam virginis infantem Iovem suo sinu fovens*[188]. Alberich hat den Tempel am Forum zweifellos nicht mehr selbst gesehen[189], da er ihn sonst nicht *latum et spatiosum* hätte nennen können, und schöpft sein Wissen demnach aus einer literarischen Überlieferung; da diese mit den Münzbildern übereinstimmt, darf man ihr Glauben schenken. Es ist jedoch zweifelhaft, ob die Gestalt dieser Statuette mit Recht als Vesta bezeichnet werden darf und nicht eher eine andere Deutung erfordert.

VIII. Die Rolle der Vestalen

An anderer Stelle[189a] ist darauf aufmerksam gemacht worden, daß die Stellung der Vestalin weder als Königstochter oder Hausfrau am Königsherd noch als eines Vergehens Verurteilte verstanden werden darf[190]. Die runde *aedes*, in der sie Dienst tut, erinnert an die alte Grabform; die rechtliche Stellung der Vestalen, die *legibus non tenentur*[191], ihr Ausscheiden aus der *patria potestas* bei Antritt ihres Dienstes *sine emancipatione ac sine capitis minutione*[192], die ihr dargebrachte Ehrerweisung durch Senken der *fasces* wie beim Vorüberziehen eines *funus*[193], ihre 'Hinrichtung' durch Sturz vom tarpeischen Felsen[194] oder

---

[187] Vgl. C. KOCH, in: RE VIII A 2 (1958), 1725.1728.

[188] Ähnlichkeit des Textes bei Alberich (10. Jhdt.) mit dem bei Mart.Cap. 1,72 ist nicht zu verkennen; Alberich geht jedoch in seiner Aussage über die des Mart.Cap. (5. Jhdt.) hinaus, kann also nicht aus ihm abgeschrieben haben.

[189] Vgl. die Maßnahmen gegenüber den römischen Kulten durch die Kaiser Gratian i. J. 382 (SEECK, Gratianus Nr. 3, in: RE VII 2 [1912], 1838) und Theodosius in den Jahren 391 und 394 (A. LIPPOLD, Theodosius I. [= Nr. 10], in: RE Suppl. XIII [1973], 891.904.908), wozu auch die Schließung des Vestatempels gehörte. Während Philocal. CIL I² p. 266 i. J. 354 die Vestalia noch erwähnt, fehlen sie bei Polem.Silv. CIL I² p. 267 i. J. 448/9 und bei Auson.fer.Rom. p. 104 PEIPER (Todesjahr 393 oder 394).

[189a] G. RADKE, Die Götter Altitaliens² 320ff.; DERS., in: ANRW I 2 (1972), 430ff.

[189] Vgl. C. KOCH, in: RE VIII A 2 (1958), 1742f.

[191] Serv.auct.Aen. 11,206.

[192] Gell. 1,12,9. Paul.Fest. 61,25ff.L. Gai inst. 1,300.

[193] Zum Senken der *fasces* vgl. Sen.contr. 6,8; sie werden bei der Ansprache an das Volk (Liv. 2,7,7. Val.Max. 4,1,1), bei der Begegnung mit einem höheren Magistrat (Plin.n.h. 7,112. Cic.Brut. 22. Dion.Hal.ant. 8,44) und bei der Begegnung mit einem *funus* (Tac.ann. 3,2,2) gesenkt; vgl. G. RADKE, in: ANRW I 2 (1972), 431.

[194] Sen.contr. 1,3,1ff. Quint.inst. 7,8,3.

durch Lebendigvergraben[195], beides unter größter Ehrerbietung seitens des *pontifex maximus*[196], sowie das Fehlen eines Totenopfers, das offenbar schon bei ihrem Eintritt in den Vestalendienst an ihr vollzogen wurde[197], haben die Auffassung begründet, es handele sich bei den Vestalen um 'lebendige Tote', denen allein deshalb auch der Zugang zu dem 'Grabe', an das die Form des Vestatempels erinnert, offenstand[197a]. Dann sind es also Mädchen, die wie die lokrischen Jungfrauen in Ilion[198] unter Beobachtung mannigfacher Tabus für ein aus gegebenem Anlaß notwendiges Opfer *pro salute populi* aufbewahrt werden: In der alten mittelmeerischen Gesellschaft wurde das Mädchen, das sich außerhalb der Ordnung ihrer Familie und Gemeinde mit einem Außenstehenden, Fremden eingelassen hatte, unter der fingierten Voraussetzung, dieser Fremde sei ein Gott gewesen, diesem Gotte durch eine 'indirekte' Tötung[199], d. h. durch Steinigung, Lebendigbegraben – zur Gleichwertigkeit beider Maßnahmen vgl. die Androhung der Steinigung bei Soph.Ant. 35 f. und die Ausführung des Einmauerns ebd. 773 ff. – oder Felsensturz – bei Danae zuerst Einschließung und dann Felsensturz (vgl. Pherek.FGrH 3 F 10 u. a.) – überantwortet, um die Übertretung der althergebrachten Lebensordnung nicht zum Schaden für die Gemeinde werden zu lassen. Diese Maßnahme war gleichsam stellvertretend auf einen kleinen Kreis junger Frauen beschränkt, die während ihres Gottesdienstes höchste Ehren erfuhren, im Falle des Bedarfes eines solchen Opfers jedoch als 'Gottesbraut'[200] aus dem Wege geräumt wurden; der ihnen jeweils

---

[195] Plin.ep. 4,11,6 f. Plut.Num.10. quaest.Rom. 96. Dion.Hal.ant. 2,67,4. Als mythisches Beispiel vgl. das Schicksal der Alope (Paus. 1,39,2), während die Einschließung der Danae eher dem zwangsweisen Priesteramt der Rea Silvia entpricht.

[196] Plut.Num. 10. Dion.Hal.ant. 2,67,4; F. Bömer, Pompa, in: RE XXI 2 (1952), 1984 vergleicht die *pompa funebris*. Nach Hor.c. 3,30,8 f. geleitet der *pontifex maximus* die Vestalin (doch wohl zum Sturz von der *rupes Tarpeia*) aufs Kapitol; er führt sie ebenso vor dem Lebendigbegraben auf dem *campus sceleratus* an der Hand (Dion.Hal.ant. 2,67,4); jede Berührung mit dem Henker wird vermieden (Plin.ep. 4,11,9. Sen.contr. 1,3,7).

[197] Das Totenopfer war offenbar schon bei Lebzeiten an ihr vollzogen worden (vgl. Plut. quaest.Rom. 96 p. 286 F.), was auch durch die Formulierung *virgines sacratas* (Isid.or. 5,26,24) zum Ausdruck kommt.

[197a] Vgl. Lucan. 1,598 *Troianam soli cui fas videre Minervam* (damit ist das Palladium im Innern des Vestatempels gemeint). G. Wissowa, Vesta, in: Myth.Lex. VI (1929–1937), 251 vermutet – m.E. mit Recht –, daß nur die *Vestalis maxima* das 'Allerheiligste' betreten darf; vgl. u. Anm. 201.

[198] Serv.auct.Aen. 1,41 (nach Annaeus Placidus). Strab. 13,600. Apollod.epit. 6,20 ff. Schol. Lykophr. 1159. Aelian.frg. 47 Hercher. Plut.ser.num.vind. 12. Aen.Tact.comm. 31,24. Die Historizität wird durch die Inschrift bei A. Wilhelm, Die lokrische Mädcheninschrift, in: JÖAI 14, 1912, 163 ff. aus dem 3. vorchristl. Jhdt. nachgewiesen.

[199] Man wagt nicht, das zu beseitigende μίασμα zu töten, ja, vermeidet sogar, es zu berühren (vgl. Plut.quaest.Rom. 96 p. 286 F.); vgl. H. Hommel, in: ANRW I 2 (1972), 397 ff. G. Radke, Polykrite, in: RE XXI 2 (1952), 1756. F. Schwenn, Die Menschenopfer bei den Griechen und Römern, RVV 15,3, Gießen 1915, 29. C. Koch, in: RE VIII A 2 (1958), 1751. *Arae humiles* beim Vesta-Opfer wie bei Mater Terra (Vitruv. 4,9).

[200] Zur Tracht der Vestalin als Brauttracht vgl. H. Dragendorff, Die Amtstracht der Vestalinnen, Rhein.Mus. 51, 1896, 281 ff.

vorgeworfene Inzest — unabhängig von seinem wirklichen Vollzug — bot demnach nur eine gleichsam 'historische' Begründung[201].

Das Musterbeispiel einer Vestalin, die sich durch ihre Verbindung mit
einem 'Gotte' außerhalb der Gesellschaftsordnung gestellt hatte, ist Rea Silvia
oder Ilia, deren Sturz in den Fluß[202] mit den zahlreichen Beispielen aus griechischer Mythologie[203] übereinstimmt; in ihnen dient die 'heilige Legende' lediglich
der Erklärung eines Kultaktes. Es geht dabei nicht um die Verletzung der
Keuschheit — auch wenn die spätere Auslegung das in den Vordergrund rückt:
Silvia fit mater; Vestae simulacra[204] *feruntur virgineas oculis opposuisse manus*
(Ov.fast. 3,45 f.) —, sondern um den Verstoß gegen die Sippenordnung; andernfalls hätte das römische Volk die Erbschaften der berühmten *meretrices* Acca
Larentia und Flora nicht so dankbar annehmen können; denn auch das Ver-
mögen der Vestalin — das legendäre Beispiel wird in der Geschichte der Gaia
Taracia geliefert — fiel bei ihrem Tode an den *populus Romanus*[205]. Wie ein
solches Opfer als Bereinigung eines Bruchs der Gesellschaftsordnung entstand,
führte es sekundär zur Abwendung einer drohenden oder schon bestehenden
Gefahr: Freiwillige Mädchenopfer schützten in Feindes- und Krankheitsnot[206].
Bei der Vestalin verbindet sich beides, wenn auch scheinbar in umgekehrter
Reihenfolge: Eine Bedrohung des römischen Volkes wird als Folge eines
Vestaleninzestes gedeutet und durch Vollzug des Opfers beseitigt. So glaube ich,

[201] Vgl. die Stimmung des römischen Volkes bei Bekanntwerden des Vestalenfrevels i. J. 114
v. Chr. bei Cass.Dio frg. 85,1 f. MELBER. Der Vorstellung, daß ein Mädchen durch eine
der Gesellschaftsordnung zuwiderlaufende Verbindung, d. h. durch ἀθεμιτομιξία, Gefahr
(vgl. Dion.Hal.ant. 2,67,5) heraufbeschworen habe, entspricht es auch, daß bei gleich-
zeitigem Vergehen mehrerer Vestalen offenbar nur eine einzige die 'Strafe', lebendig ver-
graben zu werden, erfuhr; vgl. Ascon.Cic.Mil. 32 p. 46 CL. (zu 114/3 v. Chr.) und Liv.
22,57,2 (zu 216 v. Chr.). Es wäre vorstellbar, daß die *Vestalis maxima* als diejenige galt,
die als erste an der Reihe war, geopfert zu werden, und deshalb die Bezeichnung *maxima*
trug, durch die eine besondere Fülle von Fähigkeiten ausgedrückt wurde; vgl. Neuent-
fachen des Feuers durch Auflegen des Tuches der Aemilia (Val.Max. 1,1,7. Dion.Hal.ant.
2,68,3 f.), Wassertragen in einem Siebe durch Tuccia (Val.Max. 8,1 absol. 5. Dion.Hal.ant.
2,69,1) und Flottmachen des Schiffes der Mater magna durch Claudia Quinta (Ov.fast. 4,
305 ff.).

[202] Ennius bei Porph.Hor.c. 1,2,17. Serv.Aen. 1,273; vgl. Ps.Acro Hor.c. 1.2.10; daran wird
die Vorstellung einer ehelichen Verbindung mit Anio geknüpft.

[203] Vgl. Aerope bei Soph.Ai. 1297 mit Schol. und Komaitho bei Paus. 7,19,2 ff. als Beispiele
für den Felsensturz; zur Tötung vgl. Eulimene (Parthen. 35) und die Tochter des Aristo-
demos (Paus. 4,9,4 ff.), die beide für das Wohl des Vaterlandes geopfert werden sollten,
vorher aber schon geschwängert waren, so daß beide Motive vereinigt sind.

[204] Dieses Vesta-Bild in Alba Longa ist mythisch und kann nicht für die römische *aedes Vestae*
in Anspruch genommen werden.

[205] Labeo b.Gell. 1,12,18; zu Acca Larentia, Gaia Taracia und Fufetia vgl. Gell. 7,7,1 f. W.
EISENHUT, Gaia Taracia, in: Kl.Pauly II (1967), 658 f.

[206] Vgl. die Töchter des Erechtheus (R. ENGELMANN, Erechtheus, in: Myth.Lex. I, 1 [1884–
86], 1298) und ihren Kult als παρθένοι (Suid.Phot. s. v.), ζεῦγος τριπάρθενον (Eurip.
frg. 359 bei Hesych. s. v.), Ὑάδες (Schol.Arat. 172), Ὑακινθίδες (Demosth.epitaph. 27)
sowie ferner die Leokoren (Aelian.v.h. 12,38 u. a.), die Skedasiden (Plut.Pelop. 21) und
Agraulos (Philoch. FGrH 328 F 105).

daß man die Statuette einer weiblichen Gestalt mit einem Kinde auf dem Arm nicht als Darstellung der Vesta — von dieser sah man kein Kultbild —, sondern als Hinweis auf die Vestalin zu verstehen hat.

Aus der Art der von den Vestalen verwendeten Kultmittel vermutet C. KOCH in RE VIII A 1767: „Vesta muß ein betontes Interesse am Geheimnis der Fruchtbarkeit in der Welt gehabt haben"; auch H. HOMMEL, ANRW I 2, 419f., kommt zu dem Schluß, „daß in der Tat der phallische 'Naturaspekt', dem die altertümliche Feuererzeugung beigesellt ist, der allerältesten, sozusagen prähistorischen Schicht der Vestaverehrung zugehört, während der soziale Haus- und Großfamilienaspekt erst allmählich mit der Ausbildung einer patriarchalischen Sippenorganisation aufkommen und dominant werden konnte". Wenn ich auch die Beweisführung — Feuerherstellung durch Reiben des τρύπανον auf der ἐσχάρα mit dem Geschlechtsakt verglichen, für den sogar sprachlich entsprechende Ausdrücke verwendet werden[207] — nicht nachzuvollziehen vermag, stimme ich dem Ergebnis restlos zu.

Es sei in diesem Zusammenhang auch darauf hingewiesen, daß im 'Feriale Cumanum'[208] an Geburtstagen von Mitgliedern des Kaiserhauses gerade der Vesta *supplicationes* gebracht werden.

Die Verehrung des *fascinus* im Vestalendienst[209], das Verbot der Eheschließung[210] und des Geschlechtsverkehrs der *flaminica*[211] am 15. Juni, die Verbindung mit den verschiedenen latinischen Zeugungssagen[212] und das Epitheton der Göttin selbst als *mater*[213] sind längst entsprechend gewürdigt worden. Es dürfen noch zwei Gesichtspunkte ergänzt werden: Romulus wird deshalb nicht für den Gründer des Vestalendienstes in Rom gehalten, weil das Schicksal seiner Mutter ihn die Bedrohung hatte erkennen lassen, in der eine Vestalin ständig schwebte[214]. Die zweite Beobachtung betrifft das Lebensalter der Priesterinnen, die ihren Dienst mit zehn Jahren aufnehmen und nach dreißig Dienstjahren ausscheiden können[215]; mit vierzig Jahren darf man aber für die fragliche Zeit das Ende der Empfängnisfähigkeit annehmen. Das ihnen auferlegte Keuschheitsgebot war also eine Art Herausforderung, da es gerade die Jahre betraf, in denen sie ihre Rolle als Frau zu erfüllen vermochten. Es wird sich demnach nicht um ein Reinheitstabu gegenüber dem Dienst am ewig brennenden Feuer handeln, sondern um die

---

[207] H. HOMMEL, ANRW I 2 (1972), 407ff.; vgl. Priap. 73,3f. . . . *inutile lignum utilis haec aram si dederitis, erit.*

[208] CIL I², p. 229 zu den Geburtstagen des jüngeren Drusus am 7. Oktober, der Tiberius am 16. November, des Germanicus am 24. Mai und vielleicht sogar des Augustus am 23. September (*[n]atalis Caesaris.immolatio.hostia.suppli[c]a[tio . . .]*).

[209] Plin.n.h. 28,39.

[210] Macr.sat. 1,16,18 Eheschließungsverbot an *dies religiosi* (hierzu vgl. Fest. 296,14L. *[circa Vestalia] i dies religiosi habentur*). Ov.fast. 2,561f. 5,488f.

[211] Ov.fast. 3,397. 6,231f. Gell. 10,15,30. Plut.quaest.Rom. 86.

[212] Vgl. G. RADKE, ANRW I 2 (1972), 428. H. HOMMEL, ibid., 397ff.

[213] Vgl. die Untersuchung bei A. BRELICH, Vesta, 57ff.

[214] Dion.Hal.ant. 2,65,3.

[215] Eintritt mit 10 Jahren (Gell. 1,12,1) und Ausscheiden nach einem Dienst von 30 Jahren (Gell. 7,7,4. Plut.Num. 10,1).

Bewahrung der Reinheit für die potentielle Gottesbraut: Sollte die Notwendig-
keit eintreten, eine Vestalin dem Gotte — er bleibt namenlos ebenso wie der
mögliche menschliche Partner; daß Rea Silvia mit Mars verbunden wird, ist
historisierende Legendenbildung — zu überantworten, darf sie von niemand
anderem als eben nur dem Gotte berührt worden sein oder berührt werden.
Diesem Gesichtspunkt dienen auch die Reinheitsvorschriften, die bei der Aus-
wahl eines Mädchens zum Dienst als Vestalin gelten[216].

Die Aufgaben der Vestalen[217] setzen sich aus der Bewachung des heiligen
Feuers, aus der Herstellung und Verwendung gewisser Kultmittel, der Verrich-
tung verschiedener, stets unblutiger Opfer und — der Bereitschaft zum Tode
zusammen. Ihre Captionsformel hebt den Vollzug von *sacra pro populo
Romano*[218] hervor. Man traut ihnen besondere Fähigkeiten zu[219]. Da in der
aedes Vestae ein Kultbild fehlt, erfolgt ihr Dienst nicht unter den Augen der
Göttin und ist demnach auch darin dem Dienst der lokrischen Mädchen vergleichbar[220].

IX. Der Name der virgo Vestalis

Antike[221] wie moderne[222] Erklärungen gingen vom Namen der Göttin
Vesta aus; sie vermögen jedoch nicht, eine Reihe von auffälligen Widersprüchen
aufzulösen. Nach den vorstehenden Beobachtungen scheint es ratsam, die Deutung vom Namen der *virgo Vestalis* aus zu unternehmen[223]. Da in ihrer Gestalt
der Akt der im Widerspruch zu der Gesellschaftsordnung stehenden Zeugung,
der ἀθεμιτομιξία, in besonderem Maße zum Ausdruck kommt, wird man in
diesem Bereich nach einem Etymon suchen dürfen. Daß sich der Name dann von
denen der *flamines Dialis, Martialis* u. a., die nach dem Gotte benannt sind,
dem sie dienen, unterscheidet, kann hingenommen werden, da die *aedes Vestae*
kein Bild enthält, das eine solche Beziehung zum Gottesnamen fördern oder
fordern könnte. Bildungsmäßig wäre dabei an den *fetialis*, die *feralia* oder den
lapis manalis[224] zu denken, die nicht die Zugehörigkeit zu einem Gottesnamen

---

[216] Gell. 1,12,2ff.

[217] Vgl. die Zusammenstellung bei G. ROHDE, Die Kultsatzungen der römischen Pontifices,
RVV 25, Berlin 1936, 107ff.

[218] Gell. 1,12,14.

[219] G. RADKE, Die Götter Altitaliens², 333; vgl. Cic.Font. 46. Plin.n.h. 28,13.

[220] Apollod.epit. 6,21.

[221] Nach Ov.fast. 6,299. Arnob. 3,32. Serv.Aen. 2,296 von *vi* und *stare*, nach Varro b.August.
civ. 7,24 (vgl. Serv.Aen. 1,292) von *vestire*; für Cic.nat.deor. 2,67. leg. 2,29 (vgl. Serv.
Aen. 1,292) ist Vesta ein griechischer Name.

[222] Vgl. C. KOCH, in: RE VIII A 2 (1958), 1718f.

[223] Vgl. H. HOMMEL, ANRW I 2 (1972), 404,37 „Denn die Bezeichnung *virgo Vestalis* ist ja
. . . zweifellos erst im organisierten Vestakult entstanden, nicht aber von einem alten *vesta*
= 'Herd' abzuleiten."

[224] Paul.Fest. 115,4f. L. *manalem fontem dici pro eo, quod aqua ex eo semper manet* (vgl.
Fest. 146,17ff.L. *manalis fons appellatur ab auguribus puteus perennis*). Paul.Fest. 115,

voraussetzen. Am nächsten scheint mir die Namensgeschichte des Festes der Meditrinalia zu liegen: *Meditrinalia dies dictus a medendo*[225]; *a quibus verbis etiam Meditrinae deae nomen conceptum*[226]. Nach der Bildungsform von Wörtern wie *doctrina* oder *furatrina*, „die den Inhalt des Lehrens und Stehlens bezeichnen"[227], bedeutet **meditrina* 'Heilung'; danach ist aber offenbar zuerst das Fest mit seiner Weinprobe und nachträglich erst der Name der sonst unbekannten Göttin abgeleitet. Ähnlich dürfte es bei der *virgo Vestalis* gegangen sein, was um so wahrscheinlicher dadurch wird, daß die Bezeichnung als *virgo* irgendeiner Gottheit nicht mit dem Namen eines *flamen* dieser oder jener Gottheit vergleichbar ist.

Nach den zum Wesen der *virgines Vestales* gemachten Beobachtungen wird man auf einen Stamm **u̯ers-* zurückgreifen dürfen, dem die Bedeutung 'benetzen, befruchten, zeugen' zukommt, wie er in dem Worte *verres* vorliegt. Die dem Verständnis dienlichsten Beispiele sind jedoch die Wörter *investis* und *vesticeps* — *vesticeps puer, qui iam vestitus*[228] *est pubertate; econtra investis, qui necdum pubertate vestitus est*[229] — und *curia*[230], das als **co-u̯rs-iá* 'Sippengemeinschaft' zu verstehen ist[231]. Die *virgines Vestales* sind demnach „Jungfrauen, die mit Befruchtung zu tun haben", an denen sich das Wunder der Jungfrauengeburt vollzogen hat oder vollziehen wird. Vergleichbar ist der Dienst der attischen Arrhephoren, deren Namen W. BURKERT, Griech. Rel. d. arch. u. klass. Epoche, Stuttgart 1977, 348 f., „zugleich auf Befruchtung und Nachwuchs deutet".

Die Zahl der Vestalen stellt eine Verbindung zur ältesten Gemeindeordnung her: *Sex Vestae sacerdotes constitutae sunt, ut populus pro sua quaque parte haberet ministram sacrorum; quia civitas Romana in sex est distributa partis: in primos secundosque Titienses, Ramnes, Luceres*[232]. Die mehrfach genannte Vierzahl gehört zu den vier regionalen *tribus urbanae*[233]. Später wird die

---

6 ff. L. *manalem lapidem . . . eumque, quod aquas manaret, manalem lapidem dicere.* Varro b.Non. 547 M. *manalis lapis appellatur in pontificalibus sacris . . . apud antiquissimos manale sacrum.* Dig. 33,10,3 pr. 3 *aquiminale.*

[225] Varro l.l. 6,21.

[226] Paul.Fest. 110,24 L.

[227] G. RADKE, Die Götter Altitaliens², 211.

[228] Die Formulierung *vestitus* beruht auf einer irrigen Volksetymologie.

[299] Paul.Fest. 506,1 f. L.

[230] Trotz M. LEUMANN, Latein.Laut- u.Formenlehre⁶, 134.226.291. F. SOMMER—R. PFISTER, Handb.d.latein.Laut- u.Formenlehre⁴, Indogerman.Bibliothek Reihe I, Heidelberg 1977, 195 nach P. KRETSCHMER, Lat. *quirites* und *quiritare*, Glotta 10, 1920, 149 nicht aus **cŏ-u̯ĭr-ia* entstanden.

[231] Vgl. G. RADKE, Quirinalis collis, in: RE XXIV 1 (1963), 1301.

[232] Fest. 468,3 ff. Paul.Fest. 475,12 ff. L. F. ALTHEIM, Röm.Gesch. II, Frankfurt a. M. 1953, 72 schließt daraus auf eine ursprüngliche Dreizahl.

[233] Dion.Hal.ant. 2,67,1. Plut.Num. 10.1. Nach Ambros.epist. 1,18,11. Expos.tot.mundi p. 120 RIESE waren es sieben, nach Lyd.mens.frg. 5 p. 179,27 W. zehn Vestalen, was jedoch kaum zutreffen dürfte. Nach H. HOMMEL, in: ANRW I 2 (1972), 405,50 werden auf der ebd. S. 406 abgebildeten Münze der Iulia Domna vier Vestalen und zwei Novizen dargestellt.

Sechszahl in einem praktischen Verhältnis zum Dienst gestanden haben[234]: Lehre, Arbeit, Leitung. Diese Beziehungen stimmen mit der Lage der *aedes Vestae* außerhalb des palatinischen Pomeriums[235] überein und führen auf die Zeit des Synoikismos, der dem ältesten Kalender vorausgeht[236]. So konnte der kultische Dienst einer Opferbereitschaft im Falle einer Bedrohung der Gemeinde – nun vereinigt entsprechend der Zahl der politischen Gruppen[237] – an eine ἑστία κοινή verlegt werden, wie das aus griechischen Verhältnissen bekannt ist[238]. Aus dem Dienst der Vestalen an diesem die Einheit der neuen Siedlung bestätigenden Herde wurde die Vorstellung einer Göttin, deren Aufgabe die *salus populi Romani* und die Wahrung der Fähigkeit ihrer Dienerinnen war, zu gegebener Zeit mit der Hingabe ihres Lebens der Captionsformel entsprechend für das Gedeihen der Gemeinde ein Opfer zu bringen.

X. *Vesta und die* dei penates

Je weiter die Analyse beider Kulte fortschritt, löste sich das menschlich gestaltete Bild der Gottheit auf. Wie die *dei penates* ohne eine darstellbare Erscheinung, ohne menschliches Gesicht für den *pater familias* sorgten, so standen die *optima lege*[239] ausgewählten *virgines Vestales* bereit, für die Folgen einer **ụers-tā*[240], einer 'Zeugung', die der gesellschaftlichen Ordnung zuwidergelaufen war, stellvertretend das Wohl des Volkes zu gewährleisten.

Die *dei penates* sind in Lavinium in die Aeneasüberlieferung einbezogen worden und erhielten in Rom einen Kult, dessen Bilder denen der Dioskuren mindestens ähnelten, während gelehrte Forscher, die eine solche Gleichsetzung mit Recht ablehnen (s. o. S. 350), in den Penaten *sacra* sahen, die in der *aedes Vestae* aufbewahrt wurden. Die auseinanderstrebenden Bedeutungen fanden sich schließlich wieder in der metonymischen Ausdrucksweise *penates* 'Haus', die bis in die Gegenwart weiterlebt. Ebenso strebte die ursprünglich bildlose Vorstellung einer Gottheit, die lediglich die Funktion der in ihrem Kult vereinigten

---

[234] Dion.Hal.ant. 2,67,2. Plut.Num. 10. Vgl. die Formulierung *per omnes gradus sacerdotii* auf Grabsteinen von Vestalen (CIL VI 32414. 32416. 2135 = ILS 4930. 4931. 4934).

[235] Dion.Hal.ant. 2,65,3. F. ALTHEIM, Röm.Rel.Gesch., I, Berlin–Leipzig 1931, 71 widerspricht dem.

[236] Das wird durch die Bedenken bei F. ALTHEIM, Röm.Rel.Gesch. I, 1931, 71 nicht betroffen.

[237] Nach Dion.Hal.ant. 2,65,4 richtete Romulus einen Vesta-Kult der 30 Kurien ein.

[238] Vgl. die ἑστία κοινή beim Synoikismos von Tegea (Paus. 8,53,9), Mantinea (Paus. 8,8,4. 8,9,5; vgl. die Rolle der Antinoe) und Delphi (Plut.Arist. 20).

[239] Gell. 1,12,14; die Bedeutung von *optimus* entspricht der im Namen des *Iupiter Optimus Maximus* (zu *maximus* vgl. die *Vestalis maxima*, die nicht nur ihres Alters wegen so heißt).

[240] Vgl. G. RADKE, Die Götter Altitaliens², 334.353; DERS., in: ANRW I 2 (1972), 430; DERS., Vesta, in: Kl.Pauly V (1975), 1227ff. Anerkennung dieser Herleitung bei K. OLZSCHA, Gnomon 38, 1966, 774.

virgines repräsentierte, unter griechischem Einfluß zu einer bildlichen Darstellung; nach dem Vorbild der Vesta unter den *dei consentes* und dem *signum* im Hause – in den *penates* – des Augustus wurde nach dem neronischen Brande auch im Vestatempel ein Gottesbild aufgestellt. Bis ins Mittelalter erhielt sich aber die Erinnerung an die Statuette auf dem Dach, die ein Mädchen mit Kind im Arm darstellt.

Zu dem Zeitpunkt, an dem die Penaten des Aeneas eine nationalrömische Vorstellung wurden und an dem ein Bild der Vesta dediziert werden konnte, verbanden sich Vesta und die *dei penates* zu einem gemeinsamen Kulte. Er fand seinen Platz weder im Vestatempel noch im Penatentempel an der Velia; lediglich das Opfer in Cumae an dem Tage, an dem Augustus *pontifex maximus*, d. h. *sacerdos Vestae*[241], geworden war, verbindet beide zu einer kultischen Einheit.

Die ältesten Formen religiösen Denkens, die sowohl zum Dienst der Vestalen wie zur Verehrung der Penaten geführt haben, wurden im Laufe der Jahrhunderte verschüttet und verändert, ohne daß sie ganz vergessen wurden. Mit Hilfe des sprachlichen Ausdrucks ließ sich das noch Erhaltene verdeutlichen, so daß eine uralte Schicht römischer Gottesvorstellung offengelegt werden konnte: Bei Vesta geht offenbar der – um mit H. HOMMEL a. O. zu sprechen – 'phallische Aspekt' dem 'sozialen Aspekt' ebenso voraus wie der patriarchalische dem politischen in der Verehrung der *dei penates*.

Bibliographie

A. ALFÖLDI, Early Rome and the Latins, Ann Arbor 1965, 255 ff.268 ff. = DERS., Das frühe Rom und die Latiner, Darmstadt 1977, 231 ff.241 ff.

DERS., Die Struktur des voretruskischen Römerstaates, Bibliothek der klass. Altertumswissenschaften, N.F., Reihe I, Bd. 5, Heidelberg 1974, 94.184.

DERS., Römische Frühgeschichte, Bibliothek der klass. Altertumswissenschaften N.F., Reihe I, Bd. 6, Heidelberg 1976, 138 f.

F. ALTHEIM, Römische Religionsgeschichte, Berlin 1931–33.

F. BÖMER, Rom und Troia, Baden-Baden 1951, 50 ff.

P. BOYANCÉ, Les Pénates et l'ancienne religion romaine, in: REA 54, 1952, 109 ff.

A. BRELICH, Vesta, Albae Vigiliae 7, Zürich 1949, 75 ff.

F. CASTAGNOLI, Lavinium, I. Topografia generale, fonti e storia delle ricerche, Roma 1972, 109.

G. DUMÉZIL, La religion romaine archaïque, Bibliothèque historique, Coll. 'Les religions de l'humanité', Paris 1966, 346 ff.

L. DEUBNER, Die Römer, in: P. D. CHANTEPIE DE LA SAUSSAYE, Lehrbuch der Religionsgeschichte II⁴, Tübingen 1925, 435.

L. EUING, Die Sage von Tanaquil, Frankf. Studien zu Rel. und Kultur d. Antike 2, Frankfurt/Main 1933, 29 ff.

---

[241] Ov.fast. 5,573. Auf Inschriften des 4. nachchristl. Jhdts. ist von einem *pontifex maior Vestae* (CIL VI 1741 = ILS 1243), *pontifex Vestae* (CIL VI 1779 = ILS 1259), *pontifex Vestae matris* (CIL X 1125 = ILS 2942) und *pontifex Vestalis maior* (CIL VI 499 = ILS 4151) die Rede.

W. Fauth, Römische Religion im Spiegel der 'Fasti' des Ovid, in: ANRW II 16,1, 1978, 104−186.

G. Gianelli, Il sacerdozio delle Vestali romane, Firenze 1913.
P. Grimal, Dictionnaire de la mythologie grecque et romaine³, Paris 1963.
F. Guizzi, Aspetti giuridici del sacerdozio romano. Il sacerdozio di Vesta, Napoli 1968.
D. P. Harmon, The Family Festivals of Rome, in: ANRW II 16,2, 1978, 1593 ff.
H. Hommel, Vesta und die frührömische Religion, in: ANRW I 2, 1972, 397 ff.
O. Huth, Vesta. Untersuchungen zum indogermanischen Feuerkult, ARW Beiheft 2, Leipzig 1943.

R. H. Klausen, Aeneas und die Penaten, Hamburg−Gotha 1840, 647 ff.
C. Koch, Vesta, in: RE VIII A 2 (1958), 1717 ff.

K. Latte, Römische Religionsgeschichte, Handb. d. Altertumswiss. V 4, München 1960, 89. 108 ff. (zitiert: Latte, RGG).

K. Malten, Aineias, in: ARW 29, 1931, 36.
N. Masquelier, Pénates et Dioscures, in: Latomus 25, 1966, 88 ff.
F. Münzer, Die römische Vesta bis zur Kaiserzeit, in: Philol. 92, 1937, 47 ff.199 ff.

E. Norden, Alt-Germanien, Leipzig−Berlin 1934, 98 ff.

R. E. A. Palmer, Roman Religion and Roman Empire. Five Essays, The Haney Foundation Series 15, Philadelphia 1974, 198.
J. Perret, Les origines de la légende troyenne de Rome (281−31), Paris 1942.
Chr. Peyre, Castor et Pollux et les Pénates pendant la période républicaine, in: MEFR 74, 1962, 433 ff.
G. Piccaluga, Penates e Lares, in: SMSR 32, 1961, 81 ff.
L. Preller−H. Jordan, Römische Mythologie II³, Berlin 1883, 155 ff.

G. Radke, Die Götter Altitaliens², Fontes et Commentationes 3, Münster 1979, 247 ff.320 ff.
Ders., Acca Larentia und die fratres Arvales, in: ANRW I 2, 1972, 421 ff.
Ders., Penates, in: Kl.Pauly IV (1972), 610 ff.
Ders., Vesta, ebd. V (1975), 1227 ff.
Ders., Res Italae Romanorumque triumphi, in: Klass.Sprachen u.Literaturen 6, München 1971, 84.93.
Ders., Beobachtungen zum römischen Kalender, in: Rhein.Mus. 106, 1963, 329 ff.

K. Schauenburg, Aeneas und Rom, in: Gymnasium 67, 1960, 176 ff.
Käthe Schwarz, Der Vestakult und seine Herkunft, Diss. Heidelberg 1941.

N. Turchi, La religione di Roma antica, Bologna 1939, 13 ff.

St. Weinstock, Penates, in: RE XIX 1 (1937), 417 ff.
G. Wissowa, Penates, in: Roschers Myth.Lex. III² (Leipzig 1902−1909, Nachdr. 1965), 1879 ff.
Ders., Vesta, ebd. VI (1924−1937, Nachdr. 1977), 241 ff.
Ders., Religion und Kultus der Römer², Handb. d. Altertumswiss. IV 5, München 1912, 76 ff. 156 ff.161 ff.
Ders., Gesammelte Abhandlungen zur römischen Religions- und Stadtgeschichte, München 1904, 95 ff.
Ders., Vestalinnenfrevel, in: ARW 22, 1924, 281 ff.

Janus à l'époque impériale

par ROBERT TURCAN, Lyon

Table des matières

Abréviations:

AC	L'Antiquité Classique, Louvain.
AJA	American Journal of Archaeology, New York.
ANRW	Aufstieg und Niedergang der römischen Welt. Geschichte und Kultur Roms im Spiegel der neueren Forschung, hrsg. von W. HAASE u. H. TEMPORINI, Berlin/New York, 1972 ss.
BMC	The Coins of the Roman Republic in the British Museum, by H. A. GRUEBER, 3 Vol., London, 1910. Coins of the Roman Empire in the British Museum, by H. MATTINGLY, London, 1923 ss.
CIL	Corpus Inscriptionum Latinarum, consilio et auctoritate Academiae Litterarum (Regiae) Borussicae editum, Leipzig/Berlin, 1862–1943. Ed. altera, ibid., 1893 ss.
JAC	Jahrbuch für Antike und Christentum, Münster.
JRS	Journal of Roman Studies, London.
MDAI(R)	Mitteilungen des Deutschen Archäologischen Instituts (Röm. Abt.), Mainz.
MEFR(A)	Mélanges d'Archéologie et d'Histoire de l'École Française de Rome, Paris (Mélanges de l'école française de Rome [Antiquité], Paris).
RE	PAULYS Realencyclopädie der classischen Altertumswissenschaft, Neue Bearb., begonnen v. G. WISSOWA, fortgef. v. W. KROLL u. K. MITTELHAUS, hrsg. v. K. ZIEGLER u. W. JOHN, Stuttgart, 1893 ss.

Introduction

Quoique dieu des *prima*, Janus n'est pas au premier plan de la religion romaine impériale. On l'a noté depuis longtemps[1]: paradoxalement, ce dieu autochthone, originalement romain, typique de la protohistoire italique et sans équivalent dans le monde grec, n'a pas bénéficié de la moindre dédicace dans l'*Urbs* même ni dans le Latium, où il passait pour avoir régné aux beaux temps de l'âge d'or. On faisait de lui l'archétype des souverains italiques, modèle de circonspection politique: d'où sa *gemina facies*, croyait-on. Or l'Italie n'a livré que deux dédicaces gravées en son honneur, dont une par les soins de deux esclaves qui n'étaient ni Romains, ni même Italiens[2]. C'est un fait aussi que Janus n'apparaît nulle part dans la sculpture monumentale officielle, ni isolément ni dans la compagnie des empereurs ou des grands dieux de l'Etat. Tout se passe comme si la plastique impériale l'ignorait délibérément.

En revanche, Janus Bifrons et son temple figurent occasionnellement au revers des monnaies ou des médaillons frappés à Rome, exceptionnellement (en ce qui concerne le dieu même) dans le monnayage autonome de Thessalonique, sous le règne de Trajan-Dèce. Mais la signification religieuse et politique, historique et (ou) commémorative de ces représentations monétaires varie assez sensiblement et problématiquement d'une émission à l'autre. Elle varie en fonction des circonstances, mais aussi − et corrélativement − en fonction même des polyvalences de Janus, dieu de la paix et de la guerre, du passage et des commencements (ou des recommencements), du chaos et du ciel, de la lumière solaire (ou lunaire?) et du Temps. Mais tout aussi significatives que les émergences numismatiques de Janus peuvent apparaître ses absences, là où on attendrait une allusion, une référence directe ou indirecte. Ainsi la fermeture de son 'temple' est illustrée par les frappes de Néron, mais non par celles d'Auguste, de Marc-Aurèle et de Gordien III qui ont pourtant symboliquement emprisonné la guerre derrière les lourdes portes de bronze. Inversement, le dieu est célébré par l'iconographie monétaire à des époques qui ne coïncident pas − que nous sachions − avec cette cérémonie insolite, ni même avec des phases de paix uni-

---

REL   Revue des Études Latines, Paris.
RHR   Revue de l'Histoire des Religions, Paris.
RIC   Roman Imperial Coinage, edd. H. MATTINGLY, E. A. SYDENHAM, C. H. V.
           SUTHERLAND e. a., London, 1923ss.
ZPE   Zeitschrift für Papyrologie und Epigraphik, Bonn.

[1] J. TOUTAIN, Les cultes païens dans l'Empire romain. 1ère partie: les provinces latines, I. Les cultes officiels: les cultes romains et gréco-romains, Bibl. de l'Ecole Pratique des Hautes Etudes, Sc.Rel., 20, Paris, 1906, réédit. anast., Rome, 1967, p. 247; G. WISSOWA, Religion und Kultus der Römer[2], Handb. d. Altertumswiss., V,4, Munich, 1912, p. 106; K. LATTE, Römische Religionsgeschichte, Handb. d. Altertumswiss., V,4, Munich, 1960, p. 136.

[2] CIL, XI, 5374 (Assise). Cf. V. SALADINO, Iscrizioni latine di Roselle (I), ZPE, 38, 1980, p. 162ss.

verselle: tout au contraire! Les dédicaces à Janus – qu'on trouve surtout en Afrique et en Dalmatie[3] – ne sont pas liées non plus nécessairement à cette consécration rituelle de la *Pax Augusta*.

Abstraction faite de l'épineux dossier des origines[4], à ne s'en tenir même qu'aux représentations officielles de l'époque impériale, on doit reconnaître la complexité idéologique de ce dieu déconcertant. C'est une raison majeure de s'y intéresser, quoiqu'apparemment il compte assez peu dans l'imagerie impériale: ce qui explique sans doute que le Janus des trois premiers siècles de notre ère n'ait guère suscité la recherche, ou du moins les publications. On a beaucoup travaillé – et c'est fort utile – à l'étude des témoignages littéraires, des étymologies et des épithètes cultuelles[5]; on s'est attaché surtout à la définition conceptuelle et fonctionnelle du dieu, de façon trop intemporelle parfois. On n'a pas assez fait l'histoire de Janus, notamment à l'époque impériale[6], l'histoire des figurations concrètes du dieu, restituées dans leur contexte politique et dans l'esprit du temps.

I. *Auguste et Janus*

C'est une idée courante et quasiment reçue qu'Auguste «revigora les rites de Janus», comme l'écrit J. BAYET[7] qui songeait essentiellement à Janus Quirinus. Selon R. SCHILLING[8], le dieu «devait à Auguste une survie que son rôle, effacé dès la fin de la République, avait rendue aléatoire». Le culte de Janus Quirinus a pris alors «un sens symbolique», et «c'est ce sens qu'Auguste a contribué puissamment à remettre en honneur»[9]. Auguste voulut «remettre en honneur la religion de Janus», affirme de son côté J.-C. RICHARD, qui parle à ce propos de «*revival*»[10]. Plus récemment, on a parlé d'une «restauration du culte

---

[3] J. TOUTAIN, op. cit., p. 245 s.

[4] G. DUMÉZIL, Tarpeia. Essais de philologie comparative indo-européenne, Paris, 1947, p. 98 ss.; L. A. HOLLAND, Janus and the Bridge, Amer. Acad. in Rome, Pap. and Monographs, 21, Rome, 1961; L. A. MAC KAY, Janus, Univ. of California Publications in Classical Philology, 15, 1961, p. 157 ss.; G. RADKE, Die Götter Altitaliens, Fontes et Commentationes, H. 3, Münster, 1965, p. 147 s.; G. DUMÉZIL, La religion romaine archaïque, Bibl. hist., Coll. Les religions de l'humanité, Paris, 1966, p. 322. Sur le type plastique, cf. R. PETTAZZONI, Per l'iconografia di Giano, Studi Etr., 24, 1955/6, p. 79 ss. Un article récent et très conjectural rattache les rites de Janus au culte d'un arbre comme le micocoulier et le type même du *bifrons* à la représentation de Borée: J. GAGÉ, Sur les origines du culte de Janus, RHR, 195, 1979, p. 3–33 et 129–151.

[5] G. CAPDEVILLE, Les épithètes cultuelles de Janus, MEFR(A), 84, 1973, p. 395–436.

[6] A cet égard, l'article 'Janus' de W. F. OTTO, dans la 'Real-Encyclopädie', Suppl. III (1918), col. 1181 s., est plutôt décevant.

[7] Histoire politique et psychologique de la religion romaine[2], Bibl. hist., Paris, 1969, p. 174.

[8] Janus. Le dieu introducteur. Le dieu des passages, MEFR, 72, 1960, p. 90.

[9] Ibid., p. 125.

[10] Pax, Concordia et la religion officielle de Janus à la fin de la République romaine, MEFR, 75, 1963, p. 360.

de Janus Quirinus» qui se serait inscrite «dans la propagande augustéenne du rétablissement d'une paix définitive»[11].

C'est un fait que sous Auguste on ferma trois fois le 'Janus' et que dans ses 'Res Gestae'[12], l'empereur donne à cette triple fermeture le retentissement que l'on sait; un fait aussi que l'écho de l'événement est répercuté par la littérature contemporaine[13]. Sous le seul principat d'Auguste (*ter me principe*), on connut ce bonheur trois fois plus souvent que durant le demi-millénaire antérieur de la *Respublica*[14]! Mais c'est un fait aussi que le surnom de Quirinus qu'Auguste, dans ces mêmes 'Res gestae', confère officiellement à Janus atteste une intention particulière. La version grecque traduit *Ianum Quirinum* par πύλην Ἐνυάλιον, ce qui rejoint l'équation donnée par Plutarque dans Quaest.Rom., 25,285 d. Johannès Lydus[15] rendra l'épithète par πρόμαχος, ce qui correspond à la glose de Macrobe[16] *quasi bellorum potentem* et aux explications militaires qui rattachent Quirinus à *curis*, nom prétendument sabin de la lance[17]: étymologie certainement erronée, mais significative du souci d'élucider la résonance guerrière de Quirinus dans l'idéologie augustéenne. En l'occurrence, il ne s'agit pas de savoir le sens originel de Quirinus, mais celui que lui attribuaient les contemporains de la triple clôture. Sans doute Quirinus est-il et reste-t-il dans l'optique augustéenne le dieu de la communauté civique, de la Romanité: chez Ovide[18], la protection de Janus est invoquée en faveur du «peuple de Quirinus». Mais la paix de Janus Quirinus, en tant que *Pax Romana* précisément, est d'abord celle des armes. Ce Janus est le dieu de la paix armée, obtenue et assurée par les soldats-citoyens, intention que confirme − outre les traductions grecques de l'épiclèse − le contexte même de l'énoncé dans les 'Res gestae', qui rappellent

---

[11] M. MESLIN, La fête des Kalendes de janvier dans l'Empire romain. Étude d'un rituel du Nouvel An, Coll. Latomus, 115, Bruxelles, 1970, p. 25.

[12] 13 (p. 94 s. de l'éd. J. GAGÉ).

[13] Hor., Carm. IV,15,4−9; Ep. II,1,253 ss.; Verg., Aen., I,294 ss.; VII,180, 607 ss.; R. SCHILLING, art. cit. (n. 8), p. 126; H. BAUER, Kaiserfora und Janustempel, MDAI(R), 84, 1977, p. 316.

[14] Après Numa, le 'Janus' n'avait été fermé qu'en −235: Varr., De L.L.,V,165; Liv., I,19,3; Vell. Pat., II,38,3; Suet., Aug., 22,1.

[15] De mens., IV,1 (p. 63,13 WUENSCH).

[16] Sat., I,9,16 (I, p. 39,5 ss. WILLIS). Cf. Lucan., Phars., I,62 (*belligeri limina Iani*); Stat., Silv., II,3,12 (*belligerum Iani nemus*); W. H. ROSCHER, art. Janus, dans: IDEM, Ausf. Lexikon d. gr. u. röm. Mythologie, II, 1, Leipzig, 1890−94, réimpr. Hildesheim, 1965, col. 40 s.

[17] R. E. A. PALMER, The Archaic Community of the Romans, Cambridge, 1970, p. 19, 31, 61, 168, n. 2; G. CAPDEVILLE, art. cit., p. 421 s. − Sur Quirinus et Romulus Quirinus voir G. RADKE, Quirinus. Eine kritische Überprüfung der Überlieferung und ein Versuch, ci-dessus (ANRW, II, 17.1), pp. 276−299, et D. PORTE, Romulus−Quirinus, prince et dieu, dieu des princes. Etude sur le personnage de Quirinus et sur son évolution, des origines à Auguste, ci-dessus, pp. 300−342.

[18] Fast., 1,69. Cf. R. SCHILLING, art. cit., p. 119: Quirinus, «dieu de la communauté des *Quirites*», Mars l'étant de la communauté des *milites*.

que traditionnellement la fermeture du Janus se faisait lorsque *per totum imperium populi Romani terra marique esset parta victoriis pax*[19].

Janus Quirinus est donc le dieu de la pacification victorieuse qui consacre
l'ordre impérial romain. Aussi faisait-on de Quirinus un Mars de la paix[20]. Mais
l'appellation de Janus Quirinus avait aussi une résonance romuléenne. En tant
qu'instaurateur de la *Pax Romana* et refondateur de Rome, Auguste a joué, semble-
t-il, sur cette double relation de Quirinus et à Mars et à Romulus.

Cependant Velleius Paterculus[21] et plus tard Dion-Cassius[22] qualifieront de
Geminus et non de Quirinus le Janus fermé par Auguste. L'empereur a-t-il
voulu ressusciter une épiclèse ancienne, archaïsante et désuète? C. KOCH[23] et R.
SCHILLING[24] ont fait valoir en ce sens des données de valeur inégale: la loi dite
de Numa sur les dépouilles opimes (d'après Plutarque[25], Servius[26] et Festus[27]); la
formule de *clarigatio* que prononçait le fécial en prenant les dieux à témoins[28];
un vers de Lucilius[29]. Mais J. POUCET[30] a observé que, concernant les dépouilles
opimes, Festus est seul à parler de Janus Quirinus (avec l'archaïsme du datif *Ianui*
qui, de soi, ne constitue pas une preuve d'authenticité)[31]. Quant à la déclaration
du fécial, le texte livien qui nous l'a transmise est incertain: dans *et tu Iane
Quirine*, *Iane* est une correction de PERIZONIUS pour *Iuno* (sur quoi les manuscrits sont unanimes), et le fait que Janus — dieu 'primordial' — soit invoqué
après Jupiter, contrairement à la règle liturgique, a de quoi troubler[32]. Enfin,
dans le vers fr. 22 MARX de Lucilius, la juxtaposition des noms Janus et Quirinus

---

[19] Res gestae, 13 (p. 94 de l'éd. J. GAGÉ). Cf. C. M. WELLS, The German Policy of Augustus.
    An Examination of the Archaeological Evidence, Oxford, 1972, p. 8; H. E. STIER,
    Augustusfriede und römische Klassik, ANRW, II, 2, Berlin—New York, 1975, p. 19ss.
[20] Serv., Ad Aen., I,292 (I, p. 108, 25ss. THILO—HAGEN); VI,859 (II, p. 120, 14); R. SCHIL-
    LING, art. cit., p. 122, 124s.
[21] II,38,3.
[22] LIV, 36,2 (II, p. 475, 24 BOISSEVAIN).
[23] Bemerkungen zum römischen Quirinuskult, Zeitschr.f.Relig.u.Geistesgesch., 5, 1953,
    p. 6s. (= IDEM, Religio. Studien z.Kult u.Glauben der Römer, hrsg. v. O. SEEL, Erlanger
    Beiträge z.Sprach- u.Kunstwiss., 7, Nuremberg, 1960, p. 22s); C. KOCH, art. Quirinus,
    dans: RE, XXIV,1 (1963), col. 1314s.
[24] Art. cit. (n. 8), p. 116. Cf. aussi M. GUARDUCCI, Janus Geminus, dans: Mélanges d'ar-
    chéol. et d'histoire offerts à A. Piganiol, III, École pratique des Hautes Études, VIe Sec-
    tion, Centre de Recherches historiques, Paris, 1966, p. 1608.
[25] Marc., 8,9.
[26] Ad Aen., VI,859 (II, p. 120, 7ss. THILO—HAGEN).
[27] S. v. *opima spolia* (p. 204, 17 LINDSAY).
[28] Liv., I,32,9. Cf. P. CATALANO, Linee del sistema sovranazionale romano, I, Univ. di
    Torino, Mem.dell'Ist.Giuridico, Ser. II, Mem. 119, Turin, 1965, p. 37.
[29] C. Lucilii carminum reliquiae, éd. F. MARX, Leipzig, 1904, I, p. 4, v. 22. Cf. L. A. HOL-
    LAND, Janus and the Bridge, p. 109. Dans son éd.-trad. des 'Remains of Old Latin', III,
    Londres—Cambr.Mass., 1938 (Coll.Loeb), E. H. WARMINGTON (p. 10, v. 28) distingue
    Janus de Quirinus.
[30] Recherches sur la légende sabine des origines de Rome, Univ. de Louvain, Rec. de trav.
    d'hist. & de philos., IVe Sér., 37, Louvain, 1967, p. 39s.
[31] G. CAPDEVILLE, art. cit. (n. 5), p. 420s., n. 2.
[32] Ibid. Cf. L. A. HOLLAND, op. cit., p. 60s., n. 33; p. 284s.

(après Liber, Saturne et Mars) ne démontre pas péremptoirement qu'il s'agit d'un seul et même dieu. On soupçonnerait donc l'équation Janus=Quirinus d'être augustéenne. En tout cas, on ne saurait que très conjecturalement (et non sans parti pris arbitraire) y déchiffrer une opération de rajeunissement cultuel.

Mais peut-être Auguste a-t-il au moins restauré le 'temple' du dieu biface. Réexaminant de très près le Janus des sesterces néroniens (pl. I,1–4), H. BAUER[33] a montré qu'outre la typologie des colonnes, les rinceaux et les palmettes de l'épistyle pouvaient difficilement correspondre au décor d'un édifice romain du IVe ou du IIIe siècle av. J.-C.: ces éléments attesteraient une réfection au Ier siècle avant notre ère. Virgile (Aen. 7,607ss.) ferait écho à cette rénovation augustéenne du Janus Geminus. Ce Janus compterait alors au nombre des quatre-vingt-deux temples remis en état par l'empereur. Mais il n'en cite nommément aucun dans les 'Res Gestae'[34], et l'on ne voit pas que celui de Janus ait retenu tout spécialement son attention.

Si Auguste voulut vraiment revigorer la vieille religion romaine de Janus, on peut à bon droit s'étonner que ni le dieu, ni son temple n'apparaissent jamais dans l'iconographie monétaire du premier empereur. Les raisons de cette absence peuvent s'expliquer en ce qui regarde l'effigie même du Bifrons. C'était le type d'avers des as républicains, repris par Sextus Pompée en 45–44 av. J.-C. à la gloire de son père déifié iconographiquement sous les traits du dieu[35]. Il est possible que Sextus, en rappelant cette filiation, ait voulu marquer, comme on l'a dit, une promesse de paix «et non plus de conquête sans limites»[36], Magnus s'identifiant avec un Janus gardien de *Pax*. Mais je crois plutôt que ce type d'avers renouait intentionnellement avec la tradition républicaine. La double tête restait signe de valeur en tant que caractéristique de l'as, comme sur les as coloniaux de Nîmes, de Vienne et de Lyon[37]. Mais les effigies adossées d'Octavien et soit d'Agrippa à Nîmes, soit de César à Vienne et à Lyon, y occupent la place de Janus Bifrons. Comme type pompéien et républicain, le dieu bicéphale fut en quelque sorte réprouvé, démonétisé.

Certes, Janus était associé à Concordia et à Salus le 30 mars, dans un culte qu'Ovide mentionne à cette date (Fast., 3,881) et auquel il annexe l'adoration de

---

[33] Art. cit. (n. 13), p. 315s. Toutefois, il faut observer que toutes les représentations néroniennes ne comportent pas ces particularités de décor. Beaucoup d'exemplaires (comme ici pl. I,4) nous montrent un Janus massif, dépourvu de frise et de palmettes. Certaines variantes de détail peuvent être le fait du graveur et ne constituent pas des indices indiscutables de datation.

[34] 20,4 (p. 112–114 de l'éd. J. GAGÉ).

[35] E. A. SYDENHAM, The Coinage of the Roman Republic, éd. par L. FORRER & C. H. HERSCH, Londres, 1952, p. 174, n°s 1040, 1044/5; M. H. CRAWFORD, Roman Republican Coinage, Cambridge, 1974, I, p. 487, n°s 478–479; II, p. 739 et pl. 56. Cf. J. FERGUSON, The Religion of the Roman Empire. Aspects of Greek & Roman Life, Londres–Southampton, 1970, p. 90.

[36] J.-C. RICHARD, art. cit. (n. 10), p. 335.

[37] A. BLANCHET, Traité des monnaies gauloises, Paris, 1905 (réédit. anast. Bologne, 1971), p. 429s., 434, 437; M. GRANT, From *Imperium* to *Auctoritas*², Cambridge, 1969, p. 70s., 114s., 207, 337.

l'Ara Pacis[38]. La cérémonie remontait à l'année (10 ou 11 av. J.-C.) où Auguste fit ériger des autels et des statues à Concordia, Salus et Pax; mais Dion-Cassius[39] ne cite pas le nom de Janus. D'autre part, ce même Janus est le grand absent de l'Ara Pacis. Paradoxalement, dans ce que l'on connaît ou restitue du décor, nulle part la moindre représentation du dieu ou de son «temple» ne rappelle que la paix est consacrée par la fermeture du Janus. Il est vrai qu'I. SCOTT RYBERG[40], puis E. SIMON[41] ont cru pouvoir détecter une allusion au dieu dans la frise où défilent trois victimes à immoler: la procession est ouverte par un bélier, animal sacrifié à Janus chaque 9 janvier pour les *Agonalia*[42]. Sa place, en tête du cortège, pourrait correspondre à la priorité liturgique dont bénéficient Janus et son prêtre attitré, le *rex sacrorum*[43]. Mais cette allusion qui relève de la technique rituelle ne donne aucun relief explicite et particulier au dieu Bifrons[44]. Bien loin d'avoir acquis une sorte de promotion ou de réévaluation dans la religion officielle, il est resté dans l'ombre des grands dieux et survit dans la routine d'un cérémonial. On peut se demander même si le surnom de Quirinus ne tendait pas et ne visait pas à effacer celui de Janus, à l'estomper. L'ignorance dont souffre Janus explique, en tout cas, et les interrogations d'Òvide au premier livre des 'Fastes' et les multiples exégèses qui, depuis Nigidius Figulus[45], pullulent confusément autour de son nom.

Qui sait si Ovide ne s'est pas intéressé à lui et n'y a pas intéressé ses lecteurs par quelque mauvais esprit sourdement anti-augustéen? Toujours est-il que le poète exilé par l'empereur contribuait davantage qu'Auguste à le faire connaître et remettre au goût du jour. Ovide en fait un dieu cosmique, le portier du ciel dont Jupiter lui-même est tributaire[46]: belle revanche pour le vieux Janus Geminus de l'Argilète!

---

[38] Ov., Fast., III,882. Cf. R. SCHILLING, art. cit., p. 127; J.-C. RICHARD, art. cit., p. 347, 358, n. 2.

[39] LIV, 35,2 (II, p. 475, 1—3 BOISSEVAIN).

[40] Rites of the State Religion in Roman Art, Mem.of the Amer.Acad.in Rome, 22, Rome, 1955, p. 42 et pl. XI, fig. 22b.

[41] Ara Pacis Augustae, Monumenta Artis Antiquae, 1, Tübingen, 1967, p. 15 et pl. 9,2. L'auteur rappelle aussi que l'Ara Pacis avait été consacrée un 30 janvier, mois de Janus!

[42] Ov., Fast., I,333s.; G. WISSOWA, op. cit., p. 103, 504 et n. 4; K. LATTE, op. cit., p. 135; G. DUMÉZIL, Mariages indo-européens, suivi de Quinze Questions Romaines, Bibl.hist., Paris, 1979, p. 245.

[43] Le *rex* est «comme le prêtre de Janus» (G. DUMÉZIL, Tarpeia, p. 101), mais non pas exclusivement de Janus cependant (IDEM, La religion romaine archaïque[1], p. 328; [2]p. 339).

[44] On a bien fait valoir aussi que les deux entrées du temenos de l'Ara Pacis ressemblent au passage d'un Janus (E. SIMON, op. cit., p. 9); mais cette analogie lointaine et vaguement générique ne prouve pas que Janus était nommément honoré à l'Autel de la Paix.

[45] Macr., Sat., I,9,6 et 8; A.-J. FESTUGIÈRE, La révélation d'Hermès Trismégiste, IV. Le Dieu inconnu et la gnose, Études Bibl., Paris, 1954, p. 176ss.; J. BEAUJEU, La religion romaine à l'apogée de l'Empire, I. La politique religieuse des Antonins (98—192), Paris, 1955, p. 143.

[46] Ov., Fast., I,125s.

II. La paix néronienne

Le dieu biface ne compte pas ni dans le monnayage de Tibère, ni dans celui de Caligula. Aucune fermeture du Janus n'est signalée sous ces deux règnes, non plus d'ailleurs que sous celui de Claude. Toutefois, parmi les allégories qui ouvrent la série des deniers et *aurei* de Claude, en 41–42, on relève la *Pax Augusta*[47]. Selon M. GRANT[48], le choix de ce type à cette date coïnciderait avec le deuxième centenaire d'un premier *Augurium Salutis* célébré en 160 av. J.-C. (d'après J. LIEGLE)[49]. Mais cette chronologie n'a aucune base sérieuse et assurée[50]. L'avènement de Claude coïncidait du moins ou pouvait coïncider avec le troisième centenaire du temple de Janus élevé au Forum Holitorium en −260 par les soins de C. Duilius[51]: les revers du type PACI AVGVSTAE auraient alors tendu à rappeler que l'aube d'une nouvelle ère de paix correspondait au troiscentième anniversaire de cette consécration *in Foro Holitorio*. Cependant, c'est la fermeture non pas de ce temple, mais du Janus Geminus voisin de la Curie qui scellait rituellement la paix. Il n'est donc pas évident que la célébration monétaire de la *Pax Augusta* ait comporté l'intention de marquer ce triple centenaire. La relation de Janus à la paix autorise seulement à s'interroger sur les arrièrepensées (inexplicites) du pouvoir émetteur ou de certains responsables de la monnaie 'impériale' (le type n'apparaît pas dans le monnayage de bronze dit 'sénatorial').

Le problème se pose tout différemment à l'endroit des monnaies de Néron qui commémorent la fermeture du Janus après les victoires de Corbulon. Les *aurei* représentent simplement, sans profondeur, suivant une frontalité plate et comme abstraite, la façade rectangulaire du 'temple' avec sa porte à deux vantaux bardés chacun de trois traverses cloutées[52]. Au contraire, les as, dupondius et sesterces[53] nous montrent le Janus en perspective, vu de trois-quarts, avec la

[47] RIC, I, p. 126, n°s 26 ss.; BMC, Roman Empire, I, Londres, 1923 (réédit. anast. 1965), p. 165, n°s 6 s., pl. 31, 5.

[48] Roman Anniversary Issues. An Exploration Study of the Numismatic and Medallic Commemoration of Anniversary Years 49 B.C.− A.D. 375, Cambridge, 1950, p. 72.

[49] L. Aemilius Paullus als *Augur Maximus* im Jahre 160 und das *Augurium* des Heils, Hermes, 77, 1942, p. 256 ss.

[50] Cf. J.-C. RICHARD, art. cit. (n. 10), p. 377, n. 5.

[51] E. NASH, Bildlexikon zur Topographie des antiken Rom, I, Tübingen, 1961, p. 500; F. COARELLI, Guida archeologica di Roma², Milan, 1975, p. 285 s.

[52] BMC, Roman Empire, I, p. 209, n°s 64 ss., pl. 39, 17−18. Cf. D. F. BROWN, Temples of Rome as Coin Types, Numism. Notes and Monogr., 90, New York, 1940, p. 33; G. FUCHS, Architekturdarstellungen auf Münzen der Republik und der frühen Kaiserzeit, aus d. Nachlaß hrsg. v. J. BLEICKEN & M. FUHRMANN, Antike Münzen und geschnittene Steine, 1, Berlin, 1969, pl. 11, 127−128.

[53] BMC, Roman Empire, I, p. 299 ss., n°s 156 ss.; p. 238 s., n°s 198 ss.; p. 243, n°s 225 ss.; p. 263, n°s 319 ss.; p. 273, n°s 374 s., et pl. 42,6−7; 43,8−9; 44,5−6; 47,6; G. FUCHS, op. cit., p. 46 et pl. 11,123−126. Bonne macrophotographie dans E. NASH, op. cit., I, p. 503, fig. 619.

porte tantôt à gauche, tantôt à droite: figuré dans l'espace, l'édifice a une réalité, une consistance frappantes et voulues (pl. I, 1–4). Avec ses quatre colonnes d'angle (en partie cannelées sur certains exemplaires et coiffées de chapiteaux corinthiens), le Janus n'a évidemment rien d'un temple proprement dit. Les sesterces et les as de Rome (ou de Lyon) reproduisent la porte avec des variantes plus ou moins notables. Pourvus de deux gros anneaux, les vantaux sont chacun triplement compartimentés: ce sont les fameuses portes de bronze dont parlent Virgile[54] et Procope[55]. Souvent, un grènetis semi-circulaire signale l'archivolte. Sur la face latérale, visible à gauche de l'entrée, d'autres grènetis marquent la limite inférieure ou supérieure d'une frise de rinceaux fleuris. Au-dessus de cette frise végétale, une sorte d'attique porte un élégant décor de palmettes qui couronne tout l'édifice (et que V. MÜLLER[56] a comparé à certains monuments étrusques). Bâtis en *opus quadratum*, avec des pierres de taille bien apparentes sur la plupart des exemplaires, les flancs sont éclairés tout au long par deux ou trois rangs de fenêtres quadrillées. La guirlande qui pend par devant les vantaux et dont la courbe s'arrondit inversement à celle de l'archivolte (avec un subtil effet de contraste et de croisements géométriques) évoque la fête en même temps que la victoire[57].

Contrairement à V. MÜLLER[58] et à M. GUARDUCCI[59] qui attribuaient le décor architectonique à une époque relativement haute, H. BAUER[60] ne lui assigne pas une date antérieure au milieu du Ier siècle av. J.-C. et suppose qu'il s'agit d'un édifice rénové par Auguste. La signification du type monétaire s'en trouverait renforcée d'une référence au grand ancêtre de Néron, fondateur de la 'Paix Auguste'. Jamais le Janus n'avait été célébré monétairement. Le talent du graveur néronien, qui s'est distingué ailleurs par l'originalité de son style, dans les deux séries du Port d'Ostie (PORTVS AVGVSTI!)[61] et du MACELLVM MAGNVM[62], a fixé le prestige exceptionnel de l'événement[63].

---

[54] Aen., VII,609.

[55] B.Goth., I,25 (II, p. 127, 5 s. HAURY–WIRTH, Leipzig, 1963): θύραιτε χαλκαῖ ἐφ' ἑκατέρῳ προσώπῳ εἰσίν. Plus haut (p. 126, 21), Procope décrit le 'temple' comme ἅπας χαλκοῦς, ce qui peut s'entendre d'un revêtement intérieur: cf. M. GUARDUCCI, art. cit. (n. 24), p. 1611ss.

[56] The Shrine of Janus *Geminus* in Rome, AJA, 47, 1943, p. 437s., 440.

[57] R. TURCAN, Les guirlandes dans l'antiquité classique, JAC, 14, 1971, p. 109.

[58] Art. cit. (n. 56), p. 439s.

[59] Art. cit. (n. 24), p. 1612ss.

[60] Art. cit. (n. 13), p. 315; mais cf. supra, n. 33.

[61] BMC, Roman Empire, I, p. CLXXVIs.; pl. 41,7; 46,6; 48,2; G. FUCHS, op. cit., p. 63 et pl. 12,131–132. Sur le nom de Portus Augusti, cf. J. CARCOPINO, Virgile et les origines d'Ostie², Coll.Hier., Paris, 1968, p. 645ss.; F. RICHARD, Portus Augusti, Cahiers d'Histoire, 22, 1977, p. 295–311.

[62] BMC, Roman Empire, I, p. CLXXIX, pl. 43,5–7; 46,6; K. WULZINGER, Die Macellum-Dupondien des Nero, Numismatik, 2, 1933, p. 83ss., 116ss.; G. FUCHS, op. cit., p. 12, 133–135; 13,136.

[63] B. H. WARMINGTON, Nero. Reality and Legend, Londres, 1969, p. 95, 121; W. HUSS, Die Propaganda Neros, Ant.Class., 47, 1978, p. 137. Ce prestige aura des prolongements dans l'imagerie des médaillons contorniates: A. ALFÖLDI, Die Kontorniaten. Ein verkanntes

Cette fermeture du Janus consacrait le protectorat de Rome sur l'Arménie. Comme celles d'Auguste, elle confirmait avec la paix des armes l'*Imperium Romanum*. Mais il n'est plus question de Janus Quirinus. La légende PACE P(*opuli*) R(*omani*) TERRA MARIQ(*ue*) PARTA IANVM CLVSIT fait très exactement écho à l'expression des 'Res Gestae', qui correspond d'ailleurs à la formulation technique des sénatus-consultes[64]. Mais certains as et certains dupondius[65] portent la légende PACE VBIQ(*ue*) PARTA, ce qui souligne le souci de glorifier la paix impériale comme universelle. Cette variante veut singulariser aussi une fermeture du Janus qui, en 66, avait l'avantage de se faire trois cents ans après la seule qui fût attestée durant l'époque républicaine, celle de −235[66]. Certes les monnaies commémorant l'événement ont été frappées (semble-t-il)[67] à partir de 64, et beaucoup l'ont été en 65. Or Suétone[68] situe la fermeture du Janus Geminus immédiatement après le couronnement de Tiridate à Rome, soit en 66. H. MATTINGLY[69] croit possible que la cérémonie ait été rééditée *"formerly"* en 66, après avoir été célébrée *"originally"* en 64. Mais on constate aussi que

---

Propagandamittel der stadtrömischen heidnischen Aristokratie in ihrem Kampfe gegen das christliche Kaisertum, in: Festschr.d.ungar.numism.Gesellschaft, Budapest, 1943, p. 58, 115; A. ALFÖLDI−E. ALFÖLDI, Die Kontorniat-Medaillons, Ant. Münzen & geschnittene Steine, VI, 1, Berlin, 1976, p. 42, n° 146; 169, n° 537; 203, n° 108 et pl. 22,4, 49,6−8.

[64] J. GAGÉ, éd. commentée des 'Res gestae', p. 95; A. MOMIGLIANO, *Terra marique*, JRS, 32, 1942, p. 63.

[65] BMC, Roman Empire, I, p. CLXXIX, p. 239, n°s 203 s., pl. 43,9; p. 244, n°s 227 ss., pl. 44,5.

[66] M. GRANT, op. cit. (n. 48), p. 5.

[67] BMC, Roman Empire, I, p. CLXXIV. A partir de 66, IMP précède le nom de Néron, et comme *praenomen* ce titre correspond à la XIe salutation impériale. Sur les explications qu'on a données de l'anticipation monétaire, voir maintenant G. B. TOWNEND, Tacitus, Suetonius and the Temple of Janus, Hermes, 108, 1980, p. 236 s. Néron aurait été victime des circonstances. La fermeture du Janus fut différée par l'incendie de Rome en juillet 64, puis par la conjuration de Pison et la mort de Poppée après les 'Neronia' de 65 (ibid., p. 237). Finalement, d'après G. B. TOWNEND, cette fermeture n'eut peut-être jamais lieu, malgré le témoignage explicite de Suétone, qui n'aurait tenu compte que des monnaies ou d'une source écrite faisant état des monnaies. En effet, Orose écrit (Adv. Pag., VII,9,9) que Vespasien ferma le temple de Janus *sexto demum . . . post urbem conditam*, ce qui − compte tenu des fermetures antérieures attribuées à Numa, à T. Manlius et (trois fois) à Auguste − exclurait celle de Néron. Orose dépendrait ici d'un livre perdu des 'Histoires' de Tacite (p. 238). Mais l'autorité d'Orose est au moins sujette à caution, et rien ne prouve qu'il ait bien compris ou fidèlement transcrit les termes d'un historien éminemment subtil et ambigu. Vespasien peut aussi n'avoir pas voulu reconnaître la clôture néronienne du Janus, considérant que son règne inaugurait réellement une ère de paix (p. 240), d'où le grandiose 'Templum Pacis', symbole de toute une politique. En tout cas, ni Suétone ni aucune autre source que le douteux Orose n'affirme que Vespasien ait fermé le temple du dieu biface. Aucune monnaie de Vespasien n'en témoigne directement ou indirectement. *Non liquet.*

[68] Ner., 13,4; M.-L. CHAUMONT, L'Arménie entre Rome et l'Iran, I. De l'avènement d'Auguste à l'avènement de Dioclétien, ANRW, II, 9,1, Berlin−New York, 1976, p. 123; K. R. BRADLEY, Suetonius' 'Life of Nero'. An Historical Commentary, Coll.Latomus, 157, Bruxelles, 1978, p. 91.

[69] BMC, Roman Empire, I, p. CLXXIV. Cf. G. B. TOWNEND, art. cit., p. 236.

la publicité monétaire anticipe souvent sur les événements: c'est ainsi, par exemple, que les sesterces d'Hadrien représentent le temple de Vénus et de Rome bien avant l'achèvement et l'inauguration du sanctuaire[70]. Il n'est donc pas impensable qu'on ait lancé l'image et la légende du IANVM CLVSIT pour chauffer l'opinion qui attendait la paix: ne la prépare-t-on pas aujourd'hui de la sorte à certaines solennités par la presse et les moyens audiovisuels de propagande qui répercutent les slogans jadis monnayés par les sesterces? La fermeture du Janus aurait pu se faire en 64 ou en 65. Mais on retarda intentionnellement la cérémonie afin qu'elle suivît et conclût la visite de Tiridate[71], hommage de vassalité au monarque universel: *pace ubique parta* . . . La paix mondiale ne pouvait se confondre qu'avec la paix romaine. Mais on voulut surtout que la clôture du Janus coïncidât avec le troisième centenaire d'une autre clôture, celle de −235.

Un détail de l'arc triomphal figuré au revers d'autres sesterces a été commenté en relation avec la formule TERRA MARIQ(*ue*) des monnaies au Janus. G. FUCHS[72] a voulu reconnaître les 'génies' de la Terre et de la Mer dans les deux personnages qu'on discerne au pied de l'attique, au-dessus de l'entablement, de part et d'autre du groupe triomphal. Mais cette hypothèse ne tient pas, car la mer est d'ordinaire (et en principe) personnifiée par Oceanus, la terre par Tellus, et tous deux figurent normalement couchés: or les deux prétendus 'génies' figurent debout, et sur certains exemplaires on les voit même qui s'élancent à droite et à gauche respectivement. H. MATTINGLY[73] y déchiffrait dubitativement des soldats qui participent au cortège victorieux.

Quoi qu'il en soit, Néron a revalorisé et, pour ainsi dire, repopularisé Janus à la faveur de la paix qui suivit le traité de Rhandeia (63)[74], mais on attendit 66 pour le sceller plus solennellement par une commémoration qui renouait avec la tradition républicaine, lorsque Tiridate eut salué l'empereur comme un 'Mithra'[75]. Est-ce que les prétentions héliaques de Néron avaient un rapport quelconque avec la publicité faite au dieu que Nigidius Figulus identifiait un siècle plus tôt avec Apollon[76]? N'interprétait-on pas les deux mains de la statue d'après les règles du comput digital, pour y déchiffrer les 365 jours de l'année solaire[77]? Peut-être s'agit-il d'un faux problème. Il est sûr, en tout cas, que la promotion de Janus Quadrifrons sous Domitien confirmera au dieu une sorte de stature cosmique.

---

[70] P. L. STRACK, Untersuchungen zur römischen Reichsprägung des zweiten Jahrhunderts, II. Die Reichsprägung zur Zeit des Hadrian, Stuttgart, 1933, p. 174 ss.

[71] M.-L. CHAUMONT, art. cit., p. 119 s.

[72] Op. cit. (n. 52), p. 108. Il s'agit des sesterces du type BMC, Roman Empire, I, p. 234, n°s 183 ss.; p. 265, n°s 329 ss., pl. 43,3; 46,5; 48,4; G. FUCHS, op. cit., pl. 14,142−143.

[73] BMC, loc. cit., p. 234.

[74] M.-L. CHAUMONT, art. cit., p. 116 ss.

[75] Ibid., p. 120; D.C., LXIII,5,2 (III, p. 70, 13 BOISSEVAIN).

[76] Supra, n. 45.

[77] Plin., NH, XXXIV, 33; Macr., Sat., I,9,10; Lyd., De mens., IV,1 (p. 64, 2 ss. WUENSCH); G. CAPDEVILLE, art. cit., p. 413, n. 2.

III. Janus Quadrifrons

Selon une tradition attestée tardivement les Romains en prenant Faléries (241 av. J.-C.) auraient emporté une idole de Janus à quatre têtes[78]. En admettant l'historicité et la matérialité du fait, on n'est pas forcé de supposer qu'il s'agissait originairement d'un Janus (même les hermès bicéphales de l'art étrusque ne s'identifient pas nécessairement avec le dieu romain)[79]. Mais la tradition pourrait s'expliquer en fonction du nom même de Faléries. Festus[80] nous apprend qu'en étrusque *fale* signifiait *caelum*: or on faisait précisément de Janus un dieu du ciel, au moins depuis le Ier siècle av. J.-C.[81], époque à laquelle pourrait remonter cette histoire de statue qui rappelle l'*evocatio* de la Junon Reine de Veies. Les quatre faces de ce Janus s'interprétaient comme une référence plastique aux quatre éléments, aux quatre points cardinaux, aux quatre saisons[82], ce qui corroborait l'équation Janus = *caelum*. Janus Quadrifrons pourrait fort bien aussi être une „*Erfindung domitianischer Zeit*" (G. RADKE)[83]. Mais cette „*Erfindung*" est solidaire de l'exégèse cosmologique du dieu qui s'exprimait depuis plus d'un siècle.

Servius écrit que le *simulacrum* falisque fut transféré *ad forum transitorium et quattuor portarum unum templum est institutum*. On a donc admis généralement qu'un nouveau Janus à quatre baies servait d'entrée au Forum Transitorium de Domitien, face au temple de Minerve: ce tétrapylon aurait donc abrité l'idole 'tétramorphe' dont nous parlent Macrobe, Servius, Augustin, Johannès Lydus et Isidore de Séville[84]. On a contesté cependant que le nouveau monument se fût ajouté à l'ancien[85], Stace[86] faisant état d'un double seuil (*utroque a limine grates/ Ianus agit*) et de la «double voix» (*gemina . . . voce*) du dieu bicéphale. Certes Martial ne dit pas explicitement qu'un Janus flavien fût érigé à quelques pas du vieux Janus Geminus. Mais le texte d'Epigr., X,28,3—5 n'exclut pas non plus la construction d'un tétrapylon monumental contrastant avec la modestie de l'espace occupé par le premier sanctuaire numaïque: «Main-

---

[78] Macr., Sat., I,9,13; Serv., Ad Aen., VII,607 (II, p. 171, 18 ss. THILO—HAGEN).

[79] Cf. par exemple R. PETTAZZONI, art. cit. (n. 4), p. 85 s.

[80] S. v. *Falae* (p. 78, 23 LINDSAY). Cf. HESYCH., s. v. βαλόν (= οὐρανόν); R. PETTAZZONI, art. cit., p. 84 s. Johannès Lydus affirme de Janus (De mens., IV,2, p. 65, 1 s. WUENSCH) que παρὰ Θούσκοις οὐρανὸν λέγεσθαι.

[81] A.-J. FESTUGIÈRE, op. cit (n. 45), p. 176 ss. (théorie de l'augure M. Messala).

[82] Macr., Sat., I,9,13; Serv., Ad Aen., VII,607 (II, p. 172,2 THILO—HAGEN); Lyd., De mens., IV,1 (p. 64, 4 WUENSCH); Isid., Etym., VIII,11,37.

[83] Die Götter Altitaliens, p. 148.

[84] Macr., Sat. I,9,13; Serv., Ad Aen., VII,607; Aug., CD, VIII, 8 (d'après Varron: R. AGAHD, Varronis Antiquitatum Rerum Divinarum Libri, Philol., Suppl., 24, Leipzig, 1898, rééd. anast. New York, 1975, p. 204, XVI, fr. 12; B. CARDAUNS, M. Terentius Varro. Antiquitates Rerum Divinarum, Abhandl. Akad. Mainz, 1976, I, p. 100, fr. 234); Lyd., De mens., IV, 1 (p. 64, 4 WUENSCH); Isid., Etym., VII,11,37.

[85] G. CAPDEVILLE, art. cit., p. 415, n. 4.

[86] Silv., IV,1,12 et 16.

tenant», écrit le poète, «tes seuils sont entourés des présents des Césars et tu comptes, Janus, autant de forums que tu as de visages» (et fora tot numeras, Iane, quot ora geris). On a peine à croire que la locution tot . . . quot ne vise ici que deux forums, Romanum et Transitorium[87]. Le compliment eût été plat et ne méritait pas d'être formulé! L'hyperbole − si c'en est une − n'a de sens que dans l'optique d'un spectateur qui, moyennant quatre têtes comme celles de Janus Quadrifrons, pouvait non seulement voir le Forum Transitorium, mais apercevoir à travers et par delà certains passages voûtés les Forums de César, d'Auguste, de la Paix et même le Forum Romain par le couloir de l'Argilète. Mais à l'emplacement où I. GISMONDI[88] situait le tétrapylon, je suppose que Janus Quadrifrons avait vue directement sur le Forum Transitorium au nord, indirectement sur le Forum de la Paix à l'est, le Forum de César à l'ouest, le Forum républicain au sud. Comme on n'a rien retrouvé de ce Janus, le problème archéologique et topographique reste posé[89].

Récemment, H. BAUER[90] a restitué un temple (à proprement parler) de Janus, face à celui de Minerve, et situé un Janus-passage aux confins sud-ouest du Forum Transitorium et de l'Argilète: c'est à ce Janus que Martial appliquerait le fora tot . . . quot ora précité (ce qui me paraît difficile à admettre). Quant au témoignage de Servius[91] − un Africain qui ignorait tout, paraît-il, de la topographie romaine! − H. BAUER[92] l'exclut purement et simplement en même temps que le tétrapylon, ce qui n'emporte pas la conviction.

Il reste que les travaux de Domitien ont à un certain moment concerné Janus et qu'au IVe siècle ap. J.-C. on liait la mise en valeur du Quadrifrons à l'aménagement du Forum Transitorium. Pourquoi et quand cette nouvelle présentation du dieu ʻtétramorpheʼ? Le Forum de Domitien est mentionné par Martial[93] au premier livre de ses ʻEpigrammesʼ, publié avec le second livre dans les premiers mois de 86, mais écrit sans doute antérieurement. Si l'érection d'un nouveau Janus Quadrifrons datait de 86, l'hypothèse suivante pourrait être risquée: la

---

[87] Comme le pense H. BAUER, art. cit. (n. 13), p. 317. Mais le texte de Mart., Epigr., VIII, 2,3 ss. n'a pas non plus valeur de preuve en faveur d'un Janus Quadrifrons.

[88] G. LUGLI, Roma antica. Il centro monumentale, Rome, 1946, pl. V. Cf. P. H. VON BLANCKENHAGEN, Flavische Architektur und ihre Dekoration untersucht am Nervaforum, Berlin, 1940, pl. 47; F. COARELLI, op. cit (n. 51), p. 102−103.

[89] Cf. L. A. HOLLAND, op. cit., p. 92 ss.; F. COARELLI, op. cit., p. 111; H. BAUER, art. cit., p. 301 ss.

[90] Ibid., p. 312 et Abb. 3. Le templum Iani des Mirabilia «ne peut être que le temple de César» d'après L. DUCHESNE, Notes sur la topographie de Rome au Moyen-Âge, IV. Le Forum de Nerva et ses environs, MEFR, 9, 1889, p. 352, cf. p. 353 (= IDEM, Scripta Minora, Coll. de l'Ecole Française de Rome, 13, Rome, 1973, p. 79, cf. p. 82).

[91] Ad Aen., VII,607 (II, p. 171, 20 s. THILO−HAGEN): translatum est ad forum transitorium et quattuor portarum unum templum est institutum. Cf. Lyd., De mens., IV,1 (p. 64, 4 s. WUENSCH): ἔνθεν καὶ τετράμορφον ἀπὸ τῶν τεσσάρων τροπῶν· καὶ τοιοῦτον αὐτοῦ ἄγαλμα ἐν τῷ φόρῳ τοῦ Νερβᾶ ἔτι καὶ νῦν λέγεται σεσωσμένον (= J. LUGLI, Fontes ad topographiam veteris urbis Romae pertinentes, lib. XVI, vol. VI, Rome, 1965, p. 42, n° 247).

[92] Art. cit., p. 318.

[93] Epigr. I,2,7 s.

tradition faisait du vieux Janus Geminus la première institution du règne de Numa, et dans le récit livien la construction du 'temple' suit immédiatement l'avènement du deuxième roi de Rome qu'on datait de −715 (chronologie varronnienne)[94]. En 86, on pouvait donc fêter le huitième centenaire du Janus Geminus, et l'on peut se demander si Domitien n'a pas voulu faire coïncider l'inauguration de son Janus Quadrifrons avec cet anniversaire. Deux ans plus tard, il célébrera (avec six ans d'avance) les Jeux Séculaires, fête du renouvellement et de la régénération du Peuple Romain qui sacralise un nouveau bail avec les dieux. C'est aussi l'époque où Stace[95] et Martial[96] invoquent Janus comme le père tout-puissant des années et du monde, comme le rénovateur des siècles et le maître du Temps. Quand l'auteur des 'Silves' le qualifie de *immensi reparator maximus aevi*, il donne du dieu en latin la définition même d'un Janus-Aiôn[97] qui personnifie la *renovatio temporum*, ou − comme on dira au IVe siècle pour le onzième centenaire de Rome − la FEL(*icium*) TEMP(*orum*) REPARATIO. Le développement et la popularisation des théories syncrétiques brodées autour de Janus ne pouvaient qu'encourager le culte d'un Quadrifrons, image monstrueuse du Temps cyclique et cosmique rythmé par la tétrade solaire des saisons. Malheureusement aucune allusion monétaire ne confirme sur ce point les intentions du pouvoir. Mais on dut se plaire à faire valoir le fait que l'hommage au Janus des recommencements voisinait avec l'engagement rituel d'un nouveau contrat séculaire avec les déités tutélaires de Rome. Topographiquement aussi l'érection du nouveau Janus prenait un sens symbolique. En effet, que l'on restitue au sud du Forum Transitorium un temple proprement dit ou un tétrapylon, l'édifice se trouvait sur le chemin qui menait de Mars Ultor au Forum Pacis: le Janus de Domitien servait donc réellement de passage de la guerre à la paix[98].

IV. Janus Quirinus ou Janus-Aiôn?

C'est dans le monnayage d'Hadrien qu'on trouve la première et unique représentation officielle d'un Janus Quadrifrons. Il s'agit d'un as[99] frappé entre 125 et 128 (après l'été 123 selon P. L. STRACK[100]; en 126, pour les *Decennalia*,

---

[94] Liv., I,19,2 (= J. LUGLI, op. cit., lib. XI, vol. III, Rome, 1955, p. 252, n° 5).

[95] Silv., IV,1,11 et 17s. Cf. L. A. HOLLAND, op. cit., p. 100; J. BEAUJEU, op. cit. (n. 45), p. 143.

[96] Epigr., X,28,1.

[97] Voir le commentaire d'H. FRÈRE, éd.-trad. de Stace, Silves, II[2], Paris, 1961, ad Silv., IV, 1,2, p. 136; J. BEAUJEU, loc. cit. et p. 150.

[98] R. SCHILLING, art. cit., p. 129 s.

[99] RIC, II, p. 426, n°s 662 s.; BMC, Roman Empire, III, Londres, 1936 (réédit. anast. 1966), p. 437, n° 1335, pl. 82,10.

[100] Untersuchungen zur römischen Reichsprägung des zweiten Jahrhunderts, II. Die Reichsprägung zur Zeit des Hadrian, Stuttgart, 1933, p. 80.

selon P. V. Hill[101]): avec la légende COS III, Janus y figure debout de face, la main droite serrant un 'sceptre' (ou le grand bâton dont nous parlent Ovide[102] et Macrobe[103]?), la main gauche appuyée sur la hanche (pl. I,6). Trois faces sont visibles, une frontalement, les deux autres de profil; la quatrième face (opposée à la face médiane) reste naturellement cachée. Un *aureus*[104] émis en 119–122 (à la fin de 122 ou en 123 selon P. L. Strack[105]; en 121 selon P. V. Hill[106]) porte également au revers un Janus, mais simplement *bifrons*, debout de face, tenant son 'sceptre' d'une main, l'autre sur la hanche, comme sur l'as précité, mais avec la légende PM TR P COS III (pl. I,5). Pour P. L. Strack[107], qui suit L. Laffranchi[108], l'occasion de ces représentations de Janus (les plus anciennes du dieu en pied que nous connaissions) fut un compromis de paix conclu avec les Parthes en 123. Contrairement à ce qu'affirme J. Beaujeu[109], le savant allemand ne rapporte pas ce type «à une victoire militaire en Orient» – ce qui effectivement «paraît invraisemblable» –, mais au succès de négociations qui moyennant un „*Ausgleich*" ont empêché la guerre. H. Mattingly[110] a justement souligné la nouveauté du type de Janus dans la série monétaire. Cette image signifierait-elle la fermeture du 'temple'? C'est au moins "*doubtful*", car précisément le temple ne figure pas sur les monnaies d'Hadrien. Même sans clôture officielle du Janus la représentation du dieu pourrait, il est vrai, symboliser la politique de paix à laquelle Hadrien voulut se tenir, après l'impérialisme conquérant et en partie malheureux de son prédécesseur: *et tenendae per orbem terrarum paci operam impendit*[111]. Mais l'allégorie de *Pax* sur des monnaies[112] frappées dès 117, puis de 118 à 122 suffisait à marquer explicitement cette volonté et sans aucune des ambiguïtés impliquées dans le Janus Quirinus augustéen. D'autre part, si le type simple et traditionnel de Janus Bifrons peut correspondre à l'interprétation de P. L. Strack, en revanche l'image d'un Quadrifrons trahit d'autres préoccupations que celle d'affirmer publiquement le souci d'éviter en Orient de nouveaux conflits. Autrement dit, les as émis entre 125 et 128 appellent une tout autre exégèse que les *aurei* de 119–122 (ou 123).

---

[101] The Dating and Arrangement of the Undated Coins of Rome A.D. 98–148, Londres, 1970, p. 60, 160, n°s 323/4.

[102] Fast., I,99. Cf. R. Schilling, art. cit., p. 93, n. 2.

[103] Sat., I,9,7: *Nam et cum clavi ac virga figuratur, quasi omnium et portarum custos et rector viarum.*

[104] RIC, II, p. 348, n° 62, pl. 12,225; BMC, Roman Empire, III, p. 254, n° 100, pl. 49,2.

[105] Loc. cit. (n. 100).

[106] Op. cit., p. 54, 156, n° 178.

[107] Loc. cit.

[108] Die Daten der Reisen des Kaisers Hadrian auf Grund der numismatischen Zeugnisse neu behandelt, Num.Zeitschr., NF. 19, 1926, p. 116: „*Das mag auf die Verständigung mit den Parthern anspielen*".

[109] Op. cit., p. 158, n. 1.

[110] BMC, Roman Empire, III, p. CLXVII.

[111] SHA, Hadr., 5,1 (I, p. 7, 10s. Hohl–Samberger–Seyfarth). Cf. M. K. Thornton, Hadrian and his Reign, ANRW, II, 2, Berlin–New York, 1975, p. 435.

[112] RIC, II, p. 339, n° 7; 340, n° 12; 341, n° 21.

Le dieu à quatre faces est avant tout maître des commencements et des recommencements cycliques. Cette représentation me paraît inséparable de la mystique hadrianienne de la *Renovatio temporum* et du *Saeculum aureum*[113]. Janus n'avait-il pas partagé en Italie, avec Saturne (Kronos ou Chronos, autre dieu du Temps!), la responsabilité de l'âge d'or? En 128, Hadrien allait fonder le temple de Vénus et de Rome pour le 880e anniversaire de l'*Urbs*, en tenant compte des calculs préconisés par les *genethliaci*[114]. Un cycle de 440 ans correspondait, en somme, à quatre siècles de 110 ans (selon la mesure des *Ludi saeculares*)[115]. En 128 commençait pour Rome un nouveau cycle de 440 ans, tétrade séculaire qu'on pouvait mettre en parallèle avec celle du Quadrifrons, quatre saisons de 110 ans . . . Cette préoccupation dut compter davantage que la politique proche-orientale dans l'exaltation du Janus à quatre têtes.

V. Un quatrième centenaire

Entre 140 et 144, des as et des sesterces[116] frappés à l'effigie d'Antonin le Pieux portent au revers, avec la légende TR POT COS III, le même type de Janus biface que les *aurei* émis naguère par Hadrien: la main gauche sur la hanche, un linge roulé autour du ventre, le dieu debout de face tient le même bâton que les numismates appellent traditionnellement un 'sceptre', mais qui s'identifie peut être avec le *baculum,* attribut du *viator* ou du gardien des portes et des routes[117] (pl. II,7).

J. H. ECKHEL[118] faisait rentrer ce type dans la galerie des antiquités de Rome qui illustrent monétairement la commémoration du neuvième centenaire de l'*Urbs*. H. MATTINGLY[119] reste influencé par l'opinion de celui qu'on a justement considéré comme le père de la numismatique gréco-romaine, mais qui n'a pas serré d'assez près la chronologie des émissions: "*Janus in this context seems to be rather the primitive king of Latium than the index of peace and war*". Ce "*context*", c'est l'émission contemporaine de pièces au type de la Louve et des Jumeaux, symbole de la renaissance de Rome. De son côté P. V. HILL[120] croit devoir reconnaître en Janus "*the patron of Latium*" plutôt que le dieu dont le

---

[113] J. BEAUJEU, op. cit., p. 150ss.

[114] R. TURCAN, La fondation du temple de Vénus et de Rome, Latomus, 23, 1964, p. 42—55.

[115] Censor., De die nat., 17, 9 (p. 46, 7ss. JAHN). Cf. P. BRIND'AMOUR, L'origine des Jeux Séculaires, ANRW, II, 16.2, Berlin—New York, 1978, p. 1334ss.

[116] RIC, III, p. 112, n° 644; p. 117, n° 693; BMC, Roman Empire, IV, Londres, 1940, (réédit. anast. 1968), p. 210, n° 1317 et pl. 31, 5; p. 220, n° 1369.

[117] Supra, n. 102—103.

[118] Doctrina numorum veterum, VII, Vienne, 1828, p. 16.

[119] BMC, Roman Empire, IV, p. LXXX.

[120] Op. cit. (n. 101), p. 91, 184, n° 263.

temple fermé signifie la paix; mais comme dieu du seuil, il marquerait aussi l'entrée dans un nouveau cycle séculaire . . . Plusieurs types de revers monétaires ont, certes, anticipé sur la célébration des 900 ans de Rome. Mais Janus apparaît bien avant 148 et son image n'est pas rééditée à cette date! P. L. STRACK[121] situe l'émission des bronzes au Janus en 143, mais arbitrairement, pour pouvoir rapprocher du dieu de la pacification armée la victoire de Q. Lollius Urbicus sur les Brigantes et la deuxième salutation impériale d'Antonin. Le savant allemand suppose à cette date un Janus Clausus. Historiquement, c'est possible et vraisemblable. Mais numismatiquement, c'est l'image du Janus-monument ou des portes fermées de Janus, et non pas du Janus-dieu, qui convenait à la publicité monétaire de l'événement. Idéologiquement, la politique de paix préconisée et pratiquée par Antonin le Pieux pouvait justifier la réédition du type de Janus. Mais pourquoi entre 140 et 144?

P. V. HILL[122] date ces monnaies au Janus de 140 et les impute au "900th anniversary of Rome anticipated". Mais 141 est plus proche de 140 que 148. Or l'année 141 se trouvait coïncider avec le 400e anniversaire du temple de Janus que C. Duilius avait fait élever en −260 au Forum Holitorium et que Tibère avait restauré en 17[123]. M. GRANT[124] a noté que dans la même suite monétaire des années 140−144 comptent Juventas, Honos et (parmi les médaillons) la triade capitoline. Le temple de Juventas (voué en −207) avait trois-cent-cinquante ans en 144. En 143, il y avait trois-cent-cinquante ans aussi que le temple d'Honos (et de Virtus) avait été rebâti par Claudius Marcellus (−208). Quant au temple de Jupiter Capitolin, il avait très exactement six-cent-cinquante ans en 142. Il semble donc bien que le Janus d'Antonin rentre dans une série commémorative et non pas événementielle: il consacre un anniversaire au lieu d'illustrer un fait isolé de politique extérieure.

VI. Le Janus de Commode

Evoquant la réouverture du 'temple' de Janus sous Gordien III, Aurelius Victor[125] précise qu'antérieurement 'Marcus' en avait fermé les portes: s'agit-il de Marc-Aurèle ou de M. Aurelius Commodus? Assurément du premier, car partout ailleurs, là où il parle de Marcus, Aurelius Victor désigne indubitablement Marc-Aurèle[126].

[121] Untersuchungen zur römischen Reichsprägung des zweiten Jahrhunderts, III. Die Reichsprägung des Antoninus Pius, Stuttgart, 1937, p. 77.
[122] Op. cit., p. 91, 184.
[123] Supra, n. 51; M. GRANT, Roman Anniversary Issues, p. 105.
[124] Loc. cit.
[125] Lib. de Caes., 27,7 (p. 105, 29 PICHLMAYR−GRUENDEL).
[126] Ibid., 16, 9 (p. 95, 7 P.-G.); 20, 30 (p. 100, 26). Cf. Epit. de Caes., 16, 14 (p. 153, 24).

Mais de tous les empereurs, c'est Commode qui a le plus abondamment fait valoir l'image de Janus: as et sesterces[127] de 186, *aurei*[128] de 187 et médaillons contemporains[129]. Les uns et les autres représentent le Bifrons dans son temple figuré symboliquement soit par deux colonnes coiffées de leurs chapiteaux qui supportent une arcature, soit par deux paires de colonnes où s'appuient deux archivoltes vues de biais (pl. II,8; III,9,12−13). Le dieu est statufié debout de face sur un socle quadrangulaire(?). Comme sur les monnaies d'Hadrien et d'Antonin, on l'y voit pourvu d'un grand *baculum*, la main gauche sur la hanche; un pan du manteau qui lui enveloppe le bas du corps est ramené sur son épaule gauche. Des médaillons frappés en 187 (pl. III,10), qui portent au droit l'effigie de Commode, représentent au revers le buste de Janus avec un pan de manteau sur l'épaule gauche[130]. D'autres, enfin (pl. III,11), portent à l'avers le double buste ('janiforme') de Commode drapé, cuirassé à droite et d'Hercule lauré à gauche (Jupiter suivant A. B. Cook); au revers figure la Terre étendue à gauche, la main droite appuyée sur un globe étoilé autour duquel folâtrent les quatre génies des Saisons, au-dessus de la légende d'exergue: TELLVS STABIL(*ita*)[131]. Mais la double effigie d'avers de ces médaillons n'a sans doute qu'un rapport formel extérieur et de pure apparence avec le dieu Janus.

Un médaillon publié jadis par E. GERHARD[132], et dont W. H. ROSCHER[133], J. TOUTAIN[134], J. GAGÉ[135] ont cru devoir tenir compte, est pour le moins suspect. Il s'agit d'un exemplaire du Cabinet d'Arolsen qui nous montrerait au revers debout à côté d'un enfant pourvu d'une *cornucopia*, Commode 'en Janus' tenant un cerceau à travers lequel passent les quatre Saisons. W. FROEHNER[136] écrivait sagement: «Il faudrait examiner si cette pièce n'a pas été retouchée». Pour A. B. COOK[137] aussi, *"This bizarre medaillon is, I think, merely a tooled specimen of a type first struck by Antoninus Pius in 158 A.D. . . . and sub-*

---

[127] RIC, III, p. 419, n° 460 et pl. 16,329; p. 421, n° 479; BMC, Roman Empire, IV, p. 803, n°s 568ss. et pl. 106,5.

[128] RIC, III, p. 381, n° 141; D. F. BROWN, Temples of Rome as Coin Types, p. 21, n. 19 et pl. VII,2: ici pl. III,9.

[129] F. GNECCHI, I medaglioni romani, II, Milan, 1912, p. 62, n° 94 et pl. 84,5; A. B. COOK, Zeus. A Study in Ancient Religion, II. Zeus God of the Dark Sky (Thunder and Lightning), Cambridge, 1925, p. 365s.; A. ALFÖLDI, Die Kontorniaten, p. 39s. et pl. I,7 (,,*Neujahrsmedaille*", p. 39).

[130] F. GNECCHI, op. cit., II, p. 62, n°s 92/3, pl. 84,4.

[131] Ibid., p. 66, n° 131, pl. 87,1. Cf. W. FROEHNER, Les médaillons de l'Empire romain, Paris, 1878, p. 131; A. B. COOK, op. cit., II, p. 370; J. BEAUJEU, op. cit., p. 402.

[132] Gräbervenus. Felicitas. Novus Annus, Arch.Zeit., 18, 1861, p. 137 et pl. 147,3.

[133] Art. Janus, dans: W. H. ROSCHER, Ausf. Lexikon d. gr. u. röm. Mythologie, II, 1, Leipzig, 1890—94, réimpr. Hildesheim, 1965, col. 38, 52.

[134] Art. Janus, dans: Dict.des Antiqu.gr.et rom., III, 1, Paris, 1899, p. 612.

[135] Les classes sociales dans l'Empire romain², Bibl.hist., Paris, 1971, p. 215. Cf. encore M. MESLIN, op. cit. (n. 11), p. 35, où le médaillon est appelé «monnaie» et où (n. 2) la date de 185 est déduite d'une légende IMP VII COS III: or Commode est COS III en 181 . . . En fait, le médaillon porte l'indication COS IIII!

[136] Les médaillons de l'Empire romain, p. 121, n. 1.

[137] Op. cit., p. 372.

sequently repeated by Commodus". De fait, le type est celui même des médaillons qui célèbrent Aiôn et le renouveau des âges, avec la même légende (TR P X IMP VII COS IIII), qui les date de 185. Si l'Aiôn de l'exemplaire d'Arolsen est bien *bifrons*, on peut donc se demander si la face barbue de gauche n'est pas un arrangement de graveur moderne, compte tenu du fait que beaucoup de médaillons ont été partiellement refaits ou retouchés. Ce qui n'a pas empêché les historiens de gloser sur ce détail probablement falsifié. On a voulu déceler un Jupiter Juvenis[138] dans le profil imberbe (à droite) de cet Aiôn-Janus (ou pseudo-Janus). En réalité, Janus a deux faces barbues (et c'est l'objection qu'A. ALFÖLDI[139] oppose au déchiffrement d'un Janus sur les *quadrigati* de l'époque républicaine, là où le savant hongrois identifie les *Dii Penates Populi Romani*). De toute façon, le médaillon contesté ne peut représenter un vrai Janus et c'est erronément – me semble-t-il – que J. GAGÉ[140] prête à Commode l'intention d'avoir «cherché dans l'iconographie du vieux culte romain de Janus, ou dans les vestiges d'un culte de Jupiter Juvenis, l'image double accolant une tête barbue à une tête imberbe». Plus récemment, M. MESLIN[141] a renchéri sur cette erreur. Le médaillon en question est à écarter du dossier.

Cet apurement critique de la documentation n'exclut pas pour autant une exégèse 'séculariste' du Janus commodien.

Les premières émissions au type du Bifrons enchâssé dans sa chapelle[142] datent de 186. Selon M. MATTINGLY[143], Janus doit être interprété ici comme Patulcius Clusius, dieu qui ouvre et ferme l'année, plutôt que comme *index belli pacisque*. De même, les médaillons qui pourraient, a priori, se rapporter à la fin des guerres nous référeraient *"to Janus the opener and closer of the year"*, et le numismate anglais voit dans cette imagerie commodienne du dieu biface une allusion à la réforme du calendrier[144]. Mais si l'on suit la chronologie de Dion-Cassius[145], c'est en 190–191 que l'empereur aurait changé les noms des mois de façon à faire coïncider les douze étapes de l'année avec les multiples aspects ou charismes de Commode-Hercule. Les médaillons[146] à buste biface de 187 représentent en façon de Janus le double profil humain et herculien du prince qui prétendait ouvrir un nouvel âge d'or pour les Romains. Mais est-ce bien cette identification partielle avec Hercule et cette bicéphalie mythique du pouvoir qui motiva la relance du type de Janus?

---

[138] J. GAGÉ, loc. cit. (n. 135).

[139] Die Penaten, Aeneas und Latinus. Eine archäol.-hist. Untersuchung über das Schwurgold u. d. *nummi quadrigati*, MDAI(R), 78, 1971, p. 13ss. Il est assez piquant de noter que Procope définit Janus comme «le premier des anciens dieux que les Romains en leur langue appelaient Pénates » (infra, p. 401).

[140] Loc. cit. (n. 135).

[141] Loc. cit. (n. 135).

[142] RIC, III, p. 419, n° 460; 421, n° 479; BMC, Roman Empire, IV, p. 803, n°s 568ss.

[143] BMC, Roman Empire, IV, p. CLXIII.

[144] Ibid., p. CLXXV, CLXXXI. A. ALFÖLDI (supra, n. 129) explique le type en relation avec les fêtes du Nouvel An. Cf. J. M. C. TOYNBEE, Roman Medaillons (Num.Studies, 5), New York, 1944, p. 94 et 140 ("New Year medallions").

[145] LXXII,15,3 (III, p. 297, 2ss. BOISSEVAIN). Cf. J. BEAUJEU, op. cit., p. 399, n. 3.

[146] Supra, n. 131.

En 186, il y avait peut-être cent ans que Domitien avait fait mettre à l'abri de son Janus Quadrifrons l'idole censément rapportée de Faléries[147]. Mais aucune des monnaies, aucun des médaillons de Commode ne nous présente un Janus à quatre faces, tel que celui des as hadrianiens. Si, comme on l'a supposé, Domitien a rénové le Janus Geminus à la faveur des travaux exécutés pour le Forum Transitorium[148], il pourrait s'agir d'un anniversaire. Pour M. GRANT[149], le monnayage − au sens large (y compris les médaillons) − des *decennalia* de 184−185 fêtait avec l'Aiôn aux quatre Saisons l'avènement d'un nouveau *saeculum aureum*, du fait même que cette année 184 marquait le bicentenaire des Jeux Séculaires qu'Auguste avait présidés en −17. Mais les exemplaires du Janus en son temple distyle n'apparaissent que deux ou trois ans plus tard: or, si en numismatique romaine les cas d'anticipation se vérifient et se justifient psychologiquement[150], un pareil retard sur l'événement est en contradiction avec la raison d'être même de la publicité monétaire. On peut aventurer une autre explication. En 186, il y avait exactement neuf siècles que Numa devenu roi de Rome avait institué le culte de Janus[151]. Ce peut être à cette commémoration que nous devons la série des monnaies en question. D'autant que Commode, en s'empressant (après la mort de Marc-Aurèle) de traiter avec les Barbares et d'acheter la tranquillité apparente du monde romain, pouvait se présenter comme un nouveau Numa, après un père dont les circonstances avaient fait, bien malgré lui, un Romulus guerrier. Le sénat qualifiera Commode de εἰρηνοποιός[152]. En 185, l'empereur prendra officiellement l'*agnomen* de *felix*, ce qui cadrera directement avec la *Saeculi Felicitas* exaltée la même année par l'imagerie d'Aiôn dans la série des *decennalia*. En tant que *felix*, Commode avait partie liée avec le dieu des voeux qui ouvraient l'année. Une tablette en cristal[153] porte le souhait: *ANNVM NOVVM FAVSTVM FELICEM FELICI IMPERATORI*, qui se lit autour de *strenae* parmi lesquelles on discerne des pièces de monnaie à l'effigie de Commode ou au type d'une Victoire et d'un temple (qui − contrairement à ce qu'on a prétendu[154] − n'a rien à voir avec celui de Janus). Des lampes votives − au sens propre du terme − nous montrent à côté d'une Victoire clipéophore

---

[147] Supra, n. 78; R. PETTAZZONI, art. cit. (n. 4), p. 84 s.; L. A. HOLLAND, op. cit., p. 102 s.

[148] G. CAPDEVILLE, art. cit., p. 414 ss.; H. BAUER, art. cit., p. 316 s.

[149] Roman Anniversary Issues, p. 109.

[150] Supra, p. 384.

[151] Liv., I,19,2.

[152] D.C., LXXII,15,5 (III, p. 297, 12 BOISSEVAIN). Sur ce titre, cf. A. MOMIGLIANO, *Terra marique*, JRS, 32, 1942, p. 64. Le retour apparent et temporaire de la paix a permis de relancer les slogans de la *Felicitas* et de l'*Âge d'or*: J. BEAUJEU, op. cit., p. 368 s.

[153] A. FURTWÄNGLER, Beschreibung der geschnittenen Steine im Antiquarium der königlichen Museen zu Berlin, Berlin, 1896, n° 8100; E. MAYNIAL, art. *Strenae*, dans: Dict. des antiqu. gr. et rom., IV, 2 (1911), p. 1531, fig. 6644; M. ROSTOWZEW, Römische Bleitessere. Ein Beitrag zur Sozial- und Wirtschaftsgeschichte der römischen Kaiserzeit, Klio, Beih. 3, Leipzig, 1905, p. 115, où l'auteur (n. 5) pose toutefois la question: „*Ist die Gemme sicher echt?*"; A. ALFÖLDI, Die Kontorniaten, p. 38 et pl. LXXI,2. Sur Commode *Felix*, cf. J. BEAUJEU, op. cit., p. 395.

[154] M. MESLIN, op. cit., p. 35.

l'as traditionnel au Janus bifrons[155]. Les monnaies commodiennes qui célèbrent le dieu biface appartiennent chronologiquement, idéologiquement à ce contexte de *Felicitas* et de *Renovatio temporum*. Au vrai, en 186 le neuvième centenaire de l'avènement de Numa et du culte de Janus suivait de peu le deux-centième anniversaire des Jeux Séculaires d'Auguste (en 184). Entre les deux, Commode avait reçu le surnom d''heureux', et ce bonheur était censé devoir rejaillir mystiquement sur le monde romain pacifié.

Certaines manifestations du loyalisme provincial font peut-être écho à cette 'relance' officielle de Janus. Une inscription africaine qui fait état d'un arc érigé en 188 à la gloire de Commode mentionne en même temps une statue dédiée *IANO PATRI*[156].

Cependant Commode finit par fâcher Janus. Parmi les prodiges sinistres qui annoncèrent, dit-on, la fin du règne, l''Histoire Auguste'[157] cite l'ouverture soudaine et spontanée du Janus Geminus. Le dieu avait des raisons d'en vouloir à Commode, à commencer par la réforme nominale du calendrier, à laquelle H. Mattingly[158] rapportait (à tort, je crois) le type même de Janus: en effet, le dieu y perdait l'honneur de donner son nom au premier mois de l'année! Autre faute plus grave encore: Commode avait dessein de paraître le 1er janvier 193 en gladiateur pour inaugurer un nouveau consulat, ce qui menaçait de déshonorer la grande fête de Janus[159]. Ce projet sert à Hérodien de prétexte pour faire son excursus à propos de Janus «le plus ancien dieu» (θεὸν ἀρχαιότατον) de l'Italie[160]. A lire l'historien, et à l'en croire, tout se passe comme si Janus avait voulu faire disparaître Commode afin d'éviter l'infamie que le monarque fou réservait à son jour initial et sacré. Cette interprétation dut s'imposer à l'opinion publique. D'où la légende et le type de Janus Conservator sur les pièces (pl. IV,14) que

---

[155] E. Maynial, loc. cit., fig. 6643; H. Dressel, CIL, XV, 2, p. 784 ss., n°s 6195 ss., 6208 ss.; M. Rostowzew, loc. cit., p. 115; A. Morlet, Vichy gallo-romain, Mâcon, 1957, p. 127 s., fig. 74; M. Meslin, op. cit., p. 44; T. Szentléleky, Ancient Lamps, Monum. antiquitatis extra fines Hung. reperta quae in Museo Artium Hung. aliisque museis & coll. Hung. asservantur I, Budapest, 1969, p. 135 s., à propos du n° 267; G. Heres, Die römischen Bildlampen der Berliner Antikensammlung, Schr.z.Gesch.u.Kultur der Antike, 18, Berlin, 1972, p. 86, n° 550 et pl. 59; A. Alföldi, loc. cit., p. 38 et pl. LXX,2. Souvent des tessères ou jetons en plomb à l'effigie de Janus tenaient lieu de monnaies d'étrennes: M. Rostovtsew—M. Prou, Catalogue des plombs de l'Antiquité, du Moyen Âge et des Temps Modernes conservés au Département des Médailles et Antiques de la Bibliothèque Nationale, Paris, 1900, p. 375, n° 782a; M. Rostowzew, Tesserarum Urbis Romae et suburbi plumbearum sylloge, St.-Pétersbourg, 1903, p. 297, n°s 2578–2581 et pl. IX,21–22; Idem, Römische Bleitesserae (n. 153), p. 115 s.

[156] CIL, VIII, 16417 (Hr-El-Ust, région d'El-Ghorfa, en Proconsulaire). Cf. L. A. Holland, op., cit., p. 297; AE, 1968, 609.

[157] SHA, Comm., 16, 4 (I, p. 111, 5 s. Hohl—Samberger—Seyfarth): *Ianus Geminus sua sponte apertus est*. L'ouverture spontanée du Janus signifiait la guerre et contredisait donc la propagande officielle de paix.

[158] Supra, n. 144.

[159] Herodian., I,16,3 (I, p. 108 Whittaker dans la Coll.Loeb, Londres—Cambr.Mass., 1969). Cf. J. Gagé, L'assassinat de Commode et les *sortes Herculis*, REL, 46, 1968, p. 290.

[160] I,16,1 (I, p. 106 Whittaker).

fera frapper Pertinax[161], proclamé un 1er janvier. Le dieu y figure comme sur les monnaies d'Hadrien, d'Antonin et de Commode, debout de face, s'appuyant sur un long *baculum*, et la main gauche sur la hanche. En rendant impossible l'exhibition sacrilège prévue pour les Calendes de son propre mois, Janus avait sauvé, 'conservé' l'État. Quelques mois plus tard, Dide-Julien se fera insulter par le peuple devant le temple de Janus[162], à l'instant de sacrifier au dieu, mais en vain. Ainsi le dieu reniait l'usurpateur indigne, comme il avait renié celui-là même qui avait popularisé monétairement son image . . .

VII. *Janus Bifrons ou Jupiter Biceps?*

Un très curieux denier de Géta frappé en 211 porte au revers l'image d'un dieu qui, debout frontalement, la poitrine nue, s'appuie de la main droite sur un 'sceptre' (plutôt que sur une 'pique') et serre un foudre en sa main gauche[163]. Or le personnage porte deux faces imberbes, semble-t-il, sur certains exemplaires (pl. IV,16) — même si le menton y est fortement marqué — alors que sur d'autres l'une des faces (la droite) étant barbue ferait penser à un profil jupitérien (pl. IV,15)[164]. En tout cas, ni le foudre, ni la prétendue 'pique' ne conviennent à Janus, quoique A. B. COOK[165] ait fait état d'une dédicace aquiléenne à Jupiter Dianus (ancienne forme supposée de Janus). Mais, en fait, le savant anglais veut expliquer ce curieux type monétaire en relation avec le Jupiter Ambisagrus d'Aquilée, un Jupiter «doublement sacré» (*ambisacrus*) ou *"sacred on both sides"*.

Dans le 'RIC', H. MATTINGLY et E. A. SYDENHAM reconnaissent dans cette étrange figure une intéressante association de Janus (bicéphalie) et de Jupiter (foudre); mais pour eux *"the reason for the choice of type is unknown"*[166]. P. W. FORCHHAMMER[167] voulait y constater la confusion des attributs de Jupiter *Conservator* et de Janus *Conservator* en une déité symbolisant la dyarchie de Géta et de Caracalla. Notons pourtant que Jupiter Conservator est nu et qu'il tient le foudre dans la main droite, le sceptre dans la main gauche, alors que le Bifrons de Géta a le bas du corps drapé et qu'il tient le foudre dans la main gauche. H.

---

[161] RIC, IV, 1, p. 7, n° 3 et pl. I,4; BMC, Roman Empire, V. Londres, 1950 (réédit. anast., 1976), p. 1, n° 2 et pl. I,2; cf. p. XXXIX, LXII: Janus y tiendrait le „*sceptre of majesty*" (identification sujette à caution).

[162] D.C., LXXIII,13,3 (III, p. 317, 13 s. BOISSEVAIN).

[163] RIC, IV, 1, p. 325, n° 79: *"Janus standing, holding sceptre (or spear)"*; BMC, Roman Empire, V, p. 422, n° 12 et pl. 65,8. Cf. A. B. COOK, op. cit., II, p. 327 (*"reversed spear"*); P. V. HILL, The Coinage of Septimius Severus and his Family of the Mint of Rome, Londres, 1977, p. 31, n°s 1296/7 (Janus).

[164] Cf. A. B. COOK, loc. cit., p. 327.

[165] Ibid., p. 328 (CIL, V, 783).

[166] RIC, IV, 1, p. 90.

[167] Zeitschr.f.Altertumswiss., 2, 1844, p. 1074 ss.

MATTINGLY, dans le 'BMC'[168], renoue avec cette interprétation politique: le Janus de Géta serait *"really a Jupiter biceps representing the two imperial brothers"*. Cette *"fanciful expression of the duality of the Empire"* agréait davantage à Géta qu'à Caracalla, dont les monnaies ignorent le type de Jupiter bicéphale. La tradition historiographique et l'assassinat de Géta confirment péremptoirement l'hostilité de Caracalla à tout partage du pouvoir impérial[169]. L'explication 'dyarchique' de ce type hybride reste la plus vraisemblable. Mais il ne s'agit ni vraiment d'un Janus, ni d'un Jupiter (malgré le foudre), là où les deux profils sont imberbes.

Quoi qu'il en soit, le goût des figures à deux faces distinctes, illustré un quart de siècle plus tôt par les médaillons de Commode[170], semble s'affirmer encore très officiellement sous Caracalla. Lorsqu'après son passage en Thrace il se prit (et voulut se faire prendre) pour un nouvel Alexandre, on vit en peinture des images doubles (c'est-à-dire janiformes) du prince portant sur un seul corps les deux profils unis en un seul chef du roi de Macédoine et de Caracalla[171]. Mais cette représentation n'avait qu'un lien d'analogie formelle ou plastique avec le Bifrons. Tout comme le type monétaire précité de Géta, elle restait étrangère à la religion même de Janus.

VIII. De Sévère-Alexandre à Gallien

Au IIIe siècle, le dieu des Calendes de janvier reste assez populaire, comme en témoignent les lampes d'étrennes. Les 'Actes des Frères Arvales' attestent, en 224 encore, que les sacrifices de béliers, de moutons châtrés ou de brebis *ad aras temporales* se font dans l'ordre: *Iano patri, Iovi, Marti patri, Iunoni . . . Vestae*[172]. Janus demeure dans l'*ordo* rituel le dieu des *prima*, comme Vesta la déesse des *extrema*[173]. Mais Janus ne compte plus guère dans la publicité monétaire. En 242, Gordien III rouvre les portes du Janus Geminus pour faire la guerre aux Perses[174]. Seront-elles refermées au moins pour la célébration du millénaire de Rome? Aucun texte n'en parle. Gordien III est le dernier empereur dont la tradition littéraire rapporte ce geste de l'*apertio*, rituel depuis plus de neuf siècles.

---

[168] V, p. XXXIX; cf. p. CLXXXVIII.

[169] D.C., LXXVII, 1 s. (III, p. 373 s. BOISSEVAIN); Herodian., IV, 1 et 5; SHA, Sev., 23,7; Ant. Car., 2, 4 ss.

[170] Supra, n. 131.

[171] Herodian., IV,8,2 (I, p. 412 WHITTAKER).

[172] CIL, VI, 2107.

[173] G. DUMÉZIL, Tarpeia, p. 101 s.; IDEM, La religion romaine archaïque[1], p. 185, 322 ([2]p. 191, 332); Fest., s. v. *Ordo sacerdotum* (p. 198, 30 ss. LINDSAY).

[174] Aur.Vict., Lib.de Caes., 27,7 (p. 105, 28 ss. PICHLMAYR−GRUENDEL); SHA, Gord., 26,3 (II, p. 49, 15 s. HOHL−SAMBERGER−SEYFARTH).

1. Néron: sesterce, revers (Brit.Mus. = BMC, I, p. 229, n° 157, Rome) − 2. Néron: sesterce, revers (Brit.Mus. = BMC, I, p. 263, n° 321, Lugdunum) − 3. Néron: sesterce, revers (Sammlung W. NIG-GELER, Vente 'Monnaies et Médailles', Bâle, 2−3 novembre 1967, p. 10, n° 1128, Lugdunum) − 4. Néron: sesterce, revers (ibid., n° 1129, Rome) − 5. Hadrien: aureus, revers (Brit.Mus. = BMC, III, p. 254, n° 100) − 6. Hadrien: as, revers (Brit.Mus. = BMC, III, p. 437, n° 1335)

7

8

7. Antonin le Pieux: sesterce, revers (Brit.Mus. = BMC, IV, p. 210, n° 1317) — 8. Commode: sesterce, revers (Brit.Mus. = BMC, IV, p. 803, n° 568)

9. Commode: aureus, revers (Vienne = D. F. Brown, Temples of Rome as Coin Types, pl. VII,2) −
10. Commode: médaillon, revers (Paris, Cabinet des Médailles = F. Gnecchi, I medaglioni romani, II,
p. 62, n° 92) − 11. Commode: médaillon, avers et revers (Vienne, Münzkabinett = F. Gnecchi, I
medaglioni romani, II, p. 66, n° 131) − 12. Commode: sesterce, revers (même variété que fig. 8: Vienne,
Münzkabinett) − 13. Commode: médaillon, avers et revers (Vienne, Münzkabinett = F. Gnecchi,
I medaglioni romani, II, p. 62, n° 94)

14. Pertinax: denier, revers (Brit.Mus. = BMC, V, p. 1, n° 2) − 15. Géta: denier, revers (Brit.Mus. = BMC, V, p. 422, n° 12) − 16. Géta: denier, avers et revers (Vente 'Monnaies et Médailles' Auktion 8, 27−28 juin 1978, p. 51, n° 797) − 17. Gallien: aureus, revers (Paris, Cabinet des Médailles = RIC, V, 1, p. 134, n° 45)

Des monnaies en bronze de Thessalonique frappées à l'effigie de Trajan-Dèce[175] portent au revers l'image de Janus debout à gauche, le haut du corps nu (comme dans le monnayage romain du IIe siècle ap. J.-C.), la main droite sur le front, la main gauche tenant un pan du manteau ramené sur le bas ventre. A gauche du dieu, la statue minuscule d'un Marsyas qui, la main droite levée, tient son outre sur l'épaule symbolise la *libertas* et le statut de colonie obtenu par la ville. Mais que veut signifier Janus? Avant −31, Thessalonique avait frappé des moyens bronzes à l'effigie de Janus Bifrons[176], c'est-à-dire à l'imitation des as républicains (ce fut aussi le cas à Amphipolis)[177]; mais on connaît également des bronzes de petit module avec le même type d'avers[178]. De toute façon, sur les pièces de Trajan-Dèce, le Janus du revers doit être autre chose qu'un signe de valeur. En fait, Marsyas ne personnifie pas seulement le statut colonial (attesté par les monnaies thessaloniciennes de Trajan-Dèce), mais aussi le *Ius Italicum*[179]. Janus peut donc figurer à côté de Marsyas en tant que roi mythique de l'Italie et non pas en tant que dieu de la paix (ou de la guerre), ni même en tant que dieu 'initial' des temps recommencés. Peut-être cette allusion à l'âge d'or de la protohistoire italique impliquait-elle des espérances de renouveau et de félicité, à une époque où la Macédoine était menacée par les Goths. Mais c'est avant tout le dieu de l'Italie romaine que célèbre ce monnayage colonial, le protecteur attitré de la métropole et de tous ses prolongements, fondés pour faire face aux Barbares ou à tout autre ennemi du nom romain. On a remarqué précisément que les dédicaces à Janus se trouvaient le plus souvent dans des centres militaires ou des colonies[180]. Quoi qu'il en soit, cette représentation isolée (et plutôt exceptionnelle dans le monnayage autonome du monde grec) n'a pas de lien nécessaire avec l'idéologie ou les commémorations que me semblent impliquer les Janus romains de l'époque antonine.

Janus eut pour la dernière fois les honneurs de la publicité monétaire sous le règne de Gallien. Il s'agit des *aurei* d'une émission exceptionnelle (fin 260) qui nous montrent au revers Janus debout frontalement, tenant une patère et un *baculum*, avec la légende: IANO PATRI[181] (pl. IV,17). Ce type de Janus (avec

[175] H. GAEBLER, Die antiken Münzen von Makedonia und Paionia (= TH. WIEGAND, Die antiken Münzen Nord-Griechenlands, III), 2, Berlin, 1935, p. 130, n° 67 et pl. XXIII,8.

[176] Ibid., p. 120, n°s 17, 19 et pl. XXIII,8.

[177] Ibid., p. 36, n° 41 et pl. IX,15.

[178] Ibid., p. 121, n°s 20−21 et pl. XXIII,11. Cependant, malgré son petit module, la pièce n° 20 est bien un as, puisque l'effigie double de Janus y est surmontée d'un I.

[179] C. JULLIAN, art. *Ius Italicum*, dans: Dict.des antiqu.gr.et rom., III, 1 (1899), p. 747; A. VON PREMERSTEIN, art. *Ius Italicum*, dans: RE, X, 1 (1918), col. 1250s.; B. LEVICK, Roman Colonies in Southern Asia Minor, Oxford, 1967, p. 149, 160. Les monnaies thessaloniciennes de Trajan-Dèce donnent à la ville le titre de «colonie métropole», ce qui renforçait les liens avec l'Italie. Sur les pièces au Janus, la légende MHT/PO(πολις) est inscrite au revers, dans le champ, de part et d'autre du dieu.

[180] J. TOUTAIN, op. cit. (n. 1), I, p. 246 (où il n'est pas fait état des monnaies de Thessalonique).

[181] RIC, V, 1, p. 134, n° 45; cf. L. A. HOLLAND, op. cit., p. 279, n. 68. A l'avers, Gallien est casqué et cuirassé: l'invocation de Janus est liée à la défense de l'Empire, sauvé par la *Virtus* de l'Auguste régnant et combattant.

la patère) et le titre même de *pater* sont inhabituels dans le monnayage romain. Dans la même série rentrent des quinaires d'argent et d'or, des *aurei* et des multiples d'*aurei* qui célèbrent la VIIIe puissance tribunicienne et le IVe consulat de Gallien, qui rendent hommage à sa *Virtus*, à ses victoires et à la IIIe cohorte prétorienne. R. Göbl[182] considère cette émission comme une „*Festprägung zum Konsulat und der (wahrscheinlich gleichzeitigen) Feier der in den Revlegg genannten Siege*". L'hommage à Janus pater s'expliquerait donc en fonction du 1er janvier 261, date à laquelle Gallien devait revêtir son IVe consulat. Une série immédiatement précédente (été—automne 260) avait glorifié Jupiter Ultor et Juno Regina[183]. En l'occurrence, Janus pater n'a pas été compté dans une séquence comparable aux sacrifices précités des Frères Arvales, puisque Mars n'est pas nommé par les monnaies et que Janus n'apparaît qu'après Jupiter et Junon.

Cependant cette épiclèse de *pater* que lui attribuent les *aurei* de décembre(?) 260 — qui anticipent apparemment sur le *processus consularis* du 1er janvier — relève du rituel le plus traditionnel, avec lequel Gallien renoue en un temps de crise dramatique pour le monde romain. Ce titre n'est pas que de vénération: Janus était reconnu et honoré effectivement comme le dieu père par excellence, la plus ancienne des déités latiales, le dieu des origines et, comme tel, des recommencements. En 260, après les désastres du front oriental et la capture de son père qui pouvait faire douter des charismes impériaux[184], Gallien avait repris la situation en main. Les victoires qu'il avait remportées légitimaient un regain de l'optimisme officiel[185]. En revêtant derechef un consulat le 1er janvier 261, en ouvrant l'année avec Janus, il prenait l'initiative d'un nouveau départ. L'Empire, qui avait manqué de peu l'effondrement face aux assauts conjugués des Perses, de la peste, des Barbares et des forces centrifuges, retrouvait dans le sursaut incarné par son chef l'énergie d'une renaissance. La figure de Janus pater rappelait les *Saturnia regna* et les siècles dorés du plus lointain passé italique[186]. C'était un gage d'espoir connexe aux *vota* des calendes de janvier, espoir de paix et de prospérité puisé aux sources protohistoriques de la piété romaine (que symbolise concrètement la patère à libations, attribut exceptionnel et d'autant plus significatif).

---

[182] Der Aufbau der römischen Münzprägung in der Kaiserzeit, V, 2: Gallienus als Alleinherrscher, Num.Zeitschr., 75, 1953, p. 12, c.

[183] Ibid., a—b.

[184] R. Turcan, Le culte impérial au IIIe siècle, ANRW, II, 16.2, Berlin—New York, 1978, p. 1001.

[185] L. de Blois, The Policy of the Emperor Gallienus, Studies of the Dutch Archaeol. and Histor. Society, 7, Leyde, 1976, p. 25, 27s., 133; sur l'épithète de *pater*, cf. G. Capdeville, art. cit. (n. 5), p. 410ss.; V. Saladino, art. cit. (n. 2), p. 163.

[186] Sur l'idéologie de l'âge d'or, cf. L. de Blois, op. cit., p. 23s.; J. Gagé, Programme d'italicité' et nostalgies d'hellénisme autour de Gallien et Salonine. Quelques problèmes de *paideia* impériale au IIIe siècle, ANRW, II, 2, Berlin—New York, 1975, p. 848.

IX. Survivances littéraires et festives: le Janus des antiquaires et des nostalgiques

Dans la seconde moitié du IIIe siècle[187], à une époque où la religion ou, du moins, l'imagerie officielle n'en fait plus guère de cas, Cornelius Labeo s'est intéressé à Janus. C'est d'après l'antiquaire romain que Johannès Lydus[188] énumère et commente dix de ses épithètes cultuelles. Macrobe dépend aussi de Labeo dans les 'Saturnales'[189] où sa liste de sept épithètes est suivie d'explications dont certains détails remontent à Varron. Servius Danielis[190], enfin, cite quatre surnoms qui procèdent, semble-t-il, du même fichier labéonien. L'antiquaire a exploité les *Pontificum libri* où se lisaient des listes d'*indigitamenta*. Labeo avait certes, d'une façon générale, le goût de ces recherches sur les épiclèses et les fonctions afférentes des dieux romains. Mais l'attention singulière que l'érudit latin a vouée au syncrétisme solaire[191] donnerait à penser que ce sujet ne fut pas étranger à l'intérêt qu'il portait à Janus. On s'est demandé si Arnobe n'avait pas utilisé Labeo[192]. Le polémiste africain s'en prend souvent à Janus qu'il qualifie une fois de *pater* suivant la tradition rituelle, Janus que «certains d'entre vous, écrit-il, ont identifié avec le monde, d'autres avec l'année, quelques-uns avec le soleil»[193]. Ces confusions théo-cosmologiques durent connaître un succès relatif au temps où Aurélien et ses successeurs s'efforçaient d'organiser l'hénothéisme autour du culte de Sol Invictus.

Janus était vénéré en Afrique romaine[194] et, si Arnobe revient si fort à la charge contre le dieu[195], cette insistance peut tenir au fait que les polythéistes lui restaient fidèles, surtout à l'occasion des *Kalendae Ianuariae* que les chrétiens eux-mêmes fêtaient toujours avec ardeur[196]; elle s'explique aussi en fonction du paganisme solaire qui intégrait les attributions calendaires et 'temporelles' du dieu de l'année.

[187] Sur l'époque − longtemps controversée − de Cornelius Labeo, cf. H. Kusch, art. Cornelius Labeo, dans: Reallex.f.Ant.u.Christentum, Stuttgart, 1957, III, col. 435; P. Mastandrea, Un neoplatonico latino: Cornelio Labeone, Études Préliminaires aux Religions Orientales dans l'Empire Romain, 77, Leyde, 1978; sur le Janus de Cornelius Labeo, cf. R. Agahd, op. cit., p. 117ss.; P. Mastandrea, op. cit., p. 21ss.

[188] De mens., IV, 1 (p. 63, 8ss. Wuensch).

[189] I,9,15−16. Cf. G. Capdeville, art. cit., p. 407s.

[190] Ad Aen., VII,610 (II, p. 172, 9ss. Thilo−Hagen).

[191] H. Kusch, art. cit. (n. 187), col. 432s.; J. Flamant, Macrobe et le néo-platonisme latin à la fin du IVe siècle, Études Préliminaires aux Religions Orientales dans l'Empire Romain, 58, Leyde, 1977, p. 295s.; P. Mastandrea, op. cit., p. 159ss.

[192] A.-J. Festugière, La doctrine des *viri novi* sur l'origine et le sort des âmes, Cinquantenaire de l'École biblique et archéol. franç. de Jérusalem, Mémorial Lagrange, 1940 = Idem, Hermétisme et mystique païenne, Paris, 1967, p. 294ss.

[193] Adv.nat., III, 29 (p. 186, 18ss. Marchesi): *Incipiamus ergo sollemniter ab Iano et nos patre, quem quidam ex vobis mundum, annum alii, solem esse prodidere nonnulli.*

[194] J. Toutain, op. cit., I, p. 245s.; supra, n. 156.

[195] Adv.nat., I, 36 (p. 30, 8 M.); III, 6 (p. 164, 4); III, 29 (p. 186, 18ss.; p. 187, 1s.); III, 44 (p. 201, 3); VI, 13 (p. 339, 13s.).

[196] M. Meslin, op. cit., p. 48ss.

Deux siècles plus tard, le néoplatonicien Proclus[197] consacrera un hymne à Janus Propatôr en lui associant Hécate, « mère des dieux . . . qui veille aux portes », comme Nigidius Figulus[198] lui avait associé Diana/Iana. Proclus s'inspirait donc (en partie du moins) de la tradition qui soulignait les aspects lunaires[199] du dieu. On en faisait, d'ailleurs, un fils du Ciel et d'Hécate[200]. En tant que Prothuraios, la déesse avait sa place à côté de Janus qui garde surtout chez Proclus sa qualité de dieu-ancêtre primordial.

D'après H. Jordan[201], les portes du Janus furent encore fermées au IVe siècle ap. J.-C. Elles le furent de toute façon en tant que portes d'un édifice païen, comme celles de tous les temples[202]. Mais aucun témoignage ne précise qu'un empereur post-tétrarchique ait ouvert ou fermé le Janus avant d'entrer en guerre ou pour consacrer la paix. Quand Ammien-Marcellin (XVI,10,1) écrit à propos de Constance II *quasi recluso Iani templo*, il s'agit bien évidemment d'une formule littéraire qui se réfère à un passé révolu. Les expressions de Claudien (*Et Ianum pax alta ligat*[203], *Ianus bella premens. . .*[204]) relèvent d'une phraséologie poétique traditionnelle. Mais au revers des médaillons contorniates (supra, n. 63) le Janus de Néron restait le symbole de la *Pax Romana*, et le dieu biface ouvrait toujours nominalement les fastes de l'année.

Les Pères de l'Eglise ont longtemps prêché et grondé contre les Calendes de Janvier auxquelles le nom de Janus restait attaché[205]. Le chrétien Ausone[206] invoque encore le Bifrons dans une curieuse prière à l'an neuf et au Soleil régénéré. Chose remarquable: ce culte romain a rayonné en pays grec, et au VIe siècle de notre ère, on continuait de célébrer à Philadelphie (Lydie) les fêtes du 1er janvier en suivant processionnellement une idole de Janus ἐν διμόρφῳ προσώπῳ[207]. Il demeurait le dieu 'initial' qu'il était originellement, dieu du passage et du renouveau.

A Rome, depuis que l'Empire était chrétien, le Janus restait fermé. En 537, pendant que Bélisaire défendait la ville assiégée par les Ostrogoths, des païens

---

[197] Hymn., VI (p. 31 Vogt = Klass.Philol.Studien, 18, Wiesbaden, 1957; commentaire p. 72ss.).

[198] Macr., Sat., I,9,8.

[199] L. A. Mac Kay, Janus, p. 158ss.

[200] Arnob., Adv.nat., III, 29 (p. 187, 1s. M.).

[201] Topographie der Stadt Rom im Altertum, I, 2, Berlin, 1885, p. 346.

[202] Au moins à partir de 356, si la loi de Cod.Theod., XVI,10,4 est bien de cette année-là: A. Piganiol, L'Empire chrétien[1], Hist. gén. fond. par G. Glotz, Hist. rom. IV, 2, Paris, 1947, p. 96; A. Chastagnol, La préfecture urbaine à Rome sous le Bas-Empire, Publ. de la Faculté des Lettres et Sciences Humaines d'Alger, 34, Paris, 1960, p. 148, n. 2. Mais cf. L. De Giovanni, Costantino e il mondo pagano, dans: KOINΩNIA. Collana di Studi e Testi a cura dell'Assoc. di Studi Tardoantichi, II, Naples, 1977, p. 138ss.

[203] De laud. Stilic., II, 287.

[204] De VI. cons. Hon., 637.

[205] M. Meslin, op. cit., p. 95ss.

[206] Lib. III, 5 (I, p. 48ss. de l'éd.-trad. H. G. E. White, dans la Coll.Loeb, Londres, 1968); cf. aussi VII, 9 (p. 182); 10 (p. 184); 14, 6 (p. 188); Sid. Apoll., Carm., 2, 8ss.

[207] Lyd., De mens., IV, 2 (p. 65, 11ss. Wuensch).

tentèrent d'ouvrir les portes du 'temple'[208], avec l'espoir que l'exécution du rite déchaînerait contre l'ennemi les forces mystérieuses de la guerre emprisonnées depuis deux siècles . . . Procope décrit l'idole du Bifrons – «le premier des anciens dieux que les Romains en leur langue appellaient Pénates» – comme ayant ses deux faces tournées respectivement à l'Orient et à l'Occident, dans l'axe des portes de bronze qui fermaient de chaque côté l'antique «passage» (ou Janus)[209]. On aurait donc tort d'imaginer, sur la foi des seules monnaies commodiennes (pl. II,8; III,9,12) et du médaillon de Vienne (pl. III,13), que les têtes du dieu avaient une orientation perpendiculaire à celles des arcatures.

Janus fut occasionnellement – au Ier siècle surtout – le garant de la *Pax Romana*, mais aussi et souvent une figure ambiguë du temps réitéré ou récapitulé: ses deux profils regardant le passé et l'avenir unissaient indissolublement le dieu primordial, «archaïque»[210], en qui s'enracinait la piété historique de Rome, au dieu de l'an neuf et des renaissances attendues de la 'Ville éternelle'.

Liste des illustrations

Planche I

Fig. 1 Néron: sesterce, revers (Brit.Mus. = BMC, I, p. 229, n° 157, Rome). Photo Brit.Mus., échelle 1/1.

Fig. 2 Néron: sesterce, revers (Brit.Mus. = BMC, I, p. 263, n° 321, Lugdunum). Photo Brit.Mus., échelle 1/1.

Fig. 3 Néron: sesterce, revers (Sammlung W. NIGGELER, Vente 'Monnaies et Médailles', Bâle, 2–3 novembre 1967, p. 10, n° 1128, Lugdunum). Photo aimablement communiquée par M. HANS VOEGTLI, échelle 1/1.

Fig. 4 Néron: sesterce, revers (ibid., n° 1129, Rome), Photo aimablement communiquée par M. HANS VOEGTLI, échelle 1/1.

Fig. 5 Hadrien: aureus, revers (Brit.Mus. = BMC, III, p. 254, n° 100). Photo Brit.Mus., très grossie.

Fig. 6 Hadrien: as, revers (Brit.Mus. = BMC, III, p. 437, n° 1335). Photo Brit. Mus., très grossie.

Planche II

Fig. 7 Antonin le Pieux: sesterce, revers (Brit.Mus. = BMC, IV, p. 210, n° 1317). Photo Brit.Mus., très grossie.

Fig. 8 Commode: sesterce, revers (Brit.Mus. = BMC, IV, p. 803, n° 568). Photo Brit.Mus., très grossie.

208 Procop., B.Goth., I, 25 (II, p. 126, 16ss. HAURY–WIRTH).
209 ibid. (p. 127, 4ss. H.–W.).
210 Cedren., 1 (p. 295, 10 BEKKER) = D.C., I, fr. 6, 7 (I, p. 14, 10ss. BOISSEVAIN): Δίων ὁ Ῥωμαῖος ἀρχαῖόν τινα ἥρωα Ἰανὸν λέγει διὰ τὴν τοῦ Κρόνου ξένισιν λαβόντα τὴν γνῶσιν τῶν μελλόντων καὶ τῶν προϋπαρχόντων, καὶ διὰ τοῦτο διπρόσωπον ὑπὸ Ῥωμαίων πλάττεσθαι.

Planche III

Fig. 9 Commode: aureus, revers (Vienne = D. F. BROWN, Temples of Rome as Coin Types, pl. VII,2). Photo Brit.Mus., très grossie.

Fig. 10 Commode: médaillon, revers (Paris, Cabinet des Médailles = F. GNECCHI, I medaglioni romani, II, p. 62, n° 92). Photo Bibl.Nationale, échelle 1/1.

Fig. 11 Commode: médaillon, avers et revers (Vienne, Münzkabinett = F. GNECCHI, I medaglioni romani, II, p. 66, n° 131). Photo Kunsthistor. Museum, Vienne, échelle 1/1.

Fig. 12 Commode: sesterce, revers (même variété que fig. 8: Vienne, Münzkabinett). Photo Kunsthistor. Museum, Vienne, échelle 1/1.

Fig. 13 Commode: médaillon, avers et revers (Vienne, Münzkabinett = F. GNECCHI, I medaglioni romani, II, p. 62, n° 94). Photo Kunsthistor. Museum, Vienne, échelle 1/1.

Planche IV

Fig. 14 Pertinax: denier, revers (Brit.Mus. = BMC, V, p. 1, n° 2). Photo Brit.Mus., très grossie.

Fig. 15 Géta: denier, revers (Brit.Mus. = BMC, V, p. 422, n° 12). Photo Brit.Mus., très grossie.

Fig. 16 Géta: denier, avers et revers (Vente 'Monnaies et Médailles' Auktion 8, 27—28 juin 1978, p. 51, n° 797). Négatif aimablement prêté par M. HANS VOEGTLI: photo très grossie.

Fig. 17 Gallien: aureus, revers (Paris, Cabinet des Médailles = RIC, V, 1, p. 134, n° 45). Photo Bibl.Nationale, échelle 1/1.

Funzioni politiche ed implicazioni culturali nell'ideologia religiosa di Ceres nell'impero romano

di Ileana Chirassi Colombo, Trieste

Sommario

I. Il politeismo difficile di Ceres

La problematica riguardante Ceres, l'apparentemente convenzionale dea politeistica della plebe e delle messi nel pantheon romano, offre spunti di riflessione particolarmente privilegiati per una serie di considerazioni in chiave storico-religiosa sull'interazione tra politico e sacro, o meglio sulla qualità 'sacrale' della realtà istituzionale − o viceversa − a Roma durante la repubblica prima come più tardi in età imperiale.

Dopo il punto nella ricerca di base messo dalla ricca monografia di Le Bonniec nel 1958, l'interesse specifico per la *religio Cereris*, a parte qualche contributo molto specifico di carattere per lo più antiquario, è stato praticamente nullo, se non per un problematico articolo di D. Sabbatucci negli Studia

Abbreviazioni:

ACl	L'Antiquité Classique, Louvain
BEFAR	Bibliothèque des Écoles Françaises d'Athènes et de Rome, Paris
BMC RE	British Museum, Catalogue of the Coins of the Roman Empire, ed. by H. Mattingly, London, 1923 ff.
CeS.D.I.R.	Centro Studi e Documentazione sull'Italia Romana, Atti, Milano
CIL	Corpus Inscriptionum Latinarum

Widengren[1]. In esso si pone il problema di fondo di Ceres dal punto di vista storico religioso, riassumibile in quello che potremo definire il suo 'politeismo incerto' attraverso il quale tuttavia passano le modalità della sua storicizzazione. Per spiegarci meglio, si tratta della difficoltà di Ceres di presentarsi nella realtà cultuale romana con tutte quelle solide caratteristiche funzionali che pure dovrebbero essere propie di una dea tipicamente politeistica, per di più legata al campo specifico della grande agricoltura qualificante dei cereali[2]. Come giustamente si osserva, Ceres oscilla tra la inglobante figura di Tellus (la Terra Madre dagli imprecisi contorni di „grande dea"[3], e l'ossessiva precisazione dei suoi

CRAI	Comptes Rendus des Séances de l'Accadémie des Inscriptiones et Belles-Lettres, Paris
D.	Inscriptiones Latinae selectae, ed. H. Dessau, Berlin 1892ff.
D.A.	Dialoghi di archeologia, Roma
Degrassi, I.I.	Inscriptiones Italicae, ed. A. Degrassi e. a., Roma, 1931ff.
Degrassi, I.L.L.R.	Inscriptiones Latinae Liberae Rei Publicae, ed. A. Degrassi, Firenze 1957/63
GRBS	Greek, Roman, and Byzantine Studies, Durham, N.C.
Mél.Ec.Fr.Ant.	Mélanges de l'École Française de Rome, Antiquité, Paris
Not.Sc.	Notizie degli Scavi di Antichità, Roma
PdP	La Parola del Passato, Napoli
Q.U.	Quaderni Urbinati di Cultura Classica, Roma
RHR	Revue de l'Histoire des Religions, Paris
SE	Studi Etruschi, Firenze
SMSR	Studi e Materiali di Storia delle Religioni, Roma
ZPE	Zeitschrift für Papyrologie und Epigraphik, Bonn

[1] H. Le Bonniec, Le culte de Cérès à Rome. Des origines à la fin de la République, Études et commentaires XXVII, Paris 1958. — D. Sabbatucci, La trascendenza di Ceres, in: Ex orbe religionum. Studia G. Widengren oblata, Studies in the History of Religions XXI/XXII, Leiden 1972, pp. 312—319.

[2] Per il valore del cereale come elemento qualificante di attualità in rapporto alla Demeter greca mi permetto di rinviare ad un mio contributo: I. Chirassi Colombo, I doni di Demeter. Mito e ideologia nella Grecia arcaica, in: Studi Triestini in onore di L. A. Stella, Trieste 1975, pp. 183—213.

[3] Il rapporto tra Ceres e Tellus è puntualmente analizzato da Le Bonniec nel capitolo su 'Cérès dans le cycle de Tellus' o. c., pp. 48—107. Sulla integrazione di Ceres Tellus e Demeter sulla base di una comune essenzialità ctonia che rimanda alla concezione della primordialità di un essere divino prepoliteistico, cfr. ancora F. Altheim, Terra Mater. Untersuchungen zur altitalischen Religionsgeschichte, Religionsgeschichtliche Versuche und Vorarbeiten XXII, 2, Giessen 1931, pp. 108—129. Traluce nello sfondo la proiezione del 'fantasma' della grande dea, ipostasi del femminile tellurico e materno, suscitato dal 'Mutterrecht' di J. J. Bachofen (Stuttgart 1861) rimbalzato in A. Dieterich, Mutter Erde, Leipzig—Berlin 1925, passim, come momento primordiale sempre presente a livello storico in tutte le culture a base agraria. Questa 'teologia della terra' basata sul concetto di un essere supremo femminile contende in certo senso il passo all'altra teoria dell'Essere supremo celeste e maschile che si fa avanti più o meno negli stessi anni e diventa celebre per la contesa tra l'antropologo A. Lang e padre W. Schmidt sul tema del 'monoteismo primitivo'. Per i dati della controversia cfr. R. Pettazzoni, L'essere supremo nelle religioni primitive, Torino, 1957, che li riassume in termini molto efficaci. Stranamente però le due correnti della primordialità dell'essere maschile e primordialità dell'essere femminile

indigitamenta: vedi i 'celebri' dodici dei invocati dal suo *flamen* durante il *sacrum cereale*, il Dissodatore, il Preparatore della terra, Colui che fa le porche, Colui che affonda il semme, Colui che traccia la prima aratura, l'Erpicatore, lo Zappatore, il Sarchiatore, il Mietitore, Colui che porta il grano via dai campi, Colui che lo ripone nei granai, Colui che lo tira fuori per il consumo[4].

Come si vede si tratta di un ciclo specializzato e completo che non lascia molto spazio di azione alla dea del grano intesa in senso politeistico. Ma non basta. Sappiamo da una precisa testimonianza di Tertulliano che ancora alla fine del II d.C. al Circo Massimo, proprio dove sorgeva il suo tempio, potevano essere viste sulle loro colonne tre divinità, anzi tre collettività divine specializzate, che ripropongono lo stesso frazionamento specialistico degli dei del *sacrum*: sono rispettivamente le Seiae, le Messiae, le Tutulinae, cioè le protettrici delle semine, delle messi, e genericamente di tutto il ciclo del grano dalla semina al raccolto[5]. Si affiancano ancora Seia e Segesta, ricordate da Plinio rispettivamente come la divinità della semina (*a serendo*) e delle messi (*a segetibus*) e la misteriosa dea dello spazio aperto il cui nome è vietato pronunciare *sub tecto* (Plin. XVIII,8). La peculiarità agraria e cereale di Ceres appare così frantumata e vanificata, in un processo di dissoluzione che la presenta come 'qualche cosa d'altro'.

In realtà se osserviamo più attentamente i dati, diremo che la peculiarità antica agraria di Ceres è proprio ciò che anticamente non esiste; o almeno noi possiamo solo ricostruire ipoteticamente, mentre esistono le tante divinità del grano ed esiste Tellus o Terra Mater e Ops o Fortuna (con le quali anche la stessa Ceres sarà facilmente identificata, come nella *comprecatio* ricordata da Aulo Gellio[6]). L'agrarietà, ed in particolare il rapporto con i cereali, sono uno dei 'segni' attraverso i quali si connota una divinità essenzialmente cittadina, 'politica' (prima che plebea), costruita a misura funzionale per esprimere nella dinamica interna delle forze opposte in lotta, nella rivalità dei gruppi avversi che la storio-

---

non si sono mai direttamente affrontate. Cfr. sul tema della religione della terra anche una messa a punto di O. PETTERSSON, Mother Earth. An analysis of the Mother Earth concepts according to A. Dieterich, Scripta minora Regiae Societatis humaniorum litterarum Lundensis 1965/66, 3, Lund 1967.

[4] Servio, ad Georg. I, 21 (fonte Fabio Pittore); il *sacrum* − rivolto *Telluri et Cereri*.

[5] *columnae Seias a sementationibus, Messias a messibus, Tutulinas a tutelis fructuum sustinent*, Tertul. de spect. 8,3,4. Possibile la derivazione da Varrone la cui teologia è ampiamente discussa dai padri. Vedi il rimbalzo del passo in Ag. de C.D. 4,8. Anche Macrobio accosta Seia e Tutelina a Segetia che, come in Plinio, pare sostituire le Messie del Circo. Accanto sono nominate Salus e Semonia (Sat. I, 16,6). Tutta da studiare ancora la 'religiosità' del Circo Massimo, luogo privilegiato d'incontro di un gran numero di culti sino dall'età arcaica ed 'utilizzato' sino alla tarda antichità.

[6] Gell.N.A. XIII, 23,4: *Te Anna ac Peranna, Panda te lito Pales, Neriens ac Minerva, Fortuna ac Ceres*, interessante esempio di processo di accumulazione di funzioni attraverso appropriazione di *nomina*, presente in molti politeismi come testimonianza di quella tendenza ad un sincretismo monistico che apre di solito la via alla trasformazione di una divinità politeistica in 'grande dio' o 'grande dea'. Tipico l'esempio della Isis ellenistica e romana. Da respingere per il passo citato la interpretazione in chiave etimologica proposta da PIGHI nella bella traduzione italiana (in: G. B. PIGHI, La religione romana, Lezioni 'Augusto Rostagni' III, Torino, 1967, p. 66).

grafia 'racconta' come conflitto di patrizi e plebei, quella volontà di fondare sul piano storico un tempo nuovo, attuale – quello delle leggi repubblicane secondo quel modello di fondazione del tempo nuovo, del tempo attuale, sul piano mitico così esplicitamente rappresentato dalla Demeter greca, thesmophoros ed eleusina.

Appare così abbastanza chiaro come con la fine della *respublica*, vanificate quelle istituzioni politiche, cittadine ed urbane, si vanifichi anche lo spazio proprio di Ceres che solo ora, e con modalità rovesciata, assume pienamente su di sè il carico di un rapporto agrario inteso come restaurazione più che 'invenzione'. Si giustificano così i commenti particolarmente insistenti sulla evanescenza di Ceres in età imperiale che possiamo leggere in calce agli articoli a lei dedicati nei maggiori lessici[7].

In realtà, anche lasciando da parte il caso specifico e di notevole interesse storico religioso rappresentato dal culto delle Cereres in Africa, la cosiddetta 'mancata sopravvivenza' di Ceres nella cultura e nell'ideologia di età imperiale in Roma ed in altre parti dell'impero à un dato che merita ancora la sua attenzione per le particolari prospettive che permette di cogliere.

II. Ceres dea politica ed urbana

Il primo problema che ci si presenta è quello della natura, della qualità di fondo della dea che unanimamente ci viene presentata come 'dea agraria', dea del grano, della campagna coltivata, antico nume italico della germinazione e della generazione, affine alla Kerre della tavola di Agnone[8] ed al Çerfus Martius delle tavole Iguvinae[9], integrata già in epoca molto antica nella figura della greca Demeter e 'scelta', ad un certo momento dalla plebe romana quale suo nume tutelare. Lasciando da parte le controversie, ancora non del tutto sciolte sulla composizione etnica e sociale della *plebs* romana, saltando le vecchie tesi della contrapposizione tra sfera pastorale (patrizia) e sfera agraria (plebea) che non sono più ammissibili se non nel loro valore segnico, sincronico e strutturale[10], ciò

---

[7] BIRT, in: ROSCHER, Ausführliches Lexikon der griechischen und römischen Mythologie I (1884–1890), s. v. Ceres, col. 859–866, scrive che nelle province in età imperiale il nome della dea sembra quasi scomparire. L'articolista della RE indica nelle iscrizioni l'unica fonte di informazione (s. v.): indicazioni contraddittorie dinanzi alla apparente 'sparizione' di una dea che sembra sopravvivere solo letterariamente.

[8] E. VETTER, Handbuch der italischen Dialekte, I, Heidelberg, 1953, pp. 104–107. G. DEVOTO, Il pantheon di Agnone, SE XXXV, 1967, p. 183.

[9] G. DEVOTO, Le tavole di Gubbio, Firenze, 1948 (rist. 1967) p. 47ss. La controparte iguvina di Ceres assume i connotati di un dio maschile e nazionale, al centro della vita politica del gruppo.

[10] Ad un'interpretazione di questo tipo sembra accennare anche D. SABBATUCCI nel citato articolo. Pastorale ed agrario in contrapposizione di patrizio *vs* plebeo, perdono valore storico e socioeconomico in senso diacronico per acquistarne uno nuovo di tipo strutturale, segnico.

che importa notare è il fatto della 'scelta', e della chiara 'novità' con cui il culto viene ufficialmente introdotto a Roma agli inizi del V secolo a.C. con un atto deliberato e meditato (consultazione dei 'Libri Sibyllini') in un momento di profondi mutamenti socio-economici ed istituzionali (inizi della *respublica*) che certamente avevano portato a lotte interne tra gruppi diversi proiettate nel racconto storico nella grande (e semplificata) dialettica dell'opposizione patrizi/plebei. Lotte che riguardavano certo il rapporto con il territorio, il possesso del suolo, costituito a spazio 'comune' con il quale nuove categorie, nuovi gruppi, ad esempio gli stranieri, devono entrare in rapporto[11]. Il notissimo, tanto studiato 'mito di fondazione' del tempio di Ceres, o meglio della triade Ceres Liber e Libera raccontato da Dionigi di Alicarnasso (VI,17,2−4; 99,3) ce ne dà la misura[12].

Il dittatore (patrizio) Aulo Postumio alla vigilia di una difficile guerra ed in un momento di straordinaria carestia per sterilità dei campi e mancanza di approvigionamento dall'estero (interessante precisazione del solito momento di crisi che introduce la necessità di fondazione del nuovo culto), appreso dai

---

[11] L'ipotesi di una presenza di stranieri nella composizione della *plebs* ed in particolare anche di Greci, può trovare sempre più credito sulla base dei ritrovamenti archeologici del Lazio arcaico. In particolare di notevole valore la possibilità di stabilire rapporti precisi tra la Roma di VI secolo e l'Attica contemporanea per cui l'ipotesi avanzata da C. AMPOLO di un rapporto tra il complesso della Regia nel foro ed il *prytaneion* dell'agorà di Atene, inteso su basi topografico strutturali, acquista una precisa probabilità storica (cfr. C. AMPOLO, Analogie nei rapporti tra Atene e Roma arcaica, PdP XXVI, 1971, pp. 443−457). La messa a punto dei ritrovamenti in una panoramica complessiva, soprattutto per quanto riguarda Roma, Lavinio, Graviska si trova nel volume XXXI della PdP (1977) dedicato a 'Lazio arcaico e mondo greco', passim. Acquistano così peso 'storico' le ripetute allusioni ai contatti Roma Grecia in età arcaica presenti nella tradizione romana e ritenuti da gran parte della storiografia moderna dei falsi. A cominciare da quella proiettata nel passato più lontano che ricorda un culto femminile celebrato sul Palatino e all'epoca di Evandro dal quale era escluso − come nei riti di Demeter in Grecia − l'uso del vino (Dion. I, 33). Interessante tabu che ricompare ambiguamente nell'uso romano secondo il quale le donne non possono bere mai vino, come il vino non può essere parte delle offerte in certi culti, quello della Ceres greca per l'appunto e di Bona Dea. Cfr. Serv. ad Georg. I, 344 e disputato con chiarito commento in LE BONNIEC, o. c., p. 439ss. Ma ricordiamo che, a parte l'imitazione dal rito greco, il divieto del vino ha una ragione d'essere eminentemente strutturale. Riguarda anche gli schiavi e gli uomini al di sotto dei trent'anni (Ateneo 429b), cioè un insieme di categorie e s c l u s e dalla gestione politica del potere al quale invece il vino è intimamente legato come dimostra il suo rapporto immediato nel culto e nel mito con due personaggi emblematicamente potenti: Juppiter il massimo degli dei, e Numa, il re legislatore! (cfr. G. DUMÉZIL, Vin et souveraineté, in: ID., Fêtes romaines d'été et d'automne suivi de Dix questions romaines, Paris 1975, pp. 87−97. Anche G. PICCALUGA, Numa e il vino, SMSR XXXIII, 1962, pp. 99−103). Parimenti significativi per la collocazione di Ceres nella realtà alto-repubblicana, anche gli altri cenni storiografici sui contatti con la Grecia dalla ambasceria di Tarquinio a Delfi (Liv. I, 56; Dion. IV,69) a quella dei decemviri alla metà del V per la stesura della prima legislazione scritta (volontà plebea!) (Liv. III, 31ss.; Dion. X, 52,54); alle allusioni di Cicerone agli influssi della costituzione di Solone sulle leggi delle XII tavole (De leg. II, 59). Cfr. anche M. DUCOS, L'influence grecque sur la loi des douze tables, Paris 1978.

[12] Dati in LE BONNIEC, o. c., p. 213ss.

'Libri Sibyllini' la necessità di „placare quegli dei" (ἐξιλάσασθαι τοὺς θεούς),
Ceres Liber e Libera o meglio, nell'*interpretatio* greca di Dionigi, Demeter, Dionysos e Kore, vota la fondazione di templi (ναούς) in loro onore e di sacrifici
annui „se durante la sua magistratura la città avesse potuto godere della medesima floridezza di prima" (ἐὰν εὐετηρία γένηται κατὰ τὴν πόλιν ἐπὶ τῆς ἰδίας
ἀρχῆς). Le deduzioni immediate che si possono fare sono le seguenti: la triade
appare già precostituita e garantendo raccolti ed approvvigionamento, esprime
evidentemente gli interessi di quel gruppo o gruppi che svolgono la loro attività
in questi campi, agricoltori (di un certo tipo) e mercanti. Essa è dunque intimamente legata alla città tanto che ne determina il suo stesso benessere ed indiretta-
mente permette il buon esercizio della ἀρχή, della carica istituzionale, al ma-
gistrato! Ecco perchè il console patrizio deve votare il tempio plebeo ed il
senato ratifica l'utilizzazione del bottino della guerra vittoriosa per la sua costruzione (Dion. VI,17).

La triade plebea è necessaria per la economia della *polis*, per la esistenza
della città nella sua dimensione di *res publica* alla quale assicurererà il retto
esercizio delle *archai*.

Significativamente il tempio sarà effettivamente „consacrato" (καθιέρωσεν)
non da Postumio ma da Spurio Cassio (unico patrizio della potente famiglia
plebea dei Cassî!) console durante la guerra contro i Volsci nel 493 e 'rimasto in
città' mentre il suo collega combatteva fuori. Ma questo Spurio Cassio è anche
l'autore di una prima e contrastata proposta di legge agraria e ripetutamente
accusato di *suspicio regni*, di aspirare cioè al ripristino di un potere personale e
definitivamente passato. Non protetto più dall'esercizio della magistratura, sarà
processato ed ucciso; anzi secondo una tradizione insistente, sarà fatto condan-
nare dal padre alla morte (infamante) per *verberatio* mentre le sue sostanze sa-
ranno consacrate (*consecravisse*) a Ceres (Liv. II 41,10); cioè proprio alla dea
di cui egli aveva messo in funzione per così dire l'attività ma contro la quale lo
poneva il suo comportamento antiistituzionale. Il suo *peculium*, continua ancora
Plinio (N.h. XXXIV,15), venne trasformato in una statua di bronzo della dea
con la scritta *ex Cassia familia datum*, che è anche la 'prima' statua di bronzo
(*simulacrum ex aere factum primum reperio*) vista in Roma. E'un altro tangibile
segno della 'novità' del culto introdotto: si interrompe l'uso arcaico della sta-
tuaria in terracotta e si riafferma la inviolabilità di quella *communis libertas* che
la dea inserisce nell'area della *sacrosanctitas* e Spurio aveva osato *in dubium
vocare*. Le sparse fila della contrastata tradizione su un personaggio la cui storicità è stata così tante volte messa in dubbio[13] si riannodano nella fondamentale
'storicità' del raconto mitico fissato dalla tradizione storiografica successiva (da
Livio a Valerio Massimo e oltre) per esprimere la funzione del nuovo culto.
Essa è appunto quella di garantire il funzionamento della dialettica repubblicana

---

[13] Su Spurio Cassio vedi, anche R. M. OGILVIE, A Commentary on Livy, Books 1—5,
Oxford, 1965, p. 337ss. Per la proposta agraria da ultimo M. BASILE, Analisi e valore della
tradizione sulla *rogatio* Cassia agraria del 486 a.C., in: Sesta Miscellanea greca e romana,
Roma, 1978, pp. 277—298. Secondo un'altra variante sarebbe stato bruciato vivo per ordine
del tribuno P. Mucius! (Val. Mass. VI 3,2).

nell'ambito della quale la *plebs* gioca la sua parte essenzialmente come gruppo urbano[14].

Sfuma così d'importanza il tanto dibattuto problema delle origini della triade plebea: essa non è stata importata prefabbricata dalla Sicilia, dalla Magna Grecia, dall'Etruria o da qualche località vicina della Campania o del Lazio, ma è stata certo costituita all'interno del sistema politeistico romano, espressione di una cultura già molto aperta all'influsso greco, come attestano in modo sempre più massiccio sin dall'VIII secolo i reperti archeologici del Lazio e della stessa Roma, ma capace di precise scelte individuanti.

L'attestata presenza dei nomi di Ceres e di Liber in un'iscrizione arcaica di VII a.C. su un'olla proveniente da Falerii Veteres[15], e per di più associati al cereale (farro) ed al vino secondo la 'classica' accoppiata di Demeter e Dionysos nella tradizione greca toglie qualsiasi dubbio sulla profondità di penetrazione di elementi greci nella cultura laziale arcaica e del loro ruolo attivo a livello dell' organizzazione religiosa. Ma la triade plebea si presenta comunque − anche tenendo conto della precostituita possibile assimilazione di Ceres a Demeter e di Liber a Dionysos − come una libera creazione romana, repubblicana prima ancora che plebea, ed essenzialmente 'politica', come contrapposizione alla triade regia capitolina di Iuppiter Iuno e Minerva. La contrapposizione segnalata esplicitamente anche nello schema della struttura templare che ripete − lo afferma Vitruvio − quella del tempio capitolino, si riflette in uno schema dialettico che precorre in modo significativo la *religio Cereris*: il confronto in abbinamento tra Iuppiter e Ceres.

Iuppiter è infatti presente in quella che si può considerare la sfera più peculiare della Ceres repubblicana: la tutela della *libertas* attraverso la estensione della *sacrosanctitas* (tutto ciò che rientra nella sfera del *sacrum* e del *sanctum*) a modalità del diritto pubblico esercitato dal *populus* e dalla *plebs*: *sacro sanctum . . . quod populus plebesque sanxit*, definisce ancora Cicerone (pro Balbo 14). La famosa legge Valeria Horatia − una *lex sacrata* sulla cui pregnante valenza politica ci informa una nota di Festo − destinata a stabilire quella inviolabilità delle magistrature plebee per eccellenza, edilità e tribunato, che diventa garanzia basilare per l'uso in comune dello spazio conflittuale politico, prevede per chi la violi la *sacratio* a Juppiter (*eius caput Jovi sacrum esse*) e la vendita dei suoi beni in favore del tempio di Ceres Liber e Libera (*familia ad aedem Cereris Liberi Liberaeque venum ire*). Così nel testo di Livio (III 55,7) che data la *lex* al 449 nell'ambito assegnato al grosso riordinamento legislativo dello stato[16]. Il passo

---

[14] Sul tema cfr. J. ELLUL, Réflexion sur la révolution, la plèbe et le tribunat de la plèbe, Index 3, Omaggio a Max Kaser, 1972, pp. 155 ss.; vedi anche i saggi di A. MOMIGLIANO ristampati in: ID., Quarto Contributo alla Storia degli Studi Classici e del mondo antico, Roma 1969, pp. 313−323; 419−436; 437−456. Anche J.-C. RICHARD, Les origines de la plèbe romaine, BEFAR, Roma, 1978.

[15] VETTER, o. c., n. 241; nonostante le incertezze della lettura sembra chiara la presenza di una coppia Ceres Liber legata rispettivamente al *far* ed al *vinum*. Oltre a LE BONNIEC, o. c., p. 303 ss., cfr. E. PERUZZI, Iscrizioni Falische, Maia XI, 1964, pp. 149−175.

[16] Diversamente D. Hal. VI 89−90 che 'opportunamente' pone la rivoluzionaria Valeria-Horatia in rapporto con la fondazione nuova e 'rivoluzionaria' del tempio alla triade plebea,

liviano è significativo nella misura in cui colloca esplicitamente il provvedimento (al di là delle polemiche sulla datazione) nel contesto di una situazione di tensione tra la *libertas* che è aspirazione ed appropriazione della *plebs* e la gelosa difesa delle *opes* che sono proprie dei *patres*[17]. La mediazione avviene mediante quel provvedimento che trasforma la *religio* in *lex* (o viceversa) ed è posta sotto il patrocinio di Juppiter e di Ceres, non antagonisti − dio dei patrizi e dea dei plebei − ma protagonisti di una medesima e nuova realtà politica che ha bisogno per funzionare di una rete di convenzioni irrinunciabili, cioè *sacrosanctae*.

Così non ci potrà stupire di trovare Juppiter onorato con un *epulum* − *epulum Iovis* − alle idi di settembre[18] al centro di quei Ludi Romani o Ludi Magni che un tempo avrebbero dovuto essere ludi plebei, o almeno amministrati dagli *aediles* plebei, la fondamentale magistratura sacrale, se così si può definire, della *aedes Cereris*, e solo più tardi trasferiti alla apposita magistratura (patrizia) degli *aediles* curuli[19]. Nè ci stupiamo di trovare alla stessa data, in età imperiale, ma ovviamente in campagna, in uno dei *praedia* di Plinio il giovane, una grande festa di Ceres che attira al suo tempio al giorno prefissato, *stato die*, una grande folla da tutta la regione (Plin. Ep. IX 39). − Nè sorprende trovare in apertura al famoso trattato varroniano sull'agricoltura − sia pure tenendo conto della particolare elaborazione teologica che bisogna sottendere a molte delle informazioni dell'erudito antiquario e filosofo − Juppiter e Tellus invocati come *parentes magni*. Ma sappiamo bene che, a parte le altre implicazioni, per Varrone *Cererem nihil aliud esse quam terram* (in Ag. c. D. VII,16)[20].

---

nel 493/2. Sulle *leges sacratae* in rapporto esplicito anche con la cerimonia del *sacramentum*, definizione del rito di passaggio − immissione al servizio militare sottoposto allo *iusiurandum* − cfr. G. Niccolini, Leges Sacratae, Historia II, 1928 pp. 3 ss. − Osservazioni in rapporto alla sacralità degli edili, visti come sacerdoti di Ceres, in D. Sabbatucci, L'edilità romana. Magistratura e sacerdozio, Atti della Acc. Naz. d. Lincei, S. VIII, VI, 3, 1954, pp. 255−332 (tesi accettabile solo con qualche ulteriore precisazione). La *plebs* si riserva il diritto di immettere il *sacer* nell'ambito del cosiddetto profano, di far agire la *sacrosanctitas*, ma non è affatto detto che questa fosse particolarità specifica delle sue istituzioni. Anzi, la *plebs* si limita a metterla in atto, ad estenderla, a farla agire a difesa delle sue conquiste, con un atto innovatore: *sacratae leges sunt . . . qui esse dicant sacratas quas plebs iurata in monte Sacro sciverit* (Festo 422 L.). Cfr. anche commento in appendice all'edizione di Tito Livio (Bayet−Baillet), III, p. 145; anche H. Fugier, Recherches sur l'expression du sacré dans la langue latine, Publ. de la Faculté des lettres de l'Univ. de Strasbourg CXLVI, Paris 1963, p. 439.

[17] Livio, III, 55,6. . . . *ipsis quoque tribunis ut sacrosancti viderentur − cuius rei prope iam memoriam aboleverat − relatis quibusdam ex magno intervallo caerimoniis, renovarunt, et cum religione inviolatos eos tum lege etiam fecerunt*, . . .

[18] Degrassi, I.I.XIII, 2, p. 509.

[19] Discussione del problema in Le Bonniec, o. c., p. 350 ss.

[20] Bisogna sempre tener presente l'impostazione culturale ed ideologica di Varrone. Egli compie un esplicito lavoro di riordinamento della teologia politeistica romana non privo di risonanze su certi aspetti della restaurazione religiosa di Augusto − partendo dall'applicazione del metodo allegorico di origine stoica che sfocia nell'applicazione della cd. teologia tripartita, cioè nella distinzione tra tre categorie o modi di rappresentare gli dei, il fisico, il mitico ed il politico a seconda dei destinatari del messaggio: se al filosofo, al poeta, al popolo. Sull'argomento, trattato con molta insistenza negli autori cristiani, cfr. J. Pépin,

III. La 'debolezza' agraria di Ceres e l'aiuto di Tellus e di Hercules

Si tratta di una contrapposizione dal significato strutturale e storico insieme, che si può ricondurre alla contrapposizione più pregnante del ciclo del vino al ciclo del grano: il primo è legato a Juppiter (vedi le implicazioni mitico rituali nei Vinalia di aprile e di agosto e dei Meditrinalia) come espressione di sovranità di tipo regale (rapporto con Numa), mentre il cd. ciclo del grano Fordicidia Robigalia Floralia Consualia Opiconsivia, tra le quali si inseriscono i Ceriala del 19 aprile vede una estensione abbastanza artificiosa della funzione della *dea frugum* su tutta una vasta area già densa di personaggi rappresentativi[21].

Anche se esula dagli interessi che qui ci proponiamo l'esame dei cicli agrari nei calendri romani – tema che andrebbe ripreso con più ampio spazio – la denunciata natura agraria di Ceres come elemento base del suo essere politeistico, ci obbliga ad esaminare alcuni problemi che derivano anche da un superficiale sguardo all'inserimento calendariale delle festività della dea. Il nucleo più importante, i Cerealia di aprile, si riconducono, come è stato più volte notato, originariamente al solo giorno del 19 aprile con i ludi al Circo Massimo[22]. Certamente di secondaria introduzione i ludi scenici previsti dal 12 in poi, mentre la quindicina del mese aperta dai Fordicidia vede i riti del 19 – inseriti in una sequenza di ritualismo a sfondo agrario che si sussegue sino all'apertura dei ludi *florales* con la festa per l'inaugurazione del tempio di Flora, mancante nei calendari più antichi ma certo da collegare allo stesso sistema festivo arcaico[23]. Ceres è coinvolta con Tellus, Pales, Venus (Iuppiter), Robigo, Flora, dunque un gruppo

---

Mythe et allégorie. Les origines grecques et les contestations judéo-chrétiennes, Paris, 1958, p. 276ss; G. LIEBERG, Die 'theologia tripartita' in Forschung und Bezeugung, ANRW I 4, Berlin–New York, 1973, pp. 63–115.

[21] Cfr. G. DUMÉZIL, o. c., p. 98ss. e passim. Un segno della non specializzazione di Ceres nel campo cerealicolo, almeno in origine, è dato dall'inclusione nella lista della preghiera che accompagna il sacrificio della *porca praecidanea*, in Catone della fava e della rapa, entrambi alimenti 'precedenti' l'attualità dei cereali, cibi di un tempo diverso. In particolare per l'ostilità della fava come concorrente battuta del grano di Demeter ed il valore storico-culturale di questa esclusione, cfr. I. CHIRASSI, Elementi di culture precereali nei miti e riti greci, Roma, 1968, p. 39ss.

[22] Appartengono certamente al calendario cosiddetto di Numa, probabilmente da considerare (contrariamente a quanto sostenuto da A. KIRSOP-MICHELS, A Calendar of the Roman Republic, Princeton, 1971, p. 119ss.) effettivamente prerepubblicano; anche se rimane sempre possibile una 'nuova' sistemazione da parte dei decemviri alla metà del V, considerando l'enorme importanza 'politica' della regolamentazione rituale del tempo.

[23] Possiede anch'essa un *flamen* (Varro, L.L. 7,45; CIL IX 705) e sotto molti aspetti tende ad assumere le qualità cerealicole di Ceres; il *florifertum*, festa specifica al suo *sacrarium* consiste in un'offerta di spighe (Festo exc. 91). Interessanti le modalità della riorganizzazione del culto tra il 240–238 ad opera del senato: cfr. J. CELS-SAINT-HILAIRE, Le fonctionement des Floralia sous la République, D.Hist.Anc. III, 1977, pp. 253–286. Sull'insieme dei culti di maggio-aprile ancora insostituita la vecchia monografia di W. WARDE FOWLER, The Roman Festivals of the Period of the Republic, London 1899 (rist. 1969).

dominato quasi esclusivamente da divinità femminili (eccezione Iuppiter), in una sequenza di riti certamente legati alla coltivazione dei campi in un momento segnatamente cruciale per la crescita dei vegetali; in particolare per il frumento (ma se ne occupa esplicitamente Robigo: *ne Robigo frumentis noceat*, si legge sui calendari), ai cui i Cerealia, sarebbero, secondo la minuziosa analisi agraria condotta da LE BONNIEC, la „festa propiziatoria per la formazione della spiga". Ma si tratta di un momento più complesso articolato su piani diversi, che mette in moto meccanismi di integrazione assai interessanti, ad esempio per il controllo di categorie socialmente 'imbarazzanti': le *vulgares puellae* che si riunivano al tempio della Venus Erucina fuori porta Collina proprio durante i Vinalia di Juppiter[24], o i *pueri lenoniorum* che festeggiavano il loro *dies festus* in coincidenza con i riti di Robigo[25]. Per non parlare delle *meretrices* che hanno una parte assai rilevante nel mito e nel rito dei *ludi iocosi* della *Mater florum* (Ov. Fasti, V 183) in cui il *meretricum dies* coincide con il giorno di fondazione del tempio votato *propter sterilitatem frugum*[26]. Al di là del generico e più volte sottolineato rapporto tra sessualità ed attività agricola si può osservare che, sotto questo punto di vista queste feste di fine mese chiudono un periodo in cui viene coinvolto in modo molto ravvicinato il mondo femminile. Comincia dai riti del primo aprile oscillanti tra la Fortuna Virilis e la Venus Verticordia, in cui madri e spose insieme alle *humiliores* propiziano la belleza del corpo e la buona fama (*et forma et mores et bona fama*) (Ov., Fast. IV, 156) che assicureranno loro anche il favore maschile, si conclude in certo senso con le feste matronali di maggio della Bona Dea ad Saxum (il tempio dell'Aventino restaurato da Livia, moglie di Augusto)[27]. In tutta questa lunga sequenza rituale che, anche a tenere solo conto delle notizie filtrate attraverso i 'Fasti' di Ovidio, si presenta assai ricca di elementi saldamente agganciati con una storicamente stratificata ma operante realtà culturale romana, i Cerialia appaiono piuttosto sbiaditi, assai poveri di particolari significanti, nonostante il lungo racconto mitico del *raptus*

---

[24] Ovid. Fast. IV, 865ss.; cfr. anche K. LATTE, Römische Religionsgeschichte, Handbuch der Altertumswiss. V 4, München 1960, p. 186; DEGRASSI, I.I. XIII, 2 p. 446.

[25] Il *festus puerorum lenoniorum* è segnato nei fasti prenestini, cfr. DEGRASSI, I.I. XIII, p. 448.

[26] Il tempio è votato dagli edili L. e M. Publicius nel 238 — rispondendo alla necessità di integrare nello spazio cultuale (e culturale) della *respublica* elementi stranieri assorbiti nelle nuove tribu Quirina e Velia (cfr. art. cit. in n. 23). L'esame degli elementi ludici del rituale, particolarmente interessanti per il loro carattere contraddittorio (una *venatio* di capre e pecore in circo, una distribuzione di fave e piselli al popolo, cioè una caccia per scherzo ed una . . . altrettanto scherzosa pre *frumentatio*, le vesti multicolori, l'*ebrietas* e la *saltatio*), sono tutti elementi che contraddicono sul piano del *lusus*, ripetendone contraffatti i particolari, i momenti costitutivi dei riti di Ceres del mese precedente. Compreso naturalmente il rapporto con il mondo femminile che vede correlate per opposizione anche nel rito (oltre che nella società) *matronae* e *meretrices*. Per un analisi del valore di *ludus* in rapporto ai rituali romani, cfr. G. PICCALUGA, Elementi spettacolari nei rituali festivi romani, Quaderni di SMSR II, Roma, 1965, p. 32ss.

[27] È il tempio (fondato dal Senato) che „rifugge dagli occhi maschili", fondato da una vergine dei Clausi e fatto restaurare da Livia in imitazione del comportamento del marito (*imitata maritum*). Cfr. Ov. Fast. V 150–158.

virginis, ennesima variante del ben noto mito greco della *Kores harpaghè* con il quale il poeta intende introdurre le festività per quella che, secondo il ben noto elogio, conducendo i mortali *ad meliora alimenta,* ha trasformato il mondo da selvatico in coltivato, ha fondato l'attualità[28]. Unico elemento significativamente 'romano', ricordato da Ovidio (che è anche per questa precisa circostanza unico informatore), riguarda il rito dell'*immissio* nel Circo delle *volpes* con le faci ardenti a ricordo del mito del ragazzo di Carseoli e della volpe ladra di polli[29]. Mito e rito, emblematici anche se la scarsità di confronti rende difficile coglierne il valore strutturale, ci rimandano comunque al di là del generico significato agrario: punizione della volpe animale selvatico, dannosa alla agricoltura, vedi la volpe di Carseoli che sfuggita dalle mani del ragazzino che le aveva appicato fuoco *incendit vestitos messibus agros,* „incendia i campi coperti di messi". Il suggerimento per una esegesi ci viene dalla vicina Lavinio dove Dionigi di Alicarnasso afferma di aver visto nel foro un gruppo in bronzo rappresentante la lotta di un'aquila e di una lupa contro una volpe che cerca di spegnere un fuoco che gli altri due animali vogliono invece mantenere vivo (I, 54). Il messaggio inviato attraverso l'utilizzazione degli animali simbolo è chiaro: aquila e lupa il cui valore nella tradizione romana non ha bisogno di ulteriori commenti[30], difendono il fuoco elemento indispensabile di vita culturale, segno della perennità e centralità del focolare della casa come della città, contro un animale del resto loro tradizionale nemico e qualificato in tutta la tradizione antica dalla parte dell'astuzia e dell'inganno. Il gruppo bronzeo fissa così nel tempo il messaggio di un prodigio attraverso il quale, secondo Dionigi, Enea avrebbe capito il suo destino di fondare un nuovo popolo[31]. Ceres, come Demeter, difende le *segetes* soprattutto nella loro dimensione culturale quella che usa il fuoco non come elemento distruttore ma come mezzo edificatore ed è in questa prospettiva che si condanna il cattivo uso o meglio la incapacità di usare il fuoco rivelata dal maldestro ragazzo di Carseoli che non sa di conseguenza ancora ben dominare il selvatico. Tenendo presente questa prospettiva, non ci si stupisce troppo di non vedere Ceres inserita in quello che invece appare un vero ciclo agrario, costituito con evidente finalità di dare una cerniera di sostegno ai momenti cruciali per il raccolto. Per esplicita testimonianza di Plinio sappiamo che i *dies festi,* stabiliti dagli antichi romani per queste circostanze sono: Robigalia, Floralia, Vinalia (certo, data la sequenza, i Vinalia rustica di agosto)[32]. Ma i riti di Ceres non

---

[28] Ovid. Fast. IV 395ss.; è il consueto tema dell'attualità del cereale sul quale vedi art. cit. in nota 2.

[29] Ovid. Fast. IV 680–712. È proprio il mito legato alla celebrazione dei Cerealia del 19 cioè dei *ludi* più antichi. La serie di interpretazioni date al significato delle volpi rosse e del fuoco loro appiccato è puntualmente riassunta da LE BONNIEC, o. c., p. 115ss.

[30] Cfr. D. BRIQUEL, L'oiseau ominal, la louve du Mars, la truie féconde, Mél.Ec.Fr.Ant. LXXXVIII, 1976, pp. 31–50.

[31] Già nel mondo greco è detta da Archiloco (fr. 88 WEST) πυκνὸν ἔχουσα νόον. Interessanti le caratteristiche comportamentali: si oppone agli animali 'nobili' come leone, lupo, aquila ma è amica del corvo, della gru e dei serpenti! Non accettabile l'ipotesi di GAGÉ (rec. a LE BONNIEC, in RHR, CLXI, 1962, pp. 238) che vede negli animali simboli dei popoli incontrati da Enea nel Lazio.

[32] Plin. N. H. XVIII 29.

trovano collocazione nella sequenza stabilita tra Fordicidia, Parilia, Equus
October, inizio e conclusione di un ciclo agrario saldamente connesso con una
struttura di organizzazione sociale che mette in atto l'antico sistema della
divisione per curie (Fordicidia) nel suo complesso valore di probabile modo di
articolazione socio-economico militare, ha come attori le Virgines Vestali ed il
Pontifex Maximus e come punti spaziali di riferimento il complesso ideologicamente organico del Campidoglio-Palatino, della Regia Atrium Vestae e del Campo Marzio[33].

Si tratta di un sistema certo pre-repubblicano, precedente cioè quel particolare periodo dell'organizzazione politica di Roma che trova il suo nuovo
assetto nella conflittualità permanente tra patrizi e plebei. In questo sistema la
dea agraria è Tellus non Ceres: ad essa va il sacrificio delle *fordae boves*, le
vacche gravide, esplicitamente contrario alla sfera di Ceres costantemente invece
legata al sacrificio del maiale ed alla esclusione dell'abbattimento del bove[34].

---

[33] G. DUMÉZIL nega la connessione tra l'*Equus October* ed i riti di aprile affermando l'impossibilità dell'utilizzazione del sangue dell'*equus* nel *suffimen* primaverile dei Parilia,
o. c., p. 188 ss.

[34] *Prima Ceres avidae gavisa est sanguine porcae* (Ovid. Fast. I 350 ss.). Lo stesso autore
ricorda come fosse stato proprio Pitagora ad indicare nel maiale il primo animale sacrificato
perchè nocivo all'agricoltura (Met. XV, 111−113). In realtà le implicazioni tra maiale e bove
rispetto il rito del sacrificio cruento hanno risvolti assai più complessi che qui è impossibile
accennare. Il crimine dell'uccisione del bove *in rustico opere Cereris minister* (Varro, r.r. II,
5,3) regola e fonda il rito cruento come rito della *polis* nella festa ateniese dei Buphonia o
Dipoleia (v. in proposito I. CHIRASSI COLOMBO, Morfologia di Zeus, PdP CLXIII, 1975,
pp. 249−274, in particolare p. 269−70). Particolarmente interessante, per una problematica
che solo in apparenza esula dal nostro interesse presente, il gioco etimologico usato da
Varrone per legare il vocabolo *initium* (dall'ambiguo valore) al pregnante senso sacrificale
dello *thyein* greco interpretato come sacrificio di maiali (ὗς > θῦς): *ab suillo enim pecore
immolandi initium primum sumptum videtur* (r.r. II 4,9). Sacrificio cruento ed in particolare il sacrificio del maiale (proprio di Ceres come della Demeter greca) appaiono il
primo, più antico atto sacrificale con tutta la pregnanza che esso comporta, e per questo
lo si trova ripetuto in situazioni critiche di apertura o chiusura di un ciclo, come iniziare
una pace, stabilire un patto, celebrare un matrimonio. In questo caso sposo e sposa
sacrificano insieme il *porcus* (*in coniuctione nuptiali nova nupta et novus maritus primum
porcum immolant*). Ma il sottinteso è esplicito: il *porcus* indica il sesso femminile, la „vittima sacrificata" è la *nova nupta* nel cruento sacrificio virginale che la introduce alla
sessualità normalizzata. L'analogia con il mondo greco, segnalata dallo stesso Varrone,
ha precisa conferma (cfr. a proposito dati in W. BURKERT, Homo Necans. Interpretationen
altgriechischer Opferriten und Mythen, Religionsgeschichtliche Versuche und Vorarbeiten
XXXII, Berlin, 1972, „Koremythos und Schweineopfer", pp. 283−292 cfr. anche dati
in I. CHIRASSI COLOMBO, Paides e Gynaikes. Note per una tassonomia del comportamento rituale nella cultura attica, Q.U. n.s. I, 1979, pp. 25−58, part. p. 56, n. 80.
Da segnalare, per quanto ci riguarda, l'interesse di Varrone ad indicare in Ceres una „dea
degli inizi", con tutta la possibilità semantica del termine, ma non nel senso etimologico
proposto da H. WAGENVOORT, Initia Cereris (1948), trad. ingl. in: ID., Studies in Roman
Literature, Culture and Religion, Leiden, 1956, 150−168, bensì in quello funzionale di
fondatrice di nuove situazioni. In questo senso traduce bene il termine di 'iniziazioni' dato
comunemente ai riti misterici.

Ma oltre ad individuare la presenza di un ciclo indipendente e ritualmente conseguente per Tellus, possiamo cercare ai capirne il valore: la sua assimilazione a Ceres, ad esempio in Varrone, scaturisce da quella precisa impostazione teologica che cerca un recupero dell'allegoria fisica come momento interpretativo unitario delle teologie che diversificano il pantheon pagano. L'abbinamento Tellus Ceres nella coppia delle *frugum matres* che troviamo preposta alla festa mobile delle *sementivae* occasione di un *lustrum pagi* descritto in termini abbastanza convenzionali alla fine del I libro dei 'Fasti' di Ovidio, può dipendere invece dalla volontà di 'propagandare' il più possibile la *religio* agraria di Ceres nell'ambito della 'nuova' utilizzazione del suo *numen* che si fa strada specie in età augustea[35]. È significativo comunque che a Roma le feste *sementivae*, per testimonianza esplicita di Varrone (r.r. I 1,2) si tenevano nella *aedes Telluris*. Così nella festa delle idi di dicembre è Ceres che si associa a Tellus per la celebrazione del natale del tempio, fondato sull'Esquilino nel 268 a.C.[36] Ma il tempio più antico, preesistente, è quello costruito direttamente sull'area della casa di Spurio Cassio quasi a controbilanciare la assegnazione del *peculium* alla *aedes Cereris*, quindi dare un giusto riconoscimento a chi aveva partecipato comunque a smascherare Spurio, la parte patrizia rappresentata da quel Verginius che, *quasi vaticinantem*, aveva indicato nella spartizione di terre proposta, una *regno via* (Liv. II 41,5). Si delinea così, al fondo della *religio Telluris*, una sottile dialettica nei rapporti con Ceres che, come è stato osservato, viene comunque sempre 'dopo' nelle formule rituali di invocazione. Mentre ideologicamente, Tellus per quella indeterminatezza pre o post politeistica che la rende facilmente adatta ad essere assimilata ad una grande dea, sul tipo della Magna Mater, o farsi ipostasi della immanente divina Natura delle speculazioni stoiche ed epicuree (vedi ad esempio Lucrezio)[37], si pone nella condizione ideale di offrire, a chi vuole servirsene, una piattaforma di garanzia allo immutabile ordine delle cose. La coppia Tellus-Ceres si presenta dunque in una proiezione politico-ideologica, forse molto antica, nella quale Tellus sembra costantemente 'solidificare', ancorare, il *numen* di Ceres. — Altrettanto 'ideologico' pare l'abbinamento di Hercules con Ceres in quell'offerta di scrofa gravida pane e vino mielato in cui il miele 'dolcifica' cioè media attraverso la preparazione del *mulsum* la contradditoria presenza del vino in un rituale apparentemente tutto cerealicolo (per la presenza della scrofa e del pane) ma che in realtà unisce due figure strutturalmente contrastanti. Non casuale la data del solstizio d'inverno, ricordata da Macrobio in corrispondenza con le cerimonie *arcanae* per la Diva Angerona, epiteto della 'stessa Roma'[38].

Hercules è con ogni probabilità l'Hercules Invictus dell'Ara Massima che ancora in età imperiale, attraverso la rinnovata ideologia dello eroe vincitore del selvatico, continuava a servizio dell'imperatore e dell'impero il suo culto arcaico

---

[35] Cfr. Le Bonniec, o. c., p. 56 ss.
[36] Degrassi, I.I. XIII, 2, p. 537.
[37] Lucr. II 610 (rapporto con Cybele); V 822 *genus ipsa creavit / humanum atque animal*; ancora in II 1158 *(terra) sponte sua primum mortalibus ipsa creavit*.
[38] Macrob.Sat. III 2,10; K. Latte, o. c., p. 135.

in un luogo assai prossimo topograficamente alla *aedes Cereris*[39]. Culto pre-
romuleo e di conseguenza prepolitico, affidato espressamente alle cure di un
sacerdozio gentilizio, i Potitii ed i Pinarii, ed esclusivamente maschile (le donne
non possono accedervi, Macrob. I 12,28; Plut., qu. R. 59), si presta con molte
opportunità a controbilanciare il culto politico plebeo, divenuto ʿfemminileʾ e
ʿcontadinoʾ di Ceres, memorizzando nell'assetto unitario del nuovo quadro istituzionale dell'impero il dualismo dialettico che aveva contraddistinto la dinamica
strutturale della prima *respublica*.

Del resto esaminando puntualmente le altre presenze di Ceres nel sistema
cultuale romano del periodo repubblicano, risulta chiara la modalità del suo
inserimento, in chiave eminentemente funzionale alla sua posizione politica,
mentre del tutto subordinata appare la funziona agraria che ripete il modello
ideologico della Demeter greca.

IV. Ceres e la sfera funeraria

Vediamone i punti: rapporto di Ceres con la legislazione, con il rituale
funerario e la sfera infera, con il mondo femminile.

Per il primo punto il dato più noto riguarda la famosa legge delle ʿXII ta-
voleʾ riportata da Plinio all'inizio del XVIII libro della N.H.). Secondo tale dis-
posizione chiunque fosse stato sorpreso a rubare frumento o altri cereali (*frugem
aratro quaesitam*) era destinato alla morte infamante per impiccagione se pubere,
con procedimento più grave di quanto non comportasse il caso di omicidio
(quest'ultima osservazione probabile commento pliniano o della fonte, tenendo
conto dell'uso tardo del termine *homicidium*, ma non per questo meno significativa).[40] Il passo si chiarisce solo se si tiene conto della funzione specifica cui è
chiamata la dea non in veste di *numen* dell'agricoltura. Anche se si pensa che i
contenuti delle leggi siano più antichi della trascrizione della metà del V secolo, è
ben probabile che l'inserimento di Ceres sia, in questo caso specifico, nuovo,

---

[39] Cfr. S. B. Platner—Th. Ashby, A Topographical Dictionary of Ancient Rome, London,
1929, p. 253. Hercules ha durante l'impero una vera e propria nuova teologia che lo trasforma nell'*invictus* per eccellenza, modello delle virtù imperiali, rivale di Mithra e del
Cristo. Cfr. M. Simon, Hercule et le Christianisme, Publ. de la Faculté des Lettres de
l'Univ. de Strasbourg, Sér. II, XIX, Paris, 1955, passim; e per l'*invictus* osservazioni in
I. Chirassi Colombo, Sol Invictus o Mithra (Per una rilettura in chiave ideologica della
teologia solare del Mitraismo nell'ambito del politeismo romano), Atti del Seminario Internazionale su ʿla specificità storico-religiosa dei Misteri di Mithraʾ (1978), Études préliminaires aux religions orientales dans l'Empire romain, LXXX, Leiden, 1979, pp. 649—672,
p. 666ss. Cfr. M. Jaczynowska, Le culte de l'Hercule romain au temps du Haut-Empire,
in questo stesso volume (ANRW II 17,2).

[40] Sul problema della morte infamante, senza spargimento di sangue, per il valore strutturale
e sociologico da vedere gli ʿActes du Colloque d'Ischia sur l'idéologie funéraire dans le
monde antiqueʾ (décembre 1977), in corso di pubblicazione.

cioè imposto dalla situazione sociale ed economica che sullo sfondo della fine VI inizi V a.C. agitò con ogni probabilità il Lazio arcaico riguardo i problemi della *possessio* del suolo, della proprietà individuale e collettiva, del nuovo concetto di spazio pubblico ecc.[41]. Il fatto che il furto sia punito con una pena più grave di quella prevista per l'omicidio e per di più con un tipo di morte infamante come in ogni caso in cui non sia contemplato spargimento di sangue (già il MOMMSEN, citato opportunamente da LE BONNIEC, affermava che la scure trasforma ogni condannato in vittima, cioè lo fa rientrare nella sfera del sacro!) si spiega con la 'novità' di un'infrazione che non riguarda più il diritto 'sacrale' in cùi rientra ad esempio il crimine 'inespiabile' dell'uccisione, bensì quello 'civile', 'politico', in cui il furto — ed in particolare l'attacco alla proprietà agraria — mette in rischio un sistema di rapporti nuovi — e forse non ancora ben chiariti — tra gruppi, individui, terra e produzione agraria. Ricordiamo che la pena di morte — rara nel codice decemvirale — compare ancora a difesa della proprietà agraria contro il pericolo di incantesimi, intesi ad espropriare il legittimo proprietario del raccolto che gli apparteneva (Cic. in Agost. c.D, VIII 19)[42].

Questa qualificazione di Ceres dalla parte del diritto — ed in particolare quello riguardante la proprietà e la sua trasmissione, ereditarietà — ricompare anche a proposito della sua dimensione cosiddetta 'ctonio-funeraria' (la «Cérès, déesse infernale» di LE BONNIEC). Il sacrificio detto della *porca praesentanea*, eseguito in presenza del defunto in onore di Ceres, secondo Festo (296 L. = 250 M.) e quello della *porca praecidanea* (*immolata prima*) secondo Varrone (in Non. Marcello, p. 163 M. = 240 L.) in onore di Tellus e Ceres, in caso di qualche trasgressione nel compimento del rito funebre, mettono in causa sempre l'erede[43]. Ceres si inserisce così nel complesso sistema della trasmissione ereditaria, legata alla regolamentazione dell'accesso alla proprietà individuale del suolo (vedi rapporto tra *heredes heredium*, i *duo iugera* di Romolo in Varro, r.r. II, 10,2), e l'organizzazione dello *ius manium*, ma non dei *manes* come collettività anonima, bensì nella specificità di *parentes*.

Il sottile legame che unisce in modo chiaro la trasmissione dell'eredità attraverso le regole precise che l'erede deve osservare nei riguardi di colui dal quale eredità, quindi un morto che ha ed avrà un rapporto specifico lui, può spiegare forse anche il sacrificio puramente agrario della *porca praecidanea*, prima del raccolto, per Ceres[44]. È un sacrificio privato fatto dal proprietario del fondo prima di qualsiasi tipo di raccolto, non solo dei cereali (Cato, De agr. 134) ed ha il valore quasi di una „giustificazione" preventiva nel caso che una qualsiasi trascuratezza metta in crisi, in un periodo così critico come quello della realiz-

---

[41] Cfr. recente sintesi in F. DE MARTINO, Storia economica di Roma antica, Firenze, 1979, p. 14 ss.

[42] Cfr. A. WATSON, Rome of the XII Tabel. Persons and Property, Princeton, 1957, passim.

[43] Testi in LE BONNIEC, o. c., p. 94.

[44] In un luogo Festo sembra confermare Catone sul valore solo agrario del sacrificio, 243 L. = 219 M. In un altro passo invece appare chiarissimo il rapporto con la sfera funeraria: chi non ha rispettato lo *ius manium* deve offrire un sacrificio espiatorio prima di consumare le nuove messi 290 L. = 219 M. Per uno sguardo d'insieme al ritualismo funerario cfr. J. P. JACOBSEN, Les Manes (trad. franc.), Paris, 1924.

zazione del raccolto agricolo, i buoni rapporti con gli dei e da cui dipende il suo giusto frutto.

Ancora una volta la mediazione della Ceres agraria passa attraverso un'interferenza nell'area del diritto, della normativa. Il sacrificio della *praecidanea* sembra essere soprattutto diretto ad evitare un comportamento non giusto, *quod iusta non fecisset*, o meglio correggere le conseguenze di chi trascura fare ciò che è *iustum*. Ad esempio non gettare la terra ad un morto, il che è violare lo *ius manium* in senso lato; non fare ciò che si deve verso la *familia* nel caso che una morte improvvisa l'abbia resa *funesta* (testo in Gellio, N.A. IV 6,7—9), il che rientra nella sfera del diritto privato, come il non compiere il giusto rito di inumazione per colui dal quale si eredita (Varr. in Non Marc. p. 163 M.).

L'espiazione non riguarda tanto il precipuo della 'contaminazione' per il morto in sè — concetto che pure esiste ben chiaro nella tradizione romana (cfr. Varr. l.L. V 23 ad esempio per la contaminazione gettata su tutta la casa da una morte). Si riferisce piuttosto alla violazione dello *iustum*, all'abbandono di ciò che rientra nella normativa in senso lato, nel fare *aliter quam oportuerat*[45].

Così anche l'altro fatto che ha indotto tanti a parlare delle implicazioni di Ceres con 'rituali magici di fecondità', ad insistere sulla sua natura infera e ctonia, cioè il rapporto con il *mundus*, la *deorum tristium atque inferum ianua* (Varr. in Macrob. Sat. I 16,18), può essere esaminato con ottica diversa[46].

Se accettiamo come risultato della convergenza di una serie di dati letterari e di verifiche archeologiche, la identificazione del *mundus* con il *bothros/omphalos*, centro ritualmente segnato della città nuova (la grande Roma del Campidoglio Foro), e identifichiamo il *mundus/omphalos* con l'Umbilicus Urbis trascurato monumento non distante troppo dal Miliarium aureum voluto da Augusto per indicare il centro dell'impero, il rapporto con Ceres assume un altro significato[47]. La dea collocandosi in relazione con un 'centro', centro della città, riconferma la sua vocazione eminentemente 'politica' attraverso la quale esplica poi anche quella qualità agraria e particolarmente cerealicola che segnala il suo profondo inserimento nella contemporaneità, in modo non dissimile da quello raggiunto in Grecia dalla Demeter Thesmophoros. Inoltre la localizzazione topografica del *mundus Cereris* accanto al tempio di Saturno, ed all'ara sulla quale Ceres riceveva annualmente offerte insieme ad Ops in un culto creato in età augustea[48], ripropone spazialmente la vicinanza familiare che la trascrizione mitica aveva captato, facendo di Ceres la figlia di Ops e di Saturnus cioè di Kronos e Rea[49].

---

[45] Per il rapporto tra organizzazione della proprietà e culto dei morti cfr. anche il classico saggio di J. GOODY, nel campo della 'Social Anthropology' inglese, con uno studio sui rapporti di parentela e organizzazione della proprietà in Africa: Death, Property and The Ancestors, London 1962.

[46] Dati in LE BONNIEC, o. c., p. 175 ss. Ripresi analiticamente con un preciso studio anche topografico, da F. COARELLI, Ara Saturni, Mundus, Senaculum. La parte occidentale del Foro in età arcaica, D.A. IX, 1976—77, pp. 346—377.

[47] M. VERZAR, L'Umbilicus Urbis. Il Mundus in età tardo-repubblicana, ibidem, pp. 378—398.

[48] DEGRASSI, I.I. XIII, 2, p. 493.

[49] Ovid. Met. IX 498.

Si tratta naturalmente del Saturnus romano, solo parzialmente identificabile con il greco Kronos, ricordato dalla tradizione soprattutto come antico re del Lazio e maestro di agricoltura, un'agricoltura senza fatica che contraddice quella attuale di Ceres pure implicandola come preattualità *vs* attualità[50]. Ma tale vicinanza è significativa anche sul piano rituale nella misura in cui entrambe queste divinità 'agrarie' paiono ritualmente coinvolte anche nella dinamica di un rovesciamento ricreazione dell'ordine, usato come efficace mezzo di controllo del comportamento (o comportamenti) del gruppo sociale[51].

I Saturnalia, la celebre festività di dicembre fissata già nel calendario più antico, con il loro momento centrale basato sul rovesciamento dell'ordine sociale (servi > padroni) implicano anche quella rottura dell'ordine cosmico fissata nei giorni di apertura del *mundus*, quando per tre volte l'anno si realizzava con la mescolanza dei morti con i vivi, il massimo tipo di disordine possibile in un sistema basato sulla contrapposizione tra esseri mortali ed immortali. Un disordine che è preludio e modalità per la riconferma di un ordine, accettato come l'unico ed inevitabile, secondo una tipologia mitico-rituale assai diffusa.

Anche la collocazione calendariale dei giorni di apertura del *mundus* presenta interessanti e non casuali relazioni con la sfera di Ceres.

La data del 24 agosto segue l'importante festa dei Volcanalia che tra l'altro riunisce figure femminili di sicuro interesse per i rapporti di struttura con Ceres: sono Ops Opifera, le Ninfe, Hora Quirini e Maia[52].

Il 5 ottobre segue la data della prima fissazione dello *ieiunium Cereris* (4 ottobre – Fasti Amiternini), istituito in seguito ad una serie di prodigi che sconvolsero l'opinione pubblica nell'anno 191 a.C. L'elenco tramandatoci da Livio (XXXVI 37,1–6) è significativo; buoi pacifici che salgono sul tetto di una casa in pieno centro (*in Carinis*), pioggia di pietre a Terracina ed Amiterno, tempio di Juppiter colpito dalla folgore a Minturno (il massimo degli dei che si colpisce con la sua stessa arma!) ecc. Vi si può leggere agevolmente il quadro di un preciso sovvertimento dell'ordine delle cose, cioè quella alterazione dell'ordine strutturale del cosmo che ha nell'apertura del *mundus* il momento cul-

---

[50] Per Saturnus nel mondo romano, morfologia del culto ed ideologia testimonianze cultuali in Italia cfr. anche osservazioni di I. CHIRASSI COLOMBO, Acculturazione e morfologia di culti alpini, Atti VII CeS.D.I.R. 1957–1976, pp. 157–189; specialmente p. 172ss.

[51] Il ritorno dei morti in coincidenza con le cd. feste di capodanno caratterizzate dalla creazione rituale di un tempo rovescio, sono un dato morfologico ben noto alla fenomenologia della religione, ampiamente rilevato a livello etnologico e folclorico. Per uno studio d'insieme rimando a V. LANTERNARI, La grande festa, Milano, 1972², passim.

[52] DEGRASSI, I.I. XIII 2, 500. Per le Ninfe unite a Ceres anche in rapporto alle *frumentationes*, rifornimento di grano, in 'concorrenza' già antica con le *frumentationes* del tempio di Ceres (vedi la vocazione frumentaria della *gens Minucia* patrizia risalente forse già al V secolo) e nell'ultimo scorcio della repubblica (incendio della *aedes Nympharum* da parte di Clodio), cfr. C. NICOLET, Le temple des Nymphes et les distributions frumentaires à Rome, CRAI 1976, pp. 29–51. L'abbinamento politicamente significativo ritorna in un'iscrizione ostiense della fine del secolo II (197 d.C.) che ricorda la costruzione di un *puteal* per *monitu sanctissimae Cereris et Nympharum* da parte di alcuni collegi (CIL XIV, 2 = D. 3339). (È un'altra tessera per la ricostruzione della *religio Cereris* nell'ambito della politica agraria dell'epoca di Traiano!)

minante. È abbastanza interessante rilevare che, se si può interpretare lo
ieiunium (a parte il problema della quinquennalità) come un rito di astensione
da certi cibi e ricorriamo ad un'annotazione di Plinio secondo la quale le donne
celebrando i loro digiuni avevano solo la possibilità di mangiare castagne, l'abbinamento dello *ieiunium* all'apertura del *mundus* acquista un significato logico
ben preciso: al momento della regressione cosmica rappresentata dall'apertura
del *mundus*, massimo dei *prodigia* cui è legata Ceres, segue o corrisponde un
periodo di massima regressione culturale messo in atto ritualmente[53]. Momenti
simili, a livello morfologico, sono parte del ritualismo delle feste greche di
Demeter Thesmophoros: ad Eretria le donne cucinano per la dea la carne ser-
vendosi del sole (ricreazione del tempo senza fuoco! Plut. qu.Gr. 31); a Sira-
cusa le donne celebrano le due dee „imitando il tempo antico" (purtroppo
mancano nella nostra fonte i particolari, Diod. V 4,5), ecc.

Anche la terza data dell'apertura del *mundus* cade in un momento significativo: è l'otto novembre, durante la celebrazione dei Ludi Plebei, quei ludi che
una volta si svolgevano nel tempo 'ora' occupato dai Ludi Romani o Ludi
Magni, ed erano sotto la giurisdizione degli *aediles* plebei 'ora' sostituiti dagli
aediles curuli. Senza entrare nei particolari che ci porterebbero molto lontano,
nella contraddizione delle fonti che allineano episodi e notizie apparentemente
inconciliabili, ciò che importa sottolineare è il voluto intento di ricreare una
situazione di sovvertimento dell'ordine sociale sottinteso. Essa ha il suo culmine
nella 'fantasiosa' regia della *pompa circensis* (comune sia ai Ludi Magni che a
quelli Plebei) ed il suo messaggio rivelato nello scambio di parti sottinteso dal
conferimento ai magistrati plebei da parte del senato della porpora, del trono,
dello scettro e delle altre insegne regali (D.H. VI 95). Insomma i plebei vengono
fatti temporaneamente e ritualmente re (o trionfatori) per burla. In attesa naturalmente che tutto venga riconfermato nell'ordine precedente[54].

V. *Ceres e il mondo femminile*

L'accenno all'istituzione dello *ieiunium* ci introduce alla terza sfera d'influ-
enza di Ceres: il mondo femminile. Ceres non è l'unica, nè la più importante
divinità delle donne − o almeno non lo è stata fino ad un certo punto. Dubbia
per il significato l'iscrizione arcaica che si riferirebbe al *castus Cereris*, occasione
in cui era lecito sospendere il lutto[55]. − Certo invece (o almeno molto possibile)

---

[53] Sui *prodigia* e Ceres cfr. raccolta di dati in LE BONNIEC, o. c., p. 451ss.
[54] A. PIGANIOL, Recherches sur les jeux romains, Publ. de la Faculté des Lettres de l'Univ.
de Strasbourg XIII, Paris, 1923, p. 89ss. I dati cerimoniali in Dionigi, VI, 95,4. Cfr. anche
H. S. VERSNEL, Triumphus. An Inquiry into the Origin Development and Meaning of the
Roman Triumph, Leiden, 1970, p. 225ss.
[55] Cfr. D. 3333 = DEGRASSI, I.I.L.R. 67; per l'interpretazione del *castus* come astensione dal
pane nel rituale di Cybele, anteposta significativamente nella sequenza calendariale di aprile

il rapporto del mondo femminile con il *sacrum anniversarium Cereris*, festa estiva delle matrone di cui Livio ricorda la mancata celebrazione all'epoca della battaglia di Canne perchè non c'era una matrona *expers luctus*, cioè nelle condizioni di poterla celebrare[56]. *Ieiunium* e *castus* possono inoltre ben coincidere con i *festa annua piae Cereris* celebrati per nove giorni dalle *matres* con totale astensione sessuale e corrispondenti agli *annua Cerealis tempora sacra* in cui la fanciulla dorme sola nel suo letto (Ovid. Met. X 431; Amor. III 10,1). Il riferimento immediato va con i rituali di digiuno (*nēsteia*) ben noti per i Thesmophoria delle donne greche, forse la più ripetuta festa delle città greche[57]; e, come abbiamo precedentemente detto, è qui che ben si colloca la nota di Plinio sulla sostituzione del pane con le castagne — cibo non coltivato, precedente — quindi adatto a sottolineare sul piano alimentare la ricreazione temporale del tempo caotico degli inizi (Plin. N.H. XV 92). A questa situazione caotica risponde bene anche l'astensione sessuale (eccesso, corrispondente in chiave strutturale alla sfrenatezza sessuale o all'oscenità), tenendo presente che si interrompe in questo modo, temporaneamente e sotto controllo, quell'uso regolato della sessualità che la dea ha dato insieme alla grande agricoltura ed esplicato nel matrimonio per la procreazione di figli legittimi in cui la donna è assimilata al campo da arare e l'uomo allo agricoltore[58]. Tutti questi riti rientrano bene in quei *sacra Cereris adsumpta de Graecia* (di cui parla Cicerone nella pro Balbo, 55), annoverati da Festo tra i *peregrina sacra*, culti stranieri (268 L.). Questo riconosciuto carattere greco, sottolineato soprattutto da scrittori e poeti del tardo periodo repubblicano ed età agustea (vedi Cicerone per il noto episodio di Calliphana, sacerdotessa di Demetra, importata a Roma per celebrare i riti nuovi *scientia peregrina ac externa* ma *mente domestica*, e perciò fatta cittadina) ci fa pensare ad una cosciente riutilizzazione o prima utilizzazione di temi tesmoforici come modalità di controllo del comportamento pubblico, politico, delle donne romane, ed in particolare delle matrone, sul quale ci giungono, pur attraverso sottintesi e contraffazioni, diverse informazioni 'allarmanti'. Si trattava cioè, usando un rito straniero, di far ritornare nel 'giusto' canale di un comportamento 'domestico e civile', una categoria, le donne, che forse appariva definitivamente divenuta 'estranea'. Noi sappiamo bene che nel regime integrato della polis Atene, questo era il principale scopo dei riti tesmoforici e simili.

a Ceres, cfr. i dati e le acute osservazioni di A. BRELICH, Offerte ed interdizioni alimentari nel culto della Magna Mater a Roma, SMSR XXXVI, 1965, pp. 27–42.

[56] L'identificazione del *castus* con lo *ieiunium* è respinta dal L. VIDMAN, Ieiunium Cereris quinquennale (en marge des Fasti Ostienses), ZPE 1978, pp. 87–95, sulla base di un nuovo frammento che nomina lo *ieiunium quinquennale* per il 20 ottobre del 150/55 d.C. Si tratterebbe della restaurazione dell'antico rito nel suo ritmo quinquennale (alterato ad un certo punto e trasformato in annuale come attesta la sua presenza nei Fasti Amiternini) voluto da Antonino Pio nell'ambito del recupero della religione tradizionale. La data è segnata comunque in abbinamento con quella della morte di Faustina Augusta, di cui è ben nota la 'devozione' a Ceres come attestano le emissioni monetarie sia in vita che in morte.

[57] Per il valore sociale e politico dei Thesmophoria greci, in particolare ateniesi, rimando ad un mio articolo citato in n. 34.

[58] È il celebre passo del 'De con. praec.' di Plutarco, 144; ripreso da Clemente Alessandrino (Strom. II, 2): il matrimonio è ἐπὶ παίδων γνησίων σπόρῳ.

Per Roma conosciamo una ʿcrisiʾ del mondo femminile a partire dagli inizi del II a.C . e protratta lungo tutto l'arco del secolo[59]. È in questa prospettiva che si colloca il viaggio dei decemviri ad Enna nel 133 a.C. alla ricerca della *Ceres antiquissima*, quella Ceres-Demeter che un'insistente tradizione legava cultualmente al luogo indicato nel mito come uno dei punti geografici connessi con la sparizione di Kore[60], un'altra Eleusi o un'altra Nysa dunque, ma anche il posto più vicino a Roma dove si poteva collocare lo scenario fisico del dramma divino e da dove dunque si poteva pensare di attingere forze per rinnovare il culto della dea nella *aedes* romana[61]. L'introduzione di Calliphana come sacerdotessa della dea, segno di un cambiamento nella gestione del culto, è del 95 circa: con essa si può fissare l'inizio per Roma del sacerdozio femminile pubblico per la dea, presente in forme diverse e preesistenti in altre aree italiche (vedi il sacerdozio di Ceres e di Venus nella zona dei Peligni): esso diventa subito il „massimo onore cui può aspirare una matrona romana" (Plut. de mul.virt. 26). Ma soprattutto i riti di Ceres sono o diventano gli unici *sacrificia nocturna* (insieme a quelli di Bona Dea affidati alla conduzione di una matrona di alto rango) permessi alle donne. Si tratta dei *sacra graeca* nei quali possiamo agevolmente riconoscere dei rituali tesmoforici, applicati comunque alla realtà romana (Cic. de leg II 9,21; ibid. 14−15, 35−37)[62]. La ʿellenizzazione tardivaʾ del culto di Ceres (o meglio il rinnovato e dichiarato uso del modello greco) coincide dunque con una specializzazione di Ceres nei riguardi del mondo femminile. Essa va di pari passo con la sua ʿrusticizzazioneʾ che diventa un motivo costante negli scrittori dell'ultima

---

[59] Studio d'insieme sulla portata sociopolitica dei culti ʿnuoviʾ repressi con il *senatusconsultum de Bacchanlibus* del 186 a.C. cfr. CLARA GALLINI, Protesta ed integrazione in Roma antica, Bari, 1970.

[60] Per le varianti mito-geografiche cfr. N. J. RICHARDSON, The Homeric Hymn to Demeter, Oxford, 1974 (comm.).

[61] Cic. Verr. IV, 108. LE BONNIEC spiega l'interpretazione dei decemviri alla richiesta dei ʿLibri Sibylliniʾ di placare la *Ceres antiquissima* con l'invio dell'ambasceria ad Enna, come una risposta politica alla grave situazione delle rivolte servili guidate da Eunus ed ispirate dalla dea Syria (Ceres *vs* la dea Syria!). Nonostante l'antica presenza del culto di Demeter in Sicilia, rivelata dai ritrovamenti archeologici, *thesmophorion* di Bitalemi, templi di Selinunte, Enna non pare essere storicamente il punto più antico dii presenza demetriaca: lo divenne artificiosamente più tardi nell'ambito di un precisa sistemazione politica voluta da Gelone d'Agrigento. In questo senso anche A. BRELICH, La religione greca in Sicilia, Kokalos X−XI, 1964−65, p. 51. Per i ritrovamenti archeologici dello Thesmophorion v. P. ORLANDINI, Lo scavo del Thesmophorion di Bitalemi e il culto delle divinità ctonie a Gela, in: Kokalos, XII, 1966, pp. 8−35. Per Selinunte (metopa arcaica con una triade [Demeter, Kore, Hekate?], TUSA in: Arch. Class. XXI, 1969, pp. 153−171) − cfr. anche D. WHITE, Demeter's Sicilian Cult as a Political Instrument, GRBS V, 1964, pp. 261−279.

[62] I *sacra* femminili di Ceres a Roma furono probabilmente rimaneggiati più volte, almeno a partire da un certo periodo, da quando cioè lasciata da parte la notizia della Demeter arcade sul Palatino, cominciano ad essere uno strumento importante. Alla fine del III a.C. prima menzione del *sacrum anniversarium* come festa matronale; nel 191 fondazione dello *ieiunium*; nel 133 legazione alla Demeter-Ceres di Enna; intorno al 95 accordo della cittadinanza a Calliphana di Velia; seconda metà del I a.C. probabile ulteriore intervento nei riguardi dei *nocturna sacrificia mulierum*.

metà del secolo e di età augustea nell'ambito di un'ideologia 'antiquaria' del recupero di dimensioni perdute, parte del programma di restaurazione al quale Ottaviano Augusto darà crisma ufficiale.

VI. Il rovesciamento di età imperiale; Ceres dea della campagna e delle donne

Divenuta dea delle virtù femminili e della campagna, generoso ed inesausto reservoir di *alimenta* per il corpo e per lo spirito, Ceres cessa di essere 'politica', esaurendo progressivamente questa sua dimensione man mano che si esauriscono nelle loro funzionalità politiche le istituzioni di quella Roma *polis-respublica* che trapassa alla nuova costituzionalità dell'impero. 'Rifugiatasi' in campagna diventa la dea *laeta pacis* dalla quale i coloni possono invocare quella *pax perpetua* che è condizione necessaria al proseguimento del loro duro ma insostituibile lavoro (Ovid., Fasti IV 407, ma anche Tib. I 10,45). L'agricoltura è intesa come fonte di apprendimento di *artes*, è qualificata dal *labor*, non pena ma elemento di progresso, tanto che, nella particolare proiezione di Varrone, i *Saturnia Regna*, l'età dell'oro dell'antico Lazio, sono un momento di felice agricoltura e gli agricoltori sono *ex stirpe Saturni regni* (r.r. III 1,4−5)[63]. Sapientemente gestita dalle élite di potere la apparente *renaissance* georgica condotta in mezzo a problemi socioeconomici di vasta portata, vede ad un certo punto lo stesso imperatore assumersi la corona spicea come membro di quel collegio arvalico, fondazione 'romulea', che ripristinato da Augusto si pone come chiusa sodalità elitaria strettamente legata al potere imperiale, visto in un intimo ed immediato rapporto con la *lustratio agrorum* ed i vari riti propiziatori che annualmente nel mese di maggio i nobili 'fratelli dei campi' compiono in onore della misteriosa Dia[64]. Attraverso la corona spicea l'imperatore arvale simboleggia o meglio segnala l'assunzione in prima persona del grave problema del rifornimento annuale di viveri (in particolare pane) connesso con la *cura annonae*[65]. Togliendolo definitivamente agli *aediles plebei*, ai quali già era stato sottratto da Cesare con la creazione degli *aediles ceriales*, Augusto si assumeva infatti l'incarico di garantire al popolo quello che con intraducibile vocabolo i Greci indicavano nel *biotos*, dono

[63] Per la 'dottrina' del lavoro in Virgilio cfr. R. MARTIN, Recherches sur les agronomes latins, Paris 1971 p. 185ss.; per Varrone cfr. E. NOÈ, I proemi del De Re Rustica di Varrone, Atheneum n.s. LV, 1977, pp. 289−302.

[64] Sul ritualismo degli Arvales cfr. I. CHIRASSI, Dea Dia et Fratres Arvales, SMSR, XXXIX, 1968, pp. 191−291, passim. Sulla composizione prosopografica cfr. J. SCHEID, Les frères Arvales. Recrutement et origine sociale sous les empereurs Iulio-Claudiens, Paris, 1975.

[65] Suet. V.Aug. 25; sul tema dell'*annona* vedi H. PAVIS D'ESCURAC, La préfecture de l'annone, service administratif impérial d'Auguste à Constantin, Roma, 1976, che sottolinea l'importanza anche ideologica della carica. Analoghe osservazioni in P. GROS, Aurea Templa. Recherches sur l'architecture religieuse de Rome à l'époque d'Auguste, Roma, 1976: Augusto avrebbe accettato la *cura annonae* intorno al 22 quando gli venne offerta, dopo una serie di cataclismi, la carica di *dictator clavi figendi causa*.

essenziale di Demeter, „tutto ciò che serve per vivere una vita demetriaca", il pane. Creava così una specie di 'unione mistica' tra la sua figura e l'insieme sociale che gli era affidato sfruttando elementi che ricordano molto da vicino quel concetto di 'regalità sacra' dell'età del bronzo egiziana e Vicino orientale[66]. Ne è prova il valore ominale assunto proprio dalle corona di spighe se posata sul capo dello imperatore una volta tolta dal capo della dea[67].

Racconta Tacito che un cavaliere fu condannato a morte per aver visto in sogno (ed averlo divulgato) l'imperatore Claudio *spicea corona evinctum spicis retro conversis*, con la corona di spighe, come arvale dunque, ma con le spighe rovesciate, segno di una futura *gravitas annonae* strettamente dipendente dalla persona stessa „del capo di stato". Lo stesso Tacito ci informa poi di gravi disordini scoppiati in coincidenza con difficoltà incontrate nel rifornimento di grano, nelle *frumentationes*. La pesantezza della pena − come abbiamo visto comune nella sfera di Ceres − rivela la gravità politico-istituzionale sottintesa alla divulgazione del sogno che appariva un attacco diretto all'*auctoritas* del *princeps*. Una speciale emissione monetaria, un dupondio raffigurante al dritto la testa dell'imperatore ed al rovescio la figura di Ceres velata in trono con spighe e torcia e la scritta CERES AUGUSTA, vuole forse richiamare l'attenzione sul mai rotto accordo tra la dea e chi, ora, la rappresentava[68]. Mentre Annona, personificata e staccata da Ceres di cui assume gli attributi unendoli a quelli di Fortuna, compare su un sesterzio di Nerone che reca la duplice scritta ANNONA AUGUSTI CERES S.C.[69]. Puntualmente la propaganda imperiale si servirà del mezzo monetale per segnalare nel caso specifico attraverso lo stereotipo della dea agraria, il personale intervento del *princeps* nel campo della politica agraria. Come nel caso di Domiziano, o di Traiano, che vede durante il regno una ben precisa manovra di recupero della 'religiosità' della *dea rusticorum* in un quadro in cui ben si colloca quel restauro di un rustico ma frequentatissimo tempio della dea di cui ci parla Plinio ed alla cui singolare importanza abbiamo già in precedenza accennato[70]. Comunque l'imperatore accosta l'agricoltura nella dimensione dell'ar-

---

[66] Vedi in generale la raccolta di saggi a cura di LUC DE HEUSCH, Le Pouvoir et le Sacré, Bruxelles, 1962.

[67] Tac. An. XI, 4; cfr. anche Plinio, N.H. XVIII, 6.

[68] BMC RE 136, 183.

[69] BMC RE 220, 126.

[70] Dupondio di Domiziano, reca al rovescio Annona seduta con spiga in mano, una piccola figura maschile e sullo sfondo lontana una nave; allusione al ripristino della agricoltura italica e cessazione delle importazioni. BMC RE 360, 286; per Traiano cfr. J. BEAUJEU, La religion romaine à l'apogée de l'Empire, Paris, 1955, p. 281. La 'felice' esperienza della politica agraria di Traiano, riflessa nell'epistolario di Plinio, si esemplifica nella ricostruzione ampliamento di un'antica *aedes* di Ceres resa ormai inadeguata alle sue funzioni considerando la grande frequenza da parte di una gran folla (*magnus populus*) in occasione della festa delle Idi di settembre (in coincidenza come abbiamo già notato con l'*epulum Iovis* urbano). Anche se non possiamo localizzare il luogo in cui doveva sorgere l'*aedes*, su suolo privato, in uno dei *praedia* di proprietà di Plinio, i dati che ne ricaviamo sono di notevole importanza: il tempio avrà caratteristiche 'urbane', colonne di marmo, rivestimenti oltre ad un ampio portico staccato per riparare i fedeli dal sole e dalla pioggia durante le lunghe e complesse cerimonie (*multae res aguntur*). Efficace spaccato di religio-

vale, media cioè la sua partecipazione alla sfera agraria attraverso una emblematica sodalità di alto rango (vi potevano partecipare solo membri di classe senatoria) ed il nome di Ceres appare 'ovviamente' escluso dalla lista delle divinità invocate nelle preghiere ed alle quali si offrono sacrifici. I riti della dea sono lasciati alla *pubes agrestis* di Virgilio, alla *rustica pubes* di Tibullo, i giovani della *familia* cui si contrappongono gli *iuvenes* stretti nell'élite delle borghesie municipali[71]. Ad essi la dea richiede umili sacrifici purchè ritualmente puri *parva sint modo casta*. Aggettivo quest'ultimo denso di significato che qualifica in modo esplicito il ritualismo della dea e passa ad esprimere tutto ciò che ha attinenza alla sfera religiosa e diventa modello irrinunciabile di comportamento etico: *casta placent superis*[72].

Al sottile ma insistente richiamo della *castitas* deve rispondere specialmente il mondo femminile, quel mondo femminile naturalmente che vuole qualificarsi agli occhi degli dei e degli uomini e che rimane 'in città' a difendere attraverso i riti casti di Ceres quella *mulierum fama* di cui esplicitamente si mostra così sollecito il legislatore[73]. Sono Favonia, *sacerdos Cereris publica p.R.Q.*, Casponia, Iulia Procula che assiste allo scioglimento del voto della liberta Claudia Attica nel santuario della Ceres di Anzio, le sacerdotesse che continuano a Corfinio l'antico culto (probabilmente indigeno e di ispirazione greca) di una copia femminile divenuta di Ceres e di Venus, o ancora le matrone di Sorrento, Pozzuoli, Teano, Sulmona, Capena ecc.[74]. Quest'ultima epi-

sità popolare che ci dà la misura immediata dell'importanza della posizione della dea pur divenuta da publica 'privata' (Ep. IX, 39,1): *in praediis [suis]*.
Ovvia la presenza di Ceres sui conî dell'Optimus Princeps: al dritto busto di Traiano radiato / al rovescio Ceres con *corona spicea* e mano sul *modius*, la scritta SPQR OPTIMO PRINCIPI (BMC RE 195, 921).

[71] Questa contrapposizione tra Pubes rustica (di Ceres) e Iuventus municipale (di Ercole?) formalizzata anche da una contrapposizione agricoltura/caccia in proiezione ideologica, meriterebbe un approfondimento in rapporto anche al dilagare della moda delle *venationes* ed al moltiplicarsi dei poemetti tipo il 'Kynegetikon' di Grattius. Per gli Iuvenes ed Ercole cfr. anche M. JACZYNOWSKA, Le caratteristiche delle associazioni della gioventù romana, Atti Venezia CXXXIV, 1975–76, pp. 359–381; D. LADAGE, Collegia Iuvenum, Ausbildung einer municipalen Elite?, Chiron IX, 1979, pp. 319–346.

[72] Ovid. Fast. IV, 412: *parva bonae Cereri, sint modo casta, placent*. Tib. II, 1–3. La *castitas* tende ad uscire dalla sfera rituale per diventare norma etica, obbligo 'normale' almeno per il mondo femminile: emblematica in tal senso l'ordalia delle fanciulle di Lavinio ricordata da Properzio (IV, 8,13–14): ogni anno devono scendere nell'antro di un serpente, conficcargli un'offerta in gola e: *si fuerint castae, redeunt in colla parentum*, mentre gli *agricolae* sanno che la *castitas* delle loro ragazze preannuncia un *fertilis annus*! È il condizionamento sotteso all'abbinamento *castitas* e *fertilitas*, lo stesso che si può trovare soggiacente a tanti e familiari modelli di comportamento etico e sociale riguardanti il rapporto donna e sessualità nelle culture gravitanti nell'area mediterranea. Cfr. anche J. PITT-RIVERS, The Fate of Shechem or the Politics of Sex. Essays in the Anthropology of the Mediterranean, Cambridge, 1977.

[73] Cic., de leg., l. c.

[74] Manca uno studio d'insieme sul sacerdozio femminile nel mondo romano, ed in particolare sul sacerdozio pubblico. I dati epigrafici esaminati anche superficialmente, ci informano come questo servizio fosse in realtà assai diffuso e diversificato, offrendo al mondo femmi-

grafe che reca la data del 256 d.C., ci testimonia la persistenza tenace del
doppio sacerdozio sino in età tarda, la sua esplicita ufficialità, in un periodo in
cui è ben nota la concorrenza, specie presso il pubblico femminile, dei cd. culti
orientali ed in particolare di Isis. Per questo mondo femminile che solo così, attraverso la partecipazione ai *sacra*, svolge un ruolo in qualche modo politico, Ceres
è esssenzialmente la dea protettrice del vincolo matrimoniale, usurpando in tale
direzione Juno che vi è più tradizionalmente connessa, nell'ambito di quella
precisa azione di controllo divenuto anche ideologico di cui ci ha informato
Cicerone. Si spiega così l'ambiguità rispetto il tema, attestata esplicitamente da
Servio (ad Aen. IV 58): Ceres sarebbe contraria alle nozze *propter raptum filiae*,
ma altri invece affermano il contrario, ed è citato il poeta Calvus che 'inventa' un
nuovo mito certo ben accetto al suo uditorio. Ceres non solo non è contraria ma
favet nuptiis perchè essa per prima sposò Juppiter, *quod prima nupserit Iovi*:
fonda così il 'primo matrimonio', assumendo la parte di una eroina inventrice,
figura così comune nella mitologia eroica greca ed in altre mitologie, mettendo
in atto praticamente quella che è la vita civile, identificata qui con perfetta
rispondenza strutturale, nella 'vita di città': et *condendis urbibus praesit*. Attraverso il mondo femminile Ceres riacquista quindi la dimensione 'urbana' perduta
attraverso la *rusticitas* imposta alla controparte maschile ma senza rinunciare al
messaggio ideologico di fondo che la vede sempre in rapporto ad una situazione
in qualche modo di progresso. Ma in proposito ci sono anche testimonianze più
precise: ci informa Festo che la face che compare nella *deductio* della *nova nupta*
(il corteggio nuziale che scortava la sposa alla nuova casa maritale proprio del
matrimonio religioso e patrizio per eccellenza, la *confarreatio*) veniva portata in
onore di Ceres per quella sposa che doveva essere *casta et pura* — aggettivi propri
della sua sfera —. Si aggiunge il rito dell'aspersione con l'acqua che in correlazione con il fuoco stabilisce, come espressamente dichiarato, la modalità della
comunicatio cum viro[75].

nile l'unico modo per entrare nello spazio esterno 'politico', cittadino, nella città come nel
pagus. Per il sacerdozio che ci riguarda osserviamo che l'epigrafe di Favonia da Roma si
pone già in età repubblicana (DEGRASSI l'inserisce nelle I.L.L.R. 61 = CIL VI, 2182); cosí
l'epigrafe di Munnia da Atine (Campania) (I.L.L.R. 62 = CIL X, 5073); quelle delle due
sacerdotesse di Ceres e Venus da Sulmona e zona (I.L.L.R. 65 = CIL IX, 3087 e
I.L.L.R. 66 = CIL IX, 3090). Il sacerdozio sulmonese ingloba un culto precedente nel
quale, come attesta un'epigrafe funeraria peligna, la defunta compare con il titolo di *cerfum
sacaracirix* (= *sacerdos Cererum*?). L'epigrafe è tardo-repubblicana ma nella zona il sacerdozio di Venus e Ceres è ampiamente attestato per l'epoca imperiale; ad esempio a Corfinio (vedi dati in G. COLONNA, Sul sacerdozio peligno di Cerere e Venere, ACl VIII,
1953, pp. 216—217). Ma è difficile individuare quale realtà cultuale ed ideologica si
nasconda sotto questa etichetta, e quale sia la specifica funzione locale. Casponia che ha
il titolo di *Maxima sacerdos Cereris* appartiene invece all'età imperiale (D. 3334 = CIL VI,
2181). Iulia Procula nella dedica del tempio di Anzio è solo *sacerdos* (D. 3338 = CIL X,
6640). L'epigrafe capenate citata è in Not.Sc. 1953, p. 22. Per gli altri dati cfr. DE RUG-
GIERO, Diz.Ep. II (1900), s. v. Ceres, p. 208. Da ricordare ancora la *sacerdos cerialis mun-
dalis* da Capua (CIL X, 3926): probabile riferimento al *mundus*?
[75] Festo-Paul. ep. p. 77 L.: *facem nuptiis in honorem Cereris praeferebant; aqua asperge-
batur nova nupta, sive ut casta puraque ad virum veniret, sive ut ignem atque aquam cum
viro communicaret.*

Il richiamo a Varrone è immediato, alle speculazioni dotte della sua teologia, per cui Liber e Ceres appaiono uniti sulla base dell'opposizione dialettica del *masculus* vs *femina* = *liquor* vs *ariditas*. È una Ceres che può presentarsi agevolmente anche come Libera e come Venus, facilitando quel processo di sovrapposizione e pluriidentificazione di figure divine, fatto molto diffuso nei politeismi maturi[76]. Ma la correlazione può passare anche attraverso la contrapposizione del *vino* vs. *pane* che nella ben nota offerta primiziale ricordata da Festo, diventano la *sacrima* ed il *praemetium*, il vino nuovo e le prime spighe (Festo-Paulo 423 L. = 319 M.). Tenendo conto dello stretto rapporto che unisce al vino non solo Liber ma, anzi, soprattutto Juppiter si vede bene che Juppiter può essere Liber e si chiarisce lo stretto rapporto tra Juppiter e Liber del resto 'sapientemente' annotato nei fasti degli Arvales (CIL I², 1, p. 214). Mettendo insieme i commenti di Festo e le note di Servio, la *conffarreatio*, strettamente legata alla sfera di Juppiter come attestano la presenza del *flamen dialis* e del *pontifex Maximus* e del patronato sulla cerimonia di un Juppiter Farraeus, appare, ad un certo momento, pensata come imitazione del matrimonio modello di Juppiter e Ceres che come unione del'umido e del secco possono essere, anzi 'sono' Liber e Libera.

Non ci stupisce dunque trovare Ceres con la torcia nuziale oltre la corona di spighe nelle emissioni monetarie delle imperatrici che a cominciare da Livia moglie di Augusto ripetono spesso le sembianze della dea[77].

In particolare Livia tende ad identificarsi con la dea partecipando personalmente al programma ideologico di restaurazione e ricostruzione tracciato dal marito. In un'epigrafe da Gozo (isoletta di Malta) essa è *Ceres Iulia Augusta Mater* (dedica posta da una donna, Lutatia in funzione di *sacerdos Augustae*) ove *Mater* è titolo di evidente conio augusteo come attesta la didascalia in calce ai fasti amiternini del 10 agosto, giorno di fondazione del sacrificio *Cereri Matri et Opi Augustae*[78]. A *Ceres Augusta Mater* va anche la dedica posta in un ignoto *pagus* della *regio VII* il 19 aprile del 18 d.C., ultimo giorno dei Cerialia urbani, da L. Bennius Primus *magister pagi* e da sua moglie la *magistra* Bennia Primigenia (CIL XI, 3196 = D. 3334)[79].

Onorata dalle *piae matres* e dalle *castae nuptae*, dai coloni, dalla piccola borghesia municipale e da qualche funzionario provinciale, Ceres continua, per il meccanismo ripetitivo della conservazione formale delle tradizioni cultuali, ad avere il suo *flamen*, l'antica ed importante magistratura sacerdotale di fonda-

---

[76] Varrone (ed. Cardauns): fr. 260: *Liberum et Cererem praeponunt seminibus, vel illum masculinis, illam feminis; vel illum liquori, illam vero ariditati seminum.*

[77] Aureo da Lugdunum dell'11–13 d.C., BMC RE I, 91,544. Al dritto testa di Augusto come DIVI F PATER PATRIAE, al rovescio Livia come Ceres. Antonia ed Agrippina compaiono con la corona spicea su monete di Claudio. Cfr. anche P. L. Strack, Untersuchungen zur römischen Reichsprägung des zweiten Jahrhunderts, III, Stuttgart, 1937, p. 48 ss.: significativa la presenza di Ceres sui coní delle due Faustine; cf. H. Temporini, Die Frauen am Hofe Trajans. Ein Beitrag zur Stellung der Augustae im Principat, Berlin–New York, 1978, p. 71 ss., 101 ss.

[78] CIL X, 7501 = D. 121; Degrassi, I.I. XIII, 2, p. 493.

[79] CIL XI, 3196 = D. 3334.

zione numana, a Roma almeno fino alla epoca di Vespasiano come attesta la nota iscrizione di Sextus Caesius Propertianus (CIL XI, 5028 = D. 1447). Ma è tagliata definitivamente la relazione di funzionalità che aveva creato la sua ragion d'essere nel pantheon politeistico della repubblica, nel quale, a parte il possibile influsso già antico della Demeter greca, è figura del tutto originale.

Nell'impero, nonostante alcune attestazioni di devozione che ci vengono in massima parte dal mondo provinciale (ed escludiamo l'Africa che merita come già detto uno studio a parte, specifico), il culto più significativo deve essere stato quello femminile, espresso attraverso il sacerdozio pubblico e comunque attraverso una devozione che doveva avere un alto significato ideologico. Il culto di Ceres non è certo l'unico tipo di *sacra* cui partecipino le donne, ed in particolare quelle dei livelli elitari delle strutture sociali (un discorso a parte riguarda l'inquadramento di altre categorie), ma per il suo particolare messaggio unificante a livello etico, quello di Ceres è certo significativo. Mondo femminile e mondo agrario trovano un punto di qualificazione ideologica ben preciso nel complesso mitico e cultuale di Ceres ponendosi come contraddizione della realtà politica e culturale in atto, cioè della vita urbana intesa come specchio di attualità.

Pensiamo alla testimonianza di un Giovenale, con il suo attacco così analitico allo specifico urbano che provoca per contrapposizione l'elogio di una vita rustica, vista però come malinconico ritorno dettato dalla impossibilità della vita cittadina. Come quello di Umbricius, l'amico che lascia Roma perchè non vi si può più vivere nella Satira III. Si può ormai solo ritornare in campagna, ad Aquinum dove si onora ancora Ceres Helvina posta significativamente vicino a Diana (II, 320) ma „poche donne in città sono ormai degne di toccare le sue bende" (VI, 50). Ed è a questa dea di Aquino che il poeta stesso (o uno della sua famiglia) pone con ogni ufficialità una dedica[80]. Ma donne e *rusticitas* non fanno attualità politica! In questa prospettiva trovano così precisa logica strutturale le tarde e apparentemente confuse informazioni di alcuni scolii a Virgilio e del Mythologicon Vaticano: le matrone in certi giorni fissati vanno a levare i loro gridi rituali (*exerceatur ululatus*) nei *compita*, ed i Compitalia, festa del dominio rustico e degli schiavi, si identificano con la festa *Cereris*. O addirittura le matrone sono sostituite dai *rustici* nella esecuzione di riti divenuti ormai totalmente extraurbani[81].

L'apparente confusione rispecchiata dai testi rivela in realtà la capacità del narratore di segnalare il senso ultimo, a livello semiologico, cui è andato via via adeguandosi il culto della dea uscendo dalla sua funzionalità politica e romana per divenire modello categoriale di portata assai più vasta, su uno sfondo ideologico in cui il femminile ed il rurale assumono esplicitamente gli ambigui aspetti della marginalità.

---

[80] Cfr. J. GÉRARD, Juvenal et la réalité contemporaine, Paris, 1976, p. 374 ss. Respinge con argomenti non definitivi l'autenticità della dedica di un (Iu)nius Iuvenalis, CIL X, 5382 = 2986.

[81] I testi, molto significativi, sono raccolti da LE BONNIEC, o. c., p. 413.

Tellus—Terra Mater in der Zeit des Prinzipats

von TAMÁS GESZTELYI, Debrecen

Inhalt

I. Einleitung

Die Verehrung der die ganze Natur aufrechterhaltenden und in sich fassenden 'fruchtbaren Erde', bzw. der 'Mutter Erde' nahm in der römischen Religion bei weitem keine zentrale Stelle ein. Auch die mit ihr verbundenen Denkmäler sind nur in geringer Anzahl auf uns gekommen. Diese Zeugnisse stammen überwiegend vom Ende der Republik, bzw. aus dem Zeitalter des Prinzipats. Deshalb ist es berechtigt, diese Periode in den Mittelpunkt unserer Untersuchung zu stellen, was natürlich nicht bedeutet, daß auf die frühere Geschichte des Kultes bezügliche Schluß-folgerungen aus den Zeugnissen nicht gezogen werden könnten. Im Gegen-teil: dies ist sogar sehr wichtig, um die im Prinzipat zu beobachtenden Erscheinungen besser verstehen zu können. Zur Vervollständigung des Bildes haben wir in die Untersuchung neben den Texten auch bildliche Darstellungen und Inschriften einbezogen.

II. Geschichte und Ergebnisse der Forschung

Die Anzahl der modernen Werke, die sich mit der Tellus—Terra Mater beschäftigen ist nicht bedeutend; die Mehrzahl geht darauf nur als Teil-problem irgendeiner anderen Frage ein. Die meisten Arbeiten streben nur nach der Rekonstruktion einer frühen Periode des Kultes. Im Zeichen der ethnologischen Schule am Ende des vorigen Jahrhunderts schuf A. DIE-TERICH zu Anfang dieses Jahrhunderts sein Buch unter dem Titel 'Mutter Erde'[1], das den Zielsetzungen der Schule entsprechend das Weiterleben einer primitiven Religiosität in der Antike aufzudecken bestrebt war. Die Untersuchung ist in erster Linie auf die griechischen Quellen aufgebaut, ihre Ausgangspunkte sind aber auch manche römischen Gebräuche. Diese sind: das Legen des neugeborenen Kindes auf den Boden und sein Auf-heben; die Anrufung von Tellus bei der Eheschließung; die Beerdigung der verstorbenen Säuglinge ohne Verbrennung; das Auf-den-Boden-Legen der Todkranken. Der Autor zählt zahlreiche ähnliche Bräuche bei primitiven Völkern auf. Mit Hilfe der vielen miteinander verknüpften Angaben umreißt er die Mutter Erde als die wichtigste weibliche Gottheit der primitiven Religionen. Aufgrund der so herausgebildeten Erscheinung sieht er auch in Tellus eine Muttergöttin, die einst eine sehr wichtige Rolle gespielt hat, die Erzeugerin von allem ist und zugleich nach dem Untergang alles in sich einschließt. Aber im Laufe der Differenzierung der Götterwelt verlor sie immer mehr an Bedeutung. Für die Wirkung des Werkes von A. DIE-TERICH zeugt, daß es 20 Jahre später mit einem unveränderten Text und einem Anhang mit zahlreichen ergänzenden Bemerkungen von E. FEHRLE und R. WÜNSCH wieder erschienen ist.

Weil eine reichere Literatur fehlt, kann die Veränderung des Tellus-Bildes nur in den Stichwörtern von Lexika oder Handbüchern verfolgt werden. Im ersten Viertel des Jahrhunderts erscheint das Werk von G. WIS-SOWA, 'Religion und Kultus der Römer' (RuKR)[2], von DEMS. bearbeitet der Artikel 'Tellus' in: 'Ausführliches Lexikon der griechischen und römi-schen Mythologie', Bd. 5 (Leipzig 1924) von W. H. ROSCHER (s. v.) und von J. A. HILD der Artikel 'Tellus mater' im 'Dictionnaire des antiquités grec-ques et romaines' (Paris 1919) von CH. DAREMBERG und E. SAGLIO. In diesen Arbeiten kommt es zu einer systematischen Untersuchung des Kul-

Abkürzungen:

A.E.   L'Année Épigraphique
AJA   American Journal of Archaeology
BABesch   Bulletin van de Vereeniging tot Bevordering der Kennis van de Antieke Be-
            schaving. Leiden.
BAC   Bulletin Archéologique du Comité des Travaux Historiques
Bud.Rég.   Budapest Régiségei
ILAl   Inscriptions latines d'Algérie, ed. ST. GSELL, I, Paris 1922.
JbÖAI   Jahreshefte des Österreichischen Archäologischen Instituts
JRS   Journal of Roman Studies
TAPhA   Transactions of the American Philological Association
TRF   Tragicorum Romanorum Fragmenta

---

[1] Untertitel des Werkes: Ein Versuch über Volksreligion, Leipzig–Berlin 1905.
[2] München 1912². Tellus Mater 193 ff.

tes, und zwar der mit ihm verbundenen Feste und Opferformen[3], sowie zu einem Überblick über die Wirkungskreise[4] der Göttin. Auch die Verbreitungsgebiete und manche Eigentümlichkeiten[5] ihrer Inschriften werden erwähnt und schließlich ihre häufigsten Darstellungsweisen (sitzende bzw. sich am Boden auf die Ellbogen stützende Lage).

In allen drei Zusammenfassungen ist die Wirkung der DIETERICHschen Konzeption zu erkennen: Tellus war eine Muttergöttin, die in der alten römischen Religion eine wichtige Rolle spielte, das Leben gab, den Verstorbenen empfing, die — infolge der griechischen Wirkung — neben Ceres immer mehr in den Hintergrund geriet. Dies wird auch durch die Titel betont: Tellus Mater (RuKR, Dictionnaire). In seiner zweiten, ausführlicheren Zusammenfassung wählt WISSOWA (Myth. Lex.) das Stichwort 'Tellus' und hält ihre älteste Verehrung für unpersönlich und nicht an eine Kultstelle gebunden (p. 332).

In der ersten Hälfte der 30er Jahre melden sich zwei neue Konzeptionen, die von F. ALTHEIM[6] und die von ST. WEINSTOCK[7]. ALTHEIMS Buch beschäftigt sich ausdrücklich — im Gegensatz zu seinem Titel — bloß in einem Kapitel mit der Terra Mater (Ceres und Tellus, 108ff.). Die Funktionen der Göttin untersuchend kommt er zu der Folgerung, daß sie für die griechische Mutter Erde, das heißt für Demeter charakteristisch sind; es handelt sich also, ähnlich wie bei Ceres, um Übernahme dieser griechischen Göttin. Die Übernahme haben schon in den sehr frühen Zeiten die oskischen Stämme aus Süditalien nach Rom vermittelt. Dem entsprechend existierte Tellus als alte römische Göttin nicht.

Nach dieser extremen Meinung richtete sich die Arbeit von WEINSTOCK darauf, die Frage zu klären: Was kann im Fall der Göttin als uraltes römisches Element und was als griechische Einwirkung betrachtet werden? Sein Ausgangspunkt war die Untersuchung der Feste und der Opfer, die immer zu der ältesten Schicht aller Religionen gehören. Aufgrund dieser erstreckt sich der Wirkungskreis von Tellus ausdrücklich auf die Vegetation des Ackerbaus. Die mit dem Totenkult verbundene Rolle taucht im Zusammenhang mit der *porca praecidanea* auf; diese kann aber auch als reinigender Ritus vor dem Anfang der Feldarbeiten gedeutet werden. Der

---

[3] Feriae Sementivae im Januar (der Zeitpunkt des Festes wechselt), das Opfer ist *sus plena* oder *gravida*; Fordicidia am 15. April, das Opfer ist *fordae boves*; das Gründungsfest des Tellus-Tempels am 13. Dezember, wo ein *lectisternium* gehalten wurde. Von der *succidia*, die auch im Dezember stattfand, wissen wir nichts Näheres. Vor dem Beginn der Ernte wurde die *porca praecidanea* dargebracht.

[4] Vor allem der Ackerbau, wo sie mit Ceres in enger Verbindung steht; der Totenkult; die Eheschließung; das Erdbeben.

[5] In Nordafrika ist ihre Benennung regelmäßig Tellus, und in den Donau-Provinzen Terra Mater.

[6] Terra Mater. Untersuchungen zur altitalischen Religionsgeschichte, Religionsgeschichtl. Versuche und Vorarbeiten XXII 2, Gießen 1931.

[7] Terra Mater, RE V A 1 (1934), Sp. 791ff.; DERS., Tellus, Glotta 22, 1933/34, 140ff. Beide Artikel sind im wesentlichen gleich.

nächste Gesichtspunkt ist die Natur der mit den Tellus-Festen verbundenen Göttergruppe. Aus ihren Namen wird offenbar, daß sie Helfer je einer Phase der landwirtschaftlichen Arbeit sind (z. B. Vervactor, Occator, Sarcitor usw.). Dies bewog WEINSTOCK dazu, auch die Lösung des Namens von Tellus in dieser Richtung zu suchen. So hat er den Stamm *tel- mit den Verben *tollere, tuli* in Verbindung gebracht, was auf die mit dem Wachstum der Pflanzen zusammenhängende Rolle hinweist[8]. Tellus war also keine *mater*[9], und sie hatte mit dem Totenkult nichts zu tun; die mit diesem in Verbindung stehende Terra Mater war vielmehr das Ergebnis einer griechischen Einwirkung. Tellus wurde zu einer chthonischen Macht, als sie mit der Erde identifiziert wurde. Des weiteren beschäftigt sich WEINSTOCK noch mit dem Tellurus-Problem und mit der Frage der Kultstelle.

Danach erscheint lange Zeit keine zusammenfassende Übersicht über die Frage, bis H. LE BONNIEC[10] im Laufe seiner Untersuchung des Ceres-Kultes darauf eingeht. Nach seiner Meinung ist Tellus eine große italische Göttin. Dies versucht er aber nicht mit Hilfe des vergleichenden Materials der Religionsgeschichte, sondern mit Hilfe der römischen Quellen zu beweisen. Diese Deutung spielt in der Konzeption seines Werkes eine wichtige Rolle, da er Ceres als eine sich aus einer Funktion der Tellus selbständig machende Göttin (*numen Telluris*) erklärt. Die Lösung einer unklaren Martianus-Capella-Stelle als Ceres Telluris annehmend[11] hält er Ceres für die *vis creatrix Telluris*. Ihre enge Beziehung wird auch dadurch widergespiegelt, daß ihre meisten Feste und Opfer gemeinsam sind; darin muß einstmals Tellus den Primat gehabt haben, wonach ihren Platz stufenweise Ceres einnahm. Diesen Vorgang sieht LE BONNIEC in der chthonischen Funktion von Ceres besonders bewiesen, weil sie diesen ihr als einer ursprünglich Produktionskraft ausdrückenden Göttin fremden Aufgabenbereich ausschließlich von Tellus, von der par excellence chthonischen Göttin, übernehmen konnte. Der Kultus von Tellus wurde im historischen Zeitalter zurückgedrängt, und der von Ceres machte sich durch hellenischen Einfluß selbständig.

Der neueste Lexikonartikel, der sich auf das Thema bezieht, ist im 'Reallexikon für Antike und Christentum' unter dem Stichwort 'Erde' er-

---

[8] Die etymologischen Wörterbücher der lateinischen Sprache (A. WALDE—J. B. HOFMANN[3], Heidelberg 1954, A. ERNOUT—A. MEILLET[4], Paris 1959) nehmen diese Worterklärung nicht an. Der durch sie vorgeschlagene Ursprung aus dem ai. *talam* (= flach, Ebene) läßt aber die Frage offen, warum das Wort Tellus nicht auch schon vor dem I. Jahrhundert v. u. Z. in der Bedeutung Erde gebraucht wurde.

[9] Ihr männliches Gegenstück, Tellumo, spricht auch dafür, daß sie nicht eine Muttergöttin als Gegenstück von Iuppiter sein könnte.

[10] Le culte de Cérès à Rome. Des origines à la fin de la République, Paris 1958.

[11] C. THULIN, Die Götter des Martianus Capella, Religionsgeschichtl. Versuche und Vorarbeiten III, Gießen 1907, 46ff.

schienen (Band V, Stuttgart 1962, 1113—1179). Verfasser ist ILONA OPELT. Nach der Natur des Lexikons gliedert sich der Artikel in einen nichtchristlichen und einen christlichen Abschnitt. Innerhalb des ersteren beruht die Behandlung der Tellus auf den Ergebnissen von G. WISSOWA, ST. WEINSTOCK, K. LATTE und H. LE BONNIEC. So wird die Vorstellung LE BONNIEC's von dem doppelten Charakter der *porca praecidanea* übernommen: einerseits ein *piaculum* im Falle der Verfehlung gegen die Manes, andererseits ein Voropfer vor der Ernte (1132); aber es wird die Meinung abgelehnt, daß Tellus eine ursprüngliche und beherrschende Muttergöttin gewesen sei (1147ff.); der Name Terra Mater erscheint nur unter Augustus, auf griechischen Einfluß hin. Da das Stichwort nicht 'Tellus', sondern 'Erde' ist, beschäftigt sich der Artikel auch mit den volkstümlichen Vorstellungen und Gebräuchen, die mit der Erde in Verbindung stehen.

Die vergleichende religionsgeschichtliche Untersuchung kam wieder in der Arbeit von O. PETTERSSON[12] zur Geltung. Der Untertitel zeigt, wie sehr DIETERICHs Aufsatz die Forschung noch immer beschäftigt. Der Großteil der Untersuchung bezieht sich aber auch in diesem Fall auf die griechische Mutter Erde und nicht auf die römische. Der Verfasser nimmt von den sich mit Tellus beschäftigenden Aufsätzen gar keine Kenntnis. Die Konzeption von DIETERICH hält er für völlig falsch und das römische Material für ungenügend, um daraus auf eine Mutter Erde von großer Bedeutung schließen zu können. Seine letzte Feststellung ist: Wir können über große Götter sprechen, die in einer Beziehung zu der Fruchtbarkeit stehen, aber keinesfalls über eine große Göttin, die mit der Erde identisch und Göttin der universellen Fruchtbarkeit ist.

Wie man sieht, sind die Hauptfragen der Forschung: ob Tellus eine Muttergöttin war; ob sie in Verbindung mit dem Totenkult stand; inwieweit sie als römisch bzw. italisch und inwieweit als griechisch betrachtet werden kann; was für ein Unterschied zwischen den Namen Tellus, Tellus Mater und Terra Mater gemacht werden darf. Wir halten unter den auf diese Fragen gegebenen Antworten die von WEINSTOCK für die am besten begründeten. Die ur-römische Tellus erklärt er nur aus den Quellen, die sicher mit ihr zu verbinden sind, ohne daß er sie überinterpretiert. Die Arbeit von DIETERICH hat heute unter dem Gesichtspunkt der Beurteilung von Tellus nur eine wissenschaftshistorische Bedeutung. Aus einer eingehenden Untersuchung der Quellen ergibt sich nicht, daß Tellus eine in dem Mittelpunkt des alten Glaubenslebens stehende Muttergöttin gewesen wäre[13]. Wenn gewisse Zeichen darauf hinweisen, so handelt es sich dabei

---

[12] Mother Earth. An Analysis of the Mother Earth Concepts According to A. Dieterich, Lund 1967.

[13] Die Trias, die sich an die *flamines maiores* anknüpft, weist auf die führende Rolle der männlichen Götter hin. Tellus hatte keinen *flamen*, auch kein Fest, das nach ihr benannt war, und sie spielte in dem uralten Fruchtbarkeits-Ritus der *fratres arvales* keine Rolle. Erst im III. Jahrhundert v. u. Z. bekam sie ein Heiligtum.

um eine griechische Einwirkung, womit wir in Rom schon vor dem direkten Kontakt mit den Griechen rechnen können (ALTHEIM, o. c. 129).

Die Vorstellung WEINSTOCKs wird auch dadurch verstärkt, daß im Gebrauch der Wörter *tellus* und *terra* ein Unterschied zu entdecken ist. Servius (Aen. 1,171) schreibt darüber so: *cum Tellurem deam dicamus, terram elementum.* Die Feststellung ist natürlich für die Kaiserzeit nicht mehr gültig, damals sind sie schon Synonyma. Die Texte aus dem III.—II. Jahrhundert v. u. Z. gebrauchen für die Bezeichnung der Erde ausschließlich das Wort *terra*; *tellus* bedeutete also nur die Göttin und nicht die Erde. In den frühesten Texten, die über die Erde als die Erzeugerin von allem sprechen, wird das Wort *terra* gebraucht: *Mater terrast: parit haec corpus*[14]. In diesen Fällen wird der Name Tellus selbstverständlich darum nicht gebraucht, weil er etwas anderes bedeutete. Wenn auch Tellus selbst eine *mater* wäre, wäre die Bildung einer neuen Wortfügung nicht nötig gewesen, die die Mutter Erde bedeutet. Diese erfolgt nach dem Zeugnis der Texte im II. Jahrhundert v. u. Z. Die Folge des parallelen Gebrauchs der beiden Namen und ihrer Identifizierung im I. Jahrhundert v. u. Z.[15] war ein dritter, verhältnismäßig selten vorkommender Name: Tellus Mater[16].

Falls sich die Bedeutung von Tellus ursprünglich auf die mit dem Ackerbau zusammenhängende Fruchtbarkeit beschränkt, so weist sie keine Beziehungen zum Totenkult auf. Die Auffassung der *porca praecidanea* als Reinigungsopfer (Lustration) wird auch von G. RADKE vertreten[17]. Es sind auch noch die Beziehungen zwischen Tellus und den Dei Manes im spezifisch römischen Ritus der *devotio* zu erwägen. Der römische Heerführer bringt sich selbst und das Heer des Feindes den Göttern der Unterwelt und der Erde dar. Der ursprüngliche Text der Darbringung ist uns aber nicht bekannt, nur seine Paraphrase, und diese zeigt gerade an der unter unserem Gesichtspunkt entscheidenden Stelle eine ständige Abweichung: sie nennt die Erde Terra Mater (Liv. 8,6,10), Tellus (Liv. 8,9,8; 10,28,13), Tellus Mater (Liv. 10,29,4) und auch Terra Parens (Iuv. 8,257). Dies läßt uns aber völlig in Ungewißheit darüber, welcher Name im ursprünglichen Text vorkam. Am wahrscheinlichsten ist es, daß keiner von ihnen vorkam (vgl. Inc. auct. de vir. ill. 27), sondern wie in den griechischen Fluchtexten die Darbringung auch hier ursprünglich den unterweltlichen Göttern und der Erde erfolgte und der Platz der Erde erst später durch den Namen der Göttin abgelöst wurde. Dasselbe gilt für die sogenannte *defixio*[18]. In diesem Fall geht der Ritus aber Tellus ursprünglich nichts an.

Tellus war also ursprünglich ein *numen*[18a], das bei dem Zustandebringen der Vegetation anwesend war. Weil dieser Vorgang von der Erde untrenn-

---

[14] Pacuvius TRF p. 100, vgl. Ennius A. 13—14.
[15] Varro r. r. 1,1,5; Cic. nat. deor. 3,52.
[16] Liv. 10,29; Macr. Sat. 3,29; Arnob. adv. nat. 7,22.
[17] Rez. LE BONNIEC, Gymn. 69, 1962, 143.
[18] Suet. Tib. 75,1; Aur. Vict. 33,31.
[18a] Vgl. W. PÖTSCHER, 'Numen' und 'numen Augusti', ANRW II 16,1, hrsg. v. W. HAASE, Berlin—New York 1978, 355—392.

bar ist, wurde Tellus im Laufe der Entwicklung des Gott-Begriffs mit der Erde identifiziert. Dies öffnete den Weg dazu, daß man sie mit den Eigenschaften ausgestattet hat, über die bei den Griechen Gaia verfügte.

III. Tellus—Terra Mater in der Philosophie und in der schönen Literatur

Der volle Durchbruch des griechischen Einflusses wird am offensichtlichsten durch die Quellen des I. Jahrhunderts v. u. Z. widergespiegelt, vor allem durch Varro und Lucretius. Bei ihnen steht Tellus—Terra Mater vor uns, als wenn sie die wichtigste Muttergöttin der römischen Religion wäre; sie ist das weibliche Gegenstück von Iuppiter Pater, sie beide sind die *magni parentes* (Varro r. r. 1,1,5) oder zusammen mit Caelum die *magni dei* (Varro 1. 1. 5,57). Varro identifiziert mit ihr eine Reihe von Göttern, so z. B. Ops (1. 1. 5,64), Iuno (1. 1. 5,67), Magna Mater, Proserpina, Vesta[19]. Bei Lucretius handelt es sich natürlich nicht um theologische Erörterungen, die Mutter Erde erscheint nicht als der weibliche Pol der Götterwelt, sondern als der Erzeuger und Erhalter der Natur. Er übernimmt zwar die Vorstellung, nach der das Leben von Himmel und Erde abgeleitet wird (1,250 ff., 2,991 ff.)[19a], gibt danach aber eine streng materielle Erklärung der

---

[19] Aug. c. D. 7,24. Die hier veröffentlichten etymologischen Erklärungen zeigen, daß Varro keine Ahnung davon hatte, woraus die zwischen den erwähnten Göttinnen bestehende Verbindung entsprang. Die christlichen Kirchenväter — Augustinus, Arnobius — spotteten über diese erzwungene Theologie mit Recht.

[19a] Lucrez 1,250 ff.:

postremo pereunt imbres, ubi eos pater aether   250
in gremium matris terrai praecipitavit;
at nitidae surgunt fruges ramique virescunt
arboribus, crescunt ipsae fetuque gravantur;
hinc alitur porro nostrum genus atque ferarum,
hinc laetas urbis pueris florere videmus   255
frondiferasque novis avibus canere undique silvas;
hinc fessae pecudes pingui per pabula laeta
corpora deponunt et candens lacteus umor
uberibus manat distentis; hinc nova proles
artubus infirmis teneras lasciva per herbas   260
ludit lacte mero mentis perculsa novellas.
haud igitur penitus pereunt quaecumque videntur,
quando alid ex alio reficit natura nec ullam
rem gigni patitur nisi morte adiuta aliena.

Lucrez 2,991 ff.:

Denique caelesti sumus omnes semine oriundi;
omnibus ille idem pater est, unde alma liquentis
umoris guttas mater cum terra recepit,
feta parit nitidas fruges arbustaque laeta
et genus humanum, parit omnia saecla ferarum,   995
pabula cum praebet quibus omnes corpora pascunt

Natur. Deshalb, weil die Erde bei der Herausbildung der Natur eine bestim-
mende Rolle spielte, kehrt Lucretius auch mehrmals zu ihrer Beschreibung
zurück. Hier melden sich regelmäßig drei Aufgabenbereiche: *procreat ex se
omnia* (5,319, vgl. 2,598, 994, 5,783), *ex se auget alitque* (5,322, vgl. 2,594ff.,
996), *recipit perempta* (5,320, vgl. 2,999ff.). Sie ist ein wichtiger Teil nicht
nur der lebendigen, sondern auch der leblosen Natur: urältestes Element
(2,589ff.) und Himmelskörper (2,602f.).

Beide Gott-Portraits sind Produkte philosophischer Spekulation, von
Stoizismus bzw. Epikureismus. Mit unterschiedlichen Schlußergebnissen
streben beide nach der allegorischen Deutung der traditionellen Götterwelt.
Varro ... caelum Iovem, terram Iunonem, ideas Minervam vult intellegi
(Aug. c. D. 7,28). Die Stoiker bemühen sich, die Götter mit den einzelnen
Teilen der Natur zu identifizieren, so wird die Mutter Erde zu einer
Zusammenfassung aller Göttinnen, die mit der Erde in Verbindung stehen.
Wie die Vorstellung Varros, so geht auch die des Lucretius auf die grie-
chische Philosophie zurück, was von W. S. ANDERSON[20] und von C. BAILEY
(Comm. ad loc.) ausführlich analysiert worden ist. Die Allegorisierung wird
auch durch den Dichter verstärkt:

> *concedamus ut hic terrarum dictitet orbem*
> *esse deum matrem, dum vera se tamen ipse*
> *religione animum turpi contingere parcat.* (2,658ff.)

In der Kaiserzeit leben die stoischen Spekulationen Varros weiter,
unter diesen die auffallendste: die Vesta-Terra-Identifikation[21]. Nach der
Feststellung von P. LAMBRECHTS[22] ist hier die Rede vom Feuer, das sich
der Erde verbindet. Außer den oben aufgezählten Göttinnen werden mit
der Erde noch Maia, Bona Dea, Fauna, Fatua (Macr. Sat. 1,12) und Ceres[23]
identifiziert.

Das bei Lucretius gezeichnete Terra-Mater-Bild wurde in der Literatur
der Kaiserzeit zu einer Gewohnheitsphrase (Ov. M. 2,272ff.; 15,91f. usw.).
Alle zu Gaia gehörenden Geschichten der griechischen Mythologie wurden
mit der Muttergöttin, die Erzeugerin und Ernährerin von allen ist, verbunden. So wurde sie auch Mutter der Titanen und Giganten[24]. In vielen
Beziehungen kann die hymnische Beschreibung der Erde durch den älteren

> *et dulcem ducunt vitam prolemque propagant;*
> *quapropter merito maternum nomen adepta est.*
> *cedit item retro, de terra quod fuit ante,*
> *in terras et quod missumst ex aetheris oris,*   1000
> *id rursum caeli rellatum templa receptant.*

[20] Discontinuity in Lucretian Symbolism, TAPhA 91, 1960, 1ff.
[21] Ov. F. 6,267; 460, vgl. J. G. FRAZER, ed. with comm., London 1929, z. St.; Festus, p. 320; Aug. c. D. 7,16; Serv. Aen. 1,292; 2,296; Macr. Sat. 1,23,8.
[22] Over aard en betekenis van Vesta, Mededel. Vlaamse Acad. voor Wetensch., Lett. en Schoone Kunsten, Kl. der Lett. XII 7, Brüssel 1950, 16.
[23] Firm. Mat. de er. prof. rel. 17,3.
[24] Verg. Georg. 1,277ff.; Aen. 6,58; Hor. c. 3,4,73; Ov. F. 3,799; 5,35ff.

Plinius mit der Beschreibung des Lucretius verglichen werden (n. h. 2,63, 154—159)[24a]. Auch er lehnt den traditionellen Polytheismus der Römer ab und stellt sich die Gottheit als ein völliges Geistwesen vor (2,7,14), das die ganze Natur durchdringt. Die Beschreibung der Erde spiegelt so einerseits die Gründlichkeit des Naturforschers, andererseits aber die pantheistische Auffassung wider: die Erde sorgt für die oft undankbare Menschheit mit einer unbegrenzten Güte und Geduld. Die früher erwähnten drei Hauptfunktionen sind: Mutter, Ernährer, Grab; diese bedeuten noch nicht das Wesen, sondern nur eine Einführung. Das Wesen ist die immer vielseitigere Vorstellung und der Beweis der vorher erwähnten Güte (*benigna, mitis, indulgens, ususque mortalium semper ancilla*). Dann kommt die Rede auf die noch nicht erwähnte Wohltat: *medicas fundit herbas et semper homini parturit*[25], sowie darauf, was zwar nicht freiwillig, aber eben doch den

---

[24a] Plinius n. h. 2,63,154—159: 63. (63) 154. *Sequitur terra, cui uni rerum naturae partium eximia propter merita cognomen indidimus maternae venerationis. sic hominum illa, ut caelum dei, quae nos nascentes excipit, natos alit semelque editos et sustinet semper, novissime conplexa gremio iam a reliqua natura abdicatos, tum maxime ut mater operiens, nullo magis sacra merito quam quo nos quoque sacros facit, etiam monimenta ac titulos gerens nomenque prorogans nostrum et memoriam extendens contra brevitatem aevi, cuius numen ultimum iam nullis precamur irati grave, tamquam nesciamus hanc esse solam quae numquam irascatur homini. 155. aquae subeunt in imbres, rigescunt in grandines, tumescunt in fluctus, praecipitantur in torrentes, aer densatur nubibus, furit procellis: at haec benigna, mitis, indulgens ususque mortalium semper ancilla, quae coacta generat, quae sponte fundit, quos odores saporesque, quos sucos, quos tactus, quos colores! quam bona fide creditum faenus reddit. quae nostra causa alit! pestifera enim animantia, vitali spiritu habente culpam: illi necesse est semina excipere et genita sustinere; sed in malis generantium noxa est. illa serpentem homine percusso amplius non recipit poenasque etiam inertium nomine exigit. illa medicas fundit herbas et semper homini parturit. 156. quin et venena nostri miseritą instituisse credi potest, ne in taedio vitae fames, mors terrae meritis alienissima, lenta nos consumeret tabe, ne lacerum corpus abrupta dispergerent, ne laquei torqueret poena praepostera incluso spiritu, cui quaereretur exitus, ne in profundo quaesita morte sepultura pabulo fieret, ne ferri cruciatus scinderet corpus. ita est, miserita genuit id, cuius facillimo haustu inlibato corpore et cum toto sanguine exstingueremur, nullo labore, sitientibus similes, qualiter defunctos non volucres, non ferae attingerent terraeque servaretur qui sibi ipsi periisset. 157. verum fateamur: terra nobis malorum remedium genuit, nos illud vitae facimus venenum. non enim et ferro, quo carere non possumus, simili modo utimur? nec tamen quereremur merito, etiamsi maleficii causa tulisset. adversus unam quippe naturae partem ingrati sumus. quas non ad delicias quasque non ad contumelias servit homini? in maria iacitur aut, ut freta admittamus, eroditur. aquis, ferro, igni, ligno, lapide, fruge omnibus cruciatur horis multoque plus, ut deliciis quam ut alimentis famuletur nostris. 158. et tamen quae summa patitur atque extrema cute tolerabilia videantur: penetramus in viscera, auri argentique venas et aeris ac plumbi metalla fodientes, gemmas etiam et quosdam parvulos quaerimus lapides scrobibus in profundum actis. viscera eius extrahimus, ut digito gestetur gemma, quo petitur. quot manus atteruntur, ut unus niteat articulus! si ulli essent inferi, iam profecto illos avaritiae atque luxuriae cuniculi refodissent. et miramur, si eadem ad noxam genuit aliqua! 159. ferae enim, credo, custodiunt illam arcentque sacrilegas manus. non inter serpentes fodimus et venas auri tractamus cum veneni radicibus? placatiore tamen dea ob haec, quod omnes hi opulentiae exitus ad scelera caedesque et bella tendunt, quodque sanguine nostro rigamus insepultisque ossibus tegimus, quibus tamen velut exprobrato furore tandem ipsa se obducit et scelera quoque mortalium occultat.*

[25] Vgl. Plin. n. h. 18,1,1.

Menschen zur Verfügung gestellt wird: *penetramus in viscera, auri argenti-que venas, et aeris ac plumbi metalla fodientes: gemmas etiam et quosdam parvulos quaerimus lapides, scrobibus in profundum actis.*

Die in den epischen Werken vorkommenden Gebete und Hymnen können nicht als kultische Texte betrachtet werden, sie stehen aber doch jenen sehr nahe. Es ist selbstverständlich, daß sich der Schriftsteller den in der religiösen Praxis gebrauchten Texten zu folgen bemüht. Dies wird aber durch die epischen Traditionen und durch die klassische Bildung des Verfassers modifiziert und bereichert. Die Texte beziehen sich zwar auf eine sagenhafte Vergangenheit, in ihren Details bei Vergil und Statius knüpfen sie aber doch eng an unser Zeitalter an.

Über die Rolle, die Tellus bei der Eheschließung spielte, wissen wir nicht mehr als das, was Servius zur 'Aeneis' bemerkt (4,166). Jedenfalls kann diese Beziehung mit der Vegetations-Natur der Göttin erklärt werden (WEINSTOCK, RE, Sp. 801). Wir wissen aber mehr über ihre Rolle bei der Eidesleistung. Aeneas und Latinus rufen, als sie ihr Bündnis schließen, unter anderem Terra als Zeuge (Aen. 12,176; 197). Wir kennen die bei der Eidesleistung aufgezählten Götter nicht nur aus der epischen Tradition[26], sondern auch aus den Inschriften, die in der östlichen Hälfte des Reiches zum Vorschein kamen[27]. Auf diesen kommt Gaia immer vor. Die Opferung eines schwarzen Lammes vor dem Niedersteigen in die Unterwelt können wir als eine homerische Wirkung ansehen[28]. Dieses Tier kam näm-lich früher bei Tellus nicht vor, bei den Unterwelt-Göttern aber ja. Die Erde hatte also als Unterwelt-Macht an diesem Opfer teil.

Wir sehen Tellus bzw. Terra in zwei Szenen der 'Aeneis' in einem neuen Aufgabenbereich: Sie ist die Verteidigerin eines bestimmten Gebietes bzw. seiner Bewohner. Als Aeneas auf dem Boden ankommt, der ihm vom Schicksal bestimmt war,

> . . . *geniumque loci primamque deorum*
> *Tellurem nymphasque et adhuc ignota precatur*
> *flumina* (7,135ff.).

Im kritischen Moment des Zweikampfs, den Turnus mit Aeneas kämpft, bittet er gerade um das Gegenteil: die Götter des Ortes, Faunus und Terra, sollen gegen Aeneas Hilfe leisten, dessen Volk, unwissend zwar, ihre Gott-heit doch beleidigt hatte, während er selbst sie immer verehrt hat (12,776ff.). In dieser Rolle treffen wir die Erde bei den griechischen Tragikern mehr-mals. In den 'Schutzflehenden' des Aischylos (890ff.) und in den 'Hera-kliden' des Euripides (748ff.) wenden sich die Bürger an ihre Erde, daß sie den Feind von ihnen fernhalten und die Verwüstung verhindern möge.

---

[26] Hom. Il. 3,276—80; 14,271—74; 15,36—40; 19,258—60.
[27] F. CUMONT, Un serment de fidélité à l'empereur Auguste, Rev. Et. Grecques 14, 1901, 26ff.; H. USENER, Dreiheit, Rh. Mus. 58, 1903, 17ff.; P. HERRMANN, Der römische Kaisereid, Hypomn. 20, Göttingen 1968.
[28] Aen. 6,249f., vgl. Hom. Od. 11,44f.

In der 'Thebais' des Statius meinen die Argiver, die sich gegen Theben erhoben haben, eine Stellungnahme der Tellus zu entdecken, als Amphiaraus von einer Schlucht verschlungen wurde[29]. Sie bemühen sich, den Zorn der Erde durch Opferdarbringungen und Gebet zu versöhnen (8,298 ff.)[29a]. Wir treffen eine so ausführliche, an Tellus gerichtete Zeremonie nur hier allein. Der *sacerdos* läßt einen Doppelaltar aufstellen (*geminas aras*) aus frisch gehacktem Holz (*arboribus vivis*) und aus Rasenziegeln (*adulto caespite*). Als unblutiges Opfer bringt er Blumen, Früchte und Milch vor dem Gebet dar und danach schwarze Schafe (*nigrantis pecudes*) und dunkelfarbige Rinder (*obscura armenta*). Die Tiere werden nicht geschlachtet, sondern lebendig begraben — als Parallele zum Tode des Amphiaraus. Ein zum Teil ähnliches Opfer wird durch Vergil am Grab des Anchises beschrieben (5,77 ff.). Der Unterschied liegt nur darin, daß bei ihm statt Früchten Wein und heiliges Blut vorkommen und unter den Tieren auch Schweine sind. Der Tellus mit Unterwelt-Macht werden also nicht ihre uralten Opfertiere dargebracht, sondern das, was bei Totenopfern üblich war.

Das an Tellus gerichtete Gebet gehört zu den gehobensten Teilen der 'Thebais'[30]. In seinem Text ist die Wirkung des Lucretius unverkennbar, sowohl im Gebrauch gewisser Wendungen als auch im Inhalt. Gleich der Anfang klingt bekannt: *hominum divomque aeterna creatrix*, was in seinem archaischen Ton eine Reminiszenz an die Anfangszeile der Venus-Hymne des Lucretius ist. Die schon bekannten Funktionen wiederholen sich: Sie ist Erzeugerin und Ernährerin aller Lebewesen. Es wird von ihr als Himmelskörper geredet, worin das stoische Weltbild zu erkennen ist: die Erde ist *firmum atque immobile mundi robur, rerum media*, die von den Himmelskörpern umfangen wird[31]. Wir können die Betonung ihrer Güte und Tragfähigkeit verstehen, als die Bitte an die Reihe kommt: *nos tantum portare negas, nos, diva, gravaris?* Die Leute von Argos sehen ihre Sünde darin, daß sie fremden Boden betreten. Das Wohlwollen der Tellus versuchen sie durch eine listige Argumentation zu gewinnen:

> *. . . nec te, optima[32], saevo*
> *tamque humili populos deceat distinguere fine*
> *undique ubique tuos. . .*

Die Impressivität, wie sie von VESSEY (o. c. 266) beobachtet wird, gipfelt hier, und vermutlich handelt es sich um eine Anwendung der stoischen Lehre der menschlichen Brüderlichkeit, wenn dies auch ziemlich über-

---

[29] Über die enge Verbindung von Tellus mit dem Erdbeben informiert ein Ereignis bei Florus (1,14,2): *domiti ergo Picentes et caput gentis Asculum Sempronio duce, qui tremente inter proelium campo Tellurem deam promissa aede placavit* (v. u. Z. 268).

[29a] Eine ausführliche Untersuchung dieses Details s. T. GESZTELYI, Placatio Telluris bei Statius (Thebais 8, 298—341), Acta Class. Debr. 12, 1976, 53 ff.

[30] Vgl. D. VESSEY, Statius and the Thebaid, Cambridge 1973, 267.

[31] Varro bei Aug. c. D. 7,24, vgl. Cic. somn. Scip. 17, 18.

[32] Dieses Attribut wird auch von Turnus gebraucht (Aen. 12,777).

raschend wirkt, gerade inmitten des Krieges. Ihre Bitte lautet: die Erde von Boiotia soll ihre Bewohner nicht beschirmen, sie soll den Körper der Angreifer nicht wegreißen, ohne abzuwarten, daß sie ihre Seelen ausatmen. Der Schluß ist an Amphiaraus gerichtet. Er soll, als ehemaliger Priester des Apollo, mit seiner Prophezeiung seinem Volk helfen.

Der Ritus ist offensichtlich ein schriftstellerisches Produkt, in dem die literarischen und philosophischen Muster zu erkennen sind. Die ihre Bewohner beschirmende Rolle der Erde bzw. daß sich die Bewohner um Hilfe an sie wendeten, war auch in der Wirklichkeit ein praktiziertes Verfahren. Dafür finden wir auch in den Inschriften Beispiele.

IV. Tellus—Terra Mater in der Religionspolitik der Kaiser

Das Zeitalter des Augustus bietet uns ein reiches Material an Zeugnissen. Neben den literarischen Texten erscheinen zum ersten Mal in einer bildlichen Darstellung die Gestalt der Erdgöttin und auf einer Inschrift ihr Name — in beiden Fällen auf einem staatlichen Denkmal. Damit sind zwei literarische Texte eng verbunden: die *laus Italiae* der 'Georgica' Vergils (2,136ff.) und das 'Carmen saeculare' des Horaz. Hinzu kommen zwei Kunstwerke von privatem Charakter, die aber gewiß dem Kaiserhof gehört haben: die Augustusstatue von Primaporta und die Gemma Augustea.

Von den oben erwähnten Werken entstand die *laus Italiae*, das Lob der *Saturnia tellus*, am frühesten. Diese *magna parens* unterscheidet sich in vielen Beziehungen von der *magna mater* des Lukrez. Beide sind Erzeuger der Lebewesen der Natur, aber bei Vergil ist nur von den Haustieren (*armenta, equus, greges, taurus, pecudes*) und vom *genus acre virum* die Rede, nicht von irgendwelchem menschlichen Geschlecht. Auf dieser vergilischen Erde gibt es keine schrecklichen Ungeheuer, giftige Pflanzen und gefährliche Schlangen, wie im Osten, sondern es gibt ewigen Frühling, die Rinder sind zweimal trächtig, die Obstbäume bringen zweimal Frucht. Unverkennbar sind dies die Topoi des goldenen Zeitalters, deren Bedeutung W. RICHTER[33] folgendermaßen formuliert: ,,Alles, was man vom Sagenzeitalter berichtet, geschieht in Wahrheit im Hier und Jetzt des italischen Bauernlebens. Dies alles ertönt als das politische Programm des Herrschers, wie dies später auch direkt zum Ausdruck kommt: *aurea condet saecula* (Aen. 6,292f.).''

Der Überfluß des goldenen Zeitalters strahlt vom repräsentativsten Werk der bildenden Künste aus der Zeit des Augustus, auf dem Tellus-Relief der Ara Pacis[34]. Der Schoß der mittleren weiblichen Gestalt ist voll

---

[33] Vergil, Georgica, München 1957, 206.

[34] Es hat keine Bedeutung, ob sie Tellus oder Terra Mater genannt wird, weil es sich im Fall der Darstellungen um eine moderne Namengebung handelt. Wir stimmen mit der Venus-

von Früchten, rings um sie herum sind reiche Frucht tragende Pflanzen, an ihrem Fuß sind friedliche Haustiere gelagert, im Arm hält sie zwei Kinder; alles weist viel mehr Verwandtschaft mit der Beschreibung Vergils auf, die uns an das goldene Zeitalter erinnert, als mit der Terra Mater des Lukrez. Ihre elementare Natur wird nicht so sehr betont wie bei Lukrez (2,589ff.). Auch auf dem Relief erscheinen nur Haustiere und diejenigen Schönheiten der Natur, die Vergil für Italien aufzählt: *saxa, flumina, mare.* Beide zeigen nur die Blüte, und der Gedanke des Todes, der mit der Terra Mater eng verbunden ist, fehlt bei ihnen. Es wäre natürlich ein sinnloses Bestreben, die *laus Italiae* Zeile für Zeile mit dem Tellus-Relief zu vergleichen[35]. Das Relief ist ja offenbar keine Illustration zu dem gegebenen Text, und mag es auch einen ähnlichen Gedanken ausdrücken, so haben doch beide ihre eigenen Mittel dafür gebraucht, die Gesetze ihrer Gattung einhaltend. Die Gleichheit der Gedanken wird auch durch den gleichen historischen Hintergrund unterstrichen. Der Kaiser hat in dem einen Fall im Osten (29 v. u. Z.), in dem anderen im Westen (13 v. u. Z.) die Gefahr, die Italien bedrohte, verhütet und dadurch die Voraussetzungen eines friedlichen Lebens gesichert. Dies war der Grund dafür, daß die *aurea aetas* nach Italien zurückkehrte. Die *laus Italiae* und das Tellus-Relief führen uns diese *aurea aetas* vor Augen[36].

Die personifizierte Darstellung der Tellus erscheint auf den Denkmälern der Kaiserzeit oft auf der Erde sitzend oder liegend und meist bis zum Gürtel nackt. Von diesem üblichen Typ weicht das Relief der Ara Pacis ab, wo die Frauengestalt auf einem Felsen sitzt und ihr Kopf mit einem Schleier, ihr Körper mit einem Kleid bedeckt ist. Damit scheint sie der Darstellungsweise der Kultstatuen zu folgen[37], was wir sonst selten finden. Aus Karthago kennen wir eine Variante des Reliefs[38]. Außerdem gibt es ein Wandgemälde in Herculaneum, worauf sie neben einer Sagenszene erscheint[39]: Die auf dem Felsen sitzende Frauengestalt hat ein langes Kleid an, auf ihrem Kopf trägt sie einen Blumenkranz, in der linken Hand

Interpretation von G. K. GALINSKY, Venus in a Relief of the Ara Pacis Augustae, AJA 70, 1966, 223ff., nicht überein.

[35] Vgl. VAN BUREN, The Ara Pacis Augustae, JRS 3, 1913, 134ff., M. SCHÄFER, Zum Tellusbild auf der Ara Pacis Augustae, Gymn. 66, 1959, 288ff.

[36] In diesen Fällen ist Tellus eine Personifikation, die mit der Tellus der alten römischen Religion nicht identisch ist. Dies kann eine Erklärung dafür sein, warum Tellus in der Invokation der 'Georgica' unter den angesprochenen Göttern nicht vorkommt, wogegen sie bei Varro (r. r. 1,5) auf dem 2. Platz zu finden ist. In den Reihen, wo Tellus durch die Gaben von Ceres und Liber reiche Nahrung sichert (Georg. 1,7ff.), können wir dieselbe Personifikation entdecken wie in der *laus Italiae* (vgl. V. 143), es ist also nicht über eine Göttin zu sprechen. Das Gegenteil dessen versucht F. REBELO GONÇALVES, A deusa Telure na invocação das Geórgicas (mit latein. Zusammenfassung), Euphrosyne 3, 1961, 91ff., zu beweisen.

[37] A. FURTWÄNGLER entdeckt einen ähnlichen Unterschied im Laufe des Vergleichs der liegenden und sitzenden Nil-Statuen: Antike Gemmen, II: Berlin—München 1969, 255.

[38] Über die Schwierigkeiten der Interpretation s. E. STRONG, Terra Mater or Italia, JRS 27, 1937, 124.

[39] R. HAMANN, Herakles findet Telephos, Berlin 1953.

hält sie einen Stock, unter ihrem rechten Ellbogen liegt ein Korb voll mit Früchten — es ist die Personifikation der Erde von Arkadien. Auf ihre Verwandtschaft mit dem Ara Pacis-Relief weist R. HAMANN hin (o. c. 14), indem er bemerkt, daß die personifizierte Darstellung eines bestimmten Gebietes zum Typ der Tellus-Darstellungen gehört. Wir denken, daß durch dieses Beispiel vom ikonographischen Gesichtspunkt aus die Annahme unterstützt wird, daß auf der Ara Pacis die Erde von Italien erscheint, die die Fülle sichernde *Saturnia tellus*[40].

Einen mit den vorigen übereinstimmenden Gedanken verkünden die im Jahre 17 v. u. Z. veranstalteten *ludi saeculares*. Das Ziel des Festes wird durch die Neuerungen klar ausgedrückt, die Augustus dabei eingeführt hat. Ursprünglich standen in seinem Mittelpunkt Dispater und Proserpina, da es sich um das Begräbnis des vergangenen *saeculum* handelte. Statt ihrer wurde nun dem I. O. M., der Iuno Regina, dem Apollo und der Diana und in der Nacht den Moeren, der Ilithyia und der Terra Mater geopfert[41]. Es ist besonders beachtenswert, daß auch in der Nacht nicht die Götter der Unterwelt auftraten. Die Aufgabe der Moeren war die Sicherung des guten Schicksals, die der Ilithyia die Sicherung der leichten und reichen Geburt, die der Terra Mater die Gewährleistung des Überflusses der Pflanzen und Tiere[42]. In dem Mittelpunkt dieses Festes steht also nicht das Begräbnis des vergangenen Jahrhunderts, sondern die Begrüßung des neuen, das eine gerechte Macht, gutes Schicksal und Fülle bringen wird, d. h. den Zustand des goldenen Zeitalters. Dazu ist die wohltätige Mitwirkung der Erde unentbehrlich, deshalb bekommt sie auch hier einen Platz im Kult und ebenso im 'Carmen saeculare', das für das Fest geschrieben worden ist:

> *Fertilis frugum pecorisque Tellus*
> *Spicea donet Cererem corona*
> *Nutriant fetus et aquae salubres*
> *Et Iovis aurae.*   (Hor., c. saec. 29ff.)

Diese Strophe wird oft neben das Relief der Ara Pacis gestellt, auf dem die Nebengestalten an der Seite der Tellus die Personifikationen der *aquae salubres* und der *Iovis aurae* sein können[43]. Aus den Umständen ist offensichtlich, daß es sich auch hier um die Erde Italiens handelt. Hier tritt das neue Zeitalter ein, bei der Darbringung der Opfer an den Festen erfolgt das Gebet für das römische Volk (*populus Romanus Quiritium*).

---

[40] Diese Interpretation taucht zum ersten Mal bei VAN BUREN (ob. Anm. 35) auf. Die neueste Literatur kehrt wieder zu dieser zurück: E. SIMON, Ara Pacis Augustae, Tübingen 1967, 25ff. Die Tellus=Italia Vorstellung ist im Bericht von Varro (r. r. 1,2) zu entdecken, nach der die Wand des Tempels der Tellus mit der Darstellung von Italia geziert wurde.

[41] CIL VI 32323 = ILS 5050.

[42] Vgl. E. DIEHL, Das *saeculum*, seine Riten und Gebete, II. Die *saecula* der Kaiserzeit. Ritual und Gebet der Feiern der Jahre 17 v. Chr., 88 und 204 n. Chr., Rh. Mus. 83, 1934, 355.

[43] E. SIMON, o. c. 27.

Die Terra Mater der *ludi saeculares* ist auch in ihrem Namen, auch ihrem Gehalt nach eine neue Göttin, die durch Augustus zu einem Teil der Staatsreligion geworden ist. Unter solchem Namen genoß bisher keine Göttin eine religiöse Verehrung in Rom. Sie ist mit der Tellus nicht identisch, die in der Ackerbau treibenden römischen Gesellschaft an bestimmten Tagen des Jahres öffentliche oder private Opfer bekam. Diese Änderung wollte gewiß auch Augustus, der im übrigen die Tradition pflegte, mit dem neuen Namen ausdrücken, der die lateinische Übersetzung der in den sibyllinischen Büchern vorkommenden Gaia ist. Die Inkonsequenz im Namengebrauch fängt aber schon hier an: das 'Carmen saeculare' nennt sie Tellus. Diese mangelnde Folgerichtigkeit bleibt auch im Laufe der Kaiserzeit sowohl bei den staatlichen als auch bei den privaten Denkmälern charakteristisch; so hat die Unterscheidung zwischen Tellus und Terra Mater im weiteren keinen Sinn mehr. Der neue Inhalt wird am besten durch die *laus Italiae* und das Relief der Ara Pacis ausgedrückt: Sie ist die Personifikation der die Fülle des goldenen Zeitalters sichernden Erde von Italien. Die Erhöhung der Personifikationen zu einem göttlichen Rang ist in der römischen Religion keine neue Erscheinung; sie kommt schon zur Zeit der Republik mehrere Male vor (WISSOWA, RuKR 327ff.). Auf solche Weise ist die Tellus der Ara Pacis ein ähnlich entstandener Gottesbegriff wie die ihr gegenüber befindliche Dea Roma, die eine Personifikation der Macht Roms ist.

Zwei hervorragende Werke der Periode sind die Augustusstatue von Primaporta und die Gemma Augustea. Die letztere stellt ein Ereignis aus dem Jahre 12 oder 10 u. Z. dar[44], auch für die erstere ist diese Datierung wahrscheinlich[45]. Dafür spricht bei beiden Stücken die göttliche Vergegenwärtigung des Augustus. Auf diesen beiden Bildern weist Tellus sowohl formell als auch inhaltlich gegenüber den bisherigen offiziellen Denkmälern eine Abweichung auf. Statt der sitzenden Lage stützt sie sich zu ebener Erde auf die Ellbogen bzw. auf die Seite des Thronsessels, ohne Schleier auf dem Kopf, auf der Gemme mit unbedecktem Oberkörper. Diese ihr elementares Wesen betonenden Details werden noch durch ihre Plazierung ergänzt: sie erscheint als Gegenstück zu Caelus bzw. Oceanus. Die Situation macht unzweifelhaft, daß Tellus hier nicht nur Italien[46], sondern die ganze Erde personifiziert. Das Füllhorn in ihrem Schoß und daneben die zwei Kinder weisen auf das durch den göttlichen Herrscher gesicherte und für

---

[44] A. FURTWÄNGLER, Ant. Gem. II 257f.; H. KÄHLER, Alberti Rubensi Dissertatio de Gemma Augustea, Berlin 1968, 26f; vgl. jetzt die Literaturangaben bei J. R. FEARS, The Cult of Jupiter and Roman Imperial Ideology, ANRW II 17,1, hrsg. v. W. HAASE, Berlin—New York 1981, n. 268.

[45] H. KÄHLER, Die Augustusstatue von Primaporta, Köln 1959, 16ff., hält die Verfertigung der Statue nur nach dem Tod vom Augustus für vorstellbar. Nach H. INGHOLT, The Prima Porta Statue of Augustus, II. The Location of the Original, Archaeology 22, 1969, 308, kam es zur Aufstellung dieser Statue nach den Ereignissen (im Jahre 19 v. u. Z.), die auf dem Panzer dargestellt sind — in Pergamon. Die in Rom gefundene Statue ist deren Kopie.

[46] H. KÄHLER (ob. Anm. 44) behauptet im Fall der Gemma Augustea gerade das Gegenteil. Er sieht keinen Sinn darin, daß auch Tellus neben Oikumene anwesend ist.

die ganze Erde geltende goldene Zeitalter hin. Treffend ist dafür die Feststellung von E. STRONG: *"The place assigned to her in the composition stresses
once again the universality of the Imperial Providence which has brought back
the Golden Age to the Earth"* (o. c. 120). Die in der offiziellen Ideologie der
Tellus zukommende Rolle wird im weiteren durch diesen Gedanken
bestimmt.

Sehr beliebt ist, offenbar auf die Wirkung der Statue von Primaporta
zurückgehend, die Darstellung des Kaisers auf dem Reliefschmuck des
Panzers von Statuen. Im Mittelpunkt erscheint regelmäßig Victoria. Der
Zusammenhang liegt auf der Hand: der Herrscher sichert den Wohlstand
seines Reiches durch seinen Sieg. Mit diesen Statuen beschäftigen sich
mehrere Arbeiten[47]. Ein ähnlicher Gedanke wird durch die Tellus-Bilder
der Triumphbögen und Münzen ausgedrückt[48]. Ihre Darstellung verbreitet
sich auch auf den Werken privaten Charakters, die der offiziellen Ideologie
folgen, wie auf der Patera von Aquileia[49] oder auf dem Onyx-Lekythos von
Braunschweig[50].

Zu einer selbständigen Darstellung der Tellus kommt es nach Augustus
erst wieder unter Hadrian, und zwar auf einem der wichtigsten Mittel der
staatlichen Propaganda, auf dem Geld. Vier Typen sind uns bekannt[51],
unter denen einer von den bisherigen Lösungen völlig abweicht. Tellus
steht in einer kurzen Tunika, in ihrer rechten Hand hält sie einen Pflug,
in der linken eine zweizackige Hacke, am Fuß liegen zwei Ähren. Die
Inschrift ist: TELLUS STABIL*(ita)*[52]. Im Namensgebrauch können wir
wahrscheinlich eine Archaisierung sehen, die zu Hadrians Zeit modisch
war. Eine neue Lösung ist die stehende Darstellung, auch das kurze Kleid
und die landwirtschaftlichen Werkzeuge als Attribute. Diese deuten darauf
hin, daß es sich hier um die Personifikation des Ackerbaus handelt, und
die Inschrift weist auf die Sicherung der Ruhe und Ordnung hin, die zur
Feldarbeit nötig sind. Beim zweiten Typ sitzt Tellus auf der Erde, im
langen Kleid, ihre rechte Hand hält sie auf einem Rad, mit ihrer Linken
stützt sie sich auf einen Obstkorb und hält eine Weinrebe[53]. Der dritte Typ
unterscheidet sich von den übrigen darin, daß der rechte Arm der Frauengestalt auf einem gestirnten Globus ruht. In ihrer Linken, mit der sie sich

---

[47] E. STRONG, o. c. 118f.; A. HEKLER, Beiträge zur Geschichte der antiken Panzerstatuen,
JbÖAI 20, 1919, 190ff.; G. MANCINI, Le statue loricate imperiali, Bollettino della Com-
missione Archeologica communale in Roma 50, 1922, 151ff.

[48] H. P. LAUBSCHER, Der Reliefschmuck des Galeriusbogens in Tessaloniki, Arch. Forsch. I,
Berlin 1975, 73ff.; M. GUARDUCCI, Sol Invictus Augustus, Rend. Pont. Ac. Rom. di Arch.
30—31, 1957—59, 161ff.

[49] Die neueste Literatur bei F. L. BASTET, Nero und die Patera von Aquileia, BABesch 44,
1969, 143ff.

[50] H.-P. BÜHLER, Antike Gefäße aus Edelstein, Mainz 1973, 65ff.

[51] Ihre Datierung ist nur zwischen weiten Rahmen möglich: BMC III, CXLIV: 134—37; RIC in
the Hunter Coin Cabinet II, LVII: 128—38. Über die Darstellungen: J. M. C. TOYNBEE,
The Hadrianic School, Cambridge 1934, 140ff.

[52] BMC III nr. 737—47.

[53] RIC in the Hunter Coin Cabinet II p. 110 nr. 251.

auf einen vollen Obstkorb stützt, hält sie einen Zweig[54]. Auf dem vierten kommen zu dem vorigen Bild noch die personifizierten Kindergestalten der vier Jahreszeiten[55]. Die Inschrift von allen ist: TELLUS STABIL. Im Fall der letzten drei Typen drücken das Rad, der gestirnte Globus und die Personifikationen der Jahreszeiten etwas Neues aus. Die Bedeutung dieser Elemente übersteigt die Sicherstellung des friedlichen Ackerbaus; sie bringen mehr zum Ausdruck als die bisherigen Tellus-Darstellungen, die das Eintreffen des goldenen Zeitalters verkünden. Die Emissionen hängen mit dem im Jahre 121 veranstalteten Fest des *natalis Romae* und mit der Weihe des Tempels der Venus und Roma in den Jahren 136 und 137 zusammen[56]. Rom ist das Zentrum des Weltreiches, das durch den Kaiser regiert wird, den *restitutor orbis terrarum*, den *kosmokrator*. Die durch den Herrscher geschaffene Ordnung ist zugleich die Ordnung des Weltalls, das *felix saeculum*[57]. Das Rad und die vier Jahreszeiten sind die Symbole des ständigen Umlaufs und der Erneuerung der Zeit und der Natur und gehören zu den Attributen des Aion[58]. Dieser hellenistisch-ägyptischen Gottheit kam unter Hadrian eine große Bedeutung zu, sie erschien auf Prägungen im Zodiakus mit einer Inschrift SAEC*(ulum)* AVR*(eum)*, als der Genius des goldenen Zeitalters[59]. Tellus und Aion drücken also ein ähnliches politisches Ziel aus.

Der Gedanke des goldenen Zeitalters unter Hadrian wiederholt sich mit einer Übernahme der Ausdrucksmittel auf den Münzemissionen seiner Nachfolger, des Antoninus Pius, des Commodus[60] und des Septimius Severus[61]. Eine Gelegenheit zur Ausgabe dieser Prägungen bot nicht nur der ständig vorhandene Anspruch auf die Herbeiführung des goldenen Zeitalters, sondern auch das unter Antoninus Pius im Jahre 147 anläßlich des 900jährigen Bestehens der Stadt Rom begangene Fest und die unter Septimius Severus im Jahre 204 zum letzten Mal veranstalteten *ludi saeculares*. Die Darstellung der Tellus — eine Frau, die auf der Erde sitzt, in ihrer Linken ein doppeltes Füllhorn, in ihrer Rechten eine Ähre, vor ihr zwei Kinder — erscheint mit einer Inschrift FECUNDITAS TEMPORUM unter Philippus Arabs, der im Jahre 248 das 1000jährige Bestehen Roms feierte[62].

[54] BMC III 1565—67.
[55] P. L. STRACK, Untersuchungen zur römischen Reichsprägung des zweiten Jahrhunderts, II, Stuttgart 1933, nr. 164.
[56] J. BEAUJEU, La religion romaine à l'apogée de l'empire, I, Paris 1955, 151.
[57] J. BEAUJEU, o. c. 159.
[58] Vgl. D. LEVI, Aion, Hesperia 13, 1944, 285 ff.
[59] J. BEAUJEU, o. c. 155.
[60] M. BERNHARDT, Handbuch zur Münzkunde der römischen Kaiserzeit, Halle 1926, 69.
[61] BMC V, XLIV p. 317. Die Authentizität ist zweifelhaft.
[62] J. CHARBONNEAUX, Aiôn et Philippe l'Arabe, Mél. d'arch. et d'hist. de l'École Française de Rome 67, 1960, 259 f.

V. Tellus—Terra Mater in der privaten Religiosität

Die Göttin nahm nicht nur in der kaiserlichen Propaganda einen wichtigen Platz ein, sondern sie verfügte auch in der Privatreligiosität über einen selbständigen Kultus, besonders in manchen Provinzen. Die wichtigsten Zeugnisse dafür sind die Inschriften, manche bildliche Darstellungen und Heiligtümer. Ihre Verbreitung ist in Nordafrika, in den Provinzen des Donau-Beckens und in Rom bedeutend, anderswo kommt sie nur ab und zu oder gar nicht vor.

Am stärksten ist der Kultus in Nordafrika. Da er schon Gegenstand ausführlicher Untersuchung gewesen ist[63], geben wir hier nur eine Zusammenfassung. Sein Verbreitungsgebiet ist in erster Linie die Provinz Africa Proconsularis, aber er kommt auch in Numidien und Mauretanien vor. Die Heiligtümer verdichten sich in allen drei Provinzen an der wichtigen Handelsstraße, die von Karthago ausgeht und nach Sitifis führt, besonders im Medjerda-Tal, das das wichtigste Getreideanbaugebiet in Nordafrika war. Der Name der Göttin ist, abgesehen von zwei Ausnahmen, Tellus; einmal kommen ihre beiden Namen vor (L. Leschi, Un Autel votif de Bourbaki, Lib. [Archéol.-Épigr.] 1, 1953, 87). Die Inschriften berichten über die Aufstellung von Tempeln und Statuen, von diesen kennen wir aber allein einen Tempel aus Thugga[64]. Ein bedeutender Teil der Dedikanten der Inschriften gehörte zu der munizipalen Aristokratie: es sind *aediles*[65] und *flamines*[66]. In einem Fall macht die Dedikation ein *legatus Augusti* (CIL VIII 8309). Aus den Inschriften kennen wir sieben *sacerdotes Telluris*[67], wofür es nirgendwo anders ein Beispiel gibt. Die früheste datierbare Inschrift stammt aus dem Jahre 40 v. u. Z. (CIL X 6104), die späteste aus dem Jahre 261 u. Z. (ILAfr 530); die Mehrheit von ihnen ist im II. Jahrhundert entstanden.

Das Material beweist, daß wir es in Nordafrika mit der am besten organisierten, offiziell unterstützten Tellus-Verehrung zu tun haben, die schon gegen Ende der Republikanischen Zeit begann und sicher bis zum Ende des Prinzipats existierte. Sie hatte gewiß einen örtlichen Hintergrund, den wir in erster Linie in dem Kult der Thesmophoroi sehen müssen, der noch vor der römischen Eroberung offiziell gepflegt wurde[68]. Daher kann

---

[63] T. Gesztelyi, The Cult of Tellus-Terra Mater in North Africa, Acta Class. Debr. 8, 1972, 75ff.

[64] C. Poinssot, Les ruines de Dougga, Tunis 1958, 45. Das Heiligtum wurde 261 gebaut, in einer seiner Zellen kam eine Statue des Pluto zum Vorschein, mit einem ihm gewidmeten Altar. Auf dem erhalten gebliebenen Mosaikboden ist eine Inschrift *Apona* und eine Hirsenstengel-Darstellung zu sehen. Die letzterwähnten weisen auf ihre apotropäische Rolle hin.

[65] CIL VIII 19489, 5305, X 6104.

[66] ILAfr 530, 553, A. E. 1968 nr. 596.

[67] CIL 26237, ILAl 1373—74, 2227, BAC 1928/29 163.

[68] J. Carcopino, Salluste, le culte des «Céres» et les Numides, Rev. Hist. 158, 1928, 1ff.

in diesem Gebiet die sonst ungewöhnliche Bezeichnung Cereres erklärt werden, in deren Kreis auch Tellus gehörte[69]. Demzufolge hatte ihr Kult einen Mysterien-Charakter und waren auch Pluto und Kore damit verknüpft (siehe die Funde der Heiligtümer in Thugga und Soliman). Im Laufe der Kaiserzeit war es von bestimmender Bedeutung, daß dieses Gebiet die wichtigste Getreidequelle für Rom und somit eine unentbehrliche Basis der Fülle im verkündeten goldenen Zeitalter war. Der Tellus-Kult gehörte also zum religiösen Hintergrund des politischen Programms: Der Gebrauch des alten Namens der Göttin kann damit erklärt werden, daß zu der Zeit, als sie nach Afrika eingeführt wurde, auch in Rom nur der Name Tellus in Gebrauch war, und daß nach ihrer Einbürgerung keine Änderung der Nomenklatur mehr erfolgte. Eine Unsicherheit in der Benennung zeigt sich erst an einem späten Altar, der von ihrem eigentlichen Verbreitungsgebiet weit entfernt liegt; hier kommen beide Namen vor.

Das andere, über bedeutendes Zeugnismaterial verfügende Gebiet sind die Provinzen des Karpaten-Beckens bzw. des Nord-Balkans: Dalmatia, Pannonia, Moesia Superior und Dacia[70]. Wenn wir die dortigen Verhältnisse mit denen von Nordafrika vergleichen, können wir bedeutende Unterschiede feststellen. Als Kultname wurde ohne Ausnahme Terra Mater angenommen, bis kürzlich (1974) in Intercisa ein Altar mit dem Namen Tellus zum Vorschein kam[71]. Dies spricht wieder dafür, daß der Namensgebrauch nur durch die Gewohnheit bestimmt war, nicht durch einen inhaltlichen Unterschied. Terra Mater hat keine Priesterin, und wir wissen auch nur in einem einzigen Fall von einem Tempel[72]. Die Zeit der Aufstellung der Inschriften ist die zweite Hälfte des II. Jahrhunderts u. Z. und die erste Hälfte des III. Jahrhunderts. Der Kult weist in den verschiedenen Provinzen Abweichungen auf. Das einheitlichste Gesicht zeigt er in Dalmatia, wo alle Inschriften im Bergbaugebiet in der Gegend von Ljubija zutage getreten sind[73]. Die Dedikanten sind: der *vilicus officinae ferrariae*, der *vilicus ferrariarum* oder der *procurator* des Bergwerks. Die Aufstellung erfolgt gewöhnlich *pro salute imperatoris*, was uns die Grundlage zur Datierung bietet: Sie reichen von Septimius Severus bis Gallienus, und die Altaraufstellung erfolgt immer am 21. April. Dieser Tag ist das Fest des *natalis urbis Romae*, dem Hadrian eine besondere politische Bedeutung gab. Es ist anzunehmen, daß auch die Emission der Münzen mit der Legende TELLUS STABIL*(ita)* mit diesem Ereignis zusammenhängt und daß sie die auf der Erde eingetretenen sicheren Zustände verkünden sollen. Vom Gesichtspunkt des

---

[69] Vgl. Fasti archaeologici 9, 1954, nr. 5321: das Cereres-Heiligtum von Soliman.

[70] Eine ausführliche Untersuchung s. T. GESZTELYI, The Cult of Terra Mater in the Danubian Basin Lands, Acta Class. Debr. 7, 1971, 85ff.

[71] B. LŐRINCZ, Vezető a Dunaujvárosi Muzeum római kötárához (Führer durch das römische Lapidarium des Museums in Dunaujváros), Dunaujváros 1975, nr. 55; B. LŐRINCZ—Zs. VISY, Neuere Inschriften aus Intercisa, Alba Regia 15, 1976, 202, nr. 486.

[72] CIL III 8333 = 6313.

[73] D. SERGEJEVSKI, Rimski rudnici željeza u sjeverozapadnoj Bosni (Die römischen Eisenbergwerke im nordwestlichen Bosnien), Glasnik Zemaljskog Muzeja u Sarajevu, Archeologija (Sarajevo) NS 18, 1963, 85ff.

Verständnisses der Inschriften aus ist es ein sehr wichtiger Umstand, daß
die erwähnten Eisenerzgruben von der Mitte des zweiten Jahrhunderts an
in der Sicherstellung der Verteidigungslinie des Reiches an der Donau eine
bedeutende Rolle spielten[74]. Dadurch können auch der organisierte und
offizielle Charakter des Kultes und die Tatsache erklärt werden, daß nicht
weit entfernt, aber schon auf dem Gebiet der Provinz Moesia Superior, also
auch auf Bergbaugebiet, sein einziger Tempel in dieser Region stand (s.
Anm. 72). Die Beziehung zwischen der Terra Mater und dem Bergbau ist
auch in Dacia zu entdecken. Der Altar in Domneşti wird für das Heil des
conductor pascui et salinarum geweiht[75], und in einem anderen Fall mag die
Nähe des Bergbaugebiets auf eine solche Beziehung hinweisen[76]. In Pannonia haben wir dafür keine Angaben.

Bei einem Teil der Inschriften kommt Terra Mater zusammen mit den
Schutz-Göttern des Ackerbaus vor, wie Liber Pater[77], Hercules, Silvanus[78],
oder ihr Epitheton hat solchen Charakter, wie Genetrix[79]. In manchen
Fällen ist die Dedikation ausdrücklich an die Erde der Provinz gerichtet[80].
Von diesem Gesichtspunkt aus verdient unsere Aufmerksamkeit ein in
Sopianae gefundener Altar; seine Darstellung ist bisher noch nicht völlig
geklärt worden[81]. Die Dedikation lautet: *IOM Terrae matri.* Auf der Seite
links von der Inschrift steht Iuppiter mit Szepter; auf der rechten Seite
(Taf. I 1) steht eine Frauengestalt in langem Kleid, in der linken Hand
eine Stange haltend, die genauso hoch ist wie sie selbst und an deren oberer
Spitze, nach der Aussage der Erstveröffentlichung, ein dreieckiges Blatt
zu sehen ist. Auf Grund der Dedikation kann man nur an Terra Mater
denken, obzwar man eine solche Darstellung von ihr sonst nirgends findet.
Die meisten Zweifel verursacht die Bestimmung des Gegenstandes, den sie
in der Hand hält. Der Autor der Erstveröffentlichung hielt ihn für einen

---

[74] E. Pašalić, Rolle und Bedeutung der römischen Eisenbergwerke in Westbosnien für den
pannonischen Limes, Studien zu den Militärgrenzen Roms. Vorträge des 6. Int. Limes-
kongr. in Süddeutschland, Köln–Graz 1967, 127ff.

[75] Die neueste Literatur: I. I. Russu, Inscripţii romane din judetul Hunedoara, Sargetia 5,
1968, 92.

[76] CIL III 1284—85, N. Gostar, Studii epigrafice (II), Arch. Mold. 4, 1966, 176.

[77] Liber Pater ist — wie wir es auch über Terra Mater festgestellt haben — in den Donau-
Provinzen beliebt. Drei gemeinsame Altäre kennen wir, auf denen gepaarte Gottheiten
vorkommen, und zweimal sind L. P. und T. M. miteinander verbunden: *IOM ET TERRAE
MATRI LIBERO PAT ET LIBIRE* (!) (A. Dobó, Inscriptiones extra fines Pannoniae
Daciaeque repertae ad res earundem provinciarum pertinentes, Dissert. Pannon. I 1,
Budapest 1940, nr. 450 = 1975, nr. 559), *[IO]M IV[NONI ...] TERRAE MATRI LIBERO
[PAT]* (I. Wellner, Egy aquincumi Terra Mater és Liber Pater-nek dedikált oltárkö feli-
ratához [Zur Inschrift eines der Terra Mater und dem Liber Pater dedizierten Aquincu-
mer Altarsteines. Deutsche Zusammenfassung], Bud. Rég. 23, 1973, 187f.), *IOM IVNONI
REG LIBERO TELLVRI* (ob. Anm. 71).

[78] CIL III 1152, vgl. G. Wissowa, RuKR 281.

[79] CIL III 11009, vgl. CIL VIII 8309.

[80] CIL III 1351 = 7853.

[81] O. Szönyi, Római leletekröl Pécsett, Arch. Ért. 31, 1911, 373. Über diese Frage ausführlicher s. T. Gesztelyi, Eine singuläre Terra Mater-Darstellung aus Sopianae, Acta Class.
Debr. 13, 1977, 45ff.

Spaten, aber sein mannshoher Stiel macht das unwahrscheinlich. Nach einem anderen Vorschlag ist der Gegenstand mit dem Abzeichen des Dolichenus-Kultes verwandt[82]. Völlig unerklärt bleibt aber die Beziehung zwischen der Göttin und dem Dolichenus-Kult. Der neueste Bearbeiter denkt an eine Lanze[83]. Alle Deutungsversuche sind von vornherein unfundiert, da keiner von einer genauen Anschauung des Gegenstandes ausgegangen ist, den die Frauengestalt in ihrer Hand hält, sondern nur von der ungenauen Beschreibung in der Erstveröffentlichung bzw. unter ihrem Einfluß von einer oberflächlichen Untersuchung der Photographie. An der Spitze der Stange befindet sich in Wirklichkeit kein Dreieck, sondern ein Viereck, dessen vierte Seite fehlt, weil sie vom Rahmenstück abgeschnitten ist. Irreführend ist die Zuspitzung der linken unteren Ecke des Vierecks; es ist aber völlig klar, daß es oben nicht in einer Spitze endet, sondern durch eine waagerechte Linie abgeschlossen wird. Als Analogie können wir ähnliche Darstellungen zitieren: die Münz-Serie des Aelius Caesar[84], auf deren Rückseiten eine Frauengestalt in langem Kleid steht, ihren mit einer Mauerkrone geschmückten Kopf zu dem in ihrer rechten Hand gehaltenen *vexillum* hin- oder von ihm weggewendet, mit ihrer linken Hand hält sie auf ihrer Hüfte ihr *pallium*. Die Legende lautet: PANNONIA (Taf. I 2). Die Anwesenheit der Mauerkrone bzw. ihr Fehlen ist vielleicht von keiner entscheidenden Wichtigkeit; die Provinz-Personifikationen der Münzen, die unter Hadrian geprägt wurden, zeigen ja eine sehr abwechslungsreiche Ikonographie[85]. Bei den meisten kommt keine Mauerkrone vor. Da sie das Gebiet, die Erde einer Provinz personifizieren, stehen sie nicht nur inhaltlich, sondern auch ikonographisch den Tellus-Darstellungen am nächsten (eine auf der Erde sitzende Frauengestalt mit Füllhorn und mit Obstkorb usw.). In mehreren Fällen finden wir aber eine stehende Frauengestalt (Italia, Germania, Cappadocia), was im Fall der in der Kaiserzeit entstandenen Personifikationen sehr häufig ist. So weisen die Münzdarstellungen mit dem Altarrelief sowohl in der Form als auch im Inhalt eine Verwandtschaft auf. Was die Zuspitzung der unteren linken Ecke des Abzeichens anbetrifft, bemüht es sich das Schwingen der Fahne wiederzugeben, was auch auf Münzprägungen zu beobachten ist.

Die Konsequenz dieser Deutung ist, daß Terra Mater die verteidigende Göttin der Erde eines gegebenen Gebietes, meist einer Provinz ist[86]. Die Beziehung des Aelius Caesar zur Provinz Pannonia ist bekannt: Er führte

[82] F. LÁNG, Das Dolichenum von Brigetio, Laureae Aquincenses. Memoriae V. Kuzsinszky dedicatae, 2, Budapest 1941 (Dissert. Pannon. II 11) 178, dies wird von P. MERLAT, Jupiter Dolichenus. Essai d'interprétation et de synthèse, Publ. Inst. d'art et d'arch. de l'Univ de Paris 5, Paris 1960, 172f., übernommen.

[83] F. FÜLEP—A. Sz. BURGER, Pécs római kori köemlékei (Die römerzeitlichen Steindenkmäler von Pécs. Ungarisch-deutsch), Dunántúli Dolgozatok (Publicationes Transdanubienses) 7, Pécs 1974, 18f.

[84] BMC III nr. 1919ff.

[85] BMC III, CLXXIVff.

[86] Vgl. WEINSTOCK, o. c. in RE, Sp. 806.

hier 136 mit einer außerordentlichen Vollmacht ausgerüstet gegen die Barbaren einen Krieg[87]. Dies ist die Erklärung dafür, daß die Gestalt der personifizierten Pannonia ein Feldzeichen trägt. Der Zusammenhang zwischen der Erde eines bestimmten Gebietes und den im Interesse ihrer Verteidigung geführten Kriegen kann uns bei dem Verständnis der Terra Mater-Inschriften in Pannonia weiterführen. Erst dieser Zusammenhang gibt uns Antwort auf die Frage, warum die Göttin am *limes* und in erster Linie im Lager der *legio* bzw. *cohors* (Aquincum, Brigetio, Intercisa) vorkommt und warum sie in der Dedikation so oft mit Iuppiter oder mit der capitolinischen Trias verbunden ist.

Die in Rom zum Vorschein gekommenen Denkmäler sind viel bedeutsamer als die bisherigen. Hier kann ein einheitlicher Charakter kaum festgestellt werden, und es gibt keine offizielle Organisation des Kultes. Abgesehen von einer Ausnahme (CIL VI 769) sind alle Inschriften an Terra Mater gerichtet. Am beachtenswertesten ist das auf dem Campo Verano zum Vorschein gekommene Heiligtum, aus dem auch die Kult-Statue ans Tageslicht kam[88] (Taf. II 3). Auf einem lehnenlosen Thron sitzt die Göttin, Ährenkranz und Schleier auf dem Kopf, den Körper mit einem langen Kleid bedeckt, in ihrer Linken eine Fackel, deren gegliederte Stange nur von der Erde bis zum Thron erhalten geblieben ist. Nach der Feststellung von HELBIG ähnelt das Gesicht der Göttin den Porträts der Frauen des iulisch-claudischen Hauses, das Gebäude ist aber später zu datieren. Ursprünglich war vielleicht Antonia als Ceres dargestellt, und in einem sekundären Gebrauch wurde sie zur Kult-Statue der Terra Mater. Wir erfahren also in diesem Fall nicht, wie die Göttin dargestellt wurde, höchstens soviel, was auch sonst klar ist, daß sie Ceres sehr nahe stand. Außerdem ist noch ein Heiligtum von ihr anzunehmen, südlich von den *thermae Antoninianae*, und zwar deshalb, weil hier zwei ihr gewidmete Altäre zum Vorschein kamen[89].

Die früheste Inschrift stammt wahrscheinlich aus der Zeit des Claudius (CIL VI 770); zwei sind in die erste Hälfte des II. Jahrhunderts zu datieren, auf 133[90] bzw. auf den 19. April 142[91]; die übrigen sind wahrscheinlich später. Was das Gesicht der Göttin anbetrifft, so zeugt es von der Bewahrung des agrarischen Charakters der oben erwähnten Statue, sie kann aber genauso auch mit der Unterwelt in Verbindung stehen. Dieser Aspekt der Terra Mater ist nämlich hier am bestimmtesten zu entdecken: zwei Grabaltäre wurden ihr gemeinsam mit den *dei Manes* dediziert[92]. Sie

---

[87] A. MÓCSY, Pannonia, RE Suppl. IX (1962), Sp. 554f.

[88] CIL VI 3731 = ILS 3951. W. HELBIG, Führer durch die öffentlichen Sammlungen klassischer Altertümer in Rom, II⁴, Tübingen 1966, p. 334f. nr. 1521.

[89] CH. HÜLSEN—H. JORDAN, Topographie der Stadt Rom im Altertum, I, 3, Berlin 1907, 197, 37.

[90] CIL VI 31171. M. SPEIDEL, Die equites singulares Augusti, Bonn 1965, 102.

[91] CIL XIV 67. Zwei Tage trennen sie vom Zeitpunkt der Aufstellung der Altäre in Dalmatia.

[92] CIL VI 16398, 20200. Zu diesem Aspekt gehört wahrscheinlich eine neu publizierte Inschrift: H. SOLIN, Epigraphische Untersuchungen in Rom und Umgebung, Helsinki 1975, nr. 2.

kann die eine Region der Welt bedeuten in Fällen, wo neben ihr Caelus bzw. Caelus und Mare stehen[93].

Die Stifter haben meist griechische Namen: Euhodia (CIL VI 84), Merops (CIL XIV 67), Threptus (CIL VI 769), Cerdo (CIL VI 3731). Sowohl bei diesen als auch bei denen mit lateinischem Namen ist es sicher oder wahrscheinlich, daß es sich hier um *liberti* (CIL VI 771, 772) handelt[93a]. Der Kult konnte also kaum eine Beziehung zur Staatsreligion haben, und wahrscheinlich hatte er sogar einen orientalischen Hintergrund.

Noch in einer anderen Gegend Italiens kamen mehrere der Terra Mater geweihten Altäre zum Vorschein, in Venetia und Histria. Der sprechendste unter ihnen ist der aus Aquileia (ILS 3952), der auch von einem Freigelassenen orientalischer Abstammung gemeinsam mit seinem Sohn aufgestellt worden ist. Beide nahmen an der Verwaltung der Stadt teil: Einer von ihnen ist *equ. publ. decurio Aquileiae*, der andere *sevir Aquileiae*. Unter vier Inschriften in Histria handelt es sich bei zweien ebenfalls um eine *libertina* bzw. einen Sklaven mit griechischem Namen[94]; in zwei Fällen lautet die Dedikation Terrae Histriae[95], was deshalb besonders beachtenswert ist, weil man vermuten kann, daß dieser Kult mit dem von Pannonia und Dacia in Verbindung stand, wo die Verehrung der Erde der Provinz auch zu beobachten ist.

Verstreut kamen Inschriften noch in Gallia[96], Hispania[97] und Germania[98] zum Vorschein. Man kann auf Grund dessen keinen beträchtlichen Kult voraussetzen. Zur Restaurierung der verlorengegangenen Kultstatuen kann eine kleine Terra Mater-Darstellung aus Hispania eine wichtige Hilfe geben[99] (Taf. II 4). Eine auf einem Thron sitzende Frauengestalt in einem langen Kleid, deren Arme und Kopf verloren sind, hält in ihrer Linken wahrscheinlich ein Füllhorn, in ihrem Schoß sind Früchte. Dies finden wir bei liegenden Tellus-Darstellungen sowie bei der sitzenden Gestalt der Ara Pacis. Vom Gesichtspunkt der Beurteilung des Inhalts aus, der sich hinter dem Namen der Göttin verbirgt, ist der Umstand kaum eine Nebensache, daß der Dedikant der Statue zugleich auch *genio loci* zwei *genius*-Statuen aufgestellt hat (CIL II 3525—26). Dies ist ein neues Zeichen dafür, daß in Terra Mater eine Schutz-Göttin eines bestimmten Gebiets verehrt wurde, wie es durch die Darstellung des Altars von Sopianae unmißverständlich bewiesen wurde.

---

[93] CIL VI 84 = ILS 3950, CIL VI 31171.

[93a] Vgl. H. SOLIN, Juden und Syrer im westlichen Teil des römischen Reiches. Eine ethnisch-demographische Studie mit besonderer Berücksichtigung der sprachlichen Zustände, unten in diesem Werk (ANRW), Bd. II 29,1, hrsg. v. W. HAASE, Berlin–New York 1982.

[94] JbÖAI 14, 1911, Beiblatt 194ff., Inscr. It. X, I nr. 664.

[95] Inscr. It. X, I nr. 664, CIL V 327 = ILS 3918.

[96] CIL XII 359, 3071, 4140, Gallia 2, 1944, 78 79 nr. 27.

[97] CIL II 2526, 3527.

[98] CIL XIII 8249. E. SCHWERTHEIM, Die Denkmäler orientalischer Gottheiten im römischen Deutschland, Leiden 1974, 28 nr. 28: Terra Mater = Cybele.

[99] A. GARCIA Y BELLIDO, Esculturas romanas de España y Portugal, Madrid 1949, 157f. T. 127.

Auch hinter der oft auftauchenden Magna Mater–Terra Mater-Identifikation müssen wir mehr sehen als eine philosophische Spekulation[100]. Nur so kann die Interpretatio Romana erklärt werden, nach der die germanische Nerthus mit Terra Mater gleich ist (Tac. Germ. 40); denn die rituellen Handlungen, die mit der Statue der Göttin vollzogen wurden — sie wurde auf einem von Kühen gezogenen Wagen ins Wasser getaucht —, können nur auf Magna Mater zurückgeführt werden[101]. In Nordafrika mochten die Kulte von Terra Mater und Magna Mater in einer sehr engen Verbindung miteinander stehen, zumal dort zwei Altäre zum Vorschein gekommen sind, die ihnen beiden und der Aerecura gewidmet waren[102]. Es ist denkbar, daß Augustinus auch hier Erfahrungen gesammelt hat, wenn er folgendermaßen schreibt: *Haec sunt Telluris et Matris Magnae praeclara mysteria, unde omnia referuntur ad mortalia semina et exercendam agriculturam* (c. D. 7,24). Es ist offenbar, daß es sich hier um einen Mysterien-Kult handelt, der im Fall des nordafrikanischen Tellus-Kultes ohnehin anzunehmen war, da er mit dem Kult der Thesmophoroi in Verbindung stand. Es stimmt damit überein, daß die Grundlage ihrer gemeinsamen Verehrung mit dem Ackerbau und der Fruchtbarkeit zusammenhängt. Auch eine Inschrift in Ostia[103] weist auf ihre Verbindung hin. Tellus erscheint auf der Patera von Parabiago neben Magna Mater und Attis (vgl. G. S. R. THOMAS, a. a. O. [ob. Anm. 100]) als Symbol der sich ewig erneuernden Zeit.

Mehrere Denkmäler zeugen ferner davon, daß die Verehrung der Erde im Mithraismus eine Rolle spielte, der die Elemente, aus denen das Weltall gebildet ist, vergötterte und ihnen Verehrung zukommen ließ. Ihre Darstellung folgte der sich in Rom herausbildenden Ikonographie[104]. Tellus wurde aber nicht nur als die Personifikation eines der Elemente dargestellt. Sie wurde auf der Erde liegend, mit einer Schlange, mit der Personifikation der vier Jahreszeiten und mit dem einen Zodiacus haltenden Aion zum Symbol der sich ewig erneuernden Zeit[105].

Die Darstellung der sich in der kaiserlichen Religionspolitik ausbildenden Tellus-Gestalt wurde in der sepulkralen Symbolik sehr verbreitet. Von der Mitte des II. Jahrhunderts an wurden Sarkophage in Rom gebräuchlich, deren Seiten gewöhnlich mit mythologischen Szenen geziert waren. Bei gewissen Bildtypen dieser mythologischen Szenen ist Tellus ein ständiger Begleiter. Hier tritt die Schlange zum erstenmal als Attribut

---

[100] Varro bei Aug. c. D. 7, 24; Lucr. 2, 598ff.; Macr. Sat. 1, 12, 20; 21,8; 23,20; Serv. Georg. 4,64; Aen. 7,136; 10,252. — Zu Magna Mater vgl. unt. in diesem Band (ANRW II 17,2): G. S. R. THOMAS, Magna Mater and Attis.

[101] Vgl. E. BICKEL, Nordisches Stammgut in der römischen Religion, Rh. Mus. 89, 1940, 26f.

[102] CIL VIII 5524, A.E. 1895 nr. 81. Über ihre Verbindung s. Y. ALLAIS, Djemila = Une dédicace à Cybèle, Lib. (Archéol.-Épigr.) 2, 1954, 252ff.

[103] CIL XIV 67, vgl. M. FLORIANI SQUARCAPINO, I culti orientali ad Ostia, Leiden 1962, 9.

[104] F. CUMONT, Textes et monuments figurés relatifs aux mystères de Mithra, Brüssel 1899, 98, 103, 154f., 297ff. M. J. VERMASEREN, Mithraica I. The Mithraeum at S. Maria Capua Vetere, Leiden 1971, 8ff. Brustbild von Tellus. — Zum Mithraskult vgl. unt. in diesem Band (ANRW II 17,3): R. L. GORDON, Mithraism since Franz Cumont.

[105] D. LEVI, o. c. (ob. Anm. 58), 291ff.

1. Terra Mater an einem Altar in Sopianae

2. Pannonia auf Sesterzen des Aelius Caesar

4. Sitzstatue der Terra Mater in Murcia, Spanien

3. Heiligtum für Terra Mater vom Campo Verano, Rom

auf, die ein Symbol der ewigen Erneuerung und Wiedergeburt ist[106]. Ihre Darstellung verlor die symbolische Bedeutung wahrscheinlich bald, und sie diente mit dem neben ihr oft vorkommenden Oceanus und Caelus einfach zur Bezeichnung der Weltregionen[107]. Auch auf den Grabinschriften ist das stereotype Vorkommen des Namens der Göttin in solchen Formeln zu beobachten: *Terra mater me recipit; precor, Tellus, levis ossa tegas* usw.[108]. Vom kultischen Gesichtspunkt aus können wir diesen Formeln nicht viel Bedeutung zuschreiben, aber sie können den sepulkralen Aspekt der Göttin bezeugen, ebenso wie die zwei römischen Grabaltäre (s. ob. Anm. 92).

Anhangsweise können wir über ein an Tellus gerichtetes abergläubisches Gebet sprechen. Die sogenannte 'Precatio terrae'[108a] wurde von der

---

[106] Die Untersuchung eines umfangreichen Tellus-Reliefs von Arrabona (Pannonia Superior), das zu diesem Kreis gehört, s. bei T. GESZTELYI, Tellus-Relief aus Arrabona, Studium II ed. extra ordinem facta, quae opuscula in Conventu indagatorum iuvenum Debreceniensi a. MCMLXX lecta continet, ed. J. VELIKY, Debrecen 1971. Diese Tellus-Darstellung lebt am Ende der Kaiserzeit in der Katakomben-Malerei weiter: M. GUARDUCCI, La morte di Cleopatra nella catacomba della via Latina, Rend. Pont. Ac. Rom. di Arch. 37, 1964—65, 259ff.

[107] Mit der Deutung der Szenen der Sarkophage beschäftigen sich: F. CUMONT, Recherches sur le symbolisme funéraire des Romains, Bibl. archéol. et hist., 35, Paris 1942; A. D. NOCK, Sarcophagi and Symbolism, AJA 50, 1946, 140ff.; M. A. HANFMANN, The Season Sarcophagus in Dumbarton Oaks, Cambridge 1951.

[108] Darüber ausführlicher: B. LIER, Topica carminum sepulcralium Latinorum, Philologus 62, 1903, 586ff.

[108a] Poetae Latini Minores, rec. et emend. AE. BAEHRENS, vol. I, Leipzig 1879, p. 138—140:

PRECATIO TERRAE

Dea sancta Tellus, rerum naturae parens,
Quae cuncta generas et regeneras indidem
Quod sola praestas gentibus uitalia,
Caeli ac maris diua arbitra rerumque omnium,
Per quam silet natura et somnos concipit,   5
Itemque lucem reparas et noctem fugas:
Tu Ditis umbras tegis et inmensum chaos
Ventosque et imbres tempestatesque attines
Et, cum libet, dimittis et misces freta
Fugasque soles et procellas concitas,   10
Itemque, cum uis, hilarem promittis diem.
Tu alimenta uitae tribuis perpetua fide,
Et, cum recesserit anima, in tete refugimus:
Ita, quidquid tribuis, in te cuncta recidunt.
Merito uocaris Magna tu Mater deum,   15
Pietate quia uicisti diuum numina;
Tuque illa uera es gentium et diuum parens,
Sine qua nil maturatur nec nasci potest:
Tu es Magna tuque diuum regina es, dea.
Te, diua, adoro tuumque ego numen inuoco,   20
Facilisque praestes hoc mihi quod te rogo;
Referamque gratis, diua, tibi merita fide.
Exaudi me, quaeso, et faue coeptis meis;
Hoc quod peto a te, diua, mihi praesta uolens.
Herbas, quascumque generat maiestas tua,   25

Tradition dem Antonius Musa zugeschrieben, der der Arzt des Augustus war; dies wird aber durch mehrere Ausdrücke (z. B. *maiestas tua*) ausgeschlossen. Durch einen Autor von gutem Rufe und durch Briefe, die an Maecenas, Agrippa und Augustus gerichtet und neben die 'Precatio' gestellt waren, wollte man die Glaubwürdigkeit eines botanischen Buches (Ps.-Musa, De herba uettonica) steigern. Hier handelt es sich in Wirklichkeit um ein Werk aus der späten Kaiserzeit[109].

Der Teil, in dem die Macht der Tellus gerühmt wird, knüpft eng an schon bekannte Vorgänger an, ein Vergleich mit jenen bietet aber auch viele Neuigkeiten. Die Anrede zeugt von einer neuartigen und späten Entstehung: *dea sancta Tellus*. Wir treffen Ähnliches nur auf einer Inschrift aus der späten Kaiserzeit: *deae sanctissimae Terrae matri* (CIL VI 771). Neben den traditionellen Aufgaben (*cuncta generas, praestas vitalia*) steht noch die, *diva arbitra* des Himmels und des Meeres zu sein. Die Göttin ist also hier eine Herrscherin aller Regionen. Mit einem so breiten, sich über die ganze Welt ausdehnenden Machtbereich wurden nur die größten Götter in den Hymnen ausgezeichnet. Tellus sichert die Ordnung der Natur, den Wechsel von Tag und Nacht, die Trennung der Unterwelt und des Chaos von der Oberwelt. Von den beiden anderen Elementen (*aqua, aer*) spricht auch Plinius, aber deshalb, weil er deren gefährlichen Äußerungen (*imber, grandines, fluctus, nubes, procellae)* die wohltätigen Wirkungen der Tellus gegenüberstellen will. Aus der Eigenschaft einer *caeli ac maris diva arbitra* ('Precatio terrae') folgt dagegen, daß Tellus Herrin über Wasser und Luft ist, die Winde, Regengüsse und Stürme (*ventos, imbres, tempestates*) zurückhalten, aber auch entlassen kann, damit sie das Meer aufrühren und die Sonne verdunkeln; wenn sie will, kann sie andererseits auch eine glänzende Sonne sichern. Diese Erde ist eine fürchterliche Kraft; sie kann gleichmäßig Gutes und Schlechtes tun, ein Gebet um ihr Wohlwollen ist also nötig. (Bei Plinius teilt sie ihren Segen mit einer uneingeschränkten Geduld aus, höchstens wird er vom Menschen zu eigener Gefahr verkehrt.) Die Betonung fällt hier allerdings auf ihre Segnungen: *alimenta vitae tribuis perpetua fide* (bei Plinius: *bona fide*). Ähnlich wie Lukrez kommt der Autor der 'Precatio' zu einer Identifikation mit Magna Mater, worin er ihrer *pietas*, die allen anderen Göttern vorgeht, eine Rolle

> *Salutis causa tribuis cunctis gentibus:*
> *Hanc nunc mihi permittas medicinam tuam.*
> *Veniat medicina cum tuis uirtutibus:*
> *Quidque ex his fecero, habeat euentum bonum,*   29
> *Cuique easdem dedero quique easdem a me acceperint,*
> *Sanos eos praestes. denique nunc, diua, hoc mihi*
> *Maiestas praestet tua, quod te supplex rogo.*

Text mit kurzer *adnotatio critica* auch bei R. HEIM, Incantamenta magica Graeca Latina, Jahrbb. f. class. Philol., hrsg. v. A. FLECKEISEN, Suppl. XIX, Leipzig 1893, 504f.

[109] G. SWARZENSKI, Mittelalterliche Kopien einer antiken medizinischen Bilderhandschrift, JDAI 17, 1902, 47; M. SCHANZ—C. HOSIUS, Geschichte der römischen Literatur, II[4], München 1935 (Nachdr. ebd. 1967), 395f.

zuschreibt. Auch der Abschluß des hymnischen Teils enthält eine ungewöhnliche Bezeichnung: *divum regina*.

Der kürzere Rest des Textes ist die Bitte. Hier lernen wir einen ganz neuen Aspekt der Tellus kennen: Die Person, die mit Heilpflanzen heilen will, bittet um die Hilfe der die Heilpflanzen hervorbringenden Erde, damit ihre Behandlung einen Erfolg hat[110]. Das Streben nach der peinlichen Gründlichkeit (*cuique easdem dedero quique easdem a me acceperint*), die mehrmalige Wiederholung der Bitte (*adoro, invoco, rogo, quaeso, peto, supplex peto*) und der Aufforderung zur Hilfe (*praestes, exaudi, fave, praesta, permittas*) fällt in die Augen. Diese Erscheinungen weisen darauf hin, daß man um die Wirksamkeit des Gebets sehr besorgt war, daß es zu einem praktischen Zweck diente und ein echter kultischer Text ist.

Der Kodex aus dem XI. Jahrhundert, der den Text aufbewahrt hat, illustriert auch das Gebet: Vor einem Mann, der auf's Knie fällt, sitzt Tellus in einem langen Gewand, zu ihren Füßen befindet sich eine Schlange, in ihrer Rechten ein Füllhorn. Es ist kaum zu bezweifeln, daß die Darstellung einem antiken Muster folgt. Die Göttin hat die bei den Kultstatuen übliche sitzende Haltung mit den bekannten Attributen inne.

VI. Zusammenfassung

Obwohl die Anzahl der Quellen, die sich auf Tellus–Terra Mater beziehen, nicht groß ist, ein beträchtlicher Teil von ihnen wortkarg ist und deswegen wenig über die Göttin verrät, erschließt sich uns doch, wenn wir alles ins Auge fassen, ein reiches, vielfarbiges Bild. Im Blick darauf stellt sich heraus, daß die Ansicht unzutreffend ist, eine in Rom einst mächtige Tellus-Göttin sei zunehmend in den Hintergrund gedrängt worden. Tellus war von Anfang an eine wichtige Gottheit der Lebenserhaltung. Diese Rolle hat sie auch weiterhin beibehalten, aber ihre Bedeutung hat sich gewandelt[111]. Ihre philosophische Interpretation in der späten Republik und ihre Rolle in der Religionspolitik der Kaiserzeit übersteigt weit den ursprünglichen Rahmen ihres Wirkungskreises. Potenziell ist sie wirklich die mächtigste weibliche Göttin, dies wurde aber nie realisiert, weil sie nicht ein natürliches Produkt des Glaubens war. In der privaten Religiosität fand sie nur dort einen Widerhall, wo die Tradition oder die momentane Aktualität ihr eine größere Rolle gab, als diejenige war, die sie in der alten römischen Religion erfüllt hat.

Der Name der Göttin war ursprünglich nur Tellus, und sie stand nur mit dem Ackerbau in Verbindung. In der Kaiserzeit ist kein inhaltlicher

---

[110] Ihre Heilpflanzen bringende Rolle wird auch von Plinius erwähnt (s. Anm. 25).

[111] Zu dieser Feststellung gelangt LE BONNIEC, o. c. 456 (ob. Anm. 10) im Fall des Kultes von Ceres

Unterschied zwischen den Namen Tellus und Terra Mater festzustellen, das Gesicht der Göttin ist aber nicht einheitlich. Sie bedeutet etwas anderes für die Philosophie, für die Theologie, für die kaiserliche Propaganda und für die Bewohner der Provinzen in Nordafrika oder an der Donau. Ihre Verbindung mit dem Ackerbau bleibt durchweg bestehen, daneben wird sie aber mit bestimmten Gebieten identifiziert, was in der privaten Religiosität eine Bedeutung hatte, oder mit dem ganzen Erdkreis, was in der kaiserlichen Religionspolitik eine wichtige Rolle spielte. Ihre Bedeutung und ihre Möglichkeiten waren immer durch ihre Erdgebundenheit bestimmt.

Abbildungsverzeichnis

I 1: Terra Mater an einem Altar in Sopianae. — Janus Pannonius-Museum, Pécs. F. FÜLER—A. Sz. BURGER, Die römerzeitlichen Steindenkmäler von Pécs, Pécs 1974, Taf. V/2.

2: Pannonia auf Sesterzen des Aelius Caesar. — BMC III, pl. 100/7, 101/5.

II 3: Heiligtum für Terra Mater vom Campo Verano, Rom. — Rom, Capitol, Konservatorenpalast. Photo DAI Rom. Vgl. ob. Anm. 88.

4: Sitzstatue der Terra Mater in Murcia, Spanien. — Museo Arqueológico de Murcia. Photo DAI Madrid. Vgl. ob. Anm. 99.

Mercure romain, les 'Mercuriales' et l'institution du culte impérial sous le Principat augustéen

par B. Combet Farnoux, Nice

Table des matières

Introduction

L'étude du Mercurius romain pose un problème initial qui tient à deux éléments correspondant à deux traditions d'origine différente. D'une part l'iconographie nous présente un personnage divin bien typé, identifiable par des traits et des emblèmes caractéristiques: une silhouette juvénile souvent drapée dans une courte chlamyde, le caducée dans une main, le pétase ailé comme couvre-chef, des ailettes fixées aux chevilles ou aux sandales font reconnaître la transposition romaine de l'Hermès hellénique. D'un autre côté, la tradition latine littéraire et le matériel épigraphique nous ont transmis un nom divin Mercurius d'allure fonctionnelle, à la manière de tant de divinités latines archaïques, dont la personnalité indécise se définit essentiellement par un mode d'action. Cette dénomination suggère la spécialisation du dieu dans la sphère des intérêts mercantiles et des activités marchandes[1].

Pour préciser la vocation première, saisir en quoi consiste la spécificité du dieu romain, la difficulté tient à la nature de la documentation à notre disposition: non pas que ce matériel documentaire nous induise en incertitude par sa pauvreté, mais bien plutôt sa diversité a contribué égarer l'enquête sur des voies divergentes. Certes pour l'époque républicaine nous sont parvenues seulement des indications éparses procurées par la tradition annalistique, mais ces notices brèves sont significatives. Les deux plus anciennes transmises par Tite-Live relatent la date et les circonstances de la fondation de l'*aedes Mercurii* en 495 av. J.-C.[2]. D'autres font ultérieurement mention de la participation de Mercure associé à Neptune aux cinq célébrations du lectisterne organisées au IV° siècle, de 399 à 326 av. J.-C., selon le modèle institué en 399[3], cérémonie caractéristique du *ritus graecus*. Un passage de Tite-Live rapporte encore la présence de Mercure accolé cette fois à Cérès au lectisterne des douze grands dieux, célébré selon une formule élargie et renouvelée en 217 av. J.-C., après la défaite de Trasimène[4].

---

[1] Sur 'Mercure romain' on peut consulter: G. Wissowa, Religion und Kultus der Römer, 2° éd., Hb. d. klass. Altertumswiss., IV,5, Munich, 1912 (R.K.R.), p. 304 sq.; Steuding, Art. Mercurius, dans: W. H. Roscher, Ausführl. Lex. der griech. u. röm. Mythologie II, 2, Leipzig, 1894−97, réimpr. Hildesheim, 1965, col. 2805 sq.; W. Kroll, dans: Art. Mercurius, R.E., XV, 1, 1931, col. 975 sq.; K. Latte, Römische Religionsgeschichte, Handbuch d. Altertumswiss., V, 4, Munich, 1960, p. 162−163; G. Radke, Die Götter Altitaliens, Fontes et Commentationes, 3, Münster, 1965, s. v. Mercurius, p. 213 sq.; B. Combet Farnoux, Mercure romain. Le culte public de Mercure et la fonction mercantile à Rome de la République archaïque à l'époque augustéenne, B.E.F.A.R., 238, Rome, 1980.

[2] Liv., II,21,7: . . . *Aedes Mercuri dedicata est idibus Maiis*. Liv., II,27,5−7: *Certamen consulibus inciderat, uter dedicaret Mercuri aedem. Senatus a se rem ad populum reiecit: utri eorum dedicatio iussu populi data esset, eum praeesse annonae, mercatorum collegium instituere, sollemnia pro pontifice iussit suscipere. 6− Populus dedicationem aedis dat M. Laetorio, primi pili centurioni, quod facile appareret non tam ad honorem eius cui curatio altior fastigio suo data esset factum quam ad consulum ignominiam. 7− Saeuire inde utique consulum alter patresque* . . .

[3] Liv. V,13,5−8. VII,2,1−2. VII,27,1. VIII,25,1.

[4] Liv., XXII,10,9: *Tum lectisternium per triduum habitum, decemuiris sacrorum curantibus. Sex puluinaria in conspectu fuerunt: Ioui ac Iunoni unum, alterum Neptuno ac Mineruae, tertium Marti ac Veneri, quartum Apollini ac Dianae, quintum Vulcano ac Vestae, sextum Mercurio et Cereri.*

Mais à partir de la fin de la République, et de l'époque augustéenne, le matériel documentaire se révèle divers et abondant, il comporte de fréquentes références littéraires, de nombreuses dédicaces épigraphiques et une grande variété de représentations iconographiques, telles des peintures pompéiennes, des effigies procurées par les arts plastiques, et de nombreuses statuettes votives témoignant de la piété populaire.

Cependant l'analyse des données littéraires, épigraphiques et iconographiques fournies par ce matériel documentaire relativement tardif, a abouti à des résultats décevants, faute de mettre en œuvre, pour l'interpréter correctement, une définition précise de la fonction essentielle de l'homologue latin d'Hermès dans son domaine romain[5]. Ni l'état d'une documentation hétérogène, ni les résultats des travaux antérieurs ne suggèrent d'emblée un fil directeur pour saisir la spécificité du Mercurius romain. Depuis l'essai de FRANZ ALTHEIM qui date de 1930[6], aucune étude d'ensemble n'a plus été esquissée sur le problème du Mercure romain. Certes la recherche n'est pas demeurée inactive, et des documents figurés ou épigraphiques révélés au hasard des fouilles ou des inventaires de collections ont donné lieu à des publications de détail propres à expliciter, valoriser un aspect ou une attribution du dieu, mais par la force des choses, ces essais d'interprétation d'un matériel fragmentaire détaché le plus souvent de son contexte général, se réclament d'explications anciennes.

Selon les cas, se référant à la multiplicité des aspects du personnage de l'Hermès-Mercurius, les commentateurs ont mis en vedette plus particulièrement l'un ou l'autre. Certains, prenant, non sans raison, au pied de la lettre la relation du vocable *Mercurius* avec *merx*, *mercator*, ont retenu et mis en avant le rôle de patron des marchands et des voleurs, entendu comme dispensateur de profit monétaire, de richesse, voire de fécondité. D'autres plus sensibles à la diversité de l'Hermès hellénique, ont cherché un principe d'explication du côté de la fonction de psychopompe, impliquant des attaches avec le monde souterrain, et des affinités chthoniennes[7]. Enfin toute une lignée érudite depuis Varron, se référant à l'Hermès Λόγιος hellénistique, a incliné à faire de Mercure le dieu de la parole et du discours, le Λόγος, principe divin d'action bienfaisante à l'œuvre à travers l'Univers, en conformité avec la théologie stoïcienne[8].

---

[5] Dans le domaine grec la recherche des origines d'Hermès a également nui à la cohérence du personnage du dieu, en privilégiant tour à tour parmi ses fonctions multiples, celle qui tenue momentanément pour la plus ancienne, apparaissait au gré des hypothèses, la plus apte à rendre compte de l'ensemble de ses figures et de ses rôles. Cf. L. KAHN, Hermès passe ou les ambiguïtés de la communication, Paris, 1978, p. 9−19. Cet essai neuf en rendant leur unité aux grands thèmes du mythe d'Hermès qui inspirent l'Hymne homérique à Hermès, dégage sa fonction première de dieu du passage, de la communication. Cette analyse pertinente montre que s'attachent initialement à cette fonction les pouvoirs que met en œuvre à Rome Mercure au niveau du sacré, à l'occasion de sa prise en charge de la *merx*: pouvoir de désacralisation, puissance de lier et délier, action de médiation.

[6] F. ALTHEIM, Griechische Götter im alten Rom, Religionsgeschichtl. Versuche und Vorarb., 22, 1, Gießen, 1930, p. 39−93.

[7] P. RAINGEARD, Hermès psychagogue. Essai sur les origines du culte d'Hermès, Paris, 1935.

[8] Aug., Ciu., VII,14. Varro, ed. AGAHD, Antiquitatum rerum diuinarum lib. XVI,30−31:

La simple compilation d'un matériel documentaire abondant, ordonné selon des rubriques correspondant aux attributions traditionnelles et hétérogènes d'Hermès-Mercure, ne procure pas le moyen de saisir la spécificité du dieu romain, ni ne suffit à élucider sa raison d'être et le principe de sa fonction. Les interprétations traditionnelles certes, ne sont pas erronées à proprement parler, elles sont partielles parce que s'inspirant d'aspects particuliers, — voire secondaires — du dieu, elles manquent à retrouver le principe d'unité propre à rendre compte d'un personnage divin multiple et divers. La croyance populaire, les influences helléniques, l'apport des mythographes hellénistiques, les compilations des ʿantiquairesʾ romains, et les spéculations des érudits ont pu valoriser certains aspects du dieu, mais ce sont variations en marge d'un thème procuré par le culte public romain.

Pour atteindre le principe d'explication qui nous permettra de discerner plus précisément l'originalité du Mercurius romain, en particulier par rapport à son prototype hellénique Hermès, il convient de chercher du côté du culte public instauré en 495 av. J.-C., sur l'initiative des autorités de l'*Urbs*, à l'*aedes Mercurii ad Circum Maximum*, et des *sacra publica* de cette *religio* officielle, propres à manifester l'efficacité du dieu en conformité avec la fonction première qui avait déterminé son adoption par l'Etat romain.

I. Origine et fonction première du Mercure romain

La dédicace de l'*aedes Mercurii* relatée par la tradition annalistique à la date des Ides de Mai 495 av. J.-C.[9], correspond à l'adoption d'un culte nouveau. Aucune référence annalistique, aucun recueil érudit compilé par les grammairiens et les ʿantiquairesʾ de la fin de la République, pour rassembler des faits et des usages archaïques, n'a gardé le souvenir d'une dévotion à Mercure remontant aux temps primitifs de Rome. La *religio* de Mercure n'a pas place dans le calendrier de Numa, elle ne se rattache pas au noyau originel des plus anciens dieux romains, ni ne s'intègre aux cycles rituels archaïques essentiellement agraires et guerriers, aucun flamine n'était affecté à son service.

Comme l'attestent ses plus anciennes effigies, Mercurius était la transposition latine de l'Hermès grec: le nom est romain certes, mais le personnage divin est grec, ce n'est pas le produit d'un processus d'hellénisation qui aurait prêté à une antique puissance divine latine les apparences et les traits de l'Hermès grec.

Mercurium uero et Martem sermocinandi et belligerandi administros . . . Ideo Mercurius quasi medius currens dicitur appellatus, quod sermo currat inter homines medius: ideo Ἑρμῆς *Graece, quod sermo uel interpretatio, quae ad sermonem utique pertinet,* ἑρμηνεία *dicitur; ideo et mercibus praeesse, quia inter uendentes et ementes sermo fit medius; alas eius in capite et pedibus significare uolucrem ferri per aera sermonem; nuntium dictum, quoniam per sermonem omnia cogitata enuntiantur.*

[9] Liv., II,21,7. Supra note 2.

Avant Apollon reçu officiellement en 431 av. J.-C., c'est le premier dieu proprement grec, dont l'adoption par la puissance publique soit attestée à Rome par la tradition annalistique à la charnière des VI° et V° siècles, dans la période de crise et de renouvellement qui correspond à l'instauration de la République, consécutive à la Révolution de 509.

Le *ritus graecus* s'est ordonné autour des trois divinités d'origine grecque honorées à Rome dès le V° siècle, Apollon, Hercule et Mercure. Le lectisterne de 399, la première grande cérémonie du *ritus graecus*, rapportée par la tradition annalistique, organisée selon un dispositif qui fut repris à chacune des célébrations ultérieures du IV° siècle, l'atteste clairement[10]: ces trois dieux y font figure de chefs de file, et chacun constitue l'élément significatif des trois couples étendus sur les *puluinaria*. Les divinités qui leur étaient adjointes sont moins caractéristiques, et leur participation à une cérémonie du *ritus graecus* tire son sens de leur association avec un de ces dieux. De ces trois dieux helléniques qui conféraient au lectisterne sa signification et sa portée, Mercure était le plus ancien à avoir été reçu dans le culte public romain à l'aube du V° siècle.

1. L'*aedes Mercurii* et la vocation mercantile du quartier du Grand Cirque

Le siège du culte de Mercure à Rome était l'*aedes Mercurii*, le sanctuaire fondé en 495 av. J.-C.; nous en connaissons l'existence seulement par le témoignage des textes, il n'en subsiste point de ruines, et l'archéologie n'a mis au jour aucun vestige significatif[11]. Seules les données procurées par des textes littéraires nous permettent de situer l'*aedes Mercurii* aux abords du Circus Maximus[12]. Le recoupement de ces diverses indications topographiques nous fournit le moyen de préciser la position du sanctuaire romain de Mercure: il se trouvait hors du *pomerium*[13], il faisait face au Cirque, c'est-à-dire son *pronaos* était orienté dans cette direction, et il dominait les *metae Murciae* qui marquaient l'extrémité Sud-Est de la *spina* de l'hippodrome. L'*aedes Mercurii* s'élevait donc au pied ou à mi-pente de l'Aventin, tournant le dos à la colline, au-dessus de l'extrémité méri-

---

[10] Liv., V,13,6: *Duumuiri sacris faciundis, lectisternio tunc primum in urbe Romana facto, per dies octo Apollinem Latonamque et Dianam, Herculem, Mercurium atque Neptunum tribus quam amplissime tum apparari poterat stratis lectis placauere.*

[11] F. Castagnoli, Topografia e urbanistica di Roma antica, Ist. di Studi Romani, 2° éd., Bologne, 1969, p. 75; G. Lugli, Fontes ad topographiam ueteris Urbis Romae pertinentes, VIII (Lib. XIX—XX), Univ. di Roma Ist. di Topografia antica, Rome, 1962, p. 366, n° 425 et 425 a.

[12] Ovide, Fasti, V,669—670:

> *Templa tibi posuere patres spectantia Circum*
> *Idibus: ex illo est haec tibi festa dies.*

Apulée, Métam., VI,8,2: *Si quis a fuga retrahere uel occultam demonstrare poterit fugitiuam regis filiam, Veneris ancillam, nomine Psychen, conueniat retro metas Murtias Mercurium praedicatorem* . . .

[13] G. Wissowa, R.K.R., p. 304, note 5; K. Latte, Römische Religionsgeschichte, p. 162—163.

dionale du Grand Cirque. De ce fait, le sanctuaire ne relevait pas proprement de l'Aventin − appartenance dont on avait parfois hâtivement déduit d'éventuelles affinités plébéiennes de la *religio* de Mercure −, il était en marge de la colline, et apparaît davantage comme situé dans l'orbite du Cirque, ainsi qu'en témoignent les auteurs anciens qui ont fait état de repères topographiques propres à déterminer son emplacement *ad Circum Maximum*.

Quant à la disposition générale, à l'architecture et à l'importance de l'édifice, aucune donnée de fait ne nous apporte d'indice positif. Nos sources documentaires nous mettent en mesure cependant d'établir un point essentiel en fixant avec précision la localisation du sanctuaire qui se trouvait en relation directe avec la dépression du Grand Cirque, la 'Vallis Murcia', et le Forum Boarium. Le choix de cet emplacement est significatif, car il est tout empreint d'affinités avec la fonction mercantile prise en charge par le dieu dès la fondation de son sanctuaire romain: il associe les débuts de la *religio* du Mercure romain à la liaison terrestre réalisée par les Etrusques avec leurs possessions campaniennes au temps où leur expansion imprima son premier essor au rôle de marché et de relais, et à la fonction d'échange du site de Rome à la croisée du fleuve et de la route de terre.

La vocation mercantile ancienne du Forum Boarium[14] avait été préparée par le précédent des foires au bétail qui attiraient les populations pastorales du voisinage, elle était servie par les avantages de la position au passage du Tibre, et au débouché des dépressions qui donnaient accès vers l'intérieur et vers le Sud, elle fut confirmée et valorisée par la présence étrusque. C'est au VI° siècle que le pont du Tibre et le port primitif installé sur les berges du fleuve entre la Porta Trigemina et la Porte Carmentalis[15] conférèrent au marché et au carrefour leur importance[16]. La vallée du Cirque drainée et aménagée par les Tarquins[17] ouvrait le chemin du Midi, or c'est précisément à l'extrémité Sud-Est de la Vallis Murcia que s'éleva l'*aedes Mercurii*, proche de la Porte Capène au-delà de laquelle bifurquaient les deux tracés de la route de Campanie, la Via Latina par l'intérieur, et l'itinéraire du littoral, la future Via Appia[18].

L'adoption du culte de Mercure à Rome apparaît inséparable dans le temps des transformations des structures socio-économiques et mentales imprimées à l'*urbs* par la présence étrusque. A cet égard, la découverte sur le site de Portonaccio d'une effigie d'Hermès, connu en Etrurie sous le nom de 'Turms', en association avec le groupe de terre-cuite de l'Apollon de Véies, suggère un rapprochement. Dès 1930, frappé par l'intérêt de ce document significatif, FRANZ ALTHEIM, dans une étude qui apportait beaucoup d'idées neuves mêlées à des vues parfois hasardeuses, 'Griechische Götter im alten Rom', s'efforça de démontrer le caractère proprement étrusque du Mercure romain. Son essai de dé-

---

[14] F. CASTAGNOLI, Op. cit., p. 159.

[15] J. LE GALL, Le Tibre fleuve de Rome dans l'antiquité, Publ. de l'Inst. d'Art. & d'Archéol. de l'Univ. de Paris, 1, Paris, 1953, p. 93 sq.; F. CASTAGNOLI, Op. cit., p. 71.

[16] J. LE GALL, Op. cit., p. 49, p. 53.

[17] F. CASTAGNOLI, Op. cit., p. 17.

[18] F. COARELLI, Guida archeologica di Roma, 2° éd., Milan, 1975, p. 21, p. 281.

monstration dans le cas d'Hermès-Mercure illustrait le thème général de son étude: les dieux d'origine hellénique reçus à Rome au début du V° siècle av. J.-C. auraient été transmis aux Latins par l'intermédiaire des Etrusques. Mercure serait certes bien une transposition de l'Hermès grec, mais assimilé au préalable par l'Etrurie, et ce sont les conquérants étrusques qui l'auraient fait connaître à Rome[19].

Le groupe coroplastique de l'Apollon de Véies lui apparaissait comme une preuve décisive confirmant la puissance de l'influence hellénique en Etrurie non seulement sur le plan artistique, mais aussi dans le domaine du sacré. Il ne s'agissait pas de produits d'arts mineurs, mais de statuaire monumentale exécutée par l'école de Vulca pour un sanctuaire étrusque. Comme on a retrouvé parmi les débris du groupe de terre-cuite les effigies d'Apollon et d'Hermès-Mercure, F. ALTHEIM concluait que ces divinités étaient connues des Etrusques, et qu'au temps où elles furent représentées, c'est-à-dire dans le dernier quart du VI° siècle av. J.-C., avant qu'elles fussent adoptées à Rome, elles étaient déjà l'objet d'un culte en Etrurie méridionale[20].

Cette conclusion était trop absolue, certes l'influence grecque en Etrurie et en Italie centrale est amplement démontrée dans la production artistique, et à cet égard, la recherche archéologique récente a confirmé l'apport hellénique avec la mise au jour à Rome et à Lavinium d'effigies de type grec d'Athéna-Minerve et d'Hercule datables du dernier quart du VI siècle av. J.-C.[21]. La statue de l'Apollon de Véies, pas plus que la tête d'Hermès-Mercure, n'était pas une image de culte. Façonnée certes par l'atelier de Vulca, elle n'avait pas la même destination que la statue de Jupiter réalisée dans le même temps pour le sanctuaire capitolin. Le groupe coroplastique de Véies illustrait un épisode mythologique: Apollon chassant la biche cérynienne qu'il disputait à Héraklès en présence d'Hermès-Mercure et d'Artémis-Diane[22]. Le groupe, dont les éléments devaient être alignés sur le faîte de l'édifice[23], avait valeur décorative, il n'atteste pas que le sanctuaire de Portonaccio abritait à la fin du VI° siècle av. J.-C. un culte grec d'importation rendu à des divinités helléniques tels Apollon et Hermès.

En fait, dans le même contexte étrusco-italique, à la charnière des VI° et V° siècles av. J.-C., nous trouvons le même personnage divin de l'Hermès hellénique en Etrurie sous le nom de Turms, et à Rome avec la qualification de Mercurius qui implique une vocation fonctionnelle. Ce parallélisme dans l'espace et dans le temps devait refléter des affinités profondes dans la mesure où la *merx,* la relation mercantile, assumée à Rome par Hermès sous la dénomination de Mer-

---

[19] F. ALTHEIM, Op. cit., p. 40, p. 72, p. 92—93.

[20] F. ALTHEIM, Op. cit., p. 39—40.

[21] A. SOMMELLA MURA, La decorazione architettonica del tempio arcaico, Parola del passato, 32, 1977, p. 62—128; F. CASTAGNOLI, Roma arcaica e i recenti scavi di Lavinio, Parola del passato, 32, 1977, p. 340—355.

[22] A. ANDRÉN, Architectural Terracottas from Etrusco-Italic Temples, Skrifter utg. av Svenska Inst. i Rom, 6, Text, Lund—Leipzig, 1940, p. 3—4; M. SANTANGELO, Veio, santuario di Apollo (Scavi tra il 1948 et il 1949), Bollettino d'arte, 27, 1952, p. 147—172.

[23] A. ANDRÉN, Op. cit., p. 4; M. RENARD, Les socles kalyptères du temple de l'Apollon à Véies, Latomus, 8, 1949, p. 19—29.

curius, était un mode d'échange de type nouveau, lié aux structures urbaines, dont Rome se dota à partir du VI° siècle av. J.-C., sous l'impulsion de la dynastie étrusque. F. ALTHEIM, en attribuant à l'Etrurie le rôle d'intermédiaire dans l'introduction d'Hermès à Rome[24], avait eu une intuition de départ féconde, mais il en limita la portée, et égara son étude sur des voies hasardeuses en perdant de vue que Rome était également redevable à l'Etrurie de l'adoption de la fonction mercantile, dont Hermès romain fut investi en même temps qu'il était reçu sur les rives du Tibre. Pour expliciter l'adoption de la *religio* d'Hermès-Mercurius à Rome dans ce temps, c'est l'examen du nom divin Mercurius qui nous procure le moyen le plus approprié pour définir et préciser la fonction première du dieu.

2. *Nomen Mercurii*

FRANZ ALTHEIM s'était ingénié à prouver que le nom divin Mercurius était d'origine étrusque. Déjà WILHELM SCHULZE s'était efforcé d'établir que les noms, qui en latin s'achèvent par le suffixe *-urius*, sont en relation avec des formes étrusques en u[25]. En fait cette éventualité doit être envisagée avec prudence, car les exemples allégués par W. SCHULZE n'apportent point de preuve décisive, ni ne fondent de règle générale.

Or FRANZ ALTHEIM non seulement tint pour acquise l'origine étrusque du suffixe *-urius,* mais encore entreprit de démontrer que le radical *merc-* était également étrusque. Cependant un obstacle apparemment insurmontable fermait la voie à l'attribution d'une origine étrusque au nom divin Mercurius: en Etrurie, la représentation de l'équivalent d'Hermès, sur les documents figurés est pourvue d'un nom étrusque bien attesté, 'Turms'. F. ALTHEIM n'ignorait certes pas cette difficulté, il la tourna au moyen d'une explication ingénieuse et subtile. Considérant que Mercurius était constitué sur le modèle des gentilices d'origine étrusque Titurius, Mamurius, Veturius, il concluait que c'était une forme gentilice étrusque composée à partir d'un radical étrusque *mercu-* complété du suffixe étrusque *-urius.* Mercurius aurait été le dieu d'une *gens Mercuria* ou *Mercuvia,* comme le 'deus Domitius' était le dieu propre à la *gens Domitia*[26].

Cette interprétation qui se fonde sur des analogies fragiles plus que sur des preuves irréfutables est encore acceptée par plusieurs érudits[27]. Cependant le point de vue de F. ALTHEIM n'est plus reçu unanimement comme une opinion

---

[24] F. ALTHEIM, Op. cit., p. 40, p. 71—72, p. 93.

[25] W. SCHULZE, Zur Geschichte lateinischer Eigennamen, Abh. d. kgl. Gesellschaft der Wiss. Göttingen, phil.-hist. Kl., NF 5, 5, Berlin, 1904 (Réimpr. 1966), p. 401 sq.

[26] F. ALTHEIM, Op. cit., p. 44.

[27] A. WALDE, J.-B. HOFMANN, Lateinisches etymologisches Wörterbuch, Idg. Bibl. I. Abt., 2. Reihe Wörterbücher, I, 3° éd., Heidelberg, 1954, II (M—Z), p. 74, s. v. Mercurius; F. BÖMER, Ovidius Naso, Die Fasten, Heidelberg, 1957—1958, II. (Kommentar), p. 331; G. RADKE, Die Götter Altitaliens, p. 213—216, s. v. Mercurius.

sûre[28], et même si Mercurius a des affinités étrusques, l'idée d'une relation avec la *merx* a raisonnablement prévalu.

Plus habituellement, les modernes ont été portés à tenir pour fondée la relation entre Mercurius et *merx*, et ont rattaché le nom du dieu à la racine *merc-*[29]. Déjà l'érudition latine avait esquissé le rapprochement entre le dieu Mercurius et la *merx*[30]. D'une façon générale, la recherche récente a reconnu la parenté du nom divin de l'homologue d'Hermès à Rome avec les substantifs *merx, mercatura, mercator*, et avec le verbe *mercari*[31], qui se rapportent à l'exercice des activités marchandes et des échanges mercantiles sur lesquels le dieu étendait sa protection particulière. Le nom divin Mercurius apparaît comme une forme adjective employée originellement en épithète à *deus*, composée à partir du radical *merc-*, à l'instar du vocable *merx*, et du verbe *mercari*[32]. Le terme *merx* avait deux significations, l'une concrète, l'autre abstraite. Au sens concret il désignait toute espèce de marchandise, objet de négoce, concept abstrait il définissait les relations commerciales, l'échange mercantile[33]. L'origine du terme *mers, merx-mercis*, reste obscure, et les tentatives des philologues pour rendre compte de sa formation n'ont abouti à aucun résultat satisfaisant, l'étymologie de *merx* nous échappe[34].

Mercurius originellement n'est pas un nom propre, c'est une forme adjective, qui employée initialement en épithète à *deus* définissait un aspect particulier de la puissance divine à l'œuvre dans le domaine neuf des trafics et des actes de commerce. Dans l'usage courant, on dut très tôt sous-entendre le substantif, et Mercurius prit valeur de nom propre désignant le personnage divin. Pour caractériser le *deus Mercurius*, l'élément signifiant n'était pas la désinence *-urius* propre à suggérer une éventuelle affinité étrusque, mais la racine *merc-*, qui implique les attaches du dieu avec la relation mercantile, et les activités marchandes.

Cette racine *merc-* n'est pas proprement latine, elle a été empruntée, comme l'a observé E. BENVENISTE: «. . . il n'y a pas en indo-européen de mots communs pour désigner le commerce et les commerçants; il y a seulement des mots isolés, propres à certaines langues, de formation peu claire, qui sont passés d'un peuple à l'autre»[35]. On ne sait à quel rameau linguistique appartient la

---

[28] A. ERNOUT, A. MEILLET, Dictionnaire étymologique de la langue latine. Histoire des mots, 4° éd., Paris, 1967, p. 400, s. v. *merx*; K. LATTE, Römische Religionsgeschichte, p. 163, note 4.

[29] G. WISSOWA, R.K.R., p. 304; W. KROLL, dans: R.E., Art. cit. Mercurius, col. 981–982.

[30] Festus, p. 124 M, s. v. Mercurius: *Mercurius a mercibus est dictus*; Varro, AGAHD, R. D., XVI, Frg. 31: . . . *ideo et mercibus praeesse* . . .

[31] J. BAYET, Histoire politique et psychologique de la religion romaine, 1° éd., Paris, 1957, 2° éd., Paris, 1973, p. 123; K. LATTE, Op. cit., p. 163; G. DUMÉZIL, La religion romaine archaïque, Les religions de l'humanité, 10, Paris, 1966, 2° éd., Paris, 1974, p. 425–426.

[32] J. BAYET, Op. cit., p. 123; K. LATTE, Op. cit., p. 163, note 4.

[33] A. ERNOUT, A. MEILLET, Op. cit., p. 400.

[34] A. WALDE, J.-B. HOFMANN, Op. cit., II, 3° éd., p. 78, s. v. *Merx*; A. ERNOUT, A. MEILLET, Op. cit., p. 400.

[35] E. BENVENISTE, Le vocabulaire des institutions indo-européennes, I, Économie, parenté, société, Paris, 1969, p. 140.

racine *merc,* et on ne peut exclure qu'elle se rattache à l'étrusque, c'est une possibilité que n'étaye aucun fait probant dans l'état présent de nos connaissances.

Merx et les vocables voisins formés sur la racine *merc-* s'appliquent à une forme d'échange spécifique, distincte du simple fait d'acheter et de vendre, qui ne constitue pas la caractéristique essentielle de l'acte de commerce. L'originalité de l'échange commercial, de la relation mercantile, consiste à acheter et vendre pour le compte de tiers, à s'instituer intermédiaire professionnel entre celui qui vend et celui qui acquiert, entre producteur et consommateur, entre propriétaire et client. Une part essentielle de l'intervention médiatrice du *mercator* dans l'acte de commerce, consistait à ménager l'accord sur la fixation de la valeur de l'objet de la transaction, et à en assurer le transfert en contre-partie du règlement de cette valeur réalisée en signes de richesse.

Définir le rôle du *deus Mercurius* à partir de la relation étymologique entre le nom divin et la *merx,* comme le simple patronage des activités marchandes et la protection des *mercatores,* c'est s'en tenir à une formulation commode, mais superficielle et insuffisante, qui ne rend pas compte du principe de l'action mise en œuvre par le dieu à l'occasion de sa prise en charge de la *merx.* L'analyse de la relation mercantile, dans la mesure où elle implique médiation, doit nous permettre de discerner la nature de la fonction première de Mercure, et de préciser en quoi consistait sur le plan du sacré l'efficacité de l'action dont il était l'agent en conformité avec sa spécialisation dans la *merx.*

3. Echange, médiation mercantile et fonction première du Mercure romain

La caractéristique essentielle de la relation mercantile était l'intervention au service des parties engagées dans le processus contractuel inhérent à l'opération mercantile. Le rôle du *mercator,* le service mercantile se définissait dans son principe par une médiation. A cet égard, il est significatif que l'interprétation varronienne de Mercure, dieu de la parole, à partir du vocable *Mercurius* entendu comme la contraction de la formule *medius currens*[36], procède de la fonction de médiation, dans la mesure où le langage identifié en l'occurrence avec le dieu, est l'intermédiaire explicitant la pensée, et permettant la communication entre les hommes.

Mais le problème reste d'approfondir en quoi consistait dans son principe la médiation exercée par Mercure à l'occasion du processus mercantile. De prime abord, on est tenté d'identifier la fonction du dieu à l'intervention du *mercator,* qui s'employait à mettre en contact les parties, à réaliser l'accord entre vendeur et acquéreur. Entendue de la sorte, la médiation de Mercure s'apparenterait aux bons offices d'un courtier, et c'est dans ce sens apparemment que Varron identifiant le dieu avec le langage, rend compte de l'autorité qu'il exerce sur les

---

[36] Aug., Ciu., VII,14; Varro, AGAHD, R.D., XVI, 30—31. Supra note 8.

opérations commerciales, par le fait que la parole circule à la manière d'un intermédiaire entre les vendeurs et les acheteurs[37].

L'étymologie varronienne de l'appellation latine de l'homologue d'Hermès présentée comme équivalant à l'expression *medius currens*, transformée par l'usage en *Mercurius*, est linguistiquement aberrante. Cette explication étymologique relevait du système d'interprétation symbolique d'inspiration stoïcienne que Varron mit en œuvre dans ses 'Antiquitates rerum diuinarum': dans le nom du dieu il s'ingéniait à retrouver l'essentiel de son être divin, en l'occurrence présider au *sermo*, au discours, à l'instar de l'Hermès Λόγιος hellénistique. Certes au premier examen, cette fonction d'intermédiaire divin semble résulter seulement d'une conception de Varron insérée dans des spéculations issues de la théologie stoïcienne. Cette conception aboutit à subordonner la vocation mercantile, pourtant première − attestée par la relation étymologique entre la *merx* et *Mercurius* − chez l'homologue romain d'Hermès, à la propriété de l'Hermès Λόγιος d'être le dieu du discours.

Cependant cette interprétation apparemment sollicitée dans ses modalités est fondée dans son principe, car à son point de départ elle se réclame d'un élément essentiel de l'opération mercantile, l'*interpretatio,* le marchandage destiné à établir l'*interpretium,* au terme du débat entre vendeur et acheteur sur l'estimation de la valeur, et la fixation du prix de l'objet en cause dans la transaction[38]. A ce titre Mercurius était pleinement *interpres,* et c'est cette qualité d'*interpres* qui a permis à Varron de l'assimiler à Hermès Λόγιος, et d'en faire le dieu du *sermo* dans la mesure où un rapprochement étymologique superficiel prétendait à apparenter Hermès à ἑρμηνεύς, le synonyme grec du latin *interpres*[39]. Evidemment au sens second, *interpres* correspond bien à ἑρμηνεύς entendu comme truchement, traducteur, mais au sens premier, c'était l'intermédiaire qui intervient dans la transaction pour fixer le prix accepté de part et d'autre par accord commun (*interpretium*).

La fonction de médiation de Mercurius en matière mercantile ne procède pas de son assimilation à l'Hermès Λόγιος, elle était en fait inhérente à la vocation mercantile qui avait valu son nom latin à l'homologue romain d'Hermès. En qualité d'intermédiaire divin, Hermès sous le nom de *Mercurius* aurait été en quelque sorte le *mercator* par excellence. En fait, le recours à une sorte de symbolisme assimilant Hermès, à titre de médiateur, à un équivalent du marchand, ne suffit pas à rendre compte de son affectation à la fonction mercantile. Car à Rome Hermès-Mercurius fait figure de divinité fonctionnelle, d'abord dieu de la *merx*, plutôt que dieu des *mercatores*: sa spécialisation ne

---

[37] Varro, AGAHD, R.D., XVI, Frg. 31: . . . *ideo et mercibus praeesse, quia inter uendentes et ementes sermo fit medius . . .*

[38] E. BENVENISTE, Le vocabulaire des institutions indo-européennes, I, Économie, parenté, société, Paris, 1969, p. 140: «En latin, par exemple, le terme *pretium* 'prix' est d'étymologie difficile; il n'a de rapprochement certain, à l'intérieur du latin, qu'avec *inter-pret-*; la notion serait celle de 'marchandage, prix fixé par accord commun' (Cf. *inter-*).»

[39] P. CHANTRAINE, Dictionnaire étymologique de la langue grecque. Histoire des mots, II (E−K), Paris, 1970, p. 373, s. v. ἑρμηνεύς.

procède pas d'un intérêt bienveillant pour les praticiens de la chose commerciale, mais de la prise en charge sur le plan du sacré de la relation mercantile, c'est-à-dire que de quelque façon il était à l'œuvre dans le processus même de l'échange commercial.

A cet égard, son appartenance au *ritus graecus* suggère un rapprochement significatif. En 431 av. J.-C., une *pestilentia* fut l'occasion de l'appel à Apollon, en qualité de 'Medicus', de dieu guérisseur doté d'un pouvoir purificateur conforme à la vocation du *ritus graecus*[40]. Le recours à Hermès dès l'aube du Vᵉ siècle, pour assumer la relation mercantile, n'a-t-il pas été commandé par le fait qu'à la spécificité de celle-ci répondait l'efficacité propre du *ritus graecus* sur le plan du sacré? Dépassant la portée pratique de la médiation assurée par le *mercator* entre les parties, la médiation divine exercée par Hermès-Mercurius dans le processus mercantile ne consistait-elle pas en une vertu libératoire, en une action purificatrice nécessaire à l'accomplissement et à la validité de ce mode d'échange?

4. Le don et l'origine du mode mercantile de l'échange

Pour saisir la nature de ce pouvoir d'Hermès-Mercurius à l'œuvre dans le processus mercantile, il convient de chercher du côté de l'origine des modes d'échange. L'activité commerciale est une forme — et certainement pas la plus ancienne — d'un phénomène plus général, l'échange. Toutes les sociétés, tous les groupes humains ont pratiqué l'échange, mais l'échange selon des modalités proprement commerciales, à finalité utilitaire et lucrative, se constitue et s'exerce dans certaines sociétés, à un stade donné de l'évolution de leurs structures mentales et socio-économiques.

En fait, comme l'a montré MARCEL MAUSS, dans les sociétés primitives ou archaïques, le point de départ de la circulation des richesses, le principe de l'échange, a été le don[41]. Le don en théorie était volontaire et gratuit, mais la chose offerte et reçue oblige, elle portait en elle l'obligation pour le donataire de présenter en retour un contre-don au donateur[42]. Le don issu d'une initiative libre de son auteur appelait de la part du bénéficiaire, dans la mesure où l'objet reçu à titre de libéralité l'engageait à l'égard de la personne du donateur, un

---

[40] J. GAGÉ, Apollon romain, Essai sur le culte d'Apollon et le développement du ritus graecus à Rome des origines à Auguste, Bibl. des Écoles franç. d'Athènes & de Rome, 182, Paris, 1955, p. 24, p. 71sq.

[41] M. MAUSS, Essai sur le don. Forme et raison de l'échange dans les sociétés archaïques, dans: IDEM, Sociologie et anthropologie, Bibl. de sociologie contemporaine, Paris, 1950, p. 145–279; E. BENVENISTE, Don et échange dans le vocabulaire indo-européen, dans: IDEM, Problèmes de linguistique générale, I, Paris, 1966, p. 315–316; E. BENVENISTE, Le vocabulaire des institutions indo-europénnes, I, Économie, parenté, société, Paris, 1969, p. 65sq.

[42] M. MAUSS, Op. cit., p. 147–148; T. F. CARNEY, The Economies of Antiquity: Controls, Gifts and Trade, Lawrence, Kansas, 1973, p. 59–62.

présent en quelque sorte libératoire de son côté, mais propre à lier en revanche le partenaire initial[43].

Comme le présent spontané dans son principe engendrait en fait l'obligation de réciprocité, le don initial par un jeu de va-et-vient entre groupes et individus, de dons offerts et de contre-dons compensatoires, ouvrait un circuit indéfini de transferts des biens et de la richesse à travers la société entière[44]. A partir du don s'était constitué un réseau archaïque complexe de relations, d'obligations et de droits dont la signification dépassait de beaucoup le simple échange utilitaire de biens et de produits entre individus. Le don était à la fois libre et contraignant: ainsi la richesse et la puissance imposaient-elles à leurs détenteurs de manifester leur pouvoir et leur supériorité en offrant des dons; il était par ailleurs obligatoire pour le bénéficiaire d'accepter le don, et en retour de présenter un contre-don propre à démontrer son autorité et son prestige[45].

Une forme intermédiaire qui procède encore de l'échange-don est dite «commerce des chefs»[46], elle tendait à manifester tout à la fois le prestige individuel du chef et celui de son clan, par là elle était distincte du simple échange de biens somptuaires à des fins utilitaires, et restait étrangère au souci d'un gain matériel immédiat[47]. Le jeu du don et du contre-don exprimait l'antagonisme et la concurrence dans la démonstration réciproque de supériorité.

Le don appelait en retour une contre-prestation sous peine de disqualification sociale du bénéficiaire, mais dans la pratique un délai était nécessaire pour la préparation et la présentation de cette contrepartie. Dans une phase ultérieure, quand les préoccupations utilitaires et les considérations d'intérêt matériel eurent pris le pas sur la démonstration de prestige, le système archaïque du don et du contre-don à rendre à terme fit place à la procédure d'achat-vente, en unifiant dans le contrat mercantile les deux moments complémentaires, mais initialement disjoints dans le temps, de la présentation du don et du retour du contre-don[48].

Dans le droit de la Rome archaïque, dans l'économie primitive des Latins, MAUSS avait relevé des vestiges isolés de l'échange-don[49]. La reconstitution, pour une part hypothétique, du système originel des dons obligatoires, qu'il a esquissée à partir des débris conservés par la tradition juridique et érudite, trouve une confirmation dans les indices issus de documents archéologiques et épigraphiques, relatifs à la pratique de l'échange-don dans l'Etrurie contemporaine de la Rome royale. De ce côté M. MAURO CRISTOFANI a tiré des conclusions suggestives de l'examen du problème posé par la signification de textes épigraphiques incisés ou gravés sur des objets de type somptuaire[50].

---

[43] M. MAUSS, Op. cit., p. 153, p. 155, p. 159.

[44] E. BENVENISTE, Don et échange dans le vocabulaire indo-européen, p. 315.

[45] M. MAUSS, Op. cit., p. 153, p. 161, p. 187; E. BENVENISTE, Le vocabulaire des institutions indo-européennes, I, p. 74–76.

[46] M. MAUSS, Op. cit., p. 176 sq.

[47] Ibid., p. 202.

[48] Ibid., p. 199–200; E. BENVENISTE, Le vocabulaire des institutions indo-européennes, I, p. 76.

[49] M. MAUSS, Op. cit., p. 229 sq.

[50] M. CRISTOFANI, Il 'dono' nell'Etruria arcaica, Parola del passato, 30, 1975, p. 132–152.

Il s'est attaché à élucider le sens et la valeur propres de deux formules épigraphiques *mini muluvanike* (variante *mi mulu*) et *mini turuke* (variante *mi turu*) tenues pour exprimer l'offrande et la dédicace[51]. L'étude de la répartition dans le temps de ces deux types d'inscriptions archaïques révèle que la formule *mini muluvanike* ou *mi mulu* figure du VII° au milieu du VI° au siècle av. J.-C. sur des objets appartenant au mobilier funéraire provenant de tombes, ou déposés dans un sanctuaire à titre d'offrandes dans la première moitié du VI° siècle. Puis à partir de la seconde moitié du VI°, et au V° siècle, prévaut la formule *mini turuke* ou *mi turu* qui ne semble pas synonyme de la précédente, et qui figure exclusivement sur les textes inscrits de dédicace des objets offerts à des sanctuaires. M. CRISTOFANI a conclu que la disparition de la formule *mini muluvanike* correspondait à l'abandon de la pratique réelle de l'échange-don dans les relations sociales[52].

Les objets portant la formule *mini muluvanike* illustrent la forme d'échange-don dite «commerce des chefs», propre à une phase intermédiaire ne pratiquant plus le système des prestations collectives qui engageaient la communauté, mais à laquelle le contrat d'échange purement économique était encore étranger[53]. Ces textes épigraphiques en un temps où l'usage de l'écriture était devenu familier aux classes dirigeantes de la société étrusque[54], attestent que du début du VII° au milieu du VI° siècle, le don comme principe de circulation des richesses, du fait de l'obligation de réciprocité incombant au bénéficiaire d'un présent, était d'usage courant dans les milieux de l'aristocratie[55]. Les objets nouveaux et précieux, souvent de provenance étrangère, constituaient un signe de distinction sociale; aussi entre personnages de la classe dominante, le jeu alternatif du présent et de la contre-prestation appelée en retour reflétait l'émulation dans l'affirmation de la supériorité sociale, et la surenchère dans la manifestation de la richesse[56].

La disparition de la formule *mini muluvanike*, et l'effacement de l'échange-don au milieu du VI° siècle, sont à mettre en relation avec la diffusion de la monnaie en Etrurie, au contact des Grecs, dans la période 530—500 av. J.-C.[57]. Dans la seconde moitié du VI° siècle av. J.-C., l'usage et l'apport d'espèces monétaires du côté des partenaires étrangers ont contribué à substituer l'économie de marché à l'ancienne économie du don. Le rôle de l'Etrurie archaïque dans l'évolution des modes d'échange, et dans la diffusion d'un type de relation d'échange à finalité utilitaire génératrice de richesse économique, permet de mieux saisir comment Rome encore dans l'orbite des Etrusques, a sur leur modèle, adopté Hermès au début du V° siècle, pour prendre en charge la relation d'échange mercantile.

---

[51] M. CRISTOFANI, Art. cit., p. 133—135.
[52] Ibid., p. 136.
[53] Ibid., p. 146, p. 148—150.
[54] Ibid., p. 143.
[55] Ibid., p. 143, p. 145.
[56] Ibid., p. 146.
[57] Ibid., p. 151, note 50.

Le système de l'échange-don, bien que le présent initial fût en théorie libre et gratuit, était en fait tout imprégné de contrainte, dans la mesure où le jeu alternatif de la prestation et de la contre-prestation renouvelait indéfiniment l'obligation renvoyée tour à tour d'un partenaire à l'autre. L'innovation du processus mercantile fut de préciser et d'assouplir la relation d'échange: il consistait essentiellement en un mode d'échange contractuel régi par un contrat consensuel de portée limitée, débattu et établi d'un commun accord entre des parties individuelles traitant sur pied d'égalité[58]. Le contrat d'échange mercantile dont la finalité était seulement l'utilité économique, n'était pas générateur de contrainte indéfiniment réciproque, il définissait des obligations convenues à l'occasion d'un marché, mais réservait la liberté des parties par-delà l'exécution des termes de la transaction.

Il s'agissait d'un contrat d'*emptio-uenditio* par lequel la partie disposant d'un bien, le vendeur (*uenditor*) s'obligeait à procurer à la partie demanderesse, l'acheteur (*emptor*) la libre possession à titre de maître (*dominus*) d'une chose disponible (*merx*) moyennant règlement de valeur appréciée en signes de richesse, et réalisée en espèces monétaires (*pretium*). L'exécution du contrat d'échange était subordonnée à une prestation matérielle, le transfert de la *res uendita*, et son appropriation par l'acquéreur au moyen d'une *traditio*, c'est-à-dire la translation de la *merx* du *tradens* à l'*accipiens*.

5. La médiation de Mercure et la neutralisation de l'obligation contraignante inhérente aux *res*

Or dans le système de l'échange-don, l'obligation ne résultait pas d'une convention arrêtée entre groupes ou individus, elle naissait de la contrainte inhérente à la *res,* objet de don ou de contre-don. MAUSS a clairement reconnu que le ressort des mécanismes d'obligation réciproque et automatique résidait dans les choses échangées[59]. Originellement par sa nature propre, la *res,* objet d'échange, lie celui qui la reçoit, et cela indépendamment de la forme du processus d'échange: dans l'échange-don archaïque elle liait le donataire, elle dut initialement lier tout pareillement l'*emptor* dans l'échange mercantile.

Le mode d'échange mercantile apparaît comme un instrument souple dans la mesure où il tendait à restreindre les effets du processus à l'utilité économique, et à la sauvegarde de la liberté réciproque des contractants. Mais pour en saisir exactement la portée et les limites au sortir de l'époque archaïque, il convient de ne pas perdre de vue l'antinomie de principe entre l'autonomie des parties et la force contraignante propre à la *res,* objet de transaction, sur laquelle leur volonté était sans prise, dans la mesure où la nature des choses ne pouvait être transformée par la seule décision des parties en présence. La relation des parties avec la *res,* la chose concrète, dont le transfert constituait la matière du

---

[58] B. COMBET FARNOUX, Mercure romain, p. 237sq.
[59] M. MAUSS, Op. cit., p. 148, p. 157–158, p. 177.

contrat, restait la même qu'à l'époque archaïque dans le système de l'échange-don.

En conformité avec son caractère consensuel, l'originalité de la relation mercantile consistait à éluder, sinon délier l'obligation inhérente aux *res,* dont la procédure d'*emptio-uenditio* régissait le transfert. Or comme l'a montré EMILE BENVENISTE, vendre acheter pour son compte, ce n'était pas proprement faire acte de commerce; pour qu'il y eût commerce, il fallait la présence et l'intervention d'un intermédiaire entre le vendeur et l'acheteur. Le propre de la relation mercantile, c'est la médiation entre les parties exercée par un tiers spécialisé, le *mercator*[60].

La portée de la fonction du *mercator* allait bien au-delà de la simple utilité économique réduite à la commodité d'un dispositif apte à faciliter le rapprochement entre vendeur et acquéreur: son entremise interrompt la relation d'obligation qui se nouait entre *tradens* et *accipiens,* à l'occasion du transfert de la *res,* objet de la transaction. La *res* passait du *tradens* au *mercator,* puis de celui-ci à l'*accipiens*: ainsi le *mercator* se trouvait pris en quelque sorte par délégation dans la trame du réseau d'obligations réciproques tissé entre les deux contractants; mais élargi, distendu, ce réseau était voué à se faire moins contraignant. En principe l'intervention du *mercator* lui faisait assumer l'obligation inhérente à la *res,* mais il n'était ni propriétaire de l'objet qu'il transmettait, ni bénéficiaire de la prestation qui passait par ses mains: le lien se nouait par lui, mais ne l'engageait que passagèrement puisqu'il n'était détenteur en titre de la *res,* ni au début, ni à l'issue du processus. Sur le plan pratique, le relais interposé par le *mercator* dans le circuit de l'échange, était propre à diluer, sinon à délier l'obligation[61].

Sur le plan du sacré, la prise en charge de la relation mercantile par Hermès sous le nom de Mercurius manifestait l'originalité de ce mode d'échange, en s'exerçant également dans le sens d'une médiation dont nous discernons le point d'application, la portée et les modalités d'action. Mais au niveau divin, la fonction de médiation d'Hermès-Mercurius n'était pas la transposition pure et simple de l'intervention du *mercator* dans le processus mercantile.

L'échange sous forme mercantile, parce qu'il impliquait entrée en relation, prise de contact avec l'autre, était chargé d'incertitude, générateur de risque, comme toute démarche d'ordre individuel ou collectif ouvrant sur l'extérieur: le transfert des *res* était de nature à créer indépendamment de la volonté des parties une relation de dépendance contraignante, d'autre part la forme contractuelle du mode mercantile de l'échange mettait en cause la Fides sur le plan du sacré. L'échange de type mercantile, comme toute espèce de rapport avec l'autre, devait être fondé au niveau du sacré en droit religieux. Cette dimension sacrée avait pour conséquence la nécessité de prévenir tout manquement de nature à rompre la *pax deorum* à l'occasion d'une opération d'échange pratiquée selon le mode mercantile. Dans le domaine des rapports avec l'étranger, les *Fetiales,*

---

[60] E. BENVENISTE, Le vocabulaire des institutions indo-européennes, I, p. 139–140.
[61] B. COMBET FARNOUX, Op. cit., p. 245 sq.

dépositaires et protagonistes de rites et de procédures archaïques, fondaient dans le sacré les actes de droit international[62]; parallèlement des rites spécifiques en conformité avec l'efficacité prêtée à Hermès-Mercurius en matière mercantile, devaient conditionner sur le plan du sacré l'accomplissement, et la validité des opérations d'échange mercantile.

La médiation de Mercurius dans sa fonction d'assumer la relation d'échange mercantile, consistait à garantir à la *merx* un fonctionnement en conformité avec le sacré, puis à annuler, neutraliser la puissance inhérente à la *res,* à délier l'obligation contraignante attachée aux choses. A l'échelon divin, Hermès-Mercurius libérait l'échange, et à cet égard, selon la formule d'Arnobe, il était bien *nundinarum, mercium, commerciorumque mutator*[63]. En assumant l'obligation, en déliant la contrainte inhérente aux choses de l'échange, Hermès Mercurius exerçait une action de purification et de libération, conforme à la vocation du *ritus graecus.*

6. La médiation de Mercure et la finalité lucrative du processus mercantile

La médiation exercée par Mercure était dans son principe opérative, elle avait efficacité libératoire, elle déliait l'obligation créée par la puissance contraignante émanant des *res,* et elle imprimait à l'acte d'échange la forme mercantile, en donnant le champ libre au jeu du processus contractuel de la transaction. Mais l'évolution aidant, à l'issue du IV° siècle, cette efficacité opérative initiale fut perdue de vue dans la mesure où les liens inhérents aux choses et aux structures perdirent de leur puissance contraignante d'obligation, et tombèrent en désuétude. Dans la définition et la constitution de l'acte d'échange prévalurent la relation contractuelle, et l'accord consensuel des parties, dès lors la médiation exercée par Mercure était vouée à s'identifier avec le principe contractuel propre aux débats transactionnels, et aux accords négociés.

Une fois que l'évolution des structures mentales et des rapports socio-économiques eût fait tomber en désuétude la notion d'une obligation inhérente aux choses, la compétence mercantile de Mercure s'identifia à une médiation d'ordre contractuel, en conformité avec les modalités juridiques caractéristiques de l'acte d'échange mercantile. Mais cette médiation présidait à une opération de transfert de biens existants, en soi et initialement elle n'était pas génératrice de richesse, pas plus que la forme mercantile de l'échange, consistant dans son principe en un transfert de biens équivalents appréciés à leur valeur d'usage, selon le commun accord fixé à la convenance des parties, n'était originellement productrice d'une richesse propre.

Mais l'intervention de la notion de valeur d'usage devait dans une étape ultérieure frayer la voie à celle de valeur proprement marchande avec l'introduction dans le circuit des échanges de signes de richesse, symboles des biens réels, étalons de mesure de leur valeur, substitués pour la commodité à l'un des

[62] G. Dumézil, Idées romaines, Bibl. des sc. hum., Paris, 1969, p. 68–70.
[63] Arnobe, Adu. Nat., III, 32.

termes de la transaction[64]. La forme élaborée de ces signes de richesse exprimant une notion économique abstraite et quantifiée de la valeur des choses indépendante de leur réalité, fut la monnaie dont la mise en circulation en substituant au concept ancien de la chose entendue selon la catégorie de la φύσις, c'est-à-dire à la diversité qualitative des choses, une mesure commune réduite à leur valeur d'échange, permit la création d'une richesse de type nouveau différente de celle attachée à la possession des biens concrets propres aux sociétés archaïques, terres et têtes de bétail[65]. Cette richesse nouvelle s'exprima sous la forme du profit mercantile issu du jeu de l'échange des choses, considérées sous le seul angle de leur valeur marchande, et matérialisé en espèces monétaires.

Au stade archaïque, l'échange mercantile s'est accommodé de signes prémonétaires pour exprimer la valeur[66], mais c'est l'usage de la monnaie *stricto sensu*, c'est-à-dire frappée, titrée, estampillée par la puissance publique, qui a imprimé toute sa portée révolutionnaire à ce mode d'échange, qui en a fait le principe moteur d'un système d'économie mercantile, producteur d'une forme de richesse spécifique exprimée en valeur marchande[67]. Or si l'invention de la monnaie est apparue dans le monde grec dès le VIIIᵉ siècle av. J.-C.[68], à Rome son emploi est tardif, et sa généralisation date seulement du IIIᵉ siècle, après que fut tombée en désuétude la notion archaïque de l'obligation par les choses.

Dès lors, la nature contractuelle du processus mercantile et l'accentuation de sa finalité économique, suggèrent les deux directions principales, selon lesquelles la fonction de médiation de Mercure était appelée à se renouveler en conformité avec l'orientation de l'économie mercantile. D'une part, son rôle d'intermédiaire divin le qualifiait pour être l'inspirateur et l'agent des accords négociés. D'un autre côté, dans la mesure où la relation mercantile, par-delà l'opération proprement échangiste, était génératrice d'une forme de richesse, le dieu avait désormais vocation à procurer le profit mercantile à l'aboutissement du processus, à garantir la réalisation du *lucrum*.

Les emblèmes attribués aux effigies de Mercure sont significatifs de cette évolution de la fonction du dieu. Initialement le dieu est porteur du caducée. Les modernes ont incliné volontiers à établir une relation directe entre l'affectation du caducée au Mercure romain, et son rôle de dieu du commerce[69]. En fait, le caducée avait une signification plus générale, à laquelle participait l'échange mercantile, dans la mesure où il se définissait par une relation contractuelle: il était l'insigne du héraut, du κῆρυξ, qui n'était pas seulement un porte-parole officiel, mais le témoin des accords négociés, et également le garant de la validité

[64] J.-P. VERNANT, Mythe et pensée chez les Grecs. Etudes de psychologie historique, Petite coll. Maspero, 86–87, Paris, 1974, p. 118.

[65] Ibid., p. 117–120.

[66] M. MAUSS, Op. cit., p. 178 note 1, p. 178 sq.; L. GERNET, Anthropologie de la Grèce antique, Paris, 1968: La notion mythique de la valeur en Grèce, p. 95 note 4, p. 97, p. 111 note 4.

[67] J.-P. VERNANT, Op. cit., II, p. 117; L. GERNET, Op. cit., La notion mythique de la valeur en Grèce, p. 136–137, Les nobles dans la Grèce antique, p. 341.

[68] Her., I,94; J.-P. VERNANT, Op. cit., II, p. 117 note 55.

[69] R. BOETZKES, Art. Kerykeion, dans: R.E. XI, 1, 1921, col. 340.

des transactions mercantiles. A cet égard, une disposition significative du traité de 509 entre Rome et Carthage stipule que les transactions devaient s'effectuer en présence d'un héraut, dont l'intervention était propre à conférer sa validité au processus mercantile, et à lui valoir la garantie de la puissance publique[70].

À la valorisation ultérieure de la finalité lucrative de la fonction de Mercure, correspond l'adjonction d'un second attribut, la bourse, symbole de la circulation monétaire, qui alimente le circuit de l'économie mercantile, et du *lucrum* réalisé en espèces sonnantes.

Le caducée, à titre d'insigne de Mercure, avait une portée générale, il symbolisait pleinement la fonction assumée initialement par le dieu romain, c'est-à-dire la prise en charge sur le plan du sacré de l'ensemble du processus de la relation d'échange sous forme mercantile. C'était l'emblème essentiel du dieu responsable de la *merx*, car il tirait sa signification de la dimension contractuelle qui définissait proprement le mode mercantile de l'échange, et qui était de l'ordre de la 'Fides'. La bourse était seulement un attribut circonstanciel relevant de l'ordre de la chrématistique, elle correspondait à un effet induit du processus mercantile, le profit apprécié et réalisé en espèces monétaires.

Ces symboles reflètent la dualité de la vocation reconnue au dieu romain: d'un côté, une vocation fonctionnelle première s'exerçant au niveau de la dimension contractuelle du processus mercantile, et de l'autre une vocation économique secondaire, dont l'objet procédait moins du fonctionnement de la *merx*, que de sa finalité lucrative envisagée à l'avantage des *mercatores*.

II. Les Mercuriales *et la sacralisation de la relation mercantile*

A l'efficacité purificatoire et libératoire de l'action exercée au niveau divin par Hermès-Mercurius dans sa fonction première, devaient correspondre des *sacra* propres à la *religio* romaine de Mercure, et à l'*aedes Mercurii* dédiée en 495 av. J.-C. fut attaché dès sa fondation un *collegium* à vocation sacerdotale, qui devait être dépositaire et protagoniste d'un rituel approprié à la spécificité de la relation d'échange de forme mercantile.

1. Les *Mercuriales, collegium* à vocation sacerdotale

La seconde notice relatant la fondation de l'*aedes Mercurii*[71] rapporte également que le personnage à qui reviendrait l'honneur de procéder à la dédicace du sanctuaire, aurait en même temps la charge de présider à la *cura annonae* (*prae-*

---

[70] Pol., III,22,8–9.
[71] Liv., II,27,5: . . . *Senatus a se rem ad populum reiecit: utri eorum dedicatio iussu populi data esset, eum praeesse annonae, mercatorum collegium instituere, sollemnia pro pontifice iussit suscipere.*

esse annonae), et de fonder une corporation de marchands (*mercatorum collegium instituere*). L'association de cette mission doublement profane à l'accomplissement des rites de la dédicace est insolite, la procédure rapportée par Tite-Live est inhabituelle, et suscite d'emblée un doute légitime, la tradition ne lui prête point de précédent, ni n'atteste d'autres exemples où elle ait été mise en œuvre ultérieurement.

Cette adjonction d'un *collegium* professionnel à un sanctuaire apparaît tout à fait inusitée: l'initiative attribuée au Sénat de confier à l'un des consuls en exercice, c'est-à-dire à un magistrat *cum imperio*, la responsabilité de fonder un *collegium* professionnel, est contraire à tout ce que nous savons de la doctrine et des usages romains en la matière. Sous la République, en règle générale, la puissance publique s'abstint presque constamment d'intervenir dans la vie des corporations professionnelles; il n'était besoin ni de la permission expresse, ni de l'aveu des autorités officielles pour établir un *collegium*[72]. Les *collegia* professionnels étaient alors libres de s'organiser comme ils l'entendaient; leur création, leurs statuts ne dépendaient pas d'un acte de la puissance publique, mais de l'accord des membres d'un même corps de métier. Il suffisait que trois personnes au moins, se fussent concertées pour que se constituât un *collegium*. Le fondateur, le *constitutor collegii*, était un des membres de la première heure, généralement celui qui avait pris l'initiative, et invité ses collègues à se grouper[73]. Le *collegium mercatorum* attribué à la date de 495, aurait dû être fondé par un *mercator*, or Tite-Live ne nous rapporte rien de tel.

Par ailleurs la notice de Tite-Live implique que ce *collegium mercatorum* attaché à l'*aedes Mercurii* était voué à faciliter l'accomplissement de l'autre tâche assortissant la dédicace, l'organisation de l'annone. Les commerçants groupés dans cette compagnie marchande auraient pratiqué un trafic destiné à alimenter l'annone, de la sorte ils auraient été les ancêtres des *mercatores frumentarii*. Dès le début du V° siècle, ils auraient fait figure de négociants traitant de grand commerce, occupés d'intérêts touchant à la vie même de la cité. Or les documents épigraphiques mentionnant bien plus tard sous l'Empire, les *collegia* de grands *negotiatores*, et de *mercatores* importants, n'indiquent nulle part qu'ils aient eu vocation à cultiver la religion de Mercure, à entretenir son sanctuaire, à assurer le service particulier de son culte.

Si un *collegium* fut attaché à l'*aedes Mercurii* lors de sa fondation, ce ne pouvait être une compagnie professionnelle de marchands, mais un *collegium* sacerdotal, ou une *sodalitas sacra* de *cultores*. Or précisément, deux témoignages documentaires, l'un de la fin de la République, l'autre du début du Principat, font état de l'existence à Rome au I° siècle av. J.-C. d'un *collegium Mercurialium*.

---

[72] W. Liebenam, Zur Geschichte und Organisation des römischen Vereinswesens. Drei Untersuchungen, Leipzig, 1890, p. 13–16; J.-P. Waltzing, Etude historique sur les corporations professionnelles chez les Romains depuis les origines jusqu'à la chute de l'Empire romain d'Occident, Louvain, 1895–1900. I, p. 70 sq., II, p. 247 sq.

[73] W. Liebenam, Op. cit., p. 169–170; J.-P. Waltzing, Op. cit., I, p. 74, p. 335–337; E. Kornemann, Art. Collegium, dans: R.E., IV, 1901, col. 381.

Dans une lettre à son frère Quintus datée du 9 Avril 56 av. J.-C., Cicéron rapporte incidemment que les *Capitolini* et les *Mercuriales* lors de leur séance du 5 Avril, avaient chassé de leur sein le chevalier romain, M. Furius Flaccus, connu par cette unique allusion de Cicéron qui le qualifie de malhonnête homme (*hominem nequam*)[74]. D'autre part, une inscription de Lanuvium[75] datant probablement du début du principat augustéen[76] fait mention d'un certain A. Castricius Myrio, *magister* de quatre *collegia*, Luperques, *Capitolini*, *Mercuriales*, et *pagani Auentinenses*.

Ces deux témoignages documentaires mentionnent conjointement avec les *Mercuriales*, les *Capitolini*, et ce rapprochement est propre à confirmer à la fois la vocation religieuse, et l'antiquité reculée des *Mercuriales*. En 390 av. J.-C., après l'incendie de Rome par les Gaulois, le Sénat délibéra sur les mesures religieuses à prendre pour purifier la Ville, et sur le rapport du dictateur M. Furius Camillus, par un senatus-consulte[77], décida entre autres dispositions, la création de Jeux Capitolins, et la constitution aux fins de célébrer ces *ludi* d'un *collegium* recruté parmi les habitants du Capitole et de la citadelle[78].

La procédure suivie en 390 est semblable en tout point à celle qui présida à l'établissement du *collegium* fondé en 495 en même temps que l'*aedes Mercurii*: le *collegium Capitolinorum*[79] fut constitué sur l'initiative du Sénat (*auctore senatu*) qui en confia la formation au magistrat suprême du moment, le dictateur M. Furius Camillus, ainsi institué *constitutor collegii*.

Les *Mercuriales* devaient être attachés à la *religio* de Mercure, comme les Luperques se consacraient à la célébration des Lupercales, et comme les *Capitolini* étaient voués à la préparation et à l'organisation des Jeux Capitolins. L'association des *Mercuriales* avec les *Capitolini* au dernier siècle de la République tend à confirmer leur antiquité. Evidemment les deux témoignages documentaires mentionnant conjointement ces deux *collegia* sont tardifs, mais la tradition annalistique rapporte en 495 la fondation du *collegium* attaché à l'*aedes Mercurii*, et un siècle plus tard celle du *collegium Capitolinorum* en 390. L'association des deux *collegia* au I° siècle av. J.-C. devait tenir à leur communauté de vocation et d'origine. L'antiquité reculée des *Mercuriales* peut être tenue pour certaine, au même titre que celle des *Capitolini*.

---

[74] Cic., Ad. Q. fr., II,5,2: *M. Furium Flaccum equitem Romanum, hominem nequam, Capitolini et Mercuriales de collegio eiecerunt, praesentem ad pedes uniuscuiusque iacentem*; C. NICOLET, L'ordre équestre à l'époque républicaine (321–42 avant J.-C.), II, Prosopographie des chevaliers romains, Bibl. des Ecoles franç. d'Athènes & de Rome, 207, Paris, 1964, p. 891–893, § 162– M. Furius Flaccus.

[75] C.I.L., XIV, 2105: *A. Castricius Myrio / Talenti f. tr. mil. praef. eq. / et classis mag. colleg. / Lupercor. et Capitolinor. / et Mercurial. et paga / norum Auentin. XXVI uir / . . . mo, i per plures / . . i sortitionibus / . . . dis redemptus.*

[76] A. STEIN, Art. Castricius, dans: R.E., III, 1899, (9.) col. 1777; C. NICOLET, Op. cit., II, p. 892: propose de dater l'inscription d'avant 12 av. J.-C.

[77] Liv., V,50,1.

[78] Liv., V,50,4, et V,52,11.

[79] G. WISSOWA, Art. Capitolini, dans: R.E., III, 1899, col. 1529–1530.

L'adjonction d'un *collegium* sacerdotal spécialisé apparaît à la réflexion inséparable de la fondation de l'*aedes Mercurii*, dans la mesure où ce sanctuaire abritant un dieu étranger était le siège d'un culte inédit. Mercure était la transposition d'Hermès, un dieu grec, il n'appartenait pas aux structures traditionnelles de la religion romaine issues de l'héritage latin archaïque, il n'avait pas de flamine. En un temps où le *ritus graecus* était en gestation, la fondation de l'*aedes Mercurii* dut donner lieu à l'institution d'un *collegium* à caractère sacerdotal, afin de prendre en charge le service de ce culte public.

Au dernier siècle de la République, les *Mercuriales* comme les *Capitolini* étaient des survivances, et c'est à ce titre qu'ils durent s'associer, comme l'atteste le témoignage de Cicéron: leur regroupement assurait la pérennité d'institutions en voie de décrépitude. Les *Capitolini* avaient été créés en relation avec le Capitole, pour assurer la célébration des *Ludi Capitolini*, les *Mercuriales* avaient été voués initialement au service de Mercure, service déterminé par la spécificité du mode mercantile de l'échange, dont le dieu avait la charge. Le problème, c'est de saisir quelles étaient originellement la portée et la finalité de l'action spécifique des *Mercuriales*, et de retrouver en quoi consistait le rituel dont ils étaient les dépositaires et les agents.

2. Rituel des *Mercuriales* et *sacra* de la *religio* de Mercure

Le précédent des *Fetiales*, praticiens de rites archaïques associés aux procédures d'entrée en guerre et de conclusion du *foedus*[80], est révélateur de la dimension sacrée qui s'attachait à toute démarche impliquant relation, échange entre groupes, et suggère qu'au mode mercantile de l'échange devait correspondre un rituel particulier sur le plan du sacré. Les *Fetiales* étaient les gardiens d'un très vieux droit, le *Ius Fetiale*, dont les formules et les règles devaient garantir à Rome la protection des dieux dans ses rapports avec les peuples en sacralisant les actes de déclaration de guerre, et de conclusion des traités[81]: leur mission consistait à régler et organiser les relations de la communauté romaine avec les peuples voisins, en satisfaisant aux exigences du sacré, de façon à ce que fût préservée la *pax deorum*.

L'échange des biens avant de viser à l'utilité économique, a été initialement une forme privilégiée de relation qui mettait en contact une collectivité avec une autre. L'échange dans les sociétés archaïques engageait mutuellement les collectivités prises dans leur ensemble en créant un réseau d'obligations réciproques, il donnait lieu à fêtes, célébrations de cérémonies, accomplissement de rites[82], dont l'objet ne se limitait pas au seul souci de la circulation des biens et des richesses. La relation mercantile était une forme différenciée de l'échange, elle

---

[80] G. WISSOWA, R.K.R., p. 387 note 6, p. 552 sq.

[81] J. BAYET, Histoire politique et psychologique de la religion romaine, Bibl. hist., 2° éd., Paris, 1969, p. 105; G. DUMÉZIL, La religion romaine archaïque, 2° éd., p. 579−581.

[82] M. MAUSS, Op. cit., p. 150−151; E. BENVENISTE, Le vocabulaire des institutions indo-européennes, I, Économie, parenté, société, p. 140.

mettait en présence par l'intermédiaire du *mercator* deux parties individualisées certes, mais elle était également génératrice d'obligations dont le respect ou la non-observation avait une portée collective: le principe de son fonctionnement correct résidait dans le sacré, la garantie de son bon aboutissement, comme l'exécution de tout contrat ou pacte se situait au niveau du divin. A Rome un dieu l'assumait, cette prise en charge divine par Hermès-Mercurius impliquait un mode d'action sur le plan du sacré au moyen d'un rituel approprié.

Dans la mesure où comme l'échange-don, la relation mercantile se manifestait par un transfert d'objets matériels, de biens concrets, elle déclenchait initialement le même mécanisme d'obligation par les choses. L'obligation était inhérente aux *res*, et pour qu'elle ne mît point les partenaires dans une situation de dépendance réciproque indéfiniment renouvelée, il fallait que le lien qu'elle constituait fût dissout, que fût levée la contrainte qu'elle engendrait. Le moyen de résoudre une telle relation d'obligation qui tenait à la nature des choses, ne pouvait résulter de l'accord transactionnel entre les parties, propre au mode mercantile de l'échange, il se trouvait seulement au niveau du sacré, et par là le processus mercantile, afin d'exercer ses effets, était inséparable d'un rituel.

Dans la pratique, tout se passait comme si le processus contractuel, propre à la relation mercantile, interrompait le circuit d'obligations contraignantes réciproques, engendré par le transfert des *res*, en rendant leur liberté aux parties, par-delà l'exécution des termes convenus de la transaction[83]. Mais en fait, l'accord débattu et accepté au moyen de la médiation du *mercator* avait une portée d'ordre économique seulement, en fixant la valeur des choses, objets de la transaction. Ce n'était pas l'accord établi et enregistré des parties en présence, qui neutralisait la puissance contraignante inhérente à la *merx*, mais la médiation divine assumée par Mercurius, et exercée au moyen d'un rituel, qui en quelque sorte libérait l'échange. La finalité économique caractéristique de la relation mercantile n'excluait pas l'élément religieux, au contraire même elle était conditionnée par un recours au sacré, et à cet égard MARCEL MAUSS observait justement que «les diverses activités économiques, par exemple le marché, sont imprégnées de rites et de mythes»[84].

Les modalités contractuelles de la relation mercantile rendent compte de la seconde fonction du rituel, dont les *Mercuriales* devaient être responsables: il s'agissait de garantir le bon aboutissement et la validité du processus mercantile, eu égard à sa portée collective, dans la mesure où il mettait en cause la Fides. Sur le modèle des *Fetiales*, dépositaires et experts sacrés du droit de la guerre et de la paix, les *Mercuriales* durent être initialement les gardiens des rites et des règles qui conditionnaient en matière sacrée le jeu de l'échange mercantile, de façon qu'il fût bénéfique, ni ne devînt en aucun cas dommageable à la communauté, en le préservant de tout manquement dans le déroulement de son processus propre à irriter les dieux, et à provoquer une rupture de la *pax deorum*.

Le propre de la relation mercantile, c'était de mettre en présence deux parties par l'intermédiaire du *mercator*, et le processus reposait sur une forme de

---

[83] B. COMBET FARNOUX, Mercure romain, p. 295 sq.
[84] M. MAUSS, Op. cit., p. 266.

contrat, dont le marchand était à la fois exécutant et garant. Un risque était inhérent à ce mode de transaction, que la fraude, la tromperie ou la mauvaise foi vînt compromettre l'application de la convention. Le processus mercantile, d'une façon ou d'une autre, engageait la Fides, cette notion qui fondait les rapports entre les hommes et les dieux, et qui était le principe de la cohésion de la communauté romaine, comme de son accord profond avec le divin[85].

De ce risque, nous trouvons une confirmation significative dans les 'Fastes' d'Ovide, bien que le ton ironique du passage ait masqué partiellement aux commentateurs l'apport documentaire de ce texte, dont la portée dépasse la simple fantaisie poétique[86]. Le poète sur le mode plaisant prête une prière au marchand, qui à l'occasion du *dies mercatorum* aux Ides de Mai, fait ses ablutions et ses dévotions à la source de Mercure à la Porte Capène: l'invocation du *mercator* est toute entière composée sur le seul thème de ses parjures, et de ses faux serments destinés à abuser le client[87]. Ni l'épisode, ni le personnage ne sont exempts d'une empreinte parodique, car il y a disproportion entre la cause et l'objet de l'invocation: ni les menues filouteries, ni les propos fallacieux du boutiquier ou du colporteur n'étaient de nature à compromettre la *pax deorum*. La forme pittoresque donnée par le poète à la justification du *mercator* a fait perdre de vue le fond, c'est-à-dire que l'aspect contractuel propre à l'acte mercantile faisait intervenir la Fides dans l'établissement de la transaction.

La relation mercantile, dans la mesure où elle mettait en jeu la Fides, était grosse de risques, et dans une société encore archaïque il convenait qu'elle fût sacralisée de façon à prémunir la communauté contre ces risques. Les agissements du marchand, sciemment ou imprudemment, pouvaient rompre la Fides, aussi la communauté devait se garder de tout manquement de nature à perturber l'accord entre la cité et ses dieux, à l'occasion de l'exercice de la *mercatura*.

Avec l'évolution de la société et des structures mentales, la relation d'échange mercantile, par la force des choses, dut être progressivement soustraite à l'emprise du sacré. Au mouvement qui tendait à détacher la pratique d'un processus économique de l'efficacité d'un rituel, tout concourait, la nature éminemment pragmatique des affaires traitées, l'enjeu des intérêts en cause, un

---

[85] G. DUMÉZIL, Mitra-Varuna. Essai sur deux représentations indo-européennes de la souveraineté, 2° éd., Paris, 1948, p. 64–66, p. 71–73; G. DUMÉZIL, La religion romaine archaïque, 2° éd., p. 403.

[86] Ovide, Fasti, V, 681–688, Ed. trad. et commentaire par HENRI LE BONNIEC, Coll. Poètes du monde latin, II, Bologne, 1970, p. 168 note 148; J. LE GALL, La religion romaine de l'époque de Caton l'Ancien au règne de l'empereur Commode, Regards sur l'Hist., 22, Sér. Hist. ancienne, Paris, 1975, p. 106, p. 218–219.

[87] Ovide, Fasti, V, 681–688:

> „Ablue praeteriti periuria temporis" inquit
>   „ablue praeterita perfida uerba die!
> Siue ego te feci testem falsoue citaui
>   non audituri numina uana Iouis,
> Siue deum prudens alium diuamue fefelli,
>   abstulerint celeres improba uerba noti,
> et pateant ueniente die periuria nobis,
>   nec curent superi si qua locutus ero!"

champ d'action profane. Enfin la dimension extra-romaine de la relation mercantile impliquait que la validité d'actes auxquels était partie un contractant étranger, ne pouvait être subordonnée au seul accomplissement de rites romains, voués à être aussi inadaptés que le *Ius Fetiale* en matière de relations extérieures, quand Rome eut étendu ses entreprises au-delà du cadre étroit de l'Italie centrale[88].

Mais ce fut la généralisation de l'économie monétaire dans le milieu romain à partir du III° siècle av. J.-C. qui dut abolir l'efficacité du rituel dans son principe même. La raison d'être, la finalité d'un tel rituel était d'ordre essentiellement libératoire. Or le fait décisif à cet égard, c'est qu'à partir du III° siècle, la mise en circulation d'une monnaie de forme élaborée, émise par la puissance publique, a pris le relais du rituel dans cette fonction libératoire. L'insertion de la monnaie dans le circuit de l'échange mercantile, en substituant dans les termes de la transaction aux *res* matérielles génératrices d'obligation, des signes de richesse neutres et interchangeables, annulait la relation de dépendance que créait entre les parties, le transfert de choses concrètes, l'objet du marché d'une part, et de l'autre sa contre-partie équivalente.

Evidemment, dans ses manifestations archaïques, avant d'être le monopole de la puissance publique, la monnaie était tenue pour dotée d'un pouvoir magique, dans la mesure où elle était encore liée à un clan ou à un individu[89]. Mais les espèces monétaires, une fois qu'elles furent pesées, titrées, estampillées par la puissance publique, devinrent des symboles de valeur interchangeables, neutres, non créateurs pour l'*accipiens* d'obligation par rapport au *tradens*. La monnaie, au stade où elle était devenue la chose de la puissance publique, était libératoire, pas seulement au sens économique d'acquitter une créance, d'éteindre une dette, mais pleinement dans la mesure où elle excluait l'obligation par les choses du circuit de l'échange.

Le rituel archaïque dont les *Mercuriales* avaient été institués gardiens et protagonistes à la fondation de l'*aedes Mercurii*, immuable dans son principe et ses dispositions, était voué à tomber en désuétude: sa fonction originelle fut annulée par la diffusion de l'économie monétaire. Inadapté, mais non aboli, le rituel survécut; certes l'efficacité n'en était plus exactement perçue, mais le rôle des *Mercuriales* fut d'en maintenir les formules et les modalités.

3. L'eau vive et l'efficacité purificatoire des *sacra* des *Mercuriales*

De ce rituel, le matériel documentaire parvenu jusqu'à nous, n'offre aucun vestige d'archives comparables aux ʿActes des Frères Arvalesʾ. Cependant un texte littéraire, le développement consacré par Ovide dans ses ʿFastesʾ[90] au *dies*

---

[88] G. Wissowa, R.K.R., p. 554; K. Latte, Römische Religionsgeschichte, p. 123, p. 297; G. Dumézil, La religion romaine archaïque, 2° éd., p. 581; H. Le Bonniec, Op. cit., II, p. 168 note 149.

[89] M. Mauss, Op. cit., p. 178 note 1, p. 266.

[90] Ovide, Fasti, V,671—692.

festus mercatorum des Ides de Mai, et les indices procurés par plusieurs documents épigraphiques, nous mettent en mesure de préciser dans quel esprit avait été constitué ce rituel, et quel moyen d'action il mettait en œuvre. L'essentiel des rites caractéristiques célébrés, et des dévotions particulières accomplies à l'occasion de la solennité de Mercure aux Ides de Mai, Ovide en localise le théâtre à une source, l'*Aqua Mercurii* proche de la Porte Capène[91], c'est-à-dire située dans un secteur attenant à l'extrémité Sud-Est de la vallée du Grand Cirque, et de ce fait à portée immédiate du sanctuaire *ad Circum Maximum*. Cette source inséparable de la *religio* romaine de Mercure était tenue pour posséder des propriétés divines qui se manifestaient par une action purificatoire[92]. Faute de document topographique ou de vestiges archéologiques en place, la localisation précise de l'*Aqua Mercurii* nous échappe, mais en établir l'emplacement exact importe moins à notre propos, que constater son appartenance à l'ensemble des sources d'eau vive, à vocation sacrée, jaillissant au pied du Caelius, à proximité de la Porte Capène[93].

Cette association du culte de Mercure avec l'eau vive n'était pas une particularité propre seulement à Rome où elle aurait été favorisée, sinon engendrée par la présence au voisinage de l'*aedes Mercurii* de sources investies anciennement d'un caractère sacré. La relation de Mercure avec l'eau courante n'était pas une donnée accidentelle limitée à son seul culte romain, c'était une constante d'ordre fonctionnel qui conditionnait l'efficacité de l'action du dieu à l'égard de la relation mercantile qu'il assumait. A cet égard, cinq inscriptions de Cirta publiées par M. ANDRÉ BERTHIER procurent un témoignage significatif sur la permanence de rites associés à l'eau par des *Mercuriales* provinciaux à époque impériale.

Ces textes sont gravés sur des blocs de pierre parallélépipédiques mis au jour en Septembre 1941 sur la rive gauche du Rummel à proximité immédiate du lit du cours d'eau. Ces cinq documents épigraphiques font état de l'offrande au *collegium Mercurii* par des membres de cette association de ces blocs de pierre, qualifiés par les dédicaces n° 4 et n° 5 de *scamnum*[94]. Les *scamna* étaient des sortes de banquettes qu'on trouvait en particulier dans les établissements ther-

---

[91] Ovide, Fasti, V,673—674:

> *Est aqua Mercurii portae uicina Capenae;*
> *si iuuat expertis credere, numen habet.*

[92] Ovide, Fasti, V,681—688. Supra note 85.

[93] B. COMBET FARNOUX, Mercure romain, p. 300—303.

[94] A. BERTHIER, Le culte de Mercure à Cirta, Recueil des Notices et Mémoires de la Société Archéologique de Constantine, 65, 1942, p. 131—140:

1°— *L. Iulius Victor fil. L. Iuli Victoris uotum / collegio Mercuri promisit s. p. l. a. f. d. d.*

2°— *P. Caecilius Quadratus cum Iulia Fortunae ma/ritae collegiaris libens animi s. p. f. d. d.*

3°— *Q. Claudius Nampamo uiso monitus collegio Mercu/ri libens animo collegiaris suis donauit d. d. d. s. p.*

4°— *P. Arius Processus et fili eius collegiari / Genio Amsige ex uiso capitis collegiaris suis do(nauerunt).*
   Sur le côté droit: *Scamnu.*

5°— *Q. I. Honoratianus / scamnu. col(legiaris) cum suis do(nauit).*

maux, à l'intention des baigneurs pour leur commodité. La disposition de ces *scamna*, attribués par les donateurs à leur *collegium Mercurii* sur la berge du Rummel, à portée de main de l'eau, et la mention dans l'inscription n° 4 du *Genius Amsige*, dont le nom est attesté par ailleurs dans une inscription de Sila faisant état d'une dédicace au génie de la rivière à sa source (*Caput Amsagae*)[95] suggèrent une relation entre les activités du *collegium* et le cours d'eau.

Ces textes épigraphiques attestent la présence à Cirta d'un *collegium* attaché au culte de Mercure, or la mention de tels *collegia* est peu fréquente en Afrique, et on est tenté de rapprocher des *scamna* attribués à titre de dons au *collegium Mercurii* sur le bord du Rummel, une grande cuve de marbre rectangulaire offerte aux membres d'un *collegium* de Cirta, dont l'inscription de dédicace ne définit pas davantage l'appellation par une qualification précise[96]. La nature du don, la parenté de la formule de dédicace avec les inscriptions des *scamna*, suggèrent que l'offrande était commandée par le rôle de l'eau dans les *sacra* du *collegium*, et que les *collegiarii* de Cirta bénéficiaires de cette libéralité pourraient être également les fidèles de Mercure[97].

D'autres témoignages épigraphiques confirment l'implantation du culte de Mercure à Cirta: il disposait d'un temple dans la cité[98], et une inscription de dédicace fait état de l'offrande d'une statue de bronze du dieu[99]. Les aménagements réalisés sur la rive du Rummel à l'initiative, et par les soins de membres du *collegium Mercurii*, devaient servir à l'accomplissement de rites particuliers. La référence de l'inscription n° 4 au génie de l''Amsige', et l'installation des *scamna* sur le bord de la rivière suggèrent que l'eau courante était indispensable à la célébration de certains *sacra* du *collegium*. Ces *sacra* devaient comporter la pratique d'ablutions et de rites de purification, à la façon des dévotions rapportées par Ovide dans sa notice sur l'*Aqua Mercurii* de la Porte Capène.

Cette notice d'Ovide, les *scamna* de Cirta, sont des témoignages documentaires relatifs à des manifestations particulières et locales d'une règle générale qu'un texte tardif nous rapporte, mais dont la portée a été négligée dans la mesure où sa signification première avait échappé au compilateur qui en a enregistré le libellé. Une notice transmise par Jean Lydus fait état d'une relation étroite et singulière de Mercure avec les sources: «nous savons qu'Hermès est aussi préposé aux eaux, et pour cette raison dans ses sanctuaires, on consacre des sources, ou on creuse des puits»[100]. Cette notice est unique, et au premier abord passablement déconcertante, nous ignorons chez quel auteur antérieur, et plus précisément dans quel contexte Jean Lydus avait relevé ce fait qu'il présente comme caractéristique d'Hermès-Mercure. Mais elle nous procure un élément

---

[95] C.I.L., VIII, 5884: *(g)eni(o) numinis / caput Amsagae / sacrum / C. Arruntius / Faustus Arrunti / Proculi filius / magistratus / permisso ordinis / suis pecunis fecit / itemque dedicauit / libens animo.*

[96] C.I.L., VIII, 6970: *Antius Victoricus cum / Antios Victoricu et Mausolu iuniores uiso / moniti libens animo colegiaris donaue/runt ex s. n. CC. s. p. f. d. d.*

[97] A. BERTHIER, Art. cit., p. 136.

[98] Ibid., p. 136 note 5, p. 137 note 1.

[99] C.I.L., VIII, 6962.

[100] J. Lydus, De mensibus, IV, 76.

positif qui importe au premier chef à notre propos, la prescription relative à la
présence de fontaines et de puits dans les sanctuaires de Mercure. Cette règle
était d'ordre rituel, comme l'atteste la notice d'Ovide, elle garantissait l'efficacité
des *sacra* particuliers au moyen desquels s'exerçait l'action du dieu à l'égard de la
merx dont il assumait la charge au niveau du divin.

Quelle était la signification originelle de ces rites dont l'accomplissement
exigeait la présence d'eau courante? La notice d'Ovide attribue à ce rituel une
action purificatoire, mais de quel principe procédait son efficacité, sur quoi portait son action, et de quelle nature était la souillure qu'il était appelé à effacer?

La plupart des commentateurs attentifs à la prière du *mercator*, ont prêté à
l'*Aqua Mercurii* la propriété de laver le marchand de la souillure attachée à ses
tromperies et filouteries[101]. Par-delà la formulation, sur un mode ironique, des
invocations du trafiquant avide de profit, le propos exprimé par une «voix
habituée à tromper»[102], met l'accent sur le manquement à la foi jurée, c'est-à-
dire sur la rupture de la Fides dans le jeu de la relation mercantile, dans l'exécution du contrat d'échange commercial.

En fait, le rite procède de conceptions archaïques encore suffisamment pré-
dominantes dans la société romaine des débuts de la République, au moment où
fut adoptée la relation d'échange selon le mode mercantile, pour marquer de leur
empreinte les formes et les modalités d'exécution du contrat propre à ce type
d'échange. Prendre en considération seulement le *mercator*, s'en tenir aux
paroles que lui prête Ovide, ne permet pas de saisir dans sa plénitude la portée
du rite. En effet, pour qu'il y eût échange sous forme mercantile, l'essentiel à
quoi répondait l'efficacité originelle du rituel, c'était de neutraliser les choses
constituant la matière et les termes de la transaction, d'annuler l'obligation
contraignante émanant d'elles à l'égard des parties prenantes au contrat. La
fonction première du rituel n'était pas de purifier l'agent, le *mercator*, mais de
neutraliser l'objet, la *merx*, et par là de libérer ce mode d'échange de l'obligation
par les choses propre à l'échange-don archaïque.

De toute façon, la prière attribuée par Ovide au *mercator* n'est pas un
carmen rituel, et le développement qui la précède décrit des gestes rituels autrement significatifs, parce qu'hérités d'un passé lointain, et efficaces indépendamment du discours de supplique tout empreint des motivations personnelles, et
des préoccupations intéressées du marchand. En une formule, Ovide définit
exactement la signification originelle, et l'efficacité première de ce rite d'aspersion par l'eau: . . . *lauro sparguntur ab uda / omnia, quae dominos sunt habitura
nouos*[103], «avec ce laurier, il arrose tous les objets qui doivent passer à de
nouveaux propriétaires». On s'est attaché à chercher le sens du rite du côté de la
seule purification du *mercator* coupable d'une faute personnelle de tromperie et
de filouterie, à laquelle le jeu de la transaction mercantile devait donner lieu à

---

[101] Ovide, The Fasti of Ovid, Ed. James Frazer, IV, Commentary on Books V and VI,
Londres, 1929, p. 115; F. Bömer, P. Ovidius Naso. Die Fasten, II, p. 332.
[102] Ovide, Fasti, V,680:

Et peragit solita fallere uoce preces . . .

[103] Ovide, Fasti, V,677–678.

l'occasion, et on a négligé son action première et essentielle qui s'exerçait sur les choses constituant la matière de la relation mercantile, en annulant l'obligation contraignante dont elles étaient porteuses.

Dans l'exécution du contrat d'échange mercantile, la *res* objet de la transaction devait être remise à celui qui la recevait, dégagée de ses liens, libérée des vices magiques de nature à lier l'acheteur au propriétaire antérieur, elle devait être *pura*[104], et c'était le rôle de rites appropriés d'assurer cette purification à l'occasion des transactions.

Or dans la pratique des *sacra* romains, les opérations de lustration donnaient lieu à l'emploi d'eau vive recueillie à des sources naturelles, puisée *uiuo flumine*, et non point prise à des citernes[105]. Ainsi l'aspersion au moyen de l'eau de la source de la Porte Capène constituait le rite propre à purifier les *res*, objets des transactions commerciales, en les libérant des obligations inhérentes à leur nature intrinsèque, qui faute d'être levées, risquaient de lier l'acquéreur, indépendamment des clauses convenues du contrat d'échange mercantile. Ce geste rituel libératoire n'était pas effectué seulement à l'occasion du *dies mercatorum* des Ides de Mai; toute opération commerciale, tout acte d'échange selon la procédure mercantile, devait donner lieu à une aspersion purificatoire, car Ovide spécifie que le *mercator* emportait de cette eau bénéfique dans une urne préalablement purifiée par une fumigation[106].

D'autre part, le *mercator*, intermédiaire entre les parties présentes au contrat d'échange mercantile, agent de la transmission des objets matériels de la transaction, était exposé à être lié dans sa personne par le report sur sa tête des obligations émanant des *res* dont il assurait le transfert. Il convenait donc qu'il se prémunît contre ce risque, et se dégageât des liens éventuellement créés ou transférés par le jeu du processus mercantile. Enfin dans la mesure où le contrat d'échange mercantile mettait en cause la Fides, comme dans l'exécution d'un *uotum*[107], comme dans le serment[108], le *mercator* se trouvait engager sa personne, *caput obligare*. A cet égard, il est significatif que de son laurier ruisselant de l'eau puisée à la source de la Porte Capène, il s'aspergeait les cheveux[109], c'est-à-dire le sommet de la tête, pour libérer sa personne des liens dont le transfert des objets matériels, l'engagement de la Fides, pouvaient le charger.

Evidemment, la fonction médiatrice du dieu appliquée à la relation d'échange mercantile, d'un point de vue général, consistait à assurer la bonne marche, et à pourvoir à l'aboutissement du processus mercantile, et à cet égard, la mise en œuvre du rituel correspondant manifestait l'efficacité du dieu en

---

[104] M. Mauss, Op. cit., p. 238.

[105] G. Wissowa, R.K.R., p. 219; G. Dumézil, Op. cit., 2° éd., p. 392.

[106] Ovide, Fasti, V,675—676:

> Huc uenit incinctus tunica mercator et urna
> purus suffita, quam ferat, haurit aquam.

[107] K. Latte, Op. cit., p. 46 note 1.

[108] G. Wissowa, R.K.R., p. 388.

[109] Ovide, Fasti, V,679:

> Spargit et ipse suos lauro rorante capillos.

accordant l'acte mercantile avec les exigences du sacré. Un tel rituel, compte tenu de la place qu'y tenait l'emploi de l'eau vive, avait une action purificatoire à l'égard de l'objet – la *merx* –, et de l'agent – le *mercator* – de la relation mercantile, mais son efficacité indispensable à la réalisation du contrat d'échange selon le mode mercantile, dépassait de beaucoup la portée d'une simple *lustratio*, dont l'action était d'ordre essentiellement préventif, à la manière de tant de rituels agraires archaïques.

En fait, l'essentiel de l'efficacité du rituel propre aux *Mercuriales* se situait sur un autre plan, elle n'était pas simplement d'ordre défensif et préservatif, elle était opérative, elle conditionnait le jeu et l'accomplissement du contrat d'échange selon le mode mercantile. Le rituel dans son principe n'était pas une sauvegarde, c'était une condition nécessaire pour imprimer à l'échange, qui de par la nature des choses, restait tout entier chargé des astreintes propres à l'échange-don archaïque, la forme mercantile, en laissant le champ libre au jeu de l'accord contractuel des parties par la neutralisation des *res* concrètes, objets matériels de la transaction. La destination du rituel était de délier une obligation, lever une contrainte, dissoudre une dépendance, en un mot libérer l'échange au sens fort.

Investi de la charge de la *merx*, Hermès, en tant que Mercurius était bien dans le droit fil de l'héritage sacré des Latins, une puissance divine fonctionnelle, mais l'efficacité libératoire nécessaire à la fonction mercantile, qu'il assumait, il ne la tirait pas de la tradition romaine, il la tenait, à titre de transposition d'Hermès, de ses attaches avec le *ritus graecus,* dont l'action était précisément libératoire. De cette vocation témoigne significativement la participation de Mercure à la première grande cérémonie du *ritus graecus,* le lectisterne de 399 av. J.-C. à finalité cathartique et prophylactique.

III. *La* religio *de Mercure, les* Mercuriales *et les débuts du culte impérial*

Un problème longtemps controversé reste celui de la nature de la relation associant la *religio* de Mercure aux premières formes du culte rendu à la divinité du *princeps*. Divers témoignages attestent cette relation entre les empereurs et Mercure[110]. Cette relation s'est constituée, et a pris forme dès le début du principat, et à ce sujet nous disposons de plusieurs documents qui les uns rapportent, les autres suggèrent l'identification d'Octave-Auguste avec Mercure.

Ces témoignages ont été vivement discutés. Le problème le plus controversé qui a contribué à jeter la suspicion sur l'ensemble de la documentation parvenue jusqu'à nous, a été celui de l'identification d'Octave-Auguste avec Mercure. Cette assimilation du *princeps* à une divinité est apparue à de nombreux historiens comme une innovation insolite, voire irrecevable, dans la

---

[110] J. Chittenden, Hermes-Mercury, Dynasts and Emperors, Numismatic Chronicle, Ser. VI, 5, 1945, p. 52—53.

mesure où à Rome le sens du sacré, la sensibilité religieuse, interdisaient qu'on divinisât de son vivant un homme, si éminent fût-il.

1. Critique du matériel documentaire attestant une relation entre la *religio* de Mercure et le culte impérial

A cet égard, un article critique de KENNETH SCOTT[111] illustre de façon exemplaire comment l'étude de la relation associant Octave-Auguste à Mercure avait été faussée depuis le début par le fait que le matériel documentaire rassemblé par les érudits avait été pris en considération, et interprété seulement en fonction de l'identification du *princeps* avec le dieu, prise au pied de la lettre sur la foi d'une ode d'Horace (Carm. I, 2). Depuis MOMMSEN, le point de départ des spéculations sur Auguste et Mercure a été la strophe où Horace qualifie Octave-Auguste de «fils de Maia» *almae filius Maiae*[112].

KENNETH SCOTT a observé combien les érudits depuis STEUDING jusqu'à W. DEONNA[113], parce qu'ils tenaient pour parfaitement établie l'existence d'un culte rendu à Auguste sous les apparences de Mercure, se sont répétés les uns les autres dans l'énumération des mêmes témoignages considérés comme probants, dès lors qu'ils paraissaient aller dans le même sens que l'affirmation d'Horace, sans examiner de près les sources, sans vérifier la portée, la signification et parfois même l'authenticité des documents qu'ils alléguaient comme preuves[114].

Ainsi KENNETH SCOTT au long d'une étude rigoureuse rejeta comme inadéquats la plupart des éléments du matériel documentaire invoqués précédemment à titre d'arguments propres à démontrer l'existence d'un culte rendu à Auguste en qualité de Mercure: certains sans rapport avec le problème ont été pris en considération à tort[115], d'autres sollicités par les commentateurs sont irrecevables[116], d'autres encore apparaissent extrêmement douteux, sinon faux[117]. Au terme de son examen critique, KENNETH SCOTT inclinait à recon-

---

[111] KENNETH SCOTT, Mercur-Augustus und Horaz C. I, 2, Hermes, 63, 1928, p. 15–33.
[112] Hor., Carm., I, 2, 41–44:

> *siue mutata iuuenem figura*
> *ales in terris imitaris, almae*
> *filius Maiae, patiens uocari*
> *Caesaris ultor.*

[113] STEUDING, dans: W. H. ROSCHER, Lex. II,2,1894–97, Art. cit. Mercurius, col. 2817–2818; LEGRAND, dans: Dict. des Ant., III, 2, Paris 1904, Art. Mercure, p. 1820–1821; G. WISSOWA, R.K.R., p. 93, p. 305–306; H. HEINEN, Zur Begründung des römischen Kaiserkultes, Klio, 11, 1911, p. 150 note 3; W. DEONNA, Le trésor des Fins d'Annecy, Rev. Arch., Sér. V, 11, 1920, p. 187–188; W. DEONNA, La légende d'Octave-Auguste, dieu sauveur et maître du monde, Revue d'Histoire des religions, 83, 1921, p. 35 sq.
[114] KENNETH SCOTT, Art. cit., p. 17.
[115] KENNETH SCOTT, Art. cit., p. 17–19, et p. 21–23.
[116] Ibid., p. 19–21.
[117] Ibid., p. 25–26.

naître comme probants deux documents seulement, l'ode d'Horace, et une inscription de dédicace des *scrutarei* de Cos[118].

En fait, le matériel documentaire propre à nous procurer des indices dignes de créance comporte des textes, et des représentations iconographiques. Parmi les textes, nous possédons une source littéraire, l'ode d'Horace (Carm., I, 2), puis des documents épigraphiques. Au nombre de ces derniers, les plus importants sont des inscriptions de dédicace donnant à conclure que des *collegia* de *Mercuriales* au temps d'Auguste, en Italie, et particulièrement en Campanie, se confondaient, ou avaient fusionné avec les *Augustales* pour célébrer le culte impérial[119]. Les nombreuses dédicaces à 'Mercurius Augustus'[120] ne peuvent fournir d'indication digne d'être retenue, 'Augustus' devint très tôt une épithète appliquée aux divinités comme au *princeps,* elle impliquait un surcroît de sacralité, et ne signifiait nullement que le dieu ainsi qualifié fût obligatoirement assimilé à l'empereur[121].

Quant aux documents iconographiques, nous pouvons en envisager essentiellement quatre, qui en dépit des opinions partagées auxquelles donna lieu l'interprétation de chacun considéré séparément, apparaissent propres à confirmer qu'Octave-Auguste fut représenté sous les apparences de Mercure.

1°— Une scène figurée sur le côté gauche d'un autel de Bologne[122].

2°— L'effigie de Mercure constituant un des motifs de la décoration en stuc du plafond d'une maison du quartier de la Farnésine à Rome[123].

3°— Une gemme gravée de l'ancienne collection Marlborough, représentant le portrait d'Octave-Auguste accompagné du caducée[124].

4°— La statue signée de Kléoménès représentant un Mercure orateur sur le modèle de l'Hermès Λόγιος. C'est le document dont l'identification est la moins assurée. On avait proposé à tort de reconnaître dans la tête de cette statue le portrait de Germanicus. Si on s'accorde pour y voir l'effigie d'un membre de la famille d'Auguste, on n'a pas apporté de preuve décisive en faveur de l'attribution à une individualité précise. L'interprétation proposée par certains érudits, qui ont essayé d'établir qu'il s'agissait du portrait d'Octave jeune n'a pas été unanimement acceptée[125].

---

[118] Ibid., p. 32; A. MAIURI, Nuova silloge epigrafica di Rodi e Cos, Florence, 1925, n° 466.

[119] TH. MOMMSEN, C.I.L., X, p. 109; C.I.L., IX, 54. X, 217, 232, 233, 485, 884 à 892, 1272; A. DEGRASSI, I.L.L.R.P., n° 230 = C.I.L., I (2), 1612. X, 1153; A. DEGRASSI, Iscrizioni nuove. I 'Magistri Mercuriales' di Lucca e la dea 'Anzotica' di 'Aenona', Athenaeum, 15, 1937, p. 284—287.

[120] STEUDING, dans: W. H. ROSCHER, Lex., II,2,1894—97, Art. cit. Mercurius, col. 2818.

[121] G. WISSOWA, R.K.R., p. 85 note 1; K. LATTE, Römische Religionsgeschichte, p. 324—325; J. GAGÉ, Apollon romain, p. 576.

[122] E. SAMTER, Mercurius und Minerva, Mitt. Dt. Arch. Inst. Röm. Abt., 10, 1895, p. 93—94. K. LEHMANN-HARTLEBEN, Ein Altar in Bologna, Mitt. Dt. Arch. Inst. Röm. Abt., 42, 1927, p. 163—176.

[123] O. BRENDEL, Novus Mercurius, Mitt. Dt. Arch. Inst. Röm. Abt., 50, 1935, p. 231—251.

[124] A. FURTWÄNGLER, Die antiken Gemmen. Gesch. d. Steinschneidekunst im klass. Altertum, Berlin—Leipzig, 1900, III, Pl. XXXVIII, 30; F. ALTHEIM, Römische Religionsgeschichte, Berlin, 3 Bde., 1931—33, Bd. II, p. 206.

[125] J. SIX, Octavien-Mercure, Rev. Arch., Sér. V, 4, 1916, p. 257—264; KENNETH SCOTT,

2. Insuffisance des interprétations traditionnelles de la relation de Mercure avec Octave-Auguste et le culte impérial

La signification de la relation entre Octave-Auguste et Mercure a été diversement entendue, et généralement mal saisie. Les chercheurs modernes ont engagé leurs commentaires sur des voies illusoires, et proposé des solutions sollicitées, faute d'avoir clairement discerné, et exactement défini la spécificité du Mercure romain. La raison de l'identification du *princeps* avec le personnage divin de Mercure devrait résider dans la fonction du dieu. Mais sur ce point, les appréciations des commentateurs modernes divergent profondément. Mercure a-t-il été réputé s'incarner dans Octave-Auguste à titre de dieu évergète, bienfaiteur des hommes à qui il aurait enseigné les avantages de la civilisation, ou en qualité de dieu du commerce, générateur de gain et de prospérité?

La première explication est depuis longtemps reçue avec faveur par les érudits: le Mercure appelé par Horace à descendre sur terre pour s'incarner dans la personne d'Octave, serait l'Hermès Λόγιος, dieu de l'éloquence et des arts, dispensateur de bienfaits utiles à l'organisation et à la vie de la société des hommes, assimilé depuis le III° siècle av. J.-C. au Thôt égyptien, tenu pour l'inventeur de l'écriture, des lois et de la civilisation. Cet Hermès-Thôt, à la fois Λόγος et Νοῦς, était tout ensemble un sauveur envoyé du ciel pour apporter au monde le salut avec l'ordre et la paix, et un maître de la connaissance venu révéler aux hommes les secrets des arts et des sciences.

Cette interprétation ouvrait la voie à de larges perspectives, car l'identification d'Octave à Hermès-Thôt, dieu bénéfique et sauveur, en présentant le *princeps* dans le rôle d'un βασιλεὺς σωτήρ rejoignait un thème persistant de la sibyllistique orientale[126], et le vieux problème controversé de l'influence éventuelle du culte royal hellénistique sur les débuts du culte impérial romain. Ainsi les spéculations hermétiques hellénistiques tributaires de la tradition égyptienne, auraient servi et légitimé à Rome l'identification du *princeps* avec Mercure, en tant qu'homologue de l'Hermès Λόγιος, et du Thôt égyptien. A cette interprétation dont REITZENSTEIN, dès le début de ce siècle, avait déjà formulé le principe, et tracé les grandes lignes[127], les chercheurs ultérieurs ont emprunté la substance des commentaires qu'ils ont composés sur ce thème[128].

Cette interprétation a été reçue avec une faveur persistante, dans la mesure où cette assimilation mettant en œuvre une divinité salutaire semblait traduire l'aspiration à un renouvellement, à un accomplissement attendu d'un souverain promoteur d'une ère nouvelle[129]. Un Mercure-Auguste aux affinités orientales,

Art. cit., p. 24 et notes 5, 6, 7 et 8; J. CHITTENDEN, Art. cit., p. 41; J. CHARBONNEAUX, L'art au siècle d'Auguste, Paris, 1948, p. 50–51, Pl. 59; E. BICKERMAN, Consecratio, dans: Le culte des souverains dans l'Empire romain, Fondation Hardt, Entretiens, 19, Genève, 1973, p. 3.

[126] J. GAGÉ, Apollon romain, p. 596.

[127] R. REITZENSTEIN, Poimandres. Studien z. griech.-ägypt. u. frühchristl. Litteratur, Leipzig, 1904, p. 174 sq.

[128] KENNETH SCOTT, Art. cit., p. 30; O. BRENDEL, Art. cit., p. 235, p. 245–247, p. 251.

[129] O. BRENDEL, Art. cit., p. 239.

dans le rôle de βασιλεὺς σωτήρ, paraissait répondre aux thèmes sibyllins et millénaristes alors en circulation, et qualifié pour ménager l'entrée dans un nouveau cycle dont l'annonce et l'espérance étaient entretenues par tant de prophéties ambiguës dans leur propos, leurs origines et leur destination.

Aussi les commentateurs ont retenu volontiers cette interprétation en même temps qu'ils croyaient discerner dans l'appel d'Horace à Mercure-Octave, l'aspiration à une mission de salut. Une analyse récente se rattache encore sur le fond à ce courant[130]: M. E. J. BICKERMAN, pour rendre compte de l'invocation d'Horace à l'*almae filius Maiae*, a repris ce thème de l'œuvre de renouvellement attendue d'Hermès-Mercure descendu du ciel. Par-delà la tâche de restaurer la *pax deorum*, en acceptant de se faire sous les apparences d'Octave, le vengeur du meurtre de César[131], il revenait à Mercure qui était le Λόγος, le verbe incarné, la mission d'instaurer un nouvel ordre sous les traits du *iuuenis Octauius*[132].

En fait, cette interprétation de prime abord séduisante pour l'esprit, apparaît à la réflexion peu vraisemblable, et très improbable, compte tenu du moment — les années qui suivent immédiatement Actium —. En toute occasion, Octave-Auguste a témoigné son aversion à l'égard des influences égyptiennes, et des divinités d'Alexandrie, aussi il est douteux qu'il ait accepté d'être identifié à Rome et en Italie avec un dieu, qui eût été la réplique du Thôt égyptien. Quant à Horace, il est également douteux qu'il ait fourvoyé son imagination poétique dans une direction si peu conforme aux intentions, et à la politique d'Octave qu'il approuvait et soutenait. Par conséquent il est peu vraisemblable que son appel à Mercure pour venger le meurtre de César, s'adressât à un Hermès-Thôt, et il est bien hasardeux de chercher dans cette ode la preuve qu'Horace ait vu dans ce Mercure-Octave, qu'il qualifiait des titres bien romains de *pater atque princeps*[133], un βασιλεὺς σωτήρ à la mode des Ptolémées.

La spécialisation proprement romaine du dieu dans le domaine mercantile a inspiré une autre interprétation. Dans la mesure où on a entendu communément la fonction de Mercure, en qualité de dieu du commerce, comme le patronage des activités mercantiles, et la protection des *mercatores,* on a envisagé depuis longtemps une explication dont le principe résidait dans le côté bénéfique de l'œuvre de réorganisation d'Auguste en matière de prospérité, et de développement des intérêts matériels[134]. Octave en mettant un terme aux vicissitudes des guerres civiles garantissait la paix, rendait la sécurité aux échanges, et favorisait l'enrichissement. Il y aurait gagné la reconnaissance particulière de la classe moyenne, des milieux mercantiles et financiers désormais recrutés pour l'essentiel parmi les affranchis[135], qui par gratitude intéressée auraient été enclins

---

[130] E. J. BICKERMAN, *Filius Maiae* (Horace. Odes I,2,43), Parola del passato, 16, 1961, p. 5—19.

[131] Ibid., p. 6—7, p. 14.

[132] Ibid., p. 15, p. 18.

[133] Hor., Carm., I,2,50.

[134] G. WISSOWA, R.K.R., p. 93 note 3, p. 306.

[135] R. SYME, The Roman Revolution, Oxford, 1952, p. 354; J. GAGÉ, Les classes sociales dans l'Empire romain, Paris, 1971, p. 140—142.

à identifier leur divinité protectrice avec le *princeps,* mué sous les apparences de Mercure, en une manière de *mercator* d'honneur.

A cet égard, KENNETH SCOTT rompant avec le point de vue exclusivement critique qu'il avait développé dans un premier temps, a proposé de voir dans la représentation de Mercure-Auguste sur l'autel de Bologne, un témoignage de piété offert par un homme de cette catégorie, occupé d'affaires de négoce, un *Mercurialis,* au dieu patron de ses activités, et de ses intérêts[136]. Il concluait, cette fois sans référence à la conception égyptienne d'un Hermès-Thôt, βασιλεὺς σωτήρ, que le Mercure-Auguste représenté sur ce document iconographique procurait un indice supplémentaire attestant que l'identification de l'empereur avec ce dieu doit être attribuée probablement à la classe des gens d'affaires, aux *Mercuriales*[137].

Pour étayer cette interprétation, exploitant une hypothèse formulée par KERÉNYI[138], il concluait que la scène figurée de l'autel de Bologne, où Mercure-Auguste est précédé par un personnage féminin, en attirail guerrier identifiable avec la déesse Rome ou Minerve[139], correspond à un tableau décrit dans le 'Satiricon' comme retraçant l'entrée du jeune Trimalcion à Rome, le caducée à la main, sous la conduite de Minerve[140]. Les tableaux peints sur un mur d'un portique de la maison de Trimalcion illustraient l'ascension sociale de cet affranchi enrichi qui avait placé significativement les étapes de sa carrière sous le signe de Mercure[141], et qui se réclamait de la protection particulière du dieu[142]. Selon KERÉNYI, la représentation de la réussite du parvenu millionaire se serait doublée d'une signification symbolique: Trimalcion figuré avec le caducée s'identifiait avec son patron divin, et par l'initiation il se muait en νέος Ἑρμῆς, *nouus Mercurius*[143]. La symbolique dont fait état cette interprétation n'a été confirmée par aucun élément positif, et il est tout à fait hasardeux de s'en réclamer, pour conjecturer à l'arrière-plan des *sacra* des *Mercuriales* l'action de cercles d'initiés pratiquant d'éventuels mystères hermétiques[144].

L'erreur commune, qui dès le départ, a égaré ce type d'interprétation, c'est d'avoir fait consister la fonction du dieu dans le patronage d'une catégorie socio-professionnelle, les *mercatores,* les praticiens des activités de négoce, et non dans

---

[136] KENNETH SCOTT, Mercury on the Bologna Altar, Mitt. Dt. Arch. Inst. Röm. Abt., 50, 1935, p. 225–230, et particulièrement p. 228–229.

[137] KENNETH SCOTT, Art. cit., Mercury on the Bologna Altar, p. 229.

[138] K. KERÉNYI, De teletis Mercurialibus observationes II, Egyetemes Philologiai Közlony, 47, 1923, p. 150–164.

[139] KENNETH SCOTT, Art. cit., Mercury on the Bologna Altar, p. 227–228; K. LEHMANN-HARTLEBEN, Art. cit., Ein Altar in Bologna, p. 173–174.

[140] Petrone, Satiricon, XXIX, 3.

[141] Ibid., XXIX, 3–5.

[142] Ibid., LXXVII, 4: *Interim dum Mercurius uigilat, aedificaui hanc domum . . .*

[143] K. KERÉNYI, Art. cit., p. 158 sq.

[144] J. GAGÉ, Apollon romain, p. 577–578, p. 618; J. GAGÉ, Les classes sociales dans l'Empire romain, p. 142–143.

la prise en charge au niveau du sacré de la *merx*, c'est-à-dire du mode mercantile de l'échange.

Les *Magistri Mercuriales Augustales* mentionnés dans les inscriptions de Campanie et d'Italie du sud étant issus du milieu des affranchis, on a conclu volontiers que la dévotion à Mercurius Augustus s'était instaurée chez les commerçants, et de façon générale chez les petites gens. Ceux-ci mus par une reconnaissance intéressée pour le *princeps*, qui à l'issue des guerres civiles, avait rétabli la paix et la prospérité nécessaires à leurs affaires, auraient été portés par loyalisme à l'identifier avec le dieu du commerce, promoteur de profit et de richesse.

Cette interprétation inspirée du thème d'une bienveillance également prêtée au dieu et au *princeps* à l'égard des préoccupations, et des intérêts mercantiles de cette catégorie sociale, est sollicitée, car elle déduit de ces témoignages documentaires une dévotion particulière à Mercurius Augustus, comme s'il s'agissait d'ex-votos, de manifestations individuelles de piété reconnaissante motivées par la réussite commerciale. Or ces inscriptions ne font état ni de particuliers exprimant leur gratitude à titre personnel, ni même de *mercatores* satisfaisant à une dévotion d'ordre professionnel, mais de *Magistri Mercuriales Augustales* ou de *Ministri Augusti Mercurii Maiae*, c'est-à-dire de membres responsables de *collegia* de *Mercuriales*, qui avaient la charge du rituel attaché aux *sacra* de Mercure. De toute façon, le culte impérial rendu au *princeps* n'est né ni d'une décision impériale, ni même de l'initiative individuelle de fidèles, ce fut un culte public institué par des collectivités, les cités autonomes, et mis en œuvre dans le cadre d'organismes tels les *Mercuriales*, déjà investis d'une mission d'ordre institutionnel, la célébration des rites d'un culte public.

Ainsi, comme l'avait déjà observé justement Madame CHITTENDEN à propos du problème posé par le thème du Mercure-Auguste: «Ni l'explication mercantile, ni l'interprétation philosophique ne fournissent pleinement la réponse»[145]. En fait, la raison d'être, et la signification de la relation de Mercure avec le culte impérial doivent être cherchées dans la *religio* romaine de Mercure, et dans la finalité du rituel, dont les *Mercuriales* étaient les dépositaires. A cet égard, l'explication mercantile n'est pas erronée dans son principe, elle a seulement été dévoyée constamment dans son application, dès lors que les commentateurs donnant le pas au *mercator* sur la *merx*, entendaient la fonction de Mercure comme la protection particulière de la profession marchande, non comme la prise en charge du processus mercantile. Mercurius n'était pas le 'Mercator' divin, mais la puissance divine qui donnait le champ libre au jeu de la relation d'échange mercantile, et dont l'action spécifique s'exerçait au moyen d'un rituel à finalité libératoire et purificatoire. Or compte tenu du contexte de l'ode d'Horace, l'appel du poète à l'*almae filius Maiae* doit précisément procéder de cette vocation purificatoire attachée à la fonction première du dieu romain.

---

[145] J. CHITTENDEN, Art. cit., p. 57.

1

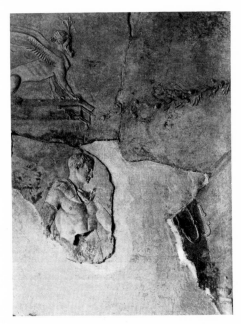

2   3

Auguste représenté sous les traits de Mercure:
1. La gemme gravée de l'ancienne Collection Marlborough
2. Statue de Mercure orateur de Kléoménès
3. Mercure—Auguste (Stuc de la maison de la Farnésine)

4

5

6

L'autel de Bologne:

4. Face antérieure   5. Face latérale gauche

6. Face latérale droite

3. Le témoignage de l'ode d'Horace (Carm. I, 2) et la vocation purificatoire de Mercurius Augustus

Un examen attentif de l'ode d'Horace est propre à confirmer que l'appel à l'intervention de Mercure, sous les apparences du *iuuenis Octauius*, était conforme à l'action libératoire et purificatoire, dont le dieu avait manifesté initialement l'efficacité à Rome dans le champ particulier de la *merx*.

Le thème général de cette ode n'est pas la divinisation indirecte d'Octave, ni son assimilation, selon l'usage hellénistique, à un βασιλεὺς σωτήρ apportant salut et régénération à un monde renouvelé. L'inspiration de l'ensemble du poème procède d'une notion romaine essentielle, la *pax deorum*, cet accord nécessaire entre le monde terrestre et le plan du sacré, accord sans lequel une communauté humaine en rupture avec le divin ne peut rien faire de légitime, ni fonder quoi que ce soit de durable.

Or le meurtre de César avait rompu profondément la *pax deorum*. Cette rupture est attestée non seulement par ses conséquences, les vicissitudes militaires, et les convulsions politiques de la guerre civile, mais elle a été rendue d'emblée manifeste par les signes qui se produisent habituellement à chaque fois qu'un désordre intolérable survient dans le cours normal de la relation entre le divin et l'humain, des prodiges, des *monstra*[146]: des perturbations atmosphériques, chutes de neige et averses de grêle, des prodiges fulguratoires frappant le Capitole et l'*Arx*, ces sites symboliques de la puissance romaine, une crue du Tibre qui au printemps 44 entraîna une inondation d'une ampleur exceptionnelle[147].

L'assassinat de César ne fut pas seulement un manquement criminel aux lois humaines, mais il a été cause d'un désordre grave dans l'accord entre la communauté romaine et ses dieux. Quand Horace interroge: *Cui dabit partis scelus expiandi, Iuppiter*[148]?, la formule n'exprime pas seulement un vœu conforme à toute morale sociale qui exige qu'il soit tiré vengeance des forfaits contraires aux lois, par le châtiment de leurs auteurs. Certes il s'agit bien que soit purifiée la souillure inhérente à un crime de sang, mais l'application des règles ordinaires du droit pénal ne saurait y suffire. L'emploi d'un verbe appartenant au vocabulaire de la technique sacerdotale, *expiare*, indique qu'il importe au moyen de *piacula* appropriés de restaurer la *pax deorum*[149], en apaisant les dieux, et au premier chef le Diuus Julius.

Le choix des divinités appelées à assister Octave dans cette œuvre de piété destinée à restaurer la *pax deorum* est significatif par la relation privilégiée qui les associait à la *gens Julia*, et les rattachait au Diuus Julius: Apollon, Vénus et Mars étendaient leur protection particulière sur les Julii et Octave devenu un des leurs par son adoption. De prime abord, l'invocation à Mercure, après en avoir appelé successivement à Apollon Vénus et Mars, semble particulièrement appropriée à

[146] Hor., Carm. I,2,6; E. J. BICKERMAN, Art. cit., p. 6–8.
[147] J. LE GALL, Le Tibre fleuve de Rome dans l'antiquité, p. 29–30.
[148] Hor., carm., I,2,29.
[149] E. J. BICKERMAN, Art. cit., p. 8.

la situation du moment, dans la mesure où son intervention pouvait apparaître comme le gage du rétablissement définitif de la paix.

Mais ce qui est le plus propre à étonner dans l'invite adressée par Horace à Mercure, c'est la mission qu'il lui propose: «Accepte d'être appelé le vengeur (*ultor*) de César»[150]. Entendue littéralement, cette formule ne correspond ni à la vocation, ni à la sphère d'action du Mercure romain. A aucun titre, Mercure ne fut un dieu guerrier ou justicier; ni la force, ni la coercition n'ont jamais fait partie de la panoplie de ses moyens d'action. *Ultor* ne fut jamais une épithète cultuelle de Mercure, et il ne saurait l'être au même titre que Mars.

«Accepter d'être appelé le vengeur de César» doit s'entendre comme assumer sur le plan du sacré la liquidation des conséquences de l'assassinat des Ides de Mars: il s'agit de rendre manifeste que la vengeance du meurtre de César est cette fois pleinement accomplie, que le Diuus Julius est désormais apaisé, et que le désordre apporté à la *pax deorum* par ce crime sacrilège est maintenant effacé.

Or la fonction première d'Hermès-Mercurius à Rome, ce fut la prise en charge de la *merx*, c'est-à-dire de la relation d'échange selon le mode mercantile, et cette fonction dans son principe ne consistait pas en un patronage symbolique, mais en une médiation opérative au niveau du sacré. En assumant le mode mercantile de l'échange, le dieu exerçait une action libératoire et purificatoire propre à neutraliser les *res*, objets matériels de transaction, à annuler les obligations et contraintes tenant aux choses, aux structures et aux personnes, à lever les obstacles au libre jeu de la relation contractuelle qui fondait le processus mercantile. L'efficacité de cette action se matérialisait par l'intermédiaire d'un rituel attaché à la *religio* romaine de Mercure, où intervenait l'eau vive comme moyen de purification.

Dans le droit fil de cette vocation première à assumer la relation contractuelle, Mercure était également *pacifer*, promoteur et garant des accords négociés, et cet aspect de sa fonction médiatrice doit rendre compte de l'allusion aux Parthes, sur laquelle Horace a clos son poème. Sur ce sujet, l'exhortation finale adressée au dieu est aussi surprenante dans sa formulation que l'appel initial le conviant à se faire le vengeur de César: «Ne permets pas que les Mèdes chevauchent impunément»[151], car Mercure n'est en aucun cas un dieu guerrier.

Le règlement de la question parthe laissé en suspens par la disparition de César faisait partie de la succession du Diuus Julius, et sur ce point qui touchait à la fierté romaine, Octave devait également relever l'héritage. L'opinion attendait de lui une expédition en Orient sur le modèle de celle préparée par César, or il s'attacha à obtenir une solution satisfaisante par les moyens de la

---

[150] Hor., Carm., I,2,43–44:

> *filius Maiae, patiens uocari*
> *Caesaris ultor;*

E. J. Bickerman, Art. cit., p. 14–15.

[151] Hor., Carm., I,2,51–52:

> *neu sinas Medos, equitare inultos*
> *te duce, Caesar.*

diplomatie, plutôt que par une démonstration militaire coûteuse et d'issue aléatoire[152]. Dans ce contexte, le recours à Mercure s'accorde avec la politique de négociation adoptée après Actium, qui devait aboutir en 19 av. J.-C. à imposer à Phraatès la restitution des prisonniers survivants et des *signa,* et la reconnaissance d'une suzeraineté romaine de principe[153].

Restauration de la *pax deorum,* règlement du problème parthe par voie amiable, deux thèmes qui nous permettent de saisir la pleine signification du recours à Mercure. L'appel formulé par Horace n'est pas un jeu poétique gratuit, il s'adressait non pas à un dieu protecteur des marchands, dispensateur de profit, ni même dans un sens bénéfique plus large à l'initiateur des hommes aux bienfaits de la civilisation, mais au Mercure romain, dans sa fonction première de médiation à l'efficacité libératoire et purificatoire propre à sacraliser les modalités contractuelles de toute relation d'échange. Quant à l'identification du *iuuenis Octauius* avec Mercure, elle implique qu'Octave-Auguste s'affirmant promoteur efficace de réconciliation, pour fonder au niveau du sacré son œuvre de pacification et de réorganisation, s'est présenté comme assumant la fonction médiatrice de Mercure.

4. Desservants des *sacra* de Mercure et *Mercuriales Augustales*

Quand furent mises en place les structures institutionnelles du culte impérial, les *collegia* de *Mercuriales,* gardiens des *sacra* propres à la *religio* de Mercure étaient voués au service de la divinité impériale en vertu de l'identi-fication précoce de la mission du *princeps* à la fonction de leur dieu. Car au niveau du sacré, c'était au moyen du rituel, dont les *Mercuriales* étaient les dépositaires et les protagonistes, que se manifestait l'efficacité libératoire et purificatoire attendue de l'action exercée par le dieu, et prêtée au *princeps.*

Un des arguments principaux invoqués dans le débat sur le problème du Mercurius Augustus est fourni par l'interprétation que proposa MOMMSEN d'un groupe d'inscriptions de Pompéi[154]. Il s'agit de dédicaces d'offrandes votives annuelles présentées par des *collegia* de desservants, des *ministri,* les uns de condition servile, les autres affranchis. Or MOMMSEN suggéra de reconnaître dans les formes successives de la titulature de ces desservants, des étapes correspondant à l'institution et au développement du culte impérial.

En 25, ces desservants étaient qualifiés simplement *ministri*[155], en 14 ils avaient le titre de *Ministri Mercurii Maiae*[156], et bientôt dans le temps où s'orga-nisait et s'affermissait le culte impérial − c'est en 12 av. J.-C., que pour la première fois une inscription fait mention de *magistri Augustales* à Nepete en

---

[152] R. SYME, The Roman Revolution, p. 301−302.
[153] Ibid., p. 388; J. GAGÉ, Op. cit., p. 548, p. 596−599.
[154] TH. MOMMSEN, C.I.L., X, p. 109, et inscriptions n° 884 sq.
[155] C.I.L., X, 884.
[156] C.I.L., X, 885, 887.

Etrurie[157] —, les *ministri* pompéiens sont désignés comme *ministri Augusti Mercurii Maiae*[158]. Enfin en 2 av. J.-C., au moment où deux témoignages épigraphiques attestent la présence à Pompéi d'un *sacerdos Augusti*[159], le titre des desservants se réduit à *Ministri Augusti*[160]. Ainsi les desservants des *sacra* de Mercure auraient pris en charge le culte d'Auguste, par ailleurs identifié à ce dieu. Avec le temps, à mesure que l'importance et le succès du culte du Genius Augusti s'affirmèrent sur le plan institutionnel, le service traditionnel de Mercure et Maia serait passé en retrait.

En fait, la compréhension des dédicaces des *ministri* pompéiens a donné lieu à controverses, et l'interprétation proposée par MOMMSEN a été discutée[161]. Cependant hautement vraisemblable, elle est communément reçue, et d'autres documents épigraphiques provenant pour l'essentiel de Campanie et d'Italie du sud procurent des indices supplémentaires propres à confirmer son bien-fondé. Si une inscription d'Abellinum probablement d'époque républicaine qualifie un citoyen de *Mercurialis*[162], une autre de Nole gravée vraisemblablement du vivant d'Auguste, fait état d'un affranchi comme *magister Mercurialis et Augustalis*[163]. De ce double titre MOMMSEN concluait que le culte de la divinité d'Auguste avait été pris en charge par le *collegium* voué au service des *sacra* de Mercure, et que les *Augustales* desservants du culte impérial constituaient avec les *Mercuriales* un seul et même corps[164]. Au fil du temps, la qualification *Augustales* aurait seule subsisté dans la dénomination officielle de ces *collegia*, tandis que la référence à leur vocation première, le culte de Mercure, tombait en désuétude.

Dans une inscription de Brindes nous trouvons également un C. Octavius *Magister Mercurialis Augustalis*[165]. D'autres témoignages épigraphiques attestent encore la présence de *collegia* de *Mercuriales Augustales* à Grumentum[166], Paestum[167], Mesagne[168].

---

[157] C.I.L., XI, 3200.
[158] C.I.L., X, 888.
[159] C.I.L., X, 837, 890.
[160] C.I.L., X, 890.
[161] E. BORMANN, Aus Pompeii, Wiener Eranos, Sect. V, I, 2a, 1909, p. 304 sq.; R. M. PETERSON, The Cults of Campania, Papers and Monographs of the American Academy in Rome, I, Rome, 1919, p. 263—265; A. VON PREMERSTEIN, dans: DE RUGGIERO, Dizionario epigrafico di antichità Romane, Rome, 1895—1916, I, p. 842, Art. Augustales; KENNETH SCOTT, Mercur-Augustus und Horaz, C. I, 2, Hermes, 63, 1928, p. 16—17; G. GRETHER, Pompeian ministri, Classical Philology, 27, 1932, p. 59—65; A. DEGRASSI, Iscrizioni nuove. I magistri Mercuriales di Luccae e la dea ʿAnzoticaʾ di ʿAenonaʾ, Athenaeum, 15, 1937, p. 284—287.
[162] A. DEGRASSI, I.L.L.R.P., n° 230. C.I.L., X, 1153, et I (2) 1612.
[163] C.I.L., X, 1272.
[164] TH. MOMMSEN, C.I.L., X, p. 142.
[165] C.I.L., IX, 54.
[166] C.I.L., X, 205, 232, 233.
[167] C.I.L., X, 485.
[168] C.I.L., X, 217.

Cette titulature double, reflet de l'adjonction du culte impérial au service des *sacra* d'une divinité, n'est pas limitée aux seuls desservants de la *religio* de Mercure. Ainsi à Tibur, le culte d'Auguste dut être célébré conjointement avec celui ancien, de l'Hercule Saxanus de la cité, et les *cultores* sont intitulés dans divers témoignages épigraphiques *Herculanei Augustales* ou *Herculanei et Augustales*[169]. Une inscription fait état d'un *magister Herculaneus et Augustalis*[170], titre parallèle dans la formulation à celui de l'affranchi de Nole. Deux inscriptions de Grumentum mentionnent aussi des *Herculanei et Augustales*[171].

Le culte impérial, dès ses débuts, a été un culte public, institué officiellement sur l'initiative, et par la décision des cités, dans les municipes de Campanie et d'Italie du sud il a été greffé sur des structures institutionnelles déjà existantes, propres à la *religio* de Mercure. Aussi le problème posé par les *ministri Augusti Mercurii Maiae* pompéiens et les *magistri Mercuriales Augustales* ne se réduit pas seulement au vieux débat formel sur le bien-fondé de l'interprétation de MOMM-SEN: sur le fond, il s'agit de reconnaître ce qui dans les *sacra* de Mercure s'accordait avec la vocation prêtée à la divinité d'Auguste, et habilitait les dépositaires du rituel attaché à la *religio* de Mercure, à prendre en charge le culte impérial.

Pour rendre compte de la relation entre le culte impérial à ses débuts et la *religio* de Mercure, l'érudition moderne a cherché volontiers un principe d'explication du côté de l'appartenance sociale, et des activités à dominante supposée mercantile des fidèles du dieu. En effet, les *ministri* pompéiens et les *Mercuriales Augustales* mentionnés par les documents épigraphiques, sont pour une bonne part des affranchis. Or de façon générale sous l'Empire, la pratique des trafics commerciaux, le jeu des opérations de banque, le maniement des intérêts financiers constituèrent un champ d'action ouvert pour l'essentiel aux affranchis[172]. De nombreux éléments en vue de cette catégorie sociale devaient leur situation matérielle avantageuse aux bénéfices issus des activités mercantiles dont ils faisaient profession.

Dans la mesure où négligeant l'essentiel, c'est-à-dire la prise en charge de la *merx*, de la relation d'échange selon le mode mercantile, les commentateurs ont réduit la fonction du Mercure romain au patronage des professionnels des activités marchandes, et au rôle de dispensateur du *lucrum*, c'est-à-dire d'une forme de richesse appréciée et réalisée en espèces métalliques, la pratique du négoce semblait devoir vouer les affranchis à entretenir une dévotion particulière et intéressée à l'égard d'un dieu générateur de richesse, qui pourvoyait à leur fortune et à leur réussite. Par ailleurs, le loyalisme envers le *princeps* aurait incité les membres de cette catégorie sociale, par une reconnaissance politique calculée, à identifier Auguste avec leur divinité d'élection[173].

---

[169] C.I.L., XIV, 3661, 3679.
[170] C.I.L., XIV, 3665.
[171] C.I.L., X, 230, 231.
[172] J. GAGÉ, Les classes sociales dans l'Empire romain, p. 142; MOSES I. FINLEY, L'économie antique, trad. par M. P. HIGGS, Coll. le sens commun, Paris, 1975, p. 74—75.
[173] KENNETH SCOTT, Mercury on the Bologna Altar, Mitt. Dt. Arch. Inst. Röm. Abt., 50, 1935, p. 229—230; J. GAGÉ, Op. cit., p. 142—143.

Les dédicaces des *ministri* pompéiens ne représentent ni des témoignages d'une piété spontanée, ni des initiatives d'ordre professionnel ou individuel commandées par une dévotion reconnaissante envers le dieu, pour la protection particulière, qu'il accordait aux entreprises et aux intérêts de ses fidèles. Ces dédicaces correspondent à des actes du culte public, à des offrandes officielles décidées par un décret des décurions, dont l'exécution par ordre des magistrats locaux, les *duouiri iure dicundo*, était confiée aux *ministri*[174]. Ces *ministri Augusti Mercurii Maiae*, comme les *magistri Mercuriales Augustales*, assumaient à la fois la charge des *sacra publica* de Mercure et de Maia, et celle des *sacra publica* d'Auguste, ils n'étaient pas des fidèles exprimant à titre individuel ou collectif leur gratitude dévote, mais des exécutants responsables au nom de la cité de la mise en œuvre d'un rituel. Indépendamment de la diversité des dénominations, *ministri* et *magistri* étaient investis institutionnellement d'une mission identique, la différence de titre devant correspondre seulement à une différence de statut: les *magistri* étaient de condition libre, à Pompéi où les dédicaces attestent la présence d'esclaves parmi les desservants, ceux-ci étaient qualifiés *ministri*.

L'apparente vocation des affranchis pour le service du culte de Mercure suggérée par ces documents épigraphiques ne tient pas à des affinités d'ordre socio-professionnel entre les *liberti* et les *sacra* de Mercure, elle était l'aboutissement d'une évolution institutionnelle dans le milieu des municipes campaniens, dont nous pouvons suivre le fil à partir du II° siècle av. J.-C. avec les *magistreis* de Délos, et les *magistri* de Capoue.

Les *magistreis Mirquri* de Délos comptaient exclusivement des membres de condition libre répartis indifféremment entre *ingenui* et *liberti*[175], de même les collèges annuels de *magistri* attestés à Capoue par une série d'inscriptions s'échelonnant entre 111 et 71 av. J.-C. étaient composés à la fois d'*ingenui* et de *liberti*[176]. Le rôle éminent et les responsabilités politiques de ces *collegia* campaniens qui dépassaient de beaucoup leur compétence proprement religieuse, tenaient au statut particulier de Capoue.

Depuis l'abolition de ses institutions, consécutive à sa reddition en 211, Capoue *urbs trunca sine senatu, sine plebe, sine magistratibus*[177], était hors du droit commun de la cité, et les douze *collegia* de *magistri fanorum* suppléaient à l'absence de magistratures régulières en assumant les fonctions politiques et administratives, qui incombaient normalement à celles-ci[178]. A partir de 58 av.

---

[174] C.I.L., X, 886, 888, 890; I.L.S., 3207.

[175] J. HATZFELD, Les Italiens résidant à Délos, B.C.H., 36, 1912, p. 154–155; PH. BRUNEAU, Recherches sur les cultes de Délos à l'époque hellénistique et à l'époque impériale, Bibl. des Écoles franç. d'Athènes & de Rome, 218, Paris, 1970, p. 585–589.

[176] J. HEURGON, Les *magistri* des collèges et le relèvement de Capoue de 111 à 71 av. J.-C., M.E.F.R., 66, 1939, p. 5–27; M. W. FREDERIKSEN, Republican Capua: A Social and Economic Study, Papers of the British School at Rome, 27, 1959, p. 80–130, plus particulièrement § 2 'The Campanian magistri', p. 83–94, et appendice (recueil des inscriptions des *magistri* de Capoue), p. 126–130.

[177] Liv., XXXI,29,11.

[178] M. W. FREDERIKSEN, Art. cit., p. 92–94.

J.-C., avec la création de la colonie de César, Capoue recouvra le statut de cité, et l'exercice des responsabilités politiques revint aux magistrats, et à la curie locale, dont l'accès était réservé aux *ingenui* qualifiés selon les critères censitaires de la naissance et de la fortune. Dès lors que les *ingenui* qui en avaient la capacité civique et financière, étaient appelés à la gestion des *honores* municipaux, le recrutement des *collegia* de *magistri fanorum* désormais réduits à leur fonction religieuse première, se trouva par la force des choses limité aux *liberti*, et même éventuellement aux *serui* financièrement aptes à satisfaire aux frais inhérents à cette charge.

Cette évolution institutionnelle apparaît indépendante d'une quelconque vocation d'ordre social ou économique prédestinant les affranchis pour le service du culte de Mercure. Et ce n'est ni l'appartenance sociale, ni la spécialisation professionnelle des desservants, qui ont déterminé l'adjonction du culte d'Auguste au service des *Mercuriales*. Que ceux-ci, au gré des époques et des cités, fussent *ingenui* ou *serui*, les *sacra* dont ils avaient la charge restaient les mêmes, porteurs sur le plan religieux d'une spécificité et d'une signification, qui ne dépendaient ni de la condition, ni des activités profanes des célébrants, mais procédaient de la fonction du dieu.

C'est dans les affinités de la vocation divine d'Auguste avec la fonction de Mercure, et au niveau de l'efficacité des *sacra* dont les *Mercuriales* étaient les gardiens, qu'il faut chercher le principe de leur affectation au service du culte impérial. Les *Mercuriales Augustales* représentent la transposition sur le plan des institutions, de l'assimilation de l'action d'Auguste avec la fonction médiatrice de Mercure, conformément à l'appel d'Horace conviant le dieu à s'incarner sous les apparences du *iuuenis Octauius*. Le rituel attaché à la *religio* de Mercure était empreint de la même finalité libératoire et purificatoire qu'on prêtait à l'action d'Auguste identifié à Mercure, comme promoteur de sacré et de purification.

Conclusion

Le problème du Mercurius Augustus a été longtemps obscurci par des considérations extérieures à la religion proprement romaine. Les spéculations sur d'hypothétiques mystères de Mercure, d'affinités hermétiques, ont négligé le caractère officiel des *Mercuriales Augustales* qui avaient la charge d'un culte public institué dans le temps même où Auguste veillait à sauvegarder le caractère national des cultes romains. Les *Mercuriales* ne constituaient pas des sociétés marginales pratiquant à l'occasion des rites ésotériques, et des *sacra* initiatiques étrangers au *mos patrius*. Une juste appréciation de la relation d'Auguste avec le culte de Mercure a été longtemps faussée par l'idée que Mercurius Augustus procédait de la conception hellénistique du βασιλεὺς σωτήρ qui aurait inspiré l'ode d'Horace.

Les commentateurs modernes ont généralement égaré leur investigation sur des voies illusoires, parce qu'ils ont perdu de vue deux faits: d'une part la spécificité de la fonction de médiation du Mercure romain qui consistait d'abord dans la prise en charge de la *merx*, plutôt que dans le patronage des *mercatores*, d'autre part le caractère romain aussi bien des *sacra* de Mercure, que du culte impérial à ses débuts à Rome et en Italie, au temps où il s'établit parallèlement à la restauration des rites et des cultes traditionnels par Auguste.

En fait de l'ode d'Horace aux *ministri Augusti Mercurii Maiae* pompéiens et aux *magistri Mercuriales Augustales*, c'est l'affirmation de la même démarche, dont le principe et la continuité procédaient de la conception romaine de la *pax deorum*, et des *sacra* au moyen desquels se manifeste la relation entre l'humain et le divin. Auguste fait figure d'incarnation de Mercure dans la mesure où comme promoteur de sacré, restaurateur de la *pax deorum*, il assumait dans le rôle de médiateur, une vocation purificatoire conforme à l'efficacité spécifique dont faisait preuve Mercure dans l'exercice de sa fonction. Mais cette action attendue au niveau du sacré était conditionnée par l'accomplissement de *sacra*, par la mise en œuvre du rituel attaché à la *religio* de Mercure, et les desservants de ce culte public, en conformité avec leur mission officielle, furent appelés à prendre en charge Mercurius Augustus.

Certes à l'époque augustéenne, ces desservants sont pour l'essentiel des affranchis, et cette circonstance a incité à voir dans le culte de Mercurius Augustus une dévotion populaire spontanée exprimant la reconnaissance au dieu dispensateur du *lucrum*, et le loyalisme à l'égard du *princeps*. En fait, l'exact accomplissement des *sacra* de Mercure n'était pas plus populaire en soi, que n'était aristocratique la célébration des rites attachés aux sacerdoces publics, dont la gestion fut attribuée par Auguste à l'ordre sénatorial et aux *equites,* car ni le statut civique, ni la condition sociale, ni l'état professionnel des desservants ne changeaient rien au caractère romain, ou à la spécificité des *sacra publica* dont ils avaient la charge. Mercurius Augustus, c'était le Mercure romain exerçant la même action à finalité libératoire et purificatoire, qu'il manifestait dans sa fonction première de médiation en assumant la *merx*, comme mode contractuel de l'échange.

Bibliographie

1. Outre les ouvrages et les articles mentionnés à la note 1:

A. Berthier, Le culte de Mercure à Cirta, Recueil des notices et mémoires de la Société archéologique de Constantine, 65, 1942, p. 131–140.

Norman O. Brown, Hermes the Thief. The Evolution of a Myth, Madison, Wisconsin, University of Wisconsin Press, 1947, 164 p.

J. Chittenden, The Master of Animals, Hesperia, 16, 1947, p. 89–114.

J. Chittenden, *Diaktoros Argeiphontes*, American Journal of Archaeology, 52, 1948, p. 24–33.

P. Devambez, Piliers hermaïques et stèles, Rev. Arch. Nelle. Sér., 1968, 1, p. 139–154.

F. J. M. De Waele, The Magic Staff or Rod in Graeco-italic Antiquity, Diss.Gent, 1927.

Hetty Goldmann, The Origin of the Greek Herm, American Journal of Archaeology, 46, 1942, p. 58–68.

L. Kahn, Hermès passe ou les ambiguïtés de la communication, Paris, 1978.

M. Leglay, Inscriptions inédites de Lambèse se rapportant au culte de Mercure, Bull. Arch. du Comité, Nelle. Sér. 3, 1967, p. 273–281.

R. Lullies, Die Typen der griechischen Herme, Königsberger kunstgeschichtliche Forschungen, 3, Königsberg, 1931.

A. D. Nock, The Lyre of Orpheus, Classical Review, 41, 1927, p. 169–171.

A. D. Nock, Varro and Orpheus, Classical Review, 43, 1929, p. 60–61.

E. Samter, Altare di Mercurio e Maia, Mitt. Dt. Arch. Inst. Röm. Abt., 8, 1893, p. 222–225.

J.-P. Vernant, Hestia-Hermès. Sur l'expression religieuse de l'espace et du mouvement chez les Grecs, L'Homme. Revue française d'anthropologie, 3, 1963, p. 12–50.

H. S. Versnel, Mercurius amongst the *Magni Dei*, Mnemosyne, Sér. IV, 27, 1974, p. 144–151.

2. Sur Mercure psychopompe:

S. Eitrem, Hermes und die Toten, Christiania Videnskabs-Selgkabs Forhandlinger for 1909, n° 5, Christiania 1909.

K. Kerényi, Hermes der Seelenführer. Das Mythologem v. männl. Lebensursprung. I. Der Hermes der klass. Überlieferung; II. Der Hermes d. Lebens u. d. Todes, Zürich, 1944.

P. Raingeard, Hermès psychagogue. Essai sur les origines du culte d'Hermès. Paris, 1935.

J. van Wageningen, De Mercurio qui „ψυχοπομπός" dicitur, Mnemosyne, Sér. II, 32, 1904, p. 43–48.

3. Sur Mercure et le culte impérial:

E. J. Bickerman, *Filius Maiae* (Horace, Odes I,2,43), Parola del passato, 16, 1961, p. 6–19.

O. Brendel, Novus Mercurius, Mitt. Dt. Arch. Inst. Röm. Abt., 50, 1935, p. 231–251.

J. Chittenden, Hermes-Mercury, Dynasts and Emperors, Numismatic Chronicle, Sér. VI,5, 1945, p. 40–57.

W. Deonna, Le trésor des Fins d'Annecy, Rev. Arch., Sér. V,11, 1920, p. 125–206.

W. Deonna, La légende d'Octave-Auguste dieu sauveur et maître du monde, Rev. Hist. Rel., 83, 1921, p. 32, p. 163; ibid., 84, 1921, p. 77.

J. Guey, Encore la 'pluie miraculeuse', Revue de Philologie, 22, 1948, p. 16–62.

K. Kerényi, De teletis mercurialibus observationes II, Egyetemes Philologiai Közlöny, 47, 1923, p. 150–164.

K. Lehmann-Hartleben, Ein Altar in Bologna, Mitt. Dt. Arch. Inst. Röm. Abt., 42, 1927, p. 163–176.

E. Samter, Mercurius und Minerva, Mitt. Dt. Arch. Inst. Röm. Abt., 10, 1895, p. 93–94.

Kenneth Scott, Mercur-Augustus und Horaz C. I, 2, Hermes, 63, 1928, p. 15–33.

Kenneth Scott, Mercury on the Bologna Altar, Mitt. Dt. Arch. Inst. Röm. Abt., 50, 1935, p. 225–230.

J. Six, Octavien-Mercure, Rev. Arch., Sér. V,4, 1916, p. 257–264.

Liste des illustrations

Fortuna

by Iiro Kajanto, Helsinki

Contents

I. Fortuna in Religion

1. Origin of the Cult of Fortuna

According to LATTE 176, the cult of Fortuna came to Rome from Latium, where she had two centres of cult, Praeneste and Antium. The Fortuna of Praeneste, the famous Fortuna Primigenia, was in origin a goddess of women's fertility. However, the transparent Latin name Fortuna influenced the nature of the goddess; she became a deity of good luck. LATTE is patently following WISSOWA 256ff., who insisted that the early Fortuna was a goddess of women.

These arguments are debatable. There is no evidence that the cult of Fortuna really came to Rome from Latium. The Roman tradition ascribed the introduction of the cult of Fortuna in Rome to Servius Tullius. The temple of Fors Fortuna on the bank of the Tiber and the sanctuary of Fortuna in the Forum Boarium, also called *virgo* or *virginalis* (p. 512) were said to be his foundations[1].

Abbreviations:

AE	Année épigraphique
CIL	Corpus Inscriptionum Latinarum; usually quoted here by the number of the volume only, II, XIII, etc.
ESP.	E. ESPÉRANDIEU, Recueil général des bas-reliefs de la Gaule Romaine, 1—11, Paris 1907—1938.
FASOLO- GULLINI	cf. Bibliography
GULLINI	cf. Bibliography
Inscr. Ital.	Inscriptiones Italiae, Vol. XIII, Fasti et elogia, 1—2, Roma 1947, 1963, curavit A. DEGRASSI.
LATTE	cf. Bibliography
RIB	The Roman Inscriptions of Britain edited by R. G. COLLINGWOOD and R. P. WRIGHT, Oxford 1965.
RIC	Roman Imperial Coinage, 1—7 and 9, London 1923—67.
RUGG.	E. DE RUGGIERO, Dizionario epigrafico di antichità romane, Roma 1886ff.
SYDENHAM	E. A. SYDENHAM, The Coinage of the Roman Republic, London 1952.
WISSOWA	cf. Bibliography

[1] For the temple of Fors Fortuna, cf. Varro, LL 6,17; Dion. Hal. 4, 27,7; Ovid, Fasti 6,773—84; Plut., fort. Rom. 5; for the temple of Fortuna in the Forum Boarium, cf. Ovid, Fasti 6,569ff.; Dion.Hal. 4,40,7; Val.Max. 1,8,11.

Literary and archeological evidence in fact suggests that these temples were of considerable antiquity. A notice in Livy shows that the temple of Fors Fortuna was in existence at least in the fourth century. According to 10,46,14, the *consul* Sp. Carvilius built 293 B. C. an *aedes* of Fors Fortuna out of the Samnite and Etruscan booty near the *aedes* of the goddess dedicated by Servius Tullius. If this is correct — which I do not doubt — the latter temple must be considerably older because even at this early date it was considered a foundation of hoary antiquity. Both temples had the same day of dedication, June 24; cf. Inscr. Ital. XIII.2, p. 473.

The sanctuary of Fortuna in the Forum Boarium may date back to the very beginning of urban life in Rome. Recent excavations have shown that sacred life in the Forum Boarium began ca. 575 B. C. when the first floor of the *forum* was laid.[2] The cult-place was originally an open area with an altar in the centre. The first temples, identifiable with the *aedes* of Mater Matuta and Fortuna, were not built until the early 5th century. These archaic temples were reconstructed by Camillus in 395 B.C. (cf. Liv. 5,19,6 on the temple of Mater Matuta). The first literary record of the sanctuary of Fortuna is from 213 B.C. According to Liv. 25,7,5, cf. 24,47,15, the sanctuary burnt down 213 B.C. but was rebuilt the next year by the *triumviri*.

There is no evidence that the cult of Fortuna in Latium and especially at Praeneste dates back to older times than it does in Rome. WISSOWA 258 certainly refers to Varro LL 5, 74 as evidence for an early cult of Fortuna among the Sabines, but this is quite unconvincing. Varro argues that a number of divine names, among them Fortuna, were borrowed from the Sabines. The reliability of his information may be gauged from the fact that his list includes Vesta, Salus, Fons, Fides.

The first record of the Fortuna of Praeneste is probably from the last years of the First Punic War. According to Val. Max. 1,3,2. the Senate forbade the *consul* Lutatius Cerco to consult the *sortes* of Praenestina Fortuna. The cult of this goddess was accepted by the Romans 204 B.C. Before engaging Hannibal near Croton, the *consul* P. Sempronius Tuditanus vowed an *aedes* to Fortuna Primigenia if he should rout the enemy that day, Liv. 29,36,8. The temple was dedicated 194 B.C. on the Quirinal hill, 34,53,5. This is one of the three shrines of Fortuna Publica Populi Romani on the hill (see p. 514). The famous temple of Fortuna Primigenia at Praeneste was probably built after the mid-second century B. C. Originally the site had a cave of the *sortes*[3]. The votive inscriptions found at the area of the temple are datable to a period between the mid-second century and the age of Sulla[4].

Even Tusculum may have had a shrine of Fortuna. Livy 21,62,8 records from the year 218 *supplicatio Fortunae in Algido* because of *prodigia*. This may mean a site near Tusculum. An inscription dedicated to Fortuna

[2] E. GJERSTAD, Early Rome III, Lund 1960, 458—62.
[3] FASOLO-GULLINI 301—24; GULLINI 778—79.
[4] FASOLO-GULLINI 284; GULLINI 762—65.

has been found at Tusculum, *M. Fourio(s) C. f. tribunos [milita]re de praidad Fortune dedet*, CIL I² 48. This is datable to ca. 200 B.C.[5] LATTE 177 erroneously equates this Fortuna with Fortuna Primigenia.

We know relatively little about the cult of Fortuna at Antium. Apart from the well-known opening of Horace's hymn on Fortuna, carm. 1,35,1 *o diva gratum quae regis Antium*, this Fortuna is recorded in two inscriptions from the Imperial age, X 6555 (Velitrae) *Fortunis Antiatibus*, and 6638c28, a. 44, *Philetus aeditus Fortunarum*, and on a coin from 21—20 B.C., RIC I p. 69 No. 96. Jugate busts and two ram's heads, depicted on the coin, show that the Fortunae were two; a famous oracle was attached to them, cf. Macrob. 1, 23,13; Suet., Cal. 57,3; Serv., Aen. 6,68. The future was divined from the movements of the images of the goddesses. LATTE 178 argues that this kind of divination was late and due to Oriental influence. All this gives us few clues as to the age of the cult at Antium.

It is probable that both in Rome and at Praeneste Fortuna was in origin a goddess of good luck. This is suggested by the very etymology of the name, obtained from the root *fortus*, cf. Portunus from *portus*, and connected with the verb *ferre*[6]. The word thus suggested 'a bringer', consequently 'a bringer of good luck, success'.

There is indeed little evidence that Fortuna was ever a goddess of women or of fertility. The oldest literally documented sanctuaries, those of Fors Fortuna, have no special relationship to women. Fors Fortuna was obviously an old name for a goddess of good luck, created before the Latin word came to have the specific meaning of 'chance'[7]. We know that these sanctuaries were especially frequented by the common people. The temple of Fors Fortuna founded by Servius Tullius was the site of a popular festival described by Ovid, Fasti 6, 773 ff.; cf. Cic., fin. 5, 70. A number of votive inscriptions found in the neighbourhood of the sanctuary founded by Sp. Carvilius were dedicated by artisans and tradespeople, CIL I² 977 *conlegia aerarior(um)*, i. e. copper-smiths; 978 *conlegiu(m) lani(es) Piscinenses*; 979 *lanies* (= *lanii*); 980 *violaries, rosaries, coronaries*. In Columella 10, 317, she appears as a patron goddess of the peasants especially at market-days. Only later, when *fors* had come to signify 'chance', was this goddess — at least in literature — identified with Tyche, the personification of blind chance (cf. p. 525), Donat., Ter. Phorm. 841 *Fors Fortuna est, cuius diem festum colunt, qui sine arte aliqua vivunt*, but the reference is very late and does not interpret the passage in Terence correctly (cf. fn 7). Fors Fortuna is otherwise little heard of in cult. A recently found but fragmentary inscription, AE 1972, 144 (regio III, Italy) records Fors Fortuna in the nominative.

---

[5] Identified by F. MÜNZER, RE VII 1, 1910, 353, with M. Furius Crassipes, *praetor* 187 and 173 B.C.

[6] WALDE-HOFMANN, Lateinisches etymologisches Wörterbuch ⁴I, Heidelberg 1965, S. 534, s.v. fors.

[7] cf. Ter., Phorm. 841 *o Fortuna, o Fors Fortuna, quantis commoditatibus, quam subito meò ero Antiphoni ope vostra hunc onerastis diem*; on the other hand, *forte fortuna* means 'by chance' Eun. 134 and 568, though LATTE 179,7 included even them here.

It is datable to the mid-first century B.C. From the period of the Severan dynasty, we have an African dedication to Fors Fortuna Propagatrix (p. 512). At the beginning of the fourth century A. D., Forti Fortunae appears on the coins issued to commemorate the deification of Galerius, RIC VI, p. 452. But it is questionable whether this deity had any real connection with the ancient goddess of the same name. Her attributes at any rate are identical with those of Fortuna at this period (see p. 519); cf. the description of the coins, ibid. p. 480; 482—83; "Fortuna st(andin)g l(eft) by wheel, r(ight) holding rudder or globe, l(eft) *cornucopiae*".

According to WISSOWA 257, the Fortuna of the Forum Boarium was a women's deity. The evidence is, however, far from conclusive. Only three ancient writers record the epithet *virgo* or *virginalis* (see p. 512 s.v. *VIRGO*), and two of them are late. In 213 B.C., the goddess of the temple was apparently simple Fortuna (see p. 504). Even if she at some period came to be conceived of as a deity of women, this has little significance because in the republican age, Fortuna was splitting up into special guardian spirits. If there was a Fortuna of women, there was also a Fortuna of men (p. 513 s.v. *VIRILIS*).

The arguments for Fortuna Primigenia as a deity of fertility are inconclusive, too. There is an old votive inscription dedicated *nationu(s) cratia Fortuna Diovo fileia Primogenia*, CIL I² 60, i. e. *nationis* (= childbirth) *gratia Fortunae Iovis filiae Primigeniae*, and a famous statue of *Iuppiter puer, qui lactens cum Iunone Fortunae in gremio sedens mammam appetens castissime colitur a matribus*, Cic., div. 2,85. But the dedication "because of childbirth" is only one instance of the causes for setting up votive offerings. The special reasons for the offerings were stated only occasionally. Moreover, is it any wonder if a deity of good luck received votive offerings for childbirth? The statue may be due to Etruscan influence (p. 509).

On the other hand, there is a great number of votive inscriptions to Fortuna from the republican period, dedicated by artisans and other common people, who had little to do with childbirth[8], CIL I², 1446—50; new finds in FASOLO-GULLINI p. 275ff. Nos. 10—45. A considerable number of the dedicators were slaves or freedmen. A slave had special reasons to venerate a goddess who could one day change his lot. But unlike Silvanus, Fortuna Primigenia was never a specific deity of slaves. Especially in the Imperial period, all social strata were represented as dedicators of votive offerings, *vir clarissimus*, XIV 2850; *[e]ques Roman[us]*, 2851; *aedil(is) curul(is)*, 2866.

2. Is Fortuna of Etruscan origin?

It is difficult to say anything certain about the ultimate origin of the cult of Fortuna in Rome. The facts of cult reviewed above suggest that

---

[8] F. BÖMER, Untersuchungen über die Religion der Sklaven in Griechenland und Rom I, Wiesbaden 1957, 143; W. EISENHUT, s.v. Fortuna, Der Kleine Pauly 2, Stuttgart 1967, 598.

Fortuna was unlikely to have been imported from Latium. Neither can Fortuna be of Greek origin. Tyche was different from old Roman Fortuna. Moreover, the cult of Fortuna seems to antedate any Greek influence upon Roman religion.

We could of course contend that Fortuna was native both in Rome and in Latium. Nevertheless, I would suggest another hypothesis. The cult may have been due, at least to some extent, to Etruscan influence. Evidence can be produced in support of this theory. Firstly, the Etruscans were notorious for the importance they attached to the idea of Fate. Though the religious life of the Etruscans is still largely shrouded in mystery, and the information supplied by Roman writers often confused and even contradictory, it seems that the chief god *tin* was thought to have two councils, one composed of six gods and six goddesses, the other, more powerful and more mysterious, comprising deities of unknown number, name, and sex. In the *interpretatio Romana*, these deities appear as *dii superiores et involuti*, even as *favores opertanei*[9]. In all probability, they were deities of Fate[10].

In addition to these general considerations, we can quote some more concrete evidence. The earliest shrine of Fortuna may have been that in the Forum Boarium (p. 504). If the dates suggested by GJERSTAD are correct, the sanctuary dates back to the period of Etruscan hegemony in Rome. Consequently, Etruscan influence should be seriously considered in discussing the origin of this particular cult. The problem of the veiled image kept in the temple is more complex (for the evidence, see p. 512 s.v. *VIRGO*). It has been connected with the *dii involuti* of the Etruscans. In this case, the veiling of the image would be a symbol of mysterious Fate[11].

Etruscan influence seems equally undeniable at half-Etruscinized Praeneste. Its famous oracle, where the future was divined by the drawing of lots, *sortes*[12], may have some connection with the *disciplina Etrusca*. In Italy, divination was an Etruscan speciality. Moreover, though prophecy

---

[9] The chief document is Seneca, nat. 2,41. In debating the Etruscan doctrine of lightnings sent by Jupiter, Seneca distinguishes three classes of them, each more destructive than the other. In hurling the lightnings of the second class, Jupiter consults a council composed of 12 deities. According to Arnob., nat. 3,40, they were called *Consentes et Complices*. The deadly lightnings of the third class were hurled *adhibitis in consilium diis quos superiores et involutos vocant*. These deities may be identical with *favores opertanei* placed by Martianus Capella, 1,45, in the first region of the Etruscan heaven, *post ipsum Iovem*, cf. S. WEINSTOCK, Martianus Capella and the Cosmic System of the Etruscans, JRS 36, 1946, 109, but cf. his fn. 46: the name *favores* is much in contrast to their destructive character.

[10] M. PALLOTTINO, Etruscologia[6], Milano 1968, 246.

[11] C. THULIN, Die Götter des Martianus Capella und die Bronzeleber von Piacenza, RGVV 3, Gießen 1906, 37—38; cf. LATTE 180.

[12] The oracle was described in detail by Cicero, div. 2,86—87; cf. Suet., Tib. 63,1; Domit. 15,2. There are references to the oracle in epigraphy, XIV 2989 *sortilegus Fortunae primigeniae*; a newly found inscription, FASOLO-GULLINI 286 No. 31, records *[Fortunae primige]niae Io[vis pue]ri sortes*.

through *sortes* was found among many primitive peoples[13], in Italy it seems to have been found only in Etruria or in places where Etruscan influence can be assumed. Besides Praeneste, we know of *sortes* at Caere[14], at Falerii[15], in Appeninus (i.e., north of Spoletium)[16], in the sanctuary of Clitumnus,[17] and at Patavium[18]. With the exception of Patavium, all these places lay within the sphere of ancient Etruscan hegemony. It is thus more natural to explain *sortes* as an Etruscan form of divination than to describe it as originally Italic[19] or even to put it down as a legacy of the invading Celts[20]. If this is so, even the Fortuna of Praeneste may owe something to the Etruscans.

There are points of contact even in the epithets of Fortuna Praenestina. It has been argued that *Iovis puer/filia* had replaced an earlier epithet *Iovia*, documented in Umbria[21]. But according to Martianus Capella, there were sons of Jupiter in Etruscan religion as well, 1,50 *vos quoque, Iovis filii, Pales et Favor*; cf. above *favores opertanei* as the Roman equivalents of the Etruscan deities of Fate. There is accordingly some possibility that the epithet may be of Etruscan origin.

The other epithet, *primigenia*, is enigmatic. WISSOWA 259 explained it literally as 'the first-born daughter of Jupiter' and ascribed it, because of its non-Italic idea of divine genealogy, to foreign influence. On the other hand, LATTE 176 argues that the epithet only suggests a privileged position (*Vorzugstellung*), not a genealogical connection. Etruscan origin is unlikely or at least unverifiable[22]. But because Τύχη Πρωτογένεια has been found in Greek inscriptions, Inscr. de Délos 1072—73 and Inscr. Cret. 3,4,14, the epithet may have been borrowed from the Greek equivalent of Fortuna[23].

---

[13] LATTE, s.v. Orakel, RE XVIII, 1, 1939, 854; T. YOSHIMURA, Italische Orakel, La Nouvelle Clio, VII—IX, 1955—57, 411.

[14] Liv. 21,62,5 *Caere sortes extenuatas* (i.e., diminished in number).

[15] Liv. 22,1,11, a similar reference.

[16] SHA 25,10,4—6, with three examples of *sortes*; 29,3,4.

[17] Plin., epist. 8,8,5 (at the Clitumnus Fons) *stat Clitumnus ipse amictus . . . praesens numen atque etiam fatidicum indicant sortes*.

[18] Suet., Tib. 14,3 *cum Illyricum petens* (scil. *Tiberius*) *iuxta Patavium adisset Geryonis oraculum, sorte tracta, qua monebatur*, etc.

[19] V. EHRENBERG, s.v. Losung, RE XIII 2, 1927, 1456,61ff.

[20] YOSHIMURA, op. cit. (fn. 13) 422—23.

[21] K. MEISTER, Lateinisch-griechische Eigennamen I, Leipzig 1916, 115.

[22] THULIN's attempt, op. et loc. cit. (fn. 11) to derive the epithet from an Etruscan divine name, is unconvincing. cf. J. CHAMPEAUX, Primigenius, ou de l'originaire, Latomus 34, 1975, 909—85, where the epithet is interpreted in the sense of '*primordial*', '*premier*'.

[23] LATTE 176,1 argues that on the contrary it was Fortuna Primigenia that had occasioned the Greek epithet. This is, however, unlikely, the influence of Roman religion on Greek cult being insignificant. The inscriptions of Delos were dedicated ῎Ισιδι Τύχηι πρωτογενείαι, which makes the Roman influence still more unlikely. Moreover, the inscription from Crete, Itanos, is too early for any real Italian influence in these districts. M. GUARDUCCI, ad loc., dates it to 215—181 B.C. S. SPYRIDAKIS, The Itanian cult of Tyche Protogeneia, Historia 18, 1969, 42—48, also dismisses the identification with Fortuna Primigenia. He derives the epithet from the mythological name Protogeneia, daughter of Erechtheus, and consideres her a protector of cities. According to a legend, Protogeneia, together with

Finally, even the statue where Fortuna is giving the breast to Iuno and Jupiter (p. 506) has been attributed to Etruscan influence, LATTE 21 and 176f.

To conclude, the evidence for Etruscan influence upon the cult of Fortuna cannot be dismissed offhand. At the beginning of the present century, Fortuna was often thought to be of Etruscan origin[24]. However, the authoritative word of WISSOWA, who derived the cult from Latium, made a speedy end of the hypothesis. It even came into vogue to minimize Etruscan influence upon Roman religion[25]. But this is going too far. There are Etruscan deities in the early pantheon of Rome, presumably Saturnus, certainly Volturnus, LATTE 20, not to speak of Etruscan influence upon the Capitoline Trias, upon funerary rites, etc.

In view of all this, it is not impossible that the cult of Fortuna owed something, or even a great deal, to the Etruscans with their well-developed ideas of Fate. However, Fortuna's Latin name implies that she cannot have been imported wholesale from Etruria. We should also remember that Fortune is not quite the same thing as Fate, especially destructive Etruscan Fate.

3. The epithets of Fortuna

It was a speciality of the Roman conception of Fortuna that she was generally conceived of as a *numen* which could manifest itself in many ways, as a guardian spirit of a single people, of a single individual, of a single locality, and even of a single day or a single event[26]. All these different aspects of Fortuna's power were signified by the epithets attached to her name. The earliest documented case seems to be Fortuna Equestris, who had a temple vowed to her 180 B.C. because of the victory in a cavalry fight, and dedicated a few years later (see the list). Fortuna was here a power which had manifested itself in the battle by turning the scales in Rome's favour. Another early and even otherwise similar case is Fortuna Huiusce Diei, 101 B.C. Here too, Fortuna's influence was limited to a single day and a single event. Other epithets of Fortuna dated to the republican period

---

a few other daughters of Erechtheus, sacrificed herself to save Athens from the invasion of an enemy, cf. Phanodemus, FHG 2,366 = Suidas, s. v. παρθένοι; PRELLER-ROBERT, Griechische Mythologie[4] 1, Berlin 1894, 201,1. But Protogeneia has not been documented as the guardian spirit of a city. Consequently, the origin of the epithet still remains obscure. At any rate, it is highly improbable that it can be put down as Italic influence. The more likely Greek influence on the Latin epithet is seen even in its form. MEISTER, op. cit. (fn 21) 115,2 explains the oldest variant *prigmogenia*, CIL I[2] 60, quoted on p. 506, ,,*als ziemlich junge Nachbildung griechischer Kompositionsweise*". Tyche Protogeneia may well have been the model here.

[24] THULIN, op. cit. (fn. 11) 37—38; W. OTTO, Fortuna, RE VII, 1 1910, 14.

[25] Cf. H. J. ROSE, On the Relations between Etruscan and Roman Religion, Studi e materiali di storia delle religioni, 3, 1927, 161—78.

[26] Cf. LATTE 182f.; LATTE, Über eine Eigentümlichkeit der italischen Gottesvorstellung, Arch. Rel. Wiss. 24, 1926, 247.

are *mala, muliebris, obsequens, respiciens, virgo, virilis*, and especially Fortuna Populi Romani, the guardian spirit of the Roman people. The great majority of the epithets were, however, from the Imperial age. I have counted more than 90 different epithets; a few are uncertain, distinguished in the list by a question mark.

The epithets are listed below. The cases relating to the guardian spirit of human beings and localities have been listed separately. I have also included here the general divine epithets of Fortuna, though they do not suggest any specific aspect of her power.

a) List of the epithets of Fortuna

α) Vis Fortunae

ADIVTRIX III 5314 (Noricum), uncertain (not extant, *nutrici Aug.* in the manuscripts). VI 179. AE 1932, 66 (Verona).

ARMIPOTENS XIII 11774 (Germ. sup.) *supera armipotens*, a. 212.

BARBATA Tertull., nat. 2,11,11 *virorum ... Fortuna barbata*; August., civ. 4,11 *sit et Fortuna barbata, quae adultos barba induat.*

BONA III 1009 (Dacia) *bona domestic(a)*; 4355 (Pann. sup.). VI 183; 184 *bona salutaris.* AE 1968, 233 (prov. Tarrac.) *bona redux.*

BREVIS Plut., quaest. Rom. 281D; probably only a literary expression, cf. LATTE 182.

CASVALIS III 10265 (Pann. inf.); on the adjective, cf. Thes. l. L. III 571,79.

CONFLVENS AE 1947, 160 (Guidonia, Italia); the epithet probably suggests 'to come in abundance', cf. Sen., ep. 45,9 *ad quem pecunia magna confluxit.*

CONSERVATRIX III 1938 (Salonae); 4289 (Pann. sup.); 4558 (Vindobona); 10400 (Pann. inf.); 14359, 26 (Vindobona). RIB 575; 968; 1449. XIII 7733 (Germ. sup.); 7741 (ibid.). AE 1949, 199 (Dalmatia) *?Fortunae conservatrici potenti* (uncertain); 1954, 273 (Rome).

CRESCENS AE 1966, 183b = 1972, 251 (Baetica) *crescens Augusta.*

DOMESTICA III 1009, cf. *BONA*; 1939 (Salonae); 4398 (Carnuntum). XI 3730 (Lorium) *?F(ortunae) d(omesticae) d(ono) d(edit).* XIV 6 (Ostia) *domestica sancta.*

DVBIA VI 975, 3, 51, a. 136.

DVX VI 2103B7, a. 214. IX 2194 (Telesia). XIII 6677a, cf. Add. p. 107 (Germ. sup.) *reg(ina) dux coh(ortis) II pr(aetoriae).* RIC III, p. 240 No. 343, age of M. Aurelius.

EQVESTRIS The temple of Fortuna Equestris was vowed 180 B.C. by Q. Fulvius Flaccus in memory of the victory of the Roman cavalry over the Celtiberians, Liv. 40,40,10; 44,9. The temple was dedicated 173 B.C., Liv. 42,10,5. It was in the neighbourhood of Circus Flaminius, cf. Vitruv. 3,3,2. But Tac., ann. 3,71, A.D. 22 relates that when the Roman *equites* vowed a gift to Fortuna Equestris for Augusta's recovery from illness, none with this title was found in Rome. A temple at Antium was discovered to have this designation. The old temple in Rome had probably fallen into decay.

FELIX VI 30871b FORT[/FELIX (unless a personal name?). This epithet is frequent on coins, RIC III, p. 65, No. 323, age of Antoninus Pius; p. 384, No. 172, age of Commodus; IV. 2, p. 16, No. 9, age of Iulianus; p. 167, No. 552, age of Iulia Domna; p. 234, No. 154, age of Caracalla; IV. 2, p. 82, No. 139B, age of Severus Alexander.

FORS FORTVNA, cf., p. 506 and *PROPAGATRIX*.

FORTISSIMA III 10992, see *Fortuna Legionis*.

GVBERNATRIX XIII 12049 (Germ. inf.) *cubern[*; 7792 (ibid.) *?cu[*.

HVIVSCE DIEI Fort(unae) huiusque diei, Fasti Pinciani, Iul. 30; *Fortunae huiusce [d]iei in campo*, Fasti Allifani; cf. Cic., leg. 2,28: *Fortunaque sit vel huiusce diei (nam valet in omnes dies)*. The temple was vowed by Q. Lutatius Catulus a. 101 at the battle of the *campi Raudii*, cf. Plut., Mar. 26,2. According to DEGRASSI, Inscr. Ital. XIII. 2, p. 488, in Rome there were two sanctuaries of this deity, *si quidem Catulus duo signa Phidiaca posuit non in aede sua Fortunae Huiusce Diei, sed in aede eiusdem deae quam L. Aemilius Paulus propter pugnam ... ad Pydnam extruxerat*, cf. Plin., nat. 34,54. VI 975 records *vicus huiusque diei*, which according to DEGRASSI refers to the sanctuary of Aemilius Paulus in Palatio.

?INVICTRIX recorded in RUGG. III 190, but XIII* 1296: *spuria vel interpolata*.

MALA Cic., nat. deor. 3,63; leg. 2,28 *araque vetusta in Palatio Febris et altera Esquiliis malae Fortunae detestataque omnia eius modi repudianda sunt*; cf. Plin., nat. 2,16.

MAMMOSA VI 975,4,42, a. 136; probably a symbol of fecundity.

MANENS RIC III, p. 386, No. 191a; p. 427, No. 534, age of Commodus.

MELIOR XI 4216 (Interamna), the word *Fortuna* restored; 4391 (Ameria) *magistra Fortunae mel(ioris) coll(egi) centonarior(um)*; 4770 (Spoletium) *maelior Aug(usta)*. XIV 2873 (Praeneste) *]elior*. AE 1937, 178 (Marengo, Gallia cis.)

MEMOR VI 190.

MVLIEBRIS The temple of Fortuna Muliebris lay at the fourth milestone of the *via Latina*, Val. Max. 1,8,4; cf. 5,2,1. Only the women who had not been married twice were allowed to enter the sanctuary, Festus, p. 242M; Tert., non. 17,3; Serv., Aen. 4,19. The legend attributed the founding of the temple to Coriolanus' mother and wife, Dion. Hal. 8,55,3; Plut., Cor. 37,2; cf. Liv. 2,40,12, A miraculous voice of the goddess was alleged to have proclaimed that the dedication had been done *rite* by the *matronae*, Val. Max., loc. cit.; Aug., civ. 4,19, etc. According to LATTE 181, in the archaic period only widows were not *univiriae*. Because Fortuna had not shown herself propitious to them, they were denied entrance to the temple. LATTE's explanation may be a little constrained, but has undoubtedly a kernel of truth. – In addition to these literary references, this variety of Fortuna is recorded only on a late coin, RIC III, p. 269, No. 683, age of M. Aurelius.

OBSEQVENS Plaut., asin. 716. I² 1509 (Cora). V 5246 and 5247 (Comum). VI 191; 975,1,26 a. 136. RIC III, p. 43, No. 139, age of Antoninus Pius.

OPIFERA XIV 3539 (Tibur).

PENAS AE 1928, 122 = 1954, 218 (isola farnese); probably an equivalent of Fortuna Domestica, cf. AE ad loc.

?POTENS AE 1949, 199, see *CONSERVATRIX*.

PRAESENS VI 181b *Augusta Praesens*

PRAESTITA Not. Scav. 1953, 240, from the verb *praestare*, but meaning not quite clear.

PRIVATA Plut., quaest. Rom. 281 E.

PROPAGATRIX AE 1909, 20 (Algiers) *Forti Fortun(ae) propagarci*, the same 1972, 794 (Maur. Caes.) *Forti Fortunae progatrici*, age of Caracalla.

REDVX, passim, see p. 517.

REGINA III 4399 (Carnuntum). XIII 6677a, see *DUX*.

RESPICIENS Cic., leg. 2,28 *respiciens ad opem ferendam*; Fronto II, p. 104 (Loeb). VI 181a *Fortunae Augustae respicie(nti)*; 975,2,6, a. 136. IX 5178 (Asculum). XI 347 (*ager* Ravennas); 817 (Mutina); 6307 (Pisaurum). XIII 6472 (Germ. sup.) a. 148. AE 1956, 243 (Köln) *dea Fo[rtuna respi-] ciens*.

RESTITVTRIX VI 30876.

SALVTARIS III 3315 (Pann. inf.). VI 184, cf. *BONA*; 201; 202. XIII 6678 (Germ. sup.); 7994 (Germ. inf.) *Fortuni[s] salutaribu[s] Aesculapio Hyg[iae]*. AE 1902, 143 (Dacia).

SERVATRIX RIB 760.

STABILIS III 5156 4a (Noricum), age of Sept. Severus.

TVTATRIX XII 4183 *Deae Fort[unae] tuta[trici] huius [l]oci*.

TVTELA VI 178.

VICTRIX VIII 5290 (Numid.) a. 294–305.

VIRGO Fortuna may be a later name of the Fortuna in the Forum Boarium (see p. 506). The day of dedication was June 11, the same as that of *Mater Matuta*, whose temple was likewise in the Forum Boarium, cf. Inscr. Ital. XIII. 2, p. 469; Ovid, Fasti 6, 569ff. This goddess was called *Fortuna Virgo* in Non. 189 M from Varro; Plut., quaest. Rom. 281 E; or *virginalis*, Arnob., nat. 2,67, who records an ancient custom to deposit the *togulae* of the brides at her shrine. For the obvious antiquity of the temple, see p. 506. A covered image was kept in the sanctuary, Ovid., Fasti 6, 570–71; Dion. Hal. 4,40,7 "a gilded wooden statue"; Val. Max. 1,8,11. Festus , p. 242 M records *Pudicitiae signum in foro boario . . . eam quidam Fortunae esse existimant*. According to Nonius, p. 189 M from Varro, and Plin., nat. 8, 194, the image was covered with a *toga undulata*. The meaning of *undulata* is obscure. According to the older writers, Varro, Dion. Hal., Ovid., Val. Max., the image represented King Servius. Plin., nat. 8, 197 and Dio 58,7,2–3, however, tell us that the statue belonged to *Fortuna*. This may well be true (cf. H. LYNGBY, Fortunas och Mater Matu-

tas kulter på Forum Boarium i Rom, Eranos 36, 1938, 42–72). The statue
was taken by Sejanus to his house. According to Pliny, loc. cit., the *togae*
survived *ad Seiani exitum*. They may have worn off as a consequence of
Sejanus' robbery, and the true nature of the statue been revealed. This
is why only later writers knew that the statue represented Fortuna.

VIRILIS known only from the *fasti* and literature, especially because of
a peculiar rite, Fasti Praenestini, April 1: *frequenter mulieres supplicant
Fortunae virili; humiliores etiam in balineis quod in iis ea parte corpor[is]
utique viri nudantur qua feminarum gratia desideratur*; cf. Ovid, Fasti
4, 145ff. At any rate, this custom must be of recent date as public baths
were built in Rome only during the second century B.C. *Fortuna Virilis*
was in origin probably the guardian spirit of men, *viri*. cf. LATTE 181, 3
for attempt to explain the genesis of the rite.

β) Fortuna hominum

AVGVSTA, AVGVSTI, AVGVSTORVM, passim, see, p. 517.

DOMVS AVGVSTI VI 196/97 *redux domus August(ae)*.

?CLAVDIAE IVSTAE VI 3679 = 30873; LATTE 182 argues that Fortuna
is here only „*ein etwas schmeichelhafterer Ersatz für Iuno*". According to
CIL, the statue on the stone represented *Fortuna*. On the other hand,
except for *Fortuna Augusti*, the *Fortuna* of an individual was always an
adjectival formation on *-ana/-iana*.

COHORTIS XIII 6677a, see *DUX*; ?7787 (Germ. sup.), fragm.

COLLEGI CENTONARIORVM XI 4391, see *MELIOR*.

COLLEGI FABRVM VI 3678 *numini Fortunae col. fa[brum]*.

CRASSIANA VI 186, age of Severus Alexander; the Fortuna of a Crassus.

FLAVIA VI 187; the Fortuna of the *gens Flavia*. The suffix *-ius/-ia* of the
gentile names had not quite lost its old adjectival meaning, cf. *via Aurelia,
Cassia, Claudia, circus Flaminius*, etc. instead of the more common
-anus/-na.

DOMVS FVRIANAE III 8169 (Moesia sup.) *Fortunae aeternae domus Furia-
nae*.

IMPERI XI 3075 (Falerii); the conjecture of BORMANN, ad loc., *Fortunae
imperi[o]*, is improbable.

IVVENIANA LAMPADIANA VI 189; the Fortuna of a Iuvenius Lampa-
dius.

LEGIONIS III 10992 (Pann. sup.) *F[o]rtun[ae] fortissima[e] leg(ionis) I
ad(iutricis) p(iae) f(idelis) S[everianae]*. XIII 6677 (Germ. sup.) *reduci
leg(ionis) XXII pr(imigeniae)*; 7996 (Germ. inf.), fragm.

OMNIVM Lyd., mens. 4,7, p. 70 W: Trajan dedicated a temple τῇ πάντων
τύχη but with the provision that every one should sacrifice alone, i. e.
to his personal *Fortuna*.

PIENTIANA VI 36753; probably the Fortuna of a Pius.

PLOTIANA AE 1926, 41 (Rome); the Fortuna of the *gens Plotia*.

POPVLI ROMANI Fortuna public(a) p(opuli) R(omani) Q(uiritium),
Fasti, May 25, and *Fortuna publica citerio[r]*, April 5; cf. DEGRASSI,
Inscr. Ital. XIII. 2, p. 437: *Tres aedes in colle Quirinali . . . Fortunae dedi-
catae fuerunt . . . Nomen omnibus videtur fuisse Fortuna Publica Populi
Romani Quiritium. Una, quippe quae proxima Urbem esset, cognomine
Citerioris distincta fuit, altera (25. 5.) cognomine Primigeniae.* This deity
is depicted on republican coins, SYDENHAM, p. 157, No. 938 FORT. P. R.
a. 49–48; p. 180, No. 1083 F. P. R., a. 43, and in the Imperial period, RIC
I p. 184 *florente Fortuna p. R.*, a. 68–69; II, p. 223, No. 5, a. 96; 224,
No. 17, a. 97. In epigraphy, however, she is rare, only RIB 1684. *Fortuna
Publica* is probably only a variety of the former, twice found in inscriptions, IX 1543 (Beneventum) *Fortunai poblicai*, which is certainly republican, though probably not from the third century, as LATTE 179, 2 seems
to hold; another case, III 1010 (Dacia).
TORQVATIANA VI 204 = 30713; the Fortuna of a *Torquatus.*
TVLLIANA VI 8706 *aedituus aedis Fortunae Tullianae*; the Fortuna of
the *gens Tullia* or a Fortuna connected with Servius Tullius.

γ) Fortuna locorum

ANTIAS, ANTIATINA, cf. p. 505.
ARELATENSIS XII 656 (Arelate) *A]relaten[sis] | Nem]ausen[sis] |
]ibus[.*
BALNEORVM Fronto, de oration. 6, p. 151, 1 (VAN DEN HOUT). II 2701 and
2763 (prov. Tarrac.) *balnearis.* VI 182 = 30708 *Fortunab(us) bal(nei)
Verul(ani).* XIII 6552 (Germ. sup.) *sancta balinearis redux*, a. 248; cf.
6592, a. 232: a votive offering to *Fortuna* because *balineu[m] vetustate
conlapsum . . . restituer(unt)*, a. 232.
SIN[GVLARIS C]OLONIAE AV[ZIENSIVM] AE 1966, 597 (Auzia,
Mauretania); the supplement *sin[gularis]* is uncertain as there is no
other example of this epithet.
GENI COLONIAE AE 1950, 233 (Berytos); notice the expression *Fortuna
Geni* instead of the usual juxtaposition of *Fortuna et Genius.*
CVRIAE AE 1957, 145; 1958, 157; 1959, 293; 1961, 255, an inscription
found in a niche in the *frigidarium* of the *thermae* at Themetra, near
Hadrumetum: *HAEC EST FORTVNA | CVRARIAE | FORTVNATAE.*
There has been some disagreement upon the interpretation of the inscription. According to its first publisher, G.-CH. PICARD, it is to be interpreted
haec est fortuna | cur(iae) Ar(r)iae | Fortunatae, cf. AE 1957, 145 and espec-
ially Rev. Arch., 1960 II, p. 36f., cf. AE 1961, 255. L. FOUCHER, Thermes
romains des environs d'Hadrumète (Institut national d'Archéologie et
d'Arts, Tunis: Notes et documents, Nouv. sér. I, 1958, p. 25), cf. AE 1959,
293, retains the form *CVRARIAE*, explaining it either as a place name or
as a gentile name. The former interpretation is quite impossible, the latter founders upon the fact that there is no example of a gentile name
*Curaria. PICARD's interpretation seems to be more acceptable. In Afri-

can towns, *curiae* with epithets derived from gentile names were not uncommon, cf. the list in CIL VIII. 5, p. 282, especially *curia Iulia felix*, 2596. Moreover, *CVRIA* was often abbreviated *CVR.*, ibid., p. 294. According to PICARD, «*les thermes appartenaient non à tous les habitants de Themetra, mais aux membres d'une seule des curies composant la cité.*»

EPHESIA RIC II, p. 399, No. 477, age of Hadrian.

FOLIANENSIS IX 2123 (Vitulanum); cf. Folianum, in the neighbourhood of Vitulanum, WEISS, RE VI 2, 1909, 2828.

HORR(EORVM) VI 188; 236 *conservatrix horreor(um) Galbianorum.*

HVIVS LOCI III 10399 (Pann. inf.). VI 216 *Ginio et Fortunae / Tutelaeque huius / loci cohortium praetoriarum.* XII 4183, cf. *TUTATRIX.* AE 1973, 417 (Vindobona) *huius [loci].*

KARN(VNTIENSIS) AE 1929, 226 (Carnuntum), a. 153? the precise form of the epithet is uncertain.

ET GENIVS MACELLI AE 1935, 51 (Macedonia).

MVNICIPI IX 2586 (Terventum).

NEMAVSENSIS XII 656, see Arelatensis.

PRAETORIA XIV 3540 (Tibur); probably the Fortuna of *praetorium.*

VIRVNIENSIS V 778 (Aquileia); the inscription has survived only in a manuscript, which gives the form *Veruniensi*, probably a Vulgar form (*e pro i*) for *Viruniensis*, cf. Virunum in Noricum. HEICHELHEIM, RE VIII A2, 1958, 1689, retains the form *Veruniensis*, arguing that it suggests a local guardian goddess.

VISENT(I) AE 1974, 329 (near Montefiascone); cf. Visentium, modern Bisenzo, near Lake Bolsena, G. RADKE, RE IX A 1, 1961, 361.

δ) Epithets of uncertain meaning

CAMCESIS VI 30709; the name may be corrupt, *CAMCESIS.* At any rate, no word or name of this type has been documented. The termination may be *-e(n)sis*; in this case, we would have here a Fortuna locorum.

VISCATA Plut., quaest. Rom. 281 E; according to LATTE 182, 1, the epithet is obscure and hardly to be connected with the magic power of the mistletoe (a suggestion of BUDIMIR, Raccolta Ramorino, Milano 1927, 147ff.). At any rate, the epithet seems to suggest Fortuna/Tyche, the Latin adjective *viscatus* meaning 'smeared with birdlime'. In a passage in Seneca's letters, the gifts of Fortune are called *viscata*, insidious, 8, 3 *Munera ista fortunae putatis? insidiae sunt. quisquis vestrum tutam agere vitam volet, quantum plurimum potest, ista viscata beneficia devitet* ... Like *brevis*, this may be a literary expression rather than an epithet of the Fortuna of popular cult.

ε) Divine epithets of Fortuna

AETERNA III 8169, see *DOMUS FVRIANAE.* XIII 6777a, see *DUX.*

COELESTIS VIII 6943 (Numidia) *Fortunae caelestis sacrum*, i. e. *sacellum.*

DEA passim.
?DIVA II 3026 (Tarrac.) *FORTVNA | DIVA*, „*aut male descripta aut inter-polata*" HÜBNER.
FILIA IOVIS (Praenestina), see p. 508.
MAGNA III 1018 (Dacia).
PRIMIGENIA (Praenestina), see p. 508.
SANCTA VI 203. X 5384 (Aquinum). XI 2997 (*ager* Viterb.). XIV 6 (Ostia) *domestica sancta*; 2568 (near Tusculum) *s(ancta) d(ea) F(ortuna)*; 2850 (Praeneste); 4281–82 (Ostia). XIII 6386a (Germ. sup.); 6592 (ibid.). RIB 968; 1029. AE 1912, 86–87 (Rome); 1968, 234 *redux sancta* (prov. Tarrac.).
SVPERA III 1014 (Dacia) *supera Aug(usta)*. XIII 6679 (Germ. sup.) *Fortunam superam honori aquilae leg(ionis) XXII*.

ζ) Identified with other deities (excluding names connected with the copula *et*)

CERERV(M) AVG. AE 1955, 160 (Tiddis, Algiers); the plural Cereres was frequent in Africa, representing Ceres and Proserpina, see WISSOWA, Ceres, RE III, 1899, 1978f.; cf. CIL VIII. 5, p. 222.
NEMESIS III 1125 (Dacia) *Deae Nemesi sive Fortunae.*
PANTHEA VI 30867 X 5800 (Aletrium); cf. 1557 (Puteoli) *post adsignationem aedis Fortunae signum Pantheum . . . d(ono) d(edit).*
STATA VI 761 *Statae Fortunae Aug(ustae)*, a. 12; scil. Stata Mater.
VENVS AE 1954, 146 (Timgad) *Fortunae Veneri Aug.*

b) Analysis of the material

The material reveals that almost all of the epithets characterized Fortuna as a benevolent power, as a protector of human beings and even of localities. There was in fact little difference between Fortuna and Genius[27]. All the varieties of Fortuna listed as Fortuna hominum, Fortuna locorum naturally belong to this category. But the majority of the epithets grouped in the section Vis Fortunae suggested a similar idea. Only a few of the epithets described her power in general, *dux, fortissima, gubernatrix, potens* (uncertain), *regina, victrix*, or even suggested a fickle, malicious power, *brevis, casualis, dubia, mala, viscata* (if correctly interpreted). But *brevis* and *viscata* were quoted only by Plutarch. These epithets may have been literary expressions and not obtained from the language of popular cult. *Casualis, dubia*, and *mala* were not very frequent, though Fortuna Mala seems to have had an old altar on the Esquiline.

Out of the other epithets of Fortuna, a number referred to her power over different spheres and aspects of life: *muliebris, virgo, virilis* manifested themselves in the life of woman and man, *barbata* and *mammosa* in the

---

[27] cf. LATTE 333; besides with Genius, Fortuna was juxtaposed even with Tutela.

development of the human body; *domestica* and *penas* protected home, *armipotens*, *equestris* and even *huiusce diei* appeared in war, whereas Fortuna Privata was conceived of as a counterpart to Fortuna Publica, as a guardian spirit of private citizens and private life. Again, epithets like *bona, confluens, conservatrix, manens, obsequens, respiciens, salutaris, stabilis,* etc. clearly suggested a benevolent and constant, not a malevolent and fickle deity.

It is thus unlikely that Hellenistic Fortuna/Tyche, the personification of blind chance, should have had any great influence upon the Roman ideas of Fortuna as an object of popular cult. It is of course possible to argue that it was precisely simple Fortuna, without any epithets, that was the Roman equivalent of Hellenistic Tyche. There is a considerable number of dedications to this entity throughout the Empire[28]. Nevertheless, if the Fortuna of popular cult was really the fickle and malevolent Fortuna/Tyche, we could have expected a greater number of epithets suggesting this aspect of her power.

The conclusion seems inevitable. Fortuna, such as she appears in Roman religious life, was not the personification of blind chance. She remained primarily the goddess of luck, the bringer of good fortune.

c) Fortuna Augusta/Augusti, Fortuna Redux

Two varieties of Fortuna came to have a very great importance during the Empire, Fortuna Augusta or Augusti, the guardian spirit of the emperor, an equivalent of his Genius, and Fortuna Redux, the power that guarded the return of the emperor from dangerous foreign journeys. Both deities were recorded in an uncountable number of votive inscriptions, coins, etc. This was in part due to the fact that the honour paid to Fortuna Augusta and Fortuna Redux was an expression of loyalty to the State and the reigning emperor.

Fortuna Aug. seems to have come into use later than Fortuna Redux. On coins, she first appears A.D. 70–71, RIC I, p. 213, No. 140. Especially in inscriptions, the name was almost invariably abbreviated. If occasionally written out, it had the form Augusta, thus VI 181a–b; VIII 15576, a. 164, etc. However, the genitive AUGVSTI was not rare on coins, the first case being RIC II, p. 31, No. 140, age of Vespasian. If there were two Augusti, the abbreviation AVGG. was used. The first example on coins is RIC IV. 1, p. 100, No. 77, A.D. 196–97.

At least by the Antonine age, the emperors had a golden statue of their Fortuna in their bed-chamber. At the transference of power to a new emperor, the statue of Fortuna was also transferred[29].

In official cult, Fortuna Redux was of greater importance. The Senate consecrated an altar to this deity near the Porta Capena in memory of Au-

---

[28] In VI, dedications to Fortuna 171—76; for the other volumes of CIL, cf. the indices.

[29] SHA 3, 12,5 *Marco Antonino rem publicam ... commendavit* (scil. *Antoninus Pius) Fortunamque auream, quae in cubiculo principum poni solebat, transferri ad eum iussit;* cf. 4, 7,3; in 10, 23,5 (age of Severus), the Fortuna has the epithet *regia.*

gustus' return from Syria, October 12, 19 B.C.[30]. Games in honour of the
emperor, *Augustalia*, were associated with the cult of Fortuna Redux.
According to the Fasti Amiternini (post 20 A.D.), they extended from October 5 to October 12. Even the day of the dedication of the altar, December 15,
was entered in the Fasti.

Fortuna Redux was from the very beginning by far the most common
variety of Fortuna on coins, the first case being RIC I, p. 85, No. 272 and
274, minted in Colonia Patricia in Spain (Augustan age). The name was
usually abbreviated RED. An otherwise undocumented form, FORTVNA
REDVCA, RIC II, p. 429, No. 697, A.D. 125–28, is worth notice. In
epigraphy, dedications to Fortuna Redux were quite as common as
dedications to Fortuna Aug. It is pointless to give here any examples. All
the indices of CIL will show them in abundance, and AE lists almost
annually new finds.

4. The iconography of Fortuna

Except for ROSCHER's Mythologisches Lexicon I. 2, 1503—08, there is no
comprehensive treatment of the representation of Fortuna in the visual
arts, and even this work is dated in some respects. The following discussion
is not exhaustive as it is based only on a limited material, on coins (SYDEN-
HAM and RIC), on the reliefs in epigraphy so far as they have been listed
in the indices of CIL, and in ESPERÁNDIEU's great collection of statues and
reliefs from Gallia and Germania (69 cases of Fortuna, some of them uncertain;
the great majority come from Belgica and Germania). But I think even this
material suffices to illustrate the normal iconography of Fortuna.

During the republic, there were coins depicting Fortuna where she did
not yet have any attributes, SYDENHAM, p. 157, No. 938, B.C. 49—48[31].
But very soon the typical attributes of Fortuna began to appear. Fortuna
was represented as a standing woman, with a rudder in her right, a cornucopia in her left hand. This picture is first found on a coin of B.C. 44—28,
SYDENHAM, p. 179, No. 1078 and p. 184, No. 1126, B.C. 40[32].

These attributes correspond to the representations of Greek Tyche.
The rudder and the cornucopia were the standard attributes of the Greek
goddes as well[33]. The rudder as a symbol of Tyche is found as early as Pindar (p. 526). Dio Chrysosthomus, 63, 7, explains these symbols thus: "The

---

[30] Aug., Res gestae 11; Dio 54,10,3; Fasti Amiternini, Oct. 12; cf. DEGRASSI, Inscr. Ital.
XIII.2 p. 519—20.

[31] The picture is described thus: "Head of Fortune r(ight), diad(emed), with cruciform ear-
ring; hair in knot and falling in two locks; jewels in hair; on l(eft) *P(opuli) R(omani)*
on r(ight) *Fort(una)*"; another case, ibid. p. 180 No. 1083, B.C. 43.

[32] In another republican variety, Fortuna was holding Victory and cornucopia, SYDENHAM
p. 186 No. 1144, B.C. 44—28.

[33] L. RUHL, s.v. Tyche, ROSCHER V, Leipzig 1916—24, 1342—44.

rudder indicates that Fortune directs the life of men; and the horn of Amaltheia calls attention to the giving of good things and prosperity[34]."

Besides standing, Fortuna was also represented as seated. Seated Fortuna was almost as common as was the standing variety. There is probably little or no difference in significance between these two types of Fortuna[35].

The rudder and the cornucopia were the essential attributes of Fortuna. The cornucopia seems to have been even more typical than was the rudder; it sufficed alone, thus RIC IV. 1, p. 155, No. 477A, A.D. 195–97: Fortuna with cornucopia in each hand; XIII 6621 (Germ. sup.): Fortuna's head between two cornucopias; 6516 (ibidem): a votive inscription to *Fortuna*, with cornucopias cut in relief on either side.

The globe was also a typical attribute of Fortuna, though not quite as common as the rudder and the cornucopia. Dio Chrysosthomus, 63, 7, explains the meaning of the globe to be "that change of fortune is easy, for the divine power is, in fact, ever in motion." It is, however, equally probable that the globe symbolized Fortune's power over the world. The rudder was often set on the globe, a clear indication of the significance of the attribute[36]. Again, if the globe was meant to serve as a symbol of Fortune's fickleness, it is hard to understand why still another symbol of fickleness, the wheel, later on should have become common (p. 520).

Besides the cornucopia, there were some other symbols of Fortuna as distributor of material blessings, corn-ears[37], and *modius*[38]. Again, *patera* was a common attribute of Fortuna on coins, where it represented the act of sacrifice, e. g. RIC III, p. 124, No. 771, A.D. 145–61; V. 1, p. 192, No. 8, age of Gallienus: Fortuna holding *patera* and sacrificing at altar. This may have suggested the blessing bestowed by the goddess[39]. Again, Esp. 8, 6458 = XIII 12049 (cf. p. 511 s. v. *GVBERNATRIX*) depicts Fortuna with a *patera* in her right hand between man and woman presenting offerings to her. The prow was also a rather common attribute of Fortuna on coins, either held by the goddess, RIC II, p. 18, No. 31, A.D. 70—72, etc., or with the rudder set on it, RIC II, p. 245, No. 4, A.D. 98—99; III, p. 128, No. 801, A.D. 145—61, etc. This attribute may symbolize Fortuna as a goddess of seafaring[40]. The anchor may be a similar symbol[41]. It appears very late on a coin, RIC V. 2, p. 466, No. 35, age of Carausius.

---

[34] Translation according to the Loeb edition.

[35] According to Ruhl, op. cit. 1343,19, sitting Fortune suggests constancy, but the evidence quoted by him is scanty. On Roman coins, seated Fortuna and wheel, the symbol of fickleness, were often found together (p. 520).

[36] CIL III 4495 (Carnuntum), A. D. 178; Esp. 5,4247 (Luxemburg); 6,4899 (Belgica); 4936 (ibid.); 4950 (ibid.); 5028 (ibid.); 5124 (ibid.), etc. On coins, RIC II p. 73 No. 487, A. D. 71, and passim.

[37] RIC II p. 223 No. 5, A. D. 96; IV.1 p. 143 No. 387, A. D. 194—95, etc.

[38] RIC IV.2 p. 34 No. 81, age of Elagabalus; VII p. 606 No. 38, age of Constantine; Esp. 3,1744 (Lugudunum): Fortuna with a *modius* on her head.

[39] Cf. H. Luschey, Φιάλη, RE Suppl. VII, 1940, 1030.

[40] Peter-Drexler, Roscher's Lexicon I.2, 1507,6.

[41] P. Stumpf, s.v. Anker, RLAC 1, Stuttgart 1950, 441.

On coins, Fortuna was often identified with other deities, usually by the adoption of their attributes. In one case, even the names of the deities were united, FORTVNA SPES, RIC II, p. 368, No. 246, commemorating the adoption of Aelius (ibid., p. 327 and 334). Both deities were depicted with their typical attributes, Spes "holding flower and raising dress"[42]. Other borrowed attributes may be the scales, RIC IV. 1, p. 27, No. 30, A.D. 193—194, the attribute of Aequitas; *caduceus*, RIC II, p. 16, No. 11, A.D. 69—71, etc., the usual attribute of Mercurius[43]; long palm, RIC IV.1 p. 137, No. 355, A.D. 193; V. 2, p. 530, No. 793, age of Carausius, suggests Hilaritas; the poppy, RIC IV.1, p. 143, No. 387, A.D. 194—195, Ceres, etc. Fortuna could even assume the typical attributes of Jupiter, the sceptre and the thunderbolt, RIC III, p. 387, No. 191b, A.D. 189. The sceptre alone was often found, e.g. RIC II, p. 398, No. 473, A.D. 138 and III, p. 229, No. 204, A.D. 168—169.

It is worth notice that at least on coins, there is no example of an identification with Isis. The typical attribute of this deity, the *sistrum*, is not found in connection with Fortuna. Neither is there any evidence of the identification in literature and epigraphy. Apuleius' 'The Golden Ass', which is quoted as testimony, has been misinterpreted (p. 551). In epigraphy, there are a few references to Isityche, XIV 2867, a votive gift to Fortuna Praenestina of *statua Antonini August(i) Apollinis Isityches Spei*. Another case is ROSTOVZEV, Tesserarum urbis Romae sylloge, Petersburg 1903, 1265: *Isity(che)*. Moreover, there are two cases of the Greek form, IV 4138 Εἰσιτύχη and L. MORETTI, Inscriptiones Graecae urbis Romae, Roma 1968, a votive inscription to Ἰσιτύχη. Because Isis and Tyche were found identified in the East as early as the late third century B. C. (p. 508 fn. 23), it is no wonder that evidence of this is found even in the West. PETER-DREXLER, op. cit., 1530—33 and 1549—55 quote a number of statues, paintings, etc. in which Fortune is depicted with the attributes of Isis. Nevertheless, it is an open question whether the goddess always represented Roman Fortuna and not Greek Tyche.

The attributes discussed so far represent Fortuna as a distributor of life's good things or as a mistress of the world. In these symbols, little or nothing suggested an unpredictable, malicious deity. There was, however, an attribute which accentuated this side of Fortuna's character, the wheel. In the statues and reliefs from Belgica and Germania, it was not very rare[44]. On the coins, it was late to appear. In contrast to the former group, where the wheel was equally divided between seated and standing Fortuna, on coins the wheel was found as an attribute of seated Fortuna, under the

---

[42] On some coins, Fortuna is depicted as raising dress, RIC III p. 185 Nos. 1328—29 (if correctly identified as Fortuna), which may suggest a similar identification.

[43] PETER-DREXLER, op. cit., 1537,57: „Die Verbindung der Glücksgöttin mit dem Gott des Handels und Wandels ist an sich verständlich."

[44] ESP. 5, 4004; 6, 4662; 4940; 8, 5945; 6007; 6318 (rudder, wheel, and cornucopia on top of each other); 7526.

seat[45], or with the goddess seated on or by it[46]. On one coin, the wheel was
held by Fortuna, RIC V. 2 p. 519 No. 647, age of Carausius. The wheel was
also an attribute of Nemesis, but judging from the frequency of the wheel
especially in statues and reliefs, where as a rule only the standard attributes
were used, the wheel cannot simply suggest an identification with this
deity[47].

II. Fortuna in Literature

It is a peculiarity of the Roman conception of Fortuna that the goddess
of popular cult and *fortuna* in literature were often very different entities.
The former Fortuna was primarily a benevolent deity, bringer of luck,
guardian spirit of human beings and localities, not unlike Genius.

In literature, the very word *fortuna* had a number of meanings, which
could suggest contradictory ideas. Moreover, Greek Tyche as a personification of blind chance had been superimposed upon native Roman notions.
It is thus necessary to analyze the meanings of the word *fortuna* in some
detail.

1. The meanings of the word *fortuna*

a) Passive meanings

Very often *fortuna*, in a passive sense, denotes an effect and not a
cause or superhuman agent. This meaning is clearest if the word was used
in the plural, thus carmen Nelei (Festus p. 352 M, 3rd century B.C.) *topper
fortunae commutantur hominibus*; Plaut., Asin. 515 *verum ego meas queror
fortunas*; Ter., Andr. 609 *servon fortunas meas me commisisse futtili*. It was,
however, very frequent in the singular, too, e.g. Plaut., fragm. 16—17 *quis
est mortalis tanta fortuna* (i.e. misfortune) *adfectus umquam*; Liv. 6,24,9
ni restituitur pugna ... fortunam cum omnibus, infamiam solus sentiam.
The word may be an equivalent of the Greek καιρός, *opportunitas*, often
construed with the gerund or the gerundive, Cic., Phil. 13,7 *laetemur decertan-
di oblatam esse fortunam*. The meaning of "state, circumstances, social
position, etc." is very common. The best definition is given by Cicero, Inv.
rhet. 2,30 *et ex fortuna saepe argumentatio nascitur, cum servus an liber,
pecuniosus an pauper, nobilis an ignobilis, felix an infelix, privatus an in
potestate sit aut fuerit aut futurus sit, consideratur*. The meaning of "posses-

---

[45] RIC III p. 240 No. 343, A. D. 175—76; IV.1 p. 324 No. 75, A. D. 211; IV.2 p. 29 No.
18, A. D. 129; IV.3, passim.
[46] Ibid., IV.1 p. 324 No. 77, A. D. 211; V. 1 p. 279 No. 128 and p. 284 No. 170, age of
Aurelian; V. 2, passim.
[47] cf. RUHL, op. cit. (fn. 33) 1342,63: an attribute of Nemesis.

sions" was frequent in the plural, Cic., QRosc. 33 *tum enim propter rei publicae calamitates omnium possessiones erant incertae, nunc deum immortalium benignitate omnium fortunae sunt certae.*

It is naturally often difficult to decide whether *fortuna* was used in a passive sense or whether it really denoted a cause or an agent beyond human control. But the number of ambiguous cases is not really very great.

b) *Fortuna* denoting chance

Latin has special words for "chance", *fors* and *casus.* In ancient definitions, a difference is usually made between *fors* and *fortuna,* cf. Nonius p. 425 M *fors et fortuna hoc distant: fors est casus temporalis, fortuna dea ipsa.* Here *fortuna* was clearly conceived of as the personification of chance. However, *fors, casus,* and *fortuna* may be used as synonyms, thus Cic., div. 2,15 *quid est enim aliud fors, quid fortuna, quid casus, quid eventus, nisi cum sic aliquid cecidit, sic evenit, ut vel non cadere atque evenire, ut vel aliter cadere atque evenire potuerit?* This meaning of the word is especially frequent in philosophical works, but the influence of Greek ideas should here be taken into account (cf. p. 529).

In ordinary language, the meaning of "chance" was at first found in the stock expression *forte fortuna,* thus Plaut., Bacch. 916 *ni illic hodie forte fortuna hic foret;* Mil. 287 *forte fortuna per impluvium huc despexi in proxumum;* Ter., Eun. 134—35 *forte fortuna adfuit | hic meus amicus* (cf. p. 505 fn. 7). Later on, the simple word *fortuna* could stand for "chance", e. g. Liv. 2,12,7 (Mucius Scaevola's attempt on the life of King Porsenna) *quo temere traxit fortuna facinus, scribam pro rege obtruncat;* notice the abverb *temere,* which accentuates the meaning of the word *fortuna.*

In a little wider sense, *fortuna* stood for the incalculable element which defies human planning especially in warfare. The frequent expressions *fortunam experiri, fortunam temptare, fortunae se* or *aliquid committere,* are an indication of the popularity of this connotation[48]. The expressions *fortuna belli, fortuna pugnae,* unless denoting the "outcome" of a battle, had a similar meaning[49].

c) *Fortuna* denoting luck. Sulla Felix

In the earliest literary documents, there is an unmistakable parallel between Fortuna of the popular cult and *fortuna* as an agent of good luck; cf. the following passages, Plaut., Poen. 973 *aliqua fortuna fuerit adiutrix tibi;* Asin. 716 *quem te autem divom nominem? Fortunam, atque opsequentem;* 718 *licet laudem Fortunam, tamen ut ne Salutem culpem;* Capt. 864 *idem ego sum Salus, Fortuna, Lux, Laetitia, Gaudium;* Ter., Eun. 1046—47 *an fortunam conlaudem quae gubernatrix fuit, | quae tot res tantas tam opportune in*

---

[48] Cf. Thes. 1. L. VI.1 1184,38; 1185,11 and 21.
[49] Thes. 1. L. II 1843,49.

unum conclusit diem; she is once called Bona Fortuna, Plaut., Aul. 100.
This epithet, and even more *opsequens* quoted from Plautus, suggests that
it was indeed Fortuna such as she was venerated at Praeneste and in Rome
who was thought of in these passages.

In later literature, *fortuna* as an agent of good luck became rarer,
being replaced by *fortuna/tyche*. But there is another, related idea of *fortuna* which was popular throughout Roman literature. *Fortuna* denoted
simple 'good luck' without a clear idea of its cause or agent. In other
words, it was a synonym of *felicitas*; cf. Serv., Aen. 3,16 *sciendum quotiens-
cumque fortunam solam dicimus felicitatem intellegi.*

This meaning is often found in a few set expressions, in particular
those in which *virtus* is supplemented or aided by luck, thus in the popular
Latin proverb *fortes fortuna adiuvat,* e.g. Ter., Phorm. 203, and its varieties,
e.g. Enn., Ann. 257 (VAHLEN) *fortibus est fortuna viris data;* cf. Thes. l. L.
VI.1 1181,72.

Fortuna denotes "good luck" in those cases, too, in which the *virtus*
and *fortuna* of a general are referred to. It was a peculiar Roman idea that
in addition to other requirements, a great general should also be attended
by good luck. Cicero argues, De imp. Cn. Pomp. 28 that a general should
possess *scientia rei militaris, virtus, auctoritas, felicitas.* But later on, discussing the last requirement, he uses *fortuna* and *felicitas* as synonyms,
47 *reliquum est ut de felicitate quam praestare de se ipso nemo potest . . .
sicut aequum est homines de potestate deorum, timide et pauca dicamus.* Cicero's
idea seems to be that gods bestowed good luck upon some outstanding generals: *ego enim sic existimo, Maximo, Marcello, Scipioni, Mario ceterisque
magnis imperatoribus non solum propter virtutem sed etiam propter fortunam
saepius imperia mandata atque exercitus esse commissos. fuit enim profecto
quibusdam summis viris quaedam . . . divinitus adiuncta fortuna.* Then he
proceeds to speak in the same vein about Pompey. It is possible that the
reference to the gods as givers of good luck was mere pious language requisite in a speech made in the Popular Assembly. The word *felicitas* was derived
from *felix,* which originally denoted 'fruitful'. Consequently, a man was
felix if he "produced" success. *Felicitas* was an innate, magic quality. But
later on, after Rome came under the influence of Greek civilization and Greek
modes of thought, this original idea grew dim and disappeared, at least
among the educated. It was equated with the Greek εὐτυχία, 'good luck',
'success', which was only a matter of observation and did not imply an
innate quality[50]. Hence the use of *fortuna* as a synonym of *felicitas* despite
the fact that the former word could not possess the original connotation of
felicitas. And on occasion, as in Cicero's speech, *felicitas/fortuna* could be
considered a gift of the gods. At any rate, there can be no doubt that
considerable importance was attached to the irrational fact of a person

---

[50] Cf. H. WAGENVOORT, Felicitas Imperatoria, Mnem. 7, 1954, 300—22; F. TAEGER, Charisma
II, Stuttgart 1960, 25; 32.

'having luck'. In the passage quoted, Cicero was only voicing ideas current in Roman society.

Besides Cicero, many other authors referred to the same ideas, e.g. Liv. 1,42,3 *in eo bello et virtus et fortuna enituit Tulli;* cf. Thes. l. L. VI.1, 1195,55 for similar passages.

Sulla's much-discussed *agnomen* Felix may be explicable in the same way[51]. The name Felix cannot be interpreted to imply a special relationship to Fortuna as his personal guardian spirit. It is equally unlikely that Sulla should have entertained any ideas of a magic *felicitas* innate in him[52]. He simply believed to be always attended by good luck, *felicitas*.

d) Personal *fortuna*

In not a few passages in Roman literature, *fortuna* represented a kind of guardian spirit of an individual or of a group of individuals, in principle not unlike Fortuna hominum reviewed in the first part of the present work. It is, however, often difficult to make a clear distinction here between *fortuna* as 'good luck' and *fortuna* as an equivalent of *genius*. Thus the very first example in Roman literature, Enn., Trag. 172 (VAHLEN) *ubi fortuna Hectoris nostram acrem aciem inclinatam dedit*, is ambiguous. But in Ammianus Marcellinus, 27,11,2 *hunc* (= Probum) *quasi genuina quaedam* (i.e. congenital) — *ut fingunt poetae* — *fortuna vehens praepetibus pinnis*, a personal *fortuna* seems to be found. There are similar references elsewhere in Amm.,[53] *fortunam eius* (i.e., of Constantius) *in malis tantum civilibus vigilasse*, 14,10,16; Valentinianus on the night before his death saw in vision his Fortuna departing *cum taetro habitu*, 30,5,18.

Besides Ammianus, the personal fortuna was of some importance in the work of Curtius Rufus, who ascribed Alexander the Great's success at least in part to his *fortuna* (cf. p. 549). Again, in Lucanus, the personal *fortuna*, especially the personal *fortuna* of Caesar, was often found (p. 550). But otherwise *fortuna* as a special guardian spirit of an individual was rare in Roman literature. Even in Ammianus and Curtius, it may owe something to the Greek ideas of a personal *tyche* (p. 527). Ammianus was in origin a Greek, and Curtius, in his biography of Alexander, followed Greek originals and models.

The *fortuna* of the Roman people or of the Roman state was more clearly a native Roman idea — cf. the importance in cult of Fortuna Populi Romani — and references to this entity were frequent, especially in historical writing. In Cicero's speeches, *Fortuna populi Romani* resisted Catilina's criminal plans, Cat. 1,15; by letting Pompey appear in the right time *Fortuna populi Romani* saved Asia for the Romans, De imp. Pomp. 45; *vel mea vel*

---

[51] cf. J. P. V. BALSDON, Sulla Felix, JRS 41, 1951, 1—10; H. ERKELL, Augustus, felicitas, fortuna, Göteborg 1952, 71—93.

[52] WAGENVOORT, op. cit. (fn. 50) 321—22.

[53] Cf. C. P. T. NAUDÉ, Fortuna in Ammianus Marcellinus, Acta classica, Proc. of the Class. Ass. of South Africa, 7, 1964, 80—83.

rei publicae fortuna protected Cicero from Clodius' attempts on his life, Milo 20; *fortuna quaedam rei publicae* kept Antony from the city, Phil. 5,29. As is natural, the Fortuna of Rome is represented as a guardian spirit of the city and of the people. In some rhetorical passages, Cicero certainly makes her appear as hard and cruel, *dura . . . mihi iam Fortuna populi Romani et crudelis videbatur, quae tot annos illum* (i.e. *Clodium*) *in hanc rem publicam insultare pateretur*, Milo 87, but this should not be taken seriously.

It is significant that Fortuna of Rome is found in Cicero only in the speeches. It was probably little more than a tribute to popular religious ideas.

There is no example in Caesar, in Sallust only one, Catil. 41,3: the Allobroges, after wavering, decide to inform the Romans of the conspiracy, *haec illis volventibus tandem vicit fortuna rei publicae*, but the word may here simply denote 'the good luck of the state'. For Livy and Tacitus, see pp. 538 and 545. Ammianus once records *Fortuna orbis Romani* 25,9,7.

e) *Fortuna/tyche*

From the very beginning, there appears a quite different idea of *fortuna*, a fickle and malicious power that causes the often chaotic ups and downs in human life, Plaut., Capt. 304 *fortuna humana fingit artatque ut lubet*; Enn., Ann. 312—13 (VAHLEN) *mortalem summum Fortuna repente/ reddidit e summo ut famul ultimus esset*; and especially a long fragment from Pacuvius, 37—46 (Loeb): *Fortuna* is *insana, caeca, bruta*, she is standing *saxo in globoso*. She is said to be *insana* because she is *atrox incerta instabilisque*, and *caeca* because *nil cernat quo sese adplicet*, and *bruta* because *dignum atque indignum nequeat internoscere*.

In the passages quoted, *fortuna* is clearly a personification of blind chance, cf. the etymology given by Isidorus, 8,11,94 *Fortunam a fortuitis nomen habere dicunt, quasi deam quandam res humanas variis casibus et fortuitis inludentem*. But this *fortuna* was not a Roman creation. On the contrary, fickle and malicious *fortuna* was the Roman equivalent of Greek *tyche*. Consequently it may be called *fortuna/tyche*[54]. To get a better idea of this entity, it may be useful to give a brief analysis of Greek tyche.

α) A history of Greek *tyche*[55]

Tyche, derived from the verb τυγχάνω, 'happen to one', was used in a passive sense (LIDDELL-SCOTT: regarded as a result) and in an active sense (LIDDELL-SCOTT: an agent or cause beyond human control). There is

[54] Cf. G. HERZOG-HAUSER, Tyche und Fortuna, Wiener Studien 63, 1948, 156—63; KAJANTO, Livy, 14—15.

[55] L. RUHL, s.v. Tyche, ROSCHER V 1309—1357; G. HERZOG-HAUSER, s. v. Tyche, RE VII A 2, 1948, 1643—89; M. P. NILSSON, Geschichte der griechischen Religion 2², München 1961, 200—210, (= Handb. der Altertumswissenschaft V.2)

thus some similarity between *tyche* and *fortuna*. Again, like *fortuna*, *tyche* often denotes 'chance', especially in the expression κατὰ τύχην; in the early period, it was often considered 'bringer of good luck'. But unlike *fortuna*, *tyche* was increasingly regarded as a personification of chance, a fickle and malicious entity. This is the popular or Hellenistic *tyche*, so called because it came to have great importance precisely in this period. Another contrast to *fortuna* is the fact that *tyche* only late became an object of cult. Greek Tyche has not the abundance of epithets which were a distinctive feature of Roman Fortuna.

Tyche is recorded for the first time in Hesiod., Theog. 360: she is a sea-nymph, daughter of Oceanus and Tethys. All the daughters of Oceanus are said to bring up the sons of men together with Apollo, 346—47. Tyche the sea-nymph, who is also recorded in hymn. Hom. Cer. I 420, is clearly a goddess of good luck[56], but soon vanished from literature.[57]

Pindar records Tyche in several passages[58]. She is, however, not a sea-nymph but a goddess who 'upholds a city', cf. fragm. 39 Τύχα φερέπολις. He has composed a hymn on her, Ol. 12, where she is Soteira Tycha, daughter of Zeus Eleutherios, guardian spirit of the city of Himera. But even in Pindar, though he spiritually belongs to the archaic period, Tyche sometimes suggests a personification of chance. Thus in fragm. 40, Tyche is argued to be 'disobedient' and 'to use a double rudder', in other words, to cause now success, now ill fortune.

Aeschylus rarely refers to *tyche*, and even then mostly in a passive sense. In an active sense, Tyche is found, e. g., Agam. 664: Tyche Soter protects the ship home-bound from Troy; Sept. 426: a messenger reveals that Capaneus threatens to destroy Thebes, and expresses the hope that Tyche might not allow this. Thus in Aeschylus, a providential idea of *tyche* prevails.

Tyche is more frequent in Sophocles. The word often denotes 'bringer of good luck'; thus OT 80 records Tyche Soter, and 1080 Oedipus declares that he will be saved from shame because he is the son of Tyche the giver of good gifts. In a few passages, however, *tyche* suggests a fickle power, Ant. 1158: *tyche* can unexpectedly raise or cast down the high and the low alike; OT 977 Iocaste reasons that man should not be afraid since he is the sport of *tyche*, with no foreknowledge of the future.

Euripides records *tyche* on an average 12 times per play[59]. Though mostly used in a passive sense, there are a great many examples of an active use, too. *Tyche* may denote 'bringer of good luck'[60], but popular *tyche* begins to grow in importance. *Tyche* is unaccountable and unpredictable, e. g.

---

[56] F. ALLÈGRE, Étude sur la déesse grecque Tyche, Paris 1889, 7.

[57] Cf. in general H. HERTER, Glück und Verhängnis. Über die altgriechische Tyche, Hellas 4, 1963, 1—10.

[58] Cf. H. STROHM, Tyche. Zur Schicksalsauffassung bei Pindar und den frühgriechischen Dichtern, Stuttgart 1944.

[59] G. BUSCH, Untersuchungen zum Wesen der Τύχη in den Tragödien des Euripides, Diss. Heidelberg 1937, 10.

[60] Thus IT 909 and El. 648, where the assistance of *tyche* is counted on.

Alc. 785ff.: no one knows what *tyche* has in mind; only the day to day life is one's own, everything else is in *tyche's* power; HF 508ff. Amphitryon complains that all his happiness was snatched by *tyche* in one day. *Tyche* is a divine being (*daimon*), more powerful than the gods, Cycl. 606—07. Not Zeus but *tyche* is the master of mankind, Hec. 488ff.

Attic orators, in particular the later ones, frequently record *tyche*. The orators had to adopt the point of view of ordinary citizens. This is why their religious ideas correspond to popular beliefs[61]. *Tyche* appears as an unaccountable entity, e. g. Demosth., prooem. 25, 2: giving good advice is easy, but to put it into effect for the most part depends upon *tyche*. This is why the blame for political failures may be laid on *tyche*. Demosthenes argues in his famous speech 'On the crown' that he was not defeated by Philip in forethought and armaments, only the generals and forces of the allies by *tyche*, 300; cf. 306. But unpredictable *tyche* may be favourable, too. Demosthenes contends, prooem. 36, 1, that *tyche* makes many things right themselves where the prudence of the people in authority would have been of little avail.

In later orators there begins to appear the idea that each man and even each state has his or her own *tyche* as a companion of life. This personal *tyche*, as it is called, seems to have originated from the old Greek belief that each man was allotted his future fate at birth[62]. On the other hand, Τύχη πόλεως was an old idea, attested as early as Pindar (see p. 526). For personal *tyche*, cf., e. g., Aeschin. 3, 157: he admonishes the Athenians to beware of the *daimon* and *tyche* who follow Demosthenes in life; cf. Demosthenes' retort, 'On the crown' 258 and 265—66. Philemon, the playwright, argues, fragm. M IV 6 that *Tyche* is neither one nor new. When a man is born, his *Tyche* is given to him together with his body. No one can have the *Tyche* of another.

The personal *tyche* of an individual did not, however, become very important, as it was soon replaced by *daimon*, who already in Plato is found as man's companion through life, Phaedo 107D. On the other hand, the *Tyche* of a city, a true guardian spirit, found general acceptance, especially in cult[63].

Tyche was a dominant figure in the literature of the Hellenistic period. Two factors contributed to her popularity. The Olympic gods were rapidly losing ground. This created a religious vacuum, which was in part filled by *Tyche*. Again, the time of Alexander the Great and of the Epigoni was a period of great upheavals. Many great states, e. g. the Persian Empire, fell to pieces, and new ones were founded instead. The success of an individual seemed often to depend more upon chance than upon his own efforts. This

[61] Cf. H. MEUSS, Die Vorstellungen von Gottheit und Schicksal bei den attischen Rednern, NJbb 139, 1889, 445ff.

[62] NILSSON, op. cit. (fn. 55) 210; MEUSS, op. cit. (above) 473 argues that the passive meaning of the word *tyche*: „Lage, jedoch ausgedehnt auf die ganze Dauer des Lebens des einzelnen oder der Existenz des Staates" was the point of departure.

[63] RUHL, op. cit. (fn. 55) 1333f.

may explain why fickle Tyche, the personification of blind chance, gained so important a position in men's minds[64].

A good idea of Hellenistic *tyche* may be obtained from the New Comedy. *Tyche* is master of everything, Menandr. fragm. 116; Philem. M IV 39; *tyche* turns everything upside down, Philem. M IV 39; *tyche* may make a rich man a beggar in one day, Philem. M IV 31; *tyche* is incalculable, Menandr. 295; hard to understand, 424; blind and wretched, 463; for one good thing *tyche* gives us three evils, Diphilus M IV 424; *tyche* delights in vicissitudes of all kind and lets a just man fall into misfortune, Menandr. 630; Reason (νοῦς) means nothing because everything is in *tyche's* power, whether it be πνεῦμα θεῖον or νοῦς; human foresight is like smoke and idle talk, Menandr. 417.

Even in the New Comedy, man's free will, however, still had some importance. Thus in one fragment Menander argues that misfortune is due to *tyche*, an intentional wrong to free choice, 359; misfortune is caused in one instance by *tyche*, in another by character, 623; why to blame *tyche* for folly, which is man's own doing? 468. The philosophers were later to develop this idea of the superiority of human mind over Fortune[65], which came to have great importance especially in Roman literature.

It is a measure of the popularity of *tyche* in the Hellenistic period that even Polybius, for all his avowed purpose to write pragmatic history, was unable to resist her[66]. Polybius frequently criticizes people who resort to that entity. In particular he dislikes attempts to ascribe to *tyche* the triumphs of his heroes, such as the Roman people, 1,63,9; 18,28,4—5 or the Scipios, 10,2,5 and 13; 10,5,8 and 9,2; 31, 30,2—3 or the Achaean league, 2,38,4–5.

Polybius, however, recognizes that everything is not reducible to rational causes. In a theoretical discussion, 36,17,1—2 he argues that "in the case of things of which it is difficult or impossible for mortal men to grasp the causes, one may justifiably refer them, in one's difficulty, ἐπὶ τὸν θεὸν . . . καὶ τὴν τύχην". As examples of events of this type he lists continuous and heavy rain and snow, drought and plague. It is probable that Polybius here follows Panaetius[67].

But despite this repudiation of *tyche*, in not a few passages Polybius himself makes ample use of the idea, even in contexts where the events are otherwise rationally explicable. His *tyche* indeed has almost all the characteristics that the New Comedy attributed to her. *Tyche* is unpredictable and

---

[64] Cf., e.g., ALLÈGRE, op. cit. (fn. 56) 87ff.; E. ROHDE, Der griechische Roman und seine Vorläufer[4], Darmstadt 1960; 296ff.; G. MURRAY, Five stages of Greek religion[3], London 1946, 130ff.; and especially NILSSON, op. cit. (fn. 55) 201—02.

[65] cf. NILSSON, op. cit. 204.

[66] Polybius' attitude to *tyche* has been eagerly discussed. I list here only a few of the more important modern works, NILSSON, op. cit. 204—06; F. W. WALBANK, A Historical Commentary on Polybius I, Oxford 1957, 16—26; P. PÉDECH, La méthode historique de Polybe, Paris 1964, 331—54.

[67] Cf. a quite similar discussion in Cicero, off. 2,19—20, which is certainly due to Panaetius: *haec igitur ipsa fortuna ceteros casus rariores habet, primum ab inanimis procellas, tempestates, naufragia, ruinas, incendia, deinde a bestiis ictus, morsus, impetus.*

unaccountable, 2,37,6; 30,10,1; she settles the great issues against expectation, 2,70,2; she is cunning and resourceful, 38,18,8; she is jealous of human happiness, 39,8,2; she may turn great success into great misfortune; this is why at the hour of success one should remember her fickleness, 38,21,3; *tyche* may be unjust, 32,4,3; but she can also punish wrongdoers, 4,81,5; 15,20,5-8; 23,10,2. In general, events of a sensational and capricious character were ascribed to *tyche*[68]. This is perhaps no more than surrendering to current usage of language. What is mere chance or coincidence becomes the work of a fickle and malicious power[69].

The greatest inconsistency, however, is the one between his rational exposition of the causes of Rome's greatness and the passages in which the rise of Rome was ascribed to the purposeful action of *tyche*, especially 1,4: *tyche* has brought about the unification of the world under Roman rule; cf. 4,2,4 and 8,2,3. It is probable that *tyche* has here a different connotation. It does not stand for a fickle entity. On the contrary, it denotes almost the same as φύσις or even εἱμαρμένη, a natural development[70]. To use here a word which normally evoked quite different ideas was of course unfortunate, but Polybius was often inaccurate in his use of language[71].

Finally, philosophical thought demystified *tyche* and gave it a rational explanation. As early as in Thucydides, *tyche* was only a name for unexpected happenings[72]. The idea was developed by Aristotle. In his Physica, 195b, 31 ff. he argued that *tyche* was primarily coincidence, the coming together of two unrelated chains of causes.[73] Again, the Stoics defined *tyche* as αἰτία ἄδηλος ἀνθρωπίνῳ λογισμῷ, Stoic.Vet.Fragm. 2, 965—67.[74] *Tyche* thus had nothing mysterious. It was a rational cause, only undiscernible for some reason.

---

[68] WALBANK, op. cit. 18.

[69] An example may illustrate the point. King Eumenes thought his power well established after the defeat of Perseus, but then the unexpected rise of the Gauls in Asia put him in great danger, 29,22,1—4. Now Polybius, before retailing the facts, argues that this is characteristic of human life and that *tyche*, if she has favoured someone, soon so to speak repents and at once wipes off all her former favours. The rise of the Gauls precisely at this hour was a coincidence, but because Polybius was not accurate in his use of language, coincidence was replaced by the well-known figure of fickle *tyche*.

[70] Cf. W. W. FOWLER, Polybius' conception of τύχη, CR 1903, 446; NILSSON, op. cit. (fn. 55) 205.

[71] WALBANK, op. cit. 25.

[72] The decisive passage is 1,140,1: "We may suffer disaster for (though a man make a wise decision) the turn of events may prove as unwise as the plans of men. And it is for this very reason that we commonly lay upon *tyche* the blame for whatever turns out contrary to our calculations." This is what he makes Perikles declare to his countrymen. *Tyche* is here no divinity, not even a superhuman agent or cause, only a name for the incalculable, the unexpected. Cf. H.-P. STAHL, Thukydides. Die Stellung des Menschen im geschichtlichen Prozess, Zetemata 40, München 1966, 77ff.; 98ff. O. LUSCHNAT, Thukydides, RE Suppl. XII, 1970, 1254, 64ff.

[73] Cf. D. Ross, Aristotle[6], London 1964, 75ff. The same definition is found in Chalcidius, comm. 159 p. 214 *fortuna est concursus simul cadentium causarum duarum originem ex proposito trahentium, ex quo concursu provenit aliquid praeter spem cum admiratione.*

[74] Cf. M. POHLENZ, Die Stoa. Geschichte einer geistigen Bewegung[3] 1, Göttingen 1964, 102.

β) Characteristics of *fortuna/tyche*

All the characteristics of the Hellenistic *tyche* were found in the Roman authors. There is in fact little difference between *tyche* and her Roman equivalent, *fortuna/tyche*. But we should keep in mind that *fortuna* also signified 'chance' and 'good luck', the same as *felicitas*. Especially the latter meaning was foreign to Greek *tyche*. This is why one cannot simply equate Roman *fortuna* and Greek *tyche*.

The present discussion is only concerned with one variety of *fortuna*, *fortuna/tyche*, the personification of blind chance. However, it is this variety of *fortuna*, not 'chance' or 'good luck', that really represents a superhuman agent. Even then *fortuna/tyche* shows all the varieties from an anthropomorphic goddess to an indistinct 'power' beyond human control.

The basic characteristic of *fortuna/tyche* was her fickleness and unreliability. *Fortuna* can make or mar human lives without regard to merits, and no one can be certain that her favour will last, cf. Sall., Cat. 8,1 *profecto fortuna in omni re dominatur; ea res cunctas ex lubidine magis quam ex vero celebrat obscuratque*; Curt. 4,5,2 *nunquam diu eodem vestigio stare fortunam*; Sen., benef. 2,28,2 *quam raro fortuna iudicat*; Tac., hist. 4,47 *magna documenta instabilis fortunae summaque et ima miscentis*; Firm., math. 1,7,42 *vides ut semper ubique fortuna dominetur? vides ut varii sint hominum mutabilesque semper eventus?* Amm. 14,11,29 *versabilis eius* (= *fortunae*) *motus expertus est, qui ludunt mortalitatem, nunc evehentes quosdam in sidera, nunc ad Cocyti profunda mergentes.*

This basic characteristic of *fortuna/tyche* was brought out by a number of symbols and epithets. Because *fortuna/tyche* was different from the Fortuna of popular cult, the goddess of good luck, Fortuna's symbols were not quite the same in literature as they were in cult. Whereas in cult, the most typical attributes, the cornucopia, the rudder, and the globe, symbolized Fortuna as the giver of material blessing and as the arbiter of human destinies (see p. 519), in literature her symbols accentuated fickleness and unreliability. Thus the wheel was a common literary attribute of *fortuna*, a symbol of her ever-changing nature, cf. Cic., Piso 22 *ne tum quidem Fortunae rotam pertimescebat*; Amm. 26,8,13 *ignorans quod quivis beatus, versa rota Fortunae, ante vesperum potest esse miserrimus*[75].

Other symbols of Fortuna's fickleness were the ideas that she was standing upon a stone, Pacuv. 37ff. (p. 525), or upon a sphere, Ovid., Trist. 5,8,7; Pont. 4,3,31; that she was winged, i. e. could easily fly away, Hor., carm. 3,29,53—54; Curt. 7,8,25; that she was roaming in the world *passibus ambiguis*, and did not stay in any place, Ovid., Trist. 5,8,15—16; that she expressed her favour or disfavour by her countenance, Hor.,

---

[75] Cf. a detailed description, consol. ad Liv. 51ff.: *nempe per hos etiam Fortunae iniuria mores | regnat et incerta est hic quoque nixa rota | hic quoque vertitur: ne quid non improba carpat | saevit et iniustum ius sibi ubique facit*, where a good number of Fortune's attributes and symbols are recorded, among them the wheel.

epist. 1,11,20 *dum licet et voltum servat Fortuna benignum*, or by her smile, Ovid., Trist. 1,5,27 *dum iuvat et vultu ridet Fortuna sereno*, and even by her thundering voice, ibid. 29 *at simul intonuit*. All these symbols were rare or unknown in cult.

Fortuna's fickleness and unreliability were accentuated by a great number of epithets, thus *caduca*, Apul. Socr. 4, p. 126; *dubia*, Sen., Agam. 146; *fallax*, Sen., Agam. 58; *fragilis*, Anth. Lat. 629, 13; *incerta*, Plaut., Capt. 245; Pacuv. 40; Sen., contr. 1,1,10; Sen., benef. 3,11,1; *inconstans*, Plin., nat. 2,22 *volubilis . . . vaga inconstans incerta varia*; Amm. 14,11,30; *infida*, Lucan. 7, 686; Stat., silvae 5,1,144 *infida levisque*; *instabilis*, Pacuv. 40; Rhet. Her. 4,32,44; Sen., contr. 1,1,5; Tac., hist. 4,47 (see p. 546); *levis*, Cic., fam. 9,16,6 *levis et imbecilla*; Publil. L 4; Sen., Med. 219 *rapida et levis*; Petron. 123, 244; Anth. Lat. 629, 1; *lubrica*, Curt. 7,8,24; Anth. Lat. 629, 13; *mutabilis*, Amm. 14,11,30; *perfida*, Anth. Lat. 629, 13; *vaga*, Cic., Milo 69 *quam vaga volubilisque*; Plin., nat. 22; *varia*, oratio Claudii, ILS 212,1,20; *velox*, Sen., Phaedr. 1143; *versabilis*, Curt. 5,8,15; Amm., 23,5,19; *volubilis*, Cic., Milo 69; Ovid., Trist. 5,8,15; Val. Max. 7, 1 pr.; Plin., nat. 2, 22; *volucris*, Cic., Sulla 91; Petron. 120, 78.

Human beings often appeared as mere sport of fickle Fortuna. Hence the frequent expressions *ludus, ludere*, thus Ovid., Pont. 4,3,49 *ludit in humanis divina potentia* (i. e. *Fortuna*) *rebus*; Hor., carm. 2,1,3 the Roman Civil Wars are described as *ludus Fortunae*; sat. 2,8,61—63 he apostrophizes Fortuna: *ut semper gaudes inludere rebus humanis*; Seneca, epist. 74,7 advises Lucilius to picture to himself *ludos facere fortunam*.

Fickle Fortuna, the personification of blind chance, showed favour and disfavour quite indiscriminately. Hence she seemed to ignore human merits. This is indeed one of the commonest charges against Fortuna, e. g. Manil. 4,96 *nec fortuna probat causas sequiturque merentes*. This characteristic of Fortuna was symbolized by one of her most common literary symbols, by her blindness. Pacuvius 41 explains why she is called blind: *quia nil cernat quo sese adplicet*. Other references to Fortuna's blindness, Cic., Phil. 13,10; Ovid., Pont. 3,1,125—26; Plin., nat. 2, 22; Apul., met. 7, 2 *caeca et prorsus exoculata*; Amm. 31,8,8, etc.

Because Fortuna was fickle, seemed to sport with human beings, and disregarded human deserts, she appeared as a malicious power. Fortuna has in fact malice attributed to her almost as often as fickleness. Thus *saevit, saeva, saevitia*, were frequent in connection with *fortuna*, e. g. Sall., Cat. 10, 1 *saevire fortuna . . . coepit*; Hor., carm. 3,29,49 *saevo laeta negotio*; Liv. 25,38,10 *saevitia fortunae*; Tac., ann. 2, 72 *saeviens fortuna*; Apul., met. 2, 13 *scaevam an saevam verius dixerim*.

Fortuna's malice was also accentuated by the epithets. These have been listed in Thes. l. L. VI. 1, 1185, 77ff., but in a great number of them the word *fortuna* was used in a passive sense. Thus *gravis* and *mala fortuna* mainly suggested 'misfortune', and *misera fortuna*, the most frequent of the cases, did so exclusively. The words quoted below were epithets of *fortuna* obviously denoting an agent beyond human control.

Acerba, Ovid., Her. 15, 59; *adversa*, Sen., Helv. 5, 4; *aspera*, Manil. 4, 565 *invidet in facie saevitque asperrima fronti*; *atrox*, Pacuv. 40; Suet., Tib. 23 (a quotation of Augustus); Anth. Lat., 629, 2 (Asclepiadii de Fortuna); *bruta*, Pacuv. 37; *carnifex gloriae*, Plin., nat. 28,39; *crudelis*, Ciris 313; Hor., sat. 2,8,61; Sen., contr. 10,3,5; Petron., 114, 8; *dura*, Verg., Aen. 12, 677; Sil., 10, 597; *furibunda*, Consol. ad Liviam 373; *gravis*, Ovid., Her. 15, 59; Pont. 4,4,5; *immitis*, Consol. ad Liviam 375; *impotens*, Val. Max. 4,5,3; Sen., Agam. 248 *superba et impotens*; Curt. 3,11,23; *improba*, Verg., Aen. 2, 80; Consol. ad Liviam 53; Sil. 5, 93; Iuv. 6, 605; Carm. de fig. 80 *improba et amens*; *inclemens*, Amm. 20,4,13; *indigna*, Verg., Aen. 11, 108; *infesta*, Val. Max. 1, 7 ext. 6; *inimica*, Ovid., Pont. 2,9,7; Val. Max. 1, 7 ext. 6; *iniqua*, Ovid., Pont. 4,6,39; Sen., contr. 7,3,1; Sen., Polyb. 2, 2; Val. Max. 4,6,2; Sen., HF 326; CE 68, 11; CE Suppl. (ENGSTRÖM) 279; *iniusta*, Sen., Polyb. 3, 4 *tam iniusta et tam violenta*; *insana*, Pacuv. 37; *insolens*, Plin., nat. 35, 201; *invida*, Sen., HF 524; Val. Fl. 2, 473—74; Claud. 5, 194; *irata et infestans*, Sen., beat. 5, 3; *laeva*, CE 506; *licentiosa*, Apul., met. 9, 31; *mala*, Plaut., Rud. 501; Sen., contr. 7,6,15 *malam fortunam timuit* (passive meaning?); Sen., prov. 2, 8; 3, 4; Apul., met. 1, 7; *peior*, Lucan. 2, 132; *malignior* Anth. Lat. 474, 7; *minax*, Iuv. 10, 52; *nefaria*, Apul., met. 11, 15; *noxia*, Claud., rapt. Proserp. 1, 94—95; *pertinax*, Curt. 5,9,4; *pervicax*, Apul., met. 7, 25; *rapax*, Hor., carm. 1,34,15; *saeva* (in addition to the passages quoted above) Sen., Oed. 786; Ps. Sen., Oct. 931; Mart. 4,18,7; CE 980, 3; *sinistra*, Sil. 9, 9; *superba*, Hor., epist. 1,1,68; Sen. (see *impotens*); *tristis*, Ovid., Her. 3, 43; Val. Max. 4, 4 pr. *tristioris fortunae incursus* (active meaning?); Lucan. 9, 1060; *violenta*, Sen. (see *iniusta*).

Finally, though in Latin literature human spirit usually counted superior to Fortune — cf., e. g., Accius, trag. 625—26 (Loeb) *nam si a me regnum fortuna atque opes | eripere quivit, at virtutem non quiit*, and see p. 534 — there are passages in which we encounter the Hellenistic idea of *fortuna/tyche* overriding all human foresight, Plaut., Pseud. 678—79 *centum doctum hominum consilia sola haec devincit dea, | Fortuna*; Liv. 44,40,3 *fortuna, quae plus consiliis humanis pollet*; Curt. 3,8,29 *omni ratione potentior fortuna*, etc. For this idea in Greek literature, see p. 528.

2. The attitude of Roman authors to *fortuna*

The attitude to *fortuna* differs greatly from one writer to another, being dependent upon the character and outlook of a writer and even upon the literary genre. If the thought and language of a writer were precise, *fortuna* usually stood for 'chance' or 'luck', whereas in works characterized by literary elaboration and rhetorical embellishment, *fortuna/tyche* with all her symbols and attributes makes frequent appearances. Cases in point are, e. g., Ovid and Seneca the Younger. Seneca in particular can scarcely have taken Fortuna seriously. Nonetheless, his pages are full of all the paraphernalia of Fortuna. As will be shown later on, this was little more than rhetorical elaboration of some simple basic ideas.

It is also worth notice that there is very little chronological development. On the contrary, the ideas and attitudes found in the Republican period were common throughout the Empire and, apart from the specific Christian writers, even later. A very late writer like Asclepiadius, Anth. Lat. 629, describes Fortuna in almost the same terms as Pacuvius (see p. 525), notwithstanding the span of several centuries which separates these two authors. Fortuna is *potens* and *nimium levis*, she is *inconstans, fragilis, perfida, lubrica*, she destroys and afflicts the good, the just and the innocent, she raises and enriches the wicked, the undeserving, and the unworthy, she carries off the young and saves the old. As a single bright aspect, it is admitted that Fortuna does not for ever harass the people whom she has forsaken.

The Roman authors were naturally well aware of the fact that Fortuna was merely the personification of an abstraction. This is revealed by Juvenal in his famous verse, *nullum numen habes, si sit prudentia: nos te | nos facimus, Fortuna, deam caeloque locamus*, 10, 365—66, and by Pliny the Elder, 2, 22, in a passage where he illustrates the great power of Fortune, the quintessence of fickleness, over men's minds[76], concluding *adeoque obnoxiae sumus sortis ut sors ipsa pro deo sit, qua deus probatur incertus*. Though it is alalways difficult to say anything determinate about the religious ideas of the educated in antiquity, it is probable that though they may have believed in a 'power' or rather an 'agent' beyond human control as a cause of some at least of the capricious ups and downs in human life, they scarcely believed in the existence of a goddess Fortuna with all her anthropomorphic features.

The following review of the attitude of Roman writers to Fortune is not exhaustive. It would exceed the limits of the present paper to discuss separately every single author. Moreover, such a discussion would be of little profit. The ideas and attitudes found in one writer will be encountered in many others, too. Especially in the Imperial period, I have selected the authors to illustrate different attitudes to *fortuna*. Authors like Juvenal, Martial, Petronius have been omitted whereas I have given considerable attention to a second-rate historian of the type of Florus. This is because Fortune is a leitmotif in his work.

a) The Republican period

In this period, the Roman writers in general made a modest use of *fortuna*. It was especially *fortuna/tyche* that was comparatively rare.

---

[76] *Toto quippe mundo et omnibus locis omnibusque horis omnium vocibus Fortuna sola invocatur et nominatur, una accusatur rea, una agitur una cogitatur, sola laudatur, sola arguitur et cum conviciis colitur, volubilis a plerisque vero et caeca existumata, vaga, inconstans, incerta, varia indignorumque fautrix*. Though probably rhetorically exaggerated, the passage may serve as a document of the importance of the idea of *fortuna* in the early Imperial period.

α) Cicero

In his philosophical works, Cicero defined *fortuna* as 'chance', cf. p. 522. In addition to the quotation from his de div., we could adduce Nat.D. 2, 93. Refuting the Epicurean idea of the world's order as a result of a fortuitous concourse of atoms, he illustrates the point by arguing that the 'Annals' of Ennius cannot be produced by throwing copies of the letters of the alphabet together into some receptacle and then shaking them out, *quod nescio an ne in uno quidem versu possit tantum valere fortuna*. And refuting the Stoic deification of abstractions, he writes, ibid. 3,61 *quo in genere vel maxime est Fortuna numeranda, quam nemo ab inconstantia et temeritate seiunget, quae digna certe non sunt deo*.

In some of his ethical works, however, *fortuna* is more than mere chance. It appears as a power beyond human control. Thus in the 'Tusculan Disputations' he makes much of the antithesis *virtus — fortuna*, which is defined as *domina rerum . . . et externarum et ad corpus pertinentium*, 5,25. According to Cicero, she is inferior to the human spirit, i.e. to *virtutes*, 2,30; 3,36; 5,2; 5,17; to *ratio*, 2,11; to *animus*, 3,78; to *consilium*, 5,25. Here Cicero anticipates Seneca, except that his *fortuna* is still devoid of the attributes and symbols of *fortuna/tyche*, which were so conspicuous in the latter's works (see p. 543).

The idea of the superiority of the human spirit to Fortune is ultimately traceable to Hellenistic philosophy (see p. 528) and especially to the Stoics. According to a Stoic tenet, "the sage is unconquered and unsubdued and unharmed and unaffected by *tyche*", Stoic.Vet.Fragm. 1,99,22; cf. 3,13,31: "the good man has no cause to fear *tyche*". In Rome, this idea became very popular, no doubt because of the tact that it admirably accorded with the native Roman appreciation of *virtus*, and in general with the character of the Roman people.

In his 'De re publica', Cicero makes a contribution to a debate of the ultimate causes of Rome's greatness. Some passages in Polybius, 1,63,9 and 18,28,4—5 (cf. p. 529) reveal that as early as the second century B.C. there were Greeks who attributed the success of Rome to *tyche*[77]. Polybius, who argued that Rome's rise to power was due to the excellence of her citizens, of course rejected the idea. The idea, however, did not die out. More than a hundred years later another pro-Roman Greek, Dionysius of Halicarnassus, wrote that many Greeks thought the growth of the Roman empire was not due to the piety or righteousness or other virtues of the Romans, but to chance and unjust *tyche*, which gave at random the greatest goods to the underserving, and openly accused *tyche* of giving the Greek possessions to the most worthless of the barbarians, 1,4,2; cf. 2,17,3—4. This passage reveals the motives of the Greeks who cherished the idea. Jealous of the greatness of Rome and humiliated by their own inferiority they found

---

[77] Cf. H. Fuchs, Der geistige Widerstand gegen Rom in der antiken Welt, Berlin 1938.

solace in the thought that the Romans were really inferior to the Greeks in so far as they owed their empire to the favour of fickle Fortune[78].

In all likelihood Cicero had these claims in mind when he made his mouth-piece Scipio declare, rep. 2,30 *(si) progredientem rem publicam* (scil. *Romanam) atque in optimum statum naturali quodam itinere et cursu venientem videris*. A few lines later Scipio (Cicero) makes his idea clearer, *intellegesque non fortuito populum Romanum sed consilio et disciplina confirmatum esse nec tamen adversante fortuna*. Cicero argues that Rome's greatness was not due to chance *(fortuito)* but to natural development through conscious effort and strong discipline. Cicero could not totally dismiss the idea that something should be accorded to Fortune, but his Roman pride prevented him from going any further[79]. He grudgingly admits that Fortune had not been against Rome.

In Cicero's speeches and letters, there are a few references to *fortuna/tyche*, all quoted on pp. 531—2, Milo 69; Sulla 91; Piso 22; Phil. 13,10. But in the great majority of passages *fortuna* represents an indistinct 'power' or simply stands for 'luck' and 'chance'. The meaning of 'luck' is clear in cases like, *quem mihi fortuna dedit amplificatorem dignitatis meae*, fam. 2,9,3; *fortuna nos iuvet*, Att. 5,9,1; *omnia sunt in te quae aut fortuna hominibus aut natura largitur*, Verr. 4,80. For *fortuna* as a synonym of *felicitas*, see p. 522. *Fortuna* as 'chance' or more generally as 'the incalculable element' is very clear in Cicero's first letter to his brother, QFr 1,1. Cicero encourages Quintus, whose term as governer of Asia had been prolonged against his wishes: Quintus had not been given a mission *in qua fortuna dominetur, sed in qua plurimum ratio possit et diligentia*, 1,1,4. Cicero means that Quintus has no great and perilous war to wage. In that event, Cicero would have had some real cause for alarm because *fortunae potestas* over them would have been prolonged together with the *imperium*. In Quintus' present duties as the governer of a peaceful province, *fortuna* had *nulla aut perexigua pars*, everything rested on Quintus' *virtus ac moderatio animi*, 1,1,5. That *fortuna* here really means the incalculable element which in war may upset the best plans, is brought out by the passages in which Cicero enumerates the unexpected contingencies of war, *nullas . . . insidias hostium, nullam proeli dimicationem, nullam defectionem sociorum, nullam inopiam stipendi aut*

[78] The problem of the success of Rome, whether it was due more to *tyche* than to *arete*, was debated by the Greeks also during the Empire, witness an early rhetorical essay by Plutarch, 'De fortuna Romanorum'. Unfortunately only the first part, in which the claims of *tyche* are set forth, has come down to us. According to Plutarch, the rescue of the twins which made the founding of Rome possible (8), the external peace prevailing during the reign of Numa (9), the fact that Hannibal received no help from home, that Antioch kept peace while Philip was warring with the Romans, and vice versa, that the Cimbri and the Teutones did not come simultaneously and with joined forces (11), the saving of the Capitol by the cry of the geese (12), and finally the death of Alexander before the proposed expedition to Italy (13), were all due to *tyche*. It is likely that the claims of *arete* were discussed in the lost part of the work and that Plutarch finally made a synthesis of the two sets of claims, cf. K. ZIEGLER, Plutarchos, RE XXI 1, 1951, 719 ff.

[79] Cf. V. PÖSCHL, Römischer Staat und griechisches Staatsdenken bei Cicero, Berlin 1936, 80.

rei frumentariae, nullam seditionem exercitus pertimescimus, quae persaepe sapientissimis viris acciderunt, ut, quem ad modum gubernatores optimi vim tempestatis, sic illi fortunae impetum superare non possent. This has close affinity withThucydides' definition of *tyche* (see p. 529 fn. 72), and reappears, though in a more succinct form, in Caesar (see p. 537). According to this idea, war was the special province of the incalculable whereas in peace-time, difficulties and contingencies were usually such that the human spirit easily proved superior to them.

β) Sallust

For Sallust, the idea of *fortuna* is of some importance. If we exclude speeches, there are two main passages relating to the influence of *fortuna* on Roman history. In Cat. 10,1, before setting out the causes that brought about the moral decay, Sallust writes: *sed ubi labore atque iustitia res publica crevit . . . saevire fortuna ac miscere omnia coepit.* Of course this *fortuna* de-notes fickle and malicious *tyche*. It has been explained as the *deus ex machina* of moral decay and as an equivalent for the law of cause and effect[80], as an attempt to sugar the bitter idea that Rome's decay was an inevitable na-tural process[81], as a mere rhetorical cliché[82], as a reference to the disap-pearance of *virtus* and the rise of *fortuna* to the role of the main historical force after Rome's moral decay had set in[83]. In view of the fact that *fortuna* is not really listed in the causes of decay in 10,2ff., the last but one interpretation seems to be correct. Cat. 53,3 may have more weight. Sallust gives some examples of the *virtus* of the ancient Romans and adds: *ad hoc saepe fortunae violentiam toleravisse.* I think this passage should be taken together with Iug. 1,1—3, where Sallust argues that the human mind (*ani-mus*), if it is dominated by *virtus*, has no need of *fortuna*; a similar idea in epist. 1,1,1—2. This is of course a Stoic commonplace (cf. p. 528). Sallust's idea in Cat. 53,3 is that the *virtus* of the ancient Romans proved superior to *fortuna* which, so far from favouring them, often caused great setbacks. It is not impossible that Sallust here wanted to answer the Greeks who attributed Rome's rise to power to the favours of Fortune (see p. 534).

In Sallust's portrayal of Marius, there are some significant remarks on *fortuna*[84]. According to him, Marius trusts to omens, Iug. 63,1; 64,1, as well as to his luck, 93,1 *fortunam . . . qua saepe prospere usus fuerat.* And Fortune favoured him even where he had neglected the necessary prepa-rations, thus at the taking of a fortress at Muluccha, 92,6 *sed ea res forte quam consilio melius gesta*; cf. 94,7.

[80] F. Klingner, Über die Einleitung der Historien Sallusts, Hermes 63, 1928, 166. O. Seel, Sallust. Von den Briefen ad Caesarem zur Coniuratio Catilinae, Leipzig—Berlin 1930, 77.

[81] W. Schur, Sallust als Historiker, Stuttgart 1934, 76.

[82] Erkell, op. cit. (fn. 51) 153ff.

[83] G. Schweicher, Schicksal und Glück in den Werken Sallusts und Cäsars, Diss. Köln 1963, 50ff.; K. Vretska, De Catilinae Coniuratione 1, Heidelberg 1976, 203f.

[84] C. D. Gilbert, Marius and Fortuna, Cl. Quart. 23, 1973, 104—07.

γ) Caesar

Caesar's attitude to *fortuna* has been the subject of a lively discussion[85]. This is in part due to the importance Caesar himself attaches to Fortune in his writings, and perhaps even more to later writers, who believed that Caesar enjoyed the special protection of Fortune or that he had his own *fortuna* as a guardian spirit. Thus Velleius, e.g., writes, *sua et celeritate et fortuna C. Caesar usus*, 2,51,2; *sequens fortunam suam Caesar pervectus in Africam est . . . ibi primo varia fortuna, mox pugnavit sua*, 2,55,1, etc. However, the word seems here to suggest 'good luck' rather than something like a *genius*; notice that it is not used as a subject. Again, in winter 48, Caesar tried to cross in a small boat from Dyrrhachium to Brundisium to fetch reinforcements. According to a story first told by Plutarch, Caes. 38,3 he encouraged the helmsman who was frightened by the violence of the storm with the words: "do not be afraid for you are carrying Caesar and Caesar's Fortune, τὴν Καίσαρος τύχην"; cf. App. civ. 2,57: almost identical[86]. The story is, however, of dubious authenticity. Suetonius, Iul. 58,2, Florus, 2,13,37, and Dio 41,46,3 in relating the incident, do not make any reference to *fortuna*. Florus, especially, is revealing, *exstat ad trepidum tanto discrimine gubernatorem vox ipsius: quid times? Caesarem vehis*. When Florus otherwise attaches considerable significance to the idea of *fortuna*, it is queer that he should have omitted to quote it here had he only found anything of the kind in his sources[87]. The majority of modern scholars have in fact rejected Caesar's saying as a legend. They hold that Caesar was a rationalist and that his writings do not reveal any belief in good luck or personal *fortuna* peculiarly his own[88].

---

[85] W. W. FOWLER, Caesar's Conception of Fortuna, Class. Rev. 17, 1903, 153—56; E. TAPPAN, Julius Caesar and Fortuna, TAPhA 58, 1927, 27, and ID., Julius Caesar's Luck, ibid. 61, 1930, 22; H. ERKELL, Caesar und sein Glück, Eranos 42, 1944, 57—69; W. H. FRIEDRICH, Cäsar und sein Glück, in: Thesaurismata. Festschr. I. Kapp, München 1954, 1—24; C. BRUTSCHER, Cäsar und sein Glück, Mus. Helv. 15, 1958, 75—83; M. GELZER, Caesar, der Politiker und Staatsman[6], Wiesbaden 1960, 176—78; G. SCHWEICHER, Schicksal und Glück in den Werken Sallusts und Cäsars, Diss. Köln 1963; F. BÖMER, Caesar und sein Glück, Gymn. 73, 1966, 63—85.

[86] But when the attempt failed, Appian represents Caesar τῷ δαιμονίῳ χαλεψάμενος ὡς φθονερῷ.

[87] Cf., however, Lucan, who, in his version of the incident, makes much of Caesar's personal relations to Fortuna, 5,580 *sola tibi causa est haec iusta timoris | vectorem non nosse tuum, quem numina numquam | destituunt, de quo male tunc Fortuna meretur, | cum post vota venit. medias perrumpe procellas, | tutela secure mea*. Here Caesar is undoubtedly represented as having a firm belief in the special protection of Fortuna. But Lucan was no historian. As will be shown later on, *Fatum* and *Fortuna* were the leitmotifs of his 'Pharsalia' (p. 549). It is not impossible that the anecdote of Caesar's words to the helmsman originated in Lucan's poem.

[88] A few older scholars still thought that Caesar believed in his own luck, thus TH. MOMMSEN, Römische Geschichte 3,6 Berlin 1875, 463 and T. RICE HOLMES, Caesar's Conquest of Gaul[2], London, 1931, 41. TAEGER, op. cit. (fn. 50) 24 and 76—78 as well as BÖMER, Der Eid beim Genius des Kaisers, Athenaeum 44, 1966, 87 and especially op. cit. (fn. 85) have recently resuscitated the idea. Holding the anecdote to be authentic, they argue that the idea

This is borne out by a review of the passages in which Caesar avails himself of the idea of Fortune. In his writings, *fortuna* mostly denotes the incalculable element in war which may upset a general's plans, e. g. BGall. 6,30,2 *multum cum in omnibus rebus tum in re militari potest fortuna. nam magno accidit casu ut . . .*, where the juxtaposition of *fortuna* and *casus* reveals that *fortuna* cannot have been conceived of as a superhuman agent. There are similar expressions in BGall. 6,35,2 *hic quantum in bello fortuna possit et quantas adferat casus cognosci possit*; BCiv. 3,10,6 *quantum in bello fortuna posset, iam ipsi incommodis suis satis essent documento*; cf. 3,68,1. It is probable that Caesar resorted to the notion partly in order to explain away misfortunes. Thus in BGall. 6,30,2ff. the escape of Ambiorix, BCiv. 3,68,1ff. a defeat at Dyrrhachium were imputed to *fortuna*. In BGall. 6,35,2 and 42,1 *fortuna* is, by inference, made to bear some of the blame for a near disaster which might otherwise attach to Quintus Cicero. On the other hand, Caesar trusts that the *virtus* of his troops will prove superior to *fortuna*, cf. BCiv. 3,73,4 *si non omnia caderent secunda, fortunam esse industria sublevandam*; BGall. 5,34,2 *nostri, tametsi ab duce et a fortuna deserebantur, tamen omnem spem salutis in virtute ponebant.*

There are no traces of *fortuna/tyche* in Caesar, not to speak of personal *fortuna*. Caesar's attitude to *fortuna* was typical of his person and profession. As a general, he had to give particular attention to the incalculable element in war. On the other hand, living in a sceptical and rationalistic age, he could not take seriously the popular ideas of the goddess Fortuna or Tyche.

b) The Augustan age

In the Augustan literature, the significance attached to *fortuna* is clearly growing, and *fortuna/tyche* is found more often than in the preceding period, especially in Horace and in Ovid's poems of exile. Nevertheless, *fortuna* was not as important an idea as it often was in the Imperial age. The absence of *fortuna* from the elegiac verse — even from Ovid's amorous poetry — is worth notice.

α) Livy

Livy attaches considerable importance to *fortuna*[89]. The very word is found ca. 500 times in his whole work. In many cases, however, *fortuna* was used in a passive sense. If conceived of as a cause of events, three different approaches can be distinguished.

Fortuna populi Romani, the guardian spirit of the nation, is found in a number of passages. In most cases, she is seen to operate in war. The Volsci

---

in question was *felicitas*, not *fortuna*. According to Bömer, Caesar himself did not probably believe in his *felicitas*, but he wanted people to think he enjoyed perpetual good luck. Because Caesar makes few references to *felicitas* in his writings (Bömer cites only BGall. 1,40,12 and BCiv. 3,26,5), even this is unlikely.

[89] Cf. J. Kajanto, God and Fate in Livy, Turku 1957, 63—100.

and Aequi had joined forces and invaded Roman territory, but fell out over the question who should appoint the commander-in-chief, and the disagreement led to a fight. Livy comments, 2,40,13 *ibi fortuna populi Romani duos hostium exercitus haud minus pernicioso quam pertinaci certamine confecit*. But this entity is often supplemented with *virtus*, the excellence of the citizens. A military tribune devises a stratagem of saving the Roman army which had been cut off in a valley. He promises to occupy a hill above the enemy, while the consul withdraws the main body of his army, 7,34,1—5. Of the rescue of his own men he says, 34,6 *nos deinde aut fortuna populi Romani aut nostra virtus expediet*. References to the Fortune of the Roman people were, however, largely found in the first decade. This suggests that Livy thought an entity of this type more appropriate to the legendary past than to later times.

In a way similar to other Roman writers, Livy's *fortuna* could represent 'luck' or 'chance' and 'the incalculable'. The former use is rare, 6,12,11 *nec dux legiones nec fortuna fefellit ducem*; 3,8,11 *tertia illa pugna eo anno fuit. eadem fortuna victoriam dedit*. But this meaning is important in cases where it is thought subject to, or supplemented by, *virtus*, e. g. 4,37,6 *ergo fortuna, ut saepe alias, virtutem est secuta*; or his comment on the unexpected surrender of the city of the Falisci, 5,26,10, due to *fortuna* and *cognitae rebus bellicis virtutis specimen*. The meaning of 'chance' is mostly confined to set phrases, *fortunam temptare*, e.g. 26,12,14 or *fortunae se* or *aliquid committere*, e.g. 9,12,11. Even the common phrase *fortuna pugnae* or *belli* suggests the incalculable element in war, e.g. 10, 43,7; 23,16,7; cf. 10,28,1 where *Mars belli* and *fortuna* are juxtaposed.

Fickle and malicious *fortuna/tyche* is not frequent in Livy. When it is found in broader contexts, it is seldom shown to be an agent working for the benefit of Rome. In most cases it is an evil power to which Roman defeats may be attributed, e.g. 23,24,6: the Cannensian defeat had been a severe blow, but it was not the only one that year, *nova clades nuntiata aliam super aliam cumulante in eum annum fortuna*; cf. similar references 23,22,1 and 25,38,10. It is natural that Livy cannot accept the claims of the jealous Greeks that the Roman Empire was built on Fortune's favour, for this is wounding to Roman pride (cf. p. 534). He is even more unaccommodating than Cicero, who admits that *fortuna* was at any rate not against Rome (ibid.). In considering *fortuna* a cause of Roman defeats Livy is readier to accept Sallust's viewpoint (p. 536). And at any rate, *virtus Romana* is superior to this malicious power, as a Roman knight, L. Marius, assures to his troops, 25,38,10 *cuius populi vis atque virtus non obruta sit Cannensi clade, ex omni profecto saevitia fortunae emersurum esse*.

β) Virgil

For Virgil *fortuna* is of a subordinate interest. The very word is lacking in the 'Bucolica'. In the 'Georgica' it is found twice, but only in a passive sense, 3,452 *praesens fortuna laborum*, and 4,209 *stat fortuna domus*, 'state', 'condition'.

Fortuna is not very conspicuous in the 'Aeneid', either. This was in part due to the fact that the 'Aeneid' was an epic poem. Since Homer did not know *tyche*, his Roman successor could not give undue attention to that entity. In the epic poetry, Fate was represented by *moira, Parca, fatum*. Again, Virgil was writing from a Stoic point of view. For the Stoic, the course of events was due to *fatum* or *heimarmene, ordo seriesque causarum* or, in a little more religious view, Providence[90]. Both the Homeric tradition and his Stoic conviction led Virgil, in his 'Aeneid', to consider *fatum* as the prime mover of events, 1,2 *Italiam fato profugus . . . venit*[91]. But Virgil could not entirely avoid the well-known figure of *fortuna*. In many cases, she seems to have been used as a simple synonym of *fatum*, thus 8,334—35 *Fortuna omnipotens et ineluctabile fatum / his posuere locis*. Servius, ad loc, certainly argues that Virgil was here following the Stoics, *qui nasci et mori fatis dant, media omnia fortunae*. According to this argument, only the great outlines of life had been preordained by Fate, everything else was the province of Fortune. But apart from the fact that this scarcely accords with the Stoic idea of Fate, a review of the passages in which the word *fortuna* occurs in the 'Aeneid' shows that Virgil used it in many different senses. In cases like the one quoted above, it cannot have a meaning different from *fatum*; cf. 12,147—50, where *fortuna, Parcae* and *fata* are found side by side without any difference in meaning. Again, the meaning of 'good luck' is evident in some cases, e.g. 2,385 *aspirat primo fortuna labori*; 4,109 *si modo quod memoras factum fortuna sequatur*. Finally, *fortuna* is sometimes an equivalent of *tyche*, especially 11,426/27 *multos alterna revisens / lusit et in solido rursus Fortuna locavit*; cf. 5,22.

Virgil, the poet, cannot be expected to hold a consistent view of an elusive idea like *fortuna*. Nevertheless, he is consistent so far as he gives that entity little consideration, and the Hellenistic variety of her even less.

γ) Horace

For Horace, *fortuna* is clearly the same as unpredictable and spiteful *tyche. Saevo laeta negotio*, she sports with human destinies, *ludum insolentem ludere pertinax*, carm. 3,29,49—50. However, one can always face the reversals due to her by resorting to *virtus*, ibid. 53—55 *laudo manentem: si celeres quatit / pinnas resigno quae dedit et mea / virtute me involvo . . .*; cf. other similar passages, sat. 2,2,126—27; epist. 1,1,68—69. Horace sometimes quotes *fortuna* in discussing historical events. In carm. 2,1,3, the Civil

---

[90] cf. Cic., de div. 1,125; M. POHLENZ, op. cit. (fn. 74) 101—106; J. M. RIST, Stoic Philosophy, Cambridge 1969, 112—32.

[91] For Virgil's idea of Fate, cf. R. HEINZE, Virgils epische Technik[4], 1957, 291—304, especially 293,3; K. BÜCHNER, RE VIIIA2, 1958, 1460—61: *fatum* is not immovable, only a possibility; G. CARLSSON, The Hero and Fate in Virgil's Aeneid, Eranos 43, 1945, 111ff.; W. PÖTSCHER, Das römische Fatum — Begriff und Verwendung, ANRW II 16, 1, ed. by W. HAASE, Berlin—New York 1978, 409—414.

Wars are imputed to *ludus fortunae*. In carm. 4,14,37—40, on the other hand, the military triumphs of Augustus and his lieutenants are ascribed to Fortuna, who *lustro prospera tertio | belli secundos reddidit exitus*. This may suggest the personal Fortuna of the emperor; the cult of Fortuna Redux and Fortuna Augusta was rapidly expanding in precisely this period (p. 517). The supposition that Horace may have been thinking of the personal Fortuna of the emperor is sustained by the fact that a few lines earlier, 33—34, he refers to Fortuna by *te* (scil. *Augustus*) *consilium et tuos | praebente divos* (scil. to Tiberius, who was waging the war for Augustus).

The most important poem where *fortuna* is found in Horace is his famous hymn on the Fortuna of Antium, carm. 1,35, a prayer for the welfare of Augustus, who was about to invade Britain, as well as of the Roman armies sent to the East[92]. But his Fortuna is not the old Roman goddess of good luck, for she is characterized thus: *praesens vel imo tollere de gradu | mortale corpus vel superbos | vertere funeribus triumphos*, which clearly suggests Hellenistic tyche. As has been pointed out[93], the verses brought to mind Servius Tullius, who, though only a maidservant's son, became a king, and L. Aemilius Paullus, whose triumph was followed by the funeral of his two sons. People of every social positions and every nationality stood in awe of Fortuna's power, 5—12, and especially her capacity to turn success into misfortune, 13—14.

δ) Elegiac poets

In Tibullus, the word *fortuna* is not found at all. *Fortuna* is rare also in Propertius. The only passage where *fortuna/tyche* seems to figure, is 1,6,25 *me ... quem semper voluit fortuna iacere*, where the malice of that power is accentuated.

For Ovid, *fortuna* is a more important subject[94]. Yet there are great differences between one work and another. The word is very rare in his amorous verses — not found at all in 'Ars amandi', only four cases in 'Amores', five in 'Heroides' — and not much more frequent in the mythological poems, the 'Metamorphoses' and the 'Fasti'. It was not until the poems of exile, 'Tristia' and 'Ex Ponto', that *fortuna* was made much of. This is comprehensible. *Fortuna* is a fickle and malevolent power that topples one from the pinnacle of glory and happiness to the depths of despair. This is precisely what had happened to Ovid, an exile in an outpost of the Empire. Hence the frequent charges against Fortuna, e.g. Pont. 2,7,15 *sic ego Fortunae telis confixus iniquis*; Trist. 1,5,27—29, quoted on p. 531. In another passage, he illustrates the idea by an original but not quite felicitous simile, Trist. 1,9,13—14 *mobile sic sequitur Fortunae lumina vulgus | quae simul inducta*

---

[92] Cf. T. OKSALA, Religion und Mythologie bei Horaz, Helsinki 1973, 26—30; W. JAEGER, Horaz c. 1,34, Hermes 48, 1913, 442—49; H. JACOBSON, Horace and Augustus. An interpretation of Carm. 1.35, Cl. Ph. 63, 1968, 106—13; E. DOBLHOFER, Horaz und Augustus, ANRW II 31, 3, ed. by W. HAASE, Berlin—New York 1981, 1959—1961.

[93] OKSALA, op. cit. 26.

[94] Cf. I. KAJANTO, Ovid's Conception of Fate, Turku 1961, 24—35.

nocte teguntur, abit: how could lights (*lumina*) be extinguished by approaching night?

But even in exile, Ovid could not entirely yield to Fortune. The very Roman idea of the superiority of the human spirit to Fortune was cherished by him, too. Thus he praises the noble conduct and the moral courage of the few who, unlike the populace, did not follow fickle Fortune and fail him in his hour of disaster. Such a friend was Celsus: *adfuit ille mihi, cum me pars magna reliquit | . . . fortunae nec fuit ipse comes*, Pont. 1,9,15—16. Again, he assures his wife that his *ingenium*, his talent for poetry, will survive the blows of Fortune, Trist. 5,14, 3—4 *detrahat auctori multum fortuna licebit, | tu tamen ingenio clara ferere meo.*

c) The Imperial period

It was in the literature of the Imperial period that *fortuna*, and especially *fortuna/tyche*, really became a weighty entity. In many authors she was even a leitmotif, thus in Florus, Curtius Rufus and Apuleius, even in Seneca.

The authors are not discussed in a strictly chronological order. After Seneca, I have grouped the historians, last of them Curtius, whose dating is uncertain. Chronologically Lucan naturally belongs to the same period as Seneca, but as a writer of fiction, I have debated him together with Apuleius. Ammianus, the sole representative of the Later Empire, will come last.

α) Seneca the Younger

In Seneca, references to *fortuna* are perhaps more numerous and worked out in more detail than in any major Roman writer[95]. This may seem unexpected. According to the Stoic doctrine adopted by Seneca in all its rigidity[96], everything that happens, down to the smallest details, has been predetermined by *fatum* or *series causarum*; cf. prov. 5,7 and especially nat. 2,35—38. It is problematic how immovable and inexorable Fate may be reconciled with a fickle power which is its very opposite[97].

It is, however, futile to expect excessive consistency in a writer like Seneca, who was not so much an original thinker as a disseminator of Stoic doctrines. A writer of this type has to make concessions to popular taste and even to popular ideas. Moreover, Seneca was a rhetorical author

---

[95] Cf., e.g., Helv. 5,3 *omnes conatus fortunae, omnes impetus prospicere*; ibid. 2,4 *ne saevitiam suam fortuna leviorem diducendo faceret*; Marc. 16,7 *at hoc iniquior fortuna fuit, quod non tantum eripuit filios, sed elegit*; prov. 4,12 *verberat nos et lacerat fortuna? patiamur*, etc. The personification is clear-cut in these and similar cases.

[96] H. O. SCHRÖDER, Fatum (heimarmene), RLAC 7, 1969, 542.

[97] G. PFLIGERSDORFFER, Fatum und Fortuna. Ein Versuch zu einem Thema frühkaiserzeitlicher Weltanschauung, Lit. wiss. Jb. NF 2, 1961, 1—30, discusses Seneca but does scant justice to the actual use of the idea of Fortune. Cf. W. PÖTSCHER, op. cit. (fn. 91) 417—419.

anxious to adorn his style with all kind of devices. *Fortuna*, with all her well-known symbols and characteristics, was a figure that could be turned to use to give the exposition of philosophical doctrines vividness and descriptive power.

The discrepancy between *fatum* and *fortuna* in Seneca may consequently be more apparent than real. In one passage, Seneca certainly seems to represent the usual view of a difference in principle between these two ideas, epist. 16,4—5 *nam et mutari certa* (i.e. *fatum, deus*) *non possunt et nihil praeparari potest adversus incerta* (i.e. *casus, fortuna*; both words used here indiscriminately). If we take this at its face value, it hardly accords with the Stoic doctrine of *heimarmene*. However, another Stoic tenet makes it possible to argue that *incerta* are *incerta* only in appearance. Even *incerta, fortuita, casus, fortuna* have been preordained by *fatum* or *series causarum*: only their causes are indiscernible to the human mind (cf. p. 529).

In another passage Seneca clearly equates *fortuna* with *fatum*, Marc. 10,5—6 *in hanc legem* (scil. that Marcia's son should die) *erat datus, hoc illud fatum ab utero statim prosequebatur. in regnum fortunae et quidem durum atque invictum pervenimus.* This is revealing. According to Seneca's Stoic convictions, everything has been predetermined, everything is *fatum*. But to give a vivid expression to all the perils and hazards to which Fate submits us, he resorts to the familiar language of *fortune/tyche*[98].

Seneca of course was not the only one who made a similar use of the idea of Fortune. The ancient Stoics, who defined *tyche* as 'indiscernible cause', also asserted that "the sage is unhurt by tyche" (p. 534). But Seneca surpasses his Stoic predecessors by uninhibitedly exploiting all the popular ideas of *fortuna/tyche*, that is her malice[99], her jealousy[100], the ambiguity of her gifts[101] etc. But it is unavoidable that in so doing, he should have detracted something of the solidity of his philosophical doctrines.

The Stoics attached particular importance to the fact that human spirit is unconquerable by Fortune. This is a central theme in Seneca. In one passage after another, he champions the superiority of Spirit over Fortune, *valentior enim omni fortuna animus est*, epist. 98,2[102]. Man has to match his strength with *fortuna*, prov. 4,12, and by so doing to show his true quality, ibid. 4,2; epist. 13,1. Sometimes, however, Seneca counsels committing oneself as little as possible to Fortune, tranq. 13,2; brev. 11,2, and advises not to despise Fortune's gifts, but to use them with moderation, vit.beat. 23,2—3.

---

[98] There are a few other similar cases of a clear identification of *fortuna* with *fatum*, e.g. Polyb. 3,4—4,1; cf. even prov. 5,4 *non trahuntur a fortuna, sequuntur illam*, where *fatum* could have been substituted for *fortuna* without any change of meaning.

[99] Cf. the passage quoted in fn. 95.

[100] Marc. 5,6 *nulla re maior invidia fortunae fit quam aequo animo.*

[101] Polyb. 9,4 *non levitas fortunae cito munera sua transferentis inquietabit*, etc.

[102] Cf. vit. beat. 4,2 *summum bonum est animus fortuita despiciens virtute laetus*; 20,3 *ego fortunam nec venientem sentiam nec recedentem*; 25,5 *totum fortunae regnum despiciam.*

Similar ideas of *fortuna* were found in Seneca's tragedies. The ideas were naturally suited to situations and characters. Thus in 'Agamemnon', the sudden reversals of Fortune, the downfall from the heights of power and glory, are an important theme, cf. 57—60; 71—72; 87—90; 100—02, etc., whereas the defiant Medea protests the superiority of the human spirit, 159; 176; 242—43; 520.

β) Tacitus

Tacitus discusses the problem of 'chance' and 'the incalculable' both in the 'Histories' and in the 'Annals'[103]. At the beginning of the former work, 1,4, he writes that he will describe the situation in Rome, in the army, in the provinces, in the whole world, *ut non modo casus eventusque rerum, qui plerumque fortuiti sunt, sed ratio etiam causaeque noscantur*. The passage has been interpreted to imply that though history admits of a causal explanation, the course of events is not predictable in all its details[104]. It is natural that this should contradict any belief in *fatum/heimarmene*, whether 'scientific', e.g. *series causarum*, or astrological. In the famous excursus, ann. 6,22, he wonders whether *fatone res mortalium et necessitate immutabili an forte volvantur*. He did not use the word *fortuna* in order presumably to avoid the undesirable popular ideas which this word inevitably suggested. Clearly *fors* is to be taken in a strictly philosophical sense. Tacitus' own convictions are not easy to ascertain. In this excursus, he is largely recording ideas and beliefs current in his time[105]. He pronounces with caution even on astrology[106], which had provoked the whole digression.

In his writing, Tacitus in fact gives *fors* and *fortuita* considerable attention. These words do not imply any superhuman 'power', only an incalculable factor or an unpredictable event[107]. Two passages are of especial interest. The common soldiers, in a critical situation, believed the low level

---

[103] Tacitus attitude to *fortuna* has been discussed, e. g., by R. von Pöhlmann, Die Weltanschauung des Tacitus, Bayr. SB, Phil. Hist. Kl., 1, 1910; H. Wurms, Das Schicksal Roms und die Götter bei Tacitus, Hum. Gymn. 47, 1936, 10—17; J. Kroymann, Fatum, Fors, Fortuna und Verwandtes im Geschichtsdenken des Tacitus in: Satura. Festschrift O. Weinreich, Baden-Baden 1952, 71—102; J. Lacroix, Fatum et Fortuna dans l'oeuvre de Tacite, REL 29, 1952, 247—64; P. Beguin, Le positivisme de Tacite dans sa notion de 'fors', Ant.Class. 24, 1955, 352—71.

[104] H. Fuhrmann, Das Vierkaiserjahr bei Tacitus, Phil. 104, 1960, 254 and 254,1.

[105] Cf. quite similar discussions in Lucan, 2,7—15 and in Curtius, 5,11,0: *fors* and *series causarum* are represented as alternative 'ultimate causes'. In none of these writers do the digressions contain any original ideas. The problem was probably debated even in rhetorical schools. cf. Quint. 3,5,12: *sitne virtus finis? regaturne providentia mundus?* listed as problems suitable for an orator.

[106] E. Koestermann, Annalen I, Heidelberg 1963, 34 and II, 1965, ad loc.

[107] Cf., e.g., hist. 1,31 *ut turbidis rebus evenit, forte magis et nullo adhuc consilio rapit signa*; other passages, 2,42; 4,29; 4,49 *causa* opposed to *fors*; ann. 1,28; 4,27 a rising of the slaves balked by *fors*; 15,38 the burning of Rome due to *fors* or *dolus principis*; hist. 4,23 *fortuita belli*; ann. 14,3 *nihil tam capax fortuitorum quam mare*, etc.

of water in the Rhine a prodigy; Tacitus comments, *quod in pace fors seu natura, tum fatum et ira dei vocabatur*, hist. 4,26. This may imply criticism of common people's belief in Fate and the Gods[108]. There is a quite similar, ironical comment upon the credulity of the populace in hist. 1,86, except that instead of *fors*, we have here the expression *fortuitae causae*.

What Tacitus otherwise writes about *fortuna* is not very momentous. In a number of passages, the word stood for 'chance' or 'the incalculable'. A general, counselling caution to his troops, argues, *initia bellorum civilium fortunae permittenda: victoriam consiliis et ratione perfici*, hist. 3,60. Clearly *fortuna* here suggests 'the incalculable'. Ann. 1,11 Tacitus reports Tiberius complaining that an emperor's duties were subject to *fortuna*, all kind of hazards.

There are a few significant passages in which *fortuna* is seen shaping the course of events. In particular he seems to ascribe the triumph of the Flavians at least in part to the workings of *fortuna*. In beginning his description of the rise of Vespasian, hist. 2,1, he writes, *struebat iam fortuna in diversa parte terrarum initia causasque imperio*; cf. 3,82 *pro Flavianis fortuna et parta totiens victoria*, which are given as reasons for a victory at the Campus Martius; 3,59: the passage over the Appennine would have been perilous *ni Vitellium retro fortuna vertisset, quae Flavianis ducibus non minus saepe quam ratio adfuit*. But in other passages, Vespasian's rise to power is attributed to *fatum*, thus Agr. 13,5; hist. 2,82; hist. 4,81 Vespasian is credited with *caelestis favor* and *quaedam inclinatio numinum*. Clearly *fortuna* in the passages quoted is more or less a synonym to *fatum*: Vespasian's triumph had been preordained. Nothing here suggests fickle and malicious *fortuna/tyche*.

Tacitus once quotes Vespasian's personal *fortuna*, hist. 4,81 *Vespasianus cuncta fortunae suae patere ratus*. This is given as Vespasian's own conviction, which may indeed be true. There are similar reported references to personal *fortuna*, e.g. ann. 14,6: after being rescued from death at sea, Agrippina informs Nero that she had been saved *benignitate deum et fortuna eius* (scil. Nero's). This shows that Fortuna Augusta, the guardian spirit of the emperor, extended her protection over the whole Imperial family. But Tacitus once makes a direct reference to the Fortune of the Roman people, hist. 3,46 *adfuit, ut saepe alias, fortuna populi Romani*. The *ut*-clause is significant. It calls to mind the age-old belief that the interests of Rome were looked after by her Fortune. Nevertheless, it is questionable whether *fortuna* here really represents the Fortuna of the popular cult. More probably it only suggests 'the good luck of the Roman people'.

Fortuna seems to signify 'good luck' even in the famous passage, Germ. 33,2 where the discord of the Germans is seen as the only hope left by

---

[108] For Tacitus' adverse judgement on the intellectual capacities of the common people, see I. KAJANTO, Tacitus on the Slaves, Arctos 6, 1970, 56—57 and Id., Tacitus' Attitude to War and the Soldier, Latomus 29, 1970, 709—10.

Fortune to the Romans *urgentibus imperii fatis*. The meaning of the latter phrase has been much discussed but need not detain us here[109].

Fickle and spiteful *fortuna/tyche* was not conspicuous in Tacitus. He seems to have avoided quoting this entity too frequently. There are certainly references to the irony of Fortune in secretly reserving despised Claudius for the throne, ann. 3,18; he opens the chapters on Sejanus' rise to power in a Sallustian phrase by *cum repente turbare fortuna coepit*, ann. 4,1; cf. Sall. Cat. 10,1 (p. 536). Even here, *fortuna* is cited more as a literary device to arouse the expectations of the reader than as a real historical cause. Fortune's fickleness is recorded hist. 4,47 (cf. p. 531) and the ambiguity of her favours is made a point of, ann. 16,1 *inlusit dehinc Neroni fortuna*, which serves as the motto of the story of a ludicrous treasure-hunt. But in comparison with, e.g., Seneca, Tacitus is very modest in his use of the idea of *fortuna/tyche*. This, as well as his obvious preference for the unambiguous terms *fors* and *fortuita*, suggests that he aimed at clarity both in thought and language.

γ) Florus

In Florus' synopsis of the Roman history, there are two leitmotifs. One is the biological conception of a people's history as analogous to an individual's life, with infancy, youth, manhood, and old age, Prooem. 4—8. Another is the rivalry of *virtus* and *fortuna* in building up the Empire[110].

This motif is struck quite at the beginning, *ut ad constituendum eius imperium contendisse virtus et fortuna videantur*, Prooem. 2. This is a contribution to the age-old debate about the ultimate causes of Rome's success. It will be remembered that Greek jealousy imputed Rome's triumph primarily to blind Tyche (p. 534).

Florus, as a Roman, naturally did not share the extreme anti-Roman point of view of the Greeks[111]. But he did not simply ascribe Rome's prosperity to *virtus*. His attitude to the problem is more complex than that of Cicero and Livy (p. 534 and 539). According to him, *virtus* had helped the sturdy and honest Romans in the old days when Rome was slowly emerging as the leading power of the Mediterranean world. The *virtus*, primarily the martial valour, of the Roman people and of the Roman leaders was put to the test in the Gallic invasions[112] as well as during the Punic wars[113]. She stood her test admirably. Fortune was no match for *virtus* in these early days. The courage of Regulus in defying death by torture even

---

[109] Cf. J. G. C. ANDERSON, Tacitus' Germania, Oxford 1970 (= 1938) 163: equal to *urgentibus imperium fatis*; cf. a similar phrase, Liv. 5,36,6, *ibi iam urgentibus Romanam urbem fatis*.

[110] Cf. A. NORDH, Virtus and Fortuna in Florus, Eranos 49, 1951, 111—128.

[111] But all Greek historians were not anti-Roman so far as to ascribe her triumphs to Tyche, cf. Polybius, Dionysius, Plutarch, p. 534—5.

[112] 1,13,2 *quod tempus populo Romano nescio utrum clade funestius fuerit, an virtutis experimentis speciosius*; cf. ibid. 8 and 19.

[113] 2,6,26 and 28, but *virtus* is here supplemented by *consilium*.

makes Florus declare that his *virtus* triumphed over Fortune, 2,2,25; cf.
2,2,22.

After this, *virtus Romana* began to decline, being increasingly replaced
by *fortuna*. After the defeat of Carthage, the Eastern peoples fell into Rome's
power *quodam quasi aestu et torrente fortunae*, 2,7,1; *fortuna* was devising
quodam casu, quasi de industria, that the Empire should expand from Africa
to Europe, and from Europe to Asia, 2,8,1. Here Florus seems to represent
a view similar to Polybius' (see p. 529). *Fortuna* was acting purposefully
to make Rome the ruler of the world. *Fortuna* is not here the equivalent
of fickle *tyche*. It may suggest 'the natural order of things' or *fatum/heimar-
mene*. But notice that Florus, by using the words *quodam, quasi*, marks *fortuna*
more or less as a metaphor. Moreover, in the latter quotation, *fortuna* is
supplemented by, or juxtaposed with, natural causes; the Roman might
expanded *ultro se suggerentibus causis*.

In the subsequent period, *fortuna* furthered the careers of Pompey,
3,5,21; of Caesar, 3,10,1; of Marius, 3,21,8. Florus quotes *fortuna* most
often in the chapter on the Civil war of Caesar and Pompey 4,2. Here *fortuna*
may even suggest malicious *fortuna/tyche*. Thus quite at the beginning,
*itaque invidens fortuna principi gentium populo, ipsum illum in exitium sui
armavit*, 4,2,1. But in the Anacephalaeosis, 3,12, Florus ascribes the Civil
wars to Rome's moral decay due to excessive riches brought to Rome from
the East[114]. Consequently, it is questionable whether *fortuna* represented
any primary cause for Florus. At any rate, there are no less than seven other
passages in this chapter in which *fortuna* appears as an agent shaping the
course of events; 4,2,30 she causes temporary setbacks to Caesar; 35 and
44 she is seen to be behind the battle at Pharsalus; 55 Fortune exacts
vengeance on Ptolemaeus for the murder of Pompey; 78 at Munda, in Hispania, Caesar did not rout the Pompeians *cetera felicitate*; the battle was
long prolonged, *ut plane videretur nescio quid deliberare fortuna*; finally,
87, Fortune hid Sextus Pompeius in Celtiberia for wars after Caesar's
death[115].

In these passages, *fortuna* is acting at one time on purpose, at another
she appears as a fickle and even spiteful power. It is thus unlikely that Florus had any clear-cut idea of *fortuna*. She was not a mere rhetorical cliché,
but neither was she conceived of as an ultimate cause behind the course
of events.

There are still two significant references to *fortuna* in Florus. In 4,3,7,
in the year 44 B.C., the committing by Fortune of the Roman empire to

---

[114] This is no original idea. It is found in Sallust, Cat. 6—13, and in Livy, praef. 8ff. and was
ultimately due to Polybius and especially Posidonius, cf. I. KAJANTO, Notes on Livy's
Conception of History, Arctos 2, 1958, 55—63.

[115] 4,2,61 is the only reference to *fortuna* in this chapter not relating to the Civil Wars, *plane
quasi de industria captante fortuna hunc Mithridatico regno exitum, ut a Pompeio pater,
a Caesare filius vinceretur*.

Caesares[116] was attended by another Civil war. And 4,7,10, Florus has reason to pass a sad comment upon the superiority of Fortune over *virtus*. The defeat of Cassius and Brutus at Philippi was due to an error: *sed quanto efficacior est fortuna quam virtus*. The contrast to older times, exemplified in the bravery of Regulus, is indeed striking.

δ) Curtius Rufus

In Curtius' history of Alexander the Great, *fortuna* is an important idea. This is only to be expected. A number of Greek historians, especially the Peripatetics, had ascribed Alexander's success to Fortune's favour[117]. Curtius had adopted this view from his Greek predecessors. This may explain why references to *fortuna* are more numerous and more detailed in his work than in Roman historians in general.

There are two ideas of *fortuna* running through Curtius' book. In the majority of passages, *fortuna* is the usual *fortuna/tyche*, a fickle goddess, whose favour is perilous either because no one can be sure that it will last or because it spoils one's character and thus leads him to ruin. The latter is an aspect to which Curtius gives particular attention. Dareus had been vitiated by Fortune, 3,2,17; cf. 18. And very soon, Fortune deserted Dareus and let him suffer all kinds of humiliations[118].

In Curtius' presentation, Dareus quotes the fickleness of Fortune when trying to persuade Alexander to conclude an alliance with him, *nunquam diu eodem vestigio stare fortunam*, 4,5,2, and in addressing his troops, 4,14,19: Alexander had only had good luck, but Fortune's favour was never stable; his rashness would sooner or later ruin him.

Dareus' prophecy did not come true, at least not immediately. According to Curtius, Fortune saw to it that Alexander's rashness always turned to glory, thus 3,6,18; 9,5,3. *Fortuna* helped him to defeat a nomadic tribe, 5,6,19; *fortuna indulgendo ei numquam fatigata* had the Bactrian prince Spitamenes murdered by his wife, 8,3,1; Fortune's favour turned even the drunken revelries of the Macedonians to glory, 8,10,18; 9,10,28, and made bad weather serve Alexander's cause, 8,13,22.

The perils of Fortune's favour are not entirely disregarded even in regard to Alexander. In a few passages, Curtius suggests that *fortuna* was ruining Alexander's character as she had ruined Dareus'. At the beginning of his career, Alexander was not yet corrupted by Fortune, 3,12,20; Alexander is himself represented as apprehensive of the fickleness of *fortuna*,

---

[116] The text is uncertain, the manuscripts, giving both *Caesarem* and *Caesares*. But the context seems to require the plural. It is not Caesar but the Imperial power that is meant here.

[117] cf. W. W. TARN, Alexander the Great II, Cambridge 1950, 95; the peripatetic view especially in Diodorus, 17; cf. also Plutarch's essay 'De Alexandri Magni fortuna aut virtute libri duo'.

[118] *Inpotens fortuna* had the *tabernaculum* prepared to Dareus' fall into the hands of Alexander, 3,11,23; Dareus was chained with golden fetters, *nova ludibria subinde excogitante fortuna*, 5,12,20.

3,8,20. But 4,7,29, Alexander's assumption of divine honours, and 8,4,24, his lack of self-control are put down as consequences of Fortune's favour.

There is another, slightly different idea of *fortuna*: Alexander is thought to enjoy the protection of his personal *fortuna*. However, in the majority of cases, references to this *fortuna* are found in speeches[119], thus 3,5,12 *Dareus cum tam superbas litteras scriberet, fortunam meam in consilio habuit*?[120] There are only three direct references to Alexander's *fortuna*: Alexander's army could have been routed while fording the Tigris, *sed perpetua fortuna regis avertit inde hostem*, 4,9,22; Alexander owed the victory at Gaugamela *maiore ex parte virtuti quam fortunae suae*, 4,16,27. In both passages, however, *fortuna* may have the usual meaning of 'good luck', the synonym of *felicitas*. In 8,6,14, the failure of a conspiracy to kill Alexander is ascribed, inter alia, to *fortuna ipsius*.

It is thus questionable whether Curtius himself thought the personal *fortuna* of Alexander an important idea. In his work, *fortuna* represented the Hellenistic *fortuna/tyche*, only favouring longer than usual one single person. Curtius' final judgement on the share of *fortuna* in Alexander's career is given in 10,5,35, *fatendum est tamen, cum plurimum virtuti debuerit, plus debuisse fortunae, quam solus omnium mortalium in potestate habuit*. In ascribing Alexander's triumphs more to Fortune than to *virtus*, Curtius comes close to the Peripatetic view of Alexander.

ε) Lucan

In a few passages, Lucan discusses the ultimate causes shaping the course of events. At the very beginning, 1,67—72, he ascribes the Civil War of Caesar and Pompey to the Stoic *heimarmene*, the *invida fatorum series*, intertwined with the idea of *nemesis* provoked by the excessive greatness of Rome. But in another passage, 2,7—15, he seems to hesitate between two antagonistic explanations, the Stoic *heimarmene* or *fatorum immotus limes* and *fors incerta*. But this is hardly more than an exercise in rhetoric; for this commonplace of Imperial literature, see p. 544.

---

[119] TARN, op. et loc. cit. (fn. 117) thought the personal *fortuna* was Curtius' main idea; this is certainly erroneous.

[120] Cf. similar passages, 4,11,15 *nihil quidem habeo venale, sed fortunam meam utique non vendo*; 4,13,9 *malo me meae fortunae paeniteat quam victoriae pudeat*; 4,16,5 *nimirum nobis quoque regis nostri fortuna vicit*; 7,7,27—28 his personal diviner foresees trouble, *vereor ne praesenti fortunae tuae sufficere non possis*, but is reassured by Alexander, *rex iussit eum confidere felicitati suae*; 7,8,24 the envoys of the Scythians try to dissuade Alexander from attacking their country, *proinde fortunam tuam pressis manibus tene: lubrica est, nec invita teneri potest ... 25 nostri sine pedibus dicunt esse Fortunam, quae manus et pinnas tantum habet; cum manus porrigit, pinnas quoque conprehende*; to this 9, 1, *rex fortuna sua et consiliis eorum se usurum esse respondet*; 7,11,27 *fortunae suae confisus*; 9,3,14 *nisi mavis errare, pervenimus, quo tua fortuna ducit* (scil., to the borders of India); after his death, 10,6,1 *militum turba cupientium scire, in quem Alexandri fortuna esset transitura* (unless 'royal position', cf. 20).

Lucan certainly gives preference for *fatum/heimarmene*. It is in line with his attachment to the Stoic doctrine that he quotes *fatum* extremely often, even more often than *fortuna*, though the reverse is more usual in Roman writers. But *fortuna* is also very common; ca. 130 examples in the whole poem.

Fortuna does not, however, often represent *fortuna/tyche*. She certainly appears as a fickle and malicious power, e.g. 2,132: the ups and downs in the career of Marius were due to her; 2,567: *Fortuna* is blind and impudent; 3,448: she often guards the guilty; 7,487: *incerta Fortuna* makes whom she will guilty; 7,686: *infida Fortuna* has deserted Pompey but not crushed his spirit; 8,21: *Fortuna* demands penalty from Pompey for her long favour. But in view of the great number of references to *fortuna*, this does not amount to much.

The personal *fortuna* is found in a number of passages. Especially Lucan seems to have credited Caesar with a *fortuna* of his own. The famous passage relating to Caesar's venture to sea in a small boat, 5,580ff., has already been discussed (p. 537). Other references to his *fortuna* are 5,301—03 *fata sed in praeceps solitus demittere Caesar | fortunamque suam per summa pericula gaudens | exercere*; 7,547 *constitit hic bellum fortunaque Caesaris haesit*; 9,244—45 *fortuna cuncta tenetur | Caesaris*. But in these passages *fortuna* may simply denote 'good luck', *felicitas*, not an entity similar to *genius*. It may even suggest Destiny; notice that *fata* and *fortuna* are juxtaposed in the first example. Another similar case is 1,226—27, where he represents Caesar as saying: *te, Fortuna, sequor . . . credidimus fatis*. There is accordingly a clear contrast between Pompey, first favoured and then deserted by fickle Fortune, and Caesar, the protégé of Fate and Fortune who aim at making him the master of the world[121]. The third protagonist of the poem, Cato, is depicted as the embodiment of Stoicism. As a true Stoic, he defies *fortuna* by resorting to *virtus*[122].

In the great majority of passages, Lucan seems to have used the terms *fatum* and *fortuna* indiscriminately[123]. For him, *fatum* was, however, the dominant idea. This is why *fortuna* often gets its colour from *fatum*, thus 7,151—52, where *fortuna* clearly does duty for *fatum*: she reveals the future by a variety of signs. In many cases, *fatum* and *fortuna* are juxtaposed and interchangeable, e.g. 7,504—05 *nec fortuna diu rerum tot pondera vertens | abstulit ingentis fato torrente ruinas*; 10,484—85 *nusquam totis incursat viribus agmen. | fata vetant, murique vicem fortuna tuetur*. In these and similar cases, the reference to *fortuna* was largely due to a desire for poetic varia-

---

[121] Cf. 3,392—94 *quantum est quod fata tenentur | quodque virum toti properans imponere mundo | hos perdit fortuna dies.*

[122] 2,242—44 Brutus is made to say to Cato: *omnibus expulsae terris olimque fugatae | virtutis iam sola fides, quam turbine nullo | excutiet fortuna tibi*; 9,881—83 *cogit tantos tolerare labores | summa ducis virtus, qui nuda fusus harena | excubat atque omni fortunam provocat hora.*

[123] Cf. W. H. FRIEDRICH, Cato, Caesar und Fortuna bei Lucan, Hermes 73, 1938, 405—11. For a slightly different view, see F. M. AHL, The Shadow of a Divine Presence in the Pharsalia, Hermes 102, 1974, 566—90.

tion. There was, however, this difference between *fatum* and *fortuna* that the latter could be easily personified, the former only occasionally, and even then in the highly poetic form of the Parcae.

ζ) Apuleius

In Apuleius' 'Metamorphoses' or the 'Golden Ass', we encounter some new ideas of *fortuna*. Firstly, Apuleius wrote in a style characterized by a superabundance of expression, by a preference for attributives, metaphors, etc. Hence an accumulation of the symbols of *fortuna*, which may at times lead to a certain clumsiness; cf. 1,16 *telum mortiferum Fortuna . . . subministraret*; 4,12 *saevum Fortunae nutum*; 7,16 *novis Fortuna saeva tradidit cruciatibus*; 7,20 *in rebus saevis adfulsit Fortunae nutus hilarior*, etc. In all these and similar cases, Fortuna is clearly a personification, a goddess.

It is, however, of still greater importance that Fortune is for Apuleius something more than a stylistic figure or a rhetorical cliché. The story of Lucius, turned by magic into an ass, in which shape he undergoes a variety of adventures and vicissitudes, and is finally restored to human form by the grace of Isis, is in a way built around Fortune. In Lucius' words, cruel Fortuna, set on persecuting him, had caused his turning into an ass. After reproving, in the age-old fashion, Fortune for her blindness, he says: *ego denique, quem saevissimus eius impetus in bestiam et extremae sortis quadripedem deduxerat*, 7,3. This cannot be dismissed as an occasional outburst of bitterness. In the subsequent story, Lucius' persecution by malicious Fortune is a recurrent theme, 7,16 and 7,17: cruel Fortuna, his insatiable tormenter, works him new pains; 7,20: her occasional favour only portends future troubles; 7,25: she does not allow a respite from trials; 8,24: Lucius is unable to flee her or to placate her by his sufferings; 9,1: he could not avoid Fortuna's machinations by wise counsel.

Finally, in accordance with a prophecy of Isis, 11,4—6, Lucius is delivered from the clutches of cruel Fortune and restored to human shape, 11,12, *deae maximae* (scil. *Isis*) *providentia alluctantem mihi saevissime Fortunam superarem*. The responsibility of Fortune for Lucius' adventures is made clear by the priest of Isis, 11,15: blind Fortune may have tormented Lucius in a variety of ways, but this deity has no power over those who have dedicated themselves to the service of Isis, *in tutelam iam receptus es Fortunae, sed videntis*. Unlike Fortune, Isis is not blind; she guards the people who faithfully serve her.

Isis is a goddess who can liberate from the power of inexorable Fate and fickle Fortune. In her prophecy to Lucius, she argues that she is able to prolong Lucius' life *ultra statuta fato tuo* ("by your Fate") *spatia*, 11,6. After being initiated into the mysteries of Isis, Lucius addresses an oration to Isis, and praises her great power over all the forces of Fate, *salutarem porrigas dexteram, qua fatorum etiam inextricabiliter contorta retractas licia, et Fortunae tempestates mitigas, et stellarum noxios meatus cohibes*, 11,25. All the great powers of Fate are here represented as inferior to Isis, *fatum | heimarmene*, Fortuna, and astrology.

Though Fortune is claimed to have been identified with Isis in the visual arts (p. 520), it is unlikely that this had anything to do with the theme of Apuleius' novel[124]. Fortuna and Isis are clearly quite different deities. Moreover, though Isis was identified with a great number of other divinities, Fortuna is not even mentioned in the list of the various identities of Isis in 11,4.

η) Ammianus Marcellinus

Ammianus' idea of *fortuna* is in a way similar to that of Apuleius. In his work, too, *fortuna* is richly furnished with attributes, e.g. 14,1,1 *Fortunae saevientis procellae tempestates alias rebus infudere communibus per multa illa dira facinora Caesaris Galli*, where the accumulation of epithets and metaphors makes the expression unduly ponderous. At any rate, in no other great Roman historian is *fortuna* more unequivocally a personification, Hellenistic *fortuna | tyche*. Her two basic characteristics, fickleness and malice, are accentuated. With her capricious ups and downs, as *mutabilis* and *inconstans*, she sports with humanity, 14,11,29—33: including a catalogue of illustrious examples; she is *versabilis*, 23,5,19; Fortune is *moderatrix humanorum casuum*, 15,5,1; she is *luctuosa et gravis*, 26,9,9; she is *inclemens et caeca*, 31,8,8; her decree is blind, 25,5,8.

Ammianus also makes ample use of metaphors and of the attributes of Fortuna in cult. A common metaphor in his work is the breeze, *incertus flatus*, 23,5,8; *aura salutis* breathed by Fortune, 19,6,1; *reflante Fortuna*, 31,13,19. There are references to the wheel of Fortuna, which causes the rotation of success and misfortune, 26,8,13 and 31,1,1. He even quotes Fortune's cornucopia, a rare feature in literature, 22,9,1 *velut mundanam cornucopiam Fortuna gestans propitia*, where the symbol is, however, qualified by *velut*. Similar qualifications are found in other cases, too[125].

The personal *fortuna* is frequent in Ammianus, especially the persnoal *fortuna* of the emperor. The relevant passages have been discussed on p. 524.

Ammianus' attitude to *fortuna* has been analyzed by ENSSLIN[126] and NAUDÉ[127]. According to the former, Fortune was no longer an evil power because she was in the service of Adrastia/Nemesis[128]. *Fortuna* was almost synonymous with *fatum*. The latter, however, claims that Ammianus' attitude to Fortune was much more traditional in that Ammianus, like his

---

[124] ROSCHER I.2, p. 1533, Apuleius' novel is quoted as evidence for the identification, but the quotation from 11,15 is incomplete and thus misleading.

[125] 19,6,1 *adspiravit auram quandam salutis Fortuna*; 25,5,8 *caeco quodam iudicio Fortunae*.

[126] Zur Geschichtsschreibung und Weltanschauung des Ammianus Marcellinus, Klio, Beiheft 16, Leipzig 1923, 69—77.

[127] Op. cit. (fn. 53) 85—88.

[128] Ammianus discussed at length this deity of just retribution in 14,11,25—26.

Roman predecessors, opposed *virtus Romana* to hostile *fortuna*, claiming the superiority of the former.

The epithets and attributes which Ammianus gives to *fortuna* make it unlikely that he really thought *fortuna* synonymous with *fatum*. For him, *fortuna* is primarily a malicious power. Though he does not quote Fortuna very often — *fortuna* is found as an agent in ca. 45 passages — he nevertheless attributes some great Roman setbacks to her. Thus he opens his description of the catastrophe of Hadrianopolis by referring to *Fortunae volucris rota, adversa prosperis semper alternans*, 31,1,1. After narrating the defeat, he compares it to the Roman rout at Cannae, and concludes, *Romani aliquotiens reflante Fortuna fallaciis lusi, bellorum iniquitati cesserunt ad tempus* 31,13,19. By this he obviously wanted to suggest that Roman defeats were at least in part due to the hostility of Fortune. This is a palliative well-known to us from Sallust and Livy (p. 539). The expression *ad tempus*, on the other hand, was meant to imply that the defeats were temporary, in time set right by the *virtus Romana*.

In 14,6,3—6 Ammianus expounds a philosophy of history borrowed from Florus (p. 546), with the ages of Rome corresponding to the ages of an individual, and with Virtus and Fortuna rivalling on building up the Empire. But otherwise *virtus* and *fortuna* are not often referred to by him, at least not in any significant passages[129].

To conclude, Fortune was not a very important idea for Ammianus. Though he describes this entity often in considerable detail, this was due more to the floridity of his style than to a conviction of the significance of *fortuna* as an ultimate cause of events.

d) Christian authors

Though Christianity as a doctrine was incompatible with the pagan ideas of Fortune, this entity did not quite disappear. The Christians were the inheritors of pagan literary traditions. However zealously they may have combated pagan mythology and derided the pagan gods, all this was so firmly embedded in ancient literature that even the Christians, inadvertently or not, paid tribute to it. This explains why Fortune, with all her age-old characteristics, survived in Christian authors, especially in the works that were not specifically Christian. On the other hand, in dismantling the pagan world of the gods, the Fathers assailed the cult of Fortuna as well. Hence a double attitude to Fortuna, on one hand as an inherited literary figure, on another as a pagan deity to be dealt with harshly and decisively.

α) Fortuna as a pagan inheritance

Fortuna is not all that rare in Christian poets. Thus Ausonius, in addressing a very old person, exploited the classical ideas of the goddess,

---

[129] 16,5,1 he quotes a saying of Democritus, *ambitiosam mensam fortuna, parcam virtus apponit*; 27,2,4, because of a success of Iovinus over the Alamanni, *hoc prospero rerum effectu, quem virtus peregerat et fortuna*, a stock expression in Roman historiography (cf. p. 539).

Par. 4,23—24 *tu novies denos vitam cum duxeris annos,* | *expertus Fortis tela cavenda deae.* The substitution of Fors for Fortuna was due to the requirements of the metre. There are also other references to *fortuna* in Ausonius[130]. A century later, we find Sidonius[131] and Dracontius[132] quoting the *fortuna* of the rulers.

It is especially in Boethius, in the very last century of the ancient Rome, that we once again encounter the old idea of a fickle, incalculable and malicious *fortuna*. In his 'Consolatio', he has particular reason to deplore the instability of Fortune. This book was written in the prison where he, a favourite of the king Theodoric, was awaiting execution because of false charges of treason. According to Boethius, fickleness is the essence of Fortuna, her *ludus*; she is turning *rotam volubili orbe*, changing *infima summis, summa infimis*, 2,2; she is constant only in her fickleness, a *caecum numen* with *ambiguos voltus*, 2,1; she is *superba, saeva, fallax, dura*, 2, carm. 1. The entire chapter two is devoted to a discussion of the fickleness and unreliability of Fortune. But Fortuna with all her symbols and attributes is here nothing but a poetic expression for the insecurity of human life and for the unreliability of worldly prosperity[133]. This is obvious from the fact that elsewhere in the book he repudiates the idea of chance as a principle underlying the universe[134], and expresses his belief in the divine world-order, 4,6. He explains chance in the Aristotelian sense as the coming together of two unrelated chains of causes[135]. But, as a Christian, he goes beyond Aristotle. According to him, the coming together, the coincidence, was due to divine Providence[136]. Here his point of view is similar to that of Augustine (see below).

Similar references to pagan ideas are rare in the Fathers. There is, however, a passage in the letters of Augustine, ep. 3,5, where he seems to ascribe the acquisition of friends to *fortunae potestas* and argues that the *verissimi sapientes* have advised us neither to fear nor to desire *Fortunae bona*. But such occasional concessions to inherited literary conventions are not of any particular importance in Augustine.

---

[130] Par. 22,13 *Fortunae . . . vertigo rotabat*; Mos. 411—12 *festinet solvere tandem | errorem Fortuna suum libataque supplens | praemia*, etc.

[131] Paneg. on Anthemius, 96 *purpureos Fortuna viros cum murice semper | prosequitur*, i. e., power is the natural destiny of people of Imperial or consular family; a similar reference to Fortuna, 213.

[132] Satisf. 215 *quod pereunt hostes, regis fortuna vocatur | quod pereunt populi, temporis ordo regit*, naturally quoted in an ironical sense.

[133] cf. 2,4 *si iam caduca et momentaria fortunae dona non essent, quid in eis est, quod aut vestrum umquam fieri queat aut non perspectum consideratumque vilescat?*

[134] 1,6 '*huncine . . . mundum temerariis agi fortuitisque casibus putas?*' . . . '*Atqui . . . nullo existimaverim modo, ut fortuita temeritate tam certa moveantur*'.

[135] 5,1 *nam proprias causas habet, quarum inprovisus inopinatusque concursus casum videtur operatus.*

[136] Ibid., *concurrere vero atque confluere causas facit ordo ille inevitabili conexione procedens, qui de providentiae fonte descendens cuncta suis locis temporibusque disponit.*

β) Christian attitude to *fortuna*

Lactantius and Augustine have dealt with the problem of *fortuna* at some length, but it has also been briefly treated by Tertullian, St. Jerome, and Paulinus of Nola. It was common to most Christian writers to point out the inconsistencies inherent in the very idea of a goddess of blind luck, to show that she was nothing but a personification of fickle chance, and to make the ancient philosophical definitions of *fortuna* as chance the starting-point of the Christian reshaping of the idea.

Tertullian, anim. 20,5 distinguishes between the pagan and Christian ideas of the powers presiding over humanity, *Deus dominus* and *diabolus aemulus* according to the Christians, *providentia et fatum et necessitas et fortuna et arbitrii libertas* according to the pagans. Here, any more than in resurr. 57,5 *ubi* (scil., in the heaven) *necessitas aut quod dicitur fortuna vel fatum?* no distinction is made between *fatum* and *fortuna*. Even otherwise, Tertullian's attitude to these pagan ideas is uncompromising. He does not seem to accord *fortuna* even that modest place in the Christian world of ideas later on allowed it by Lactantius and Augustine.

Lactantius debates *fortuna* in inst. 3,28,6—3,29. He claims that *fortuna* is nothing but an unexpected event and that those who express belief in her power, e.g. Sallust and Virgil, follow the mistaken ideas of the populace and the uneducated who make Fortuna a real goddess, distributor of good and evil to humanity, 3,29,7—8. An analysis of the pagan cult of Fortuna reveals several inconsistencies. If Fortuna is all-powerful, why is she not worshipped to the exclusion of other divinities? If she is a real goddess, why does she cause misfortune to people who devoutly worship her? 3,29,9—12; the same idea in 5,10,13.

Lactantius' solution of the problem of *fortuna* is peculiarly Christian. Taking up the idea brought forward by him at the outset of the discussion that events, the causes of which were unperceivable to them, were ascribed by the pagans to *fortuna*[137], he concludes that what the pagans called *fortuna* was in reality the unrelenting enemy of mankind, the Devil[138].

Augustine discusses *fortuna* in several connections. In a way similar to Lactantius, he points out the absurdities of the pagan concept of *fortuna*, civ. 4,18. Felicitas and Fortuna are alleged to differ in that the latter can also be evil. But as all the deities should be good, why is Fortuna sometimes good, sometimes evil? If she, as a goddess, is always good, she is the same as Felicitas. Why, then, have they different names? Felicitas and Fortuna are also argued to differ in that *felicitas* is due to good men because of their previous merits, whereas the latter has no regard for merits. But this argument leads to difficulties. How can Fortuna be good if she completely disregards human deserts? Why is she worshipped at all if she usually passes

---

[137] 3,28,6 *non dissimili errore credunt esse Fortunam quasi deam quandam res humanas variis casibus inludentem quia nesciunt unde sibi bona et mala eveniant*; a similar idea in 5,10,12.

[138] 3,29,17 *huius itaque perversae potestatis cum vim sentirent virtuti repugnantem, nomen ignorarent, fortunae sibi nomen inane finxerunt.*

by her worshippers? On the other hand, if her worshippers really obtain something from the goddess, she cannot be a goddess of blind chance.

One could argue that Augustine and other Christian authors did not fully grasp the nature of the ancient Roman goddess of Fortuna. As pointed out in the present work, Roman Fortuna was primarily a goddess of good luck. In literature, fortuna chiefly represented *fortuna/tyche*, the personification of blind chance. The Christian authors seem to have paid undue attention to the literary idea of fortuna, a thing understandable enough in these late centuries when true Roman religion had long since fallen into decay.

In a lighter vein, and ironically, Augustine argues in civ. 7,3 that the *di selecti* of the pagans having been selected quite arbitrarily, Fortuna, who grants favours quite arbitrarily, should occupy a place of honour among them, because their selection had apparently taken place by the random operation of her power.

A somewhat different line of criticism is represented by the passages in which Augustine reprehends the practice of some people to ascribe one's transgressions to *fatum*, *fortuna* or the Devil, contin. 14. In quoting *fortuna*, they claim that everything is ruled by blind chance. Augustine meets this argument by proving that those who attribute everything to chance, come to this conclusion not by chance but by the use of reason[139].

Augustine could not, however, entirely dispense with *fortuna*. In his definition of the concept, his point of departure is the ancient philosophical idea of *fortuna*. In retract. 1,2 he tells us that he now repents of having so often quoted *fortuna* in his 'Contra Academicos', a book of his pre-Christian period, inasmuch as people had the bad habit of conceiving of *fortuna* as a real goddess. He had, however, meant by *fortuna* nothing but *fortuitus rerum eventus*, an unexpected event. But from a Christian point of view, he cannot rest content with this. Even in his 'Contra Academicos', he had conceded that what is called chance (*fortuna*), may in reality be due to some hidden order of things, only its causes were unperceivable. To make the idea Christian, he had only to substitute Providence for the *occultus ordo*. This he does in the passage of retract. quoted: *quod tamen totum ad divinam revocandum est providentiam*[140].

The Christian reshaping of the idea of *fortuna* becomes still clearer in civ. 5,9. Augustine does not deny the existence of *causae fortuitae*, but argues that they were in reality hidden causes, *causae latentes*, attributable to the will of the true God or of some spirits. In civ. 4,19 he seems to represent a point of view resembling that of Lactantius, who equated the pagan *fortuna* with the secret workings of the Devil. In relating the ancient legend of the mysterious voice in the temple of Fortuna Muliebris (see p.

---

[139] Cf. lib. arbitr. 3,18 for a similar discussion.

[140] A similar definition, quaest. hept. 1,19, *cum haec ipsa tamen, quae fortuita videntur, causis occultis divinitus dentur*; cf. C. N. COCHRANE, Christianity and Classical Culture, New York 1957, 478—80.

511), Augustine suggests that Fortuna was here an instrument of malignant demons to discourage people from right living; they inspired in them the belief that it sufficed if *fortuna*, who grants favours irrespective of merit, was propitious to them. But this is naturally not quite the same as Lactantius' straightforward identification.

The other specifically Christian writers add little to the above.

Prudentius, the leading Christian poet, dealt with Fortuna in his polemic against paganism, 'Contra Symmachum'. According to him, Fortuna is a savage tyrant. Belief in her excludes belief in God because all is due to chance and is for ever turning round and round without any presiding power[141]. Prudentius does not seem to visualize *fortuna* as a real goddess here, only as 'chance'. He does not even call *fortuna* by name in this passage.

In the voluminous output of St. Jerome, there are only a few references to *fortuna*. Occasionally he argues that the idea of the world being ruled by chance was a grave error, in eccl. 9, *omnia fortuito fieri, et variam in rebus humanis fortunam ludere*. Characteristically, the passage betrays his classical learning. His real purpose was the repudiation of the principle of chance, *fortuito*, but in the age-old fashion he illustrated the idea by quoting its personification, *varia* and sporting *fortuna*[142].

Paulinus, the bishop of Nola, discusses *fortuna* in ep. 16,4. If God has created the universe and is ruling it, where is the province of *casus*, *fatum* and *fortuna*? In repudiating these pagan ideas, he makes use of the same arguments as Lactantius and Augustine. The personifications of abstractions, Spes, Nemesis, Amor, Furor, Occasio, *Fortuna lubrico male fixa globo*, were mere words, *cassa nomina*, which the pagans had erroneously considered as divine beings and furnished with corporeal shapes.

Bibliography

ANWANDER, A., Schicksal-Wörter in Antike und Christentum, Zeit. Rel. Geist. Gesch. 1, 1958, 315—27.

ARGENIO, R., La vita e la morte nei drammi di Seneca, Riv. St. Cl. 17, 1969, 339—48.

BEAUJEU, J., La religion de Juvenal, in: Mélanges Carcopino, Paris 1966, 77—81.

BEGUIN, P., Le positivisme de Tacite dans sa notion de 'fors', Ant. Class. 24, 1955, 352—71.

BÖMER, F., Caesar und sein Glück, Gymnasium 73, 1966, 63—85.

ID., Untersuchungen über die Religion der Sklaven in Griechenland und Rom I, Abhandlungen der geistes- und sozialwiss. Kl. der Akad. d. Wiss. und der Lit. Mainz 1957, 7, Wiesbaden 1957, 140—53.

BRUTSCHER, C., Cäsar und sein Glück, Mus. Helv. 15, 1958, 75—83.

---

[141] 2,875ff. *operitur nescia caeli | mens hominum saevo vivens captiva tyranno. | haec putat esse Deum nullum, namque omnia verti | casibus, et nullo sub praeside saecla rotari.* Here, too, fickleness is the basic characteristic of *fortuna*.

[142] There is a similar passage in Is. 18,45: all who forsake the Church *parant fortunae mensam* (i. e., worship her) because they do not believe that anything pertains to God *sed vel stellarum cursu* (i. e., astrological *fatum*) *vel varietate fortunae omnia gubernari*.

COCHRANE, C. N., Christianity and Classical Culture. A Study of Thought and Action from Augustus to Augustin, Oxford 1940, repr. New York 1957, 478—80.

ERKELL, H., Augustus, felicitas, fortuna, Göteborg 1952 (Diss.) 129 ff.
ID., Caesar und sein Glück, Eranos 42, 1944, 57—69.

FASOLO, F.—GULLINI, G., Il Santuario della Fortuna Primigenia a Palestrina, Roma 1953.
FOWLER, W. W., Caesar's Conception of Fortuna, Class. Rev. 17, 1903, 153—56.
ID., Fortune (Roman), Encyclopaedia of Religion and Ethics 6, Edinburgh 1913, 98—104.
FRIEDRICH, W. H., Cäsar und sein Glück, in: Thesaurismata. Festschrift I. Kapp, München 1954, 1—24 (repr. in: IDEM, Dauer im Wechsel, Göttingen 1977, 376—388).
ID., Cato, Cäsar und Fortuna bei Lucan, Hermes 73, 1938, 391—423 (repr. in: IDEM, Dauer im Wechsel, Göttingen 1977, 303—335).

GILBERT C. D., Marius and Fortuna, Cl. Quart. 23, 1973, 104—07.
GULLINI, G., Il santuario della Fortuna Primigenia a Palestrina, ANRW I. 4, 1973, 746—99.

HERZOG—HAUSER, G., Tyche und Fortuna, Wiener Studien 63, 1948, 156—63.

JEFFERIS, J. D., The Concept of Fortuna in Cornelius Nepos, Class. Phil. 38, 1943, 48—50.

KAJANTO, I., s. v. Fortuna, RLAC 8, Stuttgart 1972, 182—97.
ID., God and Fate in Livy, Annales Univ. Turkuensis Ser. B, 64, Turku 1957.
ID., Ovid's Conception of Fate, Annales Univ. Turkuensis Ser. B, 80, Turku 1961.
KROYMAN, J., Fatum, Fors, Fortuna und Verwandtes im Geschichtsdenken des Tacitus, in: Satura. Festschrift O. Weinreich, Baden-Baden 1952, 71—102.

LACROIX, J., Fatum et Fortuna dans l'œuvre de Tacite, REL 30, 1952, 248—64.
LATTIMORE, R., Themes in Greek and Latin Epitaphs, Urbana 1942, 154—56, 316—17.
LYNGBY, H., Fortunas och Mater Matutas kulter på Forum Boarium i Rom, Eranos 36, 1938, 42—72.

NAUDÉ, C. P. T., Fortuna in Ammianus Marcellinus, Acta Classica, Proc. of the Class. Ass. of South Africa, 7, 1964, 70—88.
NORDH, A., Virtus and Fortuna in Florus, Eranos 50, 1952, 111—28.

OTTO, W., s. v. Fortuna, RE VII 1, 1910, 12—42.

PASSERINI, A., Il concetto antico di Fortuna, Philol. 90, 1935, 90—97.
PATCH, H. R., The Tradition of the goddess Fortuna in Roman literature and in the transitional period, Smith College Studies in Modern Languages 3, 1922, 132—77.
PETER—DREXLER, s. v. Fortuna, in: W. H. ROSCHER, Ausführliches Lexikon der griechischen und römischen Mythologie I. 2, Leipzig 1886—90, 1503—58.
PFLIGERSDORFFER, G., Fatum und Fortuna. Ein Versuch zu einem Thema frühkaiserzeitlicher Weltanschauung, Lit.wiss. Jb. NF 2, 1961, 1—30.

SCHWEICHER, G., Schicksal und Glück in den Werken Sallusts und Cäsars, Diss. Köln 1963.

TAPPAN, E., Julius Caesar and Fortuna, Tr. Proc. Am. Philol. Ass., 58, 1927, xxvii.
ID., Julius Caesar's Luck, ibidem 61, 1930, xxii.

WISSOWA, G., Religion und Kultus der Römer², Handb. der Altertumswissenschaft IV 5, München 1912, repr. ibid. 1972, 256—68.
WURMS, H., Das Schicksal Roms und die Götter bei Tacitus, Hum. Gymnas. 47, 1936, 10—17.

Aufstieg und Niedergang der römischen Welt (ANRW)

Geschichte und Kultur Roms im Spiegel der neueren Forschung

Herausgegeben von Hildegard Temporini und Wolfgang Haase

3 Teile in mehreren Einzelbänden und Gesamtregister. Groß-Oktav. Ganzleinen

RUBRIK »RELIGION«

Herausgegeben von Wolfgang Haase

In allen drei Teilen von ANRW soll eine Übersicht über den gegenwärtigen Stand der Forschungen zu den Religionen der antiken römischen Welt und ihrer Nachbargebiete gegeben werden. Die einzelnen Beiträge sind ihrer Form nach, dem jeweiligen Thema entsprechend, entweder zusammenfassende Darstellungen oder Problem- und Forschungsberichte oder exemplarische Untersuchungen.

Im I. Teil des Werkes („Von den Anfängen Roms bis zum Ausgang der Republik") besteht die Rubrik „Religion" nur aus einer kleinen Gruppe von Beiträgen in Bd. I 2 (Berlin–New York 1972) über wichtige Aspekte der älteren römischen Religion. Im II. und III. Teil („Principat" bzw. „Spätantike und Nachleben") wird sie dagegen jeweils mehrere Bände umfassen und dem Charakter einer handbuchartigen enzyklopädischen Übersicht näherkommen. Hier wie in den anderen Rubriken werden Lücken und Ungleichmäßigkeiten des Programms zumeist Tendenzen der aktuellen Forschung widerspiegeln.

Im II. Teil behandelt die Rubrik „Religion" außer den sog. heidnischen Religionen griechisch-römischen, orientalischen und sonstigen regionalen Ursprungs (Bde. II 16–II 18) auch das späthellenistische, das „intertestamentarische" und das rabbinische Judentum im Blickfeld der römischen Welt (Bde. II 19–II 21), Gnostizismus und verwandte Erscheinungen (Bd. II 22) und das frühe Christentum vor Konstantin (Bde. II 23–II 28). Im III. Teil wird das spätantike Christentum etwa von der Zeit Konstantins an Hauptgegenstand der Rubrik sein. Darüber hinaus werden aber mehrere Beiträge auch dem byzantinischen und dem römisch-katholischen Christentum des Mittelalters und der Neuzeit bis hin zum 2. Vatikanischen Konzil hinsichtlich ihrer Beziehungen zum Alten und Neuen christlichen Rom der Antike gewidmet sein.

Walter de Gruyter · Berlin · New York

(ANRW)

Teil II: Principat

Band II 16: Religion (Heidentum: Römische Religion, Allgemeines)

3 Teilbände.

1: XII, Seiten 1–832. 1978. DM 375,–
2: Seiten 833–1773. 1978. DM 420,–
3: Seiten 1773–ca. 2300. (in Vorbereitung)

Preisänderungen vorbehalten

Walter de Gruyter   Berlin · New York